HANDBOOK OF
DEATH
&
DYING

EDITORIAL BOARD

HANDBOOK OF
DEATH
&
DYING

Clifton D. Bryant, Editor in Chief
Virginia Tech University

VOLUME ONE
THE PRESENCE OF DEATH

A Sage Reference Publication

SAGE Publications
International Educational and Professional Publisher
Thousand Oaks ■ London ■ New Delhi

For information:

Sage Publications, Inc.
2455 Teller Road
Thousand Oaks, California 91320
E-mail: order@sagepub.com

Sage Publications Ltd.
6 Bonhill Street
London EC2A 4PU
United Kingdom

Sage Publications India Pvt. Ltd.
B-42, Panchsheel Enclave
Post Box 4109
New Delhi 110 017 India

Printed in the United States of America

Library of Congress Cataloging-in-Publication Data

Handbook of death and dying / edited by Clifton D. Bryant.
      p. cm.
A Sage Reference Publication.
Includes bibliographical references and index.
ISBN 0-7619-2514-7
   1. Death—Social aspects. 2. Thanatology. I. Bryant, Clifton D.,
1932-
HQ1073.H36 2003
306.9—dc222

2003014864

03   04   10 9   8   7   6   5   4   3   2   1

Acquiring Editor:	Rolf A. Janke
Editorial Assistant:	Sara Tauber
Production Editor:	Diana E. Axelsen
Copy Editors:	Judy Selhorst (Volume I)
	Linda Gray (Volume II)
Typesetter:	C&M Digitals (P) Ltd.
Indexer:	Rachel Rice
Cover Designer:	Ravi Balasuriya

CONTENTS

Preface: A Thanatological Odyssey xv

Introduction xix

About the Editors xxiii

About the Contributors xxvii

VOLUME ONE: THE PRESENCE OF DEATH

PART I: DEATH IN CULTURAL CONTEXT 1

CONFRONTING DEATH

The Universal Fear of Death and the Cultural Response 3
Calvin Conzelus Moore and John B. Williamson

Historical Changes in the Meaning of Death in the Western Tradition 14
William R. Wood and John B. Williamson

Dealing With Death: Western Philosophical Strategies 24
Michael R. Taylor

Death Denial: Hiding and Camouflaging Death 34
Bert Hayslip, Jr.

Death, Dying, and the Dead in Popular Culture 43
Keith F. Durkin

The Death Awareness Movement: Description, History, and Analysis 50
Kenneth J. Doka

KEEPING THE DEAD ALIVE

The Spiritualist Movement: Bringing the Dead Back 57
Charles F. Emmons

Reincarnation: The Technology of Death 65

    Jane Dillon

Hosts and Ghosts: The Dead as Visitors in Cross-Cultural Perspective 77

    Clifton D. Bryant

Ghosts: The Dead Among Us 87

    Charles F. Emmons

The Malevolent "Undead": Cross-Cultural Perspectives 96

    Keith P. Jacobi

TRANSCENDING DEATH: RELIGIOUS AFTER-DEATH BELIEFS

Spirituality 110

    John D. Morgan

Religion and the Mediation of Death Fear 117

    Michael R. Leming

Christian Beliefs Concerning Death and Life After Death 126

    Donald E. Gowan

Near-Death Experiences as Secular Eschatology 137

    Tillman Rodabough and Kyle Cole

DEATH AND SOCIAL EXCHANGE

Life Insurance as Social Exchange Mechanism 148

    Dennis L. Peck

"Full Military Honors": Ceremonial Interment as Sacred Compact 159

    Timothy W. Wolfe and Clifton D. Bryant

Symbolic Immortality and Social Theory: The Relevance of an Underutilized Concept 173

    Lee Garth Vigilant and John B. Williamson

**PART II: DEATH IN SOCIAL CONTEXT:
VARIANTS IN MORALITY AND MEANING** 183

*THE SOCIAL MODES OF DEATH:
THE IMPORT OF CONTEXT AND CIRCUMSTANCE*

Historical and Epidemiological Trends in Mortality in the United States 185

    Vicki L. Lamb

Global Mortality Rates: Variations and Their Consequences for the Experience of Dying 198

    Clive Seale

To Die, by Mistake: Accidental Deaths   211

    Lee Garth Vigilant and John B. Williamson

Megadeaths: Individual Reactions and Social Responses to Massive Loss of Life   223

    Jerome Rosenberg and Dennis L. Peck

On the Role and Meaning of Death in Terrorism   236

    Lee Garth Vigilant and John B. Williamson

Death Attributed to Medical Error   246

    Jerry T. McKnight and Pat Norton

Homicidal Death   256

    Steven A. Egger and Kim A. Egger

PRE-PERSONALITY DEATHS

Pre-Personality Pregnancy Losses: Miscarriages, Stillbirths, and Abortions   264

    Jack P. Carter

Sudden Infant Death Syndrome   275

    Charles A. Corr and Donna M. Corr

DEATH AS SOCIAL ENTITY: THE SOCIAL CONSTRUCTION OF DEATH

The Evolution of the Legal Definition of Death   284

    Tillman Rodabough

Death Education   292

    Charles A. Corr and Donna M. Corr

DEATH AS INTERMISSION: THE CONTINUATION OF IDENTITY

The Postself in Social Context   302

    Jack Kamerman

PART III: DEATH AND SOCIAL CONTROVERSY   307

SUICIDE

Historical Suicide   309

    Alan H. Marks

Suicide and Suicide Trends in the United States, 1900–1999   319

    Dennis L. Peck

Suicide Survivors: The Aftermath of Suicide and Suicidal Behavior   339

    John L. McIntosh

Cross-Cultural Perspectives on Suicide 351

    David Lester

CAPITAL PUNISHMENT

A History of Execution Methods in the United States 357

    Trina N. Seitz

Capital Punishment in the United States 368

    Stephanie Picolo Manzi

Military Executions 378

    J. Robert Lilly

ABORTION

The Abortion Issue in the United States 386

    Michael C. Kearl

THE HIV/AIDS EPIDEMIC

Dying of AIDS and Social Stigmatization 397

    Robin D. Moremen

EUTHANASIA

Medical Euthanasia 405

    Gail C. Walker

Physician-Assisted Death 424

    Monika Ardelt

PART IV: PASSING AWAY: DYING AS SOCIAL PROCESS 435

DEATH AS SOCIAL PROCESS: THE APPROACH OF DEATH

Death Awareness and Adjustment Across the Life Span 437

    Bert Hayslip, Jr., and Robert O. Hansson

Dying as Deviance: An Update on the Relationship Between Terminal
Patients and Medicine 448

    Charles Edgley

DEATH AS SOCIAL PROCESS: DYING

The Dying Process 457

    Graves E. Enck

On Coming to Terms With Death and Dying: Neglected Dimensions of Identity Work 468

    Kent L. Sandstrom

THE INSTITUTIONAL CONTEXT OF DEATH

Death in Two Settings: The Acute Care Facility and Hospice   475

    Sarah Brabant

The History of the Hospice Approach   485

    Michael R. Leming

Dying in a Total Institution: The Case of Death in Prison   495

    Francis D. Glamser and Donald A. Cabana

Formal and Informal Caregiving at the End of Life   502

    Pamela J. Kovacs and David P. Fauri

VOLUME TWO: THE RESPONSE TO DEATH

PART V: FUNERALIZATION: THE SOCIAL CEREMONIES OF DEATH 511

BEFORE THE FUNERAL

The Death Notification Process: Recommendations for Practice, Training, and Research   513
    Alan E. Stewart and Janice Harris Lord

The Autopsy   523
    James Claude Upshaw Downs

A Social History of Embalming   534
    Melissa Johnson Williams

THE ORGANIZATIONAL RESPONSE TO DEATH

Fallen Soldiers: Death and the U.S. Military   544
    Morten G. Ender, Paul T. Bartone, and Thomas A. Kolditz

Death-Related Work Systems Outside the Funeral Home   556
    Watson Rogers II and Clifton D. Bryant

FUNERALIZATION IN THE UNITED STATES

The American Family and the Processing of Death Prior to the 20th Century   567
    Paul David Nygard and Catherine H. Reilly

The Evolution of the Funeral Home and the Occupation of Funeral Director   575
    Jerome J. Salomone

The American Funeral   587
    Bert Hayslip, Jr., Kenneth W. Sewell, and Russell B. Riddle

Black Funeralization and Culturally Grounded Services   598
    James L. Moore III and Clifton D. Bryant

On the Economics of Death in the United States   604
    Dwayne A. Banks

FUNERALIZATION IN CROSS-CULTURAL PERSPECTIVE

The Funeral and the Funeral Industry in the United Kingdom   611
    Brian Parsons

Practices Surrounding the Dead in French-Speaking Belgium: Rituals in Kitlike Form   619
    Florence Vandendorpe

The Native American Way of Death   631

    Gerry R. Cox

The Hindu Way of Death   640

    Anantanand Rambachan

The Muslim Way of Death   649

    Dawood H. Sultan

The Japanese Way of Death   656

    Hikaru Suzuki

The Taoist (Chinese) Way of Death   673

    Linda Sun Crowder

The Jewish Way of Death   687

    Ruben Schindler

POSTFUNERALIZATION ACTIVITIES

Obituaries   694

    Joyce E. Williams

Gracing God's Acres: Some Notes on a Typology of Cemetery Visitation
  in Western Cultures   703

    Joseph E. Boyle

Impromptu Memorials to the Dead   712

    Jon K. Reid

Death and Community Responses: Comfort, Community, and Culture   721

    William J. Hauser and AnneMarie Scarisbrick-Hauser

Monuments in Motion: Gravemarkers, Cemeteries, and Memorials as Material
  Form and Context   730

    Ann M. Palkovich and Ann Korologos Bazaronne

PART VI: BODY DISPOSITION   741

DISPOSING OF THE DEAD: ELYSIUM AS REAL ESTATE

The History of the American Cemetery and Some Reflections on
  the Meaning of Death   743

    Vicky M. MacLean and Joyce E. Williams

Pet Burial in the United States   757

    David D. Witt

DISPOSING OF THE DEAD: OPTIONS AND ALTERNATIVES

Cremation   767

    Douglas J. Davies

Body Recycling   775

    Kelly A. Joyce and John B. Williamson

The Iceman Cometh: The Cryonics Movement and Frozen Immortality   786

    Clifton D. Bryant and William E. Snizek

Disposing of the Dead: Minor Modes   792

    DeAnn K. Gauthier, Nancy K. Chaudoir, and Rhonda D. Evans

DISPOSING OF THE DEAD: OTHER TIMES, OTHER PLACES

The Social History of the European Cemetery   801

    Harold Mytum

Body Disposition in Cross-Cultural Context: Prehistoric and Modern
Non-Western Societies   810

    Keith P. Jacobi

Mummification and Mummies in Ancient Egypt   819

    Peter Lacovara and John Baines

PART VII: THANATOLOGICAL AFTERMATH   827

GRIEF AND BEREAVEMENT

The Evolution of Mourning and the Bereavement
Role in the United States: Middle- and Upper-Class European Americans   829

    David E. Balk

Social Dimensions of Grief   838

    María I. Vera

The Experience of Grief and Bereavement   847

    Robert A. Neimeyer and Louis A. Gamino

Bereavement in Cross-Cultural Perspective   855

    Paul C. Rosenblatt

THE SOCIAL IMPACT OF SURVIVORHOOD

Widowhood and Its Social Implications   862

    Felix M. Berardo

Children and the Death of a Parent 871

Eric Lichten

Parents and the Death of a Child 880

Sangeeta Singg

PART VIII: THE LEGALITIES OF DEATH 889

DEATH IN LEGAL CONTEXT

Living Wills and Durable Power of Attorney for Health Care 891

Carolyn Pevey

The Death Certificate: Civil Registration, Medical Certification, and Social Issues 899

Dennis L. Peck

Coroner and Medical Examiner 909

James Claude Upshaw Downs

DEATH, SUCCESSION, AND TESTAMENTORY INHERITANCE

The Disposition of Property: Transfers Between the Dead and the Living 917

Robert K. Miller, Jr., Jeffrey P. Rosenfeld, and Stephen J. McNamee

The Last Will and Testament: A Neglected Document in Sociological Research 926

Clifton D. Bryant and William E. Snizek

THE LEGAL REGULATION OF DEATH-RELATED ACTIVITIES

The Legal Regulation of Mortuary Science Education 934

Todd W. Van Beck

Cemetery Regulation in the United States 941

Robert M. Fells

DEATH AND LEGAL BLAME

Death and Legal Blame: Wrongful Death 950

Thomas J. Vesper

Negligent Death and Manslaughter 968

Frances P. Bernat

THE DEAD AS LEGAL ENTITY

"Thanatological Crime": Some Conceptual Notes on
Offenses Against the Dead as a Neglected Form of Deviant Behavior 974

Clifton D. Bryant

PART IX: THE CREATIVE IMAGINATION AND THE RESPONSE TO DEATH 987

ART

Death in Art 989
    Charles E. Walton

LITERATURE

Cultural Concern With Death in Literature 998
    Diana Royer

MUSIC

"Arise, Ye More Than Dead!" Culture, Music, and Death 1008
    Robert Kastenbaum

ORGANIC SCULPTURE

Dead Zoo Chic: Some Conceptual Notes on Taxidermy in American Social Life 1019
    Clifton D. Bryant and Donald J. Shoemaker

PART X: THE FUTURE OF DEATH 1027

Death in the Future: Prospects and Prognosis 1029
    Clifton D. Bryant, Charles Edgley, Michael R. Leming, Dennis L. Peck, and Kent L. Sandstrom

Index 1041

PREFACE: A THANATOLOGICAL ODYSSEY

My early encounters with death, like those of other youngsters in the United States, were sporadic and ephemeral. My first encounter with death occurred 63 years ago, when my beloved dog Scrappy was killed by a truck in front of my home. Scrappy was more than a dog, he was my pal. My grief was painful. The death of my dog and the later demises of other pets over time were traumatic experiences. With the help of playmates, I created a pet cemetery for deceased pets and other dead creatures that we found, and that served to foster notions of confronting death collectively and of ritualistic obligations to the dead. At one point, I considered converting a storage shed next to the pet cemetery into a "chapel" for funeral services. My interest in death had become more than casual.

One of my classmates in the third grade was the son of a mortician, and he often brought tombstone catalogs to school. I befriended him, and he let me look at the catalogs. They were imposing, with protective pages of tissue paper between the compelling photogravure pages of tombstone illustrations. I was fascinated by the images of marble and granite markers, and I remember them vividly even today.

The occasional deaths and subsequent funerals of family friends and distant relatives introduced me to human death. Early in my primary school years, my grandparents, over the objections of my parents, took me to the funeral of a family friend who had died. My parents were of the death-denial generation; they believed that children should be shielded from death and that the funeral experience would traumatize me. Those in my grandparents' generation, however, felt that people should confront death and learn to accept it as a natural and inevitable fact of life. I found the funeral experience, including viewing the body, to be informative and insight inspiring rather than traumatic. Like many individuals of my generation, I did not experience death in my immediate family until adulthood. However, while I was in high school the accidental deaths of several schoolmates gave death a very realistic presence for me.

Growing up during World War II gave me an even more sobering perspective on death, with the large numbers of combat deaths sustained by the U.S. armed forces. Family friends and neighbors received telegrams telling them of the deaths of sons or husbands with dreadful frequency. The ultimate tally of dead from the war, on both sides, especially as a result of massive bombing attacks such as those on German cities and the atomic bombing attacks on Hiroshima and Nagasaki, demonstrated megadeath of almost unfathomable proportions.

My intellectual interest in death, however, was not piqued until I was in college. Early in my college career, I read Evelyn Waugh's novel *The Loved One*, with its dark and biting, satirical but compellingly amusing account of a dog cemetery and a human cemetery. Some years later, I read other popular books on death, such as Leroy Bowman's *The American Funeral* (1959) and Jessica Mitford's *The American Way of Death* (1963), which proved to be informative, if not entertaining. After college, a tour of duty in the army as a military police officer provided me with training in the investigation of violent death, such as murder, and an assignment as company commander of a military police detachment (making me the de facto chief of police) at Camp Rucker, Alabama, gave me some firsthand exposure to violent deaths from automobile and airplane wrecks as well as suicides.

Early in my graduate school training, I encountered an article in a sociological journal that seized my attention. In 1958, William A. Faunce and Robert L. Fulton published an article titled "The Sociology of Death: A Neglected Area in Sociological Research" in the journal *Social Forces*. Suddenly, I (and some fellow graduate students) realized that death and dying are proper topics for scholarly investigation. One of my professors whom I had told about the article dismissed it as having little in the way of professional promise because the topic was too "doleful." One of my graduate student friends, however, shortly thereafter undertook to write a master's thesis on the funeral home as a work system.

By the time I had finished my graduate work, my scholarly inclinations led me to study and teach the sociology of work and occupations as a major specialty. But the study of work encompasses the study of death-related work, among other types of vocational endeavors. I ultimately developed an interest in funerary work, and that interest has persisted for the remainder of my career.

In 1968, as a new department head at Western Kentucky University, I inaugurated a new professional journal titled *Sociological Symposium*. As the name implies, each issue was to be a theme issue. The first issue of the journal was devoted entirely to the study of death and dying. It was very well received. Later in my career, when I came to Virginia Tech University, I had developed a more focused interest in the study of death and dying, and over a period of several years, I authored or coauthored a number of papers and articles on such topics as cryonics, last wills and testaments, taxidermy as a thanatological art form, thanatological crime, and symbolic communication between the living and the dead. As a result of my death-related scholarship, I developed a course called "The Sociology of Death," which I have now taught for 25 years, invariably to very large classes of 130 to 300 students. The exploration of death and dying has come to occupy a place of significant centrality in my scholarly agenda, and I have addressed various death-related topics—such as military combat death and execution—in some of my books and articles.

A number of extended trips to various countries in Southeast Asia (including living in two such countries, the Philippines and Taiwan, on visiting teaching appointments) afforded me opportunities to observe and study death in other cultures. I arrived in Taiwan during Ghost Month, observed funerals and cemetery behavior, and conducted a detailed study of geomancers (*feng shui* practitioners) who select grave sites for deceased persons.

In the late 1970s, I founded the journal *Deviant Behavior*, for which I served as editor in chief for 13 years. During that time, the journal published many articles that addressed various types of death, including murder, suicide, and execution.

As I reached middle age, death began to take its inevitable toll on my family and friends. Within a few short years, I lost my grandfather and grandmother, two maternal uncles, and, in 1979, my father, who died unexpectedly after surgery. Within this general time period my wife lost her grandfather, her father and mother, and her older brother. In recent years, a number of my old friends, dating back to high school, have passed away, as have numerous professional colleagues. Even several of my former students have died. As we age, death ceases to be a stranger and increasingly intrudes in our lives.

A few years ago, I served as editor in chief of the four-volume reference work *The Encyclopedia of Criminology and Deviant Behavior*. My involvement in the development of that work led me to the belief that a new reference compendium in the area of thanatology would be both timely and useful to scholars. I also felt that, rather than an encyclopedia of short and concise entries, this compendium should take the form of a collection of detailed and comprehensive essays that provide suitably informative contexts for the topics being discussed. This two-volume handbook is the result of that inspiration.

This effort has consumed the better part of 2 years and is the product of a sizable group undertaking. In this regard, a number of individuals have played signal roles, and they must be recognized and acknowledged. Rolf Janke at Sage Publications shared my original vision for the development of this compendium and greatly facilitated the process of review and contractual acceptance of the handbook as a Sage publishing project. Much appreciation goes to Rolf for adding the handbook to the Sage agenda. Sara Tauber, Rolf's assistant, has been the liaison person at Sage throughout the development of this work and has provided invaluable assistance in handling and processing entry manuscripts, overseeing many of the attendant administrative details, and troubleshooting on various problematic details of the project. Many thanks go to Sara for her efforts.

The copy editors for this project, Judy Selhorst and Linda Gray, have done an outstanding job in smoothing out the lumps and bumps in the chapters, as well as polishing and perfecting the narratives presented. The entries reflect their careful attention to detail, and I am most appreciative of their fine efforts. Diana Axelsen has served as the production editor for the handbook and has been its guiding hand as it has moved through the final stages toward publication. She has energetically pushed the project along on schedule and has creatively ensured a finished product that is attractive in design, nicely crafted in format, and impressive in appearance. My gratitude and thanks go to Diana for producing such an excellent set of books.

My four associate editors—Charles Edgley, Michael Leming, Dennis Peck, and Kent Sandstrom—all signed on early, when the handbook was barely out of its conceptualization stage, and contributed to the final plan for, and outline of, the work, thereby lending their names and good offices to the effort. Once the project was under development, they served above and beyond the call of duty, reviewing, editing, and guiding the entry manuscripts to perfection, through multiple revisions in some instances. It was challenging and labor-intensive work, but they accomplished the task with professional aplomb, making no complaints or excuses while maintaining a cheerful mien in the face of my ongoing exhortations to accelerate their editing pace. The result is a set of outstanding essays that are interesting, informative, and insightful. I owe these colleagues a commodious supply of gratitude for their splendid effort.

My assistant editor, Watson Rogers, did unstinting duty in all sorts of capacities—library researcher, computer technician and consultant, editor, author, and chief cook and bottle washer, to mention but some of his many roles. His contribution to the project was very significant, and I thank him for his tireless and creative efforts.

The more than 100 contributing authors are to be especially commended for producing such fine essays in the face of very pressing time constraints. Their work invariably exceeded my expectations and forms a comprehensive body of thanatological knowledge that will serve scholars in the field for years to come.

A number of individuals provided clerical assistance in the preparation of the handbook. Brenda Husser provided valuable computer and word-processing information and advice. Lou Henderson assisted with the computer processing of manuscripts. Barbara Townley typed some of the manuscripts and helped format some of the graphics that accompanied them. I thank them all for their invaluable services. Diane Hawk expended much time and effort in typing manuscripts, developing graphics, printing out finished entries, and discharging a wide array of clerical responsibilities in connection with the project. I am very much indebted to her for her extraordinarily helpful assistance.

Patty Bryant took on a prodigious workload as managing editor and labored mightily, sending and receiving thousands of e-mail messages, typing manuscripts, dealing with telephone traffic, proofreading, filing, developing lists and outlines, running the "mail room," handling a vast array of administrative details, and coordinating interaction with more than a hundred contributing authors and associate editors, plus the editorial staff at Sage. She accomplished all of this within the context of a grueling work agenda and a very demanding time schedule, all the while maintaining a cheerful composure and an optimistic and encouraging outlook. In this regard, she very much served as a role model for me on the project. She made an enormous contribution to the handbook, and I am extraordinarily indebted to her and owe her much love and affection in repayment.

—Clifton D. Bryant

INTRODUCTION

Death, historically a topic of major social concern, has in recent decades become a phenomenon of even more relevance. Demographic trends portend a much-increased proportion of aged individuals in the U.S. population and an attendant increase in the number of terminal illnesses and death. Technological innovations such as organ transplants and life-support systems enhance the possibility of significantly extending life expectancy, but they also raise serious sociolegal and ethical questions concerning even the very definition of death itself. The corrosion of traditional religious beliefs and values, and the concomitant eschatological scenarios that they generate, renders more traumatic the prospect of death and the final annihilation of self.

Death constitutes crisis for society as well as for individuals and groups. Various patterns of behavior and social processes have been institutionalized as coping and response mechanisms for confronting the crisis of death. Death has social consequences for the larger social enterprise as well as for immediate survivors, and societal perceptions of, and ideological posture toward, death have a major influence on culture and social structure. Death is component to the process of life, in that dying is a social as well as a physiological phenomenon. The particular patterns of death and dying characteristic to a given society engender modal cultural responses, and such institutionalized behavior has familial, economic, educational, religious, and political implications.

Historically, death has been essentially a family matter, in that kin of the deceased handled the details of processing the dead and death. Death, human and animal, is a ubiquitous event in farming cultures and is assimilated into the fabric of social life and accepted as a matter of inevitability and the natural order. In the United States, various events of the 19th century, such as the advent of arterial embalming and increasing industrialization and urbanization, however, shifted the handling of death and the dead out of the home and into the commercial sphere. After death became a commercial commodity, intimate familiarity with it tended to fade and, in time, the United States became a death-denying society, to the extent of making death a taboo and, according to some, a "pornographic"

topic, thereby effectively shielding death from public attention. After World War II—and, to some extent, because of the war—death was "rediscovered," and a new "death awareness" movement surfaced. The public took an interest in death, and books, articles in periodicals, programs on television, and movies all provided material to satisfy public curiosity and dialogue concerning the topic. Best-selling books such as Mitford's *The American Way of Death* (1963) fueled disputatious debate about the ceremonies of death, and cases such as that of Karen Ann Quinlan generated discussion concerning the dilemmas that death sometimes precipitates. The expansion and enhancement of the mass media again brought death into the home, in the form of vivid accounts of homicide, disaster, war, plagues, executions, fatal accidents, and the burdens and trials of prolonged death due to chronic disease attendant to terminal illness. Death as a topic could not be denied or contained, and the body of public information about death grew and evolved into scholarly study and research. Death studies beyond medical studies became constituent to a number of academic disciplines, especially the behavioral sciences, such as sociology, anthropology, and psychology. Other applied fields, including social work, counseling, law, family development, and law enforcement, began to take a more expansive view of the social parameters of death. The literature of many disciplinary subfields began increasingly to focus on death studies and expanded accordingly.

Because the field of death studies is multidisciplinary and subsumes a variety of specialty interests, the literature in this subdiscipline has developed and proliferated in near exponential fashion. Multiple scholarly journals are devoted to the study of death, and extensive lists of new books are published annually in the different constituent specialty areas. The mass of research and theoretical information available has become almost intellectually unmanageable. Beyond the extensive size of the literature that has been generated in this area, there are also the problems of literature overlap, conflicting findings, theoretical and conceptual ambiguity, fugitive literature, overlooked or neglected paradigms, unsubstantiated hypotheses, methodological incongruity, and exploratory redundancy to the point of unproductivity. The corpus of knowledge in the field of death studies has, in effect, become increasingly unwieldy in terms of its parameters. What is needed at this time is an attempt to aggregate, consolidate, integrate, classify, organize, and better delineate and articulate the details of the information contained in the expansive body of literature that has been generated in this field. This, perhaps, can best be accomplished in the form of a concise but comprehensive compendium of the current state of knowledge in thanatology.

In terms of constituent contribution to the body of knowledge in a given field, articles tend to be fragmentary and books are often truncated and ephemeral, whereas reference works offer the advantages of definitive summary, meaningful assessment, and productive synthesis. Reference works offer the further advantage of durability. Some encyclopedic reference works have served as the definitive arbiters in certain disciplines for decades. With the new millennium under way, this would seem to be an opportune and compelling time to stop and take stock of the literature in the field of thanatology, to arrange and synthesize that body of knowledge in a way that will be useful for scholars in the future. A properly developed reference work at this point in time will, in effect, provide direction and momentum to the study of death-related behavior for many years to come.

An appropriate understanding of death and its attendant social processes can enable individuals to confront the prospect of death itself and their own mortality, and helps them to integrate the ongoing process of death more adequately into their total life experience. The primary focus of this reference work is to acquaint the user with the social consequences of death and the behavioral mechanisms, both individual and collective, through which death is experienced. It is my hope that this compendium will provide the user with a more sensitive insight into the social parameters of death and the various ways in which our behavior and our social institutions are affected by death and dying. Additionally, I hope that it will afford the user a refined perspective on the major death-related activities, such as funeralization, bereavement, and disposing of the dead.

Many vocations address death and dying in one fashion or another. In this regard, this reference work should prove to be valuable, as a sensitizing as well as an educational resource, for prelaw and premedical students; for students who intend to pursue careers as clergy, nurses, or counselors; and for practitioners in the fields of medicine, law, law enforcement, social work, and insurance (to name only a few). Scholars and students in the fields of philosophy, management, family development, theology, psychology, sociology, education, and various heath-related fields should also appreciate the utility of this work.

In developing comprehensive reference works, there are two basic strategies. One model of encyclopedia development involves the articulation of 500 to 1,000 basic concepts and intellectual notions, and then the generation of concise entry essays for each topic. Although this approach results in inclusiveness regarding the parameters of the field and breadth of coverage in terms of the array of topics, it also has disadvantages in that the relatively brief expositions presented often display limited perspectives, and sometimes the collected entries provide a fragmented overview of the field.

A second model addresses the task of coverage through the use of a smaller number of entries that take the form of essays that are more comprehensive in context and better integrate sets of individual concepts or topics. Often several basic concepts may be intimately linked or overlapping, and these may be understood most clearly within the framework of a more elaborate context. This purpose can best be served by a handbook such as this one. In the two volumes of this handbook, the contributors address approximately 100 pivotal topics, each of which subsumes and incorporates several more basic concepts and behaviors. The essays generated to discuss these topics direct special attention to the constituent concepts and social patterns within the exploration of the larger topical concern. Each chapter is of journal-article length and addresses its general topic with appropriate detail and elaboration.

The advantage of this literary venue is that, compared with reference works that present extensive lists of topics in fragmented fashion, this model of compendium presents various subtopics and concepts in a more contextually elaborate fashion, demonstrating concept linkages and evolution, and provides enough background to ensure understanding.

This work is, by intent and design, comprehensive and inclusive in content. Topics range from autopsies to vampires, from capital punishment to suicide, from abortion to physician-assisted death, from cryonics to the spiritualism movement. Major sections of these volumes focus on the cultural context of death (social means of transcending death), the various modes (causes) of death, death and social controversy (abortion, capital punishment, euthanasia, and suicide), dying as social process, funeralization, body disposition, grief and mourning, the legalities of death, and creative responses to death (art, literature, and music).

This handbook is multidisciplinary; the contributing authors represent a diverse array of disciplines, including anthropology, psychology, social work, sociology, philosophy, theology, medicine, law, family studies, mortuary science, and history. This work is also cross-cultural; it addresses death-related behavior within a number of different religious contexts (including Christian, Hindu, Jewish, Taoist, and Muslim) and also examines such behavior in different countries and cultures (including Belgian funerals, European cemeteries, ancient Egyptian mummies, Japanese death rituals, Chinese cultural views of death, the Native American way of death, bereavement in different cultures, and body disposition in cross-cultural perspective). Various chapters also examine death-related topics in historical perspective, such as the history of the

American cemetery, historical changes in the meaning of death in the Western world, the history of suicide, historical changes in body disposition for members of the military, and the processing of death in the American family prior to the 20th century.

The two volumes of this handbook offer 103 definitive essays covering almost every dimension of death-related behavior. Leading scholars and researchers in the field of thanatology have contributed chapters, and all of the authors represent authoritative expertise in their respective areas of knowledge and practice. The essays included here constitute an insightful and well-informed synthesis of the current state of understanding in the field of death studies. As a definitive exposition, these volumes should help shape, articulate, and direct the development of the corpus of knowledge in this field well into the 21st century. It is my hope that in this regard this handbook will be a signal advancement in the evolution of the social study of death.

ABOUT THE EDITORS

EDITOR IN CHIEF

Clifton D. Bryant, Ph.D., is Professor of Sociology at Virginia Polytechnic Institute and State University (Virginia Tech) in Blacksburg, Virginia. He has been a faculty member there since 1972 and served as Department Chair from 1972 to 1982. Prior to coming to Virginia Tech, he held full-time faculty teaching appointments at Western Kentucky University (Department Head 1967–1972), Millsaps College (Department Head 1963–1967), and the University of Georgia (1960–1963). He was Visiting Professor at Mississippi State University (Summer 1985) and at the Pennsylvania State University (Summer 1958). His research appointments include Visiting Scientist at the U.S. Army Institute for the Behavioral and Social Sciences (Summer 1993), Visiting Research Scholar with the Mississippi Alcohol Safety Education Program (Mississippi State University; Summer 1985), and Visiting Research Scholar with Training and Technology Project operated by the Resource Development Office of Oak Ridge Associated Universities, Inc. (Summer 1987). His foreign teaching appointments include Visiting Fulbright Professor, Department and Graduate Institute of Sociology, National Taiwan University, Taipei, Taiwan, Republic of China (1987–1988), and Visiting Professor in the Department of Sociology/Anthropology, Xavier University, The Ateneo, Cagayan de Oro City, Mindanao, Philippines (1984–1985). He was a participant in the U.S. Department of Education's 1998 Fulbright-Hays Seminars Abroad Program in the People's Republic of China (Summer 1998) and was also a participant in the U.S. Department of Education's 1993 Fulbright-Hays Seminars Abroad Program in Hungary (Summer, 1993).

Dr. Bryant served as President of the Southern Sociological Society (1978–1979) and as President of the Mid-South Sociological Association (1981–1982). He was the recipient of the Mid-South Sociological Association's Distinguished Career Award in 1991 and the Distinguished Book Award in 2001. He is also the recipient of the Southern Sociological Society's 2003 Distinguished Contributions to Teaching Award. He has been listed in *Who's Who in America* since 1984 and in *Who's Who in the World* since 1991. He is a member of Omicron Delta Kappa, Phi Kappa Phi, Phi Beta Delta, Alpha Kappa Delta, Pi Kappa Alpha, and Alpha Phi Omega.

Dr. Bryant was founder and Chairman of the Editorial Board of *Sociological Symposium* (1968–1980). He was also the founder of *Deviant Behavior* and served as Editor-in-Chief of that journal from 1978 to 1991. He continues to serve as Chair of the Editorial Policy Board for the journal. He was editor of *the Southern Sociologist* (1970–1974). He has served as a member of the editorial board of *Criminology* (1978–1981), Associate Editor of *Sociological Forum* (1979–1980), Associate Editor of *Sociological Spectrum* (1981–1985), member of the Board of Advisory Editors of *Sociological Inquiry* (1981–1985) and also Associate Editor of that journal (1997–2000). He was a member of the Board of Editors of *Society and Animals* (1997–1999) and was Associate Editor for a special issue of *Marriage and Family Relations* (Fall 1982).

He is the author of *Sexual Deviancy and Social Proscription; Khaki-Collar Crime: Deviant Behavior in Military Context;* and *Deviant Behavior: Occupational and Organizational Bases;* editor of *The Encyclopedia of Criminology and Deviant Behavior* (four volumes); *Deviant Behavior: Readings in the Sociology of Norm Violations; The Rural Work Force: Nonagricultural Occupations in America; Sexual Deviance in Sexual Context; The Social Dimensions of Work;* and coeditor of *Social Problems Today: Dilemmas and Dimensions; Deviance and the Family;* and *Introductory Sociology: Selected Readings for the College Scene.* He has published articles in a number of professional journals, including *Social Forces, Society, Sociological Inquiry, Sociology and Social Research, Rural Sociology, Sociological Forum, American Journal of Public Health, the Journal of Sex Research, Journal of Veterinary Medical Education, Journal of Leisure Sciences, Sociological Spectrum, The Rural Sociologist, Psychological Reports, Free Inquiry in Creative Sociology, World Leisure and Recreation, Hort Technology, Anthrozoos, Applied Behavioral Science*

Review, Man and Environmental Systems, The Southern Sociologist, and *Deviant Behavior.*

He received his B.A. and M.A. degrees from the University of Mississippi, did advanced graduate work at the University of North Carolina (Chapel Hill), and received his Ph.D. degree from Louisiana State University.

MANAGING EDITOR

Patty M. Bryant has worked as an executive secretary for various corporations and agencies, including the law firm of Stennett and Stennett in Jackson, Mississippi; Orgill Brothers Hardware Corporation; Great Southern Box Corporation; Illinois Central Railroad; and the city of Blacksburg, Virginia. She has been involved in the editorial process of several journals, including *Sociological Symposium, Southern Sociologist,* and *Deviant Behavior,* for which she served as Assistant Editor and later as Managing Editor. She has traveled extensively in Asia and lived in both the Philippines and Taiwan, where she worked with Clifton D. Bryant in conducting research on Asian culture. She was involved in the editorial process (with Clifton D. Bryant) on several books, including *Deviant Behavior: Readings in the Sociology of Norm Violation, Deviant Behavior: Occupational and Organizational Bases,* and *The Social Dimensions of Work.* Most recently, she served as Managing Editor of *The Encyclopedia of Criminology and Deviant Behavior* (four volumes). She graduated from Draughon's Business College in Jackson, Mississippi, and did undergraduate work at Western Kentucky University, majoring in sociology.

ASSOCIATE EDITORS

Charles Edgley, Ph.D., is Professor and Chair of the Department of Sociology at Oklahoma State University. The author or coauthor of six books and numerous scholarly articles, he has been teaching courses on death and dying, social psychology, deviance, and sociological theory for more than 30 years. Working within the symbolic interactionist tradition, he coedited the widely acclaimed *Life as Theater: A Dramaturgical Sourcebook* as well as several articles with the late Dennis Brissett. That book represented a major contribution to dramaturgical analysis and brought together some of the first dramaturgical thinking applied to death and dying. He also coauthored (with Ronny Turner) "Death as Theater: A Dramaturgical Analysis of the American Funeral."

Michael R. Leming, Ph.D., is Professor of Sociology and Anthropology and Asian Studies at St. Olaf College. He is the coauthor (with George E. Dickinson) of *Understanding Dying, Death, and Bereavement* (1985, 1990, 1994, 1997, and 2000) and *Understanding Families: Diversity,* *Continuity, and Change* (1990, 1995). He is also the coeditor (with Raymond DeVries and Brendan Furnish) of *The Sociological Perspective: A Value-Committed Introduction* (1989) and (with George E. Dickinson and Alan C. Mermann) *Annual Editions: Dying, Death, and Bereavement* (1992, 1994, 1996, 1998, 2000, and 2002). He is the founder and former director of the St. Olaf College Social Research Center, former member of the Board of Directors of the Minnesota Coalition on Terminal Care, and steering committee member of the Northfield AIDS Response, and he serves a hospice educator, volunteer, and grief counselor. He currently directs the Spring Semester in Thailand program at Chiang Mai University. He holds degrees from Marquette University (M.A.) and the University of Utah (Ph.D.) and has done additional graduate study at the University of California at Santa Barbara.

Dennis L. Peck, Ph.D., is Professor of Sociology at the University of Alabama. He has served as a senior analyst with the U.S. Department of Housing and Urban Development and the U.S. Department of Education. He is a past President of the Mid-South Sociological Association, President-elect of the Alabama/Mississippi Sociological Association, and was honored as a Distinguished Alumnus by the University of Wisconsin–Milwaukee. Other past professional involvement includes serving as editor of *Sociological Inquiry,* book review editor for *Deviant Behavior,* and thematic issue editor for the *Quarterly Journal of Ideology, Sociology and Social Welfare,* and *Sociological Inquiry.* He was also associate editor for *The Encyclopedia of Criminology and Deviant Behavior* and has served on the editorial boards of several journals. Included among his publications are *Fatalistic Suicide; Psychosocial Effects of Hazardous Toxic Waste Disposal on Communities; Open Institutions: The Hope for Democracy; Demographic and Structural Change: The Effects of the 1980s on American Society;* and *Extraordinary Behavior: A Case Study Approach to Understanding Social Problems.* His research has been published in a wide range of professional journals, including *Sociological Spectrum; Health and Social Work; Social Science; Omega: Journal of Death and Dying; Journal of Sociology and Social Welfare; Sociological Practice; Sociological Practice Review; Sociological Inquiry; Clinical Sociology Review;* and *International Quarterly of Community Health Education,* among others. He earned his Ph.D. in sociology from Washington State University and M.S. degree in sociology from the University of Wisconsin–Milwaukee.

Watson Rogers II, M.S., is a doctoral candidate in sociology at Virginia Polytechnic Institute and State University, where he also received a master's of science degree in sociology in fall 2000. His master's thesis is titled "A Theoretical Synthesis of Telecommuting and Family Violence," and his current research interests include work, technology, the sociology of science, deviance, and thanatology.

Kent L. Sandstrom, Ph.D., is Professor of Sociology at the University of Northern Iowa. He is also the Executive Officer of the Midwest Sociological Society. He received the Faculty Excellence Award from the Iowa Board of Regents in 2000, the Outstanding Teaching Award from the University of Northern Iowa in 1999, and the Herbert Blumer Award from the Society for the Study of Symbolic Interaction in 1989. His most recent journal publications focus on how people living with HIV/AIDS manage emotions and construct vital and enduring identities. He is the coauthor of two books: *Symbols, Selves, and Social Reality: A Symbolic Interactionist Approach to Social Psychology* and *Knowing Children: Participant Observation With Minors* (Sage, 1988).

ABOUT THE CONTRIBUTORS

Monika Ardelt, Ph.D., is Associate Professor of Sociology at the University of Florida. She is also a Core Faculty Member of the Institute on Aging and a Founding Faculty Member and Member of the Advisory Committee of the Center for Spirituality and Health at the University of Florida. In 1999, she was elected as a Brookdale National Fellow to study the similarities and differences between aging and dying well. Her research focuses on successful human development across the life course with particular emphasis on the relationships between wisdom, spirituality, aging well, and dying well. She has been published in several professional journals, such as *Journal of Gerontology, Social Psychology Quarterly, Social Forces, Research on Aging, Journal of Aging Studies,* and *Journal of Religious Gerontolog*y. She received her M.A. in sociology from the Johann Wolfgang Goethe-University of Frankfurt/Main in Germany and her Ph.D. in sociology from the University of North Carolina at Chapel Hill.

John Baines, D.Phil., has been Professor of Egyptology at the University of Oxford since 1976. He has held visiting appointments in Egypt, France, Germany, and the United States. He has lectured in Egypt and Sudan, Europe, Japan, and the United States and has represented the field of Egyptology at interdisciplinary conferences and advanced seminars in archaeology, anthropology, art history, and literature, as well as publishing in journals and collected volumes over a similar spread of fields. He is coauthor with Jaromir Malek of *Cultural Atlas of Ancient Egypt* (2nd ed., 2000). He has research interests in ancient Egyptian art, religion, and literature; social theory; and anthropological approaches to ancient civilizations. He has directed epigraphic fieldwork at Abydos in Upper Egypt. His current research is on biography, elite self-presentation, and the enactment of an aesthetic high culture by the Egyptian elite.

David E. Balk, Ph.D., is Professor of Human Development and Family Science in the College of Human Environmental Sciences at Oklahoma State University. Most of his research efforts have been focused on adolescent bereavement, with some attention paid as well to program evaluation.

The National Institute of Mental Health and the William T. Grant Foundation funded some of his bereavement research proposals. He is associate editor for the journal *Death Studies* and for *Omega* and the book review editor for *Death Studies.* His professional memberships include the Association for Death Education and Counseling (ADEC); the International Work Group on Death, Dying, and Bereavement; the American Evaluation Association; and the American Psychological Association; he is a member of the Scientific Advisory Committee that the Center for the Advancement of Health formed to examine bereavement research issues. He also is a member of the ADEC Credentialing Council and Chair of the ADEC Test Committee working to develop a national exam to certify foundational knowledge in thanatology. He earned an M.A. in theology from Marquette University, an M.C. in counseling psychology from Arizona State University, and a Ph.D. in counseling psychology from the University of Illinois at Urbana–Champaign.

Dwayne A. Banks, Ph.D., has been Country Director of the Partners for Health Reform *Plus* (PHR*plus*) project in Amman, Jordan, since March 1998. PHR*plus* is a USAID-funded project providing long-term technical assistance to the government of Jordan in the areas of health insurance reform, hospital managerial reform, health policy training, and research, as well as the development of a system of national health accounts. Prior to his current assignment, he served as Assistant Professor of Public Policy at the Richard & Rhoda Goldman School of Public Policy at the University of California, Berkeley. In 1994, he was selected as an Atlantic Fellow in Public Policy, by the British government. He was a Visiting Scholar at the London School of Economics and the King's Fund Policy Institute. He has published extensively in prominent research journals such as *Health Economics, Journal of the American Medical Association,* and *Health Matrix Journal of Law and Medicine* and has authored numerous technical reports on health policy-related issues. He currently serves on the editorial board of the *Journal of Anti-Aging Medicine.* He received a Ph.D. in economics from the University of California at Berkeley, where he specialized in health care economics, industrial organization, and public finance.

Paul T. Bartone, Ph.D., teaches in the Department of Behavioral Sciences and Leadership and serves as Director of the Leader Development Research Center at the United States Military Academy, West Point. He joined the U.S. Army Medical Service Corps in 1985 as a research psychologist and has served continuously on active duty since then. He has conducted numerous field studies on psychosocial stress, health, and adaptation among military personnel and their families, covering deployments ranging from the Gulf War through Bosnia, as well as a number of peacetime disasters. A continuing focus of his research involves the search for factors, such as personality hardiness, that might account for individual and group resiliency under stress. Professional memberships include the Inter-University Seminar on Armed Forces and Society (IUS), the International Society for Traumatic Stress Studies, the American Psychological Society, the American Psychological Association (Divisions 1, 13, 19, 48, & 52), and RC01 of the International Sociological Association. He is also a member of ERGOMAS (European Research Group on Military and Society) and is the ERGOMAS coordinator for the Working Group on Morale, Cohesion, and Leadership. He has served as Division 19's Member-at-Large, representative to APA's CIRP (Committee on International Relations in Psychology), chair of the International Military Psychology Committee and is currently Division 19's Web site coordinator and liaison to the IUS. He received his Ph.D. in psychology/human development from the University of Chicago in 1984.

Ann Korologos Bazzarone, M.A., is a doctoral candidate in cultural studies at George Mason University. Her dissertation will be a study of Greek American cemeteries and their relevance in Greek American communities. She has an M.A. in archaeology from George Mason University and a B.A. in classics and ancient Greek from the College of William and Mary.

Felix M. Berardo, Ph.D., is Professor of Sociology, University of Florida. His teaching and research interests include family sociology, social gerontology, the sociology of death and survivorship, and the sociology of risk. He has published over 100 articles in professional journals and is the author, coauthor, or editor of over a dozen major book-length works. He is former editor of the *Journal of Marriage & the Family,* current editor of the monograph series on *Current Perspectives in Family Research,* and deputy editor of the *Journal of Family Issues.* He also has served as President of the Florida Council on Family Relations and as associate chair and chair of the Department of Sociology at the University of Florida. He was the recipient of the Arthur Peterson Award in Death Education and has been awarded the status of Fellow by

the Gerontological Society of America and the National Council on Family Relations. His book (with F. Ivan Nye) *Emerging Conceptual Frameworks in Family Analysis* was included among a small, selected group of works considered "classics" in family sociology and has been recognized for its long-lasting impact on the field of family science.

Frances P. Bernat, Ph.D., is Associate Professor in the Administration of Justice at Arizona State University West. She received the Governor's Spirit of Excellence Award from the state of Arizona in 1998, the 1998 President's Medal for Team Excellence from Arizona State, and the Semi-finalist Award for Innovations in American Government from the Ford Foundation/JFK School of Government at Harvard University. She is a member of the editorial board for *Women and Criminal Justice,* as well as serving as a guest editor. She has been published in over 10 professional journals.

Joseph E. Boyle, M.A., is currently finishing his doctorate in sociology from Virginia Tech, where he was awarded the graduate student teaching award in 1998. He is also an instructor of sociology and criminal justice at Brookdale Community College in Lincroft, New Jersey, specializing in criminological theory, social problems, and deviant behavior. A graduate of Rutgers University, he received his M.A. in community college education from Rowan University in New Jersey and his M.S. degree in sociology from Virginia Tech.

Sarah Brabant, Ph.D., Professor Emeritus of Sociology at the University of Louisiana at Lafayette, is a Certified Sociological Practitioner and holds additional certifications in Thanatology: Death, Dying, and Bereavement, and Family Life Education. In 1981, she designed the first course on death and dying at her university, a course she still teaches each semester. She has served as a support person for Compassionate Friends, Acadiana Chapter, since 1983; counseled persons living with AIDS through Acadiana CARES since 1988; and was appointed to the faculty of the Delta Region AIDS Education and Training Center in 1990. She was one of the founders and serves on the Board of Directors of the Grief Center of Southwest Louisiana, a local program for bereaved children. She is the author of the book *Mending the Torn Fabric: For Those Who Grieve and Those Who Want to Help Them* and has contributed over 50 articles to professional journals. Her publications on death- and grief-related issues appear in *Omega;* the *Hospice Journal; ADEC Forum; Illness, Crisis & Loss; Teaching Sociology; International Journal of Addictions; Death Studies; Clinical Sociology Review; AIDS Patient Care;* and *Journal of Gerontological Social Work.* She has presented numerous papers, workshops, and lectures on death and bereavement at the local, state, and national levels. She received her Ph.D. from the University of Georgia in 1973.

Donald A. Cabana, Ph.D., is Associate Professor of Criminal Justice at the University of Southern Mississippi, specializing in penology and capital punishment. He worked in corrections for 25 years as a warden and Commissioner of Corrections. He is the author of the book, *Death at Midnight: Confessions of an Executioner.* He received his Ph.D. from the University of Southern Mississippi.

Jack P. Carter, Ph.D., is Associate Professor of Sociology at the University of New Orleans. His teaching duties include senior- and graduate-level courses in population dynamics and issues, and the sociology of aging. He has published more than 30 articles on topics including mortality, fertility, migration, and aging in professional journals such as *Family Life, Research on Aging, Review of Comparative Public Policy, Journal of Applied Gerontology,* and *Aging,* as well as refereed monographs and a book. He earned an M.A. degree in sociology at the University of Texas at Arlington and an M.S. in demography and Ph.D. in sociology at Florida State University, with social demography and the sociology of aging as areas of specialization.

Nancy K. Chaudoir, B.A., is a graduate student in rehabilitation counseling at the University of Louisiana at Lafayette and currently serves as managing editor of *Sociological Spectrum,* the official journal of the Mid-South Sociological Association. Her interest areas include gender, deviance, and mental health counseling. She received her B.A. in sociology at the University of Louisiana, Lafayette, in 2001.

Kyle Cole, Ph.D., is Associate Director of Religionsource (www.religionsource.org) at the American Academy of Religion at Emory University in Atlanta, Georgia. Formerly, he was Assistant Professor of Journalism and directed the graduate journalism program at Baylor University. He received a Ph.D. in journalism from the University of Missouri with concentrations in mass media and society and in American political behavior. He also has 7 years of editing and reporting experience at city dailies.

Charles A. Corr, Ph.D., is Professor Emeritus, Southern Illinois University Edwardsville, a member of the Board of Directors of the Hospice Institute of the Florida Suncoast (2000–present), a member since 2002 of the Executive Committee of the National Kidney Foundation's transAction Council, and a member (1979–present) and former Chairperson (1989–1993) of the International Work Group on Death, Dying, and Bereavement. His professional publications include 22 books and more than 80 articles and chapters on subjects such as death education, hospice care, and children/adolescents and death. His most recent book (coauthored with Clyde M. Nabe and Donna M. Corr) is *Death and Dying, Life and Living* (4th ed., 2003). His professional work has been recognized by the Association for Death Education and Counseling in awards for Outstanding Personal Contributions to the Advancement of Knowledge in the Field of Death, Dying, and Bereavement (1988) and for Death Education (1996), and by Children's Hospice International in an award for Outstanding Contribution to the World of Hospice Support for Children (1989) and through the establishment of the Charles A. Corr Award for Lifetime Achievement [Literature] (1995). In addition, he has received Research Scholar (1990), Outstanding Scholar (1991), and the Kimmel Community Service Award (1994) from Southern Illinois University Edwardsville.

Donna M. Corr, R.N., M.S., took early retirement in 1977 from her position as Professor, Department of Nursing, St. Louis Community College at Forest Park, St. Louis, Missouri. She continues to write, give presentations, and offer workshops locally, regionally, nationally, and internationally. Her publications include *Hospice Care: Principles and Practice* (1983), *Hospice Approaches to Pediatric Care* (1985), *Nursing Care in an Aging Society* (1990), *Sudden Infant Death Syndrome: Who Can Help and How* (1991), *Handbook of Childhood Death and Bereavement* (1996), and *Death and Dying, Life and Living* (4th ed., 2003).

Gerry R. Cox, Ph.D., is Professor of Sociology and Director of the Center for Death Education and Bioethics at University of Wisconsin–La Crosse. His teaching focuses on theory/theory construction, deviance and criminology, death and dying, social psychology, and minority peoples. He has been publishing materials since 1973 in sociology and teaching-oriented professional journals and has published more than 50 articles, chapters, and books. He is a member of the International Work Group on Dying, Death, and Bereavement, the Midwest Sociological Society, the American Sociological Association, the International Sociological Association, Phi Kappa Phi, the Great Plains Sociological Society, and the Association of Death Education and Counseling. He studied at Ball State University, the University of Kansas, Texas A&M University, and St. Mary of the Plains College.

Linda Sun Crowder, Ph.D., is a cultural diversities consultant in Brea, California. She has published articles in the *Journal of American Folklore, Chinese America: History and Perspectives, Cakalele* (*Maluku Research Journal*), and others. Her research focuses on symbolism, public display, performance, identity, and death rituals. She an M.A. in theater arts from the University of Hawaii, an M.A. in anthropology from California State University, Fullerton, and a Ph.D. in anthropology from the University of Hawaii where she specialized in the culture areas of Southeast Asia and American Chinatowns.

Douglas J. Davies, Ph.D., is Professor in the Study of Religion and Head of the Department of Theology at the University of Durham, England. He is on the editorial board of the journal *Mortality.* His recent books include *The Mormon Culture of Salvation* (2000), *Anthropology* *and Theology* (2002), and *Death, Ritual and Belief* (2002). He holds a master of letters research degree in anthropology from Oxford University and a Ph.D. from the University of Nottingham, where he also taught for many years and was Professor of Religious Studies. The University of Uppsala conferred on him their Honorary Degree of Doctor of Sacred Theology in 1998.

Jane Dillon, Ph.D., is a sociologist and independent research scientist currently conducting studies in the fields of alternative health, international religious freedom, and the science of subliminal influentiality. She is project coordinator of several double-blind clinical trials on the effect of subliminal influence technology in vivo and in vitro. She served as Visiting Professor at Whittier College in the Department of Sociology and Co-Director of the Human Science Program at the graduate school and research facility of the California Institute of Human Science. She has presented numerous papers at academic conferences for the past 18 years, including the Pacific Sociological Association, the Society for the Scientific Study of Religion, the University for Peace in Costa Rica, and the historic 1993 Parliament of World's Religions. In addition to her comprehensive work on the reincarnationist worldview, the Western yoga movement, and the Self-Realization Fellowship, she has published articles on environmental legislation, constitutive theory, and new social movements in *Syzygy: Journal of Alternative Religions and Culture* and *The California Coast.* In 1999, she completed the groundbreaking pilot "Burn Study" in which children hospitalized with severe third-degree burns demonstrated full recovery, without grafting, in less than 30 days due to the spiritual intercession (subliminal influence) of the eminent European scientist and Celtic spiritual leader of Brittany (France). She received M.A. and Ph.D. degrees from the Department of Sociology at the University of California, San Diego.

Kenneth J. Doka, Ph.D., is Professor of Gerontology at the Graduate School of the College of New Rochelle and Senior Consultant to the Hospice Foundation of America. A prolific author, his books include several titles on living with grief in addition to *Disenfranchised Grief: Recognizing Hidden Sorrow; Living With Life Threatening Illness; Children Mourning, Mourning Children; Death and Spirituality; Caregiving and Loss: Family Needs, Professional Responses; AIDS, Fear and Society; Aging and Developmental Disabilities;* and *Disenfranchised Grief: New Directions, Challenges, and Strategies for Practice.* He has also published over 60 articles and book chapters and is editor of both *Omega* and *Journeys: A Newsletter for the Bereaved.* He was elected President of the Association for Death Education and Counseling in 1993 and received its award for Outstanding Contributions in the Field of Death Education in 1998. In 1995, he was elected to the Board of Directors of the International Work Group on Death, Dying, and Bereavement

and served as Chair from 1997 to 1999. In 2000, Scott and White presented him an award for Outstanding Contributions to Thanatology and Hospice. He participates in the annual Hospice Foundation of America Teleconference, hosted by Cokie Roberts, and has appeared on *Nightline.* He has served as a consultant to medical, nursing, funeral service, and hospice organizations as well as businesses and educational and social service agencies. He is an ordained Lutheran minister.

James Claude Upshaw Downs, M.D., is coastal Georgia's first Regional Medical Examiner. He has served as a medical examiner since 1989 and was Alabama's State Forensics Director and Chief Medical Examiner from 1998 to 2002. He has lectured extensively in the field of forensic pathology and has presented at numerous national and international meetings in the fields of anatomic and forensic pathology. He is a consultant to the FBI Behavioral Science Unit in Quantico, Virginia, having authored four chapters in their manual on *Managing Death Investigation,* and was primary author of the FBI's *Forensic Investigator's Trauma Atlas.* His professional activities have included service on numerous professional boards and committees. He has testified in state and federal court, as well as before the U.S. Senate and House of Representatives. He is on the Board of Advisors for the National Forensic Academy and the Board of Directors of the National Association of Medical Examiners. He received his doctor of medicine degree, his residency training in anatomic and clinical pathology, and held a fellowship in forensic pathology from the Medical University of South Carolina (Charleston). He is board certified in anatomic, clinical, and forensic pathology.

Keith F. Durkin, Ph.D., is Associate Professor of Sociology and Director of the Institute for Social Research at Ohio Northern University in Ada. He is a coauthor of *How Chiropractors Think and Practice* and author or coauthor of approximately two dozen research reports and monographs. His articles have appeared in *Deviant Behavior, Federal Probation,* the *Journal of Alcohol and Drug Education,* and the *College Student Journal.* He was a contributing author for the *Encyclopedia of Criminology and Deviant Behavior* and is a member of the editorial board for *Sociological Inquiry.* He received his Ph.D. in sociology from Virginia Polytechnic Institute and State University.

Kim A. Egger, B.A., is planning to begin studies for her Ph.D. in 2003. She is coauthor, with Steven Egger, of a chapter on victims of serial murder in a monograph on victimology and is the author of "Motives for Murder" in *The Encyclopedia of Homicide and Violent Behavior* and "Victims: The 'Less-Dead'" in *The Killers Among Us: An Examination of Serial Murder and Its Investigation.* For the past 12 years, she has been developing a database on serial killers that currently holds information on over 1,300 serial murderers. She has lectured at Purdue

University; University of Illinois at Springfield; Brazosport College, Texas; and the University of Houston, Clear Lake. She is currently working on an encyclopedia of serial murder with Steven Egger. She received a B.A. in psychology from the University of Illinois at Springfield.

Steven A. Egger, Ph.D., is Professor Emeritus of Criminal Justice at the University of Illinois at Springfield and is Associate Professor of Criminology at the University of Houston, Clear Lake. He was formerly interim Dean at the University of Illinois and was Project Director of the Homicide Assessment and Lead Tracking System, the first statewide computerized system in the nation to track and identify serial killers. He has worked as a police officer, homicide investigator, police consultant, and law enforcement academy director. He is the author of *Serial Murder: An Elusive Phenomenon* (1990) and *The Killers Among Us: An Examination of Serial Murder and Its Investigation* (2nd ed., 2002) and was the editor for two different monograph series. He has written numerous articles, encyclopedia entries, and chapters and given many lectures and presented academic papers in the United States and in England, Spain, Canada, and the Netherlands. He has appeared on numerous national television networks and many local television and radio stations, in addition to giving numerous interviews in the print media around the world. He is currently coediting a book on police misconduct as well as continuing his research on serial murder. He holds an M.S. degree from Michigan State University and a Ph.D. from Sam Houston State University, where he completed the first dissertation in the world on serial murder.

Charles F. Emmons, Ph.D., is Professor of Sociology at Gettysburg College, Pennsylvania. Most of his publications have been in Chinese studies and in the sociology of religion and the paranormal. His books include *Chinese Ghosts and ESP: A Study of Paranormal Beliefs and Experiences, Hong Kong Prepares for 1997,* and *At the Threshold: UFOs, Science and the New Age.* He has also been a consultant for and appeared in popular television programs on apparition experiences. His recent research examines the spiritualist and new age movements. He received an M.A. in anthropology from the University of Illinois, Urbana, and a Ph.D. in sociology (1971) from the University of Illinois at Chicago.

Graves E. Enck, Ph.D., is Associate Professor of Sociology at the University of Memphis, where he has taught courses on medical sociology, sociology of mental illness, and sociology of aging since 1974. He served as Director of the Master of Arts in Liberal Studies Program from 1999 to 2002. He has published articles in professional journals and was a contributor to the *Encyclopedia of Criminology and Deviant Behavior* (2001). He serves on the editorial board of *Sociological Inquiry.* In his current research, he is conducting a long-term study of

changes in rural health care and other community institutions as a result of the legalization of casino gambling in the Mississippi Delta. He earned his Ph.D. at Yale University in 1975, having attended as a U.S. Public Health Service trainee in medical sociology.

Morten G. Ender, Ph.D., is Associate Professor of Sociology in the Department of Behavioral Sciences and Leadership at the U.S. Military Academy at West Point, where he teaches introductory sociology, sociological theory, and courses on cinematic images of war and on the Armed Forces and society. Prior to teaching West Point, he taught in Norway, at the University of North Dakota, and at the University of Maryland. An award-winning teacher at both the University of Maryland and at West Point, he has also taught a course on the sociology of death and dying through correspondence study for the past 8 years to over 200 undergraduate students. His research areas include military sociology, social psychology, and teaching sociology, with single and coauthored articles published in *The American Sociologist, Teaching Sociology,* the *Journal of Political and Military Sociology,* and *Armed Forces and Society.* He is currently investigating the representations of children of military personnel in American films—follow-up research to his 2002 book, *Military Brats and Other Global Nomads: Growing Up in Organization Families.* He earned his M.A. and Ph.D. from the University of Maryland at College Park.

Rhonda D. Evans, Ph.D., is Assistant Professor of Criminal Justice at the University of Louisiana at Lafayette. Her research interests are in the areas of crime, deviance, and gender. Her work has appeared in a number of journals, including *Sociological Spectrum* and *Sex Roles.* She received her doctorate in sociology from Texas A&M University in 2002.

David P. Fauri, Ph.D., is Professor of Social Work at Virginia Commonwealth University (VCU) where he teaches in the M.S.W. foundation, advanced concentration courses in administration and planning, the advanced standing M.S.W. program, doctoral program, and B.S.W. program. He has been at VCU for 20 years, having previously taught or served in administrative positions at the University of Tennessee, the University of Kentucky, and Southern Illinois University. He has served on the Board of the Council on Social Work Education, has been active in leadership for the National Association of Social Workers in Virginia and Tennessee, and has served and led mental health, public social services, Parents Anonymous, and United Way boards. His practice has included planning community programs for elders and staff work in training and management analysis. Topics of his recent writing include dying and caregiving by professionals, family, and volunteers; bereavement programming; and political participation of social workers. He is currently a member of the editorial board of *Arete.*

Robert M. "Bob" Fells, J.D., has worked on behalf of the cemetery and funeral services industry since 1975 and has served as General Counsel of the International Cemetery and Funeral Association (ICFA) for the past 20 years. Also for the past 4 years, he served as the Association's Chief Operating Officer, External Affairs. In addition to these duties, he serves as President and General Counsel of the ICFA Service Bureau, Inc., a for-profit subsidiary of the association, which administers the Credit Exchange Plan for prearranged cemetery lot purchases. He is also National Coordinator and Assistant Secretary of the Cemetery Consumer Service Council, an industry-sponsored consumer assistance organization. He is contributing editor for the *ICFA WIRELESS,* a biweekly e-mail newsletter that reviews important legal and regulatory developments affecting the industry. His news column, "The Washington Report," appears each month in the ICFA magazine, *International Cemetery & Funeral Management.* He is member of the Virginia State Bar and the U.S. Supreme Court Bar and has been listed in *Who's Who in American Law* and in *Who's Who Among Emerging Leaders in America.* He is a graduate of George Mason University School of Law.

Louis A. Gamino, Ph.D., ABPP, is a Diplomate in Clinical Psychology on staff with the Scott & White Clinic in Temple, Texas, since 1980. In addition to a clinical practice specializing in bereavement-related problems, he is an Associate Professor who teaches about death and dying at the Texas A&M Health Science Center College of Medicine. Together with Ann Cooney, he is the author of *When Your Baby Dies Through Miscarriage or Stillbirth* (2002). He is editor of *The Forum,* the official (quarterly) publication of the Association for Death Education and Counseling. He also conducts empirical research on the phenomenology of grieving, from which he is developing a model of adaptive bereavement. He received his doctorate from the University of Kansas.

DeAnn K. Gauthier, Ph.D., is Assistant Professor of Sociology in the Department of Sociology and Anthropology at the University of Louisiana at Lafayette. She is also editor in chief of *Sociological Spectrum,* the official journal of the Mid-South Sociological Association. Her interest areas include deviance, gender, criminology, and death and dying. Her work appears in journals such as *Criminology, Sex Roles,* and *Deviant Behavior.*

Francis D. Glamser, Ph.D., is Professor of Sociology and a former department chair at the University of Southern Mississippi. His research areas are social gerontology and the sociology of sport, and he has published articles in various journals, including the *Journal of Gerontology, The Gerontologist, Aging and Work,* the *Journal of Aging and Religion,* and the *Journal of Sport Behavior.* He earned an M.S. degree from Virginia Polytechnic Institute and a Ph.D. in sociology from the Pennsylvania State University.

Donald E. Gowan, Ph.D., is Emeritus Robert Cleveland Holland Professor of Old Testament at Pittsburgh Theological Seminary, where he served from 1964 to 1999. He worked as a mathematician for the General Electric Co. at the Hanford Atomic Products Operation in Richland, Washington, from 1951 to 1954. He participated in the excavation of Tel Ashdod, in Israel, in 1965 and 1968, and was a visiting scholar at Mansfield College, Oxford, in 1971–1972. He has published 10 books in Old Testament studies, is the editor of the new *Westminster Theological Wordbook of the Bible,* and was coeditor of the journal, *Horizons in Biblical Theology,* from 1990 to 1998. He earned a Ph.D. from the University of Chicago in 1964 and is an ordained minister in the Presbyterian Church (U.S.A.).

Robert O. Hansson, Ph.D., is Professor of Psychology at the University of Tulsa. His research interests focus on successful aging, aging families, and coping with bereavement and loss. With Margaret S. Stroebe and Wolfgang Stroebe, he coedited a special issue of the *Journal of Social Issues* on the topic of bereavement and widowhood (Fall 1988) and *The Handbook of Bereavement: Theory, Research, and Intervention* (1993). He also coedited (with Margaret S. Stroebe, Wolfgang Stroebe, and Henk Schut) *The Handbook of Bereavement Research: Consequences, Coping and Care* (2001). He coauthored (with Bruce Carpenter) *Relationships in Old Age* (1994). He is a Fellow of the Gerontological Society of America and serves on the editorial boards of *The International Journal of Aging & Human Development, Journal of Loss and Trauma,* and *Journal of Social & Personal Relationships.* He earned his Ph.D. in social psychology from the University of Washington in 1973.

William J. (Bill) Hauser, Ph.D., is currently a research and business intelligence consultant. Prior to that, he was the Senior Vice President and Director of Market Research and Planning at KeyCorp in Cleveland, Ohio. Before going to Key in 1999, he was the Director of Business Development and Research at Rubbermaid and its toy subsidiary, Little Tikes. He is also an adjunct professor at the University of Akron, where he teaches courses in death and dying, applied sociology, and rock and roll. In 2001, he was named the University of Akron, Buchtel College of Arts and Sciences, Part-time Teacher of the Year. His current research focuses on the role that communities play in dealing with traumatic events, such as disasters. Along with AnneMarie Scarisbrick-Hauser, he is currently preparing a handbook that communities can use in responding to disasters and their aftereffects. He earned a Ph.D. in sociology from the University of Akron in 1979 and has taught at Washington University in St. Louis and at West Virginia University.

Bert Hayslip, Jr., Ph.D., is Regents Professor of Psychology at the University of North Texas. He is a Fellow of the American Psychological Association, the

Gerontological Society of America, and the Association for Gerontology in Higher Education and has held research grants from the National Institute on Aging, the Hilgenfeld Foundation, and the National Endowment for the Humanities. He is currently associate editor of *Experimental Aging Research* and editor of the *International Journal of Aging and Human Development.* His published research deals with cognitive processes in aging, interventions to enhance cognitive functioning in later life, personality-ability interrelationships in aged persons, grandparents who raise their grandchildren, grief and bereavement, hospice care, death anxiety, and mental health and aging. He is coauthor of *Hospice Care* (Sage, 1992): *Psychology and Aging: An Annotated Bibliography* (1995); *Grandparents Raising Grandchildren: Theoretical, Empirical, and Clinical Perspectives* (2000); *Adult Development and Aging,* (3rd ed., 2002); *Working With Custodial Grandparents* (2002); and *Historical Shifts in Attitudes Toward Death, Dying, and Bereavement* (in press). He received his doctorate in experimental developmental psychology from the University of Akron in 1975.

Keith P. Jacobi, Ph.D., is Assistant Professor of Physical Anthropology at the University of Alabama and Curator of Human Osteology at the Alabama Museum of Natural History at the University of Alabama. His work on human skeletal remains spans over 25 years. His academic interests include skeletal biology, paleopathology, forensic anthropology, dental anthropology, medical anthropology, history of disease and medicine, and dermatoglyphics. He has been a forensic consultant for the Alabama Department of Forensic Sciences since 1996 and on contract with the department since 2000. His research work currently involves archaic and Mississippian period warfare among Native Americans in northern Alabama, dental morphology, and dental metrics at the prehistoric site of Moundville, health in Alabama as seen through skeletal remains from early 19th-century cemeteries, and the health of the historic Chickasaw. He has published articles on the health of Barbadian slaves at Newton Plantation and the historic Maya from Tipu, Belize. His book *Last Rites of the Tipu Maya* (2000) is on the dental genetics of the historic Tipu Maya as well as prehistoric Maya. He was the recipient of the Indiana University Medical Sciences Teaching Award. He earned a Ph.D. in anthropology from Indiana University in 1996.

Kelly A. Joyce, Ph.D., is Assistant Professor in the Department of Sociology at the College of William and Mary. Her current research examines perceptions of medical imaging technologies in the United States, investigating why these techniques occupy a privileged space in contemporary medical practice. She publishes primarily in the fields of medical sociology and science and technology studies. She earned a Ph.D. in sociology from Boston College.

Jack Kamerman, Ph.D., is Professor of Sociology at Kean University in Union, New Jersey. He is the author of

Death in the Midst of Life: Social and Cultural Influences on Death, Grief, and Mourning (currently being revised), coeditor of *Performers and Performances: The Social Organization of Artistic Work,* and editor of *Negotiating Responsibility in the Criminal Justice System.* He has served as a consultant on suicide and occupational stress for New York City's Emergency Medical Services and was a member of a committee on suicide prevention at the New York City Police Department. He is currently working on a comparative study of the New York and Vienna Philharmonics during the directorship of Gustav Mahler. He received a Ph.D. in sociology from New York University.

Robert Kastenbaum, Ph.D., is a psychologist with a cross-disciplinary approach who has been active as a clinician, researcher, program developer, and educator with particular attention to gerontology, thanatology, and creativity, and Professor Emeritus at Arizona State University. He directed the first major study of the terminal phase of life in a geriatric hospital where he also introduced wine, beer, and relationship therapy programs that inspired other programs across the nation. A past President of the American Association of Suicidology, he served for many years as editor of *Omega: Journal of Death and Dying,* and *International Journal of Death and Dying.* His books include *The Psychology of Death; Death, Society, & Human Experience; Defining Acts: Aging as Drama; Dorian, Graying: Is Youth the Only Thing Worth Having?* and the forthcoming *On Our Way: The Final Passage Through Life and Death.* He and his wife Beatrice edited the first modern *Encyclopedia of Death* (1989/1993), and he served as editor of the new *Macmillan Encyclopedia of Death and Dying* (2002). His interest in music has been expressed in libretti and lyrics for the operas *Dorian, Closing Time,* and *American Gothic* and the musicals *Outlaw Heart,* and *Parlor Game.*

Michael C. Kearl, Ph.D., is Professor and Chair of the Department of Sociology & Anthropology at Trinity University in San Antonio, Texas. He publishes and teaches in the areas of social gerontology, thanatology, social psychology, family, the sociology of knowledge, and the sociology of time. His works feature titles such as *Endings: A Sociology of Death and Dying,* "You Never Have to Die! On Mormons, NDEs, Cryonics and the American Immortalist Ethos" (in *The Unknown Country: Experiences of Death in Australia, Britain and the USA,* edited by Charmaz, Howarth, and Kellehear), and "Political Uses of the Dead as Symbols in Contemporary Civil Religions" (in *Social Forces*). An early explorer of the pedagogical potential of the Internet, he is perhaps best known for his Web site "A Sociological Tour Through Cyberspace." He holds a Ph.D. in sociology from Stanford University.

Thomas A. Kolditz, Ph.D., is Professor and Head of the Department of Behavioral Sciences and Leadership at the

U.S. Military Academy at West Point, New York. An Army officer with more than 20 years of active service, his research and teaching activities span applied social psychology, personality, mentoring dynamics, and leadership development. He has published across a diverse array of academic and military journals, including *Military Review,* the *Journal of Personality and Social Psychology, Field Artillery Professional Journal,* the *Journal of Personality,* and *Perception and Psychophysics.* He holds a master's degree and Ph.D. degree in social psychology from the University of Missouri. He has also received a master of military arts and science degree from the School of Advanced Military Studies at Fort Leavenworth, Kansas, and a master's in strategic studies from the Army War College at Carlisle Barracks, Pennsylvania.

Pamela J. Kovacs, Ph.D., is Associate Professor of Social Work at Virginia Commonwealth University where she teaches social work practice and research in the undergraduate, master's, and doctoral programs. She worked as a clinical social worker for 15 years in a variety of settings, including hospice, oncology, prenatal, and other health care positions, as well as community mental health, private practice, and a college counseling center. She joined the faculty at Virginia Commonwealth in 1996. Her scholarship and service have focused on chronic illness and end-of-life care, in particular, the hospice response to HIV/AIDS, hospice volunteers, the patient, family, and professional caregiver experience of living with chronic and terminal illness, as well as how best to prepare social workers to assist persons with these life challenges. Between 1997 and 2001, she served as an evaluation mentor for the Promoting Excellence in End-of-Life Care grantees, programs funded by the Robert Wood Johnson Foundation. She is a consulting editor for *Health and Social Work.* She earns an M.S.W. from Boston College and a Ph.D. in social welfare from Florida International University.

Peter Lacovara, Ph.D., is Curator of Ancient Egyptian, Nubian, and Near Eastern Art at the Michael C. Carlos Museum of Emory University in Atlanta, Georgia. Previously, he was Assistant Curator in the Department of Ancient Egyptian, Nubian, and Near Eastern Art in the Museum of Fine Arts, Boston. He has excavated extensively in Egypt and has written on the mortuary archaeology of ancient Egypt and organized a number of exhibitions and symposia around that theme. He received his Ph.D. in Egyptian archaeology from the University of Chicago.

Vicki L. Lamb, Ph.D., is a Research Scientist at the Center for Demographic Studies, Duke University. Her former appointments were at Johnson C. Smith University and the University of South Carolina. She has numerous publications on measures of health and disability, particularly of older adults. The National Institute on Aging/National Institute of Health has funded her most recent research project on "Foods Programs and Nutritional Support of the Elderly." She is an associate editor of *Population Research and Policy Review* (Southern Demographic Association) and a member of the Scientific Review Board for *Demographic Research* (Max Planck Institute for Demographic Research). She received her Ph.D. in sociology from Duke University in 1992, with concentrations in demography of aging and life course studies.

David Lester, Ph.D., is Professor of Psychology at the Richard Stockton College of New Jersey. He is a former President of the International Association for Suicide Prevention and has written 2,000 scholarly articles and notes, mostly on thanatology, with a special focus on suicide. His latest books are *Fixin' to Die: A Compassionate Guide to Committing Suicide or Staying Alive* and *Katie's Diary: Unlocking the Mystery of the Suicidal Mind.* He has doctorates in psychology (Brandeis University) and social and political science (Cambridge University, UK).

Eric Lichten, Ph.D., is Professor of Sociology and chairs the Department of Sociology and Anthropology at Long Island University, C.W. Post Campus, where he has taught since 1981. He is a recipient of Long Island University's Trustee Award for Scholarly Achievement for his book *Class, Power & Austerity: The New York City Fiscal Crisis* (1986) and has published numerous articles in professional journals and publications. He has also received Long Island University's David Newton Award for Teaching Excellence and an "award of excellence" for "his outstanding contribution to the training of pediatric residents and health care providers" from the Child Development Center at North Shore University Hospital (Long Island, New York) and Project D.O.C.C. (Delivery of Chronic Care). His current research concerns the social problems associated with children's chronic and terminal illnesses.

J. Robert Lilly, Ph.D., is Regents Professor of Sociology/Criminology and Adjunct Professor of Law at Northern Kentucky University. His research interests include the patterns of capital crimes committed by U.S. soldiers during World War II, the "commercial corrections complex," juvenile delinquency, house arrest and electronic monitoring, criminal justice in the People's Republic of China, sociology of law, and criminological theory. He has published in a number of journals, including *Criminology, Crime & Delinquency, Journal of Drug Issues, Social Problems, Qualitative Sociology,* and the *British Journal of Criminology.* He is coauthor (with Richard A. Ball and C. Ronald Huff) of *House Arrest and Correctional Policy: Doing Time at Home* (Sage, 1988) and coauthor (with Francis T. Cullent and Richard A. Ball) of *Criminological Theory: Context and Consequences* (3rd ed; Sage, 2002). In 2003, he published *La Face cachée des GI's: Les viòls commis par des soldats américains en France, en Angleterre et en Allemagne pendant la Seconde Guerre mondiale* [The Hidden Face of the GI's: The Rapes

Committed by the American Soldiers in France, England and Germany During the Second World War]. In 1988, he was a visiting professor in the School of Law at DeMonfort University, Leister, England, and a visiting scholar at All Soul's College, Oxford University. Since 1992, he has been a visiting professor at the University of Durham, England. He received in Ph.D. in sociology from the University of Tennessee in 1975.

Janice Harris Lord, M.S.S.W., is a consultant for a number of crime victim organizations and serves as a media representative for victims. She is certified in thanatology (CT) by the Association of Death Education and Counseling and is a member of the International Association of Traumatic Stress Studies and the American Association of Pastoral Counselors. She has worked in the crime victims' movement since 1976 and was National Director of Victim Services for Mothers Against Drunk Driving for 14 years. She has written two books for the popular market—*No Time for Goodbyes: Coping With Sorrow, Anger, and Injustice After a Tragic Death* and *Beyond Sympathy: How to Help Another Through Injury, Illness, or Loss*—and has published many journal articles, curricula pieces, brochures, booklets, research reports, and other works. She served as editor of *MADDVOCATE,* a magazine for victims and their advocates, for 11 years and is a founding Advisory Board member of the National Institute of Victim Studies at Sam Houston State University. In 1994, she received the U.S. Presidential Award for Outstanding Service on Behalf of Victims of Crime from President Bill Clinton and U.S. Attorney General, Janet Reno. She received her M.S.S.W. degree from University of Texas at Arlington and is a licensed social worker and professional counselor.

Vicky M. MacLean, Ph.D., is Associate Professor of Sociology at Middle Tennessee State University where she teaches courses in social theory, qualitative research methods, community studies, and race/class/gender. She is currently researching the impact of innovative educational interventions on the development of health resiliency among adolescent African American, Latina, and Anglo females. Additional interests include neighborhood development and diversity issues, health care access, and the development of American sociology. She has taught sociology at Wake Forest University, Mary Washington College, and for the graduate federation of the North Texas University system. She has worked as an applied sociologist for the Federal Women's Program of the National Institutes of Environmental Health Sciences, the U.S. General Accounting Office, and the Texas Woman's University Institute for Women's Health. She has published on compensation, careers in science, and gender. She received her M.A. and Ph.D. degrees in sociology from Duke University.

Stephanie Picolo Manzi, Ph.D., is Assistant Professor of Criminal Justice in the School of Justice Studies at Roger Williams University. Her current research interests include policing and theories of crime causation. She has written several articles on women in policing and is serving as the research analyst for Project Safe Neighborhoods, a federally funded project designed to reduce gun violence. She is also an associate editor for *Criminal Justice Policy Review.* She received her M.A. and Ph.D. in criminology from the University of Maryland, College Park.

Alan H. Marks, Ph.D., is Professor and past Chair of the Department of Sociology, Anthropology and Gerontology at the University of Arkansas at Little Rock. He is cofounder and has served as Vice Chairman of the Arkansas Youth Suicide Prevention Commission since 1985. He also served as a scientific adviser to the National Lieutenant Governor's Association from 1985 to 1988, helping to create and participating in a video and educational materials distributed nationally. He created a high school curriculum on youth suicide prevention that has been used in Arkansas. In 1990, he won the University of Arkansas at Little Rock's Excellence Award in Public Service for his work in Youth Suicide Prevention and with the elderly. He received national news coverage when he assisted the police in Shreveport, Louisiana, in preventing a suicide by talking a man off a bridge, an event that occurred when he and the Lt. Governor of Arkansas were in Shreveport doing a radio show on suicide prevention. He and a former student, who was elected to the Arkansas Legislature, were responsible for the enactment of the Intergenerational Security Act of 1995.

John L. McIntosh, Ph.D., is Chair of and Professor in the Department of Psychology at Indiana University South Bend. He is the author, coauthor, or coeditor of six published books on suicide, including *Suicide and Its Aftermath: Understanding and Counseling the Survivors* (1987) and *Elder Suicide: Research, Theory and Treatment* (1994). He has contributed chapters to many books and articles to numerous professional journals and has made over 100 presentations at professional conferences. He also serves on the editorial boards of *Suicide & Life-Threatening Behavior, Gerontology and Geriatrics Education,* and *Crisis: The Journal of Crisis Intervention and Suicide Prevention.* He is also on the National Advisory Board of the Yellow Ribbon Suicide Prevention Program and is a past President of the American Association of Suicidology (AAS). He was the 1990 recipient of the AAS's prestigious Edwin Shneidman Award (awarded to a person below the age of 40 for scholarly contributions in research to the field of suicidology) and the 1999 recipient of AAS's Roger Tierney Award for Service. He has also been recognized by his university with awards for teaching, service, and research. His work has been reported in newspapers and magazines across the country. He received his doctorate degree from the University of Notre Dame.

Jerry T. McKnight, M.D., is Professor in the Department of Family Medicine at the University of Alabama School of Medicine–Tuscaloosa. His primary interest is training physicians for service to underserved populations. After completing his National Health Service Scholarship obligation in Tennessee, he returned to the University of Alabama–Tuscaloosa Family Practice Residency where he has spent 12 years in the training of family medicine residents in minimizing medical errors. He has been published in 18 different professional journals, manuals, and books. He received his M.D. from the University of Tennessee College of Medicine–Memphis and completed his residency at the University of Alabama–Tuscaloosa Family Practice Residency.

Stephen J. McNamee, Ph.D., is Professor of Sociology at the University of North Carolina at Wilmington. He has served as Chair of the Department of Sociology and Criminal Justice at UNC Wilmington and is the recipient of the UNC Wilmington Distinguished Teaching Award and the UNC Board of Governors Award for Teaching Excellence. His research interests include stratification, theory, and organizations. He coedited *Wealth and Inheritance in America* with Robert K. Miller, Jr., and they are completing another book, *The Meritocracy Myth.* He received his M.A. and Ph.D. degrees in sociology from the University of Illinois at Urbana–Champaign.

Robert K. Miller, Jr., Ph.D., is Professor of Sociology at the University of North Carolina at Wilmington, where he serves as Assistant Chair of the Department of Sociology and Criminal Justice. His research interests include stratification and racial and ethnic group relations. He coedited *Wealth and Inheritance in America* with Stephen J. McNamee, and they are completing another book, *The Meritocracy Myth.* He received his M.A. and Ph.D. in sociology from Temple University.

Calvin Conzelus Moore, J.D., Ph.D., is Visiting Assistant Professor of Sociology and Anthropology at Bowdoin College. Prior to pursuing his Ph.D., he practiced criminal defense law in the District of Columbia. His current research focuses on determining structural correlates of violent crime. He earned his law degree from Harvard Law School and his Ph.D. from Boston College.

James L. Moore III, Ph.D., is Assistant Professor in Counselor Education in the School of Physical Activity and Educational Services at Ohio State University. His research agenda is centered on black male issues, academic persistence and achievement, cross-cultural counseling issues in schools, counseling student athletes, and using innovative technological approaches in counselor education. He is currently working to use his research and scholarship to shape state and national public policy as it relates to preparing highly competent school counselors, improving the overall quality of school counseling, developing interventions and programs for improving the academic persistence and achievement of African American students and other people of color in public schools and higher education, and advancing the mission of the academy in the areas of teaching, service, and scholarship/research.

Robin D. Moremen, Ph.D., is Associate Professor of Sociology at Northern Illinois University. She is also a Faculty Associate in Gerontology and Women's Studies and has received numerous awards for excellence in undergraduate teaching. Her research interests include health and aging, complex organizations, HIV/AIDS, death and dying, women's health issues, and social inequality. She has published on Medicare admissions to nursing homes, the effects of third-party payers on clinical decision making, long-term care and AIDS, multicultural curriculum transformation, gender discrimination after death, and women's friendships and health. She is past Teaching Chair of the Medical Sociology Section of the American Sociological Association. Currently, she is a member of the Provost's Task Force on Multicultural Curriculum Transformation (Northern Illinois University), Undergraduate Director in the Department of Sociology (Northern Illinois University), and a nationally certified hospice volunteer. She received an M.A. degree in physical therapy from Stanford University, and M.A and Ph.D. degrees in sociology from Yale University.

John D. Morgan, Ph.D., a pioneer in the death awareness movement, brings to the podium a wide range of topics in the field of death and bereavement drawn from his work as educator, author, lecturer, and program organizer. He is presently the Program Manager of the London Ontario Grief Resource Centre, and Coordinating Secretary of Bereavement Ontario Network. In 1997, he received an award from the Association for Death Education and Counseling for his work in death education. He has spoken extensively throughout the world, has edited 18 books, and is series editor for the Death, Value, and Meaning Series, which now has over 50 volumes. His most recent project (with Dr. Pittu Laungani) is *Death and Bereavement Around the World* (five volumes). He holds a Ph.D. in philosophy from the University of Southern California.

Harold Mytum, Ph.D., is Reader in the Department of Archaeology at the University of York and for 5 years was head of the department. A major research interest is that of mortuary archaeology, with particular emphasis on historic burials and monuments. He has carried out and published fieldwork on graveyard memorials from England, Wales, Ireland, and Gibraltar. Present graveyard research is concentrated in Ireland and Wales through his Castell Henllys Field School, which is open to international students. He has also developed the methodology of graveyard recording and published *Recording and Analysing Graveyards* in 2000. He serves as archaeologist on the York Diocesan Advisory Committee responsible for the care of over 600 churches and churchyards in the diocese.

Robert A. Neimeyer, Ph.D., holds a Dunavant University Professorship in the Department of Psychology, University of Memphis, where he also maintains an active clinical practice. Since completing his doctoral training at the University of Nebraska in 1982, he has conducted extensive research on the topics of death, grief, loss, and suicide intervention. Neimeyer has published 18 books, including *Meaning Reconstruction and the Experience of Loss; Lessons of Loss: A Guide to Coping;* and *Dying: Facing the Facts.* The author of over 200 articles and book chapters, he is currently working to advance a more adequate theory of grieving as a meaning-making process. Neimeyer is the editor of the respected international journal *Death Studies* and has served as President of the Association for Death Education and Counseling (1996–1997). In recognition of his scholarly contributions, he has been granted the Distinguished Research Award (1990), the Distinguished Teaching Award (1999), and the Eminent Faculty Award (2002) by the University of Memphis, elected Chair of the International Work Group on Death, Dying, and Bereavement (1993), designated Psychologist of the Year by the Tennessee Psychological Association (1996), made a Fellow of the Clinical Psychology Division of the American Psychological Association (1997), and been given the Research Recognition Award by the Association for Death Education and Counseling (1999).

Pat Norton, Ed.D., is Program Director for the Introduction to Clinical Medicine course at the University of Alabama School of Medicine in Birmingham, Alabama (UASOM). After completing a master's degree in library science, her position was the Medical Education Coordinator within the Department of Family Medicine in the University of Alabama School of Medicine–Tuscaloosa Program. In addition to curriculum development and grant writing with the Family Medicine Department, she was placed in charge of the Standardized Patient program and assisted in clinical skills assessment activities. In her current position, she continues to participate in curriculum development as well as serving as the Director of the UASOM Standardized Patient program, providing patients for teaching, assessment, and research activities within the School of Medicine.

Paul David Nygard, Ph.D., is Associate Professor and Chair of the Social and Behavioral Sciences Department at St. Louis Community College–Florissant Valley Campus. His writings have appeared in several publications, including the *Illinois Historical Journal* and *The Encyclopedia of New England Culture.* He is President of the St. Louis Area Historical Association and a 2002 recipient of an Emerson Excellence in Teaching Award. He received an M.A. in history from Southern Illinois University Edwardsville and a Ph.D. from St. Louis University.

Ann M. Palkovich, Ph.D., is Krasnow Associate Professor at the Krasnow Institute of George Mason University. She is a biological anthropologist interested in the evolution of hominid cognition, prehistoric population dynamics, and the cultural dynamics of cemeteries. She holds an M.A. and Ph.D. from Northwestern University.

Brian Parsons, Ph.D., has worked in the funeral industry in London since 1982. His doctoral research focused on the impact of change during the 20th century on the funeral industry. He has contributed to *The Manual of Funeral Directing,* to numerous industry periodicals, and to the journal *Mortality.* He is the author of *The London Way of Death* (2000) and is active in funeral service education. He received his Ph.D. from the University of Westminster (London).

Carolyn Pevey, Ph.D., is Assistant Professor of Sociology at Auburn University–Montgomery. Her research and teaching interests include medical sociology, thanatology, gender, and religion. Currently, she is using a new faculty grant in aid to explore premenstrual syndrome among health care workers. An edited and greatly improved version of her master's thesis "Male God Imagery and Female Submission: Lessons From a Southern Baptist Ladies' Bible Class" was published with Christine Williams and Christopher Ellison in *Qualitative Sociology.* She received an M.A. from the University of Texas at Austin in 1993 and a Ph.D. from the University of Texas at Austin in 2001.

Anantanand Rambachan, Ph.D., is Professor or Religion, Philosophy and Asian Studies at St. Olaf College in Northfield, Minnesota. He is the author of several books, book chapters, and numerous articles and reviews in scholarly journals. Among these are *Accomplishing the Accomplished: The Vedas as a Source of Valid Knowledge in Shankara* and *The Limits of Scripture: Vivekananda's Reinterpretation of the Authority of the Vedas, The Hindu Vision, Gitamrtam,* and *Similes of the Bhagavadgita.* He has been very active in the dialogue programs of the World Council of Churches and was Hindu guest and participant in the last three General Assemblies of the World Council of Churches in Vancouver, Canada; Canberra, Australia; and Harare, Zimbabwe. He is a regular participant in the meetings of the Pontifical Council for Interreligious Dialogue at the Vatican. He is an associate editor for the *Encyclopedia of Hinduism,* a project that is working to produce the first, comprehensive, multivolume series treating the Hindu tradition. He is also a member of Consultation on Population and Ethics, a nongovernmental organization affiliated with the United Nations.

Jon K. Reid, Ph.D., is Professor and Chair of the Department of Behavioral Sciences at Southeastern Oklahoma State University in Durant, Oklahoma. He is a member of the 2002–2003 Outstanding Professor's Academy for Oklahoma Colleges and Universities and holds Texas licenses as a professional counselor, a marriage and family therapist, and a Certificate in Thanatology from the Association for Death Education and Counseling. He is an ordained Unitarian Universalist minister. Previous professional experiences include serving as a minister of single adults and as an outpatient therapist. He has led grief support groups in public schools, churches, and hospitals and is the bereavement consultant for Camp Fire for Boys and Girls in his community. He has been published in *Death Studies; Illness, Crises, and Loss; School Psychology International;* and the *Journal of Personal and Interpersonal Loss.* He completed a doctorate in family studies at Texas Woman's University in Denton, Texas, and a master's degree in religious education at Southwestern Baptist Theological Seminary in Fort Worth, Texas.

Catherine H. Reilly, M.A., is Assistant Professor and Reference Librarian at St. Louis Community College–Florissant Valley campus. She has presented on the subject of death in America at several professional gatherings throughout the United States and is also a founding member of the St. Louis Chapter of the Jane Austen Society of North America. She received a B.A. in history from the University of Missouri–St. Louis and an M.A. in library science from the University of Missouri–Columbia and is in the American Culture Studies program at Washington University in St. Louis.

Russell B. Riddle, M.S., is a doctoral student in counseling psychology at the University of North Texas. His interests focus on determinants of adjustment to the funeral as a ritual. He currently serves as research director for the psychology unit at Scottish Rite Children's Hospital in Dallas, Texas.

Tillman Rodabough, Ph.D., is Professor and Graduate Program Director in the Department of Sociology at Baylor University. He is also the Research Director for the Baylor Center for Community Research and Development. Active in the field of sociology, he is past President of the Southwestern Sociological Association and is currently President-elect of the Society for Applied Sociology. For the past 25 years, he has conducted research and published in the area of death and dying as well as in applied sociology. His current work in developing a Ph.D. program with emphases in applied sociology and in sociology of religion allows him to integrate both interests. Currently, he is examining through survey research and focus groups the efficacy and changing attitudes toward capital punishment, as well as the impact of different aspects of religiosity on the fear of death specifically as it relates to war and the threat of terrorism.

Jerome Rosenberg, Ph.D., is Associate Professor in the Department of Psychology and the New College Program at the University of Alabama. He teaches and conducts research in the areas of the Holocaust and genocide, human destructiveness and dehumanization, traumatic stress, humane survival, and ethics. He is a charter member of the Association of Genocide Scholars. He has served as Chair of the Alabama Holocaust Advisory Council and is currently a member of the Alabama Holocaust Commission. He has worked with Holocaust survivors and has served on the Hospice of West Alabama Ethical Review Board. He teaches in the University of Alabama Thanatology Certificate Program and serves on its planning board. He has published on the issues of dehumanization and the Holocaust. He received his Ph.D. from Florida State University in clinical psychology.

Paul C. Rosenblatt, Ph.D., is Morse-Alumni Distinguished Teaching Professor of Family Social Science at the University of Minnesota. His writing on bereavement includes five books and dozens of articles. With Beverly Wallace, he is working on an interview project dealing with African American bereavement, and with Sungeun Yang he is working on a paper on how Korean families deal with terminal illness.

Jeffrey P. Rosenfeld, Ph.D., writes on the social dynamics of inheritance, disinheritance, and will contests. Apart from writing, he has consulted to the estate tax area, statistics of income, at the Internal Revenue Service, and to the estate-planning industry. In recent years, he has become interested in the financial abuse and exploitation of older people. He is currently funded by the Bar Foundation of the State of New York to develop an elder abuse resource center to facilitate the detection and prevention of elder abuse (including financial abuse).

Diana Royer, Ph.D., is Professor of English at Miami University. Her most recent book is *A Critical Study of the Works of Nawal El Saadawi, Egyptian Writer and Activist* (2001). She has coedited anthologies on the commercialization and appropriation of American Indian cultures and on regional women writers, and currently, she is coauthoring a volume of horror film criticism. She has written articles, book chapters, and conference papers on Virginia Woolf, horror cinema, and death in 19th-century American literature. She serves as a manuscript referee for the *Woolf Studies Annual.* She holds an M.A. and a Ph.D. in English from Temple University.

Jerome J. Salomone, Ph.D., is Dean Emeritus of the College of Arts and Sciences at Southeastern Louisiana University in Hammond, Louisiana. He presently serves as Professor of Sociology and Scholar-in-Residence. He has previously taught at Louisiana State University, Nicholls State University, and the University of New Orleans, and he has held research appointments at Ohio State University. His professional involvements, among many others, have included serving as President of the Mid-South Sociological Association, editor of *Sociological Spectrum,* and member of the board of the Louisiana Endowment for the Humanities, which he chaired for 2 years. The Mid-South Sociological Association has honored him with its Career Achievement Award. His written work appears widely in a variety of sources, including *Phylon, Rural Sociology, Sociological Spectrum,* and *Philosophy and Social Science.* His book *Bread and Respect: The Italians of Louisiana* was published in 2002. He did his graduate work at Louisiana State University where he received his master's and doctorate degrees in sociology.

AnneMarie Scarisbrick-Hauser, Ph.D., is Senior Vice President of Client Information and Relationship Management at KeyCorp in Cleveland, Ohio. Prior to coming to KeyCorp in 1999, Anne was the Associate Director of the Survey Research Center at the University of Akron. She is also an adjunct professor at the University of Akron, where she teaches courses in collective behavior and emergency management. Her current research focuses on the role of human factors in dealing with traumatic events, such as disasters. In 2001, Anne was part of a select team sent to Somerset, Pennsylvania, immediately after the September 11 tragedy to observe how emergency workers responded to the traumatic situation. Along with Bill Hauser, she is currently preparing a handbook that communities can use in responding to disasters and their after-effects. She earned a Ph.D. in sociology from the University of Akron in 1991, along with degrees from the University of Limerick (Ireland) and Purdue University.

Ruben Schindler, Ph.D., is the Dean of Ashkelon College, associated with Bar Ilan University in Israel. Previously, he served as Dean of Students at Bar Ilan University. He is a founding member of the School of Social Work at Bar Ilan and served as Dean of the school for almost a decade. His research in social work education has taken him to India, where together with Alan Brawley, he wrote the book *Social Care at the Front Line* (1987). Over the years, he has published widely, exploring the interface between the secular and the sacred and Jewish and social science literature in assisting people facing crises and trauma. Prior to his current post, he spent his sabbatical at the Rutgers School of Social Work. He was raised and educated in New York and attended the City College of New York and Columbia University School of Social Work. He earned his doctorate from the Wurzwelier School of Work, Yeshiva University. He was ordained for the rabbinate by Rabbi Moshe Feinstein, a leading 20th-century scholar known for his seminal Talmudic responsa and piety.

Clive Seale, Ph.D., is Professor of Sociology in the Department of Human Sciences, Brunel University, London. His research focuses on topics in medical sociology, including work on the experience of dying and the popular media representation of illness, health, and health care. He is author or editor of numerous books, including *The Year Before Death* (1994); *Researching Society and Culture* (Sage, 1998); *Constructing Death: The Sociology of Dying and Bereavement* (1998); *Health and Disease: A Reader* (2001); *The Quality of Qualitative Research* (Sage, 1999); *Media and Health* (Sage, 2002); *Social Research Methods: A Reader* (in press); *Qualitative Research Practice* (Sage, in press).

Trina N. Seitz, Ph.D., is Assistant Professor of Sociology at Appalachian State University in Boone, North Carolina. Her professional experience includes having served 9 years as a patrol officer with the Wake County Sheriff's Department and as a death row correctional officer at the North Carolina Correctional Institution for Women. Her research interests are in the areas of the death penalty as well as extralegal social control, specifically throughout North Carolina's history. She recently submitted an article to the *North Carolina Historical Review* that examined the social and political factors that affected the state's shift in execution methods during the first three decades of the 20th century. She is a member of the North Carolina Criminal Justice Association, the American Correctional Association, the Academy of Criminal Justice Sciences, and the North Carolina Literary and Historical Society. She received her Ph.D. in sociology from Virginia Polytechnic Institute and State University, where she specialized in criminology and deviant behavior.

Kenneth W. Sewell, Ph.D., is Professor of Psychology and Director of Clinical Training at the University of North Texas. He has authored dozens of journal articles and book chapters in the areas of posttraumatic stress, psychotherapy, constructivism, bereavement, and forensic assessment. He has studied posttraumatic stress in combat veterans, sexual assault survivors, mass murder witnesses, and women diagnosed with HIV. Stemming from his work with trauma survivors, he was a collaborator in the development of the Scott & White Grief Project. This multiphase program of research is dedicated to understanding how some bereaved persons struggle with distressing symptoms for years following a loss and others seem to undergo transformative personal growth. He received his Ph.D. in clinical psychology from the University of Kansas in 1991, which included an internship with the Department of Veterans Affairs.

Donald J. Shoemaker, Ph.D., is Professor of Sociology at Virginia Polytechnic Institute and State University. His research interests include international studies of delinquency, theoretical studies of delinquency, Philippine studies, and evaluation research. In 1990, he received a Fulbright grant to study patterns of juvenile justice in the Philippines. His publications include *Theories of Delinquency* (a 5th edition is in preparation), *International Handbook on Juvenile Justice* (editor), and numerous article and book chapters on crime and delinquency. He is currently on the editorial board of the *Philippine Journal of Law and Justice* and the *Journal of Research in Crime and Delinquency.* He received a Ph.D. in sociology from the University of Georgia in 1970.

Sangeeta Singg, Ph.D., is Professor of Psychology and Director of the Graduate Counseling Psychology Program at the Angelo State University, San Angelo, Texas. She is also a licensed psychologist in the State of Texas and has practiced and taught psychology for over 20 years. She has xl • HANDBOOK OF DEATH AND DYING

published in the areas of counseling training, student personal responsibility, childhood sexual abuse, self-esteem, posttraumatic stress disorder, depression, color preference and color therapy, memory, alternative methods of healing, grief, and suicide. She received an M.A. in sociology from Mississippi State University and M.S. and Ph.D. degrees in psychology from Texas A&M University–Commerce.

William E. Snizek, Ph.D., is Distinguished Professor of Sociology at Virginia Polytechnic Institute and State University. Prior to coming to Virginia Tech in 1972, he taught at the University of South Florida and Western Kentucky University. During his tenure at Virginia Tech, he has won over 25 departmental, college, university, state, national, and international teaching awards. These include 10 Certificates of Teaching Excellence from the College of Arts and Sciences, the university's W. E. Wine Award, Alumni Teaching Award, Diggs Teaching Scholar Award, and the Commonwealth of Virginia's 1991 Outstanding Faculty Award. In 2001, he received the Delta Gamma Foundation Award for University Excellence in Teaching. He has been a Visiting Professor and Senior Research Fulbright Fellow at the University of Leiden, The Netherlands and has been employed as a consultant by numerous government business and labor groups. He has coedited five books and published over 75 refereed articles and notes in journals such as the *American Sociological Review, Social Forces, Academy of Management Review, Journal of Applied Behavioral Science, Organizational Behavior and Human Performance, Human Relations,* and *Organizational Studies.* He received his master's and doctoral degrees from The Pennsylvania State University.

Alan E. Stewart, Ph.D., is Assistant Professor in the Department of Counseling and Human Development at the University of Georgia. From 1997 to 2002, he was Assistant Professor of psychology at the University of Florida. He has established his line of research in the areas of death, loss, and trauma. Specific interests within these areas involve death notification following fatal vehicular crashes, death notification training, and the psychological effects of surviving serious crashes. He also has interests in measurement and evaluation and has created several scales for use with people who have experienced crashes: the Driving and Riding Avoidance Scale and the Driving and Riding Cautiousness Scale. Finally, he has research interests in family emotional processes and the ways in which language can be used to characterize one's family of origin experiences or to construct healing narratives in the aftermath of a trauma. He received his Ph.D. in counseling psychology from the University of Georgia in 1994 and has since completed postdoctoral training in counseling and psychotherapy at the HUB Counseling Center in Tucker, Georgia. He also completed research postdoctoral training in psychology at the University of Memphis.

Dawood H. Sultan, Ph.D., is Assistant Professor of Sociology in the Department of Sociology, Anthropology, Social Work and Criminal Justice at the University of Tennessee at Martin. From August 1998 to June 2003, he served as an instructor in the Department of Sociology at Louisiana State University (LSU). From August 2001 to May 2003, he also served as Assistant Director of International Development in the Office of International Programs at LSU. In 1999, he was selected by the University of Nebraska–Lincoln (UNL) as the recipient of its Multicultural Teaching Fellowship Award and, subsequently, spent part of the summer teaching at UNL's Department of Sociology. He is fluent in Arabic, has traveled extensively, and is published in a number of professional journals. He was born and raised in Sudan and received a B.Sc. (Hon.) in economics from the University of Gezira (Sudan) and an M.A. in development studies from the University of East Anglia (England). In 1996, he received a doctorate degree in sociology from LSU.

Hikaru Suzuki, Ph.D., is Assistant Professor of Anthropology at the School of Economics and Social Sciences at Singapore Management University. She is the author of *The Price of Death: The Funeral Industry in Contemporary Japan* (2001). This work investigates the transformation and professionalization of funeral practices in Japan. Her future research interests include the impact of globalization and marketing on everyday practices, medical institutions and professionals, the expansion of Internet recruitment systems, and the professionalization/ transformation of working culture. Prior to her appointment at Singapore Management University, she was a Freeman postdoctoral student at Wittenberg University. She received a B.A. from Beijing University, M.A. and Ph.D. degrees from Harvard University, and an M.B.A. from the University of Wisconsin–Madison.

Michael R. Taylor, Ph.D., is Associate Professor in the Department of Philosophy at Oklahoma State University, where he teaches Death and Dying, Holocaust Studies, Metaphysics and Epistemology, and Philosophy of Life. Before coming to Oklahoma State University, he held a temporary appointment as an Adjunct Assistant Professor in the Department of Philosophy at Bowling Green State University, where he taught Death and Dying and Philosophy of the Development of Persons. He has also held positions as a counselor, as coordinator of a tri-county mental health emergency service, and as Associate Director of the George F. Linn Center, a public mental health center in Ohio. His primary areas of research are social and political philosophy and ethics. He has publications in *Southwestern Philosophical Review, Proteus: A Journal of Ideas,* and *Public Affairs Quarterly.* He is a member of the American Philosophical Association, the Southwestern Philosophical Society, and the Society for the Philosophical Study of Genocide and the Holocaust. He has an, M.A. in philosophy from Bowling Green State

University and a Ph.D. in philosophy from Florida State University.

Todd W. Van Beck is President and CEO of the Commonwealth Institute of Funeral Service Education in Houston, Texas. He is an internationally known speaker and writer in the funeral service profession. He sits on the Board of Trustees of the Academy of Professional Funeral Service Practice and on the Board of Directors of the National Funeral Service Museum.

Florence Vandendorpe, Diplôme d'Etudes Approfondies, is an assistant teacher at the Institute for the Study of Family and Sexuality at the université Catholique de Louvain-La-Neuve (UCL) in Belgium. She is a sociologist whose research interests focus on symbolism and cultural representations. She carried out research at UCL for a few years, notably in the field of sociology of religion. She received her master's degree from UCL in 1994 and a postgraduate diploma at École des Hautes Études en Sciences Sociales (EHESS) Paris in 1995.

María I. Vera, Ph.D., is Associate Professor in the Department of Psychiatry at the University of Florida. In 1974, she joined the faculty of the College of Medicine at the University of Florida, where she has taught in various programs of the medical school curriculum. She has specialized in teaching and training psychiatric residents in various modalities of psychotherapy, and she has been the Director of the Family Therapy and Group Therapy Programs in the Department of Psychiatry at the University of Florida. She practices psychotherapy as a licensed Marriage and Family Therapist and Clinical Social Worker. She has extensive clinical experience in individual, family, and group psychotherapy. Her clinical interests and expertise include treatment of depression, adjustment disorders, and anxiety disorders; stress management; grief resolution; conflict and anger management; infertility counseling, couples and family conflict; divorce and stepfamily issues; domestic violence; sexual victimization; and career- and work-related issues. She has published her research in professional journals in her areas of specialty. Her undergraduate work was in sociology at Universidad Católica in Santiago, Chile. Her master's degree in social work is from the University of Kansas, and her Ph.D. is from Florida State University.

Thomas J. Vesper, J.D., is a Certified Civil Trial Attorney admitted to the bar of New Jersey in 1973. A senior partner in the Atlantic City law firm of Westmoreland, Vesper & Schwartz, he concentrates on personal injury and wrongful death cases. He served with the U.S. Marine Corps Reserve from 1969 to 1991 and was certified as a UCMJ 27(b) Trial Counsel and Defense Counsel by the Secretary of the Navy. Past President of the New Jersey Chapter of the Association of Trial Lawyers of America, he is a Diplomate and Sustaining Member of the Association of Trial Lawyers of America (ATLA), Fellow of the International Academy of Trial Lawyers, a founding member of Trial Lawyers for Public Justice, and was selected by his peers to be listed in *The Best Lawyers in America.* His litigation experience includes products liability, commercial trucking and bus crashes, negligence, professional negligence, and consumer fraud cases. He is a frequent guest lecturer for ATLA, state trial lawyer associations, bar associations, and law schools. A faculty member and past trustee of the National College of Advocacy, he has published articles and lectured on wrongful death, products liability, truck and bus accident reconstruction, discovery, case evaluation, settlement, and trial techniques. He received his legal education at Rutgers University (J.D., 1973) where he was a writer and member of the *Rutgers-Camden Law Review.*

Lee Garth Vigilant, Ph.D., is Assistant Professor of Sociology at Minnesota State University, Moorhead, where he teaches courses in social thanatology, sociological theory, and qualitative methods in social research. He has been the recipient of teaching awards at both Boston College and Tufts University, receiving in 2000 the Donald J. White Teaching Excellence Award in Sociology at Boston College and in 2001, the TCU Senate Professor of the Year Award at Tufts University. His current research is in the area of illness recovery. His past publications, in the area of race and ethnic relations, appear in the journal *Gryo Colloquium Papers* (Boston College). He received his Ph.D. in sociology from Boston College in 2001.

Gail C. Walker, Ph.D., is Professor of Psychology at Alfred University, where she has been a member of the faculty since 1981. Prior to coming to Alfred University, she was on the staff of the Cook County Office of Special Education in Chicago. She had previously been Assistant Professor of Psychology at Marian College in Fond-du-Lac, Wisconsin. Her honors include Phi Kappa Phi, Honor Scholastic Fraternity; Phi Delta Kappa, Honor Education Fraternity; nine Bi-annual Excellence in Teaching Awards (1984–2001); Citizen Ambassador to the U.S.S.R. (1989); Sears Foundation Excellence in Teaching and Campus Leadership Award (1991); Independent College Fund of New York Teaching Excellence Award (1993-1999); and the Omicron Delta Kappa leadership Award (2001). She is listed in the International Directory of Distinguished leadership (1990), Who's Who Among America's Teachers (1996, 1998, and 2000), Outstanding Americans (1998), and Directory of American Scholars (10th ed.). She has published extensively on the topic of death and dying in journals such as *Omega* and *Journal of Death Studies.* She is a member of the Foundation of Thanatology and the Association for Death Education and Counseling. She received her M.S. and Ph.D. degrees from Oklahoma State University.

Charles Walton, Ph.D., is Assistant Professor of Sociology at Lynchburg College in Lynchburg, Virginia. He has previously taught at Radford University, Virginia Tech, Roanoke College, and Mary Baldwin College. He specializes in cultural theory, deviance, and popular culture. He has published in the *Encyclopedia of Criminology and Deviant Behavior* and the *Journal of Higher Education* and contributed a chapter on contemporary theory to Shifflett and Everett's *Fundamentals of Sociology* (2003). He earned an M.S. in sociology from Virginia Commonwealth University and a Ph.D. in sociology from Virginia Tech.

Joyce E. Williams, Ph.D., is Professor of Sociology at Texas Woman's University, Denton, Texas, where she has been since 1980, serving as Department Chair for more than half that time. She is the author of three books and articles in more than a dozen journals, including *Omega, Teaching Sociology, Victimology,* and the *Journal of Marriage and the Family.* She has held faculty positions at the University of Mary Hardin-Baylor, the University of Texas at Arlington, and Trinity University. She is currently working on a history of early sociology in the United States. She holds a Ph.D. degree in sociology from Washington University in St. Louis, Missouri.

Melissa Johnson Williams is a licensed funeral director and embalmer with over 30 years practical experience. Her presentations have included practical embalming demonstrations and talks on restorative art, history of embalming, infectious disease and medical technology, and shipping of human remains. She has over 75 published articles in the *Director* (National Funeral Directors Association publication), the *American Funeral Director,* and medical journals. She is the editor of the *International Shipping Section in the Blue Book* (American Funeral Director), has contributed several new chapters to the third revised edition of the textbook *Embalming: History, Theory, and Practice,* and was a chapter contributor to the new *Textbook of Thanatology.* She serves on the Ethical Practice Committee of the Illinois Funeral Directors Association and the Board of Trustees of the Academy of Professional Funeral Service Practice and is a board member of the Funeral Directors Services Association of Greater Chicago and Autopsy Committee member of the Institute of Medicine of Chicago. She is also the founder and Executive Director of the Midwest Forensic & Mortuary Support Foundation and is a cofounder of the American Society of Embalmers. She is a graduate of Governors State University in Governors Park, Illinois, and Worsham College of Mortuary Science.

John B. Williamson, Ph.D., is Professor of Sociology at Boston College. He is coeditor (with Edwin Shneidman) of the fourth edition of *Death: Current Perspectives.* In the area of death studies, he has published articles dealing with hospice, euthanasia, suicide, and homicide. He is the author of 15 books and more than 100 journal articles and book chapters. He has written extensively in the areas of aging and aging policy, including Social Security reform, the politics of aging, the debate over generational equity and justice between generations in connection with public policy, the proposed privatization of Social Security, and the comparative study of Social Security policy. He has been elected Chair of the Youth, Aging, and Life Course Division of the Society for the Study of Social Problems and secretary/treasurer of the Aging and the Life Course Section of the American Sociological Association. He is currently on the editorial board of four journals. His books and articles have been translated into Chinese, Hungarian, Italian, German, French, and Spanish. He holds a Ph.D. from Harvard University in social psychology.

David D. Witt, Ph.D., is Professor in the School of Family and Consumer Sciences at the University of Akron. His published work includes articles in the *Journal of Marriage and the Family, Social Forces, Sociological Spectrum, American Journal of Dietetics,* and the *Professional Journal for Primary Education.* He holds M.A. (1978) and Ph.D. (1983) degrees from Texas Tech University, where his emphasis was on social theory and research in family studies.

Timothy W. Wolfe, Ph.D., is Associate Professor of Sociology and Director of Criminal Justice at Mount Saint Mary's College in Emmitsburg, Maryland. His research interests include juvenile drug dealing, chronic and violent delinquency, college student binge drinking, and social thanatology. His work has appeared in the *American Journal of Criminal Justice, Journal of Alcohol and Drug Education,* and *The College Student Journal.* He received his M.S. and Ph.D. degrees in sociology from Virginia Polytechnic Institute and State University.

William Wood, M.Div, is currently finishing his Ph.D. in sociology at Boston College. He also has an M.Div. from Union Theological seminary in New York City, where he studied religious history and philosophy.

PART I

DEATH IN CULTURAL CONTEXT

THE UNIVERSAL FEAR OF DEATH AND THE CULTURAL RESPONSE

CALVIN CONZELUS MOORE

JOHN B. WILLIAMSON

Is the fear of death universal? Anthropologist Ernest Becker (1973) seems to think so, arguing that "the idea of death, the fear of it, haunts the human animal like nothing else; it is the mainspring of human activity—activity designed largely to avoid the fatality of death, to overcome it by denying in some way that it is the final destiny for man" (p. ix). There is much about death to fear: Whether by accident, disease, or intentional infliction by another human, the path to death for all but a few fortunate humans is accompanied by pain. Death can also be a lonely and isolating experience (Feder 1976). Humans are social beings, and it is our interactions with other humans that complete our existence and give our lives meaning. Death is thus separation from everything that gives our life form; it is the loss of everything that we hold dear (Hinton 1967). The loss of a loved one to death is often one of the most emotionally painful experiences that a human can have (Gordon 2000). Even when the death is not that of a loved one, simply being a witness to death can evoke a natural horror and revulsion (Malinowski 1948). Furthermore, because of its seeming finality, death presents one of the most formidable challenges to the idea that human life has meaning and purpose. Given these facts, it should be no surprise that fear has been one of the most commonly expressed responses of humans to death.

Because the idea of death evokes a number of fears, researchers have suggested that the fear of death is actually a multidimensional concept. Hoelter and Hoelter (1978) distinguish eight dimensions of the death fear: fear of the dying process, fear of premature death, fear for significant others, phobic fear of death, fear of being destroyed, fear of the body after death, fear of the unknown, and fear of the dead. Similarly, Florian and Mikulincer (1993) suggest three components of the death fear: intrapersonal components related to the impact of death on the mind and the body, which include fears of loss of fulfillment of personal goals and fear of the body's annihilation; an interpersonal component that is related to the effect of death on interpersonal relationships; and a transpersonal component that concerns fears about the transcendental self, composed of fears about the hereafter and punishment after death. Because of the complexity of death fears, some authors suggest using the term *death anxiety* to describe the amorphous set of feelings that thinking about death can arouse (Schultz 1979).

Because of the complexity of death fears, scholars have debated whether such fears are natural or whether they are social constructs. The most common view that runs through the history of thought on death is that the fear of death is innate, that all of life tends to avoid death, and that the underlying terror of death is what drives most of the human endeavor. The anthropological, philosophical, and psychoanalytic perspectives offer evidence and rationales that the fear of death is a natural response, given all the attempts of biological organisms to preserve life. Throughout human history, fear has been the universal response to death. In 1889, the cultural anthropologist Edward B. Tylor stated, "All life fears death, even brutes which do not know death" (p. 433). Aristotle (1941) said that "plainly the things we fear are terrible things" and referred to death as "the most terrible of things" (p. 978). According to the anthropologist Ernest Becker (1973), of the various factors that influence behavior, one of the most important is the terror of death. The most common view, then, is that fear is one of the most natural reactions to encounters with death (Charmaz 1980).

On the other hand, some sociologists argue that the fear of death is not necessarily innate; rather, it is a learned reaction (Schultz 1979). Vernon (1970) states that the fear of death is the result of an individual's learning

3

experiences, and not an internal phenomenon. Charmaz (1980) notes that social and cultural conditions may give rise to the fear of death. The industrialism and individualism of modern society, for example, may create the fear of death: "The rise of individuality with the illusion of self-sufficiency fosters an emergence of the fear of death. In societies that foster individuality, fear of death logically follows" (p. 14). In traditional and rural cultures, on the other hand, the fear of death is not as strong. Such arguments seem to suggest, however, that if the cultural response in a given society is not to fear death, individuals within that culture do not respond to death with fear. This is a premise that requires empirical validation. Perhaps the most useful conception of the fear of death may be that it is a variable subject to manipulation by social context. A society's culture may offer explanations of death that either repress or encourage fears about death according to the needs of the society.

In this chapter, we explore cultural responses to the fear of death. The fact that humans are symbolic beings allows us to construct symbolic systems that preserve the meaning and significance of life in the face of death. An examination of various cultures throughout history suggests that an underlying fear of death has always been a major organizing force in human society. Because the social construction of meaning is a fundamental element of culture, an examination of the universal fear of death and cultural responses to that fear offers us an opportunity to survey the vast human experience with death, from the earliest beginnings of society to the present. In that regard, we examine here the major theoretical contributions to our understanding of the fear of death and its relation to human culture, from anthropological studies of preliterate societies to the religious, philosophical, and psychoanalytic systems of more advanced societies.

Every culture has generated a system of thought that incorporates the reality and inevitability of death in a manner that preserves the social cohesion of that culture in the face of the potentially socially disintegrating aspects of death. Early human societies developed religious systems, including ancestor worship, that bridged the divide between the dead and the living and portrayed death not as an end, but as a transition to another world that is still very much connected to the earthly one. The Greeks used reason and philosophy to deal with the fear of death. Early Jews incorporated a variety of practices into their religious beliefs surrounding cleanliness and purity to stave off unwanted death. Christians of the Middle Ages gave themselves over to the reality of death by associating the death of the body with the freeing of the spirit to spend eternal life with God. Religious systems of the Eastern world evolved ideas of continual rebirth and the attainment of freedom from the cycle of rebirth through enlightenment or nirvana. In each case, the symbolic system accords death a place in society that offers meaning to the individual and prevents the society from lapsing into complete nihilism in the face of death.

EARLY AND PRELITERATE HUMAN RESPONSES TO THE FEAR OF DEATH

Perhaps the most basic human response to death is flight from it. Herzog (1983) describes several groups of preliterate peoples in Malaysia and North India who had burial practices but simply fled, never to return to the place where one of their members died. He attributes this behavior to the sheer horror that accompanies the inexplicable change from living to dead as witnessed by tribal members. Another group of preliterate Malays, however, fled to abandon the dying, but later returned to see whether the person had died; if death had occurred, they buried the deceased with leaves. Afterward, they would desert the place, returning only years later. Herzog views this practice as an important stage in the psychological development of humans, the stage at which humans first confronted death. Only by confronting death could humans gradually begin to integrate the concept of death into their understanding of the natural scheme of existence.

Early humans did not always flee from death; at some point, they were actually confronted with the dead. Once confronted, the dead produced a mixture of emotions in the living, ranging from horror at the sight of a corpse to a combination of fear and feelings of loss for the departed (Malinowski 1948). The deaths of members of a society were thus traumatic and potentially disintegrating experiences for the group. The development of practices surrounding disposal of the corpse served to reintegrate the community by allowing members to assert some manner of control over the society's relationship with death and the dead (Malinowski 1948). Cultural practices regarding disposal of the corpse thus became important in all human societies. These practices were subject to an infinite degree of variation, but in all cases they served a similar underlying purpose: bringing what was once an incomprehensible horror within the realm of an ordered understanding of the role of death in the human experience.

Early humans understood death to be a gateway to an afterlife. The belief that humans live on after death is almost universal (Frazer 1966). According to Malinowski (1948), preliterate humans were actually incapable of imagining death as the annihilation of being. This can be attributed to the fact that humans are symbolic beings; although human bodies are confined to a series of single moments in time and space, the human mind is able to traverse many temporal and spatial dimensions simultaneously. Humans are able to imagine, reflect, and dream. Tylor (1889) notes that animism, the most preliterate form of religion, originated in primitive explanations of dreams, visions, apparitions, and other products of the imagination. Similarly, Durkheim (1915:66) says that humans' belief in the spirit world originated in early humans' attribution of equal reality to the waking world and the world of sleep and dreams. Because humans, through these mental processes, could form images of persons who had died, they could use these images and the effects that memories of the dead continued to have on the living to reason in the most elementary fashion that humans live on after death.

The prevailing attitude of early human societies toward the dead, with some exceptions, was fear. Frazer (1966) notes:

> While it would be foolish and vain to deny that [the savage] often mourns sincerely the death of his relations and friends, he commonly thinks that their spirits undergo after death a great change, which affects their character and temper on the whole for the worse, rendering them touchy, irritable, irascible, prone to take offence on the slightest pretext and to visit their displeasure on the survivors by inflicting on them troubles of many sorts, including accidents of all kinds, drought, famine, sickness, pestilence and death. (Pp. 10–11)

Evidence of this fear has been found in most preliterate societies. This is to be expected. For many millennia, life on the whole for humans has been brutal and short, yet the natural tendency of preliterate groups was to view life and health as natural, whereas sickness and death required supervening causes that required explanations (Malinowski 1948). The obvious culprits were either disgruntled dead relatives or higher-order beings who took a special interest in human affairs.

Because of fear of the dead, gods and ancestors became the objects of attempts at either appeasement or control by the living. These two goals, says Malinowski (1948), branched off in two directions: religion and magic. Religion is essentially the attempt to appease, whereas behind magic is the desire to control. Religion sustained fears of the gods and focused on efforts to supplicate them; magic purported to transfer power to the hands of the magician, giving that individual a degree of control over forces that affected human lives. In one sense, magic was intensely psychological, as it involved convincing participants of the power of its wielder. Magic also involved experimentation, however, and some of that experimentation eventually laid the foundation for more formal scientific experimentation (Malinowski 1948). In the anthropological distinctions between religion and magic, then, we can see the foundation for humanity's ongoing efforts to overcome the fear of death through the opposing tactics of belief and control.

RELIGION AND THE FEAR OF DEATH

Cultural practices surrounding death combined with ideas about what happens after death to form the basis of religion, which is one of the cornerstones of all civilizations. Malinowski (1948) asserts that religion "is as instinctual a response as the fear of death which underlies it" (p. 29). He states, "Of all sources of religion, the supreme and final crisis of life—death—is of greatest importance" (p. 29). Durkheim's (1915) simple definition of religion is "the belief in spiritual beings" (p. 44). According to Durkheim, the purpose of religion is to regulate humans' relations

with these beings through "prayers, sacrifices, propitiatory rites, etc." (p. 44). Religion sets up a fundamental distinction between the sacred and the profane. It establishes a priesthood that acts as guardian of the sacred and serves as interlocutor between the physical and spiritual worlds (Berger 1969).

Religion orders human behavior by setting up a series of taboos and prescriptions surrounding sacred objects and rites (Durkheim 1963). It thus forms one of the most elemental institutions of social order. It represents the human attempt to unite social organization with cosmic organization—to order human society, the spirit world, and the cosmic and animal world in which humans are immersed into a comprehensible reality.

Cults of the dead, mythical heroes, ancestor worship, and totemism are all forms of religion that embody a combination of social organization of the living with attempts to influence relations with the dead and that act as the gateway to a desired type of immortality. In this manner, religion addresses two of the most basic fears of humans: fear of the dead and fear of what will happen to us after we die.

Religion thus forms one of the basic elements of authority of humans over other humans (Weber 1956). The fundamental problem of society is the preservation of social order. Humans quickly realized that disorder ultimately leads, through chaos, to death. Order and organization represent a flight from death. Religion, which capitalizes on the innate fear of death, is one of the most efficient methods of achieving what Durkheim calls "mechanical solidarity," which is social order premised on the understanding that all societal members follow the same behavioral norms.

Underlying religion is power, and the foundation of all power is that of life over death. As Lifton (1979) notes, the final meaning of religion is "life-power and power over death" (pp. 20–21). Persons in positions of authority, whether priests, warriors, or kings, assume their power by controlling who will live and who will die, by playing upon the fear of members of society that to disobey authority means not only death, but also the possibility of an unpleasant afterlife. Rulers cannot rule by force alone. The combination of rule by force and rule through religious authority has been one of the most effective means of assuring the obedience of a population. Many monarchies share this characteristic (Sypnowich 1991).

Every society remains continually under threat of revolution and disintegration from below by its youth, because of the power of the sex drive (Freud 1936). Each generation must therefore be forever diligent in the transmission of rules of behavior to the succeeding generation. The collective superego uses both the fear of death and fear of the dead to enforce the rules and preserve social order. Societies have different levels of success in generating symbolic systems that are powerful enough to maintain allegiance over time. Wars, migration, and trade, as well as constant reflection by later generations on the previous generations' experiences, often lead to transformations of symbolic systems. The most enduring systems are therefore those that are best able to adapt their symbolic systems to the present set of human conditions.

KILLING, SACRIFICE, AND THE FEAR OF DEATH

Even though humans instinctively fear death, they also willfully participate in death through killing. Shapiro (1989) suggests that killing by early humans may have been a response to the fear of death. Killing is seen to enhance life, to make it eternal. Killing energizes the killer. Killing allows the killer to confront death immediately and intentionally, and with that confrontation comes a sense of power. By killing, humans master the fear of death, showing death that they are not afraid to face it, and even bring it into being. For early humans, death was a nameless and formless horror; participation in the act of killing allowed them to identify themselves with death, to give shape and form to death, and, in so doing, to begin to understand it. The power behind death thus becomes recognizable.

Killing evokes a complex set of psychological responses in humans. Killing was problematic for early humans. Even when they killed animals, they performed ceremonies as magic practices to "cancel out the event of death" and thus allay its horror (Herzog 1983). Herzog (1983) describes the practice of murdering the elderly and diseased group members in many preliterate societies; the variety of methods used included suffocation, strangulation, burying alive, feeding to wild animals, and abandonment. It was shameful in some cultures for adult children to allow their parents to die a natural death. Herzog thus suggests that a measure of guilt may have accompanied these acts even if they were viewed as necessary and life affirming.

Ceremonies performed prior to these killings may have served the psychological purpose of expiating feelings of anxiety that surrounded the murderous acts. They also may have alleviated feelings of being overwhelmed by death by suggesting that humans indeed had some authority over life and death. Once humans connected death with life and came to see that death is part of the cycle of life, that it is even required for life, participation in the act of killing may have come to be seen as an act of affirming life. The attitude toward killing progressed from one of anxiety to one in which killing was seen as pleasing to the gods (Paul 1996). Killers, particularly warriors and hunters, were glorified and given great positions of honor in society (Herzog 1983).

Killing by sacrifice allowed the priest who conducted the ceremony to proclaim mastery over death to those who witnessed the sacrifice. The symbolic language system that surrounded the sacrifice enabled the religions' adherents to believe that power over death also means power over life. According to German psychoanalyst Otto Rank (1936), the sacrifice of the other "lessens the death fear of the ego," and "through the death of the other, one buys oneself free from the penalty of dying, of being killed" (p. 170). Ritual sacrifices also had the purpose of instilling fear in those who witnessed and took part in the ceremonies. Sacrifice necessarily evoked a visceral reaction of horror and brought each witness into direct confrontation with his or her own hidden fears of death. Beneath the idea of sacrifice is power; priestly sacrifice represented the efforts of priests as a class to consolidate power in society by exploiting the group's natural fears about death.

THE BODY, CULTURE, AND THE FEAR OF DEATH

The concept of death is intricately tied to the human body. It is the body that dies. The body is corruptible; the body is the recipient of disease and subject to decay. It is the physical corpse that rots away, whereas the soul, according to many belief systems, is set free and lives forever. The body feels pain, and bodily misery is the source of most human misery. Passion is of the body; contemplation is of the soul. Man's body can thus make him a slave to passion while the contemplative power of his spirit sets him free. This basic fact is behind many religious practices, philosophical systems, and science (Heinz 1999). A major function of culture, then, is to structure pleasure fulfillment of the body in a manner that supports the continuity of society. Reason, law, religion, science, even magic—all products of the contemplative mind—discipline the body, structure bodily movements, and set restraints on the desires of the body (Jones 2001). The primary struggle throughout human history is thus that between reason and passion, between the mind and the body.

The thrust of human culture in response to death has been to overcome the limitations and pains inflicted on the soul by the body. Underlying many religious practices is the function of controlling bodily impulses, purifying the body through practices of mortification, asceticism, celibacy, and other forms of self-denial. Much of human culture, therefore, involves the establishment of rules surrounding bodily orifices. In the Old Testament creation myth, Adam and Eve sin by eating of the fruit of the tree of life. Their eyes are opened and they subsequently have sex. They also learn that they must die. Their sins thus involved the two bodily orifices that can be most subject to conscious control, the mouth and the genital organs. Their once-perfect bodies were corrupted by these acts, and Adam and Eve were required to leave the Garden of Eden and live by the sweat of their brows.

The myth of Adam and Eve sets the foundation for a system of religious practices that revolve in large part around food and sex and that may underlie practical considerations about the relationships among food, sex, cleanliness, and death. In *Purity and Danger* (1966), Mary Douglas uses the Book of Leviticus to explore ideas about pollution of the body and hygiene and their incorporation into religious ideas about uncleanness and ritual purity.

Leviticus sets forth the laws for the children of Israel, and many of those laws involve food. The laws set forth in the Old Testament Book of Leviticus are laws of God as delivered by Moses; pragmatically, they are early attempts to address the potentially corrupting effects of filth and uncleanness. The laws require priestly inspections when there is evidence of leprosy and prohibit sex when there is discharge from the penis of a male or when a women is menstruating; they set forth explicitly what foods may be eaten and prohibit the consumption of animals that die before they are killed (Porter 1976). Attempts to cleanse and purify are closely related to human societies' attempts at order, which in turn serve to defy death and chaos; as Douglas (1966) observes, "Reflection on dirt involves the reflection on the relation of order to disorder, being to non-being, form to formlessness, life to death" (p. 5). Religious categorizations of what is clean and unclean are thus further indications of humankind's attempts to build barriers to slow the encroachment of death by seeking to protect the body from the corrupting effects of filth.

The anxieties associated with sex in all societies have also been linked to the fear of death (Brain 1979). Sex is linked to aggression and causes men to kill other men; it is thus a source of disorder and death. The sexual organs are also very close to the anus, which is a source of corruption, disease, and death. The smell of sex can thus resemble that of feces and is a reminder of death. Sex itself can be a corrupting agent; filth can enter into the human body through the act of sex. Humankind became aware of germs only relatively recently, but sex has historically been the cause of numerous diseases that can lead to bodily discomfort, pain, and—in the case of diseases such as syphilis—incapacitation and death. In modern society, AIDS has solidified the link between sex and death; it has been associated with higher levels of death anxiety in gay men as well as among doctors and health workers who treat patients with AIDS (Bivens et al. 1994; Essien et al. 2000; Hayslip, Luhr, and Beyerlein 1991). It is no small wonder, then, that humans have such anxiety surrounding sex. In all societies, sex is the most regulated behavior. Rules surrounding sexuality constitute the strongest taboos in almost all human societies and are at the core of many religions.

Whereas Old Testament taboos focus on cleanliness and dietary practices (Douglas 1966), the New Testament is particularly focused on sexuality. Sexual morality became one of the cornerstones of the Christian Church. It was one of the major themes of the writings of the apostle Paul, one of the principal authors of the New Testament, who himself confessed to an ongoing struggle with the sins of the flesh. Sin is yielding to the desires of the flesh, becoming a slave to passion, and "the wages of sin is death" (Romans 6:23). The Holy Spirit, on the other hand, is the gift granted by God to help humans fight against the sins of the flesh and is the source of life everlasting. Overcoming the sins of the flesh became one of the principal paths to the freedom granted by the New Testament God, a

freedom that included not only life eternal, but also a new and perfect body to inhabit in that life. The Catholic Church subsequently placed great emphasis on sexual immorality and structured the practice of confession around expiating the Christian of impure thoughts and deeds, which were primarily of a sexual nature (Foucault 1990a). Christianity thus portrays the human body as weak and corruptible and the major source of sin, and promises those who strive to be of the spirit that they will overcome those weaknesses with eternal life and new bodies.

Christians of the Middle Ages despised the body. Mysticism thrived among the monks of that period; practitioners sought to overcome anxieties about death by ignoring the welfare of the body, allowing it to suffer and using that suffering as a path to freeing the spirit from the flesh (Carse 1980; Clarke 1978). Cultural productions of the Middle Ages reflected a desire to be free of the body completely (Helgeland 1984). There was an obsession with the macabre (DuBruck and Gusick 1999). The figure of Death was one of the most popular representations in artwork of the age (Aries 1981). The ideal human figure as represented in art was that of an emaciated saint whose eyes reflected the desire of his soul to depart from his body. The overall picture that emerges of the Middle Ages is one of an era that conceded the victory to death and used its cultural productions to express the people's overwhelming despair (Worcester 1999).

Yielding to death was that culture's particular solution to the problem of meaning in life, for giving oneself over to death could be interpreted as the supreme sacrifice. When one sacrifices the self—in particular, the body that one knows death will inevitably acquire—one is taking an absurd and meaningless death and giving it meaning. Foss (1966) suggests that the significance of sacrifice operates on two levels: First, the sacrificed leaves behind in society a memory of the sacrificial act, so that the life of the sacrificed acquires meaning in the world left behind; and second, the sacrificed gives over to death the body that is the cause of so much suffering and the primary hindrance to salvation. Making the supreme sacrifice of one's body prepares one for the transformation to new life and a new body free of the world's ills. The act of self-sacrifice thus becomes a subversion of death's power: Victory by death was turned into victory over death, for in the act of sacrifice, life achieves its supreme significance (Foss 1966).

The ancient Greek philosophers used truths evolved from rational discourse about the relationship between the body and the soul to determine practical rules concerning bodily restraint. The Greeks despaired over death precisely because life and the body offer so many pleasures (Choron 1963). They also realized that completely succumbing to the body's demands for pleasure is the path to death. The problem the Greek philosophers addressed was therefore one of controlling the body's excesses. Foucault (1990b) terms the classical Greek approach a "moral problematization of food, drink and sexual activity" (p. 51). In Greek thought, the goal was for the human not to be ruled by the passions of the body, but rather to temper the body's passions with reason.

To the Greeks, the problem of the body was not a religious one but a moral one. The body thus required attention because it was subject to abuse; bodily excesses were associated with sickness and death (Foucault 1990b). The Greeks, too, linked bodily abuse with the mouth and sex organs. Plato's *Laws* refer to three basic appetites that involve food, drink, and reproduction, and Plato notes the unique strength of the sexual desire in particular (Foucault 1990b). The goal of the Greeks, then, was the proper management of the body's desires for pleasure.

Bodily desires are also made problematic and linked to death in Eastern religions. "Desire is suffering," says Buddha, anticipating both the apostle Paul and Freud. The fear in Buddhism is not of an unpleasant afterlife. Rather, the fear is that unless freed from bodily desires, the individual will remain trapped in the birth-death cycle that prevents the self from being united with the oneness of the universe (Prabhu 1989). Oneness is the state of nirvana that Buddhists seek. Rather than fearing the annihilation of the self, practitioners of Buddhism seek such annihilation. The body and bodily desires act as hindrances to the attainment of nirvana. The body and its desires maintain the separateness of the self from the universal one as long as the individual remains enslaved to bodily passions (Toynbee 1976; Carse 1980).

The self is an equal restraint in Hinduism, in which the individual also seeks self-annihilation and union with oneness (Glucklich 1989). Whereas the Greeks emphasized thought as the path to freedom, Buddhism and Hinduism emphasize meditation (Carse 1980). "Meditation is in truth higher than thought," states a master in the Upanishads, the great Hindu philosophical/religious work. Meditation with the mind is the path to freedom and nirvana in Hinduism and Buddhism, but both Eastern and Western systems of thought reverberate the overall human theme of restraining the body's passions through self-discipline and self-denial.

The cultural practices of many human societies resonate with the idea that bodily desires are related to death and the restraint of bodily desires is the path to freedom from death, for both the individual and the society. Two psychological processes are evident in acts of self-denial, and both are guided by the idea that excesses of the body lead to death: First, self-discipline can serve the goal of increasing the individual's pleasure in the present life by making the body healthier through moderation; second, self-discipline can be interpreted as pleasing to the gods or as a path to reunion with an uncorrupted world after death occurs. Individuals and societies gravitate toward one or the other of these two interpretations and construct symbolic systems to support their choices.

Three dominant methods have evolved to enforce self-discipline. Traditional religions use external coercion to force the body into submission through the threat of punishment from the gods. The Greeks constructed a moral system guided by practical reason. Eastern religions set forth rules and practices that allow practitioners to control bodily desires through meditative practices. These are the three major routes that humans have taken in their attempts to flee from the body's death. The goal in all cases remains the same: to overcome death by achieving freedom from bodily desires.

REASON, PHILOSOPHY, AND THE FEAR OF DEATH

One of our major premises in this chapter is that human societies can exist because symbols and the objects in the worlds that they represent are organized into conceptual systems that provide coherent explanations of human existence (Samuels 1993). Human reason underlies all such efforts. The logic of existence flows from the human capacity to reason. Reason informs all but the most irrational superstitions about the causes of death (Murphy 1993). What distinguishes advanced societies from societies that are less advanced is the range of worldly phenomena accounted for within their conceptual systems and their reliance on logical proofs to validate truths about the world. The discipline of philosophy in advanced civilizations represents humankind's most rational attempts to deal with the problem of death. "Death is the true inspiring genius, or the muse of philosophy," says Schopenhauer (1957:249).

Even in philosophy, however, conclusions about death are socially grounded; the pervasiveness of a set of conditions may lead to an era in which a singular philosophical attitude toward death prevails, or the social conditions in the life of a particular individual may determine whether that person determines that death is to be feared or not feared. The ancient Greeks took philosophy to some of the greatest heights known to humankind, but their philosophy regarding death exhibits the duality that has pervaded the remainder of history: On the one hand were the materialists, who argued that the soul dissolves at death, and on the other hand were the idealists, who argued that the soul lives on independent of the body in some form after death.

Each approach was determined by the focus of the philosophical inquiry: The materialists were early scientists concerned with the organization of material phenomena in the world, and thus saw the human as tied to the change and dissolution in the material world; the idealists, in contrast, set their sights on the seemingly perfect and unchanging conceptual world that reason ordered within the human mind, and could thus discern the possibility of a world beyond material experience in which the concept of the human, as represented by the soul, could live on (Sutherland 1978). Classical Greek society itself epitomized the precarious relationship between change and decay of the material world on the one hand and universal ideals of the conceptual world on the other: It was always challenged from both within and without by the forces of decay, and yet its leaders and thinkers were also able to construct ideals, such as truth, freedom, democracy, and justice, that seemed eternal.

The duality is most evident in the logical systems of Plato and Aristotle and their respective schools of thought. To Plato, reason supported the existence of an ideal world beyond universal time and space, whereas Aristotle argued that reason can allow knowledge of the experienced world but can never prove a world beyond experience (Crescenzo 1990). Democritus, a student of Aristotle, also saw death as dissolution; he argued for learning to accept death as a part of life. Similarly, the materialist thinker Epicurus argued that religious thinking inflicts the living soul with fear of gods and fear of the hereafter (Gill 1995), but there is no need for such fear, because the soul dissolves upon death. According to Epicurus, the fear of death is the main obstacle to pleasure; individuals can achieve peace of mind by maximizing their pleasure while they are living (Rosenbaum 1993).

The rational approaches propounded by the Greeks yielded to an obsessive fear of death during the Middle Ages, but classical ideas resurfaced in Western societies during the Renaissance. People again began to think that humans are not bound by fate and death and that they can take their lives into their own hands and learn to live fully and creatively (Choron 1963). The Renaissance spirit is exhibited in the ideas of the French essayist Montaigne (1993), who argued that it is the fact of death that gives life its value. To Montaigne, life is a gift made all the more real by death.

The age of reason and science that flowered in the 16th century yielded proof of a mechanically ordered universe that operates according to logical and discernible principles. The possibility of eternity seemed to exist in the ordered, efficient operation of the world. Philosophical approaches to the fear of death often reflected the orderliness of the universe. Thus Descartes (1984) argued that we need not fear death because the mind/soul is eternal; the decay of the body need not imply the destruction of the mind. Kant (1998), reasoning from the perspective of his very orderly and circumscribed existence, argued that we cannot disprove God, freedom, and immortality, so reason supports their existence. There is no need to fear death, said Kant, because death is change.

Much of 20th-century existentialist philosophy reflects the need to find meaning in a world shaken by catastrophic wars. The great world wars brought forth death and human evil on such a massive scale as to strip human life completely of the meaning that Western culture had built around it in preceding centuries. Modern philosophers thus express a need to find personal meaning in human lives constrained by the finality of death. Martin Heidegger's (1996) concern is in demystifying death, teaching the individual to develop a proper attitude toward death and to learn to live life "authentically." Karl Jaspers (1963) argues that proofs of immortality are faulty, and also echoes the Stoic notion that individuals should deal with the horror of nonbeing by learning how to die. Jean-Paul Sartre (1992)

echoes the same notion with his arguments that individuals should accept the finitude of death and seek their freedom through the knowledge of how to die.

What can we conclude, then, about philosophical approaches to the fear of death? Underlying them all is the same mind/body duality of old, and all of these thinkers prove the limitation of human thought through their ability to consider only two options: Either death need not be feared because it is the release of an immortal spirit or death is complete annihilation of the being and can offer no further punishment to the being. The conclusions of each philosopher remain products of both his era and the social conditions unique to his life. The entire philosophical enterprise, however, can be viewed as a highly evolved human cultural response to the fundamental problem of death.

THE FEAR OF DEATH AND MODERN THOUGHT

Much of the modern project involves overcoming the historical human impotence in the face of death. Underlying the modern project is the discovery of the individual and the attempt to liberate the individual—whether from the strictures of past group practices that are no longer functional or from the limitations and miseries heaped upon the individual by the very nature of existence, including death (Giddens 1991). There are many fronts to this project, and it employs the full array of tactics accumulated through millennia of human experience and subsequently ordered by human reason (Webb 1997). Science, medicine, psychoanalysis, philosophy—are all adapted to the ultimate liberation of the individual (Momeyer 1988). Psychoanalysis seeks to balance the individual personality by providing the ego with psychological tools to cope with the reality of its ultimate dissolution (Minsky 1998). Science offers technology to protect the body against the harshness of nature, while medicine attempts to slow and even halt the processes associated with the body's natural decay and corruption (Conlin 1988).

In modernity, death recedes further and further from day-to-day human experience. Humans are no longer constantly faced with death, and when they do confront death, it is usually presented in a sanitized form, with the sting of its horror far removed from everyday reality. We witness death through the mass media, but in heavily filtered fashion. When a death is anticipated, the individual is sent to a hospital, and his or her dying is left to the care of professionals (Fulton 1977). Humans today have access to a great deal of information about the process of dying (Walters 1988). Humans still attempt to reduce the shock of death by confronting and understanding it, but individuals are more informed about the process of dying than ever before (Prior 1989). Advances in medicine have generated drugs that serve to reduce the pain and discomfort associated with death (Kothari and Mehta 1981; Kass 1971).

Progress, however, has not come without a price: Modern societies have been traumatized by confrontation with death in magnitudes not experienced in previous eras; the devastatingly efficient wars and genocides of the 20th century killed millions and revealed the persistence of great evil in humanity. All humans currently live under the shadow of potential nuclear annihilation. Modernity further fuels an existential crisis within individuals by generating knowledge of a world of overwhelming size and complexity, a world in which individual lives and projects seem increasingly meaningless (Slote 1978). The sheer scale of existence thus furthers perceptions of the pointlessness of individual lives. As a result, death anxiety has not receded, despite all human advances over the millennia.

To combat death anxiety, however, modern society produces a full array of diversions that take our minds off of death. At the core of all human endeavors, says Ernest Becker (1973), is the terror of death. Because all individuals instinctively fear their own annihilation, death confers a narcissistic need to preserve the individual's self-esteem in the face of the pointlessness of life. What humankind fears most is not extinction, says Scimecca (1979), but "extinction without meaning" (p. 67). According to Becker, society provides a "cultural hero system" that creates and perpetuates the myth of the significance of human life. Cultural hero systems provide channels that allow the individual to contribute to the human enterprise. All members of society can strive to be heroes through their contributions, however large or small, thereby allowing the gratification of narcissistic impulses and the maintenance of self-esteem. Society thus creates the illusion of the significance of life by creating heroic projects that galvanize members of the society. If the illusion is lost, despair is the result (Scimecca 1979). Heroic projects focus our attention and give life meaning and purpose.

"Culture opposes nature and transcends it," says Becker (1973:159). Transcendence is thus not an otherworldly phenomenon. Transcendence occurs with each heroic human effort to counter the devastating effects that nature has on humanity. Society itself is a transcendent being, constructed by the combined heroic efforts of all the individual humans who make up society. Culture thus offers immortality. Culture offers an opportunity to preserve the memory and works of the individual within the context of the heroic project that is society itself. Culture overcomes the fear of annihilation, the fear of being forgotten. Culture preserves an individual's productions and thus allows the individual to achieve a form of "symbolic immortality" (Lifton 1979:23).

Following Becker's ideas, Solomon, Greenberg, and Pyszczynski (2000) argue in their "terror management theory" that the awareness of mortality produces a potentially paralyzing terror in humans. We require cultural worldviews that mediate this terror by instilling in individuals the idea that they are valuable members of particular communities. Humans thus create symbolic systems that are shared among all members of given communities in order to preserve self-esteem mutually in the face of the underlying terror of death. This idea offers the needed boost to self-esteem that humans need to overcome the paralyzing fear of death. Cultural worldviews thus produce the means for death transcendence, and so are critical for helping humans to overcome the fear of death. Solomon et al. also assert that when societies are exposed to terror or the direct threat of annihilation, they embrace their worldviews even more strongly, often to the derogation of opposing worldviews. This derogation of other worldviews is necessary because alternate conceptions of reality dispute their own and challenge the underlying sense of self-esteem that their worldview is designed to protect.

Advanced societies provide a wide array of institutional structures that construct appropriate sets of goals and symbolic systems to imbue human actions with meaning and purpose (Hollach and Hockey 2001). Little time is thus left for any void through which the repressed fear of death may resurface. Modern society perpetuates elevated ideals and places noble projects before humanity, keeping members ever striving toward reform for the betterment of humankind. Eradicating diseases, feeding the hungry, sheltering the poor, controlling the population, managing resources, protecting the environment, exploring inner and outer space, developing human potential through sports, art, and entertainment—all of these projects become endowed with significance that makes those who participate in them heroes and role models for generations to come.

The institutions through which meanings are transmitted are continually subjected to critical inquiry against the objective standard of whether or not the institution extends or betters human lives. Even religion is rationalized and reconciled with philosophy and science at its highest levels and participates in rather than presides over the human project. A delicate balance is struck. Religion allows continued belief in an afterlife, but its approach is more pragmatic and this-world oriented than in the past; "love thy neighbor" translates into proactively building community, doing good, and abstaining from harming fellow human beings as the path to everlasting life. The goal of building a society that best assures that members live the longest and healthiest earthly lives possible is thus reconciled with the goal of assuring entry into a rewarding afterlife.

CORRELATES OF THE DEATH FEAR

Studies suggest that the fear of death varies even within modern cultures. Social institutions can manipulate fears about death. The fear of death has thus been found to correlate with religious affiliation, religiosity, and exposure to death education, although in each case, the correlates are complicated by the multidimensional nature of the death anxiety. Hoelter and Epley (1979), for example, found that religiosity serves to reduce certain fears about death, such as fear of the unknown, while heightening others, such as fear of being destroyed, fear for significant others, fear of the dead, and fear for the body after death. Patrick (1979) reports that Christian religions are more effective at reducing death anxiety than is Buddhism. Studies of the relationship between death anxiety and death education have yielded mixed results. For example, Davis-Berman (1998–99) found that among a sample of college students, courses on death education served to decrease the fear of death, whereas other studies have shown mixed effects of death education on death anxiety (Knight and Elfenbein 1993; Maglio and Robinson 1994).

The fear of death has also been found to vary with sex and age (Drolet 1990; Florian and Snowden 1989). Firth-Cozens and Field (1991) found that women tend to have a greater fear of death than men. Drolet (1990) suggests that older adults are better at establishing a sense of symbolic immortality than are young adults and thus may experience less death anxiety than the young. On the other hand, Roth (1978) notes that the fear of death is "widely prevalent among old people" (p. 554), although deeply repressed, and may be due to such factors as low self-esteem and the low value that modern society attaches to the aged. Cicirelli (2002) suggests that the fear of death among the aged is variable and may be related to weak religiosity, lack of social support, and low self-esteem.

The degree of advancement of a society may determine how far that society can remove the actual experience of death from the day-to-day existence of individuals. The further death can be removed from common experience, the more of an abstraction it becomes. The abstract nature of death makes the fear of it even more subject to social manipulation. Modern societies have created a variety of institutional mechanisms for removing the actual experience of death from everyday life. In addition to traditional mechanisms (such as religion), hospices, drugs, death education, psychotherapy, philosophical belief systems, and other secular mechanisms all serve to remove, sanitize, and ease the pain of the transition from life to death. It thus becomes ever easier for societal members not to fear such an abstraction.

When the veils over death that society has provided are suddenly stripped away, however, scholars have an opportunity to assess the most basic human response to death. Research findings suggest that a lingering fear of death is one of the most consistent outcomes of traumatic encounters with death (Solomon et al. 2000). Death fears have been linked to individuals' experiences of traumatic events such as air disasters and the experience of trauma surrounding the deaths of loved ones. Chung, Chung, and Easthope (2000) found, for example, that residents of a town in England near which an airliner crashed exhibited higher death anxiety than did members of a control group. Florian and Mikulincer (1993) found the fear of death to be positively related to the loss of significant others. Even exposure to death through the media has been found to increase death fears (King and Hayslip 2001–2). In each of the cases cited above, the sense of security that society had provided between death and the individual was suddenly

stripped away, and the encounter with death became direct and immediate.

One of the starkest examples of the relationship between the fear of death and trauma is provided by the terrorist attacks on the Pentagon and the World Trade Center of September 11, 2001. In that instant, all Americans simultaneously came face-to-face with death. A terror of death suddenly resurfaced from beneath the comfortable, security-generating symbolic universe that had served to repress that fear. The anthrax attacks soon after September 11 produced the same response of fear, as does the general threat of nuclear annihilation. The general response to these threats seems to suggest that fear is a natural response to the threat of death, and that direct confrontation with the possibility of death can erode the symbolic buffers that cultures erect between individuals and death.

CONCLUSION

The evidence suggests that human progress is indeed ultimately driven by the fear of death. Death, in all its complexity, finality, and absurdity, its challenge to existence, its ugliness, pain, and isolation, and its power to deprive, continues to hold sway over humankind. The anthropological record suggests that early human societies experienced death as children might—as a faceless, nameless horror that sought to deprive them of the few pleasures offered by existence. There were understandably mixed reactions to death—accept its lordship, make excuses for it, create a more powerful friend to humankind and enemy to death, avoid it, embrace it, or deny its finality. Experience with the world over time suggested a variety of means for incorporating the unwanted and yet ever-present guest into the human household. The history of humankind represents the sum total of the various experiments that have evolved to minimize the effects of death's constant presence in the midst of human society.

Death has been inextricably linked to the death of the body and the body's fallibilities—its susceptibility to disease, injury, and death. Humans have sought to blame themselves for the body's weaknesses and have established practices aimed at strengthening the body, through morality, diet, exercise, medicine, magic, and supplications to the gods. The spirit or soul, on the other hand, has come to be conceptualized in most cultures as the seat of reason, hope, truth, and immortality. Humans have dichotomized themselves and convinced themselves that if only they could be free of the body, then they could be truly free. Yet most still fear the prospect of a bodiless existence, so much so that many religions offer a new body on the other side of death.

One of the most basic responses to death in all human societies has therefore been to place restrictions on the fulfillment of bodily desires. Yet excessive self-denial of the body by an overreaching conscience can be equally harmful to the being. Societies can lean toward either too little discipline and too much self-indulgence or too many restrictions on human desire and creativity. Both paths can lead to the very death whose avoidance is sought. The theme of psychoanalysis for individuals and for societies should therefore be the same—to prevent individuals or societies from being overwhelmed by either the desires of the body or the strictures of conscience and law. The goal is to develop a healthy balance of the two forces, so the personality of the individual or society can live life with maximum success, which means maximum happiness and pleasure and minimum pain and suffering. It is this ideal that is embodied in the modern human project.

Culture is the primary vehicle through which passion and reason are mediated, and by which the pangs of death are lessened. Culture ennobles efforts at self-restraint and turns into heroes those who deny the self and face the possibility of self-annihilation for a larger cause. Through culture, the insulting banality that death confers on life is transformed through symbolism into a noble quest for being, a heroic struggle against the forces of evil. Funerals, birth ceremonies, remembrances of the dead, memorials, holy days, and other rituals, as well as art, literature, and drama, all seek to clothe the stark, absurd events of life and death within a system that gives human history meaning and purpose. Cultural productions order seemingly random and meaningless events into coherent narratives whose ultimate goal is to grant dignity to humans in the face of the utter disregard that nature seems to have for life. In sum, although death's sovereignty will persist for some time to come, the human spirit will forever struggle to deprive it of its central place in human existence.

REFERENCES

Aries, Philippe. 1981. *The Hour of Our Death,* translated by Helen Weaver. New York: Alfred A. Knopf.

Aristotle. 1941. *The Basic Works of Aristotle,* edited by Richard McKeon. New York: Random House.

Becker, Ernest. 1973. *The Denial of Death.* New York: Free Press.

Berger, Peter. 1969. *The Sacred Canopy: Elements of a Sociological Theory of Religion.* Garden City, NY: Doubleday.

Bivens, Alexander, Robert A. Neimeyer, Thomas M. Kirchber, and Marlin K. Moore. 1994. "Death Concerns and Religious Beliefs Among Gays and Bisexuals of Variable Proximity to AIDS." *Omega* 30:105–20.

Brain, James Lewton. 1979. *The Last Taboo: Sex and the Fear of Death.* Garden City, NY: Anchor.

Carse, James P. 1980. *Death and Existence: A Conceptual History of Human Mortality.* New York: John Wiley.

Charmaz, Kathy. 1980. *The Social Reality of Death.* London: Addison-Wesley.

Choron, Jacques. 1963. *Death and Western Thought.* New York: Macmillan.

Chung, Man Cheung, Catherine Chung, and Yvette Easthope. 2000. "Traumatic Stress and Death Anxiety Among Community Residents Exposed to an Aircraft Crash." *Death Studies* 24:689–95.

Cicirelli, Victor G. 2002. "The Fear of Death in Older Adults: Predictions From Terror Management Theory." *Journals of Gerontology Series B: Psychological Sciences and Social Sciences* 57:357–66.

Clarke, John J. 1978. "Mysticism and the Paradox of Survival." In *Language, Metaphysics and Death,* edited by John Donnelly. New York: Fordham University Press.

Conlin, D. Walters. 1988. "Future Health Care: Increasing the 'Alternatives.'" *Futurist* 22:13–15.

Crescenzo, Luciano de. 1990. *The History of Greek Philosophy.* London: Pan.

Davis-Berman, Jennifer. 1998–99. "Attitudes Toward Aging and Death Anxiety." *Omega* 38:59–64.

Descartes, Rene. 1984. *The Philosophical Writings of Descartes,* vol. 2, translated by John Cottingham, Robert Stoothoff, and Dugald Murdoch. Cambridge: Cambridge University Press.

Douglas, Mary. 1966. *Purity and Danger: An Analysis of Concepts of Pollution and Taboo.* London: Routledge & Kegan Paul.

Drolet, Jean-Louis. 1990. "Transcending Death During Early Adulthood: Symbolic Immortality, Death Anxiety, and Purpose in Life." *Journal of Clinical Psychology* 46:148–60.

DuBruck, Edelgard and Barbara Gusick, eds. 1999. *Death and Dying in the Middle Ages.* New York: Peter Lang.

Durkheim, Émile. 1915. *The Elementary Forms of the Religious Life.* New York: Free Press.

———. 1963. *Primitive Classification.* Chicago: University of Chicago Press.

Essien, Ekere James, Michael W. Ross, E. Ezedinachi, and Martins Meremikwu. 2000. "Measuring AIDS Fears in Health Workers: Structure of the FAIDSS Across Countries." *International Journal of Intercultural Relations* 24:125–29.

Feder, Samuel. 1976. "Attitudes of Patients With Advanced Malignancy." Pp. 430–37 in *Death: Current Perspectives,* edited by Edwin S. Shneidman. Palo Alto, CA: Mayfield.

Firth-Cozens, Jenny and David Field. 1991. "Fear of Death and Strategies for Coping With Patient Death Among Medical Trainees." *British Journal of Medical Psychology* 64:263–71.

Florian, Victor and Mario Mikulincer. 1993. "The Impact of Death-Risk Experiences and Religiosity on the Fear of Personal Death: The Case of Israeli Soldiers in Lebanon." *Omega* 26:101–11.

Florian, Victor and Lonnie R. Snowden. 1989. "Fear of Personal Death and Positive Life Regard: A Study of Different Ethnic and Religious-Affiliated American College Students." *Journal of Cross-Cultural Psychology* 20:64–79.

Foss, Martin. 1966. *Death, Sacrifice and Tragedy.* Lincoln: University of Nebraska Press.

Foucault, Michel. 1990a. *The History of Sexuality,* vol. 1, *An Introduction.* New York: Vintage.

———. 1990b. *The History of Sexuality,* vol. 2, *The Use of Pleasure.* New York: Vintage.

Frazer, James George. 1966. *The Fear of the Dead in Primitive Religion.* New York: Biblo & Tannen.

Freud, Sigmund. 1936. *The Problem of Anxiety.* Albany, NY: Psychoanalytic Quarterly Press.

Fulton, Robert. 1977. "The Sociology of Death." *Death Education* 1:15–25.

Giddens, Anthony. 1991. *Modernity and Self-Identity: Self and Society in the Late Modern Age.* Stanford, CA: Stanford University Press.

Gill, Christopher. 1995. *Greek Thought.* Oxford: Oxford University Press.

Glucklich, Ariel. 1989. "Karma and Rebirth in India: A Pessimistic Approach." Pp. 81–87 in *Death and the Afterlife,* edited by Stephen T. Davis. New York: St. Martin's.

Gordon, Rosemary. 2000. *Dying and Creating: A Search for Meaning.* London: Karnac.

Hayslip, Bert, Jr., Debra Luhr, and Michael M. Beyerlein. 1991. "Levels of Death Anxiety in Terminally Ill Men: A Pilot Study." *Omega* 24:13–19.

Heidegger, Martin. 1996. *Being and Time.* Albany: State University of New York Press.

Heinz, Donald. 1999. *The Last Passage: Recounting a Death of Our Own.* Oxford: Oxford University Press.

Helgeland, John. 1984. "The Symbolism of Death in the Later Middle Ages." *Omega* 15:145–60.

Herzog, Edgar. 1983. *Psyche and Death: Death-Demons in Folklore, Myths and Modern Dreams.* Dallas: Spring.

Hinton, John. 1967. "The Physical and Mental Distress of the Dying." *Quarterly Journal of Medicine* 32:1–21.

Hoelter, Jon W. and Rita Epley. 1979. "Religious Correlates of the Fear of Death." *Journal for the Scientific Study of Religion* 45:795–800.

Hoelter, Jon W. and Janice A. Hoelter. 1978. "The Relationship Between Fear of Death and Anxiety." *Journal of Psychology* 99:225–26.

Hollach, Elizabeth and Jenny Hockey. 2001. *Death, Memory and Material Culture.* New York: Oxford University Press.

Jaspers, Karl. 1963. *Philosophy and the World: Selected Essays.* Washington, DC: Regnery.

Jones, James W. 2001. *Terror and Transformation: The Ambiguity of Religion in Psychoanalytic Perspective.* New York: Routledge.

Kant, Immanuel. 1998. *Critique of Pure Reason.* Cambridge: Cambridge University Press.

Kass, Leon R. 1971. "The New Biology: What Price Relieving Man's Estate?" *Science* 19:779–87.

King, Jennifer and Bert Hayslip, Jr. 2001–2. "The Media's Influence on College Students' Views of Death." *Omega* 44:37–56.

Knight, Kim H. and Morton H. Elfenbein. 1993. "Relationship of Death Education to the Anxiety, Fear, and Meaning Associated With Death. *Death Studies* 17:411–26.

Kothari, Manu L. and Lopa A. Mehta. 1981. "The Trans-Science Aspects of Disease and Death." *Perspectives in Biology and Medicine* 24:658–66.

Lifton, Robert Jay. 1979. *The Broken Connection: On Death and the Continuity of Life.* New York: Basic Books.

Maglio, Christopher J. and Sharon E. Robinson. 1994. "The Effects of Death Education on Death Anxiety: A Meta-Analysis." *Omega* 29:319–36.

Malinowski, Bronislaw. 1948. *Magic, Science and Religion and Other Essays.* Boston: Beacon.

Minsky, Rosalind. 1998. *Psychoanalysis and Culture: Contemporary States of Mind.* New Brunswick, NJ: Rutgers University Press.

Momeyer, Richard W. 1988. *Confronting Death.* Bloomington: Indiana University Press.

Montaigne, Michel de. 1993. *The Complete Essays.* New York: Penguin.

Murphy, Jeffrie G. 1993. "Rationality and the Fear of Death." Pp. 42–58 in *The Metaphysics of Death,* edited by John Martin Fischer. Stanford, CA: Stanford University Press.

Patrick, John W. 1979. "Personal Faith and the Fear of Death Among Divergent Religious Populations." *Journal for the Scientific Study of Religion* 18:298–305.

Paul, Robert A. 1996. *Moses and Civilization: The Meaning Behind Freud's Myth.* New Haven, CT: Yale University Press.

Porter, J. R., ed. 1976. *Bible: Old Testament: Book of Leviticus.* Cambridge: Cambridge University Press.

Prabhu, Joseph. 1989. "The Idea of Reincarnation." Pp. 65–80 in *Death and the Afterlife,* edited by Stephen T. Davis. New York: St. Martin's.

Prior, Lindsay. 1989. *The Social Organization of Death: Medical Discourse and Social Practices in Belfast.* New York: St. Martin's.

Rank, Otto. 1936. *Truth and Reality: A Life History of the Human Will.* New York: Alfred A. Knopf.

Rosenbaum, Stephen E. 1993. "Epicurus and Annihilation." Pp. 291–305 in *The Metaphysics of Death,* edited by John Martin Fischer. Stanford, CA: Stanford University Press.

Roth, Nathan. 1978. "Fear of Death in the Aging." *American Journal of Psychotherapy* 32:552–61.

Samuels, Robert A. 1993. *Between Philosophy and Psychoanalysis: Lacan's Reconstruction of Freud.* New York: Routledge.

Sartre, Jean-Paul. 1992. *Being and Nothingness: A Phenomenological Essay on Ontology,* translated by Hazel E. Barnes. New York: Washington Square.

Schopenhauer, Arthur. 1957. *The World as Will and Idea.* London: Routledge & Kegan Paul.

Schultz, Richard. 1979. "Death Anxiety: Intuitive and Empirical Perspectives." Pp. 66–87 in *Death and Dying: Theory/ Research/Practice,* edited by Larry A. Busen. Dubuque, IA: William C. Brown.

Scimecca, Joseph A. 1979. "Cultural Hero Systems and Religious Beliefs: The Ideal-Real Social Science of Ernest Becker." *Review of Religious Research* 21:62–70.

Shapiro, Warren. 1989. "Thanatophobic Man." *Anthropology Today* 5:11–14.

Slote, Michael A. 1978. "Existentialism and the Fear of Dying." In *Language, Metaphysics and Death,* edited by John Donnelly. New York: Fordham University Press.

Solomon, Sheldon, Jeff Greenberg, and Tom Pyszczynski. 2000. "Pride and Prejudice: Fear of Death and Social Behavior." *Current Directions in Psychological Science* 9:200–204.

Sutherland, Stewart. 1978. "Immortality and Resurrection." Pp. 196–207 in *Language, Metaphysics and Death,* edited by John Donnelly. New York: Fordham University Press.

Sypnowich, Christine. 1991. "Fear of Death: Mortality and Modernity in Political Philosophy." *Queen's Quarterly* 98:618–36.

Toynbee, Arnold. 1976. "Various Ways in Which Humans Beings Have Sought to Reconcile Themselves to the Fact of Death." Pp. 13–44 in *Death: Current Perspectives,* edited by Edwin S. Shneidman. Palo Alto, CA: Mayfield.

Tylor, Edward B. 1889. *Primitive Culture,* vol. 1. New York: Henry Holt.

Vernon, Glenn M. 1970. *The Sociology of Death: An Analysis of Death-Related Behavior.* New York: Ronald.

Walters, Conlin D. 1988. "Future Health Care: Increasing the Alternatives." *Futurist* 22:13–15.

Webb, Marilyn. 1997. *The Good Death: The New American Search to Reshape the End of Life.* New York: Bantam.

Weber, Max. 1956. *The Sociology of Religion.* Boston: Beacon.

Worcester, Thomas. 1999. "In the Face of Death: Jean Dulumeau on Late-Medieval Fears and Hopes." In *Death and Dying in the Middle Ages,* edited by Edelgard DuBruck and Barbara Gusick. New York: Peter Lang.

Historical Changes in the Meaning of Death in the Western Tradition

William R. Wood

John B. Williamson

To speak of a single death is to speak biographically. In the deaths of others and in the recognition of our own mortality, death cultivates the creation of stories that testify to the quality of life lived as well as to the relative manner of death itself. To hear that one lived a good life is to combat the nonsensical specter that haunts the modern *bios.*

In some sense, death has always haunted the living. Biography underscores, in particular, a modern proclivity toward individual narrative—death as the last unavoidable chapter of an otherwise fulfilling life, death as the thief of the devoted husband, death as the end of a long period of suffering, death as the accidental drowning of a child. Modern obituaries function as the briefest of biographies from which we can deduce structure and meaning.[1] Senseless death is anathema to us.

Such individuated narratives of death stand historically in marked contrast to earlier traditions in the West. In the philosophical treatment of life as preparation for death, or the *contemptus mundi* of the early Christians, or even in the *danse macabre* of medieval and baroque Europe, death remained a question of the *psyche,* the *nous,* the soul, the species. It served not merely as an end, but also as a beginning, an illusion, a test, an immutable force of nature. Not until the rise of the natural sciences in the late 18th century did matters of life and death become fundamentally organic. In this discursive epistemological rupture, a new biomedical positivism emerged as the legitimate sentinel of life. The language of life itself, once the prerogative of theology and philosophy, became calculated, instrumental. The language of death, on the other hand, reemerged as antithetical, its only function that of nonfunction. Beginning initially with the cessation of breath (which still bore some of the ancient relation between *pneuma* and life), death moved in definition with advances in medicine to the stoppage of the heart, and then finally now to the cessation of brain activity.[2] Bodies begin to fail and break down, systems begin to malfunction. We look to our stories, perhaps, for differentiation.

The historical complement to the rise of the biographical ethos has been the gradual disappearance of death from the world of the living. In the United States and Western Europe, dying is now primarily a private and often technical affair, hidden behind the closed doors of the hospital, the mortuary, and the funeral home. For most of us, the actual witnessing of death will occur quite infrequently over the course of our lives. When it does, as in the case of the death of a friend or loved one, we find ourselves in the uncomfortable position of spectator, witnessing the sublimation of dying to the auspices of professional medical and postmortem practices. With these practices, public and private rituals of dying, burial, and care for the dead common to earlier eras fade into solitary and disconnected stories.

It is this thesis, the radical transformation of attitudes and experiences of dying in the modern world, that has underscored virtually all recent critical works on the history of death in the West.[3] Stemming largely from the

---

1. In speaking about obituaries of well-known figures, William Powers (2001) argues, "Obits are, in a sense, arguments. They make the case for why we should care about a particular life."

2. On the shift in the definition of death from cardiovascular to neurological, from the heart to the brain, see Pernick (1999).

3. Aries (1974) expresses such an attitude when he notes, "In our day, in approximately a third of a century, we have witnessed a brutal revolution in traditional feelings and ideas, a revolution so brutal that social observers have not failed to be struck by it" (p. 85).

work of French social historians, recent works on changing attitudes toward death evidence a shift away from the contracted analyses of funerary art, epitaphs, wills, and occidental literary sources that occupied much of late-19th- and early-20th-century writings on the topic.[4] Historians and other scholars have begun to address the difficult task of elucidating not only what was said about death in earlier times but also the lived experience of dying, expressed not merely in words but in ritual, gesture, and even silence.

It is certainly not the case that critical analyses of literature, wills, epitaphs, and funerary art are lacking in contemporary historiographies. Such analyses continue to serve as primary resources for those concerned with the history of death and dying. Rather, the shift lies more in the posture of social historians toward already established collections of historical knowledge. It is not at all clear, for example, that epitaphs from the 14th century speak any more definitively to ritual and belief in the medieval world than modern gravestone inscriptions speak to contemporary understandings of death and dying. Although epitaphs often help to elucidate funerary customs and religious motifs, they provide less evidence for the myriad practices, beliefs, and rituals that elude or even contradict formal transcription. As such, more recent works (by social historians or others) tend to move among disparate sources and methods, often transgressing earlier disciplinary boundaries and methodologies.

Disciplinary transgressions speak to the difficulty of the task facing historians who are concerned with establishing working parameters from which to investigate changes or shifts in cultural attitudes toward death. In the introduction to his work *The Hour of Our Death* (1981), Philippe Aries argues his methodological imperative: "If the modern observer wishes to arrive at an understanding that eluded contemporaries, he must widen his field of vision. . . . The historian of death must not be afraid to embrace the centuries until they run into a millennium" (pp. xvi–xvii). Yet we might suppose that to "widen one's field of vision" is not necessarily to engage in a millennial historiography. Indeed, among the work of his contemporaries, Aries's work stands arguably as the most chronologically ambitious.

Such a widening of vision, however, requires an epochal familiarity with prevailing ideas, theologies, art, literary themes, and cultural rituals, as well as a questioning of the usefulness of commonly accepted historical demarcations (the classical world, the medieval world, the Renaissance, and so on) in their ability to speak to historical shifts in attitudes on death and dying. Thus Aries proposes an alternative historical scheme in which death had gradually become less familiar to the living, moving initially from what he calls the "tame death" of the ancients

and the early Middle Ages to the "wild death" of the modern world. Similarly, American scholar John Stephenson has proposed in his work *Death, Grief and Mourning: Individual and Social Realities* (1985) the movement in American society from an age of "sacred death" in Puritan times to one of "secular death" and finally "avoided death" in the modern age. Often these alternative historical schemata parallel larger historical transformations in the West. Sometimes, however, they do not. In any case, the historian of death is faced with the question of a beginning and an end, a pericope for transformation that exceeds any one text, monograph, painting, inscription, or ritual.

Finally, to propose that many of the more recent historical works on death and dying share common threads is not to argue that these works are saying the same thing. Most emphatically, they are not. Specifically, most recent works on the history of death lack Aries's chronological ambition. Indeed, many take exception to Aries's (1981) insistence that "the errors [the historian] will not be able to avoid are less serious than the anachronisms to which he would be exposed by too short a chronology" (p. xvii). The examination of such a large time span has the propensity to both illuminate certain shifts and obscure others, particularly in the case of women, the poor, and the dispossessed.[5] In this case, the history of death is no less a battlefield than other social histories, one in which both method and source are central to the histories of the dying, and ultimately to how we interpret our own death. Thus in this chapter we offer only the briefest of sketches, taking into account both the major shifts that have occurred in people's experience of death and dying and the methodological and interpretive collaborations and disagreements central to this endeavor.

PHILIPPE ARIES'S HISTORY OF DEATH

The work of French historian Philippe Aries stands as arguably the most visible social history of death available to date. In *Western Attitudes Toward Death and Dying* (1974) as well as in the better-known *The Hour of Our Death* (1981), Aries proposes that death itself has, from the early medieval period onward, undergone a series of gradual yet discernible changes, which he titles "tame death," "one's own death," "thy death," and "forbidden or wild death."

This fourfold division centers directly on how people experience and understand death. As such, it stands as a peculiar history, one that often eschews more visible changes (e.g., the Reformation) in favor of less discernible shifts present in literature, art (including funerary art), liturgy, burial practices, and wills. It is characterized by the

---

4. On the contribution of the French to social studies of death and dying, see Mitchell (1978) and McManners (1982).

5. Koslofsky (2000) states: "As one reviewer of Ariès's essays has noted (and the point applies to Vovelle's schema as well), many aspects of death in pre-modern Europe, from the gruesome death presented at a public execution to the deaths of heretics, Jews or witches in the wake of mass persecutions . . . fall outside his view" (p. 6).

use or assumption of *mentalités*—attitudes that characterize particular epochs or periods of time.[6] Michel Vovelle (1983, 1990), another French historian and contemporary of Aries, has argued that the primarily French social histories of "attitudes" (*mentalités*) occupy a specific location in the overall investigations into history of death. Such investigations Vovelle divides into three categories: *mort subie* (the burden of death), characterized by works that measure the demographic levels and effects of death in particular places and times; *mort vécue* (experienced death), which seeks to explain how people have understood dying and, in particular, their own mortality; and *discours sur la mort* (discourses on death), which seek to elucidate how philosophy, religion, art, and literature have depicted death.[7] Within this tripartite division, the works of both Aries and Vovelle move among all three, but remain arguably focused on *la mort vécue,* occupied with elucidating the manner in which people have experienced and lived death (see Koslofsky 2000:5).

It was Aries's work that, in the context of French social history, first suggested the usefulness of examining *mentalités* (or attitudes) for understanding long-term changes in attitudes toward death. In Aries estimation, although each attitude (or rather loose collection of attitudes) exhibited a distinct posture toward death and dying, these shifts were also part of a larger gradual movement in the West, where death had receded from the public, visible, and highly stylized rituals of late antiquity and the early Middle Ages toward an increasingly private, individuated, and ultimately socially inchoate event.[8] Hidden from public view, and finally even from the dying person him- or herself, death had became ultimately unspeakable and unknowable. Once tame, the modern world had, in Aries's estimation, rendered death wild.

The tame death was, for Aries, not necessarily commensurate with a tame life, especially in late antiquity and the early Middle Ages, when material conditions were unimaginably horrid and death was a common event. War, famine, pestilence, and childbirth made living a perilous endeavor. A span of 30 years often constituted a full life. The decline of the Roman Empire returned urban populations to the familiarity of towns and villages. Roads declined, and people did not travel long distances, usually living in one location for the entirety of their lives. If death was "tame," it was because people died frequently, in plain view of their townsmen or fellow villagers; in such times, it would have been difficult to die a private death.

The tame death was more than mere familiarity with the spectacle of death, however. Aries (1981) argues that the tame death had been occurring for hundreds or even thousands of years. It was, in his estimation, the "oldest death there is" (p. 28). The rituals that surrounded an individual's approaching death were deeply inscribed into the actions of both the dying and those present at the death. Throughout his work, Aries often juxtaposes the highly stylized and familiar rituals of the tame death against what he understands to be the social incomprehensibility of death in the modern world. In his writings, figures from earlier eras find meaning in ritual. They understand their deaths and what is expected of them in a manner that would appear highly scripted and even unemotional today. In this oldest death, an individual's passing was usually forewarned; it was the dying person who first saw his or her own death, allowing time for preparation, contemplation, and prayer. Aries contrasts this—that the dying knew their own death when they saw it—with the modern hospital or cancer ward, where knowledge of death often comes last, or not at all, to the dying.

Not all deaths in the Middle Ages were so sanguine, however. People died suddenly, violently, or by accident. The death of children was common. Both the ancient and early medieval worlds distrusted those who had died *mors repentina,* in sudden death. Outside the familiar rituals of the tame death, a murky and uncertain world existed in which those who had perished suddenly were suspected, blamed, and potentially excluded from Christian burial. Such attitudes toward the victims of unexpected or violent death had existed for ages. As early as Homer, the shades of those who had been murdered or killed accidentally were understood to present trouble for the living. The specter of death haunts Achilles as the slain Patróklos visits him after his victory over Hektor. "Sleeping so?" Patróklos inquires of his friend. "Thou has forgotten me, Akhilles [*sic*]. Never was I uncared for in life but am in death. Accord me burial in all haste; let me pass the gates of Death" (Homer 1974:chap. 23, ll. 80–84). Virgil spoke as well of the falsely accused and murdered inhabiting the darkest part of the underworld. Their very deaths marked them as suspect and culpable. As Aries (1981) notes:

> The vile and ugly death of the Middle Ages is not only the sudden and absurd death, it is also the secret death without witness or ceremony: the death of the traveler on the road, or the man who drowns in a river, or the stranger whose body is found at the edge of a field, or even the neighbor who is struck down for no reason. It makes no difference that he was innocent, his sudden death marks him with malediction. (P. 11)

---

6. Michel Vovelle (1990) has said about *mentalités:* "It seems to me to be very much the case that we have progressed from a history of mentalities which, in its beginnings, essentially stuck to the level of culture . . . to a history of attitudes, forms of behavior and unconscious collective representations. This is precisely what is registered in the trends of the new research—childhood, the mother, the family, love, sexuality, and death" (p. 5).

7. This discussion of Vovelle is based on Craig Koslofsky's *The Reformation of the Dead* (2000:5).

8. Although the term *Middle Ages* has generally fallen out of favor, it is the term Ariès employs.

By the 12th century, perceptions of innocence and culpability were shifting beyond the boundaries of the *mors repentina*. If for at least a millennium the living had remained "as familiar with the dead as they were . . . with the idea of their own death" (Aries 1974:25), small but discernible changes began to appear that placed more emphasis on the religious significance of a person's own death. Although many of the rituals surrounding death remained familiar, the certainty with which men and women faced death was becoming increasingly individuated. Illustrations of the Parousia depicting Christ as Judge suggested that salvation was moving from a collective rite to an individual trial (Aries 1981:101). The iconography of the Book of Life (*liber vitae*), depicted in paintings as well as in the woodcuts of the *artes moriendi,* illustrated these changes.[9] Prior to the 13th century, the Book of Life had been represented largely as a collection or list of those who were to be saved, a "formidable census of the universe" (Aries 1974:32). Between the 13th and 15th centuries, however, a shift occurred, as the (now) familiar image of the Book of Life, often draped around the neck of the judged, replaced the earlier emphasis on collective salvation. The sins and deeds of human beings emerged as the currency of the Book of Life.

Aries (1974) calls this book a "personal account book." Presumably, this is an allusion to the bookkeeping techniques central to the rise of industrialization and capitalism, both of which play a central role in Aries's analysis of the eventual dissolution of ritual and meaning in the West. Even if capitalism had not yet made large inroads into Europe, Aries suggests that a historical movement toward individualism (so often linked to economic processes) was under way as early as the 13th or 14th century. Unlike the *Homo faber* central to historical materialism, however, or even Max Weber's emphasis on the relationship between Calvinistic salvation and capitalism, Aries (1974) suggests a precursor:

> In the mirror of his own death, each man . . . discover[ed] the secret of his own individuality. And this relationship—which Greco-Roman Antiquity and especially Epicureanism had glimpsed briefly and had lost—has from that time on never ceased to make an impression on our Western civilization. (P. 52)

In the 17th and 18th centuries, although death remained visible in the vestiges of public ritual, the growing division between reason and madness, portrayed so well in Brueghel's *The Fight Between Carnival and Lent* (1559), placed death increasingly within the auspices of the erotic, the phantasmagoric, and the forbidden. Already in Brueghel's painting, the world of carnival (the world of the tame death) is at odds with the increasingly austere, orderly, and rational movements transpiring within the Church and society. It remains perhaps within the later romantic rejection of the Enlightenment, and its turn toward the interior world (including the emphasis on the baroque), where burgeoning relationships among madness, the erotic, and death begin to haunt an increasingly disenchanted world.

A growing fascination with death transpired in the larger context of the removal of the dead from churchyard cemeteries located within cities. The public and visible death, including the daily reminders provided by such town cemeteries, gave way in one sense as the burial places of the dead became themselves casualties of an emerging discourse of concern over public hygiene, disease, and general disregard for the treatment of the body. In both Britain and France, from about 1750 to 1850, the dead were relocated to burial locations outside city walls. This move, however, was coupled with a less visible but nevertheless present emerging cult of the dead (e.g., involving secular cemeteries and familial tombs where one could visit the dead), as well as increasingly erotic depictions of the bodies of the dead (especially the saints), depictions that Aries (1981) calls "the confusion between death and pleasure" (p. 373).

THE CONTESTED MOVEMENT OF DEATH

For Philippe Aries, within the scope of perhaps the past hundred years, death had become wild, forbidden, excluded. Much of Aries's work on death from the 18th century onward (and perhaps the impetus for his work on death as a whole) details the movement away from death as a collective ritual and toward something unmentionable, unspeakable. From the baroque fascination with death in the 17th and 18th centuries, and the later removal of the dead from urban cemeteries in the 19th century, the dying were increasingly disappearing from the world of the living. With both the act and evidence of death removed from public view, it was not long before the dying themselves were repositioned behind the opaque veneer of hospitals, nursing homes, and mortuaries. According to Aries, by the middle of the 20th century death had become invisible, or worse. In the words of English anthropologist Geoffrey Gorer ([1955] 1965), it had become pornographic.

This thesis of Aries, this "forbidden death," is arguably at the center of the resurgence in the scholarship and

---

9. Aries (1981:107) notes that in the 15th century, the iconography of the Last Judgment was replaced by a new iconography that was popularized by the printing press in the form of books containing woodcuts, individual images that each person could contemplate in his or her own home. These books were the treatises on the technique of dying well, the *artes moriendi. Latin artes moriendi* emerged around 1475, and translations into German, English, Dutch, and French followed.

debate surrounding the history of death and dying. Virtually no contemporary work on the social history of death in the West does not reference the work of Aries, if not directly address his arguments. Perhaps because of this, or in spite of it, the dearth of scholarship is least evident in historical studies of death from the 18th century to the present. Yet within this scope, many scholars have taken exception to Aries's use of *mentalités*.[10] They have also taken exception to his lack of geographic specificity and class analysis. Perhaps most important, although it is clear that changes have taken place in people's attitudes toward death and dying over the previous three centuries, whether these changes constitute a "rupture," in Aries's terms, and whether such a rupture denotes the radical exclusion of death and aging from contemporary life, is not at all certain.[11]

What is clear is that, from the 17th century onward, death was already receding from its more traditional religious and social roles. The way in which people experienced death was changing. Part of the explanation for this is demographic. Increasing urbanization in Britain and Western Europe underscored growing anonymity, both in life and in death. It also allowed for a degree of freedom not common to provincial and rural ecclesiastical parishes. The recurring appearance of the plague, smallpox, and influenza in Britain and continental Europe between the 15th and 17th centuries ensured that death remained visible in and central to the lives of both urbanites and those living in provincial areas. But this visibility, as Aries notes, was already moving toward an increasingly individualized perception of death, if not yet in Puritan America, then certainly in both Britain and France, where the convergence of medicine, commerce, and incipit industrialization provided further discursive impetus toward a view of the individual as the emerging locus of truth in an increasingly secular world.

If death was becoming increasingly individualized, so was the fate of the body and its location after death. As Aries (1974) notes, "In the second half of the eighteenth century . . . the accumulation of the death within the churches or in small churchyards suddenly became intolerable" (p. 70). On the surface, the impetus for this newfound concern came largely in the form of newly perceived health dangers involving the close proximity of the living and the dead. In response to this health crisis, the dead, who had for so long been buried within the city walls and churches, were increasingly moved to outlying cemeteries or familial plots. Beginning in the middle of the 18th century, a massive displacement of cemeteries, particularly urban cemeteries, to outlying regions was undertaken; this displacement continued for almost a century in France. This was the case in Britain as well, where as early as 1726, Thomas Lewis had published *Churches to Charnel Houses; Being an Enquiry Into the Profaneness, Indecency and Pernicious Consequences to the Living, of Burying the Dead in Churches and Churchyards* (Houlbrooke 2000:193). In 1839, George Alfred Walker's *Gatherings From the Graveyards* painted for its audience an alarming picture of the putrescence and visible gore present in graveyards (Rugg 2000:220).

The communicability of death and decay reached a peak in the middle of the 19th century. By that time, a large number of private and commercial burial sites had emerged in both Britain and France. Such sites were located almost uniformly on the outskirts of towns or cities, away from the traditional churchyard sites (Houlbrooke 2000:193). By 1850, in Britain, private cemetery companies in effect had begun to take over from the Church the role of caretakers of the dead. As Rugg (2000) explains: "A series of Burial Acts . . . built on the success of cemetery companies by permitting the establishment of Burial Boards. . . . The Church's virtual monopoly on provision for the dead had been irredeemably shattered" (p. 221). In place of the Church arose the first professional organizations concerned solely with the disposal of the dead.

Yet within the emerging discourses on hygiene and health, more than one impetus was at work in the drive to relocate cemeteries and burial plots outside of city centers. Hygienic arguments alone do not adequately explain the transfer of cemeteries to outlying regions (Kselman 1993:167). A new relationship between the living and the dead was emerging as well, a relationship appropriate not only to health but to the individuality required of both parties. Such a relationship, contrary to the concerns of the hygienists, was evidenced not in the increased removal of the dead from the world of the living, but rather in the

---

10. As Mitchell (1978) has noted, "The French perception of the problem . . . has generally been in terms of *attitudes toward death*." This seems correct in the case of Aries's work, as well as that of Michel Vovelle. Such works, Mitchell argues, are characterized by "the famous search for a definition of *mentalités* that has guided the efforts of French historians and determined the course of their investigations. They seek not what we could precisely call an ideology of death, but they do hope to synthesize a popular conception or collective attitude, and to trace its evolution over several centuries" (p. 685).

11. Georges Minois's writings represent a challenge to Aries's proposition that the exclusion of death in France is a historically recent phenomenon. In his work *Histoire de la vieillesse* (1987), Minois argues that although death, and particularly death of the elderly, was in fact excluded from much of daily life, this exclusion was far older than Ariès realized. Minois places the rupture between accepted and excluded death not in the rise of modern medicine, or even in the rise of capitalism, but rather in the shift from oral to written cultures. Michel Vovelle, as well, has questioned Aries's insistence that the "forbidden death" was necessarily a new phenomenon. Vovelle's well-known *La Mort et l'occident: de 1300 à nos jours* (1983) was critical of both Aries's methodology and his conclusion that the exclusion of death signified a recent and radical break in French history. Vovelle proposes that, although death had indeed become alienated and invisible to most of the living, this process occurred more gradually than Ariès himself has estimated, perhaps 200 or 300 years earlier than he proposes in *The Hour of Our Death* (1981).

movement of the living to these newly relocated places of the dead. Cemeteries, for so long the anonymous grave sites of the faithful, were over time replaced with individual burial sites or plots. In and around Paris and other urban centers, such plots began to appear in number for those who could afford them. Some plots were quite exquisite or even ostentatious, but many bore nothing more than names and brief inscriptions, particularly in more urban areas (Aries 1974:49). The coffin, as well, came to be seen as "an essential element of the decent funeral, even for the poor" (Houlbrooke 2000:193). Easily accessible to the living—not for purposes of prayer or devotion, but for purposes of visitation—such plots evidenced individual characteristics almost unknown since antiquity. The acceptability of the mass grave and the anonymous burial was replaced with an emphasis on individuality, even in death. A secular sentimentality for the dead was emerging.

This sentimentality played out along several vectors. On one hand was the emerging personal relationship between the living and the deceased. By the end of the 18th century, the visitation of the dead was becoming increasingly common. Those with money could afford to bury their family members at home, on family property. Those not inclined to do so were still able to visit the deceased, buried as they were in public cemeteries. However, as Aries (1974) notes, "in order to be able to visit them, the dead had to be 'at home,' which was not the case in the traditional funeral procedure, in which they were in the church" (p. 72). The dead required homes of their own. On quite another level was the emergence of civic and national sentiment surrounding the places of the dead:

> The use of mausolea shifted memorialism of the dead to areas outside the confines of the church building. In France from the 1770s there was considerable discussion of the need for new places in which to bury the dead which would celebrate civic virtue rather than spiritual worth. . . . In England a shift away from the spiritual worth of the deceased is best reflected in the neoclassical treatment of civic and military heroes. (Rugg 2000:208)

Although the hygiene-related arguments of health officials kept the spaces of the dead at bay for perhaps a hundred years, the growing movement toward memorials—both private and public—slowly returned the dead to the inner sanctuary of the city. Devoid of either their posthumous relationship with the Church or their propensity for disease and sickness, the cemeteries, memorials, and mausoleums became in essence secularized cults of the dead. In this manner, it was the "unbelievers [who became] the most assiduous visitors to the tombs of their relatives" (Aries 1974:72).

This secularization occurred throughout Western Europe as well as in the United States. In the United States, however, there were marked differences stemming from the geographic insularity of America—what David

Stannard (1977) has called the prevalence of a "Puritan way of death" (we discuss this topic below). In the case of Europe, however, the work of another scholar, Barbara Ann Day (1992), provides a useful longitudinal index for understanding the changing expectations of life and attitudes toward death in early-modern Europe. In analyzing various common prints depicting the "stages of life," Day found that in the earliest known prints from 16th-century Amsterdam "for the most part, death was central to the Stages of Life. The very placement in [the] sixteenth century Dutch version of that theme demonstrates its function as arbiter standing on the axis of a rotating universe" (p. 694). By the 17th century, however, the centrality of death had been altered. Death had been relegated to its position under the bridge of life, instead of at the center of it. According to Day, death's descent from a superior to an inferior location, the fundamental change of both the trajectory of life and the role of death, represented a radical shift. As death sank slowly to a position below the bridge of life, the bridge itself came to act as a shield for those "privileged figures located on the rising scale of status and age" (p. 695).

Yet the figures are not privileged merely because they are shielded from death. Rather, as the prints changed from the 16th to the 17th and 18th centuries, the depiction of exactly who was walking across the bridge of life shifted as well:

> The concurrent displacement of the gleaner from earth to an underground domain and the ascendance of the bourgeoisie to the top of the pyramid function as a historical telltale that marks a major transformation in cultural attitudes. Such shifts in priority register not only separation from death, but also changes in power relations that favor the prerogative of the French bourgeoisie. (Day 1992:696)

Thus, for Day, the gradual displacement of death, first from the cosmic center to under the bridge of life and then finally disappearing altogether from prints in the late 18th century, represents the larger historical movement toward the exclusion of death. It also suggests a class distinction that was already playing out both before and after 1789; the rising bourgeoisie were growing into expectations of a longer life, a *complete* life with its various stages, that moved progressively through the world over the specter of death (Day 1992:697).

By the early 19th century the expectation of longer life was becoming more realistic, particularly for those living in urban centers. The appearance of public health offices, as well as advances in medical science, made the understanding, anticipation, and prevention of mortality an increasing reality (Rugg 2000:203). Within this movement toward an understanding of life and death as a natural phenomenon, Michel Foucault has proposed, it is in fact with the natural sciences, at the end of the 18th century, where the greatest shift in the understanding of life and death emerged. In his work *The Order of Things* (1973),

Foucault argues that by 1795, a transformation occurred (largely in the work of Cuvier) that allowed the natural sciences to introduce a precise and technical definition of life. In what Foucault terms the "era of biology," the natural sciences reorganized not around the language of the visible (Aristotelian) systems of classification, but rather around the principle of the "organic," the deduction of the living and the nonliving through the classification of biological function.

> From the moment when organic structure becomes a basic concept of natural characterization, and makes possible the transition from visible structure to designation, it must of course cease to be no more than a character itself. . . . This being so, the opposition between organic and inorganic becomes fundamental. (Pp. 231–32)

It is this fundamental shift, Foucault notes, that allowed Vicq d'Azry to exclaim in 1786, "There are only two kingdoms in nature, one enjoys life and the other is deprived of it" (p. 232).

The recognition of the difference between living and nonliving had of course existed before this rupture. Foucault's (1973) point, rather, is that the shift represented a reorganization of classifications schemes within the natural sciences that allowed for the distinctly scientific distinction between life as "that which produces, grows and reproduces" and the nonliving as "that which neither develops nor reproduces . . . the unfruitful—dead" (p. 232). The shift that allowed Cuvier to relate functions, as opposed to appearances, enjoined life as a function unto itself. Whereas "life" and, with it, death had before been inexorably enjoined with religion, and then later philosophy and even humanism, the organic definition of life rejoined nothing but the beginning of a purely technical and operational functionality. In a short time, through discursive and often unconnected processes, the idea of the natural or normal life began to replace (if it had not already) the fear and trembling of the Christian tradition. The good life, as depicted in Day's work on the stages of life, was slowly evolving into the expectations of a bourgeois class nurtured on the positivism of 19th-century life—increased life expectancy, decreased illness, urban growth, and industrialization. The belief in the movement forward in history was perhaps nowhere better expressed than in the redefinition of life itself, which, given its natural course, had nothing but death to fear.

The implication of Foucault's proposal finds the physician, rather than the priest, at the bed of the dying. Whereas the Church had, with little regard for the body, attended (perhaps not always sufficiently) to the needs of the soul, it was the state and its relation to the emerging bureaucratic organization of hospitals, clinics, health boards, and public hygiene that found the greatest interest in the body itself. Keeping track of the dead and dying, along with disease and famine, "was the beginning of a process that would eventually re-create dealing with death as a municipal and medical function, increasingly hidden from the general population" (Rugg 2000:216). Not only the act of dying, but the management of illness, disease, pestilence, and death became functions for public or semi-public bureaucratic institutions, hidden behind the veneer of daily life.

If it is true that by the 19th century "death could be viewed as a natural phenomenon, over which man appeared to have increasing control" (Rugg 2000:203), it is in this context of control where death was largely redefined through the languages of management (public hygiene and disposal of the dead) and pathology (medicine and illness). Medical inventions such as inoculation and immunization, improvements in diet and hygiene, and public health projects all contributed in the latter half of the 19th century to advances in life expectancy, decreases in infant mortality, and a general improvement in health for those lucky enough to escape class warfare, genocide, and slavery. But control over death was effected in another important way as well. Quite simply, the dying were themselves beginning to disappear from the world of the living. If the deceased had returned in their civic cemeteries and public monuments to the center of urban life, it was the dying who were, by the end of the 19th century, becoming increasingly removed from view. With the advent of the 20th century, the rise of institutions responsible for the dying and the dead would prohibit all but the most cursory of interactions between the two worlds.

To argue, as John Stephenson (1985) does, that by the end of the 19th century Europe and the United States had moved in large part to a "secular death" is to admit that such a term serves, at best, as a general indicator. To be sure, religious considerations of the fate of the soul waxed and waned—as they do today in both Europe and the United States. It is clear, however, that by the dawn of the 20th century the epiphanies of the deathbed scene, as well as the anguish of the Puritan struggle with salvation, had all but disappeared. The place of the confessor at the bedside was increasingly filled by that of the medical practitioner. The state had taken over, either directly or through the licensing of professionals, the role of the care of the dead. Death was becoming, in most aspects, impersonal, managed increasingly through bureaucratic and professionalized institutions.

THE SHORT 20TH CENTURY

In an essay originally published in 1955, anthropologist Geoffrey Gorer ([1955] 1965) argued that the treatment of death in the 20th century bore many similarities to the treatment of sex in the previous one. In the Victorian era death was openly discussed, but sex had become increasingly taboo, kept from children, performed only behind closed doors with the lights low. In Gorer's estimation, the situation had reversed itself some 100 years later. Sex was now discussed more freely, whereas death had become taboo, dirty, hidden—pornographic.

It is the contention of both Gorer and Aries that this change occurred over a short period of time, somewhere between the end of the 19th century and the middle of the 20th century. Similar to Aries, who argues that death had become shameful and forbidden, Stephenson (1985) has written of the movement in the 20th century toward "avoided death." He notes:

> The lack of open observance of mourning and the individualization of grief have aided in banishing references to death in everyday living. No longer are those who are grieving easily identified. Any public display of strong feelings is considered inappropriate today. . . . [T]he relegating of death to institutions has removed death from the home, and hidden it behind institutional walls. (P. 41)

The difference in the terms that Stephenson and Aries use is negligible. The main facets of the argument that a radical change occurred, particularly in the case of the United States, center on the following observations of historians and social scientists: a growing fear and anxiety surrounding death and aging (Becker 1973); the refusal to discuss death, particularly with the elderly, the infirm, or the dying themselves (Glaser and Strauss 1968, 1978); the removal of the elderly and the dying to nursing homes, hospitals, and hospices (Stephenson 1985); the increasing medicalization of death (Illich [1976] 1982; Aries 1981: 563–88); and the beautification and cosmetic enhancement of the dead and the professionalization of the funeral industry (Mitford 1963, 1998).

If, in the above-mentioned processes, death had indeed become excluded and pornographic, it is also Aries's contention that this exclusion of death—far above its mere secularization and increased individualization—began in earnest in the United States. Exactly why Aries believes this impetus came from America is unclear. In many ways American changes in attitudes toward death and dying in the late 18th and early 19th centuries parallel those that took place in Western Europe. In some important ways, however, they do not. In his well-known work *The Puritan Way of Death* (1977), David Stannard addresses the unique context from which American attitudes toward death emerged. According to Stannard, the Puritan tradition of death in America is important, as it led Americans to resist much of the secularization and individualization surrounding death in 18th-century Europe. Even as Enlightenment ideas took hold in urban centers toward the end of the century, the intensely individual death of the Puritans, even in vestiges, remained present. In one sense, the Puritan death *was,* as Weber argued, intensely personal and perhaps excruciatingly so. Stannard notes that "the Puritans were gripped individually and collectively by an intense and unremitting fear of death" (p. 79). On the other hand, this occurred while they were *"simultaneously*

clinging to the traditional Christian rhetoric of viewing death as a release and relief for the earth bound soul" (p. 79).

We can imagine that this experience was perhaps not so different from that of Puritans in Europe. What was different—and is worth consideration, according to Stannard—was that, in contrast to Aries's supposition that the extended family was the primary familial structure in the 17th and early 18th centuries, the nuclear family was already present and central in Puritan life in both America and England. Stannard (1977) suggests that this proposition does not seriously compromise Aries's thesis, however, "since the central idea of his argument is not really dependent upon . . . the changing structure of the individual family life" (p. 169). Aries's argument is not dependent upon this changing structure because, for Stannard, Puritan nuclear families formed interfamilial relationships that functioned in much the same way as extended family structures. Might we not suppose, however, that this difference, insignificant in Puritan 17th-century America, would gain significance as the world of Puritan New England gave way to a world of increasing industrialization, capitalism, science, and medicine? According to Aries, it is exactly in the growing relations of the nuclear family where the dead would begin to be shunned, pitied, and lied to. It was the members of the nuclear family, as much as the doctors and the institutions, who would eventually turn their heads away at the moment of death.

It is not so difficult to imagine that the relative speed and thrust of capitalism and the emerging Industrial Revolution were central to these changing attitudes. In Puritanism, the community was held close through interfamilial structures as well as through the Puritans' own understanding of themselves and their divine mission on earth (Stannard 1977:169). The speed with which the Puritan view of death lost its sway, as America moved from provincialism to "the nineteenth century attitude towards death and dying that was characterized by self-indulgence, sentimentalization, and ostentation" (Stannard 1977:171) underscores the rapid movement from an intensely religious worldview to one characterized by growing emphasis on commerce, individualism, and productivity. As Aries (1974) notes, in the 19th century

> in the United States, everything was happening as if the Romantic interval had never existed, and as if the mentality of the eighteenth century had persisted without interruption. [But] this hypothesis was false. It did not take sufficient account of American Puritanism, which is incompatible with confidence in man, in his happiness. . . . We must concede [however] that the phenomenon we have just observed occur much later than the French Enlightenment. (P. 96)

It is not merely that these phenomena occurred later, but that they occurred much more rapidly, within the contexts of three devastating wars (the Civil War and World Wars I and

II), a series of economic depressions including the Great Depression, rapid advances in medicine and science, increasing longevity, and an emerging normalized rubric of health and life. Stephenson (1985) argues that perhaps the massive carnage and loss of life stemming from World War II[12], following so closely on the losses of the Great War, produced a kind of "death overload" in which "the extensive mourning process and the sentimental approach to grief of the past were seen as old fashioned" (p. 31). If such an overload existed, perhaps it was not so much because of the wars themselves—after all, wars, plagues, and massive illness were common to modern Europe. Rather, perhaps it was within the expectation of longer and healthier lives, induced no doubt in part through the increasing medicalization and commodification of daily life, that the tragedy of war, both in the United States and Europe, became most present.

A note of caution to anyone who would seek any single explanation for Aries's tentative thesis: If a rapid change—an exclusion—of death has characterized much of the 20th century, there are still substantive differences among France, Great Britain, and the United States, for example, that require explanation. The practice of embalming, common in the United States for at least the past hundred years, has made hardly any inroads in either Britain (where cremation is common) or France. If the United States has exported its denial and exclusion of death, why has this practice that seemingly refuses to acknowledge death (a practice devoted to making the dead appear as lifelike and serene as possible) not taken hold? Similarly, the rise of memorial services in the United States, with their requisite managed, contrite emotionality, has not been imitated in other countries, where more traditional funerals are still the norm. In many respects, common characteristics exist; the institutionalization and medicalization of death, to a greater or lesser degree, stands central to all Western cultures. But within these cultures, if we assert that something like a *mentalité* of death exists, we must temper our assertion with a recognition of the enormity of difference and distinction present throughout the West.

EPILOGUE: TOWARD A NEW ACCEPTANCE OF DEATH?

In the past 30 years, "back-to-death movements" have challenged our growing alienation from and exclusion of death. Much has been written on the hospice movement in both Britain and the United States, for example, as a humane response to the growing impersonalization and dehumanization of death in hospitals and nursing homes. Death awareness, spurred on by the publication of Elisabeth Kübler-Ross's *On Death and Dying* (1969), has challenged the notion that death should remain hidden

behind closed doors. Marilyn Webb (1997) writes of the return to prepared dying—a mix of traditions from both the East and the West that seeks an alternative to the medicalized and insular institutional death. Even prime-time television, it seems, has a response to the "taboo pornography" of death in the HBO television series *Six Feet Under,* in which semimorbid humor attempts to interject the discussion and visibility of death back into the world of the living, or at least the world of the living who are able to view HBO.

Such movements, however, have their detractors as well. All of these movements are in some way mediated through the reality of commerce. Is good dying merely becoming good business? Ron Rosenbaum (1982) has said of the back-to-death movement inspired by Kübler-Ross:

> What's been lost in the general approbation of Kübler-Ross's five stages is the way her ordering of those stages implicitly serves a *behavior control* function for the busy American death professional. The movement from denial and anger to depression and acceptance is seen as a kind of spiritual *progress,* as if quiet acceptance is the . . . highest stage to strive for. (P. 34)

In a bifurcated and even schizoid culture, the effectiveness of death professionals seems reasonable. In a culture that reasons death.

When a friend's mother recently passed away—in the hospital—all anyone could think to say was "I'm sorry." Our friend later confessed that he felt dirty, used, taken advantage of. People were unable to address him directly, permitting nothing but the most hollow of phrases. He refused to engage in conversation about his mother's death with anyone who had not earned the right to participation in her life. In many deaths, including those of close family members, we have witnessed much the same thing—a medicalized and excruciatingly painful death followed by awkwardness and a sense of bewilderment.

Somewhere between the nether regions of the dying who inhabit the county hospital and HBO's guarded optimism, people are seeking alternatives. The hospice movement, although not uncontroversial, is testament to the success of social movements that are increasingly concerned not only with the question of life but also the manner of death. It is unclear, however, if such movements can continue to shoulder the burden of caring for the dying in a world increasingly defined by the attenuation of social welfare, huge gaps in the distribution of wealth, burgeoning medical costs, and a growing elderly population. If the redefinition of life that Foucault describes as the separation of the organic and nonorganic signified the beginning of the era of biology, it is the medicalization of life, so defined, that remains for most of us the likely conclusion to the biographies we seek of ourselves.

---

12. Overall, in World War II a staggering 61 million people were killed.

REFERENCES

Aries, Philippe. 1974. *Western Attitudes Toward Death: From the Middle Ages to the Present,* translated by Patricia M. Ranum. Baltimore: Johns Hopkins University Press.

———. 1981. *The Hour of Our Death,* translated by Helen Weaver. New York: Alfred A. Knopf.

Becker, Ernest. 1973. *The Denial of Death.* New York: Free Press.

Day, Barbara Ann. 1992. "Representing Aging and Death in French Culture." *French Historical Studies* 17:688–724.

Foucault, Michel. 1973. *The Order of Things: An Archaeology of the Human Sciences.* New York: Pantheon.

Glaser, Barney G. and Anselm L. Strauss. 1968. *Time for Dying.* Chicago: Aldine.

———. 1978. *Awareness of Dying.* Chicago: Aldine.

Gorer, Geoffrey. [1955] 1965. "The Pornography of Death." Pp. 192-99 in Geoffrey Gorer, *Death, Grief and Mourning.* Garden City, NY: Doubleday.

Homer. 1974. *The Iliad,* translated by Robert Fitzgerald. Garden City, NY: Doubleday.

Houlbrooke, Ralph. 2000. "The Age of Decency: 1660–1760." In *Death in England,* edited by Peter C. Jupp and Clare Gittings. New Brunswick, NJ: Rutgers University Press.

Illich, Ivan. [1976] 1982. *Medical Nemesis: The Expropriation of Health.* New York: Pantheon.

Koslofsky, Craig. 2000. *The Reformation of the Dead: Death and Ritual in Early Modern Germany.* New York: St. Martin's.

Kselman, Thomas A. 1993. *Death and the Afterlife in Modern France.* Princeton, NJ: Princeton University Press.

Kübler-Ross, Elisabeth. 1969. *On Death and Dying.* New York: Macmillan.

McManners, John. 1982. "Death and the French Historians." In *Mirrors of Mortality: Studies in the Social History of Death,* edited by Joachim Whaley. New York: St. Martin's.

Minois, Georges. 1987. *Histoire de la vieillesse.* Paris: Fayard.

Mitchell, Allan. 1978. "Philippe Aries and the French Way of Death." *French Historical Studies* 10:684–95.

Mitford, Jessica. 1963. *The American Way of Death.* New York: Simon & Schuster.

———. 1998. *The American Way of Death Revisited.* New York: Alfred A. Knopf.

Pernick, Martin S. 1999. "Brain Death in a Cultural Context: The Reconstruction of Death, 1967–1981." Pp. 3–33 in *The Definition of Death: Contemporary Controversies,* edited by Stuart J. Youngner, Robert M. Arnold, and Renie Schapiro. Baltimore: Johns Hopkins University Press.

Powers, William. 2001. "Dying to Be Read: What Obits Tell Us." *National Journal,* February 17, p. 505.

Rosenbaum, Ron. 1982. "Turn on, Tune in, Drop Dead." *Harper's,* July, pp. 32–40.

Rugg, Julie. 2000. "From Reason to Regulation: 1760–1850." In *Death in England,* edited by Peter C. Jupp and Clare Gittings. New Brunswick, NJ: Rutgers University Press.

Stannard, David E. 1977. *The Puritan Way of Death.* Oxford: Oxford University Press.

Stephenson, John S. 1985. *Death, Grief and Mourning: Individual and Social Realities.* New York: Free Press.

Vovelle, Michel. 1983. *La Mort et l'occident: de 1300 à nos jours.* Paris: Gallimard.

———. 1990. *Ideologies and Mentalities,* translated by Eamon O'Flaherty. Chicago: University of Chicago Press.

Webb, Marilyn. 1997. *The Good Death: The New American Search to Reshape the End of Life.* New York: Bantam.

DEALING WITH DEATH

Western Philosophical Perspectives

MICHAEL R. TAYLOR

Seeking means to transcend death is a widespread, if not universal, inclination among human beings. The Western philosophical tradition has developed numerous viewpoints on, and fostered various attitudes toward, our mortal nature. In this chapter, I discuss five distinct strategies that have had significant impacts on how we think about and cope with death. I offer an explanation of how these ideas get developed by some of the major philosophers and their followers, followed by a consideration of the attitudes toward death that these views are likely to engender. For a discussion of reincarnation, Plato's account is a good place to begin; I follow this with an overview of the medieval Christian understanding of death developed by Saint Thomas Aquinas. Attitudes and beliefs about death changed at the dawn of modern science, and I consider here both the dualistic theory of Descartes and the skeptical approach developed by David Hume, exploring some of the consequences of their views. Finally, the unique contribution of existentialism is exemplified by the distinctive way in which human finitude figures into the thought of Martin Heidegger. Some of the oldest accounts still have a great deal of influence; Saint Thomas and Descartes articulate ideas that still have impacts on the attitudes of many people. Plato's account of the transmigration and reincarnation of souls has fallen out of favor in the West, but it has not entirely disappeared.

THE ANCIENT GREEKS AND THE TRANSMIGRATION OF SOULS

Among the ancient Greeks, the most striking view concerning death is the idea that souls migrate into new bodies. This view was not widely held among the Greeks, but some religious sects and philosophical schools were committed to the doctrine of the transmigration of souls. Plato developed the most extensive account of these ideas in several of his dialogues. He probably borrowed some elements of his account from the Greek religions of his day, and he may also have incorporated some of the ideas of the Pythagorean philosophers (Bostock 1986:12).

Two fundamental beliefs are central to Plato's thought about death: the doctrine of recollection and the transmigration and reincarnation of souls. The doctrine of recollection amounts to the idea that the soul contains within it knowledge of the most fundamental realities, which Plato calls "Forms." The soul, according to Plato, exists eternally and is always in possession of this knowledge. The task of human beings is to recover this knowledge buried deep within the recesses of the soul. The knowledge must be recovered because it has been forgotten due to the shock of the soul's entry into the body. The ultimate meaning of human life is, in this account, the recovery of the knowledge of the true nature of things that lies hidden in the souls of every human being. It is our ignorance concerning these ultimate realities that gives rise to human evil, misery, suffering, and injustice. Recovery of the knowledge forgotten by the soul leads to harmony and justice both within the individual and, under the right circumstances, in society.

The fate of the soul depends, in Plato's view, on the success of the quest to recall the forgotten knowledge buried within each of us. This quest can succeed only if we adopt and practice the proper philosophical attitudes along with unremitting devotion to living the philosophical life. It is through the practice of philosophy that we recover from the soul knowledge of the Forms. The practice of philosophy is illustrated through the method, called *dialectic,* practiced by Socrates in Plato's dialogues. Far from being a mere irritant (although he was surely that), Socrates attempted to motivate people to care for their souls rather than for the wealth and power they saw being coveted by those around them. He tried to do this by drawing out their ideas and then submitting those ideas to examination in order to see if they could stand the test of criticism. According to Socrates, it is only by ridding ourselves of our false beliefs that we will become motivated to search for the knowledge that we truly need if we are to set our souls in good order. The souls of those who engage in the philosophical life and who recover the soul's hidden knowledge live eternally with the gods after the body dies, and their lot is immensely better than that of those here on earth.

What, then, awaits the soul when the philosophical life is not attained? Although Plato (1981:120) didn't intend what he said about this matter to be taken as the literal truth, he asserts that it is reasonable for humans to expect something very much like the following: The fate of such souls is to be reincarnated, and the nature and quality of our future incarnations depends on our conduct in our current lives. Those who have discovered the truth concerning the eternal and unchanging realities go to a blissful realm and enjoy communion with the gods and contemplation of the Forms. If we have lived good lives by conventional standards but have not recovered the knowledge within us through the practice of philosophy, then we can expect to live again in the form of some social creature (as ants, bees, wasps, or as human beings again). If, however, we have not lived good lives, we can expect to return in some less desirable form, perhaps as hawks, kites, or asses (donkeys, I presume). Plato further suggests that those who live extremely evil lives may not return at all, but instead continue to exist in eternal torment (p. 121).

In the final book of the *Republic,* Plato introduces the "Myth of Er." This is the story of a warrior, Er, who was apparently slain in battle. The bodies of the dead were collected and Er's body was placed upon his funeral pyre, but he revived and reported an extraordinary experience that he had while "dead." Er claimed to see souls coming up from the earth or down from the heavens. These souls were about to be sent back into the world and were in the process of choosing the patterns of their upcoming lives. The choices that they made concerning the lives on which they were about to embark turned out to be heavily influenced by the moral quality of their previous lives. Thus one's past life has significant consequences for one's future prospects, but it is still up to each person to decide what to make of the conditions imposed upon him or her by the upcoming life (Plato 1992:285–86).

Although I know of no evidence in support of this contention, it seems likely to me that the so-called Myth of Er is not, properly speaking, a myth. I think that it could be an account of what we today call a *near-death experience* (or NDE). A near-death experience sometimes occurs when a person is pronounced clinically dead or appears, given all empirically observable evidence, to be dead, but then regains consciousness. Occasionally a person who has undergone such an occurrence will report having had particular experiences while unconscious. Descriptions of NDEs reveal a recurring pattern, and Er's story resembles many of these reports. The structure of NDEs often

includes a sensation of leaving the body, traveling through a kind of tunnel, arriving in a place of light, and being in the presence of other (usually benevolent) beings, followed by (often unwilling) return to the revived body (Beloff 1992:263).

Most contemporary accounts of NDEs describe them in positive terms, but the further back in time we look, the more reports we find that include a requirement that the individual account for his or her life and how it was lived, along with judgment of that life. Carol Zaleski (1987) describes these older versions:

> The soul is either embraced or disowned by its guardian angel and challenged by evil spirits who look for traces of their influence; its merits or demerits, hidden during life, are now disclosed. Again, at the divine tribunal, the soul's deeds are displayed in the form of victims who come forward to testify against it. (P. 73)

NDEs have not always been perceived as entirely pleasant, and in the older accounts that Zaleski describes there is commonly a significant element of anxiety involved. Thus, although Er's experience may seem to deviate from contemporary accounts of NDEs, which tend to be uniformly positive, it squares pretty well with the descriptions transmitted by inhabitants of the ancient or medieval world. Of course, Plato may have modified Er's report to suit his own purposes.

Arnold Toynbee (1968) notes the similarity between the view of the soul as eternal and undergoing multiple incarnations and the conception widely held by Eastern philosophers, in which the soul is reincarnated in various forms until it achieves enlightenment:

> One conception of the immortality of the soul has been that souls are not only immortal but eternal: i.e. that every soul has been in existence eternally before it ever came to be embodied, and that it will remain in existence eternally after becoming disembodied once [and] for all. Of all the divers conceptions of personal immortality of the soul, this is the one that comes nearest to the Indian conception of a supra personal or a depersonalized immortality. This belief was held by some pre-Christian Greeks, but never, so far as we can judge, by more than a small sophisticated minority. (P. 86)

It is not known whether there was some common root from which the belief arose both in India and among the Greeks, but it is a remarkable view, and the timing would have been right for there to be either a common source or some kind of cross-fertilization. We simply have no knowledge of the matter.

One Platonic dialogue seems to be much less decisive about our prospects for postmortem existence. In the *Apology,* which gives an account of the trial of Socrates, Plato portrays Socrates as unwilling to commit to any very definite ideas about what awaits us after death. Socrates holds at the end of the dialogue that the good man has nothing to fear from death, because either the soul will survive or death will amount to personal annihilation. If the latter, then there is nothing after death, and so there is nothing for anyone to fear. If this is so, then there is nothing for the good man to fear. If, on the other hand, the soul survives bodily death, then for the good person what comes will presumably be something good. It is not reasonable to fear an improvement in one's condition, so, if the good man can expect something good after death, once again he has nothing to fear. In either case, death should hold no terrors for the good person (Plato 1981:43). Of course, that leaves the vast majority of us unaccounted for; few of us would think ourselves entirely good, and Socrates remains silent concerning the matter of what death may hold for the rest of us. There may be ample reason for most of us to adopt a fearful attitude toward death.

In the *Apology,* Socrates seems far from certain concerning the fate of the soul. Perhaps it continues to exist, and if the person has lived a good life, then something good can be expected. Or perhaps the death of the body amounts to the annihilation of the person. Socrates leaves the matter at that and does not attempt to decide between these alternatives. Perhaps Socrates and Plato held divergent views concerning what it is reasonable to believe about the fate of the person after the death of the body. Socrates may have been uncertain about whether the soul continues to exist, but Plato may have thought he had good reason to suppose that it continues to exist after the body dies.

Plato advocates an attitude that involves embracing our mortal nature. He defines death as the separation of the soul from the body, and he asserts that the body is a source of distraction from the pursuit of wisdom (understood as knowledge). Death thus removes a major obstacle to the pursuit of wisdom. Because philosophy is the love of wisdom, the philosopher should look forward to the time when the soul can engage in its pursuit of wisdom undisturbed by the perturbations of the body. Understood in this way, philosophy boils down to practice for death, because the philosopher attempts to pursue pure knowledge, and this pursuit can be successful only if the soul becomes separated from the body. So philosophers ought to look forward to death, not fear it (Plato 1981:100–103). An attitude of fearlessness and hopeful anticipation is, in Plato's view, the appropriate one for us to adopt toward our future demise.

Although Plato's views concerning death can be inspiring or consoling to those who have, or believe that they have, the high-powered intellect needed for grasping the Forms, they offer little solace to the rest of us. For people who are caught up in the daily business of survival there is little time left after working, paying the bills, and attending to family responsibilities to devote to achieving the contemplative philosophical life that Plato advocates. For those of us caught up in the concerns of everyday existence, Plato's ideas concerning death may not seem very comforting. The only bright spot is that we will get another chance next time around on the cycle of death and rebirth,

and yet another, until we finally achieve the knowledge harbored within our souls. Still, for those not philosophically inclined (probably the vast majority of humankind), the thought of the next life being one of philosophical contemplation of the eternal realities is unlikely to appear very attractive. Plato nowhere suggests that after death we will experience some of the things that many look forward to most, such as reunion with deceased loved ones. However, for those able to make use of them, Plato's views can take, and have taken, a good deal of the sting out of our impending demise. Socrates died well, and the Christian philosopher Boethius found immense consolation in Plato's views while awaiting his execution (see Boethius 1962).

MEDIEVAL CHRISTIANITY AND THE RESURRECTION OF THE DEAD

With the rise and spread of Christianity, Western philosophical ideas concerning the prospects for survival of bodily death underwent significant change. Medieval Christians believed not only that the soul continues to exist after the body dies, but that the body itself would, at some future time, be resurrected and reunited with the soul. This doctrine of the resurrection of bodies apparently did not originate with Christianity. If Toynbee (1968) is right, "This belief in the bodily resurrection of all dead human beings is common to Christianity and Islam, and, like the belief in judgment noted earlier, it seems to have been derived by both religions from Zoroastrianism via Pharisaic Judaism" (p. 90). Not only Muslims, Christians, and Zoroastrians held this belief; the Egyptians seem to have believed that at least some dead human bodies could be resurrected (Toynbee 1968:90).

The doctrine of resurrection receives its most sophisticated philosophical development in the hands of Saint Thomas Aquinas, who believed that in order to be a human being it is necessary to be a combination of body and soul. The soul is the principle of life and hence indispensable, but the body is also necessary if this life is to be the life of a human person. The soul by itself enjoys certain powers, such as understanding, willing, and considering, but in order to enjoy the powers of sensation, it must be united with a body. Taken together, soul and body united make up a complete human being (Aquinas 1992:93–96). In Thomas's view, no postmortem survival of the person is possible without the body, because the soul by itself does not constitute a person. Anthony Kenny (1993) points this out:

> Aquinas undoubtedly believed that each human being had an immortal soul, which could survive the death of the body and continue to think and will in the period before the eventual resurrection of the body to which he looked forward. Nonetheless, Aquinas did not believe in a self which was distinct from the body, nor did he think that disembodied persons were possible. (P. 138)

In other words, we will most assuredly undergo death, which we (in the sense of a self) will not survive. Our soul will survive this death, but our soul and our personal identity are not the same thing, and so the survival of the death of the body by the soul is insufficient for our continued existence as selves or persons.

The Thomistic picture looks something like this: When a person dies, the soul separates from the body and goes to its proper place; eventually, at the appropriate time, it is reunited with the resurrected body. The soul is, according to this account, created by God and conjoined with the body at some point during development; it is not eternal in the sense that it exists everlastingly, both before and after its embodiment. Rather, it is created and conjoined with the body. The soul remains in existence throughout the person's life and continues to exist after the person dies. The body, on the other hand, undergoes death. At some time in the future, the body is resurrected and reunited with the soul, and at that time the person is reestablished and enjoys eternal life through the grace of God. It is in this way that Christians achieve their final end, happiness, which is unobtainable in the present earthly form of existence.

There are a number of problems associated with the idea of the resurrection of the body. Imagine, for example, that cannibals have eaten someone; how can that person's body be resurrected when it is now part of other persons? Thomas assures us that "whatever is wanting will be supplied by the Creator's omnipotence" (Aquinas 1992:99). This response, however, leaves unanswered a number of troublesome questions. Will my resurrected body be in the same condition as it was when I died? For some, that would be an unpleasant prospect indeed. Will it be the feeble, infirm, frail body of old age? Or will it be the body as it was during the prime of life? Attempts to answer such questions, and others like them, seem to have a strong element of arbitrariness about them.

More important, from a philosophical point of view, issues concerning identity arise when one entertains the idea of resurrection. At the heart of this issue is the question of whether the resurrected body will be identical to the body that was conjoined with the soul during the earthly existence of the person. In part, this amounts to the question of whether the resurrected body will be made of the same "stuff" as the earthly body. Will the new body be composed of the same atoms and molecules as the original body? Will it be made of the same flesh, blood, and bone? Subject to the same vulnerability, pain, pleasure, growth, and decay? Or will it be composed of some special, spiritual kind of stuff, less subject (or even immune) to degeneration, decay, and injury? If the latter, how can it be identical to the original body rather than merely a facsimile of it, made out of some other material?

We might also wonder whether the resurrected body could be the same as the original body if there is a break between the existence of the earthly body and the resurrected one. Suppose the body dies, decomposes, and is finally reduced to its most basic constituent parts. Come resurrection day, all these parts are rounded up by an infinitely powerful and omniscient God, who reassembles them in exactly the way they were arranged before the original body decomposed. Is the reassembled body identical to the original one? Some philosophers contend that a break in the existence of an object amounts to a break in its identity. According to this view, the total destruction of a body, whether through natural decomposition or some other means, undermines the idea that the restoration of that body through the collection and reconstitution of its constituent parts is capable of preserving identity. The body of the person will be, at best, an exact replica, down to the last detail (even the last atom), but it cannot be the same, identical body (van Inwagen 1992:244).

The resurrection of the body was the mainstay of Christian belief during the Middle Ages. It is still today the official doctrine of many Christian denominations, including Roman Catholic (Clary 1998:198), Assemblies of God (Horton 1998:6), Baptist (Hendricks 1998:44), Lutheran (Lee 1998:165), and Methodist (Warren 1998:228). Despite the philosophical problems inherent in the idea of resurrection, many of the faithful still appear to reap considerable comfort from this belief. It certainly seems to fit in better with the way many people conceive of the afterlife and what they hope to get from it than do Plato's ideas about the contemplative disembodied soul.

In thinking of the world to come, few envision a soul eternally contemplating the Forms. Rather, they think of union with the divine; freedom from pain, suffering, decay, disability, and sin; and reunion with lost loved ones. In other words, they think of the afterlife as very much like life here, but freed from things that make earthly life a burden. Thinking about reunion with those loved and lost is usually imagined in bodily terms; those loved and lost people are recognizable in their bodily form. This imagined reunion is a great consolation for many people. So the belief in resurrection is, for many, more comforting than the intellectualism of Plato. It is not necessary, in the case of resurrection, to practice the life of the Platonic sage in order to achieve beatitude; a desirable form of eternal existence is available to all of the faithful. Faith does not require the great intellectual gifts necessary to apprehension of the Forms; rather, it depends on one's belief in the saving power of the Divine, and such belief seems to be open to all. In fact, approaching faith in an overly intellectual manner often results in suspicion within the community of the faithful. Faith is supposed to be a matter of the heart, not of the head.

What the faithful picture when they consider the afterlife is a relation with a personal Divine Being, reunion with deceased friends and relatives, and freedom from sin and the sufferings associated with flesh-and-blood existence. These benefits are bestowed after death; the soul survives bodily death, and its conjunction with the resurrected body is anticipated at some future time appointed by God. One need not have a superhuman intellect or pass through more lives in order to look forward to the benefits of the life to come. Such a vision helps the faithful to maintain an attitude of hope while at the same time acknowledging the reality of death.

KEEPING MIND AND BODY TOGETHER: DESCARTES AND MODERN SCIENCE

A different way of conceiving the relationship between soul and body developed as modern philosophy began to separate from its alliance with theology and place itself in the service of the emerging new science. The father of modern philosophy is generally held to be René Descartes. Descartes famously divides reality into mind and matter. Actually, according to Descartes, reality is made up of three separate substances—mind, matter, and God—each of which possesses a different essence. The essential property of divinity is perfection. In order for something to count as matter, it must possess the property of extension; that is, it must exist in space. The essential property of mind is thought (Descartes 1980:62–63). Mind and matter, having different essential properties, can be conceived apart from one another, and Descartes (1980:93) holds that what the mind can conceive as separate, God can make to exist separately in reality, so mind and body can actually exist apart, in separation from one another.

The Cartesian mind is conceived as a conscious ego that possesses capacities such as intellection, willing, imagining, affirming, and denying; Descartes uses the word *thinking* in a very wide sense to cover all of the activities of consciousness. The body, on the other hand, is matter, and its operation is fundamentally mechanical (Descartes 1980:96–97). It is the mind that possesses the characteristics traditionally ascribed to the soul; the body is basically a machine. The mind, or soul, can exist without the body, if God makes it so; as mind has an essence different from that of body, the two can be conceived separately, and what the mind can conceive as separate, God can cause to exist separately (p. 93). Given that the soul can exist in separation from the body, it can survive the death of the body, and so long as God continues to preserve it, there is no reason the soul should ever perish. So, in Descartes's view, the soul can survive the death of the body and continue to exist eternally under the influence of God's creative power.

Unlike Saint Thomas, who holds that it is essential to personhood that there be a union of both the soul and the body, Descartes associates the self—that is, personal identity—with the mind or soul. According to Descartes, I could continue to exist apart from my body, although I could not engage in a fully human existence, because the sensations that human beings undergo would no longer be fully available to me (Cottingham 1998:84–85). But, according to Descartes (1980:93), these experiences of

sensation are not part of my personal identity, and given that this is so, their lack would not obstruct my continued existence as a self in the form of a disembodied soul. The soul, then, may continue to exist in the absence of the body while maintaining personal identity, and so we can think about existence after the body dies in terms of the existence of disembodied souls. What is important for my continuing existence is the survival of my soul, and the resurrection of my body is of secondary importance or may be entirely neglected. Because our souls are the bearers of our personal identities, their continuing existence is enough to assure us that we need not die when our bodies die.

A serious drawback of this view emerges when we start to wonder how the soul and body might be related to one another. Descartes (1980:98) asserts that they are causally connected, but he makes these two separate substances so entirely distinct that it is hard to understand how they could ever be closely bound together. How can an unextended thinking substance be conjoined with a material object to begin with? The nature of extended things is to occupy space, and the soul, not possessing the property of extension, cannot be localized in space. Where, then, will the conjunction of mind and body take place? Any specification of the point of conjunction would spatially locate an unextended thinking thing. The problem here is not that the soul might fail to survive the death of the body; rather, it lies in the difficulty of our trying to comprehend how it could ever have been connected with the body in the first place. Problems along these lines have led some to attempt to dispense with the two-substance account (dualism) altogether.

But if we are not the conjunction of body and soul, then what are we? We could try to answer this question by following the path laid out by an influential branch of modern science, which aims to reduce the soul and its mental activity to states of the brain and nervous system. If this reduction should prove successful, it will eliminate the need to explain the relation between the soul and the body, for in this account there is no soul to be related to the body. We can, of course, take up this project, and indeed many very capable people have taken it up. But even though there have been numerous attempts to carry out a successful reduction, and many expressions of faith that it can be carried out, there is nothing on the horizon that suggests an emerging consensus on a plausible way to reduce mental states to brain or nervous system processes.

Why does Descartes believe himself to be warranted in asserting that he is a mental substance, anyhow? It might be held that the most that Descartes is entitled to conclude is that there is thought (Copleston 1960:105). Descartes may have supposed that if there is an activity, such as thought, there must be something engaged in that activity; that something he calls the mind, or mental substance, and he understands it to be an unextended thinking thing. But why could it not be the brain that thinks? Descartes holds that, as the brain is a material object, its essence is extension, and because extended things operate in a purely mechanical fashion, an explanation that limits itself in this way cannot adequately account for thought. At best, it can offer an account of reflex behavior (Cottingham 1998:69).

The trend toward attempting to explain the mental by appeal to the physical is very much in the spirit of Descartes's conception of what it means to be a science. Taking physics as his model, he insists on the reduction of scientific explanation to the mechanical operation of efficient causes. For Descartes, anything that counts as a science must be able to offer ultimate explanations in terms of efficient causality and mathematical laws. Given this conception of science, and the fact that the scientific enterprise soon expanded beyond the realm of physics to include biology, psychology, and social science, it is unsurprising that the new science should begin inquiries into the mind and try to bring it under the sway of scientific investigation. To accomplish this after Descartes meant that science would have to explain the mind in terms of the body, conceived as a kind of machine, and the most prominent candidate for such an explanation is the brain. There is, of course, a bit of irony here, given Descartes's own conception of the mind as a thinking thing, by which he means an immaterial, unextended substance.

Although Descartes gives us what appear to be grounds for hope that we might survive the death of the body in the form of an immortal soul, the logic of his thought helps to undermine such a hope. As the scope of science expanded beyond the mechanical and geometric physics that Descartes had in mind, it eventually crept into the areas of life and mind. But the Cartesian conception of what counts as science was never given up, and that meant that these new areas of scientific endeavor had to be able to produce the same kind of mechanical and mathematical explanations that prevailed in physics. The disenchantment of life and mind are inevitable given this model of explanation and the expansion of science. And so the grounds for hoping that the Cartesian mind might outlast the corporeal husk begin to appear shaky. Science is increasingly taken to be the paradigm for knowledge, and what science investigates is the brain; but the brain dies along with the rest of the body.

Despite the many problems associated with Cartesian dualism, something very similar to it seems to enjoy widespread acceptance among those who believe in life after death. Even if the official doctrines of their churches accept the resurrection of bodies, some people are concerned less with their resurrected bodies than with the fate of their immortal souls. Whether they subscribe to a version of the doctrine of resurrection or not, they tend to think of their personal identities as being associated with their souls and not their bodies. So it is the fate of the soul that is of most concern; if the soul continues after the body dies, and the soul is the seat of personal identity, then the person continues. This provides an additional comfort for some, who believe that they don't really have to die. They will admit, "Oh, yes! The body dies," but then quickly add the qualification "but that isn't really me; I am an immortal soul; and since the soul is immortal, I never really die." The body is, from this point of view, a disposable husk, and little interest is shown regarding its fate.

I am not sure how widespread this pseudo-Cartesian belief really is, but I suspect it has a fairly large following. It is worth noting that the people who hold this belief usually emphasize different qualities of the soul than did Descartes; whereas his emphasis was primarily on the intellectual powers associated with the soul, they see the elements of moral character as more important. Still, their view is a Cartesian one in the sense that they (usually without self-conscious realization) subscribe to a version of dualism in which body and soul are conceived as two separate and distinct substances, and in doing so they inherit most of the problems associated with that view.

Descartes gives almost no attention to the ultimate fate of the soul or the nature of its disembodied existence, but to some contemporary religious believers, these matters are all-important, for they think that their souls are headed either for heaven or for hell, destined for eternal bliss or eternal suffering. Arnold Toynbee (1968) observes that these people should be among the most anxious of those who believe in any kind of personal immortality:

> The believer in a personal immortality which he may be going to spend either in heaven or in hell, according to the verdict that will be passed, after his death, on his conduct while he was alive, ought, if he holds this belief bona fide, to be the most anxious of all; and his version of the belief in personal immortality ought to have the greatest effect of all on his present behavior. (P. 93)

And so it would seem, as such people understand themselves to live under the threat of eternal damnation. Yet they often do not seem anxious at all; rather, they are serene in their assurance that they will be the recipients of good offices in the appointments to come. This tension between what one might plausibly expect of them and their actual comportment suggests that the belief functions primarily to allay death anxiety by including the assumption that the believer will be among those destined for the heavenly side of the dichotomy. The attitude of such people toward death is generally sanguine, for they believe that they will never truly die and that good things await them when their bodies expire.

The hope that the mind or soul might be separable from the body was further undermined by the growing influence of the experimental method. In some (probably very complex) way, the experimental method relies for its results on confirmation through sense perception, and so much emphasis is placed on what is observable. An empirical experimentalism has come to be included among the fundamental ideas of science. But observability is precisely the property that the Cartesian mind lacks.

SKEPTICISM AND
THE GROWTH OF SCIENCE

As modern science grows, accumulates experimental evidence, and enjoys increasing success in manipulating and predicting events, it becomes ever more entrenched as our paradigm for what counts as knowledge or even rational belief. Along with a growing tendency to rely primarily on observation and experience comes a rise in skepticism directed toward unobservable entities such as mind and soul. No one has epitomized this skeptical attitude more thoroughly, or employed it with more devastating results, than David Hume. Although there is a tendency among scholars today to avoid the image of Hume as an unrestrained and wholly destructive skeptic, certainly he remains a model of the skepticism characteristic of modern thought. His insistence that any expectation of survival after the death of the body can find no ground in reason or experience constitutes a serious assault on the complacency of those who seek refuge from threatened annihilation in the views of Plato, Saint Thomas, or Descartes. Hume's skeptical analysis has two main prongs: an attack on the idea of substance followed by a series of arguments leading to the conclusion that expectation of survival after the death of the body is unreasonable and bootless.

Hume's attack on the soul or mind, conceived as a separate substance, is grounded in his commitment to empiricism. Basically, his position is that our ideas are copies of impressions that we receive through the senses, or compounds and combinations of these sense impressions. If we lack a sense impression, we can have no corresponding idea (Hume 1977:13). Hume next points out that we have no sense impression of the mental beyond our experience of various mental states, such as intellection, judging, willing, doubting, and emotion. These kinds of experiences exhaust our impressions of the mental; we have no impression of a separately existing substance that supports all of these mental activities or in which they inhere. As we have no such impression, we have no such idea, and hence no ground for supposing that such a thing exists; nor can we have any idea of such a substance, because an idea is a copy of an impression, and we have no such impression. Thus Hume (2000:164–65) sets out to undermine the notion of a separable substance that might go on existing after death.

The second prong of Hume's battery of arguments against immortality consists of a moral argument and a series of analogies. The moral argument examines the view that immortality is required in order for the virtuous and the vicious to receive their just rewards. In reply, Hume (1965:162–63) contends that, as every effect has a cause, and that cause has a cause of which it is the effect, so back until we reach the first cause of all, God. Given that God is, ultimately, the cause of everything, all things that happen are ordained by God, and so nothing can rightly be visited with God's punishment or vengeance. Hume also puts into question the idea of eternal damnation by invoking our intuition that in cases of just retribution there should be some relation of proportionality between the offense and its punishment. He then asks how, given that we are so morally frail, human beings could commit any offenses warranting eternal damnation (p. 164).

Finally, Hume develops a series of analogies drawn from nature to discredit the idea that the soul might survive the death of the body. One of the more interesting is the idea that the waxing and waning of the soul parallel the growth and degeneration of the body: In infancy, when the body is weak, so is the soul or mind. As the body gains maturity and strength, so does the soul. As the body slips into the degeneracy of old age, so the mind begins its slide toward senility. Finally, the body dies; if the proportionality between mind and body holds, then the next logical step would be to suppose that the mind or soul dies as well. As Hume (1965) himself so bluntly puts it, "The last symptoms which the mind discovers, are disorder, weakness, insensibility, and stupidity; the forerunners of its annihilation" (p. 165).

Hume continues his attack on the idea of immortality by pointing out that no form of life survives in conditions very different from the original ones in which it is found; trees perish in water, fishes in the air, men in the earth. Why, then, think that a change so great as the death of the body, which is the environment of the soul, would have no significant effect on the soul? Surely it would be more just to suppose precisely the opposite: that when the body dies, the soul perishes as well (Hume 1965:166).

Hume concludes his series of arguments with a consideration of change as a general feature of the universe. Everything, no matter how firm it may seem at the moment, is subject to change. It comes into being and passes away. The universe itself shows signs of its possible decay. Why suppose that one thing, the mind or soul, apart from all else found in nature, is exempt from the principle that governs all else? We do not experience its stability or resistance to change. Experience points in precisely the opposite direction: The mind is subject to serious disorders, such as those brought on by stroke, mental illness, senility, or physical injury. Judging on the basis of experience, we ought to conclude that the fate of all else within the order of nature befalls what we call the mind or soul as well. When the body dies, according to Hume (1965:166–67), so do we, including our mind or soul.

One could object, with some justice, that Hume employs an empirical standard when dismissing the likelihood of the continued existence of the soul. It is, then, little wonder that the soul fails the test, because the soul, if it exists at all, certainly does not exist as the sort of thing that might be known through empirical investigation relying on the senses. Thus the idea that we have no impression of mental substance demonstrates nothing, because if there were such a substance it would be, by its very nature, imperceptible. There is something like this seeming arbitrariness in many of Hume's arguments, and he deploys these arguments with telling effect in dismissing the intelligibility of the mind or soul and a good many other things as well. Perhaps what Hume does best is make us acutely aware of the limits of intelligibility within the framework of a thoroughgoing empiricism applied in a ruthlessly consistent way.

The appropriateness of Hume's universal application of empirical standards to all things, including supposed metaphysical entities, has been the subject of significant criticism. It seems undeniable, however, that Hume expresses a powerful strand of the modern outlook formed by the rise of the empirical sciences, their ascendance and eventual edging out of the religious point of view, and finally their hegemony over the entire intellectual landscape. Some empiricist philosophers of the 20th century saw Hume as their forerunner, and there has been a resurgence of interest in his philosophical ideas over the past hundred years. His view is representative of much of the current philosophical thinking concerning the fate of the soul after the body dies.

What kind of attitude toward our impending death is appropriate? The simple and straightforward answer, of which I think Hume would approve, is that impending death puts us in a position to accept the plain, brute, and unalterable fact of our mortality. It isn't that Hume denies the possibility of survival beyond the death of the body; he allows that anything other than an outright self-contradiction is possible. Rather, he denies that there is any basis in reason or experience for belief in survival beyond bodily death. We would do well, then, to accept our finitude and adjust our expectations to what we can reasonably hope for. What we can reasonably hope for is a relatively long, healthy, and vigorous life, and a death as free from pain as possible. If this seems like cold comfort, remember that Hume himself demonstrated the viability of his own view. By his conduct in the face of death, Hume showed us that we can live this attitude and that by doing so we can command the respect of those we love and who care for us (Mossner 1980:589–603). In Hume's account, the appropriate attitude toward death is one of humility; if we successfully cultivate this perspective on mortality, we finally come to understand that the universe is not as horrified as we are by the idea that it might have to get along without us.

EXISTENTIALISM AND DEATH: ONE'S OWNMOST POSSIBILITY THAT CANNOT BE OUTSTRIPPED

Human finitude, and particularly concern for our mortal nature, took a new turn in the 20th century, when it became a central theme in European philosophy. The German thinker Martin Heidegger made facing up to one's own death a crucial element of his philosophy. Heidegger holds that a confrontation with one's own finitude is an indispensable feature of the human project, and that without it one is unable to achieve an authentically human life. For Heidegger, many, perhaps most, of us will live inauthentic

lives, mostly due to our evasiveness concerning our own finitude. Living an authentic, fully human life involves an unavoidable confrontation with the death that is one's own.

According to Heidegger, generally and for the most part, *Dasein* (roughly, Heidegger's term for *human being*) avoids facing up to its mortal nature by means of diverting its attention away from thoughtful consideration of its death. *Dasein* finds itself thrown into a world, into a situation that it did not choose and had no hand in creating, and immerses itself in the everyday objects and projects that it encounters. Its understanding of its own conditions and projects is provided by the "they," an anonymous, public understanding that *Dasein* finds ready-made and that it is strongly encouraged to accept without question. A prefabricated understanding of and involvement in the objects and projects of the everyday divert us from confronting the nature of our finitude. By losing ourselves in everydayness, we shield ourselves from seeing that our own existence, as well as our way of existing, is not a mere given but an issue for us. Without such an understanding, authenticity, in Heidegger's (1962:303) sense of the word, is unattainable.

We tend to lose ourselves in the everyday existence of the "they," and this anonymous, public understanding discourages us from being attentive to our own finitude and the fact that we must (and will) die. This anonymous, public understanding insists that such concern is morbid, useless, or unhealthy, but it is not entirely successful in diverting *Dasein*'s attention (Heidegger 1962:223). The experience of anxiety calls us away from our involvement with the objects of everydayness and the concerns of the "they." Anxiety is similar to fear, a strong emotion that is difficult to ignore, but whereas fear has an object, anxiety does not, so it takes our attention away from involvement with things and other people and throws us back upon ourselves. As Stephen Mulhall (1996) puts it:

> In effect, then, anxiety plunges Dasein into an anxiety about itself in the face of itself. Since in this state particular objects and persons within the world fade away and the world as such occupies the foreground, then the specific structures of the they-world must also fade away. Thus anxiety can rescue Dasein from its fallen state, its lostness in the "they"; it throws Dasein doubly back upon itself as a being for whom its own Being is an issue, and so as a creature capable of individuality. (P. 110)

In this way, anxiety constitutes an opportunity for *Dasein* to divest itself of its involvement in the everyday, to rid itself (at least temporarily) of the understanding that is articulated for it by the "they," and to confront its own finitude.

The encounter of *Dasein* with its own finitude is an indispensable element of authenticity. If I respond to the experience of anxiety, then I find myself facing "that possibility which is one's ownmost, which is non-relational, and which is not to be outstripped" (Heidegger 1962:294), that is, my own upcoming death. It is one's ownmost possibility in the sense that only I can die my death, and no other can substitute for me; in this sense, death is the ultimate form of individuation. Others, of course, can die in my place, but this does not exempt me from dying my own death, it only postpones the moment when I must die. It is also isolation, in the sense that I must die on my own; no one can accompany me into my death, although they may be there beside me as I die. And this possibility cannot be outstripped; I cannot successfully avoid it, and it is not an option that I could choose to reject. By threatening to bring to a close all of *Dasein*'s possibilities, it reveals that *Dasein*'s own existence is an issue for itself.

Dasein's realization that its own existence is an issue for itself focuses attention on the fact that, for the most part, any issues that surround *Dasein*'s existence have been left in the hands of others; that is, *Dasein* has not authentically appropriated its own existence. This awareness opens up the opportunity for *Dasein* to make its existence its own rather than a mere reflection of understandings and engagements preapproved by the "they." In order to do this, *Dasein* must choose for itself its own way of life, must endorse its own engagements selected from among its genuine possibilities. Authenticity, in this sense, involves the acceptance of responsibility for that into which one is thrown (for these conditions establish, in large part, what one's genuine possibilities are), as well as for the projections one makes and the possibilities one chooses on the basis of that thrownness. This shouldering of responsibility, instead of relying on the "they" to provide understanding in these matters, is what makes authenticity a possibility for *Dasein*. *Dasein* becomes authentic when it resolves to endorse and make its own the choice of its possibilities on the basis of its own thrownness (Heidegger 1962:343–44). The attitude that we should adopt toward our own impending death is to keep it constantly before our minds, giving it the concernful attention it deserves if it is to play its role effectively in making a humanly authentic existence possible.

Heidegger incorporates human finitude, the death of the human person, into the life of *Dasein* by making death integral to authentic human existence and wholeness. He does not suggest that there might be something awaiting us after the body dies; he offers no hope of a continuation of *Dasein*'s existence after death. To find fault with Heidegger for this would be to miss the point; it is the fact of our finitude that gives us the possibility of being authentically human.

Heidegger's view of death and its importance for an authentic form of human life has been criticized for being excessively focused on the self and the meaning that death has for that self. Although Heidegger acknowledges that a human way of being is always being among others, he largely ignores the importance of being with others in his consideration of the central role played by death in the achievement of authenticity. What is important is *my* death; the death of others is a secondary matter, and may even be part of that evasiveness that prevents me from facing up to

my own finitude. In relation to his concern for death, Heidegger represents *Dasein*'s concern for and relationships with others mainly as impediments that obstruct *Dasein*'s possibilities for coming to grips with its finite nature. But the criticism loses some of its bite if Heidegger is right in his characterization of the "they" and everydayness as ways of fleeing from a confrontation with our own mortality.

CONCLUSION

All of the philosophical views that I have discussed in this chapter represent distinct ways of coming to terms with the fact that we die. Most Western thinkers have abandoned Plato's account of reincarnation, but similar ideas are still a central feature of much Eastern philosophy. None of these ideas concerning our postmortem fate has achieved hegemonic status. Hume has his adherents, as does Descartes, and theologians and philosophers continue to debate and elaborate upon the issues surrounding resurrection. These, along with Heidegger's strategy for making death meaningful even if we do not ultimately overcome it, all remain live options from the philosophical point of view. Not all philosophical problems are without solutions, but there is at present no prospect for a consensus concerning the matter of what is, ultimately speaking, in store for us when we come to our end.

REFERENCES

Aquinas, Saint Thomas. 1992. "The Resurrection of Man." In *Immortality,* edited by Paul Edwards. New York: Macmillan.

Beloff, John. 1992. "Is There Anything Beyond Death? A Parapsychologist's Summation." In *Immortality,* edited by Paul Edwards. New York: Macmillan.

Boethius. 1962. *The Consolations of Philosophy,* translated by Richard Green. New York: Macmillan.

Bostock, David. 1986. *Plato's Phaedo.* New York: Oxford University Press.

Clary, Francis X. 1998. "Roman Catholicism." In *How Different Religions View Death and the Afterlife,* 2d ed., edited by Christopher Jay Johnson and Marsha G. Magee. Philadelphia: Charles.

Copleston, Frederick. 1960. *A History of Philosophy,* vol. 4, *Modern Philosophy Descartes to Leibniz.* Garden City, NY: Doubleday.

Cottingham, John. 1998. *Philosophy and the Good Life: Reason and the Passions in Greek, Cartesian, and Psychoanalytic Ethics.* New York: Cambridge University Press.

Descartes, René. 1980. *Discourse on Method and Mediations on First Philosophy,* translated by Donald Cress. Indianapolis: Hackett.

Heidegger, Martin. 1962. *Being and Time,* translated by John Macquarrie and Edward Robinson. New York: Harper & Row.

Hendricks, William L. 1998. "A Baptist Perspective." In *How Different Religions View Death and the Afterlife,* 2d ed., edited by Christopher Jay Johnson and Marsha G. Magee. Philadelphia: Charles.

Horton, Stanley M. 1998. "Assemblies of God." In *How Different Religions View Death and the Afterlife,* 2d ed., edited by Christopher Jay Johnson and Marsha G. Magee. Philadelphia: Charles.

Hume, David. 1965. *Of the Standard of Taste and Other Essays,* edited by John W. Lenz. Indianapolis: Bobbs-Merrill.

———. 1977. *An Enquiry Concerning Human Understanding,* edited by Eric Steinberg. Indianapolis: Hackett.

———. 2000. *A Treatise of Human Nature,* edited by David Fate Norton and Mary J. Norton. New York: Oxford University Press.

Kenny, Anthony. 1993. *Aquinas on Mind.* New York: Routledge.

Lee, Daniel E. 1998. "Lutherans." In *How Different Religions View Death and the Afterlife,* 2d ed., edited by Christopher Jay Johnson and Marsha G. Magee. Philadelphia: Charles.

Mossner, E. C. 1980. *The Life of David Hume.* New York: Oxford University Press.

Mulhall, Stephen. 1996. *Routledge Guidebook to Heidegger and Being and Time.* New York: Routledge.

Plato. 1981. *Five Dialogues: Euthyphro, Apology, Meno, Crito, Phaedo,* translated by G. M. A. Grube. Indianapolis: Hackett.

———. 1992. *Plato's Republic,* translated by G. M. A. Grube; revised by C. D. C. Reeve. Indianapolis: Hackett.

Toynbee, Arnold A. 1968. "Traditional Attitudes Toward Death." In *Man's Concern With Death,* edited by Arnold Toynbee, Keith Mant, Ninian Smart, John Hinton, Simon Yudkin, Eric Rhode, Rosiland Heywood, and H. H. Price. London: Hodder & Stoughton.

van Inwagen, Peter. 1992. "The Possibility of Resurrection." In *Immortality,* edited by Paul Edwards. New York: Macmillan.

Warren, James I. 1998. "United Methodist Church." In *How Different Religions View Death and the Afterlife,* 2d ed., edited by Christopher Jay Johnson and Marsha G. Magee. Philadelphia: Charles.

Zaleski, Carol. 1987. *Otherworld Journeys: Accounts of Near-Death Experience in Medieval and Modern Times.* New York: Oxford University Press.

DEATH DENIAL

Hiding and Camouflaging Death

BERT HAYSLIP, JR.

Death anxiety is a common human attribute. May (1950) suggests that death is the most obvious symbol of the individual's fear of "nonbeing," in that each of us has a finite existence. Indeed, it has been said that all anxiety is rooted in our awareness of our own mortality (Kastenbaum 1992). In this context, Becker (1973) has similarly observed that the fear of death is universal, and indeed underlies all other fears that we as human beings have. Thus the "morbidly minded" argument (Becker 1973) regarding how humans come to fear death presumes that such fears are therefore threatening and must be defended against. Consequently, anxiety about death may be prototypical of all anxiety, emphasizing not the transcendence of death but its coexistence with loving relationships (May 1969). Recognizing death-related fears can enhance the quality of an individual's life, whereas ignoring them may lead to self-deception (Nuland 1994).

CULTURAL MANIFESTATIONS OF DEATH DENIAL

Death and dying can be understood at many levels. Although we often think of the denial of death as an individual phenomenon, cultures vary in terms of the extent to which they deny the reality of death, and individuals' responses to death are to a certain extent a function of the cultural contexts in which the individuals are born, grow, mature, and eventually die. Indeed, Kearl (1989) argues that death is socially and culturally constructed; that is, individuals' feelings and attitudes about death and dying are reflected in their particular culture's use of language, the culture's religious or funeral rituals, and the values placed on different lives in the culture (e.g., the death of a child may be seen as more tragic than the death of an older person). In addition, a culture may attach greater social value to some deaths than it does to others (e.g., a death due to cancer may be more highly valued than one due to suicide or to AIDS, or the death of a highly visible public figure, such as John F. Kennedy, Jr., may be valued more than the death of a homeless person).

Events as small as a single robbery or as large as the terrorist attacks of September 11, 2001, force individuals to reconstruct their views about life's predictability and the controllability of death. Like individuals, cultures have "thresholds" beyond which the emotional, interpersonal, political, and economic impacts of particular events are significant enough to lead cultural members to modify their daily lives. Such changes in the degree to which death is denied are therefore in part culturally driven, as when the United States mandated changes in security procedures at airports after the September 11 disaster, undermining our sense that we are immune to such tragedies. Depending on the gravity of the event, over a brief or longer period of time, a culture's sensitivity to or preoccupation with death, like that of an individual, eventually returns to "pre-event" levels, and the predictability and rationality of life and death again become normative. This normal state of affairs is characterized by the "veil of order and meaning that societies construct against chaos" (Kearl 1989:26), which is often referred to as *cultural ethos* (Geertz 1973).

A culture's stance toward death—its *death ethos,*— affects the everyday behavior of all cultural members (e.g., willingness to engage in risky behavior, the likelihood of taking out an insurance policy) as living human beings, as well as their attitudes toward a variety of issues, such as the justifiable loss of life through war, euthanasia, organ donation, reincarnation, the death penalty, abortion, and the possibility of an afterlife and resurrection (Kearl 1989). In this respect, as cultures can be characterized as death accepting, death denying, or death defying (DeSpelder and Strickland 2002; Kearl 1989), it follows that their respective thresholds regarding death vary as well, dictating the quality and quantity of their responses to natural disasters, the deaths of public figures, and the loss of life through violence. Individuals' responses to death are therefore intertwined with the death ethos of the cultures in which they are embedded.

THE DEATH SYSTEM

On the assumption that fears of death (nonbeing) are indeed universal, and given the assumption of cultural embeddedness (see above), it is important to examine how both cultures and individuals cope with threats to their mortality. At a cultural level, in the context of the construct of the "death systems" that characterize all cultures (Kastenbaum 2001; Corr, Nabe, and Corr 2000), there appear to be many manifestations of the need to deny, manipulate, distort, or camouflage death so that it is a less difficult threat with which to cope. All of the culturally relevant examples of the denial or distortion of death discussed here reflect the fact that "people conspire with one another to create cultural imperatives and institutions that deny the fact of mortality" (Firestone 1994:221)

All cultures' death systems have several functions that relate to such a stance toward death. Among the various functions of death systems, the most relevant to denial as a defense mechanism against death are (a) preventing death, (b) disposing of the dead, (c) helping make sense of death, and (d) endorsing socially sanctioned killing. For example, to the extent that persons believe that medical personnel can save lives, this represents a form of denial. This belief may be reinforced through individuals' donation of money toward medical research; that is, such donations support the belief that with enough resources, research, effort, and support, medical science can find cures for fatal illnesses or develop procedures for saving the lives of persons with acute or chronic illnesses that might kill them. Yet despite such advances, people continue to die from known illnesses (e.g., cancer, AIDS), and new illnesses develop that are beyond medicine's current ability to treat (e.g., antibiotic-resistant strains of staphylococcus). Because not every life can be saved, our sensitivity to the failure of medical science to deal with life-threatening illness becomes more acute. Thus we need some form of denial to deal with such threats to our health and well-being.

Likewise, the use of metaphors or euphemisms that serve to soften the harshness of death (e.g., *passed away, deceased, expired*) clearly represents a culturally approved attempt to deny or camouflage death's impact on our daily lives. Other cultural manifestations of denial are the displacement of the event of death from the home to the hospital, medical center, or nursing home (in contrast to the modern hospice movement) and the presumed "triumph" over death offered by the use of life-extending technology (DeSpelder and Strickland 2002). Aries (1981) discusses such a cultural perspective in his treatment of historical shifts in attitudes toward death, conceptualizing the latter as

"remote and imminent death" (emphasizing its frightening nature) and "death denied–forbidden death" (emphasizing its pornographic, filthy, or indecent nature; see Gorer [1955] 1965).

Many attitudes toward the dead demonstrate denial. For example, the separation of churches from cemeteries and efforts by embalmers to make the dead look as if they are only sleeping reflect the perception of death as something to be avoided. Additional cultural manifestations of death denial are found in the shift in focus from dead persons themselves to our responses to the deaths and dying of others; the removal of death from our presence via brief funerals, accompanied by the prescription that our emotions should be muted; and the "medicalization" of death (the view that death represents the failure of medicine to cure illness or save lives, where indeed the emphasis is on the disease or cause of death) (see Corr et al. 2000). Indeed, the construct of death denial has been normalized among social scientists by the assertions of writers such as Jaques (1965), who states that midlife crisis is initiated by the individual's fear of his or her own mortality, and Kübler-Ross (1969), who argues that persons first respond to the news of their own imminent death by denying its reality, as well as by debates about the validity of "near-death experiences" (Greyson 2000; Greyson and Bush 1992; Ring and Valarino 1998).

THE MEDIA AS AGENTS OF THE DEATH SYSTEM

It is difficult to address the culture's role in the distortion or denial of death adequately without mentioning the mass media. Indeed, the media, through news and entertainment programming, often foster and/or reinforce denial by purposefully distorting the nature of death. The news media accomplish this distortion by selectively focusing on violent or mass death and on the deaths of the famous. Other media-driven efforts to distort death's harshness are evidenced in fictionalized attempts to represent death. Movies and television programs display deaths caused by shootings and by plane and auto crashes; they portray "dramatic" deaths in hospitals and spectacularize the deaths of characters in action and horror films. Many video games portray the deaths of "victims." As Corr et al. (2000) state, the deaths displayed in the media represent a "highly selective portrait of death and life in today's society" (p. 85), as well as deaths that are "very unrealistic or fantasized" (p. 87). Indeed, a person's having been exposed to death via the media has been found to be positively related to greater death anxiety (King and Hayslip 2002), which further necessitates either complete or partial death denial to minimize intrapsychic threat. Oddly enough, to the extent that such denial is successful, it may further insulate persons from their feelings about death, leading to more distant, depersonalized, or euphemized responses to their own deaths, more generally to death itself, or to dying or dead persons. Thus the relief of one's anxiety when one engages in such distortive behaviors reinforces those very efforts to avoid thinking about one's own mortality.

DEATH DENIAL: NORMAL OR PATHOLOGICAL?

It is instructive to recognize that death anxiety and its complements, suppression and denial, exist along a continuum. For this reason, it may be difficult to distinguish between normal and neurotic components of anxiety associated with death, as they may be intermingled in most people, creating a conflict representing, ultimately, our helplessness and powerlessness in the face of death. In Freud's (1946, [1920] 1955, [1926] 1959) discussions of the dualism of life and death instincts, he concludes that when fear of death arises, the ego is depleted of libido. To protect itself, the ego uses defense mechanisms that can drive anxiety into the unconscious. The greater the extent of one's fears, the more energy one needs to defend against them, and the excessive use of defenses necessitated by high levels of anxiety compromises the ego, leading to diminished life satisfaction (Rychlak 1981; Santrock 1986). Alternatively, as people's defenses are lifted, they may come to place greater value on their lives, while at the same time becoming more consciously fearful of death (Firestone 1993). Thus some degree of conscious death anxiety may be necessary for psychological health (see Servaty and Hayslip 1996).

According to Fromm (1941), the experience of living loses it meaning if death is ignored, thus the denial of death may represent both normal and pathological efforts to come to terms with mortality and ultimate separation from others. Becker (1973), based on the work of Otto Rank, describes high levels of conscious death anxiety as relating to the breakdown of defenses, especially denial. Thus the ability to deny death is normal and consistent with the personal cultural style that Kastenbaum and Aisenberg (1976) describe as "overcoming."

COMPLETE VERSUS PARTIAL DENIAL OF DEATH

Kastenbaum (2001) proposes that death denial is better conceived in terms of "partial denial" than in terms of complete denial. Alternatives to classical, complete denial include selective attention (purposeful ignorance or avoidance of death stimuli), selective responding (hiding one's feelings from others), compartmentalizing (allowing incongruencies, such as understanding a terminal diagnosis and making long-term plans), purposeful deception (lying), and resistance (not giving up or giving in to death). Such variations are intrapsychic, but they are also expressed interpersonally (in terms of individuals' relationships with dying persons)—for example, in a "mutual pretense" awareness

context (Glaser and Strauss 1965). Death denial is also situational—it may be minimized or exacerbated by the individual's immediate situation (e.g., a hospital vs. a hospice environment). As Kastenbaum (2001) points out, although complete denial and complete awareness/ acceptance of death can exist, they are extremes and comparatively rare. Even to the extent that individuals employ forms of partial denial, efforts to cope with the threat of death must be seen in an adaptive light.

THEORETICAL PERSPECTIVES ON DEATH DENIAL: TERROR MANAGEMENT THEORY

A more recent conceptual equivalent to the analytic stance described above can be found in terror management theory (Greenberg, Pyszczynski, and Solomon 1986; Solomon, Greenberg, and Pyszczynski 1991), which asserts that because we can reflect on our own death, such knowledge terrifies us in light of our desire for survival. Denial in this case takes the form of the perception that the world is "controllable, fair, and just" (McCoy et al. 2000:39). Such culture-driven percepts permit us order amid chaos and ensure our immortality through a belief system that values history, accomplishment, and wealth. McCoy et al. (2000) suggest that in addition to denial, persons manage their anxiety about death by overestimating their time left to live, underestimating the likelihood that they will experience illnesses or accidents, and creating psychological distance between themselves and others who are dead or dying. Empirical support for terror management theory is extensive. Specifically, the "anxiety buffer" hypothesis (that internal psychological structures exist because they reduce anxiety) and the "mortality salience" hypothesis (that reminding persons of the source of their anxiety— their mortality—leads to greater use of defenses and greater liking of similarly minded persons to manage such fear) have been supported by research findings (for a review, see McCoy et al. 2000).

ACCURATELY IDENTIFYING DEATH DENIAL

Kastenbaum and Costa (1977) and Firestone (1993, 1994) have discussed the pervasive nature and natural status of death anxiety, its relationship to separation, and the role of defenses in both the individual and the institution/culture. As Kastenbaum (1998) notes, however, the difficulty in operationalizing unconscious or covert death fear is that one must infer the existence of denial as a defense on the basis of a lack of behaviors that would otherwise suggest that individuals are anxious about some aspect of death. Moreover, if death anxiety is conscious in nature, persons should be aware of such concerns and should indeed purposefully and willfully behave in ways that reflect this awareness.

With respect to the assessment of death fear, low scores on self-report measures of death fear may therefore represent low anxiety or high denial; only extremely high scores on such measures represent responses to genuine degrees of threat (Kastenbaum 1992, 1998). As noted above, Kastenbaum (1998, 2001) proposes that, rather than presuming that most persons completely deny their fears about death (a strategy that is ultimately ineffective), we should examine degrees or types of death denial. Perhaps complete denial as a defense, where the self is incapable of recognizing "death-laden reality" (Kastenbaum 1998:20), can be adaptive, but only if it is temporary (when threat is overwhelming). Thus denial should be considered as adaptive to the extent that it is not overused, and there are certainly persons for whom its overuse is indeed pathological. The question of how much denial is normal has yet to be addressed (Kastenbaum 1998, 2001). Consequently, in light of an approach to denial as a potentially adaptive coping strategy, higher scores on a measure of covert (unconscious) death fear and/or lower scores on self-report (conscious/overt) measures of death fear may represent degrees of selective or incomplete denial that may or may not benefit the individual. In this light, Firestone (2000) claims that microsuicidal (symbolically self-destructive) behaviors reflect an individual's anxiety about death typified in systematic self-cognitions ("the voice") that devalue the self, instead motivating the individual to fear living and/or becoming too attached to life.

RESEARCH PERSPECTIVES ON DEATH DENIAL

Approximately 95% of the studies that have examined death anxiety have utilized measures of conscious fear in the form of self-report questionnaires or scales (Neimeyer 1997–98). However, many of these assessment measures suffer from methodological shortcomings, such as insufficient evidence of reliability and validity. Many such studies also have utilized inadequate sampling and relied too heavily on correlation coefficients (Neimeyer 1997–98) that capitalize on chance and are often interpreted as implying causality, to the exclusion of more sophisticated statistical analysis techniques (e.g., causal modeling, factor analysis). In addition, the assessment of consciously admitted fears of death may be influenced by social desirability response bias; thus such studies may yield flawed estimates of such constructs. These shortcomings suggest that exclusive reliance on direct self-report measures of death anxiety (e.g., Lester 1991, 1994; Lester and Templer 1992–93; Templer 1970) is both conceptually and methodologically unsound.

Because death means different things to various individuals at different times, questions concerning the meaning a person attributes to death have the potential to evoke a variety of responses (Hayslip and Panek 2002). Indeed,

understanding a person's conceptions of death may be the key to predicting how that person responds to such questions. Death anxiety may be one response to questions concerning death's meaning, and such anxiety may actually be a complex mixture of responses. Fear, denial, and ambivalence are among the most frequent interpretations of orientations toward death, reflecting affective and perceptual-cognitive components (Kastenbaum and Costa 1977). In this light, it is not surprising that there is some disagreement among researchers regarding the various dimensions of death anxiety (Neimeyer 1988, 1997–98; Neimeyer and Van Brunt 1995). This inconsistency results in a lack of synthesis in the many labels, levels, and techniques researchers use to assess death anxiety (see Levin 1989–90; Neimeyer and Van Brunt 1995). Some have even criticized the interchangeable use of the terms *fear* and *anxiety* in the research; these two terms imply disparate approaches to measurement (Kastenbaum and Costa 1977). Thus death anxiety most likely is multidimensional, and the above discussion of its theoretical underpinnings suggests that such anxiety may or may not be manifested at a conscious level of awareness (Kastenbaum and Costa 1977; Lonetto, Fleming, and Mercer 1979).

In addition to the conscious (overt) and unconscious (covert) dimensions of death anxiety, many research studies have differentiated the person's fear of his or her own death from the person's other fears related to dying and have separated responses to the death and/or dying of self from responses to the death and/or dying of significant others (Collett and Lester 1969; Kalish 1976; Kastenbaum and Costa 1977; Schulz 1978). This suggests a three-factor model of death anxiety, the three factors being conscious (overt) death and dying of self, conscious death and dying of others, and unconscious (covert) death anxiety. This model follows from the assumption that in order to understand and interpret anxiety regarding death adequately, researchers must view it from many perspectives (e.g., private, public).

Kastenbaum and Costa (1977) suggest that death anxiety may reside in the unconscious, but reviews by Neimeyer (1997–98) and by Fortner, Neimeyer, and Rybarczyk (2000) fail to give much credence to this notion. For some time, scholars have stated concerns about existing self-report measures' ability to tap any dimension of death concerns other than conscious or public attitudinal concerns (see Fulton 1961; Rheingold 1967). Some psychoanalytic thinkers believe that conscious fear of death occurs when an individual experiences a serious breakdown of his or her defenses (Becker 1973), and there is some literature to suggest that the conscious and unconscious aspects of death anxiety are relatively independent of one another (Feifel and Hermann 1973; Templer 1971).

THE MEASUREMENT OF DEATH DENIAL

The measurement of the unconscious dimensions of death anxiety has been largely ignored (Kurlychek 1978-1979).

Where exceptions can be found (e.g., Pinder and Hayslip 1981; Shrut 1958; Stroop 1938), there is, not surprisingly, a lack of a uniform approach to the assessment of covert death fear. Indeed, because of the variety of methods researchers have used to tap unconscious death fear (e.g., dream content analysis, galvanic skin response, the Stroop Color Word Interference Test [Stroop 1938], the Thematic Apperception Test), it is difficult to compare results across studies. Several researchers have noted the need for studies that assess unconscious aspects of death anxiety (especially the person's concerns about his or her own death rather than the death of someone else) through the use of projective techniques (Feifel and Hermann 1973; Richardson and Sands 1986–87).

In this light, researchers have employed several indirect measures to assess death anxiety at an unconscious level. Many such techniques—such as the Thematic Apperception Test (Diggory and Rothman 1961; Lowry 1965), measurement of galvanic skin response and reaction time to the presentation of death-related versus neutral words via word-association or tachistoscopic word-recognition techniques (Alexander and Adlerstein 1958; Feifel and Branscomb 1973; Feifel and Hermann 1973; Lester and Lester 1970), and dream analysis (Handal and Rychlak 1971)—are either time-consuming or otherwise not practical for screening purposes. In addition, these methods may be threatening in themselves and may produce subject reactivity (Campbell and Stanley 1963), which can have adverse effects on reliability and validity.

In view of the methodological concerns noted above regarding the possibilities for subject reactivity and the pragmatic aspects of attempting to assess unconscious death fear, it is important to note that Shrut (1958) was the first to employ a sentence-completion technique to assess the covert aspects of this construct. However, Shrut's study treated anxiety about death as unitary, and the measures utilized to assess covert death fear lacked reliability and validity. Consequently, their use could not be supported on a conceptual or empirical basis. Nevertheless, Shrut's work provided the impetus for further research.

Hayslip, Pinder, and Lumsden (1981) and Pinder and Hayslip (1981) expanded on this perspective toward understanding fear of death by creating a scoring system for the sentence-completion method that is reliable and can differentiate groups of individuals in a manner that suggests it is a valuable approach for assessing death anxiety at an unconscious level. The scoring system comprises nine dimensions of unconscious death anxiety, each dimension yielding a separate score. Summing across all nine dimensions produces a total score. The dimensions are defined as follows:

1. Overt mention of death or dying
2. Fear of separation or isolation
3. Fear of dependency or loss of control
4. Fear of stasis or stagnation
5. Fear of loss of goals
6. Fear of injury to or disease in oneself
7. Fear of pain/suffering
8. Fear of punishment or rejection by others
9. Concern over time (futurity)

Each of these dimensions can be reliably scored (Hayslip, Galt, and Pinder 1993–94; Hayslip et al. 1981; Pinder and Hayslip 1981).

Since these initial studies were conducted, a great deal of evidence has been accumulated regarding the method's validity, as such scores have been found to be sensitive to (a) the impact of death education (Hayslip and Walling 1985–86; Hayslip et al. 1993–94; Servaty and Hayslip 1996), (b) variations in occupational choice (Lattaner and Hayslip 1984–85), (c) individual differences in communication apprehension regarding the dying (Servaty and Hayslip 1996), (d) relationships to locus of control (Hayslip and Stewart-Bussey 1986–87), and (e) the impact of terminal illness (Hayslip, Luhr, and Beyerlein 1991; Hayslip et al. 1996–97).

DEATH DENIAL AND AGE

In a study conducted with a sample of young and middle-aged adults, Hayslip et al. (1981) found that age and conscious death fear were negatively related, whereas age and covert fear were positively related. In this light, Galt and Hayslip (1998–99) expanded on the Hayslip et al. (1981) study by cross-sectionally exploring the relationship of age to levels of death fear, utilizing samples of younger and older (age 60 and over) adults and measuring death anxiety at multiple levels of awareness. Results indicated that there were reliable age differences in both overt and covert levels of death fear. In contrast to earlier findings (see Neimeyer and Van Brunt 1995), older adults reported higher levels of overt personal death fear and expressed greater conscious fears over the loss of others. On the other hand, younger adults evidenced higher levels of conscious fear of pain associated with death and scored higher regarding conscious fears of their own dying. These results suggest that cumulative differential loss experiences over the course of a lifetime may covary with an individual's lessened need to deny fears of his or her own death.

Kastenbaum (1992) advises, however, that we must not jump to the conclusion that conscious death fears decrease with age or that young adults are typically more death anxious when compared with members of older age groups. Because most of the studies in this area have been cross-sectional, differences may be due to cohort effects (see Baltes 1968), and thus may not reflect intraindividual change over time; longitudinal designs are more advantageous for investigating intraindividual change (Baltes 1968). Neimeyer and Van Brunt (1995) suggest that additional work is necessary if we are to understand the apparent negative relationship between death fear and age in adulthood. Attention to the multilevel nature of death anxiety may illuminate this relationship further, especially if older adults are found to have lower conscious but higher unconscious death fear scores, suggesting that individuals' needs to deny their fears about death vary with age because of older adults' greater experience of threats to their mortality brought about by illness, injury, and the deaths of others, such as childhood friends, siblings, parents, grandparents, and spouses.

RELATIONSHIPS BETWEEN COVERT AND OVERT DEATH FEARS

Galt and Hayslip (1998–99) also found a reciprocal relationship between conscious (overt) and unconscious (covert) levels of death fear; that is, if conscious death anxiety is higher, unconscious death fear is lower (indicating less denial), and vice versa. Indeed, negative relationships between self-reported death fears and both repression-sensitization and galvanic skin responses have been noted (Templer 1971). Greyson (1994) found that persons who had had near-death experiences scored lower on a measure of death threat, indicating that having an NDE may lessen denial, perhaps by instilling or reinforcing the belief that one can transcend the destruction of one's body and/or the belief that life will go on beyond physical death.

Hayslip, Guarnaccia, and Servaty (2002) have found evidence supporting a blended projective/psychometric measurement model that allows for the assessment of both overt and covert death anxiety to explore the factorial composition of death fear, utilizing confirmatory factor-analytic techniques (LISREL; Hayduk 1996; Jöreskog & Sörbom 1993), which are more powerful than correlational/exploratory factor-analytic techniques for ascertaining the latent structure of death anxiety (see Tabachnick and Fidell 1996; Ullman 1996). Hayslip et al. (2002) tested the robustness of a six-indicator, two-factor model of overt and covert death anxiety utilizing data from two randomly selected halves of a parent sample of 392 adults. The researchers used these data to translate a theoretical model into an empirically valid factor model, wherein the model was developed in one sample and then was cross-validated with the second sample.

In the Hayslip et al. (2002) study, in the development of both the cross-validation samples, the two-factor (overt and covert fear) and three-factor (overt-other, overt-self, and covert death fear) model fits were quite adequate, yet the ease with which the two-factor model was fit to both the first and second data sets suggests that death anxiety does appear to have a two-factor structure—that is, overt death anxiety and covert death anxiety. Consequently, on the joint basis of parsimony and the two-factor model's superiority in the first (development) sample, Hayslip et al. retained the two-factor model to represent the structure of death anxiety.

In this light, the fact that covert death fear can be identified as a separate yet interrelated dimension of death anxiety suggests that a person's conscious awareness of his or her mortality can be minimized, distorted, or denied, principally through the operation of defenses such as denial and regression or through the development of self-nourishing habits that protect the individual from existential anxiety (see Firestone 1994). The fact that the two (overt and covert) components of death anxiety are negatively related is supported by previous research (Galt and Hayslip 1998–99; Hayslip et al. 2002) as well as by Firestone's (1994) observations, which suggest that "death anxiety increases as people relinquish defenses, refuse to conform to familial and societal standards, reach new levels of differentiation of the self, or expand their lives" (p. 237). Thus the conscious awareness of one's fears about mortality is inversely related to the extent to which one's defenses effectively mask such fears. Consequently, the relationship between conscious (overt) and unconscious (covert) death fear is best thought of in dynamic rather than static terms, consistent with the degree of threat the individual experiences and the individual's need to deal with resultant anxiety through the utilization of defenses in the context of a culture that, in varying degrees, promotes the denial and/or distortion of death.

In spite of the empirical basis for the existence of death denial, it is instructive to take note of Kastenbaum's (1998) observations on the illusive nature of denial as a defense against death (see above); it may still be premature to attempt to speak definitively to the status of covert death fear without sufficient behaviorally and affectively anchored work to substantiate its existence. Methodologically, however, the use of both self-report and projective methods to assess and understand how persons cope with death anxiety represents an advantage over other methods that emphasize one approach over the other. Moreover, it can be argued that a confirmatory factor-analytic approach to this question (see Hayslip et al. 2002) is much superior to either an exploratory one or a strictly correlational strategy (see Neimeyer 1997–98; Tabachnick and Fidell 1996; Ullman 1996). That both the two-factor and three-factor models convincingly fit the data in both the developmental and cross-validation samples taken by Hayslip et al. (2002) is especially impressive given the modest internal consistency of both the Templer (1970) and Collett and Lester (1969) measures of conscious death fear.

DEATH DENIAL: WHERE ARE WE GOING?

Perhaps most important, attention to the assessment of death denial reflects Neimeyer's (1994) calls for innovation and movement in the field of death anxiety. For example, use of the Incomplete Sentence Blank to assess covert death fears is grounded in psychoanalytic theory, and given the integration of self-report and projective approaches in the measurement of death anxiety, such research lays the groundwork for further studies of an interventive (psychotherapeutic, death educative) nature, in which specific hypotheses might be tested based on the dualistic nature of death fear. Additionally, given the necessarily developmental relationship between an individual's exposure to the deaths of others and the nearness/likelihood of his or her own death (see, e.g., Devins 1979), a dualistic yet integrated conception of death fear permits a greater understanding of the temporal relationship between chronologically (age) driven experiences and the individual's need to construct defenses to maintain the illusion of immortality (see Firestone 2000; Galt and Hayslip 1998–99; Hayslip et al. 1996–97). Thus research speaking to the nature of overt and covert death fear embodies many of Neimeyer's (1994) observations regarding the development of new and more theoretically and methodologically sophisticated approaches to the study of death fears that would move the field forward so as to enhance our understanding of death attitudes.

CONCLUSION

To understand and measure the denial of death, we must attend to the nature of the responses of both cultures and individuals to the fact that all humans die. Moreover, such responses are driven by the fact that the manners in which some deaths occur are more likely than others to evoke strong denial. A step forward in our attempts to understand the denial of death would be the development of theory that integrates attitudes toward death at both individual and cultural levels. Clearly, individuals' and cultures' reactions to death are interwoven, as we observed on September 11, 2001. The events of that day not only altered Americans' sense of their own vulnerability and mortality, but threatened the stability of their relationships with others and their careers (as a person might also be threatened by a diagnosis of cancer).

It is also important to observe that the very meaning and role that death plays in shaping the cultural ethos is altered by death-related events, be they unique to individual lives or culturally symbolic in nature. For example, Americans' collective identity as citizens of a powerful nation was shaken by the events of September 11, and our responses to this change have ranged from the institutionalization of greater security measures to the embrace of our collective belongingness, grief, and spirituality, to the targeting of individuals whose appearance and/or heritage cause us to be suspicious of their motives. Such responses are best understood on multiple levels—they are at once interpersonal, sociocultural, and idiosyncratic in nature.

As researchers, theoreticians, practitioners, and human beings, we face the challenge of finding better ways to understand the dynamic interplay between individual life events and cultural change, so that we can appreciate more fully the role of the denial of death in helping to shape our own individual lives as well as our culture's death system. In many respects, this will be an ongoing endeavor, as events whose role in reinforcing the denial of death become clearer and as events that have yet to occur challenge our sense of individual and collective security. Such events may exceed our idiographic and cultural thresholds, affecting whether we respond to death by embracing it or by denying its impact on our lives.

REFERENCES

Alexander, I. E. and A. M. Adlerstein. 1958. "Affective Responses to the Concept of Death in a Population of Children and Early Adolescents." *Journal of Genetic Psychology* 93:167–77.

Aries, P. 1981. *The Hour of Our Death,* translated by H. Weaver. New York: Alfred A. Knopf.

Baltes, P. 1968. "Cross-Sectional and Longitudinal Sequences in the Study of Age and Generation Effects." *Human Development* 11:145–71.

Becker, E. 1973. *The Denial of Death.* New York: Free Press.

Campbell, D. T. and J. C. Stanley. 1963. *Experimental and Quasi-Experimental Designs for Research.* Chicago: Rand McNally.

Collett, L. and D. Lester. 1969. "Fear of Death and Fear of Dying." *Journal of Psychology* 72:179–81.

Corr, C. A., C. M. Nabe, and D. M. Corr. 2000. *Death and Dying: Life and Living.* Belmont, CA: Wadsworth.

DeSpelder, L. A. and A. L. Strickland. 2002. *The Last Dance: Encountering Death and Dying,* 6th ed. New York: McGraw-Hill.

Devins, G. M. 1979. "Death Anxiety and Voluntary Passive Euthanasia: Influences of Proximity to Death and Experiences With Death in Important Other Persons." *Journal of Consulting and Clinical Psychology* 47:301–9.

Diggory, J. C. and D. Z. Rothman. 1961. "Values Destroyed by Death." *Journal of Abnormal and Social Psychology* 63:205–10.

Feifel, H. and A. Branscomb. 1973. "Who's Afraid of Death?" *Journal of Abnormal Psychology* 81:282–88.

Feifel, H. and L. Hermann. 1973. "Fear of Death in the Mentally Ill." *Psychological Reports* 33:931–38.

Firestone, R. W. 1993. "Individual Defenses Against Death Anxiety." *Death Studies* 17:497–515.

———. 1994. "Psychological Defenses Against Death Anxiety." Pp. 217–42 in *Death Anxiety Handbook: Research, Instrumentation, and Application,* edited by R. A. Neimeyer. Washington, DC: Taylor & Francis.

———. 2000. "Microsuicide and the Elderly: A Basic Defense Against Death Anxiety." Pp. 65–86 in *Death Attitudes and the Older Adult: Theories, Concepts, and Applications,* edited by A. Tomer. Philadelphia: Taylor & Francis.

Fortner, B. V., R. A. Neimeyer, and B. Rybarczyk. 2000. "Correlates of Death Anxiety in Older Adults: A Comprehensive Review." Pp. 95–108 in *Death Attitudes and the Older Adult: Theories, Concepts, and Applications,* edited by A. Tomer. Philadelphia: Taylor & Francis.

Freud, S. 1946. *The Ego and the Mechanisms of Defence.* New York: International Universities Press.

Freud, S. [1920] 1955. "Beyond the Pleasure Principle." In *The Standard Edition of the Complete Psychological Works of Sigmund Freud,* vol. 18, edited and translated by J. Strachey. London: Hogarth.

———. [1926] 1959. "Inhibitions, Symptoms, and Anxiety." In *The Standard Edition of the Complete Psychological Works of Sigmund Freud,* vol. 20, edited and translated by J. Strachey. London: Hogarth.

Fromm, E. 1941. *Escape From Freedom.* New York: Holt, Rinehart & Winston.

Fulton, R. 1961. "Discussion of a Symposium on Attitudes Toward Death in Older Persons." *Journal of Gerontology* 16:44–66.

Galt, C. P. and B. Hayslip, Jr. 1998–99. "Age Differences in Levels of Overt and Covert Death Anxiety." *Omega* 37:187–202.

Geertz, C. 1973. *The Interpretation of Cultures: Selected Essays.* New York: Basic Books.

Glaser, B. G. and A. L. Strauss. 1965. *Awareness of Dying.* Chicago: Aldine.

Gorer, G. [1955] 1965. "The Pornography of Death." Pp. 192–99 in G. Gorer, *Death, Grief and Mourning.* Garden City, NY: Doubleday.

Greenberg, J., Pyszczynski, T., & Solomon, S. 1986. "The Causes and Consequences of the Need for Self-Esteem: A Terror Management Analysis." Pp. 189–212 in *Public Self and Private Self,* edited by R. F. Baumeister. New York: Springer-Verlag.

Greyson, B. 1994. "Reduced Death Threat in Near Death Experiences." Pp. 169–79 in *Death Anxiety Handbook: Research, Instrumentation, and Application,* edited by R. A. Neimeyer. Washington, DC: Taylor & Francis.

———. 2000. "Near Death Experiences." Pp. 315–52 in *The Varieties of Anomalous Experience: Examining the Scientific Evidence,* edited by E. Cardena, S. Lynn, and S. Krippner. Washington, DC: American Psychological Association.

Greyson, B. and N. E. Bush. 1992. "Distressing Near Death Experiences." *Psychiatry* 55:95–110.

Handal, P. J. and J. F. Rychlak. 1971. "Curvilinearity Between Dream Content and Death Anxiety and the Relationship of Death Anxiety to Repression-Sensitization." *Journal of Abnormal Psychology* 77:11–16.

Hayduk, L. A. 1996. *LISREL: Issues, Debates, and Strategies.* Baltimore: Johns Hopkins University Press.

Hayslip, B., Jr., C. P. Galt, and M. M. Pinder. 1993–94. "Effects of Death Education on Conscious and Unconscious Death Anxiety." *Omega* 28:101–11.

Hayslip, B., Jr., C. Guarnaccia, and H. Servaty. 2002. "Death Anxiety: An Empirical Test of a Blended Self-Report and Projective Measurement Model." *Omega* 44:277–94.

Hayslip, B., Jr., D. Luhr, and M. M. Beyerlein. 1991. "Levels of Death Anxiety in Terminally Ill Men." *Omega* 24:13–19.

Hayslip, B., Jr., and P. Panek. 2002. *Adult Development and Aging.* Melbourne, FL: Krieger.

Hayslip, B., Jr., M. M. Pinder, and D. B. Lumsden. 1981. "The Measurement of Death Anxiety in Adulthood: Implications for Counseling." Pp. 14–30 in *New Directions in Death Education and Counseling: Enhancing the Quality of Life in the Nuclear Age,* edited by R. Pacholski and C. A. Corr. Arlington, VA: Forum for Death Education and Counseling.

Hayslip, B., Jr., H. Servaty, T. Christman, and E. Mumy. 1996–97. "Levels of Death Anxiety in Terminally Ill Persons: A Cross Validation and Extension." *Omega* 34:203–18.

Hayslip, B., Jr. and D. Stewart-Bussey. 1986–87. "Locus of Control–Levels of Death Anxiety Relationships." *Omega* 17:41–49.

Hayslip, B., Jr., and M. L. Walling. 1985–86. "Impact of Hospice Volunteer Training on Death Anxiety and Locus of Control." *Omega* 16:243–54.

Jaques, E. 1965. "Death and the Mid-Life Crisis." *International Journal of Psychoanalysis* 46:502–14.

Jöreskog, K. G. and D. Sörbom. 1993. *LISREL 8 User's Reference Guide.* Mooresville, IN: Scientific Software.

Kalish, R. 1976. "Death and Dying in a Social Context." In *The Handbook of Aging and the Social Sciences,* edited by R. Binstock and E. Shanas. New York: Van Nostrand Reinhold.

Kastenbaum, R. J. 1992. *The Psychology of Death.* New York: Springer.

———. 1998. *Death, Society, and Human Experience,* 6th ed. Boston: Allyn & Bacon.

———. 2001. *Death, society, and human experience,* 7th ed. Boston: Allyn & Bacon.

Kastenbaum, R. J. and R. Aisenberg. 1976. *The Psychology of Death.* New York: Springer.

Kastenbaum, R. J. and P. T. Costa. 1977. "Psychological Perspectives on Death." *Annual Review of Psychology* 28:225–49.

Kearl, M. C. 1989. *Endings: A Sociology of Death and Dying.* New York: Oxford University Press.

King, J. and B. Hayslip, Jr. 2002. "The Media's Influence on College Students' Views of Death." *Omega* 44:37–56.

Kübler-Ross, E. 1969. *On Death and Dying.* New York: Macmillan.

Kurlychek, R. T. 1978–79. "Assessment of Attitudes Toward Death and Dying: A Critical Review of Some Available Methods." *Omega* 9:37–47.

Lattaner, B. and B. Hayslip, Jr. 1984–85. "Occupation-Related Differences in Levels of Death Anxiety." *Omega* 15:53–66.

Lester, D. 1991. "The Lester Attitude Toward Death Scale." *Omega* 23:67–76.

———. 1994. "The Collett-Lester Fear of Death Scale." Pp. 45–60 in *Death Anxiety Handbook: Research, Instrumentation, and Application,* edited by R. A. Neimeyer. Washington, DC: Taylor & Francis.

Lester, D. and G. Lester. 1970. "Fear of Death, Fear of Dying, and Threshold Differences for Death Words and Neutral Words." *Omega* 1:175–79.

Lester, D. and D. I. Templer. 1992–93. "Death Anxiety Scales: A Dialogue." *Omega* 26:239–53.

Levin, R. 1989–90. "A Reexamination of the Dimensionality of Death Anxiety." *Omega* 20:341–49.

Lonetto, R., S. Fleming, and W. G. Mercer. 1979. "The Structure of Death Anxiety: A Factor Analytic Study." *Journal of Personality Assessment* 43:388–92.

Lowry, R. 1965. "Male-Female Differences in Attitudes Toward Death." Ph.D. dissertation, Brandeis University.

May, R. 1950. *The Meaning of Anxiety.* New York: Ronald.

———. 1969. *Love and Will.* New York: W. W. Norton.

McCoy, S., T. Pyszczynski, S. Solomon, and J. Greenberg. 2000. "Transcending the Self: A Terror Management Perspective on Successful Aging." Pp. 37-64 in *Death Attitudes and the Older Adult: Theories, Concepts, and Applications,* edited by A. Tomer. Philadelphia: Taylor & Francis.

Neimeyer, R. A. 1988. "Death Anxiety." In *Dying: Facing the Facts,* 2d ed., edited by H. Wass, F. Berardo, and R. A. Neimeyer. Washington, DC: Hemisphere.

———. 1994. "Death Attitudes in Adult Life: A Closing Coda." Pp. 263–77 in *Death Anxiety Handbook: Research, Instrumentation, and Application,* edited by R. A. Neimeyer. Washington, DC: Taylor-Francis.

———. 1997–98. "Death Anxiety Research: The State of the Art." *Omega* 36:97–120.

Neimeyer, R. A. and D. Van Brunt. 1995. "Death Anxiety." Pp. 49–88 in *Dying: Facing the Facts,* 3d ed., edited by H. Wass and R. A. Neimeyer. Washington, DC: Taylor & Francis.

Nuland, S. B. 1994. *How We Die: Reflections on Life's Final Chapter.* New York: Alfred A. Knopf.

Pinder, M. M. and B. Hayslip, Jr. 1981. "Cognitive, Attitudinal, and Affective Aspects of Death and Dying in Adulthood: Implications for Care Providers." *Educational Gerontology* 6:107–23.

Rheingold, J. C. 1967. *The Mother, Anxiety, and Death.* Boston: Little, Brown.

Richardson, V. and R. Sands. 1986–87. "Death Attitudes Among Mid-Life Women." *Omega* 17:327–41.

Ring, K. and E. E. Valarino. 1998. *Lessons From the Light: What We Can Learn From the Near-Death Experience.* New York: Insight/Plenum.

Rychlak, J. F. 1981. *Introduction to Personality and Psychotherapy: A Theory-Construction Approach,* 2d ed. Boston: Houghton Mifflin.

Santrock, J. W. 1986. *Psychology: The Science of Mind and Behavior.* Dubuque, IA: William C. Brown.

Schulz, R. 1978. *The Psychology of Death, Dying, and Bereavement.* Reading, MA: Addison-Wesley.

Servaty, H. and B. Hayslip, Jr. 1996. "Death Education and Communication Apprehension Regarding Dying Persons." *Omega* 34:133–42.

Shrut, S. D. 1958. "Attitudes Toward Old Age and Death." *Mental Hygiene* 42:259–66.

Solomon, S., J. Greenberg, and T. Pyszczynski. 1991. "Terror Management Theory of Social Behavior: The Psychological Functions of Self-Esteem and Cultural Worldviews. Pp. 93–159 in *Advances in Experimental Social Psychology,* vol. 24, edited by M. P. Zanna. San Diego, CA: Academic Press.

Stroop, J. R. 1938. "Factors Affecting Speed in Serial Verbal Reactions." *Psychological Monographs* 50:38–48.

Tabachnick, B. G. and L. S. Fidell, eds. 1996. *Using Multivariate Statistics,* 3d ed. New York: HarperCollins.

Templer, D. I. 1970. "The Construction and Validation of a Death Anxiety Scale." *Journal of General Psychology* 82:165–77.

———. 1971. "The Relationship Between Verbalized and Nonverbalized Death Anxiety." *Journal of Genetic Psychology* 119:211–14.

Ullman, J. B. 1996. "Structural Equation Modeling." Pp. 709–812 in *Using Multivariate Statistics,* 3d ed., edited by B. G. Tabachnick and L. S. Fidell. New York: HarperCollins.

DEATH, DYING, AND THE DEAD IN POPULAR CULTURE

KEITH F. DURKIN

Fulton and Owen (1987) have observed that for members of the generation born after World War II, individuals who generally lack firsthand experience with death, the phenomenon of death and dying has become abstract and invisible. Americans, like members of many other societies, attach fearful meanings to death, dying, and the dead (Leming and Dickinson 2002). Moreover, it is has frequently been suggested that the United States has become a "death-denying" culture. A number of scholars have documented the various ways in which Americans attempt to deny death (e.g., DeSpelder and Strickland 2002; Leming and Dickinson, 2002; Mannino 1997; Oaks and Ezell 1993; Umberson and Henderson 1992). For example, we have a societal taboo against frank discussions about death and dying. When we do refer to these topics, it is normative for us to use euphemisms, such as *passed away* or *expired*. Furthermore, in the United States death typically occurs in the segregated environments of hospitals and nursing homes, and we typically relegate the task of handling the dead to professionals, such as funeral directors.

Although the United States is a death-denying society, Americans may be said to have an obsessive fascination with death and death-related phenomena. As Bryant and Shoemaker (1977) observe, "Thanatological entertainment has been and remains a traditional pervasive cultural pattern both in the United States and elsewhere, and has become very much a prominent and integral part of contemporary popular culture" (p. 2). For instance, death, dying, and the dead "regularly appear in various informational and entertainment media" (Walter, Littlewood, and Pickering 1995:581). Accordingly, the mass media have become a primary source of information about death and dying for most Americans.

In this chapter, I explore the various manifestations of death, dying, and the dead in contemporary U.S. popular culture. This discussion is not intended as an exhaustive exposition of this topic; rather, I seek to address the more prominent examples of this phenomenon. These include portrayals of death, dying, and the dead on television, in cinema, in music, and in products of the print media, as well as in recreational attractions, games, and jokes. Additionally, I explore the social import of the presence of these thanatological themes in popular culture.

TELEVISION

Nearly every American household has at least one television set, and a large percentage have several. Death and dying are brought directly into homes via the medium of television. According to DeSpelder and Strickland (2002), in an average issue of *TV Guide,* approximately one-third of the listings "describe programs in which death and dying feature in some way" (p. 35). These topics appear in soap operas, crime dramas, mysteries, documentaries, and comedies. Many of the current top-rated shows, such as *ER* and *CSI,* prominently feature death and dying. The popular "reality" show *Survivor* deals with a type of symbolic death. In fact, death and dying are the most frequently appearing social topics even in religious television programming (Abelman 1987). Recently, the unique series *Six Feet Under,* the ongoing saga of a family that owns and operates a mortuary, has proven to be compelling for many viewers.

Many people have expressed tremendous concern about the amount of violent death featured on U.S. television. According to the National Institute of Mental Health, by the time the average American reaches age 16, he or she has seen 18,000 murders on television (Kearl 1995). It has been estimated that violent death "befalls five percent of all prime time characters each week" (Gerbner 1980:66). Violent death is not limited to prime-time programming, however. The cartoons that are featured on Saturday mornings contain an average of 20 to 25 violent acts per hour, and many of these acts result in the apparent deaths of characters (Wass 1995). However, unlike in reality, cartoon characters have their deaths "reversed with no serious consequences to their bodily functions" (Mannino 1997:29).

Death has also long been a mainstay of televised news programming, but with the advent of cable television and satellite broadcasting, death coverage has taken on a new dimension. The Gulf War of 1991 was a major news event, with live coverage of the battles as they occurred. An average of 2.3 million households tuned in daily to the O. J. Simpson trial, the so-called Trial of the Century (Durkin and Knox 2001). The funeral of Diana, Princess of Wales, was seen on television "by 31 million people in Britain and two billion worldwide" (Merrin 1999:53). The tragic terrorist attacks on the World Trade Center and the Pentagon on September 11, 2001, were a media event that transpired on live television:

> Every major network, as well as many specialized cable networks (e.g., VH1 and MTV) featured live coverage of the events as they unfolded. According to Nielsen Media Research, 80 million Americans watched television news coverage on the evening of September 11th. . . . In the days following September 11th, there was around-the-clock coverage of the subsequent reaction to the attack, the rescue efforts, and the eventual military retaliation. (Durkin and Knox 2001:3–4)

CINEMA

Thanatological themes have traditionally been, and continue to be, an extremely popular element of the cinematic enterprise. For instance, death and dying feature prominently in westerns and war movies. There have also been many successful film dramas about dying, including *Love Story, Dying Young, Stepmom, My Life,* and *Sweet November.* Death has even been the topic of comedies, such as *Weekend at Bernie's* and *Night Shift.* As Kearl (1995) notes, beginning in the 1970s, a popular motif "involved attacks on humanity by the natural order—frogs, bees, sharks, meteors, earthquakes, and tidal waves" (p. 27). A vast array of movies have featured "disastrous life-threatening phenomena such as diseases (e.g., AIDS, Ebola-like virus), massive accidents (e.g., airplane crashes, nuclear plant accidents) and natural disasters" (Bahk and Neuwirth 2000:64). Ghost movies (e.g., *Truly, Madly, Deeply* and *Ghost*) as well as thrillers such as *Flatliners* have used the near-death experience as a narrative focus (Walter et al. 1995).

Many movies have a decidedly morbid focus. Young people appear to be particularly fascinated by films that feature violent deaths (Leming and Dickinson 2002). Zombie films such as *Dawn of the Dead* and *Night of the Living Dead* not only feature the undead but have scenes containing gruesome acts of violence and murder. The notorious serial killer Jack the Ripper has been featured in a large number of films, including *Murder by Decree, A Study in Terror,* and *Man in the Attic* (Schecter and Everitt 1997). A number of recent films have portrayed the activities of murderers, including *Silence of the Lambs, Hannibal, American Gothic,* and *Natural Born Killers.* In the popular *Faces of Death* series, which appeared in video rental outlets in the mid-1980s, "actual death was displayed, with images of suicides, executions, and autopsies" (Kearl 1995:28).

One specific genre of horror film, the slasher movie, has become especially popular in recent years. According to Molitor and Sapolsky (1993):

> The genre can be characterized as commercially released, feature length films containing suspense evoking scenes in which an antagonist, who is usually a male acting alone, attacks one or more victims. The accentuation in these films is extreme graphic violence. Scenes that dwell on the victim's fear and explicitly portray the attack and its aftermath are the central focus of slasher films. (P. 235)

Slasher movies feature plenty of sex and large teenage body counts (Strinati 2000). Examples include *Halloween, Friday the 13th, Nightmare on Elm Street, Slumber Party Massacre,* and *Motel Hell.* In 1981, 25 slasher movies were ranked among the 50 top-grossing films of that year (Strinati 2000). The impact of slasher films has extended far beyond the cinema; for example, the mayor of Los Angeles proclaimed September 13, 1991, Freddy Krueger Day, in honor of the killer featured in the *Nightmare on Elm Street* film series (Lewis 1997).

MUSIC

Historically, thanatological themes have been present in nearly all musical styles. For instance, folk songs about serial killers date back well into the 19th century (Schecter and Everitt 1997). Death-related themes are also present in many operas and classical musical pieces. These motifs have played a major role in the recording industry. Interestingly, one of the first recordings ever "produced for the Edison phonograph featured an actor reading the shocking confessions of H. H. Holmes, the notorious nineteenth-century "Torture Doctor" (Schecter and Everitt 1997:185). However, death became particularly prominent in the popular music of the so-called Baby Boom generation's teenage years (Kearl 1995). In the 1950s, a musical genre often referred to as "coffin songs"—songs featuring themes related to dying and grief (e.g., "Last Kiss")—became popular with young Americans (DeSpelder and Strickland 2002). The eminence of death-related motifs continues to this day. At times, this can assume remarkable configurations. For example, the funeral of Diana, Princess of Wales, produced pop artist Elton John's hit single "Candle in the Wind '97" (Merrin 1999), which is a lyrically rearranged version of an earlier John song about the dead movie icon Marilyn Monroe. Moreover, a large number of musicians have died in tragic and untimely fashion. Some examples include John Bonham, Kurt Cobain, Jimi Hendrix, Buddy Holly, Janis Joplin, John Lennon, Bob Marley, Keith Moon, Jim Morrison, Elvis Presley, Bon Scott, and Ritchie Valens.

The music that is popular with today's young people frequently has a morbid element that emphasizes death's destructive and catastrophic nature (Fulton and Owen 1987). Examples include songs about homicide, suicide, and extremely violent acts (Wass et al. 1988; Wass, Miller, and Redditt 1991). Many members of our society consider such topics to be particularly unsavory and antisocial, and, accordingly, a number of groups have been particularly vocal in their criticism of this music. For instance, as Wass et al. (1991) note, "A number of professionals, their representative organizations such as the American Academy of Pediatricians and the National Education Association, various child advocacy groups, including the Parent's Music Resource Center, and others have suggested that such lyrics promote destructive and suicidal behavior in adolescents" (p. 200).

The themes of death and destruction play an especially prominent role in two of the most popular styles of contemporary music: heavy metal and rap. Many heavy metal bands have names associated with death, such as Megadeath, Anthrax, Slayer, and Grim Reaper. Examples of heavy metal song titles include "Suicide Solution," "Highway to Hell," and "Psycho Killer." The band Guns N' Roses even recorded a cover version of the song "Look at Your Game Girl," which was written by the infamous murderer Charles Manson (Schecter and Everitt 1997).

In rap music, the violent lyrics of artists such as Snoop Dogg, Dr. Dre, Eazy-E, and Puff Daddy have generated a great deal of controversy. In fact, one of the most successful rap recording companies is named Death Row Records. Examples of rap song titles include "Murder Was the Case," "Sex, Money, and Murder," and "Natural Born Killers." The song that rapper Eminem performed at the Grammy Awards in 2001, "Stan," describes a murder-suicide. Rap music came under national scrutiny after performer Ice-T released the song "Cop Killer." The murders of rap artists Tupac Shakur and Notorious B.I.G. in recent years have also served to enhance the deadly image of this style of music.

PRINT MEDIA

Dying, death, and the dead are principal themes in much of American literature (Bryant and Shoemaker 1977). Westerns, war novels, mysteries, and true-crime books are exceptionally popular with readers. Violent death is a ubiquitous theme in popular fiction (Fulton and Owen 1987). Books about hospitals and doctors are also fairly successful (Bryant and Shoemaker 1977). Death and dying are even featured in children's stories (DeSpelder and Strickland 2002; Umberson and Henderson 1992). Newsmagazines frequently publish stories that deal with

death and dying, often featuring these stories on their covers. Even comic books have featured the exploits of notorious serial killers (Schecter and Everitt 1997).

Reports of death and dying are common in daily newspapers. The deaths of ordinary people are usually reported only in brief obituaries, unless a person has died in some sensational fashion. Newspapers report the deaths of public figures such as politicians, celebrities, and musical artists in far greater detail (Walter et al. 1995). For instance, the *Seattle Times* ran a front-page feature on the death of rock star Kurt Cobain, complete with photos of the suicide scene (Martin and Koo 1997).

In general, newspapers tend to overemphasize catastrophic causes of death (Combs and Slovic 1979). As Walter et al. (1995) observe, those dramatic deaths that are "boldly headlined and portrayed in the news media are extraordinary deaths" (p. 594). The image of the burning World Trade Center towers was featured on the front pages of many newspapers on September 12, 2001.

Newspaper depictions of death and dying are not always so explicit, however. When Umberson and Henderson (1992) conducted a content analysis of stories about the Gulf War that appeared in the *New York Times,* they found a striking absence of explicit references to death. Instead, the stories frequently employed governmentally inspired euphemisms such as "collateral damage" when discussing death. Moreover, the stories repeatedly quoted State Department and military spokespersons who talked about efforts to keep casualties to a minimum.

One form of print media that scholars have traditionally overlooked is the supermarket tabloid. The weekly circulation of the six major tabloids (*Star, Sun, National Enquirer, National Examiner, Globe,* and *Weekly World News*) is about 10 million, with an estimated readership of about 50 million (Bird 1992). As Durkin and Bryant (1995) note, these publications are full of thanatological content. Articles about murders, accidents, celebrity health scares, and dead celebrities are common, as are stories about paranormal phenomena such are reincarnation, ghosts, and near-death experiences. Health advice regarding the prevention of life-threatening medical problems can be found in some tabloids. In fact, Durkin and Bryant report that the *National Enquirer* has "received an award from the American Cancer Society for medical stories that the paper provided" (p. 10).

RECREATION

Aside from their presence in the media, dying, death, and the dead play an important role in the recreational activities of many Americans. As Bryant and Shoemaker (1977) note, many people show an "interest in, and morbid fascination with, facsimiles of the dead, the pseudo dead as it were" (p. 12). An example of this common fascination is the ever-popular wax museum. Also, the traveling museum exhibit of objects from King Tut's tomb was a nationwide sensation. In fact, actual dead bodies have sometimes been used for sideshow exhibits. According to Bryant (1989):

> For many years carnival concessionaires have displayed various kinds of odd bodies and curious corpses . . . because the public was fascinated with such unusual exhibits. A particularly morbid type of display that was common to carnivals was the exhibition of deformed fetuses in jars of formaldehyde, euphemistically known in the trade as "pickled punks." (P. 10)

In a somewhat similar vein, Bunny Gibbons, a sideshow exhibitor, displayed the "Death Car" of serial killer Ed Gein at county fairs throughout the Midwest (Schecter and Everitt 1997).

Some scholars have adopted the term *dark tourism* to refer to "the presentation and consumption (by visitors) of real and commodified death and disaster sites" (Foley and Lennon 1996:198). For example, since 1994, one of the more popular tourist attractions in Los Angeles has been the Brentwood condominium where Nicole Brown Simpson and Ronald Goldman were murdered (Schecter and Everitt 1997). Battlefields such as Gettysburg have traditionally been successful tourist attractions, as has the site of the assassination of President John F. Kennedy (Foley and Lennon 1996). During times of disaster, public safety officials often experience major problems in controlling curiosity seekers motivated by the chance to experience novel situations firsthand (Cunningham, Dotter, and Bankston 1986). Authorities have labeled this phenomenon *convergent behavior* (Bryant 1989).

Cemeteries and burial sites are also popular tourist attractions. For instance, the Forest Lawn cemetery near Hollywood is internationally known as the "cemetery of the stars" (Morgan 1968). Arlington National Cemetery in Virginia has millions of visitors annually (Bryant and Shoemaker 1977). As Frow (1998) reports, Graceland, the former home and burial site of music legend Elvis Presley, "is the object of both everyday pilgrimage and especially intense commemoration during the vigils of Tribute Week, culminating in the candle-lit procession around Presley's grave on the anniversary of his death" (p. 199). Merrin (1999) notes that when a telephone hot line was first opened for members of the public to order tickets to visit the grave of Princess Diana, it was "reported that up to 10,000 calls a minute had been attempted at peak times" (p. 58).

Games, a popular form of recreation, frequently contain thanatological themes. War toys and board games featuring characters like Casper the Friendly Ghost are popular with children. Video games such as Mortal Combat and Duke Nukem feature vivid images of violent deaths (see Funk and Buchman 1996). Several million copies of the Ouija Board, which is touted as a means of communicating with the dead, have been sold (Bryant and Shoemaker 1977). As Schecter and Everitt (1997) report,

the thanatological themes in games can assume morbid dimensions:

> Though it is unlikely to become the next *Trivial Pursuit*, a board game called Serial Killer set off a firestorm of outrage when it was put on the market a few years ago. . . . [It] consisted of a game board printed on a map of the United States, four serial killer game playing pieces, crime cards, outcome cards, and two dozen plastic victims (in the possibly ill-advised form of dead babies). (P. 31)

JOKES

Humor is a mechanism that allows for the violation of taboos regarding the discussion of death-related topics (Mannino 1997). A vast array of jokes deal with death, dying, and the dead. Thorson (1985) identifies two major varieties of death humor. The first is humor associated with the body. This includes jokes about cannibalism, funerals, undertakers, burials, and necrophilia. The second type, humor associated with the personality, includes jokes about suicide, homicide, memories of the departed, grief, executions, deathbed scenes, last words, and the personification of death.

Some jokes about death, dying, and the dead involve what has frequently been referred to as *gallows humor*. This term originated "from the genre of jokes about the condemned man or helpless victim, and is often generated by the victims themselves" (Moran and Massam 1997:5). An excellent example is Freud's classic anecdote about a man who joked on his way to the gallows. Currently, gallows humor is conceptualized as more of a philosophical posture than a specific repertoire of jokes (Van Wormer and Boes 1997). This type of humor is intentional (Thorson 1985) and tends to express "a cynical, morbid focus on death" (Sayre 2001:677).

An especially violent and cruel strain of death humor spread through American popular culture in the 1980s (Lewis 1997) and is still popular today. AIDS jokes are the classic example of this type of humor, in which the common tactic is to "specify an outgroup and make fun not only of death but also of dying people" (Thorson 1993:21). Moreover, many jokes are told about particular murderers and accused murderers (e.g., Jeffrey Dahmer and O. J. Simpson). Additionally, a variety of jokes circulate in relation to disasters such as the crash of ValuJet Flight 592 in Florida and the destruction of the space shuttle *Challenger* (see Blume 1986). Americans have also created macabre humor surrounding the Ethiopian famine, the Gulf War, and the mass suicide of the Branch Davidians. Such jokes "invite us to be amused by images of bodily mutilation, vulnerability, and victimization" (Lewis 1997:253). Controversial by its very nature, this insensitive type of humor is particularly offensive to many people (Thorson 1993); their responses ensure a dialectic, which increases the humor's entertainment value.

THE POSTSELF

Many of the manifestations of death and the dead in U.S. popular culture deal with what has been termed the *postself*. This is especially true for deceased celebrities and other public figures. The postself is the reputation and influence that an individual has after his or her death. According to Shneidman (1995), this "relates to fame, reputation, impact, and holding on" (p. 455). The postself constitutes a form of symbolic immortality, whereby "the meaning of a person can continue after he or she has died" (Leming and Dickinson 2002:143). In essence, the deceased person continues to exist in the memories of the living (Shneidman 1995). On a cultural level, this functions symbolically to blur the bifurcation between the living and the dead (Durkin and Bryant 1995).

As Frow (1998) observes, the fame of dead celebrities sometimes assumes a pseudoreligious dimension in contemporary society: "A small handful of stars and public figures experience this adoration that raises them beyond the human plane . . . [such as] Elvis, Rudolph Valentino, Lenin, Stalin, Hitler, Mao, James Dean, Kurt Cobain, Bruce Lee, Che Guevara, and Evita Peron" (p. 199). Perhaps the most prominent example of this phenomenon in recent years is Princess Diana, whose tragic and untimely death has resulted in what has been characterized as the "Diana grief industry" (Merrin 1999:51). The devoted can buy Diana dolls, books, plates, videos, stuffed animals, key chains, ashtrays, T-shirts, towels, mugs, spoons, stamps, posters, and more. Although this phenomenon has certainly been highly profitable for a vast array of entrepreneurs, some people find it particularly distasteful. For instance, British Prime Minister Tony Blair has condemned the sale of Princess Diana collectibles as the tacky exploitation of Diana's memory (Merrin 1999).

DISCUSSION

On the one hand, the contemporary United States is frequently described as a death-denying society. Numerous scholars have observed that recent generations of Americans lack the firsthand familiarity with death and dying that their ancestors had (e.g., Fulton and Owen 1987; DeSpelder and Strickland 2002; Leming and Dickinson 2002). Accordingly, many Americans express a great deal of death anxiety. On the other hand, many Americans also have an obsessive fascination with death, dying, and the dead (Oaks and Ezell 1993; Umberson and Henderson 1992). Nowhere is this paradox more apparent than in our popular culture. Television programming, movies, songs, the print media, games, jokes, and even recreational activities are fraught with thanatological content.

This seeming contradiction may be read at several levels, in that there are differential interpretations. The most obvious, albeit superficial, interpretation is that the United States is not as much of a death-denying society as many writers contend. A second explanation for the paradox is that our society is, indeed, a death-denying one, but our insulation from death causes us to crave some degree of information and insight concerning death, and we feed that craving through popular-culture depictions of death and dying. This situation would be not unlike the Victorian period in Great Britain and the United States, during which sexual Puritanism was an ideological mainstay of the value system, but nevertheless there was a significant demand for clandestine, salacious accounts of sex and sexual activity, such as smuggled "dirty" books from Europe.

Another interpretation of the contradiction between the death-denying nature of U.S. society and the saturation of death themes in the American mass media is that the treatment of death as entertainment and humor is simply an extension of, or another configuration of, death denial. By rendering death into humor and entertainment, we effectively neutralize it; it becomes innocuous, and thus less threatening, through its conversion and ephemerality in the media. This is, perhaps, the more compelling explanation.

Death is a disruptive event, not only for the individual who dies but for the larger social enterprise as well. Consequently, all societies must construct mechanisms to deal with death's problematic impacts (Blauner 1966). As Pine (1972) notes, the "beliefs and practices of the members of a society toward dying and death are largely dependent upon that society's social organization" (p. 149). Popular culture serves as a type of collective vision by which meanings are socially constructed, which in turn "greatly influences our norms, beliefs, and subsequent actions" (Couch 2000:25). It appears that the thanatological themes in U.S. popular culture function as a mechanism that helps Americans to deal with death. As Bryant (1989) notes, death, dying, and the dead "are traumatic and anxiety producing topics, and can be better confronted if they are socially neutralized" (p. 9).

Such social neutralization can help to assuage the disruptive impact of death and dying for the individual. This can occur in three related ways. First, in the context of popular culture, death, dying, and the dead are frequently reconceptualized into forms that stimulate something other than primordial terror. These phenomena may be considered fascinating, entertaining, and even humorous, depending on the social context. Bryant (1989) observes that when death is camouflaged in such a manner, "individuals can more comfortably indulge their curiosity about, and fascination with, such concerns" (p. 9). For instance, a visit to Elvis Presley's grave, to the site of the JFK assassination, to the spot where Nicole Brown Simpson and Ronald Goldman were murdered, or to the Forest Lawn cemetery near Hollywood might be considered part of a vacation. Moreover, many individuals find it thrilling to be frightened by horror and death at the movies (Leming and Dickinson 2002). Also, newspaper accounts of violent or accidental deaths may engender some voyeuristic, albeit convoluted, pleasure "or some macabre enjoyment in the misfortunes of others" (Walter et al.

1995:586). Similarly, many of the outrageous stories that appear in supermarket tabloids such as the *Weekly World News* and the *Sun* "appear to have no purpose other than catering to accident watchers" (Bird 1992:54).

Second, appreciation of many of the types of thanatological themes found in our popular culture requires some detachment on the part of the individual. Like spectators at professional wrestling matches, viewers of horror movies are required to suspend disbelief (Weaver 1991). Children or adolescents playing violent video games must detach themselves from the depictions of primal carnage occurring before their eyes. The quintessential example of this phenomenon is thanatological humor. Humor functions as a type of defense mechanism, allowing people to cope with the fear and anxiety associated with death and dying (Moran and Massam 1997; Oaks and Ezell 1993; Sayre 2001; Thorson 1993). Enjoyment of this type of humor requires us to laugh at our own mortality (Thorson 1985). As Lewis (1997) notes, the appreciation of a so-called killing joke "calls for the adoption of a playful detachment from an act of violence or suffering" (p. 264).

Finally, some observers have argued that the tremendous amount of exposure to death, dying, and the dead that we receive through our popular culture may make us more accepting of these phenomena (Oaks and Ezell 1993). This saturated environment of thanatological concerns may function to inure individuals to death and dying, thus diluting or counteracting their anxiety about these phenomena (Bryant and Shoemaker 1977). Durkin and Bryant (1995) speculate that "the inordinate amount of attention afforded to thanatological themes in the tabloids may actually help to desensitize the reader" (p. 11). Similarly, Wass et al. (1991) suggest that the ubiquitous death-related themes in popular music might help adolescents confront their anxieties about these phenomena, given that death and dying are seldom discussed in the home or the classroom.

CONCLUSION

The United States is commonly characterized as a death-denying society. Americans frequently attach fearful meanings to thanatological concerns, have taboos against frank discussions about death and dying, and relegate the task of handling the dead to professionals. Nonetheless, death, dying, and the dead occupy a prominent place in our popular culture. Thanatological themes appear frequently in television programming, cinema, the print media, jokes, and recreational activities. Dead celebrities also play an important role in our popular culture. These thanatological elements of popular culture function as a mechanism to help individuals deal with the disruptive social impacts of death and dying. They help us to redefine death as something other than a terror, and enjoyment of these themes requires some detachment on the part of the individual. It has also been argued that we may be more accepting of

death, dying, and the dead because of our frequent exposure to these phenomena through our popular culture.

REFERENCES

Abelman, Robert. 1987. "Themes and Topics in Religious Television Programming." *Review of Religious Research* 29:152–69.

Bahk, C. Mo and Kurt Neuwirth. 2000. "Impact of Movie Depictions of Volcanic Disasters on Risk Perceptions and Judgements." *International Journal of Mass Emergencies and Disasters* 18:63–84.

Bird, S. Elizabeth. 1992. *For Enquiring Minds: A Cultural Study of Supermarket Tabloids.* Knoxville: University of Tennessee Press.

Blauner, Robert. 1966. "Death and Social Structure." *Psychiatry* 29:378–94.

Blume, Delorys. 1986. "Challenger 10 and Our School Children: Reflections on the Catastrophe." *Death Studies* 10:95–118.

Bryant, Clifton D. 1989. "Thanatological Crime: Some Conceptual Notes on Offenses Against the Dead as a Neglected Form of Deviant Behavior." Paper presented at the World Congress of Victimology, Acapulco.

Bryant, Clifton D. and Donald Shoemaker. 1977. "Death and the Dead for Fun (and Profit): Thanatological Entertainment as Popular Culture." Presented at the annual meeting of the Southern Sociological Society, Atlanta, GA.

Combs, Barbara and Paul Slovic. 1979. "Newspaper Coverage of the Causes of Death." *Journalism Quarterly* 56:837–43.

Couch, Stephen R. 2000. "The Cultural Scene of Disasters: Conceptualizing the Field of Disasters and Popular Culture." *International Journal of Mass Emergencies and Disasters* 18:21–37.

Cunningham, Orville R., Daniel L. Dotter, and William B. Bankston. 1986. "Natural Disasters, Convergence, and Four-Wheel Drive Machines: An Emergent Form of Deviant Behavior." *Deviant Behavior* 7:261–67.

DeSpelder, Lynne Ann and Albert Lee Strickland. 2002. *The Last Dance: Encountering Death and Dying,* 6th ed. New York: McGraw-Hill.

Durkin, Keith F. and Clifton D. Bryant. 1995. "Thanatological Themes in the Tabloids: A Content Analysis." Presented at the annual meeting of the Mid-South Sociological Association, Mobile, AL.

Durkin, Keith F. and Kristy Knox. 2001. "September 11th, Postmodernism, and the Collective Consciousness: Some Sociological Observations." Presented at the annual meeting of the Mid-South Sociological Association, Mobile, AL.

Foley, Malcolm and J. John Lennon. 1996. "JFK and Dark Tourism: A Fascination With Assassination." *International Journal of Heritage Studies* 2:198–211.

Frow, John. 1998. "Is Elvis a God? Cult, Culture, and Questions of Method." *International Journal of Cultural Studies* 1:197–210.

Fulton, Robert and Greg Owen. 1987. "Death and Society in Twentieth Century America." *Omega* 18:379–95.

Funk, Jeanne and Debra D. Buchman. 1996. "Playing Violent Video and Computer Games and Adolescent Self Concept." *Journal of Communication* 46:19–32.

Gerbner, George. 1980. "Death in Prime Time: Notes on the Symbolic Functions of Dying in the Mass Media." *Annals of the American Academy of Political and Social Science* 447:64–70.

Kearl, Michael C. 1995. "Death in Popular Culture." Pp. 23–30 in *Death: Current Perspectives,* 4th ed., edited by John B. Williamson and Edwin S. Shneidman. Mountain View, CA: Mayfield.

Leming, Michael R. and George E. Dickinson. 2002. *Understanding Death, Dying, and Bereavement,* 5th ed. New York: Harcourt College.

Lewis, Paul. 1997. "The Killing Jokes of the American Eighties." *Humor* 10:251–83.

Mannino, J. Davis. 1997. *Grieving Days, Healing Days.* Boston: Allyn & Bacon.

Martin, Graham and Lisa Koo. 1997. "Celebrity Suicide: Did the Death of Kurt Cobain Influence Young Suicides in Australia?" *Archives of Suicide Research* 3:187–98.

Merrin, William. 1999. "Crash, Bang, Wallop! What a Picture! The Death of Diana and the Media." *Mortality* 4:41–62.

Molitor, Fred and Barry S. Sapolsky. 1993. "Sex, Violence, and Victimization in Slasher Films." *Journal of Broadcasting and Electronic Media* 37:233–42.

Moran, Carmen and Margaret Massam. 1997. "An Evaluation of Humour in Emergency Work." *Australasian Journal of Disaster and Trauma Studies* 3:1–12.

Morgan, Al. 1968. "The Bier Barons." *Sociological Symposium* 1:28–35.

Oaks, Judy and Gene Ezell. 1993. *Death and Dying: Coping, Caring and Understanding,* 2d ed. Scottsdale, AZ: Gorsuch Scarisbrick.

Pine, Vanderlyn R. 1972. "Social Organization and Death." *Omega* 3:149–53.

Sayre, Joan. 2001. "The Use of Aberrant Medical Humor by Psychiatric Unit Staff." *Issues in Mental Health Nursing* 22:669–89.

Schecter, Harold and David Everitt. 1997. *The A-Z Encyclopedia of Serial Killers.* New York: Pocket Books.

Shneidman, Edwin S. 1995. "The Postself." Pp. 454–60 in *Death: Current Perspectives,* 4th ed. edited by John B. Williamson and Edwin S. Shneidman. Mountain View, CA: Mayfield.

Strinati, Dominic. 2000. *An Introduction to Studying Popular Culture.* London: Routledge.

Thorson, James A. 1985. "A Funny Thing Happened on the Way to the Morgue: Some Thoughts on Humor and Death, and a Taxonomy of Humor Associated With Death." *Death Studies* 9:201–16.

———. 1993. "Did You Ever See a Hearse Go By? Some Thoughts on Gallows Humor." *Journal of American Culture* 16:17–24.

Umberson, Debra and Kristin Henderson. 1992. "The Social Construction of Death in the Gulf War." *Omega* 25:1–15.

Van Wormer, Katherine and Mary Boes. 1997. "Humor in the Emergency Room: A Social Work Perspective." *Health and Social Work* 22:87–92.

Walter, Tony, Jane Littlewood, and Michael Pickering. 1995. "Death in the News: The Public Investigation of Private Emotion." *Sociology* 29:579–96.

Wass, Hannelore. 1995. "Death in the Lives of Children and Adolescents." Pp. 269–301 in *Dying: Facing the Facts,* 3d ed., edited by Hannelore Wass and Robert A. Neimeyer. Washington, DC: Taylor & Francis.

Wass, Hannelore, M. David Miller, and Carol Ann Redditt. 1991. "Adolescents and Destructive Themes in Rock Music: A Follow-Up." *Omega* 23:199–206.

Wass, Hannelore, Jana L. Raup, Karen Cerullo, Linda G. Martel, Laura A. Mingione, and Anna M. Sperring. 1988. "Adolescents' Interest in and Views of Destructive Themes in Rock Music." *Omega* 19:177–86.

Weaver, James B. 1991. "Are Slasher Horror Films Sexually Violent?" *Journal of Broadcasting and Electronic Media* 35:385–92.

THE DEATH AWARENESS MOVEMENT

Description, History, and Analysis

KENNETH J. DOKA

The term *death awareness movement* refers to a somewhat amorphous yet interconnected network of individuals, organizations, and groups. This movement includes scholars, advocates, and counselors. It encompasses self-help networks such as the Compassionate Friends and professional associations such as the Association for Death Education and Counseling, the International Work Group on Dying, Death and Bereavement, and the National Hospice and Palliative Care Organization, as well as their members, affiliates, and regional and state counterparts. Most hospices and palliative care units would identify with the death awareness movement, as would many funeral service organizations. Foundations such as the Hospice Foundation of American and the Project on Death in American Society are involved, as are varied institutes and interorganizational committees and task forces. Many large organizations with broad and diffuse memberships and goals may focus some attention on end-of-life issues and on research or education concerning dying and death; for example, the American Psychological Association has a specialized task force on end-of-life issues. A number of scholarly journals (such as *Omega; Death Studies; Loss, Grief and Care;* and *Mortality*) as well as newsletters (such as *Journeys, Thanatos,* and *The Forum*) focus exclusively on issues of dying, death, and loss. Groups and individuals involved in the death awareness movement host teleconferences, symposia, conferences, training sessions, and workshops; they also publish a plethora of literature annually that is aimed at audiences ranging from children to adults and that ranges in subject matter and style from inspirational to self-help to serious clinical and scholarly work. The individuals and groups involved in this amorphous and far-reaching network—in reality a social movement—share a common focus (although not necessarily common goals, models, or methods); that focus is dying, death, and bereavement.

As a social movement, the death awareness movement had considerable success in the last half of the 20th century. From a small gathering of scholars at a 1956 professional meeting, thousands of college-level courses on the topics of death and dying are now offered. In the early 1970s, one hospice opened in Branford, Connecticut, outside of New Haven. Now more than 3,000 hospices serve almost every community in the United States. In this chapter, I explore and recount the history and trace the development of the death awareness movement. I also consider a more significant issue: Why in the past half century has there been such interest in dying, death, and bereavement?

BRIEF HISTORY OF THE ACADEMIC STUDY OF DEATH

The death awareness movement has amorphous and numerous roots, but it is perhaps best to begin here with a review of the emergence of death as a field of academic study. Much of the work done in this field has been a theoretical basis for, an inspiration to, and a reflection of the movement's organizational efforts.

Although some very early literature, including religious, philosophical, and social science writings, considers the problem of death, death studies as an area of academic interest advanced considerably with the publication of Freud's 1917 essay on mourning and melancholia. Freud's scope in the essay is broad—his concern is to distinguish between melancholia, or depression, and normal expressions of grief. This work, in which Freud defines the central task of mourning as the individual's relinquishment of emotional energy and the deceased, has long influenced conceptions of the mourning process. However, Freud's concept of the central task of mourning as learning to detach emotionally has been challenged recently by work that affirms the many healthy ways in which bonds between survivors and the deceased can continue (see, e.g., Doka 1989; Attig 1987; Klass, Silverman, and Nickman 1996).

Throughout the period between Freud's essay on mourning and the pioneering work of the mid-1950s, a number of scholars did some excellent exploratory work on death and dying (for a complete sociohistorical account, see Pine 1977). Two of these should be noted in particular. Lindemann (1944) conducted research on the survivors of Boston's Cocoanut Grove nightclub fire of 1942, which claimed more than 490 lives, as well as other groups of mourners and published the first clinical findings on acute grief. His conclusions that grief is a normal reaction to loss and a clearly identifiable syndrome with cognitive, physical, behavioral, spiritual, and affective manifestations set the tone for subsequent research on grief. In 1955, the British anthropologist Geoffrey Gorer published an essay titled "The Pornography of Death" ([1955] 1965). In that essay, Gorer became one of the first to suggest and analyze the reasons for modern society's tendency to ignore or deny death.

Pine (1977) characterizes the next period, 1958–67, as a decade of development. During this time, a number of influential works were published in a variety of fields, including medicine, nursing, philosophy, sociology, psychology, pastoral care, social commentary, funeral service, and theology. This was significant in that it firmly established the multidisciplinary nature of death studies. In a chapter of this size and mandate, I cannot do complete justice to the wide range of research published during this decade, but I want to mention here a few authors whose works are especially worthy of note, either because of their continued significance or because of their great heuristic value.

Perhaps one of the most significant books of this era was Feifel's edited volume *The Meaning of Death,* published in 1959. This book clearly established death studies as an academic discipline and offered scholars clear evidence of the wide range of issues encompassed by the study of death and dying. Whereas Feifel's work was scholarly, another influential book of this era drew from the muckraking tradition. Mitford's best-selling *The American Way of Death* (1963) was a scathing critique of both the funeral service business and contemporary funeral practice. It had far-reaching effects, spawning increased governmental scrutiny of the funeral service industry and generating research on the value of funeral rituals, the findings of which ironically tended to discount some of Mitford's criticisms and conclusions. *The American Way of Death* also generated interest in memorial societies and led to the development of local associations that would offer or arrange for members to receive dignified funeral services at reasonable cost, sometimes in conjunction with specified funeral service firms. This movement represented an early attempt on the part of Americans to organize

collectively around areas related to dying and death and to gain a sense of control over the process. Some of these societies and associations came to play a significant role in the subsequent development of the death awareness movement. For example, William Wendt, a Washington, D.C., clergyman, organized a burial society that later spawned a significant grief center and played a role in the development of professional associations concerned with death and dying.

Other work was also going on in this era. For example, Parsons (1963) published an article in which he challenged the oft-stated assumption that the United States is a death-denying culture, asserting that American patterns of death are actually active attempts at control. Saunders (1959) and Parkes (1959) began to do their work that would later underpin the work of St. Christopher's Hospice. In fact, in this period two important things occurred: First, many of the principal models that would influence subsequent academic work were developed (see, e.g., Glaser and Strauss 1965, 1968); and second, many scholars whose work or teaching would become influential in the field, such as Fulton (1961; Faunce and Fulton 1958), began their work.

Pine (1977) describes the decade spanning the late 1960s and early 1970s as a period of popularity for death studies. This is most evident in the work of Elisabeth Kübler-Ross. In her book *On Death and Dying* (1969), Kübler-Ross theorized five stages of dying, a theory that, although criticized by many subsequent scholars and unverified by research (see Corr 1993), became an overwhelmingly popular paradigm for understanding reactions to both dying and loss in general. Kübler-Ross's popularity at the time was a result of many factors. She was a charismatic advocate with a folksy charm, and, as Klass and Hutch (1985–86) note, her message was one that rejected dehumanizing technology, embraced a normal death, and saw opportunities for growth even at the end of life—all of which resonated well with American culture in the 1960s.

Kübler-Ross's work had far-reaching effects. First, and most critical, it brought the study of death out beyond the boundaries of academia and into the realm of health care workers and the lay public. Second, by doing so, it created a context for many of the organizational efforts that would emerge or move ahead in this era, such as the proliferation of hospices. Third, it generated a great deal of academic interest, stimulating research and bringing the subjects of death and dying to the attention of many in the academic community. Moreover, it created a larger context for the works of others, such as Earl Grollman (1967), who, through their writings and presentations, continued to educate professionals and the public about death and dying. In summary, the 1960s provided a firm foundation for death studies to emerge as an established academic discipline with its own models, controversies, journals, and organizations.

COMPLEMENTARY EFFORTS IN THE FIELD

As the scholarly study of death proceeded in the last half of the 20th century, it generated and was supported by a number of other efforts. In this period, journals and organizations devoted to death studies began, as did academic courses. In addition, a range of grief- and disease-related self-help organizations and networks proliferated. The growth of hospice was also a significant development in this era (I discuss hospice in greater depth below).

Journals and Associations

Among the predictable events that accompany the establishment of any academic field are the development of journals and the founding of professional associations. In 1967, Austin Kutscher, himself a widower seeking information on death and dying, developed the Foundation of Thanatology. The foundation convened a series of multidisciplinary symposia, some of which continue to the present. It also began publishing one of the first journals in the field, the *Journal of Thanatology,* in 1971. Although the journal did not survive, it demonstrated the need for a specialized journal focused on dying and death.

Omega: Journal of Death and Dying, has survived. First organized as a mimeographed newsletter, by 1970 it was formalized into a journal coedited by Richard Kalish and Robert Kastenbaum. In 1977, Hannelore Wass developed a second journal, *Death Education;* in its original form, it focused on death education, but the focus was soon broadened and the journal's name changed to *Death Studies.* Recently, the British journal *Mortality* and the new American journal *Loss, Grief and Care* (which has its roots in the Foundation of Thanatology) have emerged. It is interesting to note that none of these journals has yet developed a distinct point of view or a distinguishing theoretical perspective. In fact, all of these publications tend to share authors, similar topics, and even overlapping editorial boards. Both *Omega* and *Death Studies* are considered official journals of the Association for Death Education and Counseling. Naturally, given the multidisciplinary nature of the field, articles on death and dying are also published in academic journals associated with a wide range of other disciplines.

Professional associations in the field of death and dying began with Ars Moriendi (literally, "art of dying"), a loose network of scholars brought together by John Fryer, a psychiatrist at Temple University. Although the early history of this group and the reasons for its demise are subject to varying interpretations, one likely factor was its members' failure to agree on a vision of what the organization was to be. Some favored a group composed of leaders in the field who would come together to discuss common concerns and assist in setting standards for care of the dying and the bereaved. Others favored a broad-based professional association. Both visions were soon realized by other organizations. The Forum for Death Education, begun in 1976 and now called the Association for Death Education and Counseling, became that broad-based professional association, whereas the International Work Group on Dying, Death and Bereavement emerged as a similar but more selective group, inviting prospective members to apply for membership. Again, reflecting the nature and history of the field, these two groups have many members and leaders in common. In addition, scholars in other fields have also formed interest groups concerned with death and dying within their own professional organizations, such as the Gerontological Society of America and the American Psychological Association.

Death Education Courses

In the late 1960s, courses on death education began to be offered on college campuses. As Pine (1977) notes, the early chronology of these courses is not easy to establish, because the courses were offered by a variety of academic departments. By 1971, Green and Irish found that more than 600 courses related to death and dying were offered by colleges and universities across the United States. Five years later, Cummins (1978) found more than 1,000 such courses in the United States enrolling more than 30,000 students. In addition, thanatology content is found in the curricula of both secondary and primary schools, integrated into modules in a variety of subjects, including health science and literature. In some secondary schools, courses directly concerned with the topics of death and dying are offered as electives.

Death education continues to consolidate. In addition to courses, many colleges and universities are now developing majors, certificates, and even master's degree programs in grief counseling. The Association for Death Education and Counseling is now poised to establish a process for certifying death educators and grief counselors. Already, some members of the association who represent colleges and universities that have formalized programs have begun to discuss accreditation. These programs have been supplemented by academic centers such as the Center for Death Education and Research at the University of Wisconsin–La Crosse.

Although this growth is impressive, recent events continue to suggest the tenuous existence of death-related courses in the curricula of universities and colleges. Many of these courses, as well as death education programs and centers, are still tied to individuals rather than to departments or colleges. When a given professor retires, courses or even an entire program may be retired as well. Two examples illustrate this state of affairs. First, the Center for Death Education and Research was able to survive the retirement of its director, Robert Fulton, but it was transferred from it original home at the University of Minnesota to the home institution of Fulton's chosen successor, Robert Bendiksen at the University of Wisconsin–La Crosse. Second, although many younger leaders in the field of thanatology and palliative care received significant training through a thanatology option in New York University's doctoral program in counseling, it is questionable whether the option will survive the full retirement of its founding professor, Dr. Richard Ellis.

Self-Help Networks

Along with the growth of thanatology as a subject of academic study, there has been parallel growth in self-help movements associated with death and dying. Since the early development of Widow-to-Widow groups (see, e.g., Silverman 1986), some groups (such as Compassionate Friends, a group for bereaved parents and siblings) have focused primarily on bereavement support, whereas others (such as Mothers Against Drunk Driving and Parents of Murdered Children) have included bereavement support along with other functions, such as legal advocacy. Recent research has found that such support can be helpful to both those giving assistance and those receiving it (Lund 1999).

THE DEVELOPMENT OF HOSPICE

The major organizational effort that has taken place in the death awareness movement is the development of hospice. The remarkable history of the hospice movement has been well described by several authors (see, e.g., Stoddard 1978). Hospice represents, perhaps, one of the most successful grassroots movements in the last quarter of the 20th century. Although this movement has its roots in religious orders such as the Knights Hospitallers and the Sisters of Charity, both of which focused on caring for the dying, Dame Cicely Saunders is generally credited with opening the first modern hospice, St. Christopher's, outside of London in 1967. At St. Christopher's, she tried to create a homelike atmosphere and a holistic, family-centered way to allow dying persons to live life as fully as possible, free from debilitating pain and incapacitating symptoms.

St. Christopher's Hospice became an exemplar in both research and practice, generating seeds that would grow throughout the world. Many of the pioneers who would influence the development of hospice and palliative care visited or trained there. In the United States, the spread of the hospice movement resulted in the establishment of Hospice, Inc., in Branford, Connecticut, in 1974. Branford also had a small home-care unit, but it was Dr. William Lamers, founder of a hospice in Marin County, California, who first focused on home care as both the heart and future of hospice. Lamers believed that the best way to offer patients a homelike environment was to treat them in their actual homes. He offered a model of hospice that freed interested individuals from fund-raising for new facilities, and this home-care model quickly spread throughout the country, sponsored by a range of groups, from churches and interfaith groups to junior leagues. Hospice in the United States is thus very different from hospice in England, centering more on home care and heavily emphasizing psychosocial care and the use of volunteers (Connor 1998).

The success of the hospice movement in the United States has been impressive. In 1974, the National Hospice Organization (NHO) was formed, and by 1978, there were more than 1,200 hospices nationwide (Connor 1998). In 1982, hospices became eligible for Medicare reimbursement, and this proved a further spur to growth. Current estimates place the number of hospice programs in the United States at more than 3,000, serving 700,000 persons annually (Miller et al. 2002).

As Saunders and Kastenbaum (1997) note, the growth of hospice was a reaction to a number of trends. First, advances in technology-driven medicine focused on cure seemed to be abandoning those who were no longer responsive to treatment. Second, hospice resonated with two other themes of the era—anticonsumerism and return to nature. Both trends converged on the idea that individuals could create alternative, more natural organizations, that they could take control of their lives—and their deaths. The study of death, especially the popularity of books such as Kübler-Ross's *On Death and Dying* (1969), increased awareness of the unmet needs of the dying and bereaved.

Not everyone learned the same lesson at St. Christopher's Hospice. Dr. Balfour Mount, a Canadian physician, was impressed by the hospice, but was also convinced that the lessons of St. Christopher's need not necessarily lead to a new form of care; rather, those lessons could be applied even in the high-technology environment of the modern hospital. In his position at the Royal Victoria Hospital in Montreal, he pioneered the development of a hospital-based palliative care model. This model was successful, and in February 2000, the NHO changed its name to the National Hospice and Palliative Care Organization to reflect these two different approaches to providing the dying with humane care.

CURRENT REALITY AND REACTIONS

By the late 1990s, the death awareness movement had become relatively institutionalized. This is evident in a number of changes. For example, it has become routine for many funeral homes to offer after-care services ranging from information and referral to educational seminars to the sponsorship of counselors and therapy groups. Large-scale educational events concerning death-related topics are not uncommon, and television programs and films focused on death and dying (such as *Tuesdays With Morrie* and Bill Moyers's *On Our Own Terms*) have received widespread critical acclaim and respectable audiences. Each year, the Hospice Foundation of America produces a major teleconference titled "Living With Grief," hosted by TV journalist Cokie Roberts; this conference reaches more than 2,000 sites throughout North America and offers education to close to a quarter of a million professionals. It is now routine for government agencies to send crisis teams and grief counselors to sites of sudden and traumatic death and loss. In fact, President Clinton devoted part of his response to the shootings of 13 students and teachers at Columbine High School in 1999 to reassuring the nation that he had dispatched grief counselors to the site.

Changes in our attitudes are also reflected in the mass media, where dying and death are no longer taboo topics. News programs such as *60 Minutes* and *Dateline* frequently feature stories related to death and dying. In the aftermath of events such as the death of John F. Kennedy, Jr., or the September 11, 2001, terrorist attacks, it is not unusual to see, in both print and nonprint media, grief and trauma experts discussing common reactions to such events and offering advice. Topics surrounding death have even become part of our entertainment. One of the HBO cable television network's highest-rated series is the critically acclaimed *Six Feet Under,* which follows the lives of the members of a family who live and work in a funeral home. This program frequently shows expressions of grief, funerals, and corpses.

Naturally, such changes have generated various reactions. For example, in the aftermath of the shootings at Columbine, the popular press published a few critical pieces that challenged the value of grief counseling. There has also been a small reactive movement against death education in schools spearheaded by Phyllis Schlafly, perhaps best known for her activism against the Equal Rights Amendment in the 1970s. In 1982, Ron Rosenbaum led a scathing attack on the death awareness movement in an article published in *Harper's*. According to Rosenbaum, the death awareness movement, led by Kübler-Ross, seeks to create a cult of the dead, romanticizing the process of dying and encouraging suicide. Rosenbaum's piece mixed serious cultural criticism with personal attacks on Kübler-Ross, who, at the time Rosenbaum wrote his article, had begun to explore spiritualism. What Rosenbaum neglected to realize or to state was how distant the death awareness movement, at least within academia, had become from this former icon. Rosenbaum echoed Lofland's (1978) earlier academic critique, in which she accused what she called the "Happy Death Movement" of offering a positivist view of death that romanticizes dying and overemphasizes emotional expressiveness as therapy for the dying and bereaved. It might be stated that although many of these reactions do speak to some of the strains of popular thanatology, they are based on vast oversimplification of the many approaches and rich theoretical debate evident within the death awareness movement. In any case, the movement's place in academia, health care, self-help, and popular culture seems secure.

FACTORS UNDERLYING THE DEVELOPMENT OF THE DEATH AWARENESS MOVEMENT

Beyond simply reviewing the chronology of the death awareness movement, it is interesting to speculate on some of the factors that have influenced the easing of cultural taboos concerning death and the emergence of this movement. In earlier work, I have identified four sites or factors that have facilitated increased interest in and awareness of death in the United States (Doka 1983). The first factor involves demographic changes: As the proportion and population of the elderly have increased, interest in the field of aging has intensified, and with the study of aging has come increased awareness and study of dying and death. The prolongation of the dying process has created new strains for medical staff, new ethical issues, and new forms of care, all of which have served to increase public awareness of and interest in the discussion and organization of dying and death.

The second factor is historical. Many researchers have noted that the beginning of the nuclear age created totally new issues that complicated death and increased death anxiety. In the latter half of the 20th century and the beginning of the 21st, other issues have been raised. We have become aware of dangers to the environment. We are aware of the ever-present threat of worldwide terrorism. We have seen the emergence of a new disease—AIDS—that has devastated communities in the Western world even as it decimates Africa and threatens other developing areas. Faced as we are with the possibilities of the nuclear death of civilization, new diseases, environmental holocaust, and random terrorism, death has become a critical social concern. Support for this perspective can be found in the case of the late Middle Ages, when the widespread devastation caused by bubonic plague was reflected in a preoccupation with death, as evidenced by art, religion, and popular thought (Boase 1972; Tuchman 1978; Aries 1981).

The third factor associated with the apparent rise in death awareness is sociological and social psychological in nature. In its beginnings, the death awareness movement was aligned in goals with many of the social movements and trends of the 1960s. It asserted the rights and dignity of the dying. It proclaimed the naturalness of death. It denounced dehumanizing technology. It emphasized openness toward death and sharing with the dying. In short, its increasing popularity was aided by its identification with many social themes evident at that time.

The fourth factor is cultural. The death awareness movement has filled a void in a secular society where many segments of the population previously found no significance in the culture's understandings of death, making the topics of death and dying more acceptable and thus more meaningful. In our materialistic society, death has often been avoided or denied. The death awareness movement has been part of a broad trend toward the inclusion of spirituality and meaning making in individuals' lives. It is probably no coincidence that the movement emerged at a time when many members of the Baby Boom generation began to contemplate their parents' mortality as well as their own.

CONCLUSION

I do not mean to suggest that the death awareness movement is merely a fad or a relic of the 1960s. Although a number of factors combined in that era to cause the movement to emerge and grow, it has demonstrated respectability and durability. It has become institutionalized. This should continue as the Baby Boomers age, given that, historically, the members of this generation have actively confronted the issues they face and compelled the larger society to face them as well.

I do not mean to suggest, either, that the entities that make up the death awareness movement will remain always in their present forms. It will be interesting to see, for example, the ways in which the growth of palliative care as well as other changes in U.S. health care will affect the future of hospice. In addition, as Lofland (1978) notes, the tendency of many practitioners to emphasize emotional expressiveness as the heart of self-help groups and counseling has been challenged by critics both within and outside the field. In fact, there is a clear need for the careful evaluation of practice. There is a danger that untested and unevaluated approaches that lack theoretical depth, demonstrated by persons of dubious training, can do the movement great harm. Yet, even here, there are promising trends. As a field develops, consolidation of knowledge and moves towards certification usually emerge (Doka & Smith-Fraser 1986). As this book goes to press, the Association for Death Education and Counseling is on the verge of developing a certification process that will codify a body of knowledge and a uniform standard of practice.

It is possible to predict that in the next few decades there will be intensified interest in death and dying and an increase in the growth of the death awareness movement. Part of this growth will come simply from momentum. The establishment of large self-help networks, hospices, professional associations, and other organizational efforts, as well as the development of certification and educational programs, suggests continued focus. In short, interest breeds more interest. Part of the growth in the movement, however, will be related to demographics. Members of the Baby Boom generation are now at the verge of moving into later life. As the Baby Boomers age, they will undoubtedly continue their characteristic way of confronting the issues they face and compelling the larger society to do so; this suggests that death will continue to be a topic of interest well into the 21st century.

REFERENCES

Aries, P. 1981. *The Hour of Our Death,* translated by H. Weaver. New York: Alfred A. Knopf.

Attig, T. P. 1987. *Grief, Love and Separation.* In *Death: Completion and Discovery,* edited by C. A. Corr and R. Pacholski. Lakewood, OH: Association for Death Education and Counseling.

Boase, T. A. 1972. *Death in the Middle Ages: Mortality, Judgment and Remembrance.* New York: McGraw-Hill.

Connor, S. 1998. *Hospice: Practice, Pitfalls and Promise.* Washington, DC: Taylor & Francis.

Corr, C. A. 1993. "Coping With Dying: Lessons That We Should Learn and Not Learn From the Work of Elizabeth Kübler-Ross." *Death Studies* 117:69–83.

Cummins, V. A. 1978. "On Death Education and Colleges and Universities in the U.S. 1977." Presented at the Forum for Death Education and Counseling, September, Washington, DC.

Doka, K. J. 1983. "The Rediscovery of Death: An Analysis of the Emergence of the Death Studies Movement." In *Creativity in Death Education and Counseling,* edited by C. A. Corr, J. Stillion, and M. Ribour. Lakewood, OH: Association for Death Education and Counseling.

———. 1989. "Grief." Pp. 127–31 in *Encyclopedia of Death,* edited by R. J. Kastenbaum and B. Kastenbaum. Phoenix, AZ: Onyx.

Doka, K. J. and D. Smith-Fraser. 1986. "The Emergence of Gerontology." *ASA Connection,* July/August, pp. 1, 3.

Faunce, W. A. and R. L. Fulton. 1958. "The Sociology of Death: A Neglected Area in Sociological Research." *Social Forces* 36:205–8.

Feifel, H. 1959. *The Meaning of Death.* New York: McGraw-Hill.

Fulton, R. L. 1961. "The Clergyman and the Funeral Director: A Study in Role Conflict." *Social Forces* 39:317–23.

Glaser, B. G. and A. L. Strauss. 1965. *Awareness of Dying.* Chicago: Aldine.

———. 1968. *Time for Dying.* Chicago: Aldine.

Gorer, G. [1955] 1965. "The Pornography of Death." Pp. 192–99 in G. Gorer, *Death, Grief and Mourning.* Garden City, NY: Doubleday.

Green, B. R. and D. P. Irish. 1971. *Death Education: Preparation for Living.* Cambridge, MA: Schenkman.

Grollman, E. A. 1967. *Explaining Death to Children.* Boston: Beacon.

Klass, D. and R. Hutch. (1985–86). "Elisabeth Kübler-Ross as a Religious Leader." *Omega* 16:89–109.

Klass, D., P. R. Silverman, and S. I. Nickman. 1996. *Continuing Bonds: New Understandings of Grief.* Washington, DC: Taylor & Francis.

Kübler-Ross, E. 1969. *On Death and Dying.* New York: Macmillan.

Lindemann, E. 1944. "Symptomatology and Management of Acute Grief." *American Journal of Psychology* 101: 141–48.

Lofland, L. 1978. *The Craft of Dying: The Modern Face of Death.* Beverly Hills, CA: Sage.

Lund, D. 1999. "Grieving and Receiving Help During Later Life Spousal Bereavement." In *Living With Grief: At Work, at School, at Worship,* edited by J. Davidson and K. J. Doka. Washington, DC: Hospice Foundation of America.

Miller, G. W., J. R. Williams, D. J. English, and J. Keyserling. 2002. "Delivering Quality Care and Cost-Effectiveness at the End of Life: Building on the 20-Year Success of the Medicare Hospice Benefit." Report distributed by the National Hospice and Palliative Care Organization, Washington, DC.

Mitford, J. 1963. *The American Way of Death.* New York: Simon & Schuster.

Parkes, C. M. 1959. "Morbid Grief Reactions: A Review of the Literature." Ph.D. dissertation, University of London.

Parsons, T. A. 1963. "Death in American Society: A Brief Working Paper." *American Behavioral Scientist* 6:61–65.

Pine, V. 1977. "A Socio-Historical Portrait of Death Education." *Death Education* 1:57–84.

Rosenbaum, R. 1982. "Turn on, Tune in, Drop Dead." *Harper's,* July, pp. 32–40.

Saunders, C. 1959. "The Problem of Euthanasia." *Nursing Times,* October 9, pp. 960–61.

Saunders, C. and R. J. Kastenbaum. 1997. *Hospice Care on the International Scene.* New York: Springer.

Silverman, P. R. 1986. *Widow-to-Widow.* New York: Springer.

Stoddard, S. 1978. *The Hospice Movement: A Better Way of Caring for the Dying.* New York: Vintage.

Tuchman, B. W. 1978. *A Distant Mirror: The Calamitous 14th Century.* New York: Ballantine.

THE SPIRITUALIST MOVEMENT

Bringing the Dead Back

CHARLES F. EMMONS

DEFINITIONS AND CROSS-CULTURAL PERSPECTIVE

Although my central purpose in this chapter is to analyze the social functions of the spiritualist movement that began in the United States in the 1840s, it is appropriate that I first establish some generic definitions. These definitions will also help to provide some perspective on what is a controversial subject in Western culture by presenting it in cross-cultural context.

Spiritualism

Taken broadly, the term *spiritualism* could refer to any religious worldview that considers living things to have souls or spirits (Tylor 1871; Lowie 1924). This does not necessarily privilege human beings as the only possessors of souls. In fact, the National Spiritualist Association of Churches (NSAC) of the United States explicitly changed the wording of its "Declaration of Principles" in 2001 to refer to "souls" rather than "human souls," as the group wanted to avoid the implication that only humans have souls (Sharon L. Snowman, secretary, board of directors of the NSAC, personal communication, October 17, 2001).

More particularly, however, the term *spiritualism* connotes a focus on *contact* with the spirit world. Means of contact might be through spirit mediumship but may also include related concepts, such as spirit possession, dreams, apparitions/ghosts, paranormal physical effects (moving objects and the like), ancestor worship, divination, and synchronicities taken to represent after-death communications. Reasons for the living to encourage such communication vary; they include not only information exchange but also healing and other physical benefits.

Shamanism Versus Mediumship

On a world scale, the anthropological concept of the *shaman* has been used to refer to a religious specialist who

manipulates the spirit world in order to heal the sick (Eliade 1964; Nicholson 1987; Drury 1991). *Spirit medium* refers to a specialist who contacts spirits for information. However, sometimes shamans do mediumship as well, and the terms overlap in the literature.

Before I address the cultural variations in the concept of spirit mediumship, it is worthwhile to comment on its cultural universality. Mediumship probably exists in some form and to some degree in virtually all societies. However, it tends to be more institutionalized in societies that venerate ancestors (Emmons 1982).

In regard to the techniques used by spirit mediums, it is interesting to observe how similar they are cross-culturally. Mediums generally go into some type of altered state of consciousness, often into varying degrees of trance, bordering on or including spirit possession. Even if not in trance, they often use the help of spirit guides or "controls," spirits who work with and for the mediums, contacting other spirits and passing on their information (Emmons and Emmons 2003).

Mediumship can be analyzed from both conflict and functional perspectives. An observer taking the conflict perspective would emphasize the dynamics of inequality involved in the institution of mediumship, whereas one taking the functional perspective would emphasize the logic of mediumship within the cultural system. Another perspective is that of symbolic interaction, through which one might observe the face-to-face process of spirit medium interacting with client (sitter).

One attempt to find a general conflict theoretical explanation for direct involvement with the spirit world on the part of the living is displayed in I. M. Lewis's classic article "Spirit Possession and Deprivation Cults" (1966). Lewis writes, "Women and other depressed categories [of people] exert mythical pressures upon their superiors in circumstances of deprivation and frustration when few other sanctions are available to them" (p. 318). As we shall see later, this is a particularly useful interpretation for the activities of American spirit mediums, most of whom were women, during the spiritualist movement of the 19th century.

However, it is also important to examine the functional relationship of institutions of spirit mediumship with the rest of a culture. In the Chinese case, mediumship is an information-gathering tool; one uses it to find out what one's ancestors want in the afterlife (Emmons 1982). A Chinese person traditionally goes to a medium (e.g., a *mun mai poh*, "ask-rice woman") with a cup of rice from his or her kitchen to identify the particular family. Through the medium, the individual may discover (nowadays in Hong Kong, for example) that his or her deceased uncle wants a Mercedez-Benz with a CD player and lots of money. The family member may promise to burn an offering of a paper-and-wood effigy of such a car and some "hell bank-notes" in return for a positive outcome in the public hous-ing lottery. Lineage members are thought to help each other in both directions across the divide between this world and the next.

On a micro level, this institution may help alleviate the anxiety individuals may feel over their success, even in modern urban Hong Kong. In a broader, macro perspective, spirit mediumship and ancestor worship have been more prominent in areas of south China that have practiced large-scale wet-rice cultivation, often managed by particular lineages or clans. Ancestor worship provides solidarity by inducing cooperation among people who share ancestors back as many as five generations.

In other cases, spirit mediumship has had political, even revolutionary, significance. Lain provides a good example of this for another culture area—Zimbabwe in East Africa—in *Guns and Rain* (1985). Although the case that Lain describes is relevant to Lewis's idea of deprivation cults, historically, powerful political leaders have con-sulted more powerful mediums than have people of lower status in Zimbabwe. The same is true for China, in that mediumship and ancestor worship seem to have trickled down from exclusively elite involvement initially to the eventual involvement of lower-status groups (Emmons 1982).

For Native Americans, spirit mediumship had both personal and social movement significance, both of which can be seen in the life story of Black Elk (1988), who lived from 1863 to 1950. The Ghost Dance was a movement mainly among Plains Indians, from 1885 through 1890, in which spirits of the ancestors were to return and lead the people against white domination (Kehoe 1989). The influ-ence of Native American culture continues into the present among white spirit mediums, many of whom claim to have Native American spirit guides.

Not only are there variations in the meanings and func-tions of spiritualism across cultures, there are also signifi-cant changes within particular cultures over time (something to be aware of in the American case). For example, Morris (2000) shows that spirit mediumship in northern Thailand has been transformed through the forces of modernization in politics and mass media.

QUESTIONS FOR THE AMERICAN CASE

This is a good point at which to reflect upon the general "social problems" that death causes, as a way of preparing for discussion of more specific questions about the nature of American spiritualism. Notice that this subsection of this volume is titled "Keeping the Dead Alive," and that the subtitle of this particular chapter is "Bringing the Dead Back." Why might it be important socially to keep the dead alive and to bring them back to communicate with the living through the services of a spirit medium?

As I have noted above, spirit mediumship can be a political tool. Lewis's (1966) theory of deprivation cults stresses the use of spirit possession and mediumship by subordinate groups as a means of undermining the author-ity of dominant groups. However, elites have also used mediumship as a source of supernatural power, as in ancient Greece when kings consulted the Oracle at Delphi, even if the mediums themselves were women of low status. Could some version of this conflict approach help to explain the American spiritualist movement?

Another social reason for communicating with the dead is to provide continuity in the institution of the family. In many societies, the eldest members of a family or lineage have greater power than younger members and also pro-vide a connecting link for solidarity among their descen-dants. In the Chinese case this was particularly significant as a part of ancestor worship in the context of wet-rice cul-tivation, but it continues as a cultural survival tool with practical functions in modern urban Hong Kong as well.

Of course, American culture is quite different from Chinese culture; compared with Chinese, Americans have both less respect for elders and greater economic indepen-dence as individuals. Therefore, we should expect spirit mediumship to be less significant in the United States than it is in China and, when it exists, to be more oriented toward personal emotional concerns. In other words, we should expect American mediumship to focus on easing individuals' fears of dying and of losing their loved ones to death.

When I was doing participant observation research with a spirit medium in Hong Kong in 1980, I asked the medium to contact my aunt as an example. Returning several times for further sessions, I was recognized by some of the medium's other clients (all Chinese women) in the waiting room. Not realizing that I knew the Cantonese language, and assuming evidently that I relied on an inter-preter in the séance room, one woman in the waiting room laughed and said, "The Westerner's here again to chitchat with his auntie!" Her gentle ridicule was based on a clear cultural difference: Chinese would normally use a medium only for practical reasons, not because they missed the company of their departed relatives.

One other significant cultural characteristic is relevant to any examination of American mediumship: the domi-nance of science over religion and magic in Western societies. This is not to say that American society is completely secularized in all of its institutions. However, spirit mediumship is considered far less legitimate in modern Western societies than it is in others. This should lead us to ask how it is that spiritualism managed to flourish in the United States in the 19th century, and how it survived and even revived in the 20th and 21st centuries. (For a discussion of how spiritualism has been less condemned in Iceland than in other Western countries, partly due to its being more closely associated with a scientific attitude early on and partly due to special attitudes about religion among Icelanders, see Swatos and Gissurarson 1997.)

Interrelated with the issue of scientific legitimacy is the phenomenon of the popular culture of the paranormal that thrives in the Western mass media. What should we make of the popular entertainment context of spirit mediumship today? Case in point: A sign posted at a "psychic fair" held by a Spiritualist church in a fire station states, "Readings are for entertainment purposes only."

ORIGINS OF THE SPIRITUALIST MOVEMENT IN THE UNITED STATES

Tracing the social history of American spiritualism is a complex matter, as would be tracing the history of any diffuse religious social movement. Throughout all of its changes over the past 153 years and more, spiritualism has always had multiple associations and meanings (essential sources on this subject include Braude 1989; Cross 1981; Moore 1977; Carroll 1997; Doyle [1926] 1975; Owen 1990; Lawton 1932).

From a collective behavior perspective, the structural conduciveness (Smelser 1962) that provided fertile soil for religious social movements like spiritualism lay in the rapidly changing social climate of western New York State in the early 19th century. The Erie Canal, completed in 1825, brought economic development and a rapidly growing, mobile population to the area (Cross 1981:3–77). Not only spiritualism but several other religious and ideological movements grew to a significant degree out of western New York by 1850; these included Mormonism, Millerism (later Seventh-Day Adventism), abolitionism, and feminism.

Spiritualists today trace the beginnings of their religion to an occurrence of alleged spirit mediumship in 1848 involving the Fox sisters in Hydesville, New York, near Rochester. To be sure, this was not the only or the earliest case in the region (for others, see Doyle [1926] 1975). Although the details are variously described in the literature, the stories agree on some basic points: Margaret Fox, age 14, and Kate Fox, age 11, heard rapping noises in the family's cottage. Kate, attempting to imitate the sounds, clapped her hands and said, "Mr. Splitfoot, do as I do" (Doyle [1926] 1975:1:66). The mysterious sound followed with the same number of raps as the child's claps. A code was worked out, and this led to a message that the spirit

was that of a peddler who had been murdered in the house for his money and buried in the basement.

For our purposes, it need only be said here that the story spread as various Quakers, Universalists, and Swedenborgians promoted the sisters and their phenomena. The craze of spirit rapping and table tipping (putting hands on a table and waiting for spirits to move it) diffused rapidly within a few years, across not only the United States but Europe as well, and especially England. A confession of fraud by Margaret Fox in 1888 (which she retracted in 1889) provides to this day a foundation for the debunking of the Fox sisters' claims, although the matter is much too complicated to warrant such an easy dismissal.

As Cross (1981) points out, the Fox sisters helped create "a new religious enthusiasm" from what had been a "liberal, intellectual, somewhat rationalistic movement" in American Swedenborgianism (pp. 344–45). The spiritual ideas of Quakers, Universalists, and other "freethinkers" were also loosely connected in this emerging religious social movement.

More specifically, however, Andrew Jackson Davis was to the ideology of spiritualism what the Fox sisters were to the phenomena and practice of spiritualism. Davis, born in 1826 in Orange County, New York, had a vision in 1844 in which he met the ancient Greek physician Galen and the prominent 18th-century Swedish scientist Emanuel Swedenborg, who also wrote extensively as a mystical/spiritual philosopher (Davis 1859). From that point, Davis moved from giving psychic messages and diagnoses to actual healing. He would examine people and prescribe unusual remedies; for example, he recommended putting warm rat skins over the ears as a cure for deafness. In 1845, at age 19, he began to lecture in trance and to write books in language that was seemingly too sophisticated for someone with less than a year of formal education.

George Bush, a New York University professor and America's top expert on Swedenborg at the time, examined Davis and decided that he was an authentic marvel. Bush verified that Davis could dictate in Hebrew, Arabic, and Sanskrit, languages that Davis supposedly could not have known, but that Bush thought he might be channeling from Swedenborg or others (Moore 1977:11). A century later, social historian Whitney Cross (1981) took a less charitable view, referring to Davis as "a yokel from Poughkeepsie" and saying that "with Bush's aid [he] in considerable measure plagiarized Swedenborg's writings" (p. 344). Whatever the case, Davis became a major figure in the spiritualist movement, writing books about the spirit world and natural law, such as *The Univercoelum* and *Harmonia,* between 1848 and 1850 (Davis 1859:296–307, 420–36).

RADICAL CORRELATES OF SPIRITUALISM

Throughout the 19th century in the United States, spiritualism became associated with several radical causes in opposition to dominant institutions and powerful groups, especially mainstream churches and patriarchy. These causes included the abolition of slavery, health reform, temperance, marriage reform, reform of attitudes toward sexuality and reproductive rights, women's suffrage, and dress reform for women (Braude 1989).

Of course, spiritualists were far from unified on these issues, but there was a tendency, especially for adherents of feminist causes, to accrete to spiritualism because Spiritualist churches and assemblies were among the few places in which women could have a voice. Interestingly, spiritualism can be seen as an old example of a "new" social movement, in that it was rather broad in its class base and promoted empowerment and consciousness-raising over a wide range of interconnected issues. If feminism today is a new social movement, then spiritualism in the 19th century is an even better example of such a movement.

In fact, 19th-century advocates of women's rights risked ridicule from moderates when they spoke to spiritualist groups, as Susan B. Anthony did several times in the 1890s at Woman Suffrage Day in Lily Dale, the Spiritualist camp located about 55 miles southwest of Buffalo, New York (Braude 1989:196). Unlike more moderate feminists who had to concentrate on restricted battles they had a chance of winning, such as suffrage, spiritualists tended to be all-purpose, noncompromising radicals.

Focusing on the religious/spiritual core of spiritualism, the main issues that drew especially women to spiritualism in the first place had to do with death and the continuity of life after death. Those who rejected, for example, the idea of infant damnation (for babies who died unbaptized) sought comfort in more liberal Protestant theology, the rural cemetery movement (1850s), and the possibility of contact with the spirit world found in the emerging movement of spiritualism (Braude 1989:49–55).

One of the ironies of this situation is that in the 1850s, when spiritualism was spreading in the United States and Britain, women found a voice in the movement that they did not have elsewhere. Spiritualist women were able to speak in public in a trance state at a time when women in general, even feminists, were not. Because the spirit was in charge, women trance speakers could not easily be accused of stepping out of their legitimate passive domestic roles. This practice resulted in both the spread of spiritualism through enthusiastic audiences and some loosening of the restrictive role of women (Braude 1989: 82–98).

The downside was that the trance state fell under the medical definition of psychological abnormality. This was one of many ways in which spiritualism was labeled as deviant, part of the social control process mobilized against the spread of spiritualism as a religious social movement in the 19th century (Owen 1990:143–67). Even in the 20th century, until recently, anybody who spoke as if channeling another spirit entity was a good candidate for a diagnosis of multiple personality (or dissociative disorder).

SPIRITUALIST ORGANIZATION AND ANTIORGANIZATION

Throughout the history of spiritualism in the United States, there has been a tension between contradictory tendencies for and against organization. To a great extent, spiritualists early on were reacting against established, male-dominated Protestant churches and did not wish to create their own dogmatic structures. Carroll (1997), however, argues that spiritualism before the Civil War was more organized than has been generally believed. The more spiritualists attempted to organize nationally in the 1860s and 1870s, the more conflict they generated over issues of the validity of spirit mediumship and the status of women in the movement (Braude 1989:164–91).

Estimating the number of spiritualists in the United States at any given time is extremely difficult. Even defining what qualifies a person to be counted as a spiritualist is difficult. In 1932, the sociologist George Lawton stated that the Census of Religious Bodies in 1926 counted 50,631 enrolled members in 611 affiliated Spiritualist churches and societies, but that "no reliable index is available . . . of the number of independent" ones (pp. 143–56). Lawton estimated 10 to 15 nonenrolled for every enrolled member.

The National Spiritualist Association of Churches, first convened in Chicago in 1893, headquarters located now in Lily Dale, New York, was the largest association of Spiritualist churches in 1926 and still is today. It counted 45,000 members in 334 churches in 1890, 41,000 members in 543 churches in 1926 (Lawton 1932:146), and 2,500 members in 112 churches and associations in 2000 (National Spiritualist Association of Churches 2001). However, in 2001 there were 22 Spiritualist organizations other than the NSAC in the United States with unrecorded numbers of member churches, in addition to many other independent churches.

There is no way to test assertions that there were many millions of spiritualists in the United States in the 19th century. It is generally recognized that there was a decline in spiritualism from the 19th century to the 20th, punctuated by periods of greater interest at times of war, when more people attempted to contact relatives and friends who had died untimely deaths. Lawton's estimate for 1926 would yield fewer than a million spiritualists, less than 1% of the U.S. population at that time.

Of course, especially because of the opposition to formal organization among many spiritualists, it is necessary to consider forms of involvement aside from formal church membership. Spiritualist activities have included lectures, assemblies, summer camp meetings, psychic fairs (nowadays), classes and workshops, and home circles and séances, in addition to regular church services. Add to this the consumption of mass media on the subject (books, magazines, films, radio programs, and now popular television shows such as *Crossing Over with John Edward*).

At the height of the spiritualist craze in the 1850s, table tipping and séances around the dining room table were the equivalent of popular board games. It appears that much of this activity was taken about as seriously as the use of Ouija Boards in the late 20th century—which is to say, for the most part, not very.

FUNCTIONS OF SPIRIT MEDIUMSHIP

Allegedly, contacting the spirits of the dead has been the centerpiece of the spiritualist movement, although spiritual healing and philosophical development have been quite significant as well. One of the difficulties in attempting any sociological analysis of diffuse social movements such as spiritualism, however, is that it is even more problematic to characterize the involvement of individuals at the micro level. Whatever cultural themes apply as useful generalities at the macro level, there can be many variations on each theme and differences in value priorities within local minicultures. For much of the 19th century, these ethnographic details have been lost. However, data are available on recent mediumistic activity, based mostly on participant observation and ethnographic interviews (see Emmons and Emmons 2003; unless otherwise noted, the information about and quotations from interviews with mediums presented in the following subsections are taken from this work).

Proving the Continuity of Life

"Proving the continuity of life" is the main purpose of spirit mediumship, as expressed by most mediums today. This is formally recognized in the "Declaration of Principles" of the National Spiritual Association of Churches: "We affirm that the existence and personal identity of the individual continue after the change called death . . . [and] that communication with the so-called dead is a fact, scientifically proven by the phenomena of Spiritualism." In the 19th century, this principle was a reaction against the doctrine of infant damnation. Today mediumship functions as part of grief management, a salient theme in recent popular books about mediumship by George Anderson, James Van Praagh, and Rosemary Altea, in addition to books about after-death communications that do not necessarily involve spirit mediums.

Although mediums believe it is appropriate to bring through messages of love and advice from the dead, there is generally a taboo against forecasting a person's impending death. Mediums who feel that they are picking up such information either ignore it or encourage the living to visit or to give extra care to the person whose death is apparently imminent. A few of the 40 mediums interviewed for our study emphasized that mediumship helps people have a more positive attitude toward their own death. Spiritualist funerals provide good illustrations of the belief that death is a cause for grief but not a reason for fear or despair.

Helping and Healing

Another very commonly stated function of mediumship is to "help people," in the generic sense of providing guidance, counseling, and healing. Mediums frame this in a holistic perspective by saying, "It's all about healing," meaning that mediumship and hands-on healing, both of which are part of Spiritualist church services, are directed toward healing body, mind, and spirit.

One restriction on the physical aspect of the healing function, however, comes from mediums' fears of being accused of practicing medicine without a license. In his observations of the activities in the Spiritualist camp at Lily Dale, New York, in 1929, George Lawton (1932:337–43) recorded some very negative statements by healers and mediums about the medical profession. Such is not the case today. Instead, at public message services, mediums typically offer clear disclaimers before they bring forth any statements about the health of the living. For example, "I am not a doctor, and I cannot diagnose or prescribe. However, I think it would be a good idea for you to see your doctor to check on your liver." Most mediums' comments regarding health are positive, such as "I feel a lot of healing going on through this area," or "Make sure you keep up that walking."

Fortune-Telling

Moving along a continuum from more spiritual to more secular functions of spirit mediumship, at some point helpful advice from the spirit world turns into "fortune-telling," a derogatory label from a spiritualist perspective. This includes such things as information about relationships, career, and money. Especially when this type of advice is not taken very seriously, another function of mediumship enters: entertainment, in private readings and especially at public message services, where there is often some expectation that messages will be amusing for the rest of the "audience" (congregation).

In their 1974 study of Lily Dale, sociologists Richard and Adato (1980:191) surveyed 57 visitors, only 4% of whom mentioned the death of a relative as a reason for their coming to Lily Dale, compared with 47% who mentioned seeking "guidance and knowledge." It is difficult to know exactly what these respondents understood by "guidance and knowledge," but these data tend to confirm our recent observations that visitors are more interested in "fortune-telling" or "practical magic" than they are in "proving the continuity of life."

People who go to Lily Dale for private readings and public messages are not necessarily Spiritualists (25% identified themselves as such in Richard and Adato's study). When asked if they would like to ask questions, after the medium has already brought through some information, sitters are more likely to ask about their love lives and jobs than about dead relatives. Consequently, mediums often say that they do more mediumship on the platform (in public services) and more "psychic" message work in private readings.

Spiritualist mediums, then, present an ideology in which "proving the continuity of life" is most important. However, many of their clients do not necessarily share a Spiritualist perspective or care about mediumship at all, and may frame the activity as psychic fortune-telling. In this sense, Chinese clients go to mediums for similar reasons, "practical" ones (such as getting rich with the help of their ancestors), although the Chinese clearly frame their actions differently—that is, in terms of the system of ancestor worship and spirit mediumship.

SUBCULTURES OF KNOWLEDGE

As I have pointed out above, the concept of communicating with the dead is problematic in the United States today, with our modern, scientific, secular culture. Nevertheless, the practice of spirit mediumship has survived for more than 150 years and has been interpreted variously in different subcultures. In most of these subcultures, the key issue is, predictably, *death,* as well as the question mark that lies beyond it, what parapsychologists refer to as the issue of "survival."

In this section, I examine and compare four partly conflicting but overlapping knowledge subcultures: scientific debunking, social/behavioral science, parapsychology, and some spiritual perspectives. I approach these subcultures in order roughly from most scientific to most religious. (For a general analysis of debunking or "skepticism," parapsychology, and contemporary spirituality—the "New Age" movement—see Hess 1993.)

Scientific Debunking

In this discussion of scientific debunking, I refer especially to work by the Committee for Scientific Investigation of Claims of the Paranormal (CSICOP) and its journal *Skeptical Inquirer.* In contrast to members of the social/behavioral scientific subculture, considered next, debunkers are explicitly interested in the question of whether a particular paranormal phenomenon (in this case, a surviving soul or spirit) has an objective existence; they conclude that there is no evidence that it does. However, they are also likely to see paranormal beliefs as dangerously irrational; they do not consider that such beliefs may have positive social functions.

It is more difficult to compare debunking with parapsychology and spiritual views. However, members of all three of these subcultures have acknowledged that, at least in some instances, there have been deceptive or fraudulent practices in mediumship. The authors of some articles published in *Skeptical Inquirer* have analyzed the "cold reading" techniques of mediums who apparently assimilate information from sitters through body language and conversational cues, or by asking "fishing" questions and manipulating the conversation. Others have attacked the paranormal by attempting to demonstrate that particular phenomena can be produced through fraudulent means (such as by trick magicians).

Social/Behavioral Science

I have discussed some aspects of the perspective of the social/behavioral science subculture above, including, for example, Lewis's (1966) deprivation theory of cults and the treatment of mediumship associated with Chinese ancestor worship (Emmons 1982). These represent, essentially, conflict and functional theories of spirit mediumship.

Although most social scientists would probably deny that they take any position on the truth status of mediumistic claims, there seems to be an implicit assumption in most of the sociological/anthropological literature that otherworldly experiences have only symbolic, socially constructed, rather than objective, reality (Howell 1989). Nevertheless, some anthropologists have written about their own paranormal experiences in the field. Psychologists have usually seen trance mediumship mainly in terms of multiple personality or dissociative disorder.

Parapsychology

Parapsychology is unique in that it straddles science and the paranormal. It emerged as a field in the latter half of the 19th century out of the curiosity of scientists and spiritualists about mediumship. Moore (1977) discusses this history, including the 1882 founding of the Society for Psychical Research in London, a very prestigious organization that included eight fellows of the Royal Society (such as Alfred Russel Wallace) and literary elites such as Alfred, Lord Tennyson. In 1926, Arthur Conan Doyle (1975) wrote a sympathetic review of spiritualist mediumship and the controversies surrounding its investigation. Gauld (1982) provides an excellent more recent overview of this subject, which has received much less attention by parapsychologists in the past half century.

For those mediums who do not appear to be frauds and who provide impressive evidential material, parapsychology offers essentially two explanations: telepathy and survival of the spirit. The thorniest theoretical problem arises when the concept of super-ESP (extrasensory perception unlimited by time or space and not dependent on mental telepathy) seems to account for everything that might be thought to come from contact with the spirit world. Gauld (1982) concludes that the super-ESP hypothesis seems unconvincing in a number of cases, and that there is "a sprinkling of cases which rather forcefully suggest some form of survival" (p. 261). Other modern parapsychologists have tended to be more dismissive of spirit mediumship as evidence for survival (Emmons and Emmons 2003).

Spiritual Perspectives

That there are spiritual perspectives on mediumship might appear to be obvious, given that spiritualists have long emphasized that mediumship provides evidence for the continuity of life. However, spiritualists have also been bothered by one of the problems noted by parapsychologists: How is one to know that a medium is not accessing information through some form of ESP (telepathy with the living or clairvoyance directly of present or past events) rather than through a spirit contact?

Another problem for spiritualists is the possibility of unreliable, even deceitful, messages from the other side. Swedenborg, the intellectual ancestor of much spiritualist thought, wrote in 1748 that a person "must beware lest he believe them in anything. For they [the spirits] say almost anything" (quoted in Anderson 1993:289). Most mediums today de-emphasize the problem of visitation by evil spirits, yet they feel protected if they say a prayer and set their intention for only "the highest and best"; often, they ask for a "white light of protection" while doing mediumship (Emmons and Emmons 2003).

Other challenges to spiritualist mediumship have come from other spiritual movements that have tried to distance themselves from at least part of what mediums were doing. Although spiritualists borrowed from the Transcendentalists, Emerson and Thoreau showed disdain for spiritualism, which Emerson referred to as the "rat hole of revelation" (see Moore 1977:25, 38, 52–54). Theosophy, an outgrowth of spiritualism in the late 18th century, represented an attempt to reform spiritualism and elevate its status, partly by encouraging the channeling of a higher class of spirits (Prothero 1993).

CONCLUSION

Spiritualism is a virtually universal religious phenomenon that centers on contact with the spirit world through spirit mediums. It tends to be more institutionalized in societies that practice ancestor worship, but it can have a wide variety of functions and may be used as a source of supernatural power in politics. Spirit mediumship is especially problematic in Western societies such as the United States, due to the dominance of scientific rationality in these cultures.

Spiritualism in the United States can be seen from a variety of perspectives and has had a diffuse set of meanings over its long history. Especially in the 19th century, it represented an array of radical impulses, both sacred and secular. On the sacred side, it rebelled against infant damnation and male patriarchy in formal churches. On the secular side, it overlapped feminism, abolitionism, and other movements. Attempts to explain and test spiritual mediumship can be categorized as falling within four subcultures: scientific debunking, social/behavioral science, parapsychology, and, of course, spiritual perspectives.

Peeling away some of the social/cultural elaboration of this religious social movement, what does spiritualism say about death? The central claim of American spiritualists is that mediumship shows evidence of "the continuity of life," which is a denial of the finality of death. In the United States, this belief can help individuals and families with the grieving process when loved ones die. In other cultures, where the social organization of the wider community is more important than the grief of individuals, spiritualism may allow the dead to preserve social continuity, in terms of lineage solidarity, or give supernaturally sanctioned political power to either elites or deprived groups.

Spirit mediumship seems anachronous in modern industrial societies. The American spiritualist phenomenon changed in the 19th century from craze to social movement to organized church. In the 20th century, its culture blended with New Age channeling, psychic phenomena, and fortune-telling, although Spiritualist churches continued to exist on a small scale. Within this larger, redefined context, mediumship can be expected to flourish in an alienated mass society that shows symptoms of spiritual revival and increased interest in the paranormal.

REFERENCES

Anderson, Rodger. 1993. Review of Paul Beard, *Inner Eye, Listening Ear: An Exploration Into Mediumship. Journal of the American Society for Psychical Research* 87:287–91.

Black Elk. 1988. *Black Elk Speaks: Being the Life Story of a Holy Man of the Oglala Sioux.* Lincoln: University of Nebraska Press.

Braude, Ann. 1989. *Radical Spirits: Spiritualism and Women's Rights in Nineteenth-Century America.* Boston: Beacon.

Carroll, Bret E. 1997. *Spiritualism in Antebellum America.* Bloomington: Indiana University Press.

Cross, Whitney R. 1981. *The Burned-Over District: The Social and Intellectual History of Enthusiastic Religion in Western New York, 1800–1850.* New York: Octagon.

Davis, Andrew Jackson. 1859. *The Magic Staff: An Autobiography of Andrew Jackson Davis.* New York: J. S. Brown.

Doyle, Arthur Conan. [1926] 1975. *The History of Spiritualism,* 2 vols. New York: Arno.

Drury, Nevill. 1991. *The Elements of Shamanism.* Rockport, MA: Element.

Eliade, Mircea. 1964. *Shamanism: Archaic Techniques of Ecstasy.* Princeton, NJ: Princeton University Press.

Emmons, Charles F. 1982. *Chinese Ghosts and ESP: A Study of Paranormal Beliefs and Experiences.* Metuchen, NJ: Scarecrow.

Emmons, Charles F. and Penelope Emmons. 2003. *Guided by Spirit: A Journey Into the Mind of the Medium.* New York: iUniverse.

Gauld, Alan. 1982. *Mediumship and Survival: A Century of Investigations.* London: Paladin.

Hess, David J. 1993. *Science in the New Age: The Paranormal, Its Defenders and Debunkers, and American Culture.* Madison: University of Wisconsin Press.

Howell, Julia D. 1989. "The Social Sciences and Mystical Experience." In *Exploring the Paranormal: Perspectives on*

Belief and Experience, edited by George K. Zollschan, John F. Schumaker, and Greg F. Walsh. Dorset, Eng.: Prism.

Kehoe, Alice Beck. 1989. *The Ghost Dance: Ethnohistory and Revitalization.* New York: Holt, Rinehart & Winston.

Lain, David. 1985. *Guns and Rain: Guerrillas and Spirit Mediums in Zimbabwe.* Berkeley: University of California Press.

Lawton, George. 1932. *The Drama of Life After Death.* New York: Henry Holt.

Lewis, I. M. 1966. "Spirit Possession and Deprivation Cults." *Man* 1:307–29.

Lowie, Robert. 1924. *Primitive Religion.* New York: Boni & Liveright.

Moore, R. Laurence. 1977. *In Search of White Crows: Spiritualism, Parapsychology, and American Culture.* New York: Oxford University Press.

Morris, Rosalind C. 2000. *In the Place of Origins: Modernity and Its Mediums in Northern Thailand.* Durham, NC: Duke University Press.

National Spiritualist Association of Churches. 2001. *Yearbook.* Lily Dale, NY: National Spiritualist Association of Churches.

Nicholson, Shirley, comp. 1987. *Shamanism: An Expanded View of Reality.* Wheaton, IL: Theosophical Publishing House.

Owen, Alex. 1990. *The Darkened Room: Power and Spiritualism in Late Victorian England.* Philadelphia: University of Pennsylvania Press.

Prothero, Stephen. 1993. "From Spiritualism to Theosophy: 'Uplifting' a Democratic Tradition." *Religion and American Culture* 3:197–216.

Richard, Michael P. and Albert Adato. 1980. "The Medium and Her Message: A Study of Spiritualism at Lily Dale, New York." *Review of Religious Research* 22:186–97.

Smelser, Neil. 1962. *The Structure of Collective Behavior.* New York: Free Press.

Swatos, William H., Jr. and Loftur Reimar Gissurarson. 1997. *Icelandic Spiritualism: Mediumship and Modernity in Iceland.* New Brunswick, NJ: Transaction.

Tylor, Edward B. 1871. *Primitive Culture.* London: Murray.

REINCARNATION

The Technology of Death

JANE DILLON

According to the social historians Joseph Head and Sylvia Cranston (1977), one-half of the world's population believes in some form of rebirth, and as of 1981, according to a Gallup poll conducted in that year, 23% of Americans also claimed a belief in reincarnation. Today, few analysts of religious institutions would doubt the significance such beliefs hold for the contemporary experience.

The importance of such statistics is demonstrated in the discussion of reincarnation and death that follows, which is based on sociological research that I conducted during a 13-year period at the University of California, San Diego (Dillon 1998).[1] This qualitative ethnographic study was designed to focus on the meaning reincarnation has for Americans who believe deeply in this phenomenon and how a belief in reincarnation affects their daily activities of work, marriage, parenting, citizenship, social action, personal morality, and death. The data are based in part on extensive, in-depth interviews that I conducted with monastic and lay members of the Self-Realization Fellowship (SRF), one of the oldest and most firmly established "Eastern" religious groups in the United States.[2]

In the following sections, I present portions of these interview data to provide the reader with an overview of the Western Yoga movement that brought the concept of reincarnation to America and the meaning of the reincarnationist worldview to people who have adopted it.[3] In addition, I discuss the role of the reincarnationist perspective in the greater Western society.

THE REINCARNATIONIST PERSPECTIVE

The concept of reincarnation has traversed the continents from Asia to Europe and the oceans from the Indian to the Atlantic. Mistaken for centuries as simply a core belief of the Hindu religion known as "transmigration of souls," the representation of reincarnation as taught by Paramahansa Yogananda has attained authoritative status in the West with the universal appeal of Yogananda's work. Fitting comfortably with Western scientific, religious, and philosophical traditions, Yogananda's Kriya Yogic understanding of reincarnation has been widely accepted by millions of Westerners and is now being reintroduced to the peoples of India and Asia. Yogananda's Self-Realization movement has gained significant attention in the West over the past eight decades and is currently experiencing phenomenal growth.[4]

---

1. Dr. Dillon may be reached by phone at (760) 415-4550, by e-mail at jddrssr@aol.com, or by mail at P.O. Box 144, Cardiff, CA 92007.

2. The Self-Realization Fellowship, a nonsectarian religious and humanitarian organization, was founded in the United States in 1920 by Paramahansa Yogananda, one of India's most respected spiritual leaders. Yogananda has been widely acclaimed for his classic work *Autobiography of a Yogi,* which was first published in 1946. In 1977, the government of India honored Yogananda as one of India's great saints with the issuance of a national stamp. In 1935, Mahatma Gandhi showed his deepest respect when he requested that Paramahansa Yogananda initiate him in the advanced scientific techniques of Kriya Yoga meditation.

3. The root cause of belief in reincarnation for the modern Western world is Yoga. See especially Leviton (1993), Isherwood (1962), Worthington (1982), and Feuerstein (1989).

4. Dr. Evans-Wentz writes in the preface to Yogananda's *Autobiography of a Yogi* ([1946] 1994): "As an eyewitness recountal of the extraordinary lives and powers of modern Hindu saints, the book has importance both timely and timeless. To its illustrious author, whom I had the pleasure of knowing in both India and America, may every reader render due appreciation and gratitude. His unusual life document is certainly one of the most revealing of the depths of the Hindu mind and heart, and of the spiritual wealth of India, ever to be published in the West. . . . It has been my privilege to meet one of the sages whose life history is herein narrated—Sri Yukteswar Giri. A likeness of the venerable saint appeared as part of the frontispiece of my *Tibetan Yoga and Secret Doctrines*" (p. vii).

Issues that are frequently raised regarding reincarnation include the meaning of this important concept, how those who believe deeply in reincarnation live out their daily lives and confront the normal processes of living and dying, the process through which one is reincarnated and the form taken, whether it is possible to recall one's past lives, and the future of the reincarnationist perspective. To begin this discussion, I present several noteworthy points pertaining to reincarnation and death as a foundation for understanding the reincarnationist worldview.

First, from a reincarnationist perspective, *there is no death;* there is only a transition to another life-form. The essential Self is eternal, part of Life Itself. As is known in the field of quantum physics, time and space are relative concepts, products of our perceiving what we see as one fixed reality from the perspective of our own particular fixed time and place. From a cosmic perspective on life, there is no separation, no division; all life "flows" in one continuum, one creation, within which are infinitely diverse multiple realities and multiple dimensions that take form on the physical plane. Death, as an end to Life, in such a system is simply a misnomer, the reflection of a misunderstanding of and about Life.

Second, for those who believe in reincarnation, dying is not the economic enterprise or moneymaking business it has become in American culture. The law of reincarnation undercuts dominant Western ideology by claiming an interconnectedness, interviolability, and infinite extension of all life in the physical and other worlds for each and every individual life-form, thereby eliminating, at least theoretically, any basis for fear, denial, or confusion about death. From a reincarnationist point of view, the simple, at-home enlightenment experience that death and dying represent renders any elaborate material endeavors irrelevant.

Third, within the reincarnationist system, reincarnation is not a belief, it is a law—the law of the evolution of human consciousness. Akin to the law of gravity, the law of evolution is also derived from the laws of magnetism that operate life in the physical world.

Fourth, reincarnation is not merely an "Eastern" concept. Rather, it represents an idea that is fundamental to all the religions of the world and is found in some form in all cultures (Head and Cranston 1977). To Americans, however, reincarnation is somewhat of a novelty, having been introduced recently into the cultural mainstream during the 1960s, after centuries of repression throughout most of the Judeo-Christian Western world (Dillon 1991).

Fifth, the law of reincarnation should not be confused with "New Age" philosophy, belief in the power of crystals, past-life regression, or psychic phenomena. Rather, the basis of the concept of reincarnation is simply the idea that human life, which most religions teach is eternal, repeats itself (or reincarnates) many times throughout the course of its spiritual journey (Dass 1970). The concept and the reality of reincarnation are simple and obvious when one examines them without prejudice, as demonstrated by the extensive scientific evidence gathered by researchers such as Drs. Ian Stevensen (1974) and Raymond Moody (1975), who have documented and verified hundreds of cases of people, from adults to small children, who have been able to describe the details of previous lives they have lived, including information about people, events, and things still in evidence today.

Sixth, reincarnation and karma are inextricably linked. They are corollary laws that effectively produce each other. In other words, one makes no sense without the other. Without reincarnation, an individual would have only one human lifetime—not enough time in which to fulfill his or her karma (that is, to reap all the good and bad consequences of the good and bad deeds—thoughts, words, and actions—he or she has produced). Conversely, without karma, reincarnation would be unnecessary, as there would be nothing to come back for—no pull, no magnetism, no desires.

Seventh, the laws of reincarnation (evolution) and karma (cause and effect) are essential factors for understanding quantum physics and for explaining why units of energy behave in the manner observed. However, because reincarnation is dependent on a linear space-time continuum as it is currently understood, some quantum scientists have challenged the reincarnation concept based on an expanding knowledge of the cyclical, multidimensional, nonlocal, and nonseparative elements of life. For example, paleontologist Philip Savage (1999) proposes instead the idea of "transcarnation," a system of multiple identities within multiple dimensions, existing *all at the same time.*[5]

Eighth, individuals can try to know about their past lives through intuition, meditation, hypnosis, and psychic experiences. The problem is that there is no reliable method for discerning whether what they learn or experience in seeking such knowledge is actually related to their past lives or some form of their own fantasies or delusional imaginations. Spontaneous past-life recollection or knowing is déjà vu, and sometimes instances of déjà vu can be very convincing to those who experience them. However, déjà vu experiences are completely subjective, usually rare, and generally only hint at the identity of the person during a previous lifetime.

---

5. Philip Savage (1999) explains his concept of transcarnation versus reincarnation: "Contrary to a very common mistake, Druids never really believed in reincarnation. The famous Druidic 'metempsychosis' differs from common reincarnational systems in the sense that, in the ancient Celtic paradigm, nothing moves in a linear fashion, but in circles and cycles. Druids, like the most advanced physicists today, didn't believe in time as a separate, intangible and distinct dimension. Instead of a sequential succession of different lives, they believed in a multiple simultaneous super-existence. In this system, one may be a man and a woman in the same time. A human, an animal, a mineral and a plant as well. A drop in the ocean, a quark and a galaxy just the same. One lives now, before and later without separation. What one does (not DID) in the seventeenth century influences what one does (not WILL DO) one thousand years from now. In fact, the old Druidic system sounds very much like the theory of multiple parallel universes" (p. 54).

Finally, although reincarnation is a satisfying and comforting system, being reborn repeatedly is actually not something to be desired; coming back forever and ever is not the goal. Breaking free of the physical phase of human existence—the "wheel of transmigration"—and moving up to a higher, nonphysical consciousness is the desirable and guaranteed result of all human evolution (MacGregor 1982).

DEFINING THE PROCESS OF REINCARNATION

The overwhelming conclusion of Head and Cranston's comprehensive research on the history of the reincarnation concept is that all major civilizations and religious systems that have ever existed in the world have contained some version of reincarnation within their cultural tool kits.[6] For example, Hindus who base their teachings on the earliest known human records of the Vedas, the Upanishads, and the Bhagavad Gita cite many clear references to reincarnation in each of these sacred texts. Prominent philosopher and former president of India Sarvepalli Radhakrishnan claims an abundance of references to reincarnation even in the earliest Rig Veda. He writes, "The passage of the soul from the body, its dwelling in other forms of existence, its return to human form, the determination of future existence by the principle of Karma are all mentioned [in statements such as] 'The immortal self will be reborn in a new body due to its meritorious deeds'" (quoted in Head and Cranston 1977:36). In the Upanishads, readers find many references to reincarnation; the translation of that text by Charles Johnston, professor at Columbia University, includes statements such as the following: "Through his past works he shall return once more to birth, entering whatever form his heart is set on" (quoted in Head and Cranston 1977:39). And in the celebrated Bhagavad Gita, the most famous part of the epic poem Mahabharata, which reports the Lord Krishna's dialogue with his foremost disciple, Arjuna, a text studied by Western scientists (e.g., Oppenheimer), philosophers (e.g., Thoreau), and politicians (e.g., Hastings), students find not only innumerable references to reincarnation such as the one that follows, but also a full allegorical treatment of the doctrine itself.[7]

Such a man doth not perish here or hereafter. For never to an evil place goeth one who doeth good. The man whose devotion has been broken off by death goeth to the regions of the righteous, where he dwells for an immensity of years and is then born again on earth in a pure and fortunate family, or even in a

family of those who are spiritually illuminated. But such a rebirth into this life as this last is more difficult to obtain. Being thus born again, he comes in contact with the knowledge which belonged to him in his former body, and from that time he struggles more diligently towards perfection, O son of Kuru. (Quoted in Head and Cranston 1977:47)

Many scholars would claim that in the Orient, the acceptance of reincarnation is simply "in the air"; reincarnation is tacitly accepted, without the necessity for words or explanation (see, e.g., Polanyi 1966). Experts in Buddhism and Taoism, however, also find abundant references to the concept in the sacred texts of these religions. Edward Conze, writing of the "Buddhist scriptures," comments: "The state of a Buddha is one of the highest possible perfection. It seems self-evident to Buddhists that an enormous amount of preparation over many lives is needed to reach it" (quoted in Head and Cranston 1977:61).[8] About Taoism, Chuang Tzu writes in *The Musings of a Chinese Mystic:* "To have attained to the human form must be always a source of joy. And then, to undergo countless transitions, with only the infinite to look forward to—what incomparable bliss is that! Therefore it is, that the truly wise rejoice in that which can never be lost, but endures always" (quoted in Head and Cranston 1977:111).

Head and Cranston (1977) document similar references to reincarnation in the Egyptian Book of the Dead, the Hermetic writings, the Persian Mithra, the writings of the Zoroastrians and the Manicheans, and also in the ancient Jewish traditions of the Essenes, the Kabala, the Zohar, and the Hasidics. They also note that widespread understanding of reincarnation by leading Western writers, scientists, philosophers, and religious advocates has been documented among the early Christians, the early Muslims, the ancient Greeks and Romans, and the Native peoples of the Americas, from the Middle Ages and on through the Renaissance, the Reformation, and the ages of Enlightenment and Science. In the following subsections I offer definitions of the concepts of reincarnation, karma, magnetism, and scientific meditation and explain their meanings through reference to authoritative Western sources.

The Law of Reincarnation

Paramahansa Yogananda ([1975] 1990) defines reincarnation as

the doctrine that human beings, compelled by the law of evolution, incarnate repeatedly in progressively higher

---

6. See Head and Cranston's many publications on reincarnation: *Reincarnation: The Phoenix Fire Mystery* (1977), *Reincarnation: An East-West Anthology* (1961), *Reincarnation in World Thought* (1967), and *Reincarnation: A New Horizon in Science, Religion and Society* (Cranston and Head 1993).

7. The most recent translation and interpretation of this ancient text by Paramahansa Yogananda was published by the Self-Realization Fellowship in 1995.

8. In fact, the most well-known living embodiment of reincarnation is the most famous Buddhist of the modern world, His Holiness, the Dalai Lama of Tibet.

lives—retarded by wrong actions and desires, and advanced by spiritual endeavors—until Self-realization and God-union are attained. Having thus transcended the limitations and imperfections of mortal consciousness, the soul is forever free from compulsory reincarnation. [In Revelation 3:12 it is noted,] "Him that overcometh will I make a pillar in the temple of my God, and he shall go no more out." (P. 479)

This law of reincarnation means that all people are souls, reincarnated on earth, made in the image of God, and therefore essentially already saved (one with God). It means that human beings are attached to the world through unfulfilled material desires that force them to reincarnate in the physical plane. Souls reincarnate in order to satisfy or transmute (renounce) these desires until they consciously choose, as their only desire, union with the Divine. Reincarnation is the mechanism of evolution (change in consciousness)—the technology of death—and humans almost always (with rare exceptions) reincarnate in human form. Eventually, all souls attain Self-realization and liberation from the delusory identification of self with ego.

Reincarnationists understand that the reincarnated human soul is reborn again and again to the physical world in many different physical bodies, living in different physical environments and different social circumstances, depending on its karmic desires and needs accumulated over a very long period of time (i.e., hundreds, thousands, or perhaps even millions of lifetimes). Advanced souls reputedly *choose* their social and physical conditions at rebirth; less advanced souls are simply *drawn* to the conditions that satisfy the state of consciousness realized at the moment of previous physical death. The experience of life for the reincarnated human soul is largely determined by its own karma from that individual's behavior in previous lives, combined with a certain degree of *free will,* depending on that soul's stage of spiritual advancement.

All human beings exist at a high stage of evolution because, unlike other life-forms, human souls are given the gift of free will, which is simply the capacity to choose to move forward (closer to the Divine) or backward (away from the Divine). Reincarnation represents the law of evolution, the process of the upliftment of all souls from delusion to final liberation, which requires that souls reincarnate in different forms at different states of consciousness in all three vibratory worlds.

Reincarnationists view the system as a fair one in which all souls have certain things to learn and accomplish in each lifetime and all are given as many chances as they need or deserve to reincarnate until they "get it right." Reincarnation also is seen as the only logical explanation for certain personal experiences, such as why individuals sometimes feel instantly comfortable with certain people and in certain places—they have been with those people or in those same places before. Reincarnation explains why individuals may have unusual or extreme fears, such as fear of flying or of motorcycles; a person who fears flying, for instance, may have died in a plane crash in a previous life. Reincarnation also explains why some children are "born" with particularly developed skills or abilities (e.g., musical talent) or with unusually difficult personality traits (e.g., nasty temper)—they learned such skills or developed those traits in their recent past lives.

The Law of Magnetism

The law of magnetism encompasses two forces: attraction and repulsion. Drawing from ancient Vedic teachings, Paramahansa Yogananda ([1946] 1994) explains that human souls were originally projected as rays from the formless, nondualistic Transcendent Divine. From that moment on, the sole purpose of the human soul has been to return to God through a process of attraction. Through the process of repulsion, Spirit created the three vibratory worlds of form: the causal world of thought, the astral world of light, and the physical world of matter. Through the process of attraction, all Life is drawn back to Spirit.

Soul is the vibrationless image of Spirit manifest in the world. All aspects of the vibratory worlds, including the individual human being, are aspects of Spirit-in-form. Thus the underlying nature of all forms in all worlds is Spirit-in-form or vibration, that is, the Word of God—the *Aum.* Once it becomes a part of the vibratory worlds of Creation, the soul experiences delusion (*maya*) and eventually forgets its true identity and from whence it came (One with Spirit). Instead, the soul falsely identifies itself as separate from Spirit (which in reality it can never be) and engages in cycles of reincarnation.

Through the process of Self-realization, or when the soul *realizes* its true identity of Self made in the image of "God," the soul becomes liberated from its delusion and consciously experiences its true Self as participating in the nature of the formless Spirit (i.e., God as ever-existing, ever-conscious, ever-new Bliss). As Spirit (*Iswara*) is ultimately formless and vibrationless, so too is the soul, even in the worlds of vibration. Thus transcendence or Self-realization occurs when the soul truly identifies with (realizes) its vibrationless Self instead of with its vibratory body or ego.

The reincarnated soul seeks expression and happiness that it can ultimately attain only through reunion with Spirit, Self-realization. Thus the individual soul, regardless of in which body it resides, is seeking God (i.e., Self), whether consciously or not, and is therefore always on the spiritual path to God. When the soul realizes its true identity, thereby transcending the delusion (*maya*) that it is separate from God, the soul is instantly rejoined (as in "yoke" or *yoga*) with God. Practicing the scientific technique of Kriya Yoga is a process through which the realization of Self as one with Spirit is possible.

Souls inhabiting and constituting the physical world are involved in a process of evolution and involution whereby individual and collective consciousness is lifted or lowered according to the stage, or *yuga,* in which the world exists at any particular moment. The particular *yuga* influences how worlds are constituted and experienced by their inhabitants. This physical world, for example, evolves through 24,000-year cycles that are divided into four *yugas: Satya Yuga* (the highest or Golden Ages), *Treta Yuga* (the next highest), *Dwapara Yuga* (second lowest), and *Kali Yuga* (the lowest or Dark Age). The earth is now in the beginning of the *Dwapara Yuga,* the atomic age of electricity, continuing upward as consciousness evolves to higher states (Yukteswar [1894] 1977).

The physical world consists of four forms of matter: mineral, vegetal, animal, and human. These different forms represent fundamentally different vibrations of conscious energy. All are called soul (i.e., consciousness). Yogananda ([1946] 1994) refers to mineral forms of soul as sleeping consciousness, vegetal forms as awakened consciousness, animal forms as conscious consciousness, and human forms as self-conscious consciousness. The individual human soul evolves from existence as all other physical forms, which means it has lived in previous incarnations as animal, vegetal, and mineral forms. The individual human soul is the highest manifestation of God on the physical plane because it is *self*-conscious. Only the human soul has the conscious capacity to accomplish the purpose of all creation, which is to realize self-consciously its true identity as Soul, part of Spirit (Christ-consciousness). No other physical form has this potential for soul expression. Having evolved from these previous forms of consciousness, human souls are responsible not only for their own individual human evolution, but for the general evolution of the collective soul in all other forms, the collective animal, vegetal, and mineral evolution, including the evolution of Mother Earth Herself.

Human souls rarely, if ever, revert through reincarnation to lower physical form unless they choose to learn specific lessons that emphasize the incomparable value of human incarnation. Such reversions take place only very occasionally and only temporarily. Reincarnation is the natural process through which the soul moves from one world to another on the journey back to Spirit (according to the laws of magnetism). Reincarnation from physical to astral bodies, and back again, takes place for the individual soul as many times as necessary and/or desired. Each incarnation marks the completion of some specific goal of the soul in the physical or astral world, a process that will eventually and inevitably lead to the attainment of Self-realization and Union with Spirit (*Yoga*).

The Law of Karma

Karma represents the law of cause and effect, action and reaction, sowing and reaping. Derived from the law of magnetism that created the physical realms, karma draws all souls back to the physical world while directing all action in the social world. Karma is the fruit of one's actions. It is Newton's third law of motion applied to the social world: For every action, there is an equal and opposite reaction; for every thought, word, and deed there will be, in the future, an equal and opposite reaction.

Karma and reincarnation represent corollary principles. *The Encyclopedia of Religion* defines karma as follows:

> Action, action-influence, deed. It is the dynamic manifestation of mental and physical energy in deeds, speech or thought, inevitably producing the good, evil or neutral effect, either immediately or in the future, according as the action is good, evil, or indifferent. The effect itself becomes the cause of further effect, making the self, in the case of an individual, a process of unceasing transformation from one life to another in the wheel of transmigration, and the world, in the case of the universe, a process of perpetual becoming. (Ferm 1945:119)

To receive the effects of one's past actions, one must live long enough, perhaps through several lifetimes. And while living in the three vibratory worlds, souls forget their true identity as one with Spirit. Immersed in *maya,* or delusion, people develop desires that create more karma and thereby keep the cycles of reincarnation active until, through scientific techniques of meditation, the souls are freed from all desires except the desire to return to God.

Some view karma as a cosmic bank account, with a plus or minus balance, all created by one's own doing. Wherever one is in life, it is the result of one's own thoughts, words, and deeds, both positive and negative—whatever actions the individual put into the vibratory ether. The law of karma is the program whereby human beings reap what they sow and thereby get exactly what they deserve. Some of this is considered *good karma,* but much of it is experienced as *bad karma,* hence the statement offered by many reincarnationists, "I don't like karma."

How karma works depends upon individuals and their willingness to learn from their karmic situations, overcome the obstacles that karma brings, and eventually choose to do the right thing with the right attitude, thereby establishing either good or no karma for the future. As the Bhagavad Gita states, the goal is to act without concern for the fruits of action, without karma-creating attachment. One should perform an action only because it is the right thing to do; action performed for the fruits it produces (the results of action) represents attachment to things of this world and thereby creates more unfulfilled material desires that force the soul to reincarnate again and again. Statements such as "What goes around comes around," "An eye for an eye and a tooth for a tooth," and "Do unto others as you would have others do unto you" are all references to the law of karma, God's Divine Law of Justice.

Scientific Techniques of Meditation

Because believers in reincarnation understand this karmic process, they are highly motivated to take responsibility for their own actions, to change their behavior, and to do always what is right. According to the law of reincarnation, individuals have as many opportunities as necessary to succeed, to regain their true status as Sons of God. By acting only on the thought of pleasing God, the soul finds liberation from karmic desires and is thus released from the cycle of reincarnation. The way to achieve this goal is to employ scientific techniques of meditation. As one successful adherent notes:

> When you act for God, you are identified with Him. . . . Do the best you can and be not overly concerned with results. Leave the fruits in God's hands. If you are doing your best, your actions are bound to produce good fruit. . . . Only God exists and every one of us is only His expression. Let us always be honest, sincere, truthful, humble expressions. Let us be sweet, fragrant, understanding, willing, devoted, dedicated, intelligent, serviceful expressions of God. That covers everything—but it is a big order, isn't it? . . . The more you meditate and become anchored in the consciousness of God, the less importance you will give to externals. . . . As you go on practicing, those moments of utter stillness become longer. (Daya Mata 1990:69–75)[9]

By contacting God in the stillness of meditation, one becomes more truly the soul expression of God, moving progressively closer to final liberation, at which point all remaining karma is burned up, the cycle of reincarnation is completed, and, through the law of magnetism (the force of attraction), the individual returns to Spirit, from whence she or he came.

Self-realization, through successful meditation, brings final liberation from the laws of reincarnation and karma in all spheres of creation. The members of the Self-Realization Fellowship whom I interviewed explained that Kriya Yoga meditation is the scientific way—the fastest, surest, and most tested path—to realize that the soul is made in the image of God and already one with Spirit. Scientific meditation on God is a practice that requires control of the physical body and mind. Kriya Yoga meditation is the *science of life-force control,* and its techniques produce observable, measurable, and replicable effects on human beings. Results of Kriya Yoga meditation include the freedom to choose right action with the right attitude that leads to happiness, security, and satisfaction. Observable effects of the successful practice of Kriya Yoga include breathlessness and unblinking eyes, accompanied by feelings of peace, love, calmness, expansion, joy, bliss, and ecstasy, along with visions of light and experiences of nonphysical sound (i.e., the *Aum* vibration). One monk explained:

> To operate God's laws, the key to the meditation part is Kriya, because as we begin to practice Kriya Yoga we begin to feel the internal operation of the law of magnetism and we begin to feel those forces inwardly that we are learning about outwardly. You feel it in your spine and in your whole body. . . . You feel the whole power of it operating inside you.

For example, through the practice of Kriya Yoga, the Kriyaban learns to interiorize his or her consciousness so that he or she can, at will, shut out the distracting delusory messages brought by the senses and instead concentrate the consciousness directly and solely on the vibration of God in creation (on the Word or *Aum*). The successful Kriyaban eventually experiences a state of complete and ultimate "breathless" stillness in which the presence of God as Bliss can be felt (i.e., a state of conscious Ecstasy). This personal experience of the presence of God within is the purpose of Yoga meditation (*Yoga* meaning union with God). As one interviewee said:

> Actually, the soul *is* the presence of God within you. What you want to do in meditation is try to uncover that state of consciousness. That's why you sit there, and the more you sit there, then the worldly consciousness begins to erode and the soul consciousness comes to the fore. That's why Yogis meditate for years to get to that point. At times, without great faith, it seems useless for you sitting with your eyes closed. Sooner or later, that darkness and that restlessness starts to dissipate and other things come into view. It takes a long time.

The highest states of consciousness for the Yogi, where the soul is able to experience oneness with God, are called *samadhi.* These states of Yogic *samadhi* correlate with the Christian state of Ecstasy, the Buddhist state of Nirvana, and the general state of consciousness referred to as Enlightenment. The universal characteristics of all these states are unending Joy, Light, and Bliss Consciousness. To bring the advanced scientific techniques of the ancient Kriya Yoga tradition to the West was the specific mission of Paramahansa Yogananda, who was sent as the representative of his sacred lineage of Self-realized Masters. Students may receive these techniques, with Yogananda's blessings, directly through the organization he founded, the Self-Realization Fellowship.

WHO AM I IN THE SYSTEM?

Paramahansa Yogananda ([1929] 1981) concludes his poem *Samadhi* with these words: *"A tiny bubble of laughter, I Am become the sea of mirth itself."* The meaning of such Soul-identity, as many SRF followers have learned, is complex. Until human beings realize themselves as Soul, they go through innumerable life experiences or lessons that eventually bring them to their knees before the Divine Presence. However, during this process, those who believe in reincarnation have a framework that provides them with the satisfaction and comfort they seek to identify who they are. For example, the monks of the Self-Realization Fellowship Monastic Order provide fascinating accounts of their personal experiences "on the path" to their own

---

9. Sri Daya Mata has been president of Self-Realization Fellowship since 1955. The utter stillness she refers to in the practice of Kriya Yoga scientific meditation techniques is that cited in the Bible: "Be still and know that I am God" (Psalms 46:10).

long-awaited soul liberation. One monk, Brother T, related in an interview:

[Some years before I entered the monastic order in the 1970s], I was trying to approach an understanding of life and death and couldn't accept the premise that there was nothing after life; that all there is is what you get and after that there's a void, nothing. I also couldn't accept any belief unless it was part of a total worldview. And I know after taking that [college] class I realized I wanted a belief and worldview that would leave no questions unanswered. That would answer everything and everything had to fit. So I went shopping around and I became depressed. . . . All of a sudden, I started going into moods. Horrendous moods. I used to be carefree and free about life and not caring very much and very irresponsible. When I started approaching the subjects of life and death and realized how important it was and I wasn't getting answers, I started every now and then slipping into a "blue funk," . . . being so depressed. It was amazing because I would slip out of it and go back to my normal state and your consciousness would make excuses and you'd go back to having a good time and all of a sudden you'd get this funny feeling like things just aren't right . . . and sink down again and boy, you'd just hit the bottom. . . .

After I got in the ashram, I looked back objectively on what I had gone through and couldn't believe that I was able to make it. . . . [There have been] so many forces to keep me involved [in worldly attachments]. I had somehow, . . . suffered through it. After the ashram, I looked back and couldn't believe how I was able to . . . hang on. . . . I saw clearly that my seeming indifference in the world was actually a raft that took me across all these involvements and relationships and everything to get into the ashram. . . . I don't have to doubt now . . . I know that when I'm talking to people and doing counseling as a monastic, I have a sense of understanding of what people are going through. I know the attachments and the process of breaking the attachments. . . . I'm fortunate . . . I know very specifically what I decided and why, and what the results were and why I came to those conclusions and there is a very powerful current of feeling behind that to back it up. . . . The logic, the reason, and the feeling going in the same direction. And I've made sure those forces continue to go in the same direction.

Another monk, Brother J, noted:

I'm more myself. I'm more natural, more concerned. I feel more for others. I still see the injustices, but I know why they are there. I still feel the pain, but I understand the reasons behind it, the social reasons. I'm not saying the law of karma [should keep people from trying]. People [should] also try to help them[selves and others] and free themselves from the pain [in] which social conditions exist. So [I] don't just observe them from a detached standpoint. I will also participate to help them because it makes more sense now. I know now why they are here and why they need help if they can accept it. . . . When I took the brother vow [in the 1960s], . . . it is written as part of the vow: "[From now on] your only goal in life is to become Self-realized." That's it. And a second [goal], very closely, [is] to help others to obtain their own realization. For me, [there is] nothing bigger [and truer] than that. . . .

I share what I found . . . because it leads you to what I have. It leads me, so it should lead you. . . . Things come up [sometimes] and make you lose that Joy. But you know it is still there and you know it comes and goes. And when you know the ups and downs, you become more mature, you know what I mean? A person matures with age. Similarly, spiritually, you grow more mature on the spiritual path. So nothing shocks you [or disturbs you]. You understand. Everything's okay. You know where you are, where you are going. Everything makes sense. There's nothing to worry about. So you grow more in that state of consciousness [and Joy comes by itself].

Brother B made the following observation:

Having finally overcome bouts of sadness and doubts, I never felt sad, even though I had difficulties. . . . You see, when you feel the bliss, you see the problem and then you work at it. In other words, the sadness comes when we allow the problem, the trouble, whatever anyone says, to enter our being. But if you keep it at a distance, keep it right there, you are not affected. You see, I used to practice in the early days [the 1940s and 50s], . . . being in a plastic cylinder, a Lucite cylinder. I could see out and others could see me. But, anything negative hit the cylinder and fell to the floor. I did not allow it to penetrate me or disturb me. So I practiced that and that helped to avoid being hurt by any negative remark or situation. . . . I don't feel anything but what I feel inside, bliss. I don't let [other people's] problems penetrate me. I know what the problems are. I give them the advice they need and that's all. And I pray for them of course, [but] I don't allow it to penetrate me. . . . They usually say [they feel my love] and they feel so much better in every way. I don't try to [express love] or anything. That's up to God. I talk to them. And yes, sure, what I feel [the bliss] of course, has to come out. . . . I'm just the instrument [of God].

Past Lives

For people who desire to learn of their past lives, there are methods of investigation, such as intuition, meditation, hypnosis, and psychic readings. Yogananda ([1975] 1990) always cautions against paying too much attention to past lives, however, hinting that if God wanted us to know what we did before, He would make it easier for us to find out. Moreover, a great deal of pain can be associated with our past lives (as with our present lives), which suggests it may be preferable not to remember. Yogananda also points out that although many people might like to fantasize about their "glorious" pasts as famous historical figures, most people previously experienced ordinary and perhaps ignoble lives, immersed in the darkness of the lower age (the *Kali Yuga*) that immediately preceded the age in which they now exist. Yogananda cautions particularly strongly against using any form of hypnotism to learn about past lives, owing to the danger an individual faces in allowing someone else to control his or her conscious mind. In scientific meditation, which is central to soul liberation, the person must always *consciously* maintain the highest level of awareness, never relinquishing control of his or her mind to someone else.

Nevertheless, one male interviewee related how he had attempted to confirm the truth of reincarnation through hypnosis with a trusted colleague when they were new to the SRF in the early 1950s. Eventually this effort proved to be beneficial, but the pain this man experienced was considerable, as he relived a particularly violent death on a Viking ship during the Middle Ages. He was convinced, however, by this and other firsthand subjective experiences under hypnosis, that reincarnation is real, and he felt this knowledge was worth the effort and the pain he had to go through:

> I talked with my friend. I said, the only way I can feel happy about the tapes of some regressions is to test it myself. They're fantastic. People speaking in foreign languages and stuff, but it still bothers me . . . because I don't know those people. Maybe they're making it up. Maybe the hypnotist is giving the suggestions to say those things. I'm not completely happy with this. The only way I can be satisfied that this is genuine would be if I could play both those roles. If I could hypnotize people and get these things where I know there's no monkey business. . . . So my friend had me under hypnosis and he started jumping me ahead then about every 5 years. He'd hit an event and then go forward. Everything was going fine until one time we were in a sea battle with another Viking boat and I was fighting and had my leg cut off. . . . It bled a lot, obviously. Then they took the sword and heated it and cauterized the wound to stop the blood flow because I lost so much blood. But I died about a day later and they dumped me overboard. But the fascinating thing was when that happened, I was living it. . . . Did I feel the pain? I screamed at the top of my lungs. AHHHHHH! Then I went into shock. Can you imagine my friend? The first time he was successful with the regression, I'm dying on him. For a while he was a little panicky. . . . Then . . . , fortunately, he had enough common sense to know what to do. He moved me ahead another 5 years. . . . Well, I was up in the astral, of course. So, everything was cool up there.

Although curious about their past lives, these men, who were scientists by profession, were interested primarily in validating the reality of reincarnation. Because many SRF teachings assume the laws of reincarnation and karma, they felt a personal need to verify the reality of the laws with their own experiments.

MEANING OF REINCARNATION IN DAILY LIFE AND DEATH

How one finds the purpose of one's current incarnation, the effects reincarnation has on one's life, how one's present life will affect the future, and the importance of reincarnation as a part of one's worldview—all of these are critical issues for the individual "seeker." To document the meaning of reincarnation from the believer's point of view, I employed the folk model methodology.[10] My purpose was to analyze the interview data to determine the effects of a deep belief in reincarnation on individuals' daily lives as they conducted the normal activities of raising children, engaging in personal relationships (including marriage and divorce), working to support their families, and managing everyday responsibilities.

In the following subsections I address several of these issues, describing how people who believe in the laws of reincarnation and karma conduct their daily living and experience dying. My intention was to interview "ordinary" members of the SRF who had practiced Kriya Yoga meditation techniques for at least 10 years, because I knew that such members would necessarily believe deeply in reincarnation and yet not necessarily represent any official position of the organization. My purpose was to assess the meaning of the reincarnationist perspective in the everyday lives of ordinary people. Those interviewed represent a cross section of the mainstream American population: male and female; young and old; Protestant, Catholic, and Jewish; lower-, middle-, and upper-class status; levels of education ranging from high school graduate to professional and graduate degrees; immigrants and individuals who can trace their families on American soil back to the Revolutionary War; artists, musicians, carpenters, teachers, architects, doctors, CEOs, and surfers. Although the SRF membership includes significant percentages of blacks, Asians, and homosexuals, all of the members with whom I conducted in-depth interviewees are white and heterosexual.

Child Rearing

Reincarnationists believe that the soul has experienced many lives. When the soul is drawn to rebirth in the physical world, it chooses a specific time, place, gender, and family depending on the lessons desired or needed. The child born is thus on a specific course, with obstacles or karma to deal with. Parents are equally responsible for guiding and training their children by providing love, care, and discipline as well as by demonstrating appropriate moral and spiritual behavior.

For the study interviewees, children represent a priority, with the parents serving as God's channel. Life is an educational experience, children are souls, and the highest role of parents is to teach children about God and assist them in developing spiritual consciousness. Because parents and their children are drawn together, children and parents alike receive appropriate training in partaking of the karmic lessons of life. Of course, as children bring with

---

10. Bennetta Jules-Rosette and I developed the powerful comparative methodology we call the *folk model* based on Hugh Mehan's work on constitutive theory and the politics of representation and Roy D'Andrade's work on the folk model of the mind. See Jules-Rosette (1978), Mehan (1986), D'Andrade (1984), and Dillon (1989).

them the seeds of "good" and "bad" tendencies that distract them from the purity of soul expression, the parents' role is to assist in the achievement of the child's spiritual goal. As one parent indicated, "A father is not a judge or a disciplinarian; karma and reincarnation will take care of that. It is the parents' duty to teach reality—karma, the law of cause and effect—because life will do this eventually, but with much less mercy." Regarding the behavior of parents toward their children, another interviewee stated:

> Be a friend. Don't scold or accuse, or get angry and holler. Be interested. Talk calmly and lovingly with your arms around [your children] and assume they want to do the right thing. The parents' attitude is the most important. Don't blame or scold. You have to save the person's face.

Relationships

For believers in reincarnation, all human relationships are formed on a spiritual basis; each is a relationship between souls, and these are between equals, eternal, and eventually find fulfillment in merging with Spirit. Current friends were happy together in past lives; current enemies were enemies in the past. Social situations are designed for the individual's spiritual progress. For this reason, friends and enemies find themselves together again until all karmic binds are resolved and relationships are ended in harmony. Differences in social situations are based on karma and provide the infinite variety of relationships, cultures, and lifestyles needed and desired by all souls involved. Friendship is the foundation for spiritual relationships; the highest friendship is between spiritual master and disciple.

According to this worldview, each world of vibration is fundamentally social, meaning that people (reincarnated souls) are always and by necessity in relationship (in community) with other reincarnated souls, from this life and past lives, in this and other worlds. Within each social sphere, people act in different roles and for various purposes, always moving toward or away from the spiritual goal of eventual liberation. Until all souls have achieved final liberation, there will be social worlds in which people can evolve and develop spiritually, through relationships with others. The underlying essence of all relationships is spiritual, manifesting only on the surface as physical, emotional, psychological, sexual, economic, political, or social.

All relationships are important to pursue. Karma guarantees that as one treats others, so one will be treated. It is prudent, therefore, to use one's power wisely lest that same power be used against oneself. The law of karma also guarantees that by promoting love, peace, harmony, and kindness, one can guarantee the same in return.

Because the nature of the physical world is duality, souls, which are as One, are temporarily distinct and differentiated in social relationships. When souls reincarnate in the physical world, outward differences are apparent and particular roles are circumscribed. Social circumstances vary depending on the needs and desires that draw the souls to reincarnate. Hence the varieties of people, things, places, cultures, lifestyles, forms of government, and relationships that exist represent distinctions that people either favor or disfavor.

Death

For reincarnationists, death is not an end, nor is it destruction. Death is a very important moment that signals a new role for the everlasting soul. Death represents an intermediate state prior to another reincarnation. One's experience at death depends on one's state of consciousness at the time of death. Thus death is simply another phase of life in which the individual changes from one form of existence to the next in order to work out karma. Therefore, there is no "death" at all, only the evolution of the soul, Life.

The SRF members I interviewed expressed the belief that at the event called death, the soul withdraws from the physical body and is *born* into a body of light, the astral world of light. The soul remains in the astral world until desires draw the soul back for another incarnation into a physical body. In the astral world, individuals work as they did on earth; they meditate, serve, sleep, work, and travel with the same goal of assessing their lives and determining how to continue to learn "lessons" according to their karmic desires and purposes. The soul also works out karma on the astral plane and thus can be very active, including spiritually active, seeking God and serving His work.

For most people, however, the astral world provides a time of rest and even deep sleep. In this state, the soul is not particularly aware or conscious of itself (comparable to the lives of most spiritually unadvanced people currently on the physical planet), *until,* as one interviewee stated, "some little desire you didn't satisfy draws you back right away." Desires that bring people back may be as minor as an addict's desire for a cigarette or a drug, for which the individual needs the physical, material world for satisfaction. The soul is then drawn to parents and to the environment that best serves these needs and desires. Thus, as one man put it, "we are building our next life right now." All is a continuum, and karma is the law that ensures that the soul evolves according to desires and choices made in the past and present.

However, it is willpower, in spite of karma, that allows for soul freedom. In this view, the soul is architect of its own destiny and can change things at any moment by exercising willpower with determination and attunement with God's will. For advanced souls, death is joyous and something to look forward to. For others, there may be regrets or trepidations about their ability to let go of limitations completely. For all, however, death is actually life, and for most people life will continue in much the same way it has in the past, with another (or many other) rebirth(s) in the physical world.

A person's consciousness at the moment of death determines the future life of the soul. This means that *whatever state of consciousness one is in at the moment of death continues into the soul's experience in the next world.* Those thoughts, or state of consciousness, at death also determine where in the astral world the soul will be born. The astral world, like the physical and the causal worlds, has many planets (or "mansions"; see Cox 1988). To which of these the individual will traverse is dependent on the level of consciousness at the time of death, as well as the individual's karma. Parts of the astral world of light are permeated with bliss and calm, filled with love and joy experienced among people who remember one another. Other parts are darker (in lesser light), with less desirable experiences that are sometimes referred to as hell. For most, the soul is happier in the astral world than it was in the physical world. Individuals existing on the darker planets experience sleep, torment by their own negative states of consciousness, unhappiness, or unawareness, depending on how they lived their lives in the physical world.

In turn, *the manner is which one lives one's present life* often determines one's state of consciousness or thoughts at the time of death. This is because an individual's consciousness does not change at death; no one is made into an angel just by dying. (Angels, and saints, are made in *this life on earth* through conscious effort at realization of the Self as soul.) Thus the *ability* to hold on to the thought of God at the moment of death is important for the next life of the soul. This ability is cultivated and secured through the longtime habit of meditation, which prepares one for a high spiritual consciousness at the time of death. For these reasons, those who believe in reincarnation engage in what some observers may see as extraordinary spiritual effort.

One interviewee described death as "a graduation day," noting that even though you have passed, it is also a reminder to get busy and stay busy. If you graduate, you will reincarnate into a more spiritual environment *earlier* in the next life, such as being drawn to parents who meditate. The goal for people who expect to return again to the physical world is to return to a better environment, where they hope for peace, less violence, greater joy, less tragedy, more success, less discouragement, good habits, and less temptation; they also hope to serve as better examples than they have in their present lives. They aspire to learn spiritual principles, to learn to meditate, and to "find" God sooner in their next lives.

For those I interviewed, the fear of death does not exist. Rather, they expressed an acceptance of death, including the death of loved ones. Not denying their own sadness and loneliness at loss, these people spoke of letting go of others, of lovingly allowing them to move on. One mother stated she and her husband hope to assist their children to live without the fear of death. If they succeed, these parents believe, their children will have a much greater chance to be happy. If they do not succeed, the kids may be miserable and attached to their bodies, which will require them

to reincarnate again and again. One nun remembered the death of her father:

> I cried and cried. My father had cancer which spread to his lungs. I had to accept it. I prayed and supported him on the phone and I was able to visit him. Then he died a couple years later. My mother waited [and then died]. There was a great joyous feeling of upliftment and joy. I cried and went to [my spiritual mentor] for comfort. She said, "Now he knows there's a loving God." I was ill and couldn't go to the funeral, but I talk to them and they get these feelings. I want them to be happy. They were good people.

Another interviewee talked about when her mother passed away:

> I was emotional. The phone rang and I burst into tears. She had been ill. My only thought was to be with Dad. I didn't even think of Mother. I went home and did the arrangements. I was actually happy; I was the only one. I stayed with Dad a month. The neighbors were so loving and my sister was so sad—she had regrets. I knew where my mother was. I cried out of sentiment, not sadness.

For reincarnationists, the purpose of death is the evolution of the soul; it is an opportunity to broaden the individual. To understand the importance of death is to understand life in the world of duality: Life is sweet and death a dream. In reality, neither actually exists. Only God is, and God is Bliss Consciousness.

In *Autobiography of a Yogi* ([1946] 1994), Yogananda writes about his posthumous encounter with his revered spiritual master, Sri Yukteswar. In this intense and loving dialogue, Yogananda learned some extraordinary details about the astral and causal worlds, in which Sri Yukteswar was now playing an integral role:

> The earth-liberated astral being meets a multitude of relatives, fathers, mothers, wives, husbands, and friends, acquired during different incarnations on earth, as they appear from time to time in various parts of the astral realms. He is therefore at a loss to understand whom to love especially; he learns in this way to give a divine and equal love to all, as children and individualized expressions of God. . . .
>
> The span of life in the astral world is much longer than on earth. A normal advanced astral being's average life period is from five hundred to one thousand years, measured in accordance with earthly standards of time. . . . The astral world is free from unwilling death, disease, and old age. These three dreads are the curse of earth, where man has allowed his consciousness to identify itself almost wholly with a frail physical body requiring constant aid from air, food, and sleep in order to exist at all.
>
> Physical death is attended by the disappearance of breath and the disintegration of fleshly cells. Astral death consists of the dispersement of lifetrons, those manifest units of energy which constitute the life of astral beings. At physical death a being loses his consciousness of flesh and becomes aware of his subtle body in the astral world. Experiencing astral death in due time, a being thus passes from the consciousness of

astral birth and death to that of physical birth and death. These recurrent cycles of astral and physical encasement are the ineluctable destiny of all unenlightened beings. Scriptural definitions of heaven and hell sometimes stir man's deeper-than-subconscious memories of his long series of experiences in the blithesome astral and disappointing terrestrial worlds. . . . Man as an individualized soul is essentially causal-bodied. (P. 407)[11]

A Universal Theodicy

For most people, the *fear* of death can be more terrifying than the experience of dying itself. Because death is a universal human condition, all religious philosophies and theologies include some version of a theodicy—that part of the doctrine that explains, for better or for worse, the ultimate questions of suffering and dying. According to sociologist Peter Berger (1969), a theodicy is religion's attempt to make a pact with death:

The world of sacred order, by virtue of being an ongoing human production, is ongoingly confronted with the disordering forces of human existence in time (i.e. suffering, evil, chaos, and death). . . . *Therefore every human society is, in the last resort, men banded together in the face of death.* The power of religion depends in the last resort upon the credibility of the banners it puts in the hands of men as they stand before death or, more accurately, as they walk, inevitably, toward it. (P. 51; emphasis added)

Both Berger and Max Weber (1978) categorize the various theodicies proffered by the religions of the world. Berger (1969) does so in terms of their degree of rationality, or, in his words, "the degree to which they entail a theory that coherently and consistently explains the phenomena in question in terms of an overall view of the universe" (p. 54). Weber (1978:519–22) categorizes theodicies based on how believers psychologically relate to death in the physical world:

1. Justice will eventually prevail in the world.
2. Never mind, it will be better in heaven.
3. Retribution in this world or another is exact and inevitable.
4. Try to mollify God and improve one's chances through good works.
5. Judgment Day will take care of everyone once and for all.

Noteworthy for this discussion is that both theorists argue that the most rational, convincing, and comprehensive theodicies are those systems that include the concepts of karma and reincarnation. Of retribution, for example, Weber (1978) states:

The most complete formal solution of the problem of theodicy is the special achievement of the Indian doctrine of karma, the so-called belief in the transmigration of souls. This world is viewed as a completely connected and self-contained cosmos of ethical retribution. Guilt and merit within this world are unfailingly compensated by fate in the successive lives of the soul, which may be reincarnated innumerable times. . . . Each individual forgets his own destiny exclusively and in the strictest sense of the word. This thirst for life is the ineradicable basis of individuation and creates life and rebirth as long as it exists. Strictly speaking, there is no sin, but only offenses against one's own clear interest in escaping from this endless wheel, or at least in not exposing oneself to a rebirth under even more painful circumstance. The meaning of ethical behavior may then lie . . . in improving one's chances in his next incarnation or—if the senseless struggle for mere existence is ever to be ended—in the elimination of rebirth as such. (Pp. 524–25)

One of the most significant implications of the reincarnationist worldview is, thus, the rather substantial and comprehensive *banner it provides in the face of death* (Eliade 1954). For example, the reincarnationist theodicy that explains suffering, evil, and death is proven to be extraordinarily satisfying for those who believe it, especially in their greatest time of need, such as when a loved one dies. Believers describe feelings of love, connectedness, and joy, whereas nonbelievers experience sadness, regret, and fear. Reincarnationists also describe feelings of psychological peace and assurance in the idea that they, and all others, will attain liberation (salvation) of the soul from further incarnations, constituting a particularly significant personal religious experience (James [1902] 1961). These people know they are already liberated, if they would but realize it. They know that eventually *all* souls will be called back to Spirit. Until then, people will reincarnate over and over, according to their attachment to karmic desires, until they "learn" all the lessons their souls have chosen for them, and until they finally find God by realizing the Self within.

CONCLUSION

Reincarnationists hold a worldview that offers legitimation for certainty, surrender, acceptance, detachment, and joy when they are faced with the inevitable experiences of

---

11. Note that Yogananda also provided a dramatic demonstration of the incorruptibility of life by death in his own passing in 1952. According to a notarized statement by the mortuary director at Forest Lawn Memorial Park in Los Angeles: "The absence of any visual signs of decay in the dead body of Paramahansa Yogananda offers the most extraordinary case in our experience. . . . No physical disintegration was visible in his body even twenty days after death. . . . Our astonishment increased as day followed day without bringing any visible change in the body under observation. Yogananda's body was apparently in a phenomenal state of immutability. . . . The physical appearance of Yogananda on March 27th, just before the bronze cover of the casket was put into position, was the same as it had been on March 7th. He looked on March 27th as fresh and as unravaged by decay as he had looked on the night of his death" (quoted in Yogananda [1946] 1994:478).

chaos in life, including so-called death. In a practical sense, implications of the reincarnation theodicy also mean that those who believe in reincarnation are less likely than others to support the traditional Western death industry (which includes hospitals, doctors, priests, funeral directors, grief counselors, cemetery monuments, hospice, and drugs). As the transformation of knowledge to include a reincarnationist worldview takes place in the Western world, Western institutions will begin to reflect a newly defined spiritual context, one that is structurally based on a knowledge of the scientific laws of reincarnation and karma.

Knowledge systems, whether classified as scientific, religious, or social, ultimately rest on belief—belief in "sacred" texts, teachers, and experience. Given the substantial literature on the *transformation* of knowledge, particularly the work of Kenneth Gergen (1982), Michael Polanyi (1958), and Thomas Kuhn (1962), the task for Western society becomes the restructuring of human institutions so that they befit *reincarnated* souls, rather than simply physical beings or even saved souls who transcend to heaven and those unsaved souls who, forever, descend to hell.

Indeed, by redefining universal human experiences such as death, afterlife, and evolution, the emergent reincarnationist worldview may lead to a new paradigm, a spiritual humanism that represents a historical point of convergence between the currently opposed and dominant salvationist (one-life, one-afterlife) and secular-humanist (one-life, no-afterlife) perspectives in Western culture, science, and religion.

REFERENCES

Berger, Peter L. 1969. *The Sacred Canopy: Elements of a Sociological Theory of Religion.* Garden City, NY: Doubleday.

Cox, Harvey. 1988. *Many Mansions: A Christian's Encounter With Other Faiths.* Boston: Beacon.

Cranston, Sylvia and Joseph Head. 1993. *Reincarnation: A New Horizon in Science, Religion and Society.* Wheaton, IL Theosophical Publishing House.

D'Andrade, Roy G. 1984. "Cultural Meaning Systems." In *Culture Theory: Essays on Mind, Self and Emotion,* edited by Richard A. Shweder and Robert A. LeVine. New York: Cambridge University Press.

Dass, Ram. 1970. *The Only Dance There Is.* Garden City, NY: Anchor.

Daya Mata, Sri. 1990. *Finding the Joy Within.* Los Angeles: Self-Realization Fellowship.

Dillon, Jane. 1989. "A Folk Model of Life and Death for the Self-Realization Fellowship." Presented at the annual meeting of the Society for the Scientific Study of Religion, Salt Lake City, UT.

———. 1991. "Reincarnation and the Council of Constantinople: A Study of Early Christian Belief." Presented at the annual meeting of the Pacific Sociological Association.

———. 1998. "The Social Significance of a Western Belief in Reincarnation." Ph.D. dissertation, Department of Sociology, University of California, San Diego. Available from UMI Dissertation Services, Ann Arbor, MI.

Eliade, Mircea. 1954. *Cosmos and History: The Myth of the Eternal Return.* New York: Harper.

Ferm, Vigilius, ed. 1945. *The Encyclopedia of Religion.* Secaucus, NJ: Poplar.

Feuerstein, George. 1989. *Yoga: The Technology of Ecstasy.* Los Angeles: J. P. Tarcher.

Gergen, Kenneth J. 1982. *Toward Transformation in Social Knowledge.* London: Sage.

Head, Joseph and Sylvia Cranston, eds. 1961. *Reincarnation: An East-West Anthology.* Wheaton, IL: Theosophical Publishing House.

———, eds. 1967. *Reincarnation in World Thought.* Wheaton, IL: Theosophical Publishing House.

———. 1977. *Reincarnation: The Phoenix Fire Mystery.* New York: Julian.

Isherwood, Christopher, ed. 1962. *Vedanta for Modern Man.* New York: Collier.

James, William. [1902] 1961. *The Varieties of Religious Experience: A Study in Human Nature.* New York: Penguin.

Jules-Rosette, Bennetta. 1978. "The Politics of Paradigms: Constructing Theories of Consciousness and Society." *Human Studies* 1:92–110.

Kuhn, Thomas. 1962. *The Structure of Scientific Revolutions.* Chicago: University of Chicago Press.

Leviton, Richard. 1993. "Celebrating 100 Years of Yoga in America." *Yoga Journal,* May/June.

MacGregor, Geddes. 1982. *Reincarnation: A Christian Hope.* Totowa, NJ: Barnes & Noble.

Mehan, Hugh B. 1986. "Oracular Reasoning in a Psychiatric Exam: The Resolution of Conflict in Language." In *Conflict Talk: Sociolinguistic Investigations of Arguments in Conversation,* edited by Allen D. Grimshaw. New York: Cambridge University Press.

Moody, Raymond A. 1975. *Life After Life: The Investigation of a Phenomenon—Survival of Bodily Death.* New York: Bantam.

Polanyi, Michael. 1958. *Personal Knowledge: Toward a Post-Critical Philosophy.* Chicago: University of Chicago Press.

———. 1966. *The Tacit Dimension.* Garden City, NY: Anchor.

Savage, Philip. 1999. *Journey Into the Absolute Elsewhere.* Encinitas, CA: Unit.

Stevensen, Ian. 1974. *Twenty Cases Suggestive of Reincarnation.* Charlottesville: University of Virginia Press.

Weber, Max. 1978. *Economy and Society: An Outline of Interpretive Sociology,* 2 vols., edited by Gunther Roth and Claus Wittich. Berkeley: University of California Press.

Worthington, Vivian. 1982. *A History of Yoga.* London: Penguin.

Yogananda, Paramahansa. [1929] 1981. *Whispers From Eternity.* Los Angeles: Self-Realization Fellowship.

———. [1975] 1990. *Man's Eternal Quest.* Los Angeles: Self-Realization Fellowship.

———. [1946] 1994. *Autobiography of a Yogi.* Los Angeles: Self-Realization Fellowship.

———. 1995. *God Talks With Arjuna: The Bhagavad Gita, Royal Science of God-Realization (The Immortal Dialogue Between Soul and Spirit: A New Translation and Commentary),* 2 vols. Los Angeles: Self-Realization Fellowship.

Yukteswar, Swami Sri. [1894] 1977. *Kaivalya Darsanam: The Holy Science.* Los Angeles: Self-Realization Fellowship.

HOSTS AND GHOSTS

The Dead as Visitors in Cross-Cultural Perspective

CLIFTON D. BRYANT

All societies must confront the problems of death. The immediate and practical problems that death poses include the physical processing of the dead and the social processing of the death (grief, bereavement, and so on). The secondary problems are related to anxiety about death itself, which affects the members of the society, and to the need for an appropriate relationship between the living and the dead. In this connection, all societies project onto the dead some degree of animation. Furthermore, just as there is a social covenant among the living, there is a covenant between the living and the dead. As John Honigmann (1959), an anthropologist, notes:

> Also the remembered dead might be included within a society's limits. Living members credit the dead with ideas, poetry, and paintings. Among the deceased are the sources of inherited debts and the men who built the irrigation ditches or cleared the fields from which people still prosper. Communities that intercede with ancestors for health, rain, and prosperity strikingly show their awareness of the common interests that unite living and dead. (P. 23)

In maintaining relationships between the living and the dead, societies tend to apply one of two different socially constructed premises: They may elect to consider the dead as totally separated from the living and keep the dead alive only in a symbolic fashion, or they may consider the dead to be only substantively separated from the living and keep them alive in a literal sense.

THE LIVING AND THE DEAD

The United States is an example of a society that culturally attempts to keep the dead alive symbolically. This is accomplished through the physical immortality of products and artifacts associated with memorializing the deceased, such as buildings or structures named for

deceased persons, as well as through preservation of the artistic efforts of the deceased, such as music, artworks, and movies. Americans also keep the dead alive symbolically through elaborate socially contrived communication systems, or "death messages" (Bryant 1976), and community-level ceremonial behavior involving the dead (Warner 1959).

Among those societies that elect to conceptualize the dead as being only substantively separated from the living and work to keep the dead alive in a literal sense (at least for short periods of time) are Mexico and China. In these two societies, not only do the living sometimes keep the dead alive literally, but the dead also periodically visit the living. Many societies around the world, both today and in the past, have traditions of entertaining visits from the dead from time to time. For example, during the ancient Celtic (Irish, Scottish, Welsh) festival of Samhair (celebrated on November 1 and the progenitor of modern-day Halloween), the souls of those who had died during the preceding year returned briefly to the land of the living (Brandes 1998a:370–71), and during the annual festival of *bon* (Festival of the Dead) in today's Japan, the spirits of the dead also return briefly. The Mexican festival known as the Days of the Dead and the celebration of Ghost Month in Chinese culture offer particularly colorful examples of visitation by the dead; I examine these two traditions in turn below.

THE DAYS OF THE DEAD IN MEXICO

The Mexican culture is a culture of hospitality. Visitors to the home are warmly welcomed, and the dead are as warmly welcomed as the living. The dead visit only periodically, however—only once a year, during a series of holy days known collectively as *los Días de Todos Muertos*, or the Days of the Dead. The Days of the Dead take place over the course of three nights and two days. Many behavioral scientists have devoted extensive investigative efforts to this religious festival (e.g., Brandes 1998a, 1998b; Green 1972; Garciagodoy 1994).

The Days of the Dead begin on the night of October 31, which is known as Allhallows Eve (in the United States, this night is known as Halloween), and continues through the following two days and nights: through All Saints' Day on November 1 and All Souls' Day on November 2. The celebrations that take place during these days and nights are a cultural blend or amalgamation of traditional Spanish Catholic festivals, as practiced historically in many Catholic countries around the world, and rituals and beliefs from Mexico's pre-Spanish period (Green 1972:245). Certain elements of the Days of the Dead celebrations, especially the iconographic symbols of skulls, skeletons, and other thanatological representations, are believed to derive from various pre-Spanish sources, including Aztec, Toltec, and Maya sculptures, carvings, and other death-related representations, as well as the death-related religious rituals of Mesoamerican Indians (Brandes 1998b:186, 189–94). The iconography of the Days of the Dead also has origins in early Christian art, with its "skeletal representations of death in the abstract" (Brandes 1998b:199).

All Saints' and All Souls' Days are celebrated throughout the Roman Catholic world, including Mexico. These religious holy days have their roots in Catholic masses that originated as early as the 11th century to honor all of the saints and all of the souls in purgatory (Brandes 1998a:360). By the early 16th century, Roman Catholics in Spain and other parts of Europe had established a tradition of observing All Saints' and All Souls' Days by "visiting cemeteries, presenting offerings of flowers, candles, and food to deceased relatives; and soliciting or begging in ritualized form" (Brandes 1998a:362). The Days of the Dead as observed in Mexico are essentially similar to these Roman Catholic celebrations, with certain elements of Mexico's pre-Spanish culture blended in; in recent times, some aspects of traditional U.S. Halloween celebrations have come to be included in the mix as well.

The Days of the Dead are celebrated throughout most of Mexico and in parts of Central America. The most elaborate Days of the Dead festivities are generally found in the traditional Indian areas of Mexico, such as in the valley of Oaxaca and on the island of Janitzio in the state of Michoacán (Green 1972:245). The Days of the Dead are also observed to some extent in those parts of the United States with large Latino populations, such as Southern California, Arizona, New Mexico, and Texas. In Louisiana, which has a very large Catholic population, All Saints' Day and All Souls' Day are celebrated; in fact, All Saints' Day is a legal holiday in that state.[1]

During the Days of the Dead, the living reserve their time for their dead visitors; this is a period of great religious and familial reverence, an opportunity for family members—living and dead—to rebond. It is a signal rite of intensification, and Mexican families eagerly anticipate the festival each year. All Saints' and All Souls' Days have historically held a place of importance in Roman Catholic celebrations almost equaling that of Christmas and Easter (Brandes 1998a:360). In Mexico, the Days of the Dead festival is one of the most important of the year, as well as one of the most expensive to celebrate. For some time in advance of the occasion, families clean and prepare their homes, acquiring and storing special foods and other materials for the celebration; this might include the purchase of all new dishes to please the deceased relatives who will come to visit (Green 1972:245).

An involved sequence of events and activities occurs during these celebration days. As noted above, the rituals begin on the night of October 31, Allhallows Eve, when the family assembles in the home and makes final preparations for visits from deceased family members and more distant relatives. An altar is set up, and a variety of special foods are prepared and placed on the altar along with alcoholic beverages, tobacco, and various delicacies, such as sweets. Larger households may set up separate altars for dead children, with the alcohol and tobacco omitted but toys added to the small fruits and other foods placed there (Green 1972:245–46). Among the special foods a family is likely to prepare for this occasion are chicken dishes, chilies, fruits, moles, tamales, hot chocolate, *atole* (a gruel made of sweet corn), and breads, especially *pan de muerto,* or "bread of the dead," a special bread prepared only for the festival that often features a cross or a winged angel molded out of white dough (Day 1990:69; Green 1972:248–49).[2] Family members do not eat any of the foods placed on the altar, as these offerings are for the dead. Sometimes families spread trails of fresh marigold petals from outside the house leading into the interior and up to the altar, in order to assist the dead in finding their

---

1. Although All Saints' Day is "on the books" as a legal holiday in Louisiana, state offices are not automatically closed. Instead, the governor must declare them closed, and that does not happen every year. The current governor has not closed public offices for All Saints' Day during his tenure, but Edwin Edwards, a former governor, occasionally did so. Banks remain open on All Saints' Day in Louisiana, as do other private businesses, for the most part, although some local shopkeepers, especially in small towns, may not open for business. Although the Catholic Church observes both All Saints' and All Souls' Days, neither is designated a Holy Day of Obligation, which means the faithful are not required to attend mass on these days. All Saints' Day is set aside to recognize publicly those heroes of the church who have been officially designated saints of the church. All Souls' Day is likewise set aside to recognize publicly those who have died in the faith and are saved but publicly unrecognized as saints. Theologically, all the saved are saints, whether or not the church declares their sainthood (Jerome J. Salomone, personal communication, October 18, 2002).

2. At one point in time, family members saved the water that was used to wash the bodies of their deceased kin before they were dressed and laid out for their funerals; at some later date, this water was mixed with flour to make *pan de muerto.*

way home (Greenleigh and Beimler 1991:69). The family members prepare to stay up all night to greet their ghostly visitors.

The spirits of the dead tend to be quite punctual in their arrival (in contrast to the relatively relaxed attention to time commonly encountered in Mexican culture). Promptly at 4:00 A.M. (early on All Saints' Day), the spirits of deceased children arrive; these spirits are known as *angelitos* (little angels). The family members recite the names of remembered dead children and light tiny candles, one at a time, for each child (Green 1972:246). (The label of *angelitos* derives from Roman Catholic belief that when baptized children die without mortal sin, they do not have to pass through purgatory but instead go directly to heaven and become angels; Marino 1997:37.) The *angelitos* leave the home a few hours later, at 8:00 A.M., at which time the family members extinguish the tiny candles and remove them from the altar (or from children's altar, if there is a separate one). The deceased children's visit is over. That morning, the family attends mass at the local church (Green 1972:246). Later in the celebration, during visits to the cemetery, family members light candles and place them, along with flowers, sweets, and toys, on the graves of the dead children (Marino 1997:43).

In the afternoon on November 1, All Saints' Day, the family prepares to welcome other deceased relatives into their home. The adult spirits also arrive punctually, at 3:00 in the afternoon. The family members say the name of each deceased relative and light a candle (this time a full-sized candle) for each. The next morning at 8:00 A.M., the dead guests leave (Green 1972:246).

On that morning, which is All Souls' Day, the churches hold three masses. During the day, families visit the cemeteries where their close family members and other relatives are buried. They may put flowers and other offerings (such as lighted candles and toys) on the graves and pray. Some families may totally cover the graves of loved ones with marigold petals (Greenleigh and Beimler 1991:88). Priests may visit the cemeteries, sprinkle the graves with holy water, and say prayers for the dead (Green 1972:246). These activities go on into the evening. This is a time of family togetherness and personal closeness with the dead.

Finally, on the night of All Souls' Day, with religious commemoration completed and their responsibilities to the dead concluded, families move about the village, visiting at the homes of other families, praying at their altars and offering gifts (called *muertos*) of food from their own altars and receiving similar gifts of food from neighbors. Sometimes groups of men, wearing masks or costumes, may go about from house to house singing hymns of praise, known as *alabanzas,* for which they may receive gifts of food from the altars of the households they visit (Green 1972:246). This tradition is not unlike that of Christmas carolers going door-to-door, singing and receiving snacks in return (it also bears a resemblance to the American custom of trick-or-treating on Halloween).

Although celebrants may eat the food that has been set out on the altars or may give the food away as gifts as soon as the spirits leave, it is said that this food does not have as much taste as it might normally have, because the spirits of the deceased have eaten it. In spite of this, however, the food is eaten. Usually, families do not dismantle their home altars until November 4.

Two other dates and attendant events are connected to the Days of the Dead but are not technically components of the festival. On October 27, some families hang bread and jugs of water outside their homes as offerings to those spirits who have no surviving relatives to prepare altar offerings for them. In some villages, the custom is instead to gather such offerings and place them in a corner of the village church (Greenleigh and Beimler 1991:21–22).

There is also concern about the spirits of deceased individuals who died by accident, murder, or other violent means. These spirits are considered to be possibly malignant, inasmuch as they may have as-yet unpardoned souls. Offerings of food and beverages are set out for these spirits on October 28, but they are usually placed outside the home, to keep the spirits from coming inside (Greenleigh and Beimler 1991:22).

Although the Days of the Dead festival serves functionally as a rite of intensification, reuniting both living and dead members of a family into a cohesive whole, at least for a short time each year, it also has the latent function of neutralizing or mediating the fear of death. For adults, the fact that the dead visit their living families each year gives promise, if not evidence, of existence beyond the grave. If the dead are able to visit, then death does not have absolute finality. Many of those who celebrate these holy days hold a very sincere belief that the spirits of the dead are genuine and do, indeed, return each year to visit. Others, perhaps those of more sophisticated religious ideology, interpret the Days of the Dead on a more symbolic level. The simple observance of these holy days and the symbolic return of the dead for a short visit each year tends to reify Christian theology and reinforces the eschatological belief in spiritual life after death and ultimate resurrection.

For children, the Days of the Dead may serve to desensitize, to lessen their fear of the dead (and even of death itself). The Days of the Dead festival is a time of faith, family, and celebration. When the dead take on the form of benign visitors, it is difficult to fear them. During this time, heightened spirituality mingles with pleasurable activities and stimulating dramaturgical involvement.

To outsiders, the iconography of the Days of the Dead may appear grotesque. Traditional sweet foods associated with this celebration include candies made in the shapes of skulls, skeletons, and other death-related objects. One popular delicacy is a small confection made in the shape of a coffin. Some of these candy coffins even have plastic windows in the top through which bodies with skull heads can be seen. Some are rigged with strings that, when pulled, cause the lids to open and the corpses inside to sit up. Intended as gifts for children, these various candy items sometimes have individuals' names inscribed on them (Brandes 1998b:182).

In addition to candy skulls and skeletons, there are a variety of Days of the Dead toys and decorations featuring death-related items and themes. These include papier-mâché skeletons, and cardboard artic-ulated skeleton marionettes. Also popular are small figurines (not unlike the toy soldiers that are popular with children in the United States and Europe) that represent ordinary persons, but with one special character-istic—they are either skeletons or have skull faces. These *calavera* (skulls and skeletons) toys are made of clay and are quite fragile; they are intended only as amusing frivolities for the children and not as enduring keepsakes. Walkup (2001) describes these toys as follows:

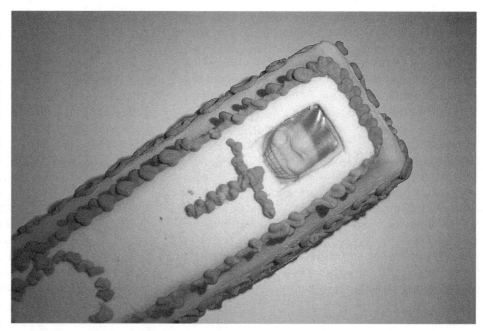

Figure 1 Sugar Candy Casket to Be Given to Children as a Treat During the Days of the Dead

SOURCE: Clifton D. Bryant collection.

> *Calavera* toys and papier-mâché skeleton figures depict specific professions, musicians, brides and grooms, bicycle riders and other subjects from everyday life. There are rich traditions in Mexican folk art that incorporate *calaveras* in many ways. (P. 23)

Other types of toys and decorative items are also associ-ated with the Days of the Dead, such as larger humorous but macabre sculptures and figurines depicting skeletal figures engaged in all sorts of activities (a skeleton riding a motorcycle, for example). The production of candy skulls and skeletons as well as other types of death-depicting, but humorous, statuary, miniature figurines, and other varieties of toys and decorative items has become something of a cottage industry in some areas of Mexico and has brought a certain notoriety to this festival. Tourists from the United States, especially, often travel to various communities in Mexico to experience especially colorful Days of the Dead celebrations. Some tour companies plan excursions in which tourists visit several different communities, even stopping at cemeteries so that the tourists can photograph the villagers lighting candles and placing offerings on the graves.

The artifacts of the Days of the Dead, with their macabre iconography, have also piqued the interest of collectors. As Brandes (1998a) observes:

> Day[s] of the Dead figurines have awakened tourists' interest in the holiday[s]. Among foreigners, they invariably appeal to the collectors' instinct. They are transported back to the United States as evidence that Mexicans really are different from mainstream Americans. (P. 182)

Many craft artisans now produce high-quality artifacts of this variety especially for sale to tourists.

Beyond the toys and sweets, during the Days of the Dead skeletons and skulls appear on signs in store windows and in newspaper ads and articles. The entire panoply of Days of the Dead iconography has been enhanced and magnified by the commercialization and growth of popular culture that now surrounds the festival.

In recent years, the Days of the Dead festival, particu-larly in urban areas and among the middle-class population in Mexico, has experienced a significant infusion of ele-ments and symbolism from American Halloween tradi-tions. Some Mexican children in the cities now go about in costume on Allhallows Eve, carrying boxes or other recep-tacles and begging for their "Halloween" (Halloween can-dies or coins). Many of the decorations in urban areas are also Halloween artifacts from the United States, such as plastic jack-o'-lanterns and manufactured costumes for children's (Brandes 1998a:372–73). These changes have not been without controversy. As Brandes (1998a) notes, "The rapid penetration of Halloween symbols into Mexico increasingly evokes Mexican nationalistic sentiments, embodied in a campaign to preserve the country from U.S. cultural imperialism" (pp. 359–60). He goes on to report that "all over Mexico today, there appears evidence of for-mal and informal resistance to the Halloween invasion from the North" (p. 375). In rural areas, however, the Days of the Dead festival retains a high degree of cultural purity.

Although the seemingly macabre death-themed iconography of the Days of the Dead festival may give some outsiders the impression that the Mexican people are fixated on death or that death-oriented themes are central in Mexican culture, most authorities assert that this is not the case. "On the contrary," Brandes (1998a) observes, "no special Mexican view of death, no uniquely morbid Mexican national character, has yielded this mortuary art. Rather, specific demographic and political circumstances originally gave rise to it, and commercial interests have allowed it to flourish" (p. 214). Like other writers, Brown (1993) characterizes the festival as "really . . . more

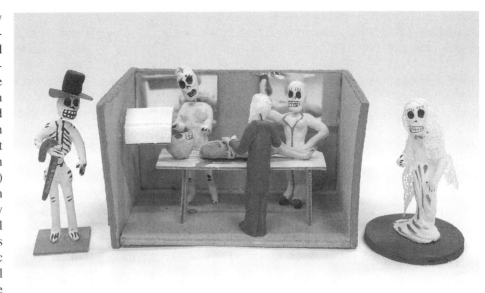

Figure 2   Operating Room With *Calavera* (Skeletal) Surgical Team and Other *Calavera* (Skeletal) Figurines, Intended as Children's Toys for the Days of the Dead

SOURCE: Clifton D. Bryant collection.

of a celebration of life than of death" (p. C9). She goes on to quote the comments of a museum curator who said: "To me, the Days of the Dead subconsciously lends itself to our times [alluding to urban violence and the AIDS epidemic]. It gives you an opportunity to feel good about someone's life, beyond mourning. It gives you a chance to affirm life by recognizing death" (p. C9).

Walkup (2001) also contends that "*los Días de los Muertos* is not in any way somber, morbid, or macabre" (p. 24). She compares the celebration activities of this festival with the practices of creating an impromptu memorial by the side of the road where a loved one has died in an automobile wreck or leaving flowers in a public place to honor a dead celebrity, such as Princess Diana. Some writers have even expressed a bit of envy toward Mexicans for their Days of The Dead. As Day (1990) reflects:

> The fastidious may regard all this as grotesque. The pious may call it pagan. But there is nothing barbaric about the Day[s] of the Dead in Mexico, even if one considers its terrifying Aztec ancestry. It occurs to me that we might have something to learn from a people who have learned to be on such easy terms with death. (P. 72)

In short, for many, the Days of the Dead are life affirming, not death embracing. To celebrate in this fashion is, on the one hand, to confront death openly and honestly and to be aware of its inevitability and its presence in the midst of life. On the other hand, celebrating the Days of the Dead is a form of wholesome death denial in that it reifies the

Christian eschatology of eternal life in another form triumphing over death. Most important, it subjectively keeps the dead alive, for if the dead come home to visit, then, indeed, death does not portend the annihilation of self with absolute finality.

GHOST MONTH IN CHINESE CULTURE

In Chinese culture, the dead have historically been considered to be only substantively separated from the living, and, accordingly, the dead are kept alive literally, in the form of ghosts.[3] Actually, *ghost* is not the appropriate term. The Chinese term *guai*, which translates literally as *ghost*, is used to refer to a "devil" or "evil spirit." In China, all disembodied spirits are known generically as *leng* or *ling wun* (Cantonese, as used in Hong Kong), and there are three major categories of such spirits (or souls) (Emmons 1982:30; for a detailed discussion of Chinese spirits, see Emmons 1982:chap. 3). These include deceased ancestors, ghosts (or *guai*, who are the spirits of deceased persons who have no relatives to worship them and care for their otherworldly needs), and gods. Gods are considered to be in the same generic category as ghosts and ancestral spirits, because most of them are assumed to have once been mortals who lived virtuous lives and subsequently became deities after death (not unlike saints in the Catholic Church; see Tong 1988). Taking into account, then, all of the dead, worshipped, uncared for, and deified, the residual

---

3. I gathered many of the observations and comments included in this discussion of Ghost Month during my fieldwork and through informal interviews during the Ghost Month celebration while I was living in Taiwan in 1987–88 and teaching at National Taiwan University as Visiting Fulbright-Hayes Professor.

number of *leng* to be reckoned with is considerable—a "host of ghosts," as it were. Concerning Chinese eschatology, Crowder (2003) explains:

> The gods and spirits are subject to negotiations like people in society because the Chinese spirit world is modeled to mirror the material one. Heaven and its pantheon of gods are organized like China's imperial government headed by the emperor and his bureaucracy of civil servants, and it must be approached systematically. Gods and spirits, having human responses and needs, require offerings to sustain their existence. Even beggar spirits must be paid off to leave the deceased alone at funerals. Because life in the spirit world requires the same items as life on earth, ritual money and paper replicas of houses and goods are burned at funerals for the deceased's spirit.

Because of the profusion of *leng* or ghosts component to Chinese eschatology, Chinese expend a significant amount of energy on the social behavior necessary to participate in the interactive interface with the deceased and to maintain the appropriate relationship between the living and the dead. In this regard, various rituals and practices that serve as interface mechanisms for the maintenance of the relationship between the living and the dead are part of Chinese culture (see Tong 1988).

The Family Altar

Chinese who are of religious persuasion have in their homes (and often in their places of business) family altars that they use for worshipping ancestors and gods. Some have two altars, one for ancestors and one for the gods. Such altars are often family heirlooms, passed down from generation to generation. Religious worship in Chinese culture is quite varied and includes, among the major non-Western faiths, Taoism, Buddhism, and Confucianism. Beyond these there are numerous folk and local patron gods, sea gods, and, in some places, animistic deities. For example, it has been estimated that throughout the island of Taiwan, more than 250 gods or deities are worshipped. (For an in-depth discussion of the pantheon of Chinese gods, see Tong 1988.) Many Chinese are polytheistic in their worship and, depending on their preferences, have effigies or figurines of several gods on their altars.

Usually also found on family altars are ancestral tablets, on which are recorded the names, titles, and death dates of deceased forebears. Some families have generic or general tablets for family ancestors who have passed from memory. As part of the worship of both gods and ancestors, families place incense pots with burning joss sticks on their altars, along with periodic offerings such as food, drink, and flowers. On several days of the month, more ritualized kinds of offerings are made, and a more formalized set of worship rites is observed on special occasions, such as particular holidays. For recently deceased relatives,

families may engage in more personalized and elaborate worship rites on their death dates, perhaps offering the favorite foods of the deceased, along with cigarettes or wine. On Chinese New Year, as well as on some other occasions, families may offer whole feasts on their altars, complete with bowls, cups, and chopsticks. On Chinese New Year, each member of the family, in order of status, kneels before the altar in a show of reverence and respect for the dead. Ghosts (of the uncared-for variety) are also worshipped at family altars, as I will discuss below. Some families also worship particular gods on a regular basis, whereas they worship others only on special occasions, such as the gods' birthdays (see "Ghostly Taiwan" 1987).

The primary interface of the living and the dead in Chinese culture, then, is in the home, with the family altar at the center of the interaction. Beyond this, the worship of the dead spreads to clan ancestral halls, where altars are also maintained, and to neighborhood temples as well as larger temples, which may be dedicated to one or more particular gods.

Burnt Offerings

Chinese eschatology differs somewhat from Western eschatology in that it includes an automatic dimension to the afterlife. This exigency confronts the soul of the deceased individual within the first week after death, in its journey through the *yin* world. During this time, the soul reaches the first obstacle on its journey, the Gate of the Demon, and finds it necessary to bribe the gatekeeper!

The existence of the dead in Hades has an economic counterpart in the world of the living—it costs money. The dead must have food and drink. They require houses in which to live, clothing, and all of the other things that are needed in life. These things must be supplied by the living, and it falls to the offspring of the deceased to assume this responsibility.

The family's economic responsibilities to the dead begin at the time of coffining and burial. Relatives may place special "spirit money" or "ghost money" (fake money produced and sold just for this purpose) in the coffin so that the deceased will have funds available for bribes and other expenses on the journey to the netherworld, or Hades.[4] As noted above, the family is also obligated to supply the deceased with the home and furnishings, as well as other supplies, he or she will need in the next world. Chinese communities have special stores where families can purchase paper effigies of all of the kinds of items their deceased loved ones will need. These include paper houses as large as trunks, gardens surrounded by walls with large gates, furniture, automobiles, clothing, and recreational items, such as radios, television sets, cameras, and even board games. Such stores also carry specialized items reflecting their particular communities, such as paper livestock and agricultural tools in rural areas for deceased farmers, and paper boats in coastal areas for fishermen. Nothing is omitted; there are

---

4. Some of this money is placed in the sleeve of the corpse's garment and later retrieved to be given to the grandchildren.

Figure 3   Ghost (or joss) money for the dead. The upper four bills are contemporary and from Chinese areas such as Hong Kong, Singapore, and Chinatown in San Francisco. Some ghost (joss) money is printed to resemble ancient money for long-deceased ancestors. The bottom left bill is a chit for new clothes for deceased ancestors at Chinese New Year. The bottom right is an offering to the god Kuang Kung for protection.

SOURCE: Clifton D. Bryant collection.

even small figures representing servants available to go with the paper houses. At the time of the funeral, usually the evening after the funeral or the next morning, the family of the deceased burns the paper house and all of the other paper items, thus sending them to the deceased so that he or she will be well housed and equipped in the next world. Presumably all of these things last indefinitely, as families do not seem to burn (and thus send) any additional or replacement items at subsequent dates.

After the funeral and burial, the family's subsequent economic responsibilities to the dead can be discharged with the burning of special types of ghost money at particular times and the making of food and drink offerings in the appropriate context. Beyond these offerings to deceased ancestors, it is also considered necessary to make similar offerings to assorted gods and wandering ghosts, as well as to various spirit soldiers, at culturally determined intervals and on specific occasions (see "Ghostly Taiwan" 1987). The spirit soldiers are the minions of a particular god (Kuang Kung), who, it is believed, sends them to protect the homes (or businesses or villages) of the living. The soldiers have to be fed and paid—thus the need for food

offerings and sacrifices of ghost money. Offerings of food to gods and ancestors are generally made inside the house, usually on the family altar, one portion offered to the gods and one to the ancestors (sometimes there are separate altars for gods and ancestors). The various figurines of the gods worshipped by the family are placed on the altar, as well as the ancestral tablets listing the names and death dates of remembered deceased ancestors (as noted above, there may also be a general tablet for unremembered ancestors) (Jochim 1986:171).

Usually, on the first and fifteenth days of the month families make offerings to both gods and ancestors in the form of food, flowers, wine, and the like. They may also make more elaborate offerings, accompanied by formal rites, on special dates, such as the death dates of relatives, the birthdays of gods, Chinese New year, and other publicly celebrated occasions and festivals. Offerings for the gods are presented facing outward, and offerings for ancestors are presented facing inward. Offerings for ghosts are presented outside of family homes (or businesses). If such an offering is for ghosts in general (such as during Ghost Month), it is placed in front of the house or place of business. If it is for a single "offending" ghost who is causing the family misfortune, it is placed on the ground outside the rear of the house, as if it were left there for a beggar.

The Hungry Ghost Month

Perhaps the most significant of all of the festivals of the dead in Chinese culture is the Hungry Ghost Month. In all Chinese communities outside of mainland China, Ghost Month, as it is popularly known, is a major celebration.[5] It is observed during the entire seventh lunar month, which generally begins sometime in August and ends sometime in September. To understand the meaning of Ghost Month, it is necessary to examine Chinese eschatology.

In Chinese culture, death is not the final annihilation of self, but an alternate, spiritual form of existence. Upon death, the soul of an individual must undertake an arduous, 7-week journey through the *yin* world or "otherworld" (Lip 1985:11–22). During this journey, the soul passes through various "gates" and "courts" where it faces trials and judgments in regard to the deceased's conduct in life on earth. The soul ultimately reaches Hades, the abode of the dead, and lives under the rule of Giam-lo-ong (in Mandarin, Yen-b-wang), the main deity of the underworld ("Ghostly Taiwan" 1987). In Hades, souls or spirits have lives not unlike those on earth. They require food and drink and money, all of which must be provided by the living; as described above, it is the responsibility of the deceased's living relatives to supply these needs. During the seventh lunar month, the gates of Hades are opened and the ancestral spirits are free to visit earth and roam about during a sort of "vacation." The spirits, although free to roam, are monitored by Ta Shih Yeh, who is the netherworld's superintendent of visiting ghosts (Tourism Bureau n.d.:47). Such spirits are of two varieties: cared-for ghosts and uncared-for ghosts. The cared-for spirits are those deceased individuals who have living relatives who make offerings of food and drink to them and send them gifts of paper money, thus providing for their needs. Those spirits with family ties are generally "quite good natured and spend their time partaking in the simple earthly pleasures of eating and drinking" during Ghost Month (Tourism Bureau, n.d.:44).

It is the second category of deceased spirits—the uncared-for ghosts—that are potentially harmful. It is only this category of spirit, or *lin,* that can appropriately be termed *ghosts,* or, more correctly, *kui* (although all spirits of deceased individuals may popularly be generically aggregated under the term *ghosts*). The uncared-for spirits are called *hungry ghosts* because, having no living descendants, they have no one to supply them with food, drink, or money in Hades; they are thus deprived, or hungry. Such ghosts may be malicious or at least mischievous and are likely to go about causing trouble—teasing humans and, in some cases, causing them harm. If the hungry ghosts are displeased or angry, they can be particularly malevolent and may bring serious misfortune or even disaster on the living (see "Ghostly Taiwan" 1987).

The most dangerous of the hungry ghosts are the spirits of individuals who died in accidents, through suicide or homicide, or as the result of other "unnatural" causes. The spirits of persons who die in these ways do not go straight to Hades. Rather, they are placed in a special limbo or purgatory where they must remain until they can lure someone else into an accident or unnatural death, at which time they report this fact to Giam-lo-ong and can enter Hades. The ghost of the newly dead victim, in effect, takes the place of the spirit that was formerly in limbo. Accordingly, it is assumed that these ghosts are actively trying to entice others into dangerous situations where they might accidentally be killed. Only the foolhardy would place themselves in potentially dangerous situations during Ghost Month; for example, many will not go swimming for fear that they might somehow be trapped underwater and drown. Motorcycle racing on the streets of Taipei, which is a widespread and dangerous pastime of many youths during most of the year, is significantly reduced during Ghost Month. During Ghost Month, the malevolent ghosts are believed to be desperately trying to promote accidents, and it is an ominous time for all. As Jochim (1986) notes, "In fact, this is a month during which no tradition-honoring Chinese would think of opening a business, buying a house, scheduling surgery, or getting married—for it is without qualification the most inauspicious time of the year" (p. 138). With the profusion of ghosts, or *lin,* both "cared for" and "uncared for," returning to the world of the living for a visit, Ghost Month is a time of general anxiety.

Although some authorities assert that the returned spirits of the deceased are invisible (Jochim 1986:138), others speak of the visiting spirits as assuming human form (e.g., Tourism Bureau, n.d.:46). When they appear as humans, it is widely believed, they resemble the living in every way save one—their feet do not touch the ground. As they walk about, they hover a fraction of an inch off the ground. During Ghost Month, many Chinese spend an inordinate amount of time looking down at the feet of other pedestrians as they walk along the street.

The principal activities of Ghost Month involve the presentation of offerings and sacrifices to the dead. Among the offerings are food, money, and entertainment. Special attention is given to the hungry ghosts. Tables are set up outside homes and places of business with offerings of food and wine for the hungry ghosts. These offerings are

---

5. In the People's Republic of China, especially during the Mao years, religious practice was suppressed or at least discouraged, and with the dilution of traditional religious beliefs and behaviors, adjunct practices, such as those related to funerals, other aspects of death, and ancestor worship, tended to decline, if not largely disappear, among significant proportions of the population. Ghost Month is not generally celebrated in that country today, and many, if not most, young people in the cities are not familiar with it.

located outside homes or businesses so that the ghosts will not go into the houses or stores and cause any trouble or harm. Also, families want to keep hungry ghosts from coming into their homes because the ghosts are likely to steal the offerings for deceased ancestors from their family altars, or otherwise interfere with the families' paying the proper respect to their ancestors and the gods (see "Ghostly Taiwan" 1987).

The offerings of food and wine for the hungry ghosts are sometimes quite elaborate, with several courses of food and various delicacies laid out. Some families may even serve up for the spirits whole pig carcasses suitable for large feasts. Usually these carcasses are only partially cooked, and after they have served their purpose as "ghost" fare, they can be further cooked for family consumption. The offerings for the hungry ghosts might also include fruit, flowers, cigarettes, burning joss sticks, and bundles of ghost money (Jordan 1985:35–56), which is burned at some point to deliver it to the ghosts for their vacation use. The offerings to the hungry ghosts serve both as a kind of protection against ghostly mischief or harm and as a kind of altruistic gesture to the unfortunate dead, out of a sense of compassion (Jochim 1986:138).

During Ghost Month, families also honor their deceased ancestors with special offerings of food, wine, flowers, and cigarettes, usually placed on their family altars. The offerings of food during this period often consist of entire meals, laid out with dinnerware and chopsticks. Joss sticks are burned constantly, and ghost money is sent to ancestors through burning. Families might make such offerings to their ancestors only on specific dates during the month, but many do so on a more frequent basis.

Beyond the offerings of food and drink and the sacrifices of ghost money to the spirits, during Ghost Month Chinese operas and puppet shows are performed on street stages to entertain the visiting ancestor spirits and ghosts. The living also find these performances enjoyable, so there are invariably big audiences (living and dead) to watch them. In another custom of Ghost Month from earlier times (perhaps still practiced in some places even today), merchants would test the money they earned during this period by putting it in a bowl of water. If it sank, it was real, human money; if it floated, it was money from a ghost (Tourism Bureau, n.d.:46).

Ghost Month reaches a climax toward the middle of the lunar month, when various specific activities occur. One of these is the festival of the "worship of good brothers," held on the 15th day of the month ("Ghostly Taiwan" 1987:9). This is also the date of the Chung Yuan Festival, a Buddhist celebration marking the end of the annual mediation period for monks and nuns. On this date, certain temples become locations for elaborate feasts for the visiting ghosts. The feasts feature large assortments of food and drink, with delicacies of every variety. Large hogs are sacrificed to be added to the fare. The temples are decorated with lanterns and other lights so the spirits will not get lost on their way. Lanterns and candles are also floated on bodies of water to appease the ghosts of those who have drowned there as well as to warn the living of the presence of the water so they will not become drowning victims. Vast amounts of ghost money are burned for the use of the spirit visitors. Frequently encountered at such temple celebrations are effigies of the god Tai-sai-ia (in Mandarin, Taoshih-yeh), who serves as a representative of the netherworld at the feasts and also supervises the ghostly visitors ("Ghostly Taiwan" 1987:29). At the temples, priests offer prayers for the deceased and conduct special religious rituals. Families may engage priests to say prayers or conduct rituals for their ancestors; some honor specific ancestors by paying for the ancestors' names to be placed in a temple for a period of time.

As noted above, Ghost Month is a time of anxiety for many individuals because of the possibility that hostile ghosts might visit misfortune upon them. It is also a time of festivities and feasting, inasmuch as the living can enjoy the special theatrical performances as well as the dead, and can enjoy the food after the spirits of the dead have had their fill. This period also gives the living an opportunity to indulge in altruism; that is, much as many Americans enjoy the satisfaction of giving to the poor at Christmastime, the Chinese "give" to the uncared-for ghosts during Ghost Month. They are also often more generous with their ancestors than usual during this time. For example, one woman told me that her family laid out extra food offerings for her deceased grandfather during this period because he had been gregarious in life, and they assumed that he might well bring guests home with him when he visited during Ghost Month.

Perhaps most important, Ghost Month's annual reenactment of dead ancestors and hungry ghosts visiting the living reinforces the notion of the continuity of the family, even in death, and the symbolic immortality of the individual. Inasmuch as the dead survive in the memories and ritualistic behaviors of the living, death itself is not so much to be feared. Even the sad plight of the hungry ghosts serves as reinforcement for the fabric of social life, for the message, as Jochim (1986) notes, is very clear: "The worst possible fate for anyone, living or dead, is to be cut off from the network of support and obligations that constitutes the Chinese family system" (p. 172).

The activities of Ghost Month are directed at remembering the dead and including them in the social fabric, as well as at eliciting amity on their part. All of these structured patterns of conduct address the special needs of the deceased and conform to the traditional obligations of the living. Such activities are social and reciprocal in nature, in that the living are motivated by love and respect for the dead as well as by the expectation of benevolence on the part of the dead. By engaging in such behavior, the living attempt to ensure some indirect control over their own lives and destiny, maintain social contacts and bonds with the dead, and perpetuate a symbiotic social structure involving both living and dead in which the deceased continue a worldly existence after a fashion, thereby diluting their own anxiety about death. The living regularly and purposefully interact with ghosts and, in doing so, effectively "deal with the dead." Through this interaction with the dead, the notion of an existence after death is reified and the prospect of death is rendered less frightening, inasmuch as ghostly interaction with the living implies the probability of a postself presence.

CONCLUSION

Many societies reanimate their dead, at least periodically. As I have discussed in this chapter, such reanimation may assume a configuration of formalized visits to the living. Such visitation rituals are particularly colorful and especially meaningful in Mexican and Chinese cultures. In both instances, the festivals or celebrations involving visits from the dead serve as rites of intensification, providing for the reinforcement of bonding between the living and the dead, thereby reifying the solidarity of the family, including members past and present.

These celebrations also function as a means of placating or rewarding the dead. The dead may have unfulfilled needs that can be met only by the living, thus the living must attend to their obligations to the dead ritualistically. The efforts of the living are not totally altruistic, however, inasmuch as there is an expectation of reciprocity—that the dead may be persuaded to help in meeting the unfulfilled needs of the living.

By annually reenacting the dramaturgical rituals of host and ghost, the living gain reassurance in regard to the validity of their religious eschatology. If the dead can come back from the netherworld to visit the living and enjoy the benefits of even a brief sojourn, then the living can expect similar opportunities and fulfillment in the future after they die. By entertaining the dead as visitors, the living mitigate their own fear of death and anticipate continued inclusion in the family circle after their earthly demise.

REFERENCES

Brandes, Stanley. 1998a. "The Day of the Dead, Halloween, and the Quest for Mexican National Identity." *Journal of American Folklore* 111:359–80.

———. 1998b. "Iconography in Mexico's Day of the Dead: Origins and Meaning." *Ethnohistory* 45:181–218.

Brown, Patricia Leigh. 1993. "Designs for a Life-Affirming Celebration in Mexico." *New York Times,* November 4, pp. C1, C8–C9.

Bryant, Clifton D. 1976. "Death Messages: Symbolic Interactional Strategies for Research on Communication Between the Living and the Dead and Dying." Presented at the annual meeting of the Southern Sociological Society, April, Miami, FL.

Crowder, Linda Sun. 2003. "The Taoist Chinese Way of Death." In *Handbook of Death and Dying,* vol. 2, edited by Clifton D. Bryant. Thousand Oaks, CA: Sage.

Day, Douglas. 1990. "A Day With the Dead: In Mexico, the Living and the Dead Celebrate Together." *Natural History,* October, pp. 67–72.

Emmons, Charles F. 1982. *Chinese Ghosts and ESP: A Study of Paranormal Beliefs and Experiences.* Metuchen, NJ: Scarecrow.

Garciagodoy, Juanita. 1994. "Romancing the Bone: A Semiotics of Mexico's Days of the Dead." Ph.D. dissertation, Department of Spanish, University of Minnesota. Available from UMI Dissertation Services, Ann Arbor, MI.

"Ghostly Taiwan." 1987. *Taiwan Grapevine,* August, pp. 9, 29.

Green, Judith Strupp. 1972. "The Days of the Dead in Oaxaca, Mexico: An Historical Inquiry." *Omega* 3:245–61.

Greenleigh, John and Rosalind Rosoff Beimler. 1991. *The Days of the Dead.* San Francisco: Collins.

Honigmann, John J. 1959. *The World of Man.* New York: Harper & Row.

Jochim, Christian. 1986. *Chinese Religions: A Cultural Perspective.* Englewood Cliffs, NJ: Prentice Hall.

Jordan, David K. 1985. *Gods, Ghosts, and Ancestors: Folk Religion in a Taiwanese Village,* 2d ed. Taipei: Caves.

Lip, Evelyn. 1985. *Chinese Beliefs and Superstitions.* Singapore: Graham Bash.

Marino, Daniela. 1997. "Prayer for a Sleeping Child: Iconography of the Funeral Ritual of Little Angels in Mexico." *Journal of American Culture* 20(2):37–44.

Tong, Fung-Wan. 1988. "Vibrant, Popular Pantheon." *Free China Review* 38:9–15.

Tourism Bureau, Ministry of Communication, Republic of China. n.d. *Festivals and Folk Arts: Taiwan Republic of China.* Taipei: China Travel and Trade.

Walkup, Nancy. 2001. "Teaching Sensitive Cultural Traditions." *School Arts,* November, pp. 23–25.

Warner, W. Lloyd. 1959. *The Living and the Dead: A Study of the Symbolic Life of Americans.* New Haven, CT: Yale University Press.

ADDITIONAL READINGS

Green, Judith Strupp. 1969. *Laughing Souls: The Days of the Dead in Oaxaca, Mexico.* Balboa Park, CA: San Diego Museum of Man.

Hernandez, Joanne Farb and Samuel R. Hernandez. 1979. *The Days of the Dead: Tradition and Change in Contemporary Mexico.* Santa Clara, CA: Triton Museum of Art.

Kelly, Patricia Fernandez. 1974. "Death in Mexican Folk Culture." *American Quarterly* 26:516–35.

Scalora, Salvatore. 1995. "Celebrating the Spirits' Return." *Americas* (English ed.), September/October.

Stepanchuk, Carol and Charles Wong. 1991. *Mooncakes and Hungry Ghosts: Festivals of China.* San Francisco: China Books and Periodicals.

GHOSTS: THE DEAD AMONG US

CHARLES F. EMMONS

FRAMING GHOSTS

Problematic is the first word to say about ghosts in modern Western society. As Buse and Stott (1999) state in the introduction to their edited volume *Ghosts: Deconstruction, Psychoanalysis, History,* "It is safe to say that to be interested in ghosts these days is decidedly anachronistic" (p. 1); they also note, "It is now frivolous to believe in ghosts" (p. 3). Of course, they go on to argue the importance of the ghost concept in theoretical realms, language, literature, and history. Nevertheless, they take for granted that the Reformation dismissed (for Protestants) the notion of ghosts returning from purgatory, and that the Enlightenment made the very idea of ghosts seem irrational to most moderns.

Whether ghosts are frivolous on any level is debatable, as we shall see. How seriously we should take ghosts, and how they represent the dead or people's ideas about the dead, are questions that depend importantly on how we frame the idea of "ghosts." Among the possible frames are normal science, parapsychology, comparative cultural studies, folklore analysis, collective behavior research, literary analysis, and mass-media and popular-culture studies.

THE VIEW FROM NORMAL SCIENCE

Because ghosts are defined as returning spirits of the dead, they fall under the perspective of surviving consciousness, or the soul, a topic considered paranormal or religious and therefore either denied or ignored by mainstream science. Currently, the most important social control agent of normal science in the United States is the Committee for Scientific Investigation of Claims of the Paranormal (CSICOP), which publishes the magazine *Skeptical Inquirer.* Articles about ghosts are not common in this publication, in contrast to articles debunking spirit mediums, which appear frequently. Perhaps this represents CSICOP's greater concern about living people (mediums) whom the organization considers to be fraudulent performers of the paranormal.

One example of a skeptical treatment of ghosts may be found in Kastenbaum's 1995 book *Is There Life After Death?* (pp. 109–39), in which the author, a clinical psychologist, plays the dual roles of "advocate" and "critic." In his role as critic in a chapter titled "No Chance of a Ghost," he presents a number of mundane explanations for ghost reports: fraud, illusion, hallucination, wishful thinking (need-determined perception), and mental illness. Then, postulating for the sake of argument that some ghost experiences may be paranormal, he argues that they may represent telepathy or some other form of ESP rather than survival of the spirit. In this discussion Kastenbaum reveals his parapsychological bent; CSICOP would not ordinarily grant the slightest possibility of anything "paranormal." So clearly, for normal science, the presence of a "ghost" represents a mistake, an illusion, or evidence of some form of deficiency in experience, not something to be taken seriously by educated and enlightened people.

PARAPSYCHOLOGY AND APPARITIONS

Parapsychology, a field that began in 1882 with the founding of the Society for Psychical Research in London, focuses largely on spirit mediumship (see Emmons 2003) but is also concerned with ghosts or apparitions (the latter term avoids the assumption that such perceptions are caused by "real" ghosts). Parapsychology may be described as a scientific perspective applied skeptically (ideally) to allegedly paranormal psychical events not accepted in normal science.

Since J. B. Rhine influenced parapsychology to move largely into the laboratory in the 1930s and 1940s, studies of spontaneous forms of psychic phenomena (known as PSI) have waned. The field has placed more emphasis on experiments concerning extrasensory perception and psychokinesis (PK) and less emphasis on studies of spirit mediums, apparitions, and hauntings. (For discussion of theoretical developments in the study of apparitions, see especially Tyrrell 1963; Rogo 1974; Rhine 1981; Emmons 1982. For recent studies of apparitions and hauntings, see Maher 1999, 2000.)

As in parapsychological studies of spirit mediumship, the stickiest issue in the study of apparitions has been the survival hypothesis, the idea that souls or spirits are responsible for the phenomena. Parapsychologists have generally explained ghosts as nonphysical, mental dramatizations of ESP images. But are these images sometimes sparked by telepathy from the dead, or do they appear only through telepathy and clairvoyance among the living? There are also physical effects in hauntings, such as moving objects and electromagnetic disturbances, that are generally separate from whatever apparitions may also occur in such places; this raises the issue of whether the agents of paranormal physical effects are living (a "poltergeist focus") or dead (Maher 2000).

To outsiders, it may seem strange that survival is such a contested issue. After all, both ESP among the living and communication with the dead qualify as "paranormal" or outside the confines of phenomena recognized by normal science. However, parapsychologists have attempted to stretch the boundaries of normal science to include the study of PSI, an as-yet unmeasured force that is postulated as the cause of measurable paranormal effects. ESP is seen as analogous to normal perception; PK is seen as analogous to normal motor activity. Survival of the spirit, however, postulates the existence of a consciousness that escapes death and exists independent of the physical body.

This viewpoint reveals that mainstream parapsychology is attempting to join mainstream science, in which the material world is all there is, and mysterious (but real) forces are merely considered to be beyond our ability to measure using current scientific instruments. In this sense there is really nothing "paranormal." Seeing ghosts as personalities who have escaped physical death goes beyond Western science and into the realm of spirituality or religion, which scientists see as a nonrational, even irrational, survival of pre-Enlightenment thinking.

This seems to leave ghosts out in the cold as far as science—even the parascience of parapsychology—is concerned. It would appear that we need to move on to social science for an analysis of the importance of ghosts in the real world. However, before we abandon the ontological question (the question of whether ghosts are "real") altogether, it is fair to say that the survival hypothesis is still suspended in parapsychology, even if most parapsychologists are loath to embrace it for fear of seeming unscientific.

It is also important to say that there are some impressive data supporting the interpretation that many apparition experiences do not have mundane explanations (including, for example, hoax, illusion, hallucination). Such "evidential cases" are essentially of two types: those in which multiple witnesses who are uncontaminated by mutual influence report the same strange events (given that it is unlikely that multiple persons would have the same hallucination independently) and those in which witnesses provide paranormal information (such as details of a death that the witness of an apparition could not have known about). In my own study of ghost experiences in Hong Kong and China, I found apparently frequent evidential cases as well as many common features of the apparition experience between China and the West in spite of cultural differences (Emmons 1982).

Thus the dismissal of questions of the existence of ghosts as "frivolous" may be rather cavalier. It would be fair to say that parapsychology has collected some interesting data about apparition experiences that are not easily discounted. However, even if adherents of normal science generally recognized such experiences as worthy of study, there would still be a shortage of testable "paranormal" theory at this point.

Hess (1993) provides a more general discussion of these issues, explaining the conflicts among the knowledge subcultures of normal science, parapsychology, and the New Age. Goode (2000:117–37) reinforces the point made here that mainstream parapsychologists cling to the model of the scientific method and prefer to explain PSI as normal. However, normal science rejects parapsychology partly because parapsychology fails to provide either consistent replication or material theoretical explanation for PSI, and partly because it is labeled as a deviant science (which isolates its work from the normal scientific community).

GHOSTS IN COMPARATIVE CULTURAL PERSPECTIVE

Having crossed the divide between natural science and the social sciences, I can now safely discuss the *social* importance of ghosts scientifically without fear of being ridiculed as "frivolous." This is typical of academic boundary maintenance regarding matters nonrational. Whereas religion has been out-of-bounds to science since the late 19th century, with parapsychology representing heresy, social scientists have been assigned the task of understanding religion and other nonrational pursuits as socially constructed natural phenomena. This means that we can take up the topic of ghosts as socially constructed dead people among us. What are they doing here, and what social roles do they play?

Answers to such questions are complex and varied. First of all, there is cross-cultural variety, with the elements connected nonetheless by some interesting cultural universals. Ghosts—that is, the returning spirits of dead humans—are commonly if not universally thought to have emotional ties to concerns in their predeath existence. Such concerns might include unfulfilled social expectations, violent death, and improper burial, but they may also involve more positive attachments to surviving relatives and friends (especially when the living need them). From a sociological perspective, one might characterize these attachments in terms of social norms and social control. For example, suicide violates social norms, and those who commit suicide may end up wandering about as ghosts. Dying before one's time or in a socially inappropriate way violates expectations. The violation may also be on the part of the living—for example, murderers or people who fail to bury the dead with respect may be haunted by ghosts acting as agents of social control. The dead among us have important jobs to do. (This is not to deny that they may play trivial roles as well, a point I return to in a later section.)

For those who are inclined to think of ghosts as trivial or frivolous, either because of childhood memories of Casper the Friendly Ghost or due to ridicule from normal science, I offer a comparative perspective on ghosts from a non-Western culture that takes ghosts seriously and for granted: China. In traditional China, as in other complex societies, there is no single, simple view of ghosts. Different beliefs, based on principles of *yin* and *yang*, ascribe to individuals anywhere from 2 to 10 different souls or soul elements (Emmons 1982:16–17). If the nature of the soul is not crystal clear, neither is the nature of the place souls go to after death. Chinese religion is an eclectic, tolerant mix of animism, Taoism, Buddhism, and Confucianism. Consequently, the Chinese heaven and hell are conceived of as consisting of various numbers of levels, annexing, for example, the Buddhist Western Paradise to the ancient concept of Supreme Heaven. The influence of Buddhism also adds reincarnation to the system, confusing some spirit mediums as to whether they can contact people's dead relatives in the other world if they died long ago and have since returned as other, living humans.

All of this eclecticism tends to blend a variety of phenomena, so that in China, "ghost stories" may include miscellaneous gods, demons, fox fairies (who change into beautiful women), and other elements. As China's dominance spread Chinese culture elsewhere in East and Southeast Asia, local folklore was also added to the mix; in Japan and Korea, for example, ghost beliefs are very similar to those in China.

One thing is certain: Among Chinese, ghosts are commonly thought to return to earth, especially during the Hungry Ghost Festival (Emmons 1982:23–26). Throughout the entire seventh lunar month, Chinese believe that hungry ghosts wander the earth in search of nourishment, especially those who have no one to worship them properly or who have died violent deaths. During this festival, food and entertainment are provided for all (living and dead), and people set out food and burn paper effigies of money and material goods (in modern Hong Kong, these goods might include automobiles) for their own ancestors on the eve of the full moon, the fifteenth day of the seventh lunar month.

This festival is only the high point of a general system of ancestor worship in which Chinese burn incense and set out food and other items, sometimes on a daily basis, on a family altar (Emmons 1982:19–20). Chinese ghosts are most important as relatives who can improve the health and financial success of their descendants in exchange for proper worship. In the past, ancestor worship was most significant among commoners in those parts of south China that practiced wet-rice cultivation, because this system supported the solidarity of the lineages or clans that tended the fields as corporate entities.

In a 1980 random-sample survey of urban Hong Kong residents, I found that an amazing 72% still practiced at least some ancestor worship (Emmons 1982). Some 53% of those practicing ancestor worship said that they believed in ghosts, compared with 43% of those who did not practice. It is somewhat surprising that the percentage believing in ghosts was not higher, given that ghosts are a central part of ancestor worship, both in China and in other cultures of the world. One possible reason the percentage reporting belief in ghosts was not higher may be that it is considered unlucky to discuss the subject. When asked whether they believed in ghosts, some of the individuals who were surveyed responded with remarks such as "Oh! Why do you ask me about such things?!" Seeing a ghost may be considered an omen of one's impending death. And, of course, improperly worshipped spirits come back as agents of social control to haunt the living who have done them wrong either before or after their death. In Chinese crime fiction, apparitions and clairvoyant dreams often provide the living with information that brings the murderer before the magistrate (Emmons 1982:22).

Complex belief sets about ghosts and various types of beings that we might attempt to categorize as ghosts are not confined to China and the rest of Asia. In the West, ancient Greece and Rome borrowed ghost concepts from other cultures, creating both cultural diversity and fluid categories of ghosts (Johnston 1999; Felton 1999:xiii). As in Japan, the Greeks and Romans also tended to blend the supernatural exploits of human ghosts with those of the gods. Moreover, there was diversity of opinion in ancient Greece and Rome about the existence of ghosts. According to Felton (1999), "Some ancient Greeks claimed to see ghosts, whereas others, such as the Epicureans, were highly skeptical, trying to find material explanations for such phenomena" (p. xiii). This parallels the modern United States, with its variety of religious and secular views of ghosts, including the debunking perspective of CSICOP and normal science. At any rate, ghosts were popular characters in Greece and Rome, especially in classical theater productions (Felton 1999:xiii–xvii).

Among the great variety of folk beliefs about ghosts in ancient Greece and Rome was the belief that ghosts would stay away from living people with freckles (Felton 1999:5). This seems to have been based on the Roman belief that freckles had negative magical value. The Greeks and Romans also apparently thought that ghosts were to be found at crossroads (a belief that is still part of modern lore). Iron was believed to provide protection from ghosts and to be useful for imprisoning them; this may be the foundation for the notion that ghosts drag chains behind them. Some Greek and Roman spirits appeared at midday, often to deliver supernatural warnings (Felton 1999:6–7). However, they were more likely to appear at night, especially at midnight, a time associated with death and dreams.

The reasons for the dead to return as ghosts in ancient Greece and Rome were similar to those in modern Western folklore. These included to extract revenge or punish the living, to reward and comfort the living, to complete unfinished business (e.g., to locate wills or treasures for the living), and to request proper burial for themselves (Felton 1999:8–12).

Anthropologists have tended to frame the discussion of ghosts and spirits in Native American societies within the framework of shamanism (see Emmons 2003). For example, Algonquian shamans known as "flyers" portrayed a mythical bird that communicated with and sometimes became possessed by the spirits of the dead (Burland 1970). However, accounts of Native American ghosts have also been interpreted in terms of social control functions and spiritual causes of illness (Henderson 1981). Honigman (1945) has reported on Navajo and Sarsi beliefs about ghosts visiting people just before death and guiding their relatives to the land of the dead, as well as characteristics of ghost experiences (e.g., the appearance of whirlwinds and balls of fire, whistling and tapping sounds).

GHOST FOLKLORE AND COLLECTIVE BEHAVIOR

Of course, there is an overlap between a cross-cultural perspective on ghosts and the study of ghost folklore. In this section, I focus on some of the literature on ghost folklore and on collective behavior studies of rumor. Rumor and folklore perspectives are useful to combine in the study of ghosts because they can both be contrasted with firsthand ghost reports, which are of interest to parapsychologists (and "ghost hunters").

In folklore studies it is generally not an issue whether the content of the lore is "true" or not. However, it is worth noting whether the people who relate the lore assume that it is true. Ghost stories told as if true are ordinarily referred to as *legends* as opposed to *tales,* which tellers and listeners assume to be at least somewhat exaggerated for dramatic effect.

Montell (1975:90), for example, found that only 3 of 175 tellers of ghost narratives in his Kentucky study indicated disbelief in ghosts. These legends came out of a "cultural matrix" in which parents and grandparents told ghost stories to frighten children into obedience, and ghost stories were part of community entertainment. Common elements in these ghost legends included night or darkness, hills, roads, houses, graveyards, and horses (as sensitive to ghosts) (pp. 90–92). Purposes for the ghosts' returning included their being upset at improper burial or post-mortem disturbance of the grave site or grave robbery, their desire for retaliation or revenge or to expose guilty

parties, their need to search for or reveal hidden money, and their desire to look in on family or friends (pp. 93–94). Note the similarities between these reasons and those mentioned above for Greek and Roman ghosts.

In contrast to the Appalachian traditional ghost lore pattern described by Montell, Ellis (2001:117–41) discusses ghost stories collected at a Pizza Hut in central Ohio in the late 1970s. Instead of being told uniformly as if they were true, these "fast-food ghost" narratives involve combinations of "amazed" and "rational" intonations that allow for varying interpretations of experience, including suspended judgment about a rational view of the world. The social context allows for safe contemplation of these possibilities.

Another approach to ghost lore is the literary/historical analysis of a large body of related material. Bennett's article "The Vanishing Hitchhiker at Fifty-Five" (1998) provides an example of this approach. As Bennett notes, more than a half century of analysis has failed to discover the origin of the "vanishing hitchhiker" stories. In fact, these stories are now more widely distributed and varied than ever before. The basic story involves a ghost who appears in corporeal form on the highway on the anniversary of her or his death and gets a ride from or gives directions to a stranger passing by in a car or carriage. Only later, upon returning to the spot where he or she last saw the direction giver or dropped off the hitchhiker, does the driver learn from someone that the individual had died previously, often by suicide or some other unnatural means. This motif also overlaps with other centuries-old motifs about road ghosts, "token-leaving phantoms" (e.g., the ghost leaves a sweater in the driver's car), ghosts who give directions, and ghosts who roam because they died unsatisfactory deaths.

Analysts in the social/behavioral science tradition are likely to look for social and psychological functions in folklore. For example, Tangherlini (1998) examines Danish legends about ghosts in which ministers deal with threats from ghosts. These legends illuminate the role of the minister and the level of respect that ministers enjoy in the community. They also underline the extent to which Danes commonly believe that ghosts represent a supernatural threat instead of being benevolent. Alan Dundes (1998) gives a fascinating psychological interpretation of "Bloody Mary in the mirror" rituals, in which "prepubescent" girls stand in front of mirrors and look for the apparition of "Bloody Mary." There are many variants, but Dundes argues that they all center on a symbolic fear of first menstruation.

In my own work, I have explored ghost stories in Hong Kong in terms of both folklore and the related collective behavior process of rumor (Emmons 1982). My basic motivation for examining Chinese ghost lore and rumors was to contrast these with firsthand reports (also collected in the study). A cross-cultural comparison between the Chinese firsthand ghost reports and those gathered in the West in the parapsychological literature indicated great similarities, both in the lack of physical features and in terms of "abnormal features of perception" (such as the ghost appearing transparent, lacking color, or lacking feet). These data, along with the presence of evidential cases (with multiple witnesses and paranormal information), gave cross-cultural support for the parapsychological theory that the apparition experience is a form of ESP rather than anything physical and is not always merely the product of hallucination. In contrast, the folklore and rumor ghosts *did* have physical features, and stories about them showed evidence of fictitious elaboration through group communication processes.

Folklore motifs about ghosts, both Chinese and Western, involve both malevolent and benevolent returns (Emmons 1982:94–108). Some Chinese examples of the malevolent include the avenging ghost of an unjustly executed man and the ghost who sucks the breath of the living. Some benevolent ones (found in both Chinese and Western lore) are the dead mother who returns to suckle her child and the ghost who comes back to give counsel. The most significant difference between Western and Chinese ghost folklore lies in the lack of Western examples involving ancestor worship. For Chinese, the tendency is to fear visits from the dead, because they tend to be associated with hungry ghosts who are restless because they have not been receiving satisfactory ancestor worship. If you take care of your ancestors properly, they tend to stay in the underworld.

Nevertheless, both Chinese and Western ghosts often act as agents of social control. Having the capacity to perform physical effects may violate the parapsychological theory of apparitions, but it makes ghosts more convincing moral agents in folklore. They punish deceitful sweethearts, spouses, and kin; they accuse or kill their murderers; and they guard buried treasures or prevent thefts. The grateful dead reward those who have buried them properly and tend their graves (in China), honor the brave, and sometimes pay howdy calls to deserving relatives.

Relatively recent Hong Kong folklore about ghosts (from the past half century) includes Japanese-occupation ghosts who haunt buildings known to have been under Japanese control during World War II. Probably second most popular are ghosts in hospitals, problematic places for Chinese in regard to death, even in healthier modern times. Cinema ghosts are also popular, especially in movie-theater bathrooms. Other categories include ghosts in live theater or Chinese opera, water ghosts of drowning victims, and ghosts who push people in front of cars. Right in front of one elementary school, a second grader received minor injuries from being knocked down by a car. Some of the children at the school attributed the accident to ghosts, because it happened during the Hungry Ghost Festival (*Yu Lan Jit*). One girl explained that such things happen during the *Yu Nan Jit* ("Run-Into-Disaster Festival"). (For fuller discussion of Hong Kong ghost folklore, see Emmons 1982:98–108.)

Many of these recently formed legends, or at least certain variants, are very close to rumors, having spread as "true" accounts among relatively small numbers of people. In my 1980 study, I traced one such ghost legend or rumor from several tellers back to the source (Emmons 1982:109–16). Several students related versions of a story about ghosts in a high-rise building on the campus of Hong Kong University. All of these versions emanated from one professor, who had told his class about the elevator ghosts. He actually intended the story as a folktale (which he made up, based loosely on previous reports about the elevator), and it contains elements typical of fictitious stories about apparitions (physical effects on the operation of the elevator and a very long conversation between the ghost and a living occupant of the elevator, something very rare in firsthand accounts). In one version of the story, the ghost in the elevator is a student who had wanted to emigrate to Canada and who had committed suicide when forced to leave school due to bad grades. The students who heard the professor tell the original story, and subsequent spreaders of the rumor, took it to be true. As a rumor, it went through all the classic changes: leveling (becoming shorter), sharpening (with essentials remaining), and assimilation (modification to fit the attitudes of the teller as well as cultural expectations). This ghost legend assimilated by taking on typical concerns of Hong Kong college students: the pressure to succeed in college, suicide due to failure, and emigration to North America.

THE GHOST AS LITERARY DEVICE

If ghosts in folklore often carry cultural meaning, demonstrating common concerns and acting as supernatural agents of social control, it is not surprising that they are used in like manner in literature. In both folklore and literature, ghosts can also have entertainment value. There are, after all, many uses for the dead.

Among the best-known examples of ghosts in Western literature are those in Shakespeare's plays, especially *Macbeth* and *Hamlet*. As Rogers (1949) notes, "Occultism in the Shakespeare plays . . . is always presented as the truth" (p. 179). Just as in traditional Chinese literature, Shakespeare's ghosts never turn out to be mere hoaxes or hallucinations uncovered at the end to appease rationality. They are integral to the pieces in which they appear and usually reinforce moral principles.

Supernatural warnings and sanctions are also prominent in Charles Dickens's *A Christmas Carol*, in which Scrooge sees the ghost of his partner Marley punished for greed and becomes resocialized in time to avoid a similar fate. If we choose, we can agree with the initially skeptical Scrooge that his visions are due merely to indigestion and conclude that his guilty conscience has transformed him in his dreams.

Smith (2001) discusses the ambiguity in Washington Irving's "The Legend of Sleepy Hollow." Although the story strongly implies that Brom Bones perpetrated a hoax in order to frighten his rival, Ichabod Crane, we are left with the possible interpretation that it really was the Headless Horseman who spirited Crane away. In spite of the cultural prejudice against a "childish" or "primitive" belief in the supernatural in Irving's time, stories that allowed for the possibility of ghosts were more exciting and popular.

Writers also use ghosts as a literary "trope"—that is, in a metaphorical, nonliteral sense. Johnson (1999) provides good examples of this in his discussion of the "specter of Communism" (Marx and Engels) and the metaphorical uses of ghosts in the novels of Breton and Bataille.

MASS MEDIA AND POPULAR CULTURE

Not all of the written forms of popular culture about ghosts stress their social control function, but many do. For example, in a group of 14 ghost stories in six American comic books collected in 1979, all 14 stories involved moral justice in the outcomes, all 14 ghosts in the stories were malevolent or conflict oriented, and in 8 of the stories the ghosts performed some type of physical effects. In one, for example, a phony psychic composer writes a piece of music supposedly channeled from the spirit of Beethoven. The ghost of Beethoven himself returns on the night of the work's concert premiere and brings down the concert hall's chandelier, which lands on the perpetrator of the fraud and kills him (Emmons 1982:95–97).

Another comic-book ghost genre involves nonmalevolent ghosts; Casper the Friendly Ghost is the best known of these (Emmons 1982:96). Casper floats and flies and does minor physical effects; he can dive under the ground but can also be captured and confined under "ghost-proof" glass. The magical, fantasy adventures in which he becomes involved are neither moralistic nor malevolent; they are only humorous.

By contrast, ghosts in some of the popular literature in Hong Kong tend to be presented for shock value more than for humor or for purposes of teaching morality. Of course, we should not take the moral lessons offered by the products of U.S. popular culture too seriously; they tend to be inserted because they suit the producers' ideas of poetic justice or for their disclaimer value (so that the producers can avoid complaints from moralists). Even in humorous Hong Kong ghost comics, the ghosts look horrible—they are never cuddly, like Casper. Hong Kong films also sometimes feature farcical, horrible-looking ghosts. There is also a ghost genre of cheap pulp fiction for adults, short stories in which the most common motif is sexual intercourse between a living male and a female ghost who appears real, even beautiful, at least on the night before the morning after. This is the traditional Chinese "fox fairy" motif.

Another aspect of the popular culture of ghosts is popular belief in ghosts. As noted earlier, in my survey of Hong Kong in 1980, I found that more than 50% of those interviewed said that they believed in ghosts (Emmons

1982:274). The traditional centrality of ghosts in Chinese culture, especially in relation to ancestor worship, makes this relatively high figure understandable. In comparison, a Gallup poll in 1978 found that only 12% of adults surveyed in the United States believed in ghosts (Emmons and Sobal 1981:304)

Unfortunately, there are no longitudinal data available to allow us to explore changes in the rates of belief in Hong Kong since 1980. In the United States, however, the Gallup Organization has asked the same question about ghost belief in subsequent years, and the data reveal steady increases: up to 25% in 1990, 28% in 1991, 33% in 1999, and 38% in 2001 (Newport 1999; Newport and Strausberg 2001). It is difficult to know how much of this change is due to the general upsurge in belief in life after death in the past few decades, but the Gallup data show very little difference in ghost belief by how important religion is to the respondent (Newport and Strausberg 2001). In fact, the 1978 Gallup data showed that belief in the paranormal tended to be higher among people who claimed to have no religion at all; of those with no religion, 23% said that they believed in ghosts, compared with 12% of all respondents (Emmons and Sobal 1981:304).

Gallup data also show increases in the proportions of Americans who believe in most other paranormal phenomena in the past decade: haunted houses, from 29% in 1990 to 42% in 2001; mental communication with the dead, from 18% in 1990 to 28% in 2001; witches, from 14% in 1990 to 26% in 2001; extraterrestrials visiting Earth, from 27% in 1990 to 33% in 2001 (Newport and Strausberg 2001). However, the proportions of those who say they believe in ESP and related phenomena have shown no increase, for the most part, and the proportion of those saying they believe in possession by the devil declined, from 49% to 41%, over the same period.

One might suspect, although it is difficult to demonstrate, that increased belief in the paranormal among Americans is related to the popularity of television shows and films that involve such subjects. One indirect indication that this may be the case is that belief tends to be much more frequent among younger people, the same group that makes up the main audience for media culture. For example, in the 2001 Gallup poll, 46% of 18- to 29-year-olds stated belief in ghosts (38% of all ages), and 58% of them believed in haunted houses (42% of all ages) (Newport and Strausberg 2001). Belief drops off dramatically over age 50 (29% of those over 50 report believing in ghosts, and 32% believe in haunted houses). However, even 29% of the older group believing in ghosts is a very high figure compared with the 12% overall who said they believed in 1978 (Emmons 1982:274). Of course, in 1978 those people who are now over 50 were 23 years younger, many of them in their 20s and 30s and consuming media about the paranormal by then.

One example of current popular media representations of ghosts may be found in Mark Nesbitt's series of five collections of ghost reports and stories titled *Ghosts of*

Gettysburg (1991, 1992, 1995, 1998, 2000). Before the publication of the first of these books in 1991, there was very little discussion in the media of ghosts in Gettysburg, in spite of the general belief in American culture that ghosts haunt scenes of violent death. Since the mid-1990s, several television programs based largely on Nesbitt's books have aired nationally; some of them have played on cable stations dozens of times.

McAdams (2000) discusses the phenomenon of the Travel Channel's including programs about the paranormal, one of which is titled *Places of Mystery.* According to McAdams, Travel Channel executives made the decision to run programs on hauntings (including one about Gettysburg) and aliens based on their concern about ratings. If it seems odd to categorize certain forms of the paranormal as travel, it is worth noting that those who program the Travel Channel recognize that real travelers watch little television, but armchair travelers like to see places of fantasy and mystery vicariously.

Real tourism also features trips to haunted places. Nesbitt runs his own "Ghosts of Gettysburg Tour," and other enterprises have arisen to offer similar kinds of experiences. "Ghost tours" may be found in many historic places, including battlefields.

The subject of allegedly haunted property intersects with another institution aside from tourism: real estate. According to an article in *Hotel & Motel Management,* New Hampshire law requires the seller of any hotel in that state to disclose the presence of any known ghosts to prospective buyers. The Seller's Property Information Report form used by the New Hampshire Association of Realtors asks, "Are you aware of any supernatural occurrences that may affect the value of the property? If yes, explain" (quoted in Marshall 2000). Whether the popularity of hauntings in the mass media makes such property more or less valuable is an empirical question.

At this writing, perhaps the most widely publicized debate about the paranormal in popular media centers on the Harry Potter books written by J. K. Rowling. Some fundamentalist Christians have condemned the books for providing children with information about the occult that might socialize them into communicating with ghosts and performing witchcraft (Breznican 2001). A Gallup poll conducted in 2000 found that only 7% of adults familiar with the Harry Potter book disapproved of them; 52% approved, and 41% no opinion. However, 12% of conservatives disapproved of the books, compared with only 2% of liberals (Jones 2000).

Clearly, the individuals on the two sides of this debate are operating from different frames. Some fundamentalist Christians see ghosts and other paranormal phenomena as real and dangerous, as being of the devil. In contrast, many people who are involved in spiritualism or new spirituality (the New Age) see the paranormal as real but substantially good. Interviews with Rowling (Breznican 2001) and with children who have read the books tend to support the frame that the Harry Potter stories are fantasy and not to be taken literally.

The debate over Harry Potter, however, highlights the question of how seriously people take the paranormal, ghosts included. In modern America, Halloween provides the prime example of pop-culture paranormal. Over the millennia, Halloween has transformed from a harvest festival during which the spirits of the dead were understood to return, analogous to the Chinese Hungry Ghost Festival (Emmons 1982:23–26), to mainly a junk-food festival for children. In polls conducted in 1985 and 1999, 69% of American adults surveyed said that someone in their families would be giving out treats on Halloween. However, 12% said that they were opposed to celebrating Halloween on religious grounds, with "these objections . . . most common among conservatives and Republicans" (Newport 1999). This seems to indicate that some Americans do indeed take Halloween seriously and literally, but negatively, as some view Harry Potter.

Another example of not seeing Halloween as a harmless fantasy can be found in an article published in *Parents Magazine* titled, "Why Halloween Scares Preschoolers" (Kutner 1994). The article's author points out that very young children have difficulty separating fantasy from reality and may therefore be frightened by extreme costumes: "Your child needs to know that ghosts are imaginary" (Kutner 1994:77). It is interesting to note that debunkers say the same thing about ghosts to parapsychologists (and the rest of us).

There is one more side to the popular culture of ghosts that deserves mention: the subculture of "ghost hunters." In my own limited participant observation in the Gettysburg area, I found that ghost hunters constitute a multifunctional interest group that combines amateur science, adventure, and sociable interaction. This subculture overlaps with the subculture of battle reenactors and comes close to being a part of parapsychology. Its relationship to parapsychology is similar to the relationship between amateur UFO study groups and more professional researchers in ufology (Emmons 1997:96–101).

A recent Internet search using the keyword *ghost* turned up 11,376 sites; the keyword *apparition* resulted in 928. About one-third of the "ghost" sites had to do with other meanings of the word *ghost,* as in *ghost town* or *Holy Ghost,* but a great many were relevant to the ghost interest subculture. These included Web sites run by ghost hunter groups organized in particular geographic areas. "Apparition" sites tended to be related to religious visions, as in the case of Marian apparitions.

Some ghost-related Web sites are organized by individuals who attempt to be "professional," in the sense that they make their livings from selling ghost books (their own and those written by others), giving ghost tours or organizing ghost outings, and selling electronic "ghost detection" equipment. Vandendorpe (1998) gives examples of such ghost-hunting devices. Many search for anomalies in temperature changes and for unexplained images on film, whereas others are designed to detect magnetic, electrical, and/or radio/microwave variations. The sellers of some devices claim that their equipment can capture electronic voice phenomena on cassettes or on digital recorders. Vandendorpe notes that although some ghost hunters are skeptical of the motives of the "professionals" (who are involved for profit), even part-time amateurs often use detection equipment, such as digital cameras for taking photographs that yield unexplained spots of light or "orbs" that may represent the presence of spirits. Sometimes their photographs contain images that are interpreted as human forms (ghosts).

Another element in the ghost hunter subculture is the use of psychics or mediums to attempt contact with the spirit world. Ghost hunting often combines psychic and technical approaches. This is in the spirit of parapsychology, attempting to bridge science and religion (or spirituality), even if ghost hunters are seldom trained parapsychologists. The few parapsychologists who actually do field studies of hauntings tend to point out that any photograph by itself is of little use as evidence without accompanying reports from witnesses.

CONCLUSION

It is clear that there are many ways of framing ghosts. In a scientifically ideal context, we ought to be able to suspend judgment and learn from them all. However, we are haunted by the ghosts of the clash between science and spirituality, between rationality and religion. It is difficult to take ghosts seriously in Western academe without becoming subject to ridicule.

If scholars and scientists were not so haunted, we might construct a theory of cultural elaboration in which we could look for some basis for ghosts in experience, then see how this experience becomes framed variously by human cultural constructions. It would still be difficult to ascertain what that basic experience is. At least debunkers and parapsychologists alike could agree that many apparition experiences are illusions, dreams, hallucinations, and other mental phenomena not necessarily related to physical reality. It is the allegedly evidential cases that become problematic.

Agreeing to suspend judgment about those cases, we could then move to an appreciation for the cultural variation in ghost cultures, finding the differences between Chinese and Western ghosts, for example, rooted in different forms of economy and social organization. At the same time, we might be impressed by how many cultural universals there are throughout world societies—for example, the use of ghosts as supernatural social control. Other patterns show up in ghost narratives collected at various times and places by modern folklorists, literary analysts, and mass-media scholars who examine ghost motifs and their social/psychological functions.

However we study ghosts, they still involve death, the dead among us, and their many uses. In spite of the official rationality brought about by and since the Enlightenment, ghosts are not really dead. Even in Western societies, with their extremes of normal science and popular culture, there is still some lingering, haunting ambiguity about death and the Headless Horseman.

REFERENCES

Bennett, Gillian. 1998. "The Vanishing Hitchhiker at Fifty-Five." *Western Folklore* 57:1–17.

Breznican, Anthony. 2001. "Supernatural Themes in 'Harry Potter' Continue to Anger Certain Conservative Christians." Associated Press, November 14.

Burland, C. A. 1970. "Algonquin Indians." Pp. 63–65 in *Man, Myth and Magic*, vol. 1, edited by Richard Cavendish. New York: Marshall Cavendish.

Buse, Peter and Andrew Stott. 1999. "Introduction: A Future for Haunting." In *Ghosts: Deconstruction, Psychoanalysis, History*, edited by Peter Buse and Andrew Stott. New York: St. Martin's.

Dundes, Alan. 1998. "Bloody Mary in the Mirror: A Ritual Reflection of Pre-Pubescent Anxiety." *Western Folklore* 57:119–35.

Ellis, Bill. 2001. *Aliens, Ghosts and Cults: Legends We Live*. Jackson: University Press of Mississippi.

Emmons, Charles F. 1982. *Chinese Ghosts and ESP: A Study of Paranormal Beliefs and Experiences*. Metuchen, NJ: Scarecrow.

———. 1997. *At the Threshold: UFOs, Science and the New Age*. Mill Spring, NC: Wild Flower.

———. 2003. "The Spiritualist Movement: Bringing the Dead Back." In *Handbook of Death and Dying*, vol. 1, edited by Clifton D. Bryant. Thousand Oaks, CA: Sage.

Emmons, Charles F. and Jeff Sobal. 1981. "Paranormal Beliefs: Functional Alternatives to Mainstream Religion?" *Review of Religious Research* 22: 301–12.

Felton, D. 1999. *Haunted Greece and Rome: Ghost Stories From Classical Antiquity*. Austin: University of Texas Press.

Goode, Erich. 2000. *Paranormal Beliefs: A Sociological Introduction*. Prospect Heights, IL: Waveland.

Henderson, J. Neil. 1981. "Comanche Ghost Sickness: A Biocultural Perspective." *Medical Anthropology* 5:195–205.

Hess, David J. 1993. *Science in the New Age: The Paranormal, Its Defenders and Debunkers, and American Culture*. Madison: University of Wisconsin Press.

Honigman, John Joseph. 1945. "Northern and Southern Athapascan Eschatology." *American Anthropologist* 47: 467–69.

Johnson, Kendall. 1999. "Haunting Transcendence: The Strategy of Ghosts in Bataille and Breton." *Twentieth Century Literature* 45:347–70.

Johnston, Sarah I. 1999. *Restless Dead: Encounters Between the Living and the Dead in Ancient Greece*. Berkeley: University of California Press.

Jones, Jeffrey M. 2000. "Even Adults Familiar With Harry Potter Books." Gallup News Service, July 13.

Kastenbaum, Robert. 1995. *Is There Life After Death? The Latest Evidence Analyzed*. London: Prion.

Kutner, Lawrence. 1994. "Why Halloween Scares Preschoolers." *Parents Magazine,* October, pp. 76–77.

Maher, Michaeleen C. 1999. "Riding the Waves in Search of the Particles: A Modern Study of Ghosts and Apparitions." *Journal of Parapsychology* 63:47–80.

———. 2000. "Quantitative Investigation of the General Wayne Inn." *Journal of Parapsychology* 63:365–90.

Marshall, Anthony. 2000. "Ghosts Are Good for Business—No Matter Where They Settle Down." *Hotel & Motel Management,* January 10, p. 18.

McAdams, Deborah D. 2000. "Trips to the Other Side." *Broadcasting & Cable,* July 31, p. 36.

Montell, William L. 1975. *Ghosts Along the Cumberland: Deathlore in the Kentucky Foothills.* Knoxville: University of Tennessee Press.

Nesbitt, Mark. 1991. *Ghosts of Gettysburg: Spirits, Apparitions and Haunted Places of the Battlefield.* Gettysburg, PA: Thomas.

———. 1992. *Ghosts of Gettysburg II: Spirits, Apparitions and Haunted Places of the Battlefield.* Gettysburg, PA: Thomas.

———. 1995. *Ghosts of Gettysburg III: Spirits, Apparitions and Haunted Places of the Battlefield.* Gettysburg, PA: Thomas.

———. 1998. *Ghosts of Gettysburg IV: Spirits, Apparitions and Haunted Places of the Battlefield.* Gettysburg, PA: Thomas.

———. 2000. *Ghosts of Gettysburg V: Spirits, Apparitions and Haunted Places of the Battlefield.* Gettysburg, PA: Thomas.

Newport, Frank. 1999. "Seven Out of Ten American Families Will Be Giving Out Treats This Halloween." Gallup News Service, October 29.

Newport, Frank and Maura Strausberg. 2001. "Americans' Belief in Psychic and Paranormal Phenomena Is Up Over Last Decade." Gallup News Service, June 8.

Rhine, Louisa E. 1981. *The Invisible Picture: A Study of Psychic Experiences.* Jefferson, NC: McFarland.

Rogers, L. W. 1949. *The Ghosts in Shakespeare: A Study of the Occultism in the Shakespeare Plays.* N.p.: Rogers.

Rogo, D. Scott. 1974. *An Experience of Phantoms.* New York: Dell.

Smith, Greg. 2001. "Supernatural Ambiguity and Possibility in Irving's 'The Legend of Sleepy Hollow.'" *Midwest Quarterly* 42:174–82.

Tangherlini, Timothy R. 1998. "'Who Ya Gonna Call?': Ministers and the Mediation of Ghostly Threat in Danish Legend Tradition." *Western Folklore* 57:153–78.

Tyrrell, G. N. M. (1963). *Apparitions.* New York: Macmillan.

Vandendorpe, Laura. 1998. "Ghost Hunters Link Data With Unexplained Images." *R&D Magazine,* June, pp. 106–7.

THE MALEVOLENT "UNDEAD"

Cross-Cultural Perspectives

KEITH P. JACOBI

Across the world and throughout time, there is a relationship between the living and the dead. An individual begins to prepare mentally for death once he or she is old enough to comprehend the concept. When a child turns to her father at the age of 4 and says, "When you are dead . . . you don't come back anymore," that realization begins the child's unfortunate walk toward death. All individuals follow similar avenues. However, different cultures march to different drummers in the ways they handle and cope with the dead. The living bury the dead, rebury the dead, pray for the dead, discuss and celebrate the dead, eat the dead, mutilate the dead, and visit the dead. Many living persons wish that particular deceased individuals were not dead and could return. Thus, to confront their own fears of their eventual death, individuals project some degree of animation on the dead. People transcend or rise above their fear of their own death by keeping the dead alive.

The term *undead* is used primarily in reference to what most people think of as the "walking dead." These undead are corporeal; that is, they are physical entities that have material substance and can be touched or felt. The types of undead that come to mind are animated corporeal bodies such as vampires, zombies, reanimated mummies, reanimated corpses, and bodies cobbled together from bits and pieces of multiple humans, such as the monster in Mary Shelley's *Frankenstein*. Usually, the corporeal undead are without souls or human sensibilities. Humans fear these undead because of their physical existence, which means they can touch and therefore physically harm the living.

There are two distinctive types of undead: (a) the *corporeal undead*, which include revenants (a generic term for the animated undead) and vampires (who are undead but have undergone a process of transformation; Barber 1988:2–3); and (b) the *corporeal living dead*, which include zombies (most notably in relation to the voodoo faith in Haiti). Zombies are not dead but appear to be, even

to doctors (Boelderl and Mayr 1995); they are individuals who have been poisoned by a concoction that includes the toxins from puffer fish (*Diodon hystrix* L., *Diodon holacanthus* L.), sea toads (*Sphoeroides testudineus* L., *Sphoeroides splengeri* Bloch), and the large *buga* toad (*Bufo marinus* L.) (Davis 1987, 1988:110). To create a zombie, one mixes these toxins with other ingredients, including the "crushed and ground remains of a human cadaver," to make a powder that can be placed in food or administered by the prick of a thorn (Davis 1988:110, 112). When an individual ingests the powder, he or she becomes a zombie, although remaining conscious of what is going on around him or her (Boelderl and Mayr 1995). For example:

> If the patient tried [*sic*] to take anything in his hand or to stand up, he feels that his limbs are powerless. The patient remains conscious. If he goes to sleep after eating, he finds that he is suffering from poisoning when he awakes and cannot move or speak. In serious cases, the patient may die while asleep. After some time, the motor nervous system is completely paralyzed and it becomes impossible to move any part of the body. The eyes do not respond and the mouth stays closed, making speech impossible. The pulse and respiration slow down. The body temperature drops. Asphyxia occurs as a result of all this and, sometimes, the patient even dies. The patient's comprehension is not impaired even in serious cases. When asked about his experiences, he can describe everything in detail after recovery. (Akashi 1880, quoted in Davis 1988:156)

Davis (1988) classifies zombies into three types. A *zombi astral* or *zombi éfface* is a zombie in which a part of the person's soul is changed by the individual who possesses it, a *zombi cadavre* or *zombi jardin* is a zombie that has been created to work for someone, and a *zombi savanne* is an individual who had become a zombie and subsequently "returned to the state of the living" (p. 301).

Unlike zombies, vampires are undead corporeal creatures, dead individuals who have returned from the grave to haunt and physically harm the living. Vampires are malevolent creatures who feed on the living to sustain their own existence because they are not alive (Boelderl and Mayr 1995). When vampires feed, they kill the living. Just as zombies return as the living dead, when a vampire kills, that act enables the deceased to become resurrected; thus the dead become reborn and alive again (Boelderl and Mayr 1995).

The term *undead* also may be used in reference to what are known as ghosts. Ghosts, however, are incorporeal; that is, they do not have a material presence. They are the disembodied and restless spirits of deceased individuals and cannot be touched, nor can they physically touch the living. Underlying belief in ghosts is the common need to confirm that once the body is dead there is a continuation of the life force in an afterlife. The souls or spirits of individuals take form as bodiless presences, or ghosts. Many cultures have traditions concerning the ghosts of ancestors. These ancestor spirits or ghosts are often known as the "living dead" only when they are held in the memory of the living (Mbiti 1970). As time progresses, memories of certain ancestors fade in the living, and eventually these individuals are forgotten and become ghosts without names (Mbiti 1970). For example, among the Lugbara of Uganda there are two types of undead ghosts. The first are ghosts who are nameless and called *ancestors.* These are dead relatives who have faded from the memories of their descendants. The second are ghosts of relatives who have recently died. The living rely on these ghosts for aid against their daily misfortunes (Middleton 1971:488).

In different cultures, people describe and perceive the presence of ghosts differently. Ghosts are often observed to be wearing white sheets—an image that undoubtedly arises from the shrouds or winding-sheets used to wrap corpses before they are placed in their graves. Ghosts come in a wide variety of shapes and kinds, however. Some are transparent. Some are lifelike apparitions of their former selves, whereas others are horribly gaunt, with empty faces, devoid of eyes and lips. Not all ghosts take human or even vaguely human form: Phantom horses frequently appear, as do phantom dogs and large birds, and ghost lore is full of accounts of ghost trains, ghost stagecoaches, and, of course, phantom ships such as the *Flying Dutchman* (Lehmann and Myers 1989:304).

These animated incorporeal undead are for the most part benevolent and benign. Many of them have died "good deaths" (Bloch and Parry 1982:16) and are helpful ghosts or spirits. Still, there are those undead whom the living do not want to return, and some cultures may create cults of the dead to help deal with the loss and fear they feel toward the deceased (Malefijt 1968). In addition, the malevolent undead may have been unsavory or vengeful people when alive—monsters in life, so they would naturally become monsters in death. They may have been people who were averted from their path to the afterlife by supernatural forces, or they may have died "bad deaths" (Bloch and Parry 1982:16). Newcomb (1940) quotes a Navajo medicine man: "After the spirit has gone there is something evil about the body which none of the Navajos understand, and of which they are afraid" (p. 75). The ancient Maya believed the underworld, or Xibalba, to be heavily populated with ugly, evil mutants. They are depicted in Maya art as "creatures that were skeletal, hermaphroditic, anthropomorphic, and zoomorphic" (Jacobi 2000:38). The names the Maya gave to the underworld spirits were of such misfortunes as "disease, old age, sacrifice and war, and were often depicted with black marks, representing decaying flesh, as well as bony bodies and distended bellies" (Schele and Miller 1986:268). In Maya art, depictions of the spirits of Xibalba show individuals with "farts so pungent that they emerge in huge scrolls, and their breath is so foul it is visible" (Schele and Miller 1986:268). These visual manifestations encapsulate the fear of the living toward ugly and malevolent spirits. The living do not want such spirits to return, but they animate the undead to provide mental and physical outlets through which they can express their own fears. One can curse at, plead with, cry out to, hate, and physically strike back at the malevolent undead; one can blame them for all of one's misfortunes (bad luck, disease, and death). The malevolent undead are a needed construct of humanity.

The cosmology of the Netsilik Eskimos includes a number of malevolent supernatural forces, some of which represent the human undead. A shaman might acquire the help of one group of spirits, the *tunraqs,* as a gift from another shaman or through the spirits' decision to associate with the shaman. The *tunraqs,* which are ghosts of dead men, could even be related to the shaman (e.g., they may include the shaman's grandfather; Balikci 1967). The *tunraqs* are supposed to be helpful spirits. They help to lessen the impacts of the actions of malevolent spirits who try to bring sickness and other types of misfortune to the Eskimos. According to Balikci (1967), even though the *tunraq* spirits are helpful, they can also be very independent: One "spirit called Orpingalik . . . used to attack his master Anaidjuq suddenly from behind and pull out his genitals; the unfortunate shaman, after much yelling, could recover these during a trance" (p. 195). Evil ghosts, such as the ghosts of men who felt that magic killed them while they were in bed, are especially feared in Netsilik Eskimo culture. When *tunraq* spirits are evil, they are the most feared of the evil spirits. If a shaman sends a *tunraq* spirit on a mission and the spirit fails in that mission, the spirit will turn on its master and could cause sickness and death to the master, his relatives, and other Netsilik in the shaman's camp. Then other shamans need to assist in turning away the evil *tunraq* with even more powerful *tunraqs* that they have enlisted to help them (Balikci 1967).

Among the Navajo, "bad deaths" include deaths caused by unforeseen acts of nature, such as lightning strikes. Kluckhohn (1967) quotes one story about such a death:

It was almost dark and that man was standing in the door of that same hogan. His wife and kids were outside getting in the sheep. All at once lightning struck that man and killed him. His wife and kids ran away and didn't even go back in the hogan to get their things. They never went back and that man is still where they left him. (P. 213)

According to Ward (1980), Navajos who die bad deaths—such as through drowning, murder, or suicide—should not be touched, therefore many of them go unburied. Violation of this taboo might force a ghost to return and harm the living.

The animation of both good and malevolent incorporeal and corporeal undead is a direct result of various event-related individual or group actions. The malevolent undead may be animated through a variety of events: An individual could die a bad death, or could misidentify a living person as someone who is dead; an individual might mistake a normal or abnormal taphonomic process for a sign of the undead returning, or strike up a discussion with a dead person about a certain topic; or an individual might neglect to pay tribute to his or her dead ancestors, or physically create a living or dead enemy through aggression, or even write about the undead.

THE MISTAKEN MALEVOLENT UNDEAD: THE MALEVOLENT UNDEAD AT FIRST CONTACT

In the early 1930s, when the Australian explorer Michael Leahy traveled to unexplored areas of Papua New Guinea to search for gold, he became the first person from the outside world to contact the inhabitants of this remote highland region. His extensive notes, photos, and film footage went unnoticed for 50 years, until Bob Connolly and Robin Anderson rediscovered them and created both a documentary film and a book titled *First Contact* (1987). The book and film include interviews with Leahy as well as his brothers and others who were on the expedition in addition to interviews with members of the Mount Hagan highland tribe who were present at first contact. The interviews with the tribe members are important because they provide recollections of what exactly the tribe's men and women believed the Leahy brothers represented. The people of Mount Hagan believed the white men were spirits, the returning ghosts of loved ones and ancestors. They even believed they recognized the white men as certain relatives:

We'd never seen white men before—that's why we thought they must be our own returning dead—and my mother thought Mick Leahy was the spirit of my dead father, who had come to take me.... One day we were digging for earthworms—well out of sight of the white man's camp. Mick . . . came up to us and took me. My mother began to cry and said, "Don't go away!" Mick took me, telling my mother, "I will look after him, and he'll grow big, and then come back and talk to you people."... My mother wasn't sure if Mick

was my dead father, and she hesitated to let me go in case they killed me. But our village was some distance away, and she had to go. But she said she would come back next morning and find out what they'd done to me. (Quoted in Connolly and Anderson 1987:160–61)

Among the tribespeople, there was no doubt that the white men were the dead. One of Michael Leahy's companions was a man named Michael Dwyer, who happened to have false teeth. One of the highlanders recounts that this white man pulled out his teeth, and "'when we saw this everyone just ran in all directions.' . . . Teeth might fall from a dead man's skull, but surely not from the living" (p. 38). When the highlanders spied on the strangers while they were bathing in the river, some highlanders at first came to the conclusion that the white men were not the returning dead, they were just men; after all, they had penises just the same as all of the tribesmen. However, while the white men bathed, the highlanders saw white foam (soap suds) surround and cover their bodies. The highlanders thought this foam "was the pus coming from a dead person's skin, like the milky part from the rotten flesh" (p. 46). When the strangers went to the river to pan for gold, it appeared to the highlanders that the white men were "sifting the gravel for their own bones" (p. 51). Even legend fueled the highlanders' fear of these malevolent white spirits. Their tribal lore included stories of "giant white beings with fangs who could crack open trees with loud explosions and who hunted men" (p. 104).

The strange appearance of Leahy's group and the shootings of Mount Hagen people that eventually took place (set off by the theft of supplies and the fact that Leahy and his companions felt that their lives and the lives of their carriers were in danger) became ingrained in the psyches of the Mount Hagen people. Even today, they keep quiet about dead relatives. They do not welcome them back from the dead as they did at first contact. They remember stories about the wild spirits that came and killed people, and these stories are the cause of much fear among the tribespeople (Connolly and Anderson 1987).

WILL THE REAL UNDEAD RISE? THE REVENANT AND THE VAMPIRE

Sometimes people animate the dead because of ignorance about taphonomic processes. Often, they mistake the details of the process of human decomposition for signs of life. The living may focus on certain aspects of a dead body and come to fear that the dead may walk again to harm the living. In the famous story of Peter Plogojowitz from the third decade of the 1700s, as recounted by Barber (1988:6–7), we get a view of how the vampire took form as a malevolent entity. Plogojowitz died and was buried. Then, some 10 weeks after his death, the village he had lived in experienced misfortune. Within the span of a week, nine other people died after an illness that lasted

24 hours. Individuals who were on their deathbeds said that Peter Plogojowitz came to them while they slept and "laid himself on them, and throttled them, so that they would have to give up the ghost" (p. 6). These accounts by several individuals who then died created fear among other villagers. They knew that certain signs would indicate if Plogojowitz were indeed a vampire. They speculated that the evidence would include a lack of decomposition, and the body may even have enlarged since its burial, due to its feasting on the living. Further, they expected that there would be obvious hair and nail growth. Plogojowitz's body was exhumed, and the following horrors were noted by the imperial provisor of the Gradisk District:

> The hair and beard—even the nails, of which the old ones had fallen away—had grown on him; the old skin . . . had peeled away and a new fresh one had emerged under it. The face, hands, and feet, and the whole body were so constituted, that they could not have been more complete in his lifetime. . . . I saw some fresh blood in his mouth, which, according to the common observation, he had sucked from the people killed by him. In short, all the indications were present that such people (as remarked above) are said to have . . . all the subjects with great speed, sharpened a stake . . . and put this at his heart, whereupon, as he was pierced, not only did much blood, completely fresh, flow also through his ears and mouth, but still other wild signs (which I pass by out of high respect) took place. (Quoted in Barber 1988:6–7)

The story of Peter Plogojowitz provides a classic example of the creation of a vampire—an undead being that is undergoing the process of transformation to a creature that might be interested in blood (Barber 1988).

As noted above, *revenant* is a generic term used to refer to all animated undead. Accounts of some of the more well-known types of malevolent undead come from Europe, but vampires are not solely a creation or construct of Eastern Europeans—vampire legends are a worldwide phenomenon. Vampires appear in one form or another in many cultures: the *obayifo* and *asasabonsam* (Ashanti) and the *asiman* (Dahomeans) of Africa; the *fifollet* or *feu-follet* of African Americans in Louisiana; the American vampires of New England; the *loogaroo* of Haiti; the *asema* of Surinam; the *sukuyan* of Trinidad; the *Dakhanavar* of Armenia; the *yara-ma-yha-who* of the Australian Aborigines; the *opyri* or *vipir, vepir, vapir,* the *obur,* and the *ustrel* of Bulgaria; the *chiang-shih* or *kiang-shi* of China; the *upír* and *nelapsi* of the Czech Republic and Slovakia; the *dhampirs* and *mulo* of the Gypsies of Eastern Europe; the *Nachtzehrer* or *Bluatsauger* of Germany; the *lamiai, empusai, mormolykiai, strige, callicantzaros,* and *vrykolakas* of Greece; the *rakshasas,* the *yatu-dhana* or *hatu-dhana,* the *pisachas,* the *bhutas, vetalas,* or *betails,* and the goddess Kali of India; the *kappa* of Japan; the *lampir* of Bosnia; the *Camazotz* of the Maya of Central America; the *Tlalteuctli, Coatlicue, Cihuacoatl, Itzpapalotl, Cihuateteo,* and *Tlahuelpuchi* of the Aztecs of Mexico; the *thaye* and *tasei* of Myanmar; the *aswang, danag,* and *mandurugo* of the Philippines; the *upier, upierzyca,* and *vjesci* of Poland; the *langsuyar, pontianak,* and *penanggalan* of Malaysia; the *Strigoi* and *Moroi* of Romania; the *uppyr* and *eretik* of Russia; the *mara* of Scandinavia; the *bruxa* of Portugal; the *Vukodlak, kosac, prikosac, tenjac,* and *lupi manari* of Croatia; the *kukuthi* or *lugat* of Albania; the *vjeshtitza* of Montenegro; the *Talamaur* of the Banks Islands in the South Pacific; the *Phi Song Nang* of Thailand; the 58 Wrathful Dieties of Tibet; and the *baobban sith* of Scotland (Melton 1994). This list, although by no means complete, illustrates the global presence of the vampire phenomenon.

The Peter Plogojowitz account shows how the decomposition of the dead plays an important part in the fears of the living. Many of the specifics of the deterioration of dead human bodies have become part of folklore. In research conducted through the Human Identification Laboratory of the Arizona State Museum, University of Arizona, Galloway (1997:140–41) defined the five stages of decomposition, beginning with remains that are fresh and progressing through early and advanced decomposition to skeletonization and finally to extreme decomposition. Galloway (1997:141), Rebmann, David, and Sorg (2000:14), Anderson (2001), and Roksandic (2002) provide definitive information on the decomposition of human remains; I summarize this information briefly below.

Fresh remains (first stage), whether they be burned or not, include flesh with little change to the surface or exterior of the body. There is no discoloration of the body. Within the body, bacteria are hard at work, decomposing tissues. No smell is obvious to humans, but dogs can detect fresh remains from a distance. No insect activity is obvious.

Early decomposition (second stage) is characterized by a change in color of the cadaver. First, the color is of a "pink-white appearance," which changes to a gray and then to green discoloration; then a brownish discoloration becomes apparent at the fingers, nose, and ears (Galloway 1997:141). There is a progression to a green color on a bloated body, and finally the color darkens from green to brown to black discoloration seen in the arms and legs. Odor from the remains is noticeable to humans and animals at a distance (Rebmann et al. 2000:14). The appearance of the body in early decomposition includes bloating from internal body gases, skin slippage, and hair loss, with some areas of the body looking fresh while other areas are bloated. After bloating, the skin can get a leathery appearance. Insects are present, helping with decomposition (Galloway 1997; Rebmann et al. 2000).

In advanced decomposition (third stage), the flesh on the body collapses due to body gases escaping, with a "caving in of the abdominal cavity, often accompanied by extensive maggot activity" (Galloway 1997:141; see also Rebmann et al. 2000). Remaining flesh can be black in color (Rebmann et al. 2000). Mummification takes place in environments conducive to this process. Moist decomposition includes beginnings of bone exposure and the development of adipocere, a soapy, crumbly material that forms from soft tissue after it has been in a water environment for a while. The odor of the remains is strong and easily discernible by humans and animals at a distance (Rebmann et al. 2000).

During skeletonization (fourth stage), the tissues undergo liquefaction. Decayed tissues liquefy and penetrate the surrounding dirt matrix. Bone becomes dry, with some remaining human grease. The odor of the remains becomes weaker. It may smell "cheesy or musty," and animals can detect this smell from a distance (Rebmann et al. 2000:14). Finally, the bone becomes a dry bone skeleton.

In extreme decomposition (fifth stage), the skeleton itself undergoes deterioration due to the natural elements. Exposure to sun will bleach bones and cause them to dry and crack. Bone will exfoliate in this fifth stage. The body may have a "musty odor," and an animal cannot detect the odor from as far away as during earlier stages (Rebmann et al. 2000).

Other signs of decomposition that figure into the folklore of the revenant and the vampire, as Glaister and Rentoul (1966) note, include the enlargement of the face, enlargement of the scrotum or vulva, the appearance of blisters of all sizes on the body, the dropping off of fingernails and toenails; the liquefaction of the eyeballs, and, perhaps most important for folklore, the exuding of a fluid mixed with blood from the mouth and nose.

The effects of decomposition, added to the manifestations of a disease, help to account for descriptions of vampires in New England. Among the signs of vampires reported by individuals in New England during the late 1700s through the later 1800s are the usual observations one might expect of a decomposing body in a grave: bloated chest, long fingernails, and blood issuing from the mouth. However, the presence of tuberculosis also played an important part in creating the vampire lore of New England. Tuberculosis is a disease that causes the sufferer to waste away. Persons with tuberculosis "'lose flesh,' despite the fact that they remained active, desirous of sustenance, and maintained a fierce will to live" (Brown 1941; quoted in Sledzik and Bellantoni 1994:271). These physical and mental characteristics helped to fuel belief in vampires among some New Englanders. People afflicted with tuberculosis desired to live but were wasting away. In addition, they coughed up blood-streaked sputum (Hetherington and Eshleman 1958); this appearance of blood at the mouth paralleled what the New Englanders knew of the vampires of Europe. Tuberculosis is also highly contagious, spreading rapidly among individuals who live in crowded conditions. If a person died of the disease, it was likely that he or she had also infected relatives or other individuals who were living in close proximity. In perpetuation of the vampire myth, it would appear that the dead individual came back as a malevolent undead being to feast off those close relatives. The victims would show evidence of this draining by appearing to waste away (Sledzik and Bellantoni 1994).

J. R. Cole (1888) describes a case involving six sisters in which such feasting by the malevolent undead was halted. Michael Bell presents this account in his book *Food for the Dead* (2001):

> In the old West Stafford graveyard the tragedy of exhuming a dead body and burning the heart and lungs was once enacted—a weird night scene. Of a family consisting of six sisters, five had died in rapid succession of galloping consumption [tuberculosis]. The old superstition in such cases is that the vital organs of the dead still retain a certain flicker of vitality and by some strange process absorb the vital forces of the living, and they quote in evidence apocryphal instances wherein exhumation has revealed a heart and lungs still fresh and living, encased in rotting and slimy integuments, and in which, after burning these portions of the defunct, a living relative, else doomed and hastening to the grave, has suddenly and miraculously recovered. The ceremony of cremation of the vitals of the dead must be conducted at night by a single individual and at the open grave in order that the results may be decisive. In 1872, the Boston Health Board Reports describe a case in which such a midnight cremation was actually performed during that year. (Pp. 161–62)

CONVERSATIONS WITH THE MALEVOLENT UNDEAD

The living often want to persuade the dead not to interfere with or harm the living. The living also often converse with the dead for other reasons, such as to describe current happenings, to ask about what the afterlife is like for the dead, to ask the dead to undertake specific actions on behalf of the living, and to create a dialogue that allows the living to understand why someone died.

Historically, among the Mandan Indians of North America a proper funeral ceremony was conducted by the village members upon the death of an individual. The body of the deceased was outfitted in clothing and supplies that represented what that individual would need if he or she were to embark on a journey of a few days' duration. The body was then wrapped in buffalo skin and placed on a scaffold in an area away from the village where there were other scaffolds. The deceased would then be considered a member of a "village of the dead" (Catlin 1975:146). Village members would visit this village of the dead daily, to mourn. Eventually, the scaffolds and the flesh of the dead would deteriorate and the skeletal remains and scaffold pieces would fall to the ground. The skulls would then be picked up and placed in a circle that included about a hundred skulls "placed some eight or nine inches from each other with the faces all looking to the center" (Catlin 1975:147). Family members of the deceased would know which skulls were those of their relations. The skull circle served as a focal point for meeting the dead, as George Catlin (1975), who studied the Indians in the 1800s, describes:

> Independent of the duties which draw the women to this spot, they visit it from inclination, and linger upon it to converse with the dead. There is scarcely an hour on a pleasant day

when some of these women may not be seen sitting or laying by the skull of their child or husband—talking to it in the most pleasant and endearing language they can use and seemingly getting an answer back. It is not unfrequently the case that the woman brings her needle-work with her, spending the greater part of the day sitting by the side of the skull of her child, chatting incessantly with it, while she is embroidering or garnishing a pair of Moccasins. Then, perhaps, overcome with fatigue, she falls asleep, with her arms encircled around it, forgetting herself for hours. Afterward she gathers up her things and returns to the village. (P. 147)

Talking to the dead is a universal practice that continues throughout the modern world. People in modern rural Alabama, and in Chicago, and in Osaka, Japan, go to cemeteries, lay offerings on or next to graves, and talk to the dead individuals buried there. One group that takes the practice of conversation with the dead to a passionate and highly involved level is the Sora of eastern India. For the Sora, conversation with the dead is a daily exercise, and participating in such conversation is a way of dealing with issues surrounding death. A conversation may be as simple as a single living individual talking to a single dead individual, or it may be very complex, involving a number of living and dead individuals. Shamans (usually female) act as mediums for the dead individuals. The discussions are synergistic: All individuals involved, both dead and alive, use these sessions to learn about each other, and, through that knowledge, both the dead and the living change. For example, they might better understand the nature of an individual's death and the feelings about that death of all the individuals, dead and alive, who may figure into the story. If a number of living participants are involved in a dialogue with several dead participants, the living often circle around the shaman, who is in a trance and provides the avenue for one or more of the dead to speak. During these sessions, the living question, argue, "persuade, cajole, tease, remind, deceive, plead," and even gossip and laugh with the dead, sometimes for hours (Vitebsky 1993:5).

Among the Sora, a dead person is known as a *sonum.* The *sonum* lives in an alternate world, a distorted world, compared with the known world of the living. In that world, "the dead keep doves as chickens and pythons as cows . . . and hunt living humans as game animals" (Vitebsky 1993:217). The *sonum* is not only an individual but a condition. A *sonum* has a dual purpose in its relationship with the living. It can be benevolent and helpful (known as an ancestor *sonum*), or it can be malevolent and punishing (known as an experience *sonum*). The Sora believe that any death or sickness is a direct result of the actions of a *sonum* (Vitebsky 1993).

An experience *sonum* does not directly kill or create a sickness for an individual. Rather, the *sonum* duplicates the symptoms of its own sickness or death and projects those symptoms and/or exact manner of death on the living. The Sora understand the *sonum*'s causing an illness or death in another person as part of the cycle of life and death. Different experience *sonums* reside in different areas, each creating its own symptoms. For example, a sun-*sonum* resides in the sun and can cause deaths due to accident or murder. An earth-*sonum* can cause death in childbirth or old age. A convulsion or epilepsy-*sonum* lives just outside a village in a "clump of bushes" (Vitebsky 1993:74) and causes convulsions and epilepsy.

Vitebsky (1993:139) relates a story that illustrates the malevolent nature of the undead in Sora society. An earth-*sonum* caused the deaths of several Sora women in childbirth. One woman named Mabmati died in childbirth and became earth-*sonum.* Mabmati duplicated the death in her niece Ra'gi, who was unmarried and pregnant. Ra'gi died in pregnancy due to an abortion gone awry; the abortion also resulted in the fetus's death. Ra'gi became earth-*sonum* and duplicated her death in her lineage-sister Gadi, who in turn duplicated the death in her sister Pui'jan.

Vitebsky (1993:164) presents a transcription of one Sora dialogue involving 19 dead persons and 3 living speakers. The Sora were trying to heal a baby stricken with diarrhea and backache caused by the lumbago-*sonum,* which is related to the sun-*sonum.* In this involved and complex dialogue, which has almost 300 speaker changes, we find out that a male *sonum* named Palda, who killed himself, is trying to kill the son of a woman named Rungkudi, who is one of the living speakers:

Palda: Hey aunt! You were happy enough to dispose of my corpse, weren't you?

Rungkudi: . . . Did your mother or father teach you to hang yourself? Did they put you up to it?

Palda: I'm not saying any of you put me up to it.

Rungkudi: So did I kill you then? Don't you try to pass on your death to your brother again. I'm not joking, if you get my boy . . . to do it I'll . . .

Palda: Only the other day I almost made him hang himself, but then I said "Hey, you, untie yourself!" I went and fetched a knife to cut him down . . . Hey, aunt, are you listening?

Palda goes on to tell the living speakers how he might be prevented from causing the death of Rungkudi's son. The ritual involves sacrificing a pig and then cutting up and burning rope. Palda leaves the dialogue and other *sonums* enter, each with issues for the living; of course, the living also have issues with the dead. One of the living, an elderly woman named Sindi, tries to prevent Rungkudi's dead daughter, Amboni, from giving her death symptoms (scars on the throat, coughing, and choking) to Rungkudi or to her living sisters.

The Sora's conversations with both the benign and the malevolent undead allow both the living and the dead to evolve. Individuals change, for the most part, in positive ways. In some cases, there is room for redemption of a *sonum.* Through their conversations with the dead, the Sora achieve a better understanding of the relationships between living individuals and dead ones. The person involved in a dialogue creates "an intimate and subtle portrait of a personality, derived from the sum of his interactions" (Vitebsky 1993:119). And when multiple living and dead individuals are involved in dialogues, the Sora people as a whole evolve, changing because they have a more defined and clearer picture of the strengths and weaknesses of the living and the histories and personalities of the dead, who become reaffirmed in the minds of the living. These conversations with the dead illustrate that the dead open relationships with the living and control those relationships. As Vitebsky (1993) notes, "The dead make the living into passive objects of *their* own activity," but the result of the dialogue is an education in life (p. 244).

THE MALEVOLENT "LIVING" VERSUS THE MALEVOLENT "UNDEAD": A NATIVE AMERICAN EXAMPLE

Throughout history, humans have been cruel in their treatment of the human body at death and after death. Decapitations and the hacking off of body parts are recorded in both the written and the archaeological record throughout the world. It is true that a good number of these decapitations and dismemberments were inflicted in the throes of battle, and some of the dismemberments happened by accident, but beyond the fact that these inflicted traumas caused death, they have another significance: Many of these dismemberments are directly related to the intent of individuals or groups to prevent the recipients of the trauma from coming back from the dead, or to prevent those individuals from attaining a particular spiritual place.

Although they were not dealing with the undead in a manner that one would equate with vampires, prehistoric and historic Native Americans had numerous methods for preventing malevolent or enemy spirits from coming back to punish the living. One of the most visible of these is found in the burial treatment of those who might have been considered threats. In most prehistoric and historic Native American interments, the individual was buried in an extended or flexed manner, on his or her back or side. Burials of individuals in a prone position—that is, lying facedown—were not as common. In fact, such burials were reserved for individuals who were different or who were enemies. At the prehistoric site of Moundville in Alabama, for example, the burials of two achondroplastic dwarves were found in the 1930s. Achondroplasia is a rare congenital malformation and is very rare in the prehistoric record. Both of the individuals were found buried facedown (Snow 1943). The unstated implication behind this mode of burial is that the living did not want these individuals to come back. Examples of similar practices have been found throughout the world. For instance, Ralph Merrifield (1987) found that in Britain during the late Roman and early Anglo-Saxon periods there were a significant number of prone burials. Merrifield asserts that the bodies were placed in this manner to ensure that the deceased did not return, as the act of prone burial separated the living from the dead and directed the dead on a journey away from the living. At the archaeological site of Mulberry Creek (1Ct27) in the Tennessee River Valley in northern Alabama, three Native American individuals were found who had been thrown in the burial pit in a haphazard fashion and covered over with dirt (Webb and DeJarnette 1942). Two of the three had projectile points embedded in their backs. These individuals were enemies to those who buried them; they were afforded the dignity of a burial, but the lack of care in how they were placed in their grave reflects disrespect.

Native Americans found that one of the most visible ways of punishing the dead was by the act of scalping. Native Americans believed that to travel successfully to an existence after death, they needed to be physically complete (Hudson 1976), and scalping precluded this. For Native Americans in the Southeast, the treatment of the body after death was of great concern. As Hudson (1976) recounts, when men were killed away from home in a raid,

> warriors would sometimes scalp one of their dead comrades themselves so that their enemies could not take the scalp. When it was possible to return and reclaim the remains of comrades fallen among the enemy, they would do so; when they could not, they wept and mourned the death of these men far more than for men who had the benefit of proper mortuary rites. It was deeply disgraceful to have one's body dismembered or left to be devoured by animals. (P. 328)

Scalping was tangible proof of an individual's success in combat. Most individuals who were scalped were already dead or died soon after the act of scalping. However, rare individuals did survive being scalped, sometimes for weeks, like one individual whose remains were found at the prehistoric site of Moundville, and sometimes longer, like another individual whose remains from the same site indicate that his scalp lesions healed totally and he lived out the rest of his life (Snow 1941). Both of these individuals would have lived what was left of their lives after their scalpings with the knowledge of their coming destiny after death and the knowledge that they would be prevented from harming the living after they died.

At the archaeological site of 1Lu59 (Bluff Creek site), excavated during the Works Progress Administration's project in the Tennessee River Valley, the burial treatment of one individual represents an interesting case of the living dealing with someone they thought to be a threat in death. As Webb and DeJarnette (1942) describe the case, the skeletal remains are of a man who was buried headless. Found across his abdomen were five human fibulae that had been sharpened to points. These fibulae may have been tools of torture used to pierce the man. In addition, evidence of a necklace made of human teeth was found in the vicinity of the individual's neck and between his elbows.

The 100 teeth that made up the necklace show evidence of holes drilled to thread cords through and grooves on the roots of the teeth to wrap cords around. It is obvious that this individual was not accorded the common treatment of a Native American at death, in that he was incomplete. This individual could have been some type of shaman, as evidenced by the necklace. The fact that the necklace included at least 10 lower-left second premolar teeth indicates that the teeth came from at least 10 different people. These teeth, although worn, show no evidence of caries development, so the deceased was not extracting teeth for the purpose of alleviating pain due to decay. All tooth classes are present: incisors, canines, premolars, and molars. All of the teeth are from adults. What did these teeth represent to the deceased individual? They were not diseased teeth. They were not the teeth of the young or of individuals who were initiates to puberty or some type of tribal fraternity. The teeth could have been the teeth of enemies, and they probably served as trophies that represented the individual's power over other living or dead individuals. The fact that this "shaman" was decapitated indicates the power the living had over this individual at his death, and their disrespect for him. The beheading was a conscious attempt to prevent the deceased from accessing the afterlife and coming back to harm the living.

When Native Americans placed additional human body parts in a burial with an individual who was complete, this represented an offering to that individual. Such human trophy elements were taken from individuals who were believed to be not worthy of being complete, or who were at least not as worthy as the individual with whom the trophy elements were buried. These unfortunate individuals were enemies or slaves. Sacrifice victims (children, tribe members, and others), in contrast, would be offered up whole, and a different status would be given to them. Regardless, the mutilated individuals would be prevented from accessing the afterlife and from coming back to harm the living. Their body parts would honor the deceased in the burial pit by virtue of being revenge. In Tennessee, at an archaeological site named Chucalissa (40SY1), which dates to the beginning of the 1400s, there are three separate burials with extra human body parts buried with them. One of the three has an individual buried with three extra human skulls (Nash 1972). Marks indicating scalping appear on two of the skulls, and one of the other skulls was painted red (Jacobi and Hill 2001). Archaeological sites in the Tennessee River Valley in northern Alabama, such as the Koger's Island site (1Lu92) and the Perry site (1Lu25), have multiple burials with deliberately placed body parts in the burial pits, specifically, skulls, hands, and feet. These skeletal offerings honor the individual; they prevent his enemies from hurting him in the afterlife and prevent those enemies from harming the living. Trophy hands and feet even accompanied some of the seven individuals who were scalped and placed in mass graves at the Koger's Island site (Bridges, Jacobi, and Powell 2000). They were

incomplete, but revenge in the form of trophy hands or feet was placed within their burial pit.

Sometimes Native Americans took the power they expressed over the dead to the level of using a human body part in a ceremony or even for everyday tasks. For example, they made simple tools out of human skeletal elements, such as a portion of human femur (Jacobi and Hill 2001). At Pinson Mound, archaeologists have found rattles made from human parietals (two parietals filled with small pebbles and fastened together with cord), decorated with elaborate designs (Mainfort 1986). These noisemakers were placed on either the arms or the legs; similar rattles made out of turtle shells were worn in the same manner (Lewis and Kneberg 1946, plates 102, 103). Native Americans also have been known to make bowls out of human skulls. At the archaeological site of Mulberry Creek (1CT27), a human skull bowl was found; it is complete with drilled holes toward the rim of the bowl that would have allowed cord to be attached so that the bowl could be hung up or suspended (Webb and DeJarnette 1942). This bowl was not found in a burial context; it most likely represents the remnants of a disrespected individual, perhaps a victim of battle, who ended up as either a utilitarian object or a ceremonial object. It is also possible that the bowl represents a Native American "attempt at keeping the legacy of some relative alive through the incorporation of a physical portion of the individual into a daily or ceremonial icon. Or, were they modifying skeletal elements of individuals who were viewed as enemies and thus exerting some kind of control or revenge over them?" (Jacobi and Hill 2001:9).

Through their actions perimortem and postmortem, Native Americans of the Southeast physically and, more important, psychologically delivered punishment to individuals who were malevolent or potentially malevolent after death. Well-known engravings by A. De Batz, Le Page Du Pratz, and Theodore DeBry (who based his work on first-person eyewitness accounts and sketches by Jacques Le Moyne) document the trophy taking and display of human remains. Drawings exist that depict individuals displaying dried scalps poles (Fundaburk [1958] 1996:48–49, ills. 113, 115), and one engraving shows the total dismemberment of a human, with nothing left but a torso. Two other engravings show trophy arms and legs hung on poles, with the remaining torsos violated in the anus with arrows and poles (Fundaburk [1958] 1996:10–11, ills. 15, 16). Native Americans who were disrespected, hated, or misunderstood during their lives would have known what would happen to their bodies at death and, in some cases, for years after. This was the inherently understood psychological punishment to the recipient. Both the physical and the psychological trauma inflicted by these actions helped Native Americans to confront their own fears of death. By continuing to use the remains of the dead, Native Americans reminded themselves of the power they had over their enemies.

THE MALEVOLENT UNDEAD AS ENTERTAINMENT: THE ANIMATED DEAD IN POPULAR CULTURE

Fear has always been a driving factor in the majority of human reactions or responses to the undead. Conversely, fascination with the dead, sometimes fascination propelled by fear, drives some humans into acceptance of, glorification of, obsession with, mimicry of, and even partnership with the undead. Since prehistoric times, humans have shown an interest in how the body works (Ackerknecht 1967, 1982; Lisowski 1967). Scientists and artists in the past fueled human fascination with the dead (and the undead) through their dissections and anatomical drawings, which provided the public with views of the inside of the human body. Hans Holbein, an artist who lived in the first half of the 1500s, produced a series of woodcuts titled *The Dance of Death.* These engravings depict a human skeleton (representing death) appearing in the lives of numerous people in all walks of life. For example, different illustrations in the series show the death skeleton standing behind the pope, playing the violin to a duchess, preventing a peddler from peddling his wares, pouring wine down the throat of a drunkard, and leading a blind man to his destiny (Holbein 1887, plates V, XXI, XXXIII, XXXIX, XLIII).

In 1543, Andreas Vesalius of Brussels, the founder of modern anatomy, created one of the greatest volumes of anatomical illustrations ever produced: *De Humani Corporis Fabrica.* Each illustration, with its accompanying anatomical labeling, is an artistic masterpiece. The title page of the volume illustrates a human dissection under way, with throngs of people straining to see, some crowding around the dissection table, others looking over their shoulders, and still others leaning over a balcony above (Saunders and O'Malley 1973:43). In the anatomical illustrations, the human body is posed in odd and striking ways. There are depictions of standing skeletons and fleshless bodies with pealed-back muscles and tendons that appear as if they are dripping or oozing off the body in the process of decomposition. The fleshless bodies also stand upright. In one illustration, a body is held upright by a rope hung around the neck; another shows a body leaning against a wall (Saunders and O'Malley 1973:103, 107). Many of the illustrations show fleshless bodies striking poses in the foreground within natural landscape scenes. In the background, towns and other structures can be seen (Saunders and O'Malley 1973:93–103). Most people today would find these depictions of fleshless figures horrific, no less than did people in the 1500s. The figures in many of the illustrations appear to walk as though alive, and although such depictions educated some of the public, others were both fascinated and frightened by them.

In the early 1800s, the vampire found its way into popular culture. Lord Byron had started a novel that was to involve a Greek vampire who fakes his own death and burial (what survives of this text today is usually referred to as "A Fragment of a Novel" or "Augustus Darvell"). The vampire's traveling companion later arrives in England and finds that the vampire is alive and feasting on Londoners (Bleiler 1966). At the time Byron was writing and plotting this novel, he was attended medically by a doctor named John Polidori. Polidori stole Byron's idea and subsequently wrote and published a story titled "The Vampyre" in an issue of the *New Monthly Magazine* in 1819 (Bleiler 1966). Even with Polidori's name on it, the public accepted the story as Byron's. The vampire soon became a popular figure. A stage play based on "The Vampyre" was produced in France in the early 1820 (Bleiler 1966), during which period the public's obsession with vampires continued. Two German operas based on Polidori's story were produced in 1828: In March, Heinrich Marschner's *Der Vampyr* was performed, and Peter Joseph Von Lindpaintner's version of the story, with the same title, was performed in September (Palmer 1992; Brown 1992).

Literature was the primary medium through which the undead continued to be part of popular culture. Thomas Preskett Prest published the amusing, campy novel *Varney the Vampire* in 1847, and Sheridan LeFanu's *Carmilla,* about a female vampire, was published in 1872. However, two novels that appeared in the 1800s rise above the rest: *Frankenstein,* by Mary Shelley, published in 1818; and *Dracula,* by Bram Stoker, published in 1897. These two works brought the malevolent undead to the mass public and created a foundation for the expanded elaboration of the undead mythos that continues to this day. These classic novels encapsulate all the centuries of humankind's fear of and fascination with the dead. From *Frankenstein:*

> It was on a dreary night of November that I beheld the accomplishment of my toils. . . . It was already one in the morning . . . when, by the glimmer of the half-extinguished light, I saw the dull yellow eye of the creature open; it breathed hard, and a convulsive motion agitated its limbs.
>
> How can I describe my emotions at this catastrophe, or how delineate the wretch whom with such infinite pains and care I had endeavoured to form? His limbs were in proportion, and I had selected his features as beautiful. Beautiful! Great God! His yellow skin scarcely covered the work of muscles and arteries beneath; his hair was of a lustrous black, and flowing; his teeth of a pearly whiteness; but these luxuriances only formed a more horrid contrast with his watery eyes, that seemed almost of the same colour as the dun-white sockets in which they were set, his shrivelled complexion and straight black lips. (Shelley [1818] 1981:42)

From *Dracula:*

> "Ah, you believe now?"
>
> I answered: "Do not press me too hard all at once. I am willing to accept. How will you do this bloody work?
>
> "I shall cut off her head and fill her mouth with garlic, and I shall drive a stake through her body." It made me shudder to think of so mutilating the body of the woman whom I had loved. (Stoker [1897] 1992:207)

The malevolent undead continue to figure as major characters in the literature of today. Public interest in the undead seems to lie with vampires in particular. Novelist Anne Rice, with her contribution to the vampire mythos through her creation of the vampire Lestat and other vampire characters (introduced in *Interview With the Vampire* in 1977 and since populating numerous sequels and other novels), keeps vampires continuously in the public eye. In her books there are good vampires and bad vampires, and all vampires are very erotic. Numerous other authors also add to the proliferation of vampire literature. Chelsea Quinn Yarbro has produced a series of books, starting with *Hotel Transylvania* (1979), that chronicle the exploits of the vampire Count Saint-Germain. Brian Lumley brings us numerous vampires and vampire conflicts in his multivolume Necroscope books and spin-offs (see, e.g., Lumley 1986). Laurell K. Hamilton has created a series of books featuring a character named Anita Blake, a vampire hunter and zombie hunter (see, e.g., Hamilton 1993), and Stephen King has included vampires in his horror fiction in *Salem's Lot* (1976). Sherlock Holmes has met Dracula (Estleman 1978) and so have the Hardy Boys and Nancy Drew (Larson and Sloan 1978). P. N. Elrod (1990, 1995) has brought us the vampires Jack Fleming, a reporter, and Jonathan Barrett, among a number of her other vampire creations. And of course there is Sonja Blue, the vampire in sunglasses created by Nancy A. Collins (1992). Numerous romance novels also feature vampires as protagonists; titles include *Vampire Lover* (Lamb 1994), *The Vampire Viscount* (Harbaugh 1995), and *Love Bites* (St. George 1995).

In Western popular culture today, we even use vampires to educate and entertain children. On the popular children's television series *Sesame Street,* a character called the Count (who bears a resemblance to Count Dracula) helps children learn about numbers. A children's book titled *Let's Count, Dracula* (Benjamin 1992) does the same thing. Beyond the vampire rabbit of *Monty Python and the Holy Grail,* a vampire rabbit named Bunnicula is a character in a popular children's book series (see, e.g., Howe and Howe 1979). In the children's book *Vampires Don't Wear Polka Dots* (Dadey and Jones 1990), teachers are vampires, and vampires are featured in at least one installment in the Babysitters Club mystery book series (Martin 1994).

In addition, vampires and other undead creatures are often featured in comic books. Anne Rice's books have been adapted by Innovation Comics, and Marvel Comics has offered vampire comic creations such as *Count Duckula, Morbius,* and *Tomb of Dracula.* Perhaps one of the most erotic female vampire creations in comics is Vampirella, whose stories are published by Harris Comics. In addition to those mentioned, numerous other vampire creations are offered monthly by various comic book publishers.

Television has brought vampires to the public in numerous series. In the late 1960s and early 1970s, the successful soap opera *Dark Shadows* featured the good/bad vampire Barnabas Collins; spin-off books by Marilyn Ross chronicling the lives of the program's characters also became popular (e.g., Ross 1968). Vampires have appeared in television in many different kinds of programs, including *The Addams Family; Count Duckula; Doctor Who; Fantasy Island; The Flintstones; Forever Knight; F Troop; Get Smart; Happy Days; Kolchak: The Night Stalker; Love, American Style; The Man From U.N.C.L.E.; The Monkees; The Munsters; The Phil Silvers Show; Rod Serling's Night Gallery; The Sonny and Cher Comedy Hour; Starsky and Hutch;* and *Tales From the Darkside* (Jones 1993). In recent years, we have become acquainted with *Buffy the Vampire Slayer,* a successful television show based on a Hollywood movie. The character of Buffy kicked her way onto television and subsequently into numerous merchandising opportunities that keep her, her associates, and good and evil vampires in our daily lives.

Hundreds of movies have been made involving vampires and other undead creatures, since the time when movies were silent and even earlier, when movies were called "2-minute trick films." An early trick film made by Georges Méliès in 1896, *The Haunted Castle,* has some familiar vampire trappings, such as a bat, a medieval castle, and a crucifix that destroys the devil (Jones 1993). The silent film *Nosferatu,* made in Germany in 1922, is the earliest screen adaptation of Bram Stoker's *Dracula* (Jones 1993). Different versions of *Dracula* and other vampire movies have been made in many different countries, showing the cross-cultural appeal of the undead in entertainment. Vampire movies have been made in the United States, England, France, Italy, Spain, Germany, Ceylon, Mexico, Malaya, Turkey, Argentina, Japan, South Korea, Philippines, Morocco, Poland, Brazil, Hong Kong, Russia, Switzerland, the Netherlands, Belgium, Singapore, India, Canada, Yugoslavia, Austria, Romania, Colombia, Thailand, Greece, Czechoslovakia, Australia, China, Finland, and Venezuela. Stephen Jones (1993) has produced an illustrated movie guide that can help you find the vampire movie of your choice, anything from the classic *Dracula* to movies with titles such as *Dracula Sucks, Mama Dracula, Love at First Bite, I Married a Vampire, Kung Fu Vampire Buster, Scream Blacula Scream, Vampires on Bikini Beach,* and *Toothless Vampires.* Vampires even appear in stage musicals, such as *Dance of the Vampires,* and stage plays; the classic Dracula story has been adapted for the stage many times.

Games and related merchandise involving the undead are popular among certain sectors of the public today. For example, Warner Bros. makes a Buffy the Vampire Slayer board game, and the U.S. Playing Card Company sells a game called Zombies. Role-playing games such as Ravenloff, by TSR, and Vampire: The Masquerade, by White Wolf, are popular. In Vampire: The Masquerade, participants create good or malevolent characters, which they role-play in scenarios monitored by a "gamemaster" or "dungeonmaster."

Obsession with the undead is widespread in modern popular culture. There are vampire- and zombie-themed rock groups, such as Desmo Donte, Type O Negative, and White Zombie. There is even a Japanese rock star who claims to believe that he is a 400-year-old vampire from the Netherlands. *Vampyre Magazine* includes a section called "The Sanguinarium Directory" that lists various vampire churches, societies, fan clubs, newsgroups, and Web sites (Melanie and Todd 2001). There are vampire boutiques, vampire corset and leather stores, vampire jewelry and cosmetics stores, and vampire art galleries. There are stores that offer casket furniture for modern-day wannabe vampires. Fangsmiths will help you to achieve the perfect vampire smile through dental filing. There is a Vampire Research Foundation and an interactive vampire dinner theater (Melanie and Todd 2001). There are underground vampire clubs and goth bars that serve a vampire cocktail known as the blood clot. At some underground vampire bars, razor blades are handed out at the door for attendees to use, possibly to participate in the dangerous behavior of exchanging blood with their loved ones.

As these numerous examples show, the undead are everywhere in popular culture. In some cultures today the evil undead are not feared; rather, they are creations in the stories told through different media. In most of these societies humans do not truly believe in the undead; rather, the undead serve as symbols for evil that is confronted and defeated by the living. However, in some cultures, even though the undead are prevalent in popular media, there remains very real belief in both the incorporeal and the corporeal undead. The undead are a necessary part of daily life in these cultures.

THE FUNCTION OF THE UNDEAD IN SOCIETIES

The idea that ghosts, vampires, zombies and other undead entities actually exist may sound silly to many of us in Western society. However, the concept of the undead is very real and serves as an important thanatological symbol in a large number of cultures. Most humans feel the need to know that there is something after death. Cultures construct variations on the concept of the undead in their attempts to help individuals understand death and the existence that is known as the afterlife.

Cultures create animated corporeal and incorporeal undead entities to help describe the processes of death as well as hoped-for outcomes/results of death. Both benign and malevolent undead function to aid humans in understanding the physical and spiritual aspects of death. Benign animated ghosts and the tangible animated undead are important only when there is a dichotomous relationship/partnership with the malevolent undead. Humans need the malevolent undead to explain things they do not understand and to take the blame for misfortune. The existence of the malevolent undead provides a way for

members of a culture to explain the unexpected deaths of loved ones, or to blame something outside themselves when bad things befall an individual or a group.

Anthropologists examine the concept of the undead across four subfields: linguistic anthropology, cultural anthropology, physical anthropology, and archaeology. Most cultures have linguistic terms for corporeal and incorporeal representations of the undead, as evidenced by the numerous names for vampires throughout the world mentioned above. Often, the terms by which undead entities are known in a culture are specific to that culture and its ways of relating to the dead. Although the concept of vampires or the undead in general is present in many cultures, explanations for the existence of the undead, the reasons given for why they help or punish the living, and the ways in which members of a society confront the undead and accept, reject, or defeat them are not the same cross-culturally.

Physical anthropologists find the undead interesting because the examination of taphonomic processes, which includes the study of decomposition of human remains, offers insights into why people in the past have viewed the undead as being in fact alive. For example, in the past, people may have viewed the bloating that is part of the decomposition of a body as evidence that an undead individual had risen from the grave and feasted on the blood of the living. Or the movement of maggots in and around a corpse may have made it look as if it were alive.

Archaeologists and physical anthropologists who are involved in skeletal analysis attempt to understand the actions of past cultures and their responses to the undead by examining human skeletal remains for evidence of certain types of trauma. Cut marks on a skull are evidence of scalping; the absence of a head, hand, or foot is a mark of mutilation. Both types of trauma, usually inflicted perimortem, shed light on a culture's belief in the necessity of entering the afterworld physically complete. If one is incomplete, one is denied access. Perimortem scalpings, decapitations, and amputations were preemptive strikes against those individuals who might, if they were whole, come back as malevolent spirits.

CONCLUSION

Children sometimes hold their breath as they pass by cemeteries to avoid inhaling the bad spirits of the dead, which could cause the children's own death. This seems like a silly superstition, but the threat of cemetery air was very real to me and my friends as we were growing up around the city of Chicago. Even though a good bit of my everyday work involves the dead, I still pause and think about that superstition when I pass the cemeteries I know from my childhood in and around Chicago. At the core of this superstition is a very real fear of the dead, of dying, and of the dead who are malevolent. Such fear of the dead, and especially of the dead who are malevolent, is pervasive in human cultures.

Spiritual constructs, both benign and malevolent, are necessary creations that once animated in the minds of humans help provide mental and physical explanations for the deaths of individuals and for the process of dying. Both benign and malevolent undead creations enable living persons to confront and transcend their own fears of death. The benign undead are important manifestations, but not nearly as beneficial as the malevolent undead to the mental and physical constitution of an individual or a group. It is the malevolent undead who help feed the fear, quiet the fear, explain the disaster, and provoke and prevent the human response.

Events in the lives of people animate the malevolent undead. Among the Navajo, strange deaths, such as a death caused by a lightning strike, were believed to create situations that might release malevolent spirits. In New Guinea, when the inhabitants of Mount Hagan first encountered the Leahy expedition, they approached with caution and fear because they saw animated ghosts. One of their first reactions was to raise their axes in shock and defense, because they thought the ghosts were probably malevolent. Then one New Guinea native recognized that one of the ghosts was in fact a relative returned from the dead. Later, after members of the Leahy expedition killed some of the New Guinea highlanders, these "ghosts," in the minds of some native inhabitants, remained malevolent.

Among Europeans and New Englanders, series of deaths from unknown causes created fear that malevolent undead entities had returned to cause disease and death. The solution for the misfortune was to exhume a body and inspect it for known signs of a vampire, and then the natural process of decomposition animated the people's beliefs in malevolent entities. The remedy in such situations was to drive a stake through the heart of the corpse or to burn the remains. Once this was done, the situation was understood.

The Mandan Indians of North America participated in conversations with the malevolent undead that helped the participants understand their own misfortunes or those of family members. Among the Sora of India, a shaman is the vehicle through which benign and malevolent spirits voice their opinions to the living while the living verbally challenge and question the dead. The resulting conversations are emotional and combative, with the malevolent undead admitting to their participation in misfortune, relating the causes of their own deaths and why they made other relations die from similar causes. From these discussions with the malevolent undead, the Sora gain understanding about why certain unfortunate events occurred, and that understanding allows them to control current and possibly future situations.

Among prehistoric and historic Native Americans of the Southeast, burial in a prone position, decapitation, scalping, trophy taking and display of human body parts, and use of human bone in utilitarian or ceremonial ways served as preemptive mental and physical deterrents toward potential and known malevolent enemies who, once dead, might return as undead bent on harming the living.

The malevolent undead are pervasive in current popular culture. They are described in literature and depicted in television programs, movies, stage plays, musicals, operas, and games. The influence of the undead can be seen in the ways some people dress, adorn themselves, cosmetically alter their teeth, listen to music, drink alcohol, use computers, and worship. The undead, malevolent or not, even take part in the education of our children. It is surprising that the malevolent undead have gained such prominence in the psyches of individuals and cultures. This prominence is evidence of human beings' continuing fear of and fascination with death, which governs and guides our actions in response to unexpected events.

REFERENCES

Ackerknecht, Erwin H. 1967. "Primitive Surgery." Pp. 631–50 in *Diseases in Antiquity,* edited by Don Brothwell and A. T. Sandison. Springfield, IL: Charles C Thomas.

———. 1982. *A Short History of Medicine,* rev. ed. Baltimore: Johns Hopkins University Press.

Akashi, T. 1880. "Experiences With Fugu Poisoning." *Iji Shimbum* 27:19–23.

Anderson, Gail S. 2001. "Insect Succession on Carrion and Its Relationship to Determining Time of Death." Pp. 143–75 in *Forensic Entomology: The Utility of Arthropods in Legal Investigations,* edited by Jason H. Byrd and James L. Castner. Boca Raton, FL: CRC.

Balikci, Asen. 1967. "Shamanistic Behavior Among the Netsilik Eskimos." Pp. 191–209 in *Magic, Witchcraft and Curing,* edited by John Middleton. Austin: University of Texas Press.

Barber, Paul. 1988. *Vampires, Burial, and Death: Folklore and Reality.* New Haven, CT: Yale University Press.

Bell, Michael. 2001. *Food for the Dead: On the Trail of New England's Vampires.* New York: Carroll & Graf.

Benjamin, Alan. 1992. *Let's Count, Dracula.* New York: Simon & Schuster.

Bleiler, E. F. 1966. "John Polidori and the Vampyre." Pp. xxxi–xl in *Three Gothic Novels,* edited by E. F. Bleiler. New York: Dover.

Bloch, Maurice and Jonathan Parry. 1982. "Introduction: Death and the Regeneration of Life." Pp. 1–44 in *Death and the Regeneration of Life,* edited by Maurice Bloch and Jonathan Parry. Cambridge: Cambridge University Press.

Boelderl, Artur R. and Daniela F. Mayr. 1995. "The Undead and the Living Dead: Images of Vampires and Zombies in Contemporary Culture." *Journal of Psychohistory* 23: 51–65.

Bridges, Patricia S., Keith P. Jacobi, and Mary Lucas Powell. 2000. "Warfare-Related Trauma in the Late Prehistory of Alabama." Pp. 35–62 in *Bioarchaeological Studies of Life in the Age of Agriculture: A View From the Southeast,* edited by Patricia M. Lambert. Tuscaloosa: University of Alabama Press.

Brown, Clive. 1992. "Der Vampyr II." P. 892 in *New Grove Dictionary of Opera,* vol. 4, edited by Stanley Sadie. London: Macmillan.

Brown, L. 1941. *The Story of Clinical Pulmonary Tuberculosis.* Baltimore: Williams & Wilkins.

Catlin, George. 1975. *Letters and Notes on the North American Indians.* New York: Clarkson N. Potter.

Cole, J. R. 1888. *The History of Tollund County, Connecticut.* New York: W. W. Preston.

Collins, Nancy A. 1992. *In the Blood.* New York: Roc.

Connolly, Bob and Robin Anderson. 1987. *First Contact: New Guinea's Highlanders Encounter the Outside World.* New York: Viking Penguin.

Dadey, Debbie and Marcia Thornton Jones. 1990. *Vampires Don't Wear Polka Dots.* New York: Scholastic.

Davis, Wade. 1987. *The Serpent and the Rainbow.* New York: Warner.

———. 1988. *Passage of Darkness: The Ethnobiology of the Haitian Zombie.* Chapel Hill: University of North Carolina Press.

Elrod, P. N. 1990. *Bloodlist.* New York: Ace.

———. 1995. *Death Masque.* New York: Ace.

Estleman, Loren D. 1978. *Sherlock Holmes vs. Dracula; or, The Adventure of the Sanguinary Count.* New York: Penguin.

Fundaburk, Emma Lila, ed. [1958] 1996. *Southeastern Indians: Life Portraits: A Catalogue of Pictures 1564–1860.* Tallahassee, FL: Rose.

Galloway, Alison. 1997. "The Process of Decomposition: A Model From the Arizona-Sonoran Desert." Pp. 139–50 in *Forensic Taphonomy: The Postmortem Fate of Human Remains,* edited by William D. Haglund and Marcella H. Sorg. Boca Raton, FL: CRC.

Glaister, John and Edgar Rentoul. 1966. *Medical Jurisprudence and Toxicology,* 12th ed. Edinburgh: E. & M. S. Livingstone.

Hamilton, Laurell K. 1993. *Guilty Pleasures.* New York: Ace.

Harbaugh, Karen. 1995. *The Vampire Viscount.* New York: Signet.

Hetherington, H. W. and Fannie W. Eshleman. 1958. *Tuberculosis: Prevention and Control.* New York: G. P. Putnam's Sons.

Holbein, John. 1887. *The Dance of Death.* London: Hamilton, Adams.

Howe, Deborah and James Howe. 1979. *Bunnicula.* New York: Avon.

Hudson, Charles. 1976. *The Southeastern Indians.* Knoxville: University of Tennessee Press.

Jacobi, Keith P. 2000. *Last Rites for the Tipu Maya: Genetic Structuring in a Colonial Cemetery.* Tuscaloosa: University of Alabama Press.

Jacobi, Keith P. and M. Cassandra Hill. 2001. *Prehistoric Treatment of the Dead: Bone Handling in the Southeastern United States.* Presented at the 70th Annual Meeting of the American Association of Physical Anthropologists, Kansas City, MO.

Jones, Stephen. 1993. *The Illustrated Vampire Movie Guide.* London: Titan.

King, Stephen. 1976. *Salem's Lot.* New York: Signet.

Kluckhohn, Clyde. 1967. *Navajo Witchcraft.* Boston: Beacon.

Lamb, Charlotte. 1994. *Vampire Lover.* Toronto: Harlequin.

Larson, Glen A. and Michael Sloan. 1978. *The Hardy Boys™ and Nancy Drew™ Meet Dracula.* New York: Grosset & Dunlap.

Lehmann, Arthur C. and James E. Myers. 1989. "Ghosts, Souls, and Ancestors: Power of the Dead." Pp. 302–5 in *Magic, Witchcraft, and Religion: An Anthropological Study of the Supernatural, 2d ed.,* edited by Arthur C. Lehmann and James E. Myers. Mountain View, CA: Mayfield.

Lewis, Thomas M. N. and Madeline Kneberg. 1946. *Hiwassee Island.* Knoxville: University of Tennessee Press.

Lisowski, F. P. 1967. "Prehistoric and Early Historic Trepanation." Pp. 651–72 in *Diseases in Antiquity,* edited by Don Brothwell and A. T. Sandison. Springfield, IL: Charles C Thomas.

Lumley, Brian. 1986. *Necroscope.* New York: Tor.

Mainfort, Robert C., Jr. 1986. *Pinson Mounds: A Middle Woodland Ceremonial Center* (Division of Archaeology Research Series No. 7). Nashville: Tennessee Department of Conservation.

Malefijt, Annemarie de Waal. 1968. *Religion and Culture: An Introduction to Anthropology of Religion.* New York: Macmillan.

Martin, Ann M. 1994. *Kristy and the Vampires* (Babysitters Club Mystery 15). New York: Scholastic.

Mbiti, John S. 1970. *African Religions and Philosophies.* Garden City, NY: Doubleday.

Melanie, Lady and Father Todd. 2001. "The Sanguinarium Directory." *Vampyre Magazine,* June, pp. 49–54.

Melton, J. Gordon. 1994. *The Vampire Book: The Encyclopedia of the Undead.* Detroit: Visible Ink.

Merrifield, Ralph. 1987. *Archaeology of Ritual and Magic.* New York: New Amsterdam.

Middleton, John. 1971. "The Cult of the Dead: Ancestors and Ghosts." Pp. 488–92 in *Reader in Comparative Religion: An Anthropological Approach,* 3d ed., edited by William A. Lessa and Evon Z. Vogt. New York: Harper & Row.

Nash, Charles H. 1972. "Chucalissa: Excavations and Burials Through 1963." Occasional Paper No. 6, Anthropological Research Center, Memphis State University, Memphis, TN.

Newcomb, Franc Johnson. 1940. *Navajo Omens and Taboos.* Santa Fe, NM: Rydal.

Palmer, A. Dean. 1992. "Der Vampyr I." P. 890 in *New Grove Dictionary of Opera,* vol. 4, edited by Stanley Sadie. London: Macmillan.

Rebmann, Andrew, Edward David, and Marcella H. Sorg. 2000. *Cadaver Dog Handbook: Forensic Training and Tactics for the Recovery of Human Remains.* Boca Raton, FL: CRC.

Rice, Anne. 1977. *Interview With the Vampire.* New York: Ballantine.

Roksandic, Mirjana. 2002. "Position of Skeletal Remains as a Key to Understanding Mortuary Behavior." Pp. 99–117 in *Advances in Forensic Taphonomy: Method, Theory, and Archaeological Perspectives,* edited by William D. Haglund and Marcella H. Sorg. Boca Raton, FL: CRC.

Ross, Marilyn. 1968. *Barnabas Collins.* New York: Paperback Library.

Saunders, J. B. deC. M. and Charles D. O'Malley. 1973. *The Illustrations From the Works of Andreas Vesalius of Brussels.* New York: Dover.

Schele, Linda and Mary E. Miller. 1986. *The Blood of Kings.* New York: George Braziller.

Shelley, Mary. [1818] 1981. *Frankenstein.* Toronto: Bantam.

Sledzik, Paul S. and Nicholas Bellantoni. 1994. "Brief Communication: Bioarcheological and Biocultural Evidence for the New England Vampire Folk Belief." *American Journal of Physical Anthropology* 94:269–74.

Snow, Charles E. 1941. "Possible Evidence of Scalping at Moundville (Part 2)." In *Anthropological Studies at Moundville* (Geological Survey of Alabama/Alabama

Museum of Natural History Museum Paper 15). University, AL: Wetumpka.

Snow, Charles E. 1943. *Two Prehistoric Indian Dwarf Skeletons From Moundville* (Geological Survey of Alabama/Alabama Museum of Natural History Museum Paper 21). University, AL: Wetumpka.

St. George, Margaret. 1995. *Love Bites.* Toronto: Harlequin.

Stoker, Bram. [1897] 1992. *Dracula.* New York: Signet.

Vitebsky, Piers. 1993. *Dialogues With the Dead.* Cambridge: Cambridge University Press.

Ward, Albert E. 1980. *Navajo Graves: An Archaeological Reflection of Ethnographic Reality* (Ethnohistorical Report Series No. 2). Albuquerque, NM: Center for Anthropological Studies.

Webb, William S. and David L. DeJarnette. 1942. *An Archaeological Survey of Pickwick Basin in the Adjacent Portions of the States of Alabama, Mississippi and Tennessee* (Smithsonian Institution Bureau of American Ethnology Bulletin 129). Washington, DC: Government Printing Office.

Yarbro, Chelsea Quinn. 1979. *Hotel Transylvania.* New York: Signet.

SPIRITUALITY

JOHN D. MORGAN

We use the term *spirit* in many ways, to refer to the vitality of a high school team, to the content of beverages, as well as to the position that there are conscious beings that are immaterial. In this last sense, the term fundamentally means independence from matter: either that the creature is an immaterial being or that there is something about the being that acts in an immaterial way, that is, in a way that cannot be fully explained by bodied functions. Other meanings of *spirit* are extensions of this idea of immateriality, which we inherited from classical thought. Because the language of Greek philosophy was a convenient tool for presenting their message, early Christians adopted the idea of an immaterial, spiritual soul, a notion not found in quite the same way either in Judaism or in non-Western philosophies. We who live in a Western culture shaped by both the language of the Greek intellectual experience and the Christian religious experience often identify the idea of spirituality with religion, but the spiritual nature of the person is broader than at least organized religion.

The literature dealing with the spiritual needs of the dying and the bereaved, or spiritual questions that persons may ask in the face of death, has grown significantly in the past 20 years. Many articles, chapters, and books deal with the spirituality of children (Coles 1990), of adolescents (Balk and Hogan 1995), of the aged (Koenig 1993), of the dying (Heyse-Moore 1996), and of the bereaved (Klass 1999). Such material has been written by nurses (O'Connor 1998), physicians (Ley 1992), and chaplains (Gilbert 2002), among others.

One might think that spirituality is a newly discovered source of special insights into the needs of the dying and bereaved, but this is not the case. The beginnings of the modern hospice movement in the United Kingdom were rooted in the Christian viewpoint of Dame Cicely Saunders, the founder of that movement. Saunders held that the spiritual needs of hospice patients, their families, and hospice staff must be not only cared for, but central to treatment (Wald 1986:26). In 1989, the International Work Group on Death, Dying, and Bereavement solidified much of the thinking up to that point with the following set of assumptions (Corless et al. 1990:34–41):

1. Each person has a spiritual dimension.

2. The spiritual orientation influences mental, emotional, and physical dimensions.

3. Dying and grieving can be times of spiritual growth.

4. Spiritual beliefs and practices are exhibited in widely different ways.

5. Spiritual needs can arise at any time or place.

6. A broad range of spiritual opportunities should be available for the dying and bereaved.

7. Joy and humor are essential parts of human spirituality.

In this chapter, I examine an argument for the spiritual reality of human beings as well as present a formulation of the idea of spirituality that I believe to be useful to those who work with dying and grieving persons.

A CLASSICAL DEFINITION OF SPIRITUALITY

Although it is evident that human beings are composed of material bodies, the idea that they cannot be described adequately in material terms is seemingly as old as the first recognition by a primitive that humans differ from other animals. All animals know—that is, they become informed by their surroundings, and they use this information as they go about satisfying their needs. Self-consciousness, however, is different from simple knowing. Human beings know that they know. This seems to be one way in which they differ from nonhuman animals. If other animals are self-reflective, they have not developed the language they need to express their self-reflexiveness in a way humans can understand. In addition, there are different levels of knowing. Nonhuman animals are aware of the tastes, colors, smells, tactile qualities, and sounds of their immediate surrounding environments, but their lack of symbolic language as a way of communicating seems to imply also a lack of abstract thought.

Language requires not only information from things, but information about things that is sufficiently abstracted from the immediate individual things that it is possible to refer to those things using symbols. For example, the sound of the word *wine* and a visual sign reading WINE refer to the same thing. This ability to know abstractly seems to be a uniquely human phenomenon. Some 25 centuries ago, Plato believed that this was the fundamental characteristic of human beings (see, e.g., Plato 1937:4490). In the abstraction of the idea "wine," the human mind is aware of the sense data received but has the ability to transcend the immediate sense data to arrive at a universal.[1] Because each person is a material being who gets its existence one moment at a time, we experience material things one experience at a time. Yet in spite of the immediacy of all experience, persons can think—that is, be aware of the commonality, the common characteristics of the individual things found in experience. Thinking, awareness of the common characteristics of things, is the fundamental example of the spiritual nature of the human being.

The question "Do you like red wine?" is easily understood by both those who like the product and those who do not. It is even understandable, by analogy, to those who have never tasted wine. The question is not "Do you like the red wine that is on your tongue at this moment?" Rather, the question is "Do you like red wine?" that is, any red wine at all. When we stop to think about it, we realize that we have never tasted "any red wine at all"; we have tasted only "this individual drop of red wine on my tongue now" or some other. In spite of the fact that all of my experiences of red wine have been in particular places and at particular times, I still understand the question "Do you like (any) red wine at all?" We can explain the fact that the human mind is aware in a way that is not limited by the immediacy of surroundings only if we hold that there is some aspect of the person that dematerializes, or spiritualizes, the data of experience. The cause of this universal idea of "wine" cannot be the individual liquids outside the mind. Each of them is individual, tied to a particular space and time. But the concept "wine" is not tied to any given space or time.

Not only does the human mind know things in an abstract way—that is, a way outside the limits of individual space and time—the human mind can also know itself. The human mind is capable of answering the question "What is a human mind?" The human mind can reflect on itself. We can, for example, give a definition of the mind as "the process by which we are aware of experience in a nonspatial or nontemporal way." Even if one were to disagree with a particular definition of thinking, the point remains that the human mind (the thinking power) is capable of defining itself, capable of thinking about what thinking is. No other material or animal capacity seems to be able to reflect back upon itself. This conceptualization beyond the limits of immediate experience is spirituality.

Free choice is also a spiritual function. By choosing, by willing, by committing oneself to a goal or a plan, one determines that something one knows abstractly, only as a future possibility, not only can exist, but can exist as a goal. The value of this goal exists only in the human will determining that it shall be. This goal is by definition something that is not yet. Deciding that one is going to make the "best apple pie ever" does not imply that the apple pie exists anywhere except in one's thoughts. The human being can commit him- or herself to that which is not yet.

The meaning that humans find in music, art, and literature, although dependent on the physical characteristics of tones, rhythm, paint, canvas, and words, is not identifiable with these tools of expression. Art, as Maritain (1966) says, is "the expression of the inexpressible" (p. 60). It is the creation, or at least the awareness, of a value that is not found directly in the material makeup of the work of art. The arts can be used to enable people to find meaning, "to overcome fragmentation in their lives" (Bailey 1986). Culture—"the ideas by which we live" (Ortega y Gasset 1944:37)—does not exist as a group of physical facts, but as human interpretations of fact, and thus is part of our spiritual heritage.

Ethics consists in doing the right thing, whether that "right thing" is perceived of as duty, as the greater balance of good over evil, or as the Will of God. Ethics is rooted in the capacity of the individual to perceive a set of possibilities outside the immediate and to compare those possibilities with their conceptualized ego ideals. The Greek word *ethos,* from which the English word *ethics* is derived, means character. Ethics is the determination of the character or person one wishes to be. Ethics understood in this way would be impossible if we were not able to understand ourselves outside the immediacy of space and time.

The spiritual nature of the person opens the door to the possibility that each of us is a part of a larger whole. We not only find the meaning in our lives in that larger whole but have some obligation to it. This is what is usually meant by religion. In this sense, the term *religion* applies not only to the usual Western or Eastern religions, but also includes philosophies and other movements in which persons find meaning in their lives. Each person asks what it is that gives meaning to life, and whether whatever he or she chooses will be a defense against the bad times that come into each life, such as death and bereavement.

---

1. The term *universal* as I use it here is taken from logic. It refers to a "oneness with respect to many," as opposed to *individual,* which refers to a single space-time phenomenon (Reese 1980:597).

TOWARD A PRACTICAL DEFINITION OF SPIRITUALITY

I believe that the following will be helpful in the analysis of spirituality. Barely skimming the surface of the history of thought, we see many definitions of what it is to be a person. These definitions range from "spiritual substance" (Plato) to "will to power" (Nietzsche), and include such awarenesses as the person as a moral creator (Kant), the person as a problem solver (James), the person as a network of relationships (Marcel), the person as worker (Marx), the person as freedom (Sartre), the person as sexual (Freud), the person as part of the Absolute (Hinduism), the person as redeemed (Christianity), and the person as destined to do the will of God (Islam).

Each of these views is intrinsically understandable. Each can be intelligently defended. Each makes a certain kind of sense. We find ourselves agreeing with many of these positions in whole or in part. Yet the diversity of viewpoints teaches us the greatest lesson of spirituality: The person is a self-creator, a being who decides in one way or another what kind of being he or she will be. Our spirituality gives each of us the particular integration of these identifying characteristics. We thus arrive at a more formal definition of spirituality: *Spirituality* refers to *the ability of the person to choose the relative importance of the physical, social, emotional, religious, and intellectual stimuli that influence him or her and thereby engage in a continuing process of meaning making* (Morgan 2002). Spirituality is not some supernaturally oriented package of ideas; rather, it is a focus on what we *can become* (Hefner 1998:540).

Another way of discovering spirituality is to examine the difference between pain and suffering. According to the International Association for the Study of Pain, pain is "an unpleasant sensory or emotional experience associated with actual or potential tissue damage, or described in terms of such damage" (quoted in Chapman and Gavrin 1993:5). It may be acute (that is, of limited duration and with a specific meaning) or it may be chronic (that is, of unlimited duration and with no specific meaning, or with a specific meaning that is already held). It is relatively easy for individuals to tolerate the pain of sunburn, minor headaches, stubbed toes, insults, or failure to receive what they perceives to be their due. In chronic pain, physical or psychological, the pain no longer operates as a signal that something is wrong. The person who is feeling the unrelieved pain of a growing tumor already knows that something is wrong.

Suffering, however, has the connotation of "perceived threat to the integrity of the self, both physical and psychological" (Chapman and Gavrin 1993:6). That is, in suffering, one has the sense of "losing it," of no longer being in control of one's own life, of helplessness and hopelessness. Callahan (1993) divides suffering into two levels: At the first level, the individual deals with uncertainty, fear, and dread; at the second, he or she deals with "the

meaning of suffering for the meaning of life itself" (p. 100). Suffering occurs when one has the sense that the level of pain has become intolerable, that one can no longer be the kind of person that one wants to be. Aside from very important individual differences in pain thresholds, a major factor in how much pain one can tolerate without disintegration into suffering is one's perception of the world, the philosophy, the sense of meaning, that one holds: one's spirituality. A Buddhist who accepts the First Noble Truth (Smith 1986:148), that life is pain, will relate to pain differently, and presumably will suffer less, than a materialist consumer who defines him- or herself only in terms of possessions. A person's philosophy can operate as a buffer against suffering. As Callahan (1993) puts it: "We are all fated to suffer and die. We are not fated to make one interpretation only of this necessity, or one response, or to have just one possibility of shaping the contours of our suffering" (p. 136).

Because humans are meaning-seeking beings, we experience spiritual pain when we have the sense that our lives may be meaningless. No one individual can tell another where to find meaning; we can only support one another in the process of meaning creation. We offer each other social support—that is, we ask each other "How are you?" and stay around long enough to hear the answer.

THE SELF AND THE OTHER

In our consciousness of our spirituality, we realize that our ego boundaries become permeable (Klass 1993:52); we realize that there is more out there than the individual person. I am on this stage of life, but I am not alone. I respond to other people, with their spiritualities. I become aware of my connections to other persons, to the environment, to our God (Graydon 1996:326).

We know that we cannot survive as loners. Exclusionary self-interest is destructive. Because primates cannot survive outside the group, whatever disrupts group bonding leads to extinction (Clark 1998:656). However, each of us must still be a unique person. As Clark (1998) notes, "Societies where a meaningful social identity is denied to the autonomous individual ultimately fail" (p. 657). The ideal is to create a human society that encourages full cooperation while at the same time encouraging the fullness of individual accomplishment.

SPIRITUALITY AND RELIGION

By *religion,* I mean an awareness that the individual is part of a larger whole and that the meaning that he or she has is found in a relationship to that larger whole. There are both descriptive and prescriptive aspects to this relationship. The descriptive aspect indicates how the universe exists and the relationship of the individual person to that universe. The opening lines of the Hebrew Bible ("In the beginning God created the heavens and the earth") provide a description of how the universe exists, and the later lines that state that the human is created in the image of the Divine are a description of the place of the individual person in that universe. The prescriptive side of this is that, given the relationship we have with the Divine, we ought to conduct our lives in a manner that will enhance that relationship rather than diminish it.

This human search for meaning is found in the traditions of the five religions of the world that account for most membership: Hinduism, Buddhism, Judaism, Christianity, and Islam. Although they may differ in many details, these traditions have some elements in common. The first of these commonalities is the idea that *the real is more than meets the eye* (Smith 1986). Although these traditions differ in the manner in which they express this truth and the foundations on which they hold the truth, they all agree that there is more to reality than physical objects. The world that we see, touch, taste, smell, and hear is only a small part of the whole. In addition, these five religions share the belief that this whole is itself the Divine, or is causally related to the Divine. In the words of Immanuel Kant, the person "is a citizen of both worlds." The human being is the bridge between the physical world and the world of the spirit, or the Divine world. This belief is founded on a revelation—that is, an event on the part of the Divine that allows the believer to enter into an awareness of the true nature of reality, something that might not happen otherwise. Underlying this thinking is the view that the Divine wills the happiness of all. Because the Divine wills the happiness of all, a pulling back of the curtain, a revelation, has occurred.

The Hebrew Bible tells us that Adam was made from the dust of the earth and that Eve was made from Adam's rib. Whether or not the Divine performed surgery in the Garden of Eden is not the point of the story, however. Rather, the point is that we are related to the earth itself, and that men and women are so related that humans of the two sexes do not achieve fulfillment apart from each other. There have been hermits in history, but even their hermitage was for the sake of the rest of the human race. The various religious traditions differ in the ways that they say it, but they agree that *the person needs to be lovingly related to others* (Smith 1986). Blending the various themes above, we have the ideas of the church, or communion of saints—that is, a fellowship through the Divine with each other.

To summarize: There is a reality outside ourselves that reveals itself to us and is a standard for us. We each create ourselves in light of that standard, and we do it in fellowship with others. However, we all fail. The major traditions differ in their formulations but agree that *we all have a need for forgiveness: peace with ourselves, our fellows, and our God* (Smith 1986). This forgiveness, or peace, among ourselves, others, and the Divine is as much of freedom from suffering as we have in this present state, because in it we find a meaning that puts all the pieces together and has withstood the test of time.

All cultures have developed ceremonies and rituals that convey these realities to the living and the dying. It is helpful to remember the points that Edgar Jackson (as cited in Rando 1984:316–17) made some years ago about the value of religion to the dying:

- It helps them control their fears and anxieties by revealing not only the tragedy and sorrow of life, but also its blessings and rich experiences.

- It emphasizes those events in the history and experience of humanity that make life seem more understandable and give more people a sense of changelessness in the midst of change, of the eternal in the midst of time.

- It helps them to turn their best thoughts and feelings into constructive action.

- It inspires those of faith to act as they believe, to fulfill their aspirations in life.

- It allows them to transform the tragic events of life through the direction of its hope and the power of its love.

- It leads to deeper sensitivity of the spirit, higher aspirations of service, and a firmer conviction that the cosmic purpose is best understood as creative goodness. Therefore, although grief is painful and disappointing, it does not lead to despair.

- When it contains a belief in immortality, it relieves some of the guilt and sorrow that would be present if it were thought that at no point in time or eternity could wrongs be righted or injustices rectified.

- It highlights tradition, giving people a longer view by allowing them to tie present sufferings to time-honored sources of spiritual strength, and thus transcend current pain.

- It gives courage in the present and direction for the future.

- It moves attention away from death and tragedy, not by denying them, but by fitting them into a larger perspective.

- Through community religious rituals, it provides evidence of group strength and comfort, and recognizes the dignity of life and the validity of feelings prompted by facing death.

THE EXISTENTIAL QUEST FOR MEANING

When the World's Fair was held in New York City in 1960, the Vatican gave the commissioners of the fair permission to transport Michelangelo's *Pietà* to New York for exhibition. People were worried. The statue was to be moved by boat, and boats do sink—not very often, but they do. If such an accident were to happen, the *Pietà* would be lost. We are often quite concerned over the loss of precious things, and many things are precious precisely because they are rare. The *Pietà* is a wonderful creation, but it is not, by far, the most precious thing in existence. The *Pietà* and similar artifacts are literally set in stone; they do not have the ability to be self-creations. Persons, however, are self-creations. Each person is a once-in-a-lifetime-of-the-universe event. Although our bodies and our instincts are structured by nature, and we are influenced by parental guidance and culture, each of us decides what *person* we shall be. Each of us is unique.

What is it to be a person? Fundamentally, a person is a subject. The definition of *subject,* from logic, is "that which has powers." The term *power* is not used here in any political sense, or in the sense of power over others. Rather, it is used in its root sense of "the capacity to do" (e.g., the power to see, the power to taste). The term *object* refers to anything that activates a person's powers. A subject is a potential seer, but unless there is a colored object (the lining of my tie), the subject will not see. The colored object (my tie) has made the subject's power to see specific. A subject is a potential seer of any color whatsoever, but becomes an actual seer of a specific colored object. A subject is a potential hearer of any sound, but because of the object now hears a specific sound. Objects get their meaning and value from subjects. Color would be meaningless if there were no seeing creatures in this world. Sounds and odors would have no meaning if there were no sensate creatures in the world.

Unfortunately, we often think of persons, ourselves and others, as objects. It was not too long ago that the common understanding of a woman was that she was "somebody's daughter," then "somebody's husband," then "somebody's mother," and then eventually "somebody's widow." A woman was defined in terms of other persons. She was thought of objectively—that is, as a thing that gets meaning from outside. When we think of persons primarily as their sexes, their races, their religions, their nationalities, their careers, their sexual orientations, we think of them as objects, as things that get their meaning from without. But a person is not an object. A person is a subject, that which creates meaning.

A subject is one who says, "Yes, but": "Yes, I am a woman, but . . . "; "Yes, I am a tennis player, but. . . . " Each of us realizes that there is more to the self that we are than a list of categories can formulate. What existentialist philosophers call the "moment of subjectivity" is the realization that no list of categories could ever possibly describe the unique person. The moment of subjectivity is the moment in which a person realizes that never before in the history of the universe did he or she exist, and never again will he or she exist. Each person is a once-in-the-life-time-of-the-universe event.

Our realization of our uniqueness has two consequences. The first is that we understand that we will never be truly known by another person. In moments of depression or sadness, we may feel sorry for ourselves, saying to ourselves, and to anyone who will listen, "Nobody really understands me." The philosopher Jose Ortega y Gasset (1956:50) uses the term "radical solitude" to describe what it is to be a person. There is something about each of us that others just cannot grasp and something about them that we cannot grasp.

The second consequence of our realization of our uniqueness is that we realize that we have a limited amount of time to be who we can be. Each person is unique, yet destined to cease to be. Nothing makes the person more conscious of his or her uniqueness than death. No one has said this better than Ernest Becker (1973):

> Yet, at the same time as Eastern sages also knew, man is a worm and food for worms. This is the paradox, he is out of nature and hopelessly in it; he is dual, up in the stars yet housed in a heart-pumping, breath-gasping body that once belonged to a fish and still carries the gill marks to prove it. His body is a material fleshly casing that is alien to him . . . the strangest and most repugnant being that it aches and bleeds and it will decay and die. Man is split in two; he has an awareness of his own splendid majesty, yet he goes back to the ground to rot and disappear forever. (P. 27)

We are unique, yet we know that we will go into the ground to rot forever. Each of us is a special self-creation, but as far as nature is concerned, we are nothing but body (Becker 1973:31). Once we have passed our genes on to the next generation, we have done our evolutionary work. The awareness that we are nothing but bodies, and bodies die, forces us to ask the question, "What kind of God would make such fancy worm food?" (Becker 1973:26).

In the process of growing up, we discover ourselves. Our culture tells us how to define ourselves, but, being self-creating beings, we stop and ask ourselves if our culture is correct in the definition it has provided. We step aside from our culture from time to time. The human condition is that we find ourselves on the stage of life knowing we have roles to play but not knowing what those roles are, or even the plot of the story. No other animal has to live this terrible condition. Nonhuman animals have instincts by which they run their lives. For Becker (1975), "Spirituality is not a simple reflex of hunger and fear, it is an expression of the will to live, the burning desire of the creature to count, to make a difference on the planet because he has lived, has emerged on it, has worked, suffered, and died" (p. 3).

ACHIEVING SELF-CONSCIOUS SPIRITUALITY

Everyone is spiritual. However, many of us adopt "short-term spiritualities" or meaning systems. Materialism is a meaning system. Consumerism is a meaning system. Marxism is a meaning system. Graydon (1996:328) suggests that the following questions may be useful for opening the door to self-conscious spirituality—that is, to an evaluation of the fruitfulness of one's meaning system or spirituality:

- When you are discouraged and despondent, what keeps you going?
- Where have you found strength in the past?
- Where have you found hope in the past?
- Who have you looked up to?
- Who inspires you?
- What does death mean to you?
- What does suffering mean to you?
- What does [religious] community mean to you?
- What does healing mean to you at this point in your life?
- What is your attitude to your death?
- Can you forgive others?
- Can you forgive yourself?
- What would bring you inner peace?
- Can you find strength in yourself?
- Do you love yourself?
- Can you perceive yourself as being loved by others, by God?
- How are you relating to yourself?
- How are you relating to others?
- How are you relating to the universe?
- How are you relating to your God?

Spiritual awareness can also be opened up in ways other than through questioning. Art therapy, music therapy, bibliotherapy, guided meditation, journaling, telling our life stories, examining photographs and other memorabilia—all of these can be effective tools for opening persons to self-conscious spirituality.

THE NEED TO BE COMFORTABLE IN OUR OWN SKINS

We will always have fundamental insecurities in our lives. Each of us is a unique being who has to make sense out of life and do it on our own. We stand on the shoulders of giants, but we still have to do it on our own, as Abraham did. And that's scary. Those who are uncomfortable with ambiguity, uncomfortable in their own skins, may believe that they need to be protected from others. To protect myself from your influence, I may want to kill you—if I can kill you, that proves how much power I have.

Each of us eventually realizes that everyone we love is going to die. We have a lot of choices when faced with this realization: We can pretend that it is not so, or we can take the energy the realization stimulates and perhaps try to make a better world. The great

contribution made by such groups as the Compassionate Friends, Bereaved Families of Ontario, the Candlelighters, and Mothers Against Drunk Driving is that they have made meaning out of chaos. We need to try somehow to create a culture in which meaning might triumph over chaos.

Once one has faced death, nothing else matters in the same way. Death has the ability to teach us to accept reality in its fullness, to accept the limits of what it is. This is the work of death education, palliative care, bereavement service. We try to make people comfortable in their own skins.

REFERENCES

Bailey, Sally. 1986. "The Arts as an Avenue to the Spirit." In *In Search of the Spiritual Component of Hospice Care,* edited by Florence S. Wald. New Haven, CT: Yale University Press.

Balk, David E. and Nancy S. Hogan. 1995. "Religion, Spirituality, and Bereaved Adolescents." Pp. 61–88 in *Beyond the Innocence of Childhood: Helping Children and Adolescents Cope With Death and Bereavement,* vol. 3, edited by David Adams and Eleanor Deveau. Amityville, NY: Baywood.

Becker, Ernest. 1973. *The Denial of Death.* New York: Free Press.

———. 1975. *Escape From Evil.* New York: Collier Macmillan.

Callahan, Daniel. 1993. *The Troubled Dream of Life: Living With Mortality.* New York: Simon & Schuster.

Chapman, C. Richard and Jonathan Gavrin. 1993. "Suffering and Its Relationship to Pain." *Journal of Palliative Care* 9(2):5–13.

Clark, Mary E. 1998. "Human Nature: What We Need to Know About Ourselves in the Twenty-First Century." *Zygon* 33:645–59.

Coles, Robert. 1990. *The Spiritual Life of Children.* Boston: Houghton Mifflin.

Corless, Inge F., Norman Autton, Sally Bailey, Marjorie Cockburn, Ronald Cosh, Barrie de Veber, Iola de Veber, David Head, Dorothy C. H. Ley, John Mauritzen, Patrice O'Connor, and Takeshi Saito. 1990. "Assumptions and Principles of Spiritual Care." In *International Work Group on Death, Dying, and Bereavement: Statements on Death, Dying, and Bereavement,* edited by Charles A. Corr, John D. Morgan, and Hannelore Wass. London, ON: King's College.

Gilbert, Richard B., ed. 2002. *Health Care and Spirituality: Listening, Assessing, and Caring.* Amityville, NY: Baywood.

Graydon, Douglas. 1996. "Casey House Hospice: Caring for Persons Living With HIV/AIDS." Pp. 325–34 in *Ethical Issues in the Care of the Dying and Bereaved Aged,* edited by John D. Morgan. Amityville, NY: Baywood.

Hefner, Philip. 1998. "The Spiritual Task of Religion in Culture: An Evolutionary Perspective." *Zygon* 33:535–44.

Heyse-Moore, L. H. 1996. "On Spiritual Pain in the Dying." *Mortality* 1:297–316.

Klass, Dennis. 1993. "Spirituality, Protestantism, and Death." Pp. 51–74 in *Death and Spirituality,* edited by Kenneth J. Doka and John D. Morgan. Amityville, NY: Baywood.

Klass, Dennis. 1999. *The Spiritual Lives of Bereaved Parents.* Washington, DC: Taylor & Francis.

Koenig, Harold G. 1993. "The Relationship Between Judeo-Christian Religion and Mental Health Among Middle-Aged and Older Adults." *Advances in Mind-Body Medicine* 9(4):33–38.

Ley, Dorothy C. H. 1992. "Spiritual Care in Hospice." Pp. 207–15 in *Spiritual, Ethical and Pastoral Aspects of Death and Bereavement,* edited by Gerry Cox and Ronald J. Fundis. Amityville, NY: Baywood.

Maritain, Jacques. 1966. *L'Intuition creatice dans l'art et dans la poesie.* Paris: Desclee, de Brower.

Morgan, John D. 2002. "Dying and Grieving Are Journeys of the Spirit." In *Heath Care and Spirituality: Listening, Assessing, and Caring,* edited by Richard B. Gilbert. Amityville, NY: Baywood.

O'Connor, Patrice. 1998. "Are We Meeting Patients' Spiritual Needs?" *American Journal of Hospice Care,* July/August, pp. 31–37.

Ortega y Gasset, José. 1944. *Mission of the University.* New York: Newton.

———. 1956. "In Search of Goethe From Within." In Jose Ortega y Gasset, *The Dehumanization of Art and Other Writings on Art and Culture.* Garden City, NY: Doubleday.

Plato. 1937. "Phaedo." In *The Dialogues of Plato,* edited and translated by Benjamin Jowett. New York: Random House.

Rando, Therese A. 1984. *Grief, Dying, and Death: Clinical Interventions for Caregivers.* Champaign, IL: Research Press.

Reese, William. L. 1980. *Dictionary of Philosophy and Religion: Eastern and Western Thought.* Atlantic Highlands, NJ: Humanities Press.

Smith, Huston. 1986. *The Religions of Man.* New York: Harper & Row.

Wald, Florence S. 1986. "In Search of the Spiritual Component of Hospice Care." Pp. 25–33 in *In Search of the Spiritual Component of Hospice Care,* edited by Florence S. Wald. New Haven, CT: Yale University Press.

Religion and the Mediation of Death Fear

Michael R. Leming

It is commonly believed that normal people are afraid to die and that death anxiety is a cultural universal. As a result, some people also assume that the threat of death should serve as a deterrent to the kinds of behaviors that are deemed to be undesirable, inappropriate, and/or threatening to the society. Such thinking seems to abound. For example, international travelers are frequently confronted with signs in some countries warning them that the possession and use of illegal narcotics is punishable by death. In many parts of the United States, people who commit murder may be sentenced to die at the hands of the state—again, the assumption is that the existence of the death penalty will deter individuals from committing such violent crimes. All capital punishment laws are based on the assumption that, because normal people fear death, the threat of capital punishment will deter the commission of heinous offenses.

Moreover, the assumption that it is normal to fear the dying process seems to permeate the American cultural fabric. In nursing homes and hospice programs, for example, it is not uncommon for neophyte caregivers, whether nurses, aides, or volunteers, to become anxious when patients express a desire to die. Inexperienced caregivers often cannot understand why patients express such a desire, and in turn they express their own need to learn how they can deter their terminally ill patients from this feeling.

The taken-for-granted assumption is that the fear of death is universal and that death anxiety is a cultural component of all societies. My purposes in this chapter are to evaluate such assumptions and to present evidence that serves to challenge this thinking.

THE ASSUMPTION OF A FEAR OF DEATH

If the fear of death were universal, it would be difficult for terrorists planning suicide attacks to overcome their own anxiety as they prepare to sacrifice their lives for the sake of their belief systems. It would also be impossible for professionals and laypersons to address the consequences of disastrous events by risking their lives to save the lives of others. If death fear were natural, then issues relating to the so-called instinct for self-preservation also would require intense examination. In fact, serious evaluation of the validity of the concept of the fear of death reveals many actions on the part of humans that demonstrate that death anxiety may not be a cultural universal.

The ancient philosopher Plato denies the universality of death anxiety, claiming that philosophy serves to prepare people for death:

> Those who really apply themselves in the right way to philosophy are directly and of their own accord preparing themselves for dying and death. If this is true, and they have actually been looking forward to death all their lives, it would of course be absurd to be troubled when the thing comes for which they have so long been preparing and looking forward. (*Phaedo* 64a, in Tredennick 1969:107)

A more contemporary example of this type of thinking comes from psychologist B. F. Skinner. When he was approaching death from leukemia, the 86-year-old Skinner said with a laugh, "I will be dead in a few months, but it hasn't given me the slightest anxiety or worry or anything. I always knew I was going to die" (quoted in Bjork 1993: 229).

If the fear of death were universal, we would not expect to find much in the way of differences when we compare populations or subpopulations of people. Such is not the case, however. Anthropological research into death-related customs and rituals has found that not all cultures hold death as something to be feared. Where death fears do exist, their intensity and form appear to vary by culture. An extensive body of cross-cultural thanatological literature suggests that people from different cultures have different views of death and dying, and that not all cultures posit that death and dying need be viewed as something to be feared (see Abdel-Khalek 2002; Lester and Becker 1993; Demmer 1998; McLennan, Akande, and Bates 1993; Reimer, 1998; Reimer and Templer, 1995–96; Roshdieh et al. 1999; Saunders 1999; Suhail and Akram 2002; Tang, Wu, and Yan 2002; Thorson and Powell 1998).

When considering death fear, many analysts begin with the premise that death per se has no meaning other than the meaning that people give it. Sociologists, for example, assume that fear of death is learned through social interaction. In U.S. culture, popular horror movies depict death—as well as ghosts, skeletons, goblins, bogeymen, and ghoulish morticians—as something to be feared. Rather than providing positive images of death and dying, these products of popular culture reinforce fearful meanings; for example, they portray cemeteries as eerie and funeral homes and morgues as scary places that are best avoided.

Sometimes people who have had traumatic death-related experiences (such as witnessing a fatal auto accident, discovering the body of someone who has committed suicide, or being present at a funeral where the emotional outbursts of some mourners created feelings of discomfort for others) develop very fearful attitudes toward death, but such occurrences are rather uncommon. Certainly, such experiences do not account for the prevalence of death fears among Americans.

As Erving Goffman (1959) observes, first impressions are important; our initial impressions tend to dominate the meanings that we attribute to situation-specific experiences. Goffman's work is germane to my argument in this chapter in that many individuals tend to maintain the meanings of death that they first learned in childhood, even when they are confronted by more positive images later in life. Fear of death is also affected by age, gender, and occupation. For example, research has shown that older people tend to have less death anxiety than do younger people. (For an overall perspective on the relationship between death anxiety and age, see Suhail and Akram 2002; Swanson and Byrd 1998; Galt and Hayslip 1998; Fortner and Neimeyer 1999; Davis-Berman 1998–99.) Studies have also found gender differences in death anxiety; men and women tend to have different types of fears related to death, and, in general, women tend to fear death more than do men (see Howze 2002; Cotton 1997; Gantsweg 2002; Suhail and Akram 2002). Thorson and Powell (1996) investigated occupational differences in levels of death anxiety and found evidence that, in general, male funeral directors tend to be more fearful of death than males in other occupational groups.

Researchers have also conducted studies concerning fear of death in people of different religions and people of different levels of religious involvement, and the findings appear to be mixed. Some analysts report an inverse relationship between religiosity and death anxiety (e.g., Alvarado et al. 1995; Chibnall et al. 2002; Suhail and Akram 2002), whereas others have been unable to establish such a relationship (e.g., Rasmussen and Johnson 1994; Shadinger, Hinninger, and Lester 1999). Researchers have also explored religious variables, documenting differences in death anxiety among people of different religious groups (see Shadinger et al. 1999; Howze 2002; Reimer and Templer, 1995–96; Saunders 1999; Swanson and Byrd 1998). In one such study, Reimer and Templer (1995–96) found that Roman Catholics have higher death anxiety than do Protestants.

In summary, death fears do not appear to be instinctive or universal. It seems that fear of life's end is learned from and perpetuated by culture. Such meanings occur because death is not an ordinary experience. In challenging the order of everyday life, firsthand encounters with death are so unusual that the prospect of the experience can be traumatic. (For discussions of the relationship between the dying and death experience and levels of individual death fear, see Cotton 1997; Straub 1997; Chung, Chung, and Easthope 2000; Evans, Walters, and Hatch-Woodruff 1999; Demmer 1998; Brubeck and Beer 1992; Ireland 1998; Hayslip et al. 1997; Firestone 1993; Mikulincer et al. 2002.)

CONTENT OF DEATH FEAR

Death anxiety is a multidimensional concept that is based on four concerns: (a) the death of self, (b) the deaths of significant others, (c) the process of dying, and (d) the state of being dead. Fears related to the process of dying can be further elaborated into concerns about dependency, pain, indignity, and isolation and the fear of leaving loved ones. Additional sources of fear include the finality of death, the fate of the body, and afterlife concerns such as divine judgment. In this model's more elaborated form (documented in Leming and Dickinson 2001), eight types of death fears can be applied to the death of self and the death of others:

The Process of Dying

1. Dependency

2. The pain in the dying process

3. The indignity in the dying process

4. The isolation, separation, and rejection that can be part of the dying process

5. Leaving loved ones

The State of Being Dead

6. The finality of death

7. The fate of the body

8. Afterlife concerns

As shown in Table 1, the content of fear is influenced by the identity of the person whose death the individual is considering. From the perspective of one's own death, one may have anxiety over the effects that one's dying (or being dead) will have on others as well as many concerns about how one's body might be treated by others. From the perspective of a survivor, concerns might include financial and emotional problems related to the death of a significant other.

Given that many factors related to the experience of death and death-related situations can engender fear, we would expect to find individual differences in types and intensity of death fear, including differences related to social circumstances and past experiences. However, with all of the potential sources for differences, repeated administrations of the Leming Fear of Death Scale yield consistently high scores for the fears of dependency and pain related to the process of dying and relatively low anxiety scores for fears related to the afterlife and the fate of the body. In one study, approximately 65% ($N > 1,000$) of the individuals surveyed experienced high anxiety concerning dependency and pain, and only 15% experienced the same level of anxiety relative to concerns about the afterlife and the fate of the body (Leming, 1979–80). Thus it is the process of dying, not the event of death, that causes the most concern. Perhaps one explanation for this finding is that many Americans are uncomfortable with death, and society does not provide a supportive environment for those undergoing the dying process. Indeed, approximately 70% of all deaths in the United States take place in hospitals and nursing homes.

RELIGION AS A MEANS OF COPING

Regardless of why death anxiety exists, perhaps a more important question is, How do people cope with such feelings and anxieties? One way has been through the practice of religion. Émile Durkheim, one of the founders of the discipline of sociology, claims that it was the fear of death and the dead that led to the creation of religion. He offers empirical support for this claim in *The Elementary Forms of Religious Life* ([1915] 1995), in which he discusses the relationship between death and the rise of religious rituals.

Table 1 The Eight Dimensions of Death Anxiety as They Relate to the Deaths of Self and Others

Self	*Others*
Process of dying	
1. Fear of dependency	1. Fear of financial burdens
2. Fear of pain in the dying process	2. Fear of going through the painful experiences of others
3. Fear of indignity in the dying process	3. Fear of being unable to cope with the physical problems of others
4. Fear of loneliness, rejection, and isolation	4. Fear of being unable to cope emotionally with the problems of others
5. Fear of leaving loved ones	5. Fear of losing loved ones
State of being dead	
6. Fear of the spirit world Fear of nothingness Fear of the finality of death Fear of not being able to achieve one's goals Fear of the possible end of physical and symbolic identity	6. Fear of ghosts, spirits, devils, and so on Fear of never seeing the person again Fear of the end of a relationship Guilt related to not having done enough for the deceased Fear of not seeing the person again
7. Fear of the end of all social relationships Fear of the fate of the body Fear of body decomposition Fear of being buried Fear of not being treated with respect	7. Fear of losing the social relationship Fear of death objects Fear of dead bodies Fear of being in cemeteries Fear of not knowing how to act in death-related situations
8. Afterlife concerns Fear of divine judgement	8. Afterlife concerns Fear of the judgement of others—"What are they thinking?"

He states that individuals construct funeral practices and then develop religious orientations and rituals to support those practices.

Death and the Origin of Religion

Symbolic interactionists assert that meanings are socially constructed. These meanings provide a knowledge base for activities and actions and provide order for those who share a common culture. Peter Berger (1969) suggests that the human world is devoid of any order other than that which is socially created. Life situations challenge the order on which social life is based. Many of these situations are related to what Thomas O'Dea (1966) refers to as the three fundamental characteristics of human existence: uncertainty, powerlessness, and scarcity.

Uncertainty refers to human activity that does not always lead to predictable outcomes. Even careful planning may not allow a person to be in a position to achieve all of his or her desired goals. To an extent, the human condition also is characterized by *powerlessness*. Many events are beyond humans' capability to change or avoid them; among these are death and natural disaster. *Scarcity* exposes humankind to inequity in the distribution of the social and environmental resources that promote life satisfaction. This unequal distribution serves as the basis for perceptions of relative deprivation and frustration. According to O'Dea (1966), experiences of uncertainty, powerlessness, and scarcity "raise questions which can find an answer only in some kind of 'beyond' itself" (p. 5). Therefore, marginal situations, which are characteristic of the human condition, force individuals to the realm of the transcendent in the search for meaningful answers.

Berger (1969) claims that death is one such marginal situation:

> Witnessing the death of others and anticipating his own death, the individual is strongly propelled to question the *ad hoc* cognitive and normative operating procedures of "normal" life in society. Death presents society with a formidable problem not only because of its obvious threat to the continuity of human relationships, but because it threatens the basic assumptions of order on which society rests. Death radically puts in question the taken-for-granted, "business-as-usual" attitude in which one exists in everyday life. (P. 23)

It is the transcendent reference, or religion, that helps an individual to maintain a reality-oriented perspective when the order of life is challenged. Contemplating death, we are faced with the fact that we will not be able to accomplish all our goals in life. We also realize that we are unable either to extend life or to control the circumstances surrounding death. It is troubling that some individuals must endure painful, degrading, and meaningless death, whereas others find more meaning and purpose during the final days of life than they experienced in the years preceding the terminal period. Finally, the relative deprivation created by differential life spans raises questions that are unanswerable.

Religious-meaning systems provide answers to the problems of uncertainty, powerlessness, and scarcity created by death. O'Dea (1966) illustrates this function of religion:

> Religion, by its reference to a beyond and its beliefs concerning man's relationship to that beyond, provides a supraempirical view of a larger total reality. In the context of this reality, the disappointments and frustrations inflicted on mankind by uncertainty and impossibility, and by the institutionalized order of human society, may be seen as meaningful in some ultimate sense, and this makes acceptance of and adjustment to them possible. (Pp. 6–7)

Religion as a Means of Providing Understanding

The anthropologist Bronislaw Malinowski (1965) calls religion the "great anxiety reliever," asserting that it functions to relieve anxiety caused by crisis. According to Malinowski, religion provides individuals with the means for dealing with extraordinary phenomena; it functions to restore normalcy.

> Every important crisis of human life implies a strong emotional upheaval, mental conflict and possible disintegration. Religion in its ethics sanctifies human life and conduct and becomes perhaps the most powerful force of social control. In its dogmatics it supplies man with strong cohesive forces. (P. 70)

Malinowski claims that "death, which of all human events is the most upsetting and disorganizing to man's calculations, is perhaps the main source of religious belief" (p. 71).

A. R. Radcliffe-Brown (1965) disagrees, claiming that religion induces fear and anxiety—such as fear of spirits, fear of God's judgment, and fear of the devil and hell—from which people otherwise would be free. According to Radcliffe-Brown, nonreligious individuals experience less death anxiety and cope better with death than do religious persons. Thus he poses an alternative perspective: "If it were not for the existence of the rite and the beliefs associated with it the individual would feel no anxiety, and . . . the psychological effect of the rite is to create in the individual a sense of insecurity and danger" (p. 81). Radcliffe-Brown argues that religion may serve to increase anxiety for the individual rather than reduce it. His contention is that religion functions to create a sense of anxiety that maintains the social structure of the society, as noted in the following:

> Actually in our fears or anxieties, as well as in our hopes, we are conditioned by the community in which we live. And it is largely by the sharing of hopes and fears, by what I have called *common concern* in events or eventualities, that human beings are linked together in temporary or permanent associations. (P. 81)

According to Radcliffe-Brown, from the point of reference of personal death anxiety, religious beliefs have dysfunctional consequences. Whereas Malinowski notes that the individual may feel anxiety on certain occasions, Radcliffe-Brown asserts that the social expectation is that people should experience anxiety on such occasions. Starting with Malinowski's reference point, attention is thus focused on the function of religion for the individual. From this perspective, patterns of social integration are contingent on psychological processes. Given that religious rituals help some individuals to find meaning in death, the social function of religion must be anxiety reduction. Malinowski (1965) illustrates this point:

> Religion in its ethics sanctifies human life and conduct and becomes perhaps the most powerful force of social control. In its dogmatics it supplies man with strong cohesive forces. It grows out of every culture, because life-long bonds of cooperation and mutual interest create sentiments, and sentiments rebel against death and dissolution. The cultural call for religion is highly derived and indirect but is finally rooted in the way in which the primary needs of man are satisfied in culture. (P. 72)

George Homans (1965) attempts to resolve this problem, declaring that both Malinowski and Radcliffe-Brown are correct in their assessments of the role religion has in promoting death anxiety. Homans argues that Radcliffe-Brown's hypothesis complements Malinowski's theory in that Malinowski's observations are at the individual level (the micro level) whereas Radcliffe-Brown's analysis is directed toward the community (the macro level). Homans argues that when individuals encounter death, the anxiety they experience is socially ascribed, or learned. With its emphasis on immortality of the soul and belief in a coming judgment, religion increases the level of death anxiety for those who adhere to religious teachings. However, once these individuals have fulfilled the requisite religious or magical ceremonies, they experience only a moderate amount of anxiety. Homans brings both these perspectives to bear in the following four propositions:

1. Religion functions to relieve anxiety associated with death-related situations.

2. Death anxiety calls forth religious activities and rituals.

3. In order to stabilize the group of individuals who perform these rituals, group activities and beliefs provide a potential threat of anxiety in order to unite group members through a "common concern."

4. This secondary anxiety may be effectively removed through the group rituals of purification and expiation.

Summarizing the relationship between religiosity and death anxiety, the following theoretical hypotheses can be derived:

Hypothesis 1: The meanings of death are socially ascribed—death per se is neither fearful nor nonfearful.

Hypothesis 2: The meanings that are ascribed to death in a given culture are transmitted to individuals in the society through the process of socialization.

Hypothesis 3: Anxiety reduction may be accomplished through social cooperation and institutional participation.

Hypothesis 4: Religious institutions foster institutional cohesiveness by giving participants a sense of anxiety concerning death and uniting them through a common concern.

Hypothesis 5: If religious institutions are to remain viable, they must also provide means for anxiety reduction.

Hypothesis 6: Through its promise of a reward in the afterlife and its redefinition of the negative effects of death upon the temporal life of the individual, religion diminishes the fear that it ascribes to death and reduces the anxieties that secular society ascribes to death.

To test the empirical validity of these hypotheses, I surveyed 372 randomly selected residents of a small midwestern city concerning death anxiety and religious activities, beliefs, and experiences (Leming 1979–80). I divided the subjects into four groups, based on the religious commitment scales developed by Charles Glock and Rodney Stark (1966) and Joseph Faulkner and Gordon DeJong (1966). Approximately 25% of the respondents fell into each category—the first group consisted of those persons who were the least religious and the fourth group was composed of those who were the most religious. I then compared the subjects' death anxiety scores on the Leming Fear of Death Scale (see the appendix to this chapter) for each of the eight different fear content areas with each of the levels of religious commitment.

As the data displayed in Table 2 indicate, the relationship found between the variables of religiosity and death anxiety was curvilinear; that is, moderate religious commitment added to the general death-related anxiety that individuals had learned from secular sources. Those subjects with moderate religious commitment received only the negative consequences of religion—this coincides with Radcliffe-Brown's identification of religion as a common concern of death anxiety. These persons acquired only the anxiety that religion is capable of producing, and none of the consolation. On the other hand, highly religiously committed individuals had the least anxiety concerning death. This supports Malinowski's argument that religion provides individuals with the solace they need to cope with death-related fears.

In summary, religiosity appears to serve the dual function of "afflicting the comforted" and "comforting the afflicted." Thus, for those with a high degree of commitment, religion relieves the anxiety it causes. The theoretical model suggests a curvilinear relationship between the two variables—those persons with moderate religious commitment experience the greatest amount of anxiety in each of the eight areas. In attempting to evaluate this relationship, I found that the theoretical model was supported, with only two curvilinear trend deviations (Leming 1979–80; see Table 2). These deviations are found among the least religious group for the factor of fear of dependency in the dying process. This finding suggests that nonreligious individuals are more concerned than religious persons about being self-sufficient and independent of others, and that they find dependency even more distressing than do persons who are more religious. In terms of the fear of isolation, there does not seem to be a relationship between death fear and religious commitment.

Education, age, and religious preference did not affect the curvilinear relationship (Leming 1979–80). With the exception of the fear of isolation, persons who held the strongest religious commitment were the least fearful. Furthermore, in each of the eight death fear areas, the strength of commitment was the most significant variable for explaining the relationship between religion and the fear of death.

Table 2 Mean Scores for the Various Types of Death Fears by Level of Religious Commitment

| | Level of Religious Commitment | | | |
| | Least Religious | | Most Religious | |
Type of Death Fear[a]	1	2	3	4
Fear of dependency in the dying process Total mean = 3.9	4.2[b]	4.10	3.85	3.75
Fear of pain Total mean = 3.7	3.80	4.00	3.65	3.50
Fear of isolation Total mean = 3.0	2.80	3.00	2.95	3.0[b]
Fear of the finality of death Total mean = 2.9	3.05	3.25	2.80	2.75
Fear of leaving loved ones Total mean = 2.8	3.05	3.25	2.65	2.60
Fear of indignity in the dying process Total mean = 2.75	2.55	2.90	2.85	2.55
Fear of the afterlife Total mean = 2.55	2.50	2.95	2.60	2.30
Fear of the fate of the body Total mean = 2.55	2.50	2.70	2.60	2.40
Combined Leming Death Fear Score[a] Total mean = 24.3	24.75	26.45	24.30	22.90

a. The possible range for the subscale scores is 1 through 6, with the values of 1 and 6 indicating low and high anxiety, respectively. For the combined Death Fear Score, the potential minimum score is 8 and the highest maximum score is 48.

b. Curvilinear trend deviation.

CONCLUSION

Death fear, or death anxiety, is not universal or inherent; like all other social values and attitudes, death-related meanings are socially constructed and transmitted from one generation to the next. People who fear death do so because they have been taught that death is something to be feared or because their life experiences have taught them to have fearful responses to death-related phenomena. On the other hand, many have little death anxiety or fear. These individuals' nonfearful responses to death are also conditioned by their social situations and experiences.

Furthermore, among those who fear death, the actual content of their fears may vary widely. Thus it is safe to assume that death anxiety is multidimensional based on four concerns: (a) the death of self, (b) the deaths of

significant others, (c) the process of dying, and (d) the state of being dead.

If the fear of death were universal, we would not expect to find many differences across populations, but this is not the case. The intensity and form of death fears vary by culture as well as by age, gender, occupation, and religion. When other factors are controlled for, religion, as a cultural system, seems to have the most influence over the salience and intensity of death fears. Religiosity appears to serve the dual function of "afflicting the comforted" and "comforting the afflicted."

Religions are systems of beliefs and practices that are related to the sacred. Religious institutions meet basic social needs in that a major function of religion is to explain the unexplainable. Religion plays a significant role in helping individuals to cope with extraordinary events, including death. Not only can religious observance assist in restoring the normative order that was in place prior to the move into disequilibrium, but high religious commitment can enable individuals to cope better with their own dying and with the deaths of loved ones. Society may derive benefits from the fears that people experience, but it also needs to foster coping strategies that people can use when faced with death-related anxieties. Religion serves to meet these social needs.

APPENDIX: LEMING FEAR OF DEATH SCALE

In this chapter, I have discussed the concept of death anxiety and factors that influence it. I have suggested that death anxiety is a multidimensional concept with at least eight areas of potential fear for the individual as he or she contemplates the deaths of loved ones and the death of self. Now, having read about death fear, you can assess your own death fear by using the Leming Fear of Death Scale (Leming 1979–80), which appears below.

Read the following 26 statements. Decide whether you strongly agree (SA), agree (A), tend to agree (TA), tend to disagree (TD), disagree (D), or strongly disagree (SD) with each statement. Give your first impression. There are no right or wrong answers.

After you have responded to the statements, add the numbers below each section and divide by the number of questions in the section to get the fear score for each area. Finally, add up the results in all eight sections to get your total Death Fear Score (maximum score is 48; minimum score is 8).

I. Fear of Dependency

1. I expect other people to care for me while I die.

SA	A	TA	TD	D	SD
1	2	3	4	5	6

2. I am fearful of becoming dependent on others for my physical needs.

SA	A	TA	TD	D	SD
6	5	4	3	2	1

3. While dying, I dread the possibility of being a financial burden.

SA	A	TA	TD	D	SD
6	5	4	3	2	1

4. Losing my independence due to a fatal illness makes me apprehensive.

SA	A	TA	TD	D	SD
6	5	4	3	2	1

(Total of 4 scores) _____ divided by 4 = _____

II. Fear of Pain

5. I fear dying a painful death.

SA	A	TA	TD	D	SD
6	5	4	3	2	1

6. I am afraid of a long, slow death.

SA	A	TA	TD	D	SD
6	5	4	3	2	1

(Total of 2 scores) _____ divided by 2 = _____

III. Fear of Indignity

7. The loss of physical attractiveness that accompanies dying is distressing to me.

SA	A	TA	TD	D	SD
6	5	4	3	2	1

8. I dread the helplessness of dying.

SA	A	TA	TD	D	SD
6	5	4	3	2	1

(Total of 2 scores) _____ divided by 2 = _____

IV. Fear of Isolation/Separation/Loneliness

9. The isolation of death does not concern me.

SA	A	TA	TD	D	SD
1	2	3	4	5	6

10. I do not have any qualms about being alone after I die.

SA	A	TA	TD	D	SD
1	2	3	4	5	6

11. Being separated from my loved ones at death makes me anxious.

SA	A	TA	TD	D	SD
6	5	4	3	2	1

(Total of 3 scores) _____ divided by 3 = _____

V. Fear of Afterlife Concerns

12. Not knowing what it feels like to be dead makes me uneasy.

SA	A	TA	TD	D	SD
6	5	4	3	2	1

13. The subject of life after death troubles me.

SA	A	TA	TD	D	SD
6	5	4	3	2	1

14. Thoughts of punishment after death are a source of apprehension for me.

SA	A	TA	TD	D	SD
6	5	4	3	2	1

(Total of 3 scores) _____ divided by 3 = _____

VI. Fear of the Finality of Death

15. The idea of never thinking after I die frightens me.

SA	A	TA	TD	D	SD
6	5	4	3	2	1

16. I have misgivings about the fact that I might die before achieving my goals.

SA	A	TA	TD	D	SD
6	5	4	3	2	1

17. I am often distressed by the way time flies so rapidly.

SA	A	TA	TD	D	SD
6	5	4	3	2	1

18. The idea that I may die young does not bother me.

SA	A	TA	TD	D	SD
1	2	3	4	5	6

19. The loss of my identity at death alarms me.

SA	A	TA	TD	D	SD
6	5	4	3	2	1

(Total of 5 scores) _____ divided by 5 = _____

VII. Fear of Leaving Loved Ones

20. The effect of my death on others does not trouble me.

SA	A	TA	TD	D	SD
1	2	3	4	5	6

21. I am afraid that my loved ones are emotionally unprepared to accept my death.

SA	A	TA	TD	D	SD
6	5	4	3	2	1

22. It worries me to think of the financial situation of my survivors.

SA	A	TA	TD	D	SD
6	5	4	3	2	1

(Total of 3 scores) _____ divided by 3 = _____

VIII. Fear of the Fate of the Body

23. The thought of my own body decomposing does not bother me.

SA	A	TA	TD	D	SD
1	2	3	4	5	6

24. The sight of a dead body makes me uneasy.

SA	A	TA	TD	D	SD
6	5	4	3	2	1

25. I am not bothered by the idea that I may be placed in a casket when I die.

SA	A	TA	TD	D	SD
1	2	3	4	5	6

26. The idea of being buried frightens me.

SA	A	TA	TD	D	SD
6	5	4	3	2	1

(Total of 4 scores) _____ divided by 4 = _____

Total Death Fear Score (addition of all 8 areas of death concern) _____

(In any given subscale, a score of 3.5 or higher means slightly fearful of death.)

REFERENCES

Abdel-Khalek, Ahmed. M. 2002. "Why Do We Fear Death? The Construction and Validation of the Reasons for Death Fear Scale." *Death Studies* 26:669–80.

Alvarado, Katherine A., Donald I. Templer, Charles Bresler, and Shan Thomas-Dobson. 1995. "The Relationship of Religious Variable to Death Depression and Death Anxiety." *Journal of Clinical Psychology* 51:202–4.

Berger, Peter L. 1969. *The Sacred Canopy: Elements of a Sociological Theory of Religion.* Garden City, NY: Doubleday.

Bjork, Daniel W. 1993. *B. F. Skinner: A Life.* New York: Basic Books.

Brubeck, Dan and John Beer. 1992. "Depression, Self-Esteem, Suicide Ideation, Death Anxiety, and GPA in High School Students of Divorced and Non-Divorced Parents." *Psychological Reports* 71:755–63.

Chibnall, John T, Susan D. Videen, Paul N. Duckro, and Douglas K. Miller. 2002. "Psychosocial-Spiritual Correlates of Death Distress in Patients With Life-Threatening Medical Conditions." *Palliative Medicine* 16:331–38.

Chung, Man Cheung, Catherine Chung, and Yvette Easthope. 2000. "Traumatic Stress and Death Anxiety Among Community Residents Exposed to an Aircraft Crash." *Death Studies* 24:689–704.

Cotton, Allison. 1997. "Is There a Relationship Between Death Anxiety and Engagement in Lethal Behaviors Among African-American Students?" *Omega* 34:233–45.

Davis-Berman, Jennifer. 1998–99. "Attitudes Toward Aging and Death Anxiety." *Omega* 38:59–64.

Demmer, Craig. 1998. "Death Anxiety, Coping Resources, and Comfort With Dying Patients Among Nurses in AIDS Care Facilities." *Psychological Reports* 83:1051–57.

Durkheim, Émile. [1915] 1995. *Elementary Forms of Religious Life.* New York: Free Press.

Evans, Jonathan W., Andrew S. Walters, and Marjorie L. Hatch-Woodruff. 1999. "Deathbed Scene Narratives: A Construct and Linguistic Analysis." *Death Studies* 23:715–33.

Faulkner, Joseph and Gordon F. DeJong. 1966. "Religiosity in 5-D: An Empirical Analysis." *Social Forces* 45:246–54.

Firestone, Robert W. 1993. "Individual Defenses Against Death Anxiety." *Death Studies* 17:497–515.

Fortner, Barry V. and Robert A. Neimeyer. 1999. "Death Anxiety in Older Adults: A Quantitative Review." *Death Studies* 23:387–89.

Galt, Cynthia P. and Bert Hayslip, Jr. 1998. "Age Differences in Levels of Overt and Covert Death Anxiety." *Omega* 37:187–202.

Gantsweg, J. Robyn. 2002. "Gender, Self-Construal, and Death Anxiety Within a Jewish Community Sample." *Dissertation Abstracts International* 62(10B):4784.

Glock, Charles and Rodney Stark. 1966. *Christian Beliefs and Anti-Semitism.* New York: Harper & Row.

Goffman, Erving. 1959. *The Presentation of Self in Everyday Life.* Garden City, NY: Doubleday.

Hayslip, Bert, Jr., Heather L. Servaty, Toni Christman, and Elaine Mumy. 1997. "Levels of Death Anxiety in Terminally Ill Persons: A Cross Validation and Extension." *Omega* 34:203–17.

Homans, George C. 1965. "Anxiety and Ritual: The Theories of Malinowski and Radcliffe-Brown." In *Reader in Comparative Religion: An Anthropological Approach*, edited by William A. Lessa and Evon Z. Vogt. New York: Harper & Row.

Howze, Alisa Renee. 2002. "Death Anxiety and Psychotherapy: An Examination of Counselor Trainees' Reactions to Death-Related Issues." *Dissertation Abstracts International,* 62(11A):3699.

Ireland, Mary. 1998. "Death Anxiety and Self-Esteem in Young Children With AIDS: A Sense of Hope." *Omega* 36:131–44.

Leming, Michael R. 1979–80. "Religion and Death: A Test of Homans's Thesis." *Omega* 10:347–64.

Leming, Michael R. and George E. Dickinson. 2001. *Understanding Dying, Death, and Bereavement,* 5th ed. Fort Worth, TX: Harcourt Brace.

Lester, David and DeAnne Becker. 1993. "College Students' Attitudes Toward Death Today as Compared to the 1930s." *Omega* 26:219–23.

Malinowski, Bronislaw. 1965. "The Role of Magic and Religion." In *Reader in Comparative Religion: An Anthropological Approach*, edited by William A. Lessa and Evon Z. Vogt. New York: Harper & Row.

McLennan, Jim, Adebowale Akande, and Glen W. Bates. 1993. "Death Anxiety and Death Denial: Nigerian and Australian Students' Metaphors of Personal Death." *Journal of Psychology* 127:399–408.

Mikulincer, Mario, Victor Florian, Gurit Birnbaum, and Shira Malishkevich. 2002. "The Death-Anxiety Buffering Function of Close Relationships: Exploring the Effects of Separation Reminders on Death-Thought Accessibility." *Personality and Social Psychology Bulletin* 28:287–99.

O'Dea, Thomas. 1966. *The Sociology of Religion.* Englewood Cliffs, NJ: Prentice Hall.

Radcliffe-Brown, A. R. 1965. "Taboo." In *Reader in Comparative Religion: An Anthropological Approach*, edited by William A. Lessa and Evon Z. Vogt. New York: Harper & Row.

Rasmussen, Christina A. and Mark E. Johnson. 1994. "Spirituality and Religiosity: Relative Relationships to Death Anxiety." *Omega* 29:313–18.

Reimer, Wilbert L. 1998. "Correlates of Willingness to Die for One's Religion and One's Country in American and Filipino Populations." *Omega* 37:59–73.

Reimer, Wilbert L. and Donald I. Templer. 1995–96. "Death Anxiety, Death Depression, Death Distress, and Death Discomfort Differential: Adolescent-Parental Correlations in Filipino and American Populations." *Omega* 32:319–30.

Roshdieh, Simin, Donald I. Templer, W. Gary Cannon, and Merle Canfield. 1999. "The Relationship of Death Anxiety and Death Depression to Religion and Civilian War-Related Experiences in Iranians." *Omega* 38:201–10.

Saunders, Sue. 1999. "A Methodological Study to Develop and Validate a Death Attitude Scale: Buddhists and Medical Students Compared." *Omega* 38:211–34.

Shadinger, Mary, Kim Hinninger, and David Lester. 1999. "Belief in Life and Death, Religiosity and Fear of Death." *Psychological Reports* 84(3, pt. 1):868.

Straub, Sandra Helene. 1997. "Fear of Death After the Loss of a Spouse." *Dissertation Abstracts International* 58(4B):1794.

Suhail, Kuasar and Saima Akram. 2002. "Correlates of Death Anxiety in Pakistan." *Death Studies* 26:39–50.

Swanson, Julie L. and Kevin R. Byrd. 1998. "Death Anxiety in Young Adults as a Function of Religious Orientation, Guilt, and Separation-Individuation Conflict." *Death Studies* 22:257–68.

Tang, Catherine So-Kum, Anise M. S. Wu, and Elsie C. W. Yan. 2002. "Psychosocial Correlates of Death Anxiety Among Chinese College Students." *Death Studies* 26:491–99.

Thorson, James A. and F. C. Powell. 1996. "Undertakers' Death Anxiety." *Psychological Reports* 78:1228–30.

———. 1998. "African- and Euro-American Samples Differ Little in Scores on Death Anxiety." *Psychological Reports* 83:623–26.

Tredennick, Hugh. 1969. *Plato: The Last Days of Socrates.* New York: Penguin.

CHRISTIAN BELIEFS CONCERNING DEATH AND LIFE AFTER DEATH

DONALD E. GOWAN

The Apostles' Creed concludes with affirmations of belief in "the resurrection of the body, and the life everlasting." In various ways, Christian communities during two millennia have reaffirmed those two clauses, but beyond this, as McDannell and Lang say in their book *Heaven: A History* (1988), "There is no basic Christian teaching, but an unlimited amount of speculation" (p. xi). In this chapter surveying Christian beliefs, then, I must necessarily be highly selective, but I must begin at the most creative moment.

Surprising new ideas concerning death and life after death appeared in Judaism during the last two centuries B.C.E. They became the basis for almost everything the early church said on the subject, and they have been reaffirmed, elaborated, and at times denied from that day to this. Any study of Christian beliefs must therefore begin with the Jewish literature produced between roughly 200 B.C.E. and 100 C.E. This literature represents a flourishing period of Jewish theology, although the works produced were not accepted as Scripture by the rabbinic Judaism of the Common Era.

THE APPEARANCE OF THE RESURRECTION HOPE

The authors of the books of the Old Testament showed little interest in life after death. They would have known of cults of the dead among their Western Asiatic neighbors, and of the Egyptian preoccupation with death, and their silence may have been partly a reaction to those beliefs and practices. Yahweh was the *living* God, and the dead were separated from him (e.g., Psalms 88:5, 10–12). They dwelt in Sheol, a kind of universal grave where everyone went, and not a place of reward or punishment (Job 3:17–19). Heaven was God's dwelling place, and only one person was said to have gone to heaven: Elijah, who did so without dying (2 Kings 2:1, 11). (Enoch also did not die; he

"walked with God; then he was no more, because God took him"; Genesis 5:24). It seems that the Israelites ordinarily accepted death without any great theological or psychological problem, and that was because they had their own sense of "immortality." Their sense of community identity was so strong that when one died at a good old age, with children, then one's true identity—character, vitality, reputation (in Hebrew, one's "name")—lived on in one's children. To die without children was thus a tragedy—then one was truly dead (Martin-Achard 1960:3–51).

The radical changes in Jewish belief that appear in documents from the second century B.C.E. onward can be easily explained. Earlier, the experience of exile had drastically disrupted communities and families, so the sense of individual identity had of necessity become stronger. The crucial question that was answered by the affirmation that there will be in the last days a resurrection of the dead was more theological than personal, however. It was the question of justice. Prior to the events of 167–65 B.C.E., it was possible to argue, as Job's "friends" did, that God's justice is always manifest within one's lifetime on earth. Suffering is always punishment for sin. But in 167, Antiochus IV Epiphanes, who ruled the region from Judea, Samaria, and Galilee in the south to Syria in the north and Mesopotamia in the east, decreed that the practice of the Jewish religion was prohibited, on pain of death (see 1 and 2 Maccabees). The reasons for that need not concern us here, but the ensuing persecution had lasting effects on theology. People were tortured to death (2 Maccabees 6–7), and when it was precisely the most faithful who were suffering the worst, it was no longer possible to say that all suffering is punishment for sin. Faithful Jews maintained their belief in a God who is sovereign and just—in spite of this awful test—by insisting that there would be in the future a resurrection of the dead, when justice for the righteous and the wicked would finally be done. The Book of Daniel, the latest book of the Old Testament, completed in 165 B.C.E., during the persecution, is the only Old Testament book to affirm explicitly the resurrection of individuals (Daniel 12:2; Isaiah 26:19 speaks of resurrection of the righteous, but may refer instead to the resurrection of the nation, as Ezekiel 37:1–14 does).

By the end of the second century B.C.E., resurrection was affirmed at greater length. The resurrection hope enabled the martyrs of 167–65 to endure, says 2 Maccabees 7, and the Wisdom of Solomon (2:12–3:9) takes up a hypothetical case of a righteous man who is attacked and killed by the wicked, but says of the righteous in general: "In the time of their visitation they will shine forth, and will run like sparks through the stubble. They will govern nations and rule over peoples, and the Lord will reign over them forever" (3:7–8). By the first century C.E. the resurrection hope had become so firmly established as a Jewish belief that when Jesus told his friend Martha that her brother Lazarus would rise from the dead, she responded, "I know that he will rise again in the resurrection on the last day" (John 11:24). The most conservative Jews of the time, the Sadducees, still considered resurrection a newfangled idea (Matthew 22:23), but they were a small minority.

Why the difficult concept of resurrection? Jews in the second century B.C.E. would have known about the Greek concept of an immortal soul, separable from the body, and a much easier way to think about life beyond the death of the body. The understanding of what it is to be human that they had inherited from ancient Israel was very different from that of the Greeks, however, and that explains it. The Jews did not think of human beings as composed of three separable parts—body, soul, and spirit—but as whole, "animated bodies," rather than "incarnated souls." The Hebrew word *nephesh,* which is frequently translated as "soul," is not used to refer to something that can be separated from the body and live apart from it. In the creation story, God is said to have formed a body, then breathed into its nostrils the breath of life and it became a "living soul," or, better, a "living person" (Genesis 2:7). To be human required having a body, as the Jews understood it, and so if there could be life after death it must involve a resurrection.

But "in what shape will those live who live in thy day?" Baruch asked (2 Baruch 49:2). In the literature of this period, Jewish authors tried out almost every possible option, and in the paragraphs that follow I try to outline these as neatly as possible. There seem to be four possible answers to the question of what happens to us when we die:

- *Annihilation:* It is simply the end.

- *Immortality:* An imperishable soul lives on without the body.

- *Resurrection:* After an intermediate period, the dead person rises to live again, in a re-created body.

- *Reincarnation*: Something of the essence of the dead person is reborn into another form of life.

The authors of the texts that I consider below occasionally spoke of the first possibility, but only for the wicked. They were much influenced by the second, especially as they dealt with the problem of the intermediate period, but did not accept it fully because of their preoccupation with the third. They show no trace of ever considering the fourth.

Where a belief in resurrection is affirmed it is not always universal in scope. Isaiah 26:19 mentions only the righteous, and Daniel 12:2 says that "many" will be raised. Although most later documents speak of a general resurrection, there are some that restrict it to the righteous. Psalms of Solomon 3:13–16 says that sinners fall to rise no more and speaks elsewhere of their destruction on the day when the righteous find life (13:10; 14:6; 15:15). 1 Enoch says that the wicked do not rise but remain where they have been, in great pain (see 91:9–10; see also 2 Baruch 30). Normally, however, the hope of resurrection meant the expectation that at some future time a dead person, after waiting in some sort of intermediate state, would rise to a new life, presumably involving a body of some sort, in order to face a final judgment.

But where do the dead wait? One of the major difficulties of the resurrection hope is the question of the "intermediate state," and the literature of the period contains a bewildering variety of opinions. Some texts imagine places in the earth (probably an extension of the Sheol concept) where the dead remain until resurrection day (e.g., 1 Enoch 22, 51; 2 Esdras 4:35, 41, 7:32; 2 Baruch 21:23, 30:2; Adam and Eve 41). Little is said about whether they are conscious. 1 Enoch 100:5 says the righteous sleep a long sleep, but Adam and Eve 41 has Adam answer God from the ground. Fairly often the righteous are said to be in the presence of God or in heaven immediately after death. This seems to be true in Wisdom of Solomon 3:1 and in Testament of Asher 6:5–6, where the soul is met at death by an angel of God or of Satan, and the former leads the righteous into eternal life. There is a garden, in 1 Enoch 60:8, where "the elect and the righteous dwell." On the other hand, the punishment of the wicked often begins immediately, rather than waiting for judgment day (Jubilees 7:29; 1 Enoch 22:11).

Most texts say that after the day of judgment the wicked will be consigned to Sheol or Gehenna for punishment. The latter word came from the Hebrew place-name Ge Hinnom, the Hinnom Valley just west of Jerusalem, which, as the city dump, was a place of everlasting fire, and fire is the typical means of torment described in these passages (e.g., 1 Enoch 48:9; 2 Baruch 85:13; 2 Esdras 7:36). Usually the place of punishment is located in the depths of the earth (e.g., 1 Enoch 90:26), but in 2 Enoch 10 and 3 Baruch 4:4–5 it is the third heaven.

For the righteous, the texts display great variety. Sibylline Oracles 4 says that resurrected men will be "as they were" (vv. 181–82) and will live on earth (vv. 187–91). 1 Enoch 51 says the earth will rejoice and the righteous will dwell on it. The Testament of Dan 5 locates the righteous in Eden and the New Jerusalem, but usually it is a heavenly existence that is expected, and, in keeping with that, the transformed nature of the resurrected body is frequently emphasized. The most interesting passage of this sort is found in 2 Baruch 49–51, which describes a two-step process: First, people are raised just as they were (50:2), then the judgment comes and the appearance of the wicked grows worse while the righteous are transformed "into every form they desire," into beings like the stars or the angels (51:10). There is a great lack of clarity about where Eden, Paradise, and the New Jerusalem are to be located; often they are heavenly, but occasionally they seem to be a part of the new creation. *Paradise* was originally a Persian word referring to a garden. It came into Hebrew as a loanword, and then moved into Greek.

Judgment is the most consistent feature of Jewish statements about life after death, and the reason is clearly the issue of justice mentioned earlier. Every eschatological passage affirms unequivocally that justice will ultimately be done, and a great court scene at the time of the resurrection was many writers' favorite way of bringing their projections of the future to a conclusion, with the deeds of the righteous and the wicked brought to light and appropriate treatment dispensed. (For detailed discussions of these texts, see Cavallin 1974; Nickelsburg 1972.)

The variety of opinions briefly surveyed above seems to justify one conclusion: No one really knew what it is like after death. Two elements of consistency are important, however. First, the question for them was not the modern one, What will happen to *me* after I die? Rather, the question was one of theodicy, whether God is truly sovereign and just. And second, in spite of the problems involved in conceiving it, resurrection of the body in the last days was the dominant form of hope. Elements of the other ideas I have briefly described reappear in Christianity.

LIFE AFTER DEATH
IN THE NEW TESTAMENT

Jesus took for granted the major beliefs about the afterlife that were prevalent in first-century Judaism and did not set out to offer his own authoritative teachings on the subject, as the writers of apocalyptic books were doing in his time. He was interested primarily in this life. The salvation he offered involved healing (to the woman with the hemorrhage: "Daughter, your faith has made you well [Greek: saved you]; go in peace"; Luke 8:48) and forgiveness (to the "sinful woman": "Your faith has saved you; go in peace"; Luke 7:50). He said that he came that people might have life and have it abundantly (John 10:10). Indeed, the eternal life of which John speaks frequently is said not to begin at death, but in the present, at the moment of decision. "Very truly, I tell you, anyone who hears my word and believes him who sent me has eternal life, and does not come under judgment, but has passed from death to life" (John 5:24).

Jesus spoke a few times of rewards and punishments in the hereafter. He said the reward for those who are persecuted for his sake will be great in heaven (Matthew 5:12;

Luke 6:23), continuing the Jewish martyrdom tradition that began in the second century B.C.E. He never described heaven, but did accept the common association of fire with the place of judgment (Gehenna, or "hell" in most English translations; Matthew 5:22, 29, 30, 10:28, 18:9, 23:15, 23; see also "furnace of fire" in Matthew 13:42). In a parable, he used the idea of two realms set aside for the righteous and the wicked after death, so as to make possible a conversation between the rich man in Hades and poor Lazarus in the "bosom of Abraham" (Luke 16:19–31). The point of the parable is that even if someone were to come back from the dead with a call for repentance it would still be possible for people to disbelieve, so it is not a teaching about what it is like after death. Given that parables sometimes include unrealistic elements to make their points (e.g., a farmer who pays all his workers alike, no matter how long they worked; Matthew 20:1–16), it would be risky to take this as necessarily representing Jesus' own thoughts about the afterlife.

Once, Jesus spoke of the Last Judgment, when the Son of Man will judge the nations for the way they have treated the hungry and thirsty, the stranger, the naked, the sick, and those in prison, saying that those judged righteous will inherit the Kingdom (eternal life), but the wicked will depart into the eternal fire (Matthew 25:31–46). He referred in passing to the resurrection of the righteous (in Luke 14:14 and also in John 5:21–29) and defended the idea against the Sadducees (in Mark 12:13–27 and parallels). He spoke of his own death and resurrection (in Mark 8:31, 9:9, 31, 10:33–34, and parallels). (The much-debated question of what Jesus *really* said—the "quest for the historical Jesus"—need not concern us, because our interest here is in what Christians believed he said.) Twice he promised that those who believe in him will be *with him* after death (Luke 23:43; John 14:2–3; "in Paradise" tells us nothing—*Paradise* had become a synonym for heaven). John emphasized, more than the other Gospels, Jesus' primary concern for life here and now (as noted above in the quotation of 5:24). In the account of the raising of Lazarus, Jesus says, "I am the resurrection and the life. Those who believe in me, even though they die, will live, and everyone who lives and believes in me will never die" (John 11:25–26). This Gospel was certainly written after some believers in Jesus had died, so it must be speaking of a life that transcends the death of the body.

Even the resurrection accounts in the Gospels and Acts do not record any teachings about the afterlife from Jesus, the only person who should know from experience. He did not talk with the disciples about death, but about what they needed to do next. Their testimony concerning Jesus certainly emphasizes his death and resurrection as the key to their good news of forgiveness, but, as one of my teachers once pointed out, their message was not, "You see, this proves it; we'll live forever." The emphasis of their preaching was that resurrection was God's vindication of Jesus, whose life had seemed to be a terrible failure, ending with the desertion of his disciples and a shameful death by crucifixion. Rather, through his resurrection, he was now proved to be the Messiah (e.g., Acts 2:32–36, 3:14–15, 10:39–42).

The first Christians were all Jews who already believed in the resurrection of the dead in the last days, but the resurrection of Jesus gave them a new basis for that hope. In Judaism it was a matter of theology: There *must* be a time when God will manifest his justice, even if it comes after death and at the end of history. For Christians it was a conclusion drawn from an event: One person has in fact been raised from the dead, and he is the first of many to come (e.g., 1 Corinthians 15:20–23). When the church spread into the Gentile world, where resurrection was a novel idea, Christians needed to say more in order to respond to disbelief and to correct misunderstandings. For our purposes, three texts will suffice as examples of early Christian thinking.

The earliest document in the New Testament is 1 Thessalonians, written circa 50–51 C.E. Christians of that time expected the last days to be imminent, and when some members of the Thessalonian church died, there was uncertainty about what to believe. Paul provided reassurance concerning the promise of resurrection and spoke of the return of the risen Christ as a time when those who are alive "will be caught up in the clouds . . . to meet the Lord in the air" (1 Thessalonians 4:13–18). This verse is the basis for the much-elaborated scenario of the "rapture" found in some branches of Christianity (see also 1 Corinthians 15:51–52).

In 1 Corinthians 15, Paul dealt with a group of questions that disturbed the Corinthian church. Some members of that church were denying that there would be a resurrection in the last days. Paul's response was based on his certainty that Christ had in fact been raised (15:3–8) and the conclusion the church had reached based on that: Christ's resurrection and the eventual resurrection of the dead are irrevocably linked (vv. 12–28). The second issue concerned the nature of resurrection. Several resuscitations are recorded in both the Old and the New Testaments— that is, cases of people who were revived but later died— but resurrection was not believed to be a similar revival of the old corpse. It would be a new creation, of a body with new qualities, and Paul tried several analogies from nature to explain what is in truth inconceivable (vv. 35–56). But note the conclusion to this longest discussion of life after death in the Bible. As in Jesus' teachings, the emphasis is on this life, not the next: "Be steadfast, immovable, always excelling in the work of the Lord" (v. 58).

The Book of Revelation, like Jewish apocalypses, is persecution literature, and like them speaks at length of heaven and hell because life on earth means suffering for the righteous. The souls of the martyrs are said to be under the altar in heaven, at rest until the victory can be won on earth (6:9–11). The Last Judgment will bring Satan's power to an end forever (chap. 20), and the righteous will enjoy eternal life—not in heaven but in the New Jerusalem, which will come down from heaven (chaps. 21–22). Once

again, the theme of life after death is used to vindicate God, as well as those who suffer because they are faithful to him. It has been noted that the New Testament says nothing to describe heaven except in Revelation, and this book has been the source of much of the later Christian speculation about what heaven must really be like. But this is apocalyptic literature, and the language of apocalypse is always symbolic, so it has been a basic error of interpretation to imagine, and even draw, pictures of the world to come based on a literal reading of this book.

DEVELOPMENT OF A DOCTRINE OF LIFE AFTER DEATH

No concept of humanity as bodies temporarily inhabited by immortal souls appears in Scripture, but in post–New Testament literature it is taken for granted. It was the prevailing view throughout the Roman world, and it was assimilated into Christian thinking, apparently without debate, in spite of the fact that it is not found in Scripture and does not fit at all well with the New Testament message concerning resurrection. Much of Christian eschatology has involved efforts to explain how both can be true. Death was assumed by all to be the separation of the immortal soul from the body, so there were no serious questions raised for centuries about whether there is life after death. Rather, the questions focused on what kind of life could be expected. With no experimental evidence available, the reflections were based on the few helpful biblical texts, on the experiences of visionaries, and, for the greatest part, on philosophical reasoning.

The motivation for affirmations about the afterlife drifted from the earlier concern, that God's justice must surely be manifested one day for the righteous and the unrighteous who had not experienced it in this life. That did not disappear, for judgment played a large role in every scheme, but the fate of the souls of believers became more and more a matter of concern. The crucial problem for those who believe that the dead will be resurrected in the last days is that of time. We die now, but the resurrection will happen in some indefinite future, and what becomes of us in the meantime? That is an especially acute question with respect to the deaths of one's loved ones (usually more so than with respect to one's own death): Where are they now? The concept of the immortal soul gave the church a way (or ways) to answer this question. Already, late in the second century C.E. Irenaeus wrote, with reference to the resurrection of Christ, that "the souls of His disciples also, upon whose account the Lord underwent these things, shall go away into the invisible place allotted to them by God and there remain until the resurrection, awaiting that event; then receiving their bodies, and rising in their entirety, that is bodily, just as the Lord arose, they shall come into the presence of God" (*Against Heresies* V.xxxi.2). From our perspective, he may seem to have been wise in adding to what he found in Scripture no more than souls "in an invisible place" during the interim before resurrection, for later writers could not restrain their curiosity about that place. Customs surrounding death for the first 1,000 years or so, however, seem to reflect the general idea that the souls of the dead were consigned to the keeping of the church until the day of resurrection (see Aries 1974:1–25). Speculation concerning the nature of heaven and hell was bound to develop during that period, of the sort that eventually appeared in Dante's *Divine Comedy* (1321) and in ecclesiastical art depicting the Last Judgment.

The church's developing "system" for the forgiveness of sins, combined with the concept of the soul, led to the development of the idea of purgatory. (For our purposes we need not delve into the philosophical efforts to define just what a soul is, as in Aquinas's theology.) The souls of unrepentant sinners were generally thought to go to a place of punishment immediately after death, with the eventual resurrection, Last Judgment, and commitment to hell added on because these were Scripture's teachings. The soul had to be defined in such a way that it could experience pain, or there would be no punishment. The souls of the saints might pass into the presence of God immediately, but few are good enough to warrant that blessing. Paul's teaching that sinners are justified by faith, fully reconciled to God by grace apart from human works of righteousness (e.g., Romans 3:21–28, 5:1–11; Galatians 3–4) had largely been forgotten, replaced by a legalistic system in which sins could be forgiven by the church, but the stain of guilt remained on the soul, which needed to be purified by penance. That system eventually became the sacrament of penance in the Roman Catholic Church. For those who died in a state of grace, but without having done sufficient penance for their minor sins, a place was provided where after death their souls could be purified—purgatory. The idea was present at least as early as the time of Gregory the Great (593–94), who wrote, "As for certain lesser faults, we must believe that, before the final judgment, there is a purifying fire (*puratorius ignis*)" (quoted in McGrath 1995:359). But the doctrine of purgatory was fully developed by Thomas Aquinas in the mid-13th century:

> To be sure, the soul is purified from this uncleanness in this life by penance, and the other sacraments, . . . but it does at times happen that such purification is not entirely perfected in this life; one remains a debtor for the punishment, whether by reason of some negligence, or business, or even because a man is overtaken by death. Nevertheless, he is not entirely cut off from his reward, because such things can happen without mortal sin, which alone takes away the charity to which the reward of eternal life is due. . . . They must then be purged after this life before they receive the final reward. (*Summa Contra Gentiles* IV.91.6)

He reaffirmed resurrection and judgment in the last days. In his commentary on 1 Corinthians 15, he wrote, "My soul is not I, and if only souls are saved, *I* am not saved, nor is any man." As the state of the soul during the interim period had been elaborated, however, resurrection and judgment functioned essentially as ratifications of the judgment of souls shortly after the deaths of individuals. Because they were in Scripture, they had to be retained, but the scenario the church had devised concerning the purgation and judgment of souls immediately after death effectively made them unnecessary. And the concept of the soul was easier for every believer to comprehend than the idea of resurrection.

The doctrine of original sin (developed largely from Romans 5:12–21) stated that the guilt incurred by the sin of Adam and Eve was passed on by procreation from generation to generation. Baptism removed that guilt, but this led the church to concern itself over the fate of infants who died unbaptized. By the Middle Ages, the concept of *limbo* had appeared, a place where unbaptized infants (and the mentally defective) do not suffer the torments of hell but are deprived of the joy of the presence of God in heaven. The concept was never as fully developed as that of purgatory.

The elaborate system of penance was a major factor contributing to Luther's break with the Roman Catholic Church. Having become completely convinced of the efficacy of Christ's redeeming death, Luther concluded that penance was contrary to Christian teaching and that purgatory was thus nothing but a human invention, or, as he put it, "illusions of the devil." Calvin also taught that purgatory "makes void the cross of Christ; that it offers intolerable insult to the divine mercy; that it undermines and overthrows our faith." For if "the blood of Christ is the only satisfaction, expiation, and cleansing for the sins of believers, what remains but to hold that purgatory is mere blasphemy?" (*Institutes* III.v.6). Both Calvin and Luther retained the belief in an immortal soul, however. Calvin wisely advised, "Moreover, to pry curiously into their intermediate state is neither lawful nor expedient. . . . It is foolish and rash to inquire into hidden things, farther than God permits us to know" (*Institutes* III.xxv.6). Unfortunately, he did not completely follow his own advice.

In the century after Luther and Calvin, the Westminster Confession of 1647 stated succinctly the beliefs held by most Protestants until recent times:

1. The bodies of men, after death, return to dust, and see corruption; but their souls (which neither die nor sleep), having an immortal subsistence, immediately return to God who gave them. The souls of the righteous, being then made perfect in holiness, are received into the highest heavens, where they behold the face of God in light and glory, waiting for the full redemption of their bodies; and the souls of the wicked are cast into hell, where they remain in torments and utter darkness, reserved to the judgment of the great day. Besides these two places for souls separated from their bodies, the Scripture acknowledgeth none.

2. At the last day, such as are found alive shall not die, but be changed; and all the dead shall be raised up with the

selfsame bodies, and none other, although with different qualities, which shall be united again to their souls forever.

3. The bodies of the unjust shall, by the power of Christ, be raised to dishonor; the bodies of the just, by his Spirit, unto honor, and be made conformable to his own glorious body. (Chap. XXXIII)

The next chapter of the Confession speaks of the Last Judgment, so the basic teaching of Scripture is reaffirmed, purged of purgatory and emphasizing resurrection, but accepting the notion of the immortal soul as orthodox Christian teaching.

The idea of a soul that represents who one really is, that can survive beyond the death of the body, is so attractive and so much easier to comprehend than resurrection into a new creation at the last days that it has long been considered, in popular religion, the essential Christian belief. Evidence of this appeared in Europe in the 1950s, when the Swiss New Testament scholar Oscar Cullmann published an article titled "Immortality of the Soul or Resurrection of the Dead" ([1955–56] 1965), in which he developed what all scholars know to be the New Testament view. In the popular press, however, he was accused of attacking one of the fundamental beliefs of Christianity.

The rise of materialism and positivism and the development of the physical sciences in the 18th and 19th centuries began to create embarrassment concerning ideas such as heaven, hell, and the soul. Cosmology left no place for heaven above and geology no place for hell below. No experimental evidence could be produced for the existence of a soul. And so beliefs that had been held for centuries began to be challenged, but challengers have not succeeded, so far, in entirely displacing them from the "instincts" (shall we say) of Christians as they face death.

CREATIVITY AND CONFUSION

Churches were founded in North America as it was settled in the 17th and 18th centuries, but it has been estimated that in 1775 only about 5% of the North American population belonged to any church (Littell 1971:37). According to Littell (1971), for most of the 19th century the United States was missionary territory, but that mission work was highly successful. By 1900, church membership had risen to 36%; by 1926, it was better than 50%. The Great Awakening of the mid-18th century and the Second Awakening from the 1790s through the 1840s, followed by the work of revival preachers throughout the century, were major factors in the growth of the Christian religion.

Revivalism is important for this discussion because the primary themes of revival preachers were the condemnation of sin and the offer of salvation from hell and for heaven. There was plenty of sin to condemn. One author described a frontier town as follows:

At New Salem everybody came on Saturdays to trade, gossip, wrestle, raffle, pitch horse shoes, run races, get drunk, maul

one another with their fists, and indulge generally in frontier happiness, as a relief from the week's monotonous drudgery on the raw and difficult farms. (Beveridge 1928:I.110)

Not to be ignored was the social message of those preachers, which led to significant reforms throughout the country. Church discipline was usually accepted by church members, and the influence of churches' ethical teachings extended beyond their membership into the larger community. The old Christian message concerning life after death became elaborated in the preaching of revivalists as part of a technique to lead sinners to repent, convert, and be saved. (It is a question whether that elaboration led to satiation and contributed in part to the decline of interest in heaven and hell, especially in the 20th century.)

Jonathan Edwards's sermon "Sinners in the Hands of an Angry God," preached during the Great Awakening, has become the classic example of a "hellfire and brimstone" revivalist sermon. It is unfortunate that Edwards is remembered primarily for this, given that he was one of the most learned men of his time in America (1703–58), a philosopher, theologian, and the third president of Princeton. But he was also a powerful orator, and the sermon reminds us that this kind of preaching was not confined to poorly educated ministers. A few examples of the depictions of hell presented by later revival preachers serve to illustrate the thinking of the 18th and early 19th centuries. Charles G. Finney (1792–1875) moved his audiences with this:

Look! Look! . . . see the millions of wretches, biting and gnawing their tongues, as they lift their scalding heads from the burning lake! . . . See! see! how they are tossed, and how they howl. . . . Hear them groan, amidst the fiery billows, as they *Lash!* and *Lash!* and *Lash!* their burning shores. (Quoted in Weisberger 1958:115)

Jedediah Burchard elaborated the idea of a lake of fire:

An ocean of liquid burning brimstone, that is daily replenished. It is walled in by great walls guarded by devils armed with pitchforks. High on the crest of the waves of fire, the damned soul is swept toward this wall, where the sinner thinks he may find at least temporary rest, but when at last he has managed to climb part way out of this sea of fire he suddenly finds himself pitchforked back and swept out by the receding tide. (Quoted in Weisberger 1958:135)

Conversion by fear seemed to have great success for about a century, but during the latter part of the 19th century many preachers found the other side—the blessings of heaven—to be more persuasive. Henry Ward Beecher (1813–87) illustrates the transition:

When I come before the Eternal Judge and say, all aglow: "My Lord and God!" will He turn to me and say . . . "You did not come up the right road. Go down!" I to the face of Jehovah will stand and say: "God! I won't go to hell! I will go to heaven! I love Thee. Now damn me if Thou canst. I love Thee!" And God shall say, and the heavens flame with double and triple rainbows, and echo with joy: "Dost thou love? Enter in and be for ever blessed." (Quoted in Weisberger 1958:170)

Elaboration of the joys of heaven included more variety than did descriptions of hell. For some, it was virtual absorption into the Divine, with little concern expressed for the preservation of personality. Others emphasized rest and eternal praise of God. Many who had absorbed the 19th-century ethos of work and progress found that to be unacceptably boring, and postulated a new life of continual activity and development. What made heaven most important for most Christians was the hope of being reunited with their families, and in spite of all that has been lost during the 20th and early 21st centuries, this seems to prevail to the present.

Three offshoots of Christianity appeared in the United States during the 19th century, and I need to discuss them here because of their creativity concerning the afterlife. I refer to them as "offshoots" because although they all honor Jesus Christ in some way, they all also include beliefs never held by any earlier church.

The first of these offshoots, the Church of Jesus Christ of Latter-day Saints, was founded in 1830 in western New York by Joseph Smith, who said that he had translated the Book of Mormon from gold plates he had discovered there and later returned to a heavenly messenger. That book, plus the Book of Doctrines and Covenants and The Pearl of Great Price, became the basis for the beliefs and practices of the new church, but Mormons believe that church leaders may receive new revelations at any time. The church has extensive teachings about the afterlife. Everyone has existed as spirit children of God before they are born into this life, and at death everyone enters into a new stage of life where the soul may develop until the resurrection. The evil are separated from the righteous and suffer from guilt and fear, but they are given a chance to accept the truths of the Latter-day Saints. The righteous live in a paradise of lakes, forests, and flowers. Family members are reunited, and infants appear as adults. Heaven is an active place, with the righteous devoted to teaching, but the ordinances of the church can be performed only in temples on earth, so church members compile genealogies to enable them to be baptized for their ancestors, who can then make progress in the afterlife. The second coming of Christ will begin the millennium, when Zion will be built on the American continent. The final judgment will lead to a fiery fate for the wicked, and the earth will be re-created as a giant crystal ball. Those who progress furthest in their development in the spirit world can become gods (Doctrines and Covenants 76:5; for sources used in this summary, see McDannell and Lang 1988:313–22).

The second offshoot, Christian Science, is based on the work of Mary Baker Eddy, author of Science and Health With Key to the Scriptures ([1875] 1994), who founded the First Church of Christ Scientist in Boston in 1879. Eddy claimed to have found the true meaning of the Bible, but her teachings are more akin to ancient gnosticism than to orthodox Christianity. God is Mind and God is All, therefore matter is "nothing beyond an image in mortal mind" (Science and Health 116:18). And "Life is God, Spirit, the divine Principle of existence. . . . Life, as so understood, does not enter existence by birth nor leave it by death. It does not come or go. It is eternal. And the individual living identities, created, by Life, God, coexist with Him, indestructible and inviolable" (Christian Science Publishing Society 1990:72–73). Sin, sickness, and death are not created by God, who is all good, so although people are in truth affected by them in this life, Christian Science sets out to prove their essential unreality by its commitment to healing (Christian Science Publishing Society 1990:109–10). Those who die pass through "a belief called death" and then, "Mortals awaken from the dream of death with bodies unseen by those who think that they bury the body" (Science and Health 429:17–18). Eddy thus seems to speak of some sort of resurrection. There is no hell for sinners after death, for she defines hell as "mortal belief; . . . that which worketh abomination or maketh a lie" (Science and Health 588:1–4). Progress is possible after death. In the dialogue in Christian Science: A Sourcebook, the answer to the question "If I were more of a sinner than you, would you get eternal life sooner than I would?" is "We both already have eternal life, since God is our real Life, but I would be more ready to see that fact and be blessed by it than you would under those conditions" (Christian Science Publishing Society 1990:106). As for heaven, it is "a divine state of Mind in which all manifestations of Mind are harmonious and immortal, because sin is not there, and man is found having no righteousness of his own, but in possession of the 'Mind of the Lord'" (Science and Health 291:13–18). Note that the familiar body/soul dichotomy is modified in these teachings, as matter is unreal, and eternal life is essentially a given, for the Life we all share is the Life of God.

The Jehovah's Witnesses, whose group represents the third offshoot of Christianity, also have distinctive beliefs about God and human destiny. The group was founded by Charles T. Russell in 1872, and after his death in 1916 Joseph F. Rutherford assumed leadership and made significant changes in Russell's teachings. Rutherford's teachings deny the Christian doctrine of the Trinity, claiming it was promulgated by Satan (Rutherford 1937:48–49). God is one and should be addressed by his biblical name, Jehovah. Jesus is not divine but was created; he is, however, Jehovah's official representative on earth. The group's primary interest is eschatology. Rutherford taught that Satan was cast out of heaven in 1914 (Revelation 12:10–12), and Jesus returned to earth and began to reign, but invisibly. The Lord came to his Temple (see Malachi 3:1) in 1918, and the saints were resurrected. The battle of Armageddon (Revelation 16:16) is imminent, and the righteous who will survive it will remain on earth forever (Rutherford 1944:354). The millennium, the 1,000-year reign of Christ on earth (Revelation 20:4), will conclude with a brief reappearance of Satan, after which most of the righteous will live forever on a transformed earth (Revelation 21–22). Only 144,000 of them will go to heaven (Rutherford 1942:100; this figure is based on Revelation 7:4, 14:1, 3). Most of the Jehovah's Witnesses' eschatology is based on a literal reading of the Book of Revelation.

During the 20th century, the teachings of the mainline churches concerning death and the afterlife changed very little, in spite of the radical cultural changes believers were experiencing. Church members tended to be left with the traditional words, with their churches providing them little help in answering the questions raised by contemporary culture. Many churches developed strong concerns about the ills of society, and social action meant a focus on this life rather than the next. Death became an issue, but because of ethical questions raised by abortion, euthanasia, and medicine's increasing ability to prolong "life" in ways that scarcely fit the biblical definition of life.

Early in the century, the Presbyterian Church in the United States made a confessional change. Showing a pastoral concern for those who have lost children in infancy, the church added a declaratory statement to the Westminster Confession, saying, "We believe that all dying in infancy are included in the election of grace, and are regenerated and saved by Christ through the Spirit, who works when and where he pleases."

Individuals continued to raise the same questions and express the same hopes, of course. In his introduction to a chapter titled "Death and Beyond," Hans Schwarz (1979) indicates his intent to find a way between two frequent temptations: "undue restraint" (asserting that "all we can say about life beyond death is that God who was good to me in life will also be good to me in death") and a "travelog eschatology" (p. 195). Although the imaginations of individuals certainly continue to produce such "travelogs," the trend has been in the direction of what Schwarz calls undue restraint.

The eschatology of what may be called, for the sake of brevity, *millennial groups* has also focused in its own way on this world and this life, more than on the life to come. The messages of many radio and television preachers, as well as the extensive printed and video material of the same kind, emphasize that current events show that we are in the last days, and they combine texts from various parts of the Bible (especially Daniel and Revelation) to create a timetable. Their intent in emphasizing this timetable is to lead people to repentance and conversion before it is too late. Heaven and hell are certainly in the picture, but they do not dominate the message, as they did in the 18th and 19th centuries. For example, in a typical book of this kind, titled *Satan in the Sanctuary,* McCall and Levitt (1973) begin by demonstrating the necessity for a third temple to be built in Jerusalem, given that the antichrist must appear there for the events of the timetable to continue (2 Thessalonians 2:4); they then describe the antichrist, the rapture, the tribulation, Christ's return, and the millennium. As for "eternity," they do little more than quote

Revelation 21:1–2, Psalms 102:25–27, Revelation 21:4–5, and Revelation 32:22 (an error on their part—the chapter and verse they mean to cite are actually 22:22). For believers, the rapture will simply take them to "be with God." For others: "You'll get a subpoena: you'll have to appear before Christ on judgment day" (McCall and Levitt 1973:103). Thus millennial groups tend to elaborate the terrors of life on earth during the last days more than they do the terrors of hell.

The question of punishment after death has been a difficult one for Christians throughout their history. Justice seems to require punishment for the wicked who have flourished during this life, and during the many centuries when torture was taken for granted as part of the system of criminal "justice," it was easy for most to assume that earthly punishments would be magnified in the afterlife. Not everyone has accepted the idea of everlasting pain, however. Some have argued for the destruction of the wicked; others have argued for their suffering and then their destruction. Eventually, universal salvation has come to be espoused by those who believe that mercy triumphs completely over justice in the divine economy. This position does raise the question, however, of how much those who have made themselves enemies of God and have embraced evil will really enjoy God's presence in another life. So another, cautious way of speaking of the fate of the wicked is to say that they will be separated from God, and thus from all that is good. John Hick (1994) has summarized effectively the now widely accepted argument against the existence of the kind of hell that was accepted for centuries: "For a conscious creature to undergo physical and mental torture through unending time (if this is indeed conceivable) is horrible and disturbing beyond words; and the thought of such torment being deliberately inflicted by divine decree is totally incompatible with the idea of God as infinite love" (pp. 200–201).

By the end of the 20th century, some theologians had rejected not only the traditional hell, but all ideas of life after death. For example, Gordon Kaufman (1968), professor of theology at Harvard Divinity School, disposes of the resurrection of Christ by calling it at best a visionary experience of the disciples, then continues: "Although contemporary reconstruction of Jesus' resurrection clarifies the ultimate convictions of Christian faith about God's nature, it completely undermines the traditional basis for hope for individual life after death" (p. 468). He continues: "God created man as a finite being. Each man has his own beginning and end, and his own particular place within the on-going movement of history" (p. 470). He also notes, "We are now in a position to dispose rather quickly of such symbols as the 'last judgment,' 'heaven,' and 'hell'" (p. 471).

Those who retain the concept have generally taken the position that Schwarz (1979) calls undue restraint, or, as McDannell and Lang (1988) put it, "From Fundamentalists to post-Christian radicals, theologians have deserted a human-oriented afterlife and have returned to the God-oriented heaven of the reformers" (p. 308). Two examples must suffice here. For the noted Roman Catholic theologian Karl Rahner (1984:118), the afterlife is a "silent emptiness," but filled with the mystery we call God and the face of Jesus looking at us. In his lectures to pastors on the Apostles' Creed, the most influential Protestant theologian of the century, Karl Barth (1960), says:

> We have no idea either of the life beyond or of the passage of this life into the other. We have only what came to pass in Jesus Christ, in his reign, which is present with us through faith, and which is declared to us. What we dare believe, is that we participate in this change, in the effects of human sanctification that occurred in the resurrection of Jesus Christ. (P. 140)

A few examples of worship materials from one denomination will illustrate this reluctance to say too much, at the congregational level. The "Brief Statement of Faith" adopted by the Presbyterian Church (U.S.A.) in 1990 uses only an allusion to Romans 8:38–39 as its conclusion: "With believers in every time and place we rejoice that nothing in life or death can separate us from the love of God in Christ Jesus our Lord." The Presbyterian funeral service is called "Witness to the Resurrection" and includes a selection of resurrection texts from the New Testament from which the pastor may choose to read. The prayers use language such as the following, however: "We enter the joy of your presence"; "Because he lives, we shall live also"; "He [she] has entered the joy you have prepared." There is one allusion to a familiar hope that is not found explicitly in Scripture: "Look forward to a glad heavenly reunion." Resurrection itself appears in a prayer that quotes the final clauses of the Apostles' Creed. The words *immortal* and *soul* do not appear, but the promise of immediate union with God is the major theme (*Worshipbook* 1970:71–86). Finally, while I was working on this chapter, I noticed, in the bulletin at the church where I worship, these words: "Then at the last bring us to your eternal realm where we may be welcomed into your everlasting joy." If one were to look further, one surely would find the word *heaven* in contemporary worship materials, but note that in these examples it appears only in the expression "heavenly realm."

The popular literature is less cautious, however, and continues to use language that theological and denominational literature either avoids or uses sparingly. *The Golden Book of Immortality* (Clark and Davis 1954), an anthology containing hundreds of quotations on death and the afterlife from the works of respected authors, provides a helpful series of examples. Immortality rather than resurrection is definitely the theme. One section of the anthology, "Easter Horizons," contains references to the resurrection of Christ, but the editors evidently were not interested in including quotations concerning the resurrection of people in the last days. Other section titles reflect the themes of many a funeral sermon, such as "Fear Death? There Is No

Death!" and "Dawn!" Author after author affirms the existence of an immortal soul that goes to be with God immediately after death. The bases for their beliefs vary, however, and it is useful to note the reasons they give (as we remind ourselves that no one can cite experimental evidence).

Authority is enough for many. Charles M. Sheldon writes: "I believe in immortality because Jesus taught it and believed it. That is all the proof I need" (in Clark and Davis 1954:188). Many authors use an argument that may or may not be religious: the value of the human personality. Robert J. McCracken argues that because man was created in the image of God, "it is surely inconceivable that death should be the end of everything for him" (p. 31). Charles R. Woodson writes: "When we survey the long and costly course personality has traveled, the belief in immortality is inescapable. Something abiding must come of personality after death, or else the whole creative process of life is utterly purposeless" (p. 42).

The quotations in this anthology reveal several of the perennial reasons human beings continue to believe in life after death, in spite of its incomprehensibility. The feeling that the human personality is so valuable that it should not, and thus cannot, die is reinforced by Christian beliefs in God's love for every person and his intent to perfect his creation—clearly not yet done. The original, convincing argument, that Jesus was in fact raised from the dead, has not been forgotten (although it has been interpreted in a great variety of ways). The justice question, the original issue for Judaism, tends to be muted now. Another factor, which I have slighted so far in this chapter, is general human misery and the ability to endure in spite of it that the promise of a better life after death has provided. With that in mind, note that there is a certain irony in the "humanist outlook" expressed by F. A. E. Crew (1968): "In a world so organized that everyone equipped to do so would be able to enjoy life at least as much as I have done, there would be very few who would hanker after an existence beyond the grave for the life lived on this earth would be complete in itself" (p. 261).

For Crew, a comfortable and satisfying life seems to be quite enough to hope for; for those who produced the words I have quoted from *The Golden Book of Immortality,* it is not. In our time, most Christians reaffirm (often without being very specific) the traditional beliefs about life after death, but others have redefined Christianity so as to exclude an afterlife. That position is partly the result of historical skepticism—doubt about the accuracy of the Gospel accounts—and partly due to the effect of a scientific worldview that finds no place for any of this. As early Christians accepted what the world taught them about the immortal soul, so contemporary Christians find it difficult not to accept what the world teaches them about the impossibility of resurrection.

The scientific worldview changed radically during the 20th century, however, and there is a small number of Christians who know something of relativity and quantum mechanics, and who find that the new science affords possibilities for new speculation about the great unknown. Two examples must suffice here to illustrate this kind of thinking. The theologian Austin Farrer (1964) writes:

> According to his [Einstein's] unanswerable reasoning, space is not an infinite pre-existent field or area in which bits of matter float about. Space is a web of interactions between material energies which form a system by thus interacting. Unless the beings or energies of which heaven is composed are of a sort to interact physically with the energies in our physical world, heaven can be as dimensional as it likes, without ever getting pulled into our spatial field, or having any possible contact with us of any physical kind. (P. 145)

Hick (1994:278–96) elaborates a similar idea.

In a recent collection of essays edited by Peters, Russell, and Welker (2002), theologians and scientists take up seriously the issues raised by what contemporary science tells us about the cosmos and about human existence, and begin to explore the possibilities for a new understanding of resurrection. One writer outlines a program:

> We must reconstruct Christian eschatology to be consistent with both our commitments to the bodily resurrection of Jesus and thus an eschatology of transformation, *and* with scientific cosmology regarding the past history and present state of the universe and its basis in such foundational theories as special and general relativity and quantum mechanics. (Russell 2002:24)

Two competing views of the future of the universe prevail today, based on notions of continual expansion or eventual contraction, both of which allow no possibility for the continuance of life billions of years into the future. The two options have been labeled "freeze or fry," and neither offers any comfort of a hope for eternal life. Theologians may deal with this in at least two ways. For one, they can claim that because the present laws of nature are God's creative work, God is free to create in new ways, and the resurrection of Christ is an indication that he intends to do so (Russell 2002:19). Another argument is that quantum cosmology allows for the possibility of multiple universes, with natural laws of which we have no knowledge (Russell 2002:5)

Continuity and discontinuity have always been a problem for the resurrection hope. What, exactly, will be raised? Early theologians struggled with the problem of the decomposition of the body and tried various solutions to the question of identity: How can one say it is the same person who will be raised? (For new approaches, see the contributions in Peters et al. 2002, especially Murphy 2002; Schuele 2002.) One scientist proposes a completely theological answer: The "pattern" that is me is perfectly preserved in God's memory until I am reembodied in the resurrection (Polkinghorne 2002:52). He also considers that what we have learned about time allows for the possibility that there is no intermediate state (p. 53). Einstein's redefinition of time may allow speculation that although for us there is an intermediate period between death and resurrection, in the world of the resurrection there is no apparent interval.

These authors admit that the dialogue between science and eschatology is currently only a program, and there is no way to predict its results. Whether it will one day offer to Christians in local congregations new ways to think about death and the afterlife remains to be seen.

REFERENCES

Aries, Philippe. 1974. *Western Attitudes Toward Death: From the Middle Ages to the Present,* translated by Patricia M. Ranum. Baltimore: Johns Hopkins University Press.

Barth, Karl. 1960. *The Faith of the Church: A Commentary on the Apostles' Creed.* London: Collins.

Beveridge, Albert J. 1928. *Abraham Lincoln 1809-1858.* Boston and New York: Houghton Mifflin.

Cavallin, H. C. C. 1974. *Life After Death. Paul's Argument for the Resurrection of the Dead in 1 Cor. 15,* Part 1, *An Enquiry into the Jewish Background* (Coniectania Biblica, New Testament 7:1). Lund, Sweden: C. W. K. Gleerup.

Christian Science Publishing Society. 1990. *Christian Science: A Sourcebook of Contemporary Materials.* Boston: Christian Science Publishing Society.

Clark, Thomas Curtis and Hazel Davis, eds. 1954. *The Golden Book of Immortality: A Treasury of Testimony.* New York: Association Press.

Crew, F. A. E. 1968. "The Meaning of Death." In *The Humanist Outlook,* edited by A. J. Ayer. London: Pemberton.

Cullmann, Oscar. [1955–56] 1965. "Immortality of the Soul or Resurrection of the Dead." Pp. 9–35 in *Immortality and Resurrection,* edited by Krister Stendahl. New York: Macmillan.

Eddy, Mary Baker. [1875] 1994. *Science and Health With Key to the Scriptures.* Boston: First Church of Christ Scientist.

Farrer, Austin. 1964. *Saving Belief.* New York: Morehouse-Barlow.

Hick, John. 1994. *Death and Eternal Life.* Louisville, KY: Westminster/John Knox.

Kaufman, Gordon D. 1968. *Systematic Theology: A Historicist Perspective.* New York: Scribner.

Littell, Franklin H. 1971. *From State Church to Pluralism: A Protestant Interpretation of Religion in American History.* New York: Macmillan.

Martin-Achard, Robert. 1960. *From Death to Life.* Edinburgh: Oliver & Boyd.

McCall, Thomas S. and Zola Levitt. 1973. *Satan in the Sanctuary.* New York: Bantam.

McDannell, Colleen and Bernhard Lang. 1988. *Heaven: A History.* New Haven, CT: Yale University Press.

McGrath, Alister E. 1995. *The Christian Theology Reader.* Oxford: Blackwell.

Murphy, Nancey. 2002. "The Resurrection Body and Personal Identity: Possibilities and Limits of Eschatological Knowledge." Pp. 202–18 in *Resurrection: Theological and Scientific Assessments,* edited by Ted Peters, Robert John Russell, and Michael Welker. Grand Rapids, MI: William B. Eerdmans.

Nickelsburg, G. W. E. 1972. *Resurrection, Immortality and Eternal Life in Intertestamental Judaism.* Cambridge, MA: Harvard University Press.

Peters, Ted, Robert John Russell, and Michael Welker, eds. 2002. *Resurrection: Theological and Scientific Assessments.* Grand Rapids, MI: William B. Eerdmans.

Polkinghorne, John. 2002. "Eschatological Credibility: Emergent and Teleological Processes." Pp. 43–55 in *Resurrection: Theological and Scientific Assessments,* edited by Ted Peters, Robert John Russell, and Michael Welker. Grand Rapids, MI: William B. Eerdmans.

Rahner, Karl. 1984. "Erfahrungen eines katholischen Theologen." Pp. 105–119 in *Vor dem Geheimnis Gottes den Menschen verstehen,* edited by Karl Lehmann. Munich: Schell & Steiner.

Russell, John Robert. 2002. "Bodily Resurrection, Eschatology, and Scientific Cosmology." Pp. 3–30 in *Resurrection: Theological and Scientific Assessments,* edited by Ted Peters, Robert John Russell, and Michael Welker. Grand Rapids, MI: William B. Eerdmans.

Rutherford, Joseph F. 1937. *Uncovered.* Brooklyn, NY: Watch Tower Bible & Tract Society.

———. 1942. *The New World.* Brooklyn, NY: Watch Tower Bible & Tract Society.

———. 1944. *Religion Reaps the Whirlwind.* Brooklyn, NY: Watch Tower Bible & Tract Society.

Schuele, Andreas. 2002. "Transformed Into the Image of Christ: Identity, Personality, and Resurrection." Pp. 219–35 in *Resurrection: Theological and Scientific Assessments,* edited by Ted Peters, Robert John Russell, and Michael Welker. Grand Rapids, MI: William B. Eerdmans.

Schwarz, Hans. 1979. *On the Way to the Future.* Minneapolis: Augsburg.

Weisberger, Bernard A. 1958. *They Gathered at the River: The Story of the Great Revivalists and Their Impact Upon Religion in America.* Boston: Little, Brown.

The Worshipbook: Services. 1970. Philadelphia: Westminster.

Near-Death Experiences as Secular Eschatology

Tillman Rodabough

Kyle Cole

Near-death experiences (NDEs) have invaded an area of concern long reserved for theologians—the study of last things. A majority of Americans believe that there is life after death. According to an August 2000 Harris Poll, 85.6% of Americans 18 years of age or older believe the soul survives after death, and 75.3% think they will go to heaven (Harris Interactive 2000). In a national survey on near-death experiences, Gallup and Proctor (1982) found that approximately 23 million Americans "have, by prevailing medical definition, died briefly or . . . come close to death" (p. 6) and about 8 million (or approximately 35%) of these have had some sort of NDEs. A recent search of the Internet for the phrase "afterlife belief" using the Google search engine garnered a list of more than 26,000 sites, and investigation of such sites quickly reveals the wide variety of opinions people have concerning what happens after death and during NDEs. Have people who claim to have had NDEs actually encountered the afterlife before death? How does this relate to the study of last things by religious scholars? Can we measure the phenomenon of near-death experience using scientific methods?

As Schwarz (2001) notes, "In its broadest sense the term 'eschatology' includes all concepts of life beyond death and everything connected with it such as heaven and hell, paradise and immortality, resurrection and transmigration of the soul, rebirth and reincarnation, and last judgment and doomsday" (p. 26). Different world religions teach that an individual's journey does not merely come to an end at death; rather, death represents a beautiful beginning that no one truly comprehends (Preuss 1971).

The afterlife has long been claimed as the domain of theology, and thereby the existence of an afterlife has been deemed primarily a matter of faith. Although the experiences of people who have come close to death or who have purportedly crossed the line between life and death have been recorded for hundreds of years, only recently have researchers attempted more organized studies of this phenomenon. Because these studies have not been conducted under the auspices of any specific dogma, this approach might be termed *secular eschatology*—the secular study of last things. We divide our discussion in this chapter into three major sections: an examination of the near-death experience using Raymond Moody's model and the findings of other researchers who have tested that model, a look at the NDE as sacred eschatology, and, finally, an examination of the NDE as secular eschatology.

NEAR-DEATH EXPERIENCES: AN OVERVIEW

The major impetus for the current secular interest in what happens at the point of death was the publication in 1975 of the book *Life After Life,* by Raymond Moody, Jr.; in this book, Moody presents his model for what he terms "near-death experiences." Three factors served to strengthen the book's appeal when it first appeared. First, Moody had impressive credentials as a philosophy professor; he held both a Ph.D. and an M.D., and he taught ethics in a medical school. Second, Elisabeth Kübler-Ross, a charismatic speaker and probably the best-known student of death and dying at the time, contributed a foreword to the book, in which she wrote, "This book . . . will confirm what we have been taught for two thousand years—that there is life after death" (p. xi). And finally, in the book Moody pieced case histories together to tell the story of a peaceful journey that helped to reduce readers' anxiety about dying.

Moody's Research

Life After Life is Moody's report on a qualitative study in which he interviewed people who had undergone near-death experiences; the book presents a composite account of what it is like to die. Moody's narrative is based on accounts from (a) persons who were resuscitated after having been thought dead, (b) persons who came close to death through severe injury or illness, (c) persons who were actually dying, and (d) persons who had severe accidents but escaped unscathed. Despite similarities, no two of the accounts are precisely alike, and a few are not even close to being like the others. No one person whom Moody interviewed reported experiencing every element in the composite, no single element is reported by every person in the sample, and the order of the elements varies.

Using the most common experiences he found in all of his research, Moody produced a scenario comprising the following 11 elements, which he pieced together into this somewhat chronological order:

- *Ineffability:* Because the events that people experience during NDEs are outside their normal frame of reference, they encounter vocabulary difficulties in expressing what has happened to them. As Moody (1975) notes, most individuals find that "there are just no words to express what I am trying to say" (p. 26).

- *Hearing the news:* During their near-death experiences, many of those Moody interviewed heard the physician in the operating room or some spectator at the scene declare them dead. One woman told Moody that during attempts to resuscitate her after a cardiac arrest, she heard her surgeon remark, "Let's try one more time, and then we'll give up" (pp. 27–28).

- *Feelings of peace and quiet:* One of the most common elements in NDEs is an overwhelming feeling of peace. A man who was wounded while he was a soldier in Vietnam said that he felt "a great attitude of relief. There was no pain, and I've never felt so relaxed. I was at ease and it was all good" (pp. 28–29).

- *The noise:* Many report some sort of auditory sensation, either pleasant or unpleasant. The descriptions vary widely—"a really bad buzzing noise," "a loud ringing," "a loud click, a roaring, a banging," "Japanese wind bells," "a majestic, really beautiful sort of music" (p. 30).

- *The dark tunnel:* Some describe a sensation of traveling rapidly through dark space, often concurrently with hearing the noise. Moody's interviewees described the space as a cave, a well, a trough, an enclosure, a tunnel, a funnel, a vacuum, a void, a sewer, a valley, a passageway, and a cylinder (p. 30–33).

- *Out of body:* Individuals often report viewing others and themselves from vantage points outside their own physical bodies. Invisible, weightless, and lacking solidness, they possess the ability to move almost instantaneously from one place to another, with physical objects presenting no barrier. Their abilities to think, see, and hear are considerably enhanced. In this state, their improved hearing is more the ability to pick up thoughts than to hear physical sounds. But because others are unable to hear or see them, persons in this state feel isolated and alone.

- *Meeting others:* As individuals move deeper into their journeys, others come to aid them in the transition to death or to tell them it is not yet their time to die. The death-threatened persons usually recognize these as relatives or friends who have died previously, or as "guardian spirits" or "spiritual helpers" (p. 55).

- *The being of light:* Many describe encountering an indescribably brilliant light that does not hurt the eyes. Most perceive this light as a being of love and warmth. "Out-of-body" persons feel an irresistible attraction to this being, or feel completely at ease, as though they are engulfed in the presence of this being. Christians sometimes identify the being as Christ, whereas Jews may call it an angel, and persons with no prior religious beliefs may simply describe it as a "being of light." Communication between the light and the person close to death takes place through direct transfer of thoughts in such a way that lying and misunderstanding cannot occur. The being of light asks, "Are you prepared to die?" or "What have you done with your life to show me?" (p. 64). The being does not ask these questions in the spirit of condemnation, but in total love and acceptance, no matter what the answers may be.

- *The life review*: The being of light answers the question by presenting a panoramic review of the person's life. These three-dimensional memories are extraordinarily rapid and in chronological order. The person close to death reexperiences the emotions and feelings associated with the life events. The being of light provokes reflection while stressing the importance of learning to love other people and acquiring knowledge. Individuals report feeling as if they are actually in these flashbacks rather than just seeing them (p. 68).

- *The border or limit:* A few of Moody's respondents described some kind of border or limit, variously interpreted as "a body of water, a gray mist, a door, a fence across a field, or simply a line" (p. 73). They wanted to cross the barrier but felt themselves drawn back to life.

- *Coming back:* The most common feelings in the initial phase of the NDE are a desire to get back into the body and regret over dying. Some of Moody's respondents reported that, at a certain point, they did not want to return, but others were glad to return to complete some unfinished, important tasks. Some felt they were allowed to return by the being of light in response to their own requests to live or because God had some mission for them to fulfill. Others felt that the prayers of loved ones pulled them back from death.

Moody notes his respondents' hesitancy to report these experiences for fear others would think them mentally unstable. Many told him that after their experiences, life became more precious to them, and the acquisition of knowledge more important. There were "no feelings of instantaneous salvation or of moral infallibility" and no "holier-than-thou" attitudes (p. 93); however, for those who had these experiences, death was no longer threatening.

None of Moody's respondents described a heaven of pearly gates and winged angels or a hell of flames. Rather, they compared death to a "homecoming," an "awakening," a "graduation," and an "escape." For the most part, the reward-punishment model of the afterlife did not appear among Moody's subjects.

In the sequel to *Life After Life,* titled *Reflections on Life After Life* (1977), Moody describes additional, less frequently discussed, elements of the NDE. Possibly as a result of the popularity of his first book, he found that people who had had NDEs where much more willing to talk openly about the topic, and he examined so many cases that he no longer kept count. These accounts included the more common elements discussed above, along with the following four additional elements:

- *Vision of knowledge:* Many reported experiencing a flash of universal insight—a brief glimpse of a realm where all knowledge seems to exist. On returning, one forgets the knowledge but remembers the feeling of knowing. This vision encouraged many survivors to continue to learn in this life after their return.

- *City of light:* Although Moody reported the lack of anything resembling the traditional concept of heaven in the first book, the phrase "a city of light" occurred in several of the new accounts. In this "city," everything, buildings and countryside, appears to be bright with brilliant light from no apparent source (Moody 1977:17).

- *Realm of dulled spirits:* Several people reported observing "dulled spirits" or "confused beings" who seemed trapped in a particular state of existence, trying to decide where to go and what to do. Some of these washed-out, dejected spirits appeared to be trying to contact people on earth who had been close to them in life, to warn them to do good to others, but the people on earth were unaware of them. There appeared to be a huge array of these spirits attached to things important to them on earth.

- *Supernatural rescues:* Moody also found instances in which people reported being rescued either before or after death by some voices or persons telling them how to get out of precarious and threatening situations. Sometimes they heard voices telling them their time had not yet come or telling them to breathe so that they might resume life.

In his second book, Moody, reinterprets the absence of a spiritual judgment in his first book. When they had been asked to look back over their lives, Moody's interviewees had felt repentant over selfish acts and satisfaction where they had shown love and kindness. One individual perceived his flashback this way: "When I would experience a past event, it was like I was seeing it through eyes with (I guess you would say) omnipotent knowledge, guiding me, because it showed me not only what I had done but even how what I had done had affected other people" (quoted in Moody 1977:45).

According to Moody, the internal judgment within the individual meshes with Scripture, "With what judgment ye judge, ye shall be judged" (Matthew 7:1). Moody (1977) notes that "nothing I have encountered precludes the possibility of a hell" (p. 36). In his more recent work, Moody (1999) also suggests that his respondents' personal adventures assured them that life continues beyond death, which need not be feared. They became certain that the most important thing they could do while alive was to learn how to love.

Other Early Research

Kenneth Ring, author of *Life at Death* (1980), wanted to collect data in a way that could be analyzed and evaluated scientifically. Ring (a psychologist with a Ph.D.) and his assistants interviewed 102 people who had "come close to death." Of these, 26% were "deep experiencers," as defined by Ring's weighted index of components experienced, 22% were "moderate experiencers," and 52% were "nonexperiencers" (pp. 33–34). This gives his total sample a 48% experiencing rate, but only 39% of those referred by medical personnel and hospitals were experiencers. Because that 39% represents a more random selection than does the total figure, which includes self-referrals, Ring notes that the 39% experiencing rate is more representative of the total population. He warns that this is only suggestive, however, given that his sample was rather haphazardly collected.

Ring examined several correlates of the NDE and found that how a person nearly dies appears to make a difference: The incidence of core experiences is greatest in connection with illnesses (56%), followed by accidents (42%) and suicide attempts (33%). However, there is a gender difference, with women having core experiences related to illness and men having core experiences related to accidents. Relative to the NDE itself, 71% of Ring's subjects used the words "peaceful" and/or "calm" to describe their experiences, 37% had out-of-body experiences, 23% experienced the darkness, 29% heard some unusual noise, 33% saw the bright light, 21% entered the light, 27% felt that they approached some kind of boundary, 57% went through a decisional phase that frequently involved flashbacks over their previous lives, 61.5% found their experience difficult to put into words, 37% had an increased appreciation of life, 24% had a renewed sense of purpose, and 24% reported that they had become more loving as a result of their experiences.

Ring, followed by other researchers (Bates and Stanley 1985), reduced Moody's 15 elements to five categories: The first stage included a strong feeling of peacefulness; the second, traveling outside of one's body; the third, traveling through the tunnel or void; the fourth, the encounter with the being of brilliant light and love; and the last and rarest stage, arriving at the final destination or "heaven." Ring uses these stages in labeling persons with various levels of experience; for example, "Stage 3" refers to a person who went through the tunnel but did not encounter the being of light. Ring and Franklin (1981–82) suggest two models regarding the stages. In the first, the five stages unfold in a predetermined sequence—an invariant model; in the second, the stages unfold in one of several distinct individually determined progressions. Of the two, their second model more closely resembles Moody's presentation; their first model was an attempt to achieve more structure and predictability.

Basically, although Ring's book is titled *Life at Death: A Scientific Investigation of the Near-Death Experience*, his work is the Moody model with frequencies. The same problems that plagued Moody—lack of a representative sampling procedure, interviewing problems, lack of ability to corroborate reports, and lack of a genuine check of alternative hypotheses—also weaken Ring's work. His contributions to research into near-death experiences consist of additional accounts and better records. In his later book, *Heading Toward Omega: In Search of the Meaning of the Near-Death Experience* (1984), Ring concludes that near-death experiencers invariably believe that that they have glimpsed life after death and that they will survive death when it comes.

Michael Sabom (1982), a cardiologist, began his investigation of NDEs with a negative view of Moody's work and became a supporter as a result of his own research. Sabom sought to determine whether variables such as social, educational, professional, and religious backgrounds made any differences in the kinds of NDEs individuals report. Also, Moody had not attempted to substantiate near-death experiencers' reports of what they "saw" happening around them when they were presumed unconscious; Sabom wanted to try to corroborate such accounts be checking medical records and other available sources.

Over a 5-year period, Sabom located 116 persons who had survived near-death experiences. Of 78 persons chosen arbitrarily from this group, 43% reported NDEs. Sabom found no social or demographic differences between those who did and those who did not report NDEs. Neither prior knowledge of the Moody model nor the cause of the near-death encounter—whether coma, accident, or cardiac arrest—affected the probability of NDE occurrence. Unlike Ring, Sabom found no correlations between how individuals nearly died and what they experienced. Both researchers used nonrandom samples, and differential biases could result from the manner in which subjects were selected.

When Sabom tested the accuracy of the autoscopic, or self-visualizing, phenomenon, he found that 26 of the 32 descriptions contained accurate but only general impressions. However, when he asked control patients with heart trouble to reconstruct their in-hospital resuscitations, 80% made at least one major error in describing their resuscitations. Asking someone to tell you what he or she remembers is different from asking someone to reconstruct a total process; the fewer details likely in the first case allow less room for error. Among his subjects, Sabom recorded 32 autoscopic descriptions; 14 entered a dark void; 17 saw a bright light; 28 saw a region of great scenic beauty; 28 reported meeting some other person; and others reported a decision to go back, a border or limit, or a

change in attitude toward death—either their own or that of others. Overall, Sabom's work is as entertaining as Moody's and provides more demographic information and statistical comparisons. Sabom concludes that medical personnel must be more respectful of "unconscious" patients, particularly where careless conversation about the grim details or the hopelessness of the situation is concerned.

Flynn (1985) examined the lives of near-death experiencers and found support for earlier findings that such persons often change their lives after their NDEs. This transformation to some degree resembles the kind of change associated with religious conversion. We now turn to the subject of the NDE as an example of the life after death promised in most religious traditions.

NEAR-DEATH EXPERIENCES AS SACRED ESCHATOLOGY

Although Moody did not interpret his findings in a sacred sense, but rather simply as descriptions of what people actually experienced, others moved quickly to make the religious connection. Maurice Rawlings (1978), a cardiologist, recorded many of the same elements that Moody found from his own interviews with patients whom he resuscitated—the out-of-body experience, the dark tunnel, the noise, the river, the dead relatives, and the being of light, along with music and the city of gold. However, additional elements piqued his curiosity. Rawlings had an experience in which he was frightened by the pleas of a man he was resuscitating, who each time he was brought back to consciousness begged, "Don't stop! . . . Each time you quit I go back to hell! Don't let me go back to hell!" A couple of days later, when Rawlings returned to ask the patient what this hell was like, all the patient could remember of his NDE was the usual pleasant, Moody-type scenario. This experience motivated Rawlings to conduct research on the negative aspects of near-death experiences.

Rawlings (1978, 1983) reports that among the one-fifth of those resuscitated with experiences to report, unpleasant experiences appear as frequently as pleasant ones. Usually, however, the unpleasant experiences related during resuscitation or immediately after are forgotten within a short period. Rawlings reasons that these experiences are so bad that the mind copes by repressing them. Also, people may be somewhat embarrassed to report any temporary sojourns in hell because of what that implies about their personal morality. Rawlings interprets the pleasant place described in Moody's writings as a prejudgment "sorting" ground; he suggests that the tolerant being of light may even be the devil in disguise, lulling the visitor into complacency. Rawlings's explanations demonstrate the ease with which these experiences can be given alternative, even opposite, interpretations.

Other writers who take a traditional Christian perspective have offered warnings about the Moody model. For example, Tal Brooke (1979) suggests that all is not as it appears. Biblical exegesis, according to Brooke, reveals that "the deceased, the dead, cannot be contacted. God has created an impassable barrier. What are, in fact, being contacted in place of the sought-after human souls are some type of deceiving spirits masquerading as the deceased" (p. 69). Brooke asserts that Moody has been seduced by the beliefs of Eastern religions. Norman Gulley (1982), a professor of systematic theology and a member of the Seventh-Day Adventist denomination, says that death is an enemy, and any other teaching is false. He asks, "If Christ did not ascend to his Father until the resurrection morning, and waited in the grave during the interim, why should we expect any other humans to rise heavenward immediately at death instead of waiting until their final resurrection?" (p. 7). Harold Kuhn (1981), another religion professor, says that the darker encounters that Rawlings has written about should not be left out of media coverage in favor of encounters that fit the more positive Moody model: "If the two types can be presented in balance, they may serve to undergird the clear teaching of our Lord concerning the final division of mankind" (p. 82). Atwater (1994) places all NDE components into four different categories: the initial experience, the unpleasant or hell-like experience, the pleasant or heaven-like experience, and the transcendent experience. He sees all of these experiences as enlightenment that comes from a higher being, whether the focus is spiritual or knowledge related.

Clearly, the writers cited above see the near-death experience as sacred eschatology to be reinterpreted according to their religious beliefs. Lorimer (1989) points out that over hundreds of years, Christianity has had a difficult time integrating the Platonic idea of the immortality of the soul with the Hebrew idea of the resurrection of the flesh. Therefore, many Christians quickly adopted the phenomenon of the NDE as proof of the existence of heaven, God, and other religious figures; the separation of body and soul; and the possibility of resurrection.

The Moody model is not inconsistent with religion; indeed, it parallels Christianity in a number of ways. Different religions, and even different people within a single religious denomination, construct different conceptions of the afterlife. Differences appear even in biblical accounts. On one hand, Jesus' words on the occasion of the raising of the daughter of Jairus, "She is not dead, but sleeps" (Matthew 9:24; Mark 5:39; Luke 8:52), have been interpreted to refer to "soul sleep"—the idea that the soul becomes unconscious at death. Similarly, in John 11:11, Jesus speaks to his disciples: "Lazarus has fallen asleep and I go to awake him." Paul refers in 1 Thessalonians 4:13 to those Christians who have already died as "those who have fallen asleep," and in Acts 7:60 he concludes his description of the stoning death of Stephen with "he fell asleep." On the other hand, the Scriptures support the idea that the dead go immediately to a place where they have a conscious existence. In Luke 23:43, for example, Jesus assures the penitent thief hanging on the cross, "Today you will be with me in paradise."

Whatever happens immediately after death, at some point the dead face one or more judgments, according to the Bible. The "sheep and the goat judgment" in Matthew 25:31–46 refers to a parable that Jesus told, suggesting that the good and bad are to be separated by God's judgment to their eternal destiny—one of bliss and honor for the servants of God and the other of terror and punishment for those who have opposed his will in the physical life.

For most religions, and particularly for Christianity, faith is important for understanding the afterlife. As this short discussion illustrates, one can paint different pictures using Scripture, depending on which verses or segments one emphasizes and how one interprets them, but the Moody model is not inconsistent with the "Today you will be with me in paradise" perspective.

Parallels in Other Literature

In this subsection, we review and examine past accounts of the experience of death and near death for elements similar to those recorded by Moody. Scrutiny of religious writings and folklore for parallels in NDE descriptions reveals the widespread appearance of these phenomena (Holck 1978). For example, the auditory sensation common to NDEs has a parallel in the Bardo Thodol (the Tibetan Book of the Dead), where the dying person is told that "the natural sound of reality reverberating like a thousand thunders simultaneously sounding, will come" (Evans-Wentz 1960:104). The sensation of being in a dark tunnel, and the accompanying or interchangeable sensations of voidness or vacuum, may relate to the voidness, *Shunyata,* described in Eastern tradition (Eliade 1967).

The out-of-body experience and the awareness of a "spiritual body" is perhaps the feature most widely shared. The Indian tribes of the Argentine and Bolivian Chaco believed that the soul "at first hovers about its old abode, the dead body and the house where the departed lived" (Karsten 1932:189). The Zoroastrian tradition holds that the soul stays near the body for 3 days, hoping to return to the body (Pavry 1965). The Bardo Thodol states that the soul stays in the place where it had lived, sees its relatives, and hears the wailings (Evans-Wentz 1960).

Members of the Church of Jesus Christ of Latter-day Saints, the Mormons, are encouraged to keep diaries, and these documents provide many interesting records of the significant events of their lives. Lundahl (1979) gives several examples of out-of-body experiences from accounts in Mormon diaries. For instance, in a diary entry dated 1838, a Mormon woman relates that her spirit left her body and she was able to see it lying on the bed and her sisters weeping. Another Mormon's diary from the early 1860s tells how a man who was badly injured in an accident was able to see his body and the men standing around it from a position in the air above; he also was able to hear their conversation. In 1898, a Mormon missionary near death reported that his spirit left his body, although he could not tell how; he said that he saw himself standing

4 or 5 feet in the air, and saw his body lying below him on the bed (Lundahl 1979).

The inaudibility and invisibility of the nonmaterial entity is illustrated by a Chippewa story about a slain chief who spoke to his wife; she could not hear him until he returned to his body. Lithuanian folklore also includes a story of a man who grieved with his family for someone who had died until he realized at his funeral 3 days later that it was his body they were grieving over and returned to life (Eliade 1967).

The common NDE element of meeting dead relatives and friends is similar to Jensen's (1963) description of primitive peoples' view of the journey into death as one in which they are reunited with departed tribal members and with the deity who receives the dead. The Siberian funeral ceremony suggests that the shaman searches through the crowd of spirits to find close relatives of the deceased to whom the soul can be entrusted (Eliade 1967). The Winnebago tribe believed that dead relatives would guide and take care of the new soul. A Chinese tradition holds that the new soul is led by a demon to ancestors, who then guide it to the happy land. In the Islamic tradition, the souls of the faithful welcome and guide the new soul to heaven. And in Lithuanian folklore, the deceased friends of the dying person come to visit and take him or her away (Eliade 1967). In Lundahl's (1979) review of Mormon near-death experiences, he relates the case of one man who reported seeing his little daughter, who had died many years earlier. Another reported being introduced to five generations of his father's people, and a 16-year-old Mormon girl reported that her departed mother had been her guide in the spirit world.

Encounters with a being of light are also found in many traditions. A passage from the Saddharma-Smrityri-pasthana Sutra (chap. 34) states that as death approaches, the dying person sees a perplexing bright light (Eliade 1967). The Bardo Thodol states, "The wisdom of the Dharma-Dhatu, blue in color, shining transparent, glorious, dazzling . . . will shoot forth and strike against thee with a light so radiant that thou wilt scarcely be able to look at it" (Evans-Wentz 1960:160). The Chaco Indians believed that upon their arrival in the afterlife, the souls of the dead encountered an ever-shining sun (Karsten 1932).

The life review, or playback of the individual's actions, is roughly paralleled in the Bardo Thodol, where "the Lord of Death will say, 'I will consult the Mirror of Karma.' . . . He will look in the mirror, wherein every good and evil is reflected. Lying will be of no avail" (Evans-Wentz 1960:166). Similar accounts of the barrier between life and death have been given by the Maori and by the Thompson River Indians of British Columbia (Eliade 1967); that is, those who have died approached some kind of barrier and returned to life. In his review of near-death experiences in Mormon writings, Lundahl (1979) found no flashbacks, but he did find the barrier and the request that the individual return to life. He relates the following typical Mormon experience. In 1891, a 15-year-old Mormon

girl, sick with scarlet fever, reported that her spirit left her body but could still hear and see her family mourning her death; went to another world, where she could hear music and singing; visited with many of her deceased family and friends; saw children singing in age-segregated groups similar to Sunday school; and was told to return to earth to finish her mission, which she did, although it was not her wish. In more recent historical research, Lundahl (1993–94) quotes full Moody-type scenarios directly from pre-1900 Mormon publications, revealing the existence of written documentation of these phenomena more than a century and a half ago.

Based on his review of religion and folklore, Holck (1978) suggests that there are similarities between contemporary NDEs and those randomly gathered from literary sources. He concludes that these phenomena are universal—a part of the experience of the human race. However, Holck asserts that whether these phenomena are archetypal, in the Jungian sense, or factual events is open to interpretation. As the above review shows, some relatively similar phenomena have happened across time and ethnic groups. If people who have NDEs actually perceive the literal contact with the afterlife that they report, these studies provide reinforcement for the religious study of last things.

NEAR-DEATH EXPERIENCES AS SECULAR ESCHATOLOGY

Looking at NDEs from a secular perspective involves taking two approaches: (a) searching for nonmetaphysical explanations for these experiences and (b) examining the experiences objectively, with no religious dogma attached. In this section we do both.

Some researchers offer a physiological explanation for the NDE. They assert that the person near death does not actually travel out of body and meet deceased relatives and religious figures; rather, these perceptions are triggered in the mind by physiological changes occurring in the organism. NDEs, therefore, become a study of last things without the sacred explanation. We do not actually see with our eyes but with our brains. Pressure against the eye produces small flashes of light when certain receptors excited by the pressure are induced to send the brain messages of perceptions that have no real object in the environment. As the brain deteriorates, changes in the central nervous system alter perception of the environment. The unconscious could be stimulated by a number of deep organismic changes, which can be separated into at least five categories: starvation and sleep deprivation, toxic metabolic products, autointoxication, anoxia, and drug use. We discuss each of these briefly in turn below.

Starvation and sleep deprivation. Starvation and sleep deprivation can interfere with psychological functioning to the point of inducing hallucinations. Symptoms of many diseases interfere with sleep and nutrition, so hospital patients could find themselves, through their inability to assimilate food or to get anything but drugged sleep, short on both, despite the best efforts of medical staff.

Toxic metabolic products. Profound psychological changes can occur as the result of toxic metabolic products in the organism. In hepatic and renal disease, for example, the liver may fail to detoxify various noxious substances, and the kidneys may eliminate only some of the organism's waste products. Extreme mental changes can occur when an individual suffers from a progressive disease of the kidneys with subsequent uremia.

Autointoxication. Disintegration of bodily tissues, as in cancer or wasting and degenerative diseases, can trigger a high degree of autointoxication. This is particularly so when psychological functioning is affected by the pathological process in diseases such as meningitis or encephalitis, or by brain tumors, head injuries, or other types of brain damage.

Anoxia. Anoxia, an insufficient supply of oxygen to the tissues of the body, occurs frequently in dying individuals. Insufficient oxygen, or excess carbon dioxide, produces an abnormal mental state. Lung diseases such as emphysema or pulmonary tumors, which reduce the body's oxygen intake, can cause anoxia. It is also caused by inadequate oxygen distribution throughout the body, as in cardiac failure or anemia, or by interference with the enzymatic transfer of oxygen at a subcellular level (Grof and Halifax 1978). Depriving the brain of oxygen has long been associated with visions and religious experiences. Australian Aboriginals at one time used near-suffocation or inhalation of smoke in religious rituals. Many religious experiences in India are aided by hyperventilation, holding the breath, obstruction of the larynx, constriction of the carotid arteries, or prolonged suspension by the feet—all of which result in brain anoxia. In a study of deathbed observations by doctors and nurses, Osis (1965) found that anoxia was the most frequently used explanation for patients' reported visions and perceptions of apparitions. Where death is caused by cardiac arrest, the tissues of the body can survive for a time by turning the oxygen present in the blood into carbon dioxide. Several minutes pass before the brain cells suffer irreversible damage. In this unusual state of consciousness, an individual can perceive that he or she is experiencing an entire lifetime in a few minutes on the clock (Grof and Halifax 1978).

Drug use. "I realized that I had died, that I, Timothy Leary, the Timothy Leary game, was gone. I could look back and see my body on the bed. I relived my life, and re-experienced many events I had forgotten" (quoted in Kohler 1963: 31–32). So Leary recounts a psychedelic experience he had in Mexico after ingesting mushrooms. Another drug user reports: "My ideas of space were strange beyond description. I could see myself from head to foot as well as

the sofa on which I was lying. About me was nothingness, absolutely empty space" (quoted in Unger 1963:113). Jane Dunlap (1961) writes of her experience on LSD, "As I watched, love which I had felt overpoweringly throughout the day multiplied until I seemed to be experiencing the sum total of love in the soul of every person who lives" (p. 184). After this experience, Dunlap says, "I feel that I am less critical and considerably more tolerant, sympathetic, forgiving, and understanding" (p. 202). Meduna (1958) notes that carbon dioxide narcosis can produce almost all of the effects of hallucinogens, and carbon dioxide buildup is a major consequence of the impairment of circulation during the dying process. Jack Provonsha (1981), a professor of ethics and an M.D. whose recognized area of authority is hallucinogenic drugs, completes his summary of the parallel between the effects of hallucinogenic drugs and Moody's model as follows: "Altered psycho-chemistry is often accompanied by heightened levels of suggestibility. The belief systems of persons taking hallucinogens thus may strongly condition the content of the experience through auto- and hetero-suggestion" (p. 15).

Stanislav Grof, a psychiatrist, and Joan Halifax, a medical anthropologist, describe the use of drug therapy with terminally ill patients in their book *The Human Encounter With Death* (1978). They found the experiences of patients under the influence of lysergic acid diethylamide (LSD) to be remarkably similar to those described in the Moody model. Grof and Halifax studied patients at Sinai Hospital in Baltimore who fit the following criteria: some degree of physical pain, depression, tension, anxiety, or psychological isolation; minimum life expectancy of 3 months; and no major cardiovascular problems, brain hemorrhage, gross psychopathology, or history of epileptic seizures. The psychedelic therapy consisted of three phases. During the preparatory period, the researchers explored the dying patient's past history and present situation and established a trust relationship with the patient and his or her family. The second phase consisted of the drug session, which lasted from 8 to 12 hours. Lying down with eyes covered, listening to music over stereophonic headphones, the patient was periodically given opportunities to communicate any feelings or insights he or she wished. Then, as the patient returned to a normal state of consciousness, relatives or close friends were invited for a "reunion" that frequently facilitated honest communication and more rewarding interaction. The third phase consisted of several postsession interviews through with the researchers intended to facilitate integration of the psychedelic experiences into the life of the dying individual.

There are many direct parallels between the psychedelic experiences that Grof and Halifax (1978) report and Moody's NDE model. For example, the patients in their study experienced the feeling of leaving the body and out-of-body travel (p. 59). Some experienced auditory sensations; for instance, one patient reported hearing "an intense humming sound of a comforting and soothing quality" (p. 97). Another described fighting her way through a "black mass" (p. 86), and one mentioned a void. Some patients had the sense of vivid and convincing encounters with the spiritual essences of various deceased relatives. Reassuring telepathic exchange introduced familiarity and joyful expectation into the previously terrifying concept of dying (p. 113). Patients reported encountering a comforting light. One man, for example, became convinced that he had died, and a brilliant source of light, whom he identified as God, appeared and told him not to fear and assured him that everything would be all right (p. 76). Patients frequently reported encountering deities and demons (p. 156). Past life review was also a frequent phenomenon; during a few minutes, persons influenced by LSD subjectively experienced entire lifetimes or even millennia (p. 186). Frequently, these psychedelic sessions included "a condensed replay and reevaluation of their entire past history from the moment of birth on" (p. 113). One patient related: "Everything that has been my life is being shown to me. . . . Memories, thousands of memories. . . . Periods of sadness and periods of nice happy feelings. . . . With the beautiful memories, everything gets very sunny. There is lots of light everywhere; with the sad ones, all gets darker. . . . It was such a beautiful life; no one would believe what a beautiful life I have had" (p. 44).

The patients experienced feelings of love, tranquility, and peace, which was one of the objectives of the LSD therapy. A 40-year-old woman commented, "I am not sad any longer that I am to die. I have more loving feelings than ever before" (p. 106). The changes in another man were dramatic. He became peaceful and serene, saying, "I feel like I might come to heaven if I die. . . . I was there" (p. 76). One woman underwent a profound spiritual transformation as a result of her LSD session that improved her remaining days (p. 64). Another similarity between these experiences and NDEs was their ineffability—that is, the experiencers noted their lack of ability to describe the psychedelic state adequately (p. 130).

Finally, Grof and Halifax (1978) were able to conduct some subjective tests of these parallels. Several patients who had undergone psychedelic sessions later experienced coma or clinical death from which they were resuscitated, and they described definite parallels between the drug sessions and the experience of "dying." They also indicated that the lessons they had learned in their LSD sessions, of letting go and leaving their bodies, proved invaluable and made the experiences more tolerable (p. 59).

If the similarities between the experiences of these patients and Moody's model of NDEs seem remarkably close, we should point out the lack of chronology in the page numbers we reference above. We have taken these examples from various places throughout Grof and Halifax's book and arranged them to coincide with the sequence constructed by Moody. This is not necessarily a naturally occurring sequence, but, as Moody (1975) notes, neither is his. The important thing to note is that most of the components of the Moody model were experienced by persons who were *not* at the point of immediate death. The

parallels were so clear that those who experienced both the psychedelic sessions and "clinical death" noticed them. An individual does not have to be at the point of death to experience such phenomena. Something occurs within the human mind that is similar across cultures and different experiences, but Grof and Halifax's drug therapy research demonstrates that it is not necessarily related to imminent death.

Tests of Metaphysical Versus Physiological Hypotheses

Rodabough's (1985) analysis of near-death experiences offers contrasting explanations for NDE accounts. Concluding that what near-death experiencers reports are actual experiences, he divides the explanations for these into metaphysical, physiological, and social psychological categories. Metaphysical explanations correspond to the sacred eschatology, physiological explanations correspond to the secular eschatology, and social psychological explanations give reasons for various components of the experience without suggesting deception. Although Rodabough assumes that simplest explanations are best and advocates the social psychological model, additional research conducted since his review was published gives credence to the metaphysical model without excluding the physiological model.

Karlis Osis and Erlendur Haraldsson focus on deathbed visions in their book *At the Hour of Death* (1977). These researchers tried to test two hypotheses that may explain such visions. According to the "death as transition" or metaphysical (sacred eschatology) hypothesis, dying persons' perceptions should be relatively coherent and should portray otherworldly messengers and environments for which there is no adequate preconception. Such afterlife visions should vary little by age, sex, religious orientation, or nationality—that is, if dying persons are seeing something that is actually there, their descriptions should cut across individual, national, and cultural differences. According to the "death as destructive" or physiological (secular eschatology) hypothesis, the content of deathbed visions should express memories and expectations stored in the brain of the individual and so should reflect cultural conditioning by family, society, and religious institutions.

To test these hypotheses, Osis and Haraldsson mailed questionnaires to physicians and nurses at hospitals in the United States northern India. They obtained 606 cases in which terminal patients reported hallucination of persons. The largest category, 47%, consisted of apparitions of the dead, and 91% of these were identified as deceased relatives of the patient. The patients' predominant reaction to their dead relatives' apparent take-away missions was one of serenity and peace. Most of these deathbed visions were of short duration. In 62% of the cases, the person died within 24 hours of the hallucination and lost consciousness in less time than that (Osis and Haraldsson 1977:62).

In their study, Osis and Haraldsson controlled for brain disease, injury, stroke or uremia, fever, and drugs. Although they do not mention the possibility of serendipitous effects of other medicines, they operated conservatively by including everything in their hallucinogenic index that might increase a patient's probability of hallucination.

Osis and Haraldsson did find that patients' degree of involvement in religion and belief in an afterlife appeared to shape the phenomena to some extent along cultural lines. For example, an Indian woman suffering a myocardial infarction saw high mountains covered with snow, but no Americans saw a snow-covered paradise. For Indians, but not for Americans, the lower echelon of heavenly personnel frequently behaved in an authoritarian manner. Americans saw figures in heavenly surroundings, whereas Indians saw them in their own sickrooms (p. 107). Some 32% of the Indian patients had negative reactions to apparitions of religious figures, but only 10% of the Americans experienced negative emotions (p. 110). Indians hallucinated fewer dead than religious figures (28% to 48%), whereas Americans hallucinated five times more dead than religious apparitions. Americans favored female apparitions, who often portrayed younger persons. As Osis and Haraldsson (1977) note, "On the whole, Christians tended to hallucinate angels, Jesus, or the Virgin Mary, whereas Hindus would most usually see Yama, the god of death, one of his messengers, Krishna, or some other deity" (p. 64). These visions were relatively independent of the individuals' reported depth of belief. It is interesting to note also that no dead clergymen and only five gurus turned up in the visions to aid patients in the transition from one world to the next.

The death as destruction hypothesis suggests that individuals' experiences should depend on hallucinogenic medical factors, psychological variables, and cultural forces, whereas the survival hypothesis suggests that otherworldly visions should be relatively independent of such factors because of their ostensibly external origin. Osis and Haraldsson (1977:171) report that the survival hypothesis (sacred eschatology) was supported to their satisfaction over the death as destruction (secular eschatology) hypothesis by the data described above. However, as this brief review demonstrates, these perceptions are culturally determined to some extent, which also gives some credibility to the secular hypothesis.

One limitation of Osis and Haraldsson's study is its reliance on the recollections of physicians and nurses; such recall is notorious for its biased selectivity. So whereas Moody constructed a subjective model, Osis and Haraldsson relied on subjective recollections to test their hypotheses. The lack of a control group with which to make comparisons also presents a problem for their study. Osis and Haraldsson describe the characteristics of terminal and nonterminal patients who saw apparitions, but they do not describe the characteristics of patients in the two

categories who did not hallucinate. If, for example, 50% of those hallucinating had fevers above 100 degrees and only 5% of those not hallucinating had fevers above 100 degrees, this contrast would implicate fever as an agent of hallucination. Without such data, some meaningful comparisons cannot be made.

As a result of Osis and Haraldsson's research, we know that some people have visions that cannot be explained by drugs, fever, and brain disturbance. We can also conclude that expectations about the afterlife affect what individuals see when they are near death. Although we do not know what actually happens to people as they are dying, systematic research such as this brings us closer.

Recent Research: A Secular Collection and Examination of Data

In this subsection we look at the other point of secular eschatology, an objective examination of the NDE without the influence of any religious dogma. In recent research, Ring and Lawrence (1993) attempted to verify NDE accounts by checking medical records and interviewing external observers. Each of Ring's research projects has moved the study of NDEs closer to more rigid scientific exploration.

In addition to surveys, interviews, and attempts to correlate certain aspects of the NDE to demographic or medical variables (Owens, Cook, and Stevenson 1990), scholars have recently used more individualist case studies. For example, Michael Sabom (1998) has employed in-depth case studies to test his earlier, more general interviews. He reports in comprehensive detail one patient's surgical procedures and the environmental setting. His account includes the patient's exact physical condition— induced cardiac arrest, deep hypothermia (a core body temperature of 60 degrees), barbiturate cerebral protection (no brain wave activity on the electroencephalogram), no brain stem response, and all blood drained from the brain in preparation for the removal of a giant basilar artery aneurysm. At this time, when she was as clinically dead as could be determined, the patient had an extended (Stage 5) NDE; she later described an unusual bone saw the surgeon was using, recounted comments made by those in the operating room during the surgery, and concluded by saying that during her NDE she was the most aware she had ever been in her life. The significance of this study is that Sabom presents detailed comparisons between what the patient reported and the surgery room notes and recall of the other participants during the time of clinical death. This research was not based on the more distant recall used in the earlier studies.

Kelly, Greyson, and Stevenson (1999–2000) require that an NDE have three features if it is to be understood to suggest the possibility of survival after the death of the body: enhanced mental processes at a time when physiological function is seriously impaired, being out of the body, and awareness of events not available by the usual senses. In a sample of people who would have died without medical attention, Owens et al. (1990) found that 62% had increased mental abilities—that is, increased speed, logic, thought, visual and auditory clarity, and control of cognition. In regard to the second feature, Kelly et al. found that 50% of those they studied who were close to death reported looking down on their bodies from positions outside themselves.

To examine the third feature, extrasensory perception, Kelly et al. focus on case studies, including Sabom's, in which the experiences of sedated patients in surgery are later verified—specifically those elements of the experiences that the patients could not have seen. Cook, Greyson, and Stevenson (1998) report one such experience in detail: A patient describing an NDE during surgery said that one of the surgeons had held his hands to his chest and "flap[ped] his arms as if trying to fly." The researchers were able to verify the patient's observation through interviews with witnesses and by examining physicians' notes. Cases in which research can verify near-death experiencers' perceptions of events outside the normal range of the physical senses are not common; each such case is thus a significant contribution. Kelly et al. (1999–2000) conclude that such research demonstrates that individuals can be aware of remote events not accessible to the ordinary senses.

In a recent report on a 13-year longitudinal study conducted in the Netherlands, van Lommel et al. (2001) provide a matched comparison between NDE patients and non-NDE patients. All 344 patients tracked by the Dutch team had cardiac arrests and were for a brief time clinically dead, with unconsciousness resulting from insufficient blood supply to the brain. All were resuscitated during a fixed period of time and interviewed. By comparing these groups, the researchers gathered reliable data about possible causes and consequences of NDEs that allowed them to conclude that the NDEs could not have been caused by medical factors. This type of careful research, employing longitudinal experimental design, combined with research using individual case studies, as described earlier, continues to advance our knowledge of NDEs.

CONCLUSION

Several conclusions may be drawn from the material we have presented in this chapter. Early attempts to gather data about near-death experiences were often limited by poor samples and problems of recall, but data gathering methods have improved steadily over time. Given the current definition of death as whole-brain death, few of these experiences have occurred while persons were dead, so most are not after-death experiences. Because so many of these accounts have not resulted from clinical death, and because those occurring apart from clinical death appear

to be little different from those related to clinical death, we may conclude that certain stimuli present in stressful situations may trigger similar perceptions in the brain. The data collection methods used by researchers investigating NDEs do not lead us to any conclusions about an afterlife. Although these NDE data may be analyzed statistically, they do not lend themselves to causal inference because they do not allow us to discard alternative explanations.

Typically, interpretations of NDEs have matched the expectations of the interpreters. Contrary to Kübler-Ross's proclamation that research into NDEs confirms the fact of life after death, the afterlife still remains a subject for religious faith and beliefs. Most skeptics could be convinced that these accounts are actual after-death accounts only if they were presented with a well-documented case of a person who had no vital signs and a flat EEG for a prolonged period who then came back to life and gave a report. Even then, many skeptics would argue that the "experience" occurred in the person's mind during the moments of death as the brain lost its oxygen supply and chemical changes took place, not during the period of the flat EEG (Goleman 1977). At present, we have no sure way of knowing.

In recent years, some researchers have organized to pursue accounts of NDEs actively and to seek explanations for them while providing support for experiencers. On its Web site, the International Association for Near-Death Studies (IANDS; at www.iands.org) says that its mission is "to respond to people's needs for information and support concerning near-death and similar experiences, and to encourage recognition of the experiences as genuine and significant events of rich meaning." Some of IANDS's stated goals are to provide "reliable information about near-death experiences to experiencers, researchers, and the public" as well as to respond to "people's needs to integrate the physical, mental, emotional, and spiritual aspects of the NDE into their daily living." To help disseminate information about NDEs, IANDS publishes the *Journal of Near-Death Studies* as well as a quarterly newsletter, *Vital Signs*. The organization's Web site had 1,466,137 hits or visits between November 18, 1998, and August 3, 2002. This ongoing emphasis should provide a wealth of data in the years to come.

Those who believe in a life after death and those who do not will find nothing in NDE studies to contradict either belief. This demonstrates that scholars need to examine research results with a critical eye, to avoid accepting any "evidence" not supported by data, no matter how desirable. No doubt, as near-death experiences continue to be recorded, as research techniques are refined, and as more accurate definitions of death are specified, our understanding of these near-death phenomena will grow. Currently, the studies we have reviewed above are the best examples available of research examining last things from a secular perspective.

REFERENCES

Atwater, P. M. H. 1994. *Beyond the Light: What Isn't Being Said About Near-Death Experiences.* New York: Carol.

Bates, Brian C. and Adrian Stanley. 1985. "The Epidemiology and Differential Diagnosis of Near-Death Experience." *American Journal of Orthopsychiatry* 55:542–49.

Brooke, Tal. 1979. *The Other Side of Death.* Wheaton, IL: Tyndale House.

Cook, Emily Williams, Bruce Greyson, and Ian Stevenson. 1998. "Do Any Near Death Experiences Provide Evidence for Survival of Human Personality After Death? Relevant Features and Illustrative Case Reports." *Journal of Scientific Exploration* 12:377–406.

Dunlap, Jane. 1961. *Exploring Inner Space.* New York: Harcourt, Brace and World.

Eliade, Mircea. 1967. *From Primitive to Zen.* New York: Harper & Row.

Evans-Wentz, W. Y., ed. 1960. *Bardo Thodol: The Tibetan Book of the Dead.* Oxford: Oxford University Press.

Flynn, Charles P. 1985. *After the Beyond: Human Transformation and the Near-Death Experience.* Englewood Cliffs, NJ: Prentice Hall.

Gallup, George, Jr. and William Proctor. 1982. *Adventures in Immortality.* New York: McGraw-Hill.

Goleman, Daniel. 1977. "Back From the Brink." *Psychology Today,* April, pp. 56–59.

Grof, Stanislav and Joan Halifax. 1978. *The Human Encounter With Death.* New York: E. P. Dutton.

Gulley, Norman. 1982. "Life After Death: What About the New Evidence?" *These Times,* April, pp. 3–7.

Harris Interactive. 2002. "No Significant Changes in the Large Majorities Who Believe in God, Heaven, the Resurrection, Survival of Soul, Miracles and Virgin Birth." Rochester, NY: Harris Interactive. Retrieved May 14, 2003 (http://www.harrisinteractive.com/harris_poll/index.asp?pid=112).

Holck, Frederick H. 1978. "Life Revisited: Parallels in Death Experiences." *Omega* 9: 1–11.

International Association for Near-Death Studies. 2002. http://www.iands.org.

Jensen, Adolf Ellegard. 1963. *Myth and Culture Among Primitive Peoples.* Chicago: University of Chicago Press.

Karsten, Rafael. 1932. "Indian Tribes of the Argentine and Bolivian Chaco." *Societas Scientiarum Fennica* (Helsinki, Finland) 4(1).

Kelly, Emily W., Bruce Greyson, and Ian Stevenson. 1999–2000. "Can Experiences Near Death Furnish Evidence for Life After Death?" *Omega* 40:513–19.

Kohler, John. 1963. "The Dangerous Magic of LSD." *Saturday Evening Post,* November, pp. 31–32.

Kuhn, Harold B. 1981. "Out-of-Body Experiences: Misplaced Euphoria." *Christianity Today,* March 13, pp. 78, 82.

Lorimer, David. 1989. "The Near-Death Experience: Cross-Cultural and Multidisciplinary Dimensions." Pp. 256–67 in *Perspectives on Death and Dying: Cross-Culture and Multi-Disciplinary Views,* edited by Joyce Berger. Philadelphia: Charles.

Lundahl, Craig R. 1979. "Mormon Near-Death Experiences." *Free Inquiry in Creative Sociology* 7:101–4.

———. 1993–94. "A Nonscience Forerunner to Modern Near-Death Studies in America." *Omega* 28:63–78.

Meduna, Ladislas Joseph von. 1958. "The Effect of Carbon Dioxide Upon the Function of the Human Brain." In *Carbon Dioxide Therapy,* edited by Ladislas Joseph von Meduna. Springfield, IL: Charles C Thomas.

Moody, Raymond A., Jr. 1975. *Life After Life: The Investigation of a Phenomenon—Survival of Bodily Death.* Covington, GA: Mockingbird.

———. 1977. *Reflections on Life After Life: More Important Discoveries in the Ongoing Investigation of Survival of Life After Bodily Death.* St. Simons Island, GA: Mockingbird.

———. 1999. *The Last Laugh: A New Philosophy of Near-Death Experiences, Apparitions, and the Paranormal.* Charlottesville, VA: Hampton Roads.

Osis, Karlis. 1965. *Deathbed Observations by Physicians and Nurses.* New York: AMS.

Osis, Karlis and Erlendur Haraldsson. 1977. *At the Hour of Death.* New York: Avon.

Owens, Justine E., Emily Williams Cook, and Ian Stevenson. 1990. "Features of 'Near Death Experience' in Relation to Whether or Not Patients Were Near Death." *Lancet* 336:1175–77.

Pavry, Jal Dastur Cursetji. 1965. *The Zoroastrian Doctrine of a Future Life.* New York: AMS.

Preuss, Arthur. 1971. *Eschatology or the Catholic Doctrine of Last Things: A Dogmatic Treatise.* Westport, CT: Greenwood.

Provonsha, Jack W. 1981. "Life After Life? Do Some People Really Die and Come Back to Life?" *Life and Health,* January, pp. 14–15.

Rawlings, Maurice S. 1978. *Beyond Death's Door.* Nashville, TN: Thomas Nelson.

———. 1983. *To Hell and Back.* Nashville, TN: Thomas Nelson.

Ring, Kenneth. 1980. *Life at Death: A Scientific Investigation of the Near-Death Experience.* New York: Coward, McCann & Geoghegan.

———. 1984. *Heading Toward Omega: In Search of the Meaning of the Near-Death Experience.* New York: William Morrow.

Ring, Kenneth and Stephen Franklin. 1981–82. "Do Suicide Survivors Report Near-Death Experiences?" *Omega* 12:191–208.

Ring, Kenneth and Madeleine Lawrence. 1993. "Further Evidence for Veridical Perception During Near-Death Experiences." *Journal of Near-Death Studies* 11:223–29.

Rodabough, Tillman. 1985. "Near-Death Experiences: An Examination of the Supporting Data and Alternative Explanations." *Death Studies* 9:95–113.

Sabom, Michael. 1982. "Recollections of Death." *Omni,* March, pp. 58–60, 103–9.

———. 1998. *Light and Death: One Doctor's Fascinating Account of Near-Death Experiences.* Grand Rapids, MI: Zondervan.

Schwarz, Hans. 2001. *Eschatology.* Grand Rapids, MI: William B. Eerdmans.

Unger, Sanford M. 1963. "Mescaline, LSD, Psilocybin and Personality Change." *Psychiatry* 26:111–25.

van Lommel, Pim, Ruud van Wees, Vincent Meyers, and Ingrid Elfferich. 2001. "Near-Death Experience in Survivors of Cardiac Arrest: A Prospective Study in the Netherlands." *Lancet* 358:2039–45.

Life Insurance as Social Exchange Mechanism

Dennis L. Peck

Legally, life insurance is justified only by the existence of an insurable interest, a reasonable expectation of gain or advantage in the continued life of another person, and no interest in his death.

—Viviana A. Zelizer, "The Price and Value of Children," 1981

In a discussion of "insurance and the law," Baker (2001) writes that insurance per se is considered a "formal mechanism for sharing the costs of misfortune" (p. 7588). In casting the conceptualization of insurance in this manner, Baker distinguishes insurance into four categories: technologies, institutions, forms, and visions. Such categories are useful for illustrating the general variety of insurance-related activities, but for purposes of this discussion the fourth category, visions, is most useful for establishing a basic conceptualization of life insurance as a social exchange mechanism.

Visions are inclusive of each of the other three categories. In the first instance, as Baker (2001) notes, technologies enhance our understanding as to the risk involved. Thus "insurance, in the sense of insurance 'technology,' refers to a set of procedures for dealing with risk. Examples include the mortality tables and inspection procedures of ordinary life insurance" (p. 7588). Visions, on the other hand, pertain to ideas about or images of a variety of business practices regarding insurance that have led to the development of the technologies, institutions, and forms. Other social visions exist as well.

Despite the fact that all forms of insurance are intended to create a sense of security, perhaps life insurance more than any other form holds a value that is secured in the imagination. Life insurance functions as a symbolic representation of a promise to be there in the future at a time of loss and/or tragedy. As numerous advertisements for insurance companies note, life insurance represents a special future gift, one that is there (or forthcoming) because the giver (the insured) really cares.

As with so many things uniquely American, life insurance emerges out of what some analysts describe as a cult of social conditioning; that is, it is part of a web of traditions, customs, and social attitudes. Such conditioning instills an attitude that money and death converge, thereby symbolizing the connection between money and life. In the words of James Gollin (1966), life insurance as a mechanism of social exchange ensures that "money—our great life symbol—is used both symbolically and in fact to abolish death" (p. 197). That is, life insurance underscores the American social belief that money is life and thus represents one important way of ensuring that death gives way to life. Thus the purchase of life insurance is a part of a symbolic process that provides the means to allow people to think that death can in fact be conquered. Insurance is *life;* at the very least, it is a living value.

But yet another vision casts some doubt on this imagined and symbolic sense of security if, for example, an insurance company should deny a claim based on suggested fraud or abuse. Moreover, people in other parts of the world do not easily understand this unique fascination with life insurance among Americans. The British and French, for example, may purchase life insurance, but, according to Gollin (1966), their purchases usually occur later in life than they do for Americans and more often take the modest form of insurance intended to cover funeral expenses. In some countries, such as Spain, widows are hesitant to accept life insurance payouts provided by their husbands' employers because of the deeply held belief that it is improper to benefit financially from the death of a loved one.

Despite these qualifications, among contemporary Americans, at least, the dominant view is that life insurance provides needed financial support for others when the holder of the policy is no longer able to provide or care for their needs. This form of insurance provides needed benefits for widows and orphans; if substantial enough, life insurance may even provide the funds essential to ensure coverage of the costs of college educations for the deceased's children. Although most individuals purchase life insurance for such assurance, it is also, in the words of one analyst, "the only effective technique of thrift for millions presumed to be too weak-minded, too indolent, or too irresolute to save money in any other way than via life insurance premiums" (Hendershot 1957:11). However, the positive values placed on the advantages of life insurance by most Americans today have not always held sway among the populace.

HISTORY OF LIFE INSURANCE AS A SOCIAL EXCHANGE MECHANISM

The modern life insurance system was born in England, where it eventually made rapid advances. Even up to the 18th century, however, the insuring of life was neither widely practiced nor generally approved in England. As Baker (2001) notes, life insurance was once perceived by the general public to be immoral because "it interfered with divine providence, equated life and money or was a form of gambling" (p. 7588). Such moral thinking had important consequences for the development of laws related to the insurance industry in the United States, as well as for the life assurance sector that had a humble beginning in 1759, obstructing the growth of life insurance as a form of social exchange. Such values later took a dramatic change of direction during the early 1840s.

The New York Life Insurance and Trust Company, founded in 1830, issued approximately 2,000 policies during its first 9 years of existence (Jack 1912:244–45). Although the extent of this activity cannot be considered intense, beginning in 1843 the American life insurance industry undertook a stage of development that has been described as an overwhelming success story. As Viviana Zelizer notes in her book *Morals and Markets* (1979), there was initially some cultural and ideological resistance to life insurance, and such resistance continues to inhibit the growth of this segment of the insurance industry in most nations other than the United States. Contrasted with other forms of insurance, such as fire and particularly marine insurance, which was a part of the economic structure of many localities dating back in time at least to the 15th-century Italian city-states, the initial American opposition to life insurance was based on a value system that rejected, as Zelizer observes, "a strictly financial evaluation of human life" (p. xi). Life was considered sacred, and Americans in general believed that the value of life—or death, as in the case of insurance—could not be determined as a fixed amount; thus "traditional economic morality and a deterministic religious ethos [in the early decades of the 19th century] condemned life insurance as a sacrilegious speculative venture" (p. xiii).

The unquestioned cultural emphasis placed on rituals of reciprocal or gift-type social exchange observed in primitive, archaic societies by anthropologists (see Mauss 1967) also was not uncommon to the experience of early industrial Western societies, including the United States. This orientation also inhibited early acceptance of life insurance as an appropriate mechanism of social exchange. Although Zelizer (1981) argues that "Christianity sacralized and absolutized human existence, setting life above financial considerations" (p. 1037), some analysts have asserted that during this time of urban development, many Americans thought that holding life insurance was potentially detrimental to a person's physical well-being and might even hasten an individual's death. For this reason, holding life insurance was deemed to be harmful to society in general. In essence, this early American ideology was based on the premise that it is wicked to insure one's life. Early efforts by government bodies to sell the idea of life insurance to the American public did little to inspire confidence in such insurance.

Later in the 19th century, however, there were also reasons to support this form of social exchange. In a discussion of problems relating to economic security in late-19th-century Europe, Whaples and Buffum (1991) note that by that time most advanced European nations had adopted some form of "public social insurance" to assist widows, the aged, the sick, and the injured (see also Jack 1912:223–30). This was not the case in the United States, where those in need of economic assistance were dependent on family members, employers, friends, and neighbors. In the rapidly changing urban, industrial environment of the time, which included growing numbers of people of diverse economic, social, ethnic, and ideological backgrounds, such assistance was not always forthcoming for those in need. The growth of industry and a strong economic base eventually led to rising income among an increasingly large and better-educated workforce. Such factors have been identified as important to the creation of ideas that led Americans to recognize a need for and to take the initiative essential to providing some form of assurance to dependent family members in case of debilitating consequences related to accident, sickness, or death.

Although some modest activity did occur in which the lives of individuals were insured under extraordinary circumstance for short periods of time, the founding of what is considered to be the first American life insurance company did not occur until 1759. This organization, known as the Corporation of Poor and Distressed Presbyterian Ministers and of the Poor and Distressed Widows and Children of Presbyterian Ministers, was established in Philadelphia by the synod of the Presbyterian Church to insure the lives of the synod's ministers and their families (American Council of Life Insurance 1996); this initial effort was followed in 1769 by the establishment of a similar organization to insure the lives of New York Episcopalian ministers (Jack 1912:244).

Despite the enthusiastic reaction to these initial efforts within the business community, it was not until the early 1840s that life insurance policies were issued to any significant extent, and even then the number of policies sold was quite small. Still, this change represented a significant transformation in economic thought (discussed at length by Fogel 2000). According to Zelizer (1978, 1979), this transformation came about as a result of shifts in cultural values and ideologies that occurred along with changes in the definitions of risk taking and gambling. Enhanced actuarial knowledge of mortality and principles relating to life insurance, better insurance rates, and an aggressive sales force first employed by the New York Life Insurance and Trust Company have also been identified as factors that may have assisted in the growth of the industry (Zelizer 1978, 1979; American Council of Life Insurance 1996; Jones [1999] 2002), although some analysts question the importance of these elements.

The Second Great Awakening

During the period known as the Second Great Awakening, with its egalitarian ethic, moral evil was equated with the institutions of the time and the idea of unselfishness was promoted. It is noteworthy that the beginning rise of the American life insurance industry corresponds roughly in time with this historical period (1800–1840), an era of religious fervor and revival (see Fogel 2000). By 1840, the U.S. population had attained a literacy rate of 90% and was witness to an active religious and political agenda intended to encourage abstinence from alcohol, improve the rights of women, redress wrongs against Native Americans, abolish slavery, address an increasing number of social problems attendant to the emergence of the urban environment, and, through education and science, advance the ideal of social justice for the working class. Committed to the broad goal of shaping the moral and political character of the nation, reform-minded religious leaders gradually asserted their influence in all aspects of life (Fogel 2000:84–120). These activities are known to have been most intense in the Northeast, where the establishment of the first life insurance organizations also began. As Zelizer (1981) states: "Gradually, the capitalization of the value of adult life and the monetary indemnation of that value became acceptable. However, the monetary evaluation of death did not desacralize it" (p. 1037).

In light of the above, it may not be coincidental that the life insurance industry really began to develop during this historical period of liberal religious revivalism. Indeed, American society in general became involved in addressing myriad social issues, led in large part by leaders of the reform-minded Methodist Episcopal Church and the emerging influence of Baptists, who promoted the idea of engaging in unselfish acts. These social-reform-minded religious leaders made a commitment to enhance the religious, moral, and political character of Americans. It was during this period that many social organizations, including insurance organizations, were created to assist members of the public in dealing with issues related to the urban crisis and social problems such as poverty, alcoholism, and prostitution. Church-affiliated individuals also became involved in the insurance industry at an early date, and, according to Gollin (1966), even today such ideologically oriented persons continue to dominate the industry at the top levels.

Other factors were operating during this period as well. Between 1820 and 1860, the growth of the U.S. economy had the effect of raising the wages of American workers, sometimes quite rapidly. At the same time the standard of living was increasing, the extent of immigration was also growing; population density intensified, and infectious diseases spread rapidly, especially within the coastal communities. Life expectancy decreased (Fogel 2000:159–63). Thus, as one might expect, early American assurance organizations were half charitable and only half insurance. It was not until 1809, when the Pennsylvania Company for the Insurance on Lives was formed, that the beginning of life insurance on a regular basis in the United States began to emerge (Jack 1912).

Cultural and Institutional Change

After the American Civil War, as Zelizer (1979) observes, the adaptation of life insurance was influenced by cultural factors such as liberal ideology, changing religious beliefs, and changed ideologies concerning risk, speculation, and gambling. Other influences included a changed industrial-based society in which the economic marketplace and the urban environment interacted with other cultural shifts to effect change in the family unit. Women and children were no longer considered to be the responsibility of the community; rather, the nuclear family assumed the obligation for their care. The symbolic meaning of life insurance changed, and the "gift of life insurance" offered assurance that future widows and orphans would have their economic needs met. Life insurance had already achieved legal recognition in 1840, when the New York State Legislature enacted a law that provided that the benefits of a life insurance policy with the wife named as beneficiary be paid directly to her, thereby exempting all claims of creditors (American Council of Life Insurance 1996:130). Factors such as these accounted for the increasingly widespread thinking among wage earners that it was the responsibility of the head of the family to ensure the welfare of dependents through the purchase of life insurance.

In 1867, the amount of American life insurance in force exceeded a billion dollars, and by 1870, fraternal organizations and commercial life insurance companies had developed rapidly, offering insurance to club members and to increasing numbers of ethnic, working-class groups whose purchasing power had increased. Rising wages among Americans, including members of the growing middle and working classes, were sufficient to warrant the purchase of life insurance protection for their families, which were experiencing modest increases in affluence. Americans' rising standard of living continued to be factor in the sale of life insurance for several decades. By 1880, the amount of life insurance in force in the United States had reached more than $1.6 billion, and by 1900, the figure was more than $8 billion (Stevenson 1927:1).

A change in cultural ideology based on an economic shift from self-sufficiency of the family unit to one of economic interdependence, along with the need for a lifetime of money income, led to the view that life insurance could be used in part to buffer the insecurities of a changing economic environment (Zelizer 1978, 1979). Although the reasons suggested for this vary considerably, the unquestioned growth of the insurance industry offers some convincing evidence of this changed view. For example, by 1843, the year often identified as the year of transition in the growth of the industry, the Mutual Life Insurance Company of New York had only 400 life insurance policies in force, equaling a total of $1,480,718. Then, in 1843 alone, the company wrote 470 policies totaling $1,640,718. By 1850, the policies in force numbered 6,242, for a total of $15,886,181 (Clough 1946:371).

The period of 1850–70 was characterized by a rapid expansion of the insurance industry; a near 50% annual increase was achieved by the end of the 1860s. Although growth in the sales of life insurance was much slower during periods of economic depression, sales increased rapidly from the end of the Civil War in 1865 through 1905. From 1864 to 1869, the prosperity of the business of life insurance was such that it has not been equaled since that period (Jones [1999] 2002:84, 116). Again drawing from Clough's (1946) historical assessment of the Mutual Life Insurance Company of New York, by the end of 1860, a total of 12,591 life insurance policies were in force in the amount of $40,159,123; by 1870, this number increased to 71,271, in the amount of $242,004,489. Then, at the end of the 19th century, the Mutual Life Insurance Company alone had 439,440 life insurance policies in effect, totaling $1,139,940,529 (pp. 371, 373, Tables 47, 49). As noted above, the *total* life insurance in force at the beginning of the 20th century was in excess of $8 billion. By 1925, this total amount had grown to $79 billion (Stevenson 1927:3). In that same year, the expenditures paid for death losses totaled only $493,391,370. Four and a half decades later, at the end of 1945, approximately $163 billion of commercial and fraternal life insurance was in force among the general population of the United States. As Dublin and Lotka (1946:144–45) note, this was more than twice the amount in force during the mid-1920s, but to this total can be added another $129 billion of U.S. Government Insurance (begun in 1917) and National Service Life Insurance (started in 1940) that was in force for the veterans who had served during the two world wars.

GIFT GIVING, SOCIAL EXCHANGE THEORY, AND LIFE INSURANCE

Gift Giving

In primitive, nonindustrial societies such as those observed by Marcel Mauss (1967) and other analysts, gift giving and gift exchange were instruments of social organization that helped to bind a social group together. In contemporary U.S. society, life insurance fills an economic void, replacing the moral exchange conducted among family members and friends to meet group members' economic needs. Earlier forms of exchanges, although they serve many functions, such as maintaining personal relationships and fulfilling social obligations, no longer remain viable within contemporary large-scale economic systems (Titmuss 1971:72). However, like the modern forms of social security that Titmuss (1971:209) has evaluated, life insurance expresses cooperation and may also serve as a renaissance of the theme of the gift.

Gift giving and gift exchange may be characterized as representing a number of group sentiments and individual motives. Titmuss (1971) identifies two such reasons for gift giving: The first includes economic purposes intended "to achieve a material gain or to enhance prestige or to bring about material gain in the future," and the second is predominantly social and moral, in that the gifts are intended "to serve friendly relationships, affection and harmony between known individuals and social groups" (p. 216). The primary function of gift giving and the future expectation of reciprocal gifts in preindustrial societies may not have been solely economic in nature, but such exchange was an important part of the social and moral intent of the members of these societies. In preindustrial societies gifts were much more functional than economic in that they served religious, magical, sentimental, and moral purposes.

Social Exchange: The Gift of Life Insurance

Exchange theory is often criticized for its reductionist approach, given that the outcomes of social exchange "are conditioned to reduce society immediately to the interplay of individual interests" (Manis and Melzer 1978:143). The formal ideas attributed to social exchange theory thus hold little utility for the analysis of social organizations and thereby diminish the theory's usefulness for assessing the complex social processes in which humans participate that lead to the decision to provide the gift of life insurance beyond what is referred to as a "preordained" type of scheme (Lindesmith, Strauss, and Denzin 1988:18–19). Nevertheless, taking the theory in its simplistic form, viewing life insurance as a form of social exchange allows one the opportunity to appreciate the utility of the gift, although the act requires one to imagine how the recipient will conceptualize its worth. Thus the basics of social exchange theory may be useful for explaining some portion of the dynamics involved in the process of an individual's deciding to provide the gift of life insurance.

If life insurance does emerge as a product of the cult of social conditioning, as former insurance agent James Gollin (1966) has proposed, then a portion of the behavioral psychology advocated by George Homans and B. F. Skinner is present. Reward and punishment stimuli serve as the foundation of an exchange of activity occurring between two people. The reward (life insurance) is predicated on the behavior of only one actor, but the gift giving is not intended as a reciprocal gesture, except, perhaps, for the power that exists in the imagination of the giver.

In contemporary industrial and postindustrial society, gift exchange does not hold the same importance it had in the past, but a gift in the form of life insurance does signify an element of altruism at the same time it represents a calculated form of economic behavior. As Zelizer (1978) observes, during the late 19th century, life insurance was surrounded with religious symbolism, advertised more for that value than for its monetary benefit: "Life insurance was marketed as an altruistic, self-denying gift rather than as a profitable investment" (pp. 599–600). A major difference from the past uses of gift giving is that life insurance does not establish any future basis for reciprocity. Rather, like any altruistic gift, the purchase of life insurance is a response to the perceived social and economic needs of others, providing an advantage for others rather than oneself. The gift provides future security while demonstrating an altruistic motive and fulfilling a moral and social obligation to those who are important in one's face-to-face relationships.

From 1830 to 1850, life insurance was promoted as a morally accepted means by which husbands could protect the futures of their wives and children. It was within this same time frame, as Zelizer (1981) notes, that "life insurance took on symbolic values quite distinct from its utilitarian function, emerging as a new form of ritual with which to face death" (p. 1037). Life insurance eventually came to be equated with peace of mind, based on the assurance that those who are insured can meet their ends secure in the knowledge that they have fulfilled their moral obligation to take care of their family members.

THE MODERN CONCEPT OF CHILDHOOD AND LIFE INSURANCE

Americans are often described as child centered, in that in U.S. society great concern is generally expressed over the care and well-being of children. But children have not always benefited from this kind of attention. Indeed, the concept of childhood is a fairly recent phenomenon, and its discovery holds relevance for any discussion of life insurance.

Until the Middle Ages, children were depicted in art as though they were small adults, without any of the unique characteristics that we ascribe to children today. Over the next several hundred years, a new concept of childhood began to emerge. These changes are evidenced, for example, by the nursing methods used in 14th-century Italy and by the use of the color white for the burial clothes of children, as a testament of their innocence, practiced in 15th- and 16th-century England. The art and literature of 16th- and 17th-century England depict the special characteristics of children through the use of distinctive costumes and the solicitous behavior of parents toward their children. Finally, a growing literature in the late 16th and the 17th centuries questioned the traditional exploitative treatment of children and their characterization as miniature adults. Increasingly, children began to be viewed as essentially innocent and dependent, in need of social training; they needed to be controlled, guarded both physically and morally, and educated in preparation for adulthood (Empey and Stafford 1991:21–45).

The first European settlers brought the concept of childhood to the American colonies, although the concept eventually underwent considerable change. In essence, the factors that created the modern urban society also were instrumental in producing the modern concept of childhood, especially among the growing middle- and upper-class portion of the developing industrial nation. It was the labor-saving technology introduced by the Industrial Revolution that allowed this change to take effect. For the first time in Western history, children were no longer an essential component of and productive force in the labor market. By the late 19th century, the segregation of society based on age had became a reality (Empey and Stafford 1991).

As children and their parents achieved greater emotional attachment, children's worth in the marketplace diminished. This process began initially among families of the urban middle class, but eventually the social value of the lower-class child changed as well. This perception of the child was to have important implications for the insurance industry.

Zelizer has thoroughly documented the relationship between the concept of childhood and life insurance. She begins her seminal article "The Price and Value of Children" (1981) with the following statement:

> On March 14, 1895, the *Boston Evening Transcript* stated, "No manly man and no womanly woman should be ready to say that their infants have pecuniary value." (P. 1036)

The newspaper was attacking the widespread contemporary practice of parents insuring their children. I discuss the significance of this newspaper statement below.

Life Insurance for Working-Class Children

Whereas most life insurance companies directed their attention toward adult males of middle-class families, in 1875 the Prudential Life Insurance Company targeted children under the age of 10 as insurees. What may surprise some is that these were not the children of well-to-do families, but children whose families were part of the expanding working class.

Since its inception in England, the practice of issuing life insurance for children has been fraught with controversy. In an intriguing analysis of this segment of the insurance industry, Zelizer (1981, 1985) traces the effect of the changing cultural definition of children and the relationship of this change to the purchase of life insurance for children, first by lower-class parents and then later by members of the middle class. In evaluating this phenomenon, Zelizer (1981) asserts that "one important variable was the cultural redefinition of the value of children. As children's lives became economically worthless but emotionally priceless, their deaths became [defined as] a social problem" (p. 1050).

During the mid-19th century, when the children of urban middle-class families were embraced as members of the new, nonproductive world of childhood, the children of working-class families not only retained the economic value they had in the past, but their value actually increased. While middle-class children enjoyed the benefit of formal education in preparation for the future, working-class children's economic value rose because of rapid industrialization and the new occupations it produced. The children of working-class families became a much-needed component of a productive workforce.

This economic situation, the large number of working-class families and their factory-employable children, and the assertiveness of the insurance industry combined to create an environment that was conducive to the introduction of a new marketing innovation. In 1875, a major life insurance company began to insure the lives of children under the age of 10. In 1879, two other major companies entered into the industrial insurance market. By 1895, $268 million of life insurance was in force; 1.5 million children were insured in 1896, and by year's end in 1902 more than 3 million children were insured. This was but the beginning. By 1928, more than 37% of the life insurance policies issued by the big three companies were for children.

Such innovative practices did not take root without acquiring detractors. Social and legal encounters between representatives of the "child-saving movement" and the insurance industry emerged soon after the practice of insuring children began. As the Progressive movement, of which the child savers were a part, surged ahead with its social reform agenda directed toward diminishing the exploitation of the children of poor families by removing them from industrial factories and placing them in schoolrooms, state legislatures and major newspapers assailed the practice of insuring children as harmful to the public interest (Zelizer 1981:1040–45, 1051).

Despite the outpouring of public protestations and moral indignation directed toward the practice of insuring the lives of lower-class children as unscrupulous, sordid, profane, speculative, the illegal wagering of life, commercially exploitative, against public policy, potentially dangerous to the well-being of children, and expensive for working-class parent, the commercial interests of this practice were eventually upheld in three major court decisions dating back to the 1850s. With these decisions, the crusade of the moral entrepreneurs was defeated, and the moral and legal rights of parents to insure the lives of their children were upheld. Zelizer (1981:1046) identifies the 1858 court case of *Mitchell v. Union Life* (45 Maine 105, 1858) as significant in upholding this pecuniary bond between parent and child.

Life insurance for children held a strong appeal among working-class families, and the sales tactics of the insurance industry were effective in thwarting the child-saving component of the Progressive movement. The insurance companies' strategy was to address the changing value of children by claiming to promote the welfare of children, and they initially marketed this form of insurance as symbolic concern, as a token of love and affection for the dead child rather than as insurance for the working child (Zelizer 1981:1047).

Although Zelizer (1981) acknowledges that one indicator of the changing value of children was the growing public concern throughout the 1800s and early 1900s with children's deaths and with providing decent Christian burials for children, she also argues that, "ultimately, the debate over child insurance was a debate on the value of poor children, a public assessment of their emotional worth" (p. 1047). The mourning of children became a focal concern among members of the middle class during the period from 1820 to 1875; within this context, Zelizer notes, "The acceptance of children's insurance suggests that after 1875 lower-class parents adopted middle-class standards of mourning young children" (p. 1049).

Ultimately, sales of child life insurance were destined to increase as a result of yet another change in marketing strategy. In moving from an emphasis on burial insurance to an emphasis on the creation of an education fund, the insurance companies promoted child insurance as an attractive child-centered investment among the middle-class. In the late 19th and early 20th centuries, children's value as economically worthless but emotionally priceless led to a view of child life insurance as symbolizing respect for the dead child. Later in the 20th century, however, this valuation symbolized an action of love and respect for the living child (Zelizer 1981:1052).

UNEQUAL OPPORTUNITY LIFE INSURANCE

The Legacy of Minority Life Insurance

The legacy of the American life insurance industry is replete with opportunities for bias against racial minorities, reflective of the social orientations of a past cultural ethos. Racial bias in the history of the life insurance industry is best demonstrated through the backstage insights of individuals who worked within the institution. One such analyst quotes a major insurance corporation official: "We are glad to accept whatever Negro business comes our way. But we don't go out looking for Negroes to insure" (Gollin 1966:100).

If the above statement appears harsh, it is, according to Gollin (1966), also a reflection of a reality of the insurance industry. Selling life insurance involves risk taking on the part of the insurer, and in this area life insurance companies established norms early on to allow them to avoid insuring individuals considered to be at risk of high mortality rates, whether because of age, occupation, morals, or race/ethnicity. Although such evaluations strongly suggest that white-owned life insurance companies did not curry favor among the black population, some analysts argue that the facts indicate otherwise. Stuart (1940:43) notes, for example, that in 1923 approximately one-sixth of all blacks in the United States were holders of policies issued through the Metropolitan Life Insurance Company of New York.

In contrast, James Gollin (1966), a former insurance sales agent, argues that minorities long experienced discrimination in the life insurance industry because of agency prejudice. Such discrimination was not necessarily based on concrete actuarial risk factors; rather, the numerical rating point scale used to calculate risk for blacks and other minorities included race as an adverse factor. Although the insurance companies used a standard rating scale, their estimation of risk for minorities, Gollin asserts, was based on racial bias rather than financial risk. Another explanation some analysts offer for the reticence of life insurance companies to sell insurance to blacks is based on the findings of studies of death rates that indicate men employed in occupations associated with lower-income groups have shorter life expectancy (Stuart 1940:55–56; see also Dublin and Lotka 1946).

The eventual entrance of blacks into the insurance arena as company owners was prompted by other factors as well. For example, as Stuart (1940) has documented, when white agents made their weekly visits to the homes of Negro policyholders to collect premiums (known as debits), their behavior was often less than commendable. Stuart notes: "Their haughtiness, discourtesies, and not infrequent abuses of the privacy of the home were resented, but to a great extent tolerated until the organization and entry of Negro companies into this field" (p. 36). The insults, abuses, and violations of the privacy of the homes of black policyholders by white agents, especially in the American South, were well-known in every black community, and such practices helped to stimulate the creation of black-owned industrial life insurance companies.

The distasteful practices of white insurance agencies had important and positive long-term economic consequences for black American entrepreneurs. As Stuart observed in 1940:

There are comparatively few types of business in which the Negro businessman has even a reasonable chance to succeed. . . . Among the lines of business and personal service in which colored operators and proprietors may be free from extra racial obstacles . . . [are] barber shops and beauty parlors, food service establishments, journalism, hotels, undertaking and life insurance businesses. (P. xxv)

Stuart lists the names of the 46 Negro life insurance organizations then operating in the District of Columbia and 24 U.S. states. Of these companies, 29 included the phrase *life insurance* in their names; *burial insurance* was the major component of 2 of the companies' names. In 1940, the "Afro-American Life Insurance Company" of Jacksonville, Florida, was one of 26 Negro companies located in the southern portion of the United States. Careful readers may recognize the significance of the wording of the name of this firm.

Growth of a Minority Industry

Black life insurance companies grew out of the church relief societies of the 1787–1890 period and the Negro fraternal benevolent burial associations that flourished in the United States from 1865 to 1915. Consistent with the fact that blacks were primarily involved in the labor-intensive industrial marketplace, most of the insurance sold first through benevolent societies and later through black-owned insurance companies covered the areas of health and accident. In reality, this form of industrial insurance was intended to provide modest benefits for the disabled and a decent burial for the deceased.

As Stuart (1940:37, 40–44) documents, the rapid growth of industrial life and disability insurance among members of the black community can be attributed in part to black insurers' sensitivity in making prompt payments to claimants. Although in the past ordinary life insurance policies accounted for only one-sixth of the total policies sold by black insurance companies to black Americans, there was rapid growth in this area, as the following numbers show. In December 1920, the total life insurance in force in what Stuart refers to as "the important Negro companies" was $86,039,131. By December 1937, 17 years later, the amount had increased to $340,816,707. Although this figure placed American blacks very high in comparison with the populations of many nations of the world, it represented only a fraction of all the life insurance in force among members of the U.S. black community. Indeed, as noted earlier, during 1937 the Metropolitan Life Insurance Company was said to hold one-sixth, or $690 million, of all black-held policies in the United States. Thus the estimated total amount of black-held life insurance in force at the time was more than $1.3 billion. This figure placed American blacks just behind the nations of Sweden and Australia in life insurance coverage.

During this period of growth for the black life insurance industry, and despite the critical view of some industry analysts, many Americans were beginning to feel that it was important to have some amount of life insurance, no matter how small the policy worth. The first weekly premium policy was issued in the United States in 1873, but such policies found their greatest market in the black community. Clearly, black insurers took what Taylor and Pellegrin (1959) identify as a humanitarian approach; their goal was to service the basic needs of the black community. Indeed, it was through the determined efforts of individuals such as the low-status "debit man," who serviced the needs of these low- to middle-income families, that this substantial portion of a vast industry was created and nurtured. Since 1983, yearly life insurance purchases in the United States have exceeded $1 trillion (American Council of Life Insurance 2002), and minority-owned life insurance companies represent an important component of this industry.

ECONOMICS AND THE VALUE OF HUMAN LIFE

> Certainly we can't predict the future. But there are steps you can take to prepare for it. Life insurance is a tool that enables people to guarantee the financial security of those they love. By providing compensation for beneficiaries at death, life insurance preserves the monetary value of a human life when other lives depend on it. (All Quotes Insurance 2002)

Dominant social values often are expressed in economic terms, and, as Starlard (1986) succinctly states, this includes the value placed on human life. This issue is especially important in relation to decisions to insure the lives of individuals whose social value is measured in economic terms relative to the financial needs of others.

The value of a man (or life), as Dublin and Lotka (1946:3–5) note in a book by that same title, may be compounded by practical and tangible qualities as well as by the aesthetic and sentimental values held by family members, friends, and business associates. All of these values represent different ideas, depending on the persons holding them and the person on whom the values are placed. Those who have an interest in the insured's continued existence, especially family members (such as spouse and children), place a high value on that individual. In this area, the value of a human life may even be considered priceless. Placing such metaphysical issues aside, however, it is the survivors' financial interest in the life of one whose earnings and role as head of the family provide stability for the family that serves as the very foundation of life insurance. Thus, as Dublin and Lotka note, "A fixed principle of the life insurance business . . . requires that the person insuring the life of another shall have a financial interest in the continuance of the life insured" (p. 5). It is through life insurance that the economic value of a person on whom family members are dependent is protected (Dublin and Lotka 1946:159).

Symbolically, life insurance is a gift intended to ensure that survivors are able to maintain a lifestyle similar to that they had during the life of the insured. Life insurance is the purchase of futures. It is planning for the future, albeit a future in which the insured will not share. In receiving the largesse provided through a life insurance policy, family members can avoid the loss of any status achieved for the family by the insured—that is, any status in the community that he or she achieved prior to death. Such status is, according to Starlard (1986), one of inequality, an inequality often based on sex, age, and, as Gollin (1966) and Zelizer (1981) note, race. In addition, as noted above, the use of life insurance by lower-class parents to assure their family welfare in the event of the loss of their working children was at one time an area of considerable controversy in American society (Zelizer 1981).

The inequality of the sexes in terms of life insurance is reflected in the greater numbers of policies sold to men versus women as well as in the amounts for which policies are written. Women are far less likely than men to have life insurance policies, and women who do have life insurance generally have policies that pay considerably less than most men's policies. Age is a factor in light of life expectancy at either end of the age continuum; those who are younger pay relatively low premiums, whereas premiums are quite high for older insurees. Race is a relevant factor only in the context of groups targeted by the industry as potential buyers of life insurance policies. In this area, many black Americans in the past were similar to today's French and British, who are inclined to purchase small amounts of insurance for burial purposes only. Working-class American laborers in the past generally held small amounts of disability and burial insurance, paying the premiums weekly to insurance agents who stopped by their homes to "collect the debit."

The historical debate as to the economic value of human life continues, given that this value orientation now includes notions related to aesthetic and sentimental values. Although the present debate is focused on public policy issues directly related to human health and safety, central to this debate is the valuation of human life. Known as the "human capital approach" to valuing human life, this debate has a long history, dating back to the late 17th century. At present, the debate pertains to risk and cost-benefit analyses used to evaluate programs that attach monetary values of risks to life. In recent years this debate has included arguments concerning the value of lives lost owing to lack of occupational safety and human negligence (see, e.g., Dardis 1980; Landefeld and Seskin 1982; Miller 1990).

OTHER DYNAMIC ASPECTS OF LIFE INSURANCE

Despite most Americans' strong acceptance of life insurance, some reservations of the past continue to the present. As one critic notes: "Life insurance can do a great deal of good for the policyholder and his family. But, strange as it may seem, it can do him considerable harm, and his family and beneficiaries as well" (Hendershot 1957:9). Some critics have expressed concern that the industry overcharges for premiums and achieves excessive, nontaxable profits by limiting the amounts of coverage provided; they assert that such practices represent harm to both individual purchasers and the entire society. Gollin (1966), for example, refers to the insurance industry as "the worst-managed Big Business in America" (p. 141). Other charges that have been leveled against the industry in the years since it was established concern the practice of paying high commissions to sales personnel, the use of premiums for lobbying purposes, the presence of nepotism in hiring and internal managerial conflicts of interest, and, during the late 19th century, the writing of tontine policies, a practice that placed policyholders into a form of gambling pool (Jones [1999] 2002:104–5). (Tontine insurance was not a true form of insurance, however; see Jack 1912:196.)

Drawing on one frequent theme promoted at annual insurance conventions, Gollin (1966), who was once a successful life insurance agent, summarizes the industry propaganda in the following manner: "Life insurance is the greatest concept society has ever produced; all life insurance men have a great mission" (p. 139). Taylor and Pellegrin (1959) also identify this theme; they report that advocates of the humanitarian approach to the sale of life insurance hold a religious fervor for the occupation and believe that through their efforts they render a great service to all people, regardless of their socioeconomic class status.

That the insurance industry is successful is not in dispute, but, its acknowledged growth and fiscal vitality notwithstanding, the real reasons for the wealth of the industry may lie elsewhere. Reflecting on the preceding half century, Gollin (1966) offers a personal insider assessment of the reasons for the success of the life insurance industry: "Better medical care, a higher standard of living, and a prosperous economy—not any outstanding effort on the industry's part—are the real reasons for the industry's great post-war success" (p. 154).

Despite the fact that state regulation of the life insurance industry began as far back as the 1850s (Jones [1999] 2002:77), it appears that yet another element is critical to the industry's success. As Gollin (1966) observes:

> Life insurance companies are so powerful that they help write the laws under which they're regulated. As a result the laws don't regulate them very well. Neither ownership nor customer groups influence management behavior, so the industry is largely exempt from the checks and balances that govern our business industry. (P. 135)

And despite charges of extravagance, inefficiency, and lack of business acumen on the part of industry leaders, the fact that some companies used policyholder premiums to make investments in speculative ventures, and the pressures of certain regulatory mandates, the past failures of the life insurance industry are not necessarily attributed to these problems. Rather, industry setbacks may have been the results of the more general collapse of financial markets experienced during economic depression and caused, at least indirectly, by the passage of the regulatory New York State Law of 1851 (Jones [1999] 2002). One example of such a collapse occurred during the 1870s, when a large number of newly formed companies ceased to exist (Zelizer 1979; see also American Council of Life Insurance 1996:108). Lack of sales was responsible for some of these failures, but it is also probable that some companies failed because they were unable to meet the $100,000 deposit required by the New York State Legislature. In general, these companies were located outside the boundaries of New York State, which led to yet another charge that the large life insurance companies influenced the shaping of industrywide regulations to protect their own interests against competition. Yet another, less controversial, conclusion is that the New York State Insurance Code was passed in the public's best interest, with the intent of placing the life insurance industry firmly under state regulation (Jones [1999] 2002:119–21).

The criticism that life insurance companies make huge profits by investing the premiums paid by clients may hold some salience during limited periods of intense media coverage and public scrutiny of insurance company activities. Such inquiry has periodically led to the creation of state legislative investigative committees. However, with few exceptions—such as the 1869 Supreme Court opinion affirming state regulation of insurance, the New York Insurance Code of 1906, the federally legislated McCarran-Ferguson Act of 1945, and the Tax Reform Act of 1884—the life insurance industry appears to be free of intense regulation. Regulatory efforts generally have only a modicum of success given the effectiveness of the insurance lobby interests in the legislative process (American Council of Life Insurance 1996:130–34; Jones [1999] 2002:102–7). There is little reason to believe the situation has changed during the past half century. As Jones ([1999] 2002:80–126) has noted recently, during the period of 1950–80 a slow and deliberate liberalization of prohibitions previously placed on the industry took place, and many of the strict controls and compliance regulations that were created during the 1920–50 period were removed.

CONCLUSION

The evolution of the life insurance industry in the United States has included experiences that have differed from dynamics elsewhere in the world, particularly in Western Europe and Scandinavian countries, where the concept of life insurance developed slowly over the period of several hundred years. Perhaps the success of life insurance in the United States can be attributed to the spirit of capitalism (and Yankee ingenuity), as Fingland A. Jack (1912) has suggested: "It is to modern capitalism more than anything else that we owe the insurance fabric as it stands to-day" (p. 245). But if life insurance has become an important capitalist enterprise, it is important to note also that the industry may not have been possible without the new science of life contingencies (Jack 1912:216–22).

Despite the fact that in the past the idea of benefiting financially from the death of loved ones was not culturally acceptable, with the beginnings of life insurance the value of human life became measurable. As this valuation gained general public acceptance, the future of the American life insurance industry was assured.

From its most humble beginning in the late 18th century, and despite the scandals that were uncovered during the late 18th and early 19th centuries, the American life insurance industry represents a story of extraordinary success. In 1759, the first American life insurance company was founded, and it was joined in 1770 by its first competitor. By 1800, the number of extant life insurance companies doubled in size, to total four. Thereafter, the potential for and growth of the industry has been shown to be quite dynamic.

The rapid growth of the insurance industry in the United States is clear from a review of the data. A selective listing of the number of U.S. insurance companies by year and number illustrate the nature of the industry: in 1850, there were 48 companies; in 1870, 129; in 1880, 59; in 1900, 84; in 1925, 379; in 1950, 649; in 1955, 1,107; in 1975, 1,746; in 1985, 2,261; and in 1990, 2,195. At the end of 1995, there were 1,715 insurance companies operating in the United States (American Council of Life Insurance 1996). One of these, the New York Life Insurance Company, founded in 1845, enjoys the status of being a *Fortune* 100 company (see All Quotes Insurance 2002). Operating revenues of more than $13 billion allow the company to create surplus and investment reserves of more than $8.7 billion. This latter figure represents the funds that finance growth and protect the interests of the holders of the company's policies. However vast the number, this amount only brings this particular company into standing as *one* of the strongest in the industry.

The total figures for the U.S. life insurance industry are even more enlightening, if not astonishing. With the acceptance of life insurance among the growing middle class throughout the 20th century, and especially during the second half of the century, life insurance as an investment form has not only served to protect the future lifestyles of policyholders' family members, it has enhanced the growth of the American economy. For example, in 1900, there was a little more than $7.5 billion of life insurance *in force* in the United States. By 1950, life insurance *purchases* in the United States exceeded $28.7 billion. In 1995, Americans *purchased* approximately $1.6 trillion worth of individual and group life insurance; for that same year there was more than $12.5 trillion worth of life insurance *in force* (American Council of Life Insurance 1996:10). In 2001, the amount of *new* life insurance coverage exceeded $2.7 trillion. During that same year, more than $16.2 trillion in

individual and group life insurance was *in force* in the United States (American Council of Life Insurance 2002).

Although some individuals prefer to invest their money in a variety of markets outside the insurance industry, most Americans tend to take for granted the purchase of life insurance as one of the essential aspects of life. Wives expect their husbands and the fathers of their children to plan for the future. A part of this planning includes the provision of the gift of life insurance, a form of social exchange intended to assure that widowed spouses and orphans will remain economically functional should the head of household die.

There appears also to be a legacy involved in the purchase of life insurance. To quote the eminent scholar who serves as editor in chief of this handbook: "The main point of the entry should be: The bad news is you are dead, but the good news is that your heirs get a big chunk of money, and thus, your life had meaning." Need any more be stated?

REFERENCES

All Quotes Insurance. 2002. "Life Insurance." New York: Cyber Financial Network. Retrieved November 3, 2002 (http://www.allquotesinsurance.com).

American Council of Life Insurance. 1996. *Life Insurance Fact Book: 1996*. Washington, DC: American Council of Life Insurance.

———. 2002. *Life Insurance Fact Book: 2002*. Washington, DC: American Council of Life Insurance.

Baker, T. 2001. "Insurance and the Law." Pp. 7587–91 in *International Encyclopedia of the Social and Behavioral Sciences,* vol. 11, edited by Neil J. Smelser and Paul B. Baltes. Amsterdam: Elsevier.

Clough, Shepard B. 1946. *American Life Insurance: A History of the Mutual Life Insurance Company of New York, 1843–1943*. New York: Columbia University Press.

Dardis, Rachel. 1980. "The Value of a Life: New Evidence From the Marketplace." *American Economic Review* 70:1077–82.

Dublin, Louis L. and Alfred J. Lotka. 1946. *The Money Value of a Man.* New York: Ronald.

Empey, LaMar T. and Mark C. Stafford. 1991. *American Delinquency: Its Meaning and Construction,* 3rd ed. Belmont, CA: Wadsworth.

Fogel, Robert William. 2000. *The Fourth Great Awakening and the Future of Egalitarianism.* Chicago: University of Chicago Press.

Gollin, James. 1966. *Pay Now, Die Later.* New York: Random House.

Hendershot, Ralph. 1957. *The Grim Truth About Life Insurance.* New York: G. P. Putnam's Sons.

Jack, Fingland A. 1912. *An Introduction to the History of Life Insurance.* New York: E. P. Dutton.

Jones, Daniel Lee. [1999] 2002. "Organizing Risky Business: The Social Construction and Organization of Life Insurance, 1810–1980." Ph.D. dissertation, University of Arizona. Ann Arbor, MI: UMI Dissertation Services, ProQuest.

Landefeld, J. Steven and Eugene P. Seskin. 1982. "The Economic Value of Life: Linking Theory to Practice." *American Journal of Public Health* 72:556–66.

Lindesmith, Alfred R., Anselm L. Strauss, and Norman K. Denzin. 1988. *Social Psychology,* 6th ed. Englewood Cliffs, NJ: Prentice Hall.

Manis, Jerome G. and Bernard N. Melzer. 1978. *Symbolic Interaction: A Reader in Social Psychology,* 3d ed. Boston: Allyn & Bacon.

Mauss, Marcel. 1967. *The Gift: Forms and Functions of Exchange in Archaic Societies.* New York: W. W. Norton.

Miller, Ted R. 1990. "The Plausible Range for the Value of Life: Red Herrings Among the Mackerel." *Journal of Forensic Economics* 3(3):17–39.

Starlard, Gwendolyn. 1986. "Life Insurance Purchase: A Measure of the Social Value of Life." *Free Inquiry in Creative Sociology* 14:105–8.

Stevenson, John Alford. 1927. *Life Insurance: Its Economic and Social Relations.* New York: D. Appleton.

Stuart, M. S. 1940. *An Economic Detour: A History of Insurance in the Lives of American Negroes.* New York: Wendell, Malliet.

Taylor, Lee M. and Roland J. Pellegrin. 1959. "Professionalism: Its Functions and Dysfunctions for the Life Insurance Occupation." *Social Forces* 38:110–14.

Titmuss, Richard M. 1971. *The Gift Relationship: From Human Blood to Social Policy.* New York: Pantheon.

Whaples, Robert and David Buffum. 1991. "Fraternalism, Paternalism, the Family and the Market: Insurance a Century Ago." *Social Science History* 15:97–122.

Zelizer, Viviana A. 1978. "Human Values and the Market: The Case of Life Insurance and Death in 19th-Century America." *American Journal of Sociology* 84:591–610.

———. 1979. *Morals and Markets: The Development of Life Insurance in the United States.* New York: Columbia University Press.

———. 1981. "The Price and Value of Children: The Case of Children's Insurance." *American Journal of Sociology* 86:1036–56.

———. 1985. *Pricing the Priceless Child: The Changing Social Value of Children.* New York: Basic Books.

"Full Military Honors"

Ceremonial Interment as Sacred Compact

Timothy W. Wolfe

Clifton D. Bryant

> HERE RESTS IN
> HONORED GLORY
> AN AMERICAN
> SOLDIER
> KNOWN BUT TO GOD
>
> —Inscription on the Tomb of the Unknown Soldier,
> Arlington National Cemetery

If Ulysses S. Grant was correct in his observation that "war is hell!" then soldiers live on the edge of hell. The warrior's duty is to wage war or be prepared to do so. Behind the facade of military parade pageantry and the pomp and circumstance of formal reviews and ceremonies; behind the military bands blaring martial music, the shrill clarion call of the bugle, and the staccato beat of the drums; behind the military costumes and the rainbow of colored ribbons and decorations—behind all these lies the existential truth of the military experience. Constituent to this truth are the ennui of garrison duty and the psychological trauma of combat. Gallantry in action and the unselfish heroic bravery of the battlefield belie the ubiquitous reality of combat death and dismemberment.

The universal soldier has historically and stoically faced the prospect of death with studied equanimity, enduring the anxiety, fear, and uncertainty that precede battle.[1] Almost overriding soldiers' fear of combat death is their concern about the fate of their remains. There can be dignity in dying, but there is no dignity in having one's corpse left on the battlefield, at the mercy of the elements, unattended, uncared for, and unconnected to others. Soldiers cannot easily accommodate or assimilate the prospect of their abandoned bodies lying in desolation, subject to desecration, deterioration, desiccation, or disintegration. Confronted with this foreboding scenario, soldiers enter into an unspoken, but implicit, compact with their nation and their comrades. They will readily sacrifice their lives for their country, their people, or their comrades in arms, as long as they are secure in the knowledge that their remains will be reverently tended and that they will be laid to rest with proper respect, honor, and sincere ceremonial recognition of their supreme sacrifice—with "full military honors," as it were. This is a compact that the nation dutifully fulfills.

THE DEAD AS RESIDUE OF WAR

A product of war is death and the dead are its by-product. Prompt disposal or disposition of the dead is essential for several compelling reasons. Bodies deteriorate rapidly,

---

1. The term *soldier* technically refers to a member of the U.S. Army, whereas the Navy has sailors, the Marine Corp has marines, and the Air Force has airmen and airwomen. However, in this chapter we use *soldier* in a generic sense, to refer to any member of the military from any and all branches. It is less cumbersome than *service member* or *military member* (although we use these terms sometimes), and it reflects our personal biases resulting from our own service in the U.S. Army.

especially in hot weather, and there is the immediate concern with aesthetic consideration. The stench of death can affect even hardened soldiers and can have severe impacts on their morale as well as their sensibilities. Dead bodies attract animals and insects, and the attendant desecration of the dead by such creatures can also be profoundly disturbing to the living, as well as an insult to the memory of the dead. Of course, health considerations also make disposition of the dead an important priority. Disease propagated by decaying bodies, insects, and water pollution can threaten the living and may ravage whole armies if left unchecked. If not removed, the dead can even become a handicap to movement and maneuver. Finally, the living need to identify the dead before deterioration renders this impossible.

Battlefield exigencies can necessitate the disposal of the dead in ways that are highly distasteful. For example, in his historical account of the American invasion of Tarawa in World War II, Hoyt (1978) describes this scene:

> The mopping up on Tarawa was easy enough. On the fourth day it was the stink that bothered the men. Some 5,000 dead bodies lay rotting in the sun. The Marines could deal with the Japanese rapidly, and they did. The enemy bodies were collected in piles, hauled out to sea in Higgins boats, and dumped into the water. In its way it was not an unfitting end for these sailor-soldiers of an island kingdom. (P. 149)

Failure to remove the dead, or to bury them promptly, is to run the risk of having bodies simply disintegrate into unrecognizable remains that commingle with the earth. In World War I, during the siege of Verdun in France there were almost a million deaths on the battlefields around the town, and the months-long battles prevented the prompt removal of bodies. Webster (1994) describes the end result: "In what may be the most grisly statistic ever, fewer than 160,000 identifiable bodies were recovered. The rest were impossible to recognize or had simply been swallowed up by the explosions and mud" (p. 36).

After the war, a French national cemetery was established at Louvemont, France, near the battlefields. A huge ossuary was constructed and filled with fragments of skeletal material recovered from the surrounding areas. The bones are arranged in alcoves built into the ossuary walls. They are identified only by the sector of the Verdun battlefield from which they were recovered. Even today, more than 80 years later, bones are still found in the ground around Verdun and placed in the ossuary (Webster 1994).

In the view of the urgency of disposing of the mass of dead bodies after a battle, the thought arises that burning the bodies on funeral pyres might resolve the problem. This arrangement has been and continues to be used in cases of mass death, particularly where the deaths have been caused by disasters or epidemic disease. The burning of bodies like refuse, however, is considered to be a repugnant option for fallen warriors. Instead, throughout history,

---

GRASS

Pile the bodies high at Austerlitz and Waterloo.
Shovel them under and let me work—
      I am the grass; I cover all.

And pile them high at Gettysburg
And pile them high at Ypres and Verdun.
Shovel them under and let me work.
Two years, ten years, and passengers ask the conductor:

      What place is this?
      Where are we now?

I am the grass.
Let me work.

—Carl Sandburg, 1918

---

with few exceptions, battlefield burial (or burial at sea for sailors) has become institutionalized as the appropriate disposition of the bodies of war dead.

For untold centuries, however, the practice of battlefield burial was not institutionalized as an official and standardized function of the military. Instead, various informal procedures evolved. In the time of the Caesars, for example, Roman legionnaires would have small sums deducted from their pay as dues to a burial club. This burial club would arrange for and pay the expenses of members' funerals should they be killed in battle (Robinson 1971:18, 31). Alternatively, after battles the Roman legionnaires would compel captured warriors and/or civilians to bury the Roman dead.

In many other cases, fellow soldiers or buddies would simply bury their comrades as a matter of final respect and affectionate responsibility. Most frequently, the impetus for battlefield burial was command decision because of exigency. Sometimes, however, such burials were accompanied by relatively elaborate military ceremonial behavior. The ceremonies might be traditional or impromptu. Historian John Wright (1975) describes the military burial ceremonies that the American troops conducted during the Revolutionary War:

> Military Funerals were conducted with dignity and solemnity. Those slain in battle were buried where they fell, the most honorable resting places for a soldier. Men who died in camp were buried on the color line, in front of camp, their bodies facing the enemy. (P. 24)

Wright goes on to detail a particular ceremony held for a slain lieutenant colonel, an artillery officer from South Carolina; it involved an honor guard with reverse muskets, flags, muffled drums and musical instruments, a marching formation, and three volleys fired over the grave.

In most instances, however, the commander of a military unit would simply order the burial of the dead (including the fallen enemy soldiers) as an expedient means of disposing of the problem. As American Civil War historian James Robertson, Jr. (1988) notes, "A necessary task after every battle was the burial of the dead; and with the summer's heat working rapidly on hundreds of corpses, the gruesome and nauseous job was done with haste rather than reverence" (p. 225). In such circumstances, the dead might be buried in rows, trenches, or even mass graves. Retreating enemies might necessarily have to leave their dead behind. Sometimes, according to Robertson, civilians were impressed to bury the dead. In instances of inadequate or shallow burial, the graves might be washed out by heavy rains, and sometimes hogs would root out the bodies (p. 225).

By the time of the Napoleonic Wars, fought by mass armies of up to a million men, the huge death tolls of battles greatly exacerbated the problem of after-battle body disposal (we discuss the history and evolution of military funerals in greater detail in a later section). Insight into the need for reestablishing equilibrium after death is requisite to an understanding of military funeralization, however.

THE NEED TO REESTABLISH EQUILIBRIUM

When an individual passes from the world of the living to the world of the dead, this event creates disruption and social disequilibrium, not only for the relatively small group of persons directly involved with the deceased (e.g., immediate family, other members of the military unit) but for the larger social entity. The groups to which the deceased formerly belonged are obviously no longer the same groups after his or her demise. If the deceased was someone of special importance, perhaps a leader or some kind of celebrity, the disruption and social imbalance that results from his or her death is even greater. War represents, then, a time of tremendous social upheaval, as the specter of death is always present and potentially disruptive.

Obviously, it is important that there be in place a cultural (or subcultural) response to death that can dilute the fears of individuals or otherwise assist them in coping with death while also maintaining a degree of social stability and cohesion. Indeed, some students of death and dying contend that it is imperative that cultures develop social mechanisms for dealing with the disruption and anxiety that death precipitates (Riley 1983:192). It would appear

that such a mechanism exists in the military in the form of burial with "full military honors." Such ceremonial behavior helps to mitigate soldiers' fears and anxieties inasmuch as it bestows a degree of symbolic immortality. It also provides closure to the soldier's life, helps to restore group equilibrium, and fulfills the social compact.

Within the complex of fears with which soldiers must cope are fear of an unnoted death, fear of a lost or mutilated corpse, and fear of dying in a far-off land. All of these fears are made more manageable for soldiers through the promise that, in the event of their deaths, their comrades will make every effort to locate and retrieve their corpses, to care for and treat their bodies with reverence, to return them home (or to a suitable military cemetery), and to place them into the aggregate of fallen warriors. Although this is clearly not a "fair exchange," in the sense that infinite honor and respect cannot restore life, it is a significant social exchange insofar as it affords important symbolic rewards for soldiers and their families.[2] As one marine graves registration officer put it, "We want everybody accounted for, that will make the healing process quicker" (quoted in United Press International 1991). An enlisted Army graves registration specialist has described his job as follows:

> We're the guys who send our soldiers home. We're the ones who get them out of here so their families can have them back again. All the parents and relatives don't accept the fact their son or daughter might be dead until they see the remains. I feel like I've done something for them and their families. (quoted in Lamb 1991)

Throughout humankind's existence, people have developed various social arrangements and behavioral configurations to assist them in their efforts to understand, accept, and transcend death and dying. One of the most important and universal cultural responses to death involves the social creation, assembly, and manipulation of death symbols and, thus, the very conceptualization and meaning of death itself. The military, as a formal organization and social institution, has developed over time its own symbolic approach to the need to confront death and dying.

In effect, although soldiers face the possibility of death and the very real chance that their bodies may be mutilated in far-off lands, the U.S. military guarantees that every possible effort will be made to locate and secure their corpses, return them home in the best possible condition, and provide for them funerals and places of interment that are compelling and memorable in terms of dignity and honor (Risch 1989).[3] The implications of the changes that

---

2. The family, along with the fallen soldier, is also honored in a military funeral, which confers special status on the members of the family and especially the parents. During World War II in the United States, any mother who had a son (or daughter) serving in the military was entitled to display a small banner with a blue star in the window of her home. When a mother lost a son (or daughter) in the service, she would proudly and sadly display a banner with a gold star. The designation of "Gold Star Mother" carried a special prestigious status and elicited appropriate empathy and sympathy from other members of the community.

3. Note that viewing the corpse is a historically important social funerary custom in U.S. society.

have occurred over time in the military's handling of the dead are significant, both for individuals and for the larger social entity. Death in the military context is unique.

DEATH IN THE MILITARY CONTEXT

Changes over time in the nature, extent, and consequences of war have necessitated certain structural changes in the military's handling of body disposition and burial practices (Risch 1989). For example, the increasing numbers of dead, the fact that fields of battle have become farther away from soldiers' homes, and the increasing destruction and devastation wrought by modern weaponry have altered the nature and consequences of death in warfare. Before we examine specifically the changing military response to death, we believe it is appropriate to consider death in the military within an understanding of the special circumstances and considerations that confront those who engage in battle.

The Importance of Comrades

The U.S. military has identified the crucial factor that successfully motivates intelligent and rational human beings to risk their lives: It is well documented that American soldiers (as well as soldiers from the Middle East, Asia, and Europe)[4] fight and die not so much for political ideas, or love of country, or any other such lofty abstractions, but instead for their comrades in arms—their buddies (Henderson 1985). The fact that motivation for fighting is to be found in the intimate, interpersonal relationships among soldiers provides a potentially important insight regarding how soldiers cope with death and dying. A major impetus for soldiers facing death in battle is their concern for one another (Coser 1956; Elder and Clipp 1988; Henderson 1985).

It has also been well documented that the emotional bonds formed in combat, especially if the survivors have witnessed many deaths, not only help to sustain soldiers during the stressful time of combat but can last an entire lifetime. In fact, one important way in which combat soldiers can learn to cope with their residual postmilitary trauma is by maintaining ties with members of their former units. As Elder and Clipp observe (1988): "The loss of comrades in battle frequently reinforces social bonds among surviving members of a unit. These relationships and their social support can lessen the psychological impairment of combat trauma" (p. 178). In addition to providing the motivation to risk life and limb, as well as the social support needed to cope with past trauma, comradeship provides symbolic immortality. As Elder

and Clipp write: "The sacrifice of life in the spirit of comradeship ensures a measure of immortality as the fallen live through the memories of survivors" (p. 180). They further comment:

> When men fight for each other and their common survival, they also, in this sense, die and suffer wounds for each other. Some pledges in life become commitments between the living and the dead, between survivors and the memory of fallen comrades. There is an insistent obligation to remember, honor, and preserve the highest meaning of their sacrifice. Remembrance of the men who died unifies war comrades in a community of memory. (P. 183)

The Fear of Mutilation and an Unnoted Death

Not only do soldiers have to face the ever-present specter of death, they have to face the possibility that their dead bodies may be mutilated, lost, or even completely destroyed. As Dinter (1985) notes:

> Even more revealing is the disproportionately strong psychological effect of the bayonet, or the Moroccan soldiers at Cassino who mutilated their victims, and were therefore particularly feared by the defending German soldiers. We are deeply afraid of losing our physical integrity by being mutilated. This fear is so great that mutilation even after death still scares us. Fear of mutilation is certainly greater than the fear of death itself. (P. 25)

In addition to the fear of death itself, and the possibility that their corpses may be mutilated if not completely lost or missing, soldiers in combat must contend with the fear of unnoted death. This fear is not so much one of no longer being alive as it is a fear of being forgotten forever. Put differently, an unnoted death means that the postself career— that is, the reputation and symbolic social presence that an individual has after death—may never proceed or grow, so to speak, for the fallen warrior. The importance that Americans place on keeping the memories of the dead alive is illustrated by our society's emphasis on publicly and properly noting individual deaths, remembering the dead through various types of memorials, and marking the final resting places of the dead to ensure their symbolic presence in the social entity.

The anxiety that soldiers face, then, as they contemplate the possibility of an unnoted death, an unmarked grave, and the lack of symbolic presence in the social entity, is burdensome indeed. The U.S. military, correctly recognizing this set of fears, has addressed the task of ameliorating or at least minimizing these concerns and providing some means of assuring soldiers, their families, and society at large that those who serve their country will not be forgotten.

---

4. After World War II, American behavioral scientists who examined and analyzed data based on the combat behavior of German soldiers and small unit solidarity convincingly demonstrated that interpersonal relationships in small military units—the primary group—are significant influences on individual behavior (Shils and Janowitz 1948).

As war itself has evolved, so too has the military's response to the death and dying of its members. In the next section, we discuss certain aspects of the military history of the United States, with particular attention to the numbers of war dead, modes of body disposition, and funeral customs. Space limitations necessitate our limiting the amount of detail we can present in this historical discussion. Our intent here is to provide an overview of how military customs and practices of body disposition have changed over time, with an emphasis on the social import of such changes.

THE MILITARY RESPONSE TO DEATH

Historical Changes

When death comes to a military member—obviously not an uncommon situation during time of war—the body is handled and disposed of in prescribed ways, and there are customs in place to respond to the emotional and psychosocial needs of the deceased's loved ones and, indeed, the functional needs of society. Today, soldiers who are killed in combat and veterans of the military are given not just "decent" burials but "inspiring funeral service[s] of great dignity" (Hinkel 1970:168). As we have noted, over time the American military has changed the ways in which it responds to the death of a members. Today's military funeral—complete with a flag-draped casket, the playing of "Taps," and a rifle or canon salute—has evolved slowly. The Civil War and World War I serve as important historical markers in this regard.

Several factors are responsible for the changes in the way the U.S. military responds to death; these include the locations of battlefields vis-à-vis soldiers homes, the numbers of war dead, and the military's institutional ability and inclination to process the dead. As we have mentioned, the earliest wars in which the United States was involved were typically fought relatively near the homes of soldiers.

In the war of the American Revolution (1775–83), fought mostly by provincial troops and state militias (Addington 1994:12), the American soldiers were typically not very far from their homes, and the families of those who died could reasonably be expected to make whatever funeral arrangements they desired. This first U.S. war saw some 100,000 men fight throughout the entire war effort, but there were never more than 35,000 American troops fighting against the British at any one time. The loss of life for gaining independence was quite high, as some 25,000 American soldiers died in this war (Addington 1994:19). Although there were no formalized or routinized military funeral customs at this time, fallen soldiers, especially officers, were interred with respect and dignity ("Horses of Arlington" 1971:24).

The next major war in which the United States was involved was the Anglo-American War of 1812 (1812–15). In this campaign, the American Army made a rather poor showing, as mobilization of troops was poorly handled and military leadership was relatively weak. American troops traveled farther from their home bases than they did during the Revolutionary War, but the American losses were relatively light, with only 7,000 dead as a result of the war (Addington 1994:35). The handling of the dead in this conflict was again left to the idiosyncratic inclinations of unit commanders or to whatever prior arrangements individual soldiers had made. At this time, there were still no institutionalized arrangements for formal military burials or ceremonial observance of interments. The battlefield often became the graveyard. Writing about the U.S. military's burial practices even up to the Civil War, Risch (1989) notes in her history of the Army's Quartermaster Corps:

> The return of the remains of deceased officers was an exception to the general practices followed in campaigns. Most officers and all enlisted personnel who died in battle were buried where they fell. For the most part, too, burial sites went unmarked and no records were kept other than the report of those killed in action. (Pp. 463–64)

After the War of 1812 and before the Civil War, the United States was involved in a war with Mexico over Texas (1846–48). This war saw soldiers from the East traveling to Texas and points south and west. Some 14,000 U.S. troops died as a result of this campaign, but only 2,000 of those deaths resulted from actual combat. The majority of deaths were caused by exposure, disease, and capital punishment meted out for desertion and war atrocities (Addington 1994:61). At this time there still were no formalized structures or procedures in place for processing and disposing of the war dead. It has even been reported that some 750 unidentified American soldiers were simply buried in a mass grave in Mexico City (Addington 1994).

Although in more recent times the mass interment of war dead has occasionally been carried out as a temporary measure, until more permanent and appropriate steps could be taken (i.e., until the bodies could be identified and prepared for shipment home for "proper" burial), the idea of permanently burying soldiers en masse is unthinkable in contemporary America. For example, in June 1980 the Veterans Administration announced plans to exhume the bodies of 627 unknown Civil War soldiers from individual graves for reinterment in a mass grave in an effort to make room for new burials. The headstone for the mass grave was to read "NOW WE ARE ONE." Because these were unknown soldiers and burial space in national cemeteries is in increasingly short supply, the VA fully expected that it could accomplish this movement of bodies without any problems. However, many people were so outraged that the plan had to be scrapped (Kearl and Rinaldi 1983:701). In the United States we have come to expect that most persons, especially "respectable" persons, will be buried in their own individual graves with their own markers. However, we do tolerate mass burial for the indigent, as in the case of Potter's Field in

New York City. We treat the most marginal members of our society differently, even in death.

Embalming

The Civil War (1861–65) marked the beginnings of some important changes in the way the military responded to death and dying. Two particularly important developments took place: (a) embalming came into practice, and (b) the military established formal mechanisms for keeping better records concerning death as well as providing markers at burial sites. As Risch (1989) writes:

> The Civil War forced changes in the traditional policies governing burial and records. Recognizing that the War Department would be called upon to answer an increasing number of inquiries concerning the fate of individual volunteers, the Secretary of War took steps to preserve records. His first action, taken in September 1861, was aimed at the maintenance of records at Army hospitals. To preserve accurate permanent records of soldiers who died at Army hospitals, he directed the Quartermaster General to place blank books and forms for such record purposes at every general and post hospital of the Army. He also ordered him to furnish headboards for soldiers' graves. Proper execution of the forms provided became the duty of the commanding officer of the military corps or department in which the individual died. (P. 464)

Although only relatively few soldiers made arrangements to have their bodies embalmed, not long after the Civil War embalming became very popular. According to Leming and Dickinson (1994):

> It was not until the time of the Civil War that embalming was promoted to temporarily preserve the body for return to the soldier's home. Some reports credit this practice to a military doctor by the name of Thomas Holmes. (P. 454)

Embalming was available prior to this time—anatomists, artists, and medical personnel were known to embalm bodies for their particular uses—but embalming to preserve bodies so that they could be transported long distances for burial was not a practice before this time. As DeSpelder and Strickland (1992) report:

> Embalming the dead came into use in the years after the Civil War. President Lincoln's funeral procession, which traveled from Washington, D.C., to Springfield, Illinois, was a public event that increased awareness of the new practice of embalming. (P. 208)

Pine (1975:16) notes that as Lincoln's funeral procession progressed through many portions of the Northeast and Midwest, people along its path became aware that it was possible to keep and view the dead for long periods of time. Although buried in 1865, Lincoln's body was so well embalmed that when it was later viewed after exhumation in 1899, it was proclaimed to be in a perfect state of preservation.[5] For such reasons, embalming became an increasingly important aspect of the American way of death.

Prior to the Civil War, U.S. war dead were not embalmed, but there are accounts of unembalmed dead soldiers from the Seminole Indian War in Florida and the Mexican American War being returned home for burial. During the Civil War, as previously mentioned, civilian embalmers did embalm thousands of soldiers on both sides and arrange for their shipment home for burial. During World Wars I and II, with few exceptions (such as some cases in which U.S. airmen in England were embalmed by English civilian embalmers), no embalming was performed on dead U.S. servicemen. In the latter stages of the Korean War, many dead soldiers were embalmed and shipped home. During the Vietnam War, dead soldiers at first were flown to the Philippines to be embalmed at a U.S. military facility, but later the U.S. military established embalming facilities in Vietnam (Johnson 1971). These mortuaries were very efficient; the time between a soldier's death and his body's return to the United States averaged 72 to 96 hours.[6] When the body arrived back in the United States, it was restored, cosmetized, dressed, and casketed. A military escort accompanied the body by the fastest available transportation to the individual's hometown, where it was turned over to the family's funeral director (or the family) to be buried with "full military honors" (Kuehnert 1970).

In addition to the use of embalming, the Civil War saw another important change in the U.S. military as the country first experienced death on a tremendously large scale. Some 254,000 Confederate soldiers and 370,000 Union soldiers died during the war, for a total combined loss of approximately 624,000, the largest number of American military deaths ever. In many Civil War battles, soldiers fought and died far enough from their homes that long-distance transportation was necessary if a fallen soldier was to be buried in the family cemetery. Typically, soldiers who were killed, whether blue or gray, were buried near the field of battle. During this period, the military did not have specialized units that were responsible for handling and processing the dead; that was to come later.

---

5. Lincoln's casket was exhumed by grave robbers, but their efforts were thwarted before they could depart with the body. Authorities then opened the casket to determine whether the body was still present and intact. They found Lincoln's embalmed body to be in an excellent state of preservation.

6. The Vietnam conflict saw some significant technical improvements in the handling of large numbers of war dead. For example, during the 1968 Tet Offensive, the U.S. mortuary at Da Nang, which normally processed about 350 remains per month, had to process more than 1,000 remains per month for 3 consecutive months. In order to deal with this tremendous increase, the mortuary used refrigerated trucks to store bodies until the embalmers could do their job and implemented procedures to increase the pace of properly preparing a corpse (see Grafe 1969). Despite the overwhelming challenge, workers at the mortuary rose to the occasion. All of this serves to illustrate the importance placed on properly caring for and preparing the remains of American soldiers for return home and subsequent interment.

Military Deaths Move Abroad

After the Civil War, the government of the United States was engaged primarily in expanding and controlling territory west of the Mississippi. The next military situation of significance for the nation involved a dispute with Spain, the Spanish-American War of 1898. Although this war originated over public concern regarding how the Spanish were treating rebellious Cubans, it quickly spread to the Far East, specifically the Philippines. Although the United States had hastily recruited and trained volunteers, scattering troops to Cuba, Puerto Rico, and the Philippines, the death toll was relatively light, with only 3,000 American lives lost (Addington 1994:128), and most of these to disease and bad food. As a result of this conflict, Cuba received its independence, and Puerto Rico and the Philippines became American territories. The trend of American soldiers fighting farther and farther away from home obviously continued in this war. The principle of returning war dead to their native soil that was established during the Civil War continued to be honored in this war, too. To the greatest extent possible, fallen soldiers were shipped home for interment in either private or military cemeteries, depending on the wishes of their next of kin (Risch 1989:689).

Military Cemeteries

It was not until after the Civil War that the U.S. National Cemetery System began to emerge (Risch 1989). One of the spoils of war for the Union was the Custis-Lee mansion, Arlington House, which was to become Arlington National Cemetery. Some have even suggested that Union soldiers intentionally buried their dead comrades on the property of the Custis-Lee mansion so that it could never be given back to its rightful owners.

As we have noted, another significant aspect of the Civil War was the volume of war dead it produced; this was the costliest war, in terms of human lives, that the United States has ever experienced. World War I also serves as an important historical marker, as it resulted in large numbers of war dead who were an ocean away from home. Although the creation of national military cemeteries began during and after the Civil War (at Gettysburg, for example, where Lincoln dedicated the cemetery with the speech we today know as the Gettysburg Address), it was after World War I that the U.S. government sought to institutionalize the creation, beautification, and maintenance of such cemeteries.

The American Battle Monuments Commission was established by law in March 1923, for the express purpose of

> commemorating the services and achievements of United States Armed Forces where they have served since April 6, 1917 (the date of U.S. entry into World War I) through the erection of suitable memorial shrines; for designing,

> constructing, operating and maintaining permanent U.S. military cemeteries and memorials in foreign countries. (American Battle Monuments Commission 1971:8)

This agency now administers and maintains 23 cemetery memorials and 11 monuments in foreign countries as well as 3 memorials in the United States. Interred in the 23 cemeteries are some 124,888 American men and women who served in the armed forces (30,912 dead from World War I, 93,226 from World War II, and 750 from the Mexican War). These burials represent about 39% of the dead from World Wars I and II. It is interesting to note that "the decisions that these servicemen be laid to rest in foreign soil on or nearby battlefields where they fell were made by next of kin" (American Battle Monuments Commission 1971:8).

In addition to these burials, memorial tablets located at the cemeteries list the names of 91,591 military personnel who were missing in action or lost or buried at sea in World Wars I and II and the Korean War (American Battle Monuments Commission 1971:8). According to the American Battle Monuments Commission (n.d.):

> These burial grounds unquestionably are the most beautiful and meticulously maintained shrines of their nature in the world. No others combine such fitness of design, beauty of landscaping and memorial features and immaculate care. (P. 2)

It should also be noted that these cemeteries are visited by 15 million people each year.

Beyond these foreign U.S. military cemeteries, the Veterans Administration has established and maintains 118 national military cemeteries on U.S. soil. Arlington National Cemetery, which contains the graves of 250,000 armed services personnel, civilian political officials, war correspondents, and journalists as well as the graves of some 3,800 former slaves, is the most famous, but there are other such cemeteries in 39 states (and Puerto Rico) (Leming and Dickinson 2001:411–13).

Any honorably discharged veteran, along with his or her spouse (and/or one dependent child), can be interred in one of these cemeteries (with grave lines or vault and grave marker) free of charge. At the burials conducted at these cemeteries, "families may be provided with a dignified military funeral ceremony, including folding and presenting the United States burial flag, the playing of Taps, and memorial certificate of appreciation signed by the President of the United States" (Leming and Dickinson 2001:411–13). The United States honors its promises to members of the armed services.

Other Changes in the Military's Handling of the Dead

The Great War, as World War I has been called, lasted from 1914 to 1918. The United States, however, did not become involved in the war militarily until 1917. Despite this late entry, a significant number of American lives were

Figure 1   Sentinel at the Tomb of the Unknown Soldier at Arlington Cemetery

SOURCE: Photo by S. H. Kelley; reprinted courtesy of Military District of Washington News Service.

lost—more than 170,000, according to some analyses (Clark 1931:1). The number of soldiers from all nations who died in this war is estimated to be greater than 8.5 million (Matloff n.d.:113). This war was so costly and utterly devastating to the nations involved that many hopefully claimed it was "the war to end all wars." As we all too painfully know, that was not the case.

Several important changes in the military's handling of the dead occurred as a result of World War I. For one, the Graves Registration Service component of the Quartermaster Corps was officially instituted in 1916; its mission was the retrieval, identification, and disposal of the dead. (The Quartermaster Corps had assumed some of these responsibilities during the Civil War, but it was not until World War I that the Graves Registration Service was formally established.) The Graves Registration Service was charged with returning the dead to their native soil to the greatest extent possible and also with establishing permanent overseas U.S. military cemeteries. The next of kin of fallen soldiers were given the option of having the bodies of their loved ones returned home for interment or laid to rest in an overseas military cemetery (Risch 1989). Several military funeral customs also had their beginnings during World War I.

The Preeminent Military Memorial

Perhaps the best-known American memorial was born out of World War I—the Tomb of the Unknown Soldier.

This soldier, "known but to God," was interred in Arlington National Cemetery in 1921 (Mossman and Stark 1971). Since that time, unknown soldiers from other U.S. wars have also been interred in this tomb. Since its inception, millions of people have visited this memorial to pay their respects. More than five million tourists go to Arlington annually to see this "unique monument to America's honored dead" (Bryant and Shoemaker 1977:21).

Later Wars, Later Losses

Only a quarter of a century after World War I, the United States was once again drawn into a worldwide war. This time, American losses would be even greater than in the previous world war: Some 400,000 troops died fighting in both the European and Pacific theaters (MacCloskey 1968:52). Several significant outcomes, in terms of the military's response to death and the dead, resulted from this war. Additional overseas military cemeteries were established to handle the large volume of war dead, and the graves registration function of the military improved in terms of efficiency as forensic techniques were developed that aided in the identification of the dead. As MacCloskey (1968) notes:

World War II was fought over vast areas of the globe and under circumstances that made recovery, evacuation, and identification much more difficult than during World War I. In

Figure 2   Military Funeral of NASA Astronaut Captain Laurel Blair Salton Clark, Who Died on February 1, 2003, When the Space Shuttle *Columbia* Broke Up During Reentry

SOURCE: Photo by Tom Mani; reprinted courtesy of Military District of Washington News Service.

spite of the many difficulties created by technological advances in warfare, the unknowns were only 3.7 per 100 recoveries. Improvements in the organization and operation of the various graves registration units in the worldwide theaters of operation reduced the number of temporary burial sites, which, in turn, facilitated the final disposition of the dead. Dental records and fingerprint charts were used to aid in the identification. (P. 52)

Since World War II, the United States has been involved in two large-scale military conflicts (in Korea and Vietnam) and one relatively minor military conflict (in the Persian Gulf). The loss of life for the U.S. armed forces in Korea was approximately 54,000 troops; American losses in Vietnam were approximately 58,000 (*Information Please Almanac* 1992:306).

Having presented this overview of the historical and social evolution of death customs in the military context, we now turn our focus to contemporary military funerals.

CONTEMPORARY MILITARY FUNERALS

The evolution of the U.S. military's response to death is a compelling story. Today, a U.S. military funeral is an impressive and moving ceremony. In this section we address contemporary military funerals, examining traditional interment (i.e., earth burial) as well as burial at sea.

Military Honors

Military honors are of two basic types: standard honors and full honors. Standard military honors are provided at the funerals of enlisted members of the armed services by the particular branches in which they served (i.e., Army, Navy, Air Force, or Marine Corps). These honors include a bugler, a firing party, a casket team, and a military chaplain (if desired). Burial flags are also provided; for active-duty members, the particular branches provide the flags, whereas the Department of Veteran's Affairs provides flags for veterans. In a funeral with standard honors, three rifle volleys are fired by seven riflemen, "Taps" is played by a military bugler, and a casket team performs the formal folding of the American flag that draped the casket.

In a funeral with full honors, all of the above takes place, and in addition an escort platoon, a color guard, and a military band are present. The size of the escort platoon varies according to the rank of the deceased. Funerals with full military honors are provided for commissioned officers and warrant officers. In addition,

> officers buried in Arlington Cemetery are entitled to use of the caisson. Officers in the rank of colonel and above in the Army and the Marine Corps are entitled to a caparisoned (riderless) horse. General officers are also entitled to a cannon salute (17 guns for a four-star general, 15 for a three-star, 13 for a two-star, 11 for a one-star). Each service has variations to these funeral honors.
>
> The president of the United States is entitled to a 21-gun salute, while other high state officials receive 19 guns. (Arlington National Cemetery n.d.)

The Ladies of Arlington

One of the most interesting features of military honors at Arlington National Cemetery is the support provided by the Ladies of Arlington. This volunteer group of ladies (plus one gentleman) is committed to seeing that no one is interred at Arlington without at least one mourner present. Most of the Arlington Ladies (there are approximately 60) volunteer about one day a month. Many of them have buried loved ones at Arlington themselves. To become an Arlington Lady, one must be the wife or widow of a service member and be referred by a current Arlington Lady.

The Arlington Ladies make certain that no one is ever buried alone, and that all are buried with honor. The Arlington Ladies attend the funerals of all U.S. Army, Navy, and Air Force members, be they privates or generals, whether they receive standard or full honors. The Marine Corps does not have volunteers in the Arlington Ladies group, but a representative of the commandant of the Marine Corps is present at each funeral of a marine.

Another organization that provides support and assistance to the bereaved is the Tragedy Assistance Program for Survivors (TAPS), a national nonprofit organization serving families, friends, and military service members who have been affected by active-duty military deaths. TAPS offers a variety of services, including peer support, crisis response and intervention, grief care and counseling resources, casework assistance, long-term survivor wellness services, and community and military education and outreach. All of these services are available 24 hours a day free of charge. (More information is available on the organization's excellent Web site at http://www.taps.org.)

Burial at Sea

Soldiers are typically buried in the ground (or, alternatively, they may choose to have their ashes placed in a columbarium), but sailors have the option of being buried at sea. This ancient death practice has its roots in necessity. As we have noted above, corpses require disposition. In the past, it was not always practical for those at sea to wait until their ships returned to port before they disposed of their dead, so an alternative had to be found.

As with earth burial, military honors can be rendered during burial at sea. The Naval Historical Center (1999) gives this description of burial at sea services:

> Personnel participating or attending the services must wear the Uniform of the Day. When a chaplain of appropriate faith is not available, the service may be read by the commanding officer or an officer designated by him/her. The committal service is as follows:
>
> - Station firing squad, casket bearers and bugler.
>
> - Officer's call. Pass the word "All hands bury the dead" (the ships should be stopped, if practicable, and colors displayed at half-mast).
>
> - Assembly.
>
> - Adjutant's call (Call to Attention).
>
> - Bring the massed formation to Parade Rest.
>
> - Burial service.
>
>   The Scripture (Parade Rest).
>
>   The prayers (Parade Rest, heads bowed).
>
>   The Committal (Attention, Hand Salute).
>
>   The Benediction (Parade Rest, heads bowed).
>
> - Fire three volleys (Attention, Hand Salute).
>
> - Taps. Close up colors. Resume course and speed at the last note of Taps (Hand Salute).
>
> - Encasing of the flag (Attention).
>
> - Retreat (Resume normal duties).

THE SOCIAL FUNCTIONS OF MILITARY HONORS

Various social needs result from death, including the need to reestablish social equilibrium, the need to mitigate the fears that attend death, the need to find ways of transcending death, and the need to find meaning in death. Military honors speak to these needs. Military funerals and honors as social processes must be viewed and understood in terms of several contextual elements. In this regard, the funeral fulfills various social functions and communicates different social messages.

IN FLANDERS FIELDS

In Flanders fields the poppies blow
Between the crosses, row on row
That mark our place; and in the sky
The larks, still bravely singing, fly
Scarce heard amid the guns below.

We are the Dead. Short days ago
We lived, felt dawn, saw sunset glow,
Loved and were loved, and now we lie
In Flanders fields.

Take up our quarrel with the foe;
To you from failing hands we throw
The torch; be yours to hold it high.
If ye break faith with us who die
We shall not sleep, though poppies grow
In Flanders fields.

—Lieutenant Colonel John McCrae, 1915

Military Honors as Distinctive Subcultural Funeralization

Funeralization often mirrors the subcultural background of the deceased. Funeral ceremonies and behaviors may reflect the religious, ethnic, regional, vocational, and/or avocational linkages of the dead individual. Thus Catholic funerals, Chinese funerals, funerals for firefighters, and funerals for members of the Masonic lodge all have distinctive characteristics; there are even unique funeral services and practices for individuals with strong hobby interests (a model railroader, for example, might be buried in a locomotive engineer's cap).

The military as a vocation and work system has its own highly singular subculture, and the military funeral is simply an extension of this subculture. Death does not necessarily disengage the individual from his or her religion, ethnic origin, avocation, or vocation. The funeral conveys continuity of membership and affiliation, and gives permanence to seminal social identity, such as nationality and occupation. Thus the military funeral of a U.S. serviceman or servicewoman eternalizes the deceased as an American soldier forever. Furthermore, the military funeral serves to strengthen the linkages between the living and the dead. It allows for a type of continuity or perpetuity such that all soldiers, dead or alive, share a connection or common bond. Thus, in an important and symbolic sense, soldiers do not die; they transfer to the Army Eternal.

Military Honors as Group Intensification

The military is a social group, as are its constituent, subordinate units. Membership in these units is a paramount dimension in military life, as it can lead to esprit de corps, loyalty, and group identity. The military is a fraternity, and the members are brothers. They live together, they fight together, and sometimes they die together. Just as soldiers may sacrifice their lives for their comrades in arms, so too will those comrades accompany their dead to the grave. The military funeral symbolizes participation in the group and group fealty. The honor guard symbolizes the unit, the playing of "Taps" articulates the group lament in musical mode, and the three volleys of gunfire represent both the experience of battle and the formal salute calling attention to the death of a soldier. Soldiers are not alone in battle, and they are not alone as they are interred.

Military Honors as Aggregation and Incorporation

The anonymity of the individual in the mass military is neutralized by the mechanism of the subordination and submersion of self into the larger social entity—often the military unit or units. The individual becomes merely a constituent part of the corporate entity, and individual meaning and fulfillment derive from group existence and collective accomplishment. In effect, the whole is greater than the sum of its parts. Accordingly, soldiers continually seek the security and satisfaction of collective unity and incorporation into the group entity.

The ubiquitous themes of aggregation and incorporation are always evident in military culture, as evidenced by the braggadocio of clichés such as "Rangers never die—they just go to hell and regroup!" These themes are universal and are found in all militaries. It is for this reason that warriors make every effort to find their fallen comrades and bring them together to rest collectively side by side for eternity. The U.S. military has sought to accomplish this goal by establishing military cemeteries both here and abroad. The dead soldiers have been collected from the battlefields where they fell, and from temporary grave sites, gathered together, and reinterred with great dignity to lie together, side by side as comrades in arms forever. Beyond the "regrouping" of collective burial, there is also the element of incorporation into larger entity of "fallen warriors"—the band of brothers, united and consolidated into one, forever. In effect, "Now we are one."

The element of incorporation of the military dead has even come to be a component of the theology and mythology in some societies, such as Japan. In his historical account of the battle for Tarawa in the South Pacific during World War II, Hoyt (1978) writes of the Japanese naval forces:

> They had been trained and exhorted in the tradition of bushido. They did not think of survival, but of dying honorably for the emperor, and taking with them as many of the enemy as possible. Then, after death, their souls would assemble at the Yasukuni shrine, that holiest of places for the warriors of Japan, and they would have eternal rest and eternal glory. (P. 69)

Military Honors as Symbolic Immortality and Memorialization

The military funeralization process, with its distinctive ceremonial characteristics and embellishments, serves to certify the deceased as a fallen warrior; it publicly legitimates the ultimate sacrifice, provides public announcement and celebration of the individual's death, and memorializes the social fact of the soldier's demise. The individual will be remembered and revered always for having laid down his life for his country. Thus the memory of the fallen soldier is indelibly fixed in the collective consciousness of the society. In addition, the memorialization serves to reintegrate the dead into the family unit. Family members come to visit the grave site; they may even enjoy picnics in the cemetery and, in a sense, include the deceased in family affairs.

An account from World War II, although specifically referring to how Japanese soldiers viewed death, provides a fine example of how warriors from around the world and throughout time have created meaning and coped with the prospect of death:

> Those who died . . . were generously rewarded. Their spirits went to Tokyo's celebrated Yasukuni Shrine—The Patriots Shrine or Shrine of the Righteous Souls—where they began a better life mingling with the spirits of other heroes and achieved a closeness to the Emperor beyond their aspirations while alive. (Feifer 1992:119)

Arlington, preeminent among American military cemeteries, is our Yasukuni. Burial there, or in any of the other American military cemeteries, here or abroad, "offers perpetual testimony of the concern of a grateful nation that the lives and services of members of the Armed Forces will be appropriately commemorated" (MacCloskey 1968:182).

Military Honors as a Social Exchange Mechanism

The fate of soldiers is to do battle with their countries' enemies and, if necessary, lay down their lives as sacrifice to that purpose. As Alfred, Lord Tennyson phrased it:

> Theirs not to make reply,
>
> Theirs not to reason why,
>
> Theirs but to do and die.

Faced with the prospect of possible ignominious death, the desecration of their corpses, and burial in lonely and anonymous graves, soldiers are comforted—and, perhaps, to some degree compensated—by the knowledge that in the event of their deaths, every attempt will be made to recover and protect their corpses, and they will be accorded full military honors in death. These honors, will recognize them as soldiers, reflect their affiliation with their brethren warriors,

aggregate them with their fallen comrade in arms, incorporate them into the battalion eternal, and memorialize and glorify them as fallen warriors forever. Thus full military honors can be conceptualized as a social exchange—the trading of life for eternal reverence and honor.

CONCLUSION

In dealing with its dead, the U.S. military has responded to changes in the nature and intensity of war. Whereas once war dead could be accommodated through impromptu means, modern warfare and mass armies have necessitated the introduction of formalized units and specialized techniques and procedures to recover, identify, and process the dead. In addition, military funerals have evolved from informal rituals to tightly choreographed formalized ceremonies that bestow military honors on those who have served their country. Although death resulting from service to the nation is obviously an event that soldiers hope and seek to avoid, the military's response to soldiers' deaths provides an exchange mechanism that diminishes, to some extent, the fear and finality of death. As Theodore O'Hara wrote so eloquently in 1847 (quoted in MacCloskey 1968:183):

> On Fame's eternal camping ground
>
> Their silent tents are spread
>
> And Glory guards, with solemn round,
>
> The bivouac of the dead.

After a battle, the military imperative is to regroup—to reassemble and reorganize. Only then can the soldiers bivouac, or encamp and rest with their comrades. In death, when soldiers receive full military honors and are ceremonially interred in military cemeteries, they simply regroup with their fallen comrades and lie in honored rest among them in the Bivouac Eternal.

REFERENCES

Addington, Larry H. 1994. *The Patterns of War Since the Eighteenth Century,* 2d ed. Bloomington: Indiana University Press.

American Battle Monuments Commission. 1971. "American Memorials and Overseas Military Cemeteries." *Mortuary Management,* December, pp. 8–12.

———. n.d. *World War II Commemorative Program.* Washington, DC: American Battle Monuments Commission.

Arlington National Cemetery. n.d. "Ceremonies." Arlington, VA: Arlington National Cemetery. Retrieved April 2, 2003 (http:// arlingtoncemetery.org/ceremonies/military_funerals. html).

Bryant, Clifton D. and Donald J. Shoemaker. 1977. "Death and the Dead for Fun (and Profit): Thanatological

Entertainment as Popular Culture." Presented at the annual meeting of the Southern Sociological Society, April 1, Atlanta, GA.

Coser, Lewis. 1956. *The Social Functions of Conflict.* New York: Free Press.

Clark, John M. 1931. *The Costs of the World War to the American People.* New Haven, CT: Yale University Press.

DeSpelder, Lynne Ann and Albert Lee Strickland. 1992. *The Last Dance: Encountering Death and Dying,* 3d ed. Mountain View, CA: Mayfield.

Dinter, Elmar. 1985. *Hero or Coward: Pressures Facing the Soldier in Battle.* Totowa, NJ: Frank Cass.

Elder, Glen H., Jr. and Elizabeth C. Clipp. 1988. "Wartime Losses and Social Bonding: Influences Across 40 Years in Men's Lives." *Psychiatry* 51:177–98.

Feifer, George. 1992. *Tennozan.* New York: Ticknor & Fields.

Grafe, William T. 1969. "1968 Tet Offensive: A Tough Job." *Mortuary Management,* September, pp. 11–20.

Henderson, William Darryl. 1985. *Cohesion: The Human Element in Combat.* Washington, DC: National Defense University Press.

Hinkel, John V. 1970. *Arlington: Monument to Heroes.* Englewood Cliffs, NJ: Prentice Hall.

"The Horses of Arlington." 1971. *American Funeral Director,* August, pp. 24–26.

Hoyt, Edwin P. 1978. *Storm Over the Gilberts: War in the Central Pacific: 1943.* New York: Van Nostrand.

Information Please Almanac, 45th ed. 1992. Boston: Houghton Mifflin.

Johnson, Edward C. 1971. "A Brief History of U.S. Military Embalming." *The Director,* September, pp. 8–9.

Kearl, Michael C. and Anoel Rinaldi. 1983. "The Political Uses of the Dead as Symbols in Contemporary Civil Religions." *Social Forces* 61:693–708.

Kuehnert, David A. 1970. "From the Field to the Funeral Director: The Story of the U.S. Army Mortuary System." *The Director,* April, pp. 2–3, 9.

Lamb, David. 1991. "Graves Registration." Los Angeles Times, February 9, p. A4.

Leming, Michael R. and George E. Dickinson. 1994. *Understanding Dying, Death, and Bereavement,* 3d ed. Fort Worth, TX: Harcourt Brace.

Leming, Michael R. and George E. Dickinson. 2001. *Understanding Dying, Death, and Bereavement,* 5th ed. Fort Worth, TX: Harcourt Brace.

MacCloskey, Monroe. 1968. *Hallowed Ground: Our National Cemeteries.* New York: Richards Rosen.

Matloff, Maurice. n.d. *World War I: A Concise History of "The War to End All Wars" and the Road to the War.* New York: David McKay.

McCrae, John. [1915] 1919. "In Flanders Fields." In John McCrae, *In Flanders Fields, and Other Poems.* London: G. P. Putnam's Sons.

Mossman, B. C. and M. W. Stark. 1971. *The Last Salute: Civil and Military Funerals 1921–1969.* Washington, DC: U.S. Department of the Army.

Naval Historical Center. 1999. "Burial at Sea." Washington, DC: Naval Historical Center. Retrieved April 2, 2003 (http://www.history.navy.mil/faqs/faq85-1.htm).

Pine, Vanderlyn R. 1975. *Caretaker of the Dead: The American Funeral Director.* New York: Irvington.

Riley, John W., Jr. 1983. "Dying and the Meanings of Death: Sociological Inquiries." *Annual Review of Sociology* 9:191–216.

Risch, Erma. 1989. *Quartermaster Support of the Army: A History of the Corps 1775–1939.* Washington, DC: U.S. Army, Center of Military History.

Robertson, James I., Jr. 1988. *Soldiers Blue and Gray.* Columbia: University of South Carolina Press.

Robinson, H. Russell 1971. "Caius Largennius." Pp. 17–31 in *The Universal Soldier: Fourteen Studies in Campaign Life A.D. 43–1944.* Garden City, NY: Doubleday.

Sandburg, Carl. [1918] 1919. "Grass." In *Modern American Poetry and Modern British Poetry: An Introduction,* edited by Louis Untermeyer. New York: Harcourt, Brace and World.

Shils, Edward A. and Morris Janowitz. 1948. "Cohesion and Disintegration in the Wehrmacht in World War II." *Public Opinion Quarterly* 12:280–315.

United Press International. 1991. "Marines Facing a Lot of Reality." February 5.

Webster, Donovan. 1994. "Out There Is a Bomb With Your Name." *Smithsonian Magazine,* February, pp. 26–37.

Wright, John W. 1975. "Military Funerals in the Continental Army." *American Funeral Director* 98:24.

ADDITIONAL READINGS

"American Memorials and Overseas Military Cemeteries." 1972. *Mortuary Management,* December, pp. 8–14.

Aries, Philippe. 1981. *The Hour of Our Death,* translated by Helen Weaver. New York: Alfred A. Knopf.

Bartone, Paul T. and Morten G. Ender. 1994. "Organizational Responses to Death in the Military." *Death Studies* 18:25–39.

Becker, Ernest. 1973. *The Denial of Death.* New York: Free Press.

Blauner, Robert. 1966. "Death and Social Structure." *Psychiatry* 29:378–94.

Borden, Penn. 1989. *Civilian Indoctrination of the Military: World War I and Future Implications for the Military-Industrial Complex.* New York: Greenwood.

Bowman, Leroy. 1959. *The American Funeral: A Study in Guilt, Extravagance, and Sublimity.* Washington, DC: Public Affairs.

Carlson, Doug. 1992. *Punchbowl: The National Memorial Cemetery of the Pacific,* 2d ed. Aiea, HI: Island Heritage.

Carlson, Peter. 1995. "And the Slain Lay in Rows." *Washington Post Magazine,* July 30, pp. 10–17, 24–27.

"The Cemetery at Tanggok." 1970. *American Funeral Director,* February.

Garb, Ronald and Avraham Bleich. 1987. "Bereavement in Combat." *Psychiatric Clinics of North America* 10: 421–36.

Gorer, Geoffrey. 1965. *Death, Grief and Mourning.* Garden City, NY: Doubleday.

Habenstein, Robert W. and William M. Lamers. 1960. *Funeral Customs the World Over.* Milwaukee, WI: Bulfin.

Harrah, Barbara K. and David F. Harrah. 1976. *Funeral Services: A Bibliography of Literature on Its Past, Present, and Future, the Various Means of Disposition, and the Memorialization.* Metuchen, NJ: Scarecrow.

Huntington, Richard and Peter Metcalf. 1979. *Celebrations of Death: The Anthropology of Mortuary Ritual.* Cambridge: Cambridge University Press.

Johnson, Edward C. 1969. "The Value of Restorative Procedures and Viewing." *The Director,* September, pp. 8–9.

Kastenbaum, Robert J. 2001. *Death, Society, and Human Experience,* 7th ed. Boston: Allyn & Bacon.

Kimbel, Steve. 1971. "Some Who Lie in Arlington Were Not Wartime Heroes." *The Director,* January, pp. 40–43.

Kuehnert, David A. 1970. "The U.S. Army Mortuary System in Vietnam." *The Director,* April, pp. 2–3.

Marion, John Francis. 1977. *Famous and Curious Cemeteries.* New York: Crown.

Mitford, Jessica. 1963. *The American Way of Death.* New York: Simon & Schuster.

"Mortuary Affairs Program." 1972. *Champion Expanding Encyclopedia of Mortuary Practice,* January, pp. 1709–12; February, pp. 1713–16.

Mosse, George L. 1990. *Fallen Soldiers: Reshaping the Memory of the World Wars.* New York: Oxford University Press.

Oaks, Judy and Gene Ezell. 1993. *Dying and Death: Coping, Caring, Understanding,* 2d ed. Scottsdale, AZ: Gorsuch Scarisbrick.

Parson, Erwin R. 1986. "Life After Death: Vietnam Veteran's Struggle for Meaning and Recovery." *Death Studies* 10: 11–26.

Pine, Vanderlyn R. 1972. "Social Organization and Death." *Omega* 3:149–53.

Proffitt, Nicholas. 1983. *Gardens of Stone.* New York: Carroll & Graf.

Rendon, Leandro. 1970 "Care of Remains of Deceased in the Armed Forces." *Champion Expanding Encyclopedia of Mortuary Practice,* April, pp. 1641–44.

Singer, J. David and Melvin Small. 1972. *The Wages of War 1816–1965: Statistical Handbook.* New York: John Wiley.

Sloane, David C. 1991. *The Last Great Necessity: Cemeteries in American History.* Baltimore: Johns Hopkins University Press.

Steere, Edward and Thayer M. Boardman. 1957. *Final Disposition of World War II Dead: 1945–51.* Washington, DC: U.S. Department of the Army, Office of the Quartermaster General.

Strub, Clarence G. 1972. "Embalming Progress Through the Centuries." *Casket & Sunnyside* 101(13).

Sudnow, David. 1995. "Death, Uses of a Corpse, and Social Worth." In *Death: Current Perspectives,* 4th ed., edited by John B. Williamson and Edwin S. Shneidman. Mountain View, CA: Mayfield.

Sulzberger, C. L. 1966. *The American Heritage Picture History of World War II.* New York: American Heritage.

Toynbee, Arnold, ed. 1969. *Man's Concern With Death.* St. Louis, MO: McGraw-Hill.

Umberson, Debra and Kristin Henderson. 1992. "The Social Construction of Death in the Gulf War." *Omega* 25:1–15.

U.S. Army. 1958. *Interment of the Unknowns: World War II and Korea.* Washington, DC: Military District of Washington.

Van Crevald, Martin. 1989. *Technology and War: From 2000 B.C. to the Present.* New York: Free Press.

Van Crevald, Martin. 1991. *The Transformation of War.* New York: Free Press.

Wass, Hannelore and Robert A. Neimeyer, eds. 1995. *Dying: Facing the Facts,* 3d ed. Washington, DC: Taylor & Francis.

Williamson, John B. and Edwin S. Shneidman, eds. 1995. *Death: Current Perspectives,* 4th ed. Mountain View, CA: Mayfield.

Woodward, David. 1978. *Armies of the World: 1854–1914.* London: Sidgwick & Jackson.

World War II From an American Perspective: An Annotated Bibliography. 1983. Santa Barbara, CA: ABC-CLIO.

SYMBOLIC IMMORTALITY AND SOCIAL THEORY

The Relevance of an Underutilized Concept

LEE GARTH VIGILANT

JOHN B. WILLIAMSON

The study of symbolic immortality begins with the seminal contributions of the social psychiatrist Robert Jay Lifton (1974, 1976, 1979), whose ideas have had notable impacts on the psychological literature on identity formation in life and on the thanatological literature on the continuity of identity beyond death (Mathews and Mister 1987; Shneidman 1973). According to Lifton, healthy individuals seek a sense of life continuity, or immortality, through symbolic means. When people lack such a sense of continuity, they experience psychic numbing and profound emotional difficulty, as Lifton (1968) has shown in his analysis of the survivors of the first atomic attack.[1] Overall, Lifton's studies have demonstrated how and why the attainment of a sense of symbolic immortality is an essential requisite for mental health and the realization of a vital and enduring self.

Unfortunately, because sociologists have largely neglected Lifton's insights, an important gap exists in the literature on identity construction and its continuation after death. In this chapter we seek to fill that gap, particularly by highlighting the central features of Lifton's theory of symbolic immortality, its application in sociological research, and its relevance for sociological theories of identity construction.

WHEN "DEATH'S ENTICING ECHO MOCKS": THE WORK OF SYMBOLIC IMMORTALITY

Lifton coined the term *symbolic immortality* to refer to the universal human quest to achieve a sense of continuity in the face of the incontrovertible evidence that *we will die*.[2] According to Lifton (1974, 1979), the knowledge that we will die forces us to confront and transcend our fears of finitude in symbolic ways; in particular, we rely on various modes of symbolic immortality. These modes connect us to the past and future, linking us to those who have gone before us and to those who will live on after us and remember our contributions (Lifton 1979). Most important, Lifton asserts that the pursuit of symbolic immortality gives meaning to our existence by preserving our connection to others in material ways in this life while ensuring our continued symbolic connection to others once we have left this mortal coil. Lifton proposes that we do this by drawing on five modes of symbolic connectedness or immortality, which he identifies as biological, creative, transcendental, natural, and experiential transcendence.

The first mode of achieving a sense of symbolic immortality, the biological, is perhaps the most ubiquitous means of ensuring our connection to the future. At the genetic

---

1. Lifton (1974) notes that psychic numbness is an adaptive strategy employed under extreme social conditions such as genocide, mass deaths, and situations of incredible violence. Lifton defines psychic numbness as "a form of de-sensitization . . . an incapacity to feel or to confront certain kinds of experience, due to the blocking or absence of inner forms or imagery that can connect with such experience" (p. 683).

2. For the heading of this section, we have adopted a line from W. H. Auden's poem *Death's Echo*.

level, this mode connects us to the past through our families of orientation and to the present and future through our families of procreation, in both their biological and their social manifestations (e.g., significant others, children and other kin, and friends). For Lifton (1979), a chain of continuous biological and social attachments mark this type of symbolic immortality mode, as in the sense of living through our children, their children, and our culture. Moreover, at the biosocial level, this mode includes our connectedness to our *species-being* by way of friendships, culture, imagined communities, and the norms and values that give us a sense of collective social identity.[3]

The second mode of achieving symbolic immortality is through creative acts. Lifton observes that the creative expression of symbolic immortality is most commonly associated with art, literature, and music, in the sense that artists' works live on after their creators have died. Lifton also points to the scientific enterprise and the building of cumulative knowledge, where the work of one researcher might be carried forward by others, as another expression of creative immortality. In addition, Lifton (1979:22) directs special attention to deep interpersonal relationships, where the bonds of the communicative act are long lasting and profound, as in the relationship between parent and child, psychotherapist and patient, or teacher and student. Such relationships embody the potential for creative immortality.

Lifton's third mode of achieving a sense of symbolic immortality, the expression of theological or religious imagery, is grounded in the idea of "life-power"—that is, the ability to overcome death through the power of religion or spirituality. Lifton (1979) posits that all of the great world religions have this one thing in common: the quest to get beyond the inevitability of death. He states: "Whatever the imagery, there is at the heart of religion a sense of spiritual power. That power may be understood in a number of ways—dedication, capacity to love, moral energy—but its final meaning is life-power and power over death" (p. 20). And eschatology—belief in a kingdom to come and that death is not the end—is the cornerstone of all major religions.

The fourth mode of achieving a sense of symbolic immortality is through natural means. By *natural means,* Lifton (1979) refers to our connectedness to the natural world around us, the sense that after our mortal demise, the world itself, with its trees, oceans, and clouds—all that constitutes the earth—will remain.

The fifth and final mode of experiencing a sense of immortality is the most important for Lifton; he refers to it as the experience of transcendence. It is a mode entirely different from the other four in that it is grounded in "a psychic state—one so intense and all-encompassing that time and death disappear" (Lifton 1979:24). As a psychological state, the mode of experiential transcendence involves moving beyond or transcending the mundane and profane, and individuals can experience it in all four of the previously described modes. Thus one might experience a sense of transcendence through a deep spiritual experience, such as a baptism and being born again in the Christian sense or being in a mystical trance—a signature feature of many religions. Other methods of achieving transcendence include epiphanic experiences such as giving birth and rapturous encounters such as might be attained through the use of psychedelic drugs or other substances that produce mundane-transcending sensations. The mode of experiential transcendence also includes the ecstatic transcendence that is derived from orgasm. Here, according to Lifton (1979), "the self feels uniquely alive—connected, in movement, integrated—which is why we can say that this state provides at least a temporary sense of eliminating time and death" (p. 26). What is unique about experiential transcendence is that when one is immersed in the experience, be it orgasmic ecstasy, drug-induced euphoria, or spiritual rapture, one feels as if one has overcome death because of the immediacy and intensity of the event.

Lifton proposes that the five modes described above constitute the mechanism whereby people are able to reduce death anxiety by achieving a sense of mastery over mortality, and this mastery is essential for psychological wellness. Additionally, these five death-transcending strategies play an important role in countering what Lifton (1979) refers to as "death-equivalent experiences." These experiences serve as antecedents to some of the common psychological and social disorders that are rooted in feelings of stasis, separation, and disintegration. By *stasis,* Lifton refers to a life without a sense of purpose—the experience of "going nowhere fast"—which, for example, forms the basis of many midlife crises.[4] By *separation,* Lifton means the loss of connectedness to a larger community or the loss of the love connection to other human beings, and this death equivalent, along with stasis, can be the basis for certain types of depression, a state of both physical and psychic stasis (p. 182).[5] Lifton describes *disintegration* as the absence of those ethical principles that individuals use to organize—or ground—human experience within a historical-cultural context (p. 101). In the absence of those unifying and organizing principles, be they based in religion or grounded in ideology, disintegration is likely to occur, and for sociologists, social

---

3. In Marxian terms, *species-being* refers to our connection to the human community. For a discussion of nationalism as an expression of a type of "symbolic family," see Anderson (1991).

4. For Lifton (1979), a midlife crisis, as related to the static feeling of "going nowhere fast," "is a crisis in ultimate life projects. . . . Men and women break away from marriage and families, seeking to take advantage of a 'last chance' for loving and caring relationships previously denied them" (p. 87).

5. It is interesting that Lifton (1979), a social psychiatrist, and David Karp (1996), a sociologist, both define depression as a disease of disconnection.

disintegration, or anomie, is the antecedent for societal pathologies.[6] So, then, people's use of death-transcending strategies becomes inextricably linked to their need to reduce these death equivalents and to maintain their psychic health by giving a sense of purpose to their existence.

The five modes of death transcendence that Lifton identifies are not the only paths to achieving a sense of symbolic immortality. Several analysts have proposed other possible methods of preserving the self after death. Edwin S. Shneidman's (1973, 1995) work on the development of the concept of the postself is particularly noteworthy. As Shneidman describes it, the postself consists of a person's reputation and continued influence after death. Shneidman (1995) delineates five ways in which the self can live on after death: (a) in the memories of those who are still living; (b) through the interactions others have with the deceased's creative works (art, music, books, and so on), (c) in the bodies of others, as in the case of organ transplants; (d) in the genes of the deceased's progeny; and (e) in the cosmos. It is important to keep in mind that a central difference between the postself and the symbolically immortalized self is that the postself often assumes an identity of its own—an identity completely unplanned for, or wholly unexpected, by the self when it was alive.[7] However, as intriguing as discussions of the postself are, our focus in this chapter is on the work of symbolically immortalizing the self in life and not on postmortal identity.

SOME PREVIOUS RESEARCH ON SYMBOLIC IMMORTALITY

The empirical literature on symbolic immortality, although relatively small, includes examinations of many of the theoretical assumptions of Lifton's work. These empirical studies span the range of inquiry, from research concerning the biological means of achieving immortality to meditations on the quest to achieve a sense of symbolic immortality through the vocation of teaching. Researchers conducted many of the earlier studies to explore the thesis that symbolic immortality is a requisite for healthy psychological development (Kastenbaum 1974; Mathews and Mister 1987; Schmitt 1982). Other work on this concept, however, has focused on the avenues to symbolic immortality available to different groups of people (Moremen and Cradduck 1998–99; Schmitt 1982).

In concert with Lifton's biological mode of achieving symbolic immortality, Robert Kastenbaum (1974) conducted an early study to examine whether the fear of death compels people to reproduce in order to ensure their continuity. He found that 90% of the respondents in his study agreed with the sentiment that "people who have children and grandchildren can face death more easily than people who have no descendents to carry on." Although this is certainly not an index of fear as an impetus for procreation, this rate of response clearly speaks to the importance of the biological mode of achieving a sense of immortality. Moreover, Kastenbaum's findings are consistent with other empirical and historical evidence on the important role that progeny play in individuals' achievement of a sense of symbolic immortality.[8] Providing further support for Kastenbaum's work is Rubinstein's (1996) observation of the phenomenon of "lineal emptiness" in many of the childless women in his study of 160 women at a Philadelphia geriatric center; Rubinstein's findings speak volumes about the importance of the biological mode in achieving a sense of immortality. The women in Rubinstein's study viewed having offspring as one way to leave a legacy and support future generations—a quest that was propelled by both egoistic and altruistic motives. In another study, Drolet (1990) found that the sense of symbolic immortality becomes stronger with age, and that achieving that sense can help to decrease the fear of death in established adults and "thus possibly can contribute to the enhancement of life for the individual, as well as for society at large" (p. 159).[9]

Other researchers have examined the attainment of a sense of symbolic immortality through creative activities (Blacker 1997; Cortese 1997; Goodman 1996; Lifton, Kato, and Reich 1979; Schmitt and Leonard 1986; Talamini 1989). Two studies concerning involvement in sports as a creative route to achieving symbolic immortality are noteworthy. The phenomenon of organized sports, especially on the university and professional levels, offers a unique arena in which to study the work of immortalizing the self. Through their involvement in professional sports, athletes can make history by taking part in extraordinary plays or by breaking long-standing records. It is this unique opportunity to "leave one's mark" that makes the study of symbolic immortality in sports so profound. According to Schmitt and Leonard (1986), participation in organized sports provides athletes with unique death-transcending opportunities, through "(1) role-support, (2) engrossment through participation and communication, (3) comparison through measurement and records, and (4) recognition through awards and commemorative devices" (p. 1093). By *role-support,* Schmitt and Leonard refer to the support that others, including teammates, fans, and society in general, give to athletes that enables them to maintain their status in life and beyond. Moreover, role-support enables greater sociality in athletes'

---

6. Lifton (1979:110) asserts that both ideology and religion are organizing principles for humans that serve essentially the same function: to satisfy our quest for "utopian perfection." For an example of the condition of anomie, see Durkheim's classic meditation *Suicide* ([1897] 1951).

7. This is often the case with celebrities who die young, such as James Dean, Jimi Hendrix, and John Lennon—their postself identities are more popular in death than the individuals were in life.

8. See Lauwaert's (1994) study of the historical significance of childbirth as a mechanism for achieving a sense of symbolic immortality in China.

9. See Mathews and Mister (1987) for a study that uses a different instrument to measure the same need for symbolic immortality.

interactions with fans and in their communications with the media, in print, television, and now cybervision. The comparison of athletes through their records is another way in which their immortality is ensured, because new athletes, commentators, and fans use the achievements of others as measuring rods for current performances. Thus athletes who have died or retired are remembered long after their playing days are over. And, of course, commemorative halls such as the Baseball and Football Halls of Fame, as well as the trophy cases that line the walls of most high school and university gymnasiums, speak to the enduring immortality of previous generations of athletes.

In another study that looked at participation in sports as a creative mode of achieving a sense of symbolic immortality, Cortese (1997) applied Schmitt and Leonard's model to the experiences of amateur intracollegiate boxers. Cortese found that the same opportunities for a sense of symbolic immortality existed in the amateur ranks through role-support, participation and communication, comparisons of records, and commemorative awards. He notes that although the manifest function of the bouts in which the boxers in his study took part was charity fund-raising, the athletes themselves were keenly aware of their opportunities for symbolic immortality through titles, awards, and commemorative ceremonies. Moreover, the opportunities they had to win commemorative awards, such as championship trophies for winners and Notre Dame boxing jackets for all finalists, played a crucial role for the participants, both as a catalyst for their participation in the charity bouts and for immortalizing their postselves in the memories of others. Finally, for these athletes symbolic immortality was ensured in another way, as all of their bouts were immortalized in the print media, which published "tidbits of the personal histories of each fighter, often pointing to academic and personal achievements" (Cortese 1997:360).

The quest for symbolic immortality in other creative activities, such as through vocation, is another arena that has drawn some attention, albeit scant, from scholars concerned with death-transcending strategies. In her meditation on the profession of medicine as a route to achieving a sense of symbolic immortality, Palgi (1996) observes, "The most appealing feature of the medical professional self is that it has the potentiality of connecting with something that immortalizes, a life outside of the physician's own, a life that may outlive the healer" (p. 229). In a sense, doctors live on in the lives and memories of their patients, and this form of creative immortality, according to Palgi, is one of the peripheral benefits of medicine.

Fortunately, the vocational path to symbolic immortality is not limited to healers; researchers have examined other professions whose practitioners also have the potential to live on in the memories of others. For example, David Blacker (1997) has analyzed pedagogy as a route to immortality, reasoning that

> the ultimate payoff of education lies in the human interconnectedness it mends, nurtures, and gives birth to; its enduring value consists in its ability to "live in" those particular Others who are so connected, to make the extension any genuine ethic requires: beyond our narrower and more immediate projects and toward the Other. (P. 61)

Lessons taught, skills learned, and in-class interlocutions continue long after pedagogy stops. According to Blacker (1997, 1998), the work of education assures teachers that their pedagogical efforts will be transferred to other generations of pupils in the great chain of knowledge and learning. As the popular aphorism "Each one teach one" implies, education connects students and teachers in a cycle that is perpetual, where the memories of both the teacher and the lesson are conjoined. Teaching, much like the work of healing, bestows on its practitioners a creative sense of surpassing death—a feeling that the ultimate payoff of the work is found in the eternal connections that both student and teacher have to the ideas that are explicated, interrogated, and modified in pedagogical praxis.

Within the larger context of achieving a sense of symbolic immortality, a small body of research extends the discourse by considering the idea of identity preservation. David Unruh's (1983) work on strategies of identity preservation between dying individuals and their loved ones is of particular import here. His study of individuals' quests to preserve their identities beyond the is of particular interest for sociologists because Unruh describes the process as one that is grounded in interactions between dying individuals and their survivors. He identifies three strategies that the dying employ to preserve their identities after death: (a) attempts to *solidify identity*, in which the dying record, in memos, journals, and letters, aspects of their identities that they would like to preserve; (b) the *accumulation of artifacts*, in which dying persons collect artifacts and mementos that come to stand as symbols of their personal histories; and (c) the *distribution of artifacts*, typically to close friends and family members through wills and testaments, that attest to the identities of the deceased and assist survivors in their reminiscences of the lives of the deceased.[10] In addition, Unruh outlines four

---

10. Attempts at solidifying identity (Unruh 1983) for postself preservation might well be interpreted as a type of "facework," or impression management, within the microinteractionist tradition of Erving Goffman (1959, 1967). We would argue that the dual labor of impression management and maintaining face, whether through journals, letters, personal artifacts, or other such devices, are signature features of the quest to preserve the postself identity and achieve a sense of symbolic immortality.

Regarding the accumulation of artifacts, Sandstrom (1998), in his work among male AIDS sufferers, also points to the importance of signifying artifacts in efforts to preserve the "vital and valued self" in the face of death. Accordingly, Sandstrom notes, the dying may "dedicate themselves to collecting artifacts or to writing journals that will be passed on to friends and family, or the wider public. They hope that this will allow their experiences or 'stores' to live on in the memories of others" (p. 365).

strategic ways in which survivors might act to preserve the identities of their deceased loved ones:

1. *Reinterpreting the mundane,* or giving new meaning to memories of ordinary past experiences with the deceased

2. *Redefining the negative,* or idealizing less desirable aspects of the deceased's personalities or lived experience

3. *Continuing to bond,* or doing certain activities that stimulate reminiscence about the deceased

4. *Using sanctifying symbols or artifacts* that come to serve as "sacred" representations of the deceased

As a significant departure from the quest to achieve a sense of symbolic immortality, this model of preserving a post-self identity beyond the grave is an interactional one that requires certain actions on the part of the dying or deceased and responses to those actions from the living—a relational requisite between the deceased and their survivors that is not explicit in Lifton's work.

A few sociological researchers have documented and analyzed the quest to achieve a sense of symbolic immortality and to preserve the self in the face of death among the chronically ill and dying (Charmaz 1991; Marshall 1975a, 1975b, 1986; Sandstrom 1998). In his work among men living with AIDS, Sandstrom (1998) found that the quest to achieve a sense of symbolic immortality was omnipresent. Many of Sandstrom's respondents grounded their post-mortal selves in their occupations and artistic endeavors, whereas others secured their immortalized selves in eschatological hopes and spiritual beliefs. Similarly, Charmaz (1991) found that concerns about immortality were heightened among her population of sufferers of chronic pain, especially when death seemed imminent. She observed that achieving a sense of immorality offered meaning and purpose to the lives of her respondents.

Our review of the literature on symbolic immortality suggests that an understanding of the individual's quest for symbolic immortality might enrich the knowledge of identity formation and maintenance in life as well as the quest for identity continuity after death. Unfortunately, the relevance of this quest to core themes in sociological theory remains underdeveloped. In order to facilitate this understanding, we link symbolic immortality to some key concepts in social theory in the following section.

SYMBOLIC IMMORTALITY WITHIN SOCIOLOGICAL THEORY: USE VALUE

The quest to achieve a sense of symbolic immortality is a deeply sociological one, and in this section we connect this pursuit to some key concepts in the major streams of sociological thought: structuration, symbolic interactionism, and phenomenology.[11] Our aim here is to broaden the existing literature on symbolic immortality by linking it to some key identity concepts in sociology.

The Immortal Self in Structuration Theory

Anthony Giddens, founder of the structuration perspective, has done more than any other sociologist in recent decades to bridge the chasm between *agency* and *structure* that has marked the science since its inception. Giddens (1984) asserts that "the basic domain of study of the social sciences, according to the theory of structuration, is neither the experience of the individual actor, nor the existence of any form of societal totality, but social practices ordered across space and time" (p. 2). These social practices, mediated by both individual choice and societal influence, have profound sway over the development of the self in late modernity, and the development of the self in late modernity is for Giddens (1991) a reflexive project in which the individual is continuously adjusting aspects of his or her biography to dynamic social changes. Giddens asserts that the self in late modernity is a self that is marked by existential anxieties. These anxieties emerge from the globalizing tendencies of economies of signs that continue to erode those primordial and *gemeinschaften* caring structures that historically functioned to build trust and inoculate against existential uneasiness.[12] Modernity, as Giddens (1991) notes, "introduces an elemental dynamism into human affairs, associated with changes in trust mechanisms and in risk environments" (p. 32).[13] Consequently, it is reflexivity, or the self-monitoring aspect of self-identity, that is principally responsible for reducing those anxieties inherent to the late modern period. But more than this, reflexivity is the mechanism by which the late-modern self is constructed, for, as Giddens (1991) notes, "we are not what we are, but what we make of ourselves" (p. 75). Thus a structuration perspective might well interpret the quest to achieve a sense of symbolic immortality as part of the reflexive project of the self in late modernity: a project that works to reduce existential anxiety through (a) attempts at "colonizing the future" through "strategic life planning," (b) addressing existential questions, and (c) creating a sense of ontological security in the "protective cocoon" that achieving a sense of symbolic immortality offers.

The quest to achieve a sense of symbolic immortality through creative, biological, religious, natural, or transcendental means can be understood as an attempt to colonize the future through strategic life planning. The work of

---

11. These theoretical traditions are certainly not the only links to the symbolic immortality concept. See Schmitt and Leonard (1986:1089) for other possible connections of the symbolic immortality concept to sociological theory.

12. For another important analysis of the self in late modernity, see Lash and Urry(1994). As Lash and Urry define them, economies of signs are postindustrial economies in which symbols, images, information, and desires are the primary exchange commodities.

13. For a similar meditation on the self in late modernity, see Lifton (1993).

colonizing the future, which Giddens (1991) defines as the "creation of territories of future possibilities" (p. 242), is itself embodied in the quest for a sense of symbolic immortality, because, as previously noted, symbolic immortality is about gaining the assurance that one's identity will continue long after one's corporeal demise. Symbolic immortality, as a death-transcending apparatus, colonizes the future by assuring that one's self-identity will remain an active part of the future, whether through an aesthetic act, a religious quest for an eternal soul, or by biological means, through progeny. But more than providing a mere assurance of transcending death, the quest for a sense of symbolic immortality might also reduce the fears and uncertainties inherent to life in the late-modern age. By forcing us to confront death's inevitability and certainty, the quest to continue after death necessarily embodies some important existential questions around human connectedness.[14] Moreover, existential questions—which, according to Giddens (1991:55), are questions concerning (a) the nature of one's existence and being, (b) the finite and sentient nature of human life, (c) the existence of others, and (d) the "continuity of self identity"—lie at the very heart of the quest to achieve a sense of symbolic immortality. Answers to these existential questions play a significant role not only in assuaging death anxiety (see Lifton 1974), but in building a sense of ontological security (Laing 1965; Giddens 1991). The strategic life planning involved in procuring one's continuation after death creates a sense of mastery over the usual anxieties associated with severing one's connectedness to the human community.

The Immortal Self in Symbolic Interactionism

Symbolic interactionism, as a branch of social psychology, is expressly concerned with the *self:* principally, how the self is created through social interactions, how it interprets those interactions, and how it manipulates symbols to form those interpretations (Mead 1934).[15] The founder of symbolic interactionism, Herbert Blumer (1962), reasons that human interaction is "mediated by the use of symbols, by interpretation, or by ascertaining the meaning of one another's actions. This mediation is equivalent to inserting a process of interpretation between stimulus and response in the case of human behavior" (p. 180). Within the confines of Blumer's definition of symbolic interaction, the work to immortalize the self becomes the work of

manipulating symbols and signs in social interaction for the purpose of continuing the self after death—a self that, according to George Herbert Mead (1934:140), *is* a social structure that arises *in* social interaction. Consequently, the work involved in achieving a sense of symbolic immortality—whether it is the labor involved in creative activity, the time and care spent in giving moral guidance to one's progeny, or the hours spent cultivating the soul in spiritual mediation—is work that is deeply social and that involves the manipulation of language, symbols, and signs, in communicative praxis with others, to engender a sense of achieving that immortal identity for the self. In essence, the immortalized self cannot exist outside the confines of the symbolic interactions that will ensure its continued existence. Recalling Unruh's (1983) analyses of identity preservation, we find that if and how one will be remembered are questions that are essentially grounded in strategic encounters and planning, which are processes of symbolic interaction. Thus the achievement of a sense of symbolic immortality, under the terms of symbolic interactionism, is contingent on the existence of a "generalized other" (Mead 1934:154), whomever or whatever that generalized other is.[16] In effect, it is the generalized other, which Mead (1934:154) defines as the reference group that gives a person his or her unity of self, that ensures that an individual will achieve a sense of symbolic immortality. It is only through social interaction, where meanings, ideas, and emotions about death and the continuity of the self are internalized and sought out, that an individual is ensured a sense of symbolic immortality and the continuation of the postself identity. Consequently, the very quest to arrive at this sense of immortality is one that is deeply social and entrenched in symbolic interaction.[17]

The quest to achieve a sense of symbolic immortality also involves a great deal of self-interaction. By *self-interaction,* Mead (1934) means a reflexive process of the "turning-back of the experience of the individual upon himself" (p. 134) through internal conversations, whereby the individual examines his or her own biography to find value and meaning in his or her life. An individual's internal conversations concerning postself identity and memory in the minds of generalized others are an essential aspect of the quest to achieve a sense of symbolic immortality. The question "How will I be remembered?" and the negotiation with others to ensure that memory begin with an internal conversation on the postself identity. This interactional quest to achieve a sense of symbolic immortality is linked

---

14. Giddens (1991) defines *existential questions* as those concerning "the basic parameters of human life, and are 'answered' by everyone who 'goes on' in the contexts of social activity" (p. 55).

15. For one of the best explications of this branch of social psychology to date, see Charon (2001).

16. In the previous example of education and pedagogy as a creative route to achieving a sense of symbolic immortality, the "generalized other" might be the teacher's pupils. Similarly, for an individual using the theological route to achieving a sense of symbolic immortality, the generalized other could very well be the religious community itself or a particular cleric.

17. It is important to mention that although individuals might share common symbols, their interpretations, or "definitions of the situation" (Thomas 1923, 1928), might vary considerably. For instance, the middle-aged professor might well interpret his pedagogical praxis as a route to achieving a sense of symbolic immortality, whereas his unresponsive students might interpret the same interaction as merely a route to good-paying jobs.

to the most innate and natural of all human needs: the desire for meaningful social interactions within—and beyond—the confines of the corporeal. As Mead (1938) notes:

> Human society is not at home in the world because it is trying to change that world and change itself; and, so long as it has failed to so change itself and change its world, it is not at home in it as the physiological and physical mechanism is. There is a need for salvation—not the salvation of the individual but the salvation of the self as a social being. . . . Apart from the instinctive love of life, is that demand for immortality any more than an assertion of the continuous character of the social value which the individual as a social being can embody in himself? (P. 477)

The "salvation of the self as a *social* being" is exactly what the quest to achieve a sense of symbolic immortality is all about. Mead connects this instinctive quest for immortality to our most basic need for social interaction in this life and beyond.

The quest to preserve the self by achieving a sense of symbolic immortality might also be interpreted as a form of biographical labor. In particular, it embodies the work of legitimating biography (Hewitt 1989), life review (Butler 1963), and self-objectification (Marshall 1986). Marshall (1986) posits that the work of legitimating one's own biography, related to what he calls an "awareness of finitude" (p. 139), is an attempt to rewrite aspects of one's biography and personal history so as to arrive at a final meaning, or a closing chapter, to life. Moreover, he notes that legitimation of biography intensifies with age, and this process reaches its peak when the individual concludes that he or she has only a few more years to live. The work to achieve a sense of symbolic immortality and, by necessity, the biographical legitimations that occur might well be understood as status passage control, what Marshall posits as people's attempts to "seek not only to make sense of themselves as dying but also to gain whatever control they can over the dying process, death itself, and in some cases, the afterlife" (p. 124). Similarly, Robert Butler's (1963) notion of the life review, or the attempt by an individual who is dying or close to death to make sense of his or her past life and choices, is another type of biographical work designed to help the individual find meaning and purpose to a past life while reducing death anxiety. All of these practices are means by which the self experiences objectification—practices that offer "a sense of continuity to personal experience" (Hewitt 1989:185).

Finally, the work of symbolic immortality, inasmuch as it incorporates the tools of impression management (Goffman 1959, 1967) in building a positive postself identity, personifies a type of "biographical work" (Gubrium and Buckholdt 1977) wherein individuals, through mindful reflexiveness, take into account the perceptions that other people have of them, accept or alter those perceptions through the conscious manipulation of interactional props, and, in so doing, negotiate new public biographies (Gubrium and Buckholdt 1977) for current interactions and for future encounters that others will have with their postselves.

The Immortal Self in Phenomenology

Phenomenological sociology, which traces its roots to the German social philosopher Edmund Husserl, is principally concerned with describing the world as seen through the consciousness of individuals. Alfred Schutz (1962) reasons that the phenomenological task is that of describing the "life-worlds," or consciousness, of individuals. He argues that "our problem, however, is not what occurs to man as a psychophysiological unit, but the attitude he adopts toward these occurrences—briefly, the subjective meaning man bestows upon certain experiences of his own spontaneous life" (p. 120). In essence, Schutz asserts that the goal of phenomenology is to understand the meanings or typifications that people attribute to their experiences. Phenomenology places a premium on discovering how individuals construct and interpret the social world in their minds. Although only in-depth phenomenology can uncover the meaning behind the work to achieve a sense of symbolic immortality for an individual—for instance, the catalyzing motives that drive an individual to acquire this sense—phenomenology does propose some essential concepts that underscore this drive.

In purely phenomenological terms, the work to achieve a sense of symbolic immortality is seen as a by-product of an individual's symbolic universe, or those symbols that an individual uses to "refer to realities other than those of everyday experience" (Berger and Luckmann 1966:95). This universe, in addition to containing the entire biography and social history of the individual, helps the individual to organize and make sense of biographical experiences in the process of meaning making. And it is the meaning-making function of this universe that is important to the quest to achieve a sense of symbolic immortality. For Berger and Luckmann (1966), achieving a sense of symbolic immortality is certainly under the purview of a person's symbolic universe, because the primary role of the symbolic universe is to assuage death anxiety—a latent benefit that the achievement of symbolic immortality certainly provides. Commenting on the foremost function of the symbolic universe, Berger and Luckmann propose:

> The legitimation of death is, consequently, one of the most important fruits of symbolic universes. . . . All legitimations of death must carry out the same essential task—they must enable the individual to go on living in society after the death of significant others and to anticipate his own death with, at the very least, terror sufficiently mitigated so as to not paralyze the continued performance of everyday life. . . . It is in the legitimation of death that the transcending potency of symbolic universes manifests itself most clearly, and the fundamental terror-assuaging character of the ultimate legitimations of the paramount reality of everyday life is revealed. (P. 101)

If applied to the work of achieving a sense of symbolic immortality, an individual's symbolic universe, according to Berger and Luckmann, is principally responsible for situating the death phenomenon within the biographical complex, transforming it from a taken-for-granted reality to an active and omnipresent aspect of biography and sociality that the individual must address. And the quest to achieve a sense of symbolic immortality, whether through biological, creative, religious, natural, or experiential transcendence means, is the mechanism that the symbolic universe employs in dealing with death apprehension.

Finally, one wonders, from a phenomenological perspective, if the quest to achieve a sense of symbolic immortality is a distinctly modern phenomenon linked to the need, whether real or perceived, to preserve our individualism. Georg Simmel, in an essay titled "Individual and Society in Eighteenth- and Nineteenth-Century Views of Life," was the first sociologist to distinguish the new individualism that was born during the Industrial Revolution. Simmel (1950) argues: "The new individualism might be called qualitative, in contrast with the quantitative individualism of the eighteenth century. Or it might be called the individualism of uniqueness [*Einzigkeit*] as against that of singleness [*Einzelheit*]" (p. 81). For Simmel, there was something unique about the industrial personality: Those with this personality measure their individualism not by comparing themselves with social others for sameness, but rather by contrasting their personal uniqueness to that of others for difference. This new individualism is one that defines the self through peculiarities and singleness (Simmel 1950:82). This simple observation on the new personality that emerged in industrial societies raises a profound implication for the quest to achieve a sense of symbolic immortality; namely, is the quest to acquire a sense of symbolic immortality merely the personality's reaction against death's erosion of that unique identity—the qualitative personality?

The existential phenomenology of Jean-Paul Sartre proposes an answer to this quandary. In an incisive essay titled "My Death," Sartre (1956:693) suggests that the distinctive feature of the dead life is how it strips the once vibrant, or qualitative, personality of its uniqueness and singularity. The peculiar feature of the dead life is the homogeneity it represents: You can live your life as you like and express your unique individuality at will, but upon death, your agency—that qualitative individualism—is lost forever. For Sartre, the dead life marks the erosion of the individual's personality in order that the individual may be reconstituted with the whole dead collective. Although Sartre does recognize the possibility of living on in the memories of others as a "reconstituted life," the inevitable fate for most personalities is a homologation into the quantitative, dead life identity (p. 693). And it is this that might impel many individuals to seek a sense of symbolic immortality for their unique, qualitative personalities—to defeat the anxieties of what the dead life personifies: to be forgotten! Accordingly, Sartre notes:

Thus the very existence of death alienates us wholly in our own life to the advantage of the Other. To be dead is to be prey for the living. This means therefore that the one who tries to grasp the meaning of his future must discover himself as the future prey of others. . . . In this sense, to die is to be condemned no matter what ephemeral victory one has won over the Other; even if one has made use of the Other to "sculpture one's own statue," to die is to exist only through the Other, and to owe him one's meaning and the very meaning of one's victory. (Pp. 695–96)

The individual's quest to achieve a sense of symbolic immortality might well be a reactionary stance against the problems posed by the dead life. Why become prey for the living when you can sculpt your own immortalized postself through one, or all, of the five death-transcending paths? Why lose your unique qualitative personality in death by becoming one of the dead masses? In essence, from a phenomenological point of view, our pursuit of a sense of symbolic immortality is grounded in our need to preserve our unique consciousness and individuality, and to be remembered as we wish.

CONCLUSION

In this chapter, we have argued that the quest to achieve a sense of symbolic immortality has a great deal of importance to sociology and is an area that is easily applicable to some core ideas in social theory. Our treatment of the quest to achieve a sense of symbolic immortality in various sociological traditions shows the relevance of this underutilized concept to theories on the development of the self in late modernity. The work to achieve a sense of symbolic immortality is work that is deeply sociological and that bears profound implications for our understanding of the development of the social self, both in this life and beyond. Thus, as long as individuals are actively working to procure a sense of immortality for their postmortal selves, their identities do not cease to exist after their corporeal demise. Moreover, their corporeal demise does not preclude postmortal interactions with loved ones left behind. Sociological theories on the development of the self have important contributions to make to our understanding of the quest to achieve a sense of symbolic immortality.

Finally, in analyzing the relevance of this concept to sociological theory, we have encountered questions to which sociological inquiry should attend. One of the gifts of sociology is the attention it pays to issues of social inequality by posing both critical and reflexive questions on the roles of race, ethnicity, class, gender, and other such social identities. The sociology of the quest to achieve a sense of symbolic immortality must, of course, consider the impact that the aforementioned social identities are having on actualizing that goal. It is not surprising, then, that sociology's failure to consider the immortalized postself seriously has left open and unexplored questions concerning access barriers to a sense of symbolic immortality by race, ethnicity, social class, and gender. Nowhere is this omission as prominent as in the current scholarly literature on symbolic immortality. This gap in the literature suggests that inequality issues are irrelevant to the quest to achieve a sense of symbolic immortality.[18] And yet, as death notices in newspapers suggest, social inequalities—particularly those associated with gender—tend to persist even after death (Kastenbaum, Peyton, and Kastenbaum 1977; Moremen and Cradduck 1998–99; Spilka, Lacey, and Gelb 1979). Still, only scant attention is paid to these critical issues. Thus the sociology of the quest to achieve a sense of symbolic immortality might also make a substantial contribution here. Some possible questions for future research are as follows:

1. Do we find the same drive to achieve a sense of symbolic immortality across all human societies, or are there differences by nationality, culture, or subculture? For instance, do individuals in postindustrial societies express different motives and drives for their quest to achieve a sense of symbolic immortality than do individuals in industrial and/or agrarian societies?

2. How do structural factors such as race, ethnicity, social class, and gender affect people's quests to achieve a sense of symbolic immortality?

3. What happens when the pathways to a sense of symbolic immortality are unavailable to large groups of people because they have certain social identities (e.g., race, ethnicity, class, gender, disability, sexuality)?

4. The work to achieve a sense of symbolic immortality has been described as an individual's quest for self-preservation beyond life. From a sociological point of view, the question arises: Is the need to achieve a sense of symbolic immortality ever expressed as a collective or an institutional need? If so, how are collective quests to achieve a sense of symbolic immortality different from or similar to the ways individuals pursue this goal? Moreover, are the motivations to achieve a sense of symbolic immortality similar at the collective and individual levels?[19]

These are but a few of the questions that remain unexplored—areas that have been the historical purview of sociological inquiry. Thus herein lies the goal of a sociological theory of the quest to achieve a sense of symbolic immortality: that we might better understand the need for, and work toward, identity preservation in this life and beyond, and the many social impediments that individuals and groups encounter as they strive to achieve this end.

REFERENCES

Anderson, Benedict. 1991. *Imagined Communities: Reflections on the Origin and Spread of Nationalism,* rev. ed. London: Verso.

Berger, Peter L. and Thomas Luckmann. 1966. *The Social Construction of Reality: A Treatise in the Sociology of Knowledge.* Garden City, NY: Anchor.

Blacker, David J. 1997. *Dying to Teach: The Educator's Search for Immortality.* New York: Teachers College Press.

———. 1998. "Education as Immortality: Toward the Rehabilitation of an Ideal." *Religious Education* 93:8–29.

Blumer, Herbert. 1962. "Society as Symbolic Interaction." In *Human Behavior and Social Processes: An Interactionist Approach,* edited by Arnold M. Rose. Boston: Houghton Mifflin.

Butler, Robert. 1963. "The Life Review: An Interpretation of Reminiscence in the Aged." *Psychiatry* 26:65–76.

Charmaz, Kathy. 1991. *Good Days, Bad Days: The Self in Chronic Illness and Time.* New Brunswick, NJ: Rutgers University Press.

Charon, Joel M. 2001. *Symbolic Interactionism: An Introduction, an Interpretation, an Integration,* 7th ed. Upper Saddle River, NJ: Prentice Hall.

Cortese, Anthony J. 1997. "The Notre Dame Bengal Bouts: Symbolic Immortality Through Sport." *Journal of Sport Behavior* 3:347–63.

Drolet, Jean-Louis. 1990. "Transcending Death During Early Adulthood: Symbolic Immortality, Death Anxiety, and Purpose in Life." *Journal of Clinical Psychology* 46:148–60.

Durkheim, Émile. [1897] 1951. *Suicide: A Study in Sociology,* translated by John A. Spaulding and George Simpson. Glencoe, IL: Free Press.

Giddens, Anthony. 1984. *The Constitution of Society: Outline of the Theory of Structuration.* Cambridge: Polity.

———. 1991. *Modernity and Self-Identity: Self and Society in the Late Modern Age.* Stanford, CA: Stanford University Press.

Goffman, Erving. 1959. *The Presentation of Self in Everyday Life.* Garden City, NY: Anchor.

———. 1967. *Interaction Ritual: Essays on Face-to-Face Behavior.* Garden City, NY: Anchor.

Goodman, David G. 1996. "Symbolic Immortality in Modern Japanese Literature." Pp. 205–20 in *Trauma and Self,* edited by Charles B. Strozier and Michael Flynn. Totowa, NJ: Rowman & Littlefield.

Gubrium, Jaber F. and David R. Buckholdt. 1977. *Toward Maturity.* San Francisco: Jossey-Bass.

Hewitt, John. 1989. *Dilemmas of the American Self.* Philadelphia: Temple University Press.

Karp, David. 1996. *Speaking of Sadness: Depression, Disconnection, and the Meaning of Illness.* Oxford: Oxford University Press.

Kastenbaum, Robert J. 1974. "Fertility and the Fear of Death." *Journal of Social Issues* 30(4):63–78.

18. In an article dated September 11, 2001, titled "Novel Auction Offers Chance to Buy Immortality," Reuters reported on the opportunity that many individuals have seized upon to buy "literary immortality" by paying for the privilege of having a best-selling author name characters in a forthcoming novel after them. Some bidders, according to the article, have paid in excess of $9,000 for this privilege to achieve a sense of symbolic immortality. As trite as this example may appear, it does illustrate how social class inequities might act as a barrier to individuals' achievement of a sense of symbolic immortality. To put it another way: There are some routes to achieving a sense of symbolic immortality that are simply unavailable to the masses.

19. Professor Kent Sandstrom, who reviewed several versions of this chapter as we prepared it for publication, brought this question to our attention.

Kastenbaum, Robert J., S. Peyton, and B. Kastenbaum. 1977. "Sex Discrimination After Death." *Omega* 7:351–59.

Laing, R. D. 1965. *The Divided Self: An Existential Study in Sanity and Madness.* Harmondsworth: Penguin.

Lash, Scott and John Urry. 1994. *Economies of Signs and Space.* Thousand Oaks, CA: Sage.

Lauwaert, Françoise. 1994. "Semence de vie, germe d'immortalité." *L'Homme* 34(129):31–57.

Lifton, Robert Jay. 1968. *Death in Life: Survivors of Hiroshima.* New York: Random House.

———. 1974. "On Death and the Continuity of Life: A 'New' Paradigm." *History of Childhood Quarterly* 1:681–96.

———. 1976. *The Life of the Self.* New York: Touchstone.

———. 1979. *The Broken Connection: On Death and the Continuity of Life.* New York: American Psychiatric Press.

———. 1993. *The Protean Self: Human Resilience in an Age of Fragmentation.* New York: Basic Books.

Lifton, Robert Jay, Shuichi Kato, and Michael R. Reich. 1979. *Six Lives, Six Deaths: Portraits From Modern Japan.* New Haven, CT: Yale University Press.

Marshall, Victor W. 1975a. "Age and Awareness of Finitude in Developmental Gerontology." *Omega* 6:113–29.

———. 1975b. "Socialization for Impending Death in a Retirement Village." *American Journal of Sociology* 80:1124–44.

———. 1986. "A Sociological Perspective on Aging and Dying." Pp. 125–46 in *Later Life: The Social Psychology of Aging,* edited by Victor W. Marshall. Beverly Hills, CA: Sage.

Mathews, Robert C. and Rena D. Mister. 1987. "Measuring an Individual's Investment in the Future: Symbolic Immortality, Sensation Seeking, and Psychic Numbness." *Omega* 18:161–73.

Mead, George Herbert. 1934. *Mind, Self, and Society: From the Standpoint of a Social Behaviorist.* Chicago: University of Chicago Press.

———. 1938. *The Philosophy of the Act.* Chicago: University of Chicago Press.

Moremen, Robin D. and Cathy Cradduck. 1998–99. "'How Will You Be Remembered After You Die?' Gender Discrimination After Death Twenty Years Later." *Omega* 38:241–54.

Palgi, Phyllis. 1996. "Reflections on the Self of Homo Hippocraticus and the Quest for Symbolic Immortality." Pp. 221–30 in *Trauma and Self,* edited by Charles B. Strozier and Michael Flynn. Totowa, NJ: Rowman & Littlefield.

Rubinstein, Robert. 1996. "Childlessness, Legacy, and Generativity." *Generations* 20(3):58–60.

Sandstrom, Kent L. 1998. "Preserving a Vital and Valued Self in the Face of AIDS." *Sociological Inquiry* 68:354–71.

Sartre, Jean-Paul. 1956. *Being and Nothingness: A Phenomenological Essay on Ontology.* New York: Washington Square.

Schmitt, Raymond L. 1982. "Symbolic Immortality in Ordinary Contexts: Impediments to the Nuclear Era." *Omega* 13:95–116.

Schmitt, Raymond L. and Wilbert M. Leonard III. 1986. "Immortalizing the Self Through Sport." *American Journal of Sociology* 91:1088–1111.

Schutz, Alfred. 1962. *Collected Papers,* Vol. 1, *The Problem of Social Reality.* The Hague: Martinus Nijhoff.

Shneidman, Edwin S. 1973. *Deaths of Man.* New York: Quadrangle.

———. 1995. "The Postself." Pp. 454–60 in *Death: Current perspectives,* 4th ed., edited by John B. Williamson and Edwin S. Shneidman. Mountain View, CA: Mayfield.

Simmel, Georg. 1950. *The Sociology of Georg Simmel,* edited and translated by Kurt H. Wolf. New York: Free Press.

Spilka, B. M., G. Lacey, and B. Gelb. 1979. "Sex Discrimination After Death: A Replication, Extension and Difference." *Omega* 10:227–33.

Talamini, John T. 1989. "After the Cheering Stopped: Retirement Patterns of Major League Baseball Players." *Free Inquiry in Creative Sociology* 17:175–78.

Thomas, William I. 1923. *The Unadjusted Girl.* Boston: Little, Brown.

——— (with Dorothy S. Thomas). 1928. *The Child in America.* New York: Alfred A. Knopf.

Unruh, David R. 1983. "Death and Personal History: Strategies of Identity Preservation." *Social Problems* 30:340–51.

PART II

DEATH IN SOCIAL CONTEXT

VARIANTS IN MORALITY AND MEANING

HISTORICAL AND EPIDEMIOLOGICAL TRENDS IN MORTALITY IN THE UNITED STATES

VICKI L. LAMB

The purpose of this chapter is to provide an overview of the major trends in causes of death in the United States from colonial times to the end of the 20th century. During this period, many changes have occurred in the types of diseases and conditions that have caused death, differentials in patterns of death, and life expectancy. The chapter is divided into five major sections. The first three of these address particular time periods: the colonial period through approximately 1790, the 19th century, and the 20th century. Each of these sections begins with a discussion of available sources of mortality data and then covers the major causes of death and the differences (e.g., by age, sex, race, social class) in death rates. Each section also presents information on the role and contribution of medicine to the death rates in each time period. The fourth major section examines two additional topics that span the entire U.S. historical period: war casualties and deaths, and disaster deaths. In the final section, I discuss the historic changes in the U.S. patterns of death within the context of the theory of epidemiologic transition.

Brief definitions of a number of the demographic terms employed used throughout the chapter are in order. The terms *death rate* and *mortality rate,* which are used interchangeably, refer to number of deaths per unit of the population, such as deaths per 100,000 persons. *Case-fatality rate* refers to the proportion of persons having a particular disease who die from that disease. For example, the case-fatality rate for smallpox might be 15% in a particular year. *Life expectancy* is the number of years an individual is expected to live from birth based on the age-specific death rates of that time or year. Thus the lower life expectancy estimates for the earlier periods are partially due to extremely high death rates for infants and children, in addition to higher death rates at the older ages.

THE COLONIAL PERIOD THROUGH THE NEW REPUBLIC: 1600–1790

Records of mortality rates, causes, and differentials are limited in coverage for the United States before the late 1800s. Information on deaths and causes of death in colonial America comes from personal journals, diaries, and letters as well as from newspaper accounts and other public records. Thus information about mortality trends from colonial times through the mid- to late 19th century is based on data collected in smaller geographic units, such as cities and reporting states. Deaths were not regularly reported or recorded in all areas, particularly infant and child deaths. As a result, we have little understanding of infant and child death rates in colonial times.

The available resources indicate that there were regional differences in mortality patterns within the colonial states, and it is unlikely that there was a national mortality pattern for colonial America. The major causes of death were infectious diseases, thus the differences in death rates across the colonies were due to differences in rates of disease transmission and survival, immunity to disease, and the use of effective methods of treating or preventing the spread of disease.

Between 1600 and 1775, smallpox was both universal and fatal in Europe and North America; it was a major cause of death in colonial America (Duffy 1953). Smallpox is a highly communicable viral disease that causes 3 to 4 days of high fever and rapid pulse with intense headache and back pain, followed by skin eruptions that eventually develop into pustules. Once infected, the person either dies or survives with an extended period of immunity. The virus typically is passed from host to host, but it can also remain infectious for months on inanimate objects, including bedding and clothing.

In the urban centers of the Old World—Europe, Africa, and Asia—children were most susceptible to the spread of smallpox. In Britain, it was considered a childhood disease (Fenn 2001; Marks and Beatty 1973). Persons who reached adulthood were usually immune and less likely to be affected by the spread of the disease. Smallpox was brought to the colonies primarily from the British Isles and the West Indies. Port settlements, such as Boston and Charleston, were particularly vulnerable to outbreaks of smallpox. The irregular arrival of trade and passenger ships meant that the spread of the disease was sporadic, resulting in periods in which the disease was not present in regions of colonial America. The periodic smallpox epidemics in North America affected persons of all ages, not just children, and the disease was greatly feared.

At the time, the common perception was that smallpox was more deadly in America than it was in Europe. However, historic evidence indicates that death rates from smallpox were actually lower in the colonies than in England (Duffy 1953). One of the factors contributing to the lower death rate was the more widespread use of variolation, or inoculation, which was first used in 1720 (Duffy 1953). Variolation was the introduction of pus from persons infected with the disease into incisions in healthy persons. The healthy person would typically contract a relatively mild case of smallpox. Chances for survival were much greater for those inoculated; their case-fatality rate was 2–3%, compared with an estimated 10–50% death rate for those who contracted the disease naturally (Duffy 1953). Unfortunately, inoculated persons were fully contagious with the smallpox virus, and unrestricted variolation could lead to greater spread of the disease, particularly in unaffected areas. The practice was used on a very limited basis in England, and thus the case-fatality rate there was higher.

The use of variolation was a point of controversy and debate in the colonies. Cotton Mather (1663–1728), a Bostonian theologian interested in scientific and medical matters, was highly supportive of the practice of variolation. To demonstrate the benefits of the practice, Mather and others collected data on a widespread smallpox epidemic in Boston in 1721. Mather reported to the Royal Society of London, of which he was a member, that of those who contracted the disease naturally, 1 in 6 had died, whereas of the almost 300 who were inoculated, only 1 in 60 had died (Duffy 1953).

Smallpox was not the only disease that threatened the American colonists. There were periodic outbreaks of yellow fever in coastal regions, brought from Africa to the West Indies to North America. Yellow fever is an infectious disease that is transmitted by mosquitoes, not native to North America, which probably bred in water barrels on slave ships from the West Coast of Africa (Duffy 1953). The disease is characterized first by high fever and flushed face, lips, and tongue. Within a few days, temperature drops below normal, the skin takes on a yellowish hue, and bloody, black vomiting occurs. Death occurs due to liver and kidney failure and extreme toxemia. According to Duffy (1953), the case-fatality rate from yellow fever in colonial America varied between 12% and 80%. The first outbreak of the disease in North America probably occurred in 1693, brought to Boston by a British ship from Barbados (Duffy 1953; Marks and Beatty 1973). Charleston, Philadelphia, and New York were struck with yellow fever numerous times in the 1700s. In 1796, New Orleans had its first outbreak of yellow fever. The disease was puzzling to the colonists because infected persons who moved to new locations did not transmit the disease. In addition, the disease would "miraculously" disappear during the cooler fall and winter months, particularly in the northern colonies. Although some had suggested the connection between mosquitoes and the transmission of yellow fever (and other diseases) at earlier times, it was not until the end of the 19th century that experiments by the U.S. Army Yellow Fever Commission proved this to be so (Marks and Beatty 1973).

Other contagious and infectious diseases that caused sickness and death in colonial times included malaria, dysentery, respiratory diseases (pneumonia, influenza, and other respiratory infections), typhoid fever, typhus, diphtheria, scarlet fever (which was often confused with diphtheria), measles, whooping cough, mumps, and venereal diseases. Only a few trends are mentioned here. Malaria, spread by mosquitoes, was endemic and appeared annually in the warm months. The disease caused great sickness, debilitation, and death, but the death rate for malaria was much lower than that for smallpox or yellow fever. Dysentery also was endemic to the American colonies, resulting in debilitating sickness and death for persons of all ages. Respiratory diseases occurred consistently in the winter months, although few data are available to allow us to document their negative effects on human life. Diphtheria primarily affected young children. Between 1735 and 1740, there was a widespread epidemic of a deadly form of diphtheria that killed hundreds of children and numerous adults in New England, New York, and New Jersey. Throughout the second half of the 18th century, waves of diphtheria threatened the colonies. Measles epidemics were noted in New England from 1759 to 1772, in Charleston in 1722, and in Philadelphia in 1778.

Infections associated with cuts, amputations, and other medical "care" were a constant problem and cause of death during the colonial period due to lack of knowledge about germs and the spread of disease. Another common cause of death was newcomers' failure at "seasoning"—that is, at adapting to the new disease environment of the colonies. This was a notable problem in the southern colonies; it has been estimated that in the 1600s as many as 40% of new arrivals in that region did not survive their first year (Gemery 2000).

Colonial Response to Infectious Disease Epidemics

Because epidemics were so widespread when they occurred, they severely disrupted the colonists' daily lives. For example, Duffy (1953) describes what happened when the 1721 smallpox epidemic was sweeping through Boston: "For the next few months, business was at a stand-still. All intercourse was shunned, and the streets were deserted with the exception of wagons carrying the dead and of a few doctors and nurses visiting the victims" (p. 50). Public offices, such as those that housed general assemblies, legislatures, and various courts, were closed for the duration of an epidemic or moved to outlying areas, away from the urban centers. Legislation was passed to address the seriousness of outbreaks of obviously contagious diseases, primarily through the isolation of sick or infected individuals. Eventually all the colonies enacted laws requiring quarantine periods of from 10 to 20 days for ships with affected passengers. Laws also were passed that required those who were affected by contagious disease to be quarantined at home or in quarantine hospitals or "pest houses" so that they were isolated from the general population. Massachusetts was the most successful colony in regulating and enforcing the isolation of contagious diseases, and thus in reducing the spread of such diseases (Duffy 1953).

Colonial physicians did little to help those suffering from infectious and epidemic diseases because such conditions were widely considered to be God's punishment for sinful ways. For this reason many doctors argued against the practice of variolation to quell the fatal effects of smallpox. During epidemics it was not uncommon for public and/or religious officials to designate a day for public prayer and fasting to appeal to God's grace to spare the population from further spread of disease.

There was little formal medical education in the colonies before the Revolutionary War. Most medical practitioners received training through apprenticeships. The few who had formal medical degrees were primarily educated in Europe. The Medical School of the College of Philadelphia, which later became the Medical School of the University of Pennsylvania, was founded in 1765. In 1768, a medical school was established in King's College in New York City, which later became Columbia University. Toner (1874) estimated that at the beginning of the Revolutionary War there were approximately 3,500 medical practitioners in the colonies, of whom only 400 had received formal medical training and only 50 had received M.D. degrees from the two medical schools that had been established in the colonies.

Native North American Mortality Trends

There were few serious epidemic diseases in North America prior to European settlement (Thornton 2000).

One possible reason for this is that the Native North Americans had few domesticated animals, to which a number of the Old World infectious human diseases can be traced. In addition, there were no large centers of population concentration, which means that the relatively high overall population density necessary for the transmission and survival of epidemic diseases did not exist (Thornton 2000). Some infectious diseases were present among Native North Americans, including tuberculosis and treponemal infections, such as syphilis. It has been estimated that the life expectancies of Native North Americans were similar to those of people living in Europe at the time. According to Thornton (2000), "Life expectancies for Native Americans—generally in the 20s and 30s—were kept relatively low by famine, nutritional deficiency diseases (e.g., pellagra), warfare, parasites, dysentery, influenza, fevers, and other ailments, besides tuberculosis and treponemal infections" (p. 15).

The colonization of North America brought a host of new diseases to the continent that the native population had never before experienced, including smallpox, typhoid, diphtheria, scarlet fever, whooping cough, pneumonia, malaria, and yellow fever (Duffy 1953; Thornton 2000). Having no natural immunity, the Native North American populations were devastated by the introduction of Old World infectious diseases, particularly during the 16th and 17th centuries.

A number of direct and indirect depopulation effects were associated with European colonization. Estimates vary widely regarding the numbers and proportions of the native population that were killed directly due to the introduction of Old World infectious diseases. Indirect postepidemic effects included declines in births due to lower fecundity because of disease and loss of marital partners. Death rates may also have increased after epidemics due to food shortages (especially if epidemics occurred during important agricultural periods) and to mothers' inability to feed and care for their infants and other children (Thornton 2000). Nondisease mortality effects on the native population of European colonization included deaths via wars and genocide, enslavement, tribal removals and relocations, and the resultant changes in Native American culture, organization, and subsistence patterns (Duffy 1953; Thornton 2000).

African American Mortality Trends in Colonial America

Information on the demographic trends of Africans brought to the colonies, and their offspring, is limited. Because of the slave trade, the records of Africans brought to the colonies are more complete than information about European immigration. However, much less is documented regarding the births, deaths, and marital unions of Africans in the colonies during this time. Slaveholders, when documenting economic transactions associated with slavery, did not identify individuals by name, or may have recorded only given names (Walsh 2000). Marital unions between slaves were not recognized in any colony except Massachusetts. Some plantation records listed minor children with mothers, but husbands or fathers were rarely identified (Walsh 2000).

The data on mortality trends during the colonial period are particularly sparse. It is generally believed that mortality rates for Africans were higher than those for white colonists. As noted above, new arrivals were vulnerable to deaths due to "seasoning," and, according to Walsh (2000), "the traditional belief was that one-third of all black immigrants died during their first three years in the New World" (p. 206). Other factors associated with higher death rates for Africans and African Americans include insufficient nutrition, shelter, and access to medical care. Death rates for Africans tended to be lower than those for whites in the summer and fall, presumably due to the Africans' greater genetic protection against malaria (Walsh 2000), but winters were particularly hard on Africans, especially in the northern colonies, in part due to their vulnerability to respiratory diseases, such as pneumonia, influenza, and pleurisy.

Regional Mortality Trends

General mortality trends varied during the colonial period. In New England during the early 1700s, death rates were much higher in urban areas than they were in small towns, with estimated annual deaths per 1,000 persons ranging from the 30s to the 40s in urban areas and from 15 to 25 in small towns (Gemery 2000). Urban death rates declined to converge with rural death rates in the early 19th century.

In terms of regional differences, mortality rates were lowest in New England and highest in the South. The middle colonies had mortality trends that closely resembled those of New England. The lower death rates in the New England colonies were due in part to the colonists' success in legislating and enforcing quarantine laws to reduce the spread of infectious and contagious disease. The higher mortality rates in the South reflect the warmer disease environment and the greater number of immigrants, among whom there were many deaths due to "seasoning" (Gemery 2000; Wells 1992).

Population Growth During the Colonial Period

Although epidemics and other factors brought death to many, the North American population grew at a steady rate. As Benjamin Franklin observed, compared with Europeans, the colonists tended to marry at younger ages and to have larger families. Such patterns of marriage and fertility led to steady population growth. Life expectancy for the colonists has been estimated to be higher than

that of their European counterparts because of lower population density (lessening the spread of epidemics), less travel and migration (reducing exposure to new contagious diseases), and better nutrition and standard of living. Studies of differences in stature between native-born American adult males and those in European countries in the mid-1700s point to sufficient nutritional support in that the American natives had a height advantage of 5 to 7 centimeters (Steckel 1999). Evidence also indicates that there were virtually no social class differences in adult height by the time of the Revolutionary War, which meant that everyone in the American colonies, including the poor and slaves, had adequate access to nutrition (Steckel 1999). There were much greater class differences in stature in Europe at the time. However, the average adult male in colonial America was taller than the average upper-class male in England.

THROUGH THE 19TH CENTURY: 1790–1900

The first U.S. Census, taken in 1790, marked an important advance in the routine collection of demographic data in the United States. However, the census did not collect mortality information until the mid-1800s, and even then the information was "incomplete, biased, and uneven" (Haines 2000:328). The U.S. population continued to increase at a rate of around 3% annually from 1790 to 1860 due to immigration, high fertility, and decreases in mortality patterns (Haines 2000). During the rest of the 19th century the population growth rate slowed to approximately 2.3%, primarily due to reduced fertility rates. In 1800, the average number of births for white women was 7.04; by 1900, the rate had declined to an average of 3.56 (Haines 2000:308, table 8.2).

During the 19th century the major causes of death continued to be infectious and contagious diseases. The threat of smallpox was reduced with the discovery of the benefits of vaccination using the relatively safe cowpox virus, credited to Edward Jenner in the late 1700s. Yellow fever was ever present during the summer months; it reached epidemic proportions in the 1840s and 1850s and in 1878. Typhus, typhoid fever, scarlet fever, and tuberculosis continued to be major causes of death and sickness in the 19th century.

The United States had its first cholera epidemic in 1832, brought by immigrants from England. Cholera is caused by bacteria that are usually spread through feces-contaminated water and food. Extreme diarrhea, vomiting, stomach cramps, and extreme dehydration characterize the disease, and the case-fatality rate is very high when treatment is unavailable. Cholera epidemics occurred in the United States from 1832 through 1873, in part due to filth and poor public sanitation, especially in urban areas.

Studies of human stature and other data (e.g., genealogical records and death registration systems in several large cities) suggest an increase in mortality rates in the 1840s and 1850s. One factor that contributed to the increased death rates was the transportation revolution that was occurring in the United States between 1800 and 1860. During this time, interregional migration and trade increased, there was a trend toward greater urbanization along with a shift from farming to employment in factories, and the public school system expanded (Haines 2000; Steckel 1999). The result of these changes was a disease environment in which there was increased interpersonal contact and greater exposure to infectious and contagious diseases. Many of the diseases prevalent at the time (e.g., cholera, diarrhea, tuberculosis, most respiratory infections, measles, and whooping cough) can negatively affect nutritional status, particularly among children, which in turn can inhibit the body's ability to grow and develop at normal levels and remain healthy. There was a decline in average height for men born in the 1820s and 1830s in the United States until the latter part of the 19th century; this trend points to reduced nutritional sustenance (Haines 2000; Steckel 1999). Class differences in height were evident among Union soldiers in the Civil War, suggesting socioeconomic differences in nutritional support (Margo and Steckel 1983). Farmers had the greatest height advantage, and laborers had the least.

Because the only mortality data available are inadequate or incomplete, there has been some debate among demographers regarding the beginning of a pattern of sustained mortality decline during the 19th century. Most of the evidence points to a trend of mortality decline beginning in the latter part of the 19th century, after the end of the Civil War. At that time, death rates began a continuous decline with few fluctuations. Advances in medical science did not have great impacts on the initial decline in mortality rates until the 20th century. Instead, the observed increase in life expectancy has been attributed to an improved standard of living (better diet, nutrition, and shelter) and to advances in public health practices. For example, in 1854, John Snow identified a public water pump as the source of a cholera outbreak in London. This discovery led municipal authorities to work toward greater access to pure water and sewage disposal. Boston and New York City began piping in water via aqueducts prior to the Civil War, and other large municipalities instituted public works programs at the end of the 19th century to improve water supplies (Haines 2000). The new science of bacteriology contributed to the understanding of the importance of water filtration and the addition of chemicals to purify public water. Because large cities could command the resources necessary to institute public health reforms, by 1900 the 10 largest cities in the United States had better mortality rates than did cities with populations of 25,000 (Haines 2000). However, better water and sewer systems were not the sole cause for the decline in mortality in the United States. As Haines (2000) notes, there were many factors:

Other areas of public health activity from the late nineteenth century onward included vaccination against smallpox; the use of diphtheria and tetanus antitoxins (from the 1890s); more extensive use of quarantine (as more diseases were identified as contagious); the cleaning of urban streets and public areas to reduce disease foci; physical examinations for school children; health education; improved child labor and workplace health and safety laws; legislations and enforcement efforts to reduce food adulteration and especially to obtain pure milk; measures to eliminate ineffective or dangerous medications (e.g., the Pure Food and Drug Act of 1906); increased knowledge of and education about nutrition; stricter licensing of physicians, nurses, and midwives; more rigorous medical education; building codes to improve heating, plumbing, and ventilation systems in housing; measures to alleviate air pollution in urban settings; and the creation of state and local boards of health to oversee and administer these programs. (Pp. 336–37)

Mortality Differentials

During the 19th century there were significant differentials in mortality rates in the United States. For most ages, males had higher death rates than did females. However, female deaths sometimes exceeded male deaths between ages 20 and 50 due to the hazards of childbearing, frontier life, and vulnerability to disease-causing organisms (Haines 2000). Urban death rates were higher than those in rural areas due to greater population density and crowding, the greater probability of unsafe drinking water, and the accumulation of garbage and waste. These mortality differences began to diminish at the end of the 19th century with the institution of public health reforms.

There is evidence of emerging social class differences in mortality rates at the end of the 19th century, with the lowest death rates for white-collar types of occupations and the highest for laborers and servants (Haines 2000). During the 1800s, the mortality rate for adult African slaves was close to that of the free population, indicating that adult slaves received adequate nutrition and support (Steckel 2000). However, the children of slaves fared much worse. Estimates based on information from plantation records and other documents indicate that infant and child death rates for slaves were roughly double the rate for the free population (Steckel 2000). The major causes for the excess infant and child deaths were poor prenatal conditions, low birth weights, inadequate diets, and childhood diseases.

There is little information available on the health of free blacks, but the evidence indicates that winters were particularly harsh for African Americans, particularly in the North, due to their "maladaptation to cold and little inherited immunity to respiratory infections such as pneumonia and tuberculosis" (Steckel 2000:461). In the latter part of the 19th century, when the United States was experiencing a long-term decline in mortality rates, African American adult mortality showed little improvement. However, child mortality rates were greatly reduced.

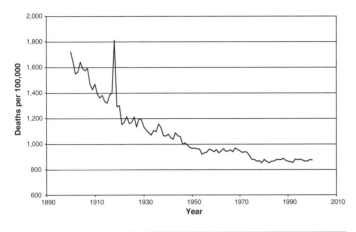

Figure 1   Crude Death Rates, United States, 1900–2000

SOURCES: Hoyert et al. (2001), Minino and Smith (2001), and National Center for Health Statistics (1996).

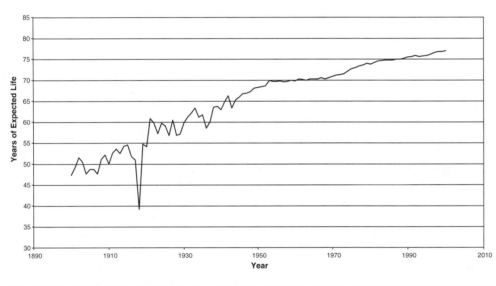

Figure 2   Average Life Expectancy at Birth, United States, 1900–2000

SOURCES: Hoyert et al. (2001), Minino and Smith (2001), and National Center for Health Statistics (1996).

20TH-CENTURY TRENDS: 1900–2000

The individual states and the federal government were slow to develop vital registration systems to record demographic events such as marriages, births, and deaths. In 1900, the federal government began publishing annual mortality statistics based on the newly established death registration system (Hetzel 1997). The initial death registration area included 10 states and the District of Columbia, plus 153 cities not in the death registration

states. The population covered by the 1900 death registration area included greater proportions of urban and foreign-born persons than did the U.S. population as a whole (Haines 2000). Through the years, additional states were added to the death registration system, and by 1933 the system covered all of the United States (Hetzel 1997). The data presented in this section are based on those collected in the federal death registration system.

The most dramatic improvements in mortality rates that have taken place in the United States occurred during the 20th century. Figure 1 shows the remarkable decline in death rates from 1900 to 2000. In 1900, the crude death rate was estimated to be 1,719 deaths per 100,000 persons; by 2000, that figure had dropped to 874 deaths. The most prominent spike in the graph was caused by the influenza pandemic, which in 1918 resulted in a death rate of 1,810 deaths per 100,000 persons. This pandemic resulted in the death of half a million Americans (Kolata 1999:5).[1] Other spikes visible in Figure 1 reflect smaller influenza outbreaks in the early part of the 20th century. With the decline in death rates came a corresponding increase in life expectancy, as shown in Figure 2, which reflects the remarkable mortality improvement in the United States over the 20th century. In 1900, the average life expectancy at birth was 47.3 years, whereas in 2000 it was estimated to be 76.9 years.

For the first half of the 20th century, the long-term decline in mortality rates was paralleled by a trend in decline of deaths due to infectious diseases, whereas mortality due to noninfectious diseases remained constant. Declines in infectious disease mortality rates were due primarily to declines in deaths due to influenza, pneumonia, and tuberculosis, which together accounted for 60% of infectious disease deaths (Armstrong, Conn, and Pinner 1999). During the second half of the century, declines in infectious disease deaths slowed to an annual rate of 2.3% until about 1980, when there was a reversal (Armstrong et al. 1999). Deaths due to infectious diseases increased at an annual

---

1. The influenza pandemic of 1918 was one of the most devastating plagues ever to sweep across the globe, possibly exceeding the death toll of the Black Plague of the 14th century in terms of the number of humans killed within a period of similar duration (Kolata 1999:185). Estimates of worldwide deaths from influenza in 1918 range from 20 million to more than 100 million (Kolata 1999:7).

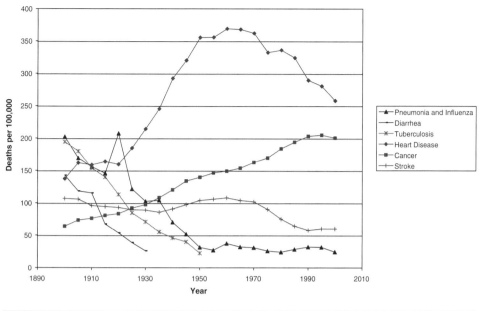

Figure 3   Trends in Selected Causes of Death, United States, 1900–2000

SOURCES: Minino and Smith (2001) and National Center for Health Statistics (2003).

increase in life expectancy in the 20th century can be attributed to reductions in infant and child mortality. Arriaga (1984) estimates that reductions in mortality for persons up to age 20 contributed almost 60% to the gains in life expectancy. Mortality rates for young to middle-aged adults also improved over the 20th century. Gains in mortality rates for ages 20 to 39 have been estimated to contribute 17% to increased life expectancy.

Since the late 1960s, death rates for American adults age 65 years and over have experienced a rapid decline. The most notable mortality improvements have been for persons 85 years old and older. The decline in heart disease deaths has been a contributing factor in the positive trend in old-age mortality. In the second half of the 20th century, medical science shifted its research focus to a greater understanding of diseases of old age. The resulting research has led to greater awareness of disease causes and symptoms, and this has had two direct effects. First, medical knowledge and practice have greatly improved. Tests are now available to detect the early onset of numerous chronic diseases, such as heart disease and various types of cancers, as well as to determine genetic predispositions for certain degenerative conditions. In addition, advances have been made in therapies to treat or slow the progress of chronic diseases, such as medication to control high cholesterol and hypertension. Second, medical research has uncovered lifestyle factors that are associated with certain diseases and chronic conditions. Thus public awareness of the ill effects of particular lifestyle behaviors—such as tobacco use, high-fat diets, and lack of exercise—has grown. An additional factor that has contributed to the improvement in old-age mortality is the establishment of Medicare in 1965. Virtually all Americans aged 65 years and older are eligible for health insurance coverage through the federally supported Medicare program, which covers hospitalization (Part A) and can also include medical insurance for outpatient and physician services (Part B).

Figure 4 shows the differences in life expectancy by sex for Americans through the 20th century. Throughout this period, life expectancy for females was higher than that for males. In 1900, females had a 2-year life expectancy advantage over males. The differential increased on a fluctuating basis up to 5.6 years in 1917 and 1918, after which it dropped to just 1 year in 1920. After fluctuating until about 1950, the differential steadily

rate of 4.8% until the mid-1990s, when they again began to decline. The AIDS epidemic was the reason for the increase in infectious disease deaths that began in 1980.

Public health advances in the 20th century continued to reduce the spread of infectious disease. In addition, medical science played a significant role in changing the most prevalent causes of death and extending life expectancy. Germ theory, advanced by Pasteur in the 1860s, became an accepted part of medical science, and surgical practices became safer as a result of Halsted's work at Johns Hopkins University at the end of the 19th century. As Easterlin (2000) has stated, "In the last half of the nineteenth century there was a revolution in knowledge of methods of disease control" (p. 637).

Changes in the most common causes of death shifted from infectious and contagious diseases to debilitating and chronic conditions in the 20th century, as Figure 3 illustrates. In 1910, heart disease was the leading cause of death in the United States (except during the influenza pandemic), and in the 1930s cancer emerged as the second most common cause of death, with stroke as the third most common. The rate of deaths for heart disease was highest in the 1960s and 1970s, which accounts in part for the stagnant trend in life expectancy during that period (see Figure 2). Since that time, heart disease death rates have been declining.

Mortality Differentials

During the first half of the 20th century mortality rates dropped for all ages, with strong health improvements for the younger ages. With the control of infectious and contagious diseases, children gained a greater probability of achieving adulthood by the 1950s. Indeed, much of the

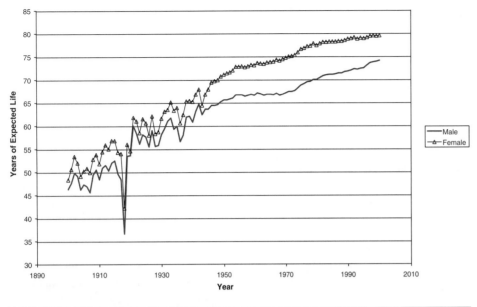

Figure 4   Life Expectancy at Birth by Sex, United States, 1900–2000

SOURCES: Hoyert et al. (2001), Minino and Smith (2001), and National Center for Health Statistics (1996).

widened until it reached 7.8 years in the late 1970s. More recently, differentials in male and female life expectancy have been declining.

The small difference between male and female life expectancy at the beginning of the 20th century was due to females' vulnerability to infectious diseases and high maternal mortality rates. At the beginning of the century the maternal mortality rate in the United States was much higher than that in European countries, but the U.S. rates include indirect causes of maternal death, such as pneumonia during pregnancy (Loudon 2000). The U.S. rates were highest between 1915 and 1920, peaking at 916 maternal deaths per 100,000 births in 1918 (Guyer et al. 2000). The influenza pandemic contributed to this high rate. Maternal mortality rates remained high in the 1920s and early 1930s, primarily because many women received no care or inappropriate care for birth complications or were subject to inappropriately performed medical interventions. Beginning in 1936 there was a steep decline in maternal mortality until 1956, when the rate was reduced from 582 to 40 deaths per 100,000 live births (Guyer et al. 2000). The reduction in maternal deaths has been attributed to improvements in obstetrical care and the use of drugs to fight infection as well as the development of more appropriate methods to deal with delivery problems in hospital births and the use of trained midwives for home births (Guyer et al. 2000; Loudon 2000).

The widening gap between female and male life expectancy later in the 20th century was due to increased male disadvantage in deaths due to heart disease and, to a lesser extent, cancer, in addition to the decline in maternal mortality (Nathanson 1984; Waldron 1993). Explanations for the female mortality advantage tend to be of two types: biological and behavioral/environmental (Nathanson

1984). For example, females have protective hormonal advantages regarding heart disease, and men are more likely to engage in risky behavior or lifestyles that lead to higher death rates due to lung cancer, accidents, and other violent deaths (Waldron 1993). At the end of the 20th century, American males continued to have higher mortality rates, although the differentials are narrowing. In 1999, the age-adjusted mortality rates for males were higher than those for females for 12 of the top 15 causes of death. The mortality rates were similar for stroke and kidney disease, and females had higher death rates due to Alzheimer's disease. The narrowing of the gap between males and females in terms of life expectancy was due to greater male improvements in mortality for heart disease, cancer, suicide, and homicide (Hoyert et al. 2001).

Throughout the 20th century there were large race differentials in mortality rates, although the trend was toward a reduction of these differences. Figure 5 shows the trends in life expectancy for whites and nonwhites from 1900 and for blacks from 1970 (when data on blacks began to be collected and estimated routinely for mortality statistics). In 1900, average life expectancy for whites was 47.6 years and that for nonwhites was 33.0 years, a difference of 14.6 years. By 1990, the life expectancy for whites was estimated to be 76.1 years, whereas it was 71.2 years for all nonwhites (5.1 year difference) and 69.1 years for blacks (7.0 year difference). The black-white differential in 1999 was 5.9 years, and in 2000 black life expectancy was estimated to be 5.6 years less than that for whites. As these figures show, the black-white gap in life expectancy has been declining. The most recent declines have been due to greater improvements in black mortality rates for homicide, cancer, stroke, and HIV disease. However, the continued gap between whites and blacks in life expectancy exists because of excess mortality for blacks compared with whites in the top five leading causes of death, in addition to deaths due to homicide, hypertension, septicemia, kidney disease, and diabetes (Hoyert et al. 2001).

Part of the black-white life expectancy gap is also due to differences in survival during the first year of life. Birth certificates have recorded race of child since the early part of the 20th century. The infant mortality rate (IMR) is the number of deaths of infants before their first birthdays per 1,000 live births. Figure 6 shows the trend of black and

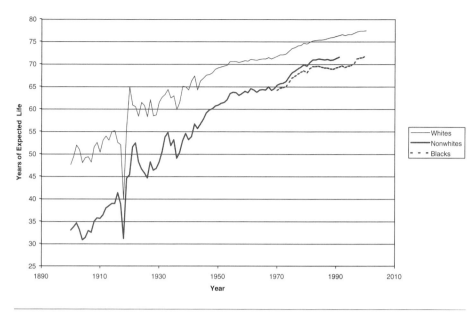

Figure 5 Life Expectancy at Birth by Race, United States, 1900–2000

SOURCES: Hoyert et al. (2001), Minino and Smith (2001), and National Center for Health Statistics (1996).

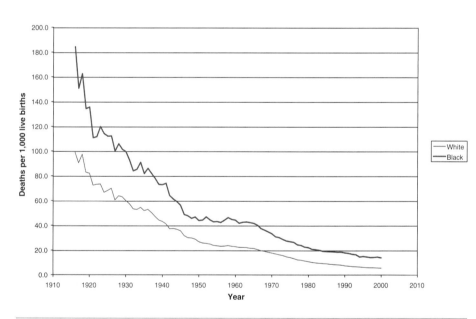

Figure 6 Infant Mortality Rates by Race, United States, 1916–2000

SOURCES: Minino and Smith (2001), Murphy (2000), National Center for Health Statistics (1986), and U.S. Bureau of the Census (1975).

outcomes (such as low birth weight) (Hummer 1993; Hummer et al. 1999).

Sex and race differentials for life expectancy at birth since 1970 show that white females have the longest life expectancy, topping at around 80 years since 1997 (see Figure 7). Life expectancy for black females is second highest, although the rates are converging with those of white males. Black males are most disadvantaged in terms of life expectancy. The trend in life expectancy for black males was stagnant and declining somewhat during the late 1980s into the 1990s. Only in recent years has there been a marked improvement in black male life expectancy. The black male disadvantage is primarily due to excessive deaths for youth, teens, and adults up to age 65, in which the age-specific black male death rates are roughly double those for white males (Anderson 2001). In 1999, homicide and unintentional accidents were the first and second most common causes of death for black males for age groups 15–19, 20–24, and 25–34.

WAR CASUALTIES AND DEATHS

A separate topic affecting U.S. mortality trends not yet addressed is deaths associated with wars waged by Americans. Since the beginning of settlement in the New World, Americans have fought in wars and service members have died. Table 1 presents the estimated numbers of battle deaths associated with all U.S. wars from the American Revolution to the first Gulf War. The table displays the numbers of casualties associated with battle deaths as well as noncombat deaths of service members during wartime. The most deadly war, in terms of the proportions of combatants killed in battle, has been the Civil War, in which Americans fought Americans. An estimated 6.34% of Union soldiers and 7.10% of Confederate soldiers died in combat.

white IMRs for the period 1916 to 2000. In 1916 there were more than 85 excess black infant deaths compared with white infant deaths. The differential has declined over the century, but there remains a disproportionate number of black infant deaths. Recent research has found that much of the black-white gap in infant mortality is due to differences between blacks and whites in terms of socio-demographic factors (such as income and mother's education), maternal health, prenatal health care, and birth

Table 1 Battle Deaths in America's Wars

	Number of Service Members	Number of Battle Deaths	% Battle Casualties	Number of Other Deaths in Service[a]	% Other Deaths in Service[a]
American Revolution (1775–83)	217,000	4,435	2.04		
War of 1812 (1812–15)	286,730	2,260	0.79		
Indian Wars (ca. 1817–98)	106,000	1,000	0.94		
Mexican War (1846–48)	78,718	1,733	2.20	11,550	14.67
Civil War (1861–65)					
Union	2,213,363	140,414	6.34	11,550	0.52
Confederate	1,050,000	74,524	7.10	59,297	5.65
Spanish-American War (1898–1902)	306,760	385	0.13	2,061	0.67
World War I (1917–18)	4,734,991	53,402	1.13	63,114	1.33
World War II (1940–45)	16,112,566	291,557	1.81	113,842	0.71
Korean War (1950–53)	5,720,000	33,686	0.59	20,560	0.36
Vietnam War (1964–75)	9,200,000	47,410	0.52	42,788	0.47
Gulf War (1990–91)	2,322,332	148	0.01	1,149	0.05
Total	42,348,460	650,954	1.54	325,911	0.77

SOURCE: U.S. Department of Veterans Affairs (2001).

a. "Other deaths in service" refers to the deaths of service members who died while on active duty but whose deaths were not attributable to combat, regardless of the location or cause of death.

Before the end of the 19th century, wars were fought without the benefit of much scientific preventive medical support or practice, because medical knowledge had not progressed regarding the understanding of germ theory (Bayne-Jones 1968). However, medical personnel did try to influence the health and well-being of troops. Because hundreds of soldiers died of smallpox during the first 2 years of the Revolutionary War, General George Washington and the Continental Congress decided that all new recruits should be inoculated against the disease, and smallpox deaths were greatly reduced. Washington, Dr. Benjamin Rush, and others emphasized the importance of cleanliness of person and environment, yet most soldiers did not heed their recommendations. Many died from diseases that were caused by filthy encampments and inadequate food and clothing. It has been estimated that for every soldier who died in combat in the Revolutionary War, 10 died from disease (Bayne-Jones 1968). The causes of death were primarily infectious and contagious diseases, including typhus, dysentery, and smallpox (until inoculation was enforced).

By the War of 1812 all U.S. soldiers were vaccinated against smallpox with the inert cowpox virus. However, throughout the 19th century many soldiers died during wartime from diseases such as typhus, dysentery, diarrhea, and pneumonia due to unsanitary camp conditions and unsafe food and water. It has been estimated that for every

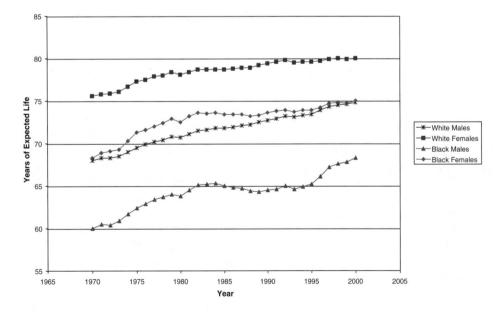

Figure 7 Life Expectancy at Birth by Race and Sex, United States, 1970–2000

SOURCES: Hoyert et al. (2001), Minino and Smith (2001), and National Center for Health Statistics (1996).

Table 2   Selected Disaster Deaths in the United States

Type of Disaster/Year	Location	Estimated Deaths
Hurricanes (most deadly)		
1776	NC to Nova Scotia	4,170
1856	Last Island, LA	400
1893	GA, SC	1,000
1900	Galveston, TX	6,000–8,000
1915	TX, LA	275
1919	FL, LA, TX	600
1926	FL, AL	243
1928	Lake Okeechobee, FL	1,836
1935	Florida Keys	408
1938	NY, New England	600
1944	NC to New England	390
1955	NC to New England ("Diane")	184
1957	LA, TX ("Audrey")	390
1969	MS, LA, AL, VA, WV ("Camille")	256
1972	FL to NY ("Agnes")	117
Tornadoes (most deadly)		
1840	Natchez, MS	317
1880	Marshfield, MO (24)[a]	99
1884	MS, AL, NC, SC, TN, KY, IN (60)	800
1896	MO, IL (18)	255
1899	New Richmond, WI	117
1902	Goliad, TX	114
1903	GA	98
1905	Snyder, OK	97
1908	LA, MS, AL, GA (18)	310
1913	NE, IA (8)	181
1917	Mattoon, IL	101
1925	MO, IL, IN	689
1927	Poplar Bluff, MO	98
1932	AL, MS, GA, TN (33)	334
1936	Deep South (17)	419
1944	WV, PA, MD (4)	153
1947	Woodward, OK	181
1952	AR, TN (28)	204
1953	Waco, TX	114
1953	Flint, MI	116
1953	Worcester, MA	90
1965	Midwest–Great Lakes (?)	256
1971	MS, LA, AR, TN (10)	121
1974	13 states (148)	330
Winter storm (worst)		
1888	East Coast	400
Earthquakes (most deadly)		
1906	San Francisco	500
1933	Long Beach, CA	117
1964	AK	117
Terrorist attack		
2001	New York City; Arlington, VA; Shanksville, PA	2,850

a. Numbers in parentheses indicate numbers of tornadoes.

soldier who died in combat during the Mexican War, 7 died of diseases, primarily dysentery (Bayne-Jones 1968).

During the Civil War, disease casualties were vast for both the Union and Confederate armies. As was the case in earlier wars, such casualties were primarily due to unsanitary conditions, inadequate food and clothing, and the soldiers' lack of immunity to contagious diseases. Many disease-related deaths were caused by intestinal disorders, such as diarrhea, dysentery, and typhoid fever. Other causes of death included respiratory diseases, such as pneumonia and bronchitis, as well as measles (and secondary complications resulting from measles), smallpox (from volunteers who were not vaccinated), and tuberculosis. During the short Spanish-American War, close to 2,000 persons died from disease, primarily typhoid fever, compared with fewer than 400 deaths in battle (Bayne-Jones 1968).

The knowledge and practice of preventive medicine flourished at the beginning of the 20th century, resulting in better conrol of personal and environmental conditions associated with the occurrence and spread of contagious and infectious diseases. Sanitary conditions and preventive health measures were much improved by World War I, yet even then the total number of deaths to soldiers due to disease was equivalent to the total number of battle deaths, because of the worldwide influenza pandemic in 1918 at the end of the war.

DISASTER DEATHS

In addition to diseases and war, American mortality trends have been influenced by natural and human-made disasters. Table 2 presents selected data on deaths due to disasters in the United States. Hurricanes are annually a threat to the Gulf and East Coasts. The most deadly hurricane on record, which killed an estimated 6,000 to 8,000 people, occurred in Galveston, Texas, in 1900. Tornadoes cause many problems in the southern, central, and midwestern states. In 1884, an estimated 60 tornadoes struck from Mississippi to Indiana, causing 800 deaths. Earthquakes have also caused numerous deaths. The most deadly earthquake to date, which left 500 persons dead or missing, took place in San Francisco in 1906. The most devastating disaster the United States has seen was the terrorist attacks on September 11, 2001, in which hijacked airplanes were crashed into the World Trade Center towers in New York City as well as into the Pentagon in Arlington, Virginia, and a field in a rural area in Shanksville, Pennsylvania. In all, close to 3,000 persons were killed.

CONCLUSION

Omran (1971) has formalized the patterned shifts in disease trends and causes of mortality, and the resulting impacts on life expectancy and population growth, in the theory of epidemiologic transition. This transition consists of three major stages: (a) "the age of pestilence and famine," when mortality is high and fluctuating; (b) "the age of receding pandemics," when mortality declines progressively as epidemics decrease in frequency and magnitude; and (c) "the age of degenerative and man-made diseases," when mortality continues to decline and eventually approaches stability at a relatively low level (Omran 1982:172).

In the United States, the first stage of the epidemiologic transition extended until the middle of the 19th century. Up to that time, unpredictable and somewhat uncontrollable epidemics were the major causes of death. Other causes of death and disease included parasitic and deficiency diseases, pneumonia, diarrhea and malnutrition complexes for children, and tuberculosis and childbirth complications for women. Fewer peaks and fluctuations of mortality rates characterize the early phase of the second stage, although mortality levels remained quite elevated. Infant and childhood mortality rates remained high, as did mortality for female adolescents and women of childbearing age. As this stage continued, death rates began a steady decline. Declines in U.S. mortality rates occurred in the late 1800s. Through the 20th century, improvements were first gained in the reduction of infectious disease deaths. Later, maternal mortality rates as well as infant mortality rates progressively fell and reductions also were realized in childhood mortality rates.

The third stage reflects even further improvements in survivorship, especially in the advanced older ages. Infant mortality rates drop, and childhood mortality accounts for less than 10% of total mortality, whereas deaths to persons over the age of 50 represent at least 70% of total deaths. The U.S. entered the third stage during the early part of the 20th century. The epidemiologic transition favors the young over the old and females over males. Survival chances improve markedly for children of both sexes and for females through their childbearing ages. By the third stage, the female age-specific mortality risks are lower than those for males for all ages. An outcome of these mortality differentials is a further imbalance in the sex ratio, with fewer males than females, especially at the older ages.

A question that remains is whether the United States has entered a fourth stage of the epidemiologic transition, with further declines in deaths due to chronic diseases and continued increases in life expectancy, particularly at the older ages. Omran did not anticipate such dramatic mortality improvements in his original framework.

An additional factor that possibly points to a new stage is the increasing presence of infectious diseases. There are unprecedented numbers of new infectious diseases (e.g., Legionnaires' disease, HIV/AIDS, Ebola virus, and severe acute respiratory syndrome, or SARS), infections such as tuberculosis and malaria are reemerging, and some reemerging pathogens are generating antimicrobial-resistant strains (Barrett et al. 1998). Factors that have contributed to the recent rise and spread of infectious diseases include increased urbanization and crowding, greater travel to Third World countries and remote areas, global climate changes, and the overuse of antibiotics and pesticides (Olshansky et al. 1997). The escalation of infectious diseases is a growing concern at both national and global levels because the long-term impacts of this trend are unknown.

REFERENCES

Anderson, Robert N. 2001. *Deaths: Leading Causes for 1999* (National Vital Statistics Reports, vol. 49, no. 11). Hyattsville, MD: National Center for Health Statistics.

Armstrong, Gregory L., Laura A. Conn, and Robert W. Pinner. 1999. "Trends in Infectious Disease Mortality in the United States During the 20th Century." *Journal of the American Medical Association* 281:61–66.

Arriaga, Eduardo E. 1984. "Measuring and Explaining the Change in Life Expectancy." *Demography* 21:83–96.

Barrett, Ronald, Christopher W. Kuzawa, Thomas McDade, and George J. Armelagos. 1998. "Emerging and Re-Emerging Infectious Diseases: The Third Epidemiologic Transition." *Annual Review of Anthropology* 27:247–71.

Bayne-Jones, Stanhope. 1968. *The Evolution of Preventive Medicine in the United States Army, 1607-1939.* Washington, DC: Government Printing Office. Retrieved April 5, 2003 (http://history.amedd.army.mil/booksdocs/misc/evprev/default.htm).

Duffy, John. 1953. *Epidemics in Colonial America.* Baton Rouge: Louisiana State University Press.

Easterlin, Richard A. 2000. "Growth and Composition of the American Population in the Twentieth Century." Pp. 631–75 in *A Population History of North America,* edited by Michael R. Haines and Richard H. Steckel. New York: Cambridge University Press.

Fenn, Elizabeth. 2001. *Pox Americana: The Great Smallpox Epidemic of 1775–82.* New York: Hill & Wang.

Gemery, Henry A. 2000. "The White Population of the Colonial United States, 1607–1790." Pp. 143–90 in *A Population History of North America,* edited by Michael R. Haines and Richard H. Steckel. New York: Cambridge University Press.

Guyer, Bernard, Mary Anne Freedman, Donna M. Strobino, and Edward J. Sondik. 2000. "Annual Summary of Vital Statistics." *Pediatrics* 106:1307–17.

Haines, Michael R. 2000. "The White Population of the United States, 1790–1920." Pp. 305–69 in *A Population History of*

North America, edited by Michael R. Haines and Richard H. Steckel. New York: Cambridge University Press.

Hetzel, Alice M. 1997. *History and Organization of the Vital Statistics System.* Hyattsville, MD: National Center for Health Statistics.

Hoyert, Donna L., Elizabeth Arias, Betty L. Smith, Sherry L. Murphy, and Kenneth D. Kochanek. 2001. *Deaths: Final Data for 1999* (National Vital Statistics Reports, vol. 49, no. 8). Hyattsville, MD: National Center for Health Statistics.

Hummer, Robert A. 1993. "Racial Differentials in Infant Mortality in the U.S.: An Examination of Social and Health Determinants." *Social Forces* 72:529–54.

Hummer, Robert A., Monique Biegler, Peter B. de Turk, Douglas Forbes, W. Parker Frisbie, Ying Hong, and Starling G. Pullum. 1999. "Race/Ethnicity, Nativity, and Infant Mortality in the United States." *Social Forces* 77: 1083–1118.

Kolata, Gina. 1999. *Flu: The Story of the Great Influenza Pandemic of 1918 and the Search for the Virus That Caused It.* New York: Farrar, Straus & Giroux.

Loudon, Irvine. 2000. "Maternal Mortality in the Past and Its Relevance to Developing Countries Today." *American Journal of Clinical Nutrition* 72(Suppl.):241S–46S.

Margo, Robert A. and Richard H. Steckel. 1983. "Heights of Native-Born Whites During the Antebellum Period." *Journal of Economic History* 43:167–74.

Marks, Geoffrey and William I. Beatty. 1973. *The Story of Medicine in America.* New York: Scribner.

Minino, Arialdi M. and Betty L. Smith. 2001. *Deaths: Preliminary Data for 2000* (National Vital Statistics Reports, vol. 49, no. 12). Hyattsville, MD: National Center for Health Statistics.

Murphy, Sherry L. 2000. *Deaths: Final Data for 1998* (National Vital Statistics Reports, vol. 48, no. 11). Hyattsville, MD: National Center for Health Statistics.

Nathanson, Constance A. 1984. "Sex Differences in Mortality." *Annual Review of Sociology* 10:191–213.

National Center for Health Statistics. 1986. *Vital Statistics of the United States 1981,* vol. 2, *Mortality.* Hyattsville, MD: National Center for Health Statistics.

———. 1996. *Vital Statistics of the United States 1991,* vol. 2, *Mortality, Part A.* Hyattsville, MD: National Center for Health Statistics.

National Center for Health Statistics. 2003. *Leading Causes of Death, 1900–1998.* Retrieved April 25, 2003 (http://www.cdc.gov/nchs/data/statab/lead1900_98.pdf).

Olshansky, S. Jay, Bruce Carnes, Richard G. Rogers, and Len Smith. 1997. "Infectious Diseases: New and Ancient Threats to World Health." *Population Bulletin* 52(2).

Omran, Abdel R. 1971. "The Epidemiologic Transition: A Theory of the Epidemiology of Population Change." *Milbank Memorial Fund Quarterly* 49:509–38.

———. 1982. "Epidemiologic Transition: Theory." Pp. 172–75 in *International Encyclopedia of Population,* vol. 1, edited by John A. Ross. New York: Free Press.

Steckel, Richard H. 1999. "Nutritional Status in the Colonial American Economy." *William and Mary Quarterly* 56:31–52.

———. 2000. "The African American Population of the United States, 1790–1920." Pp. 433–81 in *A Population History of North America,* edited by Michael R. Haines and Richard H. Steckel. New York: Cambridge University Press.

Thornton, Russell. 2000. "Population History of Native North Americans." Pp. 9–50 in *A Population History of North America,* edited by Michael R. Haines and Richard H. Steckel. New York: Cambridge University Press.

Toner, Joseph M. 1874. *Contributions to the Annals of Medical Progress and Medical Education in the United States Before and During the War of Independence.* Washington, DC: Government Printing Office.

U.S. Bureau of the Census. 1975. *Historical Statistics of the United States, Colonial Times to 1970,* Bicentennial ed., *Part 1.* Washington, DC: Government Printing Office.

U.S. Department of Veterans Affairs. 2001. "America's Wars" (Fact Sheet). Retrieved April 5, 2003 (http://www.va.gov/pressrel/amwars01.htm).

Waldron, Ingrid. 1993. "Recent Trends in Sex Mortality Ratios for Adults in Developing Countries." *Social Science & Medicine* 36:451–62.

Walsh, Lorena S. 2000. "The African American Population of Colonial America." Pp. 191–239 in *A Population History of North America,* edited by Michael R. Haines and Richard H. Steckel. New York: Cambridge University Press.

Wells, Robert V. 1992. "The Population of England's Colonies in America: Old English or New Americans?" *Population Studies* 46:85–102.

GLOBAL MORTALITY RATES

Variations and Their Consequences for the Experience of Dying

CLIVE SEALE

The statistical distribution of mortality varies considerably, both historically and across regions of the world. Most obviously, life expectancy has risen over time, yet people in some countries can expect to have much longer lives than people in others. Within countries there are marked differences in the age distribution of death for different groups; for example, life expectancy is influenced by gender and by socioeconomic differences. Additionally, there is variability among regions of the world in different causes of death, and there are great differences among countries in the availability of formal health care. Given the combination of these factors with cultural variations that affect matters as diverse as family size, gender and filial roles, beliefs about how health professionals should behave, and religious customs, it is clear that there is potentially a great deal of variation in people's experiences of dying and of care before death.

My purpose in this chapter is to map out some of this variation, initially by reviewing available statistical data about the matters I have mentioned and then by addressing the consequences of these patterns for the experience of dying in different parts of the world. I draw also on some qualitative data about the experience of dying. Toward the end of the chapter, I consider future prospects, given the continuation of present trends.

LONGEVITY

In 1995, average life expectancy at birth worldwide was 65 years, having risen from just 48 years in 1955. The World Health Organization (WHO 1998a) has predicted that average life expectancy will rise to 73 years by 2025; by that date,

WHO estimates, no country will have an average life expectancy of less than 50 years. Reductions in infant mortality and in early childhood deaths are responsible for most of this increase. In 1955, the infant mortality rate (IMR) worldwide is estimated to have been 148 per 1,000 live births; by 1995 the IMR was 59, and WHO (1998a) predicts that it will reach 29 by 2025. Mortality rates for children under 5 years old have shown similar declines (WHO 1998a).

Underlying these global figures is considerable diversity. Table 1 displays life expectancy and infant mortality rates for the major regions of the world from 1995 through 2000. The country with the highest life expectancy and lowest IMR during this period was Japan (80 years and 4.3), and the country with the lowest life expectancy and highest IMR was Ethiopia (37.5 years and 169.3) (WHO 1998b). Table 1 shows the impact of these changes (as well as the impact of reductions in fertility rates that tend to follow reductions in mortality rates) on the age structures of populations. Broadly speaking, under the circumstances of such a demographic transition, the proportion of elderly people in populations rises, and the experience of dying is increasingly a feature of old age.

However, global mortality figures mask the fact that the picture of improvement is not universal. In 16 countries, average life expectancy decreased in the period from 1975 through 1995 (WHO 1998a). In particular, the trend in certain Eastern European countries stands in sharp contrast to that in other developed countries, showing a considerable divide between the newly independent states of the former Soviet Union and the rest of Europe. In the Russian Federation itself, life expectancy for males dropped from 64.3 in 1985–90 to 57.5 in 1994; for females, the figures went from 74.4 to 71.3 (Pearce et al.

| Table 1 | Life Expectancy, Infant Mortality Rates, and Age Structures of Populations Globally |

	Distribution by Age Groups (%) (1996)			Life Expectancy at Birth (1995–2000)	Infant Mortality Rate per 1,000 Live Births (1995–2000)
	0–14	*15–64*	*65+*		
Africa	43.7	53.2	3.2	53.8	85.6
America	28.8	63.2	8.0	72.4	27.7
Asia	31.5	63.1	5.4	66.2	56.0
Europe	18.9	67.1	14.0	72.6	11.6
Oceania	25.9	64.5	9.6	73.9	24.2
World	31.1	62.3	6.6	65.6	56.8

SOURCE: WHO (1998b).

1997). These declines reflect increases in particular causes of death, influenced by deterioration in the public health services as well as worsening material and social conditions, with high alcohol consumption playing a major role in mediating the stress of these conditions. Middle-aged males seem to have borne the brunt of this worsening mortality picture, with increases in deaths from cardiovascular disease, accidental poisonings, and suicide, and, most strikingly, large increases in death by homicide, so that by 1993–94 Russia overtook the United States as the country with the highest homicide rate (Whitehead and Diderischen 1997; Okolski 1986). Since 1994, however, mortality rates have improved in Russia, and by 1998 they were back at the levels they had been in the early 1980s (Shkolnikov, McKee, and Leon 2001). A similar decline followed by a rise to previous levels has been experienced in Romania, and for quite similar reasons, with the exception that an epidemic of pediatric AIDS (stemming from some disastrous practices by health care providers specific to the 1980s) played a part, adding yet more premature death to that caused in middle-aged adults by cirrhosis and cardiovascular disease (Dolea, Nolte, and McKee 2002).

Additionally, AIDS is having a serious impact on overall life expectancy in some African countries, where the spread of this disease has been greatest so far. In Uganda, for example, where AIDS is the leading cause of death for young adults, life expectancy at birth in 1995–2000 was 41.4 (WHO 1998b), whereas once it was 56.5 years (Gilks et al. 1998). In the nine African countries with adult HIV prevalence of 10% or more,

life expectancy by 2010–15 will be 47 years on average, compared with the 62.4 years that would have been the case without AIDS. Because of transmission to infants, there will also be rises in infant mortality in such countries (UNAIDS 1998a). Figure 1 shows changing life expectancies in African countries, illustrating the impact of AIDS. UNAIDS (2002) has expressed concerns that this experience in Africa may be repeated over the next few years in countries in South and East Asia, where the epidemic is at an earlier stage.

In spite of these reversals, the overall trend worldwide is toward longer life and the aging of populations. This has particular consequences for the experience of dying, as this experience becomes increasingly merged with the general problems of old age. The trend toward longer life also has consequences for the experience of bereavement, as death occurs to people who have often been excluded already from participation in mainstream social and family life, so that they are to a degree "socially dead" and already mourned for before they are biologically dead. Additionally, the aging of populations has consequences for the sources of care on which dying people can draw. Other factors, however, also play a part in influencing the experience of dying. These include cultural differences in the living arrangements and social status of elderly people, the roles played by gender and social inequalities, the nature of health services available to elderly and dying people, and the changes in the

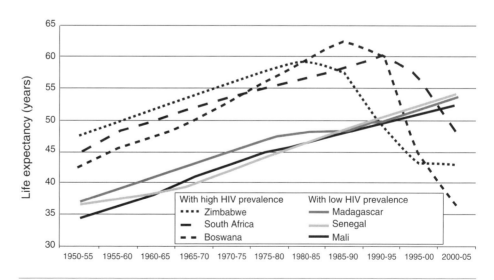

| Figure 1 | Changes in Life Expectancy in Selected African Countries With High and Low HIV Prevalence: 1950–2005 |

SOURCE: UNAIDS (2002).

causes of death that have led to the increases in longevity already reviewed. In all of these areas there are marked differences between "developed" and "developing" countries.

CAUSES OF DEATH

As is well-known, the demographic transition that most developing countries undergo involves a shift in causes of death, broadly speaking, from a predominance of infectious diseases in pretransition societies to degenerative conditions in countries that have experienced the transition. Historically, in European countries, typhoid, cholera, typhus, measles, diphtheria, whooping cough, and smallpox were major causes of death. Epidemics caused surges of mortality compared with present-day patterns, which are less volatile. Nonepidemic infectious diseases, such as pneumonia, bronchitis, tuberculosis, and enteritis, then became more important, before the present time, when the degenerative diseases of cancer, heart disease, and stroke are the major causes of death in developed European societies (McNicoll 1986).

China in the early 1980s presents an example of a country midway through the epidemiological transition (Jamison et al. 1984). This country gained 27 years in overall life expectancy in the years between 1960 and 1980 (this figure controls for the huge surge in mortality caused by the famine period around 1960). IMR dropped from 290 in 1940–45 to 65 in 1975–80. Rural areas lagged behind urban areas in the transition from a predominance of parasitic and infectious diseases to degenerative diseases. One example of a disease that was once an important cause of mortality but that had declined in importance by the early 1980s is neonatal tetanus, which is estimated to have killed up to 10% of infants in pre-1949 China but was a rarity by 1981. Malaria control measures had reduced the proportion of the population living in areas endemic for the disease from 70% in the early 1950s to around one-third by 1979. Childhood pneumonia was estimated to be at around one-fifth its former level in the early 1960s, once the control of acute respiratory diseases became a priority for health services. Tuberculosis, although still an important public health concern, had declined considerably as a cause of death, being one of several diseases in which mass immunization campaigns had made an impact. Table 2 shows the distribution of deaths by major causes in selected rural and urban areas of China in 1982. The data displayed in the table demonstrate the difference made by the urban factor in the transition to degenerative diseases as causes of death, as well as the continuation of infectious diseases, TB and respiratory disease, as smaller but still important causes of death, particularly in rural areas. Chinese life expectancy at birth in 1996 stood at 69.9; IMR was 37.6 (WHO 1998b), suggesting further movement along the epidemiological and demographic transitions since the early 1980s.

Table 2   Percentage Distribution of Deaths by Major Causes for Selected Urban and Rural Areas of China, 1982

	Urban	Rural
Cerebrovascular diseases	22.3	15.4
Heart diseases	21.1	23.7
Malignant tumor	20.6	15.3
Respiratory diseases	8.7	11.5
Digestive diseases	4.4	5.7
Pulmonary tuberculosis	2.0	4.2
Trauma	3.3	3.0
Infectious diseases[a]	2.2	3.5

SOURCE: Hayase and Kawamata (1991).

a. 1975 figures.

By way of contrast, Tanzania in the 1990s presents an example of a country somewhat further back in the demographic transition whose progress in reducing mortality has been set back considerably by AIDS. In 1996, Tanzanian life expectancy stood at 51.4; IMR was 80.1 (WHO 1998b). According to a 1997 report from the Tanzania Ministry of Health concerning selected areas of the country, HIV/AIDS was the leading cause of death among adults ages 15–59, with the spread of pulmonary tuberculosis having increased dramatically in the previous decade due to the effects of HIV infection on immunity. Infectious disease accounted for between half and two-thirds of deaths occurring to 15- to 59-year-old men, whose death rates were now as important in causing public health concern as infant mortality had been in previous decades. Maternal mortality (which still accounts for more than half a million deaths each year worldwide, particularly in Asia and Africa; WHO 1998a) accounted for 8–10% of deaths of women ages 15–49 in these areas of Tanzania. It was only among the elderly—who were of course a lower proportion of the population than in posttransition countries—that stroke, cancers, and chronic heart failure were predominant causes of death, although acute febrile illness and pneumonia still caused death in significant proportions of elderly Tanzanians.

In spite of the continuing progress in most societies toward and through the demographic transition, the picture worldwide in 1997 showed that infectious and parasitic diseases remained the cause of about one-third of all deaths (WHO 1998a). The most common infectious diseases causing death were acute lower respiratory infections (7.1% of deaths worldwide), tuberculosis (5.6%), diarrhea (4.8%), HIV/AIDS (4.4%), and malaria (between 2.9% and 5.2%). The diseases more commonly associated with the degenerative conditions prevalent in posttransition societies included 29% of deaths worldwide caused by circulatory diseases. Of these, the most common were coronary heart disease (13.8% of all deaths), cerebrovascular disease (8.8%), and other heart diseases (5.7%). Cancers accounted for 12% of deaths worldwide in 1997, with lung cancer being the most common, followed by colon and rectum, liver, and breast cancers (WHO 1998a).

Optimistic predictions suggest that, in spite of the impact of AIDS, there will be continuing progress at a global level away from infectious disease as a cause of death and toward degenerative disease as more countries undergo the transitions characteristic of developing countries. Nevertheless, infectious disease will be a major cause of mortality for many decades to come, particularly in the world's poorest countries (Heuveline, Guilot, and Gwatkin 2002). Additionally, the prospect of unforeseen reversals to the pattern of transition (demonstrated, for example, by the impact of AIDS and by the surges of mortality in Eastern Europe since the fall of communism) should not be discounted. As I will show below, we know a considerable amount about the experience of dying from degenerative conditions in Western societies, but less has been recorded about the needs and dying trajectories of those whose deaths are caused by infectious diseases.

POPULATION STRUCTURES

Although the effects of AIDS and the changes experienced in Eastern Europe suggest modifications to the picture of worldwide improvements in longevity, it is nevertheless the case that the aging of populations is the norm in most countries around the world. This trend has implications for the sources of care on which people can draw as they approach the ends of their lives. The pattern of demographic transition undergone by most developing countries involves a decline in fertility as well as in mortality rates, as the increased chances of surviving childhood are taken into account by potential parents. This creates a population structure in which there is a low proportion of younger members compared with elderly people. The age structures in different regions of the world are displayed in Table 1, which shows that Europe has the highest proportion of elderly people in its population, and Africa has the lowest. Predictions for the future draw particular attention to Latin America and Southeast Asia, which in 1998 were expected to see increases of up to 300% in the older population by 2025 (WHO 1998a). Globally, WHO (1998a) estimates that the proportion of people age 65 and older in relation to people age 20 and younger will shift from 16/100 in 1998 to 31/100 by 2025.

Because old age is associated with increased levels of disability (see below), these changes in population structures have prompted concern among some observers about societies' ability to meet the health and social care needs of elderly people (e.g., Ogawa 1986). Insofar as these needs merge with needs for care of the dying, similar considerations apply. As a reflection of these forces, research has emerged in developed countries that has demonstrated an exceedingly high cost of health care for elderly people in their last year of life (Culler, Callahan, and Wolinsky 1995; Experton et al. 1996). Some 30% of the health care

expenses of retired people in Western industrialized countries are incurred in the last year of life (Felder 1997). WHO (1998a) has expressed particular concern about the impacts of these changes in developing countries, where health and social care budgets already face difficulties. In relation to informal family care, demographic changes may be accompanied by a loosening of filial ties, as Hossain (1999) notes in a review of population aging in Bangladesh; Hossain expresses particular concerns about the situation of elderly Bangladeshi women. Other commentators have suggested that the general social status and power of elderly people decline in these circumstances (McNicoll 1986; Hull and Jones 1986). As McNicoll (1986) puts it, "Gerontocratic control in a family system, to take one instance especially important in many African societies, is inconsistent with too many gerontocrats" (p. 18). The relevance of these concerns for the "slippery slope" argument within debates about euthanasia as a social policy should not be ignored, and the relatively disadvantaged position of elderly women is of relevance here (Seale and Addington-Hall 1995; Markson 1995).

GENDER DIFFERENCES IN LONGEVITY

Gender differences in longevity, which are particularly evident in developed countries, mean that females come to outnumber males as age increases. In pretransition societies, apart from the fact that there are fewer elderly people anyway, this gender difference is less marked, with some societies showing higher rates of female mortality, particularly for the very young and at childbearing ages. Ware (1986) has argued that in such societies decisions about the allocation of scarce resources, such as food and medicine, often discriminate against the survival of female infants, although outright infanticide is probably rare. The effects of multiple childbirths on those women who survive their own childhoods also contribute to high female mortality. But as societies become relatively more affluent and fertility decreases, women are increasingly likely to survive to old age, and they commonly outlive men. In their historical and cross-national review of the ratios of women to men, Guralnik, Balfour, and Volpato (2000) largely rule out the role played by improvements in children's health as a causative factor, instead claiming that changes in the probability of survival in middle age and late life explain many of the gender differentials that exist. Because of the common marriage pattern in most societies that involves older men marrying younger women, women are also more likely to experience widowhood in old age, and so are likely to approach death alone.

Sri Lanka is an example of a society where mortality rates for women in relation to men have reversed over time. Life expectancy for Sri Lankan females in 1945–47 was 43.1 years; for men it was 44.8. Mortality in childhood was higher for girls than for boys, with the exception of the first year of life, during which male mortality was greater. In the main childbearing years of early adulthood (15–24), women were at their greatest disadvantage, with this continuing at a lesser level for older childbearing years (25–44). However, for the ages beyond 45, men were more likely to die than were women. By 1970–72 a gender transition had occurred, with life expectancy for women being 66.7 and that for men being 63.8. Although mortality at ages 1–4 was still greater for girls than for boys, for all other age groups it was either the same for females and males or much improved for females (Ware 1986).

In the United Kingdom, by contrast, life expectancy has been greater for females than for males at least since 1871, which is the earliest point at which official statistics enable calculation of gender differences in life expectancy (Gray 1993). By that time, death from infectious diseases had declined considerably from earlier levels, and birthrates had been falling steeply since the 1860s, indicating a society going through the latter stages of demographic transition. By 1995, life expectancy in the United Kingdom was 74 for males and 79.2 for females (Eurostat 1997). This difference, of 5.2 years, is exceeded in some other developed countries, but the most dramatic sex differences in favor of women are to be found in some Eastern European countries, due to the excessive impact on male mortality of the social changes reviewed above. In Estonia, for example, in 1995 life expectancy was 61.7 years for men, compared with 74.3 for women (Eurostat 1997). In 1994, these figures for the Russian Federation were 57.5 and 71.3, respectively, a difference of 13.8 years (Pearce et al. 1997). Although gender differences of this magnitude may be only a temporary phenomenon in these countries of the former Soviet Union, their example suggests that there are some circumstances that justify a reversal of the public health concern over excessive female mortality applicable to developing countries.

SOCIOECONOMIC DIFFERENCES

Socioeconomic variations in mortality within countries (bearing in mind that some really large inequalities occur between countries), with the richer and more educated possessing a variety of advantages that translate into longer lives, are also relevant to any consideration of the experience of dying. The adequacy with which different countries document the benefits of high socioeconomic status varies, but there are good reasons to believe that it is a universal phenomenon. Where material conditions are poor, differential access to food, hygienic living conditions, and health care are major influences. Wilkinson (1996) suggests that the persistence of inequalities in richer societies, where a basic level of access to these things is reasonably well established for all, is due to psychosocial factors, excess mortality in the worse-off being caused by physiological effects of stress arising from social exclusion. A more conventional explanation stresses the contributory role of class-related patterns of health behavior, as well as some continuing effects of material deprivation (Townsend and Davidson 1982). In the United States, racial differences in mortality that run in parallel with material deprivation and social exclusion have been particularly evident (Whitehead and Diderischen 1997; U.S. Congress 1993).

Although this means that age at death is likely to be differentiated systematically within societies, the roles of cultural differences among socioeconomic groups in attitudes toward the care of elderly people, or toward dying, have been less well documented. However, it is likely that in some developed countries there is variation in how people from different socioeconomic backgrounds feel about the extent to which they can control dying and plan for death. People's attitudes about such matters may influence their views concerning the desirability of euthanasia or hospice care, for example, as well as the desirability of an open awareness about the presence terminal disease (Seale 1998).

IMPLICATIONS OF DEMOGRAPHIC CHANGES

Mortality differences, then, are considerable, both within and between societies. The key features of these for an understanding of the experience of dying are rising life expectancy, causing an aging of the population, coupled with the changing pattern of diseases causing death, within which there are considerable gender and class differences. The demographic and epidemiological transitions mean that dying comes increasingly to be a part of the more general experience of old age and its concomitant disabilities. There is large variation, however, in the extent of this transition worldwide, perhaps limiting the applicability of Western models of terminal or palliative care. A consideration of some of the differences in the dying trajectories involved in different diseases may help to illustrate this point.

Dying Trajectories and Needs

Some scholars have stated that the shift from infectious to degenerative disease involves a lengthening of dying trajectories (e.g., Lofland 1978; Hull and Jones 1986). Coupled with advances in medical science's capacity to predict death at an early stage in some diseases, this has led to the emergence of a particular category of experience, that of "terminal illness," around which has developed the expertise of hospice and palliative care in some developed countries. This simple story requires some modification, which can begin with an assessment of what is known about the prevalence of disability and symptoms, as well as the length of dying trajectories, in the time before death.

Surveys of nationally representative samples of elderly people and of people in the last year of life in the United Kingdom are a useful starting point. British government surveys have shown, broadly speaking, that the prevalence of disability reflects the aging of the population over time. Since the General Household Survey (GHS) began in 1972, the proportion of adults reporting a long-standing illness that limited their daily activities rose from 15% of people living in private households to 22% in 1996. At each time point, women have been somewhat more likely than men to report this, and the prevalence of limiting long-standing illness, unsurprisingly, shows a sharp rise with age, so that among people age 75 and over, 52% report such illness (Office for National Statistics 1998a). Studies in the United States have found similar patterns (Feldman 1986).

The perception that increased life expectancy may bring with it a greater burden of disability toward the end of life led some researchers to calculate a new statistic of "healthy life expectancy" (HLE) to modify the traditional life expectancy statistic. Between 1976 and 1994 in the United Kingdom, when life expectancy rose by more than 4 years for males and more than 3 for females, HLE showed almost no change (Office for National Statistics 1998b). As a result of this increased level of disability, 30% of people age 85 or older surveyed in the 1996 GHS needed help at home in climbing the stairs, 24% needed help with bathing or showering, 8% needed help with dressing and undressing, and smaller proportions needed assistance with other self-care activities (Office for National Statistics 1998a).

According to the World Health Organization's (2000) report on world rates of healthy life expectancy (which WHO calls "disability adjusted life expectancy," or DALE) in 1999, people in poorer countries "lost" some 14% of their lives to disability, compared with 9% in richer countries. The top 5 nations in terms of DALE were Japan (74.5 years), Australia (73.2), France (73.1), Sweden (73.0), and Spain (72.8). The United States ranked 24th (70.0 years) for a variety of reasons, including the poor health of some members of minority groups and high levels of violence. All of the bottom 10 countries were in sub-Saharan Africa, reflecting the effects of HIV/AIDS.

The symptoms and restrictions experienced by people in the last year of life have been recorded in three U.K. surveys that have described people dying in 1969, 1987, and 1990 by means of interviews with surviving relatives and others who knew the deceased. The first two of these studies, conducted by Cartwright, Hockey, and Anderson (1973) and Seale and Cartwright (1994), used nationally representative samples, permitting comparisons over time. On both occasions, respondents were asked to say which of a number of areas of restriction had been experienced by the people who died. These included such activities as getting in and out of the bath, dressing and undressing, and washing. The major changes concerned the length of time that such restrictions were experienced. In 1969, 30% had needed help with at least one of these activities for a year or more. By 1987, the proportion had risen to 52%. In this respect, the figures support those from the GHS.

Table 3 Symptoms Experienced in the Last Year of Life in Britain, 1990 (in percentages)

	Cancer	Heart Disease	Stroke
Pain	88	77	66
Breathlessness	54	60	37
Nausea and vomiting	59	32	23
Difficulty swallowing	41	16	23
Constipation	63	38	45
Mental confusion	41	32	50
Pressure sores	28	11	20
Urinary incontinence	40	30	56
Bowel incontinence	32	17	37
N	2,063	683	229

SOURCE: Addington-Hall (1996).

Respondents were also asked, on both occasions, to report whether the deceased experienced certain symptoms at all during the last 12 months of life, and, for symptoms reported at this stage, how long they were experienced. The major changes since 1969 again concerned the duration of some of the symptoms: Mental confusion, depression, and incontinence were all experienced over longer time periods by people in the later study. When they had controlled for age, the researchers found that these increases were all related to the greater proportion of people age 75 or older in the 1987 study.

Recalling that cancer, heart disease, and stroke have become increasingly prevalent as causes of death as infectious diseases have declined in importance, the analyses conducted for these separate groups in the third survey (Addington-Hall 1996) are of interest. This 1990 survey, the Regional Study of Care for the Dying (Addington-Hall and McCarthy 1995), was not nationally representative, but its large size permits comparison of these different leading causes of death, as shown in Table 3. Pain, nausea and vomiting, difficulty swallowing, constipation, and pressure sores are more prevalent among people dying from cancer. Breathlessness is a particular problem for people with heart disease, whereas mental confusion and incontinence affect a high proportion of people dying from strokes. Overall, cancer caused, on average, a larger number of symptoms, and respondents considered a larger proportion of these to have been "very distressing" for the dying person. However, the duration of symptoms in cancer was less than for other conditions (Addington-Hall, Altmann, and McCarthy 1998). This pattern was also found in the earlier study of deaths in 1986 (Seale and Cartwright 1994), which suggests that an experience of longer-term disability was more typical in people not dying from cancer, who also tended to be a little older, on average, than those dying from cancer.

Researchers have conducted studies of dependency, symptoms, and needs for care in the period before death in the United States (Hunt et al. 1991; Kai et al. 1993;

Dudgeon and Kristjanson 1995; Andershed and Ternestedt 1997), Germany (Bickel 1998), Finland (Hunt, Bonett, and Roder 1993), and Australia (Karlsen and Addington-Hall 1998). Equivalent information is lacking, however, for patterns of dying in countries at earlier stages of the epidemiological transition. This means that death from infectious diseases and other causes prevalent in developing countries, as well as death in younger groups, is not well described. An exception is AIDS, for which there are descriptions of Western populations before the advent of effective antiretroviral therapies (Sims and Moss 1991). However, it is likely that these Western AIDS deaths were dissimilar from typical patterns in, say, African countries, where people progress more rapidly to death due to the presence of other uncontrolled diseases such as TB, pneumonia, and salmonellosis infections, without living long enough to experience the pattern of coinfections experienced in the West (Gilks et al. 1998; UNAIDS 1998b; Nunn et al. 1997). It is also possible that, in the future, increased availability of life-preserving drugs will change the experience of this disease in poorer countries, although there remain a variety of obstacles to this. Additionally, studies of populations in developed countries rely on the contrast between the less healthy and the average, healthy adulthood that is the norm in richer countries. Morbidity data, reflecting the prevalence of debilitating but not life-threatening disease or malnutrition, which is the norm for many in developing countries (Hull and Jones 1986), might reduce this sense of contrast between states of health and illness.

Finally, the assumption that degenerative disease creates longer dying trajectories might be questioned if comparative data were available. This may be obviously true if the point of comparison is with cholera, pneumonia, or trauma, but tuberculosis and AIDS both cause considerable long-term debilitation, dependency, and symptoms, even in an environment that precipitates an earlier death from these causes in some countries. For example, Gilks et al. (1998) report a World Bank estimate that, on average, a Tanzanian adult with AIDS has 17 episodes of illness requiring more than 280 days of care; they point out the particular strain that such chronic illness places on poor families when the sufferer may be a parent with dependent children or other dependent relatives.

CARE OF DYING PEOPLE

Households and Family Structure

On the whole, sick people turn first to their families for help, so it is important to know about any factors that change the availability of such informal care. In developed countries, the aging of populations is generally accompanied by decreasing family size and a growing propensity of elderly people to live in households separate from their children. Because of gender differences in longevity and marriage patterns, this commonly leaves many elderly widows living alone toward the end of life, dependent on nonresident caregivers for assistance if they get sick. A notable exception to the trend toward living alone in old age is Japan, where, in spite of the high proportion of elderly people in the population, the proportion of elders who live alone is small. In the 1980s, for example, only 10% of Japanese age 65 and older lived alone in private households, compared with 30% in the United Kingdom, 31% in the United States, and 40% in Sweden (U.S. Congress 1993). Cultural preferences regarding appropriate family relationships lie behind the Japanese pattern and may well apply also in many less developed countries.

On the whole, data on the household structures of elderly people are unavailable for developing countries, but data on the extent of single-person households, a rough proxy indicator of the proportion of elderly living alone, are available for some. In Bangladesh, the Philippines, and Thailand, for example, single-person households are rare (generally less than 3% of all households) and their proportion has not increased over time (Young 1986). Remember, however, that in developing countries death is less confined to the older years, so a profile of elderly households is relevant to a smaller proportion of those needing care when dying. In developing countries, concerns about family care for the dying may be offset by concerns about care for the dependents of people who have died, something that has become less relevant in developed countries because of the demographic factors outlined, but also because of relatively sophisticated systems of social insurance that are unaffordable in developing countries. With the pattern of mortality from AIDS in Africa, this has been a particularly pressing concern; as the number of orphans increases, these children are experiencing various forms of social and educational deprivation and abuse as a result of the lack of adults to care for them (UNAIDS 1998a, 2002).

U.K. data on elderly households show trends over time that follow a pattern similar to that seen in the few other countries where such data are available (for example, Australia, Canada, Japan, and the United States; see Young 1986). In 1996–97, 15% of households in the United Kingdom consisted of a single person above pensionable age living alone; in 1961, this figure was only 7% (Office for National Statistics 1998b). At the more recent date, approximately four times as many elderly women as elderly men lived alone. The 1996 GHS found that 87% of people age 65 and over were living either alone or with only a spouse (Office for National Statistics 1998a); this proportion has also been steadily increasing over time (Grundy 1996). Grundy (1996) also reports surveys showing reductions since 1962 in the proportion of elderly parents with at least one child living within 10–15 minutes' travel. These changes have had significant consequences in terms of the sources of informal help and care that people can draw upon as they approach death. A 1987 survey of the last year of life found that people living alone were in a particularly unfortunate situation concerning potential sources of help. They were the least likely to have any children or siblings alive and were most likely to be widowed or divorced and old; they were also the group most likely to progress to institutional care (Seale and Cartwright 1994).

Institutional Care and Place of Death

The widespread trend toward institutional care for elderly people is very much a phenomenon of developed countries, adopted as a solution to the shortage of informal care available in families. This shortage of available family care has been caused both by demographic factors and by features of the social organization of advanced industrialized societies that often separate elderly people from mainstream social and family life. The Japanese example suggests that demographic pressures alone are inadequate to explain the growth of institutional care, for in Japan relatively low proportions of the elderly are in institutions in spite of the country's large numbers of elderly people. In the early 1980s, for example, 4% of the Japanese population age 65 and over lived in institutions, compared with 6% in the United States and 11% in the Netherlands (U.S. Congress 1993). Data from Australia, Canada, the United Kingdom, and the United States show that the elderly living in institutions are predominantly female (Arber and Ginn 1991; Young 1986).

Although most people who enter residential institutions for the elderly will eventually die there, these are not generally perceived as places primarily devoted to the care of "dying" people. That is more normally the perception of hospices, although caring for "the dying" is also seen as a legitimate part of general hospital care. A large proportion of people in developed societies die in hospitals, rather than at home or, indeed, in hospices. Table 4 shows the proportions of deaths that occur in hospitals for selected countries. Data on place of death are available only for countries where statistical surveillance is well developed, which means that countries with high proportions of

such deaths tend to keep track of the figures. Nationally representative figures for African countries, for example, are unavailable. Such countries are likely to show marked rural/urban differences in the proportions of hospital deaths, and overall the proportion is likely to be low.

In countries with high rates of deaths occurring in hospitals, the rates have been rising steadily for many years. In 1960, for example, only 50% of people in England and Wales died in hospitals (General Register Office 1962), compared with the 66% shown in Table 4 for the United Kingdom as a whole in 1996. However, there are indications that the trend toward hospital deaths tends to level off once figures of 60–70% are reached (Brameld et al. 1998; Hunt et al. 1991). This is partly because there is a residual core of sudden deaths, but also because deaths in other institutions, such as residential homes and hospices, increase; in addition, there is often an increase in the successful provision of supportive community care for those who wish to die at home, something that in some countries may be determined by the ability to pay for such care (Dudgeon and Kristjanson 1995).

It has become part of the professional ethic of specialists in terminal care that a supported death at home is generally preferable to a death in hospital, and much of the effort of community hospice services is devoted to achieving this outcome. Researchers have noted the effects of community care and specialist hospice provision on place-of-death figures in the United States (Pritchard et al. 1998) and in that country specifically in relation to AIDS deaths, where hospital deaths have declined for whites, gay men, and men in general, although not for injecting drug users or children (Kelly et al. 1993). Studies in Sweden (Andershed and Ternestedt 1997) and Australia (Hunt et al. 1993; Hunt and McCaul 1998) have recorded shifts toward hospice as a place of death in recent years. Research in the United States (Stearns et al. 1996) and Australia (Brameld et al. 1998; Hunt et al. 1993) has found that people in their 80s and above have lower rates of hospital care, or of death in hospital, than do the "younger" elderly. This is largely due to alternative institutional provision in these countries rather than a greater proportion of home deaths. A pattern of frequent, short, nonterminal stays in the hospital in the last year of life may also develop in such countries (Brameld et al. 1998).

In a review article, Grande, Addington-Hall, and Todd (1998) note many of these features and make the additional point that gender makes a difference in all of this, given that, for the reasons outlined earlier, women in these countries tend to be disadvantaged in their ability to draw on informal family care as they approach death and are therefore less likely to die at home. Significantly, Grande et al.'s review covers 12 U.S. papers, 14 Australian, 10 Italian, 3 Swedish, and 1 each from Switzerland, Israel, and Canada. Place of death is not a topic that has been studied systematically outside developed countries.

In several Anglophone countries, but particularly the United Kingdom and the United States, a critique of the quality of care for the terminally ill arose in the 1950s and

Table 4	Proportion of Deaths Occurring in Hospitals for Selected Countries, 1996
Country	*Proportion of Deaths (%)*
Romania	18
Republic of Korea	23
Soviet Union[a]	24
Spain	30
Italy	37
Poland	47
France	50
United States	60
United Kingdom	66
Japan	67
Canada	73
Sweden	79

SOURCE: WHO (1988, 1998b).

a. 1988 data.

1960s, fueled by a general readiness to question scientific and professional authority and by widespread concerns about rights to individual autonomy in the face of institutional power (reflected also in critiques of institutions for the mentally ill, for example). The institutionalization and apparent medicalization of care for the dying were criticized for their dehumanizing emphasis on curative efforts at the expense of palliative care, and place-of-death statistics became a symbol around which these dissatisfactions coalesced.

Health Care Systems

Care specifically aimed at dying people and their families in developed countries has been marked in recent decades by the rise of the hospice movement and, most recently, the development of palliative care as a medical and nursing specialty (for details on the spread and character of this movement, see Seale 1998; Clark, Hockley, and Ahmedzai 1997). In addition to imparting a new vigor to strictly medical efforts to palliate the symptoms of terminal illnesses (chiefly cancer, but also motor neurone disease and AIDS), this movement has stimulated a concern with the psychosocial well-being of patients and their families that has led to an extension of traditional medical expertise. Nurses, by successfully claiming particular psychosocial skills, have gained a significant degree of autonomy from medical dominance in this arena of health care, assisted also by the formation of community support teams to advise lay caregivers in their homes. More recently, some have asserted that the palliative care approach is relevant to preterminal phases of terminal disease (Doyle 1996) or to additional diseases such as stroke, heart disease, and dementia, or could be applied in the context of nursing home care (Field and Addington-Hall 1999; Clark et al. 1997). To express such ambitions, however, is not to underestimate the palliative components that already exist in the health care specialties that serve these groups.

The appeal of hospice and palliative care in developed countries can be understood within a broader cultural context. The tendency to plan for and control major life events is already an important feature of self-identity in late-modern societies (Giddens 1991), although it is particularly concentrated among more educated groups and may be stronger in Anglophone countries than elsewhere (Seale 1998). Life planning, saving, taking out insurance against sickness as well as death (Benjamin 1986), and investing in schooling or training can all be engaged in with more confidence if mortality is predictably placed at the end of the life course (Chernichovsky 1986). Gradually, dying too becomes subject to this wish for control, and hospice and palliative care practitioners provide a relevant expertise to assist this. Comparison of cancer deaths in hospitals and hospices has revealed the relative success of hospice patients in planning the manner of their deaths, with hospitals showing higher proportions of deaths resulting from unplanned, emergency admissions (Seale and Kelly 1997). The shift in professional attitudes and practices toward open disclosure

of prognosis that has occurred in developed Anglophone countries (Novack et al. 1979; Seale and Cartwright 1994) has served to promote patients' desire for control while additionally opening up a new arena for psychosocial expertise (Kübler-Ross 1969).

The rising support in many developed countries for euthanasia, as an alternative means to relieve suffering and dependency toward the end of life and to control the manner and timing of death, is a reflection of similar forces (for a review of the literature on this subject, see Seale 1997). Although the hospice and euthanasia movements clash at the level of public debate because of religious differences, for individual patients they offer very similar opportunities for control and self-direction near death (Seale, Addington-Hall, and McCarthy 1997). Significantly, calls for medically assisted euthanasia are not heard in developing countries, where the suffering of dying people is of a different nature, but nevertheless considerable and in some cases occurs over lengthy periods (as noted earlier). The desire for medical assistance in this may also, paradoxically, reflect a general dependency on medically delivered solutions to suffering, which are not shared in developing countries. Justice (1995), for example, describes a culturally sanctioned method of fasting to death in Banares, India, where there is no medical involvement.

There is evidence to suggest that the largely Anglophone phenomena of hospice or palliative care and support for euthanasia are somewhat alien to the cultures of some developed countries. The cases of Japan and, to a lesser extent, Italy are relevant here. Important underlying factors seem to include respect for the traditional authority of the medical profession coupled with relatively strong religious observance, as well as a lesser emphasis on individual autonomy and greater reliance on intrafamilial support during disruptive life events. Studies suggest that the Anglo-American practices of informing most patients with cancer of their disease, of stressing the benefits and opportunities of open awareness of dying, and of involving patients rather than their families in decision making would be culturally inappropriate in countries such as Japan and Italy (Long and Long 1982; Kai et al. 1993; Surbone 1992; Gordon 1990). Japanese prohibitions against organ transplantation (Lock 1995) arise from religious considerations that may also explain the absence of a significant movement to support euthanasia. Nevertheless, Anglophone models of palliative care are increasingly spreading to European and other non-Anglophone developed countries. This is particularly marked in Eastern Europe, where the changes of political climate have led to a host of initiatives to relieve terminal suffering (Luczak 1997).

Where resources support the provision of specialist services for dying people, then, awareness of cultural differences can help practitioners to determine the appropriate form of such services. In developing countries there is the additional factor of scarce resources to consider. In practice, most debate about health care in developing countries is confined to concerns with the appropriate balance between prevention and cure, or between hospital and community services (Okolski 1986; Northrup 1986; Hull and Jones 1986); issues of palliative and terminal care, which might be considered luxuries affordable by richer countries, are rarely addressed. People in developing countries may see the involvement of religious authorities in issues of dying as more appropriate than the involvement of health services. Nevertheless, examples do exist. Western-style hospice care has developed in certain cities in India, for example, although access to such care tends to be confined to wealthier clients, and such initiatives have had to struggle against entrenched professional attitudes and working practices that are reminiscent of the situation 50 years ago in U.K. and U.S. health care (Burn 1997). The 11 cancer centers in India reach less than 10% of terminally ill cancer patients, and only 16,000 of the estimated 350,000 people with cancer pain are treated for their pain each year (Stjernsward 1997). Medical initiatives coexist with models of palliative care for the poor that draw more on religious traditions than on medicine, as seen in Mother Teresa's work.

Community palliative care initiatives in developing countries are likely to be funded at low levels and may focus on relieving the social care needs that arise from extreme poverty exacerbated by illness rather than on relieving medical conditions. This has been the experience of community initiatives in relation to AIDS care in some African countries (WHO 1994) and particularly Uganda (Gilks et al. 1998), which have attended to medical and nursing aspects of terminal AIDS care only insofar as this has been affordable. In relation to palliative cancer care, sub-Saharan Africa "remains isolated from hospice knowledge" according to Hockley (1997), with the exception of South Africa and Zimbabwe, where there are nascent hospice movements. Where palliative care initiatives exist in developing countries, they must deal with a variety of problems, including "an inadequate public health infrastructure, poor administrative systems, the lack of oral morphine and restrictions on opioid prescribing, the general poverty of patients, and poor educational opportunities for health professionals" (Haber 1999:1303).

The World Health Organization's Cancer Pain and Palliative Care Program represents a pragmatic approach to the difficulties of providing palliative care in developing countries, where a combination of poverty and cultural differences militate against the wholesale application of Western models. By prioritizing pain relief as an essential core component of a global campaign, WHO initiatives are able to concentrate on removing obstacles to the availability of opioids and promoting a low-cost approach to relieving this core distressing symptom of terminal disease (Stjernsward 1997).

CONCLUSION

A number of issues arise from this review that are important if we are to understand the implications of changing causes of death and life expectancies for the future experience of dying. I have described the aging of populations worldwide and have pointed out the consequences this can have for availability of care for elderly people toward the end of life, in both developed and developing countries. Gender differences in longevity, social status, and living arrangements have implications for the experience of old age and the availability of care toward the end of life, and these differ internationally. The experiences of dying people merge with the more general experience of old age in countries that have experienced the demographic transition. This may have consequences for the relationship between services specializing in the care of dying people and services specializing in the care of elderly people.

Different patterns of life expectancy and disease burden around the world require us, too, to question the extent to which Western models of terminal and palliative care are applicable in developing countries. The care needs and dying trajectories of diseases commonly causing death in developing countries may be rare in other countries and may not be of the sort that are appropriately met through existing models of palliative care. Even if applicable, should such services attract resources in poorer countries with high levels of preventable disease? Considering richer, developed countries, there is evidence that in some there are cultures and communication practices between health care workers and their clients that are at variance with those in which palliative care originally developed.

The sudden, perhaps temporary, declines in life expectancy that have been seen in some Eastern European countries suggest that we should exercise caution in assuming that in the future there will be a general passage of all countries through the demographic and epidemiological transitions experienced by richer countries of the world. In particular, the spread of AIDS and its impact on populations in Africa and some other regions where governments have been slow to implement preventive measures and are too poor to afford drug therapies will continue for some decades to come. This disease has a somewhat unpredictable future trajectory, but it is already clear that it has a very considerable impact on the experience of dying, on the lives of survivors, and on the economies of the countries worst affected.

REFERENCES

Addington-Hall, J. M. 1996. "Heart Disease and Stroke: Lessons From Cancer Care. Pp. 25–32 in *Managing Terminal Illness,* edited by G. Ford and I. Lewin. London: Royal College of Physicians.

Addington-Hall, J. M., D. Altmann, and M. McCarthy. 1998. "Variations by Age in Symptoms and Dependency Levels Experienced by People in the Last Year of Life, as Reported by Surviving Family, Friends and Officials." *Age and Ageing* 27:129–36.

Addington-Hall, J. M. and M. McCarthy. 1995. "Dying From Cancer: Results of a National Population-Based Investigation." *Palliative Medicine* 9:295–305.

Andershed, B. and B. M. Ternestedt. 1997. "Patterns of Care for Patients With Cancer Before and After the Establishment of a Hospice Ward." *Scandinavian Journal of Caring Sciences* 11:42–50.

Arber, S. and J. Ginn. 1991. *Gender and Later Life: A Sociological Analysis of Resources and Constraints.* London: Sage.

Benjamin, B. 1986. "Implications of Levels and Differentials in Mortality and Morbidity for Insurance and Pension Schemes." Pp. 165–74 in *Consequences of Mortality Trends and Differentials,* edited by United Nations. New York: United Nations.

Bickel, H. 1998. "The Last Year of Life: A Population-Based Study on Decedents. I. Living Arrangements, Place of Death, and Utilization of Care." *Zeitschrift für Gerontologie und Geriatrie* 31:193–204.

Brameld, K. J., C. D'Arcy, C. D. J. Holman, A. J. Bass, J. P. Codde, and I. L. Rouse. 1998. "Hospitalisation of the Elderly During the Last Year of Life: An Application of Record Linkage in Western Australia 1985–1994." *Journal of Epidemiology and Community Health* 52:740–44.

Burn, J. 1997. "Palliative Care in India." Pp. 116–28 in *New Themes in Palliative Care,* edited by D. Clark, J. Hockley, and S. Ahmedzai. Buckingham: Open University Press.

Cartwright, A., L. Hockey, and J. L. Anderson. 1973. *Life Before Death.* London: Routledge & Kegan Paul.

Chernichovsky, D. 1986. "Interactions Between Mortality Levels and the Allocation of Time for Leisure, Training, Consumption and Saving Over the Life Cycle." Pp. 126–31 in *Consequences of Mortality Trends and Differentials,* edited by United Nations. New York: United Nations.

Clark, D., J. Hockley, and S. Ahmedzai, eds. 1997. *New Themes in Palliative Care.* Buckingham: Open University Press.

Culler, S. D., C. M. Callahan, and F. D. Wolinsky. 1995. "Predicting Hospital Costs Among Older Decedents Over Time." *Medical Care* 33:1089–1105.

Dolea, C., E. Nolte, and M. McKee. 2002. "Changing Life Expectancy in Romania After the Transition." *Journal of Epidemiology and Community Health* 56:444–49.

Doyle, D. 1996. *Dilemmas and Directions: The Future of Specialist Palliative Care.* London: National Council for Hospice and Specialist Palliative Care Services.

Dudgeon, D. G. and L. Kristjanson. 1995. "Home Versus Hospital Death: Assessment of Preferences and Clinical Challenges." *Canadian Medical Association Journal* 152:337–40.

Eurostat. 1997. *Demographic Statistics 1997.* Luxembourg: Office for Official Publications of the European Communities.

Experton, B., R. J. Ozminkowski, L. G. Branch, and Z. L. Li. 1996. "A Comparison by Payer/Provider Type of the Cost of Dying Among Frail Older Adults." *Journal of the American Geriatrics Society* 44:1098–1107.

Felder, S. 1997. "Costs of Dying: Alternatives to Rationing." *Health Policy* 39:167–76.

Feldman, J. J. 1986. "Work Ability of the Aged Under Conditions of Improving Mortality." Pp. 185–91 in *Consequences of Mortality Trends and Differentials,* edited by United Nations. New York: United Nations.

Field, D. and J. M. Addington-Hall. 1999. "Extending Specialist Palliative Care to All?" *Social Science and Medicine* 48:1271–80.

General Register Office. 1962. *The Registrar General's Statistical Review of England and Wales for the Year 1960,* Part III, *Commentary.* London: Her Majesty's Stationery Office.

Giddens, A. 1991. *Modernity and Self-Identity: Self and Society in the Late Modern Age.* Cambridge: Polity.

Gilks, C., K. Floyd, D. Haran, J. Kemp, B. Squire, and D. Wilkinson. 1998. "Sexual Health and Health Care: Care and Support for People With HIV/AIDS in Resource-Poor Settings." Health and Population Occasional Paper, Department for International Development, London.

Gordon, D. R. 1990. "Embodying Illness, Embodying Cancer." *Culture, Medicine and Psychiatry* 14:275–97.

Grande, G. E., J. M. Addington-Hall, and C. J. Todd. 1998. "Place of Death and Access to Home Care Services: Are Certain Patients Groups at a Disadvantage?" *Social Science and Medicine* 47:565–79.

Gray, A. 1993. *World Health and Disease.* Buckingham: Open University Press.

Grundy, E. 1996. "Population Review (5): The Population Aged 60 and Over." *Population Trends* 84:14–20.

Guralnik, J. M., J. L. Balfour, and S. Volpato. 2000. "The Ratio of Older Women to Men: Historical Perspectives and Cross-National Comparisons." *Aging—Clinical and Experimental Research* 12:65–76.

Haber, D. 1999. Review of *New Themes in Palliative Care. Social Science and Medicine* 48:1301–3.

Hayase, Y. and S. Kawamata. 1991. *Population Policy and Vital Statistics in China.* Tokyo: Institute of Developing Economies.

Heuveline, P., M. Guilot, and D. R. Gwatkin. 2002. "The Uneven Tides of the Health Transition." *Social Science and Medicine* 55:313–22.

Hockley, J. 1997. "The Evolution of the Hospice Approach." Pp. 84–100 in *New Themes in Palliative Care,* edited by D. Clark, J. Hockley, and S. Ahmedzai. Buckingham: Open University Press.

Hossain, M. R. 1999. "Population Aging in Bangladesh and Its Perspectives." *Man in India* 79(1–2):111–22.

Hull, T. H. and G. W. Jones. 1986. "Introduction: International Mortality Trends and Differentials." Pp. 1–9 in *Consequences of Mortality Trends and Differentials,* edited by United Nations. New York: United Nations.

Hunt, R. W., M. J. Bond, R. K. Broth, and P. M. King. 1991. "Place of Death in South Australia: Patterns From 1910 to 1987." *Medical Journal of Australia* 155:549–53.

Hunt, R. W., A. Bonett, and D. Roder. 1993. "Trends in the Terminal Care of Cancer Patients: South Australia, 1981–1990." *Australian and New Zealand Journal of Medicine* 23:245–51.

Hunt, R. W. and K. McCaul. 1998. "Coverage of Cancer Patients by Hospice Services, South Australia, 1990 to 1993." *Australian and New Zealand Journal of Public Health* 22:45–48.

Jamison, D. T., J. R. Evans, T. King, I. Porter, N. Prescott, and A. Prost. 1984. *China: The Health Sector.* Washington, DC: World Bank.

Justice, C. 1995. "The 'Natural' Death While Not Eating: A Type of Palliative Care in Banaras, India." *Journal of Palliative Care* 11:38–42.

Kai, I., G. Ohi, E. Yano, Y. Kobayashi, T. Miyama, N. Niino, and K. Naka. 1993. "Communication Between Patients and

Physicians About Terminal Care: A Survey in Japan." *Social Science and Medicine* 36:1151–59.

Karlsen, S. and J. M. Addington-Hall. 1998. "How Do Cancer Patients Who Die at Home Differ From Those Who Die Elsewhere?" *Palliative Medicine* 12:279–86.

Kelly, J. J., S. Y. Chu, J. W. Buehler, D. Boyd, J. Singleton, L. Lieb, A. Hirozawa, B. Dahan, L. Conti, G. Beckett, J. Bareta, C. Wold, J. Letourneau, T. Baumgartner, J. Baldwin, K. Edge, E. J. Fordyce, M. L. Deciantis, and A. Shields. 1993. "AIDS Deaths Shift From Hospital to Home." *American Journal of Public Health* 83:1433–37.

Kübler-Ross, E. 1969. *On Death and Dying.* New York: Macmillan.

Lock, M. 1995. "Contesting the Natural in Japan: Moral Dilemmas and Technologies of Dying." *Culture, Medicine and Psychiatry* 19:1–38.

Lofland, J. 1978. *The Craft of Dying: The Modern Face of Death.* Thousand Oaks, CA: Sage.

Long, S. O. and B. D. Long. 1982. "Curable Cancers and Fatal Ulcers: Attitudes Toward Cancer in Japan." *Social Science and Medicine* 16:2101–8.

Luczak, J. 1997. "Palliative Care in Eastern Europe." Pp. 170–94 in *New Themes in Palliative Care,* edited by D. Clark, J. Hockley, and S. Ahmedzai. Buckingham: Open University Press.

Markson, E. W. 1995. "To Be or Not to Be: Assisted Suicide Revisited." *Omega* 31:221–35.

McNicoll, G. 1986. "Adaptation of Social Systems to Changing Mortality Regimes." Pp. 13–19 in *Consequences of Mortality Trends and Differentials,* edited by United Nations. New York: United Nations.

Northrup, R. S. 1986. "Decision Making for Health Care in Developing Countries." Pp. 135–49 in *Consequences of Mortality Trends and Differentials,* edited by United Nations. New York: United Nations.

Novack, D. H., R. Plumer, R. L. Smith, H. Ochitill, G. R. Morrow, and J. M. Bennett. 1979. "Changes in Physicians' Attitudes Toward Telling the Cancer Patient." *Journal of the American Medical Association* 241:897–900.

Nunn, A. J., D. W. Mulder, A. Kamali, A. Ruberantwari, J.-F. Kengeya-Kayondo, and J. Whitworth. 1997. "Mortality Associated With HIV-1 Infection Over Five Years in a Rural Ugandan Population: Cohort Study." *British Medical Journal* 315:767–71.

Office for National Statistics. 1998a. *Living in Britain: Results From the 1996 General Household Survey.* London: Her Majesty's Stationery Office.

———. 1998b. *Social Trends 28.* London: Her Majesty's Stationery Office.

Ogawa, N. 1986. "Consequences of Mortality Change on Aging." Pp. 175–84 in *Consequences of Mortality Trends and Differentials,* edited by United Nations. New York: United Nations.

Okolski, M. 1986. "Relationship Between Mortality and Morbidity Levels According to Age and Sex and Their Implications for Organizing Health Care Systems in Developed Countries." Pp. 150–64 in *Consequences of Mortality Trends and Differentials,* edited by United Nations. New York: United Nations.

Pearce, D., T. Griffin, J. Kelly, and L. Mikkelsen. 1997. "An Overview of the Population in Europe and North America." *Population Trends* 89:24–36.

Pritchard, R. S., E. S. Fisher, J. M. Teno, S. M. Sharp, D. J. Reding, W. A. Knaus, J. E. Wennberg, and J. Lynn. 1998. "Influence of Patient Preferences and Local Health System Characteristics on the Place of Death." *Journal of the American Geriatrics Society* 46:1242–50.

Seale, C. F. 1997. "Social and Ethical Aspects of Euthanasia: A Review." *Progress in Palliative Care* 5:141–46.

———. 1998. *Constructing Death: The Sociology of Dying and Bereavement.* Cambridge: Cambridge University Press.

Seale, C. F. and J. M. Addington-Hall. 1995. "Dying at the Best Time." *Social Science and Medicine* 40:589–95.

Seale, C. F., J. M. Addington-Hall, and M. McCarthy. 1997. "Awareness of Dying: Prevalence, Causes and Consequences." *Social Science and Medicine* 45:477–84.

Seale, C. F. and A. Cartwright. 1994. *The Year Before Death.* Aldershot: Avebury.

Seale, C. F. and M. Kelly. 1997. "A Comparison of Hospice and Hospital Care for People Who Die: Views of Surviving Spouse." *Palliative Medicine* 11:93–100

Shkolnikov, L., M. McKee, and D. A. Leon. 2001. "Changes in Life Expectancy in Russia in the Mid-1990s." *Lancet* 357:917–21.

Sims, R. and V. Moss. 1991. *Terminal Care for People With AIDS.* London: Edward Arnold.

Stearns, S. C., M. G. Kovar, K. Hayes, and G. G. Koch. 1996. "Risk Indicators for Hospitalization During the Last Year of Life." *Health Services Research* 31:49–69.

Stjernsward, J. 1997. "The WHO Cancer Pain and Palliative Care Programme." Pp. 203–12 in *New Themes in Palliative Care,* edited by D. Clark, J. Hockley, and S. Ahmedzai. Buckingham: Open University Press.

Surbone, A. 1992. "Truth Telling to the Patient." *Journal of the American Medical Association* 268:1661–62.

Tanzania Ministry of Health. 1997. *Policy Implications of Adult Morbidity and Mortality* (End of Phase 1 Report). Dar es Salaam: Tanzania Ministry of Health.

Townsend, P. and N. Davidson. 1982. *The Black Report.* Harmondsworth: Penguin.

U.S. Congress, Office of Technology Assessment. 1993. *International Health Statistics: What the Numbers Mean for the United States.* Washington, DC: Government Printing Office.

UNAIDS. 1998a. *AIDS Epidemic Update: December 1998.* Geneva: UNAIDS/World Health Organization.

———. 1998b. *HIV-Related Opportunistic Diseases* (UNAIDS Technical Update). Geneva: UNAIDS.

———. 2002. *Fighting AIDS: A New Global Perspective.* Geneva: UNAIDS.

Ware, H. 1986. "Differential Mortality Decline and Its Consequences for the Status and Roles of Women." Pp. 113–25 in *Consequences of Mortality Trends and Differentials,* edited by United Nations. New York: United Nations.

Whitehead, M. and F. Diderischen. 1997. "International Evidence on Social Inequalities in Health." Pp. 44–68 in *Health Inequalities,* edited by K. Drever and M. Whitehead. London: Her Majesty's Stationery Office.

Wilkinson, R. 1996. *Unhealthy Societies: The Afflictions of Inequality.* London: Routledge.

World Health Organization. 1988. *World Health Statistics.* Geneva: World Health Organization.

World Health Organization. 1994. *AIDS: Images of the Epidemic.* Geneva: World Health Organization.

———. 1998a. *World Health Report.* Geneva: World Health Organization.

———. 1998b. *World Health Statistics.* Geneva: World Health Organization.

———. 2000. "WHO Issues New Healthy Life Expectancy Rankings: Japan Number One in New 'Healthy Life' System." Press release, June 4. Retrieved April 8, 2003 (http://www.who.int/inf-pr-2000/en/pr2000–life.html).

Young, C. M. 1986. "The Residential Life-Cycle: Mortality and Morbidity Effects on Living Arrangements." Pp. 101–12 in *Consequences of Mortality Trends and Differentials,* edited by United Nations. New York: United Nations.

To Die, by Mistake: Accidental Deaths

Lee Garth Vigilant

John B. Williamson

Accidents will happen.

—Elvis Costello

On the evening of October 2, 1996, an AeroPeru Boeing 757, Flight 603, with 61 passengers and 9 crew members aboard, took off from Lima, Peru. Flight 603, however, did not make it to its final destination in Santiago, Chile. In fact, the aircraft and its passengers were doomed from the very moment of takeoff. Earlier that day, the airline's maintenance crew had taped over the plane's left-side static ports while they washed the fuselage of the plane, and, by mistake, they had failed to remove the protective covering after they were through. This seemingly insignificant oversight was actually a dangerous blunder, because with the plane's static ports covered, the flight crew would be flying without essential information, such as altitude, wind speed, and temperature. From the moment of takeoff, the plane's instruments were communicating the wrong airspeed and altitude, and, because Flight 603 was a night flight, the pilot and copilot were indeed "flying blind." When the instruments falsely indicated excessive speed, the crew slowed the plane to a near stall, and when the altimeter falsely indicated that the plane's altitude was too high, the crew compensated by dropping the elevation to a perilously low level. For nearly 30 minutes, as the cockpit voice recordings of Flight 603 indicate, the pilot and copilot struggled to make sense of the erroneous information the instruments were communicating (MacPherson 1998). Eventually, Flight 603 crashed into the ocean at more than 300 miles per hour, killing everyone on board. At impact, the plane's altimeter read an altitude of 9,700 feet (MacPherson 1998).

This air disaster, and the 70 accidental deaths that resulted, was most certainly preventable. The flight crew should have caught the maintenance crew's mistake during the visual check, the so-called walk-around, that the pilot and copilot perform as part of their preflight ritual. That we refer to this tragic event as an *accident,* and the resultant deaths as *accidental,* is particularly telling, especially given our knowledge of the determining cause.

By definition, accidental deaths are usually unforeseen, violent, and unexpected. Such deaths are unintended, the result of chance, and culpability is not a matter of simple assignment. But what does it mean to label a death an "accident," really? Are there situational characteristics that are common to all accidental deaths? The problem of labeling any death an "accident" begins with the very implications that the word *accident* imbues. If the standard criterion for an accidental death is *lack of intentionality,* how is that to be determined after the fact? In essence, the ex post facto assumptions surrounding accidental mortality are always the same, irrespective of circumstance: (a) that the deceased did not want to die, (b) that the deceased did not intentionally bring death upon him- or herself, and, ultimately, (c) that the deceased may bear little if any responsibility for his or her own death and the deaths of others involved in the incident. These assumptions raise important thanatological questions for the very meaning of the word *accident* and its application to accidental mortality, questions that we address in this chapter.

We consider here several issues in the discourse on accidental mortality. We begin with an analysis of the various meanings and problematics of the phrase *accidental death.* We then consider the occurrence and causes of some of the major accidental death categories in the United States, before turning to an overview of the problem of labeling accidental deaths and special consideration of the notion of subintentional mortality. We conclude with a brief discussion of bereavement and grief recovery in the case of accidental death.

WHAT IS AN ACCIDENTAL DEATH?

If we label all of life's unpleasant events as accidents, then we come to perceive ourselves as the playthings of fate and we cultivate a philosophy of carelessness and irresponsibility.

—John J. Brownfain, "When Is an Accident Not an Accident?" 1962

When we refer to tragedies such as that of Flight 603 as accidents, we mean to imply that these were unintentional occurrences. Accidental deaths occur by chance, without intention or design, and are unexpected and unusual (DeCicco 1985:141). Accidents and accidental deaths are nondeliberate, unplanned, and undesirable occurrences. Yet we are less than precise, both legally and connotatively, when we employ the terms *accident* and *accidental death* to describe all situational outcomes that lack intentionality (Bennett 1987; Suchman 1961). For one thing, the term *accident* conjures the idea that the occurrence of death was unavoidable (Kastenbaum 2001), even if, as in the case of Flight 603, it was the result of human incompetence and error. For another, the very idea of an "accidental death" is troubling both legally and philosophically: In legal terms, it makes us less accountable for the culpability of our actions and choices when serious injuries and death are the end result; philosophically, it involves a certain level of "bad faith" (Sartre 1956), because by reducing death to fate and chance, individuals can deny any responsibility for the final outcomes of their choices and actions (Brownfain 1962, as cited in Thygerson 1977). We too often apply the label of "accidental death" to outcomes that were completely preventable, if not expected, and this is certainly the case with autocide and subintentional suicide (Tabachnick 1973).

Recognizing the verbal and conceptual slippage common to the application of the concepts of "accident" and "accidental death," the medical sociologist Edward Suchman (1961) has sought to tighten the definitions of these labels even further. Suchman asserts that in deciding whether to label an event "accidental," we should examine three particular conditions: (a) the degree of expectedness (Was the event unanticipated?), (b) the degree of avoidability (Could the event have been prevented?), and (c) the degree of intentionality (Was the outcome intended?) (p. 244). However, Suchman extends these conditions by outlining what he calls the "antecedents" or "symptoms" of accidents to constrict further the usage and application of the term *accident*. In determining whether an event might be considered an accident after it has met the aforementioned criteria, Suchman suggests, we should look at four additional factors: (a) the degree of warning (the less forewarning, the greater the likelihood of an accidental occurrence), (b) the duration of occurrence (the more quickly a phenomenon occurs, the more likely it is to be labeled an accident, because greater speed of occurrence

reduces the likelihood and degree of control), (c) the degree of negligence (the more recklessness associated with the event, the less likely it is to be labeled an accident), and (d) the degree of misjudgment (the more misjudgments, the less likely the outcome is to be labeled an accident).

If we were to apply Suchman's rules to the tragic example of Flight 603, the question of whether this event was an accident would undoubtedly be cause for debate. Certainly, the parameters of expectedness and intentionality are satisfied: No one expected, or intentionally planned, the tragic outcome that befell Flight 603. However, a close examination of the events of the day and of the cockpit voice recordings suggests some serious shortfalls. With regard to *avoidability,* this incident was completely preventable. Human error and oversight caused the crash of Flight 603. In addition to the inexcusable error of the maintenance crew, the flight crew neglected a crucial warning during the takeoff procedure. The first indication that something was wrong with the plane's altimeter came immediately after takeoff, and the copilot brought the problem to the attention of his captain at that time (MacPherson 1998). In terms of degree of warning, had the pilot simply made the decision then to return to the airport, events would not have unfolded as they did. Moreover, there were other misjudgments; for example, upon realizing that something was wrong with the instruments, the crew should have disengaged autopilot for the duration of the flight. Finally, in terms of negligence, or dereliction of duty, if the pilot and copilot had performed their prescribed preflight visual inspection, they would certainly have noticed the masking tape covering the plane's left-side static ports.

To refer to the crash of Flight 603 as "an accident" is to ignore many important details and to suggest that what happened was the result of fate or chance. As Kastenbaum (2001) so eloquently says:

> It is a dangerous misrepresentation to classify as accidents fatal events that were shaped by human error, indigence, and greed. "Accident" implies that nothing could have been done to prevent the loss of life—thereby contributing to lack of prevention in the future. (P. 239)

Fate did not cause the crash of Flight 603; human negligence, oversight, and misjudgment did. Yet we use the concept "accident" ineptly to describe incidents caused by human error even when science itself does not recognize chance or fate as the causes of social occurrences and "accidents" (Hacker and Suchman 1963). Perhaps the label "accident" offers a measure of consolation to survivors while simultaneously protecting the injured or deceased from any liability for what their errors have wrought. Perhaps the concept "accidental death" reminds us that we are not always in control of the outcomes or proceedings in our lives, and this, for many, is comforting. Whatever the rationale for applying the concept of "accident" or "accidental death" to social outcomes, this much is certain:

The label "accident" is an ex post facto admission of the built-in fallibility of human interactions and human choices. Nevertheless, this label often obscures the social antecedents that lead to death and serious injury: the human errors that account for 60% to 80% of all accidents (Perrow 1984). Thus, mindful of this phenomenon, in the next section we report not only on the epidemiology of accidental deaths but also on the causes of, and countermeasures taken to prevent, "accidental" mortality.

THE OCCURRENCE OF ACCIDENTAL DEATHS: CAUSES, SOLUTIONS, AND COUNTERMEASURES

Accidents have consistently ranked among the principal causes of death in the United States (see Table 1), yet, compared to the other leading causes of death for all age groups, such as heart disease, malignant neoplasms, and diabetes, accidental mortality receives scant attention. This might be due in part to the fact that "unintentional injury" statistics include many subcategories (see Table 2), but in any case, the impact of accidental deaths on society is undeniable. As Table 1 shows, in 2000 there were 93,592 unintentional deaths in the United States, making accidents the fifth leading cause of death and the leading cause of death for all Americans between the ages of 4 and 33 (Minino and Smith 2001). Moreover, accidental injuries and deaths place a tremendous strain on the nation's economy through wage and productivity losses, administrative expenses, medical costs, property damage costs, and employer overhead. The National Safety Council (2002) has estimated that in 2000, the average cost of a single traffic fatality was $1 million, the cost for each unintentional death in the home was $780,000, and the average cost of each work-related death was $980,000.

It is certainly not a stretch to say that accidental death is a major social problem, yet Americans in general do not perceive it as such. Most Americans, especially the young, continue to underestimate their risks of dying from accidental causes (Glik et al. 1999). Perhaps this is because of a certain sense of invincibility, or because of a perception that accidents are fateful events over which individuals have little or no control. Whatever the reason, Americans tend to see other causes of death as potentially much more likely to affect them than accidental causes.

Iatrogenic Mortality: Medical Mistakes and Accidental Deaths

The statistical picture of the occurrence of accidental deaths in the United States neglects an entire category of unintentional mortality: accidental deaths due to medical mistakes. Such deaths are a major social problem, yet they are only now coming to public attention and under the purview of political scrutiny. Although reported figures are much debated and disputed by some (e.g., Hayward and

Table 1	Leading Causes of Death in the United States, 2000	
Rank	*Cause of Death*	*Number of Deaths*
1	Heart disease	709,894
2	Malignant neoplasms	551,833
3	Cerebrovascular diseases	166,028
4	Chronic lower respiratory diseases	123,550
5	Accidents (unintentional injuries)	93,592
6	Diabetes mellitus	68,662
7	Influenza and pneumonia	67,024
8	Alzheimer's disease	49,044
9	Nephritis	31,613
10	Septicemia	31,613
11	Intentional self-harm (suicide)	28,332
12	Chronic liver disease	26,219
13	Hypertension and renal disease	17,964
14	Pneumonitis due to solids or liquids	16,659
15	Assault (homicide)	16,137

SOURCE: Minino and Smith (2001).

Hofer 2001; McDonald, Weiner, and Hui 2000; Leape 2000), iatrogenic mortality, or deaths caused by doctor mistakes, accounts for between 44,000 and 98,000 deaths per year in the United States, a problem of epidemic scale (see Kohn, Corrigan, and Donaldson 2000). Yet, to date, nowhere in the statistics on accidental deaths compiled by the Centers for Disease Control and Prevention (CDC) do we find a category called "accidental deaths due to medical mistakes" (see Table 2).

If there were a category for these accidental deaths, iatrogenic mortality would surpass all other accidental mortalities on the list, including deaths caused by automobile crashes. Moreover, as Kohn et al. (2000) suggest in a volume produced for the Institute of Medicine, iatrogenic mortality could easily be among the 10 leading causes of death, surpassing accidental deaths (42,000), breast cancer (43,000), and AIDS (16,000). Finally, this accidental mortality type is a very expensive burden on the economy, with yearly costs between $17 and $29 billion. Among the many recommendations that Kohn et al. make for reducing the incidence of iatrogenic mortality are the following:

1. The creation of research and pedagogical tools that might bring knowledge of this crisis to the medical forefront

2. The creation of mandatory and voluntary error-reporting systems

3. The raising of standards of care through the establishment of oversight organizations and professional groups

4. The instillment, at the delivery level, of a culture of safety among health care practitioners

Motor Vehicle Accidental Mortality

Table 2 outlines the subcategories of unintentional deaths in the United States for all ages, all races, and both sexes for the year 1999. What immediately stands out in these CDC data on accidental injuries is that motor vehicles were involved in an astonishing 42% of all accidental deaths in 1999—three times as many accidental deaths as the next category on the list, falls. Motor vehicle–related accidents account for a huge proportion of all accidents in the United States and a rapidly increasing proportion of accidents globally (Grant and McKinlay 1986; Nantulya and Reich 2002; Peden et al. 2001; Roberts, Mohan, and Abbasi 2002). The scope of the problem is immense: In the United States, there is a traffic fatality every 12 minutes and a disabling injury related to motor vehicles every 14 seconds, making motor vehicle accidents the leading cause of death and injury for the young, with the 15–24 age group most affected (National Safety Council 2002; Lang, Waller, and Shope 1996; Williams and Wells 1995). The National Highway Traffic Safety Administration (NHTSA 2001a) reports that, *on average,* about 115 persons die each day in motor vehicle accidents. Yet it is important to note that the fatality rate for motor vehicle accidents in the United States is currently at an all-time low and continues to decline, with the exceptions of alcohol-related and motorcycle crashes (NHTSA 2001a). Even so, the number of automobile deaths, approximately 40,000 yearly, is still high.

The demographic picture of automobile fatalities in 2000 shows that 68% of those who died were males; that 16- to 24-year-olds—the age group with the largest number of crashes—were 24% of fatalities; that the intoxication rates of male and female drivers who died in crashes were 20% and 11%, respectively; and that the rates of seat belt use for male and female drivers involved in fatal crashes were 43% and 29%, respectively (NHTSA 2001a). Some researchers have linked the pronounced difference between males and females in motor vehicle death rates to socialization, asserting that males are socialized to engage in more risky, health-endangering practices than are females (Lang et al. 1996; Veevers and Gee 1986; Vredenburgh and Cohen 1996) and have increased driving exposure (Farmer 1997; Massie, Campbell, and Williams 1995). In addition to gender differences, some studies have found a relationship between social class ranking and accidental mortality risk, with higher death rates among the poor for most categories of accidental death, including automobile accidents (Baker et al. 1992; Hippisley-Cox et al. 2002; Nantulya and Reich 2002). But what factors account for the high number of "accidental" motor vehicle deaths in the United States each year?

It was Herbert Heinrich (1959) who initially proposed that as much as 85% of all accidental injuries and deaths in industry may be attributed to "unsafe acts" by individuals, and only 15% to "unsafe conditions." This controversial statement started a long-standing debate—which is yet to be resolved fully—among safety management professionals (Hagglund 1980; Jeffries 1980). In hindsight, it seems that Heinrich should have applied his theory to automobile fatalities and injuries, and not to industrial accidents,

Rank	Cause of Death	Number of Deaths
1	Motor vehicle	40,965
2	Falls	13,162
3	Poisoning	12,186
4	Unspecified accidents	7,459
5	Suffocation	5,503
6	Drowning	3,529
7	Fire/burn	3,471
8	Natural/environment	1,923
9	Other land transport	1,867
10	Pedestrian	1,502
11	Other transport	1,408
12	Other specified causes, classified	1,310
13	Other specified causes, not elsewhere classified	955
14	Struck by or against	894
15	Firearm	824
16	Machinery	622
17	Pedal cyclist, other	185
18	Cut/pierce	74
19	Overexertion	21
Total		97,860

Table 2 Unintentional Injuries in the United States, 1999

SOURCE: Centers for Disease Control and Prevention (2002).

because a statistical breakdown of the causes of motor vehicle crashes shows three things that lend support to his initial conclusion: (a) Most such "accidents" are in fact avoidable, (b) most involve a great many misjudgments, and (c) many are the results of gross negligence or "unsafe acts."

Every automobile accident can be reduced to three possible causes: (a) environmental factors and driving conditions (i.e., weather and the state of the roadway), (b) automobile problems (which may be due to poor maintenance or equipment failure), and (c) problems with the driver (poor health, risky decision making, risky practices, and so on) (Haddon 1968; Haddon, Suchman, and Klein 1964; Tabachnick 1973). According to the NHTSA's (2001a) statistical portrayal of motor vehicle accidents in the United States in 2000, the vast majority of all traffic fatalities in that year were due to driving while intoxicated or driving at excessive speeds (40% and 29%, respectively). Thus we can conclude that gross negligence and unsafe acts on the part of drivers—namely, driving while intoxicated and speeding—account for the vast majority of traffic fatalities in the United States.

The link between alcohol consumption and traffic fatalities is unquestionable (Brewer et al. 1994; Haberman 1987; Winn and Giacopassi 1993). According to the National Highway Traffic Safety Administration (2001a), there is, on average, an alcohol-related traffic fatality every 32 minutes; such deaths make up about 40% of the total traffic fatalities yearly. More than 1.5 million Americans were arrested for driving under the influence in 1999

(NHTSA 2001a); such drivers are at substantially greater risk of dying in automobile crashes than are drivers who are not so impaired (Brewer et al. 1994). In fact, the NHTSA (2001a) notes that in 2000, "about 1,400 fatalities occurred in crashes involving an alcohol-impaired or intoxicated driver who had at least one previous DWI conviction" (p. 12); these deaths represented 8% of all alcohol-related fatalities. According to the NHTSA (2001a), 30% of Americans will be involved in alcohol-related "accidents" at some point in their lives.

Alcohol-related traffic deaths are not the sole purview of intoxicated automobile drivers; intoxicated bicycle and motorcycle riders have many fatal accidents as well. In a study that looked at 1,711 fatally injured bicyclists age 15 years and older who were tested for alcohol, Li and Baker (1995) found that an astonishing 32% were positive for alcohol at the time of their deaths, and 23% were legally intoxicated. Among fatally injured motorcyclists in the year 2000, 28% were intoxicated when they died (i.e., they had blood alcohol concentrations of greater than 0.10) (NHTSA 2001a; Shankar 2001).

Excessive speed is another risk factor that contributes to the roughly 40,000 traffic fatalities yearly. According to the NHTSA (2001a), in 2000 speeding was a factor in 29% of all traffic fatalities, contributing to the deaths of more than 12,000 individuals. The NHTSA places the economic costs of speeding-related accidents and fatalities at around $27.4 billion per year. Speeding is a risky behavior especially associated with younger male drivers—that is, those in the 15–24 age group. In 2000, 34% of male drivers ages 15 to 24 who were fatally injured in crashes were speeding (NHTSA 2001a). The problem of speeding is even more severe among motorcyclists. In 2000, there were 2,862 motorcycle fatalities, representing 7% of all traffic deaths; 38% of those deaths were attributed to excessive speeds (NHTSA 2001a). In fact, the NHTSA (2001a) reports that a motorcycle riders is 18 times as likely as a passenger in an automobile to die in a crash. Finally, it is important to note that intoxication and speeding go hand in hand. The NHTSA (2001a) reports that 40% of all alcohol-related traffic deaths in 2000 involved drivers who were speeding; only 13% of *sober* drivers killed in automobile crashes for the same period had been speeding.

The third risk factor associated with traffic fatalities is seat belt and child restraint usage—or, rather, the lack thereof. According to NHTSA (2001b) figures, seat belts have saved approximately 135,000 lives since 1975; they saved 11,889 lives in 2000 alone. The use of child restraints (specifically designed for children under 5 years old) has saved 4,816 lives during the same period, 316 lives in 2000. In fact, the NHTSA asserts that the use of safety belts could have saved *an additional* 9,238 lives in 2000. Moreover, in a recent study on the effectiveness of seat belt usage in preventing accidental deaths in children ages 4 through 14, Halman et al. (2002) found that in the front seat of a car, an unbelted child was nine times more likely to sustain a fatal injury than was a belted child; in the rear

seat, an unbelted child was twice as likely as a belted child to be fatally injured. Cummings et al. (2002) report that seat belt usage reduces the risk of accidental death in an automobile accident by 65%; that figure rises to 68% when seat belts are used in conjunction with air bags. These researchers also note that seat belts alone provide much greater protection against accidental deaths than do air bags alone; air bag use by itself provides only an 8% reduction in the likelihood of dying in a crash.

A final factor contributing to traffic fatalities is sleep deprivation (see Coren 1996a, 1996b, 1996c). Coren (1996c) estimates that sleep deprivation results in about 25,000 accidental deaths and 2.5 million disabling injuries each year in the United States. He notes that the impacts of sleep deprivation are most obvious during the shift to daylight savings time in the spring, when, as a nation, Americans lose an hour of sleep. In a study of traffic fatalities during the week following the shift to daylight savings time in the spring and the shift back to standard time in the fall, Coren (1996a) found a 6.5% short-term increase when daylight savings time began, but no measurable difference in fatalities when it ended.

What can society do to lower the number of automobile fatalities? This question is one that is growing in significance, not just in the United States, but around the globe. The World Health Organization estimates that by 2020, road traffic accidents will move from being the ninth leading cause of health care burden to the third leading cause, replacing such causes as HIV/AIDS, diarrheal diseases, war, and cerebrovascular disease (Peden et al. 2001). Currently, automobile crashes are the leading cause of injury deaths and the tenth leading cause of all deaths around the globe (Peden et al. 2001). Clearly, this social problem demands a treatment strategy with global reach.

Until now, the primary strategies that societies have employed to lower death rates from vehicular crashes have taken the forms of technological advances (safety restraints, air bags, and the like) and driver education. Although the employment of safety equipment has been particularly effective in reducing deaths from vehicular crashes, driver education has not. In fact, in a study of the effects of high school driver education, Vernick et al. (1999) found that such training did not reduce motor vehicle crash rates for young drivers. Rather, that early licensure, which is the goal of school-based driver education courses, was actually associated with increased risk of crash involvement. Vernick et al. suggest that society should look to other treatment strategies for reducing traffic death rates.

To date, the best treatment strategy has been the enforcement of traffic laws, because, at the end of the day, people continue to underestimate their risk of dying in an automobile crash (O'Neill and Mohan 2002; Williams, Paek, and Lund 1995). The National Safety Council (2003) has called for the primary enforcement of seat belt laws (which so far exist in only 18 states) and for the adoption by all states of graduated licensing policies that require individuals to go through three steps to licensure: a learner's permit, then a provisional license, and then a full license. The most effective treatment strategies implemented thus far to reduce the numbers of motor vehicle–related deaths have been as follows: technological improvements in vehicle safety; strict traffic law enforcement; passage of safety laws such as mandatory helmet provisions for motorcycle riders, which result in near-perfect compliance in states that have them; and the lowering of the definition of "legally drunk" to .08 blood alcohol concentration in many states (see Mothers Against Drunk Driving 2002). Aside from these, very few strategies have proven to have any significant effects on the rates of motor vehicle–related accidental deaths.

Deaths Due to Accidental Falls

Falls are the second leading cause of accidental mortality in the United States, with more than 13,000 deaths in 1999 (CDC 2002). This mortality type overwhelmingly affects the elderly, accounting for 70% of accidental deaths to persons over 75 years of age (Fuller 2000). In 1999, about 9,600 persons over 65 years old died of injuries sustained in falls, making it one of the leading causes of accidental death among people in this age group (CDC 2002; Fos and McLin 1990). Moreover, accidental falls were responsible for more than 250,000 hip fractures in 1996, resulting in costs exceeding $10 billion (Fuller 2000).

Statistics on accidental falls show that men are more likely than women to die of falls. Some 60% of falling deaths occur at home, 30% occur in public places, and 10% occur in hospital settings (CDC 2002), and the causes of falling deaths vary by setting. For example, in hospital settings, one of the primary causes of falling is physiological disorientation and dizziness resulting from polypharmacy (i.e., the use of four or more medications) (Morse, Tylko, and Dixon 1987); when falls take place in work settings, a common reason is worker error, usually the misapplication of equipment or machine (Copeland 1989). The risk factors associated with falling injuries are very different for the young and the elderly: Accidental falls among the elderly are most often associated with what Stevens et al. (1991–92) refer to as *intrinsic risk factors,* or causes internal to the individual, such as chronic pain, musculoskeletal and neuromuscular diseases, and the presence of polypharmacy, whereas among the young, falling is most often attributed to *extrinsic risk factors,* such as environmental conditions or hazards and risk-taking behaviors. Given that the causes are different, the problems of falling among the elderly and the young demand different treatment solutions. For instance, for elderly persons, a few simple improvements in home design might reduce the potential for accidental falls (e.g., installation of slip-resistant surfaces in the bathroom or of wall-mounted light switches that the older person can reach without standing on a ladder) (for a more complete list of suggestions, see Rollins 2000). Because most of the accidental falls that

affect younger adults occur at workplaces and are due to some combination of unsafe acts and unsafe working conditions, efforts to prevent such falls have largely focused on improving the effectiveness of communication of the risk of injury on the job (Haskins 1980; Lauda 1980; Reamer 1980). For young children, a simple prevention measure is the use on public playgrounds of "energy-attenuating surfaces" that absorb and cushion the impacts of falls. Parents can also help protect their children from life-threatening falls by keeping appliances and furniture away from open windows in their homes, especially in high-rise apartment buildings (Baker et al. 1992).

Accidental Suffocation

Mechanical suffocation and asphyxiation were responsible for some 5,503 accidental deaths in 1999, and many of these deaths were, for the most part, completely preventable. Moreover, this accidental death category largely affects children under 1 year old, who account for around 40% of the accidental suffocation deaths in the United States (Baker et al. 1992). Any small object in the vicinity of a child is potentially dangerous, as it can lead to accidental suffocation by ingestion. Foods such as popcorn, grapes, nuts, and hard candy all pose potential risks for children less than 1 year of age (National Safety Council 2002). Deaths in this category are not limited to the very young, however; individuals over 65 years of age have one of the highest accidental food-choking rates, with more than 2,500 deaths annually (Baker et al. 1992). Accidental suffocation is also a hazard for many farmers whose work takes them into large storage bins for grains. Suffocations in such bins have been increasing in number in recent years due to the facts that larger and larger grain facilities are being built and many operators of these facilities work alone (Loewer and Loewer 2002).

One of the most prevalent causes of accidental deaths under the suffocation and asphyxiation heading receives little public attention in the way of prevention strategies: death by accidental autoerotic asphyxiation. Autoerotic asphyxiation (the application of cerebral hypoxia through self-strangulation, self-hanging, or manual strangulation among sexual partners to enhance orgasm) takes the lives of more than 1,000 Americans yearly, representing close to 20% of all deaths by accidental suffocation (Byard and Bramwell 1991; Byard, Hucker, and Hazelwood 1990; Michalodimitrakis, Frangoulis, and Koutselinis 1986). It has been speculated that the true number of accidental deaths by autoerotic asphyxia might well be much higher than reported, both because it is easy to mistake such deaths for attempts at suicide or homicide and because some officials may systematically mislabel such deaths as suicides to allow the families of the deceased to avoid the social stigma attached to the act of autoerotic asphyxia. Statistics on deaths owing to accidental autoerotic asphyxia show that males are overwhelmingly more likely than females to be victims of this form of death, with a male:female ratio of about 50:1. The typical male victim is a solitary masturbator between the ages of 12 and 25 (Cooper 1996; Gosink and Jumbelic 2000).

The typical autoerotic death scenario involves a young male who employs a strangulation procedure to the neck, usually self-hanging from a standing or seated position, while masturbating. Unfortunately, when loss of consciousness accompanies hypoxia, the victim loses control over voluntary movement, and accidental death is likely to follow. Many practitioners of autoerotic asphyxia employ "safety devices" such as knives to cut their nooses or slipknots to protect against the possibility of accidental death by losing consciousness (Cooper 1996). These escape mechanisms often do not protect against the loss of consciousness, however, and because the practitioner is usually alone, the risk of accidental death is high.

As we have noted, accidental death by autoerotic asphyxiation has yet to receive the same kind of attention to prevention afforded other accidental causes of death, even though it accounts for nearly 20% of all accidental suffocations. Perhaps this is a result of the stigma that accompanies sexuality in general in the United States, and particularly sexual practices that many perceive to be deviant and dangerous.

SOME SPECIAL PROBLEMS WITH THE LABEL "ACCIDENTAL": CASES OF SUBINTENTIONAL SELF-DESTRUCTION AND DISGUISED SUICIDE

We have already shown that the statistical picture of accidental deaths in the United States is incomplete because every year between 44,000 and 98,000 iatrogenic mortalities go uncounted. In addition to this issue, the statistical picture of accidental deaths is faulty in that it may include (a) incidents of subintentional self-destruction (i.e., cases that are neither suicide attempts nor strictly "accidental" deaths) and (b) cases of suicides disguised as accidents.

Subintentional self-destruction is death that results from practices that can reasonably be expected to lead toward death (Tabachnick 1975; Smith 1980; Shneidman 1973). Unlike suicide, where there exists in the mind of the person a clear *intention* to die, in subintentional self-destruction the person lacks immediate (or sometimes any) intentionality about the possibility of death, despite the fact that his or her behaviors are reckless, making the possibility of accidental death omnipresent (Tabachnick 1975; Smith 1980). Consequently, if death is the final outcome of such a person's actions, it does not conform to a strict definition of suicide because the individual lacked complete intentionality. Nor does such a death fit the parameters of an accident, because it was probably expected, was totally avoidable, and involved a great deal of misjudgment, negligence, and forewarning. Consider, for example, a man who sits on the wall of a balcony of a

10th-story apartment and then falls to his death. We naturally assume that this death was an accident, and maybe rightfully so because of the lack of intent, despite the reckless abandon involved in the behavior. Yet surely at some point the victim entertained the possibility of falling. Can we really call this an accidental death without violating the spirit of the concept "accident"?

Certainly, many of life's events involve risk, some greater than others. But the more risk an action entails, the more likely a self-destructive outcome. Perhaps in some cases the label of "subintentional death" is more appropriate than "accident" because it speaks to the level of obvious risk the deceased chose to ignore. Other frequently cited behaviors that might be described as subintentionally self-destructive are parasuicide (where a person might make a false "suicide attempt" as a cry for help, but with no intention of dying); polydrug abuse; participation in high-risk activities, such as Russian roulette or speeding or driving recklessly under conditions that pose a clear danger; and failure to follow a doctor's advice concerning life-saving medication (Lester 1988; Kreitman et al. 1969; Tabachnick 1975). To date, there are no consistently effective ex post facto mechanisms available that will allow us to differentiate subintentional self-destruction and unsuccessful parasuicide from true accidental or suicidal deaths (Peck and Warner 1995). Ironically, the situations that compel individuals to take part in subintentional self-destructive behaviors are often the same as those that may be the impetus for suicide; they often include a sense of hopelessness, helplessness, alienation, and isolation (Cole 1988; Smith 1980).

The problem of suicides disguised as accidental deaths also confounds the statistical picture of accidental mortality in the United States (Schmidt et al. 1977; Lester 1990; Pokorny, Smith, and Finch 1972). Although it is debatable whether many disguised suicides are counted as accidental deaths in certain subcategories of causes of accidental deaths (Lester 1985), there appears to be strong evidence that deaths in motor vehicle crashes include a number of suicides. In a decade-long study at the Los Angeles Suicide Prevention Center on the self-destructive impetus behind many automobile crashes, Tabachnick (1973) found that 25% of the victims of single-car crashes in his sample were suffering from depression and expressed feelings of hopelessness and helplessness around the time of their "accidents." In another study, Phillips (1979) found a peak in car accident fatalities (an increase of 31%) in California 3 days after a highly publicized suicide story ran in the news media. He concludes that vehicular suicides are probably included within the statistical picture of accidental vehicle deaths. In a replication of Phillips's study, Bollen and Phillips (1981) found a 35–40% increase in motor vehicle fatalities on the third day after a publicized suicide story in Detroit, lending support to the third-day peak theory. These authors also conclude that vehicular suicides might well be hidden in the statistical picture of automobile deaths. Finally, Pokorny et al. (1972) conducted an intensive review of the personalities, emotional states, and social factors of individuals involved in crash fatalities and came to the conclusion that 4 out of the 28 fatalities they observed were likely suicides.

BEREAVEMENT AND RECOVERY AFTER ACCIDENTAL DEATHS

The unexpectedness, suddenness, and often violent character of accidental deaths compound the difficulties that the survivors of the deceased face in their bereavement and grief recovery processes. The survivors of loved ones who die accidentally do not have the periods of anticipatory grief that those who lose loved ones in other ways often experience. In cases of acute mortality, such periods of grief may last weeks, months, or years, and may enhance survivors' coping abilities and bereavement recovery (Dane 1991; Hill, Thompson, and Gallagher 1988; Huber and Gibson 1990). The shock and traumatic emotions that accompany the news of accidental death, common features of this type of bereavement, might last for weeks (Hogan, Morse, and Tason 1996; Sanders 1982–83). Raphael (1983) lists four possible features of accidental deaths that can make survivors' grieving process more intense than that associated with death from chronic or acute illness: (a) the possibility of an accompanying traumatic stress response because of the shocking and unexpected nature of the news that a loved one is dead, (b) the possibility that learning of the violent nature of the death may compound the survivor's trauma and shock, (c) the possibility of seeing the loved one in a dehumanized state (e.g., attached to life-support machinery) before death, and (d) the possibility of the need to identify a body that may have been severely damaged by the accident. In fact, Reed and Greenwald (1991) found that the survivors of accident victims in their study experienced more shock and emotional distress than did the survivors of suicide victims.

In addition, there is the problem of guilt associated with accidental deaths. Especially among the parents of children who have died accidentally, self-blame and guilty feelings are common occurrences (Rosof 1994). In one study, Miles and Demi (1991–92) found that 78% of accident-bereaved parents reported feeling guilty for the deaths of their children, and Thompson and Range (1992–93) found that self-blame was more common among parents who had lost children to accidental death than among those who had lost children to suicide. According to Miles and Demi (1991–92), a signature feature of the guilt that accident-bereaved parents experience concerns *death causation;* that is, they think about how their parental decisions (to allow their children to drive or to go out at night, for example) might have inadvertently led to their children's deaths. Because of the suddenness of accidental death, which freezes the relationship in time, such parents often also feel *parenting guilt* that stems from unresolved fights, emotional problems, or simply their fear that they

did not say "I love you" frequently enough to their children (Miles and Demi 1991–92; Rosof 1994). Such feelings of guilt are not the sole province of parents of children who die in accidents, of course. Lehman, Wortman, and Williams (1987) found that 53% of the accident-bereaved spouses in their sample believed that if they had done something differently, their spouses would be still be alive.

Although the topic of bereavement in accidental death has received considerable attention in the thanatological literature, the issue of recovery, especially for the survivors of situations involving accidental deaths, has received only scant attention. In one of the few studies to date, Foeckler et al. (1978) interviewed drivers who had survived a collision involving a fatality; they found that one-third of their respondents reported experiencing depression, disturbed thinking, and other psychic pains that continued from a month to several years after the accident, and 55% reported personal crises in their lives directly related to their involvement in the accidental fatality. Lehman et al. (1987) looked at long-term effects on accident victims' survivors and found that as many as 80% of the survivors in their sample continued to ruminate about the vehicle crashes that took the lives of their spouses and children even some 4 to 7 years later, and "appeared to be unable to accept, resolve, or find any meaning in the loss" (p. 218).

Detachment seems to be a signature feature of bereavement for the survivors of loved ones lost to accidental death, and this coping mechanism carries with it profound implications for close relationships. The survivors of those who die by accidental means often withdraw emotionally in the face of insurmountable grief and their inability to explain or make sense of the suddenness of the loss. This tendency toward detachment can have adverse effects on marital and other relationships. Sometimes, the sudden loss of a child through accidental death can create a "polarization effect" between the child's parents, either strengthening or dissolving the marital bond (Lehman et al. 1989).

Men and women often experience the grief of accidental deaths differently. Men, for instance, have a stronger tendency toward detachment in sudden bereavement. As Reed (1993) notes:

> Men tend to feel the loss as a void and seek solitude. On the other hand, women tend to feel the loss as isolation and seek support from others. Women may therefore be extra sensitive to the distance between spouses precisely at the time the man is seeking solitude. (P. 218)

These differences in styles of grieving naturally lend themselves to marital discord. So, then, what factors can affect recovery in the case of sudden bereavement? Or, to put the question another way, what can we do to make accidental death bereavement more bearable?

The grief that accompanies accidental death is intense and extremely painful, especially in cases where the survivors are unable to find meaning in the experience and where the level of survivor-victim attachment was high

(Reed and Greenwald 1991). Religion can play an important role in assuaging the impact of such intense grief, and this is the first recovery resource that might assist the survivors of accidental death. According to Reed (1993), religion can help the suddenly bereaved through the grieving process in three ways. First, religious institutions provide crucial emotional support for the bereaved through friendship networks that mimic primordial ties. Second, religious beliefs often strengthen self-esteem in individuals by creating new self-awareness and building up self-worth (Reed asserts that the strongest predictor of bereavement outcome is the psychological resource of self-esteem). And finally, religion enhances "existential certainty" by offering meaning for seemingly meaningless deaths and by reassuring the bereaved of the certainty of an afterlife while giving meaning to life and living.

Friendship networks, which are an implicit part of membership in religious and other social institutions (as Reed notes), are important resources for the suddenly bereaved. Because the mourning process typically extends for 8 months or longer (Hardt 1978–79), detachment and communicative isolation are potential problems for the survivors of victims of accidental death. Sanders's (1982–83) research on grief recovery points to the importance of support systems (friends, religious institutions, family members, and so on) that remain in place for *months* after an accidental death to counter the harmful implications of social isolation, alienation, and detachment so common to sudden bereavement. Long-term support systems are important resources for grief recovery in general, and in cases of accidental death their importance is magnified. With more than 95,000 accidental deaths each year in the United States, it is not a stretch to suggest that grief recovery is a feature that deserves further attention. More research on the range of factors that might assist survivors in coping with the grief of accidental deaths and on the problems that men's and women's differing styles of grieving pose for close relationships would be especially valuable.

CONCLUSION

Accidental death is a common feature of life, affecting tens of thousands of Americans yearly, yet the subject of accidental deaths does not receive nearly as much attention from the public as do the other leadings causes of death. Perhaps, as we have argued in this essay, the word *accident* is linked too closely with the idea of fate, and this impedes our understanding of the antecedents of "accidents" as well as our ability to arrive at effective treatment strategies to reduce the occurrence of accidental mortality. Edward Suchman (1961) understood this quandary well. He notes:

> When the public is willing to accept the same type of preventive program for accidents as it demands for the communicable diseases, we may expect to witness tremendous gains in

removing accidents from its current position as one of the major causes of death and disability. (P. 249)

Obviously, we have yet to achieve such a preventive program. Until we do, we can expect accidental deaths to remain a leading cause of mortality. Perhaps a name change is in order, from "accidental deaths" to "deaths by mistakes—human mistakes." Perhaps such a change in terminology would help us to see accidental deaths as the problems of human error and fallibility that they are. Until we take that perspective, we will continue to make the dubious link between accidents and fate, ultimately denying the possibility of strategic human intervention to prevent the occurrence of untimely death.

REFERENCES

Baker, Susan P., Brian O'Neill, Marvin J. Ginsburg, and Guohua Li. 1992. *The Injury Fact Book,* 2d ed. New York: Oxford University Press.

Bennett, Ross C. 1987. "Predictors in Accidental Deaths." *Transactions of the Association of Life Insurance Medical Directors of America* 70:46–53.

Bollen, Kenneth A. and David P. Phillips. 1981. "Suicidal Motor Vehicle Fatalities in Detroit: A Replication." *American Journal of Sociology* 87:404–12.

Brewer, Robert D., Peter D. Morris, Thomas B. Cole, Stephanie Watkins, Michael J. Patetta, and Carol Popkin. 1994. "The Risk of Dying in Alcohol-Related Automobile Crashes Among Habitual Drunk Drivers." *New England Journal of Medicine* 331:513–17.

Brownfain, John J. 1962. "When Is an Accident Not an Accident?" *Journal of the American Society of Safety Engineers,* September, p. 20.

Byard, Roger W. and Nigel H. Bramwell. 1991. "Autoerotic Death: A Definition." *American Journal of Forensic Medicine and Pathology* 12:74–76.

Byard, Roger W., Stephen J. Hucker, and Robert R. Hazelwood. 1990. "A Comparison of Typical Death Scene Features in Cases of Fatal Male and Female Autoerotic Asphyxia With a Review of the Literature." *Forensic Science International* 48:113–21.

Centers for Disease Control and Prevention. 2002. "1999 United States Unintentional Injuries, All Ages, All Races, Both Sexes." Office of Statistics and Programming, National Center for Injury Prevention and Control, CDC. Retrieved from WISQARS (CDC's Web-based Injury Statistical Query and Reporting System) (http://www.cdc.gov/ncipc/wisqars/).

Cole, David A. 1988. "Helplessness, Social Desirability, Depression, and Parasuicide in Two College Student Samples." *Journal of Counseling Psychology* 56:131–36.

Cooper, A. J. 1996. "Auto-Erotic Asphyxiation: Three Case Reports." *Journal of Sex and Marital Therapy* 22:47–53.

Copeland, Arthur R. 1989. "Accidental Deaths Due to Falls at Work." *American Journal of Forensic Medicine and Pathology* 10(1):17–20.

Coren, Stanley. 1996a. "Accidental Death and the Shift to Daylight Savings Time." *Perceptual and Motor Skills* 83:921–22.

Coren, Stanley. 1996b. "Daylight Savings Time and Traffic Accidents." *New England Journal of Medicine* 334:924.

———. 1996c. *Sleep Thieves: An Eye-Opening Exploration Into the Science and Mysteries of Sleep.* New York: Free Press.

Cummings, Peter, Barbara McKnight, Frederick Rivara, and David C. Grossman. 2002. "Association of Driver Air Bags With Driver Fatality: A Matched Cohort Study." *British Medical Journal* 324:1119–22.

Dane, Barbara O. 1991. "Anticipatory Mourning of Middle-Aged Parents of Adult Children With AIDS." *Families in Society* 72:108–15.

DeCicco, Jack M. 1985. "Accidental Deaths: The Legal View." *Transactions of the Association of Life Insurance Medical Directors of America* 68:138–47.

Farmer, Charles M. 1997. "Trends in Motor Vehicle Fatalities." *Journal of Safety Research* 28:37–48.

Foeckler, Merle M., Frances H. Garrard, Catherine C. Williams, Alice M. Thomas, and Teresa J. Jones. 1978. "Vehicle Drivers and Fatal Accidents." *Suicide and Life-Threatening Behavior* 8:174–82.

Fos, Peter J. and Carlen L. McLin. 1990. "The Risk of Falling in the Elderly." *Medical Decision Making* 10:195–200.

Fuller, George F. 2000. "Falls in the Elderly." *American Family Physician* 61:2159–68.

Glik, Deborah C., Jennie J. Kronenfield, Kirby Jackson, and Weiyang Zhang. 1999. "Comparison of Traffic Accident and Chronic Disease Risk Perceptions." *American Journal of Health Behavior* 23:198–209.

Gosink, Paul D. and Mary I. Jumbelic. 2000. "Autoerotic Asphyxiation in a Female." *American Journal of Forensic Medicine and Pathology* 20:114–18.

Grant, Karen R. and John B. McKinlay. 1986. "Appropriate Technology Applied to a Western Epidemic: The Case of Motor Vehicle Accidents." *Prevention in Health Services* 5:29–55.

Haberman, Paul W. 1987. "Alcohol and Alcoholism in Traffic and Other Accidental Deaths." *American Journal of Drug and Alcohol Abuse* 13:475–84.

Hacker, Helen A. and Edward A. Suchman. 1963. "A Sociological Approach to Accident Research." *Social Problems* 10:383–89.

Haddon, William, Jr. 1968. "The Changing Approach to the Epidemiology, Prevention, and Amelioration of Trauma: The Transition to Approaches Etiologically Rather Than Descriptively." *American Journal of Public Health* 58:1431–38.

Haddon, William, Jr., Edward A. Suchman, and David Klein. 1964. *Accident Research: Methods and Approaches.* New York: Harper & Row.

Hagglund, George. 1980. "Causes of Injury in Industry: The 'Unsafe Act' Theory." Pp. 18–23 in *Readings in Industrial Accident Prevention,* edited by Dan Petersen and Jerry Goodale. New York: McGraw-Hill.

Halman, Stephen I., Mary Chipman, Patricia C. Parkin, and James G. Wright. 2002. "Are Seat Belt Restraints as Effective in School Age Children as in Adults? A Prospective Crash Study." *British Medical Journal* 324:1123.

Hardt, Dale Vincent. 1978–79. "An Investigation of the Stages of Bereavement." *Omega* 9:279–85.

Haskins, Jack. 1980. "Effects of Safety Communication Campaigns: A Review of the Research Evidence."

Pp. 264–72 in *Readings in Industrial Accident Prevention,* edited by Dan Petersen and Jerry Goodale. New York: McGraw-Hill.

Hayward, Rodney A. and Timothy P. Hofer. 2001. "Estimating Hospital Deaths Due to Medical Errors: Preventability Is in the Eye of the Reviewer." *Journal of the American Medical Association* 286:415–20.

Heinrich, Herbert W. 1959. *Industrial Accident Prevention: A Scientific Approach,* 4th ed. New York: McGraw-Hill.

Hill, Connie D., Larry W. Thompson, and Dolores Gallagher. 1988. "The Role of Anticipatory Bereavement in Older Women's Adjustment to Widowhood." *Gerontologist* 28:792–96.

Hippisley-Cox, Julia, Lindsay Groom, Denise Kendrick, Carol Coupland, Elizabeth Webber, and Boki Savelyich. 2002. "Cross Sectional Survey of Socioeconomic Variations in Severity and Mechanism of Childhood Injuries in Trent 1992–1997." *British Medical Journal* 324:1132–34.

Hogan, Nancy, Janice M. Morse, and Maritza C. Tason. 1996. "Toward an Experiential Theory of Bereavement." *Omega* 33:43–65.

Huber, Ruth and John W. Gibson. 1990. "New Evidence for Anticipatory Grief." *Hospice Journal* 6(1):49–67.

Jeffries, Jim W. 1980. "Unsafe Acts vs. Unsafe Conditions." Pp. 24–25 in *Readings in Industrial Accident Prevention,* edited by Dan Petersen and Jerry Goodale. New York: McGraw-Hill.

Kastenbaum, Robert J. 2001. *Death, Society, and Human Experience,* 7th ed. Boston: Allyn & Bacon.

Kohn, Linda T., Janet M. Corrigan, and Molla S. Donaldson, eds. 2000. *To Err Is Human: Building a Safer Health System* (Committee on Quality of Health Care in America, Institute of Medicine). Washington, DC: National Academy Press.

Kreitman, N., A. E. Phillip, S. Greer, and C. R. Bagley. 1969. "Parasuicide." *British Journal of Psychiatry* 115:747–48.

Lang, Sylvia W., Patricia F. Waller, and Jean T. Shope. 1996. "Adolescent Driving: Characteristics Associated With Single-Vehicle and Injury Crashes." *Journal of Safety Research* 27:241–57.

Lauda, Robert. 1980. "A Communication Gap in Safety." Pp. 257–63 in *Readings in Industrial Accident Prevention,* edited by Dan Petersen and Jerry Goodale. New York: McGraw-Hill.

Leape, Lucian L. 2000. "Institute of Medicine Medical Errors Figures Are Not Exaggerated." *Journal of the American Medical Association* 284:95–97.

Lehman, Darrin R., Eric L. Lang, Camille B. Wortman, and Susan B. Sorenson. 1989. "Long-Term Effects of Sudden Bereavement: Marital and Parent-Child Relationships and Children's Reactions." *Journal of Family Psychology* 2:344–67.

Lehman, Darrin R., Camille B. Wortman, and Allan F. Williams. 1987. "Long-Term Effects of Losing a Spouse or Child in a Motor Vehicle Crash." *Journal of Personality and Social Psychology* 52:218–31.

Lester, David. 1985. "Accidental Deaths as Disguised Suicides." *Psychological Reports* 56:626.

———. 1988. "Toward a Theory of Parasuicide." *Corrective and Social Psychiatry and Journal of Behavior Technology Methods and Therapy* 34:24–26.

———. 1990. "Accidental Death Rates and Suicide." *Ativitas Nervosa Superior* 32:130–31.

Li, Guohua and Susan P. Baker. 1995. "Alcohol in Fatally Injured Bicyclists." *Journal of Safety Research* 26:255–56.

Loewer, Otto, Jr. and David H. Loewer. 2002. "Suffocation Hazards in Grain Bins." Document Fact Sheet AEN-39 of the Agricultural Engineering Department, University of Kentucky, Cooperative Extension. Retrieved April 9, 2003 (http://www.cdc.gov/niosh/nasdhome.html).

MacPherson, Malcolm. 1998. *The Black Box: All New Cockpit Voice Recorder Accounts of In-Flight Accidents.* New York: William Morrow.

Massie, Dawn L., Kenneth L. Campbell, and Allan F. Williams. 1995. "Traffic Accident Involvement Rates by Driver Age and Gender." *Accident Analysis and Prevention* 27:73–87.

McDonald, Clement J., Michael Weiner, and Sui L. Hui. 2000. "Deaths Due to Medical Errors Are Exaggerated in Institute of Medicine Report." *Journal of the American Medical Association* 284:93–95.

Michalodimitrakis, M., M. Frangoulis, and A. Koutselinis. 1986. "Accidental Sexual Strangulation." *American Journal of Forensic Medicine and Pathology* 7:74–75.

Miles, Margaret S. and Alice S. Demi. 1991–92. "A Comparison of Guilt in Bereaved Parents Whose Children Died by Suicide, Accident, or Chronic Disease." *Omega* 24:203–15.

Minino, Arialdi M. and Betty L. Smith. 2001. *Deaths: Preliminary Data for 2000* (National Vital Statistics Reports, vol. 49, no. 12). Hyattsville, MD: National Center for Health Statistics.

Morse, Janice M., Suzanne J. Tylko, and Herbert A. Dixon. 1987. "Characteristics of the Fall-Prone Patient." *Gerontologist* 27:516–22.

Mothers Against Drunk Driving. 2002. "MADD Says Nation Must Make the Drunk Driving Issue a Top Priority." Press release, April 22. Retrieved April 9, 2003 (http://www.madd.org/news/0,1056,4163,00.html).

Nantulya, Vinand M. and Michael R. Reich. 2002. "The Neglected Epidemic: Road Traffic Injuries in Developing Countries." *British Medical Journal* 324:1139–41.

National Highway Traffic Safety Administration. 2001a. *Motor Vehicle Traffic Crash Fatality and Injury Estimates for 2000.* Washington, DC: U.S. Department of Transportation.

———. 2001b. *Traffic Safety Facts 2000: An Overview.* Washington, DC: U.S. Department of Transportation.

National Safety Council. 2002. "Estimating the Costs of Unintentional Injuries, 2000." Itasca, IL: National Safety Council. Retrieved April 9, 2003 (http://www.nsc.org/lrs/statinfo/estcost0.htm).

———. 2003. "Report on Injuries in America, 2001." Itasca, IL: National Safety Council. Retrieved April 9, 2003 (http://www.nsc.org/library/rept2000.htm).

O'Neill, Brian and Dinesh Mohan. 2002. "Reducing Motor Vehicle Crash Deaths and Injuries in Newly Motorising Countries." *British Medical Journal* 324:1142–45.

Peck, Dennis L. and Kenneth Warner. 1995. "Accident or Suicide? Single-Vehicle Car Accidents and the Intent Hypothesis." *Adolescence* 30:463–72.

Peden, M. M., E. Krug, D. Mohan, A. Hyder, M. Norton, M. MacKay, and C. Dora. 2001. *A 5-Year WHO Strategy on Road Traffic Injury Prevention.* Geneva: World Health Organization. Retrieved April 9, 2003 (http://www.who.int/violence_injury_prevention/).

Perrow, Charles. 1984. *Normal Accidents: Living With High-Risk Technologies.* New York: Basic Books.

Phillips, David P. 1979. "Suicide, Motor Vehicle Fatalities, and the Mass Media: Evidence Toward a Theory of Suggestion." *American Journal of Sociology* 84:1150–74.

Pokorny, Alex D., James P. Smith, and John R. Finch. 1972. "Vehicular Suicide." *Suicide and Life-Threatening Behavior* 2:105–19.

Raphael, Beverly. 1983. *The Anatomy of Bereavement.* New York: Basic Books.

Reamer, Fred. 1980. "Toward More Effective Communications in Safety." Pp. 273–80 in *Readings in Industrial Accident Prevention,* edited by Dan Petersen and Jerry Goodale. New York: McGraw-Hill.

Reed, Mark D. 1993. "Sudden Death and Bereavement Outcomes: The Impact of Resources on Grief Symptomology and Detachment." *Suicide and Life-Threatening Behavior* 23:204–20.

Reed, Mark D. and Jason Y. Greenwald. 1991. "Survivor-Victim Status, Attachment, and Sudden Death Bereavement." *Suicide and Life-Threatening Behavior* 21:385–401.

Roberts, Ian, Dinesh Mohan, and Kamran Abbasi. 2002. "War on the Roads." *British Medical Journal* 342:1107–8.

Rollins, Gina. 2000. "Preventing the Fall: Designs on Building Safe Homes for the Elderly." *Safety and Health,* September. Excerpts retrieved April 9, 2003 (http://www.nsc.org/issues/ifalls/falfalls.htm).

Rosof, Barbara D. 1994. *The Worst Loss: How Families Heal From the Death of a Child.* New York: Henry Holt.

Sanders, Catherine M. 1982–83. "Effects of Sudden vs. Chronic Illness Death on Bereavement Outcomes." *Omega* 13:227–41.

Sartre, Jean-Paul. 1956. *Being and Nothingness: A Phenomenological Essay on Ontology.* New York: Washington Square.

Schmidt, Chester W., John W. Shaffer, Howard I. Zlotowitz, and Russell S. Fisher. 1977. "Suicide by Vehicle Crash." *American Journal of Psychiatry* 134:175–78.

Shankar, Umesh G. 2001. *Motorcyclist Fatalities in 2000* (DOT Publication No. HS 809 387). Washington, DC: U.S. Department of Transportation.

Shneidman, Edwin S. 1973. *Deaths of Man.* New York: Quadrangle.

Smith, D. F. 1980. "Subintentional Suicide Among Youth." *Health Education,* September/October, pp. 44–45.

Stevens, Victor J., Mark C. Hornbrook, Darlene J. Wingfield, Jack F. Hollis, Merwyn R. Greenlick, and Marcia G. Ory. 1991–92. "Design and Implementation of a Falls Prevention Intervention for Community-Dwelling Older Persons." *Behavior, Health, and Aging* 2:57–73.

Suchman, Edward A. 1961. "A Conceptual Analysis of the Accident Phenomenon." *Social Problems* 9:241–53.

Tabachnick, Norman, ed. 1973. *Accident or Suicide? Destruction by Automobile.* Springfield, IL: Charles C Thomas.

———. 1975. "Subintentional Self-Destruction in Teenagers." *Psychiatric Opinion* 12(6):21–26.

Thompson, Karin E. and Lillian M. Range. 1992–93. "Bereavement Following Suicide and Other Deaths: Why Support Attempts Fail." *Omega* 26:61–70.

Thygerson, Alton L. 1977. *Accidents and Disasters: Causes and Countermeasures.* Englewood Cliffs, NJ: Prentice Hall.

Veevers, Jean E. and Ellen M. Gee. 1986. "Playing It Safe: Accident Mortality and Gender Roles." *Sociological Focus* 19:349–60.

Vernick, Jon S, Guohua Li, Susanne Ogaitis, Ellen J. MacKenzie, Susan P. Baker, and Andrea C. Gielen. 1999. "Effects of

High School Driver Education on Motor Vehicle Crashes, Violations, and Licensure." *American Journal of Preventive Medicine* 16(Suppl.):40–46.

Vredenburgh, A. G. and H. H. Cohen. 1996. "High-Risk Recreational Activities: Skiing and Scuba. What Predicts Compliance With Warnings?" *Journal of Safety Research* 27:134–35.

Williams, Allan F., N. N. Paek, and A. K. Lund. 1995. "Factors That Drivers Say Motivate Safe Driving Practices." *Journal of Safety Research* 26:119–24.

Williams, Allan F. and JoAnn K. Wells. 1995. "Deaths of Teenagers as Motor-Vehicle Passengers." *Journal of Safety Research* 26:161–67.

Winn, Russell G. and David Giacopassi. 1993. "Effects of County-Level Alcohol Prohibition on Motor Vehicle Accidents." *Social Science Quarterly* 74:783–91.

MEGADEATHS

Individual Reactions and Social Responses to Massive Loss of Life

Jerome Rosenberg

Dennis L. Peck

Examples of events that have led to massive loss of life, or megadeaths, abound. Such catastrophes include natural as well as human-made tragedies, such as epidemics, air and sea disasters, mining disasters, fires, cyclones, droughts, floods, earthquakes, hurricanes, tornadoes, volcanic eruptions, wars, and campaigns of genocide. All of these kinds of disasters are relevant to any discussion of megadeaths, and in the following sections we provide examples of each. In addition to examining the types of events that lead to the phenomenon of megadeath, we attempt to demonstrate the magnitude of the consequences of megadeath that result from community responses to both natural and human-made disasters (that is, the actions of humans directed against humans that cause deaths in large numbers).

COMMUNITY DISASTERS

Although events such as the Great Fire of London in 1666, the April 16, 1845, fire that took place in Pittsburgh, Pennsylvania, and the Great Chicago Fire of October 8–10, 1871, pale in comparison to many of the events we review in the sections to follow, these tragedies are no less significant in terms of loss of life and property. The Great Fire of London was a 5-day ordeal during which an area of more than 436 acres was completely destroyed; the fire consumed 87 churches and 13,200 houses. Although it is likely that many lives were lost, only six known dead were reported. As minimal as the loss of life may have been, however, this destructive fire had far-reaching financial consequences for the residents of London; as a result of the fire, thousands of individuals experienced financial

ruin, and many of them came to be incarcerated in debtors' prisons.

The 1845 Pittsburgh fire destroyed approximately one-fourth of that city. The source of the fire was a single frame building, but within 5 hours, 56–60 acres of the city were inundated. Of the 1,200 buildings destroyed, 700 were dwellings. The other 500 included a variety of businesses, factories, professional offices, and cultural and educational facilities.

Chicago grew in a short period of time from a small trading outpost to a city of approximately 330,000 people. When the devastating fire occurred in 1871, Chicago was the fourth-largest city in the United States. Much of the city proper was destroyed in the fire, and it has been estimated that 250 to 300 persons died. The leaders and residents of Chicago responded to the tragedy of the fire much as had other communities that had faced similar experiences: They set out to rebuild the city.

On August 27, 1883, a volcanic eruption on the island of Krakatoa, located between Sumatra and Java, caused a 120-foot tidal wave that covered the coastal areas of Java, killing at least 36,417 people and destroying 165 villages. The volcanic eruption caused extreme long-term damage to the environment as well, including a lowering of temperatures in the area. Temperatures did not return to normal levels until 5 years later.

On May 31, 1889, the small industrial city of Johnstown, Pennsylvania, was overwhelmed by disaster when a wall of water 35–40 feet high, let loose by the failure of the South Fork Dam located 14 miles away, crashed down upon the city. Traveling at more than 40 miles per hour, the floodwaters approached the city within 57 minutes after the dam break was noted, sending 20 million tons of water downstream toward Johnstown. Within less than 10 minutes, 4 square miles of the Johnstown downtown area was destroyed; within a matter of a few hours of the dam break, 2,209 people died, including 99 whole families, 396 children under the age of 10, and 777 unidentified victims. Some 1,600 homes were lost, and 280 businesses were destroyed.

On September 8, 1900, Galveston, Texas, experienced a hurricane that is recorded as one of the most devastating hurricanes ever to strike the U.S. mainland. The winds and rising floodwaters were responsible for the loss of approximately 8,000 lives.

One of the most famous tragedies involving massive loss of life is the sinking of the ocean liner Titanic. On April 14, 1912, only 5 days after commencing her maiden voyage from Southampton, England, to New York City with 2,227 passengers and crew aboard, the Titanic struck an iceberg and sank. Only 705 people survived; the loss of life was 1,522. The tragic loss of so many lives on the Titanic, a ship that had been considered unsinkable, had and continues to have long-term effects on the global community.

In 1957, the area around Chelyabinsk, Russia, was exposed to a catastrophic amount of radiation when an atomic weapons complex built during the late 1940s experienced a malfunction and a radioactive waste containment unit exploded. Untold thousands of people have been affected by the radioactive fallout from this accident.

In 1984, the worst industrial disaster in history occurred when a Union Carbide plant making pesticides in Bhopal, India, released toxic methyl isocyanate gas into the air. The total damage attributable to this event may never be determined, but on November 16, 1990, the state government of Madhya Pradesh submitted a compensation claim to the Supreme Court of India on behalf of the families of 3,828 dead victims, 40 victims with permanent total disability, 2,680 persons with permanent partial disability, 1,313 individuals who suffered temporary disability from permanent injury, 7,172 people with temporary disability, 18,922 persons with permanent injury with no disability, and 173,382 persons with temporary injury but with no disability.

Megadeath events such as those noted above affect social understandings of death and dying as well as the grief, bereavement, and mourning processes, as these are shaped by death experiences and reactions at both individual and societal levels. Both individuals and societies are clearly affected by the loss of life in numbers so large as to be beyond the scope of normal comprehension. Megadeaths present countless problems for individuals and societies alike as they attempt to find adequate social responses to such great loss of life and the aftereffects of tragedy. Normative responses seem inadequate for dealing with such losses.

INHUMANITY TO HUMANKIND

When death is expected, the anticipated event sets the dynamics for how people respond. Although grief and mourning represent basic, normal human responses, on occasion people are confronted with events that produce such great loss that individual grief and mourning must give way to participation in some collective form of mourning. Clearly, natural disasters are the results of random acts of nature over which humans can exercise little if any control. Human-made disasters, in contrast, such as war and genocide, challenge the human ability to cope.

During World War I (1913–18), for example, it is estimated that approximately 8.5 million military casualties and millions more civilian deaths occurred. During World War II, the military death toll was 20 million; in total, more than 50 million people, including the victims of wartime atrocities, died. The Nazi Holocaust of this period represents an extraordinary example of genocide that led to the demise of more than 6 million Jews and approximately 5 million more deaths among other portions of the civilian population, including political dissidents, homosexuals (an estimated 50,000 to 500,000), Roma Gypsies (an estimated 400,000), and Jehovah's Witnesses (an estimated 2,500 to 5,000). In addition, 150,000 German citizens were identified by their own government as "life not worthy of life" and were exterminated (Friedlander 1995:14).

It is estimated that between 800,000 and 1 million people died during the Armenian genocide of 1915. In Russia during the 1930s, 20 million victims are thought to have died during the Stalinist reign of terror. In 1994, between 800,000 and 1 million persons, mainly Tutsis, were killed during the Rwandan war of genocide, and more than 3 million people are estimated to have died during the Cambodian genocide period of the 1970s.

In East Timor during the period 1975–99, an estimated 200,000 Catholics were victimized in a Muslim purge initiated by the Indonesian army. In Bosnia from 1995 to 1999 Serbian Orthodox Christians victimized 200,000 Muslims in a government-sponsored campaign of ethnic cleansing. Even more recent examples of genocide occurred in Kosovo during 1998–99 and in the Democratic Republic of the Congo beginning in 1997 to the present. The number of Muslims killed in Kosovo is yet unknown; the Serbian Orthodox Christians displaced 400,000 Muslims. In the Congo, the government army and rebels have killed an estimated 1.7 million Congolese citizens.

Responses to Megadeath and the Impact Ratio

Events such as those described above place great demands on the resources of individuals, communities, and nations as they are called upon to cope with the enormity of this kind of loss. The effort to find meaning is an important component in individuals' attempts to locate appropriate responses to such loss of human life. Victor Frankl (1983), reflecting on his experiences during the Holocaust, has written of the search for the meaning of life and death under conditions of extreme depravation. Such meaning is elusive, but the search for meaning may nonetheless be as important as the conclusions that are reached. A variety of responses develop at the individual psychological level, prompted by anger, sorrow, grief, bitterness, and hate; at the societal level, responses may include the need to exact a form of retribution on behalf of the community. This effort also includes identifying appropriate methods by which to memorialize the losses associated with the tragic event. Such memorials can serve to symbolize the collective conscience of a nation as well as the individual feelings of survivors.

The nature and the cause of death as well as certain characteristics of the deceased inform our responses to death. That is, when someone dies, we give special consideration to the age of the person who died, the conditions under which the death occurred, the intent or randomness of the death, our ability to assess responsibility and accountability for the death, the social and political climate under which the death occurred, and our relationship to the person who died. Individual relationships and shared membership in some larger entity appear to be critical to the search for an appropriate response. It is also important whether the cause of death is an intrinsic aspect of the life cycle (such as growing old), a disease, an accident, or an intentional or unintentional act stemming from human malice or negligence. When death results from causes beyond human control, we still seek to identify causal and explanatory factors that serve our purpose. During the Middle Ages, for example, it was not uncommon for leaders of the Church to blame the spread of bubonic plague on heretical influences; they perceived the plague to be a supernatural punishment meted out by a sacred force.

Although the term *megadeaths* is usually used to refer to large numbers of deaths, it is important to recognize that the term may also be applied when the numbers of lives lost are relatively small but they represent a significant proportion of the population at risk. This concept, which Rossi and Wright (1981) call the "impact ratio" (the ratio of loss to available resources), represents an important dimension for understanding the extent of the trauma that persons and communities experience during and in the aftermath of disaster. As Robert Bolin (1985) notes, the impact ratio of a disaster is the proportion of those affected in the community compared to the proportion not affected. When a disaster affects large numbers of people and they experience the effects of the disaster for a long time, the impact ratio is large. Kai Erikson (1976) refers to this phenomenon as a "collective trauma" because of the destruction and loss of communality it entails. Identification with the tragic events and individual and collective perceptions of those events are crucial elements in human responses to megadeaths. How do humans cope with tragedy of such great magnitude? We evaluate this issue below within the context of the body of knowledge that has been generated to give meaning to the social psychology of megadeath.

PSYCHOSOCIAL RESPONSES TO DISASTER

The literature on the psychosocial aspects of individual and collective human reactions to disastrous events of any magnitude is too large to allow us to provide an adequate overview in this chapter. However, we can demonstrate the significance such events have in the lives of those who survive them by selectively drawing on a small portion of this rich body of knowledge. In this section we offer a narrow but significant example in the form of a clinical case study of community reaction to one particular disaster. This case provides some insights that can help us to understand human responses to large-scale tragedy, the impact ratio, and megadeath.

The flooding disaster that occurred in Buffalo Creek, West Virginia, in February 1972 is a classic example of an event with a high impact ratio. After days of rainfall, the entire Buffalo Creek area was devastated by rushing floodwaters within a short period when an artificial dam became saturated and gave way; the dam had been formed by the deposit of coal waste into a mountain stream. The result of this flooding was tragic in terms of life and property lost (125 people died and 5,000 were left homeless), but the secondary consequences for the survivors added to their losses. Lifton and Olson (1976) describe five survival patterns exhibited by Buffalo Creek residents in the aftermath of the disaster: (a) death imprint (memories and images of the disaster as these were associated with death) and death anxiety, (b) death guilt (the sense of self-condemnation over having survived while others died), (c) psychic numbing (a diminished capacity to feel anything), (d) impaired human relationships (conflict over need or nurturing and suspicion of others), and (e) search for the significance surrounding the disaster (the attempt to provide form to and explanation for the near-death disaster experience).

The Buffalo Creek episode is also an example of a case in which corporate negligence led to unnatural disaster. Bolin (1985) asserts that the effects of this event should be considered within the context of a human-made disaster. The secondary effects of the flooding on the members of the Buffalo Creek community, which was irreparably destroyed, are described in legal terms as "psychic impairment." The manifestations of this impairment, as identified above, were the result of what Lifton and Olson (1976:2) refer to as "indelible images" imprinted in the memories of primary and secondary victim survivors. Such victims, according to Bolin, either directly or indirectly experienced physical, material, and personal losses from the disaster. The unnatural disaster caused by human error at Buffalo Creek became, in the minds of some survivors, a natural event as fearful dreams and thoughts and anxiety became part of their normal reality. Perceptions of failure attributed to abortive efforts to save others permeated the thoughts of survivors, as did anger directed toward the coal mining company that deposited its waste in that mountain stream and also was the primary employer of Buffalo Creek residents.

Psychological manifestations such as those described above are usually expected to disappear within a 6-month period following disastrous events, especially if victims have support systems available, but when such an event has a high impact ratio, survivors can have numerous additional problems in living and negative psychological effects (Bolin 1985). According to Lifton and Olson's (1976) clinical analysis, the survivors at Buffalo Creek manifested many negative postdisaster symptoms, including apathy, social withdrawal, and depression. Along with an almost total constriction in their living patterns, many Buffalo Creek victims exhibited symptoms characteristic of a psychological "disaster syndrome" in which they continued, over the long term, to exist in the stunned state they experienced at the time of the flood. Such a numbing condition lowers an individual's level of energy, diminishes emotional feelings toward others, induces physical problems, and reduces memory capacity. As people in this state experience grieving, their once positive and constructive relationships become impaired. The need for mutual support remains high, but the process of everyday living becomes burdensome. Personal feelings are easily bruised, and anger and suspicion permeate relationships at all levels; often, the perceptions survivors hold of others become manifested through anger. Life is burdensome and generally less than satisfactory.

As noted above, the fifth type of survival pattern that Lifton and Olson (1976) describe is a condition that encompasses the individual's struggle to find significance in or meaning for the disaster. This struggle for definition should not be underestimated, for unless survivors can find acceptable explanations that give significance and meaning to the disaster, they are unlikely to be able to find similar significance and meaning for living. Without psychological resolution of the aftereffects of disaster, victims are, in Lifton and Olson's words, "locked in their death anxiety, survivor guilt, numbing . . . [with] impaired human relationships, bound to the disaster itself and to its destructive psychological influences" (p. 8). In the current psychosocial vernacular of the mental health profession, the survivors of the Buffalo Creek disaster may be said to suffer from posttraumatic stress disorder (PTSD) in their individual-level reactions to this high-impact-ratio event.

WAR: THE ULTIMATE MEGADEATH EVENT

Ground combat, the traditional method used when one military force conducts aggressive initiatives against another, often results in megadeaths. Modern warfare, popularized by Napoleon, reflects the ability of the human species to inflict almost incomprehensible damage that results in the deaths of very large numbers of people. During World War I, for example, during the battle of the Somme, the Allied armies incurred more than 57,000 casualties,

including 19,240 deaths among the British forces. The German army is estimated to have sustained more than 6,000 casualties, either killed or wounded, in this same battle (Middlebrook 1971:245).

Despite the magnitude of such numbers, perhaps the greatest loss of life attributed to military battle in modern history was sustained by the German Sixth Army during and in the aftermath of the battle of Stalingrad during World War II. In late 1941, the rapid advance of the German army led to the occupation of Stalingrad. However, their success over the retreating Russian defenders also had major negative consequences for the Germans, for the German army's support components were unable to keep pace and maintain an adequate supply line. The Russian army later surrounded Stalingrad, besieging the Germans. Hitler ordered his troops to dig in and defend Stalingrad, to fight to the last man and the last bullet. The Germans were able to evacuate by air only 25,000 wounded and critical specialist troops out of the 270,000 men who made up the Sixth Army. Depleted of food, medical supplies, and ammunition, the remnants of the surrounded German force surrendered to the Russians on February 2, 1943. Only 120,000 men survived to be taken prisoner. At the end of hostilities in 1945, a mere 5,000 German prisoners of war out of the original Stalingrad forces had survived to be sent home to Germany (Beevor 1998).

Although millions of military personnel and innocent civilians perished during World II, a limited number of wartime air raids produced what might be considered the most horrifying megadeaths of the war. Martin Middlebrook (1981:28) reports, for example, that 51,509 British civilians were killed as a result of German bombing raids conducted in the skies of the United Kingdom. Even more devastating were the combined military initiatives conducted by American and British bombers over Hamburg, Germany. During a period that lasted several days, the incendiary bombs used during the Hamburg raid created a firestorm that caused the deaths of approximately 45,000 civilians; some estimates range as high as 100,000 deaths (Caidin 1960:282; Middlebrook 1981:28).

The air war conducted over Japan during 1944–45 resulted in even higher death tolls. According to Kerr (1991:273), 112,000 deaths are thought to have occurred as the result of incendiary bomb air raids on six Japanese cities: Kawasaki, Kobe, Nagoya, Osaka, Tokyo, and Yokohama. Later, on August 5 and August 9, 1945, respectively, the atomic bombs dropped by the U.S. Air Force on Hiroshima and Nagasaki resulted in the deaths of 83,000 civilians (70,000 in Hiroshima, 13,000 in Nagasaki; Kerr 1991:271, 273). This megadeath toll led to the surrender of the Japanese forces.

Survivors of War

Robert Bolin (1985) identifies war as a prime example of human-made disaster, and Max Clelland (1982) argues that a war does not end when the shooting ceases. Rather, wars live on in the daily experiences of survivors and their dependents as well as in the collective memories of entire nations. There would seem to be little question that the greatest numbers of deaths occur under conditions of war and that these deaths are, by their very nature, intentional. This intentionality makes all those involved, from combatants to the civilians on the home front, an immediate part of the process and, in the aftermath of war, survivors.

The framing element for all individual reactions and social responses to megadeath is an important concept for survivors, whether at the individual or the collective level. Robert Lifton (1980) defines a survivor as one who has encountered, been exposed to, or witnessed death and has remained alive. This definition is broad enough to include, in the case of war, the perception of a nation that has participated in combat as a survivor, in the sense of national identity. Whatever forms individuals' and nations' responses to the massive losses of war may take, they are only for the living, those who identify as survivors. The dead do not know or care how they are remembered, yet it is their loss that demands responses from the living. Survivors need to find ways to cope with their grief and memories, somehow justify their losses, and attempt to bring closure to their experience of loss.

Individual and public responses to the massive losses that come with war take many forms and involve language, physical entities, and commemorations. The greater the scope of the loss, the more extensive, numerous, and meaningful the individual and collective responses will be. This reality has a long history, as Schwartz notes:

> Primitive societies intuitively knew the value of cultural ceremonies that mark the end of hostilities. Rites of passage were provided for the soldiers and the society to make the transition from the regression of combat to the structure of integrated living. These rituals acknowledged and sanctioned the otherwise forbidden acts of war. They thanked the soldier for his protection, forgave him his crimes and welcomed him back to life. (Quoted in DeSpelder and Strickland 1999:484)

In contemporary society, we recognize that memorials to and commemorations of the dead are essential for effectively creating a sense of closure. Most memorials dedicated to those lost in war express national and/or religious symbols that convey the real or perceived magnitude of the loss and also serve to reify the collective memories and bereavement of the survivors. As John Davies (1993) notes, the symbolic possibilities for war memorials are wide-ranging and may take iconographic, epigraphic, and topographical form. He also observes that war memorials are probably the most widespread kinds of monuments found among the European and American statuary that exists in national capitals, state capitals, small towns, and anywhere else people gather to remember and, as a community-sponsored obligation of survivorship, to honor the dead.

Since 1775, Americans have participated and lost their lives in a number of wars of at least 5 years' duration. The

Table 1	American War Casualties	
Date	*Conflict*	*Casualties (Dead)*
1775–83	American Revolution	4,435
1812–14	War of 1812	2,260
1846–48	Mexican War	13,283
1861–65	Civil War	558,052
1898	Spanish American War	2,446
1914–18	World War I	116,708
1941–45	World War II	407,316
1950–53	Korean War	33,651
1959–75	Vietnam War	58,168
1991	Gulf War	293

SOURCE: Data from "America's Wars" (2002).

greatest loss of American life occurred during the American Civil War (1861–65), when more than 558,000 military casualties occurred. As Table 1 shows, with the exception of the first Gulf War, American military casualties have been high in every war in which the United States has been a participant. In responding to these losses, communities have created hundreds of memorials across the United States and around the world. All of these memorials embody the intentions expressed by General John Logan in 1868 in General Order No. 11, which established the Memorial Day holiday:

> If other eyes grow dull, other hands slack, and other hearts cold in the solemn trust, ours shall keep it well as long as the light and warmth of life remain to us. (Quoted in Merchant 1994)

The importance of collective survivorship and collective responsibility of commemoration can be seen at Arlington National Cemetery, where a sign near the visitors' center reads as follows:

> WELCOME TO
> ARLINGTON NATIONAL
> CEMETERY
> OUR NATION'S MOST
> SACRED SHRINE
>
> PLEASE
> CONDUCT YOURSELF
> WITH DIGNITY AND RESPECT
> AT ALL TIMES
>
> *PLEASE REMEMBER*
> *THESE ARE HALLOWED GROUNDS*

As Backer (1996) notes, we usually think of a shrine as a concrete object or a particular kind of building, but any public place that symbolizes dedication and commemoration can be a shrine. The collective sense of survivorship and the physical artifacts that symbolize our losses are representative of efforts not only to honor those who paid the ultimate price for freedom but to preserve a legacy of the past. Arlington National Cemetery is so conceived as a shrine, a place where people gather to honor both individuals and a concept memorialized in a sprawling landscape (Kammen 1993). Across the United States, memorials have been established to honor Americans who have died while in the service of their country; some of the groups honored include prisoners of war and those missing in action, victims of terrorism, war correspondents, and members of the armed forces lost in the Korean War, World Wars I and II, the first Persian Gulf War, and the Vietnam War, as well as in military operations in Somalia and El Salvador.

In addition to the many physical memorials that have been established to commemorate large losses of life, some special days have also been set aside for remembrance. Memorial Day and Veterans Day in the United States are two examples. Each such day has its own rules of observance, as set out for Memorial Day by General John Logan in General Order No. 11, issued on May 5, 1868:

> Gather around these sacred remains and garland the passionless mounds above them with the choicest flowers of springtime. . . . let us in this solemn presence renew our pledges to aid and assist those whom they have left among us as sacred charges upon the Nation's gratitude, the soldier's and sailor's widow and orphan. (Quoted in Merchant 1994)

This declaration acknowledges the social need for remembrance. On a Web site devoted to the history and observance of Memorial Day, Merchant (1994) lists the following appropriate ways of observing the day:

- By visiting cemeteries and placing flags or flowers on the graves of our fallen heroes
- By visiting memorials
- By flying the U.S. flag at half-staff until noon
- By participating in the National Moment of Remembrance at 3 p.m. to pause and think about the meaning of the day, and for "Taps" to be played
- By renewing a pledge to aid widows, widowers, and orphans of our fallen dead, and to aid disabled veterans

Acts such as these symbolize the obligations of a nation to its citizens who have sacrificed their lives. In General Order No. 11 and other such declarations, we can also identify a common language of social loss and human sacrifice that provides meaning beyond the loss of human life. Important ideals are represented in symbolic words such as *ultimate sacrifice, no greater love, heroes, tragic loss,* and *guardians of freedom.* These words express the public sentiment and, in a collective sense, both define and inform community responses to massive human loss as well as the perceptions of survivors.

GENOCIDE

Much debate surrounds the term *genocide* and its appropriate definition, but for the purposes of this chapter the definition provided by Raphael Lempkin, which is included as part of the United Nations Convention on the Prevention and Punishment of the Crime of Genocide of 1948 (Article II), is useful:

> In the present Convention, genocide means any of the following acts committed with intent to destroy, in whole or in part, a national, ethnical, racial, or religious group, as such: killing members of the group; causing serious bodily or mental harm to members of the group; and deliberately inflicting on the group conditions of life calculated to bring about its physical destruction in whole or in part. (United Nations, as reprinted in Charney 1999:578)

Although the records are incomplete, many historical examples of genocide exist. During the Middle Ages and the Renaissance, males and females alike were suspected of being witches and were persecuted in many parts of the world, including Western Europe, South America, and the Salem, Massachusetts, colony in North America. These infamous witch trials served as an important mechanism for enacting a measure of social control. It has been estimated that from 50,000 to 100,000 accused witches were burned at the stake or otherwise executed.

Another case of genocide that is not widely acknowledged is the intentional extermination of Native peoples by immigrating settlers in North and South America, Australia, and Tasmania (see Robinson 2001). Tens of millions of Native Americans have been counted as victims at the hands of European explorers and settlers who immigrated to the Americas. In Australia, perhaps 720,000 out of a population of 750,000 Aborigines estimated to be living there in 1788 were decimated by disease and by murder at the hands of white European immigrants.

The 20th century has been recorded as the bloodiest period in history, and it may also become known as the century of genocide. It was from his study of genocide, especially the Holocaust, that Lifton (1980) identified and defined his concept of the survivor. Unlike in war, where many of the lives lost are those of combatants, in genocide the population under attack is composed of civilian innocents who have been targeted for extermination. The examples of 20th-century cases of genocide shown in Table 2 clearly establish the massive loss of life that genocide represents. Two examples—the Armenian genocide and the Holocaust—stand out because of the extensive documentation that exists. We use these examples below to examine the magnitude of genocide as well as community responses to such megadeath events.

The Armenian Genocide: 1915–1916

The Armenian genocide, which was carried out by the government of the Ottoman Turks, was intended to

Table 2   Examples of Genocide in the 20th Century

Date	Victims	Location	Perpetrators	Approximate Loss of Life
1915–16	Armenians	Turkey	Muslim government	1.5 million
1917–87	Public	Soviet Union	Communist government	47 million
1940–45	Jews, Romanies, and others	Poland	German army	11 million
1937	Public	Nanking, China	Japanese army	320,000
1949–87	Public	China	Communist government	35.2 million
1975–79	Public	Cambodia	Khmer Rouge	1.7 to 2 million
1975–99	Catholics	East Timor	Muslims	200,000
1994	Tutsis	Rwanda	Hutus	800,000 to 1 million
1995–99	Muslims	Bosnia Herzegovina	Serbian Christians	200,000
1998–99	Muslims	Kosovo	Serbian Christians	400,000 displaced; number of deaths unknown

SOURCE: Adapted from Robinson (2001).

establish a pure Islamic Turkish state. The Armenians of the Ottoman Empire and Turkey were Christian, whereas the Young Turks and their followers where Muslim. The genocide was systematic, beginning with the removal of Armenians from the Turkish military forces. Once disarmed, the Armenian former soldiers were relocated to labor camps and then killed. Armenian political and intellectual leaders were also rounded up and killed. Finally, the remaining Armenians were rounded up, informed that they would be relocated, and then marched into the desert. They were denied food and water, and many also were robbed and killed by marauding bands of criminals and special guard units. At the Black Sea, the Armenians were loaded onto barges that were then sunk.

The consequence of this program of ethnic cleansing was that out of a population of approximately 2 million, 1.5 million Armenians were killed. To this day, the unwillingness of the Turkish government even to acknowledge the Armenian genocide creates a major void in the efforts of survivors and their descendants to bring some closure to bear on their loss. Nevertheless, like the survivors of massive wartime losses, Armenians have sought to create basic forms of remembrance and commemoration rooted in their ethnic identification. Their primary responses have been physical memorials and an annual Day of Remembrance.

The major memorial to the Armenian genocide is located in Yerevan, in Soviet Armenia. The monument consists of two parts, a round memorial sanctuary and the Obelisk of Rebirth. The Memorial Hall is composed of 12 basalt stiles placed in a circle around an eternal flame. The Obelisk of Rebirth, a narrow pyramid shape reaching toward the sky, symbolizes the revival of Armenia. In 1998, the basalt wall that lines the memorial's walkway was inscribed with the names of the major sites in which the genocide occurred (Abdalian 1999).

The Holocaust: 1940–1945

The most documented and memorialized genocide in human history is the Holocaust, the attempted extermination of the Jews of Europe by the Nazi regime. The Holocaust represents the most systematic effort in history to exterminate an entire people. It was well planned and orchestrated by its perpetrators to take advantage of the most technically advanced resources available to establish a series of killing centers. Utilizing a common pesticide gas (Zyklon B) for mass killing, crematoria with specially designed chimneys for the disposal of large numbers of bodies, and other economically and technically advanced means of efficient extermination, the Nazis killed more than 25,000 Jews in each day of operation. Through these methods and others, the Nazi regime killed more than 6 million Jews. In addition to the genocide against the Jews, the Nazis executed more than 5 million other people who did not fit their "Aryan" ideal, including Sinti-Romanies (so-called Gypsies), Jehovah's Witnesses, homosexuals, religious and political dissidents, and persons who were crippled or mentally ill—German citizens who, as Friedlander (1995) notes, were identified as "life unworthy of life" (p. 14).

In attempting to understand the Holocaust by focusing on the victims and especially on the survivors, Lifton (1980) created the concept of individual and collective survivorship, thereby laying a foundation for an understanding of the nature of social responses to megadeath. The very nature and definition of genocide lead us to identify immediately with the victims, because they are part of a collective whole that was identified by the perpetrators along ethnic, religious, or racial lines. Survivors, according to Lifton, bear direct responsibility for remembrance and commemoration.

Sybil Milton (1999) identifies two basic types of Holocaust memorials: the unintentional and the intentional. Unintentional memorials are those made up of the remnants of former concentration and extermination camps and cultural ghettoes. Currently there are more than 100 such memorials with attendant museums located in Austria, the Czech Republic, France, Germany, Italy, the Netherlands, and Poland. These memorials preserve the contents of these camps from the time of their active participation in genocide, including electrified fences, barracks, gas chambers and crematoria, jails, and railroad tracks, among other artifacts. Each year, survivors, their children, and their children's children, Jews and non-Jews alike, visit Auschwitz/Birkenau to engage in the March of the Living.

Yom HaShoah, an annual worldwide Jewish holiday, has been established to commemorate the victims and survivors of the Holocaust. Also known as Holocaust Remembrance Day, Yom HaShoah (*Shoah* is the Jewish word for the Holocaust) is relatively new to the Jewish calendar, and little agreement exists on the best way to mark this day of commemoration. However, many Jews hope that by encouraging the observation of this day, they will help to deepen the world's understanding of the Holocaust tragedy.

In locations where remains of the Holocaust no longer exist or never existed, intentional memorials have been erected. The Warsaw Ghetto and the Treblinka death camp, both destroyed prior to the end of World War II, continue to hold a substantial legacy. At the Warsaw Ghetto, a statue honors those who died during the uprising that took place there, and in Treblinka, a semicircle of stones surrounds a monument situated where a gas chamber once stood, each stone representing an entire community destroyed during the Holocaust. There are many intentional memorials, but the largest and perhaps most important are Yad Vashem, the Holocaust Martyrs' and Heroes' Remembrance Authority, located in Jerusalem; the Ghetto Fighters' House, also located in Israel; the United States Holocaust Memorial Museum in Washington, D.C.; and the Simon Wiesenthal Center, located in Los Angeles. These memorials and other symbols impart the strong message throughout the community and especially to future generations: "Never again."

More recent genocides include those that took place in the killing fields of Cambodia (where there are thousands of mass graves), in Rwanda, and in the infamous ethnic cleansing conducted in Bosnia against Muslims by Serbian Christians. Although these events have yet to be recognized officially with public memorials, the victims of the Cambodian genocide are honored to a limited extent at the S-21 prison located in Phnom Penh.

EPIDEMICS AND DISASTERS

Some ecologists have identified diseases and concomitant epidemics that arose in the past owing to lack of scientific knowledge and ability to control them as nature's way of balancing the growth of population. In any case, when diseases become epidemic and result in megadeaths, there is always some form of social reaction, even if that reaction is later defined as having been misplaced.

Similar to epidemics, disasters strike in rapid fashion, and people's reactions to these events that disrupt community equilibrium are no less dramatic. In this section, we focus on responses to epidemics and disasters, both natural and human-made. Epidemics and disasters are often viewed as inevitable, especially those that involve diseases or events that are beyond human knowledge and control. In addition, disasters that result from mismanagement or lack of insight regarding the risks of particular actions may serve as tragic examples of nonreaction, but these also represent an important part of the human experience.

Epidemics

Two major epidemics account for the highest numbers of mass deaths recorded worldwide. The first of these, the Black Death (bubonic plague) of 1347–51 killed approximately half of the population of the European continent. The plague was responsible for an estimated total of more than 137 million deaths. Although, unlike other causes of mass death, epidemics such as the bubonic plague do not usually stimulate the establishment of memorials, they do result in societal responses. For example, in the case of the Black Death, religious leaders responded by linking the epidemic to visions of the Apocalypse. Others cast the blame for the terrible scourge on such despised groups as Jews, prostitutes, homosexuals, and other so-called immoral and heretical influences (Aiken 2001:60).

In 1918–19, a highly contagious virus known as Spanish influenza was responsible for the deaths of 20 million people worldwide; approximately 850,000 of these victims were residents of the United States. This airborne form of influenza spread rapidly, and with devastating effects. Some communities were especially vulnerable; for example, 60% of the Eskimo population living in Nome, Alaska, died within a matter of days. One-fifth of the global population was infected, as was 28% of the U.S. population.

The United States has seen at least 11 epidemics of major proportion. Among these recorded epidemics, the one that best exemplifies the scope of global response to a pandemic disease is the spread of HIV (human immunodeficiency virus), which causes AIDS (acquired immune deficiency syndrome). From the time HIV/AIDS was identified in 1981 to December 1998, according to estimates by the United Nations and the World Health Organization, worldwide more than 13.9 million people died from AIDS; more than 400,000 of these deaths occurred in the United States ("Pestilence" 2002).

Among the many social responses to the loss of lives from AIDS, two of the most important are the commemorations represented by the Names Project Memorial Quilt and World AIDS Day. The original Names Project began in San Francisco in 1987, when a group of people set out to commemorate the lives of friends lost to this disease. As of this writing, the AIDS Memorial Quilt includes more than 44,000 individual memorial panels (each 3 by 6 feet), each of which commemorates a single life. Collectively, the quilt symbolizes a worldwide loss of lives from the HIV/AIDS pandemic (AIDS Memorial Quilt n.d.). World AIDS Day, established in 1988, is a day set aside each year to commemorate those who have died from the disease,

Table 3   Major U.S. Epidemics

Date	Location	Estimated Loss of Life	Type of Epidemic
1793	Philadelphia	>4,000	Yellow fever
1832	New York City	>3,000	Cholera
1832	New Orleans	4,340	Cholera
1848	New York City	>5,000	Cholera
1853	New Orleans	7,790	Yellow fever
1878	Southern states	>13,000	Cholera
1916	Nationwide	>7,000	Polio
1918	Nationwide	>500,000	Spanish influenza
1949	Nationwide	2,720	Polio
1952	Nationwide	3,300	Polio
1981–June 2001	Nationwide	457,667	AIDS

SOURCE: Adapted from "Major U.S. Epidemics" (2002); Fact Monster (www.factmonster.com). Copyright 2002 Family Education Network, July 16, 2003.

celebrate the living, and renew a pledge to fight the pandemic ("World AIDS Day Commemorations" n.d.).

Although the initial commemorations of AIDS victims began among members of gay communities in the United States where the AIDS virus was first identified, as more knowledge of the disease has become available the memorial responses no longer target a single group, and various forms of commemoration have been established worldwide. Another social response to the AIDS pandemic has taken the form of attempts to educate the global public regarding the risks associated with the virus that causes the disease.

Natural Disasters

In 1887, nearly 2 million Chinese died when the Hwang Ho River overflowed its 3,000-mile banks. In 1931, a similar flooding of the area was responsible for the drowning deaths of 4 million Chinese, and in 1938, the Hwang Ho flooded again, leading to the drowning deaths of almost a million people.

Deaths attributed to earthquakes are not infrequent, although generally the numbers of recorded deaths are not large. Exceptions have been documented, however. The deadliest earthquake on record occurred in China on January 23, 1556, when 830,000 people died. More than 200 years later, on July 27, 1976, the second deadliest earthquake (magnitude 8.0 on the Richter scale) was recorded in Tangshan, China. The resulting loss of life was 255,000 (although some have estimated the loss to be as high as 655,000). On March 25, 2002, an earthquake of 6.1 magnitude killed 1,000 people in the Hindu Kush region of Afghanistan. On January 26, 2001, a total of 20,023 deaths occurred in Gujarat, India, as the result of an earthquake of magnitude 7.7. Earlier in that same month, a magnitude 7.7 earthquake killed 852 people in El Salvador.

Measuring 8.3 on the Richter scale, the April 18, 1906, San Francisco earthquake occurred at 5:13 A.M. The fire that followed the earthquake burned for 4 days, during which time it is estimated that 3,000 people died from all causes related to the quake, including the initial earthquake, the extensive multiple fires that resulted, a major aftershock, and the collapse of buildings. The financial damage of this disaster was approximately $500 million in 1906 dollars. However, the rebuilding of the city soon began, as the resolve of its people was put into action. On April 23, 1906, the governor of California stated, "The work of rebuilding San Francisco has commenced, and I expect to see the great metropolis replaced on a much grander scale than ever before" (quoted in Museum of the City of San Francisco, n.d.). (For more information on the numbers of deaths caused by various natural disasters, see the appendix to this chapter.)

Airplane Disasters

Since the end of World War II, worldwide air traffic has increased dramatically. In addition to the numbers of aircraft in the skies, the size of aircraft has increased, so that far greater numbers of people travel on a single airplane. As with any advances in science and technology, the advances in air travel have had some negative consequences; one such consequence is that with larger aircraft, a larger loss of life is incurred when a crash takes place.

The cumulative loss of lives in airplane disasters numbers in the thousands, a small proportion of total population compared with other forms of mass death, but the effects of these kinds of events on the world community appear to be exacerbated by the fact that it is often the case that an airplane crash accounts for a significant number of deaths in a single event as well as within a matter of minutes. Table 4 lists the 10 deadliest airplane crashes to date. Some of these were the result of mechanical failure and human error; others were caused by terrorist activity.

TERRORISM

Terrorist bombings and other forms of sabotage represent yet another source of megadeaths. We use two examples of recent acts of terrorism in this section to illustrate significant community responses in reaction to massive loss of life owing to terrorist acts. The April 19, 1995, bombing of the Murrah Federal Building in Oklahoma City, Oklahoma, stunned the entire nation. Americans were not accustomed to experiencing domestic terrorism, and the

Table 4   Ten Deadliest Airplane Crashes

Date	Location	Loss of Life	Cause
March 27, 1977	Tenerife, Canary Islands	583	Runway collision; 2 planes
August 12, 1985	Mt. Osutaka, Japan	520	Crash into mountain
November 12, 1996	New Delhi, India	349	Midair collision; 2 planes
March 3, 1974	Ermenonville, France	346	Crash after takeoff
June 23, 1985	Off coast of Ireland	329	Explosive device in cargo hold
August 19, 1980	Riyadh, Saudi Arabia	301	Fire in cargo hold
July 3, 1988	Persian Gulf	290	Surface-air missile
May 25, 1979	Chicago, Illinois	273	Engine drop and damage
December 21, 1988	Lockerbie, Scotland	270	Bomb detonation in cargo hold
September 1, 1983	Sakhalin, Island, Russia	269	Russian Air Force fighter shoot-down

SOURCE: Adapted from "The 10 Deadliest Airplane Crashes" (1999).

bombing left 168 people dead and a nation overwhelmed with grief. This significant loss of life and property was, until September 11, 2001, identified as the worst terrorist attack ever to occur on U.S. soil.

The attacks on the twin towers of the World Trade Center in New York and on the Pentagon are now secure in American history as the most devastating terrorist acts ever to be perpetrated on U.S. soil. With a loss of approximately 3,000 lives and extensive financial strain, the events of September 11, and the aftermath of these attacks on the symbols of democracy and capitalism, have produced a social response that indicates a strong need to commemorate this day. On December 18, 2001, the U.S. Congress enacted House Joint Resolution 71 as Public Law 104-89, establishing Patriot Day as a day of remembrance for the victims of the September 11 attacks. Many state legislatures either have passed or currently are considering similar resolutions. The days that states have already proposed to commemorate September 11 include Emergency Providers and Armed Forces Day (Alaska), Remembrance Day (Connecticut), Florida Rescue Worker's Day, Firefighters and Emergency Medical Personnel Day (Kentucky), Maryland Day of Temperance, Pledge of Allegiance Day (Michigan), Heroes Day (New Jersey), National 911 Day (Pennsylvania), 911 Heroes Day (South Carolina), Emergency Worker's Day (Tennessee), and Virginia Police, Fire, and Rescue Services Memorial Day. Other states have plans to create permanent memorials dedicated to the victims of September 11, 2001, financed either with state funds or through tax-deductible donations. Other sponsored activities conducted at the local level on or about September 11, 2002, to commemorate the first anniversary of the terrorist attacks included high school and college events such as performances and displays of memorial artwork, museum offerings, and public discussions pertaining to such issues as the difference between a freedom fighter and a suicide bomber.

CONCLUSION

It is difficult at best to summarize the research findings and general facts available pertaining to megadeath events and the resultant reactions of individuals and communities to these events and the processes leading to such catastrophes, but perhaps a focus on one recent event can serve to demonstrate the importance that remembrance holds for communities large and small. President George W. Bush's encouragement that we go on with our lives in the aftermath of the tragedy of the events of September 11, 2001, seemed, to Americans in particular, extraordinary. But as astonishing as the events of that day were, and as vivid as they remain in our minds, life does indeed seem to go on. And this orientation may offer us important insight into why collective commemorations not only identify the historical past but represent important cultural artifacts.

For some Americans, the events of September 11, 2001, will forever be forged in memory. In the minds of others, however, the tragedy may eventually come to be perceived merely as an event in history—an event that, like so many others, has little direct or personal meaning. We create memorials to recognize those whose lives were lost, and these memorials serve an important social function: Without them, the events might soon fade from memory and eventually enter into total oblivion. The efforts that individuals and organized groups make to ensure that memorials are erected or state or national days of remembrance are created give notice that megadeath events are social facts. Such facts represent an important part of the human legacy, no matter how tragic they may be. Time may heal the individual wounds endured directly or indirectly by all who constitute the body politic, but memorials, symbolic as they are, ensure that we never forget. This, too, represents our legacy.

APPENDIX

Natural Disasters (Selected Major Storms and Other Disasters)

Type of Disaster/Date	Location	Estimated Loss of Life
Cyclones		
1864	Calcutta, India	70,000
1942	Bengal, India	40,000
1960	East Pakistan	6,000
1963	East Pakistan	22,000
1965	East Pakistan	47,000
1965	Karachi, Pakistan	10,000
1970	East Pakistan	200,000
1971	Orissa, India	10,000
1977	Andhra Pradesh, India	20,000
1991	Southeast Bangladesh	131,000
1999	Orissa, India	9,573
Hurricanes		
1776	Nova Scotia	4,170
1780	Barbados, West Indies	20 to 22,000
1856	Last Island, Louisiana	400
1893	Savannah, Georgia	>1,000
1900	Galveston, Texas	6 to 8,000
1919	Florida Keys, Louisiana, and Alabama	>600
1926	Southeast Florida	243 (costliest hurricane in U.S. history; $84 billion)
1926	Cuba	650
1928	Southeast Florida	1,836
1930	Dominican Republic	8,000
1963	Haiti and Cuba	7,000
1974	Honduras	8,000
1998	Caribbean, Florida Keys, and Gulf Coast	600
1998	Honduras, Nicaragua, and Guatemala	11,000
Typhoons		
1906	Hong Kong	10,000
1934	Japan	4,000
1949	Off Korea	Several thousand
1958	Honshu, Japan	5,000
1959	Fukien Province, China	2,334
1960	Fukien Province, China	1,600
1984	Philippines	1,300
1991	Central Philippines	3,000
Earthquakes and tidal waves		
1201	Near East and Mediterranean	1 million
1556	China	830,000
1933	Japan	3,000
1988	Armenia	25,000
1998	Papua New Guinea	2,000
Floods		
1099	Netherlands and England	100,000
1889	Johnstown, Pennsylvania	2,000
Volcanic eruptions		
A.D. 79	Mount Vesuvius	20,000
1883	Indonesia	36,380

APPENDIX Continued

Type of Disaster/Date	Location	Estimated Loss of Life
Famines		
1845–49	Ireland	1.5 million
1959–61	Northern China	30 million (world's deadliest famine)
1967–69	Biafra	1 million
Avalanches		
1910	United States	118
1962	Peru	4,000
Blizzards		
1888	Dakota and Montana Territories and Central Plains	235
1888	U.S. East Coast	400
1950	Eastern U.S.	383
1977	Buffalo, New York	29
1993	Eastern U.S.	270
1996	Eastern U.S.	187

SOURCE: Adapted from "Natural Disasters" (2002); Fact Monster (www.factmonster.com). Copyright 2002 Family Education Network, July 16, 2003.

REFERENCES

Abdalian, Rouben P. 1999. "Armenian Genocide Memorial in Yerevan, Armenia." Pp. 102–4 in *The Encyclopedia of Genocide,* edited by Israel Charney. Santa Barbara, CA: ABC-CLIO.

AIDS Memorial Quilt. n.d. "History of the Quilt." Retrieved December 10, 2002 (http://www.aidsquilt.org/history.htm).

Aiken, Lewis R. 2001. *Dying, Death, and Bereavement,* 4th ed. Mahwah, NJ: Lawrence Erlbaum.

"America's Wars: Casualties and Veterans." 2002. Factmonster, Family Education Network. Retrieved December 11, 2002 (http://www.factmonster. com/ipka/A0004615.html).

Backer, Dan. 1996. "Arlington National Cemetery." Retrieved December 4, 2002 (http://xroads.virginia.edu/~cap/ arlington/text.html).

Beevor, Antony. 1998. *Stalingrad, the Fateful Siege: 1942–1943.* New York: Viking.

Bolin, Robert. 1985. "Disaster Characteristics and Psychosocial Impacts." Pp. 3–27 in *Mental Health: Selected Contemporary Perspectives,* edited by Barbara J. Sowder. Rockville, MD: National Institutes of Health.

Caidin, Martin. 1960. *The Night Hamburg Died.* New York: Ballantine.

Charney, Israel, ed. 1999. *The Encyclopedia of Genocide.* Santa Barbara, CA: ABC-CLIO.

Clelland, Max. 1982. *Strong at the Broken Places.* New York: Chosen.

Davies, John. 1993. "War Memorials." Pp. 112–28 in *The Sociology of Death,* edited by David Clark. Oxford: Blackwell.

DeSpelder, Lynne Ann and Albert Lee Strickland. 1999. *The Last Dance: Encountering Death and Dying,* 5th ed. Mountain View, CA: Mayfield.

Erikson, Kai T. 1976. *Everything in Its Path: Destruction of Community in the Buffalo Creek Flood.* New York: Simon & Schuster.

Frankl, Victor. 1983. *Man's Search for Meaning.* New York: Washington Square.

Friedlander, Henry. 1995. *The Origins of Nazi Genocide: From Euthanasia to the Final Solution.* Chapel Hill: University of North Carolina Press.

Kammen, Michael. 1993. *Mystic Chords of Memory: The Transformation of Tradition in American Culture.* New York: Vintage.

Kerr, E. Bartlett. 1991. *Flames Over Tokyo.* New York: Donald I. Fines.

Lifton, Robert J. 1980. "The Concept of the Survivor." Pp. 113–26 in *Survivors, Victims, and Perpetrators: Essays on the Nazi Holocaust,* edited by Joel E. Dimsdale. New York: Hemisphere.

Lifton, Robert J. and Eric Olson. 1976. "The Human Meaning of Total Disaster: The Buffalo Creek Experience." *Psychiatry* 39:1–18.

"Major U.S. Epidemics." 2002. Factmonster, Family Education Network. Retrieved December 10, 2002 (http://www. factmonster.com/ipka/a0001460.html).

Merchant, David M. 1994. "Memorial Day." Retrieved December 4, 2002 (http://www.usmemorialday.org).

Middlebrook, Martin. 1971. *First Day on the Somme.* New York: W. W. Norton.

———. 1981. *The Battle of Hamburg.* New York: Charles Scribner's Sons.

Milton, Sybil. 1999. "Museums and Memorials of Genocide." Pp. 423–27 in *The Encyclopedia of Genocide,* edited by Israel Charney. Santa Barbara, CA: ABC-CLIO.

Museum of the City of San Francisco. n.d. "Timeline of the San Francisco Earthquake: April 18–23, 1906." Retrieved

December 24, 2002 (http://www.sfmuseum.net/hist10/06timeline.html).

"Natural Disasters." 2002. Factmonster, Family Education Network. Retrieved December 18, 2002 (http://www.factmonster.com/ipka.html).

"Pestilence." 2002. Factmonster, Family Education Network. Retrieved December 11, 2002 (http://www.factmonster.com/ipka/A0769027.html).

Robinson, B. A. 2001. "Mass Crimes Against Humanity and Genocides: A List of Atrocities 1450 CE to the Present." Kingston: Ontario Consultants on Religious Tolerance.

Retrieved December 7, 2002 (http://www.religioustolerance.org/genocide2.htm).

Rossi, Peter and James Wright. 1981. *Social Science and Natural Hazards*. Boston: Abt.

"The 10 Deadliest Airplane Crashes." 1999. *News & Record*. Retrieved December 24, 2002 (http://www.news-record/ae/firstflight/10wright22.htm).

"World AIDS Day Commemoration." n.d. Global Treatment Access Campaign. Retrieved December 10, 2002 (http://www.globaltreatmentaccess.org).

On the Role and Meaning of Death in Terrorism

Lee Garth Vigilant

John B. Williamson

"Murder," wrote Karl Heinzen ([1849] 1978), "is the principal agent of historical progress" (p. 53). This rather macabre statement speaks volumes about the power that violence and terror wield in political discourse. Moreover, this lesson, which a host of terror groups the world over—at last count, more than 600 (Long 1990)—have learned very well, underscores the important role that death plays in attempts to initiate political change.

In the past two decades the world has seen an unprecedented increase in terrorism as a mechanism of asymmetrical political communication between powerful nation-states and less powerful fringe groups that have been marginalized (Simon 2001). In using terrorism as a form of low-intensity, asymmetrical warfare, these less powerful groups have applied death in the form of political murders, suicide bombings, and large-scale killings as the principal mechanism for achieving their goals of liberation and communication. During the past two decades, Americans have increasingly endured violence at the hands of both state-sponsored and fringe-group terror organizations in retaliation for political policies that these organizations deem unfair and repressive (McGuckin 1997). The point is poignantly conveyed whether we invoke the examples of the 1993 and 2001 attacks on the World Trade Center towers in New York, which together killed some 3,000 individuals and injured thousands more; the 1995 bombing of the Alfred P. Murrah Federal Building in Oklahoma City, which took the lives of 168 individuals; the 1983 bombing of the U.S. Marine barracks in Beirut, which resulted in 241 deaths; or the bombing of Pan Am Flight 103 en route over Lockerbie, Scotland, which killed 270 individuals. These events are memorable and profound in part owing to the use of mass-mediated images of death and destruction by terror groups to communicate their political aims. These events raise profound thanatological questions concerning the use of death as a political device, questions that seem to have grown in significance since September 11, 2001.

What role does death play in terrorism, and what meaning should we attach to the increasing lethality of acts of terrorism around the globe? These questions are at the heart of this essay on the thanatological implications of the role and meaning of death in acts of terror—questions that have been largely ignored by a rather extensive body of literature on terrorism (Crenshaw 1992; Miller 1988). The importance of these questions to contemporary discourses on terrorism cannot be overstated, especially at a time when images of terror and politically inspired lethal acts seem to be omnipresent and increasing. To consider the role and meaning of death in acts of terrorism is to study horror in extremis—the very reason terrorism is one of the oldest mechanisms of state-sponsored oppression and an oft-chosen pathway for the liberation of powerless groups of people. Perhaps an examination of the role and meaning of death in terrorism will ultimately lead us to an understanding of the raison d'être of politically motivated violence and other acts of terror.

We begin this chapter with an interpretation of the distinct role that death plays—and the meaning it communicates—in terrorism. We then explore the various manifestations of death by terrorism, from political violence to apocalyptic and religious terror, to the emergence of technologies of mass death and the inevitability of their application in new forms of terrorism, such as biological and chemical warfare. We close the chapter with an examination of the role and meaning of death in the shadow of the events of September 11, 2001.

THE ROLE AND MEANING
OF DEATH IN TERRORISM

In an essay titled "The Role of Death in War," Theresa Wirtz (1992) notes that the real horror of war is revealed in the way it rationally exploits human mortality for political ends. Wirtz asserts that the engine of war is *surplus death,* or the "amount a system can lose and still maintain tolerable levels of social stability and biological maintenance" (p. 12). A system's survival would be seriously threatened if the system were to incur losses beyond the point of surplus death, so losses beyond the point of surplus naturally lead to a rational consensus to end the conflict. According to Wirtz, the strategic aim of all warfare, then, is to exploit the enemy to the state of *assured limitation,* the point where it would be virtually useless or impossible to extract further deaths. This strategic goal of all warfare has led to the development of precision-guided weapons capable of producing megadeath and mass destruction, such as nuclear weaponry and chemical and biological agents, to supplement the usual arsenal of battleships, submarines, fighter jets, and armed soldiers. The underlying rationality of war is how military technologies can now achieve massive deaths in the most efficient and lethal manner. Yet such military technologies, which are designed for the express purpose of increasing enemy body count, are usually not available to less powerful and less developed nations or to nonstate factions. How, then, are these groups to engage in political conflicts with more powerful nation-states? The answer to this quandary is terrorism, or what many scholars of terrorism refer to as *low-intensity* or *asymmetrical warfare* (see Klare and Kornbluh 1988).

Although it is difficult to establish an all-encompassing definition of the concept of terrorism, owing to the presence of irreconcilable political ideologies and interstate antagonisms (Chomsky 1991) as well as simple conceptualization problems (Gibbs 1989), most attempts at a definition have in common the central roles that fear and terror play in conveying ideas. Accordingly, Cooper (2001) defines terrorism as "the intentional generation of massive fear by human beings for the purpose of securing or maintaining control over other human beings" (p. 883). Central to this definition is the aim of control. A terrorist group controls its target audience by generating widespread and crippling fear in the public through violent acts of death and destruction (Gibbs 1989). The same force that is at work in conventional warfare—namely, the strategic attempt to reduce an adversary's surplus death—is likewise at work in the deployment of terrorism, but with a major difference: In conventional warfare, under the rules of the Geneva convention, it is no longer morally acceptable for combatants to generate terror by perpetrating death on noncombatants. That is, in conventional warfare, surplus death does not include the deaths of noncombatant civilians such as women, children, and the elderly. However, terrorist groups, because of their inability to engage the military forces of major nation-states, number

civilian noncombatants among the surplus deaths of their targeted enemies. Thus, by redefining the notion of innocence and by narrowing the parameters of victimhood (see Wilkins 1992), terrorists are able to justify the strategic killing of civilians in their asymmetrical conflicts with more powerful nation-states.

Of course, the ultimate hope of every terrorist group is that the more powerful adversary will respond to the crippling fear inflicted on its population by acknowledging the terrorist group's grievances and acquiescing to its demands. It is important to mention that the infliction of mass death is not the prime aim of some terrorist groups; rather, they use other means to inflict fear in order to persuade their enemies to give them what they want. In fact, there have been instances in which terrorists have made deliberate and extreme efforts *not* to kill civilians or law enforcement personnel. For instance, in the early years of the Front de Liberation du Quebec, the group's targets for bombings were inanimate symbols of Anglo-Canadian dominance, such as the Royal Canadian Legion building, the mailboxes of upper-class Anglo-Canadians, and television transmission towers. Moreover, the group usually bombed these targets in the middle of the night, to minimize the potential for human casualties (see Fournier 1984). The vast majority of terror groups today, however, do use lethal levels of violence against their targets, and so it is crucial that we understand the important role death plays in terrorism.

Death plays a crucial part in terrorism because terrorists view the production of death and the fear that accompanies it as their principal mechanism for liberation. Consequently, death performs five key roles in terrorism: (a) as a communicative device in political discourse, (b) as a mechanism for controlling the masses, (c) as a strategy for liberating the oppressed, (d) as a generator of public sympathy, and (e) as a spectacle for mass (media) consumption.

Death as Political Communication

The first and most important role that death plays in terrorism is that of communicative medium between less powerful nation-states or nonstate factions and more powerful, militarily superior governments. Terrorist organizations typically resort to violence and death when their groups' efforts at influencing political or social changes are ignored or hampered by unresponsive nation-states.

In a study of the political context of terrorism in the United States, Christopher Hewitt (2000) found that violent acts of terrorism were more likely to take place when unresponsive presidential administrations (rather than sympathetic ones) were in power. In effect, disempowered groups see death and violence as mechanisms of last resort; they employ terrorism only after they believe they have exhausted other, more legitimate, means of political communication and persuasion. Death is at once the message and the medium they use to influence the direction of political discourse; as such, death functions as a communicative device (Schmid and de Graaf 1982).

As Crelinsten (1992) explains, terrorist victimization in the form of death serves three specific functions as a communication device: an attention-getting function, a symbolic function, and an instrumental function. Terrorist groups use public killings to bring attention to their causes or concerns; these actions are designed to capture the attention of their intended audiences, usually politicians or industrial leaders. Regarding the symbolic communicative function of terrorist victimization, Crelinsten states, "For those who identify with the victim because of something the two hold in common, the function of victimization is to warn them that they might be next" (p. 213). That is, the killing of a politician, a diplomat, or a businessperson might serve notice to other individuals with the same social status that they too could be marked for victimization. Of course, the more prominent and powerful the victim, the greater symbolism his or her death by terrorism has, and the more likely the terrorist group is to garner attention. In the absence of prominent or powerful victims, terrorist groups resort to mass killings and other forms of victimization; indeed, innocent bystanders are now the chief targets of terrorist groups around the world (Weimann and Winn 1994). The instrumental communicative function of terrorist violence is clear: By killing the right person or groups of people, as in the case of political assassinations, terrorist groups attempt to speed political changes and influence official discourse, hoping that these events will result in systemic changes on both political and social levels.

Death as a Mechanism for Controlling the Masses

Lethal violence is the principal mechanism of social control employed by terrorist groups. According to Gibbs (1989), terrorist groups employ death and extreme violence as *deterrent social control* to manage the behavior of target populations through intimidation and to influence the direction of political policies. Through extreme acts of violence, terrorists hope to instill crippling fear in the general populations of targeted nations and to force the governments of those nations to adopt repressive measures in the name of "national security," in hopes that this will cause the governments to lose legitimacy and fall (Gibbs 1989). Moreover, when repeated episodes of violence result in the deaths of innocent, noncombatant victims, a situation is created in which people lose confidence in their government's ability to perform its most basic function, that of the protection of its citizenry. Thus terrorist groups use violent death, which is connected to the quest for power and influence, to control people and to sway the course of political policies that they deem to be repressive and unfair. According to Hoffman (1998), "All terrorism involves the quest for power: power to dominate and coerce, to intimidate and control, and ultimately to effect fundamental change" (p. 182).

Why is the threat of death or extreme violence so effective in controlling populations? The answer is simple. Terrorist groups have learned well how to manipulate their targets' thanatophobic tendencies. The threat of death is an effective mechanism of social control and political persuasion because of human beings' omnipresent and omnipotent death anxieties (Zilboorg 1943; Wahl 1965; Becker 1995). Death anxiety is a natural part of the human condition. We fear death, and we try our best to delay our mortal demise, despite its inevitability. As Becker (1995) puts it, "The fear of death must be present behind all our normal functioning, in order for the organism to be armed toward self-preservation" (p. 35). Terrorists thus exploit people's natural inclination toward self-preservation by mass-producing death and the widespread terror and panic that the threat of death creates.

It is important to note that terrorists do not undertake mass killings to instill fear and panic in the immediate victims of terror; rather, they seek to create those feelings in the hearts of the witnessing public. Thus terrorist acts are successful when the public reacts to them with panic and fear (Freedman 1983; Oots and Wiegele 1985). In a succinct essay on the role of terror in terrorism, Lawrence Freedman (1983) notes:

> The sudden transformation of the human target from free agent to vulnerable victim assaults the sense of autonomy of the spectator. . . . In psychoanalytic terms, it is as though an irresistible impulse from the id assaults the personification of the social representative of the superego. These manifestations of unconscious psychic institutions arouse not only fear but also the sense of the uncanny: the terrorist is seemingly omnipotent. (Pp. 399–400)

Death by terrorism assaults our sense of ontological security (Giddens 1991), those feelings of order and stability that are closely linked to the ritual of having a daily routine. The shock, confusion, and sheer panic of the experience of violent death, especially when death is random and apparently pointless, upset our routine and shatter our sense of security and safety. Death by terrorism reminds us that we are all potential victims in waiting, and that leads to conditions of panic that deeply affect the routines of daily life. Fear of a terrorist attack can severely alter our mundane rituals and behaviors, and this is precisely what makes death by terrorism so potent: It brings to the fore our death anxieties, spreading the contagion of fear and panic, which upsets our sense of security. Terrorists use widespread fear as a form of psychological control. By forcing those they target to reassess their mundane rituals, their ways of thinking, and their freedom of movement, terrorists use the natural fear of death to exert a certain level of control.

Thus a symbiotic, mutually dependent relationship exists among terrorism, death anxiety, and feelings of helplessness and loss of control. In order for terrorism to terrorize, it must activate and play upon our death anxiety. But simply activating our death anxiety is not enough—after all, tens of thousands of people are injured and killed in automobile accidents yearly, but that fact does not prevent the vast majority of motorists from getting behind the wheel. Rather, most drivers have some sense of control over the possibility of serious injury or death while driving, and so are convinced that they will not be the next accident fatalities. They are confident in their ability to drive safely and thus avoid serious traffic incidents. Perhaps it is a sense of personal immortality that assuages an individual's potential fear of dying in an accident and keeps him or her on the road. But the case of terrorism is fundamentally different from that of taking everyday risks like driving. Terrorism works because it destroys completely the facade that individuals have control over their environment and their mortality: We cannot know how to avoid death by terrorism because terrorists purposefully exploit our sense of ontological security by randomly selecting new targets—human targets. And this realization, that we are all potential targets for death by terrorism, is one that is potentially crippling.

Death as a Strategy for Liberating the Oppressed

Some oppressed groups view inflicting death and extreme forms of violence on their perceived enemies as a route to retribution and a sense of power. These groups see the threat of death by terrorism as a leveling mechanism: It gives the privileged a taste of what life is like for the oppressed masses. What their victims see as vindictive and senseless deaths, such terrorists view as a calculated strategy for liberation, revenge, and retaliation. Terrorism for liberation purposes, or what Kastenbaum (2001) refers to as "upward-directed terrorism," is the principal weapon of the disenfranchised and powerless. Frantz Fanon (1968), in his psychiatry of colonial oppression, understood this lesson well. He asserts that "violence is a cleansing force" (p. 94) for the oppressed, a mechanism that frees the subjugated from the mire of despair, hopelessness, and powerlessness. In the terrorist's mind, death by terrorism is the ultimate reprisal for—and expression of—the hopelessness and despair of the oppressed's existential condition. It conveys only too clearly to the oppressor a people's longing for liberation in the midst of dashed hopes, unfulfilled expectations, and entrenched deprivation—the very roots of rebellion, violent terror, and death (Gurr 1970).

As a strategy for liberation, terrorism, lethal and otherwise, is appealing for another reason. As a tool of liberation, terrorism offers oppressed people a new identity and selfhood, transforming their collective self-image from one of vassal to freeman, and this new collective consciousness is one grounded in resistance (Camus 1956). But there are problems with this strategy. For one, when oppressed groups carry out acts of terrorism they run the risk of losing the moral high ground (King 1958). Equally as important, as Kelman (1973) suggests, using violence as

a mechanism for liberation might actually be a self-defeating strategy in the long run:

> Violence can offer a person the illusion that he is in control, that he is able to act on his environment, that he has found a means of self-expression. It may be the only way left for him to regain some semblance of identity, to convince him that he really exists. The sad irony is that violence is a response to dehumanization that only deepens the loss that it seeks to undo; it is an attempt to regain one's sense of identity by further destroying one's sense of community. (P. 58)

Although the use of terrorism is often psychologically and emotionally appealing for oppressed groups, it results in a sad perpetuation of oppression, because violence often begets violence, and death often begets death, on both sides—a lesson that many asymmetrical conflicts, such as the Israeli/Palestinian discord, have historically validated. Moreover, as a strategy for liberation, the use of this form of violence often leads to discord and carnage among the members of terror groups themselves (Kastenbaum 2001:231).

Death as a Generator of Public Sympathy

Lethal terrorist acts can serve to generate public sympathy for the terrorists' cause; McClenon (1988) refers to this role of terrorism as "terrorism as persuasion." Following the terrorist attacks on the Pentagon and World Trade Center on September 11, 2001, *Newsweek* magazine and other news media outlets showcased photographs of fringe groups among Palestinian refugees who were celebrating the success of the Al Qaeda operatives ("America Under Attack" 2001). As shocking as the photographs appear, the symbolism they convey is unmistakable. Terrorist groups use death as a seductive instrument of persuasion to galvanize support among their oppressed constituencies. The leader of the Hindustan Socialist Republican Army of the 1930s expressed this seduction well in a manifesto aptly titled "The Philosophy of the Bomb":

> Terrorism instills fear in the heart of the oppressors; it brings the hope of revenge and redemption to the oppressed masses. It gives courage and self-confidence to the wavering; it shatters the spell of the subject race in the eyes of the world, because it is the most convincing proof of a nation's hunger for freedom. (Charan [1930] 1978:139)

Historically, death by terrorism has been the chosen instrument of political interlocutions between less powerful fringe groups and controlling nation-states. The threat of death conveys to the oppressor the experience of subjugation. But more than mere political communication between the oppressed and oppressor, lethal terrorist acts served to build collective solidarity among the downtrodden and demoralized. The examples of the African National Congress (ANC), the Euskadi ta Askatasuna

(ETA), the Irish Republican Army (IRA), and the Palestinian Liberation Organization (PLO) are particularly noteworthy here. The broad public support that these organizations enjoy from their respective constituencies, in spite of their historical use of suicide bombings and political assignations, is powerful evidence of the seductive and persuasive influence of death by terrorism. For instance, opinion surveys among Palestinians in the late 1980s found that between 86% and 95% held a positive image of terrorists, and 61% approved of the use of violence as a route to liberation (Hewitt 1992). Similarly, among Basques, 66% held a positive image of ETA, even though the vast majority disagreed with its use of violence (Hewitt 1992). In fact, the use of violence and death as a form of political communication does not, by itself, discredit a terrorist group among its primary constituency, even when noncombatant civilians are the direct targets of violence, as in the case of Palestinian terrorists. The violence that marks the Israeli/Palestinian conflict, where civilians are deliberately targeted for death, is especially instructive of this. Hewitt (1992) notes, "Such atrocities do not discredit the cause for which they fight; neither do they tarnish their patriotic image" (p. 187).

As the popular aphorism "One man's terrorist is another man's freedom fighter" suggests, terrorist groups, by championing the causes of oppressed peoples through death and extreme violence, become revolutionary patriots to many. Moreover, the experiences of the IRA, the ANC, and the PLO suggest that yesterday's terrorists often become today's peacemakers and tomorrow's prime ministers (Goertzel 1988). The transformation of some major terrorist groups from murderous organizations into internationally recognized political parties and governments is proof that the use of violence to build sympathy and win support for political ends is sometimes successful. Nelson Mandela of the ANC, Yasser Arafat of the PLO, Gerry Adams of the IRA, and Yitzhak Shamir of the Zionist movement that preceded the establishment of the state of Israel have one thing in common: At one point in their political lives, they were all considered terrorists, anathema of nations such as the United Kingdom and the United States, who championed the liberation of their constituencies through terrorist organizations that employed acts of extreme violence and death. This point underscores the difficulty of arriving at consensus on who exactly should be considered a terrorist.

Our definitions of terrorism are socially constructed, politically mediated, and perpetually shifting. Descriptions of terrorism are themselves framed by the media, by politics, and by culture. Here, the concepts of "frame" and "frame reflection" (Goffman 1974; Gamson 1992; Schön and Rein 1994) are most applicable. When sociologists employ the concept of "frame," they are referring to the conscious manipulation of images, stories, statements, and ideas to shape and sway public opinion on an issue or to influence the interpretation of some event for public consumption. Although the mass media are today the principal site for framing battles (Ryan 1991; Gamson 1992), all of social life, from politics to sports to entertainment, is concerned with the creation and proliferation of selected impressions and premises. Thus a person might be perceived simultaneously as a "terrorist" in one frame and as a "freedom fighter" in another. In the former frame, his actions are interpreted as callous, irrational, and murderous, whereas in the latter they are seen as sacrificial, as calculated acts of martyrdom. A case in point is the debate about the proper frame to use in describing those who die, and kill others, by detonating explosives they have strapped to themselves. Are the people who use this method of asymmetrical warfare and method of generating public sympathy "suicide martyrs" or "homicide bombers"? Both of these descriptors represent skillful attempts at framing this use of violence to sway public opinion.

The suicide bombing is perhaps the most potent symbolic communiqué among the many forms of death that terrorists use to galvanize public support and sympathy for their political ends. Modern suicide bombings, as acts intended to generate fear and sympathy, began in Lebanon with the Shiite terror group Hezbollah. Hezbollah's primary targets, beginning in 1983, were Western military and diplomatic personnel, targets that offered an effective route to public sympathy and media exposure (Dobson and Payne 1987; Simon 2001; Long 1990). For Hezbollah, suicide bombings were appealing because they represented a cost-efficient way to achieve the greatest number of enemy casualties with minimal cost and risk to the organization. As Ganor (2000) notes, the following six factors made suicide bombings the new modus operandi of terrorist organizations such as Hezbollah:

1. They added to casualties and damage inflicted on enemies.

2. They attracted wide media attention.

3. They were easy to undertake.

4. They were difficult to counteract once personnel were in place.

5. They required no escape planning.

6. They ensured that perpetrators would not be interrogated about organizational secrets.

But more important than the benefits accrued to the terrorist organization itself was the potential of suicide bombings to strengthen collective solidarity around political aims and generate sympathy for those who sacrificed their lives for the cause. It is here that death by terrorism's potential as a generator of public sympathy is most strongly felt.

For the members of extreme Islamic terrorist groups such as Hamas and Hezbollah, to die committing an act of terrorism is the highest form of death (Hoffman 1995). Such a death gives the perpetrator immediate access to paradise, increased social status for his family, and the assurance that he will be remembered as a *shahid,* or a jihad (holy war) martyr (Ganor 2000). Moreover, the family of the suicide bomber, according to Ganor (2000), "is showered with honor and praise, and receives financial reward for the attack (usually *some thousands* of dollars)" (p. 2). The suicide bomber himself is believed to enter paradise to the welcome of 72 virgins, his personal servants for eternity, according to some interpretations of the Koran. Furthermore, the sympathy that his actions elicit from others is manifest in the social and economic support his family receives after his death and the martyrdom status conferred upon his memory.

It is important to note that although suicide bombings are most often associated with extremist Islamic groups, other groups have adapted and mastered the use of terrorist death by suicide as a generator of public sympathy and fear. Before September 11, 2001, by far the most effective use of terrorist suicide bombing was made by the Liberation Tigers of Tamil Ealam (LTTE), or the Tamil Tigers. The Tamil Tigers have successfully carried out more than 200 suicide bombings that have killed and injured thousands of military personnel and innocent civilians since the onset of its terror campaign (Schweitzer 2000). The LTTE's drive for an independent state within Sri Lanka has led to the assassinations of heads of state such as former Indian Prime Minister Rajiv Gandhi. Furthermore, like Hamas and Hezbollah, the LTTE has effectively galvanized popular support from among the Tamil minority by creating a sympathetic mythos around its suicide bombers as martyrs; part of this mythos is that each wears a capsule of cyanide around his neck, just in case his mission fails (Roberts 1996). The LTTE continues to receive broad public support from its Tamil constituency despite its use of suicide bombings that have injured and killed thousands of innocent bystanders of the Sinhalese majority.

Death as Macabre Spectacle for Mass (Media) Consumption

There is undeniably a mutually beneficial relationship between terrorist actions and media coverage (Weimann 1990; Paletz and Schmid 1992; Brown and Merrill 1993; Hoffman 1998), and death plays a significant role in ensuring its continuation. Terrorists, as we have argued elsewhere in this essay, use death and violent acts to attract attention to their political and ideological causes, and here death functions as political communication. But the use of death as a vehicle for political communication would not be possible without human beings' natural curiosity about the macabre and the media's tendency to exploit that inclination. The popular news media aphorism "If it bleeds, it leads" expresses this situation well. Commenting on the use of death as a public spectacle for mass consumption, May (1974) writes:

> In the case of terrorism, of course, we are talking about a festival of death, a celebration that has its own priest and victims and that carries with it the likely risk that the priest himself

will be a victim. The rest of us become celebrants in this liturgical action through the medium of the media. Thus, the media respond to the human thirst for celebration, the need for ecstasy, the desire to be lifted out of the daily round. Through violent death, their horror before it and their need to draw near it, men are momentarily relieved of that other death which is boredom. (P. 297)

The extreme acts of violence and death that terrorists perform become spectacles for the consuming masses. But our consumption of these spectacles and, by extension, our understanding of the messages conveyed, are made possible by the media. Terrorism is media spectacle par excellence, or, as Jenkins (1975) notes, "Terrorism is theatre" (p. 4). It is like theatrical performance in that it is aimed at an attentive and rapt audience and not at the immediate victims of terror; their dead bodies are but message conduits for the larger target audience. Thus terrorist organizations' use of death and other extreme forms of violence frequently assumes theatrical proportions. Sloan (1981) refers to this as "theatre of the obscene," where the attributes of improvisational performances are on display and "the ultimate plot and the conclusion of the drama are determined by how the performers interact in the environment where they have been placed" (p. 23). And like all performances, as Karber (1971) notes, the terrorist theater involves an actor (terrorist), an audience (victims and target public), a skit or message (e.g., suicide bombing, hostage taking), and feedback (a response from those targeted). Nevertheless, it would be a mistake to presume that terrorism would end if media coverage of terrorist acts ceased. In fact, the vast majority of terrorists carry out their violent acts without any thought about media coverage, and, of course, state-sponsored terrorists try to avoid the media altogether (Simon 2001). Still, the media facilitate the effectiveness of terror messages by aiding in the symbolic communication between terrorist and public, and the availability of graphic pictures of death caused by terrorism increases the likelihood that the public will partake visually in this orgy of the macabre.

DEATH BY TERRORISM: A GROWING GLOBAL PROBLEM

By all reasoned assessments, death by terrorism seems to be an expanding global problem (Hoffman 1998; Cooper 2001; Johnson 2001; Simon 2001). Many Americans saw terrorism as a very serious threat to national security long before September 11, 2001 (Kuzma 2000). In report on the future of terrorism published in 2000, the National Intelligence Council notes that "between now and 2015 terrorist tactics will become increasingly sophisticated and designed to achieve mass casualties" (p. 50). The report ends with a solemn warning that the trend in terrorism is toward "greater lethality." Why is that so, and what forms of violence should we expect?

The trend toward greater lethality is of particular interest here because it has implications for each of the five functions of death by terrorism discussed above. We can point to three reasons for this solemn prognosis: (a) the prevalence of widespread psychic numbing, (b) the use of weapons of mass destruction, and (c) the increasing influence of religiously justified violence.

With regard to psychic numbing (Lifton 1974), the media play a significant role in fueling the movement among terrorist groups toward more spectacular, more lethal, and more destructive violent acts. Terrorist acts are becoming more lethal in part because they have to be to get our attention. We have become desensitized to images of death, destruction, and suffering by our constant exposure to such images, which have long been part of our normal entertainment repertoire.

It is interesting how often Americans invoke the word *surreal* to describe their perception of the events of September 11, 2001, as if to suggest that they could not distinguish between televised news images of the real event and a Hollywood portrayal of some fictional catastrophe. We have become so desensitized to simulated violence, destruction, and death that it is now difficult for us to distinguish the real from the unreal, and this may have profound effects on our ability to empathize with people who are suffering. In an essay titled "The New Violence," Charles Strozier (1995) expresses this situation well when he observes that a new disturbing trend in violence is having a particular impact on the American psyche. He notes that our mass media are saturated with stories and descriptions of violent behavior and extreme brutality, and that we are living with more violence in our immediate context, whether that violence is simulated, as in movies and video games, or real, as in the homicide rate or the nightly news (pp. 192–93). This situation naturally results in a form of psychic numbing, a form of immunization against the trauma of witnessing graphic scenes of death and destruction.

The bar has now been raised to such a high level that the amount of violence and destruction necessary to cause us to act is obscene. We need look no further than Rwanda's state-sponsored genocide of 1994 for evidence of the "new" form of psychic numbing that fuels the increasing lethality of terrorism. In one of the most horrific examples of state-sponsored terrorism ever perpetrated, Hutu extremists butchered more than 800,000 Tutsi civilians in a span of 100 days while the United States and the rest of the free world—with full knowledge of the genocide—idly observed the events on television (Klinghoffer 1998; Uvin 1998).

Today's terrorists must increase the lethality of their attacks in order to elicit attention for their political concerns and to create fear and panic on the part of a desensitized public. Killing and maiming a few individuals is not enough, because it is not likely to draw sustained and protracted media attention; in addition, terrorists must now compete for media attention with a litany of other "normal" violence, such as murders and robberies. Terrorists now have to engage in spectacular feats of intimidation just to get an average level of coverage in the media, which are saturated with the noise and clutter of both simulated and real violence. To reach a desensitized audience such as the American public, terrorists must carry out increasingly memorable and shocking events, akin to what Schweitzer (1998) calls "superterrorism," in terms of the numbers of deaths generated and the level of damage inflicted to property. Terrorism, by all reasonable assessments, is now largely a game of numbers, and that is precisely why the use of weapons of mass destruction ("dirty bombs" or biological and chemical weapons) is inevitable.

In the drive to greater lethality in terrorist acts, the use of weapons of mass destruction is particularly alluring. The potential of such weapons to increase body counts as well as fear and panic in the public makes their future use inevitable. Historical evidence has already borne out the effectiveness of biological agents in meting out megadeaths, such as in the deliberate infection of Native Americans by British forces during the French and Indian War (1754–67) through the distribution of smallpox-tainted blankets and handkerchiefs (Christopher et al. 1997). Bioterrorism, by design, produces large numbers of death, and a single act carried through correctly could potentially result in millions of casualties (U.S. Congress 1993). Moreover, many colorless, odorless, and tasteless toxic agents can freely and easily pass through any number of security measures (e.g., metal detectors and X-ray machines) without detection, and thus may have reasonably high likelihood of reaching the target audience (Simon 1997).

Most frightening, perhaps, is the enormous number of deaths that a small quantity of such biological agents can cause. A kilogram of anthrax, for example, dispersed under the right wind conditions, can wipe out an entire metropolitan area (Danzig and Berkowsky 1997). Certainly, the anthrax letters that were mailed on the East Coast in the months following the September 11 attacks show the lethality of *Bacillus anthracis* and its potential as a weapon of mass destruction as well as a cause of public fear and panic. The dangers of anthrax as a form of bioterrorism were demonstrated decades before the 2001 incidents, however, in the Sverdlovsk anthrax outbreak of 1979. Although the official Soviet death count for that incident was 64, U.S. intelligence puts the number closer to a thousand (Meselson et al. 1994; Guillemin 1999). The deaths in Sverdlovsk were initially thought to have been caused by the eating of anthrax-contaminated meat products. However, in later epidemiological investigations, Meselson et al. (1994) and Guillemin (1999) found that the outbreak was in fact the result of an accidental release of an aerosol form of the anthrax pathogen from a military facility. The release of virulent pathogens is a most efficient killing mechanism, and the threat that terrorists will eventually use such a weapon is one that is likely to persist into the future.

The final reason for the increasing lethality of terrorism is the increasing influence of extremist religious views. In the past decade, we have seen several paradigmatic illustrations of the intensifying lethality of terrorism, beginning with the first attempt to bring down the World Trade Center towers in 1993 and culminating in the horrific events of September 11, 2001. Between these two terror acts were many others, including the bombing of the Murrah Federal Building in Oklahoma City, which took the lives of 168 people; the Aum Shinrikyo's sarin attack, which resulted in 12 deaths and more than 4,000 injuries; and the 1998 bombings of U.S. embassies in Kenya and Tanzania, which resulted in more than 200 deaths and at least 5,000 injuries. We remember these particular terror events more than any others because of the lethality involved. Very few, however, have made the salient connection between these events and the religious beliefs used by the perpetrators to justify their actions. Yet religion, more than political ideology, is now the principal justification for terrorism, and the most terrifying and lethal terrorist acts of the past decade have been religiously motivated (Hoffman 1995, 1998).

Aum Shinrikyo's sarin attack on the Tokyo subway system is a prime example of the way terrorists use their religious views as justification for carrying out the most horrific and lethal attacks (Schweitzer 1998). But why is there a link between religion and death by terrorism, or between religion and the increasing lethality of terrorism? Hoffman (1998) posits three reasons religious terrorism is more lethal than terrorism conducted for other reasons, noting that religion provides the perfect justification for the use of lethal violence. First, those who use violence in the name of religion interpret what they do as a "sacramental act" (p. 94). That is, "holy terror" is *just* because it punishes the enemies of Allah, or Jesus, or whatever other divine being the terrorist believes in. Religious terrorists are not constrained by any conventional moral calculus, nor do they abide by secular rules of appropriate conflict engagement. Antiabortion terrorism in the United States, in which fundamentalist Christian terrorists, acting without conventional moral restraints, bomb abortion clinics and assassinate abortion providers at will, stands as a perfect example (Nice 1988; Wilson and Lynxwiler 1988; Jenkins 1999). Here, as elsewhere, the religious imperative in terrorism removes all psychological barriers to murder because the targets of the violence are not innocent victims but rather infidels, sinners, and evildoers (Hoffman 1995). Second, Hoffman (1998) notes, unlike political terrorist groups, which might appeal to the public for sympathy or support, religious terrorists "seek to appeal to no other constituency than themselves" (p. 95). If you are not with them, then you are against them, and thus a likely target for violence and death. Finally, religious terrorists see themselves as outsiders and bearers of the truth who must employ violence to preserve the moral order. As Hoffman observes, this peculiar mixture of a sense of alienation and the belief that it is their duty to fight to preserve a disintegrating moral order makes the use of violence and death all the more likely and appealing for such terrorists. Al Qaeda's September 11, 2001, attack on the United States stands as resounding evidence of the lethality of religious terrorism.

SEPTEMBER 11, 2001: THE LAUNCH OF SUPERTERRORISM

The events of September 11, 2001, stand as a portent of deaths to come, while concomitantly representing the first act of superterrorism. Americans will remember the attacks on the Pentagon and the World Trade Center as the most successful demonstration of public terror in the history of upward-directed terrorism. The actions on that fateful day, when Al Qaeda operatives killed close to 3,000 innocent civilians, will define a generation much as have other tragic events in American history. But unlike other catastrophic events, the events of September 11, 2001, marked a change in warfare, both symmetrical and asymmetrical, because it was the first time that a foreign army (Al Qaeda) deliberately and successfully targeted ordinary American civilians for mass death on their home turf. To find a somewhat comparable example, one would have to go back to the 1941 attack on Pearl Harbor by Japan's Imperial Army, but the 2,388 people who died as a result of the Pearl Harbor attack were overwhelmingly military personnel. September 11, 2001, was the first time that a foreign regime successfully planned and implemented an act of superterrorism that was directed at innocent, noncombatant American civilians. Al Qaeda struck at the very lifeblood of American commerce, the twin towers of the World Trade Center in New York City, and at the very heart of the American security apparatus, the Pentagon. Its operatives transformed passenger airplanes, 757s and 767s, into flying bombs, each carrying about 24,000 gallons of jet fuel that fed the fires in the Trade Center's twin towers to well over 1,500 degrees Fahrenheit (Ashley 2001). But for the structural integrity of the buildings, which remained standing long enough for large numbers of people to be evacuated, the death toll would most certainly be higher.

The events of September 11, 2001, represent superterrorism par excellence, and this is a fact that can never be overstated. The bombings brought the entire nation to a halt, disrupting major transportation and commerce networks. Fear and panic were ubiquitous and omnipresent in the weeks following the attacks, completely shattering Americans' sense of security on both national and ontological levels. Images of death, destruction, and despair emanated from every media outlet, a media spectacle that surpassed all previous media spectacles, with nonstop coverage and nonstop speculation. In essence, the first act of superterrorism demonstrated only too well the various roles of death, destruction, and extreme violence in asymmetrical warfare.

Now, the question is, What next? What will the next act of superterrorism be like? If the history of terrorism and the role of death in it are any guides, the answer to this question is a most solemn one: September 11, 2001, stands as a disquieting augury of yet more destructive superterrorism and megadeath to come.

CONCLUSION

In this essay we have outlined the five functions of death in acts of terrorism by positing the following: Death by terrorism plays the roles of communicative device in political discourse, control mechanism for the masses, route to liberation for oppressed people, generator of public sympathy, and media spectacle for mass consumption. We have also discussed the growing threat of asymmetrical warfare and the trend in terrorism toward greater lethality and mass destruction. Moreover, we have connected the trend of greater lethality and the various functions of death in terrorism to the events of September 11, 2001.

To understand the role and meaning of death in terrorism is to begin to understand, if only slightly, why asymmetrical warfare is so seductive to people whose existential condition is marked by alienation, entrenched deprivation, and hopeless misery. By studying the role and meaning of death in terrorism, we can begin to understand the catalyzing suffering that drives some groups of people to engage in this morally repugnant form of warfare; we may also begin to come to terms with our own fears of being victims—the very fears that make terrorism so effective in the first place. Perhaps further discourse on the role and meaning of death in terrorism, for both perpetrator and victim, might lead to a better understanding of the very social conditions that give rise to asymmetrical warfare, situations that make the strategic use of lethal acts so appealing to many.

REFERENCES

"America Under Attack." 2001. *Newsweek,* special ed., September.

Ashley, Steven. 2001. "When the Twin Towers Fell." *Scientific American: Explore,* October 9. Retrieved April 15, 2003 (http://www.sciam.com/article.cfm?articleid=000b7feb-a88c-1c75-9b81809ec588ef21).

Becker, Ernest. 1995. "The Terror of Death." In *Death: Current Perspectives,* 4th ed., edited by John B. Williamson and Edwin S. Shneidman. Mountain View, CA: Mayfield.

Brown, David J. and Robert Merrill. 1993. *The Politics and Imagery of Terrorism.* Seattle, WA: Bay.

Camus, Albert. 1956. *The Rebel: An Essay on Man in Revolt.* New York: Vintage.

Charan, Bhagwat. [1930] 1978. "The Philosophy of the Bomb." In *The Terrorist Reader: From Aristotle to IRA and the PLO: A Historical Anthology,* edited by Walter Laqueur. New York: Meridian.

Chomsky, Noam. 1991. "International Terrorism: Image and Reality." In *Western State Terrorism,* edited by Alexander George. New York: Routledge.

Christopher, George W., Theodore J. Cieslak, Julie A. Pavlin, and Edward M. Eitzen. 1997. "Biological Warfare: A Historical Perspective." *Journal of the American Medical Association* 278:412–17.

Cooper, H. H. A. 2001. "Terrorism: The Problem of Definition Revisited." *American Behavioral Scientist* 44:881–93.

Crelinsten, Ronald D. 1992. "Victims' Perspective." Pp. 208–38 in *Terrorism and the Media: How Researchers, Terrorists, Government, Press, Public, and Victims View and Use the Media,* edited by David L. Paletz and Alex P. Schmid. Newbury Park, CA: Sage.

Crenshaw, Martha. 1992. "Current Research on Terrorism: The Academic Perspective." *Studies in Conflict and Terrorism* 15:1–11.

Danzig, Richard and Pamela B. Berkowsky. 1997. "Why Should We Be Concerned About Biological Warfare?" *Journal of the American Medical Association* 278:431–32.

Dobson, Christopher and Ronald Payne. 1987. *The Never-Ending War: Terrorism in the 80's.* New York: Facts on File.

Fanon, Frantz. 1968. *The Wretched of the Earth.* New York: Grove.

Fournier, Louis. 1984. *F.L.Q.: The Anatomy of an Underground Movement.* Toronto: NC Press.

Freedman, Lawrence Z. 1983. "Why Does Terrorism Terrorize?" *Terrorism* 6:389–401.

Gamson, William A. 1992. "Media Images and the Social Construction of Reality." *Annual Review of Sociology* 18:373–93.

Ganor, Boaz. 2000. "Suicide Terrorism: An Overview." Herzliya, Israel: International Policy Institute for Counter Terrorism, Interdisciplinary Center. Retrieved April 15, 2003 (http://www.ict.org.il/articles/articledet.cfm?articleid=128).

Gibbs, Jack P. 1989. "Conceptualization of Terrorism." *American Sociological Review* 54:329–40.

Giddens, Anthony. 1991. *Modernity and Self-Identity: Self and Society in the Late Modern Age.* Stanford, CA: Stanford University Press.

Goertzel, Ted. 1988. "The Ethics of Terrorism and Revolution." *Terrorism* 11:1–12.

Goffman, Erving. (1974). *Frame Analysis: An Essay on the Organization of Experience.* Cambridge, MA: Harvard University Press.

Guillemin, Jeanne. 1999. *Anthrax: The Investigation of a Deadly Outbreak.* Berkeley: University of California Press.

Gurr, Ted R. 1970. *Why Men Rebel.* Princeton, NJ: Princeton University Press.

Heinzen, Karl. [1849] 1978. "Murder." In *The Terrorism Reader: From Aristotle to the IRA and the PLO: A Historical Anthology,* edited by Walter Laqueur. New York: Meridian.

Hewitt, Christopher. 1992. "Public's Perspective." Pp. 170–207 in *Terrorism and the Media: How Researchers, Terrorists, Government, Press, Public, and Victims View and Use the Media,* edited by David L. Paletz and Alex P. Schmid. Newbury Park, CA: Sage.

———. 2000. "The Political Context of Terrorism in America: Ignoring Extremists or Pandering to Them?" *Terrorism and Political Violence* 12:325–44.

Hoffman, Bruce. 1995. "'Holy Terror': The Implications of Terrorism Motivated by a Religious Imperative." *Studies in Conflict and Terrorism* 18:271–84.

———. 1998. *Inside Terrorism.* New York: Columbia University Press.

Jenkins, Brian M. 1975. *International Terrorism: A New Mode of Conflict.* Los Angeles: Crescent.

Jenkins, Phillip. 1999. "Fighting Terrorism as if Women Mattered: Anti-Abortion Violence as Unconstructed Terrorism." Pp. 319–48 in *Making Trouble: Cultural Constructions of Crime, Deviance, and Control,* edited by Jeff Ferrell and Neil Websdale. New York: Aldine de Gruyter.

Johnson, Larry C. 2001. "The Future of Terrorism." *American Behavioral Scientist* 44:894–913.

Karber, Phillip. 1971. "Urban Terrorism: Baseline Data and a Conceptual Framework." *Social Science Quarterly* 52:521–33.

Kastenbaum, Robert J. 2001. *Death, Society, and Human Experience,* 7th ed. Boston: Allyn & Bacon.

Kelman, Herbert C. 1973. "Violence Without Moral Restraint: Reflections on the Dehumanization of Victims and Victimizers." *Journal of Social Issues* 29(4):25–61.

King, Martin Luther, Jr. 1958. *Stride Toward Freedom.* New York: Harper & Brothers.

Klare, Michael and Peter Kornbluh. 1988. *Low-Intensity Warfare.* New York: Pantheon.

Klinghoffer, Arthur J. 1998. *The International Dimension of Genocide in Rwanda.* New York: New York University Press.

Kuzma, Lynn M. 2000. "The Polls-Trends: Terrorism in the United States." *Public Opinion Quarterly* 64:90–105.

Lifton, Robert J. 1974. "On Death and the Continuity of Life: A 'New' Paradigm." *History of Childhood Quarterly* 1:681–96.

Long, David E. 1990. *The Anatomy of Terrorism.* New York: Free Press.

May, William F. 1974. "Terrorism as Strategy and Ecstasy." *Social Research* 41:277–98.

McClenon, James. 1988. "Terrorism as Persuasion: Possibilities and Trends." *Sociological Focus* 21:53–66.

McGuckin, Frank, ed. 1997. *Terrorism in the United States.* New York: H. W. Wilson.

Meselson, Matthew, Jeanne Guillemin, Martin Hugh-Jones, Alexander Langmuir, Ilona Papova, Alexis Shelokov, and Olga Yampolskaya. 1994. "The Sverdlovsk Anthrax Outbreak of 1979." *Science* 266:1202–8.

Miller, Rueben. 1988. "The Literature of Terrorism." *Terrorism* 11:63–87.

National Intelligence Council. 2000. "Global Trends 2015: A Dialogue About the Future With Nongovernment Experts." Washington, DC: National Intelligence Council. Excerpts retrieved April 15, 2003 (http://www.cia.gov/terrorism/global_trends_2015.html).

Nice, David. 1988. "Abortion Clinic Bombings as Political Violence." *American Journal of Political Science* 32:178–95.

Oots, Kent and Thomas Wiegele. 1985. "Terrorist and Victim: Psychiatric and Physiological Approaches From a Social Science Perspective." *Terrorism* 8:1–32.

Paletz, David L. and Alex P. Schmid, eds. 1992. *Terrorism and the Media: How Researchers, Terrorists, Government, Press, Public, and Victims View and Use the Media.* Newbury Park, CA: Sage.

Roberts, Michael. 1996. "Filial Devotion in Tamil Culture and the Tiger Cult of Martyrdom." *Contributions to Indian Sociology* (New Series) 30:245–72.

Ryan, Charlotte. 1991. *Prime Time Activism: Media Strategies for Grassroots Organizing.* Boston: South End.

Schmid, Alex P. and J. de Graaf. 1982. *Violence and Communication: Insurgent Terrorism and the Western News Media.* Beverly Hills, CA: Sage.

Schön, Donald A. and Martin Rein. 1994. *Frame Reflection: Toward the Resolution of Intractable Policy Controversies.* New York: Basic Books.

Schweitzer, Glen E. (with Carole C. Dorch). 1998. *Super-terrorism: Assassins, Mobsters, and Weapons of Mass Destruction.* New York: Plenum.

Schweitzer, Yoram. 2000. "Suicide Terrorism: Development and Characteristics." Herzliya, Israel: International Policy Institute for Counter Terrorism, Interdisciplinary Center. Retrieved April 15, 2003 (http://www.ict.org.il/articles/articledet.cfm?articleid=112).

Simon, Jeffrey D. 1997. "Biological Terrorism: Preparing to Meet the Threat." *Journal of the American Medical Association* 278:428–30.

———. 2001. *The Terrorist Trap: America's Experience With Terrorism,* 2d ed. Bloomington: Indiana University Press.

Sloan, Stephen. 1981. *Simulating Terrorism.* Norman: University of Oklahoma Press.

Strozier, Charles B. 1995. "The New Violence." *Journal of Psychohistory* 23:191–201.

U.S. Congress, Office of Technology Assessment. 1993. *Proliferation of Weapons of Mass Destruction: Assessing the Risks* (OTA Publication No. ISC 559). Washington, DC: Government Printing Office.

Uvin, Peter. 1998. *Aiding Violence: The Development Enterprise in Rwanda.* West Hartford, CT: Kumarian.

Wahl, Charles W. 1965. "The Fear of Death." In *Death and Identity,* edited by Robert Fulton. New York: John Wiley.

Weimann, Gabriel. 1990. "Redefinition of Image: The Impact of Mass-Mediated Terrorism." *International Journal of Public Opinion Research* 2(1):16–29.

Weimann, Gabriel and Conrad Winn. 1994. *The Theater of Terror: Mass Media and International Terrorism.* New York: Longman.

Wilkins, Burleigh T. 1992. *Terrorism and Collective Responsibility.* New York: Routledge.

Wilson, Michele and John Lynxwiler. 1988. "Abortion Clinic Violence as Terrorism." *Terrorism* 11:263–73.

Wirtz, Theresa. 1992. "The Role of Death in War." *Peace Review* 4(3):10–13.

Zilboorg, Gregory. 1943. "Fear of Death." *Psychoanalytic Quarterly* 12:465–75.

Death Attributed to Medical Error

Jerry T. McKnight

Pat Norton

Humans inherently make mistakes. Sometimes these mistakes are foolish; most of the time, mistakes teach us lessons. In most instances, the world in general does not learn of individual humans' mistakes. In the worst cases, however, mistakes lead to bodily harm or death, events that are frequently reported in the news media. Important examples include the 1984 chemical spill in Bhopal, India; the nuclear mishap at Three Mile Island, Pennsylvania, in 1979; and the recent case of the installation of defective tires on Ford Explorers. Human errors also occur in the medical profession, and these errors can be costly in terms of loss of life and other consequences of human tragedy. In this chapter, our chief focus is on deaths stemming from medical errors; we address current trends in the numbers and types of errors that occur, how the public perceives medical errors, the effects of such errors on society, and why the prevention of these errors is not easily achieved. We begin, however, with a brief discussion of some industrial accidents that have resulted from human error.

INDUSTRIAL ACCIDENTS

Human error has led to some of the most notable industrial accidents over the past 20 years. One of the largest of these was the 1984 disaster at the Union Carbide plant in Bhopal, India, which resulted in at least 3,000 deaths, approximately 500,000 injured, and the closing of the factory (Gottesfeld 1999). The immediate cause of the accident was water seeping into a chemical storage tank, which caused an uncontrollable chemical reaction; however, the longer-term cause was a lapse in safety standards and maintenance procedures at the plant over a period of months prior to the accident. In addition, the plant itself had been constructed using low-quality materials, and plant staff were poorly trained and largely inexperienced. India does not have any laws in place requiring the kinds of chemical release prevention and emergency response measures that would have prevented this accident or greatly reduced its deleterious impact.

In 1979, the nuclear reactor at Three Mile Island experienced a partial meltdown. Although no one died as a direct result of this accident, more than 2,000 personal injury claims were filed based on the negative health influence of gamma radiation exposure (Public Broadcasting Service 1998). The meltdown was the result of more than 2 hours of misreading of the machinery by workers at the plant. Once the problem was discovered, the plants' crew and engineers took an additional 12 hours to reach a consensus on appropriate corrective action.

The separation of treads on the Firestone tires that Ford Motor Company installed on its Explorer model SUV led to a series of accidents beginning in the mid-1990s and increasing in frequency through 2001, when consumer complaints led to a recall of the tires and lawsuits against both Firestone and Ford. Although some data suggest that the Explorer's design increased the likelihood of vehicle rollover in a crash, Firestone bore the brunt of the responsibility for the accidents for distributing poorly manufactured tires. An investigation by the National Highway Transportation Safety Board led to allegations that Firestone had used substandard rubber in tires when supplies of higher-quality rubber ran low, employed lackadaisical inspection practices, had workers puncture air bubbles on the insides of tires, and used poorly trained workers when its union labor force went on strike. Both Ford and Firestone issued recalls and were charged in class-action suits seeking recovery of inspection and replacement costs and, in some instances, damages for deaths and/or injuries resulting from wrecks caused by the separation of the tire treads.

All of these results of human error are tragic, but they are easy to relegate to the category of "things that happen to others." Most people do not work in or live near a chemical or nuclear plant. Most individuals do not own dangerous cars. It is almost a certainty, however, that at some point every individual will interact with the medical community, whether through hospitalization or a routine visit to the doctor's office. Americans have historically held medical professionals in high regard, but these individuals are, after all, only human, and they make mistakes. The sensationalized nature of the popular and news media coverage of medical errors serves notice that we could easily be the next victims.

MEDICAL ERRORS

Medical errors are an integral part of medical practice, in both hospital and clinic settings. With the advent of free-standing surgical centers where many outpatient surgical procedures are performed, the arena of medical errors has grown. Medical errors extend also to nursing homes, home health care settings, and local pharmacies. Due to aggressive reporting of newsworthy medical errors, most Americans are well aware of the dangers associated with interfacing with the medical system. As pharmacology, medical procedures (both diagnostic and therapeutic), and other interventions have advanced, the risks of medical errors have increased. The problem of medical errors is both cause for concern and part and parcel of the human experience within medical practice.

PUBLIC PERCEPTIONS

For some time, many Americans have been aware that medical errors occur, but the full extent of the problem was first delineated for the public at large by a report produced by the Institute of Medicine's Committee on the Quality of Health Care in America in 1999. The IOM committee's findings are compiled in a volume titled *To Err Is Human* (Kohn, Corrigan, and Donaldson 2000), which reports that as many as 98,000 people die each year in U.S. hospitals due to medical errors. Moreover, because this figure does not include outpatient deaths, the actual number of medical error–related deaths may be much higher. Prior to publication of the IOM report, many books and articles had been produced that tended to increase patient anxiety. Some of these include *The Incompetent Doctor: Behind Closed Doors* (Rosenthal 1995), which discusses the types of mistakes doctors make and the medical profession's seeming inability to self-regulate; *The Unkindest Cut: Life in the Backrooms of Medicine* (Millman 1977), which details 2 years of sociological observations at a private, university-affiliated hospital in the United States, focusing on conversations and actions in the operating rooms, in the emergency department, at morbidity and mortality conferences, and at various hospital meetings; and *The Medical Racket: How Doctors, HMOs, and Hospitals Are Failing the America Patient* (Gross 1998), which is highly critical of all the entities named in its title. These books and others

are promoted to a public that is often unable to distinguish between true warning calls and sensationalist reporting.

Books of this ilk often promote increased anxiety in medical patients and their families, although perhaps unintentionally. In addition, they help to feed suspicion in the minds of many, effectively creating an "on guard" type of attitude in both patients and physicians. Such suspicion and distrust on the part of either or both parties can create an atmosphere of "negative energy" in physician-patient encounters. Often, these negative emotions impair doctors' ability to follow their instincts and the patients' ability to heal. Such stress has the potential to create adversarial relationships between patients and their health care providers, and this unfortunately increases the risks to patients. For example, when a doctor senses that a patient is suspicious or aggressive, he or she is likely to order more tests and ask for more consultations for that patient. Although such increased thoroughness may seem like a good idea, each additional test or consultation carries its own attendant risks for the patient.

HMOs

Health maintenance organizations, or HMOs, constitute a special category that deserves mention in any discussion of medical mistakes leading to death. We have all heard and read news stories about cases in which HMOs have withheld care from particular patients. Actually, patients are free to obtain any medical treatments they want, but because most cannot afford to pay for any treatments themselves, seeking care from providers outside their insurance coverage is not always a viable option.

The concept of HMOs has existed for many years, but HMOs were not formally established and defined as legal entities until passage of the federal HMO Act in 1963. This legislation, which was amended in 1976, 1978, and 1981, served to establish HMOs' legitimacy as a means of providing low-cost medical care to the U.S. population. The federal government has also provided funds for the development of HMOs. Over time, HMOs have shifted from being nonprofit organizations to being for-profit businesses; as a result, many HMO owners and administrators have made huge profits.

HMOs established the "gatekeeper" concept in medicine. In such a system, the gatekeeper—a primary care physician, usually a family physician, internist, or pediatrician—sees each patient initially and then makes appropriate referrals to other specialists or subspecialists. The main problem with this system is that it can make it appear that the primary care physician is keeping patients from seeing specialists; this is ultimately an uncomfortable role for primary care physician, because it tends to place physician and patient in adversarial roles. The more correct, appropriate, and comfortable role for the primary care physician is that of "gateway." In such a role, the primary care physician willingly refers patients to appropriate consultants when needed, serving as a conduit or facilitator of patients' health care needs.

The HMOs' use of primary physicians as gatekeepers grew more dangerous with the implementation of a payment system called *capitation.* Under this system, primary care physicians are paid a flat fee per patient per month (insurance companies refer to this as "per covered life per month"). A primary care physician is given a specific amount of money per month based on a patient's age and medical condition (i.e., if a physician receives $15 per month for a given patient, this would total $180 for all the care provided that patient for a given fiscal year). This system allows HMO physicians to make money without actually seeing every patient. Doctors with "panels" of healthy patients make money without seeing their patients often, whereas doctors with panels of sick patients can go through the pay per service equivalent in just a few office visits. The result of the use of the capitation system is that many sicker patients in HMOs may not receive adequate numbers of office visits. The HMOs created a system in which withholding care from patients is in the physician's financial interest.

Unfortunately, more than a few patients have been harmed by their HMOs. In a book titled *Do HMOs Cut Costs . . . and Lives?* (1997), Dr. Emerita Gueson presents an angry attack on HMOs, citing many examples of their failures to help patients. The book's title is clearly a rhetorical question, as in the book's dedication Gueson lists a number of patients and their families whom she describes as victims of a failed health care system.

Recently, a consumer-led revolution against perceived problems in the health care insurance industry has resulted in proposed legislation that would make HMOs more legally liable for their errors. In the past, HMOs were virtually immune from prosecution, but negative public opinion (as evidenced by the many satirical cartoons and bitter jokes about HMOs) has led to some changes. Although the HMO concept has a certain appeal, it seems that as private companies, HMOs are concerned primarily with making money. As a physician, one of us often tells his patients that health insurance companies in general "are not in it for your health." One health care plan manager that one of us has spoken with indicated that it is more cost-effective for his company if a patient goes into the hospital and dies suddenly of a heart attack rather than receives a lot of expensive tests. As a businessman, he is correct, but such words are chilling. Doctors and patients must always be aware of the malevolent forces that work together to impede the healing process.

LEGAL ISSUES AND
THE CULTURE OF BLAME

While we were writing this chapter, the news was reported that Dick Schapp, a longtime sports journalist, had died from complications after hip surgery. This led to questions as to the exact cause of death, what series of events led to this conclusion, and what might have been done to prevent Schapp's demise. Unfortunately, the simplicity of these questions belies the need for further analysis of a series of events, many of which may have been unavoidable.

In the early 1990s, the authors who reported on the Harvard Medical Practice Study called for improved patient safety (Brennan et al. 1991). Since that time, however, little has been done systematically nationwide in this regard. It is apparent that the medical industry is at least 10 years behind other industries in safety innovation. In most industries the reporting of safety problems is encouraged, but in the medical industry a cloak of silence and the potential for litigation arising from acknowledgment of mistakes hinders such reporting. Thomas Krizek (2000) asserts that improvement in health care quality is inhibited by five factors: (a) inadequate data on the incidence of adverse events, (b) inadequate practice guidelines or protocols and poor outcome analysis, (c) a culture of blame, (d) a need to compensate "injured" patients, and (e) difficulty in telling the truth. We discuss each of these factors throughout this chapter.

Krizek suggests that the principles that W. Edward Deming introduced in Japan in his work on quality controls for the automotive and electronics industries might be applicable to medicine. Deming promoted his belief that it is the worker performing the task who, when appropriately empowered, is best able to identify and correct errors. Deming proved that workers could produce nearly defect-free products with the aid of well-defined protocols, early error identification, and continuous data collection. These principles have yet to be instituted on a mass scale in medicine.

FAILURE ANALYSIS

Failure analysis needs to be a part of any quality control mechanism aimed at creating a safer, more efficient environment, particularly in certain industries, such as aviation, and in the military. In aviation, the Federal Aviation Administration and the National Transportation Safety Board (NTSB) oversee safety and failure analysis. When a nonmilitary plane crashes, the NTSB sends an investigation team to the crash site in an effort to find the cause. This is no different from the TQI (total quality improvement) or CQI (continuous quality improvement) analyses that many industries use in managing production. The NTSB is not concerned about potential litigation, but solely about the cause of the crash. This is not to say that the pilots' union does not protest vigorously any findings of pilot error; however, the independence of the NTSB allows it to investigate and report findings in an impartial and objective manner.

Medicine has the equivalent of an investigation process after a death—the autopsy, or postmortem examination.

Autopsy (literally, "seeing with one's own eyes") is a valuable tool for determining the cause of a patient's death, but this once-common procedure is now a rarity at many hospitals. It has been shown that the rate of discordance between clinical diagnoses and autopsy results is large, despite the technological advances that have been made in medicine. Even with the advent of magnetic resonance imaging (MRI), magnetic resonance angiography (MRA), CT scans, computer-enhanced angiography, sophisticated diagnostic ultrasonography, nuclear scans, and sophisticated diagnostic endoscopy, as well as increased precision in laboratory tests and culture techniques, medicine is still an imprecise science, and diagnosticians still miss many diseases.

Burton, Troxclair, and Newman (1998) reviewed the postmortem examinations of 1,105 patients between 1986 and 1995 at the Medical Center of Louisiana in New Orleans and found that cancers were misdiagnosed before death in 44% of the patients. The research team found 250 malignant tumors in 225 patients with 111 cancers misdiagnosed or undiagnosed. Only 34% of the cancers were clinically suspected prior to death. Undiagnosed cancer was the cause of death in 57% of those patients who eventually died of cancer. The hospital in Burton et al.'s study had a high rate (42%) of autopsy for a modern hospital owing to significant cooperation from the local medical examiner. In most areas of the United States, autopsy rates are less than 10% at teaching hospitals and less than 5% at community hospitals (Marwick 1995). These rates differ significantly from those of the 1960s, when autopsies were performed in more than 50% of deaths. The medical profession has been lulled into a false sense of security by the availability of high-tech diagnostic tools and has virtually lost the opportunity to know with certainty the cause of death in most cases. As George Lundberg, former editor of the *Journal of the American Medical Association,* has stated, "Low tech autopsy trumps high tech medicine in getting the right answer" (quoted in Tanne 1998).

There are probably multiple reasons for the decline in autopsy rates. The most significant of these is that most doctors either do not ask to perform or insist on performing autopsies. To take the most positive view of this, doctors assume that they know the causes of their patients' deaths and doubt that autopsies will add any new or useful information. A more negative view is that, in this highly litigious climate, doctors really do not want to know (or have anyone else find out) if they misdiagnosed or mistreated their patients. Another plausible reason for the decline in autopsy rates is that deceased patients' families do not understand the importance of the procedure, either because of general lack of education or because doctors fail to inform them. The autopsy is an important, and underutilized, quality assurance and educational tool that allows physicians to monitor medical diagnostics and therapeutics (Burton et al. 1998).

THE SCOPE OF THE PROBLEM

Although there are no clear epidemiological data available on the numbers of deaths caused by medical error, a disturbing trend appears to be emerging. If the numbers reported in the literature are close to correct, the problem of death due to medical error is staggering. And these numbers do not take into account those medical errors that lead to prolonged hospital stays, preventable hospital stays and clinic visits, and disability. Although many Americans have been aware for years of certain dangers associated with encountering the medical system, it is only recently that publicity about medical errors has pushed the magnitude of this problem into the public's collective consciousness.

The single defining newsworthy event in this regard was the release in the fall of 1999 of the Institute of Medicine report mentioned previously (see Kohn et el. 2000). The Institute of Medicine was established in 1970 by the National Academy of Sciences to be an adviser to the federal government on issues of medical care, research, and education. The IOM report indicated that preventable adverse events are a leading cause of death in the United States. The IOM estimated that, extrapolating from data gathered in two studies for the 33.6 million hospital admissions in 1997, between 44,000 and 98,000 Americans die each year as a result of hospital errors. This places deaths in hospitals due to preventable errors between the fifth and eighth leading causes of death in the United States. This death toll is greater than that due to motor vehicle accidents (43,485), breast cancer (42,297), or AIDS (16,516). The national costs of these preventable deaths, which include lost income, lost household production, disability, and health costs, are estimated to be between $17 and $29 billion. Only limited data are available on medical errors in outpatient settings (clinics, outpatient surgical and diagnostic centers, and nursing homes) and pharmacy errors; if complete data were available, the number of preventable deaths due to errors could potentially approach the third or fourth leading cause of death. To put these statistics in another perspective: More than 6,000 lives are lost in workplace injuries each year (U.S. Bureau of Labor Statistics 1999), and the IOM estimates that in 1993 medication errors caused approximately 7,000 deaths (Kohn et al. 2000).

One of the leading studies to provide some insight into the magnitude of the problem of medical errors was the Harvard Medical Practice Study, in which researchers reviewed more than 30,000 randomly selected discharges from 51 hospitals in New York State in 1984 (Brennan et al. 1991). According to Brennan et al. (1991), the proportion of adverse events that occurred in these hospitals was 3.7%, and 58% of these errors were deemed to be preventable. Death resulted in 13.6% of these preventable adverse events. These findings have been corroborated by Gawande et al. (1999), who reviewed 15,000 randomly selected hospital admissions in Colorado and Utah for adverse surgical events in 1992. They found that the incidence of these events was 2.9%, of which 54% were deemed preventable. In this study, 5.6% of the surgical adverse events led to patient death.

Steel and his colleagues (1981) conducted a prospective study of 815 consecutive patients to determine the degree of iatrogenic illness in a general medical service at a university hospital. They found that 36% of the patients developed iatrogenic illnesses, and that 9% of all patients in the sample developed iatrogenic illnesses that threatened their lives or produced serious disability. In 2% of the cases, the hospital- or health care provider–induced illness either caused death or contributed to the patient's death.

In 1997, Andrews et al. published a report on their study of 1,047 patients admitted to two intensive care units and one surgical unit at a large teaching hospital. The researchers found that 45.8% of the patients in their sample had adverse events and that 17.7% of those events produced either serious disability or death. Andrews et al. conclude that each day a patient was hospitalized increased his or her risk of suffering an adverse event by 6%. Dubois and Brook (1988) studied 182 deaths in 12 hospitals and found that as many as 27% of the deaths might have been prevented. McGuire et al. (1992) studied 44,603 patients who underwent surgery at a large medical center and found that of the 749 who died, 7.5% of the deaths were judged to have been preventable.

The data cited above indicate that the risks of dying in a hospital setting due to medical error are not insignificant. Most of the studies we have mentioned focused on death as the end-point statistic, but some researchers have reported on disability and increased hospital stays as a result of preventable adverse errors. Krizek (2000) studied a sample of 1,047 patients admitted to three surgical units and found that 480 patients (45.8%) experienced adverse events. In total, 2,183 errors occurred in these patients, of which 462 (21.2%) were deemed potentially threatening to life or limb. Of the 480 patients, 175 (17.7%) experienced at least one serious error. Krizek reports that the average length of stay for patients who did not have adverse events was 8.8 days, compared with 23.6 days for patients who experienced adverse events and 32 days for those who experienced serious adverse events.

TYPES OF MEDICAL ERRORS

Hospital Errors

The primary author became acutely aware of hospital mistakes when he first went into practice after finishing residency training. He found the hospital setting to be unpleasant, and he struggled with the hospital environment when seeing patients there. Unfortunately, some of the hospital personnel interpreted his efforts to deal with problems as his trying to blame them, and this soon created a bunker mentality of "him versus them." One of his wiser, more experienced colleagues took him aside one day and

explained that "the hospital is part of the disease and must be managed accordingly, just as the patient's disease must be managed." This was quite a revelation. Since that time, he has taken his colleague's advice and worked to manage the hospital as if it were part of the patient's disease complex, because, very practically, it is.

Due to the complexity of both medical practice and the illnesses that patients can have, medical professionals can make myriad errors. Additionally, the numbers as well as the types of errors that can occur are multiplied by the fact that patients, particularly hospitalized individuals, are the recipients of numerous procedures and treatments. For example, it has been estimated that on any given day in a hospital intensive care unit, more than 170 different activities occur to and around an individual patient. The potential for error is further compounded by the ready availability of advanced technological modalities, which translates into greater use of diagnostic and therapeutic interventions.

In one case, errant technology led to a patient's death when the computer program controlling a radiation machine that was being used for therapy malfunctioned as the machine was being electronically positioned over the patient, and the machine delivered an overdose of radiation to the patient's head. The patient experienced an epileptic-like seizure and died 3 weeks later (Saltus 1986). In another case that we know of, a patient who was pacemaker dependent was given an MRI. The MRI reprogrammed the pacemaker, causing it to malfunction and resulting in the patient's death. Some may find it hard to believe that such errors actually happen in medicine, but because medicine is primarily people serving people, it is by nature a highly fallible, mistake-prone industry.

Deadly errors rarely occur in isolation. It is generally held that if a patient experiences an error early in the course of a hospitalization, he or she will usually experience a series of errors, none of which is self-correcting. This has been termed the "cascade effect" (Mold and Stein 1986). It is usually not the case that medical errors are made by lone individuals working in isolation, and studies have shown that those who make errors are usually not incompetent health care workers. In Krizek's (2000) study, he found that only 37.8% of the time was a single individual responsible for an error, and when an individual was responsible, he or she was part of a system that ultimately either augmented the error process or failed to impede the error. Most of the time, medical errors are simply mistakes.

In a book titled *How to Get Out of the Hospital Alive* (1997), Dr. Sheldon Blau and Elaine Fantle Shimberg detail Blau's personal hospitalization for heart disease and subsequent coronary artery bypass surgery at the hospital in which he practiced. It was a hospitalization, not unlike many, that was filled with errors and near misses. Blau and Shimberg explain how hospitals function and give many practical suggestions for having a successful hospitalization. They highlight the weaknesses of hospitals in an attempt to give patients more control over their environment within the hospital setting.

Medication Errors

At one time, doctors treated cardiac dysrhythmias more aggressively than they do today, giving patients a host of medications whether they had heart disease or not. A particular one of these medications was so good at suppressing premature ventricular contractions that it was called the "PVC killer." Doctors would prescribe this medication and see their patients' PVCs disappear practically before their eyes. Although there was a vague awareness that such medications may have side effects, most doctors believed the benefits outweighed the risks. Then came the Cardiac Arrhythmia Suppression Trial, which found increased mortality to be associated with the use of all of these medications (Cardiac Arrhythmia Suppression Trial Investigators 1989). As it turned out, these PVC killers were in fact patient killers, and physicians stopped prescribing them virtually overnight.

Americans use a great many prescription drugs; according to the National Wholesale Druggists' Association (1998), approximately 2.5 billion prescriptions were dispensed in U.S. pharmacies in 1998. Along with our extensive use of medications is an increasing trend in medication errors, which account for a significant portion of all preventable medical errors resulting in death. Phillips, Christenfeld, and Glynn (1998) have determined that the incidence of death from medication errors in the United States increased 257% from 1983 to 1993. They conclude that in 1983, medication errors caused 1 in every 539 outpatient deaths and 1 in every 1,622 inpatient deaths. In comparison, in 1993, medication errors increased to 1 in every 131 outpatient deaths and 1 in every 854 inpatient deaths. Outpatient prescriptions increased 139% during this time, and outpatient deaths due to medication errors increased 257%.

Unfortunately, one problem with retail pharmacies is that they generally have become so busy that pharmacists have less time to interact with patients than was the case in the past. The paradox is that both physicians and pharmacists today are better trained than ever, but because they are also busier than ever, sometimes patients get shortchanged. The problem of lack of pharmacist-patient communication is compounded by the growth of mail-order and Internet pharmacy services, whether patients choose to use them to save money or because they are required to do so by their insurance companies. It is easy to imagine how such long-distance filling of prescriptions could occasionally produce errors with catastrophic results.

Although Phillips et al. (1998) do not draw any conclusions from their study, an understanding of the time frame during which it was conducted might prove enlightening. During the period of 1983 through 1993, there was a virtual explosion in the numbers of medications and medication classes available. Because of this proliferation in numbers and types of medications, as well as Americans' increased use of outpatient medications (related to the aging of the population as well as the development of more aggressive treatments for arthritis, hypertension, heart disease, and diabetes), the potential number of interactions and adverse side effects increased to the point of becoming unquantifiable.

As the anecdote about PVC killers related above shows, medical professionals need to be aware that jumping on the bandwagon of new medications might not be in their patients' best interests. The fact that FDA approval does not necessarily correlate with a medication's safety has been driven home quite clearly. The old saying in medicine that "one needs to use new medications before they develop side effects" has certainly been illustrated by several FDA-approved drugs. In March 2000, history of a dubious sort was made when Rezulin (troglitazone) and Propulsid (cisapride) were recalled within the same week by their perspective companies, under FDA agreement, because of deaths associated with their use.

Lesar, Briceland, and Stein (1997) analyzed 289,411 medication orders written in a tertiary care teaching hospital and determined the rate of significant error to be 1.81%. In such a setting, as few as 30 and as many as 60 different steps take place by the time a patient is given a medication, and even an error rate as small as 1–2% can potentially lead to significant problems. Children are at increased risk from medication errors because of their size and their lack of maturity-related organ development. A review of 101,002 medication orders at two children's hospitals revealed 27 potentially lethal prescribing errors (Folli et al. 1987). Raju et al. (1989) studied medication errors in neonatal and pediatric intensive care units in a 4-year prospective study and found the frequency of iatrogenic injury to be 1 in every 33 admissions. Although most adverse drug events are nonlethal, some that can be classified as near misses involve inaccurate doses, inappropriate medications, or medication interactions that are potentially lethal.

It is likely that the majority of adverse drug events, even those causing death, take place without the knowledge or recognition of the health care team. The most common adverse drug events are associated with cardiovascular agents, anticonvulsants, antihypertensives, and nonsteroidal anti-inflammatory medications.

Many medication errors occur due to miscommunication. Unfortunately, in the time-compressed world in which health care professionals work, it is relatively easy for them to write medication orders that are not completely legible. It is also easy to misplace decimal points— for example, it is not difficult to write 20 mg when one means to write 2.0 mg. In his book titled *Drug Death: A Danger of Hospitalization* (1989), Hoffmann gives an account of a death that resulted when a patient's dose of the anti-gout medication colchicine was interpreted as 10 mg instead of 1.0 mg. When giving verbal orders, it is easy to misspeak and say "5.0 mg of epinephrine" instead of "0.5 mg"—Hoffmann tells of such a mistake that caused the death of a patient in a nursing home. It is also easy for nurses and other health care workers to misunderstand verbal orders; Hoffmann relates a case of a near miss that occurred to a hospitalized patient when she was given 60 mg of theophylline per hour instead of 16 mg per hour. Fortunately, most errors of this kind are detected by vigilant and experienced individuals and so are prevented from causing catastrophic events.

Another common problem stems from the fact that many medications that are otherwise quite different have similar-sounding names (Davis, Cohen, and Teplitsky 1992). When Prilosec, an ulcer and acid reflux medication, was first introduced, its name was Losec. However, handwritten prescriptions for Losec were frequently interpreted as being for Lasix, a diuretic, and the FDA mandated a name change (Cohen 2000). Examples of other sound-alike drugs are Coumadin (an anticoagulant) and Kemadrin (an anti-Parkinson's medication), Taxol (an anticancer drug) and Paxil (an antidepressant), and Zebeta (an antihypertensive) and Diabeta (an antidiabetic medication), not to mention Celexa (an antidepressant), Celebrex (an antiarthritic), and Cerebrex (an anticonvulsant) (Cohen 2000).

With the increasing availability of new medications, physicians are not always able to keep abreast of the knowledge required to use them appropriately. Even physicians' mandatory continuing education is unlikely to keep them adequately informed about all the possible interactions and serious side effects of the many new drugs being added to the market each year. It is virtually impossible for any physician to predict all of the multiple potentially life-threatening effects of drug interactions involving new medications. Fortunately, any given potentially lethal interaction does not happen 100% of the time. Unfortunately, serious adverse drug events are most likely to happen to the sickest patients, those who can least tolerate them. This is a variation of Murphy's Law that is well recognized in medicine.

Technical and Diagnostic Errors

One kind of diagnostic error that can occur is illustrated by a case in which one of us was involved: A hospital emergency department physician called the attending physician and said that he had a patient with abdominal pain whose blood pressure was 90/60. The emergency department doctor wanted to admit the patient and let the other doctor see the patient in the morning. The attending physician, however, thought there was something a little odd about the situation and decided to examine the patient himself. When he arrived in the emergency department, he examined the patient's abdomen and found that the patient had an expanding abdominal aortic aneurysm that was about to burst. The patient was immediately sent to a referral hospital for aortic aneurysm repair. This case turned out well, but it likely would not have if the attending physician had relied solely on the judgment of the emergency department physician.

Another form of diagnostic error is the failure to diagnose a curable, but potentially lethal, condition properly, so that it can be treated medically. An example would be the failure to biopsy a cervical lymph node and thus miss a diagnosis of Hodgkin's disease or other curable cancer. Misreading an abnormal mammogram or failing to biopsy a breast nodule and so missing a diagnosis of cancer are both potentially lethal errors. Even though radiologists are well trained, it is not uncommon for them to miss important X-ray abnormalities. Also, research has shown that different radiologists interpret the same X rays differently in a small portion of cases (Herman et al. 1975).

Herman et al. (1975) found that radiologists can miss important findings by misreading radiographs. In one case that we know of, a 45-year-old woman who had been coughing for 2 months had a chest X ray, and a radiologist read it as normal. In reality, however, the woman had a lung mass that turned out to be cancer, from which she died 8 months later.

Sometimes surgeons commit fatal errors by failing to remove cancerous tissue completely during breast lumpectomies or other cancer surgeries, and sometimes fatal errors stem from inaccurate biopsies of malignant tissues. Pathologists occasionally make the error of failing to see cancer cells on microscopic specimens. Unfortunately, in some cases cancer cells look very much like cells from tumors that are benign. If a cancerous tumor is misdiagnosed as benign, the cancer will not be effectively treated, and if a benign tumor is misdiagnosed as cancerous, the patient will be subjected to overly aggressive treatment for a benign condition. The latter happened in the case of one woman who underwent bilateral mastectomy when she did not have breast cancer ("Mastectomy Patient" 2003). It is obviously tragic enough to lose a breast due to cancer; it is a disaster to lose healthy breasts due to diagnostic error.

Pathology and cytology errors account for a small but significant portion of medical errors that have caused death. For example, it is not uncommon for abnormal Pap smears to be read as normal. Because there is a gradual transition from healthy cells to cancerous cells on cervical cytology, and because there may be thousands of cells on any one Pap smear slide, it is quite possible for a cytologist to overlook abnormal cells. Historically, another reason for misinterpretation of Pap smears was that labs were requiring cytologists to read too many slides. Before government regulation limited the number of slides any given cytologist can be required to read to 80 per day, many cytologists were reading hundreds of slides per day. Such practices are dangerous because operator fatigue may result in misinterpretation of Pap smears.

Although pathologists do not misread many microscopic specimens, erroneous readings of even a small number of slides within the course of a year can lead to devastating results. In one case with which we are familiar, a patient's skin biopsy that was initially read by a pathologist as normal tissue was later read by another pathologist as cancer. This error prevented timely treatment of a lethal skin cancer. The second pathologist later admitted sheepishly that the previous pathologist had been "let go" because of a number of "misreads." Such incidents are indeed frightening to both patients and physicians.

Kronz, Westra, and Epstein (1999) reviewed 6,171 cancer cases referred to Johns Hopkins Hospital over a 21-month period and found that 86 (1.4%) of these cases were misdiagnosed. In 80 of the cases, the new diagnosis altered the treatment plan, and in 81 cases it altered the prognosis. The diagnosis was changed from malignant to benign in 20 of the cases, and in 5 cases the diagnosis was changed from benign to malignant.

It is important to remember that a second opinion may significantly alter the treatment and disease course of a specific cancer. It is known that pathologic diagnosis is not an exact science. Studies have shown that there can be significant disagreement among pathologists in the diagnosis of a particular sample of cells on a slide. Many hospitals automatically seek second opinions within the institution on significant pathology, and if there is disagreement, an outside expert is consulted for a final determination. Most histologic specimens are read by general pathologists. These pathologists may have expertise in specific tumors, but may not be expert in the type of tumor that any one patient may have.

Another reason misdiagnosis sometimes occurs is that many biopsies are taken with thin needles because this technique is relatively uninvasive. One problem with the so-called thin-needle biopsy is that the pathologist is forced to work with a very small tissue sample, and this can result in a greater margin of error than would be the case with a larger sample. Additionally, the smaller the tissue sample biopsied, the greater the chance that abnormal tissue has been missed. Biopsy results from a small sample may give the patient and doctor a false sense of security that nothing abnormal is present when in fact the abnormal tissue has simply not been biopsied.

Surgical Errors

In one case of surgical error related to us by a colleague, a surgeon performing a laparoscopic cholecystectomy (gallbladder removal) punctured an iliac blood vessel with a trocar upon entering the abdomen. The usual procedure is to place the trocar (a piece of metal with a sharp point) into the abdomen through the abdominal wall. This requires several pounds of manual force to accelerate the trocar through the abdominal wall and a deftness of manual dexterity to stop the trocar immediately after it enters the abdominal cavity. The trocar allows the surgeon a portal through which to insufflate and distend the abdominal cavity with inert gas so that he or she can adequately view the intra-abdominal contents. Sometimes scar tissue within the abdomen causes the structures to be adhered or displaced, which then places vital organs in harm's way. In this particular case, the patient died because the injury to the blood vessel was not recognized and corrected.

Surgical errors are among some of the most catastrophic of medical mistakes. Because of their nature, surgical errors are disproportionately associated with serious or lethal outcomes (Gawande et al. 1999; Krizek 2000). Unfortunate surgical events take many forms, including the puncturing of intestines or blood vessels and the accidental tying off of such organs as the ureter (a duct that carries urine away from the kidney). These events in and of themselves are not necessarily errors, however; the errors occur when such mishaps are not recognized and quickly repaired or corrected.

Krizek (2000) found that of the 2,183 errors that occurred during and after surgery in his sample, surgical technical errors constituted only 10.5% of the total errors but 17.9% of the serious errors. The medical literature is replete with examples of surgical mishaps that occurred when laparoscopic surgery was introduced in the late 1980s and early 1990s. It is also well-known that surgeons in training and surgeons who are inexperienced in given procedures make more technical mistakes than do more experienced surgeons.

Additional surgical errors include wrong-site operations. Since 1996, there have been more than 150 reports of operations in the United States in which surgeons operated on the wrong arm, leg, kidney, or side of the brain, and even on the wrong patient (Altman 2001). Such errors prompted the Joint Commission on Accreditation of Healthcare Organizations (JCAHO) to issue its second alert in 3 years on this particular topic. The JCAHO now suggests that both the patient and the surgeon mark the correct site for surgery and also mark the site that should not be touched, because there have been two cases in which the correct limb was marked but the wrong one was not and the wrong one was operated on.

Policy Errors

Government policies can influence the health of a given population, such as when they allow unsafe practices to continue. For example, in France in the mid-1980s, the Ministry of Health permitted the use of blood that was potentially contaminated with HIV when the government clearly should have known the risks that this involved. Our government is not completely innocent in this regard. In the early 1980s, the restrictions placed on blood donors were reduced; this error in government policy will most likely cost lives.

ADMITTING ERRORS

The prevention of error in medical practice is based on the concept of the "robust individual." That is, the prevention of medical error relies on the presence of high-quality individual health care workers who can recognize and correct errors along the way as they happen. In essence, error interception is an intrinsic part of the job description of every health care professional. Medical practice has developed an aura of infallibility, which is absurd when one recognizes that the service of health care is performed by human beings, who are quite fallible. In short, people make mistakes. The attitude of society and medicine is the name, blame, and shame game, in which the person who committed an error is singled out, blamed, and punished. This strategy creates a culture in which health care workers are reluctant to admit their errors or flaws for fear they will be blamed and punished, a culture that is counterproductive to the long-term prevention of medical error.

CONCLUSION

Medicine is the only major industry in the United States that has yet to evaluate fully how it can prevent errors and improve safety. Medicine has not yet been willing or able to develop a system of full disclosure of errors, which is a necessary first step in developing a preventive strategy. Although some institutions and specialties have made some initial forays into error prevention, it is apparent to most observers that these efforts fall short of a comprehensive analysis leading to a national effort at medical error prevention.

It is axiomatic that health care consumers want the safest possible health care system. However, establishment of such a system would require full error disclosure by both health care workers and institutions, followed by failure analysis. This analysis would focus on why errors occur in an effort to develop systems for error prevention, rather than blaming and punishing the last person involved in the error process. Errors generally do not occur in isolation; rather, errors are the end results of a flawed system. Although full error disclosure is absolutely prerequisite to overall improvement in safety, there will be no such disclosure within the present culture. Nor will such disclosure occur without some level of legal protection in place for health care professionals; no one will admit error if there is a reasonable possibility that he or she will be sued. Health care consumers cannot have it both ways: They must choose between full error disclosure, which will lead to improved safety, and the freedom to sue the individuals involved when errors occur. The question the public needs to answer is, Do we want the safest health care system possible?

REFERENCES

Altman, Lawrence K. 2001. "The Doctor's World: The Wrong Foot, and Other Tales of Surgical Error." *New York Times,* December 11, p. F1.

Andrews, Lori B., Carol Stocking, Thomas J. Krizek, Lawrence Gottlieb, Claudette Krizek, Thomas Vargish, and Mark Siegler. 1997. "An Alternative Strategy for Studying Adverse Events in Medical Care." *Lancet* 349:309–13.

Blau, Sheldon Paul and Elaine Fantle Shimberg. 1997. *How to Get Out of the Hospital Alive: A Guide to Patient Power.* New York: Macmillan.

Brennan, Troyen A., Lucian L. Leape, Nan M. Laird, Liesi Hebert, A. Russell Localio, Ann G. Lawthers, Joseph P. Newhouse, Paul C. Weiler, and Howard H. Hiatt. 1991. "Incidence of Adverse Events and Negligence in Hospitalized Patients: Results of the Harvard Medical Practice Study I." *New England Journal of Medicine* 324:370–76.

Burton, Elizabeth C., Dana A. Troxclair, and William P. Newman III. 1998. "Autopsy Diagnoses of Malignant Neoplasms: How Often Are Clinical Diagnoses Incorrect?" *Journal of the American Medical Association* 280:1245–48.

Cardiac Arrhythmia Suppression Trial Investigators. 1989. "Preliminary Report: Effect of Encainide and Flecainide on Mortality in a Randomized Trial of Arrhythmia Suppression After Myocardial Infarction." *New England Journal of Medicine* 321:406–12.

Cohen, Michael R., ed. 2000. *Medication Errors: Causes, Preventions, and Risk Management.* Boston: Jones & Bartlett.

Davis, Neil M., Michael R. Cohen, and Benjamin Teplitsky. 1992. "Look-Alike and Sound-Alike Drug Names: The Problem and the Solution." *Hospital Pharmacology* 27:95–110.

Dubois, Robert W. and Robert H. Brook. 1988. "Preventable Deaths: Who, How Often, and Why?" *Annals of Internal Medicine* 109:582–89.

Folli, Hugo L., Robert L. Poole, William E. Benitz, and Janita C. Russo. 1987. "Medication Error Prevention by Clinical Pharmacists in Two Children's Hospitals." *Pediatrics* 79:718–22.

Gawande, Atul A., Eric J. Thomas, Michael J. Zinner, and Troyen A. Brennan. 1999. "The Incidence and Nature of Surgical Adverse Events in Colorado and Utah in 1992." *Surgery* 126:66–75.

Gottesfeld, Perry. 1999. "Fifteen Years After Bhopal, Lessons Learned but Not Exported." *Seattle Post-Intelligencer,* December 9.

Gross, Martin L. 1998. *The Medical Racket: How Doctors, HMOs, and Hospitals Are Failing the American Patient.* New York: Avon.

Gueson, Emerita T. 1997. *Do HMO's Cut Costs . . . and Lives?* Bensalem, PA: Theresevision.

Herman, Peter G., Donald E. Gerson, Samuel J. Hessel, Barry S. Mayer, Murray Watnick, Barry Blesser, and David Ozonoff. 1975. "Disagreements in Chest Roentgen Interpretation." *Chest* 68:278–82.

Hoffmann, Richard P. 1989. *Drug Death: Danger of Hospitalization.* Springfield, IL: English.

Kohn, Linda T., Janet M. Corrigan, and Molla S. Donaldson, eds. 2000. *To Err Is Human: Building a Safer Health System.* Washington, DC: National Academy Press.

Krizek, Thomas J. 2000. "Surgical Error: Ethical Issues of Adverse Events." *Archives of Surgery* 135:1359–66.

Kronz, Joseph D., William H. Westra, and Jonathan I. Epstein. 1999. "Mandatory Second Opinion Surgical Pathology at a Large Referral Hospital." *Cancer* 86:2426–35.

Lesar, Timothy, Laurie Briceland, and Daniel S. Stein. 1997. "Factors Related to Errors in Medication Prescribing." *Journal of the American Medical Association* 277:312–17.

Marwick, Charles. 1995. "Pathologists Request Autopsy Revival." *Journal of the American Medical Association* 273:1889, 1891.

"Mastectomy Patient Had No Cancer." 2003. *Los Angeles Times,* p. A23.

McGuire, Hunter H., Jr., J. Shelton Horsley III, David R. Salter, and Michael Sobel. 1992. "Measuring and Managing Quality of Surgery: Statistical vs. Incidental Approaches." *Archives of Surgery* 127:733–38.

Millman, Marcia. 1977. *The Unkindest Cut: Life in the Backrooms of Medicine.* New York: William Morrow.

Mold, James W. and Howard F. Stein. 1986. "The Cascade Effect in the Clinical Care of Patients." *New England Journal of Medicine* 314:512–14.

National Wholesale Druggists' Association. 1998. *Industry Profile and Healthcare Factbook.* Reston, VA: National Wholesale Druggists' Association.

Phillips, David P., Nicholas Christenfeld, and Laura M. Glynn. 1998. "Increase in US Medication-Error Deaths Between 1983 and 1993." *Lancet* 351:643–44.

Public Broadcasting Service. 1998. "Three Mile Island: The Judge's Ruling." Retrieved April 17, 2003 (http://www.pbs.org/wgbh/pages/frontline/shows/reaction/readings/tmi.html).

Raju, Tonse N. K., Susan Kecskes, John P. Thornton, Maureen Perry, and Susan Feldman. 1989. "Medication Errors in Neonatal and Pediatric Intensive-Care Units." *Lancet* 334:374–76.

Rosenthal, Marilynn. 1995. *The Incompetent Doctor: Behind Closed Doors.* Philadelphia: Open University Press.

Saltus, Richard. 1986. "Man Killed by Accident With Medical Radiation; 2 Hurt by Flaw in Therapy Machines." *Boston Globe,* June 20, p. 1.

Steel, Knight, Paul M. Gertman, Caroline Crescenzi, and Jennifer Anderson. 1981. "Iatrogenic Illness on a General Medical Service at a University Hospital." *New England Journal of Medicine* 304:638–42.

Tanne, Janice Hopkins. 1998. "News: Cancer Diagnosis Is Often Missed." *British Medical Journal* 317:1033.

U.S. Bureau of Labor Statistics. 1999. *National Consensus of Fatal Occupational Injuries, 1998.* Washington, DC: U.S. Department of Labor.

HOMICIDAL DEATH

STEVEN A. EGGER

KIM A. EGGER

The history of the United States and the character of its people include a violent component in which the taking of human life has played an important role. Violence was common in the North American continent even before the nation was formed. The systematic destruction of Native American societies by Europeans who settled in the New World reflects the notion that might makes right. The Revolutionary War took a deadly toll on both sides of the conflict. The Civil War provides yet another example of extreme violence and megadeath. The lawlessness of the western frontier and the glorification of gunslingers and mob "justice" are further evidence of the deep roots of violence in the American culture. As the history of the United States has unfolded, this violence, which has often taken the form of murder, has been well documented.

Murder is defined as the taking of the life of one person by another; *homicide* is a synonym for *murder*. The U.S. Department of Justice's Bureau of Justice Statistics (1989) defines homicide as the causing of the death of one human being by another without legal justification or excuse. A broader definition would include the killing of one human being by another through a direct action or an act of omission, regardless of justification. In Western society, criminal statutes divide homicides into killings that are culpable or blameworthy and those that are not culpable; those that fall into the latter category are not considered crimes against the state.

Humans hold a fear of death regardless of their spiritual or religious convictions. Simply put, humans do not desire their lives to end. Thus the idea that someone would take the life of another is anathema to the human mind. Although some analysts of this problem take exception to this orientation, most support this cultural value, arguing that all human life has worth. This would include those analysts who argue that the state should refrain from exacting justice through the taking of life, even in cases of homicide.

The United States has the highest rate of homicide in the Western world even though both the rate and incidence of homicides declined throughout the nation during the final decades of the 20th century. The U.S. homicide rate is high for a number of reasons. Some analysts argue that the high rate of homicide can be attributed to the relative ease of availability of handguns and widespread use of alcohol, whereas others contend that socioeconomic issues and the overall strength of the U.S. economy are partially responsible. Government officials and other social scientists assert that the high rate of homicide can be attributed to the illegal use of controlled substances, such as marijuana and cocaine, and the enormous profits to be gained from the sale of illicit drugs.

In 1966, Wertham argued that the homicide problem could be reduced, but that we need to take a long-range perspective on the problem if we are to have any chance of bringing violence under control. Violence is a part of cultural ideology and the social fabric of U.S. society; it is also an institutional fact. Thus violence is inherent in the structure of Americans' relationships. As Wertham states:

> An equitable socio-economic structure of societies must be the basis for bringing about a universal revulsion against violence. If the individual—all individuals—and society becomes the integrated entity, which they truly are in a fully developed civilization, motives for killing will yield to habits of nonviolence, and nobody will have to be afraid any longer of violent interference with his life and that of his children. (P. 356)

Before we can develop any measure of prevention other than punishment, however, it is clear that we must learn more about violence in general and about how we might bring new insight into the phenomenon of violence to bear on the homicide problem. In the discussion that follows, our focus on the homicide problem is intended to demonstrate both the scope of the problem, including the psychological and sociodemographic characteristics associated with this phenomenon, and the limits of available knowledge.

THE CLASSIFICATION OF HOMICIDES

In most U.S. jurisdictions, homicides are classified into six categories. The first is *first-degree murder,* or premeditated murder undertaken with deliberation. To be considered murder in the first degree, the act must have been intended prior to the event's taking place. In the prosecution of first-degree murder, the state is required to establish legally that the act was intentional and not spontaneous. Second, the state must prove that the act was deliberate—that is, that the act of murder was not impulsive. If the state can demonstrate that planning occurred, even if only momentarily, that is sufficient to establish the second element of first-degree murder.

The second legal category is *second-degree murder.* Here the state must establish malice aforethought, but without premeditation or deliberation. Malice can be expressed without provocation or it can be implied when murder results from negligence or unthinking behavior on behalf of the perpetrator.

The third homicide category, *voluntary manslaughter,* occurs when a life is taken without malice. In this instance, the legal distinction is that the act was voluntary but the perpetrator did not intend to kill the victim. One example of voluntary manslaughter is a murder committed in the heat of passion (as in the case of a "love triangle"), without planning or deliberation. It is lack of malice that differentiates voluntary manslaughter from second-degree murder.

Involuntary manslaughter, the fourth category of homicide, is charged when negligent behavior results in a death. A frequently used example of this kind of homicide is an accidental death caused by a driver who was under the influence of either drugs or alcohol.

The fifth legal category, *justifiable homicide,* is acceptable under the law when one individual kills another in an act of self-defense. In the United States, individuals are considered to be justified in taking the life of another in defense of themselves or their property. Thus justifiable homicide is homicide that is considered unavoidable under the criminal law in specific situations, such as when a person uses force in confronting an armed robber to protect him- or herself, others, or property.

The final category, *excusable homicide,* is not clearly distinct from the other categories, especially in those jurisdictions where the term *justifiable* in the context of self-defense is used synonymously with *excusable.* In legal terms, however, an excusable homicide is a homicide that results from the occurrence of an accident or misfortune during the commission of a lawful act by a person acting without criminal intent and employing usual and ordinary caution (Holmes and Holmes 1994:3).

Table 1   Murder and Nonnegligent Manslaughter in the United States, 1991–2000

Year	Number	Rate per 100,000
2000	15,517	5.5
1999	15,522	5.7
1998	16,914	6.3
1997	18,208	6.8
1996	19,650	7.4
1995	21,610	8.2
1994	23,330	9.0
1993	24,530	9.5
1992	23,760	9.3
1991	24,700	9.8

SOURCE: Fox and Zawitz (2001).

THE EXTENT OF HOMICIDE IN THE UNITED STATES

In the year 2000, according to the Federal Bureau of Investigation's *Uniform Crime Reports,* 15,517 officially recorded homicides occurred; the rate per 100,000 was 5.5. This number is virtually unchanged from that recorded in 1999, when 15,522 instances were reported (rate = 5.7). These figures represent a 21% reduction from that recorded during 1996 (*n* = 19,650; rate = 7.4) and a reduction of 37.2% from that recorded for 1991 (*n* = 24,700; rate = 9.8). Of the murders recorded during 2000, 44% occurred in the South, the country's most populous region; 21% occurred in the Midwest, 21% in the West, and almost 14% in the Northeast. The South and Northeast each recorded a 2.4% increase. The West recorded a decrease of 3.4%, and the Midwest experienced a decrease of 2.9%. Homicides occurred most frequently during the month of July and least often in the month of February (Federal Bureau of Investigation 1992, 1997, 2001).

The national murder rate per 100,000 in the year 2000 (5.5) represents a decrease of 25.6% from that recorded during 1996; it is 43.7% lower than that for 1991. The year 2000 murder rate in U.S. metropolitan areas was 5.9 murders per 100,000 population. For that same year, the murder rate for both rural counties and cities located outside metropolitan areas was 3.8 per 100,000 (Federal Bureau of Investigation 1992, 1997, 2001).

Table 1 displays the numbers and rates of homicides in the United States for the years 1991 to 2000. As the table shows, there was a 37% decrease in the number of homicides and a 44% decrease in the rate of homicide over this period. For 12,943 of the 15,517 murders reported during the year 2000, local U.S. law enforcement agencies have provided information on the age, sex, and race of both victims and offenders, the types of weapons used, the relationships of victims to offenders, and the circumstances surrounding the murders. According to these data, 76.2% of homicide victims were male. The greatest proportion (89.7%) of victims were age 18 and over, with approximately 45% of the victims 20 to 34 years of age. Where race is known, 49% of the victims were white and 48.5% were black, with all other races accounting for the remaining 2.5%.

The data relating to offenders indicate that in the year 2000, 14,697 offenders, or 90.2% of the offenders for whom information is known, were male. Of these, 91.3% were age 18 and over. Of all offenders, 69.1% were ages 17 through 34; 51.4% were black, 46.1% were white, and the remainder were persons of other races. The data also reveal that murder tends to be intraracial: Black offenders killed 93.7% of black murder victims and white offenders killed 86.2% of white victims. In addition, males were most often the offenders against both other males (88.5%) and females (90.8%) (Federal Bureau of Investigation 2001).

People use a number of weapons to kill one another. The most frequently used weapon of homicide in the United States in the year 2000 was a firearm, representing 65.6% of the total. Handguns specifically were used in 51.2% of cases, and other firearms were employed in 14.2%. Knives or other cutting weapons were used in 13.5% of the murders; personal weapons, such as hands, feet, or fists, were used in 7%; blunt objects, such as hammers and clubs, were used in 4.7%; and other dangerous weapons, such as explosives or poisons, were used in the remainder of the cases (Federal Bureau of Investigation 2001). Table 2 presents a breakdown of the weapons used in homicides in the United States over the same 10-year period shown in Table 1; the data indicate that very little has changed over time.

Data on murders in the year 2000 show that in about 44% of the cases the victims knew the perpetrators, and 13.4% of perpetrators were related to their victims by family ties. Of all female victims, the proportion killed by husbands or boyfriends was 33%; of all male victims, 3.2% were killed by wives or girlfriends. Victims were killed by strangers in 13% of the murders, and in 42.6% of the murders the relationships between the victims and their killers were not known. As to the circumstances of the killings, 29.4% were attributed to arguments and 16.7% were committed in conjunction with other felonious acts.

U.S. law enforcement agencies have been less than effective in solving homicides over the past 25 years. The rate of clearance (the proportion of homicide cases solved) was 79% in 1976, and by the year 2000 the clearance rate had declined to 63.1%. This decline in clearance rates may be a result of the increases in stranger-to-stranger homicides, drive-by shootings, and gang-related and drug-related killings recorded in recent years.

Persons under 18 years of age were responsible for 5.3% of the murders that were cleared during the year 2000, representing the lowest proportion of juvenile involvement in major crimes. Of the 13,227 arrests for murder made during 2000, 51.3% of those arrested were under 25 years of age; the age group 18 to 24 accounts for 42% of the arrest total. Almost 90% of those arrested were males. Blacks accounted for 48.8% of murder arrests and whites accounted for 48.7%, with other races making up the remainder. The number of arrests for murder in 2000 was 24.2% below the number recorded for 1996 and 41.3% below that recorded for 1991.

MOTIVES FOR HOMICIDE

Some analysts of the homicide problem argue that one should consider victim precipitation when attempting to establish motive for murder. In some cases, determining how the victim's actions or situation contributed to his or her demise may prove useful, but this information can provide only a partial explanation for the homicide—that is, unless self-defense is involved.

The Root Causation of Violent Behavior

Many researchers have addressed the causes of crime by identifiable motives in numerous research monographs and journal articles. Beginning with the classical and neo-classical philosophical writers, many individuals have brought important insights to bear on this topic. Among the earliest of these analysts were Cesare Beccaria and Jeremy Bentham, both of whom offer important insights, arguing that people act rationally and exercise free will in choosing to commit crimes.

In the scientific arena, biologists have long explored the roots of violent behavior in the search for physical explanations. One early pioneer in this area was Cesare

		Other Types of Guns	Knives	Blunt Objects	Unknown or Other Types of Weapons
Table 2		Weapons Used in Homicides in the United States, 1991–2000 (in percentages)			
Year	Handgun	Other Types of Guns	Knives	Blunt Objects	Unknown or Other Types of Weapons
2000	51.2	14.2	13.5	4.7	16.4
1999	51	14	13.1	5.8	15.8
1998	52.1	12.8	13.3	5.3	16.5
1997	53.3	14.4	13	4.7	14.7
1996	54.6	12.9	13.7	4.7	14.1
1995	55.8	12.4	12.7	4.5	14.6
1994	57.8	12.2	12.7	4.1	13.2
1993	57	12.6	12.8	4.4	13.2
1992	55.4	12.8	14.5	4.6	12.7
1991	53	13.3	15.8	5	12.8

SOURCE: Adapted from Fox and Zawitz (2001).

Lombroso, who, in the late 1800s, developed ideas relating to the concept of the biological, or "born," criminal. Although these early ideas quickly lost support, a great deal of the scientific literature addresses the problem of criminal behavior from psychological, psychiatric, and sociological points of view, with each discipline approaching the problem from a different level of analysis. Researchers working from each of these perspectives have attempted to offer explanations from criminal behavior that focus on different aspects of life experiences and social processes.

Although establishing the motives that lie behind the behavior that leads to homicide is not yet an exact science, one way to advance that understanding is to examine different types of homicide as these are currently known to relate to the factor of motive. The FBI's *Crime Classification Manual* (Douglas et al. 1992), or *CCM,* lists four categories of homicide: personal cause homicide, criminal enterprise homicide, sexual homicide, and group cause homicide. We discuss the dynamics involved in homicides in each of these categories in turn below.

Personal Cause Homicide

According to the *CCM,* personal cause homicide is one the most common forms of murder committed worldwide (Douglas et al. 1992). Defined as murders committed as the result of emotional conflicts, personal cause homicides can be divided into several subtypes. One of these is erotomania homicide, in which the perpetrator holds a fantasy about a public figure and stalks that person before killing him or her. An example is the case of Mark Chapman, who shot former Beatle John Lennon in front of the New York City apartment building in which Lennon lived. After the murder, it was discovered that Chapman had built a rich fantasy life around John Lennon, imitating him and at times even believing that he *was* Lennon. Chapman's delusions led him to kill Lennon because Lennon's existence threatened Chapman's fantasy life (Douglas et al. 1992). We discuss several other subtypes of personal cause homicide briefly below.

Domestic Homicide

In domestic homicide, the victim and the offender are members of the same family or household, including extended the family. The murder of a wife or girlfriend by her husband or boyfriend is an example of this type of homicide. Such a death may result from an escalation of an ongoing situation of domestic abuse or battering, or may take place suddenly when the offender becomes angry with the victim for not performing an activity to the offender's satisfaction, or may occur when the offender attempts to stop the victim from leaving the relationship. During the 1970s, many states passed new domestic violence laws in reaction to data on the numbers of women who had been killed when they attempted to leave their abusive husbands.

Child abuse resulting in the death of the child is yet another example of domestic homicide. Poverty and parental job loss, marital problems, and mental illness are thought to be contributing factors in the death of hundreds of children each year. According to a vast amount of evidence compiled by researchers in mental health and related fields, child abuse is one of the leading causes of infant and adolescent death in the United States; approximately 2,000 children die annually across the nation as the result of abuse ("Abuse a Leading Cause" 1995). Deaths stemming from the abuse of elderly family members are also included in this category, although few data are available on such homicides.

Argument/Conflict Homicide

Research has shown that there is a strong relationship between the use of alcohol and other drugs and domestic homicide. Alcohol and the presence of handguns is often a lethal combination, and both factors play major roles in argument/conflict homicide. In one study, Goldstein (1995) found that alcohol use was related to at least one-half of recorded homicides. When alcohol or other drugs and guns are present, an argument between acquaintances, or even between strangers, may quickly escalate into a violent confrontation. When combined with anger, interpersonal conflict may lead to the death of one or more of the parties to the conflict. In the year 2000, more than one-fourth of all homicides in the United States resulted from arguments. Other examples of argument/conflict homicides are killings stemming from road rage incidents, bar fights, neighborhood disagreements, and arguments over money or property.

Authority Homicide

Authority homicide is the murder of an individual in a position of authority over the killer. Cases in which individuals murder their former bosses are representative of this category of homicide. This type of crime may also escalate into mass murder, as when perpetrators kill innocent bystanders as well as their authority targets. The murders of political and religious figures also fall within this category of homicide. For example, the assassination of Afghan Northern Alliance leader Ahmad Shah Masood in September 2001 by the followers of Osama bin Laden may be understood as an authority homicide. Masood's enemies considered his death to be essential because he represented a threat to the goals of the Taliban and bin Laden, and he was a central figure in efforts to unite forces against the Taliban.

Revenge Homicide

Revenge homicide is the killing of a person in retaliation for real, imagined, or perceived wrongs the victim committed against the killer or against some other person the killer deems to be important. The victim of a revenge homicide may not have been aware of the situation that led to his or her death, but investigators may be able to discover a link between the killer and the victim and thus establish what triggered the killing. For example, an individual who is convicted of a crime may fixate on a court witness against him and vow revenge against that person, although the witness may never know of this vow.

Nonspecific Homicide

Homicides that are classified as nonspecific are perhaps the most difficult types of murders to comprehend. They do not fall into any of the other categories because they seem senseless—they have no apparent motive. Victims of such homicides often appear to be chosen at random; they may simply have been in the wrong place at the wrong time. Some homicides are classified as nonspecific because the killers have committed suicide or been killed by the police, so all questions about motive remain unanswered.

Extremist Homicide

Extremist homicide is murder committed because of the killer's ideological, political, religious, or socioeconomic beliefs. Although individuals commit homicide for such reasons, the ideologically oriented groups with which they are affiliated may not sanction murder as a legitimate means of promoting social change. One example of a perpetrator of extremist homicide is Joseph Paul Franklin, who targeted mixed-race couples across the United States in the late 1970s. Most of Franklin's gunshot victims were African American males; his white victims were all females. When Franklin was caught in September 1980, it was discovered that he had a history of associating with the American Nazi Party and the Ku Klux Klan, both extremist groups that advocate the murder of nonwhites. In contrast are the extremist homicides perpetrated by individuals whose religious views lead them to bomb abortion clinics and murder persons who assist in performing abortions. Although some of these individuals might consider themselves to be affiliated with the Roman Catholic Church, which is opposed to abortion, the Church does not advocate the murder of those who engage in this procedure.

Mercy and Hero Homicides

This category encompasses two related kinds of homicide. Hero homicides are murders committed by individuals who place their victims in life-threatening situations in order to "rescue" them; when a rescue fails, a homicide is the result. In mercy homicide, the killer's intent is to release the victim from a terminal condition that is painful or degrading. Such murders are often described as tragic because the victims are usually terminally ill persons and their killers are either family members or intimate friends.

In these cases, the victims' suffering or fear of the late-stage disease process serves as the catalyst for killing. Other persons may also be involved in this type of so-called murder. For example, the former medical pathologist Jack Kevorkian assisted many terminally ill persons in fulfilling their wishes to die, although at Kevorkian's criminal trial, he indicated in his testimony that he medicated these patients to relieve their suffering, not to kill.

Newspapers frequently carry stories about health care workers who have been responsible for the deaths of patients. In cases of hero homicide, the killers are usually health care workers who have histories of saving patients through their heroic actions when patients suddenly go into respiratory failure or cardiac arrest. Eventually, investigations of patient deaths may reveal patterns that revolve around particular shifts and eventually around specific workers, but such killings may continue for many years before any patterns are uncovered. Victims of hero homicide are frequently the elderly, the critically ill, and the very young—that is, the most vulnerable patients. When health care workers are detected as the perpetrators of hero homicide, they are often labeled either as serial killers or as "angels of death." Individuals commit this kind of murder because of their need for recognition and excitement. Examples of such killers are two nurses, Genene Jones of Texas and Lynn Majors of Indiana, who apparently began killing their patients in their attempts to establish themselves as medical heroes.

Criminal Enterprise Homicide

Criminal enterprise homicide, the second major category of homicide, is defined as murder committed for material gain, to secure territory, or to exchange favors. Murders committed as part of organized criminal activity and murders for hire are examples of this kind of criminal activity. Murders that result from kidnapping and product tampering are also included in this general category, as are murders carried out for profit from insurance benefits, inheritance, or other monetary gain.

Felony murder, defined as any death that occurs during the commission of another violent crime, also falls within the category of criminal enterprise homicide. Also included are cases in which a person has knowledge that someone is going to be killed but does not inform the potential victim or the authorities, as are witnesses to this kind of crime. Criminal enterprise homicides also include deaths that result from drug deals, gang violence, and the hiring of someone to murder and dispose of another.

Sexual Homicide

Sexual homicides are those murders that include a sexual component in the sequence of events leading to the victims' deaths. The sexual meanings and elements involved may be unique to the offender, and the sexual activity may occur before, during, or after the murder.

Such activity may be actual sexual activity or symbolic sexual activity, such as the insertion of objects into the victim's body. Many serial murders fall into this category. Homicides involving children who fall prey to pedophilic killers and women who are murdered during the act of rape are included in the sexual homicide category.

When sexual homicide perpetrators have more than one victim, they are categorized as serial murderers. Some sexual predators have been described as charming and convincing in their relationships with others; some target particular victims only because they fit the killers' preferred types (this was the case with Ted Bundy and Jeffrey Dahmer, for example). Although the serial killer's sexual gratification represents the primary motive, the brutality of the attack is also important. The victim of a sexually motivated serial killer is culpable only in that he or she entered the area where the killer operates; the reason behind the victim's death is the killer's fantasy-driven homicidal desire.

Sadistic homicide, a form of sexual homicide, involves bondage, torture, and humiliation, all aimed at fulfilling the killer's personal sexual desires. The sexually sadistic murderer is gratified in a sexual way by the victim's response to torture. The sadistic killer's appetite for bondage as part of the sex act escalates over time, ultimately resulting in murder. Sadistic killers are usually intelligent white males who methodically target and stalk their victims. After abducting a victim, the sadistic killer prolongs the torture as long as possible before murdering the victim in a particular way that is tied to sexual fantasy. Serial killers do not always work alone; for example, in 1979, Roy Norris and Lawrence Bittaker, former prison inmates who shared a common interest in the torture and rape of teenage girls, together abducted and killed at least five girls in California.

Sadistic killers are not always roaming strangers, nor is the sexual component of their crimes always obvious. Michael Swango, a doctor, poisoned some of his patients in order to watch them suffer. After numerous close calls, including a brief stint in jail for poisoning his coworkers, he was arrested and convicted of murder; he is currently imprisoned in New York State. Another case involving a sadistic killer recently came to light in Manchester, England, where Harold Shipman, a trusted family physician, is believed to have murdered more than 200 of his patients over a number of years (he has been convicted of killing 15). Many have speculated about the reasons Shipman committed the murders, and some have theorized that Shipman was addicted to watching his patients die of drug overdoses. However, psychological sadism seems to be the most likely reason Shipman killed. In the final analysis, both Swango and Shipman may have relished the power of life and death they held over their patients.

Group Cause Homicide

Group cause homicide is murder committed by two or more individuals as a result of their shared ideology or belief system. In group cause homicide, the group defines the motives for the deaths of victims. Murders committed by members of cults, paramilitary groups, and other extremists on behalf of their groups fall within this category. Cultist group homicide is exemplified by the Manson murders of the 1960s. The murder of *Wall Street Journal* reporter Daniel Pearl in 2002 by a group of Islamic extremists also can be categorized as a group cause homicide, as can the murders committed in 1995 by Oklahoma City bomber Timothy McVeigh and his coconspirators.

The September 11, 2001, terrorist attacks on the World Trade Center towers in New York City and Pentagon are also cases of group cause homicide. Unlike some cases in the category of extremist homicide, described above, in group cause homicide, the group with which the killers are associated always supports the murders that are committed on its behalf. The primary goal that groups have in carrying out actions such as the September 11 attacks is to inflict as much death and destruction as possible in order to terrorize. The victims are completely random and are unaware of the immanent threat.

Every murder is committed for a particular reason. The reason may be a bizarre fantasy in the killer's mind, or it may be as simple as one or more of the four Ls: love, lust, lucre, and loathing. Many victims of homicide meet their ends at the hands of persons known to them, but among the victims killed by strangers, the most vulnerable are those who exist on the periphery of society. Steven A. Egger (2002) refers to these individuals as the "less-dead," the homeless, drug addicts, prostitutes, homosexuals, the elderly, runaways, and hitchhikers. When such devalued individuals die, their absence is less likely to be noticed; when they are murdered, their deaths are less vigorously investigated.

METHODS OF HOMICIDE

In the year 2000, 15,517 murders and nonnegligent manslaughters in the United States were reported to the Federal Bureau of Investigation, which issues annual reports on crime statistics. In many of these cases, the methods by which the murders were carried out have been determined, but in many others the methods are less clear or were never unreported. In this section, we focus on the ways in which people kill one another.

Homicides are most often committed with guns, especially handguns. According to the Federal Bureau of Investigation, 6,686 homicides were committed with handguns; this amounts to a little over 43% of the total. Long guns—that is, rifles and shotguns—are used far less often in homicides than are handguns. The .30-06, the rifle used most commonly for hunting, is easily available to those who choose to use this type of weapon to commit murder. In 2000, the Federal Bureau of Investigation identified 864 homicides in which a rifle or shotgun was used.

Cutting and sharp, pointed instruments such as knives, ice picks, machetes, and axes are often used in murders.

Knives, which range widely in sizes and styles, are the most commonly used among these instruments. Inner-city juveniles often carry switchblade knives and may, on occasion, use them in committing murders. Striking instruments such as tire irons, bats, batons, and golf club are also sometimes used in homicides.

Sometimes killers use their hands to strangle their victims, crushing the trachea and blocking oxygen to the mouth and nose. In some cases such killers may want their victims to suffer, and so cause the victims to move in and out of consciousness by applying differing amounts of pressure to their necks (this is reportedly a "technique" favored by serial killers, who frequently strangle their victims). In other cases, such as when a killing occurs in the heat of passion, strangled victims die in a short period of time. Murderers may kill with their hands in other ways as well; for example, they may physically beat their victims to death. Sometimes killers use their feet, kicking their victims and causing them to die as a result of blunt force trauma.

Arson

Arson, which is frequently committed for profit or revenge, is also often used to conceal the fact that a homicide has occurred. Fire marshals estimate that more than 1,000 lives are lost each year in the United States due to arson fires. Arsonists use a variety of materials, including incendiary devices, gasoline, and kerosene. Arsonists may also be considered terrorists with extremist motivation. When people die as the result of an act of arson, it is considered murder.

Other Methods

Murderers who use poison generally do so by placing the poison in their victims' food or by tampering with over-the-counter drugs. Many liquid poisons are slow acting and thereby cause prolonged agony when ingested. Numerous substances, some well-known and some rare, are poisonous to humans; such substances may take the form of liquid, gas, or powder. Some of the better-known poisons include lye, carbon monoxide, various acids, copper sulfate, cyanide, and arsenic. Poisoning is used in murders relatively infrequently today, probably because, with advances in toxicology and laboratory techniques, most poisons are much more easily detected than they were in the past.

Causing a victim to asphyxiate, perhaps by inhaling an airborne chemical, a deadly gas, or an airborne pathogen, is an effective method of committing murder. Murderers have been known to use carbon monoxide to kill in this way and then stage the murder scenes to look as though the victims committed suicide.

Ligature asphyxiation is another method of homicide. The ligatures most often used are of two main types: The first is rope, and the second is some other form of elongated material, such as wire, rope, or a piece of cloth (often, in sexual murders, the piece of cloth is from the victim's underclothing). Hanging is not often a method of homicide, but the use of an elongated ligature to strangle is common.

The injection of a lethal drug directly into the victim's bloodstream is yet another method of homicide. In many instances, killers who work in medical establishments use this method, either in their workplaces or elsewhere. For example, Harold Shipman, the English doctor mentioned above, made house calls to his patient victims, injecting them with lethal doses of morphine and diamorphine in their own homes.

Some killers use force to drown their victims. A recent case of murder by drowning that received a great deal of attention was that of Andrea Yates, who, in June 2001, drowned her five children, four boys and a girl ages 6 months to 7 years. At her trial, the defense claimed that Yates was suffering from postpartum depression and thus was insane at the time of the killings, but the Texas jury thought otherwise, finding her guilty of murder and sentencing her to life imprisonment.

Mechanical and chemical explosive devices are also sometimes used to kill. One commonly used kind of device causes an explosion through the burning of combustible fuels such as natural gas, liquefied petroleum gas, gasoline, kerosene, and lubricating oils. The bomb that destroyed the Alfred P. Murrah Federal Building and killed 167 people in Oklahoma City, Oklahoma, in April 1995 was such a device. On September 11, 2001, commercial aircraft were turned into bombs in the terrorist attacks on the World Trade Center in New York City and the Pentagon in Virginia. Approximately 3,000 lives were lost in this act of mass homicide.

The examples we have presented above demonstrate the capacity for innovation of those who are intent on taking the lives of others. In the future we will undoubtedly witness even more creative ways to kill.

CONCLUSION

In this chapter, we have discussed conceptual categories of killing as well as many of the methods used to take human life. Although the analysis of conceptual categories is useful for advancing our understanding of homicidal behavior, knowledge concerning specific motives for such behavior remains more elusive. We still do not fully understand why some murderers target strangers, as in the case of serial murder. It is also difficult to understand how the killing of loved ones evolves, as it were, from emotional arguments. Yet domestic homicides are frequent occurrences, as are the deaths of individuals who become involved in confrontations with strangers (as in cases of so-called road rage).

The history of the United States is written in the blood of those who have died at the hands of many different types of killers. Although the reasons for homicide change over time, the United States continues to experience the highest rate of homicide in the Western world. With the evolution of culture, the human species has excelled at devising improved methods of killing. As science and technology advance, murderers will continue to create new techniques for killing. Such progress does not seem to change.

When one human takes the life of another, not only is the victim's being obliterated, but the existence of future generations is denied. More than 2000 years ago, it was said of murder that to take a single life is to kill an entire world; that is, not only does the victim cease to exist, but his or her possible descendants are denied existence as well. In Western culture we often appear to be inured to violence, but death by homicide is very real to the victim's survivors. Murder has direct effects on the victim's loved ones, friends, and coworkers, who must come to terms with the fact that the victim is gone forever.

REFERENCES

"Abuse a Leading Cause of Death for Small Children, Study Finds." 1995. *Miami Herald,* April 26, p. 1-A.

Douglas, John E., Ann W. Burgess, Allen G. Burgess, and Robert K. Ressler. 1992. *Crime Classification Manual: A Standard System for Investigating and Classifying Violent Crimes.* New York: Lexington.

Egger, Steven A. 2002. *The Killers Among Us: An Examination of Serial Murder and Its Investigation,* 2d ed. Upper Saddle River, NJ: Prentice Hall.

Federal Bureau of Investigation. 1992. *Crime in the United States 1991.* Washington, DC: U.S. Department of Justice.

———. 1997. *Crime in the United States 1996.* Washington, DC: U.S. Department of Justice.

———. 2001. *Crime in the United States 2000.* Washington, DC: U.S. Department of Justice.

Fox, James A. and Marianne W. Zawitz. 2001. *Homicide Trends in the United States.* Washington, DC: U.S. Department of Justice, Bureau of Justice Statistics.

Holmes, Ronald M. and Stephen T. Holmes. 1994. *Murder in America.* Thousand Oaks, CA: Sage.

Goldstein, Paul J. 1995. "The Drugs/Violence Nexus: A Tripartite Conceptual Framework." Pp. 11–36 in *The American Drug Scene: An Anthology,* edited by James A. Inciardi and Karen McElrath. Los Angeles: Roxbury.

U.S. Department of Justice, Bureau of Justice Statistics. 1989. *Crime Book.* Washington, DC: Government Printing Office.

Wertham, Fredric. 1966. *A Sign for Cain: An Exploration in Human Violence.* New York: Macmillan.

PRE-PERSONALITY PREGNANCY LOSSES

Miscarriages, Stillbirths, and Abortions

JACK P. CARTER

Researchers examining the psychological effects of miscarriages, stillbirths, and abortions on parents often consider the impacts of miscarriages and stillbirths in the same studies, and many include neonatal deaths as well. Induced abortions are almost always treated independently in research, in recognition of the basic differences between abortion and the other two types of pregnancy loss. The research literature generally assumes some degree of distress or grief following miscarriages and stillbirths because of the involuntary and unexpected nature of these types of embryonic or fetal demise, sometimes severe enough to represent serious psychological pathologies. Induced abortions, on the other hand, are voluntary pregnancy terminations, and thus may result in different sorts of psychological responses. Although researchers have examined guilt, anxiety, stress, and depression as possible consequences of all three forms of pregnancy termination, most of them expect to find greater similarity of psychological responses among parents who have experienced miscarriage and stillbirth compared with those who have experienced abortion.

NONINDUCED PREGNANCY LOSS

Length of Gestation

In the research literature on psychological reactions to miscarriage and stillbirth, authors generally agree that a spontaneous pregnancy loss within 20 weeks of gestation is termed a *miscarriage,* and one after 20 weeks is a *stillbirth.* Once a live birth has occurred, death within the first 28 days is termed a *neonatal* death, and death from an unidentifiable cause within the first year is said to result from *sudden infant death syndrome* (SIDS). Some studies have focused solely on the impacts of miscarriages or stillbirths, some have combined the two, and others have examined various combinations of miscarriages, stillbirths, neonatal deaths, and SIDS deaths. Some scholars have analyzed the reactions of individuals who have experienced different types of pre- and postbirth losses, without attempting to determine the differences in the impacts of the various types. The presence of overlapping foci in this research is justified by the fact that researchers who have examined the independent effects of these various forms of pregnancy loss/infant death have found a high degree of similarity in the effects on the parents involved. In studies of parents' responses to miscarriage and in studies comparing the impacts of miscarriages and stillbirths, researchers have found that the intensity of response is unrelated to the length of gestation at the time of loss, because significant parental bonding occurs during the early stages of pregnancy (Prettyman, Cordle, and Cook 1993; Jackman, McGee, and Turner 1991; Thomas and Striegel 1994–95; Lasker and Toedter 1991). Peppers and Knapp (1980), for example, found no differences in the patterns and intensity of grief among parents who had experienced miscarriage, stillbirth, and neonatal death. Murray and Callan (1988) found no significant differences in depression and self-esteem between parents who had experienced stillbirths and those who had experienced neonatal deaths, although those who experienced stillbirths were somewhat better off psychologically. In a study of 220 bereaved families, Vance et al. (1995) discovered differences only in the degree of negative response to stillbirth, neonatal death, and SIDS. They found that, compared with the mothers in 226 control families, the bereaved mothers had significantly higher relative risk for anxiety for all three types of losses after 2 months and 8 months, and significantly higher relative risk for depression for all three after 2 months and for neonatal death and SIDS after 8 months. At 8 months, the depressive symptoms for stillbirth were still higher for the bereaved mothers than for controls, but the difference was not statistically significant.

The findings of studies such as those just cited make it seem reasonable for researchers to emphasize the similarities among different types of pregnancy losses and to examine their effects individually or together. However, some scholars assert that the temporal factor actually has a significant effect on parents' levels of psychological distress. For example, Goldbach et al. (1991) compared parents' reactions to miscarriages and perinatal deaths and found that grief was more intense following the later losses. These authors posit that researchers who have found length of gestation to have negligible effects have mostly used retrospective designs, interviewing mothers to determine their levels of grief months, or even years, after their losses. Goldbach et al. suggest that their contradictory findings are due to methodological differences between their study and earlier studies, such as their use of the Perinatal Grief Scale, an 84-item Likert-type scale, to measure levels of grief and their practice of interviewing both father and mother soon after the parents' loss. Although Neugebauer et al. (1992) found equal levels of depression in women who had experienced early and late miscarriages, they further found, because they knew the psychological histories of their respondents, that the women who had late losses exhibited greater increases in symptoms of depression than did those with early losses.

Psychological Impact

Until around 1970, almost no research had examined the psychological impacts of early pregnancy loss because investigators generally assumed that parents experience little serious sense of loss following miscarriage. Since that time, studies of the impacts of miscarriage on parents have typically found miscarriage to be a traumatic event that causes some degree of psychological or emotional distress. It is now well established that postmiscarriage grief can be severe, and that parents' bereavement reactions are often as intense as those following the death of a loved one of any age (Lasker and Toedter 1991; Peppers and Knapp 1980).

Researchers in this area make the distinction between normal and pathological grief that has been accepted for decades in the literature on mourning in general. *Normal grief,* which is also referred to as *acute* or *typical grief,* is a syndrome that is characterized by a particular set of psychological and physiological symptoms. These symptoms begin at the time of the loss and remain in effect for some period of time. The bereaved passes through a series of stages, the last of which involves resolution and recovery. There is some disagreement among scholars in this area regarding the time frame for completion of acute grief, with estimates ranging from 2 months or less to a year or more, but all agree that it does end. Early symptoms of the typical grief reaction include somatic distress, such as reduced strength, digestive problems, shortness of breath, trouble sleeping, difficulty swallowing, feelings of emptiness, and a tendency to sigh frequently. The ensuing stages

are characterized by psychological reactions that include guilt, anger, helplessness, anxiety and stress, and depressive symptoms (Lindeman 1944).

Pathological grief, also known as *morbid grief reaction,* is a distortion or postponement of acute grief. One form of pathological grief—chronic or prolonged grief—is bereavement of unlimited duration that often involves the same phases as acute grieving, but at intensified levels, and highly exaggerated psychological symptoms. Excessive and ongoing forms of these symptoms militate against the achievement of acceptance and resolution. Another type of pathological grief is delayed grief, which is exhibited by people who do not appear to feel grief following a loss. Delayed grief is characterized as pathological because, in most cases, after a relatively short period of time, it is followed by chronic grief. In addition, symptoms of "distorted grief"—such as hyperactivity, alienation, hostility, or severe depression in the absence of a sense of loss—that occur during the nonreactive period are viewed as pathological (Lindeman 1944).

Some researchers who have studied parents' severe grief following miscarriages have focused on pathological grief as a whole, whereas others have examined chronic and delayed grief independently. Researchers have found that morbid grief reactions following early pregnancy loss can cause indefinite and negative changes in relationships with close family members and friends, unwillingness or inability to resume normal activities, increased abuse of alcohol and drugs, and other negative psychosocial consequences (Corney and Horton 1974; Raphael 1977). Lasker and Toedter (1991) conducted a 5-year longitudinal study (one of the few such studies undertaken to date) to examine both chronic and delayed grief following pregnancy loss or infant death. They found higher rates of both types of pathological grief among parents who had suffered miscarriages compared with parents who had experienced stillbirths or neonatal deaths, although rates for both were still significant after perinatal loses. Lasker and Toedter attribute this finding to the relative lack of support accorded parents who suffer early pregnancy losses.

Some studies have examined different dimensions of miscarriage-related grief independently or in various combinations. Several researchers have found guilt to be a part of the typical grieving experience of parents following a miscarriage. Parents in mourning after miscarriage often blame themselves for the loss, believing that they failed to care for and protect the fetus adequately, that their ambivalence about the pregnancy perhaps subconsciously contributed to spontaneous termination, or that the loss is some sort of retribution for their lifestyle, habits, or ambitions. Most scholars agree that unresolved guilt can predominate and complicate the normal process of grieving (Dunn et al. 1991; Leppert and Pahlka 1984; Stack 1984).

It is common for early pregnancy loss to produce anger in parents. Women often direct such anger at themselves, feeling that they are responsible because their bodies' perceived betrayal has resulted in tragedy. The anger following miscarriage may be more intense than that following stillbirth or neonatal death (Stirtzinger and Robinson 1989; Toedter, Lasker, and Alhadeff 1988). Normal grieving after a miscarriage can also include anger directed at physicians and other medical personnel for a number of reasons. Many women who have miscarried feel that health care professionals were insensitive, treating them in an uncompassionate and routine fashion, refusing to acknowledge the symbolic importance attached to the removal of non-viable tissue, and "abandoning" them by releasing them from the hospital soon after treatment. Indeed, researchers have found that physicians tend to avoid women who have suffered miscarriages and to overprescribe mood elevators for them (Stirtzinger and Robinson 1989; Peppers and Knapp 1980; Wall-hass 1985).

Studies that have focused on postmiscarriage anxiety and stress have consistently revealed elevated levels of these dimensions of grief in parents (Day and Hooks 1987; Prettyman et al. 1993; Johnson and Puddifoot 1996). The criteria for acute stress disorder (ASD) are intense negative emotions that include dissociative symptoms and reliving the trauma for up to 4 weeks. Posttraumatic stress disorder (PTSD) is characterized by the continuation of these symptoms after a month. Citing what they see as similarities between grief-related behaviors in response to miscarriage and ASD and PTSD, Bowles et al. (2000) suggest that more research should examine the relationship between miscarriage and these serious syndromes, which can impair sufferers' psychological and general functioning. Based on their analysis of anecdotal evidence, Bowles et al. assert that up to 10% of women may experience ASD within 4 weeks of having a miscarriage, and up to 1% exhibit the symptoms of PTSD a month afterward.

Numerous studies have found that depressive symptoms increase significantly following miscarriages, and many researchers have concluded that this psychological impact poses the most serious public health concern relative to other manifestations of grief after early pregnancy losses. In some North American studies, women have been found to exhibit significantly elevated depression levels shortly after miscarriage and significantly reduced but still pathological levels after 6 months (Neugebauer et al. 1992, 1997; Robinson et al. 1994). Neugebauer et al. (1992, 1997) have conducted studies utilizing research designs that employed women who had not experienced recent reproductive losses as comparison groups, in order to establish the "relative risk" of depression. They found that the depression scores of miscarrying mothers in their sample were three and one-half to four times those of mothers in the control groups after 2 weeks and two and one-half to three times higher after intervals of 6 weeks and 6 months.

Some British studies, however, have questioned the significance of depressive responses relative to anxiety (Prettyman et al. 1993; Thaper and Thaper 1992). In a longitudinal study using standardized measures, Prettyman et al. (1993) found pathological anxiety in 41% of respondents 1 week after miscarriage and in 32% at 12 weeks. By contrast, they found rates of clinical depression to be 22% at week 1, dropping to levels comparable to those in the general population by week 6.

Research addressing the intensity and nature of grief following stillbirth has drawn the same distinctions noted above between normal (acute or typical) and pathological grief, which includes chronic and delayed grief. These studies have typically included respondents who have experienced stillbirths and others who have suffered other types of pregnancy loss, such as miscarriage, neonatal death, and, in some cases, SIDS. Whereas the above-cited research on the psychological impacts of miscarriage included only samples of parents who had suffered early pregnancy losses, in this section I also examine studies in which the respondents had experienced these various types of losses, as long as a significant number of study participants had experienced stillbirths. Ample empirical evidence, as cited above, indicates that parents' psychological reactions to stillbirths and losses involving neonates and infants are similar.

Research conducted in several countries has produced relatively consistent results regarding chronic grief as a reaction to stillbirth. Studies conducted in the United States, Great Britain, Australia, and Canada have found that 20–50% of parents exhibit symptoms of grief within a year of a perinatal loss, with the proportion falling to between 10% and 30% after a year (Lasker and Toedter 1991; Forrest, Standish, and Baum 1982; LaRoche et al. 1984; Nicol et al. 1986). In a Swedish study that specifically examined grief following stillbirth, Laurell-Borulf (1982) found chronic grief in 31% of respondents 12 to 14 years following the loss. Far fewer studies have focused on delayed grief following stillbirth, but Lasker and Toedter (1991) did find a rate of delayed grief of more than 13% among parents who had experienced perinatal death.

Following up on Lasker and Toedter's (1991) study, Lin and Lasker (1996) conducted research to examine the proposition that the conventional categories of grief (acute, chronic, and delayed) are inadequate to capture the complexity of the grieving process following perinatal loss. After examining their respondents at the time of the loss as well as 1 year and 2 years afterward, they questioned whether the "normal grieving pattern"—of temporarily high levels of grief following the loss that eventually give way to low levels—is typical at all. They found several bereavement patterns among their respondents that were not consistent with the conventional concept of pathological grief. For example, some respondents who exhibited "chronic grief" at 1 year appeared to recover by the second year, some showed little or no initial grief and never developed chronic grief, and some exhibited levels of grief that worsened significantly between the first and second years. The validity of Lin and Lasker's conclusions is supported by the fact that they are based on an analysis of the data from Lasker and Toedter's (1991) earlier study, which were collected from 138 women and 56 of their partners over a 5-year period. Furthermore, Janssen, Cuisinier, and Hoogduin (1996) assert that there is practically no consistency across studies in the operationalization of the various types of grief. Similarly, DeFrain (1991) asserts that it is best for family therapists not to try to differentiate between acute and pathological grief in their patients after perinatal death because the distinction is usually blurred, because acute grief sufferers often have irrational thoughts (sometimes including thoughts of suicide), and because all forms of grief stemming from pregnancy loss constitute serious crises that must be addressed.

Parents often experience guilt following perinatal loss. DeFrain (1991) cautions family therapists to be aware of and sensitive to this common and irrational guilt while counseling the bereaved. Forrest et al. (1982) found that many mothers who have had stillbirths and perinatal losses blame themselves for their inability to keep the fetus alive.

Research has also revealed that parents experience elevated levels of anxiety and stress as a result of stillbirth and perinatal loss. Vance et al. (1995) tracked changes in the independent effects of stillbirth, neonatal death, and SIDS on levels of anxiety and depression in parents at intervals of 2 and 8 months after the loss. They found significant differences between mothers who had stillbirths and mothers in comparison groups, with mothers who had experienced losses being five times more likely to exhibit severe anxiety at 2 months and three times more likely at 8 months. They also found significantly higher levels of anxiety for fathers at 2 and 8 months after stillbirth. Similarly, in an Australian study, Boyle et al. (1996) found that 33% of mothers who had perinatal losses were anxious after 2 months, 15% were anxious after 15 months, and 14% were anxious after 30 months—a proportion that was still twice that found in control groups. Studies focusing on stress as a bereavement response have consistently found dramatic elevation of stress following perinatal loss (Leon 1986; Stack 1982). Dyregrov and Matthiesen (1987) equate the psychological impact of perinatal death to the symptoms of PTSD, described above.

Parents often exhibit depressive symptoms following stillbirth or perinatal loss. Vance et al. (1995) found that, following a stillbirth, mothers in their sample were almost seven times more likely to be depressed after 2 months compared with mothers in a control group, and about two and one-half times more likely after 8 months. They also found lower but significant levels in the fathers in their sample at 2 and 8 months after the loss. Other researchers who have examined depression following perinatal death have noted similar patterns, such as Murray and Callan (1988) and Boyle et al. (1996), who found significant reductions in depression over time, but still at a level three times higher than that found in comparison groups after 30 months.

Other Pregnancy/Fertility-Related Factors

Researchers have examined variables related to couples' pregnancy and reproductive histories other than length of gestation to determine if any of these may be related to level of distress following miscarriage. Some

have focused on whether the pregnancy was planned or unplanned as an indicator of attitude toward the pregnancy (i.e., whether it was wanted or unwanted) and have found that early loss of an unplanned pregnancy generated higher levels of distress. In their discussions of their findings, these researchers have cast doubt on the assumption that all unplanned pregnancies are unwanted and have speculated that ambivalence toward a pregnancy may result in guilt-driven distress when a loss occurs (Prettyman et al. 1993; Thaper and Thaper 1992). In contrast, Neugebauer et al. (1992, 1997) found this factor to have no significant effect on the severity of parents' reaction to a loss. However, in these later studies, unlike those cited above, the investigators had data on respondents' attitudes toward their pregnancies as well as their psychological histories, and they also utilized comparison groups. Thus, although they did find that women who had lost pregnancies were equally distressed whether the pregnancies were wanted or unwanted, their more detailed findings revealed that symptom levels after the loss of an unwanted pregnancy did not increase compared with those of a control group, because these women were already highly distressed before the loss. Therefore, the apparent inconsistency in these findings may be due to the difference in their independent variables. Indeed, Prettyman et al. (1993) note that they would like to have known how many of the unplanned pregnancies in their sample were unwanted as well as the nature of their respondents' preloss psychological states.

Neugebauer et al. (1992, 1997) and Jackman et al. (1991) are among the majority of researchers who have found no apparent effect of previous miscarriage on distress, although some have found that elevated symptom levels resulted (Friedman and Gath 1989; Thaper and Thaper 1992). Among the small number of investigators who have examined this variable, some have claimed that previous infecundity has a significant impact on postmiscarriage psychological impact (e.g., Slade 1994), whereas others have found no effect (e.g., Friedman and Gath 1989).

Very few researchers have investigated the impacts of attitude toward the pregnancy and previous infecundity on psychological responses to stillbirths and neonatal deaths. Regarding the former, Kennell, Slyler, and Klaus (1970) and Benfield, Leib, and Vollman (1978) found that positive feelings toward the pregnancy caused more intense grief for one or both parents. Murray and Callan (1988) found previous infecundity to be associated with more intense reactions. Some researchers who have studied the effects of previous stillbirths or losses of neonates have found significant effects on levels of responses (Lasker and Toedter 1991; Peppers and Knapp 1980; Lin and Lasker 1996), whereas others have reported finding no impacts (Benfield et al. 1978; Nicol et al. 1986).

Demographic Variables

In the postmiscarriage grief research, the gender of parents has received relatively little attention, because researchers have generally assumed that male partners are much less affected than women. Indeed, some researchers, such as Leppert and Pahlka (1984) and Stirtzinger and Robinson (1989), have concluded that men's grief after miscarriage is less intense than that of their partners. However, Johnson and Puddifoot (1996; Puddifoot and Johnson 1997) suggest that fathers' levels of grief and stress are similar to those of mothers. They convincingly support their assertion that qualitative research incorporating personal semistructured interviews can reveal men's true feelings about miscarriage. They conclude that men often fail to acknowledge these psychological responses because of normative assumptions that the father is less emotionally attached to the fetus than is the mother as well as social expectations that define the man's appropriate primary role as being supportive of his distraught partner.

A number of studies have consistently found that age, socioeconomic status, and marital status have negligible impacts on levels of distress following miscarriage (Prettyman et al. 1993; Neugebauer et al. 1992, 1997; Toedter et al. 1988; Thaper and Thaper 1992). Some studies have produced contradictory findings regarding the effect of number of living children on intensity of response to miscarriage: Prettyman et al. (1993) found no effect of childlessness, whereas Toedter et al. (1988) and Neugebauer et al. (1992, 1997) report that parity is a significant factor (the latter finding, however, was produced by studies with relatively robust designs). Prettyman et al. (1993) studied responses to miscarriage after 1, 6, and 12 weeks, with no comparison group, and their sample size had shrunk from an initial 65 to 50 by the time the final questionnaire was administered. In their 1992 and 1997 studies, Neugebauer et al. interviewed 232 and 229 women, respectively, who had miscarried, and somewhat larger numbers in comparison groups of women who had not experienced recent pregnancy losses. The researchers were thus able to study the effects of parity on postmiscarriage distress after 2 weeks and 6 months, and to report authoritatively not only the finding that a strong negative relationship existed, but also more detailed findings, such as that the percentage of childless miscarrying women with severe symptoms was 11 times that of women in the childless comparison group and that miscarrying women with several children exhibited distress levels similar to those of comparison group women with children.

Researchers who have investigated reactions to stillbirth and perinatal loss agree that both mothers and fathers grieve. Most have found that women's grief is more intense or lasts longer because of the physical attachment to the fetus, and that men grieve less or differently due to their being socialized to avoid open expression of intense emotion and to play a supportive role in the grieving process (Murray and Callan 1988; Benfield et al. 1978; LaRoche et al. 1984; Vance et al. 1995). DeFrain (1991) asserts, however, that fathers and grandfathers suffer as much as their female counterparts; they simply express their grief less openly. It seems reasonable that

DeFrain's qualitative study, conducted from a family therapy perspective, might well have uncovered repressed male grief. Furthermore, Vance et al. (1995) caution that their findings might reflect men's greater tendency to internalize grief and to express it differently than women do; this does not necessarily mean that men's grief is any less intense than women's.

Researchers have consistently concluded that neither parents' age nor their socioeconomic status has any significant effect on the level of grief following stillbirth (LaRoche et al. 1984; Lasker and Toedter 1991; Nicol et al. 1986; Benfield et al. 1978). Lasker and Toedter (1991) found that distress after late pregnancy loss was lessened by the presence of living children, whereas other researchers have reported no significant effect of this variable or the opposite impact (e.g., LaRoche et al. 1984; Laurell-Borulf 1982).

Previous Emotional/Mental Distress

Apparently, a history of emotional or mental problems significantly increases the probability of a morbid grief reaction following miscarriage. Friedman and Gath (1989) found that women who required psychiatric treatment after early pregnancy losses had high scores on measures of emotional "neuroticism." They also found that a documented history of previous depression or other personality disorder was strongly associated with pathological bereavement. Both of these findings have been corroborated by other studies (Prettyman et al. 1993; Neugebauer et al. 1997; Hall, Beresford, and Quinones 1987).

Similar findings have been reported regarding grief after perinatal loss and depression before the pregnancy. Lasker and Toedter (1991) found prior depression to be one of the strongest predictors of chronic grief, with respondents who exhibited depressive symptoms before their pregnancies experiencing the most intense grief after 2 years.

Level of Support

There is general agreement among researchers that levels of social support of all kinds are relatively low for miscarriage sufferers compared with those who mourn other types of losses. Day and Hooks (1987) and Forrest et al. (1982) have demonstrated the need for such support. Stirtzinger and Robinson (1989) assert that support in the form of rituals, a normatively prescribed period of mourning, and any other recognition of the loss represented by miscarriage is virtually nonexistent. There is no body, and thus no funeral or mementos for the parents, and prevailing social standards may constrain them from telling even family and friends about the loss of a pregnancy of which only they may have been aware (Leppert and Pahlka 1984; Hall et al. 1987; Robinson et al. 1994). Furthermore, respondents in many studies have reported that when they sought support after miscarriage from family, friends, and health care professionals, they consistently received responses that were insensitive, evasive, or unhelpful, even though a lack of support is clearly a risk factor for psychological morbidity (Day and Hooks 1987; Stack 1984; Stirtzinger and Robinson 1989).

There is some evidence to indicate that in recent years our collective consciousness has been raised regarding the importance of support of all kinds for lessening the intensity and duration of parents' grief following stillbirth or neonatal death. For some time, researchers have documented the emergence of a new cultural ethos that emphasizes the invalidity of the old belief that treating a late pregnancy loss as an inconsequential and unimportant event will lessen the mother's distress. Some hospital neonatal units have developed programs that include perinatal loss counselors and policies that research indicates should provide positive forms of support for the bereaved. These policies include the recommendation that physicians interact compassionately and at length with parents in such cases. In addition, the policies recommend that staff encourage the parents of a deceased infant to hold their baby, to keep photos and other mementos, to arrange for a funeral or other disposition of the remains, and to join support groups (Pauw 1991; Murray and Callan 1988; Nicol et al. 1986). Research evidence has led family therapists to recognize the importance of strong spousal and family support, and support groups, for the recovery of parents following a pregnancy loss (Thomas and Striegel, 1994–95; Nicol et al. 1986; Rowe et al. 1978; Day and Hooks 1987; DeFrain 1991). The Australian government has initiated similar policies, including the creation of a "rural pregnancy loss team" that flies to remote parts of the country to assist grieving parents after perinatal loss in all of the ways noted above, including setting up local support groups (Knowles 1994).

INDUCED ABORTION

Psychological Impact

Although debates arise concerning the public policy implications of many different kinds of research findings, few areas of inquiry are as openly controversial and politicized as that of the psychological impact of the intentional termination of pregnancy. Even within the body of research reported in established scientific journals, distinctly political references to sociopolitical movements that seek to restrict or expand women's access to legal, medically safe abortions are common, as is the questioning of other researchers' methodology (which some view as the healthy functioning of the organized skepticism that allows us to have confidence in scientifically generated knowledge). The literature reveals widely divergent findings regarding the severity and frequency of serious psychological distress after induced abortion.

Most recent research into the psychological impact of abortion employing large samples, pre- and posttests,

standardized measures, longitudinal designs, and comparison groups has found that a majority of women who have had abortions do not regret having done so or experience severe psychological problems. For example, Major et al. (2000) assessed levels of distress preabortion and postabortion, at 1 hour, 1 month, and 2 years, in a sample of 882 women, 442 of whom remained in the sample for the full 2 years. They found that rates of depression among these women were comparable to those in the general population, and most respondents reported that they were satisfied with their decisions to abort and had few regrets. Russo and Zierk (1992) followed 5,295 women for 8 years after they had abortions and concluded that opting for an abortion increased the respondents' self-esteem and improved their well-being. Russo and Zierk's study is also one of a number that have found that women who terminated pregnancies were no more negatively affected psychologically than women who bore and raised their babies (Zabin, Hirsch, and Emerson 1989; Lydon et al. 1996). After reviewing 225 articles, Dagg (1991) concluded that a minority of women who abort are adversely affected, whereas most women who seek but are denied abortions have lengthy psychological difficulties, and their children often have serious problems until, and sometimes well into, adulthood. Dagg notes that most studies have found that a large majority of women experience positive responses following abortions; for example, Lazarus (1985) found that 17% of respondents in one study experienced guilt, whereas 76% felt relief and happiness.

Some authors, however, claim that severe, long-term mental pathological disorders often result from the decision to abort. Speckhard and Rue (1992) assert that experiencing an elective abortion can cause PTSD, and that, in this context, it should be called "postabortion syndrome" (PAS). They cite several publications to support their position (e.g., Barnard 1990; Vaughn 1991; Rue 1985; Speckhard 1987) and attack studies that have found minimal negative effects as being ideologically driven and methodologically flawed. A forceful response to Speckhard and Rue's 1992 article was forthcoming and understandable, given the fairly strong consensus that has developed regarding this area of inquiry. In an article published in the *Journal of the American Medical Association* that same year, Stotland (1992) reviewed the relevant literature and asserted that PAS is a "myth" based on anecdotal evidence and a small number of studies reported in religious and nonspecialty publications. In another 1992 literature review, Wilmoth, de Alteriis, and Bussell, although at least somewhat critical of all the research in this area, characterized the "pro-choice" studies as more methodologically robust, by far, than those of PAS advocates, who typically have studied only women who have complained of serious problems long after their abortions. In a study that followed 5,300 women for 8 years, Russo and Dabul (1997) found that abortion did not cause long-lasting severe trauma. Major et al. (2000) similarly found that the rate of PTSD 2 years after an abortion was 1%, compared with 48.5% and 46% for rape and child abuse victims, respectively, and 10.5% for the general population.

Pregnancy/Fertility-Related Variables

Contradictory findings and professional disagreements aside, there is almost total agreement among researchers that some women do experience pathological psychological sequelae following abortion, and that it is important to identify the potential risk factors for such an outcome. Not surprisingly, the woman's attitude toward the pregnancy—that is, whether she felt any commitment to it or was ambivalent about the decision to abort—has been found to be related to negative reactions (Lydon et al. 1996; Miller 1992). Other studies have shown that women who assign blame for their pregnancies, either to themselves or to their partners, are at greater risk of postabortion distress (Mueller and Major 1989; Major and Cozzarelli 1992). Most abortions are performed during the first trimester, but some are performed later, and several studies have found that second-trimester abortions, including those done because of fetal anomalies, cause relatively high rates of severe psychological reaction (Stotland 1992). Researchers who conducted a study in the Netherlands similarly found that advanced gestational age produced extreme grief as opposed to the generally positive responses to most abortions (Hunfeld, Wladimiroff, and Passchier 1994).

Demographic Variables

Within the extensive research literature on abortion, there is a noticeable dearth of studies investigating the impacts on the men involved (Major and Cozzarelli 1992). U.S. researchers who have examined gender issues related to abortion have typically pointed out that women are the final authority in the abortion decision and that men sometimes suffer psychological distress but tend not to express or acknowledge that distress; in addition, researchers usually study only men who complain of distress (Rue 1985; Coyle and Enright 1997). In a Swedish study, Kero et al. (1999) found that their 75 male respondents had wanted their partners to abort, but a majority experienced contradictory feelings after the abortion, such as relief, release, anxiety, grief, guilt, and anguish. Johansson et al. (1998) report that in Vietnam, men are recognized as being the family decision makers, and, although some consider abortion to be immoral, they prioritize their responsibility to control family size.

Because most of the subjects in studies on abortion are relatively young women, researchers often do not consider age as a variable, but Major et al. (2000) did find that younger women in their sample had the most negative feelings about abortion. Various dimensions of socioeconomic status, such as employment status, educational attainment, and income, have been shown to be positively related to well-being and self-esteem following an abortion, and the number of children a woman has is positively associated with the probability of postabortion distress (Russo and Dabul 1997; Russo and Zierk 1992; Major et al. 2000).

Researchers who have examined the effects of religion on adjustment after an abortion have found that high religiosity and affiliation with a conservative or fundamentalist religion are clearly risk factors for psychological problems and regret (Miller 1992; Congleton and Calhoun 1993). Russo and Dabul (1997) found somewhat higher levels of distress in practicing Catholic women, but they attribute this finding to lower preabortion self-esteem in these particular women, rather than to religion.

Personal History and Characteristics

One of the issues researchers have addressed is the question of whether the severe psychological symptoms exhibited by some women after abortion are the result of the abortion per se, the result of preexisting psychological conditions, or products of the life satisfaction or general coping capabilities the women exhibited before pregnancy. Those who conduct such studies assert that pre- and posttest designs are essential for determining the possible risk factors for negative postabortion reactions. Major et al. (2000) found that women who were depressed or who expressed regret 2 years after their abortions typically had histories of depression before they became pregnant. Russo and Dabul (1997), who, as noted above, followed 5,300 women for 8 years after their abortions, found that the most powerful indicators of postabortion emotional/mental health were psychological history and level of self-esteem before the pregnancy. Mueller and Major (1989) note that a history of depression was common for postabortion depressive women in their sample. They also found that a woman's level of coping self-efficacy—that is, her degree of self-confidence in her ability to cope with adjusting to new experiences—was a significant determinant of her psychological well-being. In their review of a large number of studies addressing these issues, Major and Cozzarelli (1992) found widespread empirical support for the claim that much of the distress some women experience after abortion is not a direct consequence of the procedure. Russo and Denious (2001) note that in addition to prepregnancy mental health and personal coping capabilities, researchers should pay attention to the impacts of women's life histories on their responses to abortion. In their sample, a significant number of postabortion depressive respondents had life histories that included rape, sexual abuse, battery, and other circumstances that led to preexisting depression and low life satisfaction. Russo and Denious also point to the possible counterproductive effects on counseling practices and public policy of misattributing such women's psychological problems to their having had abortions.

Level of Support

The importance of social, professional, and societal support for women deciding to abort is noted in most of the relevant research literature. Miller (1992) found that independent women who did not feel the need to have the approval of family members, partners, or friends but had mutually supportive relationships with stable partners were least likely to experience postabortion distress. Major and Cozzarelli (1992) report that the studies they reviewed showed the woman's partner to be the source of social support that most significantly affected her adjustment; support from parents and friends was less important.

Professional counseling and therapy have been found to be effective in averting long-term problems for women who experience distress after abortion. Congleton and Calhoun (1993) found that counseling that included recognition of the abortion as a loss for which grieving was appropriate and encouraged the establishment of support groups to facilitate communication among similarly distressed women reduced the intensity and duration of symptoms. These authors also point out that some well-intentioned counseling approaches that prescribe self-forgiveness to relieve guilt or remorse may engender those responses rather then dispel them. They base this assertion on research findings that have shown that retrospectively altering a woman's view of her abortion in this manner can result in her perceiving it as an act for which she should feel guilty. Similarly, Russo and Denious (2001) assert that therapy based on enabling women with postabortion problems to reappraise the event is often beneficial; however, counseling that uses the same approach but encourages women to reconceptualize their abortion experiences in ways that portray them as victims (e.g., as having been duped or misinformed by abortion providers) can cause psychological harm. Counselors who take such an approach may be harming their clients unintentionally, or they may be interested in creating martyrs and spokespersons for the anti-choice movement.

Most socialized adults desire society's approval or support for their actions, at least implicitly. The abortion decision represents a dilemma for Americans, because U.S. society is conflicted regarding this issue. Abortion is legal, and thus "normative." Since 1973, there have been an average of 1.5 million abortions a year in the United States (Dagg 1991). Approximately 20% of American women of reproductive age have had abortions (Russo and Denious 2001; Major and Cozzarelli 1992), yet, still, relatively widely held moral sanctions persist against abortion, even among some who support its legal status. One result of these conflicts is the lack of recognition that a loss has occurred; another is the common practice of not discussing it. In fact, one of the reasons partner support is especially important for women's postabortion well-being is that usually the partner is told about the abortion; in comparison, women tell much smaller proportions of their friends or parents, and practically nobody else. One reason women typically keep their decisions to abort secret is their knowledge that they may encounter active opposition or criticism from normal sources of support, or even from strangers. Some studies have shown that these nonsupportive

reactions create a higher risk of postabortion distress than no support at all (Major and Cozzarelli 1992). Women who are confronted and harassed by protesters when they arrive at and leave abortion clinics report feeling intense nonsupportive social condemnation, and they are more likely than other women to experience severe psychological problems (Russo and Denious 2001).

Although the principal sources of support in America for women who have had abortions appear to be the women's spouses/partners, there is some societal support from the judicial/criminal justice system and an ongoing high-profile public debate that serves to remind American women that a majority of their fellow citizens support their right to legal abortions. International comparisons show that the United States falls in the middle of a continuum regarding societal support for those who chose to abort. For example, in Ireland, abortion is illegal and socially unacceptable, whereas in Japan abortion has long been legal and accepted, and rituals exist to help resolve parents' postabortion distress. Fletcher (1995) describes the frustration of Irish pro-choice activists who cannot persuade women who have had abortions to speak out publicly because of their society's strong social/normative prohibitions, which make them reluctant to confide in anyone regarding their decision. The activists assert that as long as women remain silent, anti-choice factions are free to claim that there is no demand for abortion and therefore no need to amend the constitution to allow them. In Japan, abortion is a common form of birth control, and because of the tradition of remaining in contact with dead ancestors in this Buddhist-based culture, parents ritually maintain bonds with their aborted fetuses. The ritual, *mizuko kuyo,* which involves small statues representing the spirits of aborted fetuses, ensures that the "dead children" will be cared for in the afterlife and thus helps to resolve parents' grief (Klass and Heath 1996–97).

DISCUSSION

Due largely to differences in methodology and research design, the literature reveals differential findings regarding the effects of specific variables on levels of distress following both miscarriages and stillbirths and differing conclusions with respect to the generally accepted ways of categorizing these psychological responses. There is, however, almost total agreement that parents typically experience some degree of grief following these types of pregnancy losses and that, in some cases, the distress is long-term and pathological. There are striking differences between these findings and those from research on the psychological impact of induced abortion. Most of the latter studies have found that a majority of women who elect to terminate pregnancies do not experience negative psychological impacts; that stress caused by an unwanted pregnancy is often alleviated by an abortion;

that many who have experienced abortion report positive impacts, such as relief, happiness, and heightened self-esteem and well-being; and that in the minority of cases in which extreme, long-term postabortion distress occurs, the distress is often not attributable to the abortion per se.

Some research indicates that certain variables have similar effects on the psychological impacts of all three types of losses, the most striking being the significant effect of a history of psychological problems on postloss adjustment and the importance of support for helping individuals to avoid severe distress and for assisting those who experience extreme grief reactions. There is widespread agreement that at least some parents exhibit the symptoms of serious negative psychological reactions to all three types of loss, whatever the facilitating factors; for those people, the availability of all forms of support is essential for the resolution of their distress. Much of the literature emphasizes the similarity between miscarriages and stillbirths in regard to almost universal negative initial parental psychological responses and significant rates of morbid grief reactions in contrast to the responses of those who chose to abort. However, when the focus is on those individuals who respond to pregnancy loss with severe long-term grief, miscarriage and abortion bear some important similarities. For example, those who are distressed following a miscarriage or abortion often find less support than do parents who experienced a stillbirth. In both cases, the absence of fetal remains and the common perception that early pregnancy losses should be relatively easy to cope with too often mean that support is not forthcoming from the usual sources, and parents who have suffered such losses are often reluctant to seek professional assistance. Those who suffer serious postabortion emotional problems, although relatively small in number, may face the greatest challenge in resolving their grief (Ney et al. 1994). The low level of support following miscarriages usually takes the form of insensitivity to, or a lack of appreciation of, the parents' sense of loss and attendant grief. Although this is also true regarding abortion, those who abort must also face the possibility of active opposition and even confrontation and condemnation. The process of psychological resolution for these individuals can be further complicated because they may think that others see compassionate support for an elected loss as unnecessary or inappropriate, or they may worry that mourning the loss implies that their decision to abort was wrong, creating additional guilt.

Research investigating the psychological impacts of all three types of pre-personality losses has indeed revealed some important differences in the frequency, intensity, and nature of responses. As DeFrain (1991) notes, however, they all have one thing in common: Parents can come to accept the event and recover from the emotional distress that results from any pregnancy loss, but they will still have somewhat painful memories, as they would following the loss of any loved one.

REFERENCES

Barnard, C. A. 1990. *The Long-Term Psychosocial Effects of Abortion.* Portsmouth, NH: Institute for Pregnancy Loss.

Benfield, D. G., S. A. Leib, and J. H. Vollman. 1978. "Grief Response of Parents to Neonatal Death and Parent Participation in Deciding Care." *Pediatrics* 62:171–77.

Bowles, S. V., L. C. James, D. S. Solursh, M. K. Yancey, T. D. Epperly, R. A. Folen, and M. Masone. 2000. "Acute and Post-Traumatic Stress Disorder After Spontaneous Abortion." *American Family Physician* 61:1689–96.

Boyle, F. M., J. C. Vance, J. M. Najman, and M. J. Thearle. 1996. "The Mental Health Impact of Stillbirth, Neonatal Death, or SIDS: Prevalence and Patterns of Distress Among Mothers." *Social Science & Medicine* 43:1273–82.

Congleton, G. K. and L. G. Calhoun. 1993. "Post-Abortion Perceptions: A Comparison of Self-Identified Distressed and Nondistressed Populations." *International Journal of Social Psychiatry* 39:255–65.

Corney, R. T. and F. T. Horton. 1974. "Pathological Grief Following Spontaneous Abortion." *American Journal of Psychiatry* 131:825–27.

Coyle, C. T. and R. Enright. 1997. "Forgiveness Intervention With Postabortion Men." *Journal of Consulting and Clinical Psychology* 65:1042–46.

Dagg, P. K. B. 1991. "The Psychological Sequelae of Therapeutic Abortion-Denied and Completed." *American Journal of Psychiatry* 148:578–85.

Day, R. D. and D. Hooks. 1987. "Miscarriage: A Special Type of Family Crisis." *Family Relations* 36:305–10.

DeFrain, J. 1991. "Learning About Grief From Normal Families: SIDS, Stillbirth, and Miscarriage." *Journal of Marital and Family Therapy* 17:215–32.

Dunn, D. S., K. R. Goldbach, J. N. Lasker, and L. J. Toedter. 1991. "Explaining Pregnancy Loss: Parents' and Physicians' Attributions." *Omega* 23:13–23.

Dyregrov, A. and S. B. Matthiesen. 1987. "Stillbirth, Neonatal Death and Sudden Infant Death Syndrome (SIDS): Parental Reactions." *Scandinavian Journal of Psychology* 28:104–14.

Fletcher, R. 1995. "Silences: Irish Women and Abortion." *Feminist Review* 50:44–56.

Forrest, G. C., E. Standish, and J. C. Baum. 1982. "Support After Perinatal Death: A Study of Support and Counselling After Perinatal Bereavement." *British Medical Journal* 285:1475–79.

Friedman, T. and D. Gath. 1989. "The Psychiatric Consequences of Spontaneous Abortion." *British Journal of Psychiatry* 155:810–13.

Goldbach, K., R. C. Dana, S. Dunn, L. J. Toedter, and J. N. Lasker. 1991. "The Effects of Gestational Age and Gender on Grief After Pregnancy Loss." *American Journal of Orthopsychiatry* 61:461–67.

Hall, R. C., T. P. Beresford, and J. E. Quinones. 1987. "Grief Following Spontaneous Abortion." *Psychiatric Clinics of North America* 10:405–20.

Hunfeld, J. A. M., J. W. Wladimiroff, and J. Passchier. 1994. "Pregnancy Termination, Perceived Control, and Perinatal Grief." *Psychological Reports* 74:217–18.

Jackman, C., H. M. McGee, and M. Turner. 1991. "The Experience and Psychological Impact of Early Miscarriage." *Irish Journal of Psychology* 12:108–20.

Janssen, H. J. E. M., M. C. J. Cuisinier, and K. A. L. Hoogduin. 1996. "A Critical Review of the Concept of Pathological Grief Following Pregnancy Loss." *Omega* 33:21–42.

Johansson, A., N. T. Nga, T. Q. Huy, D. D. Dat, and K. Holmgren. 1998. "Husbands' Involvement in Abortion in Vietnam." *Studies in Family Planning* 29:400–413.

Johnson, M. P. and J. E. Puddifoot. 1996. "The Grief Response in the Partners of Females Who Miscarry." *British Journal of Medical Psychology* 69:313–28.

Kennell, J. H., H. Slyler, and M. H. Klaus. 1970. "The Mourning Response of Parents to the Death of a Newborn Infant." *New England Journal of Medicine* 283:219–25.

Kero, A., A. Lalos, U. Hogberg, and L. Jacobsson. 1999. "The Male Partner Involved in Legal Abortion." *Human Reproduction* 14:2669–75.

Klass, D. and A. O. Heath. 1996–97. "Grief and Abortion: *Mizuko Kuyo,* the Japanese Ritual Resolution." *Omega* 34:1–14.

Knowles, S. 1994. "A Passage Through Grief: The Western Australian Rural Pregnancy Loss Team." *British Medical Journal* 309:1705–8.

LaRoche, C., M. Lalinec-Michaud, F. Engelsmann, N. Fuller, M. Copp, and M. McQuade-Soldatos. 1984. "Grief Reactions to Perinatal Death: A Follow-Up Study." *Canadian Journal of Psychiatry* 29:14–19.

Lasker, J. N. and L. J. Toedter. 1991. "Acute Versus Chronic Grief: The Case of Pregnancy Loss." *American Journal of Orthopsychiatry* 61:510–22.

Laurell-Borulf, Y. 1982. "Long-Term Adjustment After an Emotional Crisis." Pp. 156–82 in *Krislonsning I Langtidsperpektive.* Lund, Sweden: Studentlitteratur.

Lazarus, A. 1985. "Psychiatric Sequelae of First Trimester Abortion." *Journal of Psychosomatic Obstetrics and Gynecology* 4:141–50.

Leon, I. G. 1986. "Psychodynamics of Perinatal Loss." *Psychiatry* 49:312–24.

Leppert, P. C. and B. S. Pahlka. 1984. "Grieving Characteristics After Spontaneous Abortion: A Management Approach." *Obstetrics and Gynecology* 64:119–22.

Lin, S. X. and J. N. Lasker. 1996. "Patterns of Grief Reaction After Pregnancy Loss." *American Journal of Orthopsychiatry* 66:262–71.

Lindeman, J. L. 1944. "Symptomology and Management of Acute Grief." *American Journal of Psychiatry* 9: 143–49.

Lydon, J., C. Dunkel-Schetter, C. L. Cohan, and T. Pierce. 1996. "Pregnancy Decision Making as a Significant Life Event: A Commitment Approach." *Journal of Personality and Social Psychology* 71:141–51.

Major, B. and C. Cozzarelli. 1992. "Psychosocial Predictors of Adjustment to Abortion." *Journal of Social Issues* 48(3):121–42.

Major, B., C. Cozzarelli, M. L. Cooper, J. Zubek, C. Richards, M. Wilhite, and R. H. Gramzow. 2000. "Psychological Responses of Women After First-Trimester Abortion." *Archives of General Psychiatry* 57:777–84.

Miller, W. B. 1992. "An Empirical Study of the Psychological Antecedents and Consequences of Induced Abortion." *Journal of Social Issues* 48(3):67–93.

Mueller, P. and B. Major. 1989. "Self-Blame, Self-Efficacy, and Adjustment to Abortion." *Journal of Personality and Social Psychology* 37:1059–68.

Murray, J. and V. J. Callan. 1988. "Predicting Adjustment to Perinatal Death." *British Journal of Medical Psychology* 61:237–44.

Neugebauer, R. J., J. Kline, P. O'Connor, P. Shrout, J. Johnson, A. Skodol, J. Wicks, and M. Susser. 1992. "Determinants of Depressive Symptoms in the Early Weeks After Miscarriage." *American Journal of Public Health* 82: 1332–39.

Neugebauer, R. J., J. Kline, P. Shrout, A. Skodol, P. O'Connor, P. A. Geller, Z. Stein, and M. Susser. 1997. "Major Depressive Disorder in the 6 Months After Miscarriage." *Journal of the American Medical Association* 277: 383–88.

Ney, P. G., T. Fung, A. R. Wickett, and C. Beaman-Dodd. 1994. "The Effects of Pregnancy Loss on Women's Health." *Social Science & Medicine* 38:1193–1201.

Nicol, M. T., J. R. Tompkins, N. A. Campbell, and G. J. Syme. 1986. "Maternal Grieving Response After Perinatal Death." *Medical Journal of Australia* 144:287–89.

Pauw, M. 1991. "The Social Worker's Role With a Fetal Demise and Stillbirth." *Health and Social Work* 16:291–97.

Peppers, L. G. and R. J. Knapp. 1980. "Maternal Reactions to Involuntary Fetal/Infant Death." *Psychiatry* 43:155–59.

Prettyman, R. J., C. J. Cordle, and G. D. Cook. 1993. "A Three Month Follow-Up of Psychological Morbidity After Early Miscarriage." *British Journal of Medical Psychology* 66:363–72.

Puddifoot, J. E. and M. P. Johnson. 1997. "The Legitimacy of Grieving: The Partner's Experience at Miscarriage." *Social Science & Medicine* 45:837–45.

Raphael, B. 1977. "Preventive Intervention With the Recently Bereaved." *Archives of General Psychiatry* 34:1450–54.

Robinson, G. E., R. Stirtzinger, D. E. Steward, and E. Relevski. 1994. "Psychological Reactions in Women Followed for 1 Year After Miscarriage." *Journal of Reproduction and Infant Psychology* 12:31–36.

Rowe, J., R. Clyman, C. Green, C. Mikkelsen, J. Haight, and L. Ataide. 1978. "Follow-Up of Families Who Experience a Perinatal Death." *Pediatrics* 62:166–70.

Rue, V. M. 1985. "Abortion in a Relationship Context." *International Review of Natural Family Planning* 9:95–121.

Russo, N. F. and A. J. Dabul. 1997. "The Relationship of Abortion to Well-Being: Do Race and Religion Make a Difference?" *Professional Psychology: Research and Practice* 28:23–31.

Russo, N. F. and J. E. Denious. 2001. "Violence in the Lives of Women Having Abortions: Implications for Practice and Public Policy." *Professional Psychology: Research and Practice* 32:142–50.

Russo, N. F. and K. L. Zierk. 1992. "Abortion, Childbearing, and Women's Well-Being." *Professional Psychology: Research and Practice* 23:269–80.

Slade, P. 1994. "Predicting the Psychological Impact of Miscarriage." *Journal of Reproductive and Infant Psychology* 12:5–16.

Speckhard, A. C. 1987. *Post-Abortion Counseling.* Portsmouth, NH: Institute for Pregnancy Loss.

Speckhard, A. C. and V. M. Rue. 1992. "Postabortion Syndrome: An Emerging Public Health Issue." *Journal of Social Issues* 48(3):93–119.

Stack, J. M. 1982. "Grief Reactions and Depression in Family Practice: Differential Diagnosis and Treatment." *Journal of Family Practice* 14:271–75.

Stack, J. M. 1984. "The Psychodynamics of Spontaneous Abortion." *American Journal of Orthopsychiatry* 54:162–67.

Stirtzinger, R. and G. E. Robinson. 1989. "The Psychological Effects of Spontaneous Abortion." *Canadian Medical Journal* 140:799–805.

Stotland, N. L. 1992. "The Myth of the Abortion Trauma Syndrome." *Journal of the American Medical Association* 268:2078–79.

Thaper, A. K. and A. Thaper. 1992. "Psychological Sequelae of Miscarriage: A Controlled Study Using the General Health Questionnaire and the Hospital Anxiety and Depression Scale." *British Journal of General Practice* 42:94–96.

Thomas, V. and P. Striegel. 1994–95. "Stress and Grief of a Perinatal Loss: Integrating Qualitative and Quantitative Methods." *Omega* 30:299–311.

Toedter, L. J., J. N. Lasker, and J. M. Alhadeff. 1988. "The Perinatal Grief Scale: Development and Initial Validation." *American Journal of Orthopsychiatry* 58:435–39.

Vance, J. C., J. M. Najman, M. J. Thearle, G. Embelton, W. J. Foster, and F. M. Boyle. 1995. "Psychological Changes in Parents Eight Months After the Loss of an Infant From Stillbirth, Neonatal Death, or Sudden Infant Death Syndrome: A Longitudinal Study." *Pediatrics* 96:933–38.

Vaughn, H. 1991. *Canonical Variates of Post-Abortion Syndrome.* Portsmouth, NH: Institute for Pregnancy Loss.

Wall-hass, C. L. 1985. "Women's Perceptions of First Trimester Spontaneous Abortion." *Journal of Obstetrics and Gynecology* 14:50–53.

Wilmoth, G. H., M. de Alteriis, and D. Bussell. 1992. "Prevalence of Psychological Risks Following Legal Abortion in the U.S.: Limits of the Evidence." *Journal of Social Issues* 48(3):37–66.

Zabin, L. S., M. B. Hirsch, and M. R. Emerson. 1989. "When Urban Adolescents Choose Abortion: Effects on Education, Psychological Status, and Subsequent Pregnancy." *Family Planning Perspectives* 21:248–55.

SUDDEN INFANT DEATH SYNDROME

CHARLES A. CORR

DONNA M. CORR

In this chapter, we examine the phenomenon of sudden infant death syndrome (SIDS), which is the leading cause of death for infants between 1 month and 1 year of age in the United States. We begin by describing some of the typical experiences of parents, grandparents, and other family members when a SIDS death occurs. We then present a formal definition of SIDS and a discussion of its incidence. We go on to describe SIDS-related research and the "Back to Sleep" campaign, which appears to have reduced the number of U.S. SIDS deaths by about half during the 1990s. We also examine some typical experiences and tasks for first responders, other professionals, and volunteer helpers in cases of SIDS deaths. Finally, we explore bereavement, education, and support after a SIDS death and close with a brief conclusion. Following the chapter text, we provide a list of three sources for further information about SIDS.

EXPERIENCES OF FAMILY MEMBERS IN A SIDS DEATH

Most often, the parents of a child who dies from SIDS are relatively young and happy to have had this newborn come into their lives. They may be from any religious, ethnic, cultural, or socioeconomic background. Some parents who lose a child to SIDS have had other children previously, but equally often the child who is lost is the couple's firstborn.

Usually, the baby who dies from SIDS is between 2 and 4 months of age. Often, the infant has displayed no evidence of any special health or developmental problems and in his or her parents' view is a healthy, happy baby. Frequently, a physician has seen the child not long before the SIDS death, either for a routine checkup or for an examination associated with a slightly elevated temperature and other symptoms suggesting a mild viral infection. As a result, the parents later report that they felt no special anxiety about the health or future of their child.

On the day of the death, the child may have been a bit fussy or may simply have been put down for a nap or for a night's sleep. Many times, the child's parents later recall that they were grateful that the child was sleeping, so that they could have a few hours' break from caring for the infant's needs as well as an opportunity to give their attention to other responsibilities or just get some rest. But when they next checked on the infant, they immediately recognized that something was wrong.

Typically, the baby is found lying on his or her stomach, as if asleep. But the parents notice that everything is still, much too still; there are no movements or signs of breathing. When the parents pick the baby up, there is no response. It is a terrifying and terrible moment.

Often, parents try to initiate cardiopulmonary resuscitation (CPR) in an attempt to restart the baby's heart and breathing. Frequently, they call 911 or other emergency telephone numbers to reach out for assistance. An emergency operator may tell them how to perform CPR or suggest other things they can do, even as emergency medical technicians and paramedics are dispatched to the family's location.

The parents may alternate between periods of vigorous action and agitated conversation and times of shock and stricken silence. When first responders arrive, they may ask the parents and any other people present to step back and give the professionals some room to attempt to save the baby's life. As those efforts call forth no response from the infant, the parents may gradually begin to weep and become quieter and quieter. Sometimes, they may withdraw a bit further from the scene of the attempted rescue, perhaps turning to each other or remaining apart; in other instances, they may urge the emergency workers to make more and stronger efforts at resuscitation. The baby's parents may at this point reach out to their own parents or other relatives and friends to share what has happened and to seek assistance in such practical matters as providing transportation to the hospital or staying with other children in the home.

Soon after it becomes clear that the baby cannot be revived, a physician will likely examine the baby, either at the scene or at a local hospital. After the infant has been pronounced dead, the physician will usually explain to the parents that an autopsy will be required to determine the cause of death. The doctor may suggest that it seems likely the baby died from sudden infant death syndrome. Before they leave their child, the parents may be given an opportunity to spend some time with the baby in private and to hold his or her lifeless body.

In the days that follow, the parents will learn that SIDS is neither predictable nor preventable. Unless there is evidence to the contrary, they will be reassured that they did nothing to cause this terrible event and there was nothing they failed to do that might have avoided it. Ordinarily, at this point, the parents are still stunned by the swiftness and finality of what has happened. They may find themselves going over and over the events of the previous hours and days, as well as the details of the child's last visit to a pediatrician.

In the midst of their own pain, it may be difficult for each parent to comfort the other or for both to console the dead child's siblings, grandparents, or others affected by the death. Some parents may find it difficult even to talk about the baby's death with others, including those who have many questions and some who may suspect foul play on the part of the parents. Other parents who lose a child in this way may find that they have a need to talk incessantly about the baby and about his or her death. Most parents find that disposing of the baby's toys, clothing, and other items is a very difficult task; they may not be able even to think about it for some time.

Eventually, a postmortem examination and a thorough investigation will be conducted, and a diagnosis of SIDS will be confirmed. If the parents can discuss the diagnosis with the pathologist or medical examiner, this may help to settle some matters and answer some of their questions, but it is difficult for most SIDS parents not to experience much uneasiness and guilt. Historically, society has often treated parents as if they deserve all or a significant portion of the blame when an infant dies suddenly and unexpectedly. Indeed, parents often blame themselves or each other for many different reasons, such as the following: because they believe that one or both of them somehow contributed to the death or failed to protect the child from death; because they believe that one or both of them failed to live up to their own expectations or to those of society in their roles as parents; because they assume that the death is some form of retribution or punishment for their having violated a moral or religious standard; because of something they did or did not do at the time they discovered that their child was dead; or just simply because they are alive and they do not believe it is normal for a parent to outlive his or her child. In the aftermath of a SIDS death it is not at all appropriate for the parents to take on such blame and guilt. Therefore, it is extremely important in all cases of SIDS deaths that those who are in a position to do so tell the parents repeatedly that they are *not* responsible for the death of their child and that, given the current state of knowledge, no one could have prevented the death.

Many other events follow from the life-changing impact of a SIDS death. Most often, there will be a funeral or memorial service and a burial or cremation. Everyone affected by the death will engage in some type of mourning process or efforts to cope with what has happened and with its many implications. Older siblings of the dead child will need information and support as they, too, try to cope with the death and with what it means for them and for their family. The parents may need to think carefully about whether or not they should consider the possibility of a subsequent pregnancy. Even children who are born into a family after a SIDS death will eventually need someone to explain to them why the absence of an older brother or sister they never knew is such an enduring presence in the family's life.

Much of this will be awkward and difficult. No one in the family's circle can go back to the familiar routines of life as it was before this death. So much that had previously seemed clear and bright as the parents looked to the future with their precious infant may now appear confusing and unsure. The family can develop "new normals," and life can be good again, but it will never be the same as it was before.

DEFINITION OF SIDS

Sudden infant death syndrome—often referred to as SIDS, but also termed *crib death* in the United States and *cot death* in some other English-speaking countries—is technically defined as "the sudden death of an infant under one year of age which remains unexplained after a thorough case investigation, including performance of a complete autopsy, examination of the death scene, and review of the clinical history" (Willinger, James, and Catz 1991:681). Three aspects of this definition are worth noting. First, an accurate diagnosis of this syndrome requires a thorough investigation, including a painstaking autopsy (preferably performed by a medical examiner or forensic pathologist who is experienced in diagnosing infant deaths), along with a careful examination of the historical and circumstantial situation in which the death occurred (including interviews with parents and others involved in the care of the infant, collection of items from the scene of death, and meticulous evaluation of all the information obtained). Hasty or incomplete diagnoses can sometimes confuse SIDS with deaths resulting from child abuse or other causes (American Academy of Pediatrics 2001). This can compound the burdens placed on parents and other survivors of SIDS if they are wrongly accused of child abuse, just as it may cloak abusive situations under the more benign diagnosis of SIDS.

Second, a diagnosis of SIDS is essentially a "diagnosis by exclusion"—that is, a diagnosis that one makes by

Table 1 Infant Deaths, Infant Death Rates, SIDS Deaths, and SIDS Death Rates, United States: 1980 and 1990–99

	1980	*1990*	*1991*	*1992*	*1993*	*1994*	*1995*	*1996*	*1997*	*1998*	*1999*	*2000*
Infant deaths	45,526	38,351	36,766	34,628	33,466	31,710	29,583	28,487	27,692	28,371	27,937	27,987
Infant death rates[a]	12.6	9.2	8.9	8.5	8.4	8.0	7.6	7.3	7.2	7.2	7.1	6.9
SIDS deaths	5,510	5,417	5,349	4,891	4,669	4,073	3,397	3,050	2,705	2,822	2,648	2,151
SIDS death rates[a]	1.5	1.3	1.3	1.2	1.0	0.9	0.8	0.7	0.6	0.7	0.7	0.5

SOURCES: U.S. Bureau of the Census (2001), Hoyert et al. (2001), and Minino and Smith (2001).

a. Deaths of infants under 1 year old per 1,000 live births.

ruling out all other possible causes and then recognizing the distinctive patterns of this cluster of events. A "syndrome" is precisely that—a familiar constellation of events arising from an unknown cause. This is perhaps the most frustrating aspect of SIDS, because we all want to believe that every event has a cause, and we are likely to find it difficult to accept that modern medical and scientific techniques are currently unable to tell us what that cause is for SIDS. In fact, SIDS deaths may result from more than one cause acting jointly or separately, but the main point of an exclusionary diagnosis is that no conclusive explanation of the cause(s) of SIDS has yet been established, either in general or in particular cases.

Third, it is also the case that at present no definitive diagnostic indicators unmistakably identify recognized abnormalities in an infant that are sufficient to cause a SIDS death. Nevertheless, some biological, clinical, and historical or circumstantial markers are commonly found in this syndrome, including (a) tiny red or purple spots (minute hemorrhages or petechiae) on the surface of the infant's heart, in the lungs, and in the thymus; (b) an increased number of star-shaped cells in the infant's brain stem (brain stem gliosis); (c) clinical suggestions of apnea or pauses in breathing and an inability to return to normal breathing patterns; and (d) circumstantial facts such as a peak incidence at 2 to 4 months of age declining rapidly almost to nonoccurrence beyond 1 year of age. Markers such as these, when identified by a competent, thorough, and experienced physician, justify the recognition of SIDS as an official medical cause of death.

INCIDENCE OF SIDS

During most of the 1980s, SIDS accounted for the deaths of approximately 5,500 infants per year in the United States (Corr et al. 1991; see Table 1). From 1988 to 2000, however, death rates from SIDS fell by more than 62% (from more than 1.4 to just over 0.5 deaths per 1,000 live births) in the United States, and the number of SIDS deaths declined to 2,151 in 2000 (Minino and Smith 2001). This reduction in SIDS deaths has contributed to the lowest infant mortality rate—6.9 infant deaths per 1,000 live births in 2000—ever recorded in the United States.

In terms of the overall number of live births each year, the three leading causes of death in infancy (that is, during the first year of life) are congenital malformations, disorders related to short gestation and low birth weight, and SIDS. Approximately two-thirds of all infant deaths occur during the perinatal and neonatal periods (at the time of birth and during the first 28 days of life, respectively), mostly as a result of complications related to pregnancy and birth, as well as developmental problems. SIDS is the leading cause of death in the United States among infants between 1 month and 1 year of age, with a peak incidence from age 2 months to 4 months.

Researchers have drawn attention to other aspects of the incidence of SIDS deaths, but the variables examined have not yet been sufficient to establish differential diagnoses, screening procedures, or preventive measures for SIDS. In fact, SIDS is a sudden and silent killer, often associated with sleep, but apparently involving no suffering. Characteristically, SIDS deaths show a pronounced peak in number during the colder fall and winter months of the year, especially during January through March in the United States and 6 months later in the Southern Hemisphere. Epidemiological studies suggest that SIDS is somehow associated with a detrimental prenatal environment, but infants who are at risk for SIDS cannot be distinguished from those who are at risk for many other health problems. In general, at-risk infants include those with low birth weight or low weight gain and those whose mothers were less than 20 years of age, were anemic, had poor prenatal care, smoked cigarettes or used illegal drugs during pregnancy, and had histories of sexually transmitted disease or urinary tract infection. But none of these factors is sufficient to predict how, when, why, or if SIDS will occur.

SIDS appears in families from all social and economic groups, although African American infants are two to three times more likely to die of SIDS than are Caucasian American babies, and Native American infants are approximately three times more susceptible than whites. Approximately 60% of all SIDS deaths involve male infants; about 40% occur among female infants. The largest portion of SIDS deaths (approximately 70%) occurs in infants between 2 and 4 months of age, with most (approximately 90%) taking place by 6 months of age.

SIDS-RELATED RESEARCH

It is extraordinarily difficult to conduct research on SIDS; researchers who attempt to do so face many problems that have long frustrated scientific investigators (Hillman 1991). For example, there are no living patients to study because the first symptom of SIDS is a dead baby. In addition, risk factors for SIDS are not sufficiently strong or specific enough to permit researchers to identify high-risk groups as subsets of the general infant population in which they can follow the natural history of the disease with smaller numbers of subjects. And there are no naturally occurring animal models for SIDS. As a result, SIDS is currently unpredictable and unpreventable, although it is possible to modify some risk factors for SIDS deaths.

In terms of causes, most researchers believe that babies who die of SIDS are born with one or more conditions that make them especially vulnerable to stresses that occur in the normal developmental life of an infant, including both internal and external influences. The leading hypothesis for study is delayed development of arousal, cardiorespiratory control, or cardiovascular control.

Meanwhile, research based on epidemiology and pathology has dispelled numerous misleading and harmful myths about SIDS (for example, it is not contagious and does not run in families) while also ruling out many factors that have been thought at various times to be the causes of SIDS. For instance, we now know that SIDS is not the result of child abuse. Likewise, SIDS is not caused by vomiting and choking, minor illnesses such as colds or infections, or immunizations such as those involved in the DPT (diphtheria, pertussis, and tetanus) vaccines. Nor is SIDS the cause of every unexpected and sudden infant death.

THE "BACK TO SLEEP" CAMPAIGN

In the early 1990s, the findings of a research study conducted in Tasmania suggested that infants might be at less risk for SIDS if they were put down for sleep on their backs (supine) or sides, rather than on their stomachs (prone) (e.g., Dwyer et al. 1995). That idea ran contrary to the long-held view that infants should be put down to sleep prone in order to reduce the risk that they might regurgitate or spit up fluids, aspirate them into their airways, and suffocate. Some health care professionals and laypersons still seem to believe that prone sleeping is best for an infant, but the latest research suggests that infants who sleep on their stomachs are at far greater risk of SIDS than they are of other problems.

In April 1992, the American Academy of Pediatrics (AAP) Task Force on Infant Positioning and SIDS concluded that it is likely that infants who sleep on their backs and sides are at least risk for SIDS when all other circumstances are favorable (for example, when the child is sleeping on a firm mattress and is not overheated, without loose bed covers or soft toys nearby). As a result, the AAP recommended that "healthy infants, when being put down for sleep [should] be positioned on their side or back" (p. 1120).

In June 1994, the U.S. Public Health Service, the AAP, the SIDS Alliance, and the Association of SIDS and Infant Mortality Programs jointly initiated the "Back to Sleep" campaign across the United States. This campaign employs literature, the mass media, and other avenues to raise professional and public awareness about the importance of infant sleep positioning as a way to reduce SIDS deaths (Carolan and Fernbach 1994; Willinger 1995). One example of a local organization's simple but effective implementation of the campaign comes from SIDS Resources, Inc., in Missouri, which distributes to new mothers tiny, infant-sized T-shirts with the following direction printed on the front: "THIS SIDE UP . . . while sleeping."

Subsequently, the AAP (1996, 2000) revised and strengthened its recommendation by emphasizing that supine is the preferred position for infant sleep, both at night and during naps. The AAP has acknowledged that it is acceptable to allow infants to sleep on their sides, because that is significantly better for them than sleeping on their stomachs, but side sleeping without proper support is a less stable position for an infant and thus is less preferred than back sleeping.

Dramatic and sustained reductions in SIDS deaths in the United States and many other countries have been associated with initiatives like the "Back to Sleep" campaign. Together with other proactive interventions, such as good prenatal care (proper nutrition, no smoking or drug or alcohol use by the mother, and frequent medical checkups beginning early in pregnancy) and the maintenance of a smoke-free environment after the baby is born, these initiatives have had the effect of greatly lowering the risk that infants will die from SIDS.

Unfortunately, initiatives like these have not been applied equally among all racial and cultural groups in the United States. For example, less-than-optimal prenatal care is all too prevalent in some sectors of our society. Moreover, researchers have found that African American mothers are "still significantly more likely to place their infants prone" (Willinger et al. 1998:332). This reluctance to place infants on their backs for sleep appears to be directly correlated with the less significant declines in SIDS death rates among African American infants compared with infants in other groups in the United States (Willinger et al. 2000).

TYPICAL EXPERIENCES AND TASKS FOR FIRST RESPONDERS, OTHER PROFESSIONALS, AND VOLUNTEER HELPERS

First responders in the case of a possible SIDS death may include an emergency medical dispatcher or 911 operator, who is likely to be the first person to hear a parent or other family member's plea for help; police officers or sheriff's deputies; firefighters; and emergency medical technicians, paramedics, and ambulance drivers. Most of these will be paid professional emergency service providers, although some may be volunteers, family members, and friends. First responders may also include staff members in an emergency or critical care department of a hospital, clinic, or other setting to which the infant is brought for help. Other professionals who may become involved in the case of a SIDS death include the medical examiner or coroner, a pathologist, a local prosecuting attorney, members of the clergy, and funeral service personnel. Staff at a local or regional SIDS counseling center may also play a role in helping bereaved parents and family members.

In the remainder of this section, we draw on the work of Guist and Larsen (1991), who have described three distinct but interwoven areas of responsibility for first responders, other professionals, and all other persons who take part in interventions related to a possible SIDS death. These three areas encompass clinical tasks, legal tasks, and human tasks that carry through from the first moment of the crisis until well into long-term follow-up. Although these types of tasks overlap and all have some role to play throughout the SIDS experience, for the most part each type of task has a prominent role at a particular point in the changing situation associated with SIDS.

Clinical Tasks

Whatever the circumstances, the primary clinical tasks of anyone to whom a possible SIDS infant is presented are the same as those called for in any instance in which a child is reported to be without pulse and not breathing. Because the crisis may involve the death of an infant and the cause of the crisis is unknown, these immediate clinical tasks are action oriented and practical in nature. First responders will hear the family's initial plea for help and mobilize intervention resources in response to that plea. Those who arrive at the scene or make the initial face-to-face contact with the family and child will strive to proceed in a calm and deliberate way, projecting an attitude of confidence and efficiency and exhibiting concern. Without making assumptions as to what is wrong or why the infant may have died, first responders will make a prompt physical assessment of the infant and the scene. They will also begin basic life-support measures or continue such measures if they have already been initiated. At the same time, they will try to obtain a history of the events that led to the call for help and determine what may be the best plan of intervention. Often, emergency responders will quickly transport the infant to a hospital emergency department (frequently in the company of at least one parent).

At first glance, it may appear obvious to experienced professionals that the baby is already dead and may have been dead for some time. Nevertheless, they will want to ensure that every reasonable effort is made to resuscitate the infant and that no option that might offer some life-saving potential is overlooked. Once CPR is initiated, it is usually continued until the infant is pronounced dead by some proper authority.

To fulfill these clinical tasks, first responders need to be prepared to respond to a sudden, unexpected infant death at any time. This requires that they be competent in the technical skills of life support, proficient in the use of the equipment involved, and aware of how to conduct themselves at the scene.

In a case of SIDS, clinical tasks normally culminate in an autopsy, the purpose of which is to arrive at the most accurate determination of the cause of death possible, so that medical personnel can communicate that diagnosis to the parents and appropriate officials in the most effective ways.

Legal Tasks

Legal tasks that apply at the outset to first responders in a SIDS case arise from established policies regarding the care and transportation of victims of sudden infant death and their family members. These policies typically provide guidelines for such matters as who responds to pediatric medical emergencies, what is to be done at the scene, by whom, how and where the infant is to be transported, who may or should accompany the transport, who is contacted to investigate the death, and who is responsible for pronouncing death. Even if the infant has been moved from the position in which he or she was first discovered and the parents or other adults present have difficulty recalling how events took place, the first responders' careful observation of the scene and accurate reporting on its details are essential to the investigation that follows.

In a SIDS case, a thorough and sensitive investigation by a medical examiner or coroner is essential to determine the actual cause of death, to rule out child abuse, and to protect the public from criminal behavior. Where it is applicable, "sudden infant death syndrome" is the appropriate medical language for a medical examiner or forensic pathologist to enter as cause of death on the death certificate (as opposed to less precise terminology, such as "cardiorespiratory arrest" or "undetermined cause"), and the finding should be reported as such to appropriate officials.

Human Tasks

Guist and Larsen (1991) note the importance of compassion in the human tasks carried out by all who become involved in a SIDS death:

> No one can prevent the pain a family will feel or protect them from experiencing grief following the sudden, unexpected death of an infant. If the professionals who assist with the infant and interact with the infant's family are compassionate and knowledgeable, there is potential for the surviving family to achieve a more healthful outcome from this difficult experience. (P. 155)

In large part, the human tasks that need to be accomplished in a SIDS case have to do with the ways in which the clinical and legal tasks are carried out. The human tasks for first responders and other professionals arise from their knowledge about the very painful impacts of cases of sudden infant death, the diverse ways in which individuals from different religious or cultural backgrounds may respond to such losses, and the resources available in the community that might help families coping with SIDS deaths (such as local or regional counseling services or support groups for bereaved parents). With this background in mind, first responders will seek to obtain essential information about what happened to the infant in ways that are least disturbing to the parents or other adults involved. It is not the role of first responders to fix blame for what may have happened or to focus on what the parents or a caretaker may have done or failed to do. The human tasks for first responders are to listen and observe, offer understanding and support, and take care not to make family members feel guilty about the death of the baby.

First responders can best obtain needed information and respect common responses to these difficult situations by asking open-ended questions and practicing active listening. It is especially important that they recognize that parents may blame themselves for what has happened in ways that are not realistic, and that they should not take parents' statements of self-blame as reliable acknowledgments of responsibility. While resuscitation efforts continue and until death is properly pronounced, it is essential that first responders keep the parents and other family members informed and assure them that everything that can be done is being done. Throughout, as Guist and Larsen (1991) note, "extreme care must be taken by the emergency responders not to suggest by word, facial expression, tone of voice, or nonverbal actions that any blame or suspicion is being attached to any individual. The family may misinterpret the slightest gesture or casual comment" (p. 147).

Whenever possible, first responders should display sensitivity to the family's needs by allowing at least one parent to accompany the infant during transport in an ambulance. For family members cannot come along in the ambulance, first responders can help to arrange assistance with transportation from a neighbor, relative, or other emergency responder. It is not acceptable for professionals to permit a distraught parent to drive from the scene to the hospital alone. If other children are at the scene, first responders may need to help make arrangements so that they are not left unattended; these professionals can also provide the children with a short explanation of the situation in an age-appropriate manner.

Many of the care providers who become involved in a SIDS death will have only brief contact with the infant's family members. For that reason, smooth transitions from one care provider to another are essential. Whenever emergency responders are withdrawing from the situation, family members need to know who is leaving and who will be available to provide them with continued support. In particular, it is important that care providers create a bridge between first responders and those who will provide long-term, continuing support, such as members of the clergy, funeral directors, and other counseling personnel. It is also important for all who provide care to remember that even when bereaved parents and other family members have forgotten many details of the event, they will frequently remember those whom they perceived as being especially helpful, as being unsupportive, or as making the experience more painful.

Once death has been pronounced, the emphasis in the human tasks of care providers will be on helping the parents and other family members meet their own needs in a situation for which they likely will have had no previous experience. For example, helpers can provide a quiet, private place in which the parents can express their grief and be with other loved ones. They can encourage the parents to help wash and clothe the body of their infant if they wish to do so, as well as to see, hold, or simply be with the infant, perhaps in the company of the child's siblings and other family members. Helpers can be company for the parents and other family members in these circumstances, if it seems appropriate. Helpers can also take care to handle the infant's body as though the child were still alive, and not as an impersonal object. For example, a helper can wrap the infant in a blanket and carry him or her to the parents, rather than taking the parents to a room in which the infant's body is lying on a table without any attendant or supervision. Whether or not they choose to see or hold their infant, the parents may wish to cut a lock of the baby's hair or keep other mementos, such as the child's blanket. Helpers might also take it upon themselves to take photographs of the infant, either to give to the family before they leave to go back home or to include in the infant's medical record, so that the pictures might be available to the parents if they should come to want them at a later time.

Helpers should be prepared to acknowledge and legitimate a wide variety of feelings and responses on the part of the infant's parents, siblings, and other family members. Grief and mourning are highly individual experiences for persons of all ages and backgrounds. There is no right or wrong way in these matters; nothing is to be excluded or ruled out of bounds unless it causes emotional or physical harm to the bereaved family members or others. Helpers can also provide oral and printed information about SIDS, about infant death, and about loss and grief. In addition, they can offer practical assistance in matters such as arranging for transportation back home, contacting other family members, and calling a funeral home. Further, they can arrange for spiritual support and make appropriate referrals for follow-up with a local SIDS support network. By acting in sensitive and knowledgeable ways, members of the clergy, funeral service personnel, and experienced SIDS counselors can do much to ensure that this very difficult time in the lives of SIDS parents and families is not made worse. Through their actions, they can demonstrate awareness that the short life of the infant was and remains an important part of the life of the family.

Helpers can also work to make certain that the family is told the preliminary cause of death as soon as possible and that the parents are provided with a postmortem report as soon as it is available.

Finally, it is appropriate for first responders, professionals, and all others who become involved in a SIDS death to acknowledge their own responses to such a shocking event. Helpers should honor their own honest reactions and appreciate their individual coping strategies; they should have ready access to resources for additional support and should be willing to draw on those resources as needed.

BEREAVEMENT AFTER A SIDS DEATH

Any sudden, unexpected death threatens our sense of safety and security because it forces us to confront our own mortality. This is particularly true in an infant death, because the death of a very young child is often perceived as a disruption of the natural order of things. According to this view, children are not supposed to die, and adults are expected to predecease their offspring. The lack of a discernible cause, the suddenness of the tragedy, and the involvement of the legal system also help to make a SIDS death especially difficult for all those it touches, leaving a great sense of loss and a need for understanding on the part of others. As many have noted, a SIDS death is "a cosmic slap in the face" to parents, grandparents, other adults, and siblings who had previously delighted in the child's birth and growth, and had plans for his or her future.

In addition to tasks that all bereaved persons face in coping with the losses they have experienced and their grief reactions to those losses, individuals who are bereaved by SIDS face additional challenges associated with the death of a child, a sudden death, and a death for which there is no known causal explanation (National SIDS Resource Center 1997). No postdeath intervention can be expected simply to dismiss such difficult challenges. However, classification of an infant's death as an instance of SIDS—naming it as an occurrence of a recognizable syndrome—may help provide some partial framework for understanding. This diagnosis can also go a long way toward diminishing unrealistic guilt on the part of survivors, who might otherwise think that they somehow contributed to the death or that they could have done something to prevent it. SIDS survivors, especially parents and grandparents, are likely to require a great deal of information about the syndrome and extended support in their bereavement.

Contact with others who have experienced similar deaths may be particularly useful. Sometimes this can be arranged on a one-to-one basis, but most often it is achieved through one of the many mutual-support groups that have sprung up across the United States in recent years. As a general rule, a SIDS-specific group is likely to have the most to offer to those affected by a SIDS death, but when such a group is not available, an organization for bereaved parents and family members (such as the Compassionate Friends, Bereaved Parents of the USA, or Empty Arms) or a broader bereavement support group sponsored by a local community agency (e.g., a hospice program, a funeral home, or a religious organization) can be helpful.

Explaining a SIDS death to a surviving child or subsequent sibling demands empathy, skill, and role modeling in grief. An older child in the family can be told in simple, concrete, age-appropriate terms that the baby's body simply stopped working, that the doctors and others who were involved do not know exactly why that occurred, and that no one was able to make the baby's body work again. To these messages should be added very clear communications such as the following:

- Nothing that you did or said or did not do or say, or that any of the rest of us did or did not do, caused your little brother or sister to die.

- The doctors and researchers are working as hard as they can to try to find out the cause of this type of death and to learn how to prevent it.

- Until that happens, although there are many things that we do not know about this type of death, we do know that it results from a medical problem, it is very rare, and it never happens to older children like you or to adults, so you should not worry about those possibilities.

- We are very sad and have many strong reactions to the death of your brother or sister, and we know that you are likely to have similar reactions, so you should not be surprised if they occur.

- We will share our reactions with you, and we want you to share your reactions with us at any time now or in the future so that none of us is alone in our grief.

- We love you and will be here to take care of you and to talk with you whenever you want to do so about this sad event.

EDUCATION AND SUPPORT RELATED TO SIDS

There is a great need at many levels in our society for education and support in relationship to SIDS and its implications. First responders, day-care providers, funeral directors, clergy, and all others who become involved in SIDS deaths need to understand the differences among the clinical, legal, and human tasks that we have described. Helpers also need to recognize how priorities shift among these tasks from the time the crisis occurs to the time when the call for help is first answered and on to the time of follow-up. Counselors of all kinds must appreciate the special needs of those who are bereaved by SIDS. They are likely to have distinctive needs for information, both about SIDS and about their own grief reactions and coping processes (Fuller,

Barnickol, and Mullins 1991). For example, counselors should know how to validate the experiences of SIDS survivors, enable them to obtain access to medical resources, and introduce them to other SIDS survivors or bereavement support groups.

Counselors also need to help individuals who are affected by a SIDS death to be patient with family members and others who are experiencing their own unique bereavements. Parents and close family members are especially likely to welcome assistance in determining how to manage important dates and milestones in the future and in addressing questions related to a subsequent pregnancy when that is a possible option. Adult survivors may need help in explaining SIDS losses and grief reactions to siblings and other children along the lines we have suggested above.

When parents who have experienced a SIDS death subsequently have another baby, they may wish to consider using an electronic home monitor that detects when a baby stops breathing and sounds an alarm. Although the presence of such a device may be consoling for the family, there is no evidence that using a monitor can prevent SIDS. In general, physicians recommend the use of such monitors only under special circumstances (e.g., the infant has experienced one or more severe episodes when breathing stopped and resuscitation or stimulation was required, the infant was born prematurely and has demonstrated apnea or temporary pauses in breathing, or the infant is a sibling of two or more SIDS infants). Furthermore, parents who opt for using a monitor need to know how to operate and maintain it properly if it is not to become an additional burden on them. They also need to appreciate the very real possibility of false alarms, and they need to know how to resuscitate their baby if the monitor does indicate a dangerous halt in breathing.

SIDS support groups and bereavement support groups in other settings (e.g., those sponsored by religious institutions, hospice programs, or other community organizations) may need guidance in meeting the special needs of those affected by SIDS. More broadly, the general public needs to be more fully informed about SIDS and about how the needs of those who have been bereaved by SIDS can be met in the most effective ways, especially in relation to the distinctive features associated with the death of a child and with a sudden death.

As in all deaths, often the most important thing that friends, coworkers, and others who have contact with a family affected by SIDS can do is simply be present—that is, not withdraw from the family. Friends can expect that the aftermath of the event will be difficult for family members and may play itself out in different ways over what may seem to them to be—but in fact is not—an unusually lengthy period of time. They can help just by listening attentively as individual family members go over the events of the death repeatedly and work through their specific reactions to their loss. In direct contacts and in expressing condolences in writing to a SIDS family, it is wholly appropriate for friends to share their shock and sadness over the death of the infant (family members will likely be experiencing similar feelings) as well as their frustration in not knowing what to say or do about this inexplicable death (family members will share these reactions also).

Bereaved family members often appreciate it when others share any memories of the infant and/or legacies from his or her short life—especially insights or experiences of which the family members may not have been aware and that they might want to add to their own store of memories. Families are also ordinarily grateful when friends show a real willingness to help out in practical ways (not just saying, "Call me if you need anything"). Such help might include assistance with grocery shopping, preparing food, doing laundry, cutting the lawn, or temporary child care for surviving children. It is very important that others not say, "I know how you feel" in a well-intentioned but misguided effort to reach out to members of a SIDS family, or speak in ways that unintentionally minimize the loss (e.g., "You really hadn't gotten to know the baby very well" or "You can always have another baby"). Nothing can replace the infant who died; another child is just that—a separate person, not a substitute for a SIDS baby.

CONCLUSION

Sudden infant death syndrome is a challenge to everyone it touches, whether they are parents and family members of an infant whose death is caused by SIDS, first responders and others who become involved in supporting those parents and family members, medical examiners and forensic pathologists who are called upon to determine that the death did result from SIDS, members of bereavement support groups who offer their services to a SIDS family, friends and coworkers who interact with a SIDS family after the death, or students and members of the public who hear about the puzzling subject and simply wish to understand it better. We can all hope that a day will come soon when the cause or causes of SIDS will be known, when it will become possible to screen for those infants who are at high risk for SIDS and other causes of sudden, unexpected death in infancy, and when it will be possible to prevent these deaths. In the meantime, it is essential that we strive to improve the understanding of this phenomenon and its implications as much as possible and to share that understanding as widely as we can. Improvement in the assistance offered to family members and others affected by SIDS is critical, as is an expansion of efforts to reduce the risk of SIDS through the "Back to Sleep" campaign and other initiatives described in this chapter, along with advances in research, education, and bereavement support.

SOURCES OF FURTHER INFORMATION

Additional information about SIDS is available from the following organizations:

- Association of SIDS and Infant Mortality Programs, c/o Minnesota Sudden Infant Death Center, Children's Hospitals and Clinics, Suite 605-C, 2525 Chicago Avenue South, Minneapolis, MN 55404; telephone (612) 813-6285; fax (612) 813-7344; Web site www.asip1.org

- National Sudden Infant Death Syndrome Resource Center, 2070 Chain Bridge Road, Suite 450, Vienna, VA 22182; telephone (703) 821-8955; fax (703) 821-2098; Web site www.sidscenter.org

- Sudden Infant Death Syndrome Alliance, 1314 Bedford Avenue, Suite 210, Baltimore, MD 21208; telephone (800) 221-7437 or (410) 653-8226; fax (410) 653-8709; Web site www.sidsalliance.org

REFERENCES

American Academy of Pediatrics, Committee on Child Abuse and Neglect. 2001. "Distinguishing Sudden Infant Death Syndrome From Child Abuse Fatalities." *Pediatrics* 107:437–41.

American Academy of Pediatrics, Task Force on Infant Positioning and SIDS. 1992. "Positioning and SIDS." *Pediatrics* 89:1120–26.

———. 1996. "Positioning and Sudden Infant Death Syndrome (SIDS): Update." *Pediatrics* 98:1216–18.

———. 2000. "Changing Concepts of Sudden Infant Death Syndrome: Implications for Infant Sleeping Environment and Sleep Position." *Pediatrics* 105:650–56.

Carolan, Patrick L. and Kathleen L. Fernbach. 1994. "SIDS and Infant Sleep Positioning: What We Know, What Parents Need to Know." *Topics in Pediatrics* 12(3):15–17.

Corr, Charles A., Helen Fuller, Carol A. Barnickol, and Donna M. Corr, eds. 1991. *Sudden Infant Death Syndrome: Who Can Help and How*. New York: Springer.

Dwyer, Terence, Anne-Louise Ponsonby, Leigh Blizzard, Neville M. Newman, and Jennifer A. Cochrane. 1995. "The Contribution of Changes in the Prevalence of Prone Sleeping Position to the Decline in Sudden Infant Death Syndrome in Tasmania." *Journal of the American Medical Association* 273:783–89.

Fuller, Helen, Carol A. Barnickol, and Teresa R. Mullins. 1991. "Guidelines for Counseling." Pp. 158–79 in *Sudden Infant Death Syndrome: Who Can Help and How*, edited by Charles A. Corr, Helen Fuller, Carol A. Barnickol, and Donna M. Corr. New York: Springer.

Guist, Connie and Judy E. Larsen. 1991. "Guidelines for Emergency Responders." Pp. 140–57 in *Sudden Infant Death Syndrome: Who Can Help and How*, edited by Charles A. Corr, Helen Fuller, Carol A. Barnickol, and Donna M. Corr. New York: Springer.

Hillman, Laura S. 1991. "Theories and Research." Pp. 14–41 in *Sudden Infant Death Syndrome: Who Can Help and How*, edited by Charles A. Corr, Helen Fuller, Carol A. Barnickol, and Donna M. Corr. New York: Springer.

Hoyert, Donna L., Elizabeth Arias, Betty L. Smith, Sherry L. Murphy, and Kenneth D. Kochanek. 2001. *Deaths: Final Data for 1999* (National Vital Statistics Reports, vol. 49, no. 8). Hyattsville, MD: National Center for Health Statistics.

Minino, Arialdi M. and Betty L. Smith. 2001. *Deaths: Preliminary Data for 2000* (National Vital Statistics Reports, vol. 49, no. 12). Hyattsville, MD: National Center for Health Statistics.

National SIDS Resource Center. 1997. *The Death of a Child/The Grief of the Parents: A Lifetime Journey*. Vienna, VA: National SIDS Resource Center.

U.S. Bureau of the Census. 2001. *Statistical Abstract of the United States: 2001*. Washington, DC: Government Printing Office.

Willinger, Marian. 1995. "Sleep Position and Sudden Infant Death Syndrome." *Journal of the American Medical Association* 273:818–19.

Willinger, Marian, Howard J. Hoffman, Kuo-Tsung Wu, Jin-Rong Hou, Ronald C. Kessler, Sally L. Ward, Thomas G. Keens, and Michael J. Corwin. 1998. "Factors Associated With the Transition to Nonprone Sleep Positions of Infants in the United States: The National Infant Sleep Position Study." *Journal of the American Medical Association* 280:329–35.

Willinger, Marian, L. Stanley James, and Charlotte Catz. 1991. "Defining the Sudden Infant Death Syndrome (SIDS): Deliberations of an Expert Panel Convened by the National Institute of Child Health and Human Development." *Pediatric Pathology* 11:677–84.

Willinger, Marian, Chin-Wen Ko, Howard J. Hoffman, Ronald C. Kessler, and Michael J. Corwin. 2000. "Factors Associated With Caregivers' Choice of Infant Sleep Position Study, 1994–1998: The National Infant Sleep Position Study." *Journal of the American Medical Association* 283:2135–42.

THE EVOLUTION OF THE LEGAL DEFINITION OF DEATH

TILLMAN RODABOUGH

The practice of medicine was in its infancy in ancient Egypt thousands of years ago (Ghalioungui 1963), and the problems associated with defining death medically may have originated in that time, from people's witnessing various forms of death. When a person's breath and heartbeat cease, he or she often appears to be sleeping, and the ancient Egyptians referred to death as "protracted sleep." The mythology of the early Greeks also referred to this observed relationship: Hypnos, the god of sleep, was the brother of Thanatos, the god of death (Ghalioungui 1963).

A few thousand years later and a few hundred years ago, medicine had evolved little. The field of medical education was limited to the teaching supplied by mentors already in the medical profession, a few books about medicine, and rudimentary medical schools. In the next few hundred years, medical education blossomed into a widespread world of well-equipped, technologically advanced medical schools educating many new doctors each year. As medicine moved beyond the time when a black bag contained most of the physician's tools to a period when hundreds of instruments and machines are available to facilitate the support and recovery of human life, the definition of death underwent a number of changes.

As technology has improved the ability of medical personnel to prolong life, the line between life and death has become increasingly blurred. Yet there have always been reasons that a sharp demarcation between the two has been desirable. For example, in 1564, a Spanish anatomist named Vesalius is said to have conducted an autopsy in front of a crowd in Madrid. When he opened the thorax of the nobleman who had been his patient, the man's heart was still beating. As a result of this debacle, Vesalius was compelled to leave Spain (Reis n.d.). Similarly, a century ago, avoiding premature interment was the major reason people were concerned with determining an individual's time of death. Such guarantees against burying the living

as tying strings between bells and the fingers of the recently dead (so that the bells would ring if they "awoke") and the practice of the "death watch" to make sure a person was actually dead (Congdon 1977) became unnecessary with the invention of the stethoscope in the mid-1800s. Later, the widespread practice of embalming had the unintended function of precluding premature burial, because the expulsion of blood under pressure at the beginning of the embalming process would notify the embalmer that the heart was still functioning. The certification of death, required by the state, verifies for society that one of its members is gone. This certification serves as a signal for the family to reorganize life without the deceased person and for societal institutions to do such things as pay insurance, stop social security payments, and record the death in mortality statistics.

HISTORICAL DEFINITIONS OF DEATH

According to *Black's Law Dictionary,* death is "the ending of life; the cessation of all vital functions and signs" (Garner 1999:11). This definition seems clear enough until one considers all the components of death and their implications. First, deaths can be divided into several types. *Local death* refers to the death occurring constantly in all parts of the living body, where individual cells are being constantly cast off and replaced by new ones. *General death* refers to the death of the body as a whole—that is, somatic or systemic death—and tissue death. *Systemic death* refers to the absolute cessation of the functioning of the brain, the circulatory organs, and the respiratory organs as well as the complete loss of all vital actions. The whole body dies first and the tissues later (see the On-Line Medical Dictionary at http://cancerweb.ncl.ac.uk/omd/). Today, death is as much a legal matter as a medical one

(Mathieu 1988). Determining when a person is dead is not always easy, because the answers change over time.

Death occurs at a number of different levels. Somatic death, the death of the organism as a whole, usually precedes the deaths of individual organs, cells, and parts of cells. This death is marked by cessation of heartbeat, respiration, movement, reflexes, and brain activity. The precise time of somatic death is sometimes difficult to determine, because such transient states as fainting, trance, and coma can closely resemble it (Frederick 2001). Below, I discuss some of the various signs that have been taken as indicators of death, taking them in order roughly from past to present.

Soul Departure

The departure of the soul is perhaps the oldest definition of death; it is certainly one of the oldest ways of viewing death. According to this concept, death occurs when the spirit or the soul leaves the body. But what is the spirit or the soul? Some use the terms *spirit* and *soul* as synonyms, whereas some use the two words to refer to separate entities. Although some individuals working in the parapsychology tradition have recorded what they believe to be energy outbursts from bodies at the time of death, such findings are difficult, if not impossible, to verify scientifically. The question of such phenomena might best be left to religious tradition.

The idea that a soul leaves the body at death is the source of some controversy in debates between centralists and decentralists. Centralist theory focuses on the individual's vital force, the breath and blood of the individual, and where it resides (Powner, Ackerman, and Grenvik 1996). From the centralist perspective, a single organ, the heart or the brain, is responsible for life (Veatch 1976). Decentralists, in contrast, believe that life is present throughout all organs, tissues, and cells of the body (Powner et al. 1996). Decentralist theory focuses more on the loss of the soul than on the cessation of body fluids as the major contributor to death—a view highly influenced by religious thought (Lamb 1985).

Decay

A sure sign of cell death, decay appeared as an unintentional indicator during the long wakes and delayed funerals of the past. In earlier times, bodies were kept warm through the application of mustard poultices. This practice helped to maintain life in those mistakenly identified as dead and hastened putrefaction in those actually dead. Thus living persons whose heartbeat and respiration were undetected could revive. The cool mortuaries of today make such mistakes more difficult to discover until embalming begins. As noted above, blood expelled from the body under pressure when an incision is made to begin the embalming process is a sure indicator of a beating heart. The process rarely ever gets that far, however, because current methods of detecting life (or determining death) are much more sophisticated than those of the past.

Respiration

Probably the most widely recognized indicator of death used for the longest period of time was simply the cessation of breathing. A few generations ago, the term *suspended animation* was applied to persons who appeared to have stopped breathing for a period of time and then resumed breathing or "came back to life." Respiration had not actually ceased in such cases; rather, it was simply so shallow that it was not easily detected with available technology. To make certain that a person had died before entombment, someone would hold a piece of glass or a feather to the individual's nostrils to determine if breath was absent. Apparent lack of respiration is a poor indicator of death, but it was the best indicator available for many years.

Heartbeat

The heart held central position for scientists from the 17th century into the 20th century, because observations from decapitations and other traumatic casualties confirmed that organs seemed to lose function sequentially, with the heart continuing to beat after the lungs and brain ceased to function (Pernick 1988). The traditional cardiopulmonary standard was the measure used during most of the 20th century to determine the presence of life. Because heartbeat can be faint and difficult to detect, this indicator was combined with others, such as changes in the eyes, insensibility to electrical stimuli, rigor mortis, pallor, hypostasis, and relaxation of the sphincters. That is, death would be considered to be indicated if the body has no detectable heartbeat, the eyes are dilated, there is no physiological response to electric shock, the body stiffens and is pale, blood settles in the bottom of the body, and the bowels and bladder release their contents.

Prior to the 1960s, death was understood and diagnosed primarily through these cardiopulmonary criteria (Byrne 2000). Until the 20th century, physicians had few administrable remedies for illness; some patients got well despite such "treatments" as bloodletting and prescriptions of whiskey as much as because of them. New frontiers were forged in technology during the 20th century with the development of such life-saving equipment as the defibrillator and the ventilator. For a physician to diagnose death, all forms of reanimation now had to fail (Powner et al. 1996). Many first began to question seriously the legal definition of death in 1967, the year of the first successful human heart transplant. If the heart could be bypassed or entirely replaced, it might not be the "seat of life" (Lyons 1970). The definition of death had to evolve again.

PROBLEMS CREATED BY PAST DEFINITIONS OF DEATH

Medical definitions of death are influenced by philosophy, theology, and technology, as well as by political and social priorities (Powner et al. 1996). The medical technology available today raises many questions that were never considered a century ago, questions concerning such issues as when heroic efforts to save a life should stop, when the transplantation of tissue from a given individual becomes legal, and how some insurance claims and wills can be settled. The historical definitions of death, as discussed above, were less than adequate for addressing such issues.

Heroic Efforts

Today, physicians have many tools to use in trying to keep an individual alive, including the injection of chemicals, manual stimulation, electroshock, surgical invasion, and mechanical supports. Medical technology is improving constantly, pushing back the line of death. The first result of a determination that death has occurred is the release of the physician and the patient's family from continuous and burdensome efforts to continue treatment. The question becomes, When should a physician stop such efforts?

Transplantation

Up until the mid-20th century, death determination was relatively straightforward. A person was defined as dead when his or her respiratory and circulatory function ceased. However, with the advent of modern medical technology and the ability to support individual organs even when other systems fail, death became more difficult to define. Before medicine made these technological advancements, a person died all at once. When scientists realized that the part of the brain that controls respiration might be destroyed while ventilators maintain respiration, the need to harvest organs for transplantation helped to prompt a reassessment of the legal definition of death (Freer 2001). Transplant medicine is dependent on "beating-heart cadavers" and the current definition of death. Many health care professionals like to think that the significance of death is not found in the death of the body, but in the death of the person. However, depending on the definition of death, the death of the body may precede the death of the person.

Inheritance

The definition of death can add to the complications faced by children in the multitude of recombined families that exist today. For example, when both parents in a "blended" family die in an automobile accident, what each of their children will inherit is frequently determined by which parent died last—particularly if there is no will. Given the growing divorce and remarriage rates, it is likely that many parents who are in their second or later marriages will die in accidents, some together with their current spouses. This is a problem that appears to be likely to increase rather than decrease in the future.

Insurance

Life insurance has nothing to do with life but everything to do with death and who receives how much money after an individual dies. The line where legal death occurs becomes especially critical when injured or ill persons are placed on life support long enough to determine whether they will resume normal life functions on their own. Suppose a person's life insurance policy expires while he or she is on life support, and the body is later determined to be nonviable and is disconnected from life support. Was the person dead when placed on life support, did he or she die while on life support, or did death occur only when the person was disconnected from the life-support machinery? The answers to such questions can make a considerable difference financially to family members and to insurance companies.

Obviously, earlier definitions of death left many questions unanswered, so with more sophisticated technology the definition of death evolved further.

NEW DEFINITIONS OF DEATH

Organs to be transplanted must be alive, and, in most cases, the donor must be dead. At any given time, large numbers of persons across the United States are waiting for organ transplants. For example, according to the United Network for Organ Sharing (UNOS), which provides daily updates on its Web site (http://www.unos.org), as of June 30, 2002, more than 82,000 individuals were registered on national waiting lists for transplants. Of these, 52,686 individuals were waiting for kidney transplants; the rest were waiting for liver transplants (17,515), pancreas transplants (1,313), kidney-pancreas transplants (2,526), intestine transplants (197), heart transplants (4,161), lung transplants (3,789), and heart-lung transplants (212). Additionally, many people are waiting for transplants of blood and blood components, skin grafts, grafts of bone and connective tissue, and transplants of eye and ocular components.

The line between life and death becomes especially critical in situations involving potential organ donors. Organs die at different rates, and some can survive for some time, depending on how death is defined. Brain cells may survive for no more than 5 minutes after somatic death, whereas heart cells can survive for about 15 minutes and kidney cells for about 30 minutes (Frederick 2001). When "the life of one depends upon the death of another"

(Byrne 2000), the line between life and death is especially important. Waiting too long after a donor's death to harvest an organ can affect the quality of the organ, and the health and life of a transplant patient is directly connected to the viability of the transplanted tissue. According to the National Kidney Foundation (2002), 22,953 kidney transplants took place in the United States in 2000. These operations brought extended life to some and improved the quality of life for many more. According to data on the UNOS Web site, from 1992 through 2001, 44,288 patients on transplant waiting lists died while waiting for organs. The need to facilitate the harvesting of organs for transplantation has contributed to changes in the legal definition of death.

Brain Death

According to *Black's Law Dictionary,* brain death is "the bodily condition of showing no response to external stimuli, no spontaneous movements, no breath, no reflexes, and a flat reading (usually for at least 24 hours) on a machine that measures the brain's electrical activity" (Garner 1999:11). The cessation of brain function has become the criterion for death determination not only because it is more sophisticated than prior criteria but because it allows doctors to harvest more and better organs for transplantation. The term *brain-dead* was coined in 1965 when surgeons performed a renal transplant using organs donated from a patient with no recorded brain waves (Powner et al. 1996).

Incorporating brain death into consideration along with the cessation of respiration and circulation led Vincent Collins to develop the "dying score" to determine the occurrence of death (Lyons 1970). Collins stressed the importance of heart, brain, and lung functioning as a whole rather than as independent parts. According to this definition, death is caused by the failure of the main organs combined. Collins's dying score was based on five physiological functions: cerebral, reflex, respiratory, circulatory, and cardiac. Each was scored from two to zero, according to its presence, potential, or absence. A score of five was the dividing line, with five or higher indicating life and less than five indicating possible to imminent death. This system represented a further move toward the quantification of death.

Two particular historical events have forever changed the legal definition of death. The first occurred in 1968, when a group of physicians, theologians, lawyers, and philosophers on the Harvard University faculty formed the Ad Hoc Committee of the Harvard Medical School to Examine the Definition of Brain Death (1968). This committee established the following medical criteria (known as the Harvard criteria) for a diagnosis of irreversible coma:

1. Unreceptivity and unresponsivity, in which there is a "total unawareness of externally applied stimuli."

2. No movements or breathing for at least one hour while observed by physicians (this means no spontaneous respiration and no spontaneous muscle movement).

3. No reflexes, such as eye movement or tendon reflexes. The usual reflexes are absent in response to a neurophysiological examination, such as the pupil constricting when a light is shined in the eye.

4. A flat electroencephalogram (that is, when electrodes attached to the scalp record electrical activity on a paper printout or digital display, rather than the normal peaks and valleys, the device records an essentially flat line). There is no circulation to or within the brain (without the oxygen provided by circulating blood, the brain quickly dies).

These criteria were soon adopted widely as the criteria for brain death, and most physicians accepted brain death as equivalent to patient death. This definition became extremely important as the all-encompassing definition of death because no case has yet been found in which a person meeting all of these criteria has ever regained brain function even with continued respiration. A diagnosis of brain death allows medical personnel to turn off the patient's respirator.

The second event occurred in 1981, when a presidential commission was created to establish a definition of death. This commission used the Harvard criteria to conclude that in order to come to a diagnosis of death, physicians must establish the absence of brain activity (Burnell 1993; Medical Consultants 1981). No bodily functions can occur spontaneously without the help of the brain, so death occurs at the moment the brain activity necessary to control autonomous biological functions ceases. Patients are medically and legally dead when these criteria are met, and no further medical treatment is required (McCuen and Boucher 1985). The current determinant of death is variously worded in state statutes as "total and irreversible cessation of brain function," "no spontaneous brain function," "irreversible cessation of the functioning of the entire brain, including the brain stem," or something similar. The President's Commission for the Study of Ethical Problems in Medicine and Biomedical and Behavioral Research merged all of the state statutes into the Uniform Determination of Death Act (UDDA).

For physicians to declare a person brain-dead, they must monitor the patient's brain function for an appropriate period of time in the intensive care unit of a hospital (Mathieu 1988). The criteria for brain death are absence of eye response, absence of verbal and motor response to pain, and loss of brain stem reflexes (Campbell 1992), which include pupil responses, corneal reflexes, caloric response to stimulation, cough reflexes, and response to hypercarbia.

The two landmark reports described above moved medicine away from the traditional standards of heartbeat and respiration in defining death. Today, all 50 states and the District of Columbia follow the UDDA in recognizing whole-brain death as a legal standard of death. This standard of irreversible cessation of all functions of the entire brain does not replace the cardiopulmonary standard, however; rather, the UDDA recognizes either standard—whichever applies first (DeGrazia 1998). The consequence is that a person can be legally dead even if his or her cardiopulmonary system continues to function. If the brain is dead, any artificially induced heartbeat merely pumps blood through the dead body.

Several types of death are recognized under varying circumstances: heart-lung death, brain death, higher-brain death, and biological death (the ceasing of all cellular activity). Other permutations include irreversible loss of cellular brain structure, loss of both brain and spinal cord function, and varying interpretations of "higher-brain death," meaning the neocortex or the sensory cortex, above the brain stem or the cerebrum, and the cerebral cortex. Youngner, Arnold, and Schapiro (1999) raise some important issues about brain death in their edited volume examining contemporary controversies surrounding the definition of death. As they point out, whatever the standards for determining death, once those standards have been met, a person is dead. Without a brain stem, the body is merely a hopeless collection of organs, incapable of human vitality. The diagnosis of brain death has been shown to be inconsistent from one hospital to another and from one physician to another, and Youngner et al. ask how the public can or should be told that the line between life and death is somewhat imprecise even for physicians, that some brain functions are important but others can be ignored, and that whole-brain death can be abandoned in favor of brain stem death.

Pronouncing Death

Only physicians can determine the success or failure of specific treatments and make diagnoses and prognoses; therefore, only physicians must determine whether death has occurred. Only competent patients can permit or refuse treatment (Childress 1981). Defining death is an important legal factor and must not deny the rights of a patient. A dying patient who does not meet the criteria for brain death but who has decided that he or she would rather die has a legal right to prepare advance directives. The most common of these is the living will—a document written by the patient and directed to his or her family members, physician, clergyman, and lawyer, describing the patient's wishes concerning his or her treatment and death. A patient's written request not to be kept alive by artificial means or heroic measures is not complete unless the patient has signed and dated it in front of a witness, who must also sign the document (Brody 1993). Many states have passed "natural death acts" that give legal status to living wills. However, if some members of a patient's family are opposed to following the "no heroic measures" directions set out in a living will, some physicians will keep the patient alive, erring on the side of caution to avoid legal repercussions and lawsuits. Although the terms of a living will are not legally binding on the patient's family

members, most families respect the wishes of their loved ones as laid out in such documents.

Public attitudes toward end-of-life decisions in the United States have moved in the direction of giving individuals the opportunity to decide what should happen to them at the end of their lives. Although there are some limitations, such as denial of physician-assisted suicide in most states, persons do have the right to make decisions about their care as long as they are competent. Even if a person is no longer competent, his or her wishes will be honored if he or she has previously prepared a living will or has given durable power of attorney for health care to a surrogate who can make medical decisions.

If no such plans have been made, the decision-making responsibility for patients declared incompetent is passed on to the family, a hospital committee, or the courts. If family members are available and know the wishes of the patient, they decide; if technical expertise is needed, the committee decides; and if no one has clear responsibility, the courts decide. In this case, the "best interests of the patient" serve as the guide for making decisions.

Different people may certify death (legally declare that death has occurred) under various circumstances. Typically, when an attending physician is present, he or she pronounces the death and states the official time of death. The physician must complete and sign the death certificate, certifying the cause and place of death, and the certificate must be recorded with whichever state entity is in charge of keeping vital statistics; in many states this is the department of health. States use the registration of death certificates to calculate death rates, which are part of the archival record of particular importance to statisticians and demographers in determining population characteristics. These records, combined with data from the U.S. Bureau of the Census, allow government officials to determine needs and allocations for specific geographic areas of the population. Most important, official certification of death is needed before certain hospital procedures can be performed, such as autopsies, organ transplantation, and the removal of all medical therapy or life-support devices (Mathieu 1988).

When an individual dies at home or in some other non-medical location, a person other than a physician may declare that death has officially occurred. Most frequently, this is the coroner or the person designated to fill a comparable position in the state or county where the death has taken place. In some states, and in certain counties in other states, this person must possess a medical degree, but in some locales this may be a person with no medical expertise who works in the sheriff's office.

PROBLEMS CREATED BY THE NEW DEFINITIONS OF DEATH

Today, the brain-death definition of death needs to be clarified, an action that has become increasingly difficult to take because of competing interests. The Uniform Determination of Death Act states that once irreversible cessation of circulatory, respiratory, and brain function has occurred, death is to be announced. The announcement of death is to be made in accordance with the standards of the hospital, which means that the determination of death is basically left in the hands of individual hospitals. Because physicians faced a problem with defining death due to controversy surrounding organ transplantations, the American Medical Association recommended an extension to the Uniform Determination of Death Act in 1996 that required at least two doctors not involved with any related transplants to pronounce a patient dead (Kress 1998).

The term *brain death,* however, can refer to several conditions. *Whole-brain death,* as discussed above, refers to the irreversible destruction of all neural structures within the brain. *Neocortical death,* in contrast, refers to the destruction of "the cerebral cortex—the most highly differentiated brain cells, considered to be of critical importance for intellectual functioning" (Kastenbaum 2001:39).

Higher-Brain Death

The whole-brain death discussed above is the irreversible destruction of all neural structures within the brain. This, the most conservative definition, includes both hemispheres and the cerebral cortex, the cerebellum, and the brain stem. Some have argued that the whole-brain standard is inadequate and assert that the standard should be irreversible cessation of the capacity for consciousness, which can be met prior to whole-brain death that includes the death of the brain stem. Neocortical death allows spontaneous respiration and heartbeat but not consciousness, thus, according to the higher-brain-death standard, a person is considered dead when the upper region of his or her brain is inactive. A patient in a permanent coma or a permanent vegetative state and a child with anencephaly, therefore, meet the higher-brain, but not the whole-brain, standard of death (DeGrazia 1998).

The term *persistent vegetative state* (PVS) refers to a clinical condition of complete unawareness of self and the environment accompanied by sleep-wake cycles. People in this state have suffered neocortical injuries; this region of the brain has been destroyed by either disease or trauma. Hypothalamic and brain stem autonomic functions are at lease partially preserved, along with cranial-nerve and spinal reflexes. Persons in a vegetative state show no sustained, purposeful responses to any stimuli—visual, auditory, tactile, or noxious. They do not comprehend language or show bladder or bowel control. A diagnosis of PVS is made if the above conditions are present 1 month after any of the following three major causes: brain injury, degenerative or developmental or metabolic brain disorders, or severe congenital malformations of the nervous system (Multi-Society Task Force on PVS 1994). The question is, When is the patient dead "enough" without having a

possibility of living a complete, functional life (Smith 1993)? A person in an irreversible coma is a person who has sustained such brain damage that there is no possibility of his or her returning to any form of consciousness.

The outcome of PVS depends on its cause. It is unlikely that an individual will recover consciousness from a post-traumatic PVS after 12 months, from a nontraumatic PVS after 3 months, and from degenerative or metabolic disorders or congenital malformations after some amount of time between 3 and 12 months. Remaining life span for those with PVS usually ranges from 2 to 5 years, with survival longer than 10 years quite unusual (Multi-Society Task Force on PVS, 1994).

Using organs from those who have suffered higher-brain death would greatly benefit many individuals who are dying as they wait for organ transplantation, but persons in a persistent vegetative state can regain consciousness again at any time. Therefore, a protocol has been set according to which patients in a vegetative state cannot be declared brain-dead until they have been in this state for 12 months (Moon 2002). This may delay the availability of some organs for transplants, by pushing back the legal line between life and death, but it provides protection against the premature taking of human life. Therefore, the more conservative standard, whole-brain death, is the most frequently used biomedical definition today in regulatory documents. The certification of death is delayed as long as there is any observable functioning in any area of the brain, and this sharply reduces the possibility of error. There is a tendency to blur the distinction between "cannot recover" and "already dead," but use of the standard of whole-brain death minimizes the possibility that anyone will have organs harvested for transplants while he or she is still alive.

If higher-brain death were the only criterion for determining death, then people in PVS and children with anencephaly would be considered dead. Anencephalic infants are those born without part of the skull and with either a dysfunctional forebrain or no forebrain at all. These babies can survive for days or even months because of their functioning brain stems, but they never gain consciousness. Many fewer anencephalic children are born than there are people in a persistent vegetative state; this is one of the reasons there are fewer organs available for transplant for babies and young children. It often takes a long time for anencephalic children to be declared whole-brain-dead, and because of this their organs are frequently not usable for transplantation. Because of the scarcity of suitable organs for transplant, half of the children waiting for transplants die before organs can be found (Kothari and Mehta n.d.).

Until a few years ago, many physicians and researchers thought that within a few weeks of brain death, the entire body system would undergo general collapse (Kastenbaum 2001). They had to revise their view, however, given the evidence provided by striking instances in which pregnant women who had suffered traumas resulting in brain death were maintained on life support for months to provide crucial time for their fetuses to develop.

Eelco Wijdicks recently surveyed brain-death criteria throughout the world and found the presence of guidelines concerning brain death in 70 of the 80 countries responding, as well as legal standards on organ donation present in 55 (cited in American Academy of Neurology 2002). Uniform agreement existed on the neurological examination used to determine brain death, but there were variations in the numbers of physicians required, their levels of experience, their specialties, and their academic ranks, as well as in the confirmatory tests to be used. The differences in existing protocols might be the results of the collective decisions of task forces. Wijdicks observes that the guidelines used in many countries seem unnecessarily complicated, and he recommends that some international standardization be considered.

Not everyone is satisfied with the way the legal definition of death has evolved; for example, some observers, such as Byrne (1988), have expressed discomfort with the variabilities involved in declarations of death. They suggest that under the current definition of death, the life of one patient is risked to benefit another. They seem to advocate an "all or nothing" approach: A person is either all dead or all alive, with no in between. They note that when organs are to be removed from the deceased, it is best to err on the conservative side. If any part of the person can be treated as alive, then that person is alive and cannot have his or her organs removed. Byrne (1988) asserts that brain-related criteria for death are not based on valid scientific data, because the Harvard Medical School's committee published its criteria without making any reference to scientific reports or patient data. He notes that the Harvard criteria deal only with the cessation of function, not the destruction of the brain or the organism, and he concludes that death should not be declared until the entire brain and the respiratory and circulatory systems are destroyed (see also Evers and Byrne 1990).

On the other end of the debate is the question of whether medical personnel improperly subject the relatives of brain-dead organ donors to the prolonged living-death existence of their loved ones until potential recipients can be located. As medical technology has advanced, the numbers of possible donor sources have increased; these now include live human donors, cadavers, animals, and fetuses along with anencephalic infants and brain-dead donors (Banks 1995). However, the use of each kind of source presents its own unique ethical problems. How to maintain viable body parts while assuring that the donor is dead is only one of many issues. For example, the FBI recently investigated charges that the University of Texas Medical Branch was selling donated body parts and was not testing body parts used for surgical study or transplant for infectious diseases (Lozano 2002). Clearly, many factors must be balanced in the life-and-death equation represented by organ transplantation.

CONCLUSION

Although the legal definition of death has been comparatively stable for more than 20 years now, new technological advances and philosophical conflicts will require that the definition be more exact in the future, resulting in individuals' being pronounced legally dead a little earlier or a little later. No matter which way the legal line between life and death moves, the intent will be to protect not only the lives of dying persons but the lives of those who may benefit from their deaths.

REFERENCES

Ad Hoc Committee of the Harvard Medical School to Examine the Definition of Brain Death. 1968. "A Definition of Irreversible Coma." *Journal of the American Medical Association* 205:337–40.

American Academy of Neurology. 2002. "Diagnostic Criteria for Brain Death Vary Worldwide." Press release. Retrieved April 25, 2003 (http://www.aan.com/press/press/releases/01080002_diagnostic.htm).

Banks, Gloria J. 1995. "Legal and Ethical Safeguards: Protection of Society's Most Vulnerable Participants in a Commercialized Organ Transplantation System." *American Journal of Law and Medicine* 21:45–110.

Brody, Eugene B. 1993. *Biomedical Technology and Human Rights*. Brookfield, VT: Dartmouth.

Burnell, George M. 1993. *Final Choices: To Live or to Die in an Age of Medical Technology*. New York: Plenum.

Byrne, Paul A. 1988. "Understanding Brain Death." Omaha, NE: Vital Signs Ministry. Retrieved May 12, 2003 (http://www.vitalsignsministries.org/vsmbraindeath.html).

———. 2000. *Beyond Brain Death*. Norwell, MA: Kluwer Academic.

Campbell, Alastair. 1992. *Practical Medical Ethics*. Auckland, New Zealand: Oxford University Press.

Childress, James F. 1981. *Priorities in Biomedical Ethics*. Philadelphia: Westminster.

Congdon, Howard K. 1977. *The Pursuit of Death*. Nashville, TN: Abington.

DeGrazia, David. 1998. "Biology, Consciousness, and the Definition of Death." Institute for Philosophy and Public Policy, College Park, MD. Retrieved April 25, 2003 (http://www.puaf.umd.edu/IPPP/winter98/biology_consciousness.htm).

Evers, Joseph C. and Paul A. Byrne. 1990. "Brain Death: Still a Controversy." *Pharos of Alpha Omega Alpha* 53:10–12.

Frederick, Calvin J. 2001. "Death and Dying." In *Microsoft Encarta Online Encyclopedia*. Retrieved April 25, 2003 (http://encarta.msn.com).

Freer, Jack. 2001. "Brain Death." In *Ethics Committee Core Curriculum*. UB Center for Clinical Ethics and Humanities in Health, Buffalo, NY. Retrieved April 25, 2003 (http://wings.buffalo.edu/faculty/research/bioethics/mandeth.html).

Garner, Bryan A., ed. 1999. *Black's Law Dictionary*, 7th ed. Eagan, MN: West Group.

Ghalioungui, Paul. 1963. *Magic and Medical Science in Ancient Egypt.* New York: Barnes & Noble.

Kastenbaum, Robert J. 2001. *Death, Society, and Human Experience,* 7th ed. Boston: Allyn & Bacon.

Kothari, Manu and Lopa Mehta. n.d. "Death: Design and Definition." In Manu Kothari and Lopa Mehta, *Living, Dying.* Retrieved January 30, 2002 (http://www.healthlibrary.com/reading/living/chp4.html).

Kress, Jack M. 1998. "Xenotransplantation: Ethics and Economics." *Food and Drug Law Journal* 53:353–84.

Lamb, David. 1985. *Death, Brain Death and Ethics.* Albany: State University of New York Press.

Lozano, Juan A. 2001. "UT Branch Recalls Body Parts." *Waco Tribune-Herald,* August 7, pp. 1B, 3B.

Lyons, Catherine. 1970. *Organ Transplants.* Philadelphia: Westminster.

Mathieu, Deborah, ed. 1988. *Organ Substitution Technology.* Boulder, CO: Westview.

McCuen, Gary E. and Therese Boucher, eds. 1985. *Terminating Life: Conflicting Values in Health Care.* Hudson, WI: Gary E. McCuen.

Medical Consultants on the Diagnosis of Death to the President's Commission for the Study of Ethical Problems in Medicine and Biomedical and Behavioral Research. 1981. "Guidelines for the Determination of Death." *Journal of the American Medical Association* 246:2184–86.

Moon, Louisa. 2002. "Defining Death." Retrieved January 30, 2002 (http://www.miracosta.edu/home/lmoon/wk3death/html).

Multi-Society Task Force on PVS. 1994. "Medical Aspects of the Persistent Vegetative State: First of Two Parts." *New England Journal of Medicine* 330:1499–1508.

National Kidney Foundation. 2002. "25 Facts About Organ Donation and Transplantation." Retrieved April 25, 2003 (http://www.kidney.org/general/news/25facts.cfm).

Pernick, M. 1988. "Back from the Grave: Recurring Controversies Over Defining and Diagnosing Death in History." In *Death: Beyond the Whole-Brain Criteria,* edited by Richard M. Zaner. Dordrecht, Netherlands: Kluwer Academic.

Powner, David J., Bruce M. Ackerman, and Ake Grenvik. 1996. "Medical Diagnosis of Death in Adults: Historical Contributions to Current Controversies." *Lancet* 348: 1219–23.

Reis, Carlos Eduardo. n.d. "Brain Death." In *Neurology,* Medcenter Solutions do Brasil. Retrieved April 25, 2003 (http://www.medstudents.com.br/neuro/neuro5.htm).

Smith, George P. 1993. *Bioethics and the Law.* Lanham, MD: University Press of America.

Veatch, Robert M. 1976. *Death, Dying, and the Biological Revolution: Our Last Quest for Responsibility.* New Haven, CT: Yale University Press.

Youngner, Stuart J., Robert M. Arnold, and Renie Schapiro, eds. 1999. *The Definition of Death: Contemporary Controversies.* Baltimore: Johns Hopkins University Press.

DEATH EDUCATION

CHARLES A. CORR

DONNA M. CORR

*D*eath education is in many ways an awkward phrase that may convey undesirable meanings to some who hear or read it. One of its faults lies in the implication that it refers to a type of education intended for or aimed at those who are already dead. Alternatively, some may incorrectly think that it refers to explaining to living people what the state of death is really like. We begin this chapter by illustrating the proper meaning of the term *death education* by listing and discussing briefly some of the many subjects that fall within the scope of education about dying, death, and bereavement. After that, we look at several examples of death education in action, four central dimensions of this type of education, and its principal goals. We also offer some comments concerning who might be interested in death-related education and who might find themselves functioning as death educators, and we conclude with some observations concerning lessons about life and living that can be learned from the study of dying, death, and bereavement.

WHAT DOES IT MEAN TO TALK ABOUT "DEATH EDUCATION"?

The phrase *death education* is actually a shorthand expression for education about any death-related topic. Pine (1977, 1986) provides reviews of the early history of death education in the United States in two helpful articles. Currently, this type of education reaches across a broad range of topics, such as those found in college textbooks in the field (e.g., Corr, Nabe, and Corr 2003). These include the following:

Encounters with death: This topic area includes the numbers of deaths in given populations, death rates, causes of death, average life expectancy, locations of death, and experiences with particular types of death, such as deaths from long-term degenerative diseases (diseases of the heart;

cancers; neuromuscular diseases such as amyotrophic lateral sclerosis, known as Lou Gehrig's disease; and dementing diseases such as Alzheimer's disease) and their differences from deaths caused by communicable diseases.

Attitudes toward death: This area includes death anxiety as well as individuals' attitudes about their own dying or death, about the dying or death of someone else, or about what happens after death.

Death-related practices: This topic area covers practices related to death within a given death system (e.g., contemporary American practices), such as language about death, the media's relationship with death, and human-induced forms of death (including accidents and homicide).

Dying: This area includes the ways in which people die as well as the ways in which they cope with dying and help those who are coping with dying. It also includes societal programs that are concerned with caring for the dying or end-of-life care, such as hospice programs and programs of palliative care.

Bereavement: This area includes death-related losses, the grief that follows a death, mourning or coping with loss and grief, anticipatory grief and mourning, disenfranchised grief, ways to help those who are coping with loss and grief, and societal programs concerned with caring for persons who are coping with loss and grief (such as support groups for the bereaved, hospice bereavement follow-up programs, and aftercare programs in the funeral industry).

Funeral practices and memorial rituals: This area includes different forms of body disposition, cemeteries, memorial sculpture, and memorial photography.

Experiences with death among different developmental cohorts or different cultural groups: This area includes death experiences among particular groups, such as children, adolescents, adults, and the elderly or Hispanics, African Americans, Asian or Pacific Islander Americans, and Native Americans.

Coping with HIV/AIDS: This area includes coping with infection from the human immunodeficiency virus and deaths resulting from acquired immune deficiency syndrome.

Suicide: This area includes common patterns in suicidal behavior, attempts to explain or improve understanding of such behavior, interventions designed to prevent or minimize suicidal behavior, the impact of suicide on bereaved survivors, and rational suicide (the concept itself, as well as arguments for and against this type of suicide).

Assisted suicide and euthanasia: This area covers what assisted suicide and euthanasia mean in themselves, for individuals, and for societies, along with moral and religious arguments pro and con.

Legal issues: This area includes such death-related legal issues as advance directives (living wills and durable powers of attorney in health care matters); definition and determination of death; organ, tissue, and body donation; and disposition of the property of a deceased individual.

Religious, philosophical, or spiritual views: This area concerns various views about the meaning of death and its place in human life.

Near-death experiences: This area includes near-death experiences and various paranormal experiences of the bereaved.

This list is inevitably incomplete, but it illustrates the broad and diverse spectrum of subjects covered by death education.

EXAMPLES OF DEATH EDUCATION IN ACTION

We can best illustrate the many different types of educational efforts that have to do with some of the subjects we have just described by offering several examples of death education in action.

Example 1: Life Experiences and Death Education

A book titled *The Dead Bird* (Brown 1958) describes a situation in which some children come across a dead bird in a field. Although its body is still warm, the children realize that the bird is no longer alive. Its eyes are closed, they are not able to feel the beating of its heart, and its body gradually becomes cold and still as they touch it. So they decide to have a funeral for the bird, "the way grown-up

people did when someone died." They dig a grave in the woods, line it with warm sweet ferns, wrap the bird in grapevine leaves, and put the wrapped bird in the ground, placing more ferns and flowers on top of its body. Then they sing a song and cover the grave with dirt and more flowers. Finally, the children put a stone on top of the grave—on which they have written "HERE LIES A BIRD THAT IS DEAD"—and plant some flowers around it. "And every day," the story tells us, "until they forgot, they went and sang to their little dead bird and put fresh flowers on his grave."

This story has many interesting features. Because the bird does not act or feel like the living animals they have known, the children promptly realize that it is dead. They are sad for the bird, but they are also pleased in a way that they can act out a funeral and burial ceremony, thereby trying out and imitating some adult behaviors they have previously observed. Those points, and the story itself, provide interesting materials for informal death education. The general form of this event is immediately recognizable. It might apply not only to wild animals, but to pets or companion animals in a home, such as dogs, cats, fish, small caged animals (such as gerbils and hamsters), and birds (such as parakeets and songbirds). Children of any age may encounter and learn about death when unplanned events take place in their own life experiences, and, as in the case of the story related above, this may happen without any direct input from adults.

Example 2: Informal Death Education in the Home

Perhaps the most common type of informal death education occurs in people's homes and/or within religious or cultural groups when parents, grandparents, religious or cultural leaders, and other adults convey messages to children and adolescents about death-related events. For example, children learn important lessons as they observe how adults act when someone known to them is dying, when a death occurs, or when a significant other is bereaved. Unfortunately, some adults teach children that they should not talk about such events, but many other adults involve children and adolescents in caring activities while also addressing their own needs.

Informal death education of this type can become a bit more structured when proactive adults create opportunities to talk about death (Corr 1984a). Earl Grollman offers a guidebook for such interactions in *Talking About Death: A Dialogue Between Parent and Child* (1990), which includes a read-along-together section as a basis for such a dialogue, guidelines for adults to use in explaining death to a child, and suggestions about various types of additional resources. Another way in which adults can create opportunities for death-related interactions with children is to provide them with books about death-related topics that they can read by themselves or along with an adult. An extensive body of this type of literature is now available that addresses a broad range of death-related topics and is designed for young readers of nearly all ages and reading abilities (Corr, 2000, 2001, 2002a). For example, a brief list, with selections limited to literature intended for preschool and elementary school readers, might include the following:

- Simple stories about animals or cartoon characters, such as *Aarvy Aardvark Finds Hope* (O'Toole 1988), *Badger's Parting Gifts* (Varley 1992), *The Fall of Freddie the Leaf* (Buscaglia 1982), *Lifetimes* (Mellonie and Ingpen 1983), *Liplap's Wish* (London 1994), *Thumpy's Story* (Dodge 1984), *Timothy Duck: The Story of the Death of a Friend* (Blackburn 1987), *Tough Boris* (Fox 1994), and *When Dinosaurs Die: A Guide to Understanding Death* (Brown and Brown 1996)

- Activity books, such as *Saying Goodbye* (Boulden 1989) and *When Someone Very Special Dies* (Heegaard 1988)

- Books in which children encounter the death of an animal, such as *The Accident* (Carrick 1976), *Charlotte's Web* (White 1952), *The Dead Bird* (Brown 1958), *I'll Always Love You* (Wilhelm 1985), *Mustard* (Graeber 1982), *The Tenth Good Thing About Barney* (Viorst 1971), and *When Violet Died* (Kantrowitz 1973)

- Books in which children encounter the death of a grandparent, such as *Animal Crackers* (Marshall 1998), *The Happy Funeral* (Bunting 1982), *My Grandpa Died Today* (Fassler 1971), *My Grandson Lew* (Zolotow 1974), *Nonna* (Bartoli 1975), and *Why Did Grandpa Die?* (Hazen 1995)

- Books in which children encounter the death of a parent, such as *Daddy's Chair* (Lanton 1991), *The Mother Tree* (Whitehead 1971), *Rachel and the Upside Down Heart* (Douglas 1990), and *The Rag Coat* (Mills 1991)

- Books in which children encounter the death of a sibling or peer, such as *Am I Still a Big Sister?* (Weir 1992), *Dusty Was My Friend* (Clardy 1984), *I Had a Friend Named Peter* (Cohn 1987), *Meggie's Magic* (Dean 1991), and *A Taste of Blackberries* (Smith 1973)

Among other titles for young readers are books with explicit religious or spiritual themes, such as *Annie and the Sand Dobbies* (Coburn 1964), *The Next Place* (Hanson 1997), *Psalm Twenty-Three* (Ladwig 1997), *Water Bugs and Dragonflies* (Stickney 1985), and *What's Heaven?* (Shriver 1999), as well as books that offer Native American perspectives, such as *Annie and the Old One* (Miles 1971), *Beyond the Ridge* (Goble 1993), and *The Great Change* (Horn 1992). Some of these books and other similar titles might well be used in formal or informal ways in various programs of religious instruction for children of different ages.

The Barklay and Eve Activity and Coloring Books Series (Carney 1997–2001) is a fine series of eight books in which two young dogs ask questions about and explore issues of loss and sadness associated with such topics as funerals, sitting shivah, cremation, hospice, organ donation, and pet loss. And *Dog Heaven* and *Cat Heaven* (Rylant 1995, 1997) describe the delights that these

animals might hope to find in their own special heavens. (Annotated descriptions and full bibliographic information about all of the books mentioned in Examples 1–3 as well as many other children's books can be found in Corr 2000, 2001, 2002a.)

Example 3: Teachable Moments

A third kind of informal death education can be seen in two additional children's books: *We Remember Philip* (Simon 1979) and *Rudi's Pond* (Bunting 1999). Each of these tells the story of children who have death-related experiences; the son of the children's grade school teacher dies in *We Remember Philip,* and a classmate of the children dies in *Rudi's Pond.* With the cooperation of their teacher and assistance from the school principal and other adults, the children in *We Remember Philip* share a scrapbook and memories of Mr. Hall's son and plant a tree as a class memorial. Similarly, while Rudi is ill, his special friend and their other classmates make a "Get Well Rudi" banner for his room at the hospital. After his death, their teacher helps them write poems about Rudi and staple them together to make a book. In addition, their school principal encourages them to make a more lasting memorial in the form of a pond under a big tree in the schoolyard. In these examples, life events enable young children to learn important lessons about death and loss while they also support those around them who are struggling with different death-related challenges.

Although both Examples 1 and 3 arise directly from life experiences and depict different forms of commemorative activities, they differ in that the cases in Example 3 involve the death of a human being (a classmate, a peer, a friend, or the relative of someone the children know well and look up to) rather than the death of a wild animal. Example 3 also puts before us "teachable moments," unplanned life events from which important lessons can be drawn (Carson 1984; DeSpelder and Strickland 1995). In these teachable moments, adults play important roles in helping to explain some of the events to children and in guiding some of the activities. We could mention many other teachable moments here as well, such as those immediately following the terrorist attacks on the World Trade Center and the Pentagon on September 11, 2001, with their accompanying widespread media coverage. All of these kinds of life events provide individuals with opportunities to learn important lessons about dying, death, and bereavement, especially from events in which some people serve as guides and mentors to others (and perhaps especially to children) in drawing out those lessons.

Example 4: Formal Death Education in Middle Schools and High Schools

Death-related instruction can now be found in various forms in many middle schools and high schools across the

United States (Stevenson and Stevenson 1996; Weeks and Johnson 1992). Sometimes this takes the form of units in courses on biology, literature, current affairs, contemporary moral issues, or other subjects. In many secondary schools, however, death education rises to the level of a full-scale course that may be taught in various departments, including religion departments in parochial schools. Typically, formal courses on death and dying involve textbooks, reading assignments, lectures, class discussions, assigned projects, tests, and grades. Depending on the school, the instructor, the goals of the course, and the population it serves, this type of course may be similar to a college course in its topical scope, or it may focus on issues of special relevance to adolescents, such as helping them to understand and preparing them to cope with losses related to the leading causes of death in their age group—motor vehicle accidents, teen suicide, homicide, and HIV/AIDS. Often, courses of this type are associated with bereavement support groups in schools. Such courses might also be linked to peer counseling programs as part of efforts to minimize the likelihood of human-induced deaths among students or to address the consequences of such deaths (Wass, Miller, and Thornton 1990).

Example 5: Death and Dying Courses at the College or University Level

Formal courses on death and dying are now well established at many colleges and universities in North America. They are even more likely to be found in such settings than in secondary schools. These courses typically cover subject areas such as those listed near the beginning of this chapter. The staffing of such courses often depends on the expressed interests of specific instructors. As a result, they may be taught in many departments and schools, such as psychology, philosophy, religious studies, sociology, health education, nursing, and social work. Depending on how the courses are offered, their audiences may include individuals who have had prior experiences with death-related losses, individuals who are currently involved with ongoing death-related experiences, individuals who plan to enter into or are currently involved in some relevant form of work that touches on some aspect of death and loss (such as nursing, social work, special education, or volunteering with a hospice program), individuals who may wish to prepare themselves to cope more effectively with some death-related situation in the future, or individuals who are simply curious about what the subject involves (and who perhaps wonder why a "death and dying" course is one of the most popular classes on campus, as it often it). As noted earlier, a number of leading textbooks are available for such courses (e.g., Corr et al. 2003; DeSpelder and Strickland 2002; Kastenbaum 2001; Leming and Dickinson 2002), as is literature about how they might be organized (e.g., Corr 1978).

Example 6: Other Forms of Death Education at the College or University Level

In addition to broad survey courses on death and dying at the college level, there are also many more specialized educational programs in this broad field. For example, the Kings College Centre for Education About Death and Bereavement at Kings College in London, Ontario, has many offerings available, as the center's Web site shows (http://www.deathed.ca). These include academic courses on bereavement and grief, palliative care, suicide, and spiritual, philosophical, and ethical issues in death and bereavement, as well as certificate offerings on crisis response, communication with the dying and bereaved, grief support groups, and creative responses to death and bereavement. The same Web site also provides information about many other death-related educational offerings at a long list of academic and other institutions in North America. For example, Hood College in Frederick, Maryland, offers a program in thanatology that includes a new master of arts degree, a certificate in thanatology, and a summer institute in this field, with courses such as "Developmental Perspectives in Thanatology," "Historical and Multicultural Perspectives in Thanatology," and "Mourning and Principles of Counseling the Bereaved." Through its Hospice Education Department, Madonna University in Livonia, Michigan, also offers a unique university-based hospice program, with degrees in hospice education at the associate, bachelor, and master's levels; concentrated course work in several cognate fields such as pastoral ministry, nursing, and education; and a master's-level certificate program in bereavement. Courses in death education may also be offered not just as part of specific degree, academic major, or certificate programs, but as part of graduate education curricula for members of such professions as nursing, medicine, social work, funeral service, the law, and the clergy.

One further example of this type of specialized death education is found in credit-bearing, college-level courses on children and death of the type now being offered at a number of institutions of higher education. At first glance, it might seem that death-related topics involving children and adolescents are not sufficiently robust to sustain full-term college courses, but in fact, such courses have available to them a broad range of subject matter. The areas such courses might explore include the historical-cultural situation of children and adolescents in our society in relationship to matters involving dying, death, and bereavement; the formation of death-related thoughts and attitudes during childhood and adolescence; strategies, tactics, and resources for death-related education and counseling for children and adolescents; child and parental bereavement; how bereaved children, siblings, peers, and adult family members can be helped by support groups and individual interventions; understanding and helping seriously ill and dying children, as well as their family members and caregivers; and special issues that are unique to adolescents in coping with death, such as adolescent suicide and becoming a bereaved parent during adolescence. Once again, there are text resources for such courses (e.g., Adams and Deveau 1995; Corr and Balk 1996; Corr and Corr 1996) as well as literature describing how they might be organized (Corr 1984b, 1992, 2002b).

Example 7: Death Education for Adults Outside Colleges and Universities

Adult education in the field of dying, death, and bereavement takes many forms. Among the most familiar of these programs are the following:

- Continuing education courses, workshops, and conferences for professionals whose work is likely to involve interactions with dying or bereaved persons, such as nurses, physicians, social workers, funeral directors, lawyers, and members of the clergy

- Clinical pastoral education designed for ordained pastors and chaplains and typically offered in health care institutions

- A wide variety of educational offerings sponsored by hospice programs, either for their own professional and volunteer lay staff members or for the communities they serve

- Programs designed to build skills or enhance teamwork in postvention after a large-scale disaster or traumatic loss (such as that experienced in connection with the September 11, 2001, terrorist attacks)

Two specific examples of community-based death-related education are evident in Widow-to-Widow programs and the Stephen Ministries. Widow-to-Widow programs began in the Boston area with a focus on a public health (as opposed to an illness or mental health) perspective, the key idea of bereavement as transition, and confidence in the value of "mutual help" offered by those who have been previously bereaved (Silverman 1986). This type of program is perhaps now best known through the Widowed Persons Service of the AARP (information on this service is available from AARP Grief and Loss Programs, 601 E Street, NW, Washington, DC 20049; telephone [800] 424-3410 or [202] 434-2260; Web site http://www.aarp.org). The Stephen Ministries organization is a Christian, transdenominational ministry that provides leadership training through 7-day courses, print and other resources, and ongoing support for Stephen Leaders in enrolled congregations and other organizations. In turn, Stephen Leaders prepare members of their organizations to be Stephen Ministers who will provide direct, one-to-one care to troubled individuals who are coping with issues concerning dying, death, or bereavement. (More information is available from Stephen Ministries, 2045 Innerbelt Business Center Drive, St. Louis, MO 63114-57765; telephone [314] 428-2600; Web site http://www.christcare. com.)

As these examples show, death education programs for adults are diverse, and each takes its own particular form. The audiences to which programs are addressed shape them in important ways, as do the particular subjects they emphasize, the goals they are intended to serve, and the instructional resources on which they draw. This can be seen clearly in statements of assumptions and principles about death-related education, such as the separate statements published by the International Work Group on Death, Dying, and Bereavement (1991a, 1991b) for professionals in health care and human services and for volunteers and nonprofessionals. Still, all forms of adult education in the field of dying, death, and bereavement—including special programs on public television presented by Bill Moyers and others—are linked together by a shared concern about the losses and the challenges associated with death and by a desire to improve interventions to aid those who encounter such losses and challenges.

DIMENSIONS OF DEATH EDUCATION

As the seven examples presented above illustrate, death-related education may be conducted in many different settings and many different ways. What these examples all have in common is the emphasis they place on one or more of the four central *dimensions* of death education: what people know, how they feel, how they behave, and what they value (Corr 1995). These are the cognitive, affective, behavioral, and valuational dimensions of death education—distinguishable but interrelated aspects of this educational process.

Death education is most obviously a *cognitive* or intellectual enterprise because it provides factual information about death-related experiences and tries to help individuals to understand or interpret those events. For example, we all know that how we live can put us at risk for death, but we may not realize that *nearly half of all deaths in the United States arise from or are associated with behaviors*, such as the use of tobacco (cigarettes, cigars, or chewing tobacco), diet and activity patterns, and the use of alcohol, firearms, illegal drugs, and motor vehicles (McGinnis and Foege 1993).

In addition to providing information, the cognitive dimension of death education can also suggest new ways of organizing or interpreting the data of human experience. A good example of this kind of cognitive reorganization took place during the early 1980s, when some physicians recognized that they were being confronted with a relatively rare form of skin cancer (Kaposi's sarcoma, which had previously been confined largely to a specific group of elderly males) in an unusually high number of young adult men. This helped to identify a new disease and cause of death, AIDS and HIV.

The *affective* dimension of death education has to do with feelings, emotions, and attitudes about dying, death, and bereavement. For example, a wide range of feelings are involved in experiences of loss and bereavement. Consequently, it is appropriate for education in this area to try to sensitize those who are not bereaved to the depth, intensity, duration, and complexities of grief following a death. To date, awareness of the complex nature of grief has not been communicated effectively to the public at large. As a result, many people still seem to think—erroneously—that a few days or weeks should be a more than adequate period for a bereaved person to "forget" or "get over" the death of an important person in his or her life. In fact, mourning a significant death is far more like an ongoing process of learning to live with a great loss than it is like solving a problem once and for all. Sharing and discussing grief responses is an important part of the affective dimension of education in the field of dying, death, and bereavement.

In another aspect of its affective dimension, death education seeks to appreciate the feelings that are expressed in interactions between those who have and those who have not yet encountered death in any personal form. For example, many bereaved persons have told us that when someone who is not bereaved says to them, "I know how you feel," the claim seems insensitive and arrogant. How could someone who has not experienced their loss possibly know how they feel? To the bereaved, such statements (however well intentioned they may be) seem to diminish the uniqueness and poignancy of their loss. When those who have not encountered death in any personal form have such perceptions pointed out to them, they can come to appreciate more fully both their own feelings and the feelings of those who are bereaved.

Death education also has a *behavioral* dimension, as it explores why people act as they do in death-related situations, which of their behaviors are helpful or unhelpful, and how they could or should act in such situations. For example, contemporary Americans tend to try to avoid contact with situations involving dying, death, and bereavement, both in public and in private. Often, this is because they do not know what to say or what to do in such situations. Frequently, they pull back from contact with the dying or the bereaved, leaving people alone in very stressful circumstances, without support or companionship at a time when they may be in greatest need of sharing and solace.

By contrast, the modern hospice movement has shown that much can be done to help those who are coping with dying. Similarly, research on funeral rituals and on support groups for the bereaved has shown ways in which individuals and society can assist those who are coping with bereavement. This behavioral education points out the great value that is found simply in the *presence* of a caring person. It advises potential helpers not so much to talk to grieving persons as to *listen* to them. It can help individuals develop skills in interacting with persons who are experiencing or who have experienced a significant loss. One basic behavioral lesson from death education is this: "Be comfortable with your uncomfortableness" when you are in the presence of someone confronting a death-related challenge. It may be sufficient just to be present, sit quietly, and do nothing else when that is really all there is to do.

The *valuational* dimension of death education has to do with how it can help to identify, articulate, and affirm the basic values that govern human lives. Life as we know it is inextricably bound up with death. We would not have *this life* if death were not one of its essential parts. Life and death, living and dying, attachments and losses, happiness and sadness—neither alternative in these and many other similar pairings stands alone in human experience. Death provides an essential (and inescapable) perspective from which humans can try to achieve an adequate understanding of their own lives.

Much of what we have already said directs attention to that which is valued: courage, endurance, resilience, concern for others, love, and community. Such values often come sharply into focus when adults are asked what they will tell their children about death and how they will respond to the moral problems of our time. Most bereavement experts recommend that adults not attempt to hide death from children; adults should not portray life as an unending journey without shadows or tears. Hiding death from children, even if we really could do that, will not prepare them to cope effectively with future losses, a pervasive aspect of the human experience. Death education encourages adults to introduce children to the realities of life and death in ways that are appropriate to their developmental levels and capacities. Death education also nurtures and supports mature values that will enable children to live wisely and cope with death constructively.

Reflecting on values is also closely related to many of the death-related challenges that confront us at the beginning of the 21st century: the threat of nuclear warfare and terrorism, epidemics and their prevention, famine and malnutrition, dislocation of populations, capital punishment, abortion, assisted suicide, euthanasia, and all of the quandaries posed by modern medicine and its complex technologies.

GOALS OF DEATH EDUCATION

When education is well planned, the educator always has in mind some general goals and specific objectives that he or she hopes to accomplish for and with those who are engaged in the activity. For example, college courses are commonly designed to encourage critical thinking in order to help individuals learn to judge for themselves the value, meaning, and validity of subjects they address. Education about dying, death, and bereavement incorporates these broad aims and typically links them to more limited purposes (Corr 1995).

We were challenged to think about our own goals shortly after we first began teaching a course on death and dying. With no advance notice, we received the following letter from a person who had not been in our course and whom we did not know:

October 16, 1975

Dear Dr. Corr,

   Want to thank you for your course "Death and Dying."
      Not having been in your classroom, you might wonder what prompts me to write this letter.
      My mother was one of the most dedicated Christians we in our lives have ever known.
      She became very ill and it took 54 days, in and out of an Intensive Care Unit, for her to die.
      Doc and I spent as much time as humanly possible at her side.
      One day she looked at me with her beautiful soft brown eyes and said, "Why didn't anyone teach me how to die? We are taught at our mother's knee how to live but not how to die."
      Hope your course will help people through this experience because we will all have a turn unless the Rapture comes first.

God bless you,
Dr. and Mrs. S. Koerner

We appreciated Mrs. Koerner's kind words about our course, but we were also a bit perplexed: How should we evaluate her comments? Should we really take credit for teaching people how to die, as Mrs. Koerner seemed to think we were doing? That challenged us to say exactly what it was that we sought to accomplish in our courses. As we return to this issue from time to time, we now think there are several basic goals in this type of education:

Above all, education about dying, death, and bereavement seeks *to enrich the personal lives* of those to whom it is directed. In the end, as the ancient Greek philosopher Socrates is reported to have said, "the really important thing is not to live, but to live well" (Plato 1948, *Crito:*48b). Death education contributes to this goal by helping individuals to understand themselves more fully and to appreciate both their strengths and their limitations as finite human beings.

A second goal of death education is *to inform and guide individuals in their personal transactions with society.* It does this by making them aware of services that are available to them and options that they might or might not select in such matters as end-of-life care, funeral practices, and memorial rituals.

A third goal of death education is *to prepare individuals for their public roles as citizens.* It does this by clarifying some important social issues that face society and its representatives, such as advance directives in health care, assisted suicide, euthanasia, and organ and tissue donation.

A fourth goal of death education is *to support individuals in their professional and vocational roles.* Those whose work involves teaching young people about death, caring for the dying, or counseling the bereaved can benefit from the perspectives offered by a well-grounded death education.

A fifth goal of death education is *to enhance the ability of individuals to communicate effectively about death-related matters.* Effective communication is essential when one is addressing death-related topics, which may be challenging for many people (Strickland and DeSpelder 1995). Principles that can guide effective communication are at the heart of education about dying, death, and bereavement.

A sixth goal of death education is *to assist individuals in appreciating how development across the human life course interacts with death-related issues.* Children and adolescents, as well as young, middle-aged, and older adults, face issues that are dissimilar in many ways, and they are likely to differ in the ways in which they confront and cope with dying, death, and bereavement.

WHO MIGHT BE INTERESTED IN DEATH-RELATED EDUCATION?

There once was a time when those who were teaching or otherwise taking part in courses on death and dying repeatedly heard from others that such courses must be "morbid." But that is not at all true if the word *morbid* is meant to suggest an experience that is gloomy, dark, melancholy, gruesome, sinister, macabre, or even perverse. In actual fact, the root meaning of the word *morbid* is "unhealthy," whereas death-related education is vital and healthy; it is sometimes sad, but often cheerful. As we used to say, "At our university, courses on death and dying are alive and well!"

People do not seek out education about dying, death, and bereavement in order to become depressed. Their personal interests correspond roughly to the goals that we have just identified for death-related education. For example, some have personal concerns that they wish to address. Like the children described earlier in Examples 1 and 3 who encountered a dead bird, a dying classmate, and a bereaved teacher, many become interested in death-related education because they are seeking help and guidance in coping with personal experiences. Death-related education is not counseling, but it can and should be sensitive to the concerns of those who seek such education. Education in this field can provide information about death-related experiences, point the way to resources that might be useful, and provide a supportive environment in which individuals can work through their issues, whether those issues arise from events in the past or events that are current and ongoing.

Some people come to death-related education because they hope to prepare themselves to be effective in future involvements, either personal or vocational. Those who observe the aging of a beloved grandparent or who anticipate the decline of a significant other who is currently in the early stages of a degenerative disease often want to try to ready themselves for the death-related challenges they may face in the future. Similarly, those who are entering or who are already engaged in a relevant form of work, such as nursing, medicine, social work, funeral service, the ministry, the law, or volunteer service, often seek to develop or improve their skills for helping others.

Some proactive individuals are simply curious about the implications of dying, death, and bereavement and want to understand more fully what these realities mean for their own lives or for the lives of those around them, such as their children. These individuals appreciate how privileged we are to live in a society and at a time when death rates are lower than they have ever been in human history and average life expectancies are higher than ever before. Such people appreciate that although we have many advantages, we also have some responsibilities to live this life that is now ours with honesty and integrity. They know that attempting to push death out of the mainstream of life serves only to falsify the basic premises on which we live. We should not and need not become preoccupied with death, but we can attend to it in a proportionate way as one of the central dimensions of life. And we can do that with the assistance of death-related education.

WHO MIGHT BECOME A DEATH EDUCATOR?

The short answer to this question is: anyone. That is, anyone who becomes involved in any of the many types of educational activities related to dying, death, and bereavement—those we have noted in this chapter as well as others too numerous to mention here—might be thought of as a death educator. If we think of this type of education in a more formal way, however, a death educator is a person who has undertaken to prepare in specific ways for this role and who actually conducts informal or formal programs of death-related education. Such a person might be a member of one of the many academic and professional fields we have mentioned, but it has been our experience over many years that individual interests (frequently, but not always, interests precipitated by personal encounters with significant death-related losses), more than general academic or professional background, are most often the biggest factor leading individuals to engage in this type of education.

One prepares to conduct death-related education by (a) acquiring knowledge about various topics in this field; (b) exploring one's own death-related attitudes; (c) developing effective communication skills, which include the ability to listen actively and respond constructively to the real needs of those who come to take part in this educational process; and (d) being willing to work cooperatively with other individuals, groups, and societal entities toward achieving the goals of death education (Corr 1984a). It is particularly important for those who wish to

engage in death-related education to be aware of their own attitudes toward these subjects (insofar as that is possible), to try to recognize their own limitations, and to be prepared to offer support to individuals who may be struggling with personal death-related challenges or refer them for specialized professional assistance when that becomes appropriate or necessary (Attig 1992; Mahon, Goldberg, and Washington 1999). In this, educators need to realize that subjects related to death are not just objective topics that can be addressed in a distanced and depersonalized manner, as Kastenbaum (1977) has pointed out in an article with the ironic title "We Covered Death Today."

The following are three useful sources from which individuals can obtain guidance and assistance related to education about dying, death, and bereavement:

- Association for Death Education and Counseling, 342 North Main Street, West Hartford, CT 06117-2507; telephone (860) 586-7503; fax (860) 586-7550; fax on demand (860) 586-7533; Web site http://www.adec.org; e-mail info@adec.org

- Center for Death Education and Bioethics, Soc/Arc Department, 435NH, University of Wisconsin, LaCrosse, WI 54601; telephone (608) 785-6781; fax (608) 785-8486; e-mail CDEB@uwlax.edu

- Kings College Centre for Education About Death and Bereavement, 266 Epworth Avenue, London, ON, Canada N6A 2M3; telephone (519) 432-3491; fax (519) 432-0200; Web site http://www.deathed.ca; e-mail jmorgan@julian.uwo.ca

DEATH-RELATED EDUCATION AND LESSONS ABOUT LIFE AND LIVING

The most fundamental thing that one learns from education about dying, death, and bereavement is that in many ways it is really education about life and living (International Work Group on Death, Dying, and Bereavement 1992). As the list of topics we provide at the beginning of this chapter makes obvious, this form of education is about living people who are encountering death in various ways (for example, in the form of a life-limiting or life-threatening disease); experiencing or exploring various death-related attitudes; coping with dying or with loss, grief, and mourning; organizing and attending funerals or memorial services; helping children or adolescents cope with death; contemplating suicide or being affected by someone else who attempts or completes a suicide; debating the morality of assisted suicide and euthanasia; filling out advance directives; making decisions about becoming living organ donors or donating the organs and tissues of loved ones who have died; disposing of the property of someone who has died; examining religious or philosophical beliefs about death; or exploring the meaning of near-death experiences.

Many who teach about or study issues related to dying, death, and bereavement have identified for themselves some of the lessons about life and living that have emerged from that work. For example, the ways in which life and death, living and dying, are inexorably intertwined quickly reveals that humans are finite, limited beings. This has many implications for how we live, because it teaches us that although there are many things in life that we can control, there are many others that we cannot (even though we may sometimes be able to influence their outcomes). Death-related education reveals some specific things we can *control* even as it shows us many of the *limitations* that make our control less than complete.

Also, as we study death-related topics we recognize that in the end it is always an individual person who must deal with these particularized experiences: No one else can die our death or experience our grief. In this sense, death is always marked out by its unique individuality. But studying dying, death, and bereavement also teaches us that being human means being involved in community and being inescapably linked to other persons. We turn to others for assistance when we are dying or bereaved, and our deaths have impacts on those with whom we have formed attachments. Thus we learn that life and death involve both *individuals* and *communities*.

Again, although we often act as if we were invulnerable and might want to believe that we are, life and death both make our vulnerability to pain and suffering all too obvious. Still, we also learn from our studies of dying, death, and bereavement that this vulnerability is not the same as helplessness. We come to realize that most human beings have powerful coping capacities and are amazingly resilient. In fact, some persons respond to death-related challenges in ways that are ennobling and even awesome. Thus human beings find themselves endowed with both *vulnerability* and *resilience*.

Beyond this, our studies of death-related topics reveal the importance of quality in living and the human search for meaning. One man who was facing his own imminent death founded an organization called Make Today Count (Kelly 1975). In doing this, he implicitly recommended that we all should try to "make today count" for ourselves by striving to maximize the quality of our own lives right now and by appreciating that even though life is transient it can be meaningful and good. In addition, our studies show us that when death challenges the value of life, humans work hard to find sources of inspiration and religious or philosophical frameworks within which enduring meaning can be established. So *quality in living* and the *search for meaning* are significant issues for those who are coping with death as well as for those who are simply living their day-to-day lives.

Sometimes, we find these (and other) lessons about life and living to be evident throughout our programs in death-related education. At other times they are less obvious, lying just below the surface of our studies, but they are always there when we look closely at what we are doing. Those who are involved in death-related education can enrich their studies by bringing to light lessons like these about life and living.

As they look back on a course on death and dying, college students often say things like, "The class materials were about death and dying, yet I believe they are necessary instruction for 'life and living'" or "It is only when one is able to face the certainty of death that one can truly live." We agree, and that is why we gave to our textbook in this field the title *Death and Dying, Life and Living* (Corr et al. 2003) and why we have been especially impressed by the following quotations, one from the former president of France and the other from a Canadian medical sociologist:

> Never perhaps has our relationship with death been so poor as in these times of spiritual barrenness, where human beings, in their haste to exist, seem to sidestep the mystery. They do not realize that in so doing they rob the love of life of an essential source. (Mitterand 1995:9)

> Death is no enemy of life; it restores our sense of the value of living. Illness restores the sense of proportion that is lost when we take life for granted. To learn about value and proportion, we need to honor illness, and ultimately to honor death. (Frank 1991:120)

REFERENCES

Adams, David W. and Eleanor J. Deveau, eds. 1995. *Beyond the Innocence of Childhood*, 3 vols. Amityville, NY: Baywood.

Attig, Thomas. 1992. "Person-Centered Death Education." *Death Studies* 16:357–70.

Carson, Ute. 1984. "Teachable Moments Occasioned by 'Small Deaths.'" Pp. 315–43 in *Childhood and Death*, edited by Hannelore Wass and Charles A. Corr. Washington, DC: Hemisphere.

Corr, Charles A. 1978. "A Model Syllabus for Death and Dying Courses." *Death Education* 1:433–57.

———. 1984a. "Helping With Death Education." Pp. 49–73 in *Helping Children Cope With Death: Guidelines and Resources,* 2d ed., edited by Hannelore Wass and Charles A. Corr. Washington, DC: Hemisphere.

———. 1984b. "A Model Syllabus for Children and Death Courses." *Death Education* 8:11–28.

———. 1992. "Teaching a College Course on Children and Death: A 13-Year Report." *Death Studies* 16:343–56.

———. 1995. "Death Education for Adults." Pp. 351–65 in *A Challenge for Living: Dying, Death, and Bereavement,* edited by Inge B. Corless, Barbara B. Germino, and Mary A. Pittman. Boston: Jones & Bartlett.

———. 2000. "Using Books to Help Children and Adolescents Cope With Death: Guidelines and Bibliography." Pp. 295–314 in *Living With Grief: Children, Adolescents, and Loss,* edited by Kenneth J. Doka. Washington, DC: Hospice Foundation of America.

———. 2001. "Death-Related Literature for Children and Adolescents: Selected, Annotated, and With Guidelines and

Resources for Adults." Pp. 378–401 in *Hospice Care for Children,* 2d ed., edited by Anne Armstrong-Dailey and Sarah Zarbock. New York: Oxford University Press.

Corr, Charles A. 2002a. "An Annotated Bibliography of Death-Related Books for Children and Adolescents." *Literature and Medicine* 21:147–74.

———. 2002b. "Teaching a College Course on Children and Death for 22 Years: A Supplemental Report." *Death Studies* 26:1–12.

Corr, Charles A. and David E. Balk, eds. 1996. *Handbook of Adolescent Death and Bereavement.* New York: Springer.

Corr, Charles A. and Donna M. Corr, eds. 1996. *Handbook of Childhood Death and Bereavement.* New York: Springer.

Corr, Charles A., Clyde M. Nabe, and Donna M. Corr. 2003. *Death and Dying, Life and Living,* 4th ed. Belmont, CA: Wadsworth.

DeSpelder, Lynne Ann and Albert Lee Strickland. 1995. "Using Life Experiences as a Way of Helping Children Understand Death." Pp. 43–54 in *Beyond the Innocence of Childhood,* vol. 1, edited by David W. Adams and Eleanor J. Deveau. Amityville, NY: Baywood.

———. 2002. *The Last Dance: Encountering Death and Dying,* 6th ed. New York: McGraw-Hill.

Frank, Arthur W. 1991. *At the Will of the Body: Reflections on Illness.* Boston: Houghton Mifflin.

Grollman, Earl A. 1990. *Talking About Death: A Dialogue Between Parent and Child.* Boston: Beacon.

International Work Group on Death, Dying, and Bereavement. 1991a. "A Statement of Assumptions and Principles Concerning Education About Death, Dying, and Bereavement for Professionals in Health Care and Human Services." *Omega* 23:235–39.

———. 1991b. "A Statement of Assumptions and Principles Concerning Education About Life-Threatening Illness, Death, Dying, and Bereavement for Volunteers and Non-Professionals." *American Journal of Hospice and Palliative Care* 7(2):26–27.

———. 1992. "A Statement of Assumptions and Principles Concerning Education About Death, Dying, and Bereavement." *Death Studies* 16:59–65.

Kastenbaum, Robert J. 1977. "We Covered Death Today." *Death Education* 1:85–92.

———. 2001. *Death, Society, and Human Experience,* 7th ed. Boston: Allyn & Bacon.

Kelly, Orville. 1975. *Make Today Count.* New York: Delacorte.

Leming, Michael R. and George E. Dickinson. 2002. *Understanding Dying, Death, and Bereavement,* 5th ed. Fort Worth, TX: Harcourt.

Mahon, Margaret M., Rachel L. Goldberg, and Sarah K. Washington. 1999. "Discussing Death in the Classroom: Beliefs and Experiences of Educators and Education Students." *Omega* 39:99–121.

McGinnis, J. Michael and William H. Foege. 1993. "Actual Causes of Death in the United States." *Journal of the American Medical Association* 270:2207–12.

Mitterand, François. 1995. "Preface." Pp. 9–12 in Marie de Hennezel, *La Mort intime: Ceux qui vont mourir nous apprennent à vivre.* Paris: Éditions Robert Laffont.

Pine, Vanderlyn R. 1977. "A Socio-Historical Portrait of Death Education." *Death Education* 1:57–84.

———. 1986. "The Age of Maturity for Death Education: A Socio-Historical Portrait of the Era 1976–1985." *Death Studies* 10:209–31.

Plato. 1948. *Euthyphro, Apology, Crito,* translated by F. J. Church. New York: Macmillan.

Silverman, Phyllis R. 1986. *Widow-to-Widow.* New York: Springer.

Stevenson, Robert G. and Eileen P. Stevenson. 1996. *Teaching Students About Death: A Comprehensive Resource for Educators and Parents.* Philadelphia: Charles.

Strickland, Albert Lee and Lynne Ann DeSpelder. 1995. "Communicating About Death and Dying." Pp. 37–51 in *A Challenge for Living: Dying, Death, and Bereavement,* edited by Inge B. Corless, Barbara B. Germino, and Mary A. Pittman. Boston: Jones & Bartlett.

Wass, Hannelore, M. David Miller, and Gordon Thornton. 1990. "Death Education and Grief/Suicide Intervention in the Pubic Schools." *Death Studies* 14:253–68.

Weeks, Dwayne and Catherine Johnson. 1992. "A Second Decade of High School Death Education." *Death Studies* 16:269–79.

THE POSTSELF IN SOCIAL CONTEXT

JACK KAMERMAN

For ordinary mortals, constructing a posthumous reputation is lonely work. We hope that our families and friends will remember us as we wish them to remember us, and we take steps to cultivate those memories. It is only under special societal circumstances that the mechanisms for producing posthumous reputations are institutionalized. For example, it is only in particular occupations under particular cultural and historical conditions that societies generate roles and institutions through which our reputations survive us.

Edwin Shneidman's (1973) notion of the postself is a psychologistic idea that captures the human concern for how others will see us and continue to be touched by us after we are dead. He wrote, "The postself relates to the concerns of living individuals with their own reputation, impact, influence after death—those personal aspects that still live when the person does not" (p. 45). In this formulation, the postself is the product of an individual's thoughts about how others will remember him or her and, in some cases, an individual's efforts to cultivate those images. In addition, Shneidman (1980:105–10) used the postself as a therapeutic tool in helping dying patients work through their relationships with those in their immediate circle.

From a sociological view, even these individual efforts are to at least some extent socially grounded. In a more obvious way, societies institutionalize in certain occupational roles the mechanisms through which reputations survive the lives of individuals. This usually takes place when such an "investment" has commercial potential, when it serves the interests of people with power, and when it is consonant with already existing cultural knowledge and values. Statuses and roles survive individual incumbents, and organizations survive the people who populate them. On an even larger scale, particular societies in particular periods generate the roles, the types of organizations, and the underlying cultural values and assumptions that make the survival of reputations more or less likely.

The major focus of this chapter is the rootedness of the postself in the social, cultural, and historical contexts in which it is inevitably embedded. This focus is organized on the three levels of analysis just suggested—the individual, the occupational, and the societal, with the latter two receiving greater attention (Kamerman 1998:5–11). Although these three levels are interrelated, and some concepts straddle more than one level, separating them still makes analytic sense.

The sociologically relevant literature on the postself is demarcated by three conceptual benchmarks: Edwin Shneidman's (1973) delineation of the concept of the postself, Raymond Schmitt and Wilbert Leonard's (1986) discussion of the postself as it is tied to occupational roles, and Gary Alan Fine's (2001) analyses of the societal apparatus through which the posthumous reputations of public figures are formed and reformed. Because the literature that focuses specifically on the social grounding of the postself is limited, this review will be supplemented by suggestions about the directions in which this analysis might be taken.

THE POSTSELF AS AN INDIVIDUAL ACCOMPLISHMENT

Shneidman's concept of the postself came out of his work with the dying. It is centered in the individual and is future oriented. It is also exemplified by the projections of all persons who think about how others will remember them after they die. In death-denying societies such as the United States, "prematurely" musing about one's own death and its consequences is often considered morbid. In fact, in societies whose cultures make a confrontation with death problematic, even the dying are discouraged from speaking with friends and family about death, and so, in effect, are hindered in their attempts to negotiate their postselves.

In Shneidman's view, the postself is future oriented. It is constituted by how individuals want particular people in their immediate circles to remember them as well as by whatever steps those individuals take to cultivate that remembrance in those people. A therapist may use this final investment in how others see us to help dying patients work through present difficulties in relationships with those close to them.

Even though the focus of Shneidman's concept is on the individual and those in the individual's immediate circle, people of course operate in social environments. Consequently, the terms and rules of constructing the postself and, to an extent, even the likelihood of a person's worrying about being remembered are influenced by social forces. In the last half of the 20th century, the preoccupation of Americans with their own self-interest, what sociologists term the value of self-fulfillment (Henslin 2001:53), combined with the decline in the certainty of some form of survival after death guaranteed by religion to create the conditions that made the postself a much more important project for the individual. As Fred Davis (1979) observed in relation to nostalgia, "Nostalgia [in the 1970s] became, in short, the means for holding on to and reaffirming identities which had been badly bruised by the turmoil of the times" (p. 107). If that was true in the 1970s, consider the United States after September 11, 2001—how the victims of the collapse of the World Trade Center should be remembered has become a daily news story, death is an everyday conversational subject, and self-fulfillment flourishes on a grander scale than ever. These factors should make us hang on to life more tenaciously than ever, and consequently should make warding off the disappearance of our selves more important and more problematic than ever before.

In this social environment, where, in addition, as some sociologists have suggested, work is central to the way we see ourselves (Kearl 1989:247–48), the logical extension of the attention social scientists have paid to work should also have included a focus on the postself. Yet with the exception of Schmitt and Leonard 1986 article, and not much beyond that apart from Kearl, the extent to which our views of our posthumous reputations are tied to our occupational roles has not been exploited by sociologists nearly as much as it deserves to be.

THE POSTSELF AND OCCUPATIONAL ROLES

Schmitt and Leonard (1986:1093) point out that the postself may be seen both as the personal, idiosyncratic musings of individuals about how they will be remembered by friends and family and as the product of how the public wishes to remember the incumbents of particular occupational roles (in the case of their research, sports figures). Schmitt and Leonard acknowledge that they might have studied other occupations, but they chose to focus on professional sports because this social world most clearly possesses the four social conditions that promote the construction of the postself: the opportunity for role-support, engrossment through participation and communication, comparison through

records, and recognition through awards and commemorative devices.

Role-support, most simply, is the support expressed by fans and by their publicists, the media. The media and the world of nonprofessional sports are also the mechanisms through which fans become involved, or engrossed, in the careers of figures in professional sports. In professional sports, records are carefully kept. As Schmitt and Leonard (1986) note, "The competitive world of sport facilitates *the comparison of sport acts through its emphasis on measurement and records*" (p. 1095). This feature is enhanced by such relatively recent technological developments as the instant replay. In effect, an individual can compete across time and space as was the striking case of the magazine that attempted to decide the greatest heavyweight boxing champion of all time by having great boxers' cyberselves compete in virtual matches. Finally, the sports world is particularly adept at commemorating the achievements of its heroes with awards, trophies, monuments, and membership in those occupational pantheons, halls of fame. After all, as Schmitt and Leonard suggest, "the postself requires that *one's acts be recognized and remembered*" (p. 1096). This is certainly true for public figures in occupational worlds.

The positing of necessary conditions for occupationally grounded postselves provides a framework into which other occupations may fit. Occupations in the creative arts can also be analyzed in this way. For example, a number of researchers have attempted to analyze the reputations of classical composers (Simonton 1997) and performers (Holcman 2000:5–13). For sociologists, the most important work on the posthumous reputations of composers was done by John Mueller (1951:182–252) and Kate Hevner Mueller (1973), who studied with considerable quantitative precision the reputations of classical composers as reflected in the programs of major American symphony orchestras. The Muellers' formula, in its final version, defines the representation of a composer in the programs of an orchestra in a given season as the ratio of the number of minutes devoted to the works of that particular composer to the total number of minutes for all works played in that season. In the language of our times, reputations are defined quantitatively in classical music in the same way records are kept in sports, although, admittedly, both the Muellers' work and the reputations of most classical composers have less currency than do the reputations of figures in sports. In any case, this is a long way from the more personal actions of Johannes Brahms, among several other composers, who destroyed a number of his early works so that posterity would not take them into account in its calculations. The reputations of artists are measured in the society at large (and probably among artists themselves to a greater extent than they would be willing to admit) by the monetary value of the sale of their works at exhibitions and auctions. The reputations of authors are measured by the sales of their books, and their position and longevity on the lists of best-sellers published by the *New York Times* constitute a sort of record book. More than one author checks the Web site of the most popular on-line bookseller, which lists the position of each book in relation to other books in the Web site's sales, to find out how he or she is doing in the marketplace.

In relation to the postself, occupations in the performing arts come even closer than composing to occupations in sports. For symphony conductors, members of an occupation with relatively few practitioners and with an almost inevitable emphasis on individual achievement, their recorded legacies become tangible repositories of their postselves. When a conductor dies, music reviewers in fact describe the conductor's last recording of a work as the way in which he or she wanted to be remembered. In addition, of course, to crasser motives, the Austrian conductor Herbert von Karajan tried to manage his posthumous reputation by rerecording as many major symphonic works as he could before he died, so that these final interpretive statements would reflect the way he wanted to be remembered by his public. The recording industry gauges these reputations, both before and after conductors' deaths, by the sales of compact discs and the industry awards particular recordings garner.

After a conductor's death, the issuance of memorial albums and the retention of already issued albums in the catalog become the currency of reputations. In an interesting variation, the publicity agents of the actor Rudolph Valentino, who died leaving not-yet-released films behind, hired actresses to wail on cue outside the funeral home where his body lay in order to keep up interest in the upcoming release of his films.

The cultivation of a postself related to a social role is a specific example of the negotiation of identity that takes place throughout an individual's life. In addition to being tied to occupational roles, the cultivation of the postself may be tied to family roles. For example, in a study of the survivors of police officers who committed suicide in New York City between 1934 and 1940, I found that the families of Roman Catholic officers negotiated more acceptable versions of the cause of death so that the officers could be buried in Catholic cemeteries and so that the cause of death was masked within the family, or at least cast in a less unacceptable light (Kamerman 1993). Of course, occupational and family roles may be linked, such as when the survivors of soldiers who have been disgraced or whose heroism in combat went unacknowledged during their lifetimes try to salvage the soldiers' reputations by securing for them posthumous pardons or medals, respectively.

The social dimension of the postself is made clear when it is linked to the occupational roles and occupational subcultures to which it is tied. Studies such as the Muellers' may exist in the world of the sociological study of music, and not directly in the lives or worlds of musicians, but they do point to the importance of reputations to a society and to the institutionalized mechanisms, such as record

books, through which these reputations are formulated. They are taken into account as practitioners of those occupations contemplate their place in history. To be a professional baseball player, for example, is to know that, because records are so carefully kept, any records one sets might stand or be broken. The institutionalization and quantification of reputations takes the decision about our postselves, to at least some extent, out of our hands. In short, postself roles are impersonal structures with very personal consequences.

These examples also highlight the extent to which quantification has become the language used to define the postself and the fact that the postself in these occupations is increasingly managed by professionals for commercial purposes. Just as these negotiations of identity that the postself represents should be seen in relation to these occupations and occupational subcultures, these occupations and occupational subcultures in turn should be seen in the societal and historical contexts in which they are embedded.

POSTHUMOUS REPUTATIONS AND SOCIETY

Although in the strictest sense, the postself is the image we construct for ourselves and posthumous reputations are constructed by others, in reality the distinction is harder to draw. As individuals, we may enlist others in formulating the images we wish to be remembered by and turn over to them the task of steering those images after we die. In any case, after we die, control of those images is in the hands of our family and friends (Stone 1988). In the case of public figures, the situation is even cloudier. The professionals who manage the images of public figures in life usually continue to manage their images in death. In some cases, libraries and archives may be used to put together papers or possessions in a way that builds the images we have chosen. Just as often, such organizations include or excise documents based on whether or not they promote a public image for a given individual that resonates with the organizational image and serves the organization's goals.

In an important series of studies, Gary Alan Fine (2001; see also Bromberg and Fine 2002) carefully studied the production of difficult, in the sense of stigmatized or "tarnished," reputations of public figures in the arts and in politics. Although Fine's work seemingly focuses on individuals, these persons are more accurately seen as public figures whose significance tells as much about the values and institutions of a society as it does about their biographies. In addition, although Fine studies reputations in disrepair, most of his findings seem applicable to the reputations of all public figures.

Fine (2001:7–8) delineates three models that are used to evaluate historical figures: the objective, the functional, and the constructed. The objective model assumes that reputations are based on what people have actually done.

The functional model assumes that reputations are formed "in response to the functional needs of society" (p. 8). The constructed model holds that although reputations may be influenced by the objective reality and by the functional needs of society, they are "a result of the socio-political motives of groups that gain resources, power, or prestige by the establishment of reputations" (p. 8). These partial explanations must be taken together to explain how reputations are formed. For Fine, the study of reputations centers on the question of what significance reputations have for the societies in which they are produced and on the question of how the production of these reputations is actually managed. Fine answers that reputations help a society define itself, and reputations are managed by "reputational entrepreneurs," individuals who, in the arts for example, "take it as their responsibility to burnish or tarnish the reputations of particular artists" (p. 12). That is, particular versions of reputations need sponsors. That means that different sponsors may promote different versions of a reputation. In addition, reputations emerge and submerge over time. Reputational entrepreneurs direct their efforts at specific audiences, and those audiences, of course, may change over time. In sum, as George Herbert Mead (1938) succinctly puts it, "How many different Caesars have crossed the Rubicon since 1800?" (p. 95).

Technology is an important factor in defining the character of reputations and their production. In contemporary society, the mass media are crucial to the formation and distribution of reputations. As Fine (2001) points out, "The media help to determine whom we should know about and care about" (p. 3). If Caesar and Mead were alive today, Mead might also ask which networks have the rights to coverage of the crossing. Certainly for public figures, the media function as both the venue for the display of reputations and a factor in the motivation for worrying about reputations. For the postself musings of public figures, the extent of the meaning of the postself is critical. As with television ratings, the question becomes not simply how people will remember you, but how many people will remember you. The rise in the number and popularity of televised award shows tends to anchor the reputations of public figures in the awards they receive. You can win an occupationally grounded, but in effect national, award such as the Academy Award in front of tens of millions of viewers, or you can win a nominally national award that crosses occupational lines, such as the Presidential Medal of Freedom. In both cases, you become a national figure. These awards become a permanent record of your achievement that will outlast you.

The opening of cyberspace has broadened, and to an extent diluted, the meaning of the term *public figure*. Not only are public figures in the traditional sense commemorated on Web sites maintained by private and government organizations, but personal Web sites, made possible by advances in technology and motivated by the values of self-fulfillment and individualism, commemorate ordinary

people who also become their own small-scale reputational brokers.

The pace and the violence of social change in a society influence the character of and the concern for the ways in which we will be remembered after death. As mentioned above, the events of September 11, 2001, should both trigger nostalgia and brew concern for our reputations in an uncertain future. People tend to sentimentalize the past (Bettmann 1974), and also worry about the future. An era of rapid social change and a culturally diverse population put the reputations of public figures in jeopardy by shifting the bases on which we evaluate their achievements. Was Thomas Jefferson one of the founding fathers or one of the foundling fathers? Such changes have analogous effects on individuals' thinking about how they will be remembered. To the extent to which our sense of self is hinged to our occupations, the public image of those occupations may put our desired postself at risk.

The dominant ideas of the time also influence the production of postselves. In the course of the past century, Americans came to see themselves as figments of history—that is, as victims of forces beyond their control. Perhaps as a result, their identities were consciously seen as being grounded in entities larger than themselves: the occupations in which they work, the organizations to which they belong, their gender, their race, their ethnic heritage. The irony of this view in a society that at the same time places such a powerful emphasis on the individual is striking. These two conflicting views make an individual's certainty of leaving the mark he or she wishes to leave more problematic. Both the construction and the study of posthumous reputations are also influenced by the underlying metaphors that have currency in a given period. The places of particular figures in music history, for example, depend on the assumptions current in the eras in which the evaluations take place (Allen 1962).

The confluence of technological changes, social changes, ideas, and social values provides the societal backdrop against which people work out their legacies.

SUMMARY

Some of the ways in which societies intrude on the postselves of individual members and some of the circumstances under which societies invest in postself roles have been discussed. Some of the factors that influence both the character of the postself and the process by which posthumous reputations are formed and reformed have also been delineated. The importance of studying the postself as a window on society should be obvious: People's lives are socially grounded, and so too are their deaths. Unfortunately, however, this apparently isn't obvious. Schmitt and Leonard's (1986) work, buried in sociology journals at least 6 feet below public attention, has gone virtually unnoticed since its publication in the 1980s. Fine's

(2001) work, because it was collected in book form and because it deals with figures who carry with them considerable notoriety and celebrity, seems to be doing better, although it is too early to tell how it will fare in the long run. The study of the reputations of organizational leaders is also the study of organizational image and its management. The metamorphosis of J. Edgar Hoover parallels the metamorphosis of the public and organizational images of the FBI. It is also a study of changing cultural values.

Fine focuses on "difficult reputations." The field might be extended to reputations that carry no stigmatic baggage with them. Autobiographies might be studied using the concept of the postself as an analytic focus. Biographies and biographers might be studied to gain a better understanding of reputational entrepreneurship. The study of the postself tied to occupations might also be extended beyond the narrow range of occupations studied so far. The survival of criminals in total institutions might be studied, using as a focus the influence where you die has on how you will be remembered (Kamerman 1988:44–46). This would be the posthumous counterpart to the study of how these institutions affect an individual's self-image in life (see, for example, Collins 1998.) Another possible way of linking the postself to occupational roles is to think of how people want to be remembered after they retire, an experience that resembles death in a number of important ways (Kamerman 1988:71–72). Once a sports figure or opera singer, for two examples, retires, the part of that person's life that he or she wants to be remembered for, and will likely be remembered for, in any case, is over. The manner and timing of an individual's retirement influences that person's "posthumous" reputation. This is certainly true in occupations with typical careers of short duration, such as professional boxing or ballet. These suggestions barely scratch the surface; for more, see Schmitt and Leonard's (1986:1103–6) underutilized suggestions for future research.

Although to a great extent neglected by social scientists, the way we deal with our survival in the memories of others has not escaped the attention of novelists and poets. As Edgar Lee Masters wrote in "The Village Atheist":

> Immortality is not a gift,
>
> Immortality is an achievement.
>
> And only those who strive mightily
>
> Shall possess it.

To which sociologists finally attending to the postself and its social context need only add, in the interests of completeness, not poetry, "Immortality is in the eye of the beholder."

REFERENCES

Allen, Warren Dwight. 1962. *Philosophies of Music History: A Study of General Histories of Music 1600–1960.* New York: Dover.

Bettmann, Otto L. 1974. *The Good Old Days—They Were Terrible!* New York: Random House.

Bromberg, Minna and Gary Alan Fine. 2002. "Resurrecting the Red: Pete Seeger and the Purification of Difficult Reputations." *Social Forces* 80:1135–55.

Collins, William C. 1998. "'It's Not Your Fault!' A Message to Offenders From Criminal Justice and Corrections." Pp. 87–93 in *Negotiating Responsibility in the Criminal Justice System,* edited by Jack Kamerman. Carbondale: Southern Illinois University Press.

Davis, Fred. 1979. *Yearning for Yesterday: A Sociology of Nostalgia.* New York: Free Press.

Fine, Gary Alan. 2001. *Difficult Reputations: Collective Memories of the Evil, Inept, and Controversial.* Chicago: University of Chicago Press.

Henslin, James M. 2001. *Sociology: A Down-to-Earth Approach,* 5th ed. Boston: Allyn & Bacon.

Holcman, Jan. 2000. *Pianists: On and Off the Record. The Collected Essays of Jan Holcman,* edited by Donald Manildi. College Park: University of Maryland.

Kamerman, Jack. 1988. *Death in the Midst of Life: Social and Cultural Influences on Death, Grief, and Mourning.* Englewood Cliffs, NJ: Prentice Hall.

———. 1993. "The Illegacy of Suicide." In *Suicidology: Essays in Honor of Edwin S. Shneidman,* edited by Antoon A. Leenaars. Northvale, NJ: Jason Aronson.

———. 1998. "The Social Construction of Responsibility." Pp. 3–14 in *Negotiating Responsibility in the Criminal Justice System,* edited by Jack Kamerman. Carbondale: Southern Illinois University Press.

Kearl, Michael C. 1989. *Endings: A Sociology of Death and Dying.* New York: Oxford University Press.

Mead, George Herbert. 1938. *The Philosophy of the Act,* edited by Charles W. Morris. Chicago: University of Chicago Press.

Mueller, John H. 1951. *The American Symphony Orchestra: A Social History of Musical Taste.* Bloomington: Indiana University Press.

Mueller, Kate Hevner. 1973. *Twenty-Seven Major American Symphony Orchestras: A History and Analysis of Their Repertoires Seasons 1842–43 Through 1969–70.* Bloomington: Indiana University Press.

Schmitt, Raymond L. and Wilbert M. Leonard II. 1986. "Immortalizing the Self Through Sport." *American Journal of Sociology* 91:1088–1111.

Shneidman, Edwin S. 1973. *Deaths of Man.* New York: Quadrangle.

———. 1980. *Voices of Death.* New York: Harper & Row.

Simonton, Dean Keith. 1997. *Genius and Creativity: Selected Papers.* Greenwich, CT: Ablex.

Stone, Elizabeth. 1988. *Black Sheep and Kissing Cousins: How Our Family Stories Shape Us.* New York: Times Books.

PART III

Death and Social Controversy

HISTORICAL SUICIDE

ALAN H. MARKS

The desire to commit suicide and the psychological and social pressures that help shape the suicidal context have varied over time by place, social position, and belief system. In many cases it may be fairly easy to understand the motivation that prompted the act, but understanding the dynamic processes that lead to self-intentioned death is certainly more challenging.

The suicidal death of an individual or a group of people has such important implications that a case of suicide often raises questions about the very quality of life experienced by someone who chooses to die. Suicide is the ultimate rejection of life. In addition, the act of suicide forces others to examine the meaning of life, including their own. Perhaps this is why Western society has generally condemned suicide. Socrates claimed that "the unexamined life is not worth living"; it may also be suggested that the examined life is not worth living.

The act of suicide creates an awareness of the tension that exists between individual rights and the degree of social control the community can legitimately exert over its members. Suicidal behavior encompasses individual psychotic episodes, rational calculation of the positive and negative aspects of living, and institutional forces that are, under certain conditions, actively promoted.

Attitudes toward suicide, which vary widely, are often associated with social position. Albert Bayet (1922) asserts that the moral judgments pertaining to suicide are of two kinds. The first of these, *morale simple,* based on religion and superstition, represents the simple primitive thought of the common man. The second is a more sophisticated view that evaluates the social consequences of an act; this *morale nuancée* is more prevalent among the better educated, or those who are capable of dealing with complex, ambiguous situations. The suicidal act is viewed within a social context, and social judgments are based on reason, an examination of the death, and consequences of the act. As rational thought increases and education improves in a society, heightened awareness and acceptance of suicidal behavior also occurs, even as the influence of religion, superstition, and magical thinking

that condemns such behavior decreases (Fedden [1938] 1972:16–17).

Structural considerations regarding suicide influence a society's acceptance of suicidal behavior. Obligatory suicide is rare in Western societies, but portions of a population may, in times of stress and crisis, be compelled to commit suicide. In non-Western cultures, obligatory suicide appears to be more common. Historically, the Indian custom of suttee and the ritualistic suicides of Japanese soldiers and kamikaze pilots during World War II serve as classic examples. When suicides occur within the context of institutional expectations, the people involved hold the greater good of the community to be more important than the life of the individual, and such suicides are identified as altruistic in nature and reinforcing of communal solidarity. Robin Fedden ([1938] 1972:18–26) describes several examples of institutional suicide; among the more interesting are customs that required widows, servants, and soldiers to sacrifice themselves when their masters died to ensure that they could be of service to those masters in the next life.

Personal reactions to life conditions, as opposed to societal obligations, are more common elements in most suicides. In these cases, suicidal behavior is a rejection of communal solidarity and represents the ultimate extension of individual expression over communal claims on the person. Of course, there exists also a hybrid form of suicidal behavior that incorporates elements of both institutional and personal influences. Examples of such cases are the terrorist suicide bombers of the Middle East, who are influenced by both religious ideology and political considerations.

HISTORICAL OVERVIEW

Primitive Reactions to Suicide

Magic and elementary forms of religious practices that have been identified in African tribes and among Australian aborigines eventually established a tradition of penalty against suicide that was later to have a direct effect in other parts of the world, especially in Western societies. Primitive societies considered suicide committers to be persons who had been wronged by the community, and they believed, for this reason, that the spirits or ghosts of such persons would seek revenge. Thus the corpses of suicide committers were often desecrated, because it was thought that a disfigured body would be transformed into a disfigured ghost, which could do no harm to the living. Sometimes the remains of suicide committers were disbursed in order to make it difficult for their ghosts to reconstitute themselves, thereby preventing them from exacting vengeance on the community. Occasionally, suicide victims' bodies would be removed from close proximity to the community to prevent the ghosts from finding their way back to do harm.

Similarly primitive practices later became accepted customs in England, where suicides were branded with what Hoffman and Webb (1981) refer to as "marks of ignominy" (p. 374). It was believed that burying a suicide committer at a crossroads, driving a stake through the body, and placing a stone over the face would keep the spirit of the deceased confined, and just in case it were to arise, the spirit would become confused and not know which road to take to get back to its home (Fedden [1938] 1972:34–38).

Attitudes of the Ancient Greeks

In ancient Greece the act of suicide was generally held in low regard, in large part because of the works of four individuals whose views of suicide stemmed from their positions as priests, historians, and philosophers: Pythagoras (born circa 570 B.C.), Plato, (427–347 B.C.), Aristotle (384–322 B.C.), and Mestrius Plutarch (circa A.D. 45–125). All were opposed to suicide, and all were influenced by the religious beliefs of their times. Louis Dublin (1963) identifies the reasons these Greek thinkers were opposed to suicide:

> Pythagoras and Plato regarded the individual as a soldier of God. . . . Pythagoras, therefore, forbade men "to depart from their guard or station in life without the order of their Commander"—that is of God. . . . Plato also objected to suicide as an unnatural act, since man is his own closest friend and thus has no right to injure himself; moreover, suicide was cowardly and an offense against the State, which thus lost a citizen. . . . Aristotle [agreed] . . . since men owe their lives to their country, for them to abandon life voluntarily is equivalent to a criminal neglect of their civic duty. Plutarch believed . . . true courage is shown in the manly endurance of suffering and that suicide, being an act of flight, is an act of cowardice and a deed unworthy of man. (P. 111)

Plato considered man to be God's property, and, as such, man had no right to do away with something that was not his (his life). Plato thought that anyone who committed suicide would be contradicting God's will and would lose the chance for a good life after death (Choron 1972:108–10).

Plato argued that the state should, with a few exceptions, punish those who commit suicide, saying that "the graves of such as perish thus must, in the first place, be solitary . . . further they must be buried ignominiously in waste and nameless spots . . . and the tomb shall be marked by neither headstone nor name" (quoted in Choron 1972:110).

Aristotle supported Plato, describing suicide as a cowardly act that deprives the state of a citizen. For Aristotle, anything not granted by the state was forbidden by it. As the state did not grant people the right to self-destruction, if they committed suicide they were considered to be criminal. Whereas Homer considered suicide to be an alternative when life loses its meaning, Aristotle viewed suicide as an amoral act because it treats the victim unjustly (Choron 1972:110). Some of the arguments traceable to these early thinkers still hold within the contemporary experience, particularly those relating to the individual's responsibility to God, to community, to family, and to him- or herself.

After Aristotle, a shift in ideology began to emerge. Epicurus (341–270 B.C.) and Zeno (336–265 B.C.), for example, advocated the strengthening of individuals' ability to adapt to the changes inherent in life in order that they would be able to come to terms with death. Moreover, Epicurus thought that philosophers should take a more active role in influencing behavior. According to Epicurus:

> Two great afflictions of man are the fear of the gods and the fear of death, this most terrifying of all ills is nothing to us, since as long as we exist, death is not with us, but when death comes, then we do not exist. Once this is understood, nothing stands in the way of man's happiness, which consists of peace of mind and the health of the body. (Quoted in Choron 1972:113)

Zeno, founder of the school of philosophy known as Stoicism, believed that virtue is tantamount to the highest good. Basing his philosophy on the premise that one should live in harmony with nature, Zeno believed that the gods inevitably fix nature and the future, the universe is ruled by divine reason, and humanity has the capacity to be reflective and rational. For the "wise man," or the person committed to reason, suicide is essentially a matter of pragmatics rather than a moral issue; one must be evaluative regarding life's options. Indeed, Zeno thought that suicide may be reasonable in some instances, and his own life ended in suicide (Rosen 1975:10).

Stoicism marks a significant turning point in Greek cultural perceptions and evaluations of suicide. Stoicism also had a significant influence on the development of Roman thought and behavior, as I note in the following subsection.

Attitudes Toward Suicide Among the Ancient Romans

The Stoics recommended suicide as a viable course of action if it is taken as an escape from evil. George Rosen

(1975) quotes the Stoic philosopher Diogenes Laertius as follows: "The wise man will for reasonable cause make his own exit from life on his country's behalf, or for the sake of his friends, or if he suffer intolerable pain, mutilation, or incurable disease" (p. 10). Seneca (4 B.C.–A.D. 65), a leading Stoic philosopher, argued:

> The eternal law has decreed nothing better than this that life should have but one entrance and many exits. Why should I endure the agonies of disease and the cruelties of human tyranny, when I can emancipate myself from all my torments? No one is obliged to live. . . . If life pleases you, live. If not, you have a right to return whence you came. (Quoted in Dublin 1963:114)

Contemplating old age, health, and suicide, this same philosopher wrote:

> I will not relinquish old age if it leaves my better part intact. But if it begins to shake my mind, if it destroys its faculties one by one, if it leaves me not life but breath, I will depart from this putrid or tottering edifice. I will not escape by death from disease so long as it may be healed, and leaves my mind intact. I will not raise my hand against myself on account of pain, for to do so is to be conquered. But if I know that I must suffer without hope of relief, I will depart, not through fear of the pain itself, but because it prevents all for which I would live. (Quoted in Dublin 1963:114–15)

Motivated by a sense of honor to avoid humiliation, capture, and slavery, the Romans made frequent use of suicide. During the civil war between Caesar and Pompey, Vulteius's army was surrounded. After repulsing numerous attacks, it became clear that escape was impossible. Vulteius encouraged his men to kill themselves rather than suffer the humiliation of being taken prisoner, and more than a thousand men did so.

Marcus Aurelius (A.D. 121–180) believed suicide to be an appropriate action if carried out in a reasonable, rational, nonhistrionic way. Among the Romans, mass suicides, hysterical suicides, and suicides due to imitation and suggestibility were not infrequent occurrences. Rosen (1975) relates the story of the young women of Miletus, who hanged themselves in great numbers. In response, the Milesians passed a law requiring that woman who committed suicide be transported to the burial site naked, with the rope wrapped around her neck. Given the public perception of shame and disgrace associated with such a display, the epidemic stopped.

Anton J. L. Van Hooff (1990) reports on the incidence of suicide among the ancient Greeks, Romans, and Barbarians. Among these data are supposed mythology, unsubstantiated reports, and valid cases of suicide. Referring to these valid cases as "hard reports," Van Hooff presents figures on individual cases and on single incidents of mass suicide, reporting a total of 960 cases involving 9,639 individuals. Among these 960 cases were 564 events that included 8,256 self-killings verified as actual suicides.

Van Hooff (1990) notes that most of the information available about ancient times, especially among the Romans, probably reflects the perceptual biases of the recorders, who were more interested in the activities of the elite than in accurately reporting the incidence of suicidal behavior, especially among those of lesser social stature. As a result, suicide among the lower classes and women, especially older women, was likely underreported. Indeed, the data indicate that the ratio of males to females in Roman suicides was 24 to 1. An analysis of Greek suicide data, which Van Hooff believes are more accurate than the Roman data, indicates a ratio of fewer than 2 men to every 1 woman. Van Hooff notes that "old women are even less visible than women in general" (pp. 21–22) in these data. Only 5 reports of old women committing suicide were confirmed, compared with 49 confirmed reports on old men (pp. 31–33). The motivations for suicide among the lower classes, slaves, and women, Van Hooff notes, reflect the sense of despair common among minorities and the powerless.

Suicide Methods in Ancient Societies

According to some analysts, the method an individual uses to commit suicide depends on a variety of factors, including the level of technology available and the intentionality to commit suicide. As the data in Table 1 indicate, the Romans and Greeks sometimes committed suicide by starvation. This was considered a noble way to die—to starve oneself required determination and demonstrated perseverance. Suicide by starvation was not considered to be an impulsive act, and suicides of this nature were often celebrated as public events, in that the committers announced their decisions to die. Van Hooff (1990) reports that in ancient Greece and Rome 8% of those who committed suicide used this method. Most of these were older men.

The social significance of suicide in ancient times was also associated with the use of weapons such as knives, swords, daggers, and other cutting instruments. Men were more likely than women to commit suicide by using such

Table 1 — Methods of Suicide Used in Ancient Rome and Greece, by Gender

Method	Male %	Female %
Weapons	46	25
Hanging	13	34
Jumping	13	22
Poison	9	8
Starvation	9	7
Provocation	5	—
Fire	4	4
	N = 439	N = 158

SOURCE: Adapted from Van Hooff (1990:44).

instruments. Soldiers sometimes died by falling on their swords, by stabbing themselves, or by cutting their throats or other veins, or they would solicit a servant or friend to carry out the act. On occasion, physicians were called in to assist or to oversee the procedure. Women, on the other hand, most often chose to die by hanging or jumping (Van Hooff 1990:44).

In some cases, individuals who were intent on dying precipitated their deaths by provoking others into attacking them. Prisoners sometimes insulted or refused to cooperate with their captors, and soldiers sometimes purposely maneuvered themselves into hopeless battlefield situations. During periods in which Christians were persecuted, some Christians voluntarily surrendered themselves to the authorities, knowing they would be executed. Van Hooff (1990) reports one interesting account of mass suicide that occurred when Philip V conquered the city of Abydus in 200 B.C.: "The men stabbed their wives and children and after that themselves. Others burned themselves, jumped into wells, or hanged themselves" (p. 63). Such "suicides of siege" were not uncommon.

Suicide by fire, although rare, was almost always a dramatic public event that occurred as a result of circumstances beyond the immediate control of the victim. When an army overran and burned a city, for example, some of the defenders would throw themselves onto the fire rather than face capture.

The Romans held suicide by hanging to be a desperate unmanly act. An assumption of Roman law at the time was that if persons accused of crimes hanged themselves during the proceedings, they were probably guilty of the offenses with which they were charged. Grieving a person who died in this way was therefore considered inappropriate, because the action was thought to be an admission of guilt by one who was considered an enemy of society (Van Hooff 1990:69). Among the Greeks, in contrast, hanging elicited a less negative reaction, and Greek women were more likely than Roman women to hang themselves.

Jumping to one's death was considered a desperate act of despair, grief, shame, and humiliation. Van Hooff asserts that hanging and jumping represent base actions that disfigure the body, and, for this reason, suicide by jumping was thought to violate notions relating to the individual's dignity. Consequently, these methods of suicide were understood to be fit only for women, slaves, and those in the lower classes. Aristocrats, especially Roman aristocrats, were much more apt to employ the blade as a method of choice.

Motivations for Suicide

As the data displayed in Table 2 indicate, the ancient Greeks and Romans committed suicide for a number of reasons. According to Van Hooff (1990), each society held its own paradigm of suicide. In ancient Greece and Rome, shame, despair, and grief accounted for the majority of suicides. Additional reasons included exhibitionistic or

Table 2	Motivations for Suicide Among the Ancients
Motivation	*Percentage*
Shame (*pudor*)	32
Despair	22
Grief (dolor)	13
Necessity	6
Devotion	6
Loyalty	5
Unbearable physical pain	5
Total	89

SOURCE: Adapted from Van Hooff (1990:85).

ostentatious behavior, hatred, being tired of living, madness, a desire to bring a curse upon another person or country, and guilt (Van Hooff 1990:85). Among the leading motivations for suicide was necessity—that is, suicide was the only alternative in dire circumstances. In some cases, necessity took the form of the person's being ordered to commit suicide by the emperor. Suicides for which the motivation was devotion were those associated with dying for one's country, whereas those committed out of loyalty were associated with personal relationships, loyalty either to a leader or to a group.

Fedden ([1938] 1972:50–53) describes four major reasons individuals in ancient times employed suicide: (a) to preserve honor, (b) to avoid old age and infirmity, (c) to escape sorrow and bereavement, and (d) to serve ritualistic and sacrificial purposes. Although Fedden offers examples of each type, he asserts that the available data are skewed toward suicide among members of the upper class. He also notes that some of the common reasons given for suicide today were rare in ancient times:

> What is particularly interesting is that two types common today—suicide from economic change, and suicide from depression—are extremely rare, too rare in fact to form categories of their own. . . . Poverty, it seems, only becomes an adequate cause for suicide in a highly developed commercial or capitalistic civilization, where all values are apt to be chained to a money basis, and loss or lack of money means loss of respect, prestige, and a hundred other things. . . . A man's family, functions, and character could usually discount an empty purse [in ancient times]. (Pp. 53–54)

Van Hooff (1990) found that shame and despair accounted for a majority of suicides among the ancients. Shame is a personal emotional state, whereas despair relates to feelings of hopelessness, a state of mind often brought about by military defeats or calamities.

Most of the motivations for suicide found in ancient history continue to be documented in the literature. Considering the vast cultural, social, technological, and economic changes that have taken place during the past 20 centuries, it is perhaps remarkable that many often-cited reasons for suicide remain consistent. This suggests some continuity in the human condition and in the general problem of social structure and culture shaping the lives of people and the definitions and philosophies they construct to deal with living and dying. The reasons for suicide do not vary, but there is variation in the proportion of a population that is motivated toward such behavior as a result of social conditions and personal reasons.

Sanctions Against Suicide

The ancient Greeks and Romans evaluated the act of suicide in part based on the reason for the act. Suicide committed for patriotic reasons or for reasons of loyalty and fidelity was to be admired. Suicide to avoid infirmity and old age was tolerated, whereas suicide committed for less noble reasons was condemned as an act of cowardice or insanity.

Sanctions against suicide took many forms. Sometimes the bodies of suicide victims would be disfigured, such as by cutting off the hand that delivered the fatal wound. Other restrictive sanctions existed as well. In Italy, for example, suicide was a crime if committed by slaves, soldiers, or criminals. The property rights of the state and its claim on its citizens were a practical economic consideration, and individuals who attempted suicide but failed to die were imprisoned.

Roman law may have unintentionally encouraged suicide among those who were to be executed by the state. With execution, the state confiscated the estate of the deceased, thus, to avoid pauperizing their families, some condemned persons died at their own hands. Suicide under these conditions also provided committers an opportunity to preserve some measure of dignity, so that their families could retain their social status.

Attitudes Among Ancient Jews

Although Jews have been persecuted throughout much of history, suicide rates in this group have never been high. Dublin (1963) attributes the low rate of suicide among the Jews of antiquity to their belief in the sacredness of life, stating, "Suicide for Jews is unthinkable—and it is unthinkable because throughout the Old Testament runs the theme of the sacredness of life" (p. 102). In addition, one of the unintended consequences of persecution is that it promotes social cohesion and social solidarity within the persecuted group. These two factors have served to buffer Jews against suicidal behavior.

During the postbiblical era, however, the incidence of suicidal behavior among Jews increased. This was a time of political ferment, internal conflict, and a conflict with Rome that promoted violence. One of the largest mass suicides ever recorded occurred at Masada in A.D. 73, when Eleazar ben Jair, the leader of the Zealots, who had been under siege by the Romans, sensed that defeat was inevitable and encouraged the 960 men, women, and children remaining at Masada to commit suicide rather than be captured and executed, raped, and sold into slavery.

Josephus, the Jewish historian and warrior of the first century A.D., made no moral judgments about the events at Masada. He simply referred to it as "a miserable necessity." However, Dublin (1963) claims that Josephus expressed admiration for the sacrifice by members of the Masada garrison and the contempt the residents held for death. During the siege of Jotphata, in which the Romans were defeating Josephus's forces, his followers urged Josephus to commit suicide, indicating they would follow his example. However, Josephus espoused the traditional Jewish view about suicide:

> Oh, my friends, why are you so earnest to kill yourselves? Why do you set your soul and body, which are such dear companions, at such variance? It is a brave thing to die in war, but it should be by the hands of the enemy. It is a foolish thing to do that for ourselves, which we quarrel with them for doing to us. It is a brave thing to die for liberty; but still it should be in battle and by those who would take the liberty from us. He is equally a coward who will not die when he is obliged to die. What are we afraid of when we will not go up and meet the Romans? Is it Death? Why then inflict it on ourselves? Self-murder is a crime most remote from the common nature of all animals, and an instance of impiety against God our Creator. (Quoted in Dublin 1963:104–5)

Martyrdom Among the Early Christians

The early Christians thought that if Jesus died for mankind's original sin and baptism cleansed the individual's soul of sin, and if the way to get into heaven was by avoiding sin, then it made sense to commit suicide before one sinned. The longer one lived, the greater the chance that one would commit sins, so killing oneself before one could sin guaranteed entrance into heaven and eternal peace. For these reasons, many early Christians committed suicide or offered themselves up to be martyred.

During periods of religious persecution, many Christians willingly met their fate. George Howe Colt (1991) describes many instances in which early Christians offered themselves up for execution. Volunteering for certain death is suicide, but for the early Christians it was also a road to martyrdom. Although the actual number of persons martyred in this way is not known, estimates range from 10,000 to 100,000 (Colt 1991:156). Because there were so many deaths, and because of the changing status of the Church within the Roman Empire, theologians began to rethink the relationship between suicide and martyrdom, and what had once been acceptable, even encouraged, was later condemned.

SANCTIONS AGAINST SUICIDE IN THE MIDDLE AGES

It is possible to identify two distinct sets of sanctions against the taking of one's own life in Western society; one stemming from the early position of the Church in this matter and one from the sociolegal prohibitions that emerged by the middle of the 14th century in England, an influence that was to have lingering effects on Western societies, including the United States, well into the latter half of the 20th century. In this section, I present an overview of the ecclesiastical canons and the sociolegal common law that defined suicide as self-murder to demonstrate the emerging control of social institutions over the behavior of citizens.

Ecclesiastical Canons Prohibiting Suicide

In 313 A.D., the Edict of Milan established Christianity as a legitimate and recognized religion within the Roman Empire, and by 325, Christianity had evolved to become the official religion of the empire. According to Fedden ([1938] 1972), prior to the third century, the religious standards of the Church were not in opposition to suicide. This position changed during the early Middle Ages, and for the next thousand years the Church's attitude toward suicide can be described as hostile and condemning.

The Church's moral interpretation of suicide began with Saint Augustine's treatise *The City of God,* which was written from A.D. 413 to 426 After Augustine's views and position statements were published, the Church moved to install sanctions against suicide. In 451 A.D., the Council of Arles, the first religious body to address this issue, declared suicide to be an act of diabolical possession. According to Minois (1999:29–30), the Council of Arles prohibited suicide for slaves and servants. In A.D. 563, the Council of Braga ordained that no religious rites were to be celebrated at the tomb of one who had taken his or her life and that no mass should be said for the repose of the soul; in addition, the body of a suicide victim was not to be treated with respect, because such a person was considered to have died in mortal sin. In 673, the English Council of Hereford denied burial rites to those who killed themselves. Twenty years later, in 693, the Council of Toledo declared that suicide attempters would be excommunicated (Colt 1991:158). In 1284, the Synod of Nimes denied burial in holy ground to those who committed suicide (Dublin 1963). Thomas Aquinas synthesized the arguments against any tolerance for suicide in his *Summa Theologica* (as cited in Grollman 1971:24):

1. Suicide is against the natural inclinations of preservation of life and charity toward self.

2. Suicide is a trespass against the community.

3. Suicide is a trespass against God, who gave man life.

By the middle of the 5th century, the Christian Church had established a position in opposition to suicide; by the 13th century, with the work of Thomas Aquinas and others, the Church had developed a sophisticated rationale against suicide and had initiated acts of devaluation toward those who would commit suicide. These actions also were intended to cast shame and guilt on the family members of suicide committers. Such policies of social ostracism and condemnation continued into the 18th century. Confiscation of property, degradation of the corpse, and refusal of burial in consecrated ground were some of the expressions of this religious disapproval (Choron 1972; Rosen 1975; Phillips and Flora 2001).

According to Minois (1999:34), the Fourth Lateran Council (1215) mandated that the faithful must confess their sins at least once a year. Until A.D. 1000, confession of sins, penitence, and pardon were all conducted as separate processes. After the integration of these procedures during the 11th century, officials of the Church reasoned that this method would serve to buffer despair and inhibit suicidal behavior. Moreover, Church leaders believed that because priests had the power of absolution, no sane person would entertain thoughts of committing suicide. Suicide during this period continued to be understood as an act of diabolical possession. As Minois states, "There was no such thing as a sane suicide" (p. 41).

Between A.D. 400 and 1400, suicide was rare. Choron (1972) attributes this rarity to the severe sanctions the Church imposed and to the unified belief that the faithful would be rewarded with heaven. However, among the persecuted, including heretics, Jews, and Muslims, suicide was not rare (Choron 1972:24–25), and Christians considered to be sane who committed suicide received no mercy from the Church or community. Their corpses were often dragged through the streets, hanged, disfigured, and mistreated in numerous other ways as well (Minois 1999:34–39).

Social rank emerged as an important factor in suicide during this same period. According to Minois (1999), "Ordinarily suicide in the Middle Ages concerned the world of laborers (laboratories) above all others. It was peasants and craftsman who died by their own hand, often following a brutal worsening of their conditions" (p. 41). In many communities the property of a suicide committer was confiscated, so when someone died, surviving family members had a vested interest in the determination of the cause of death.

During the 15th century in Europe, a shift in worldviews began to take place, and a reawakening of intellectual curiosity began to take root. With these new perspectives, people's understanding of the role of human beings in relation to others, to society, and to God underwent changes as well. As Choron (1972:26–28) notes, many thinkers began to discuss the topic of suicide. In *Utopia,* for example, Sir Thomas More reiterated the historical viewpoint that man had the right to dispatch himself if he considered life unbearable. In a direct, revolutionary repudiation of the Church's position, John Donne argued in *Biothanato* that God is merciful enough to forgive the sin of suicide. And in *The Anatomy of Melancholy,* published in 1628, Robert Burton argued that God can forgive suicides; he also made a plea for tolerance of those who commit suicide, pointing out that individuals differ in their reactions to life circumstances. Despite such passionate pleas for constraint, civil and criminal views of suicide also underwent a change in orientation during this period.

Sociolegal Sanctions

According to Hoffman and Webb (1981), societies had penalties for suicide in place before the first laws prohibiting suicide were created in the late Middle Ages, during the early part of the 14th century (see also Rosen 1975). By the middle of that century, suicide as a legal form of murder was a part of the common law. As Hoffman and Webb note, as a felony, "the crime of suicide required both majority age and a sound mind. These same elements were part of the legal definition of attempted suicide, which was a misdemeanor" (pp. 372–73). First known as *felo-de-se,* or "felon of self," the crime of suicide was thought to involve a breach of trust between a human being and his or her lord. The common law definitions of self-murder were determined by the punishments specified for the act of suicide (Hoffman and Webb 1981:373–77).

From the 13th through the 18th centuries, two types of punishment were administered in cases of suicide. The first type dealt with the body, whereas the second dealt with the property of the committer. Prior to the establishment of the English common laws of suicide during the late Middle Ages, the goods of those who committed suicide were transferred to their local lords. Once suicide was legally declared a felony crime, the issue of forfeiture of the deceased's property to the state was firmly established. Hoffman and Webb (1981) note that perhaps the most important case in the establishment of suicide law was the 1565 case of *Hales v. Petit,* in which one Mr. Justice Brown ruled that suicide was criminal as "an offense against nature, and a thing most horrible. Also, against God, because a breach of the commandment; and against the king in that he has lost one of his mystical members" (p. 376).

During the period from 1580 to 1620, civil and religious authorities raised many questions about the crime of suicide. The results of this sociolegal debate included severe condemnation and punishment through the confiscation of property directed toward those confirmed in the courts as having committed suicide. But, as the noted English jurist Sir William Blackstone later observed:

> No part of the personnel estate was surrendered before a finding of felo-de-se . . . was rendered after some type of inquisition. Consequently, forfeiture could be avoided if the inquisition authorities pardoned the offense by not finding felo-de-se and instead finding insanity or some other mitigating circumstance. In cases where no pardon was granted, all property was forfeited. (Quoted in Hoffman and Webb 1981:375)

This firm legal position on suicide may have been intended to capture the attention of commoners and aristocrats alike, but rank had its privileges. Suicides among the clergy and the nobility often were hidden or excused as acts of insanity, which allowed for the normal ceremonies and burials to take place without concern for the violation of sacred custom (Minois 1999:142–44). To demonstrate the extent of this class bias, Minois (1999:142–47) cites as one example the official determination that 6,701 English suicides occurred from 1485 through 1714. As Minois notes, this particular study is unique, given that the social class positions were known for each of the 6,701 suicide committers. Of the cases involving peers and gentlemen brought before the court, 67.2% were judged to have committed suicide, whereas 99% of the servants and apprentices, 94.1% of the laborers, 93.5% of the craftsman, and 86.6% of the yeomen were found guilty of violating the laws prohibiting suicide (Minois 1999:145). The suicide laws aside, the intervention of influential persons often helped to protect the reputations of nobles and clerics who died at their own hands and, in so doing, the status of the families of the deceased, who also avoided forfeiture of property to the crown. Such intervention secured the goodwill of the community toward these influential persons, but it also served to undermine the moral foundation of religious and secular arguments against suicide.

The 19th century is noteworthy in the history of suicide because it began an era of reform in opposition to suicide laws. No longer was suicide deemed simply a moral and legal issue. Some observers have noted that changes in suicide laws appear to correspond to shifts in the political economy. Two important issues can be identified: First, laws requiring the forfeiture of the property of suicide committers were thought to be an effective deterrent to suicide, and second, the transfer of property to the state through such forfeitures represented a source of wealth and power for the state (Hoffman and Webb 1981:377). However, the results of the suicide laws may not have been as beneficial to the state as anticipated.

From the 14th through the 18th centuries in England, despite official sanctions against those believed to be in violation of the suicide laws, "few offenders were arrested, prosecuted, convicted, or punished" (Hoffman and Webb 1981:377). If a coroner's jury found that a committer was sane at the time of the suicidal act, the deceased could be denied Christian burial and his property could be confiscated, but the evidence reveals that coroners' juries most often returned verdicts of temporary insanity in such cases. Fedden ([1938] 1972) observes that by the end of the 18th century, a finding that a suicide was other than the act of an insane person was extremely rare, a fact that generated much criticism from the leading legal minds of the period.

Within this context it is again important to note that the suicide laws were directed toward citizens of lesser social stature. Given that the coroners' juries charged with determining whether a sane person had violated the law by committing suicide were made up of individuals of that same low social status, the public may have unwittingly been positioned to obstruct application of the suicide laws.

Whatever the reasons, limited numbers of suicide cases were determined to be the actions of sane individuals. Those who were found to have been insane when they killed themselves received decent Christian burials, and their families avoided forfeiture of property and were able to collect the benefits of any existing life insurance policies.

As indicated above, the severity of the suicide law penalties and public resistance to the enforcement of these laws ultimately led to their abolition. The movement to reform the suicide laws that took place throughout the 19th century was a part of a much greater effort to reform or abolish those common laws considered to be antiquated and inconsistent with the rise of the English capitalist investment-oriented economy. This property-based reform of the laws sought to establish new and greater citizen rights, and this included the rights of those who took their own lives. As a significant part of this reform movement, passage of the Right to Burial Act of 1823 and the Abolition of Forfeiture Act of 1870 was to have great effects on the families of suicide committers by establishing their rights of inheritance (Fedden [1938] 1972; Hoffman and Webb 1981).

THE EMERGING ROLE OF SOCIAL SCIENCE

The 19th century is notable for other changes as well, in that observers of human behavior began to apply the scientific method to their studies. Émile Durkheim ([1897] 1951) is acknowledged for his scientific approach to the study of social problems such as suicide, but it was Morselli's treatise *Suicide: An Essay in Comparative Moral Statistics* ([1879] 1903) that laid the groundwork for the theoretical and empirical methods that Durkheim used so effectively. Indeed, Durkheim's emphasis on the social forces that influence behavior provided a level of analysis beyond that of individual motivation or psychological reductionism. According to Durkheim, society deals with behavior such as suicide through mechanisms of social integration and regulation. Identifying four types of social conditions (altruistic, egoistic, anomic, and fatalistic), Durkheim argued that the rate of suicide varies inversely with the degree of social integration and regulation.

In *Suicide and the Meaning of Civilization* ([1881] 1970), Masaryk also employed the scientific method to understand the role of society and culture in determining the nature of human behavior. His contribution to understanding suicide lies in his emphasis on the nature of religion and a personal search for self-identity in humankind's attempts to reconcile the old agrarian feudal social order with a newly emerging capitalist-oriented economy and the advent of the industrial era. This emergence of the application of the scientific method to the study of social problems filled an important void by providing the kind of knowledge essential for understanding the effects of social change and even promoting change in societal organizations. Armed with the new concepts, theories, and data being created in the developing social and behavioral sciences, members of the Progressive movements of the late 19th and early 20th centuries promoted new ideas that continue to enrich the thinking of ordinary people.

CONTEMPORARY ATTITUDES TOWARD SUICIDE

The contribution of statistical methods and theory construction and the emerging objectiveness of the social science method established the foundation for a value-neutral understanding of suicidal behavior. In the view of some analysts, increases in education, the decreasing influence of religion, and the psychosocial and psychiatric paradigms used to explain suicidal behavior also have tempered formerly condemnatory attitudes toward suicide.

However, some evidence suggests that centuries of condemnation of suicide have had long-term effects, especially among orthodox Christians and frequent church attendees, who appear to be particularly intolerant of suicide. In a survey conducted in 1973, I found that among respondents who scored high on religious orthodoxy, 25% agreed with the statement "Man has the right to take his own life," whereas 70% of those who scored low on orthodoxy agreed with this statement (Marks 1973). Among frequent church attendees, 21% agreed with the statement, whereas 56% of those who had not attended church within the previous 30 days agreed. Ginsberg (1971) found that people in Reno, Nevada, thought of suicide as something that happens to people and not as something anyone intends. Among these respondents, suicide was associated with shame but not blame. In a survey conducted in Arkansas in the late 1980s, I found that the majority of those interviewed (69%) did not believe that an individual has the right to commit suicide (Marks 1988–89). The majority of the respondents in that study also associated mental illness and immoral behavior with suicide.

Although findings such as these are useful, these studies are limited in what they reveal and the extent to which the results can be generalized. Recent reports based on national survey data are perhaps more enlightening regarding public attitudes toward suicide. Indeed, the results of some relatively recent polls suggest that Americans are becoming increasingly tolerant of suicide. For example, euthanasia, physician-assisted suicide, and the role of the state in regulating behavior are all topics of discussion and debate. Rational suicide, once a taboo topic, also is being discussed openly. Public opinion polls may be useful for helping social scientists to ascertain trends in people's attitudes toward suicide and related topics.

Recent national polls pertaining to suicide (and euthanasia) have included questions regarding the role physicians should be allowed to play, if any, in assisted suicide. Polls that employ the word *suicide* rather than *euthanasia* generally show a lower level of acceptance of suicide among the U.S. population. By way of example: In the year 2002, Oregon was the only state that had legalized physician-assisted suicide. An ABC News/Beliefnet Poll conducted March 13–17, 2002, with a sample of 1,021 adults described the conditions under which the Oregon physician-assisted suicide law can be used and asked respondents whether or not they favor such laws. In this poll, 46% of the respondents said that they favor legalization of physician-assisted suicide, whereas 48% said they are opposed to such legalization. In a Harris Poll taken December 14–19, 2001, interviewees were asked, "Do you think that the law should allow doctors to comply with the wishes of a dying patient in severe distress who asks to have his or her life ended, or not?" In that case, 65% responded that they believe physician-assisted suicide should be allowed, whereas 29% of the respondents were opposed (Polling Report 2002).

Still, Americans appear to be less likely to support suicide for reasons other than terminal illness. The fact that people often make moral judgments as to the conditions under which suicide may occur only enhances the difficulty of creating a rationale through which we can understand suicidal behavior. At issue is whether the state, a professional group, or any individual should be allowed to determine whether and under what conditions suicide may be permissible. These are essential issues that will undoubtedly become increasingly important in the future.

CONCLUSION

The religious, legal, and social propriety of self-intentioned death has been under scrutiny for the full span of recorded history, and the public debate that first began over suicide late in the 16th century continues to the present. Once considered a crime, suicide has been decriminalized, in part as the result of philosophies that were first developed during the 16th century. This official decriminalization, however, has failed to silence secular and religious debates over the nature of suicide: whether it is an act of derangement or whether it may, under certain conditions, actually be a symbolic act of dignity and grandeur. In an epilogue to his book *History of Suicide* titled "From the French Revolution to the Twentieth Century, or, From Free Debate to Silence," Minois (1999:302–28) argues that despite the vast array of knowledge generated through the efforts of social and behavioral scientists, the central question surrounding the right to engage in self-destructive behavior has yet to be settled. In the early years of the 21st century the suicide question remains, albeit under the guise of a different issue. The case of human suffering and euthanasia has become the central focal point of public debate and social conflict concerning individual rights and the collective good. On this matter Minois states:

In spite of everything that the moral and political authorities can do, the problem of suicide is recurring today through the extreme case of euthanasia. Moral leaders continue to assert that suffering, even excruciating, incurable suffering, has a positive value; political leaders fear backsliding. This is why thousands of human beings who are dehumanized by intolerable suffering are condemned to live. (P. 328)

Minois concludes his powerful work on the history of suicide by raising a question that seems to capture the essence of a pressing contemporary issue. Despite its long historical legacy, the act of self-destruction remains a matter of secular, legal, and religious concern and will undoubtedly continue to serve as a focal point of interest. The question that Minois raises is this: "In the difficult mutation that values are undergoing today, should not debate on bioethics also work to create a thanato-ethics?" (p. 328).

Perhaps the philosophy of Stoicism may yet serve us well in our attempts to understand what continues to be a most contentious issue. Thus, for those individuals committed to reason, suicide may indeed be a matter of pragmatic thinking rather than a moral issue. In some instances, suicide may be a reasonable alternative to living.

REFERENCES

Augustine, Saint. 2000. *The City of God.* New York: Modern Library.

Bayet, Albert. 1922. *Le Suicide et la morale.* Paris: Felix Alcan.

Choron, Jacques. 1972. *Suicide.* New York: Charles Scribner's Sons.

Colt, George Howe. 1991. *The Enigma of Suicide.* New York: Summit.

Dublin, Louis I. 1963. *Suicide: A Sociological and Statistical Study.* New York: Ronald.

Durkheim, Émile. [1897] 1951. *Suicide: A Study in Sociology,* translated by John A. Spaulding and George Simpson. Glencoe, IL: Free Press.

Fedden, Robin. [1938] 1972. *Suicide: A Social and Historical Study.* New York: B. Blom.

Ginsberg, G. P. 1971. "Public Conceptions and Attitudes About Suicide." *Journal of Health and Social Behavior* 12:200–207.

Grollman, Earl A. 1971. *Suicide: Prevention, Intervention, Postvention.* Boston: Beacon.

Hoffman, Dennis E. and Vincent J. Webb. 1981. "Suicide as Murder at Common Law." *Criminology* 19:372–84.

Marks, Alan H. 1973. "A Regional Comparison of Attitudes Toward Suicide and Methods of Self-Destruction." Ph.D. dissertation, Department of Sociology, University of Georgia.

———. 1988–89. "Structural Parameters of Sex, Race, Age, and Education and Their Influence on Attitudes Toward Suicide." *Omega* 19:327–36.

Masaryk, Thomas. [1881] 1970. *Suicide and the Meaning of Civilization,* translated by William B. Weist and Robert G. Batson. Chicago: University of Chicago Press.

Minois, Georges. 1999. *History of Suicide: Voluntary Death in Western Culture,* translated by Lydia G. Cochrane. Baltimore: Johns Hopkins University Press.

Morselli, Henry (Enrico). [1879] 1903. *Suicide: An Essay in Comparative Moral Statistics.* New York: Appleton.

Phillips, Daniel W. and Shawn Flora. 2001. "History of Suicide." Pp. 516–18 in *Encyclopedia of Criminology and Deviant Behavior,* vol. 4, *Self-Destructive and Disvalued Identity,* edited by Charles E. Faupel and Paul M. Roman. Philadelphia: Brunner-Routledge.

Polling Report. 2002. "Health Policy." Retrieved December 22, 2002 (http://www.pollingreport.com/health1.htm#assisted%20Suicide).

Rosen, George. 1975. "History." Pp. 3–29 in *A Handbook for the Study of Suicide,* edited by Seymour Perlin. New York: Oxford University Press.

Van Hooff, Anton J. L. 1990. *From Autothanasia to Suicide: Self-Killing in Classical Antiquity.* London: Routledge.

SUICIDE AND SUICIDE TRENDS IN THE UNITED STATES, 1900–1999

DENNIS L. PECK

A noted thanatologist has observed that death has cultural, economic, medical, and social implications and effects (Blacher 1987). This is no less true of events caused by those who intentionally take their lives. As a subarea of thanatological study, suicide, or self-induced death, has a different connotation from those deaths that result from natural processes, accident, or even homicide. All the ingredients, such as emotional pain, grieving, and sense of loss are the same among survivors, but suicide represents a death form that in many ways continues to be shrouded in mystery.

Long the subject of scholarly analysis, suicide remains a matter of vexation. Identified as one of the most researched topics of the past 275 years, suicide continues to be intensely scrutinized and remains a subject of considerable and varied community reaction and debate. As we progress well into the new millennium, suicide undoubtedly will remain a controversial topic on which social, religious, medical, legal, and scientific perspectives will continue to provide important albeit conflicting perspectives.

These conflicting perspectives are brought to bear on the definition of suicide as well, as discussed long ago by Émile Durkheim ([1897] 1951:41–46), who defined suicide as "all cases of death resulting directly or indirectly from a positive or negative act of the victim himself, which he knows will produce this result" (p. 44). Although he was not completely satisfied with this working definition, Durkheim was quick to point out that it humanizes such behavior and takes the behavior out of the category of, to use Durkheim's words, "the monstrous phenomena" because this definition "gives us at once an idea of the place of suicide in moral life as a whole" (p. 45). More recent support for the lack of consensus or an agreed-upon definition emanates from Jack D. Douglas (1967:350–83), who observes that interested students of suicide frequently disagree on how to define this concept. From an extensive review of the pertinent literature, Douglas identifies six fundamental dimensions of meaning to be found in definitions of suicide found in the Western world (p. 351):

1. The initiation of an act that leads to the death of the initiator

2. The willing of an act that leads to the death of the willer

3. The willing of self-destruction

4. The loss of will

5. The motivation to be dead (or to die), which leads to the initiation of an act that leads to the death of the initiator

6. The knowledge of an actor that the actions he or she initiates tend to produce the objective state of death

In light of all the methodological implications involved, one could also make a quick reference to Christine Quigley's *Death Dictionary* (1994), which defines suicide as "an act of active or passive self-destruction; one who kills oneself. . . . suicidal behavior is self-destructive activity" (p. 147).

Although committers may determine the manner, the time, and the place at which they will die, the living are always affected in some way, whether the death is attributed to emotional stress, economic problems, health-related matters, supposed contagion, or even intense emotions such as anger. On the social level, suicide inflicts grief and remorse on survivors. The issues of church burial, social stigma, and pity also represent pragmatic considerations with which the living must contend. However, it would seem that society is the greatest loser, for the act of suicide deprives the body politic of valuable members.

Such issues are not new; suicide has long been a subject of great debate. Concerning philosophical, theistic, social, and legal issues, the debate pertains, on the one hand, to whether or not one is entitled to take one's own life. But there also exists the strongly held belief that one who commits suicide commits a sin, an immoral and antisocial act. In this view suicide is considered a form of individual expression that Western society is reticent to condone. The moral questions that arise are tied to religious dogma and, in addition, involve legal definitions that have far-reaching consequences for those left behind. Observations based on published works indicate that social reactions to suicide vary from glorification to indifference to severe societal condemnation. In this regard, it may be stated that suicide rates vary inversely with the degree of social condemnation of such behavior.

Although suicide has been and probably always will be a part of the human condition, moral philosophers of the past argued against suicide because they believed this act degraded human worth. Thus a suicidal person was once classified as "a felon against himself" (Quigley 1994:3). As Margaret Pabst Battin (1982) observes:

> Suicide was treated as a felony offense in early English and continental law; it was subject to harsh civil as well as religious penalties. . . . France relaxed its sanctions against suicide at the time of the 1789 revolution; suicide remained a felony in England until 1961, and has been a criminal offense in many states of the United States. (P. 17)

In this area, the view was that the public good should take precedence over the individual, and anything that harmed the public good was considered immoral. Immanuel Kant, for example, believed that suicide is morally wrong, stating that "to use the power of a free will for its own destruction is self-contradictory" (quoted in Dobrin 1988:194). According to Kant, suicide is morally wrong because it annuls the condition of all other duties. That is, a dead person is unable to fulfill his or her responsibilities to others. Some may reason that people commit suicide because of an inappropriate moral conception, believing that the purpose of life is to live in a happy state. Kant, who believed otherwise, presented another perspective:

> It is not necessary that whilst I live I should live happily; but it is necessary that so long as I live I should live honorably. . . . as a rule, those who labor for this happiness are more liable to suicide. . . . having been deprived of [pleasure] only given way to grief, sorrow and melancholy. (Quoted in Dobrin 1988:194)

Thomas Aquinas condemned the act of suicide as contrary to natural law, which established that each person should engage in a love of self. Augustine likewise condemned the act of suicide as contrary to God's Sixth Commandment, whereas Aristotle thought suicide is wrong because it is harmful to the social entity superior to the individual, namely, the state (see Dobrin 1988:193–95; see also Battin 1982:49–53). These moral philosophers believed in natural law; events such as suicide are either right or wrong based on how they fit into the unfolding natural scheme of things. Thus the goals of society are inherent in nature,

based on God's scheme. Citing a publication from 1824, Leonard (2001) states, "Nineteenth-century religious writings opposed suicide, equating such deaths with an imperfect acceptance of God's will" (p. 462). Drawing from early analysts of this problem, Leonard refers to the suicidal act as "self-murder," such as during periods of profound "passion, anger, pride, resentment, revenge, [or] disappointment" (p. 462). It is therefore important to constrain those who would engage in an act of self-murder and thereby serve as improper examples for others (e.g., the problem of contagion).

Such condemnations are not restricted to those who hold Christian beliefs. According to Andriolo (1998:47), ancient Hinduism condemned suicides committed by individuals who were viewed as motivated by worldly, self-centered desires or fears. On the other hand, suicides committed as expressions of religious sacrifice and self-transcendence were glorified (suicides by those who had achieved enlightenment or an understanding of the true reality and their placement or position within this reality). In general, this accepted second view of suicide was accorded to adult males. According to Andriolo, only those women who followed their husbands in death by committing suicide were accorded noble status. Known as sati or suttee, this practice involved the self-immolation of a widow on her husband's funeral pyre.

But members of contemporary society are not bound to natural law, nor do they currently appear to be committed to reestablishing what Durkheim ([1897] 1951) viewed as the diminished bonds of traditional society. Indeed, the evolution of industrialization and the birth of modern society encouraged a breakdown of the bonds of traditional life and the enhancement of individual expression; the emphasis on individualism continues to hold sway in postmodern society. Yet, and despite the historic cultural changes that have led to the present emphasis on individualism, the state nonetheless maintains an interest in the well-being of its citizens, especially in matters involving life and death (Battin 1982; Szasz 1999; Leonard 2001).

USES OF OFFICIAL STATISTICS: THE BEGINNING

Other than a reliance on church documents, the recording of births and deaths and other forms of official record keeping conducted in European cities and states can be traced as far back as the early 1500s (Vold 1958:162–65). The first numerical study of death records is attributed to John Graunt, whose 1662 work *Natural and Political Observations Upon the Bills of Morality* laid the foundation for the establishment of an empirically based science. The efforts of these data recorders, known in England as *political arithmetic* and in Germany as *moral Statistiks,* also began what was destined to become a continuing effort to standardize procedures for the recording of vital statistics. Thus what became known as *moral statistics* were first employed by analysts who were interested in the study of social problems such as poverty, juvenile delinquency, and crime (Vold 1958). Given the historical interest in the morality of such behavior, the moral philosophers also cast their attention toward the suicide problem.

The moral issues relating to suicide soon experienced a drastic new phase of analysis. With the increasing availability of various forms of official statistics during the late 18th century, those with a moral interest in the suicide phenomenon found these statistics increasingly useful for research and theory development (Douglas 1967:7–12). It was within this cultural context that suicide was considered as a moral problem, and this moral premise was to serve for a time as the foundation for all understanding on which the moral statisticians operated for much of the 18th and 19th centuries. And it was within this moral cultural climate that the sociologist Émile Durkheim was to create and then publish his classic treatise *Suicide: A Study in Sociology* in the year 1897, as he sought to examine the issue of free will versus determinism. It was through his study of suicide that Durkheim was to argue convincingly on behalf of the scientific study of human behavior. As Pfohl (1994) notes, "Durkheim's work on suicide represents what might be considered the intellectual culmination of the moral statistics tradition begun during the eighteenth century" (p. 256).

Since Durkheim's time, social scientists have argued that the usefulness of official statistics is generally limited outside of the specific purposes for which they are gathered. However true this assessment may be, perhaps the most difficult problem for behavioral and social scientists is that suicide data mirror the limitations found in all kinds of officially recorded statistics. That is, given ongoing efforts to improve the reporting of data, the recorded categories used over time are not consistent. In the United States, for example, although all states were not admitted to the death registration until 1933, in 1929, the federal government printed a specific table in the *Statistical Abstracts* that included rates for both sex and race. Then, in 1930, the mortality data published by the U.S. Bureau of the Census were at the time categorized as "white" and "colored." By 1931, the Census Bureau had refined these statistics even more, reporting "white," "Negro," "Indian," "Chinese," "Japanese," "Mexican," and "other" race categories. By the 1980s, enhancement of the categories recorded included "Asian," "American Indian/Pacific Islander," and "Hispanic." Table 1 displays Census Bureau data from 1900 forward, but for the reasons cited above, some of the information presented in Tables 2 and 3 covers the period beginning in 1930.

Comparisons of data reported over the past two decades present similar challenges. A recent example can be drawn from data reported by the National Center for Health Statistics, which changed the recording categories for its annual *Health, United States* publication in 2001 from those found in the year 2000 publication. This particular

change is rather dramatic, given that in the 2000 publication "Asian" is listed as a single category, whereas the 2001 publication includes the category "Asian or Pacific Islander." Similarly, in *Health, United States, 2000,* "American Indian or Pacific Islander" appears, whereas in the 2001 publication the category is "American Indian or Alaska Native." Because of this categorical switch, significant changes appear in the data reported for both crude and age-adjusted suicide rates. Moreover, in addition to the "Hispanic" category found in the year 2000 publication, the more recent publication includes the category "white, non-Hispanic," thereby creating another noteworthy change in the categorical data.

The moral, philosophical, social, legal, and religious issues surrounding self-destructive behavior continue to be debated during the early portion of the new millennium. In the following sections, I present an overview of historical and contemporary suicide trends in the United States, along with a series of tables that show how official recording patterns are reflective of social change.

HISTORICAL DOCUMENTATION OF THE SUICIDE PROBLEM: 100 YEARS

Table 1 displays general data recorded during a 100-year period; with the exception of the final decade of the 20th century, the table shows the beginning and midpoint of each decade as a matter of parsimony. These early data clearly point to where the major problem lies: Suicide is primarily a male problem.

During the 1930s, suicide continued to be primarily a white problem, especially among males. In 1930, for example, the overall suicide rate was 15.6 ($n = 17,383$); 600 of these deaths were minority, or "colored," as they were recorded in the mortality statistics (U.S. Bureau of the Census 1930:252). Of this total, 454 were "colored" males, compared with the 13,865 events documented for white males.

The suicide rate for males was highest in 1931; for females the highest rate occurred during the early 1940s. Combined for both sexes, the recorded suicide rate reached an early-20th-century peak in 1908 and 1932, when a crude rate of 18.6 was recorded. From this peak, the crude suicide rate declined to a low of 9.6, recorded in 1957. After that time, however, the rate of suicide increased upward, to 12.7 in 1975; since 1975, it has been at a lower and often declining rate.

But, as the data in Table 1 indicate, the crude rate of recorded suicide is, with few exceptions, markedly consistent. At the end of the 20th century, for example, the crude suicide rate for 1999 (10.6) was not significantly different from that recorded in 1900 (10.2). However, the suicide rate does show dramatic variations, especially around 1905, 1910, 1915, the 1930s, and for 1940. With the exception of these periods, the suicide rate has been fairly consistent, ranging between 10.2 and 12.7.

Table 1   Crude Suicide Rates for Males and Females, Selected Years, 1900 to 1999

Year	Rate	Male Number (Rate)	Female Number (Rate)	Total Number
1900	10.2	1,568	468	2,036[a]
1905	13.5	2,208	732	2,940
1910	15.3	5,621	1,662	7,283[a]
1915	16.2	7,712	2,299	10,011[a]
1920	10.2	6,364	2,426	8,790
1925	12.0	9,297	2,912	12,209
1930	15.6	14,319	4,004	18,323
1935	14.3	13,942	4,272	18,214
1940	14.4	14,466	4,441	18,907
1945	11.2	10,754	4,028	14,782
1950	11.4	13,297 (17.8)	3,848 (5.1)	17,145
1955	10.2	12,961 (16.0)	3,799 (4.6)	16,760
1960	10.6	14,539 (16.6)	4,502 (4.9)	19,041
1965	11.1	15,490 (16.3)	6,017 (6.1)	21,507
1970	11.6	16,629 (16.8)	6,851 (6.6)	23,480
1975	12.7	19,622 (18.9)	7,441 (6.8)	27,063
1980	11.9	— (18.6)	— (5.5)	26,869
1985	12.3	— (20.0)	— (5.2)	29,453
1990	12.4	— (20.4)	— (4.8)	30,906
1991	12.2	— (20.1)	— (4.7)	30,810
1992	12.0	— (19.6)	— (4.6)	30,484
1993	12.1	— (19.9)	— (4.6)	31,102
1994	12.0	— (19.8)	— (4.5)	31,142
1995	11.9	— (19.8)	— (4.4)	31,284
1996	11.6	— (19.3)	— (4.4)	30,903
1997	11.4	— (18.7)	— (4.4)	30,535
1998	11.3	— (18.6)	— (4.4)	30,575
1999	10.7	23,458 (17.6)	5,741 (4.1)	29,199

SOURCES: U.S. Bureau of the Census (1975:58, 414; 1977, 1999, 2000), National Center for Health Statistics (1978, 2000), and Hoyert et al. (2001).

a. Data reported in U.S. Bureau of the Census (1921) indicate the number of deaths by suicide for the years 1900, 1910, and 1915, respectively, are as follows: 1900, 3,534 deaths; 1910, 8,590 deaths; 1915, 11,216 deaths.

Throughout the final decade (1990–99) of the 20th century, suicide rates steadily declined for males (20.4 to 17.6) and females (4.8 to 4.1), whites (13.5 to 11.7), nonwhites (7.0 to 6.0), and blacks (6.9 to 5.6) (McIntosh 2001). One consistent pattern, however, has been that throughout the entire 100-year period, the suicide rates for males have far exceeded those for females.

OVERVIEW OF THE CONTEMPORARY SUICIDE PROBLEM

Throughout the 1990s, suicide was consistently one of the leading causes of death for many age-specific categories in the United States. In 1998, suicide was ranked among the 10 leading causes of death, and among males it was the eighth leading cause of death. In 1999, according to the National Center for Health Statistics, suicide was the tenth leading cause of death; among white males grouped by age-specific categories (15–19, 20–24, and 25–34), suicide was the second leading cause of death (Anderson 2001). Such forms of intentional self-harm were ranked somewhat lower as a causal factor for older age categories, ranking as the fourth, fifth, and eighth leading causes of death among the age groups 35–44, 45–54, and 55–64, respectively. In the area of death cause counting, with the exception of 1999, when it was the eleventh leading cause of death among Americans, suicide has ranked among the 10 leading causes of mortality in the United States since 1975.

In reviewing the data reported in Tables 1, 2, and 3, the most obvious observation is that white males experience the highest rate of suicide. This holds without exception. The same is true for the second observation: That is, black males always rank second, followed by white females and, finally, black females. This sequence has been seen without exception over a 100-year period.

Looking at the specific rates reported in Tables 2 and 3, the highest rates of suicide were recorded for 1930, 1935, and 1940; this observation holds for males of both races as well as for white females. Suicide rates declined significantly for white males during the years following the Great Depression and the period encompassing World War II. Of interest are the high rates recorded during the 1940s, a time when lower rates might be expected given the vast number of individuals who served in the U.S. military forces during this period.

Although the social gender gap may be narrowing in many aspects of life, as many analysts have suggested, the suicide rates for males far exceed those for females in the United States and in all English-speaking Western societies. Most suicides are committed by males, and, with some variation, suicide rates tend to rise as age increases, with rates highest among elderly white males. White males die at their own hands at almost twice the rate of black males (U.S. Bureau of the Census 1997:102). In the United States, since 1980, suicide rates have increased in only two age groups: among those 15–19 years old and among those 65 years and older.

Historically, age-specific rates of suicide in the United States have been highest among the elderly, especially older males. However, suicidal behavior has increased

Table 2   Suicide Rates by Race and Sex, Ages 15 and Over, Selected Years, 1930 to 1975

Year	Total (Rate) Both Sexes	White Male	White Female	Black and Other Male	Black and Other Female
1930	18,323 (22.1)	36.4	10.4	11.3	3.6
1935	18,214 (19.6)	31.8	9.8	10.8	3.9
1940	18,907 (19.2)	31.3	9.6	10.4	3.1
1945	14,782 (15.1)	25.6	8.2	8.5	2.1
1950	17,145 (15.6)	26.0	7.4	10.4	2.4
1955	16,760 (14.5)	24.5	6.9	9.6	2.3
1960	19,014 (15.9)	25.7	7.6	11.7	3.1
1965	21,507 (16.1)	25.3	9.2	12.9	4.8
1970	23,480 (16.2)	25.3	9.6	13.4	4.3
1975	27,063 (17.0)	27.0	9.6	16.0	4.6

SOURCES: Adapted from National Center for Health Statistics (1978:40) and U.S. Bureau of the Census (1978).

among elderly persons and terminally ill individuals regardless of gender. During the 1980–99 period, males accounted for 81% of the suicides among elderly persons 65 years of age and older.

In 1980, suicide was the tenth leading cause of death among Americans ($n = 26,869$); in 1999, a total of 29,199 persons were officially known to have died as a result of their own actions. Depending on the source cited, in 1999 suicide was ranked as either the tenth or eleventh leading cause of death. Among males, suicide was ranked seventh and eleventh among the top causes of death in 1980 and 1999, respectively. However, this act of self-destruction is not listed among the highest-ranked causes of death among white women. The same is true for blacks of either sex as well as for American Indian/Alaska Native females (Kramarow et al. 1999; Hoyert et al. 2001).

According to the U.S. government's *Annual Summary Reports,* during the first half of the 1990s the numbers of suicides recorded each year increased while the rates remained relatively stable. For example, during the 1990–95 period, the rates of suicide for all races and sexes were 11.5, 11.4, 11.1, 11.3, 11.2, and 11.0, respectively (U.S. Bureau of the Census 1997:95, table 128). During 1996, 29,280 persons (rate = 11.6) died in self-inflicted episodes, and in 1997, the number of suicides increased to 30,535 (rate = 11.4); 19,491 homicides were committed during that same year. In 1998, 30,575 suicides (rate = 11.4) were officially recorded, 24,538 of which were male; 22,174 of the male committers were white (Murphy 2000:59). These numbers are substantial when compared with those related to other social problems, such as homicide; in 1998, there were 1.5 times as many suicides ($n = 30,575$) as there were homicides ($n = 18,272$; rate = 6.8). In 1999, of the 29,199 officially reported suicides (rate = 10.7), a total of 21,107 were white males. The 1999 data indicate a similar comparison situation, with the number of suicides officially recorded as 29,199

(rate = 10.7) and the number of homicides 16,889 (rate = 6.2) (Anderson 2001:10).

Suicide and Age

The data on suicide mortality by age are particularly interesting. For the period 1950–70, for example, in descending order, the highest rates for white males were in the 65 and over age group; for the black and male category, the age groups 55–64 and 65 and over had the highest rates for 1950 and 1960, but the rates declined considerably in 1970, a time during which the 35–44 age group was at greater risk. For white females, the age categories 45–54 and 55–64 were at greatest risk during the 1950–70 period, a time when black and other females had the lowest risk of all race and sex groups; the 45–54 age group recorded the highest rate during 1950 and 1970— during 1960 this distinction fell to the 65 and over group (U.S. Bureau of the Census 1974).

This pattern of age and race continues to the present, although some variation occurs within age groups. Although it is well established that the suicide rates increase with age, according to the National Center for Injury Prevention and Control (2000), the period 1980–90 was the first decade since the 1940s that the suicide rate among the elderly rose. Nevertheless, older adult males have consistently had the highest suicide rate of all age groups since 1933, the first year all states reported mortality data.

For the 1990–97 period, a total of 42 suicides were officially recorded for the 5–9 year age group. This is a highly unusual documentation, given the cultural bias and aversion in the United States to any consideration that suicide may occur within the youngest age groups as well as among members of particular religious groups. By the ages 10–14, however, the figures increase dramatically throughout the ascending age ranks. Taking cultural factors into consideration, most recent recording techniques collapse the 5–9 age group with the 10–14 group, making a 5–14 age category.

In 1998, suicide was the eighth leading cause of death in the United States and the third leading cause of death among young people. As the National Center for Injury Prevention and Control (2000) has noted, suicide is a serious public health problem among young people: Between 1990 and 1997, the rate of suicide increased 109% for 10- to 14-year-olds and 11% for 15- to 19-year-olds.

Suicide ranked as the third leading cause of death among the young ages 15–24 in 1999 ($n = 3,901$; rate = 10.3), placing this youthful age category slightly

Table 3   Death Rates for Suicide by Race and Sex, 1930–99

	1930	1935	1940	1945	1950	1955	1960	1965	1970	1975	1980
Total											
AASR	—	—	—	—	13.2	—	12.5	—	13.1	12.7	12.2
CSR	21.6	20.1	19.5	15.1	11.4	10.2	10.6	11.1	11.6	13.0	11.9
White male											
AASR	36.4	31.8	31.1	—	18.1	—	25.7	25.3	18.2	—	18.9
CSR	—	—	23.5	25.6	19.0	24.5	17.6	—	18.0	—	19.9
Black male											
AASR	11.3	10.8	—	—	6.3	—	11.7	12.9	9.9	—	11.1
CSR	—	—	4.6	8.5	7.0	9.6	7.2	—	8.5	10.6	10.8
White female											
AASR	10.4	9.8	9.6	—	5.3	—	7.6	9.2	7.2	—	5.7
CSR	—	—	7.3	8.2	5.5	6.9	5.3	—	7.1	7.3	5.9
Black female											
AASR	3.1	3.9	3.6	—	1.5	—	1.9	4.0	2.9	—	2.2
CSR	—	—	2.1	2.1	1.7	2.3	2.0	—	2.9	2.7	2.4

lower than the national rate (10.7) for all age groups. Only accidents ($n = 13$, 656; rate $= 36.2$) and homicides ($n = 4{,}998$; rate $= 13.2$) ranked higher. Still, the well-documented idea that suicide is a leading cause of death among youth may be somewhat misleading, particularly for those under the age of 14. The public health revolution and improvements in medical care have contributed to a significant decline in youthful mortality previously attributable to infectious diseases, and this trend, in turn, has increased the relative importance of violent forms of death such as suicide. This same explanation may hold for other age groups as well.

Nevertheless, recorded increases in age-specific death rates for suicide under the age of 24 for most categories by race and gender have been noted during the past several decades. In addition, the age category 25–34 has shown marked increase in suicide rates for both race and sex categories since 1950. Although the official rates for youthful suicide may be in part an artifact of recording procedures, the age-specific rates indicate that suicide risk is directly correlated with advancing age. As noted, suicide is nonexistent under the age of 5, virtually nonexistent at 5–9 years of age, and rare at ages 10–14. However, for the years of late adolescence and early adulthood, white male suicide in particular increases with frequency about 8 to 10 times at ages 15–19, doubles in frequency in the 20–24 year age group, and is 1.5 times as great in the 25–34 age group (Peck 1979:3–4). A similar conclusion can be made for the final years of the 20th century. Beginning with the 15–24 age group, the rate of suicide ranges between 18.5 and 24.0 for youth, young adults, and adults; the rate modestly declines among the middle adult age groups and then dramatically increases among the elderly.

Refinement of the data allows us to appreciate more fully the magnitude of the suicide problem, as the information in Table 2 shows. Rather than crude suicide rates, Table 2 displays data for the 1930–75 period that clearly demonstrate that the suicide problem is better understood through age-specific categories of 15 years of age and older. Although these kinds of data have not been a regular feature of official reporting publications such as the *Statistical Abstracts of the United States*, even more refined age-specific data are currently available in the National Vital Statistics Reports published by the National Center for Health Statistics, which provide final data for given years. One example of this important adjustment to the reporting procedure is shown in Table 5, in which a larger number of racial, gender, and age categories are documented.

That the highest rates of suicide are recorded among males, especially young adult and older males, also is consistent with recorded gender differences in attitudes toward suicide. In general, younger males are more likely than younger females to engage in impulsive behavior, and this impulsivity has been linked to self-destructive types of behavior, such as cigarette smoking, alcohol use, and risk taking (Langhinrichsen-Rohling et al. 1998). The Centers for Disease Control and Prevention apparently supports this contention, suggesting that family-related problems and ease of access to alcohol, illicit drugs, and firearms are major factors in the rising rates of suicide among the young, especially young black males.

Such behaviors also are thought to be significant predictors of suicide ideation and attempts. That is, males appear to be more accepting of suicide than are females, and males are more likely than females to agree that an individual has

Table 3 (Continued)

	1985	1990	1991	1992	1993	1994	1995	1996	1997	1998	1999
Total											
AASR	12.5	12.5	11.4	11.1	11.3	11.2	12.0	11.7	11.4	11.3	10.6
CSR	12.4	12.4	12.2	12.0	12.1	12.0	11.9	11.6	11.4	11.3	10.7
White male											
AASR	19.9	19.9	18.1	—	—	—	18.6	18.0	17.4	18.3	—
CSR	22.0	22.0	19.0	—	—	—	21.4	19.3	20.3	20.3	19.1
Black male											
AASR	11.3	12.4	7.0	—	—	—	—	—	—	10.5	—
CSR	10.8	12.0	6.3	—	—	—	11.9	11.4	10.9	10.2	10.0
White female											
AASR	5.3	4.8	5.3	—	7.6	—	7.2	—	—	4.4	—
CSR	5.6	5.3	5.5	—	5.3	—	7.1	4.8	4.9	4.8	4.5
Black female											
AASR	2.1	2.4	1.5	—	1.9	—	2.9	—	1.9	1.8	—
CSR	2.8	2.3	1.7	—	1.6	—	2.6	2.0	1.9	1.8	1.6

SOURCES:U.S. Bureau of the Census (1973, 1974, 1999); National Center for Health Statistics (1991:99–100, table 35; 1994, 2001); Murphy (2000); Peters, Kochanek, and Murphy (1998); and Anderson (2001).

the right to commit suicide. Moreover, young adults and adults over the age of 60 are more likely to be tolerant of suicide than are middle-aged people (for a review of this literature, see Parker, Cantrell, and Demi 1997).

SOCIAL FACTORS ASSOCIATED WITH SUICIDE

Sex/Gender Differentials

The first and perhaps most notable sociological theory developed to explore social factors as these relate to suicidal behavior was that proposed by Émile Durkheim ([1897] 1951). Strong social ties such as those created through work, marriage, having children, religious affiliation, and engaging in community activities and commitments protect against suicide, according to Durkheim, who demonstrated that suicide rates are relatively low and even decrease during the stages of the life cycle between late adolescence and old age.

An interesting aspect of suicide is the male/female difference. Although females are more likely to attempt suicide, males commit suicide more frequently than females for all age groups. The difference between males and females is greatest in the 15–24 age category; female suicides reach their highest proportion (relative to male suicides) in the 25–39 age group. Among 20- to 24-year-olds, males are four times more likely than females to commit suicide. Although the white male ratio of suicide to that of minority males and females is considerably higher, the rates for females and nonwhites have risen more sharply than those of white males, especially since 1960.

In the wake of documented increases in the rates of suicide among nonwhites, females, and young persons, efforts at explanation tend to identify low self-esteem, shame, status worth, goal commitment, personal responsibility, low achievement, and role conflict as factors contributing to abnormal behavior. In one interesting study, Cumming, Lazer, and Chrisholm (1975) found that for all age categories, employed married women are more protected against suicide than are unemployed women who are single, widowed, or divorced. Such findings are contrary to the hypothesized role conflict or role overload model proposed by some analysts. Cumming et al. state, "These findings are compatible with the proposition that for married women the benefits of working far outweigh the costs, and that these benefits increase somewhat when the climate of opinion favours married women entering the labour market" (p. 467).

Consistent with the history of this phenomenon in the United States, however, white males and, more recently, white, non-Hispanic males represent the groups at greatest risk of suicide. Moreover, the data do not support the assertion that the current trend in the increase in suicide rates is not as great for males as it is hypothesized to be for professional women. This hypothesized relationship is based in part on the multiple roles that women in professional positions must play (Carlson and Miller 1981). The stress of a career, role and status conflict, caring for a family, and lack of personal time are all issues that professional women contend with on a daily basis. Other analysts suggest that the suicide rate for older women is changing more than that for males, especially when socioeconomic factors such as labor force participation in nontraditional occupations are controlled (e.g., Newman, Whittemore, and

Newman 1973; Yang and Lester 1988; Alston 1986; Lester and Yang 1992). Recently, Mayer (2000) found additional evidence in support of the hypothesized relationship between women's attainment of greater education and professional advancement and the suicide rate. He states, "With increased equality for men and women in white-collar employment and political representation, female suicide rates *are* rising" (p. 372).

Beginning with Durkheim's ([1897] 1951) analysis, it is noteworthy that the least advantaged members of society experience more modest rates of suicide than do those who hold greater advantages in the areas of education and labor force participation. Although U.S.-based research findings in this area appear to be quite mixed, there is some evidence that the highest rates of suicide occur among individuals, both males and females, who occupy high-status occupations. For example, research has found that among single female psychologists (Mausner and Steppacher 1973), physicians (Rose and Rosnow 1973; Frank and Dingle 1999), chemists (Li 1969), and nurses (Hawton and Vislisel 1999), rates of suicide are at least equal to if not greater than rates for males.

Various lifestyle factors have also been cited as contributing to suicidal behavior, especially among males. Examples of these factors include increased rates of divorce, unemployment, and alcohol and drug use and abuse (Appleby 2000). In addition, some analysts assert that suicide may be statistically underrepresented, because some suicides—such as "autocides" (Quigley 1994:3), or suicides disguised as vehicle accidents—are not identified as suicides. Selzer and Payne's (1962) research on alcohol use and autocide provides some support for this contention, and Peck and Warner (1995) report that some of the deaths attributed to vehicle accidents, especially single-car accidents, may result from suicidal intent on the part of the drivers.

Marital Status

Since Durkheim ([1897] 1951) conducted his seminal work, analyses of the effects of marital status on the suicide rate have focused on the buffering effect of marriage, especially for males. Research findings in this area have shown consistent patterns since the time of Durkheim, thereby firmly establishing his initial sociological efforts as a road map for all others to follow. Although one may argue that contemporary efforts do not offer major sociological insights beyond Durkheim's contributions, some scholars have made significant refinements to the original ideas presented in Durkheim's seminal research effort. Examples of these efforts include the work of Stack (1996–97, 1998) and Appleby (2000), among others.

As Stack (1998) notes, research that has explored the relationship between marriage and emotional well-being has found that men benefit more from marriage than do women. Again, such findings support those first reported by Durkheim ([1897] 1951), who recognized the buffering effect of the marital social bond. But divorce affects as many women as it does men. The same is true of whatever financial problems are attendant to unemployment or underemployment. Still, none of these factors seems to affect the female suicide rate in the same manner as it does for males. The problem of alcohol and drug abuse, a major contributing factor in male suicide, also provides an interesting comparison. Although female consumption of both alcohol and drugs is believed to have increased during the recent past, female suicide rates have remained relatively stable (Appleby 2000).

Newman et al. (1973) and Steffensmeier (1984) suggest that the increases in female labor force participation and female suicide during the 1970s may be related, given the role conflict experienced by employed, career-oriented women as well as the vast and varied changes in sex roles in the home and the workplace. Stack (1978) asserts that such changes may lead to status and role conflict stemming from the responsibilities inherent in the roles of homemaker, spouse, parent, and employee. Thus enhanced labor force participation may diminish rather than enhance status integration for females, leading, in turn, to a higher suicide rate.

Many analysts also argue that women's full-time involvement in the labor market serves as a buffer against suicide (e.g., Appleby 2000). Certainly, significant changes took place in the economic, political, and social structure of American society over the course of the final decades of the 20th century. These changes generally have been applauded within the context of the gains achieved by women and members of racial minority groups. The employment structure opened, leading in turn to opportunities previously unavailable to most members of such groups. Challenges to this structure were supported by increased educational achievement and changing social perspectives toward opening career opportunities. Such would be the situation, it is argued, for understanding an increased rate of suicide among professional females and racial minorities. Such factors may also include the notion of cultural scripts as these affect the current suicide rates and the potential any change in these traditional scripts may hold for female and minority suicide rates.

Perhaps it is true that along with social change and enhanced exposure to other less desirable situations, life chances may have evolved for those previously relegated to less challenging positions in the labor force. A society with diminished opportunities for employment may be a causal factor in enhancing the levels of individual stress among the unemployed as well as the employed. This may be particularly true in an unsteady economic climate in which job loss becomes a major concern. As Henry and Short (1954) note, dramatic economic change leads to significant social change and diminished life chances.

Race

The reporting of suicide and compilation of suicide rates for and among racial groups did not begin in the

United States until 1929. As Table 3 shows, the crude rates for minorities were at the time collapsed into a single "black and other" category. However, by 1950, more refined categories became common (see Table 4), and by the 1980–85 period, "Asian/Pacific Islander" and "American Indian/Alaska Native" categories were documented. By 1985, the suicide rates for Hispanics served notice of yet another significant change in both the composition of the American population and subsequent recording procedures (see Table 5). The elaboration of the recording procedures, as shown in Tables 4 and 5, is a clear demonstration of the changing composition of the population of the United States. Perhaps more important, these data suggest that an important social transformation has again occurred in the mixture of individuals who actively participate in the American experience. This experience may include positive aspects as well as some not so positive, such as an increased rate of suicide. The data shown in Table 4 are noteworthy, especially the high suicide rates recorded for the white, American Indian/Alaska Native, and white, non-Hispanic male categories. However, in any given year white males have accounted for as much as 73% of all suicides and, combined, white males and females may account for 90% of the total number of suicides.

Although data for a 1- or 2-year period cannot be taken to suggest a trend, the data for 1998–99 are instructive for placing the suicide problem within a public health context. In Table 5, the suicide rates and rankings of cause of death are displayed for age-specific groups by race and sex. As the table shows, for males, suicide is ranked among the 10 leading causes of death, especially among the youngest age-specific categories. However, youthful females also are well represented, especially for the 5–14, 15–24, and 25–44 age categories. If we disregard ages 5–14, the age categories that might be of greatest interest with regard to educational achievement and, more specific to these data, occupational achievement would be cause to review the rankings of cause of death more closely for ages 15–24 and 24–44. Again, and without exception, suicide is highly ranked as a cause of death for white, black, and white, non-Hispanic as well as Hispanic males.

Consistent with the thesis of the inadequacy of official data, some observers contend that among American blacks in particular, rates of suicide may be substantially higher than the official records indicate (see, e.g., Peck 1983–84). To augment this argument, some analysts suggest that an upward trend in suicide exists among minorities, especially blacks. Indeed, Burr, Hartman, and Matteson (1999) assert that this may be the case, based on their finding that higher economic status among black males and suicide appear to be significantly related. In 1998, the Centers for Disease Control and Prevention reported that suicide is increasingly a problem among black youths 10–19 years of age. According to the CDC, for the 1980–95 period, the rate of suicide among black youths increased 114%, from 2.1 to 4.5 per 100,000. Note that the official data mprovide some support for this claim, as shown in Tables 3, 4, and

5. However, it is also noteworthy that the suicide rate for black males increased up to the year 1990 and then declined throughout the 1990s. As shown in Tables 4 and 5, the data for white, non-Hispanics are rather dramatic, demonstrating that the suicide rate was highest among this racial group throughout the entire decade of the 1990s.

Religious Affiliation

Durkheim ([1897] 1951) considered the institution of religion to be an important mechanism of social influence and control that exercises integrative effects on individuals to a greater or lesser degree. Accordingly, differences are observed in the suicide rates of different religious groups, with Protestant, Catholic, and Jewish victims ranking in that order. When the information is known, religion is a recorded category on the certificate of death. However, such data are difficult to secure from the public record, so little information on this important topic is available. An exception is one of my own studies, in which the findings were consistent with those first reported by Durkheim (Peck 1979). If the greater or lesser effects of religion and the interactive effect of level of education combine, thereby discouraging life-destructive behavior based on the strength or weakness of the social bond afforded by religious institutions, the data suggest that suicide rates are highest among Protestants, followed by Catholics and Jews, in that order. More recently, Burr et al. (1999) found that church membership appears to have some positive effects for African Americans, but church membership does not seem to offer the same protection against self-destructive behavior among young black males.

Social Status and Occupation

In a review of the literature published in 1982, Arthur G. Bedeian noted that the research findings on occupation and suicide available up to that time were mixed and so inconsistent as to be almost useless. The problems he identified in the studies he reviewed included small sample sizes and, perhaps more important, numerous methodological problems. Contemporary analysts suggest that such problems continue to the present. The issue they raise concerns the valid assessment of the social status concept and the occupation variable, and the relationship of these terms to suicide. Analyses of comparable data sets are certainly useful, but the analysis of trends and bringing cumulative insight and knowledge to bear on issues relating occupation to suicide are no less critical to this understanding.

The literature on the relationship between social status/occupation and suicide can be traced back at least as far as the work of Durkheim. Durkheim ([1897] 1951) evaluated the relationship of occupation to suicide within the European experience and found that the suicide rate had a direct relationship with social class. This finding strongly suggests that the higher the socioeconomic status, the higher the suicide rate. That is, suicide rates are

(text continued on p. 331)

Table 4 Crude Death Rates by Race and Sex, Selected Years, 1950 to 1999

Year	Both Sexes M	F	White M	F	Black M	F	Asian/Pacific Islander M	F	American Indian/ Alaska Native M	F	Hispanic M	F	White, Non-Hispanic M	F
1950	17.8	5.1	19.0	5.5	6.3	1.5	—	—	—	—	—	—	—	—
1955	16.0	4.6	17.2	4.9	6.1	1.5	—	—	—	—	—	—	—	—
1960	16.5	4.9	17.6	5.3	7.2	1.6	—	—	—	—	—	—	—	—
1965	16.3	6.1	17.5	6.6	7.8	2.5	—	—	—	—	—	—	—	—
1970	16.8	6.6	8.0	7.1	8.5	2.6	—	—	—	—	—	—	—	—
1975	18.9	6.8	20.1	7.4	10.6	3.3	—	4.7	—	—	—	—	—	—
1980	18.6	5.5	19.9	5.9	10.3	2.2	8.8	4.3	20.9	4.7	—	—	—	—
1985	20.0	5.2	21.6	5.6	11.0	2.1	8.4	3.4	20.3	4.4	11.0	1.6	22.3	6.1
1990	20.4	4.8	22.0	5.3	12.0	2.3	8.7	3.8	20.9	3.7	13.7	2.2	23.1	5.4
1995	19.8	4.4	21.4	4.8	11.9	2.0	9.4	4.0	19.6	4.2	13.1	1.9	22.3	5.1
1996	19.3	4.3	20.9	4.7	11.4	2.0	9.3	4.0	19.9	5.6	12.0	2.1	22.0	5.0
1997	18.7	4.4	20.2	4.8	10.9	2.0	10.5	3.6	20.9	4.2	11.2	1.6	21.5	5.3
1998	18.6	4.3	20.3	4.7	10.2	1.8	10.2	3.6	21.1	5.4	11.0	1.8	21.6	5.2
1999	17.5	4.0	19.1	4.4	10.0	1.7	9.7	—	19.6	4.8	10.7	1.7	20.4	4.8

SOURCE: Adapted from National Center for Health Statistics (1978:40; 2000).

NOTE: Preliminary data reported for 1999.

Table 5 Death Rates for Suicide for the 10 Leading Causes of Death in Specified Age Groups by Race and Sex, 1998 and Preliminary 1999 Data

Category	Age Group (in years)	Rank	Number	Rate 1998	Rate 1999[a]
1. All races, both sexes	All ages	8	30,575	11.3	10.7
	5–14	6	324	0.8	0.6
	15–24	3	4,135	11.1	10.3
	25–44	4	12,202	14.6	13.9
	25–34	—	—	13.8	13.4
	35–44	—	—	15.4	14.3
	45–64	8	8,094	14.1	13.4
	45–54	—	—	14.8	14.1
	55–64	—	—	13.1	12.3
	65 and older	—	—	16.9	15.9
	65–74	—	—	14.1	13.5
	75–84	—	—	19.7	18.2
	85+	—	—	21.0	19.2
2. All races, males	All ages	4	—	18.6	17.6
	5–14	4	241	1.2	1.0
	15–24	3	3,532	18.5	17.1
	25–44	3	9,700	23.5	22.3
	25–34	—	—	22.9	22.2
	35–44	—	—	24.0	22.4
	45–64	8	6,201	22.4	21.2
	45–54	—	—	23.1	21.9
	55–64	—	—	21.3	20.1
	65 and older	—	—	34.1	32.1
	65–74	—	—	26.2	25.0
	75–84	—	—	42.0	38.3
	85+	—	—	57.8	55.0
3. All races, females	All ages	—	—	4.4	4.1
	5–14	6	83	0.4	0.3
	15–24	4	603	3.3	3.1
	25–44	4	2,502	6.0	5.6
	25–34	—	—	4.9	4.7
	35–44	—	—	6.9	6.3
	45–64	9	1,893	6.4	6.0
	45–54	—	—	7.0	6.6
	55–64	—	—	5.5	5.2
4. White, both sexes	All ages	8	27,771	12.4	11.7
	5–14	4	274	0.9	—
	15–24	2	3,434	11.6	—
	25–44	4	10,837	15.9	—
	45–64	8	7,546	15.5	—
	65+	—	—	—	—
5. White males	All ages	8	22,174	20.3	19.1
	5–14	3	205	2.9	—
	15–24	2	2,934	19.3	17.8
	25–44	3	8,594	25.2	23.8
	45–64	7	5,786	24.2	22.9
	65+	—	—	36.6	34.5
	65–74	—	—	29.9	26.7
	75–84	—	—	44.7	40.8
	85+	—	—	62.7	59.7
6. White females	All ages	—	—	4.7	4.4
	5–14	6	69	0.5	—
	15–24	3	500	3.5	3.2
	25–44	4	2,243	6.6	6.2
	45–64	9	1,760	7.1	6.7
	65+	—	—	5.0	4.6
7. Black, both sexes	All ages	—	—	5.7	5.6
	5–14	6	69	0.5	—
	15–24	3	488	8.6	—
	25–44	7	934	8.6	—
	45–64	9	1,760	7.1	—
8. Black males	All ages	—	—	10.2	10.0
	5–14	7	23	0.7	—
	15–24	3	425	15.0	14.3
	25–44	6	781	15.2	15.3
	45–64	—	—	11.1	10.1
	65–74	—	—	11.4	11.5
	75–84	—	—	12.5	13.7
	85+	—	—	—	—

(Continued)

Table 5 (Continued)

Group	Age Group (in years)	Rank	Number	Rate 1998	Rate 1999[a]
9. Black females	All ages	—	—	1.8	1.7
	5–14	6	63	2.2	—
	15–24	—	—	2.2	2.0
	25–44	—	—	2.7	2.5
	45–64	—	—	2.2	1.8
	65+	—	—	1.2	1.5
10. Hispanic, both sexes	All ages	—	—	—	—
	5–14	6	28	0.5	—
	15–24	3	439	8.3	—
	25–44	6	755	7.8	—
	45–64	10	301	6.9	—
11. Hispanic males	All ages	9	1,429	9.4	9.1
	5–14	6	18	—	—
	15–24	3	368	13.4	11.9
	25–44	6	651	13.0	13.1
	45–64	9	240	11.5	11.9
	65+	—	—	20.0	17.4
12. Hispanic females	All ages	—	—	1.8	1.7
	5–14	6	10	—	—
	15–24	4	71	2.8	2.0
	25–44	7	—	2.2	2.5
	45–64	—	—	2.7	2.5
	65+	—	—	2.5	2.2
13. White, non-Hispanic males	All ages	—	—	21.5	20.2
	15–24	—	—	20.2	18.7
	25–44	—	—	26.7	25.3
	45–64	—	—	25.1	23.7
	65+	—	—	37.3	35.3
14. White, non-Hispanic females	All ages	—	—	5.2	4.8
	15–24	—	—	3.6	3.4
	25–44	—	—	7.2	6.7
	45–64	—	—	7.4	7.0
	65+	—	—	5.2	4.7
15. American Indian/Alaska Native males	All ages	7	—	21.1	19.6
	15–24	—	—	41.8	36.6
	25–44	—	—	33.3	29.5
	45–64	—	—	11.3	16.0
	65+	—	—	—	—
16. American Indian/Alaska Native females	All ages	—	—	5.4	4.8
	15–24	—	—	—	—
	25–44	—	—	8.0	8.3
	45–64	—	—	—	—
	65+	—	—	—	—
17. Asian/Pacific Islander males	All ages	7	—	9.1	9.0
	15–24	—	—	10.9	10.3
	25–44	—	—	11.9	12.0
	45–64	—	—	10.2	12.4
	65+	—	—	21.0	13.9
18. Asian/Pacific Islander females	All ages	—	—	3.3	3.4
	15–24	—	—	2.7	4.4
	25–44	—	—	4.0	4.0
	45–64	—	—	4.3	4.1
	65+	—	—	7.2	6.5

SOURCES: Adapted from Hoyert et al. (2001:26–40, tables 8–9, July 24, 2000 [see also errata with revised p. 45]) and National Center for Health Statistics (2001:217–19).

a. Preliminary data for 1999 refer to the rate per 100,000; N = 29,199.

highest among the highest-income groups. As Durkheim notes:

> The liberal professions and in a wider sense the well-to-do classes are certainly those with the liveliest taste for knowledge and the most active intellectual life. Now, although the statistics of suicide by occupations and classes cannot always be obtained with sufficient accuracy, it is undeniably exceptionally frequent in the highest classes of society. (P. 165)

Durkheim also found that for a number of European nation-states the suicide rates were relatively high among professional groups devoted to letters, members of the army, and an intellectually elite group of public officials (p. 166).

Two generations after Durkheim's work was published in Europe, the empirical assessment of the occupation and social status relationship to suicide was well under way in the United States. For example, Elwin H. Powell (1958) posed the following:

> Based on the postulate that self-destructiveness is rooted in social conditions, the argument . . . is that occupation provides function and determines the individual's social status which is an index to his conceptual scheme. The conceptual system is the source of anomie, which is a primary variable in suicide. Therefore, suicide is correlated with occupation. (P. 133)

Schmid and Van Arsdol (1955) conducted a 5-year study (1948–52) of completed and attempted suicide in Seattle, Washington, but in their published report they are vague concerning the important effect of occupation on suicide. According to these analysts, "'White collar' occupations and professions have lower suicide rates of both completed and attempted suicide than persons employed in 'blue collar' occupations." However, they also state that "because of incompleteness of data on occupations, additional comparisons and conclusions are not warranted" (p. 280).

Powell's (1958:134) analysis of data from Tulsa, Oklahoma, for the 1937–56 period does offer support, however. For some reason, Powell combined professional-managerial and sales-clerical groups, and thereby reported a higher annual rate of suicide (24.6) for these combined groups than was found for manual workers (19.6). Taking this unique assessment further, Powell's study data indicate the average rate of suicide during this 20-year period was 35.1 for the professional-managerial category, whereas the rate for unskilled laborers was 38.7. Only the retired had a higher rate of suicide (83.4). Within the white-collar category, pharmacists had the highest rate of suicide (120), followed by physicians (83), nurses (38), lawyers (36), engineers (15), and accountants (7). Among blue-collar occupations the highest rate of suicide was found among cab drivers (86.9), followed by welders (25), machinists (17), truck drivers (12), mechanics (10), and carpenters (5).

During this same time period, Durkheim's contention pertaining to social class and suicide received some support from Henry and Short's (1954) study and from Ruth S. Cavan's earlier Chicago study, which was reported in 1965 (as cited in Maris 1969:120). Both these projects demonstrate the existence of high suicide rates among professionals and those of higher education.

In Warren Breed's (1963) New Orleans study of white male suicide ($n = 105$) for the 1954–59 period and Ronald W. Maris's (1969) Chicago study ($n = 2,153$) covering 1959–63, an inverse relationship was found between social status and suicide; that is, the higher the social class status, the lower the suicide rate, and the lower the social class status, the higher the suicide rate. Breed was interested in occupational status mobility, especially downward mobility, with its attendant problems associated with reduced income, unemployment, and other occupation- and business-related problems. Only half of the subjects in his sample ($n = 52$) were employed at the time of their deaths. It may be noteworthy that Breed concludes his occupational mobility and suicide commentary by stating that his findings support the anomie thesis suggested by Powell. In Breed's words, "Anomic suicide can and does occur during integrated conditions as well as during anomie, and low-achievement [work] performances promote suicide in good [economic] times or bad" (p. 188).

Breed's findings warrant some support from others, according to Ira M. Wasserman (1992), who conducted a review of the economy, work, and suicide literature and concludes that it must be assumed that certain groups of people are more prone to suicide. And it is this assumption that bears directly on the relationship between suicide and occupation or unemployment. Some social groups experience increases in their suicide rates when short- or long-term economic changes occur. These changes, in turn, affect certain occupational and work groups and individuals with high levels of psychological and psychiatric morbidity.

Maris (1969:121–35) applied a socioeconomic status (SES) score to his Chicago data in addressing the relationship between occupation and suicide, and found suicide rates to be highest among lower-status occupational groups. For example, the suicide rate per 100,000 for laborers was 50.6; among service workers the rate was 46.4, and for operatives and kindred workers the rate was 23.3; the rate was moderate among middle-status groups, such as craftsmen, foremen, and kindred workers (20.9) and sales workers (19.8), and lowest among upper-status groups—professional, technical, and kindred workers (14.8), managers, proprietors, and officials (15.8).

The findings reported by these early analysts are distinguished from those reported by contemporary scholars who address the occupation and suicide relationship in that earlier analyses were more comprehensive in their assessment of socioeconomic status. The early analysts established SES by including occupation as well as an occupational prestige score, a score that takes amount of income and level of education into consideration. Using 1950 census data and a detailed occupational classification scheme, Labovitz and Hagedorn (1971) identified the suicide rates for numerous specific occupations, of which the 15 with the highest rates are listed in Table 6. It is

Table 6 Fifteen Occupations With Highest Suicide Rates, 1950

Occupation	Rate
1. Managers, officials, and proprietors (manufacturing)	64.8
2. Policemen, detectives, sheriffs, bailiffs, marshals, and constables	47.6
3. Managers, officials, and proprietors (wholesale and retail trade)	47.3
4. Dentists	45.6
5. Cooks, except private household	42.2
6. Mine operatives and laborers	41.7
7. Guards and watchmen	38.2
8. Architects	37.5
9. Authors, editors, and reporters	37.0
10. Barbers, beauticians, and manicurists	36.0
11. Machinists and job setters, metal	34.5
12. Locomotive engineers	34.2
13. Carpenters	32.7
14. Insurance agents and brokers	32.4
15. Physicians and surgeons	31.9

SOURCE: Adapted from Labovitz and Hagedorn (1971:68).

interesting to note that the lowest rate among the 15 job categories shown is for physicians and surgeons, who had a suicide rate of 31.9; the five highest rates are for managers, officials, and business proprietors (manufacturing, 64.8; the trade industry, 47.3), law enforcement personnel (47.6), dentists (45.6), and cooks (42.2). The remaining categories represent a combination of professional and blue-collar occupations.

The significance of these data from 1950 may easily be dismissed given that the Labovitz and Hagedorn study is dated. However, contemporary analysts have also criticized the occupation-related research studies conducted since the time of Bedeian's (1982) literature review, arguing that the general occupation categories are not specific enough or study samples are too small for the findings to warrant serious consideration or to enhance our understanding of the suicide problem (for a review of these criticisms, see Stack 2001). Refinement of the rates of suicide by occupational categories offers more specific information, and it is toward this issue that I now turn.

Specificity of Occupation

As indicated above, gender-based research findings confirm that for both males and females in the United States, the highest rates of suicide occur among individuals in high-status occupations. Among female psychologists (Mausner and Steppacher 1973), physicians (Rose and Rosnow 1973; Frank and Dingle 1999), chemists (Li 1969), and nurses (Hawton and Vislisel 1999), rates of suicide are equal to if not greater than rates among males. Bedeian's (1982) review of the literature pertaining to three occupational categories—health care providers, managerial and professional workers, and military and paramilitary personnel—is useful to any discussion of this issue.

Bedeian found that among health care providers, such as physicians, dentists, pharmacists, and nurses, the research data lead to mixed conclusions. For example, the belief that physicians have a high suicide rate can be attributed to a few published county- and statewide studies that have received extensive coverage from the news media. Attempting to lay to rest misconceptions pertaining to physician suicide, Bedeian provides a survey of the literature and argues that although psychiatrists might have a higher-than-expected rate of suicide, physicians in general do not commit suicide at higher rates than other males. Thus medical specialty appears to be a significant variable, especially among psychiatrists.

Bedeian further asserts that similar arguments can be made in the cases of dentists, pharmacists, and nurses. Only limited data are available, and these come from only a few studies, each of which concludes that dentists and pharmacists experience high suicide rates. Bedeian argues that only one thorough study of the suicide problem among dentists had been conducted, and the conclusion based on the findings of that study was that the suicide rate for dentists was comparable to that of the general white male population. This conclusion is not supported by Stack (1996), who, using the 1990 National Morbidity Detail File, reports a high suicide rate among dentists (for a table of selected occupation data based on information gathered by the U.S. government for the 1990 21-state morbidity file, see Stack 2001:501). Nurses, according to Bedeian, rank lowest of any occupational group investigated up to the time of his review. However, and again based on a limited sample size and time period, suicide was found to be higher than expected for female Air Force personnel, psychologists, physicians, and chemists.

Wasserman (1992) reports occupational data for white males who died in the state of Washington from 1950 through 1979. As shown in Table 7, Wasserman calculated these data using a proportionate mortality ratio (PMR = tabulated deaths for an occupation, divided by the expected deaths for an occupation, times 100). According to Wasserman, the PMR measure standardizes the age, sex, and racial characteristics of occupational groups. Based on the PMR, Wasserman speculates that the high suicide rates found for health care professionals may be related to their ready access to drugs and other methods of self-destruction, whereas the high rates of suicide among sheepherders, wool makers, and students may be attributed to the stress and isolation these individuals experience. Wasserman also attributes the low rates of suicide for occupational categories such as the military (86) and clergymen (25) to selection factors and the procedures employed to screen individuals with psychiatric problems. Although no empirical support was available for Wasserman's contentions, he nevertheless hypothesizes that strong

Table 7 Proportionate Mortality Ratios for Selected Occupations

Occupation	Proportionate Mortality Ratio
Sheepherders and wool workers	264
Dentists	236
Hairdressers and cosmetologists	227
Veterinarians	223
Tool and die workers	194
Physicians	75
Mechanical engineers	175
Medical and dental technicians	163
Draftsmen	160
Body and fender repairmen and auto painters	152
Barbers	151
Students	125
Army/Air Force/Marine Corps personnel	86
Cooks, candy makers, and chefs	79
Navy/Coast Guard personnel	78
Road graders, pavers, machine operators	76
Building and construction contractors and foremen	64
Lumber/log/sawmill truck drivers	63
Purchasing agents and buyers (not inclusive category), sales managers	41
Airplane pilots and navigators	40
Disabled, retarded, institutionalized, and unemployable	31
Clergy	25

SOURCE: Adapted from Wasserman (1992:533).

religious beliefs among clergymen may explain the low rate of suicide found in this occupational category.

One important advance beyond the limitations of single-state studies such as Wasserman's is found in the work of Kposowa (1999), who used the National Longitudinal Mortality Study 1979–89 to estimate the effects of occupation and industry on suicide deaths. In this evaluation Kposowa notes:

> It was found that employees in mining, business and repair services, wholesale and retail trade, and construction had the highest risks of suicide. Those employed in transportation, manufacturing, and personal services had intermediate risks. Persons in administration and in the professions had smaller risks. (P. 650)

Apparently, the standard was set by Labovitz and Hagedorn's (1971) publication on occupational suicide. Despite the passage of several decades, this standard has yet to be replicated. It is also of interest that comparable national data sets have not been forthcoming since that time. The recent proliferation of more sophisticated statistical analyses of data such as those contained in the National Longitudinal Mortality Study 1979–89 and the 21-state 1990 National Morbidity Detail File aside, contemporary analyses of the effects of occupation on the rate of suicide appear to offer little additional information that leads to a greater understanding of this long-standing problem. Yet, and despite the conceptual and methodological issues and problems related to small sample sizes identified in the literature, the reporting of occupation and the relationship of this variable to suicide continues to generate considerable interest. Still, it may be stated that however noteworthy current efforts are, their significance can be recognized only when the findings are cast within a framework of implications, such as those reported by Alston (1986) for the nursing profession, and social policy recommendations. Some scholars have taken up this evaluative effort in the past (e.g., Bedeian 1982; Alston 1986); more of this kind of effort is undoubtedly needed.

The Economy and Suicide

The empirical findings reported by Henry and Short (1954), as these relate to economic vicissitudes, are especially noteworthy. The economic boom of the 1990s and the apparent bust of the earliest portion of the new millennium may hold some importance for any assessment of suicide rates among those in professional labor force positions, especially females and minority group members. This condition, according to Durkheim ([1897] 1951), became endemic within environs in which industrial-based economic progress freed individuals from all or most social and moral constraints. Durkheim's explanations of anomic suicide, a society in transition, and the dissolution of the normative constraints as a whole address what appears to be a general social malaise. Although Durkheim's views pertain to the Western European experience at the end of the 19th century, we may have been witness to a similar social condition at the end of the 20th century. And, as Henry and Short (1954) have noted, suicide rates decline during times of economic prosperity and increase during economic decline. This theoretical explanation may also help us to understand why Burr et al. (1999) found that when measured along multiple dimensions, such as economic and social standing, the racial inequality experienced by black males may place them at an increased risk to engage in self-destructive behavior.

Investigating the relationship between economic cycles and the suicide rate, Henry and Short (1954) hypothesized (a) that the suicide rate is inversely related to the business cycle and (b) that this relationship (correlation) between the suicide rate and the business cycle is higher for high-status groups than for low-status groups. Although Maris (1969:133) has criticized this theory, the robust economic boom of the 1990s may be described as an egoistic

Table 8   Suicides, by Sex and Method, 1930–99

	1930		1940		1950		1955		1960		1965		1970	
	M	*F*	*M*	*F*	*M*	*F*	*M*	*F*	*M*	*F*	*M*	*F*	*M*	*F*
Total	14,319	4,004	14,466	4,441	13,297	3,848	12,961	3,799	14,539	4,502	15,490	6,017	16,629	6,851
Firearms and explosives	6,088	647	6,310	763	6,571	806	6,808	955	7,879	1,138	8,457	1,441	9,704	2,068
Poisoning	3,458	2,083	2,086	2,461	2,461	1,508	2,189	1,240	2,631	1,699	3,179	2,816	3,299	3,285
Hanging and strangulation	2,748	520	2,776	778	2,759	833	2,689	902	2,576	790	2,453	744	1,204	837
Other	2,025	754	1,843	814	1,506	701	1,275	702	1,453	875	1,401	1,016	1,204	667

environment, an environment characterized by a lack of civility and major breaches in social decorum. If a robust economic egoism promoted one type of deviance, then the transition to economic bust may, as Henry and Short demonstrated, again be expressed as long-term anomie (see also Powell 1958; Breed 1963; Pfohl 1994:260–61). Thus it may not be surprising that the suicide rates for females remained relatively stable or declined in some racial groups during the final two decades of the 20th century, during which the United States experienced a period of economic prosperity. Only the future will allow us an opportunity to assess whether the appropriate effect predicted by Henry and Short and strongly suggested by Wasserman (1992) is taking place during the early 21st century.

Lethality of Method/Method of Choice

The lethality of the suicide methods that individuals choose has long been of interest to analysts of the suicide phenomenon. In the contemporary experience, firearms and other forms of explosive devices represent the leading method of choice, but this has not always been the case. From 1900 through 1911, poisoning was recorded as the most commonly used method for 10 years out of this 11-year period. Only during 1910 did firearms emerge as the method of choice. In 1912, firearms were officially recorded as the most common method of suicide, and from that date to the present, firearms and explosives have continued to place first on the list of methods used, with poisoning and gases representing the second leading method of choice for most of the 20th century.

As shown in Table 8, the primary methods of choice are truly lethal, suggesting the strong intent of the committers. Over time, increasingly refined recording procedures have led to greater specificity in the available data about the means individuals select in their attempts to actualize their self-destructive behavior. Noteworthy are the race and sex variables that are currently combined prior to their being reported for general use by the public. This collapsing of race and sex categories is especially important given the difficulty in comparing/controlling the race and sex categories over time, such as comparing the 1990s with the 1930–90 period. However, a Web site coordinated by the American Association of Suicidology currently provides a more consistent set of data, and these are shown in Table 8 for the year 1999. This is not to say that data pertaining to the previously standardized methods of choice are unavailable, but that the reporting refinement now available for the compendium period 1980 to the present makes it difficult to know whether the data listed under such categories are comparable over time. On a yearly basis the *Statistical Abstract of the United States* now presents suicide methods of choice in a "both sexes" category as well as in "method, white" and "method, black" categories. An example of this new classification schema is shown in Table 8 for the year 1995.

Although females are thought to be more likely to attempt suicide, it is estimated that males are four times more likely to die as a result of their attempts. In 1998, for example, 73% of the recorded 27,648 white suicides were male. During that same year, 57% of suicides (nearly 3 out of every 5) involved the use of firearms. The differences noted for 1998 were not unusual as firearms continued to represent the method of choice. In 1999, firearms were used in 56.8% of total suicides. The specific data are equally noteworthy in that of the 21,107 white males (rate = 19.1) who committed suicide that year (out of 29,199 total suicides), 14,479 chose firearms (61.7%). Among the young (*n* = 2,315), 59.3% selected firearms as the method of choice; the old used firearms (*n* = 3,921) in 71.4% of the events and females (*n* = 2,120) selected firearms 36.9% of the time. In 1999 firearms accounted for almost 57% (*n* = 16,599) of the 29,199 officially recorded suicides (Hoyert et al. 2001).

Whereas poisoning and gases represented the first suicide method of choice for females recorded prior to and throughout the 1970s, in 1999 the methods that made up this category, now divided into separate categories for solid and liquid poisons (30%) and gas poisons (6%), ranked second and fourth, with the category of hanging, strangulation, and suffocation representing the third method of choice among females. This difference is again noteworthy given that coroners and medical examiners have documented a significant change during the past two decades: That is, females have increasingly selected more lethal methods to commit suicide.

Table 8 Suicides, by Sex and Method, 1930–99 (Continued)

	1975		1980		1985		1990		1995	1999	
	M	*F*	*M*	*F*	*M*	*F*	*M*	*F*	*Both Sexes*	*M*	*F*
Total	19,625	7,441	20,505	6,364	23,145	6,308	24,724	6,182	31,284	23,458	5,741
Firearms and explosives	12,185	2,688	12,937	2,459	14,809	2,554	16,285	2,600	18,147[a]	14,479	2,120
Poisoning	3,297	3,129	3,319	2,456	3,319	2,385	3,221	2,203	5,217[b]	3,827	2,066
Hanging and strangulation	2,815	846	2,997	694	3,532	732	2,422	756	5,217[c]	4,490	937
Other	1,325	778	1,574	755	1,485	637	1,530	623	2,417	1,662	618

SOURCE: U.S. Bureau of the Census (1967:168, table 246; 1982-83:81, table 121; 1992:88, table 121; 1996), Hoyert et al. (2001), and McIntosh (2001).

a. Handguns (includes 3,700) and other unspecified firearms.
b. Includes drugs, medicaments, and biologicals; either solid or liquid substances; gases and vapors.
c. Includes suffocation.

The lethality of methods of self-harm employed also seems to be useful for understanding the differential rates of suicide. In general, males employ more violent means, such as firearms, piercing instruments, hanging, and jumping, whereas females attempting suicide are more likely to take nonfatal overdoses of drugs (e.g., Peck 1984, 1985–86; Canetto and Sakinofsky 1998; Appleby 2000). Such findings may provide some important insights into the organizational structure of gender role expectations.

Suicide and Region of the United States

In general, suicide rates are higher than the national average in the western states and lower in the midwestern and eastern states. Although it may be important for researchers to explore the interaction of a market economy over time when assessing the fluctuating suicide rates by region of the country, some fluctuations are found in the year-by-year data reported by region. The highest rates of suicide are found in the north-central and western portions of the United States. These regions include Minnesota, Iowa, Missouri, North and South Dakota, Nebraska, Kansas, and the contiguous states of California, Oregon, and Washington as well as Alaska and Hawaii. States in the Mountain region include Nevada, Arizona, and New Mexico, all of which are home to many elderly retirees. Areas that are relatively ecologically and socially isolated, such as Montana and Wyoming, also record rates that far exceed the national average.

In 1990, the eight Mountain states reported the highest overall regional suicide rate (18.5), which was much higher than the national average (12.4). Only Florida (16.1) fell within the range (15.3 to 20.9) recorded for the Mountain region of the United States. The lowest rates were recorded in the Northeast. In 1994, a similar pattern was noted—that is, the Mountain states (rate = 18.3), consisting of Montana (18.5), Idaho (17.7), Wyoming (22.5), Colorado (16.8), New Mexico (18.3), Arizona (18.8), Utah (15.3), and Nevada (23.4), combined for an overall rate of

18.3, compared with 12.0 at the national level. No other state fell within the range of the rate recorded for the Mountain region of the country. Again, the lowest rates were recorded in the Northeast and the Midwest.

In 1996, the Mountain zone states, along with Alaska, South Dakota, and West Virginia, recorded the highest suicide rates in the nation. However, for this same year a total of 30 states had suicide rates higher than the national rate of 11.6. The lowest rates, all below 9.0, were recorded in Connecticut, Rhode Island, Massachusetts, New York, and New Jersey. Washington, D.C., had the lowest rate of all jurisdictions (6.4). This pattern held throughout the decade and up to 1997, the last year for which data are available (U.S. Bureau of the Census 2001).

Gender Role Scripts and Suicide

Historically, as Girard (1993) notes, the ascribed status of women and blacks has impeded the achievement of members of both groups, and, as a consequence, these groups have lower suicide rates than those found in the general population. But "when ascriptive barriers to achievement-oriented careers become less stringent as in the 1960s for blacks and throughout the twentieth century for European women, corresponding race and sex differences in suicide risk decrease" (p. 557). Thus middle-aged women appear to be following what Canetto and Sakinofsky (1998) refer to as "cultural scripts theory," which suggests that "cultural expectations about gender and suicidal behavior function as scripts; individuals refer to these scripts as a model for their suicidal behavior and to make sense of others' suicidal behavior" (pp. 19–20). Essentially, Girard asserts that the differential rates of suicide among men and women are related to sex roles. This contention is partially supported by Canetto and Sakinofsky's analysis of cultural scripts theory.

It is also noteworthy, as Andriolo (1998) points out, that this kind of interpretation directs itself to gender role differences. If sex differences are typecast according to motives and meanings, as Girard (1993) argues, then the meanings attributed may function as a disservice to women. In this context, such analysis is replete with cultural scripts.

Canetto and Sakinofsky (1998) assert that there is a sex paradox in suicide. They argue that females generally experience much more suicidal ideation and are more prone to attempt suicide than males, but females have a much lower rate of suicide than do males. If women are not as inclined to suicide as are males, the question that begs an answer is, Why?

Based on his review of the literature, Stack (1998) notes that there is little or no support for the thesis that the degree of gender inequality in the workplace and politics would moderate the relationship between marriage and suicide acceptability, because such inequality would not likely affect the degree of marital satisfaction. In moving beyond this point, Girard (1993) offers a partial explanation, suggesting that gender differences in suicide rates, especially among older people, are correlated with role identity and the relationship between role identity and vulnerability to threats to an individual's self-concept. Employing what is referred to as "contingent-identity theory," Girard argues that the male self is strongly related to occupation, problems related to job performance, and economic security. Although women are increasingly oriented toward developing careers outside the home, Girard asserts, most women's sense of achievement is based not on occupational success but on "cooperation, social interdependence, and parenthood."

Although this may explain sex differences in suicide rates among older males and females, middle-aged women up to about age 54 are at high risk for suicide. Girard suggests that this vulnerability may be related not to the stress inherent in women's involvement in the labor market, but to the stress women feel in relation to the fortunes and misfortunes of their children. Again, the gender paradox in suicidal behavior discussed by Canetto and Sakinofsky (1998) is instructive. To be at risk of suicide may be to hold such an ideation and even to engage in such behavior, but this does not necessarily lead to completion of the suicide act.

CONCLUSION

Although the study of suicide is encumbered with numerous difficulties of a conceptual and methodological nature, perhaps no other contemporary social problem receives more critical attention. As a result, some important research has been conducted, but there is no consensus that allows for the successful application of the knowledge obtained so far to render a solution to the problem.

At present, and despite more than 275 years of analysis, the subject of suicide continues to elicit intense interest, strong emotions, and social misconceptions. At the same time, one important lingering question has yet to be answered: Should the state have the right to prohibit its citizens from choosing the manner in which they die? At issue

is whether a right-to-die law should be enacted, a law that allows suicide to take place. At this time, some countries, such as Great Britain, allow suicide, but in most assisted suicide remains punishable by imprisonment (Ames 2002).

In 1982, Margaret Pabst Battin stated that "recent development in patients' rights advocacy tend to suggest the reawakening of a stoic or eighteenth-century liberal view of suicides" (p. 30), suggesting that contemporary Western culture was at the time entering a period of renewed interest in issues surrounding the topic of suicide. These issues, according to Battin, included changes in moral attitudes toward self-destructive behavior, professional prevention strategies, and legal determinations of suicide. More than 20 years later, these issues continue to hold the public's attention.

Perhaps the intensity of this contemporary polemic can be attributed in part to the efforts of Jack Kevorkian, a retired medical examiner whose attempts to bring the issue of assisted suicide to the public's attention gained national notoriety during the 1990s. More recently, debates in the United States—between the many people who appear to support the establishment of laws allowing assisted suicide or a declared personal choice to commit suicide and representatives of the state who oppose this position—have again demonstrated the moral, legal, social, and religious significance of the suicide event.

The questions Battin raised in 1982 continue to be significant. Is suicide wrong because human life is of intrinsic value, or because the act of suicide is harmful to society, or perhaps because permissive attitudes may lead to abuse? Or is suicide a natural right? That is, should persons have the right to end their lives as they so choose despite whatever objections may be raised by any individual or by the state? Such questions call attention to this statement by Thomas Szasz (1999):

> For a long time, suicide was the concern of the Church and the priest. Now it is the business of the State and the doctor. Eventually we will make it our own choice, regardless of what the Bible or the Constitution or Medicine supposedly tell us. (P. xii)

Although these words emphasize the rights of the individual, currently the "right to die" proponents appear to be losing the legal battle to allow individuals to choose the time and manner in which they may select an officially sanctioned alternative to living a less-than-desirable existence. Sometime in the future, however, this social movement may have its intended legal effect, and perhaps an unintended effect on the suicide rate as well.

Clearly, white males continue to dominate the suicide statistics, and, although some variation is observed in the rates among women and minorities, these rates remain relatively constant. Self-destructive behavior does appear to be associated with interpersonal and intrapersonal factors attendant to the committers' efforts to influence or to control their environment. But this finding, reported extensively in the literature, may not be useful as a powerful explanation specific to suicide because the same kind of information can be used to explain a variety of deviant and nondeviant behaviors. We will be able to understand individuals' motivations for suicide only when researchers have developed a consistent base of information and when these data are made available to clinicians and public health officials who seek to enhance the personal well-being of all members of the public. When this understanding develops, those who are charged with making the social policies intended to deal with this significant public health problem may be able to perform their work more successfully.

At present, the findings reported on minority and female suicide are mixed. Some occupations appear to expose women to greater risk of suicide, but as increased numbers of women redefine their cultural scripts by relating these scripts to those traditionally reserved to males, the hypothesis to consider is that women will also experience a similar degree of success and failure. A transition from the traditional female cultural script of homemaker and family nurturer could, given women's evaluation of their success and failure in the labor market, lead to increased rates of suicide.

Although it is clear that the social, political, and economic changes that took place throughout the final 30 years of the 20th century have held important consequences for women and minorities, including enhanced educational opportunities, professional training, and career development, many of the analyses that have been conducted to assess the effects of labor market participation on female and minority suicide rates have produced mixed results. Perhaps scholars need to evaluate cultural factors other than labor market participation to explain the apparent discrepancy between the hypothesized relationships and the available data.

REFERENCES

Alston, Maude H. 1986. "Occupation and Suicide Among Women." *Issues in Mental Health Nursing* 8:109–19.

Ames, Paul. 2002. "Right-to-Die Proponents Lose Battle in European Court." *Tuscaloosa News,* May 1, p. 1E.

Anderson, Robert N. 2001. *Deaths: Leading Causes for 1999* (National Vital Statistics Reports, vol. 49, no. 11). Hyattsville, MD: National Center for Health Statistics.

Andriolo, Karin R. 1998. "Gender and the Cultural Construction of Good and Bad Suicides." *Suicide and Life-Threatening Behavior* 28:37–49.

Appleby, Louis. 2000. "Suicide in Women." *Lancet* 355: 1203–04.

Battin, Margaret Pabst. 1982. *Ethical Issues in Suicide.* Englewood Cliffs, NJ: Prentice Hall.

Bedeian, Arthur G. 1982. "Suicide and Occupation: A Review." *Journal of Vocational Behavior* 21:206–23.

Blacher, Richard S. 1987. "The Art and Science of Thanatology." Pp. 317–22 in *Principles of Thanatology,* edited by Austin H. Kutscher, Arthur C. Carr, and Lillian G. Kutscher. New York: Columbia University Press.

Breed, Warren. 1963. "Occupational Mobility and Suicide Among White Males." *American Sociological Review* 28: 179–88.

Burr, Jeffrey A., John T. Hartman, and Donald W. Matteson. 1999. "Black Suicide in U.S. Metropolitan Areas: An Examination of the Racial Inequality and Social Integration-Regulation Hypotheses." *Social Forces* 77:1049–51.

Canetto, Silvia Sara and Isaac Sakinofsky. 1998. "The Gender Paradox in Suicide." *Suicide and Life-Threatening Behavior* 28:1–23.

Carlson, G. A. and D. C. Miller. 1981. "Suicide, Affective Disorder, and Women Physicians." *American Journal of Psychiatry* 138:1330–35.

Centers for Disease Control and Prevention. 1998. "Suicide Among Black Youths" (fact sheet). Atlanta, GA: Centers for Disease Control and Prevention. Retrieved March 22, 2002 (http://www.cdc.gov/od/oc/media/fact/suicidby.htm).

Cumming, Elaine, Charles Lazer, and Lynne Chrisholm. 1975. "Suicides as an Index of Role Strain Among Employed and Not Employed Married Women in British Columbia." *Canadian Review of Sociology and Anthropology* 12:462–70.

Dobrin, Arthur. 1988. "Suicide: A Typology." *Case Analysis* 2:185–200.

Douglas, Jack D. 1967. *The Social Meanings of Suicide.* Princeton, NJ: Princeton University Press.

Durkheim, Émile. [1897] 1951. *Suicide: A Study in Sociology,* translated by John A. Spaulding and George Simpson. Glencoe, IL: Free Press.

Frank, Erica and Arden Dingle. 1999. "Self-Reported Depression and Suicide Attempts Among U.S. Women Physicians." *American Journal of Psychiatry* 156:1887–94.

Girard, Chris. 1993. "Age, Gender, and Suicide: A Cross-National Analysis." *American Sociological Review* 58:553–74.

Hawton, Keith and Lida Vislisel. 1999. "Suicide in Nurses." *Suicide and Life-Threatening Behavior* 29:86–95.

Henry, Andrew F. and James F. Short, Jr. 1954. *Suicide and Homicide.* New York: Free Press.

Hoyert, Donna L., Elizabeth Arias, Betty L. Smith, Sherry L. Murphy, and Kenneth D. Kochanek. 2001. *Deaths: Final Data for 1999* (National Vital Statistics Report, vol. 49, no. 8). Hyattsville, MD: National Center for Health Statistics.

Kposowa, Augustine J. 1999. "Suicide Mortality in the United States: Differentials by Industrial and Occupational Groups." *American Journal of Industrial Medicine* 36:645–52.

Kramarow, E., H. Lentzner, R. Hooks, J. Weeks, and S. Saydah. 1999. *Health and Aging Chartbook. Health, United States, 1999.* Hyattsville, MD: National Center for Health Statistics.

Labovitz, Sanford and Robert Hagedorn. 1971. "An Analysis of Suicide Rates Among Occupational Categories." *Sociological Inquiry* 41:67–72.

Langhinrichsen-Rohling, Jennifer, Peter Lewinsohn, Paul Rohde, John Seeley, Candice M. Monson, Kathryn A. Meyer, and Richard Langford. 1998. "Gender Differences in the Suicide-Related Behaviors of Adolescents and Young Adults." *Sex Roles* 39:839–54. Retrieved October 7, 2001 (http://www.findarticle.com/cf_0/m2294/11-12_39/53590321/p1/article.jhtml?term=%22suicide-relatedbehaviors%22).

Leonard, Edward C., Jr. 2001. "Confidential Death to Prevent Suicidal Contagion: An Accepted but Never Implemented, Nineteenth-Century Idea." *Suicide and Life-Threatening Behavior* 31:460–66.

Lester, David and Bijou Yang. 1992. "Social and Economic Correlates of the Elderly Suicide Rate." *Suicide and Life-Threatening Behavior* 22:36–47.

Li, F. B. 1969. "Suicide Among Chemists." *Archives of Environmental Health* 19:518–20.

Maris, Ronald W. 1969. *Social Forces in Urban Suicide.* Homewood, IL: Dorsey.

Mausner, J. S. and R. C. Steppacher. 1973. "Suicide in Professionals: A Study of Male and Female Psychologists." *American Journal of Epidemiology* 98:436–45.

Mayer, Peter. 2000. "Development, Gender Equality, and Suicide Rates." *Psychological Reports* 87: 367–73.

McIntosh, John L. 2001. "U.S.A. Suicide: 1999 Official Final Statistics." American Association of Suicidology. Retrieved March 22, 2002 (http://www.suicidology.org/displaycommon.cfm?an=1&subarticlenbr=21).

Murphy, Sherry L. 2000. *Deaths: Final Data for 1998* (National Vital Statistics Reports, vol. 48, no. 11). Hyattsville, MD: National Center for Health Statistics.

National Center for Health Statistics. 1978. *Facts of Life and Death* (DHEW Pub. No. PHS 79-1222). Hyattsville, MD: Public Health Service.

———. 1991. *Health, United States, 1990.* Hyattsville, MD: Public Health Service.

———. 1994. *Health, United States, 1993.* Hyattsville, MD: Public Health Service.

———. 2000. *Health, United States, 2000.* Hyattsville, MD: Public Health Service.

———. 2001. *Health, United States, 2001.* Hyattsville, MD: Public Health Service.

National Center for Injury Prevention and Control. 2000. *Fact Book for the Year 2000.* Atlanta, GA: Centers for Disease Control and Prevention. Retrieved March 22, 2002 (http://www.cdc.gov/ncipc/pub-res/factbook/suicide.htm).

Newman, J., K. Whittemore, and H. Newman. 1973. "Women in the Labor Force and Suicide." *Social Problems* 21:220–30.

Parker, Lillian Davenport, Cecilia Cantrell, and Alice S. Demi. 1997. "Older Adults' Attitudes Toward Suicide: Are There Race and Gender Differences?" *Death Studies* 21:289–98.

Peck, Dennis L. 1979. *Fatalistic Suicide.* Palo Alto, CA: R&E Research Associates.

———. 1983–84. "Official Documentation of the Black Suicide Experience." *Omega* 14:21–31.

———. 1984. "Lethality of Suicide Method Among a Youthful Sample of Committers." *Psychological Reports* 55:861–62.

———. 1985–86. "Completed Suicides: Correlates of Choice of Method." *Omega* 16:309–23.

Peck, Dennis L. and Kenneth Warner. 1995. "Accident or Suicide? Single-Vehicle Car Accidents and the Intent Hypothesis." *Adolescence* 30:463–72.

Peters, Kimberly D., Kenneth D. Kochanek, and Sherry L. Murphy. 1998. *Deaths: Final Data for 1996* (National Vital Statistics Reports, vol. 47, no. 9). Hyattsville, MD: National Center for Health Statistics.

Pfohl, Stephen. 1994. *Images of Deviance and Social Control.* New York: McGraw-Hill.

Powell, Elwin H. 1958. "Occupation, Status, and Suicide: Toward a Redefinition of Anomie." *American Sociological Review* 23:131–39.

Quigley, Christine, ed. 1994. *Death Dictionary.* Jefferson, NC: McFarland.

Rose, K. and I. Rosnow. 1973. "Physicians Who Kill Themselves." *Archives of General Psychiatry* 29:800–805.

Schmid, Calvin F. and Maurice D. Van Arsdol, Jr. 1955. "Completed and Attempted Suicides: A Comparative Analysis." *American Sociological Review* 20:273–83.

Selzer, Melvin L. and Charles E. Payne. 1962. "Automobile Accidents, Suicide, and Unconscious Motivation." *American Journal of Psychiatry* 119:237–40.

Stack, Steven. 1978. "Suicide." *Social Forces* 57:644–53.

———. 1996. "Suicide Risk Among Dentists: A Multivariate Analysis." *Deviant Behavior* 17:107–17.

———. 1996–97. "The Effect of Labor Force Participation on Female Suicide Rates: An Analysis of Individual Data From 16 States." *Omega* 34:163–69.

———. 1998. "Gender, Marriage, and Suicide Acceptability: A Comparative Analysis." *Sex Roles* 38:501–20.

———. 2001. "Suicide and Occupation." Pp. 499–503 in *Encyclopedia of Criminology and Deviant Behavior,* vol. 4, *Self-Destructive and Disvalued Identity,* edited by Charles E. Faupel and Paul M. Roman. Philadelphia: Brunner-Routledge.

Steffensmeier, R. H. 1984. "Suicide and the Contemporary Woman." *Sex Roles* 10:613–31.

Szasz, Thomas. 1999. *Fatal Freedom: The Ethics and Politics of Suicide.* Westport, CT: Praeger.

U.S. Bureau of the Census. 1921. *Statistical Abstract of the United States: 1920.* Washington, DC: Government Printing Office.

———. 1930. *Mortality Statistics.* Washington, DC: Government Printing Office.

———. 1967. *Statistical Abstract of the United States: 1967.* Washington, DC: Government Printing Office.

———. 1973. *Statistical Abstract of the United States: 1973.* Washington, DC: Government Printing Office.

———. 1974. *Statistical Abstract of the United States: 1974.* Washington, DC: Government Printing Office.

———. 1975. *Historical Statistics of the United States: Colonial Times to 1970,* pt. 2. Washington, DC: Government Printing Office.

———. 1977. *Statistical Abstract of the United States: 1977.* Washington, DC: Government Printing Office.

———. 1978. *Statistical Abstract of the United States: 1978.* Washington, DC: Government Printing Office.

———. 1983. *Statistical Abstract of the United States: 1982–83.* Washington, DC: Government Printing Office.

———. 1992. *Statistical Abstract of the United States: 1992.* Washington, DC: Government Printing Office.

———. 1996. *Statistical Abstract of the United States: 1996.* Washington, DC: Government Printing Office.

———. 1997. *Statistical Abstract of the United States: 1997.* Washington, DC: Government Printing Office.

———. 1999. *Statistical Abstract of the United States: 1999.* Washington, DC: Government Printing Office.

———. 2000. *Statistical Abstract of the United States: 2000.* Washington, DC: Government Printing Office.

———. 2001. *Statistical Abstract of the United States: 2001.* Washington, DC: Government Printing Office.

Vold, George B. 1958. *Theoretical Criminology.* New York: Oxford University Press.

Wasserman, Ira M. 1992. "Economy, Work, Occupation, and Suicide." Pp. 521–39 in *Assessment and Prediction of Suicide,* edited by Ronald W. Maris, Alan L. Berman, John T. Maltsberger, and Robert I. Yufit. New York: Guilford.

Yang, Bijou and David Lester. 1988. "The Participation of Females in the Labor Force and Rates of Personal Violence (Suicide and Homicide)." *Suicide and Life-Threatening Behavior* 18:270–78.

SUICIDE SURVIVORS

The Aftermath of Suicide and Suicidal Behavior

JOHN L. MCINTOSH

Historically, one of the most neglected areas of suicidology (i.e., the scientific study of suicide) has been the issue of the aftermath of suicide and suicidal behavior. As this discussion will show, this disregard has lessened in recent years, particularly for the topic of "survivors of suicide." Still largely ignored is the aftermath for those who have made nonfatal attempts on their own lives and for their significant others. In this chapter, I provide a review of the literatures on these topics and suggest some directions for future research on this important component in the full range of suicidal behavior.

In the suicide literature, Albert Cain edited a pioneering work in 1972 titled *Survivors of Suicide*. The chapters in this volume outlined the issues of grieving associated with the loss of a loved one to suicide. As I will show below, Cain and the other contributors to *Survivors of Suicide* discussed the psychological and social factors associated with the aftermath of deaths by suicide. Up to that time, however, there had been almost no research investigations of this topic, so the contributors presented much conjecture and extrapolation from theory and other information. More than any other publication, this book established the term *suicide survivor* in the lexicon of suicidology. In his foreword to the book, Edwin Shneidman, the founder of the American Association of Suicidology and cofounder of the Los Angeles Suicide Prevention Center, referred to the "*survivors* of suicide, [as] . . . *the* largest mental health casualty area related to suicide" (p. ix). The importance of this topic was thus highlighted among the many dimensions of suicidal behavior by perhaps the most eminent figure in the field. Shneidman had previously coined the term *postvention* to refer to work with those who remain behind after a death by suicide. Within the other dimensions of suicide prevention, including prevention and intervention,

postvention involves any issues of the aftermath of suicide deaths or other suicidal behaviors.

Despite Shneidman's strong words about suicide survivors and the appearance of Cain's book, only a small number of researchers, clinicians, and other suicidologists studied or wrote about this topic for some years after *Survivors of Suicide* was published. In this chapter, I will show that although they have continued to attract less attention than warranted, the research, clinical, and other literatures in this area have grown considerably in the past 15 years. These significant recent advances notwithstanding, our knowledge of survivors in many ways remains only a few steps beyond the level of understanding that existed 30 years ago when Cain's seminal effort appeared.

It is important at this initial point to continue a bit more on the topic of the words employed in this chapter. In one of the first full volumes devoted to the topic following Cain's book, a book edited by Dunne, McIntosh, and Dunne-Maxim (1987), I defined the issue of "survivors" by stating that "the death is the result of suicide, and the lives [being considered] are those of the family and friends who remain after a person commits suicide" (McIntosh 1987a:xvii). Thus survivors of suicide are those who have lost a significant other to a death by suicide. The focus is on the aftermath of the suicide death—that is, on the lives of these individuals and the resulting psychosocial effects of their loved one's suicide. Although the term *suicide survivor* has been employed with some clarity, the terminology is imperfect and can create confusion. This confusion arises primarily among persons who are not members of the suicidology community. The suicide literature includes other confusing, awkward, and even offensive terms. For example, *successful suicides* are those whose acts end fatally, whereas those who remain alive are *unsuccessful,*

AUTHOR'S NOTE: This chapter draws together and expands on literature I have previously reviewed (in McIntosh 1987b, 1987c, 1993, 1999). To limit the numbers of references cited herein, I often refer readers to these and other reviews for specific studies.

as they failed at their attempts. In other words, those who have made suicide attempts that did not have fatal outcomes are often seen as having "survived" their acts. Thus the term *survivors of suicide* is not ideal. A few other expressions have emerged in reference to those who have lost loved ones to suicide, but none is used as widely as *survivors*. In Australia, for example, survivors of suicide are often referred to as the *bereaved of suicide,* a more precise wording that avoids the confusion that occurs elsewhere with the term *survivor.* However, the reality is that the term *survivors of suicide* is now so widely utilized among the suicidology community that, at least to members of that community, the term does not generally produce misunderstanding.

EPIDEMIOLOGICAL ASPECTS OF SUICIDE'S AFTERMATH

A major problem in the suicide survivor literature is the lack of epidemiological investigations. Such studies are important to quantify the problem, because numbers often determine whether an issue receives attention and, particularly, needed resources, including funds for treatment, research, and prevention efforts. In order to examine the extent to which suicide survivorship is a mental health issue deserving of focused attention and support, researchers must initially determine the number of individuals involved. Eventually this will also involve calculating the "cost" of suicidal behavior and its effects on society and individuals.

Although suicidologists have identified the need for such research for some time, no national epidemiological study has been conducted to clarify the probable number of individuals who have been affected by the suicides of loved ones. In this void, I have advanced estimates of the number of survivors in the U.S. population as a basic and vitally needed figure (McIntosh 1989). Utilizing these conservative figures, and updating them to the most currently available data, we can estimate that 1 of every 62 Americans is a survivor of suicide, a conservative total of 4.4 million in 1999 (McIntosh 2001). If there are 6 survivors on the average for each suicide (Shneidman 1969), the more than 29,000 annual suicides produce an estimated 175,000 survivors each year—a pace of 6 survivors every 18 minutes (on average, there is a suicide every 18 minutes), more than 480 per day. On the other hand, based on one small study, Callahan (1989) has suggested a rate of suicide survivorship of 5.5% (and perhaps even higher), which would imply that there were more than 15 million survivors in 1999. Thus Callahan and others have suggested an even higher ratio than Shneidman's 6:1, but without a high-quality epidemiological investigation, the estimate will have to suffice ("Interaction" 1996) as a conservative indication of the number of suicide survivors.

It is, perhaps, understandable that even basic information about suicide survivors would be missing given the long-term neglect of this topic described above. Surprisingly, the extent to which the aftermath of suicide attempts is a problem has been entirely ignored, despite the constant discussion and study of suicide attempters throughout the history of suicidology. Although no official statistics are compiled for suicide attempts, a large literature describes the many investigations that have been conducted concerning those who make nonfatal suicide acts, including the epidemiology of suicide attempts. The U.S. Surgeon General's *National Strategy for Suicide Prevention* presents estimates that there are between 8 and 25 suicide attempts for every completed suicide in the United States and that each year 650,000 persons are treated in emergency care settings following suicide attempts (U.S. Department of Health and Human Services 2001). Although some of these individuals represent multiple attempts, these estimates obviously suggest that the number of attempters in the population is far larger than the number of survivors. Larger still are the numbers of persons whose lives are affected by the suicide attempts of their family members or friends. If each suicide affects at least 6 others, it seems logical that this figure would be a conservative one for the number affected by suicide attempts. The ratio is probably even more conservative than for suicide survivors, because suicide attempters are younger as a group than those who die by suicide, and as a result the number of individuals affected is likely to be larger. However, using the figure of 6 individuals from each attempt, that would mean that the lives of more than 4 million Americans are affected by suicide attempts each year. If these annual figures were cumulated over time to account for a "lifetime" risk, the number would be substantial.

SURVIVORS OF SUICIDE

At least three distinct subtopics exist with respect to the bereaved of suicide. A growing research literature that attempts to delineate the characteristic aspects of suicide bereavement has emerged over the past 30 years, along with a body of personal accounts by individual survivors of suicide. Finally, descriptions of clinical and other therapeutic interventions that assist survivors in their efforts to heal following the loss of significant others have also appeared. I discuss each of these topics briefly below to portray a shared primary goal of researchers, clinicians, support group leaders and facilitators, and survivors themselves: to understand suicide bereavement, including its commonalities and individual differences.

Research on Survivors of Suicide

Just as epidemiological information is needed, researchers must conduct methodologically sound research investigations if they are to obtain the community support and allocation of resources required to improve our understanding of suicide survivorship and assist in the healing process. As several scholars have noted in detail, early research investigations on survivors of suicide were marred by a number of methodological problems that limited the usefulness of the findings and their ability to portray suicide survivorship fully (for critiques, see McIntosh 1987b, 1999; Calhoun, Selby, and Selby 1982; Henley 1984). However, these studies served the important role of initially describing various aspects of suicide survivor grief.

Most glaring among the limitations and problems of these early studies was their inability to show how suicide grief is different from bereavement associated with other modes of death. The basic reason for this limitation was that the studies lacked comparison groups—that is, the researchers included only suicide survivors in their samples. At the time of Calhoun et al.'s (1982) review, not a single study had included a comparison or control group. Differences in grieving require that researchers include comparison groups, applying to them the same methods, procedures, and measures as they apply to suicide survivors. Despite this problem (and others), these exploratory, descriptive, non–comparison group studies advanced the knowledge base about the experience of surviving suicide. They particularly helped to demonstrate the variability in experiences as well as probable common aspects of suicide survivorship. I describe some of the findings of these studies below in the context of the larger research literature.

Early Non–Comparison Group Literature

A number of scholars have published reviews of the body of research on survivors of suicide (Calhoun et al. 1982; Clark and Goldney 2000; Cleiren and Diekstra 1995; Ellenbogen and Gratton 2001; Foglia 1984; Hauser 1987; Henley 1984; Hiegel and Hipple 1990; Jobes et al. 2000; Jordan 2001; McIntosh 1987c, 1993, 1999; Ness and Pfeffer 1990; Rudestam 1992; van der Wal 1989). Apparently, the first comprehensive compilation and review of the existing literature appeared in Cain's (1972a) introduction to his classic edited book *Survivors of Suicide* (see McIntosh 1999). In his "clustered and capsuled" portrayal, Cain noted nine reactions that are all included in what Dunne (1987:143) would later call the "survivor syndrome" (see also Dunne and Wilbur 1993). Reflecting some of the compiled psychodynamic considerations, Cain described these reactions as follows: reality distortion, tortured object-relations, guilt, disturbed self-concept, impotent rage, search for meaning, identification with the suicide, depression and self-destructiveness, and incomplete mourning (pp. 13–14). Cain also noted in the scant literature behaviors such as anniversary reactions associated with the death, preoccupation with the phenomenon of suicide and involvement with prevention efforts, and feelings of shame, stigma, and abandonment.

Calhoun et al.'s (1982) review 10 years later added few issues to Cain's list, although the number of empirical studies had increased and the findings of those studies supported the set of reactions noted earlier. The review and subsequent research yielded some additions to the survivor syndrome. The lack of comparison groups precluded Calhoun et al. from making any definitive statements regarding how suicide survivors and their survivor syndrome might differ from or be similar to the grief and bereavement observed among survivors of other modes of death. However, Calhoun et al. expanded Cain's list of reactions to include several categories and a number of new reactions. They organized the findings into affective (i.e., emotional), cognitive, behavioral, physical, and family interaction reactions. In most cases, a number of researchers had reported these reactions among suicide survivors. These additional reactions included relief, shock and disbelief, health-related problems as well as more physician visits and even higher mortality rates, and possible negative effects on the family system.

One of the most interesting elements of Calhoun et al.'s review is the authors' best guess as to a list of reactions that might eventually be determined to be unique aspects of suicide survivorship. Recognizing the tremendous methodological limitations in the research, Calhoun et al. noted that they believed enough consistency was present to support three cautious generalizations. Specifically, they said, suicide survivorship may be unique in survivors' "search for an understanding of the death," greater feelings of guilt, and "the lower levels of social support" they were likely to receive (p. 417) compared with other bereaved persons.

Evidence was lacking to show that this list of reactions for a possible suicide survivor syndrome represents unique aspects of suicide survivor grief. The reactions listed may well be common to grief following suicide, but at the time of their compilation, research verification regarding their uniqueness to suicide bereavement did not exist. Calhoun et al. could only conclude that how much bereavement associated with suicide differs from bereavement associated with other modes of death was unclear, and that the uniqueness of suicide survivorship may be limited to a small subset of reactions.

In my own work, I have suggested that these findings might be interpreted differently. Perhaps a larger set of reactions *is* unique to suicide's aftermath, not simply in their appearance, but in the quality of their appearance. In other words,

> a reaction that is labeled the same by suicide survivors and those from other causes who are interviewed may indeed occur for both, but there may be facets and issues associated with that reaction that are unique to bereavement from one cause as compared to another. For example, suicide survivors and accident survivors may both feel some degree of guilt for actions they performed or those they might not have performed which they associate with some degree of responsibility for the death of their loved one. However, the amount and subjective aspects of guilt may differ generally for suicide as opposed to accident survivors. (McIntosh 1999:164)

At the time of Calhoun et al.'s review, without comparison groups, research regarding this interpretation did not exist, and, in fact, such an approach is virtually nonexistent even in the current comparative research literature. Among many critical research needs is a focus on qualitative as well as quantitative aspects of specific bereavement reactions.

Comparison Group Literature

Since Calhoun et al. (1982) published their review of exploratory investigations, researchers have conducted a growing body of studies with stronger methodological characteristics. A decade after Calhoun et al.'s review, which was devoid of comparison group studies, I reviewed 14 published studies that included such groups (McIntosh 1993). By 1999, I had found and reviewed an additional 16 investigations that had appeared in the published literature. These 30 studies (and several more since 1999) all included various survivors of other modes of death in comparison groups, were methodologically more sound than previous studies, and represented an impressive array of relationship or kinship relations between the deceased and the survivors. Although methodologically superior to the early research with respect to the addition of control/comparison groups, research investigations that directly compare survivors of various causes of death often suffer from their own methodological flaws (for a detailed consideration, see McIntosh 1987b; see also Cain 1972b; Calhoun et al. 1982; Henslin, 1971). These problems include the use of selective samples (e.g., college students or support group attendees), the use of retrospective designs (with researchers often asking survivors to recall feelings from many years earlier), the inclusion of small numbers of individuals, the use of nonstandardized instruments of unknown reliability and validity, the omission of measures of emotional closeness to the deceased, and the omission of many important relationship categories of survivors. Although methodologically still limited, such direct comparison group studies are able to address possible bereavement differences and similarities between survivors of suicide and survivors of loved ones lost through accidental and natural deaths.

In previous work I have summarized the overall body of research (McIntosh 1993, 1999) and concluded that all the investigations examined have had methodological problems. Despite these issues, collectively, their results suggest the following six points: (a) Evidence supports findings of a generally nonpathological bereavement reaction to suicide; (b) more similarities than differences are observed between suicide survivors and those bereaved by other modes of death, particularly when suicide survivors are compared with accidental death survivors; (c) there are possibly a small number of grief reactions or aspects of grieving that may differ or are unique for suicide survivors (and these unique reactions, along with the larger number of others, may constitute a nonpathological but definable "survivor syndrome"), but the precise differences and unique characteristics are not yet fully apparent; (d) the course of suicide survivorship may differ from that of other survivors over time, but (e) by some time after the second year, differences in grief seem minimal or indistinguishable across survivor groups; and (f) the kinship relation of the survivor to the suicide as well as the precise closeness and quality of the relationship and the time that has passed since the suicide seem to be important factors in bereavement.

In addition to these general summary findings, as might be expected, some aspects of grief have been found to differ for suicide survivors compared with survivors of deaths by other modes, whereas other reactions have not been differentially observed between these groups. Unfortunately, these results have not necessarily been consistent across studies of survivors of the same kinship relations or across kinship relations. As this would indicate, the research literature contains many inconsistencies and contradictory findings. It should also be noted that among reviewers of the research literature, some disagree with my interpretations and those of others that the findings do not clearly show unique differences between suicide bereavement and that following deaths by other causes (e.g., Ellenbogen and Gratton 2001; Jordan 2001). These writers believe that the existing evidence is compelling enough to support assertions of differences. For instance, Jordan (2001) finds the qualitative evidence strong enough to support three "themes" with respect to suicide bereavement. The first two are among those given by Calhoun et al. (1982) in their cautious generalizations, whereas the third is not. These three themes of suicide grief are (a) the greater struggle to find meaning in the loss of the loved one; (b) greater feelings of guilt, shame, responsibility, and blame; and (c) greater feelings of rejection, abandonment, and anger toward the deceased. Jordan also reviews the findings on social networks and argues that the bereaved of suicide receive less social support (the third of Calhoun et al.'s generalizations) and have more disruptions of social interactions than do survivors of other deaths. Ellenbogen and Gratton (2001), on the other hand, believe that when studies examine the differences between various kinds of bereaved groups, they ignore the variety of individual differences among suicide survivors. In other words, these authors encourage researchers to attempt to determine whether there are definable patterns of bereavement within the population of suicide survivors. The existence of such discernible and distinct subpopulations might explain the inconsistencies and contradictions in the research literature.

Any search for a single suicide survivor syndrome, whether in a clinical or an experiential bereavement context, will yield only partial consistency among the unique and shared reactions observed. In addition to, and in combination with, the emotional closeness of the bereaved to the deceased, one of the reasons for the variability in bereavement reactions is the variability in relationships or kinship relations of the individuals. The majority of comparison group investigations, therefore, have involved survivors of a single relationship category to the individuals they survive (e.g., parents only, widows only), and rightfully so. Although there have been exceptions (i.e., studies that have combined survivors of all relationships into a single group), studies throughout the history of research on this topic have largely examined groups with a single form of kinship relation. Each type of relationship likely involves somewhat distinct grief and bereavement aspects. Specific relationship studies seem most likely to reveal findings that will enhance our knowledge and understanding of survivor issues. Although many of the reactions noted in the early research are probable in all survivors, the kinship relation may alter not only the reactions but also the specific set of reactions experienced. It is also important to remember that the entire set of reactions noted here will occur in few individual survivors, and all bereaved will not necessarily experience these reactions to the same degree. As I have reviewed the research on relationships in detail in earlier publications (McIntosh 1987b, 1993), I will address only the most prominent issues here (for specific references, see McIntosh 1999).

Parent survivors (of a child's suicide). Parents play special roles in the lives of their children, and they and society have specific expectations of the responsibilities of parents toward their children. These expectations and responsibilities are important factors in the experience of parents of children who die by their own hands. Although present in studies of nearly all relationships, guilt and its related dimensions (such as shame and stigma) are perhaps the most prominent aspects of grief found among parents who have lost a child to suicide. The literature on attitudes toward parents of suicides underscores the belief that these parents are blamed and held responsible for their children's deaths and that they are liked less than parents whose children died by other means. Although not all of the few studies of parents have found consistent results for these reactions when parent suicide survivors are compared with parents of children lost through other modes of death, present findings often support this difference. Similarly, the issue of lack of support from others is prevalent in the accounts of parents, but research findings with comparative groups are equivocal on this aspect in some studies; in still other studies it has not been included in those grief aspects examined. Finally, as is the case with all modalities of death, both positive and negative outcomes in family adaptation occur, although parents surviving a suicide may more often experience negative adaptation, both in the family and in the relationship with the other parent.

Spouse survivors. As the marital relationship is often the most important relationship in a person's life, the death of a spouse has potentially major social, psychological, financial, and even health ramifications for the surviving spouse, and particularly so when the death is by suicide. Nearly all studies of spouse survivors are of widows—that is, wives whose husbands died by suicide. This undoubtedly reflects the much higher levels of suicide by men and perhaps also the fact that women are more likely than men to agree to participate in research. Both early and more recent comparative studies have frequently found more similarities than differences for spouse survivors of suicide and accidental deaths. Specific study results have indicated differences between spouses who survive suicide and those who survive other modes of death, but there has not been much consistency in the particular aspects of grief for which differences have been observed. That is, some studies have found differences that have not been observed in other investigations. This includes aspects such as guilt, shame, stigma, and social support following the death. One important factor in the bereavement outcome may be the nature and quality of the marital relationship at the time of the spouse's suicide.

Child survivors (of a parent's suicide). The issue of the age of the survivor (as well as the suicide) has frequently been noted in survivor studies, but this issue is particularly salient when children survive the suicide of a parent (obviously, it is also important when the suicide was a sibling or other family member). It should be noted that the vast majority of studies of child survivors have focused on children who are mental health clients, and this aspect may confound to some degree the findings reported. Particularly, the vulnerability and high risk of child survivors for mental health symptoms is commonly observed. Among the other aspects of grief that emerge in descriptions of child survivors of parental suicide are the guilt that children feel, the identification of the child with the deceased parent, and the distortions and often misleading information provided to children by other family members about the death. It is worth noting here that studies of adult children who have survived the suicide of a parent have thus far not been conducted (or at least published), although the issues in such cases are detailed in several personal accounts appearing in Stimming and Stimming's (1999) edited volume on child survivors. Stimming and Stimming summarize some possible common themes among the accounts they collected, including identification with the parent, feelings of abandonment, the children's anxiety over their own risk of future suicide, lack of opportunity to know other adult child survivors with whom they can share their experiences, and effects on their own family relationships (with spouses and children) and work relationships. Although this set of commonalities is not unique to adult child survivors, the dimensions and characteristics of the reactions might well reveal special aspects on closer investigation.

Sibling survivors. When children die, not only do their parents become survivors, but in most cases deceased children had siblings who also become survivors. Children in this group, sometimes called "forgotten mourners," have rarely been studied, and the subject of sibling survivors seems to receive little attention. The few studies of siblings that have appeared have, like those of child survivors of parent suicide, focused on psychopathology. When sibling survivors in these studies have been compared with controls, they have shown mixed results concerning the vulnerability of sibling survivors to psychiatric illness and symptoms following the suicide. One difference that has been reported, however, is a longer period of strong grief symptoms among those who survived the suicide of an adolescent sibling. Some siblings have reported experiencing rapid emotional and social maturity following the suicide. Issues of identification and guilt are also obvious possible aspects of responses among sibling survivors. No research has yet examined bereavement effects among siblings of various ages, particularly where the suicides involve adult siblings. As is the case for other kinship relations, many more studies of sibling survivors are required before definitive conclusions can emerge.

Therapist survivors (of a client's suicide). Individuals with mental health problems, particularly depression, are at elevated risk for suicide. Obviously, many persons with mental health problems, especially serious ones, are actively involved in therapy. Thus the probability that therapists at some time in their careers will eventually experience the suicide of a client is fairly high. The topic of therapists as survivors of client suicides has been largely ignored in the suicide literature (although this is changing; see, e.g., information on the efforts of the American Association of Suicidology's Therapist Survivors Task Force on the association's Web site at http://www.suicidology.org). Existing information suggests that the suicide of a client often has a significant effect on the therapist, both personally as well as professionally. Among often-mentioned issues are concerns about lawsuits, doubts about professional competence, depression, and the usefulness of talking to other therapists who have also experienced client suicide. As is a common theme, therapist survivors have thus far not been adequately studied for us to understand how they are affected by client suicides.

Suicide Survivors Literature: Personal Accounts

Researchers combine the responses of many study participants to present their findings in brief summaries or small numbers of generalizations. In the process of showing "typical" or "average" reactions, however, researchers often make it appear that all survivors (overall or of a particular relationship to the deceased) exhibit similar grief reactions and bereavement processes. Thus research findings give us a general impression of the responses of *groups* of survivors, but they cannot provide us with the rich detail, complexity of information, and variety of *individual* survivor experiences. This is best and most poignantly accomplished when survivors are allowed to tell their own stories. Personal accounts also permit listeners or readers to show empathy and help to normalize reactions and assist survivors in understanding that they

are not alone in their grief. My latest review of the literature includes a table of personal accounts that had appeared up to that time (McIntosh 1999:160), and others have appeared subsequently (e.g., Linn-Gust 2001, sibling; Stimming and Stimming 1999, multiple adult child survivors). These personal accounts come from suicide survivors in a wide array of kinship relations. When one reads personal accounts of the aftermath of suicide, one most often finds that they echo the generalities presented in this chapter, but the authors relate particular circumstances, events, and difficulties that are not represented in characterizations based solely on group results.

Finding the "Gift" Following a Suicide

Although no research studies have reported any findings on this issue and its incidence among survivors, those who have contributed to the personal experience literature have often mentioned finding a "gift" after a suicide. Many survivors express their wish to find meaning in the death of their loved ones. This is a subissue of understanding the loss that has often been noted by researchers and writers on this topic. Iris Bolton (1983), a pioneer in the area of suicide survivorship, was told by a psychiatrist and friend shortly after Bolton's son's suicide that there "is a gift for you in your son's death" (p. 16). Although this statement outraged and perplexed Bolton at the time, she subsequently found the gift and has shared it with countless others over the years. One aspect of the "gift" emerged in her book *My Son . . . My Son . . . ,* in which she shares her own experiences and feelings about her son's death and the effects it had on her. This book has been of tremendous help to many survivors, particularly parent survivors. Bolton also completed an advanced degree focusing on the topic of suicide, and she now shares her experience and knowledge internationally in presentations. Her practical and invaluable suggestions for survivors have been widely disseminated (see Dunne et al. 1987:289–90). Other survivors have likewise discovered "gifts" in the suicide deaths of their loved ones. For example, after their daughter's suicide, Jerry and Elsie Weyrauch founded the Suicide Prevention Action Network (SPAN), an extremely active national advocacy group that works to promote legislation to provide funding for and research on the topic of suicide and suicide survivors (see the organization's Web site at http://spanusa.org). Following their son's death, Dale and Dar Emme founded a youth suicide prevention program designed to empower and get help for those who are troubled or suicidal; this international organization is called the Yellow Ribbon Suicide Prevention Program of the Light for Life Foundation (see its Web site at http://www.yellowribbon.org).These are but a few examples of the ways in which some survivors of suicide have worked to benefit others who have shared their experience and at the same time healed themselves and found meaning in their loss. This aspect of the bereavement reactions of some survivors deserves more formal study.

Postvention: Therapy and Support for Suicide Survivors

As is true for many aspects of suicide survivorship, no definitive data exist regarding the numbers, proportions, or characteristics of survivors of suicide who seek or require postventive care. Over time, a variety of resources have been developed and have increasingly become available for survivors who seek assistance in dealing with their loss (for discussions of these resources, see chapters in Dunne et al. 1987). Although general bereavement resources such as support groups are available in many communities, and some suicide survivors will benefit from them, one clear theme of the personal experience literature is that suicide survivors benefit most from group support settings that are homogeneous with respect to the mode of death (i.e., that include only suicide survivors). Although there is no empirical support for this claim (it has not been investigated directly), some survivors have described their discomfort and feelings of being different, of not fitting in, as members of survivor groups in which the modes of death were mixed. Such feelings likely arise from the feelings of guilt, shame, and stigma so often observed among suicide survivors. Following their loss, survivors of suicide sometimes seek or are referred to traditional individual or group therapy services in their communities that specifically address suicide bereavement. In other cases, survivors seek, and often find, self-help and support groups, some of which are led by mental health professionals and others of which are facilitated exclusively by individuals who are themselves suicide survivors (a list of such resources in local communities throughout North America may be found on the American Association of Suicidology's Web site, at http://www.suicidology.org). Although limited information exists about these various resources (see, e.g., Rubey and McIntosh 1996), anecdotal evidence testifies to the tremendous assistance survivors receive from them in their healing process. In a promising recent evaluation study that incorporated several desirable research characteristics, Pfeffer et al. (2002) provided a group intervention for children who were survivors of relatives' suicides to one group and not to another. The researchers found that the group intervention (which focused on the children's reactions to their relatives' deaths as well as on strengthening the children's coping skills) lessened the distress of children who had lost a parent or sibling to suicide compared with those who did not receive the intervention. More such research-based evaluations and outcome evidence are sorely needed.

SURVIVORS OF SUICIDE: RESEARCH, THERAPY/SUPPORT, AND EDUCATIONAL NEEDS

Thus far in this chapter I have summarized our current knowledge of the varied facets of suicide survivorship. As can be seen, answers to many questions are beginning to emerge, but clearly much information remains unknown or uncertain. The need is great for further research and clinical attention to suicide survivors to expand our understanding of and ability to intervene effectively with suicide survivors. The knowledge base on survivors has expanded significantly since Cain's (1972b) pioneering effort, but Cain (1972a) noted many of the issues and needs indicated here in his introduction to *Survivors of Suicide*. The limitations that Cain noted 30 years ago persist to the present (for review and discussion of these limitations, see McIntosh 1987b).

Basic Information Needs

Definition and precision of the term "suicide survivor." In work published more than 15 years ago, I stated that among the most basic issues with the widest implications for this field is agreement on nomenclature surrounding suicide survivors (McIntosh 1987b). In the most general sense, the meaning of the term *suicide survivor* can now be considered resolved (as discussed above). However, scholars must learn to apply the concept of "suicide survivor" with far greater precision and specification, to delineate clearly the populations investigated and served. The general definition of *suicide survivors* noted earlier includes the affected family and friends of those who die by suicide. As I have pointed out elsewhere, "This broad definition may include many family relationships (immediate and extended family) and nonfamily relationships (friends, therapists, coworkers, fellow students, etc.), from those emotionally close to those remote from the suicide, and individuals greatly and hardly affected by the death" (McIntosh 1987b:264). And as I have observed in relation to the personal accounts noted above, each relationship category represents a group and individuals within the group who have vastly different survivor experiences. At a minimum, researchers and clinicians must indicate precisely what subpopulations they have studied or assisted to indicate the possible limits of generalizability of their findings (e.g., findings for parent survivors may not apply well to children who survive a parent's suicide). In addition, it is important to determine how far the concept of "affected by the death" extends. For instance, how much (qualitatively and/or quantitatively) does a person need to be affected by someone else's suicide to be considered a "survivor"?

Epidemiological information. As noted earlier, a vital need exists for epidemiological and demographic investigations to determine the number and characteristics of survivors in the general population. That is, Who are those we call suicide survivors? and How many survivors are there? More specifically, what are the distributions and numbers of suicide survivors by age, sex, race, relationship to the deceased, time since the death? If the bereaved individuals who make up this special group are to receive the research, services, and funding they deserve, researchers must compile the data needed to arrive at fundamentally sound estimates of the numerical dimensions of the population at risk. Methodologically sound investigations of the population are needed to provide this information.

Family history information. The clinical literature includes many studies regarding the family history of suicidal behavior in populations such as depressives or schizophrenics. Similarly, investigations of nonclinical populations of survivors are needed. Such research could help clarify the risk of suicide among survivors of suicide and the incidence of suicide among the generations of a family (and may potentially lead to a better understanding of social and biological factors associated with suicide).

Clarification of Bereavement Reactions and Experiences of Suicide Survivors

Determination of suicide survivor syndrome characteristics. The features of suicide survivors' grief reactions must be determined through carefully conducted empirical research and clinical observation. From a biopsychosocial perspective, information is needed about the broad range of psychological and behavioral aspects as well as social, physical, and health changes. This information may identify survivor subgroups with differential needs with respect to postvention.

Comparison to bereavement by other modes of death. Nearly all contemporary research designs include comparison groups and should continue to do so. Descriptions of how suicide survivors' grief and bereavement differ from and are similar to those for other sudden (accidental, natural, and homicide) and nonsudden deaths can be derived only from such designs. Once again, the results of such investigations may guide interventions with suicide survivors, including traditional therapy and mutual support groups.

Study of the variety of relationships. Not only do we need to understand how suicide survivorship differs from and is similar to that from other causes of death, we need better knowledge of how reactions to suicide are affected by the relationship of the survivor to the suicide. Although some researchers have begun to explore certain basic relationships, as reviewed briefly above, investigations into a number of potentially important relationships are also needed. Such relationships might include the following: "parents of child or adolescent suicides; parents of adult suicides; adolescents and children as survivors of parental, sibling, or friend suicide; widows and widowers; grandparents; unmarried lovers, including individuals in gay and lesbian relationships . . .; closest friends and confidants compared to acquaintances and casual friends; therapists; those who discovered the suicide" (McIntosh 1987b:267). Each of these relationships has the potential to produce relatively unique aspects in the grieving experience.

Focus on effective coping strategies. At least as important as identifying bereavement reactions of suicide survivors is the determination of successful coping mechanisms that survivors employ to deal with their grief and loss. Such information may inform better intervention and help for the bereaved.

Role of social and familial networks. Another important but largely unstudied aspect of coping with suicide is the social support network of the survivor (see also Jordan 2001). It remains to be determined how such networks react under various survivor circumstances and how a network's extensiveness may affect a survivor's reactions, their intensity and duration, and recovery. As noted earlier, one of Calhoun et al.'s (1982) generalizations was that suicide survivors receive less social support than do other survivors. Another facet of this issue is how the family system is affected by a suicide death with respect to contacts, closeness, and communication. Special, but commonly occurring, social settings in which suicides occur also need to be investigated with respect to systemic effects as well as individual reactions. Families are one such system, and in addition to families, schools and universities, work settings, therapy groups, and other systems are among those that should be investigated. Thus far, research regarding social and support networks, familial and nonfamilial, among suicide survivors has been inadequate.

General Research and Methodological Issues

Research with survivors of deaths, and particularly suicide deaths, involves a number of primarily methodological issues. Recent individual studies have been more methodologically sound than earlier studies, but there are still many needs and issues to be addressed in future research. Among these are the following:

1. Research should be based in theory (e.g., general bereavement models and concepts, such as complicated grief, disenfranchised grief, or traumatic grief; coping; trauma and PTSD; stress and life change; attachment).

2. Researchers should attempt to replicate important findings with different populations and settings.

3. Researchers should utilize better sampling methods and include larger numbers of survivors in their study samples.

4. Researchers should develop and use better measures of general and specific aspects of bereavement (standardized instruments with desirable psychometric properties of reliability and validity determined).

5. Researchers should undertake systematic study of the entire range of kinship relations (both familial and others, including therapists), using, whenever possible, similar methods and measures.

6. Studies should include measures of the emotional closeness or even the strength of the bond or attachment between the survivor and the suicide (i.e., not all

individuals, even within specific kinship relations, are as close to or as affected by the loss; see, e.g., Reed, 1993).

7. Researchers should use longitudinal ("follow-up," rather than the more common retrospective) research methods to determine the time course of bereavement, including potentially critical periods in the bereavement process. There is a particularly great need for studies that begin early in the bereavement process (respecting and recognizing this sensitive and difficult time) and proceed over an extended period of months or even years.

8. In addition to bereaved comparison groups among other modes of death, studies should include nonbereaved control groups whenever possible, as well as participants who do not belong to the often-studied and readily available clinical, college student, and support group populations (i.e., findings based on these groups may or may not generalize to all survivors).

9. Whenever possible, research designs should include control features for potentially confounding factors that may contribute to suicide survivor reactions and hamper clear interpretation of the primary factors under investigation (e.g., emotional closeness or attachment of the survivor to the deceased, time elapsed since the death, relationship of the survivor to the deceased, the sex and/or age of the survivor, and the sex and/or age of the deceased) (with respect to closeness, see, e.g., Reed 1993).

10. Studies should attempt to determine the impacts of a broad range of general factors in addition to kinship relations, including, for example, "the age of the deceased; the age of the survivor at the time of the death; sex, racial/ethnic, socioeconomic differences; family vs. friend differences; cultural differences (including the effects as a result of grief and mourning practices, religion, rituals, attitudes toward suicide, etc.); support group attendees vs. nonattendees vs. therapy client differences; those who discover the body of the suicide; and differences in the survivor experience in the case of the various methods employed in the suicide (i.e., violent vs. nonviolent, such as firearms and hanging vs. drugs)" (McIntosh 1987b:271).

11. Researchers should extend and continue studies of attitudes toward suicide survivors to determine what factors affect perceptions of and attitudes toward survivors. In a related but new direction for this research, Peterson, Luoma, and Dunne (2002) investigated survivors' perceptions of the clinician who treated their loved one who died by suicide. The results of such studies have implications for treating the suicidal as well as for issues after a suicide. A particularly interesting set of findings relates to differences between family members who did or did not file legal actions against the treating therapist.

Postvention: Clinical, Therapeutic, and Support Issues

A number of issues remain to be resolved with respect to therapy and support for survivors of suicide.

The terminology and description of postvention. Just as terminology issues exist in the larger context of suicide survivors, terms used in postvention circumstances are also problematic. Several terms are currently employed to refer to group settings intended to aid suicide survivors. The use of consistent terminology from the larger bereavement literature would benefit communication and clarification of the operation of such suicide support groups. For instance, in the larger literature, groups that involve professionals are called *mutual help support groups,* whereas those conducted and run by survivors are referred to as *mutual help groups.* Clear designation of these mutual aid groups and their various forms is important, as is differentiation of these groups from traditional therapeutic methods. That is, mutual aid is not "therapy" in the traditional sense of the term as used by clinicians. However, it is clearly the case that mutual aid groups can have therapeutic effects (see, e.g., Dunne 1987). More formal professional communication of the variety of approaches being employed with suicide survivors is needed (e.g., therapy, support groups, self-help groups). Dissemination of the specific details of these approaches—in traditional therapy and support settings, in publications, and in presentations at professional meetings—is desirable; these details should include information about features and approaches that are beneficial as well as those that do not work well. This would facilitate the development of model approaches for survivors that may advance society's ability to meet suicide survivors' needs through the provision of services and support.

Evaluation and efficacy efforts. Perhaps the most crucial aspect of postvention approaches and their proliferation is the need for evaluation. Only a small number of formal efficacy, evaluation, or outcome studies have been conducted for suicide survivor groups and postvention approaches (for a review, see McIntosh 1999:171–72; also, for a recent study, see Constantino, Sekula, and Rubinstein 2001), but models for such research appear in the general literature on mutual aid groups (for some examples, see McIntosh 1987b:275). Both mutual aid groups and traditional therapy approaches for suicide survivors would benefit greatly from a large growth in such research as a formal aspect of providing services. Immediate as well as long-term follow-up measures are needed to demonstrate the effects of assistance to survivors. Crucial questions exist in postventive care that can be answered only through formal evaluation. For instance: What approaches are most effective and helpful, and for which subgroups of survivors? Under what circumstances would therapy as opposed to support be indicated? When in the grieving process is therapy or support most helpful? How soon after the loss should a survivor enter into postvention care? Would all survivors benefit from therapy or support, or are both unnecessary for some survivors? Is the involvement of professionals essential in mutual help settings? If so, in what capacity should professionals be involved? Should professionals or facilitators who work with support groups also be survivors themselves? Without evidence from evaluation studies, postventive efforts cannot advance, nor can they gain acceptance within the larger mental health provider system.

Needs Related to Personal/Qualitative Accounts of Suicide Survivors

Variety in data sources. Although relatively controlled, traditional research investigations are an ideal embraced by the professional community, the use of multiple methodologies and sources of information is desirable. This is particularly true given that current levels of knowledge regarding suicide survivors are not well advanced. Varied sources may provide a wealth of information about the survivor experience and identify issues in need of closer and more controlled scrutiny. In the introduction to his seminal volume, Cain (1972a:24) suggested the use of such diverse data sources as autobiographies, poetry, court cases, and coroner's anecdotes. Similarly, continued expansion of the personal accounts of suicide survivors, as described earlier, is needed as well. Conspicuously missing from the qualitative/personal experiential literature are clinical case studies of suicide survivors. Particularly desirable in this regard would be detailed case information on survivors who have experienced difficult or problematic grief. To date, the experiential literature (i.e., personal accounts) has almost exclusively been written by or about individuals who, although they have experienced bereavement process difficulties, rarely if ever could be considered "pathological" in their grief. Given that most suicide survivors seem to belong to this latter category, their personal accounts remain crucial to the body of knowledge. However, the clinical community requires cases across the entire range of experience to inform therapy and supportive interventions.

Descriptions of personal experiences in postventive settings. Few survivors have published accounts of their therapy/support group experiences and how these approaches benefited them. Eleanora Betsy Ross's (1997) depiction of the Ray of Hope program she developed in the late 1970s following her husband's suicide remains one of the few highly detailed program descriptions. It would be valuable to have survivors' detailed accounts of their experiences in therapy and/or support groups, particularly to see how they would portray "the progression, changes, frustrations, lessons learned, and 'stages' of healing that likely resulted over time" (McIntosh 1999:159, 161).

Training and Education Needs

Education and training are logical areas to include when confronting a problem, and they seem appropriate prescription components in this context as well. However, virtually no empirical evidence has been collected that clearly demonstrates the effectiveness of training or education programs with respect to postvention. Such

evaluative efforts are themselves essential in the design and implementation of educational programs. With evaluation as a crucial component, therefore, the following are some areas in which special efforts for training and education seem warranted.

Caregiver training. Caregivers and members of gatekeeper groups who frequently come into contact with suicide survivors (e.g., law enforcement personnel, emergency and medical personnel, coroners and medical examiners, funeral directors, clergy, teachers, mental health professionals) need training to sensitize them to the issues of suicide and survivors. Ideally, these individuals would receive such training as part of their professional curricula. In some cases this training would involve teams of professionals to help groups of survivors (e.g., students in a school in which a suicide has occurred). In some instances, caregiver training is also a recognition that persons in certain occupation groups (e.g., police officers, emergency personnel) are likely to become involved with suicidal individuals and so become survivors themselves. Thus training should include discussions of coping with one's own survivorship, and postvention services should be readily available for these professionals.

Public education efforts. Although caregivers may encounter suicide survivors more frequently than do most members of the general public, education of the population at large also seems warranted. Such education should include the identification of available community resources as well as general information regarding mental health services and suicide.

THE AFTERMATH OF SUICIDE ATTEMPTS

Unlike the extensive (by comparison) literature that exists on the aftermath of death by suicide for surviving significant others, almost nothing has been written regarding the effects of attempted suicide on the lives it touches. The literature on unsuccessful suicide attempts (or "parasuicides") is long-standing and extensive (e.g., Kreitmann 1977; Maris, Berman, and Silverman 2000:chap. 12). However, this large body of research has focused largely on therapy and intervention for the attempter following the nonfatal attempt as well as on the prevention and risk of future suicidal acts and death by suicide (e.g., Arensman et al. 2001; Stewart, Manion, and Davidson 2002; Suokas et al. 2001). Almost completely missing from consideration and study have been the variety of effects of an attempt on the life (and feelings, cognitions, and social world) of the attempter and his or her significant others. A small number of studies have examined the subjective experiences of parents of adolescent attempters (Wagner et al. 2000) and greater problems among friends of adolescent attempters (e.g., Hazell and Lewin 1993; Ho et al. 2000). Other than these few investigations, however, there is no body of research similar to the one that exists concerning suicide survivors on this topic, despite the substantial numbers of individuals involved with suicide attempt behaviors annually and cumulatively (as noted earlier). The pain, stress, emotional and social turmoil, shame and stigma, and other logically common aspects of life following a nonfatal suicide attempt may often be unaddressed or poorly addressed.

Unlike the now visible and growing personal accounts published by some suicide survivors, few discussions of such issues are available (an exception is Heckler 1994) for inquiring attempters or their loved ones seeking normalization and guidance in their struggle with an attempt's sequelae. Efforts similar to those that assist suicide survivors, both professionally and therapeutically as well as with respect to self-help approaches, might well benefit attempters and their significant others as well. As is true for suicide survivors, given the large numbers of people affected by suicide attempts, this topic deserves concerted research efforts to determine the scope of the problem and what issues and factors are most important following suicide attempts. In these cases, however, we not only have "survivor-victims" in the loved ones for whom assistance in healing is needed, we also have the individuals whose behavioral acts created the situation. These attempters are, obviously, alive. Information about their subjective experiences and efforts to deal with their pain and "return to life" (Heckler 1994) is potentially valuable to other attempters as well. The significant others in the lives of suicide attempters would also benefit from information on the practical and subjective experiences of others who have dealt with and recovered from such attempts.

CONCLUSION

For many years, researchers ignored the topic of suicide's aftermath. However, the literature on suicide survivors and our understanding of the experience of suicide survivorship is now growing annually. Still almost entirely ignored is the issue of the effects on attempters' loved ones following nonfatal suicide attempts. More and better designed studies have begun to be conducted that will help us to quantify and place suicide grief in the larger context of bereavement from all modes of death. This research has been supplemented by highly detailed individual accounts that personalize suicide grief and portray survivors' variety of experiences in ways that are not possible in group research finding reports. There is certainly a need for substantial further expansion of this body of knowledge in the areas of research, education, therapy/support, and postvention. The existing literature has raised awareness of this important aspect of suicidal behavior and has led to the establishment of therapy and support interventions. Long overdue, greater attention to the issues and individuals affected in the aftermath of suicide and suicidal behavior will further increase our understanding and, more important,

assist survivors in their efforts to confront their loss, or the ramifications of a suicide attempt, and heal.

REFERENCES

Arensman, Ella, Ellen Townsend, Keith Hawton, Sandy Bremner, Eleanor Feldman, Robert Goldney, David Gunnell, Philip Hazell, Kees van Heeringen, Allan House, David Owens, Isaac Sakinofsky, and Lil Traskman-Bendz. 2001. "Psychosocial and Pharmacological Treatment of Patients Following Deliberate Self-Harm: The Methodological Issues Involved in Evaluating Effectiveness." *Suicide and Life-Threatening Behavior* 31:169–80.

Bolton, Iris (with Curtis Mitchell). 1983. *My Son . . . My Son . . . : A Guide to Healing After a Suicide in the Family.* Atlanta, GA: Bolton.

Cain, Albert C. 1972a. "Introduction." Pp. 5–33 in *Survivors of Suicide,* edited by Albert C. Cain. Springfield, I: Charles C Thomas.

———, ed. 1972b. *Survivors of Suicide.* Springfield, IL: Charles C Thomas.

Calhoun, Lawrence G., James W. Selby, and Lisa E. Selby. 1982. "The Psychological Aftermath of Suicide: An Analysis of Current Evidence." *Clinical Psychology Review* 2:409–20.

Callahan, Jay. 1989. "Epidemiology of Suicide Attempts and of Survivors." Presented at the annual meeting of the American Association of Suicidology, San Diego, CA.

Clark, Sheila E. and Robert D. Goldney. 2000. "The Impact of Suicide on Relatives and Friends." Pp. 467–84 in *The International Handbook of Suicide and Attempted Suicide,* edited by Keith Hawton and Kees van Heeringen. New York: John Wiley.

Cleiren, M. and Rene Diekstra. 1995. "After the Loss: Bereavement and Other Types of Death." Pp. 7–39 in *The Impact of Suicide,* edited by Brian Mishara. New York: Springer.

Constantino, Rose E., Kathleen Sekula, and Elaine N. Rubinstein. 2001. "Group Intervention for Widowed Survivors of Suicide." *Suicide and Life-Threatening Behavior* 31:428–41.

Dunne, Edward and M. M. Wilbur. 1993. "Survivors of Suicide" (pamphlet). Washington, DC: American Association of Suicidology.

Dunne, Edward J. 1987. "Surviving the Suicide of a Therapist." Pp. 142–48 in *Suicide and Its Aftermath: Understanding and Counseling the Survivors,* edited by Edward J. Dunne, John L. McIntosh, and Karen Dunne-Maxim. New York: W. W. Norton.

Dunne, Edward J., John L. McIntosh, and Karen Dunne-Maxim, eds. 1987. *Suicide and Its Aftermath: Understanding and Counseling the Survivors.* New York: W. W. Norton.

Ellenbogen, Stephen, and Francine Gratton. 2001. "Do They Suffer More? Reflections on Research Comparing Suicide Survivors to Other Survivors." *Suicide and Life-Threatening Behavior* 31:83–90.

Foglia, Barbara B. 1984. "Survivor Victims of Suicide: A Review of the Literature." Pp. 149–62 in *Suicide: Assessment and Intervention,* 2d ed., edited by Corrine L. Hatton and Sharon M. Valente. Norwalk, CT: Appleton-Century-Crofts.

Hauser, Marilyn J. 1987. "Special Aspects of Grief After a Suicide." Pp. 57–70 in *Suicide and Its Aftermath: Understanding and Counseling the Survivors,* edited by

Edward J. Dunne, John L. McIntosh, and Karen Dunne-Maxim. New York: W. W. Norton.

Hazell, Philip and Terry Lewin. 1993. "Friends of Adolescent Suicide Attempters and Completers." *Journal of the American Academy of Child and Adolescent Psychiatry* 32:76–81.

Heckler, Richard A. 1994. *Waking Up Alive: The Descent, the Suicide Attempt, and the Return to Life.* New York: Ballantine.

Henley, S. H. A. 1984. "Bereavement Following Suicide: A Review of the Literature." *Current Psychological Research and Reviews* 3:53–61.

Henslin, James M. 1971. "Problems and Prospects in Studying Significant Others of Suicides." *Bulletin of Suicidology* 8:81–84.

Hiegel, S. M. and J. Hipple. 1990. "Survivors of Suicide: Victims Left Behind: An Overview." *TACD Journal* 18:55–67.

Ho, Ting-Pong, Patrick W. L. Leung, Se-fong Hung, Chi-chiu Lee, and C. P. Tang. 2000. "The Mental Health of the Peers of Suicide Completers and Attempters." *Journal of Child Psychology and Psychiatry and Allied Disciplines* 4:301–8.

"Interaction: Survivors of Suicide." 1996. *Newslink* (publication of the American Association of Suicidology) 22(3):3, 15.

Jobes, David A., Jason B. Luoma, Lisa Anne T. Hustead, and Rachel E. Mann. 2000. "In the Wake of Suicide: Survivorship and Postvention." Pp. 536–61 in Ronald W. Maris, Alan L. Berman, and Morton M. Silverman, *Comprehensive Textbook of Suicidology.* New York: Guilford.

Jordan, John R. 2001. "Is Suicide Bereavement Different? A Reassessment of the Literature." *Suicide and Life-Threatening Behavior* 31:91–102.

Kreitmann, Norman. 1977. *Parasuicide.* New York: John Wiley.

Linn-Gust, Michelle. 2001. *Do They Have Bad Days in Heaven? Surviving the Suicide Loss of a Sibling.* Atlanta, GA: Bolton.

Maris, Ronald W., Alan L. Berman, and Morton M. Silverman. 2000. *Comprehensive Textbook of Suicidology.* New York: Guilford.

McIntosh, John L. 1987a. "Introduction." Pp. xvii–xix in *Suicide and Its Aftermath: Understanding and Counseling the Survivors,* edited by Edward J. Dunne, John L. McIntosh, and Karen Dunne-Maxim. New York: W. W. Norton.

———. 1987b. "Research Therapy and Educational Needs." Pp. 263–77 in *Suicide and Its Aftermath: Understanding and Counseling the Survivors,* edited by Edward J. Dunne, John L. McIntosh, and Karen Dunne-Maxim. New York: W. W. Norton.

———. 1987c. "Survivor Family Relationships: Literature Review." Pp. 73–84 in *Suicide and Its Aftermath: Understanding and Counseling the Survivors,* edited by Edward J. Dunne, John L. McIntosh, and Karen Dunne-Maxim. New York: W. W. Norton.

———. 1989. "How Many Survivors of Suicide Are There?" *Surviving Suicide* 1(1):1, 4.

———. 1993. "Control Group Studies of Suicide Survivors: A Review and Critique." *Suicide and Life-Threatening Behavior* 23:146–61.

———. 1999. "Research on Survivors of Suicide." Pp. 157–80 in *Before Their Time: Adult Children's Experiences of Parental Suicide,* edited by Mary Stimming and Maureen Stimming. Philadelphia: Temple University Press.

———. 2001. *U.S.A. Suicide: 1999 Official Final Data.* Washington, DC: American Association of Suicidology.

Ness, D. E. and Cynthia R. Pfeffer. 1990. "Sequelae of Bereavement Resulting From Suicide." *American Journal of Psychiatry* 147:279–85.

Peterson, Erin M., Jason B. Luoma, and Edward Dunne. 2002. "Suicide Survivors' Perceptions of the Treating Clinician." *Suicide and Life-Threatening Behavior* 32:158–66.

Pfeffer, Cynthia R., Hong Jiang, Tatsuyuki Kakuma, Judy Hwang, and Michele Metsch. 2002. "Group Intervention for Children Bereaved by the Suicide of a Relative." *Journal of the American Academy of Child and Adolescent Psychiatry* 41:505–13.

Reed, Mark D. 1993. "Sudden Death and Bereavement Outcomes: The Impact of Resources on Grief Symptomatology and Detachment." *Suicide and Life-Threatening Behavior* 23:204–20.

Ross, Eleanora Betsy. 1997. *Life After Suicide: A Ray of Hope for Those Left Behind.* New York: Plenum.

Rubey, Charles T. and John L. McIntosh. 1996. "Suicide Survivor Groups: Results of a Survey." *Suicide and Life-Threatening Behavior* 26:351–58.

Rudestam, Kjell E. 1992. "Research Contributions to Understanding the Suicide Survivor." *Crisis* 13:41–46.

Shneidman, Edwin S. 1969. "Prologue: Fifty-Eight Years." Pp. 1–30 in *On the Nature of Suicide,* edited by Edwin S. Shneidman. San Francisco: Jossey-Bass.

Stewart, S. Evelyn, Ian G. Manion, and Simon Davidson. 2002. "Emergency Management of the Adolescent Suicide Attempter: A Review of the Literature." *Journal of Adolescent Health* 30:312–25.

Stimming, Mary and Maureen Stimming, eds. 1999. *Before Their Time: Adult Children's Experiences of Parental Suicide.* Philadelphia: Temple University Press.

Suokas, Jaana, Kirsi Suominen, Erkki Isometsa, Aini Ostamo, and Jouko Lonnqvist. 2001. "Long-Term Risk Factors for Suicide Mortality After Attempted Suicide: Findings of a 14–Year Follow-Up Study." *Acta Psychiatrica Scandinavica* 104:117–21.

U.S. Department of Health and Human Services. 2001. *National Strategy for Suicide Prevention: Goals and Objectives for Action.* Rockville, MD: Public Health Service.

van der Wal, J. 1989. "The Aftermath of Suicide: A Review of Empirical Evidence." *Omega* 20:149–71.

Wagner, Barry M., Christine Aiken, P. Michelle Mullaley, and James J. Tobin. 2000. "Parents' Reactions to Adolescents' Suicide Attempts." *Journal of the American Academy of Child and Adolescent Psychiatry* 39:429–36.

CROSS-CULTURAL PERSPECTIVES ON SUICIDE

DAVID LESTER

Culture provides a set of rules and standards that are shared by members of a society. These rules and standards shape and determine the range of behaviors that are considered appropriate under prescribed conditions. Such cultural artifacts influence the behaviors of persons of different nationalities and ethnicities as well as other subgroups within a nation. In looking at cultural influences on behavior, one important difference across cultures that comes immediately to light is the difference in rates of suicide.

One of the most interesting phenomena in suicidology is the national variation found in suicide rates. As the data displayed in Table 1 show, suicide rates for males around the world vary from a high of 73.8 per 100,000 per year in Lithuania to a low of 1.1 per 100,000 in Azerbaijan. For females, the rates range from 14.8 in Hungary to 0.2 in Azerbaijan. Our current knowledge of worldwide trends in suicide is somewhat limited because many African, Middle Eastern, and Central and South American countries do not report their suicide rates to the World Health Organization.

For all but one of the nations shown in Table 1, the male suicide rate is higher than the female suicide rate. The lone exception is China, where women have a higher suicide rate than men; in the period 1990–94, the rate for women in China was 33.6 per 100,000 per year versus 24.2 for men (Phillips, Liu, and Zhang 1999). However, the Chinese government documents suicide fatalities only in selected regions of the nation, so the reported suicide rates are not completely valid.

The differences observed in national suicide rates are large and generally stable over time, as the data displayed in Table 2 demonstrate. Although the rates have fluctuated over the years shown, within each of the nations listed the rates in one year are positively associated with the rates in other years.

Although some observers have raised questions about the accuracy of official suicide rates in various nations—given, for example, the different evaluation and recording procedures of coroners and medical examiners in different countries (e.g., Douglas 1967)—research has shown the suicide rates of immigrant groups in both the United States and Australia to be strongly associated with the suicide rates in the immigrants' home nations (Sainsbury and Barraclough 1968). For example, in 1959, Ireland's suicide rate was relatively low, 2.5 per 100,000; in that same year, Irish immigrants to the United States, who encountered the same medical examiners as did members of other immigrant groups, also had the lowest suicide rate of all immigrant groups from European countries, only 9.8 (Dublin 1963).

Male suicide rates increase with age in most nations of the world, whereas for females, the distribution of suicide rates by age varies with the level of economic development of the nation (Girard 1993). In wealthy nations, such as the United States and Sweden, female suicide rates tend to peak in middle age. In poorer nations, such as Venezuela, suicide rates are higher for elderly women, and in the poorest nations, such as Thailand, the peak shifts to young adult women (Girard 1993).

EXPLAINING NATIONAL DIFFERENCES IN SUICIDE

Conklin and Simpson (1987) used factor analysis to examine the association of sociodemographic and economic variables with national suicide rates. These researchers identified two clusters of variables that appear to be associated with national suicide rates: One cluster was made up of variables concerning religion (these had the highest loading from Islamic countries), and the second cluster was made up of variables concerning economic development. Conklin and Simpson found that predominantly Muslim nations with low levels of economic development had the lowest rates of suicide.

In my own similar study of suicide rates in 72 countries, I identified 13 independent orthogonal factors for the social variables, only one of which, economic development, was associated with suicide rates (Lester 1996). This factor had high loadings from such social variables

Table 1 Suicide Rates Around the World, by Sex

Country	Year[a]	Males	Females
Albania	1998	6.3	3.6
Argentina	1996	9.9	3.0
Armenia	1999	2.7	0.9
Australia	1997	22.7	6.7
Austria	1999	28.7	10.3
Azerbaijan	1999	1.1	0.2
Belarus	1999	61.1	10.0
Belgium	1995	31.3	11.7
Belize	1995	12.1	0.9
Brazil[b]	1995	6.6	1.8
Bulgaria	1999	24.1	8.1
Canada	1997	19.6	5.1
China[b]	1998	13.4	14.8
Costa Rica	1995	9.7	2.1
Croatia	1999	32.7	11.5
Cuba	1996	24.5	12.0
Czech Republic	1999	25.7	6.2
Denmark	1996	24.3	9.8
Ecuador	1995	6.4	3.2
Estonia	1999	56.0	12.1
Finland	1998	38.3	10.1
France	1997	28.4	10.1
Germany	1998	21.5	7.3
Greece	1998	6.1	1.7
Hong Kong	1996	15.9	9.1
Hungary	1999	53.1	14.8
Iceland	1996	20.8	3.7
India	1998	12.2	9.1
Ireland	1996	19.2	3.5
Israel	1997	10.5	2.6
Italy	1997	12.7	3.9
Japan	1997	26.0	11.9
Kazakhstan	1999	46.4	8.6
Kuwait	1999	2.7	1.6
Kyrgyzstan	1999	19.3	4.0
Latvia	1999	59.6	13.1
Lithuania	1999	73.8	13.6
Luxembourg	1997	29.0	9.8
Macedonia	1997	11.5	4.0
Malta	1999	11.7	2.6
Mauritius	1998	21.9	7.8
Mexico	1995	5.4	1.0
Moldova	1999	27.6	5.1
Netherlands	1997	13.5	6.7
New Zealand	1998	23.7	6.9
Norway	1997	17.8	6.6
Poland	1996	24.1	4.6
Portugal	1998	8.7	2.7
Romania	1999	20.3	4.4
Russia	1998	62.6	11.6
Singapore	1998	13.9	9.5
Slovakia	1999	22.5	3.7
Slovenia	1999	47.3	13.4
South Korea	1997	17.8	8.0
Spain	1997	13.1	4.2
Sweden	1996	20.0	8.5
Switzerland	1996	29.2	11.6

Country	Year[a]	Males	Females
Tajikistan	1995	5.1	1.8
Turkmenistan	1998	13.8	3.5
Ukraine	1999	51.2	10.0
United Kingdom	1998	11.7	3.3
United States	1998	18.6	4.4
Uzbekistan	1998	10.5	3.1

SOURCE: World Health Organization (2002, 2003). Reprinted with permission from the World Health Organization (WHO).

a. Most recent year for which WHO data are available.
b. Data for selected regions only.

as low population growth and high gross domestic product per capita.

Physiological Differences

One possible explanation for differences in national suicide rates is that people of different nationalities differ in their physiology. For example, there are clear differences in the frequencies of particular genes in individuals from the different nations of Europe (Menozzi, Piazza, and Cavalli-Sforza 1978). Thus the people in different nations and cultures may differ in their genetic structures. In addition, recent research on identical twins and adopted children has shown that the likelihood that particular individuals will develop certain psychiatric disorders has a strong genetic basis. Differences in inherited tendencies to develop psychiatric disorders, particularly affective disorders, or to develop brain concentrations of serotonin, the neurotransmitter believed to be responsible for depression, may be partially responsible for differences in the suicide rates of nations and cultures.

Few researchers have explored how physiological differences may account for national differences in suicide rates, but one study that examined the association between physiological factors and cross-national suicide rates found that the suicide rates of nations were associated with the proportions of their populations with blood types O, A, B, and AB. The higher the proportion of people in a nation with type O blood, the lower the suicide rate (Lester 1987a).

Psychological/Psychiatric Differences

The major psychological factors that have been found to be associated with suicidal behavior are depression, especially hopelessness, and psychological disturbance, such as neuroticism, anxiety, or emotional instability. Psychiatric disorders appear to increase the risk of suicide, with affective disorders and alcohol and drug abuse leading the list. Nations may differ in the prevalence of these conditions among their populations, and such differences could help to account for differences in suicide rates. For example, the people of different nations clearly do differ in their rates of consumption of alcohol (Adrian 1984), as well as in levels of depression generally (Weissman and Klerman 1977).

Table 2	Suicide Rates for Selected Countries, 1901, 1950, and 1990		
Country	*1901*	*1950*	*1990*
Australia	11.9	9.3	12.9
Belgium	12.7	12.9	19.0
England/Wales	9.6	10.2	7.8
Finland	6.1	15.6	30.3
Germany	20.8	18.8[a]	17.5
Ireland	2.9	2.6	9.5
Italy	6.2	6.5	7.6
Netherlands	5.8	5.5	9.7
New Zealand	10.2	9.2	13.5
Norway	5.5	7.4	15.5
Portugal	4.3	10.1	8.8
Scotland	5.3	5.3	10.5
Spain	2.0	5.4	7.5
Sweden	13.1	14.9	17.2
Switzerland	22.4	23.5	21.9
United States	10.4	11.4	12.4

SOURCE: World Health Organization (1956, 2002, 2003). Reprinted with permission from the World Health Organization (WHO).

a. This rate is for West Germany.

Social Composition

Moksony (1990) suggests that one simple explanation for national differences in suicide rates is that national populations differ in the proportions of people within them who are at risk for suicide. For example, in developed nations, suicide rates are typically highest among the elderly, especially elderly males. Therefore, those developed nations that have high proportions of elderly males will have comparatively high suicide rates.

Societal Differences

The most popular explanations for differences in suicide rates between nations focus on social variables, which may be viewed in two ways: (a) as direct causal agents of the suicidal behavior or (b) as indices of broad social characteristics that differ between nations.

Émile Durkheim ([1897] 1951) hypothesized that suicide is related to social integration, or the degree to which the people are bound together in social networks, and social regulation, defined as the degree to which people's desires and emotions are regulated by societal norms and customs. According to Durkheim, egoistic and anomic suicides result from too little social integration and too little social regulation, respectively, whereas altruistic and fatalistic suicides result from too much social integration and too much social regulation, respectively. Sociologists since Durkheim's time have argued that altruistic and fatalistic suicides are rare in modern societies; that is, suicide rarely results from excessive social integration or regulation. Rather, suicides increase in modern societies as social integration and social regulation decrease (see, e.g., Johnson 1965).

Some international studies have found suicide rates to be associated with such variables as low church attendance, amount of immigration and interregional migration, and divorce (e.g., Stack 1983). Some scholars view these associations as suggesting a positive relationship between broken relationships and suicidal behavior. For example, divorce may be associated with suicide at the societal level because divorced people have higher suicide rates than do married, widowed, or single people.

Other investigators have suggested that divorce and immigration are indicators of a broader and more basic social characteristic that plays a causal role in suicidal behavior (Moksony 1990). In the United States, interstate migration, divorce, church nonattendance, and alcohol consumption all intercorrelate highly, supporting the proposition that "social disorganization" is useful for explaining suicide rates. In this case, regions of the world with high rates of divorce may have high rates of suicide for those in all marital statuses. This been found to be true in the United States, where states with higher divorce rates also have higher suicide rates across all marital statuses—single, married, divorced, and widowed (Lester 1995).

CULTURAL INFLUENCES ON MOTIVES FOR SUICIDAL BEHAVIOR

Suicidal behavior is differently determined and has different meanings in different cultures, as Hendin's (1964) study of suicide in Scandinavian countries has demonstrated. Hendin found that Danish mothers used guilt arousal as a primary disciplinary technique to control aggression in their sons, and this resulted in a strong dependency need in the sons. This marked dependency was the root of depression and suicidality after adult experiences of loss or separation. Hendin found that fantasies about reuniting with these lost loved ones were common in those who committed suicide.

Hendin found that Swedish parents placed strong emphasis on performance and success, which resulted in ambitious children for whom work was central. Suicide in Hendin's Swedish sample typically followed failure in performance and was linked to damage to the individuals' self-esteem.

At the time Hendin conducted his study, the suicide rate in Norway was much lower than that in Denmark. Although Hendin found strong dependence on mothers among the sons in his samples in both countries, he found that Norwegian children were less passive and more aggressive than Danish children. Alcohol abuse was more common among the Norwegians, and Norwegian men were more open about their feelings—able to laugh at themselves and to cry more openly. Norwegian boys strove to please their mothers by causing no trouble, and they did not worry unduly about failure, typically blaming others for their personal failures and retreating into alcohol abuse.

Counts (1988) illustrates the ways in which a culture can determine the meaning of the suicidal act in her account of suicide among females in Papua New Guinea. In Papua New Guinea, female suicide is a culturally recognized way of imposing social sanctions. Suicide also holds political implications for the surviving kin and for those held responsible for the events leading a woman to commit suicide. In one such instance, the suicide of a rejected fiancée led to the imposition of sanctions on the family that had rejected her. Counts describes this woman's suicide as a political act that symbolically transformed her from a position of powerlessness to one of power.

Cultures also differ in the degree to which they condemn suicide. It has been argued that one explanation for the low suicide rate among African Americans is that African Americans in general consider suicide to be unacceptable behavior (Early 1992). Murder rates are much higher for African Americans than they are for other racial/ethnic groups in the United States; African Americans are both murderers and murder victims at rates disproportionate to African Americans' representation in the population at large. It has been noted that a large proportion of murders involving African American victims are precipitated by the victims; that is, the victims play some role, conscious or unconscious, in bringing about their own demise (Wolfgang 1957). It is possible that African American culture views death through victim-precipitated murder as more acceptable than suicide (Gibbs 1988).

ETHNIC DIFFERENCES IN SUICIDE RATES

Within a nation, different ethnic groups often differ in their suicide rates. In the United States, whites have higher suicide rates than blacks (13.0 per 100,000 vs. 6.8 in 1992); the same is true in those African nations that report suicide rates, such as Zimbabwe (17.6 vs. 6.9 in 1983–86) and South Africa (18.4 vs. 3.0 in 1984) (Lester 1998). In the United States, whites and Native Americans have higher suicide rates (13.2 and 13.3, respectively, in 1980) than do Filipino Americans (3.5); the suicide rates of African Americans (6.1), Chinese Americans (8.3) and Japanese Americans (9.1) fall in between these extremes (Lester 1998). The suicide rates of the various Asian ethnic groups in the United States parallel the rates in the groups' nations of origin.

Some aspects of ethnic and national differences in suicide are culturally invariant, whereas other aspects vary widely. For example, the suicide rates of Chinese populations in different regions of the world—such as mainland China, Hong Kong, Singapore, Taiwan, and the United States—show striking differences. The suicide rate in Taiwan in 1984 was 10.9; in Hong Kong, 9.2; and for the Chinese in Singapore, 14.6. The methods Chinese people use to commit suicide also vary by location, with poisoning the most common method in Taiwan, jumping and hanging most common in Hong Kong, and jumping used most often in Singapore. However, suicide rates for males and females have been found to be almost identical in these different Chinese populations—1.4 (Lester 1994).

CHOICES OF SUICIDE METHODS

The methods of committing suicide that people choose also tend to differ from culture to culture. DeCatanzaro (1981) has documented several culturally unique methods of suicide, such as the method of hanging used in Tikopia, in which the individual ties a noose around his or her neck, secures the end of the rope, and then runs to another part of the house. Firth (1961) has written about the traditional method of suicide in Tikopia, which is to swim out to sea and drown, timing the act so as to minimize, maximize, or leave to chance the prospects of rescue. Two other culturally distinct suicide methods, each of which has its own culturally determined motive, are suttee, an ancient Indian custom in which a widow commits suicide by throwing herself on her husband's funeral pyre (motivated by grief), and seppuku, a Japanese form of ritual disembowelment (motivated by shame).

The use of firearms is currently the most common method of suicide in the United States and Canada, whereas in Switzerland, where residents typically own firearms as part of their participation in the civilian militia, hanging is the most common method of suicide. Despite the case of Switzerland, research indicates that increased availability of a method for suicide is associated with an increase in its use for suicide. For example, Killias, van Kesteren, and Rindlisbacher (2001) found that in nations where large proportions of the population own guns, higher numbers of suicide are committed with guns. However, they also found that rates of gun ownership have no association with total suicide rates. This suggests that if guns are not freely available, people who want to commit suicide will use guns less often and other methods—such as poisons, hanging, stabbing, jumping, and drowning—more often. Burvill and his colleagues (1983) found that immigrants who committed suicide in Australia shifted over time from using the most common methods of suicide in their home nations to using those most common in Australia.

Sometimes a particular method of suicide is so widely used that it comes to symbolize the act of suicide in general. For example, in England in the early 20th century, the expression "to take the pipe" came to mean committing suicide by any method. The expression came from the most common method of suicide at the time in England, which was by inhaling toxic domestic gas fumes; the gas, used for lighting and heating homes, was brought into houses by means of pipes. This method remained the most commonly used in England until the 1960s, when a switch from coal gas to natural gas made the gas piped into homes less toxic.

EFFECTS OF CULTURAL CONFLICTS

Another important issue in the study of suicide across cultures in recent years has been the effect of the influence of Western culture on suicidal behaviors in less modern cultures. Van Winkle and May (1986) examined suicide rates among three Native American groups in New Mexico—the Apache, the Pueblo, and the Navajo—and concluded that the high suicide rate among the Apache was associated with Apaches' low social integration and high acculturation into mainstream U.S. society. The Navajo, who had the greatest geographic and social isolation from whites, also had the lowest suicide rate. Among the Pueblo, Van Winkle and May found that the most acculturated individuals had the highest suicide rates. In Taiwan, Lee, Chang, and Cheng (2002) found that aboriginal groups with lower levels of assimilation had higher suicide rates than did those groups that were more assimilated into the mainstream culture. These studies indicate that when people from different cultures encounter each other, the problems of acculturation can result in stress and its consequences, including increased rates of suicidal behavior, especially in less dominant cultural groups.

The Assumption of Cultural Invariability

It is important also for scholars to replicate research findings about suicide in cultures other than those in which particular results have first been observed. For example, Stack (1992) found that divorce had a deleterious effect on the suicide rates in Sweden and Denmark, but not in Japan. Stack offers four possible reasons for this finding: The divorce rate in Japan may be too low to affect the suicide rate, Japanese family support may be strong enough to counteract the loss of a spouse, ties between couples may be weak in Japan, and the cultural emphasis on conformity in Japan may suppress suicidal behavior.

In a comparison of depression and suicide among psychiatric patients in mainland China and the United States, Chiles and his colleagues (1989) found that suicidal intent was predicted better by depression for psychiatric patients in China and better by hopelessness for psychiatric patients in the United States. Compared with the Chinese patients, the American patients had considered suicide at earlier ages, made more prior suicide attempts, more often communicated their suicidal intent, and more often viewed suicide as an effective solution.

Subcultures

Wolfgang and Ferracuti (1967) examined the role that a subculture of violence plays in producing high murder and assault rates, and Gastil (1971) has argued that such a subculture of violence pervades the southern portion of the United States. Marks and Stokes (1976) refer to this subculture as an explanation for the greater use of firearms in suicides in the South compared with the rest of the United States.

Platt (1985) examined electoral wards in Edinburgh, Scotland, which differed in their rates of attempted suicide, to see whether they had different norms for suicidal behavior—that is, if they differed in their subcultures of suicide. Those living in wards with the highest suicide rates had more intimate contact with suicidal individuals and held different life values than did those in other wards; for example, they had a greater expectation that married couples would quarrel and that men would fight in public. However, Platt was unable to find to his satisfaction that the wards differed in their subcultures of suicide.

A study of the subcultural factors in teenage suicide documented several suicides in a group of adolescents, all of whom had poor relationships with their parents, poor self-images, a fascination with heavy metal music and the fantasies engendered by that music, and histories of heavy drug use (Lester 1987b).

CONCLUSION

There are large differences between cultures in the incidence of suicidal behavior, and culture influences the methods used for committing suicide and the reasons for doing so. Although the differences in suicide rates across nations and cultures may be explained in part by physiological differences between different groups of people, the more plausible explanations involve psychological and social variables, such as the abuse of alcohol and levels of social integration and social regulation. When competing cultures interact, members of the less dominant culture may experience increased stress (and, as a result, may commit suicide at increased rates).

It should be noted also that in culturally heterogeneous societies such as the United States, Canada, and Australia, we cannot assume that suicides are similar in rates, methods, motives, and precipitating factors across different subcultural groups. Those working to prevent suicide in such societies must take cultural influences into account (Sue and Sue 1990; Zimmerman and Zayas 1993).

REFERENCES

Adrian, M. 1984. "International Trends in Alcohol Production, Trade and Consumption, and Their Relationship to Alcohol-Related Problems, 1970 to 1977." *Journal of Public Health Policy* 5:344–67.

Burvill, Peter, M. McCall, T. Woodings, and N. Stenhouse. 1983. "Comparison of Suicide Rates and Methods in English, Scots and Irish Immigrants in Australia." *Social Science & Medicine* 17:705–8.

Chiles, John A., Kirk Strosahl, Zheng Yan Ping, Mark Clark, Kathryn Hall, Ron Jemelka, Brian Senn, and Cathy Reto. 1989. "Depression, Hopelessness and Suicidal Behavior in Chinese and American Psychiatric Patients." *American Journal of Psychiatry* 146:339–44.

Conklin, George H. and Miles E. Simpson. 1987. "The Family, Socioeconomic Development and Suicide." *Journal of Comparative Family Studies* 18:99–111.

Counts, Dorothy A. 1988. "Ambiguity in the Interpretation of Suicide." Pp. 87–109 in *Why Women Kill Themselves,* edited by David Lester. Springfield, IL: Charles C Thomas.

DeCatanzaro, Denys. 1981. *Suicide and Self-Damaging Behavior.* New York: Academic Press.

Douglas, Jack D. 1967. *The Social Meanings of Suicide.* Princeton, NJ: Princeton University Press.

Dublin, Louis I. 1963. *Suicide: A Sociological and Statistical Study.* New York: Ronald.

Durkheim, Émile. [1897] 1951. *Suicide: A Study in Sociology,* translated by John A. Spaulding and George Simpson. Glencoe, IL: Free Press.

Early, Kevin E. 1992. *Religion and Suicide in the African-American Community.* Westport, CT: Greenwood.

Firth, Raymond. 1961. "Suicide and Risk Taking in Tikopia." *Psychiatry* 24:1–17.

Gastil, Raymond. 1971. "Homicide and a Regional Culture of Violence." *American Sociological Review* 36:412–27.

Gibbs, Jewelle. 1988. "Conceptual, Methodological, and Sociocultural Issues in Black Youth Suicide." *Suicide and Life-Threatening Behavior* 18:73–89.

Girard, Chris. 1993. "Age, Gender, and Suicide." *American Sociological Review* 58:553–74.

Hendin, Herbert. 1964. *Suicide and Scandinavia.* New York: Grune & Stratton.

Johnson, Barclay D. 1965. "Durkheim's One Cause of Suicide." *American Sociological Review* 30:875–86.

Killias, Martin, John van Kesteren, and Martin Rindlisbacher. 2001. "Guns, Violent Crime, and Suicide in 21 Countries." *Canadian Journal of Criminology* 43:429–48.

Lee, C. S., J. C. Chang, and A. T. A. Cheng. 2002. "Acculturation and Suicide." *Psychological Medicine* 32:133–41.

Lester, David. 1987a. "National Distribution of Blood Groups, Personal Violence (Suicide and Homicide) and National Character." *Personality and Individual Differences* 8:575–76.

———. 1987b. *Suicide as a Learned Behavior.* Springfield, IL: Charles C Thomas.

———. 1994. "The Epidemiology of Suicide in Chinese Populations in Six Regions of the World." *Chinese Journal of Mental Health* 7:21–24.

———. 1995. "Explaining the Regional Variation of Suicide and Homicide." *Archives of Suicide Research* 1:159–74.

———. 1996. *Patterns of Suicide and Homicide in the World.* Commack, NY: Nova Science.

———. 1998. *Suicide in African Americans.* Commack, NY: Nova Science.

Marks, Alan H. and C. Shannon Stokes. 1976. "Socialization, Firearms and Suicide." *Social Problems* 23:622–29.

Menozzi, P., A. Piazza, and L. Cavalli-Sforza. 1978. "Synthetic Maps of Human Gene Frequencies in Europeans." *Science* 201:786–92.

Moksony, Ferenc. 1990. "Ecological Analysis of Suicide." Pp. 121–38 in *Current Concepts of Suicide,* edited by David Lester. Philadelphia: Charles.

Phillips, Michael R., Huaqing Liu, and Yanping Zhang. 1999. "Suicide and Social Change in China." *Culture, Medicine and Psychiatry* 23:25–50.

Platt, Stephen D. 1985. "A Subculture of Parasuicide?" *Human Relations* 38:257–97.

Sainsbury, Peter and Brian M. Barraclough. 1968. "Differences Between Suicide Rates." *Nature* 220:1252.

Stack, Steven. 1983. "The Effect of Religious Commitment on Suicide." *Journal of Health and Social Behavior* 24:362–74.

———. 1992. "The Effect of Divorce on Suicide in Japan." *Journal of Marriage and the Family* 54:327–34.

Sue, Derald W. and David Sue. 1990. *Counseling the Culturally Different.* New York: John Wiley.

Van Winkle, Nancy W. and Philip A. May. 1986. "Native American Suicide in New Mexico, 1959–1979." *Human Organization* 45:296–309.

Weissman, Myrna M. and Gerald L. Klerman. 1977. "Sex Differences and the Epidemiology of Depression." *Archives of General Psychiatry* 34:98–111.

Wolfgang, Marvin E. 1957. "Victim-Precipitated Criminal Homicide." *Journal of Criminal Law, Criminology and Police Science* 48:1–11.

Wolfgang, Marvin E. and Franco Ferracuti. 1967. *The Subculture of Violence.* London: Tavistock.

World Health Organization. 1956. "Mortality from Suicide." *Epidemiological and Vital Statistics Report* 9(4):243–87.

———. 2002. "Mental Health: Suicide Rate." Retrieved May 31, 2003 (http://www5.who.int/mental_health/main.cfm?p= 0000000149).

———. 2003. "WHO Mortality Database." Retrieved May 31, 2003 (http://www3.who.int/whosis/menu.cfm?path=mort).

Zimmerman, James K. and Luis H. Zayas. 1993. "Suicidal Adolescent Latinas." Pp. 133–43 in *Women and Suicide,* edited by Silvia Canetto and David Lester. New York: Springer.

A History of Execution
Methods in the United States

Trina N. Seitz

It certainly seems strange that a nation so advanced in science and engineering . . . should not be able to invent something better than the crude electric chair. Perhaps it is that every country chooses the method of execution most suitable to the temperament of its people.

—Charles Duff, *A Handbook on Hanging,* 1928

The penalty of death as a formal sanction for certain crimes has been applied in the United States throughout much of the nation's history. Although the death penalty is employed by half of the countries in the world, the United States is unique in that over time and across the country, the methods used to mete out this punishment have undergone continual change. In no other country have the formal methods of execution been more frequently redesigned, improved upon, and modified.

In this chapter, I provide a historical review of how methods of state-sanctioned death have developed over time in the United States, beginning with a brief discussion of modes of execution during the colonial and preindustrial periods and then turning to extralegal modes of execution, such as lynching. I then present an overview of the electrification of America and the nation's subsequent adoption of the electric chair as primary mode of execution. The focus then shifts to the adoption of lethal gas as an execution method in some states. The final method discussed is also the latest method of execution, lethal injection.

EXECUTION METHODS IN THE
COLONIAL AND PREINDUSTRIAL PERIODS

Given that the United States was founded by British colonists, it is not surprising that the execution methods used in the colonies in the 17th century and in preindustrial America in the 18th century closely paralleled those found in England and Western Europe in those times

(Bedau 1997; Johnson 1998; Masur 1989). Western European methods of execution prior to the mid-1800s included drawing and quartering (a process by which the condemned was half hanged, disemboweled, and then cut into quarters), burning alive, beheading (by axe, guillotine, or Halifax gibbet), pressing, disembowelment, and breaking on the wheel (a process in which the accused was tethered to a wooden wheel and struck repeatedly with a club) (Abbott 1994; Engel 1996; Johnson 1998). Although hanging was the traditional and preferred method of execution during the early colonial era, instances of executions by less traditional methods did occur.

The North Carolina General Assembly of 1715 mandated "that the laws of England are the laws of this Government, so far as they are compatible with our way of living and trade" (N.C. Laws 1715, c. 31, §5, quoted in Coates 1937:204). These laws included types of punishment and, within those, the sanction of death by mutilation, dismemberment, or various other deeds. In 1771, the English king's chief justice for the province of Carolina issued the following order concerning a condemned man: that the offender be "drawn . . . to the place of execution, where you are to be hanged by the neck; that you be cut down while yet alive, that your bowels be taken out and burnt before your face, that your head be cut off, your body be divided into four quarters, and this to be at His Majesty's disposal" (quoted in Coates 1937:206). Engel (1996) relates the only known instance of "pressing to death" ever recorded in early America: In 1692, Giles Cory suffered death by pressing in Massachusetts when he refused to enter a plea in court to the charges he was a

357

wizard. Pressing, or *peine forte et dure,* was a punishment in which the condemned lay on his or her back and a wooden slab was then placed on the body. Weights or stones were placed on the slab, and more were added until the condemned either suffocated or was crushed under the increasing pressure (Abbott 1994). In cases of pressing it was not uncommon for sharp stones or pieces of wood to be placed underneath the prisoner's body to provide further torture (Abbott 1994).

On April 11, 1712, three slaves (recorded as "Negro Robin," "Negro Claus," and "Negro Quaco") were put to death in what is now New York City for allegedly murdering the owner of one of the three (Hearn 1997). Each man was executed in a different manner—Robin was gibbeted alive (i.e., suspended in an iron cage to die of starvation or exposure to the elements; Abbott 1994), Claus was broken on the wheel, and Quaco was burned at the stake (Hearn 1997).[1] Accounts from New York also tell of blacks' being roasted alive, usually for the alleged murder or rape of a white victim (Hearn 1997; see also Dray 2002). These accounts are consistent with those from Virginia and Massachusetts, where black slave women were regularly burned alive for any number of offenses, such as murder or attempting to flee from servitude (Harries and Cheatwood 1997).

By the late 18th century, hanging was by far the preferred method of execution in the United States. Hangings were public events, rife with religious speeches (Johnson 1998). Those who delivered these sermons spoke with a blend of civil and religious authority, demanding repentance from the condemned and righteousness from those in attendance (Masur 1989). Hanging was, and still is, a rather simple procedure. In early America, the condemned prisoner was merely transported to a selected execution site and hanged from a noose suspended from a tree or other fixture. More often than not, a wooden scaffold was constructed in the town square, providing easy access for those wishing to attend the event. The scaffolds built for hangings also frequently had religious overtones. Biblical passages (in the Book of Deuteronomy, for example) speak of a hanging tree from which condemned persons were exposed to the public after execution, and early American scaffolds (as well as a scarce few still in operation today) were often built to emulate the tree referred to in Scripture (Grossman 1998; Johnson 1998).

Modern scaffolds are tall wooden structures. When a hanging takes place, the condemned prisoner stands on a trapdoor on the scaffold platform, below a horizontal beam to which a rope is affixed. The rope is secured around the prisoner's neck, and, on cue, the executioner pulls a lever that opens the trapdoor. The condemned falls a predetermined distance below the platform until the rope is taut; this sudden deceleration, ideally, breaks the neck of the condemned quickly and cleanly. British executioner William Marwood refined the modern process of hanging in 1874 (Abbott 1991, 1994; Duff [1928] 1974). As Abbott (1994) explains:

> He [Marwood] pointed out that by adjusting the length of rope to the weight of the body, the neck would be dislocated and the death almost instantaneous. . . . the most important innovation was his use of the long drop: "Weigh carefully and give as long a drop as possible," was his maxim, a principal now employed by hangmen all over the civilised world, and, if for nothing else, thousands of condemned men owe their ease of dispatch to Marwood. (P. 261)

On the surface, the adoption and use of the "hanging drop" in early U.S. history may seem unremarkable, but on closer examination, we can see that this was most likely the first early American attempt at refining death by hanging. Conventional hanging, which consisted of merely securing a noose around the neck of the prisoner and then dangling him or her from a short rope, resulted in a slow and agonizing death. At times, the condemned would literally strangle to death for upward of half an hour, understandably creating quite a spectacle for those in attendance.

The numbers in attendance at an execution could easily grow into the thousands, and by the mid-1800s, the presence of many rowdy, intoxicated spectators had begun to overshadow the political intent of public hangings. Following English practice, many U.S. states began conducting hangings within the confines of prison walls. This served two purposes. First, it provided a controlled environment in which to put a prisoner to death. The numbers of official witnesses were reduced to a few dozen, minimizing the likelihood of riots, drunken brawls, and cheering as the condemned strangled to death. Second, it accommodated changing standards of decency regarding the spectacle of overt violence; public hangings had begun to be viewed as repulsive. As middle-class sensibilities evolved, many people espoused more humanistic views toward prisoners and punishment, and attendance at public hangings was no longer considered socially acceptable. Thus the removal of hangings from public view paralleled changes in the social climate (Johnson 1998; Masur 1989).

Firing squads were used intermittently along with hanging for executions in the preindustrial United States. The first documented use of this method is the 1608 execution of George Kendall, "a councillor of Virginia" (Grossman 1998). The traditional protocol for death by firing squad was rather uncomplicated: The condemned prisoner was tethered to a post or other fixture, blindfolded, and then shot to death by an assemblage of marksmen (Bohm 1999; Grossman 1998). The firing squad is an all-but-obsolete mode of execution in the modern United States, but two states (Utah and Idaho) still offer the method as an option (Bohm 1999).

The contemporary protocol for execution by firing squad in Utah includes a five-man rifle team, of which all

---

1. The Halifax gibbet and the gibbet are two different methods of execution, although they share similar names.

members are volunteers. The condemned is seated in a chair, secured, and fitted with a black hood over the head and face. A small white target is then pinned to the prisoner's chest, indicating the position of the heart. The rifle squad is positioned behind a curtain approximately 23 feet from the prisoner; the curtain is outfitted with small portals that allow the members of the rifle team to aim their weapons—deer rifles of their choosing—all but one of which contain live rounds (Gill 1996; Bohm 1999). The team members do not know which rifle is not armed with a live round. In theory, this technique provides a psychological buffer—as Bohm (1999) notes, "The rifle with blanks maintains the fiction that none of the shooters will know who fired the fatal shot" (p. 73). This strategy is questionable, however, because firing a blank or dummy round results in little or no recoil of the weapon (Bohm 1999).

The 1977 firing squad execution of Utah prisoner Gary Gilmore stands as one of the most memorable in American history for several reasons. First, Gilmore's execution was the first to be conducted after the U.S. Supreme Court's reinstatement of the death penalty in 1976. Second, Gilmore adamantly resisted what could have been a lengthy appeals process and strenuously urged the state of Utah to execute him. Some later likened his execution to a state-sanctioned suicide (Eadie and Trombley 1995). The state of Utah also executed another prisoner, John Taylor, by the same method in 1996 (Rick Halperin, personal communication, March 15, 2001; Harries and Cheatwood 1997). Taylor opted for death by firing squad over lethal injection, fearing he would die "flipping around like a fish out of water" if he chose the latter procedure (Gill 1996). Shortly after Taylor's execution, Utah legislator Sheryl Allen introduced a bill in the state legislature that would mandate that all executions be carried out by lethal injection, eliminating the use of the firing squad altogether. Allen introduced the bill largely because of her desire to help Utah maintain its image as a "progressive" state, but many other legislators believed that eliminating the firing squad would contradict traditional Mormon beliefs regarding blood atonement for sins (Gill 1996). To this day, Utah continues to allow condemned inmates the choice between execution by firing squad and by lethal injection. (Information on the methods of execution used across the United States is available on the Death Penalty Information Center's Web site at http://www.deathpenaltyinfo.org.)

LYNCHING AS A MODE OF EXTRALEGAL JUSTICE

Lynching, or "the execution of a person without authority or process of law," was a salient component of early American justice (Peretti and Singletary 1981:227). This is especially true of the years immediately following the Civil War and continuing into the first three decades of the 20th century (Dray 2002; Johnson 1998; Lane 1997). Although evidence exists that some lynchings have involved whites suspected of crimes, this form of vigilante violence was usually rooted in racism and was typically reserved for African Americans and other minorities (Lane 1997). Between 1885 and 1930, a period some have described as the "lynching era," at least one African American was lynched per week in the United States by violent, "hate-driven" white mobs (Cutler 1969; Dray 2002; Johnson 1998:37; Lane 1997). In 1892, some 230 lynchings were reported; in more than 160 of these, the victims were African Americans. Although lynching occurred in nearly every state in the Union, the southern states accounted for nearly 80% of all incidents (Lane 1997). Some scholars have estimated that nearly 3,700 African American men, women, and children were lynched over the course of the era.

Lynching was a violent and dehumanizing process, often including excessive mutilation and desecration of victims' bodies. African Americans were lynched for any number of reasons, ranging from suspicion of murder or rape of a white victim to vaguer offenses, such as "acting like a white man" and other "violations of racial etiquette" (Cutler [1905] 1969; Dray 2002; Johnson 1998:34). Lynchings were usually carried out by armed mobs seeking instant "justice" for what they perceived as breaches of the white establishment. As Lane (1997) notes:

> Mass lynchings of this kind followed certain communal rituals: a prominent site was selected close to the alleged crime, the victim was given time to pray, hanged, and then shot up or burned after death—more rarely before—with the first match, or shot, ceremonially awarded to the injured person or family. (P. 151)

In 1911, a lynching victim was tied to a stake on the stage of a Livermore, Kentucky, opera house. Those who purchased tickets were afforded the "privilege of shooting at him from the seats" (Lane 1997:151). Other accounts make reference to special "excursion trains" that transported large crowds to the sites of lynchings (Dray 2002; Johnson 1998:35; Lane 1997:151). In 1893, thousands traveled by train to Paris, Texas, to witness the killing of a retarded African American man. The victim was tortured for over an hour with hot irons, some of which were "thrust down his throat" (Lane 1997:151). In approximately one-fourth of all lynching cases, the victims were castrated, dismembered, or burned to ashes—body parts were often sold as souvenirs, and whatever remained of the victim was left at the scene as a warning to other African Americans in the community (Lane 1997:151).

RIDING THE LIGHTNING: THE ELECTRICAL AGE OF EXECUTION

By the beginning of the 20th century, the majority of legal executions in the United States were conducted by hanging within prison walls. Aside from a smattering of small-town public hangings (the last two being in 1936 and 1937), execution as a form of punishment was largely a private practice (Bessler 1997; Masur 1989). The advent of the harnessing of electricity at the end of the 19th century, however, dramatically changed execution methodology.

In 1886, New York Governor David Hill, who was disturbed by an unusual number of bungled hangings, appointed a three-member panel of upstanding citizens to look into more humane and expeditious execution methods (Bernstein 1973; Denno 1994). This commission, which came to be known as the "New York Commission," was convened a year after Hill had delivered this message to the state legislature:

> The present mode of executing criminals by hanging has come down to us from the dark ages, and it may well be questioned whether the science of the present day cannot provide a means for taking the life of such as are condemned to die in a less barbarous manner. (Quoted in Denno 1994:566; see also *In re Kemmler* 1890:444)

At the same time, a fierce rivalry was in progress between George Westinghouse and Thomas A. Edison, two major figures who had much to gain by being responsible for "electrifying American cities" (Bohm 1999:74; see also Denno 1994). One member of Hill's commission, Dr. Alfred P. Southwick, had recently witnessed an incident in which an elderly drunkard had been killed instantly when he accidentally touched the terminals of a live electrical generator (Penrose 1994). Southwick solicited Edison, already considered an American icon, to advise the commission on whether electrocution could be a viable, humane method of execution. Although Edison was a staunch opponent of capital punishment, he agreed to assist the commission.

On June 4, 1888, following a favorable recommendation by the New York Commission, the New York State Legislature passed the Electrical Execution Act. The state would execute any criminal condemned to death after January 1, 1889, "by causing to pass through the body of the convict a current of electricity of sufficient intensity to cause death" (New York Electrical Execution Act of 1888, cited in Denno 1994:573). By mid-1889, *electrocution* had not yet been deemed the official term for the procedure. In fact, New York attorney Eugene Lewis suggested several alternative names, including "electricide" (Bernstein 1973:55). Edison also suggested names for the electric chair itself, including "dynamort," "electromort," and "ampermort" (Bernstein 1973:55).

On August 6, 1890, William Kemmler, a convicted murderer who had bludgeoned a female acquaintance to death, was the first condemned prisoner to die by electrocution in the United States. Prior to his execution, the New York State Court of Appeals concluded that death by electrocution does not constitute cruel and unusual punishment, as Kemmler's counsel had argued (Denno 1994; Driggs 1993). Furthermore, the U.S. Supreme Court affirmed that "punishments

are cruel when they involve torture or a lingering death; but the punishment of death is not cruel. . . . It implies there is something inhumane and barbarous, something more than the mere extinguishment of life" (*In re Kemmler* 1890:447; cited in Driggs 1993:1177). In short, execution by electrocution did not violate the U.S. judicial position on cruel and unusual punishment, and Kemmler was executed in New York's electric chair at Auburn Prison.

Reaction to the country's first execution by electrocution was divided. One witness, George Westinghouse, reported the following day that "the job could have been done better with an axe" (quoted in Driggs 1993:1178; see also Bohm 1999; Metzger 1996). Newspaper headlines following the execution read "Far Worse Than Hanging" and "It Was Cruel" (quoted in Driggs 1993:1178), and some newspaper editorials called for the immediate abolition of capital punishment. Not all responses were negative, however. An article in *Illustrated America* urged, "Let us give the system a fair trial. In spite of what the correspondents have told us, the first experiment in electrocution was not so horrible as many hangings have been" (quoted in Driggs 1993: 1178–79). Southwick, who later acquired the nickname "Old Electricity" for his role in championing the electric chair, made the following statement:

> There is nothing against the system at all and the fact is there has been a great deal of senseless, sensational talk about the execution. . . . In fact, a party of ladies could sit in a room where an execution of this kind was going on and not see anything repulsive whatsoever. No sir, I do not consider that this will be the last execution by electricity. . . . There will be lots more of them. It has been proven that the idea was correct and I think the law is the best one. The execution was a success. (Quoted in Neustadter 1989:84)

On a national level, the electric chair enjoyed a large degree of popularity as an efficient method of execution. As Driggs (1993) notes, "Within a generation the electric chair had ceased to be controversial" (p. 1179). By 1949, 26 states were using electric chairs, and between 1930 and 1972 electrocution became the most common method of putting criminals to death in the United States (Bohm 1999; Denno 1994; Price 1998). From 1900 to the present, more than 4,000 men and women have been put to death in electric chairs (Bedau 1997). As Penrose (1994) states, "In its heyday, [the electric chair] was by far the most popular means of execution" (p. 35).

The electric chair is an intriguing piece of technology designed to put condemned persons to death quickly and efficiently. Johnson (1998) quotes one warden's remark about the electric chair, made in an interview just prior to a 1990s execution: "It's the biggest chair you'll ever see" (p. 169). Johnson adds, "The electric chair is larger than life, a paradox that no doubt derives from its sole purpose as an instrument of death" (p. 169). Usually made of oak or other hard, durable wood, the chair itself is merely a thick piece of furniture. The condemned inmate is placed in the chair and his or her arms and ankles are secured with thick leather straps that buckle much like a belt. The inmate's head, which has been shaved to provide for smooth conductivity of electrical current, is also secured with a strap. The calf of one of the inmate's legs has also been shaved, and an electrode is placed on the smooth surface of the skin of the leg. A leather skullcap is placed on the top of the head, with a sponge soaked in a saline solution (or brine) placed between the scalp and the skullcap to serve as a conductor and to prevent excessive burning of the scalp during the process (Notley 1993). Johnson (1998) describes the procedure as it took place in one particular execution; the steps taken are fairly uniform from state to state:

> The execution team worked with machine precision. Like a disciplined swarm, they enveloped Jones, strapping and then buckling down his forearms, elbows, ankles, waist, and chest in a manner of seconds. Once his body was secured, with the electrode connected to Jones's exposed right leg, the two officers stationed behind the chair went to work. One of them attached the cap to the man's head, then connected the cap to an electrode located above the chair. The other secured the face mask. This was buckled behind the chair, so that Jones's head, like the rest of his body, was rendered immobile. . . . The cap and mask dominated his face. The cap was nothing more than a sponge encased in a leather shell, topped with a metal receptacle for an electrode. . . . it resembled a cheap, ill-fitting toupee. (Pp. 176–77)

Theoretically, the voltage sent through the condemned's body by the electric chair causes immediate unconsciousness and death. In most cases, execution protocols call for two bursts of electricity, the first at 1,700 to 2,500 volts at 5–7 amperes for a period of 60 seconds (Abbott 1994; Bennett 1897; Johnson 1998). If the inmate has not expired from this first burst of current, the executioner is instructed to repeat the process at a lower voltage for a short period of time. Then, after allowing the body to cool for 3 minutes, the attending physician checks for cardiac activity or other obvious signs of life (Johnson 1998; see also Trombley 1992).

Almost from the inception of electrocution as an execution method, there have been reports of botched or otherwise unsuccessful executions. The Kemmler execution in 1890 was reported to have sent witnesses "running out of the room in horror," with others "losing control of their stomachs and fainting" as Kemmler roasted to death in the chair (Neustadter 1989:85). Penrose (1994) reports that Kemmler's electrocution was complete with "heaving chest, gurgles, foaming mouth, bloody sweat, burning hair and skin, and the smell of feces" (p. 42). Although depictions of executions in Hollywood motion pictures are often overly dramatic or factually inaccurate, the film *The Green Mile* (based on the novel by Stephen King) contains a scene similar to that just described. In the film, the acts of a malicious, overzealous correctional officer cause the agonizing and protracted death of an inmate condemned to die by electrocution. As the inmate writhes in pain, witnesses leave the execution chamber in horror, some becoming ill and obviously panicked at the sight of the horribly disfigured prisoner.

In 1893, the New York execution of William Taylor was similar, as reported by prison staff and other witnesses. Taylor stiffened so violently against the straps of the electric chair that "the front legs of the chair collapsed" (Abbott 1994:114–15). Taylor was then removed from the chair until a failed generator could be repaired. Drugs were administered to the unconscious prisoner to alleviate his suffering until the execution could be completed, but he died before the repairmen could complete their work. Later that day, the generator was fixed, and the dead inmate was strapped into the electric chair and administered a 30-second jolt of electricity to "comply with the death sentence" handed down by the courts (Abbott 1994:115; Hearn 1997).

In a 1992 lawsuit filed on behalf of condemned inmates in the state of Virginia, lawyers for the plaintiffs raised several possibilities as to the causes of disfigurement of the body during electrocution. Notley (1993) summarizes the key points addressed in the lawsuit, one being that "the human skull is a very poor conductor of electricity. Human skin is also a poor conductor, but sweat on the outside of the skin is an excellent conductor" (p. 66). Given that most prisoners are nervous prior to execution, there is a high probability that they perspire excessively. As Notley continues, "Electrical current seeks the path of least resistance. Therefore, a greater portion of electrical current passes along the prisoner's skin than through his skull, body, and brain as it travels to the electrode on his leg" (p. 66). The end effect is the severe burning of the prisoner's skin "at extreme temperatures while he is awake and conscious for an indeterminate period" (p. 66). Because perspiration appears to amplify the burning effects of electrocution, the execution protocols in several states include references to preventing the condemned inmate from engaging in excessive exercise prior to the procedure.

Execution by electrocution received both favorable and unfavorable responses throughout the 20th century. Some argued that it was a hideous display of torture, whereas others asserted that it was the most civilized means available by which to dispatch the condemned. Sometimes relying on inexperienced personnel and resorting to the use of defective or inadequate apparatuses, states muddled through decades of executions by electricity, learning by trial and error (Madow 1995; Penrose 1994). Some early-20th-century pundits viewed electrical executions as barbaric, and observers have speculated that some early uses of the electric chair may have been purposefully sabotaged to create disfavor for this mode of execution among the general public. Homer Bennett, a 19th-century physician, wrote in 1897:

> But the law stood as it was, and after a time the feeling died out, and there was the usual revulsion, and with more complete understanding of the subject and with the perfected machinery and appliances at their command, there was

nothing more heard of the frightful tortures and the burning of flesh, and time, science, and common sense finally triumphed in the Empire State.... Such, in substance, is the history of the introduction and establishment of electrocution up to the present time, and its practical demonstration so far as shown by actual use, where this method has been once used, has doomed any older method into oblivion. (P. 129)

The electric chair used to execute William Kemmler in 1890 was destroyed by inmates during a 1929 riot at Auburn Prison (Penrose 1994).

DISFIGUREMENT AND THE ADVENT OF LETHAL GAS

In the history of execution in the United States, clear-cut boundaries separating the use of one method of execution from widespread change to another are rare. At times, several methods have been in use within given eras, as was the case with the firing squad and hanging, and then with hanging and the electric chair. There is similar overlap in the use of electrocution and the use of lethal gas. Although the electric chair was invented during the late 19th century, only 20 years passed before yet another method of execution was introduced.

Until the 1930s, the electric chair was used primarily in eastern and southern U.S. states (Harries and Cheatwood 1997). Most western states held fast to their traditional methods of execution—death by hanging and by firing squad. In 1921, the Nevada State Legislature passed that state's "Humane Death Bill," which was championed by Dr. Allen McLean Hamilton, a toxicologist (Farrell 1994; Kruckman 1921). The new law allowed condemned prisoners to choose the manner in which they died—a development that at times appeared to cause confusion and last-minute changes of heart (Kruckman 1921). The law also introduced a new choice of execution method—death by lethal gas. Although witnesses claimed that death by firing squad and hanging appeared instantaneous, the idea of gas had a humane appeal, given the medical profession's use of gases during surgery and other procedures (Kruckman 1921).

The idea of using cyanide gas for executions reminded many war-weary Americans of the consequences of the use of mustard and chlorine gases during the recently ended World War I (Bohm 1999). In the years immediately following World War I, Major D. A. Turner of the U.S. Army Medical Corps studied reports of the effects of lethal gas on army personnel. He concluded that death by gas was agonizing, including the onset of panic as the heart and lungs seized, as well as the protrusion and swelling of the tongue (Abbott 1994). As one Nevada newspaper reported, "As is well known in connection with the lethal gases used during the war, the slightest diffusion of these elements caused widespread havoc" (Kruckman 1921). Nevada Governor Emmet Boyle opposed capital punishment, but

he signed the "Humane Death Bill" because he was confident that it would be struck down by the courts as allowing cruel and unusual punishment (Bohm 1999). This, of course, proved to be an unfortunate miscalculation. Lethal gas was first employed in an execution on February 8, 1924, when Gee Jon was put to death.

The initial theory behind the use of lethal gas as an execution method predates the 20th century. In fact, several 19th-century antigallows activists debated whether chloroform or other gas should be administered to condemned inmates prior to hanging, to anesthetize them (see Peck 1848). This was suggested as a "courteous" solution to the suffering often experienced by those who died by the noose. As Peck wrote in 1848, "Manners, then, are necessary to man because of his possessing a conscious soul" (p. 283). Some observers believed that gas represented a method by which the condemned could be put to sleep humanely, without disfigurement to the body by burns from electrocution or decapitation caused by a bungled hanging.

During the initial discussions of the use of lethal gas in Nevada, several suggestions were made as to how the element could be introduced to the condemned inmate. Some advocates proposed administering "a sleeping potion" in the food of the condemned prior to the execution, and then, during the subsequent slumber, the gas could be administered unbeknown to the inmate (Kruckman 1921). One newspaper writer presented an interesting juxtaposition of medicine and justice:

It is anticipated the gas will be administered much as gas is administered to a patient in a dental chair or to a person preparing for a surgical operation. In other words, it will be a form of anesthesia, and the administrator will probably be an expert anesthetician chosen from among physicians or male nurses. Those who favor this method of dealing death declare it is absolutely painless. (Kruckman 1921)

Perhaps the most perplexing obstacle to be overcome if this new method of execution was to be employed successfully was the containment of the gas. As Major Turner and the press had noted, lethal gas has horrific consequences when dispersed throughout an uncontrolled environment, such as a battlefield. In wartime uses, lethal gases were not highly concentrated in specific areas, and so the soldiers exposed to it usually died protracted, agonizing deaths. Those who proposed using gas for executions, however, posited that if the gas were contained and administered in a highly concentrated dose, the condemned would succumb quickly and without suffering (Abbott 1994).

Prior to the first execution by gas in 1924, the state of Nevada conducted tests on vermin, cats, and pigs, which were placed in crates and locked in an airtight compartment to which the gas was introduced. As a result of the tests, authorities agreed that these conditions were favorable to a successful execution by lethal gas, and Gee Jon was executed in the modified butcher shop of the Carson

City State Prison (Farrell 1994; Noel and Rucker 1997; Eddy 1924). Doctors witnessing the execution claimed that Jon "died apparently painlessly, death being confirmed six or so minutes after the gas had been pumped into the chamber" (Noel and Rucker 1997:161; see also Farrell 1994).

The geographic dispersion of the use of the lethal gas chamber for executions is interesting. After Nevada's first seemingly successful use of this method in 1924, several western states that had not adopted the electric chair selected lethal gas as their preferred execution method. The reasoning appears fairly clear—several prison officials, especially in Colorado and Arizona, found the reported disfigurement from electrocution distasteful; they preferred a method that left the body intact for the family to view. As Noel and Rucker (1997) note, "Neither the state nor prison officials wanted to turn over to the relatives of the deceased a mutilated corpse" (p. 26). After a few western states adopted lethal gas, use of the method curiously jumped to the East Coast when North Carolina adopted it in 1935 (Harries and Cheatwood 1997). In the period from 1910 to 1935, North Carolina had sent 172 condemned prisoners to the electric chair (North Carolina Department of Correction 1998). Although surrounded by "electrocution states," officials in North Carolina espoused a more reformist, progressive social ideology than was typically found in other parts of the South. The state's relatively liberal political and social climate, coupled with the public's growing distaste for the graphic accounts that accompanied electrocutions, likely contributed to the shift to lethal gas.

From 1937 through 1939, Wyoming, Missouri, Oregon, and California adopted the method; each of these states later contracted with Eaton Metal Products in Denver, Colorado, to design their gas chambers (Harries and Cheatwood 1997; Noel and Rucker 1997). Gas chambers could be ordered with one, two, or three seats, and usually cost around $3,500 to build and install (Noel and Rucker 1997). Eaton Metal Products designed and constructed all of the lethal gas chambers used in the United States except the one utilized in the state of North Carolina. In that case, North Carolina borrowed blueprints from Eaton, which eventually received a patent for its gas chamber design in 1957 (Noel and Rucker 1997).

In states that use lethal gas, the design of the equipment is fairly uniform. The condemned sits in a chair contained in an airtight compartment with windows through which witnesses may view the procedure. A metal container located beneath the seat of the chair contains a pound of cyanide pellets. At the warden's directive, execution team personnel turn keys on a control panel outside the chamber to release the pellets into a solution of sulfuric acid and water. The resulting mixture forms hydrocyanic gas, also known as prussic acid. The fumes from the gas, which resemble wisps of smoke, rise upward, and the inmate breathes the fumes. Death results ultimately dies from hypoxia, or the inability of the body's cells to process oxygen (Leuchter 1988; North Carolina Department of Correction 1998). Once death has been pronounced, ammonia is introduced to the chamber to neutralize the hydrocyanic gas. Prison staff don protective clothing and then enter the chamber to remove the body of the deceased. Prior to removal, the body is washed down with water to further assure that no cyanide residue remains (North Carolina Department of Correction 1998).

The safety of prison staff during gas executions posed serious concerns during the years the chambers were heavily used. Because the gas is dispersed in such a concentrated manner, staff had to take precautions to assure that they and any witnesses were not exposed to the fumes or the elements used. Most gas chambers are equipped with gas detectors, emergency-breathing apparatuses, warning alarms, exhaust fans, and resuscitators for personnel working near the area. As Fred A. Leuchter (1988), a designer of execution equipment, has remarked: "Execution gas chamber design requires the consideration of many complicated problems. A mistake in any area may, and probably will, cause death or injury to witnesses or technicians" (p. 9). On January 30, 1998, Ricky Lee Sanderson was executed in North Carolina's gas chamber. Sanderson had elected to die by lethal gas even though the state had also offered him the choice of lethal injection. During the removal of Sanderson's body from the gas chamber, one staff member tripped and dislodged the air tank of another. As one reporter noted, "The worker wasn't injured, but the incident gave prison officials a scare" (Price 1998:2).

By 1973, 13 states were using lethal gas, but this method never quite gained the popularity of electrocution (Price 1998). Although gas chambers had been developed and adopted with the expectation that they would provide a relatively humane method of execution, reports abounded across the country concerning the unnecessary suffering of condemned prisoners who died by lethal gas. Death in a gas chamber does not occur immediately, as originally had been expected—in fact, several executions by lethal gas have taken 15 to 20 minutes (Radelet 1998).

THE AGE OF LETHAL INJECTION

Through the latter decades of the 20th century, U.S. states continued to use the electric chair, hanging, the firing squad, and the gas chamber. By the mid-1950s, there was a sharp decline in the number of executions conducted in the United States. Public support for capital punishment waned, with national approval rates dropping as low as 40% in some polls by the early to mid-1960s (Harries and Cheatwood 1997). These developments were related primarily to changes in political and social focus stemming from discord over the Vietnam War and the civil rights movement. In addition, the country was in turmoil over racial tensions, and the disproportionate numbers of blacks being executed called the integrity of the justice system into question. By 1967, the Legal Defense Fund had called for an unofficial national moratorium on executions until the racial disparities in the system could be corrected (Johnson 1998; Welsh 1998b). In 1972, the U.S. Supreme Court found the death penalty to be unconstitutional in its current form because of the arbitrary way in which it was applied (*Furman v. Georgia* 1972). Several states revised their death penalty procedures, and capital punishment was constitutionally reinstated in 1976 (*Gregg v. Georgia* 1976). Shortly after capital punishment was reinstated, a new method of execution made its debut.

Lethal injection is not an idea unique to the United States. In fact, Great Britain's Royal Commission on Capital Punishment (1953) considered the idea several decades ago in its search for an alternative to hanging. The commission states in its report:

> We have pursued our inquiry into the question whether there is any other method, as yet untried, that could be relied on to inflict death as painlessly and certainly as hanging but with greater decency, and without the degrading and barbarous associations with which hanging is tainted. Only two suggestions were made to us deserving serious consideration. One is the use of lethal gas in a way that does not need a gas-chamber. The other is execution by means of a hypodermic injection of a lethal drug. (P. 256, sec. 735)

In the end, the Royal Commission was dissuaded from supporting the use of lethal injections, in large part because of stern objections voiced by the British Medical Association. That group's steadfast position on lethal injections reads, in part:

> No medical practitioner should be asked to take part in bringing about the death of a convicted murderer. The Association would be most strongly opposed to any proposal to introduce, in place of hanging, a method of execution which would require the services of a medical practitioner, either in carrying out the actual process of killing or in instructing others in the technique of the process. (Quoted in Royal Commission on Capital Punishment 1953:258, sec. 743)

Hanging remained the primary method of execution in Great Britain until 1965, when capital punishment in that country was abolished for all crimes except "extraordinary civil offenses" such as treason (Grossman 1998:1).

The idea of using lethal injection as a method of execution surfaced from time to time in the United States prior to the actual adoption of this method. In 1973, Ronald Reagan, then governor of California, posed an interesting analogy between execution by lethal injection and the euthanasia of farm animals:

> Being a former horse farmer and horse raiser, I know what it's like to try and eliminate an injured horse by shooting him. Now you call the veterinarian and the vet gives it a shot [injection] and the horse goes to sleep—that's it. I myself have wondered if maybe this isn't part of our problem [with capital punishment], if maybe we should review and see if there aren't even more humane methods now—the simple shot or tranquilizer. (Quoted in Welsh 1998a:76)

In 1977, shortly after the reinstatement of capital punishment in the United States, Utah death row inmate Gary Gilmore waived all appeals and was voluntarily executed by firing squad. Soon afterward, Florida electrocuted John Spenkelink for the rape and murder of a 3-year-old girl. The pace of executions accelerated, and the constitutionality of existing methods was called into question. Debate arose concerning the design and implementation of an execution method using lethal injection, with a focus on the chemicals that such a method should employ. Several suggestions were proffered. Nearly 100 years earlier, the New York Commission of 1886, in debating alternative methods to hanging, had briefly considered injections of cyanide. This idea was quickly rejected due to medical ethics, and the possibility of cyanide injections was never seriously considered again (Welsh 1996).

Shortly after the Gilmore execution in Utah, Oklahoma Senator Bill Dawson initiated a bill geared toward implementing executions by lethal injection. In consultation with Dr. Stanley Deutsch, head of Oklahoma University School of Medicine's Department of Anesthesiology, the legislator helped to develop a protocol for the new procedure. The process entailed the administration of a quick-acting barbiturate, then the introduction of a paralytic agent to stop cardiac function. Oklahoma adopted the new method into law on May 11, 1977. In an unrelated move, Texas also passed lethal injection legislation the following day (Welsh 1996). Texas legislators made clear their reasoning in voting for the change—as one representative noted, "Electrocution is a very scary thing to see. . . . I voted for a more humane treatment because death is pretty final. That's enough of a penalty" (quoted in Welsh 1996:78). Another asserted that the death penalty should be "swift and sure punishment, not something that takes away the dignity of the state" (quoted in Welsh 1996:78).

Although two states had adopted lethal injection as a method of execution, no one was executed using the new procedure in the 1970s. By 1981, five states had legislation permitting the use of lethal injection, despite the fact that medical ethicists voiced strong aversion to the use of medical technology in exacting the ultimate punishment. Oklahoma inmate Thomas "Sonny" Hayes was scheduled to be the first to die by the new method on September 9, 1981, but the World Medical Association and Amnesty International intervened by issuing scathing statements regarding the imminent participation of medical professionals in executions, and Hayes's execution was eventually delayed. His sentence was later commuted to life in prison (Welsh 1996:79). In December 1982, Charles Brooks, Jr., became the first inmate to die by lethal intravenous injection at Huntsville Prison in Texas. Since that time, more than 600 inmates have been put to death by lethal injection. Of the 38 states with death penalty statutes, 37 have since adopted the method, as has the federal government (see the Death Penalty Information Center Web site, http://www. deathpenaltyinfo.org).

The increase in the number of states adopting lethal injection during the 1980s and 1990s was related in part to several botched executions by gas and electrocution. Perhaps the most widely publicized of these was the gas chamber death of Jimmy Lee Gray on September 3, 1983, at Parchman, Mississippi. Eight minutes into the process, prison officials had to clear the viewing room because "Gray's desperate gasps for air repulsed witnesses" (Radelet 1998:1). Gray's attorney later remarked, "Jimmy Lee Gray died banging his head against a steel pole in the gas chamber while reporters counted his moans" (quoted in Radelet 1998:1). On April 22, 1983, Alabama executed John Evans in the electric chair. Sparks and flames erupted from the electrode on his leg, and smoke was seen pouring from underneath the face hood. On May 4, 1990, Florida executed Jesse Tafero in that state's notorious electric chair, dubbed "Old Sparky." A synthetic sponge was used under the skullcap rather than the standard natural sponge, and this miscalculation resulted in 6-inch flames erupting from Tafero's head during the first moments of the execution. After three jolts of electricity were required to stop Tafero's heart, witnesses were reported to have been repulsed (Radelet 1998:1). Finally, Virginia's 1990 electrocution of Wilbert Lee Evans caused concern in that state about the use of the electric chair. During the first moments of the procedure, "blood spewed from the right side of the mask on Evans' face, drenching his shirt with blood" (Radelet 1998:2). The autopsy concluded that the loss of blood was caused by Evans's extremely high blood pressure during the execution.

Lethal injection in no way resembles the traditional methods of execution in this country. Most lethal injection execution chambers are equipped with a gurney, complete with sheets and padded headrest. Although some correctional facilities use programmed, automated machines to carry out lethal injections, others still retain intravenous poles and manual injection systems. By design, the process of death by lethal injection is quick and efficient. The inmate is usually administered a sedative an hour prior to the execution. At the time of the execution, correctional officers and execution team staff escort the inmate into the death chamber. The condemned is laid supine on a gurney and is secured with leather straps to prevent movement. Trained prison staff or medical personnel then secure intravenous lines in both of the prisoner's arms—this standard procedure is used to ensure that the drugs are administered in the event one line becomes obstructed or unusable (Amnesty International 1998).

At the signal of the warden, medical personnel begin the introduction of sodium thiopental, a barbiturate that induces sleep almost immediately. Following this first injection, Pavulon (pancuronium bromide) or a similar paralytic agent is introduced. This agent stops the inmate's respiratory function and collapses the lungs. A final injection of potassium chloride is then introduced; this ceases cardiac activity and ultimately causes cardiac arrest. The "ideal" lethal injection execution takes no more than 7 minutes; however, initiation of some executions has been delayed by up to 45 minutes due to problems locating suitable veins (Finks 1983; Radelet 1998). In some respects, lethal injection is the quintessential execution method. The process is no longer overtly violent, and there is no disfigurement of the inmate's body during the procedure. Johnson (1998) remarks on the process:

> Lethal injection, then, offers a paradoxical execution scene. A supine inmate, seemingly at rest, appears to drift off into a sleep that merges imperceptibly with death. This is, in its essentials, the ideal modern death—a death that occurs in one's sleep, painlessly. The reality may well be completely different. The interval on the gurney, reminiscent of rest but actually a case of forced restraint, can certainly be considered a kind of torture of its own; and once the drugs are introduced, what follows may well be a death by slow suffocation—likewise, a kind of torture. All of this unfolds before us as we congratulate ourselves on our humaneness and, more macabre still, as the immobilized offender comes to realize the deception of execution by lethal injection and, unable to struggle, recognizes his inability to communicate his distress to the world. (Pp. 46–47)

Johnson's perspective here sheds light on the sociological import of death rituals within the institution of punishment. Although the result of any execution is always death, the medicalized dramaturgics employed during lethal injection procedures sets up a psychological barrier between those dispensing the punishment and the act itself (Haney 1997; Lofland 1975). These techniques also function to allow participants and witnesses to maintain an impression of order and control over the event (Haines 1992; Lofland 1975).

CONCLUSION

Across the United States, five methods of execution are still employed: hanging, firing squad, lethal gas, electrocution, and lethal injection. Although almost all of the 38 states with death penalty statutes have adopted lethal injection (either as an alternate method or as their sole method), some states hold fast to their traditional electric chairs, gallows, and gas chambers. The exact numbers of legal executions carried out by these and other methods in the United States remain debatable. Bedau (1997) and Johnson (1998) both estimate that since 1608, some 20,000 individuals have been legally put to death in America.

The act of execution has always been laden with social meaning, and the method of execution itself has generally been the focal point of the procedure. In colonial America and the preindustrial United States, executions were public spectacles. The methods of execution used were inherently violent and brutal; human pain and suffering were considered necessary components of these events, which symbolized the absolute power of the state (Johnson 1998). By the mid-1800s, reformists and members of the middle class began to espouse more humanistic ideologies regarding cruel and violent forms of punishment (Masur 1989). This shift in social perceptions of how statesanctioned death should appear culminated in more mechanically efficient execution methods, such as the electric chair and the gas chamber. In essence, methods of execution are symbolic of societal values and, more important, of how American society maintains its desired image as civilized.

Lethal injection has now become what Johnson (1998) refers to as the quintessential execution method. Nearly all evidence of the prisoner's humanity is muted by the sterile nature of the procedure. This modernized method of execution virtually eliminates any indications of pain, discomfort, and violence, and reduces the execution process to what Lynch (2000) labels "a sterile and efficient waste disposal process" (p. 23). Unlike more unpredictable methods of execution, such as the gas chamber, the lethal injection process is designed in such a way as to buffer the psychological and emotional components of meting out state-sanctioned death.

Some have mused that in the future, society may employ more Socratic means of execution—that is, the condemned would be wholly responsible for the onset of his or her death, without explicit supervision or participation from penal personnel. The division of labor in the processes of modern executions alleviates the degree or amount of responsibility of any one individual for taking a life, but "self-induced" executions would all but eliminate the psychological and emotional trauma experienced by those charged with carrying out such tasks. This idea brings to mind the euthanasia procedures associated with Jack Kevorkian, whereby terminally ill patients are given ultimate dominion over the time and place of their deaths. The physician merely inserts the intravenous line—it is the *patient's* actions that begin the introduction of the lethal cocktail (see Kevorkian 1985).

Given the trend toward social distancing in regard to executions, others have speculated that the future of executions lies in the total obliteration of the condemned by way of dematerialization. This idea, although somewhat difficult to fathom, suggests a complete eradication of the criminal body that leaves no trace of evidence that a life was terminated. Although the future of execution methods is open for debate, the continued adoption, retention, and use of lethal injection provide evidence that this method has become the preferred standard in applying death as punishment in the United States.

POSTSCRIPT

In the context of the above discussion, it is important to mention two recent decisions of the U.S. Supreme Court regarding capital punishment, although these decisions are not related directly to specific methods of execution. On June 20, 2002, the Court reversed a Virginia Supreme Court decision and held that the execution of mentally retarded inmates violates the Eighth Amendment clause prohibiting cruel and unusual punishment (*Atkins v. Virginia* 2002; see Death Penalty Information Center 2002). Prior to this most recent decision, the U.S. Supreme Court had only once before heard arguments regarding execution of the mentally retarded, and at that time the Court held that putting mentally impaired prisoners to death did not "categorically" violate the ban on cruel and unusual punishment (Grossman 1998:204; see also *Penry v. Lynaugh* 1989).

On June 24, 2002, the Court held that in a capital case the jury, not the presiding judge, must decide critical sentencing issues, such as the weight to give aggravating circumstances (*Ring v. Arizona* 2002). The Court held (in a seven-to-two decision) that a defendant's right to a trial by jury is violated if the judge alone determines what issues may increase the maximum penalty for a crime (see Liptak 2002).

REFERENCES

Abbott, Geoffrey. 1991. *Lords of the Scaffold.* London: Robert Hale.

———. 1994. *The Book of Execution: An Encyclopedia of Methods of Judicial Execution.* London: Headline.

Amnesty International. 1998. *Lethal Injection: The Medical Technology of Execution* (Document No. ACT 50/01/98). London: Amnesty International.

Atkins v. Virginia, 260 Va. 375, 534 S.E. 2d 312, 2002.

Bedau, Hugo. 1997. *The Death Penalty in America: Current Controversies.* New York: Oxford University Press.

Bennett, Homer C. 1897. "Electrocution and What Causes Electrical Death." *American X-Ray Journal* 1(6):127–36.

Bernstein, Theodore. 1973. "A Grand Success." *IEEE Spectrum* 10(1–6):54–58.

Bessler, John D. 1997. *Death in the Dark: Midnight Executions in America.* Boston: Northeastern University Press.

Bohm, Robert M. 1999. *Deathquest: An Introduction to the Theory and Practice of Capital Punishment in the United States.* Cincinnati, OH: Anderson.

Coates, Albert. 1937. "Punishment for Crime in North Carolina." *North Carolina Law Review* 17:204–32.

Cutler, James E. [1905] 1969. *Lynch-Law: An Investigation Into the History of Lynching in the United States.* Montclair, NJ: Patterson Smith.

Death Penalty Information Center. 2002. "Mental Retardation and the Death Penalty." Washington, DC: Death Penalty Information Center. Retrieved June 11, 2003 (http://www. deathpenaltyinfo.org/article. php?scid=28&did=176).

Denno, Deborah. 1994. "Is Electrocution an Unconstitutional Method of Execution? The Engineering of Death Over the Century." *William & Mary Law Review* 35:551–692.

Dray, Philip. 2002. *At the Hands of Persons Unknown: The Lynching of Black America.* New York: Random House.

Driggs, Ken. 1993. "A Current of Electricity Sufficient in Intensity to Cause Immediate Death: A Pre-Furman History of Florida's Electric Chair." *Stetson Law Review* 22:1169–1209.

Duff, Charles. [1928] 1974. *A Handbook on Hanging*. Yorkshire, Eng.: EP.

Eadie, Bruce (Prod.) and Stephen Trombley (Dir.). 1995. *The Executioners* (documentary videotape). New York: A&E Home Video.

Eddy, Elford. 1924. "Death Gas Kills Slayer!" *San Francisco Call*, February 8, pp. 1, 3.

Engel, Howard. 1996. *Lord High Executioner: An Unashamed Look at Hangmen, Headsmen, and Their Kind*. Willowdale, ON: Firefly.

Farrell, Michael. 1994. "Execution by Poison Gas and Lethal Injection." *Criminologist* 18:201–4.

Finks, Thomas O. 1983. "Lethal Injection: An Uneasy Alliance of Law and Medicine." *Journal of Legal Medicine* 4:383–403.

Furman v. Georgia, 408 U.S. 238, 1972.

Gill, James. 1996. "Going Before the Firing Squad." *Times-Picayune* (New Orleans), January 28, p. B7:3.

Gregg v. Georgia, 428 U.S. 123 (1976).

Grossman, Mark. 1998. *Encyclopedia of Capital Punishment*. Santa Barbara, CA: ABC-CLIO.

Haines, Herb. 1992. "Flawed Executions, the Anti–Death Penalty Movement, and the Politics of Capital Punishment." *Social Problems* 39:125–38.

Haney, Craig. 1997. "Psychological Secrecy and the Death Penalty: Observations on 'the Mere Extinguishment of Life.'" *Studies in Law, Politics, and Society* 16:3–69.

Harries, Keith and Derral Cheatwood. 1997. *The Geography of Execution: The Capital Punishment Quagmire in America*. Lanham, MD: Rowman & Littlefield.

Hearn, Daniel Allen. 1997. *Legal Executions in New York State, 1639–1963*. Jefferson, NC: McFarland.

In re Kemmler, 136 U.S. 436, 1890.

Johnson, Robert. 1998. *Deathwork: A Study of the Modern Execution Process*, 2d ed. Belmont, CA: West/Wadsworth.

Kevorkian, Jack. 1985. "Medicine, Ethics, and Execution by Lethal Injection." *Medicine and Law* 4:307–13.

Kruckman, Arnold. 1921. "Will Use Lethal Gas on Convicts." *Pioche* (Nevada) *Record*, August 19, p. 3.

Lane, Roger. 1997. *Murder in America: A History*. Columbus: Ohio State University Press.

Leuchter, Fred A. 1988. *The Leuchter Report: An Engineering Report on the Alleged Execution Gas Chambers at Auschwitz, Birkenau, and Majdanek, Poland*. Toronto: Samisdat.

Liptak, Adam. 2002. "A Supreme Court Ruling Roils Death Penalty Cases." *New York Times*, September 16 (Reprinted by the Death Penalty Information Center). Retrieved June 11, 2003 (http://www.deathpenaltyinfo.org/article.php?did=304&scid=17).

Lofland, John. 1975. "Open and Concealed Dramaturgic Strategies: The Case of the State Execution." *Urban Life* 4:272–95.

Lynch, Mona. 2000. "The Disposal of Inmate #85271: Notes on a Routine Execution." *Studies in Law, Politics, and Society* 20:3–34.

Madow, Michael. 1995. "Forbidden Spectacle: Executions, the Public and the Press in Nineteenth-Century New York." *Buffalo Law Review* 43:461–562.

Masur, Louis. 1989. *Rites of Execution: Capital Punishment and the Transformation of American Culture, 1776–1865*. New York: Oxford University Press.

Metzger, Thom. 1996. *Blood and Volts: Edison, Tesla, and the Electric Chair*. Brooklyn, NY: Autonomedia.

Neustadter, Roger. 1989. "The 'Deadly Current': The Death Penalty in the Industrial Age." *Journal of American Culture* 12(3):79–87.

Noel, Thomas J. and Kevin E. Rucker. 1997. *Eaton Metal Products: The First 80 Years—A Story of Vision and Commitment*. Denver: A. B. Hirschfeld.

North Carolina Department of Correction. 1998. "North Carolina Department of Correction and the Death Penalty" (press release). Raleigh: North Carolina Department of Correction.

Notley, Katherine R. 1993. "Virginia Death Row Inmates Sue to Stop Use of Electric Chair." *Executive Intelligence Review* 20(9):65–67.

Peck, G. W. 1848. "On the Use of Chloroform in Hanging." *American Whig Review* 2 (September):283–96.

Penrose, James F. 1994. "Inventing electrocution." *American Heritage of Invention and Technology* 9(4):35–44.

Penry v. Lynaugh, 492 U.S. 302, 1989.

Peretti, Peter O. and Deborah Singletary. 1981. "A Theoretical-Historical Approach to Black Lynching." *Social Behavior and Personality* 9:227–30.

Price, Jay. 1998. "Proposed End of Gas Chamber Renews Execution Debate." *News & Observer* (Raleigh, NC), October 5. Retrieved May 12, 2003 (archives at http://www.news-observer.com).

Radelet, Michael L. 1998. "Post-Furman Botched Executions." Washington, DC: Death Penalty Information Center. Retrieved May 12, 2003 (http://www.deathpenaltyinfo.org/article.php?scid=8&did=478).

Ring v. Arizona, 200 Ariz. 267, 25 P. 3d 1139, 2002.

Royal Commission on Capital Punishment. 1953. *1949–1953 Report* (Presented to Parliament by Command of Her Majesty, September, 1953). London: Her Majesty's Stationery Office.

Trombley, Stephen. 1992. *The Execution Protocol: Inside America's Capital Punishment Industry*. New York: Crown.

Welsh, James. 1996. "Execution by Lethal Injection." *Lancet* 348:63.

———. 1998a. "The Medical Technology of Execution: Lethal Injection." *International Review of Law, Computers, and Technology* 12:75–98.

———. 1998b. "The Medicine That Kills." *Lancet* 351:441.

Capital Punishment in the United States

Stephanie Picolo Manzi

Although a majority of the crimes once punishable by death in the United States are no longer punishable in that manner, as of late 2002, 3,697 men and women were housed on death rows in American prisons. The United States remains the only Western democracy that takes the lives of individuals who have been convicted of what are known as capital offenses. In this chapter, I provide some historical background on the use of the death penalty in the United States and a demographic breakdown of the population of those who are at present sentenced to death. I conclude the chapter with an overview of some of the controversial issues related to the use of capital punishment, including the execution of mentally retarded persons and the execution of individuals who are innocent of the crimes for which they have been convicted.

HISTORY AND BACKGROUND OF CAPITAL PUNISHMENT IN AMERICA

When the first European settlers arrived in colonial America, they brought with them the British tradition of capital punishment. The earliest recorded use of the death penalty in the New World was in the colony of Virginia in 1622, when one Captain George Kendall was executed for the crime of treason. The death penalty was accepted as just punishment for a variety of offenses in the American colonies, but there are two striking differences between the use of the death penalty in Britain at the time and the use of the death penalty in the colonies. The first difference is found in the number of crimes for which the death penalty could be imposed. By 1760, Great Britain considered more than 100 offenses to be punishable by death, whereas the laws of the majority of the colonies listed fewer than a dozen capital offenses each. The numbers of capital crimes varied from colony to colony, but in most cases the laws describing capital offenses were accompanied by biblical quotations that were understood to justify the use of the death penalty. Crimes that carried a sentence of death in the colonies included, but were not limited to, witchcraft, rape, perjury, adultery, and murder. The rationale behind the relatively small number of crimes punishable by death in colonial times was the colonies' constant need of able-bodied workers to farm the land and participate in construction (Bohm 1999).

The second difference between Britain and colonial America in terms of capital punishment is seen in the methods of execution employed. Whereas in Britain such methods as drawing and quartering, beheading, and breaking on the wheel were still in use, the colonies utilized hanging, a method that the colonists considered to be relatively humane (Costanzo 1997).

EFFORTS TO ABOLISH THE DEATH PENALTY

Although the founding fathers accepted the death penalty, many colonists were opposed to its use. In this regard, the movement to abolish the death penalty can be traced to the effort of the Quakers in Pennsylvania and, more specifically, to Benjamin Rush, a physician and one of the signers of the Declaration of Independence. The Quakers, who were opposed to capital punishment, were instrumental in the passage of the Great Act of 1682, which limited the use of the death penalty to the crimes of treason and murder. Rush, who would later found a movement to abolish capital punishment, argued not only that the use of the death penalty brutalize society, but that putting people to death was an improper use of state power (Costanzo 1997). Rush drew his ideas from the positivist writings of Cesare Beccaria, whose treatise *On Crimes and Punishment* ([1767] 1975) has been credited with influencing European thought concerning the death penalty, leading to a reduction in the number of crimes punishable by death in European countries as well as the reduction of barbarism in criminal law and procedure in general. Beccaria believed that the death penalty does not serve as a deterrent to crime because it is much too quick a punishment. He thought that the threat of long-term imprisonment would be much more effective in preventing future crime.

As a result of the work of abolitionists such as Benjamin Rush and Benjamin Franklin, several trends developed. In 1793, William Bradford, Pennsylvania's attorney general, proposed that the law recognize gradations of murder based on a person's culpability. First-degree murder would include any willful, deliberate, premeditated killing or a murder that occurred during the commission of an arson, rape, robbery, or burglary. His proposal, which was formally adopted in 1794, restricted the use of the death penalty to first-degree murder only (Randa 1997). A second noteworthy trend was the removal of executions from the public eye. Pennsylvania was the first state to do so in 1834 when it carried out an execution within the walls of a correctional facility. However, this trend was slow in producing the desired goal; the last public execution in the United States occurred in Missouri in 1937 (Bohm 1999).

The abolitionists also were responsible for the movement toward discretionary death penalty statutes and total abandonment of the penalty in other states. In 1838, Tennessee became the first state to eliminate mandatory death sentences for capital crimes, thereby allowing jurors to choose to implement other sentences. In 1846, the Michigan State Legislature voted to allow a sentence of death only for treason, giving Michigan the distinction of being the first state to effectively eliminate use of the death penalty. Rhode Island and Wisconsin repealed their death penalty laws for all crimes in 1852 and 1853, respectively (Bedau 1982). Over the next several decades other states, including Iowa, Maine, and Colorado, followed suit. During this same time most jurisdictions began limiting the types of crimes punishable by death to treason and murder (Schabas 1997).

Support for the movement to abolish the death penalty decreased from the early 1920s until the 1940s, as social scientists wrote of the social need for this form of punishment as a deterrent to crime (Bohm 1999). The execution rate in the United States continued to increase, peaking in 1935, when 199 people were executed. Following the mid-1930s, the numbers of executions declined as public support for the use of the death penalty decreased and as social action groups, such as the NAACP's Legal Defense Fund, sought to appeal every capital conviction (Lifton and Mitchell 2000). Finally, in 1972, executions were temporarily halted while the U.S. Supreme Court decided on the constitutionality of capital punishment.

THE CONSTITUTIONALITY OF THE DEATH PENALTY

Prior to 1968, the challenges brought before the U.S. Supreme Court regarding the use of the death penalty were related mostly to methods of execution. In these cases, the Court upheld the states' use of firing squads, electrocution, and even second attempts if the first ones failed.

From 1968 through 1972, the death penalty issues the Court addressed began to change. In *U.S. v. Jackson* (1968) the Supreme Court ruled as unconstitutional a provision in the federal death statute that allowed a capital defendant to escape a death sentence either by waiving his or her right to a jury trial or by pleading guilty. That same year, in *Witherspoon v. Illinois* (1968), the Court rejected the practice of "death qualifying" a jury during the penalty phase of a capital case, stating that to do so is to deprive the defendant of an impartial jury on the issue of sentence.

By 1970, several other aspects of the death penalty were under challenge. In the companion cases *McGautha v. California* and *Crampton v. Ohio* (1970), the defendants, both tried for murder and convicted, argued that their sentences violated the due process clause of the 14th Amendment to the U.S. Constitution, inasmuch as the juries had "unfettered discretion" in imposing a sentence of death. Neither jury had been given guidelines to follow, and the defendants argued that this omission constituted a fact of arbitrary and capricious sentencing. Also in question was whether a two-stage trial, or what is known as a bifurcated jury, is necessary in a capital case. In a two-stage trial, the jury determines only guilt or innocence in the first phase, and in the second phase the same jury determines the sentence. By a vote of six to three, the Supreme Court upheld the death sentences of both defendants. Scholars believe that with this decision the justices condoned laws that allow unfettered discretion as well as trials in which both guilt and sentence are determined by one jury during one deliberation (Bohm 1999).

In 1972, in the consolidated cases of *Jackson v. Georgia, Branch v. Texas,* and *Furman v. Georgia* (hereafter referred to as *Furman v. Georgia* 1972), the defendants challenged their death sentences because the juries in their trials were afforded complete discretion in determining whether to impose the sentence of death. Furman had been convicted of murder and Jackson and Branch had been convicted of rape. The Supreme Court granted certiorari to answer the question, "Does the imposition and carrying out of the death penalty in these cases constitute cruel and unusual punishment in violation of the Eighth Amendment?" (*Furman v. Georgia* 1972). By a vote of five to four, the Court reversed and remanded all three sentences of death. The majority opinion stated that the death penalty had been imposed in such an arbitrary and discriminatory manner in these cases that it constituted cruel and unusual punishment.

The *Furman* decision is noteworthy because in it the Supreme Court established that the death penalty per se is not unconstitutional, but that the manner in which the sentence is imposed may be unconstitutional. The Court suggested that states rewrite their capital punishment statutes to ensure the removal of the kind of juror discretion they found in *Furman*. As a result of *Furman*, the statutes that allowed for the use of the death penalty in 37 states, the District of Columbia, the military, and the federal government were deemed unconstitutional, and the death sentences of more than 600 prisoners were vacated (they became sentences of life imprisonment) (Bohm 1999). To avoid total abolition of the death penalty, many states passed new statutes. Some states attempted to remove the problematic juror discretion issue by mandating that a capital sentence be imposed automatically on a person convicted of any crime on a prescribed list. Others established specific guidelines to which judges and juries were required to adhere. Finally, some legislators believed that they might satisfy the Supreme Court by expanding the methods of execution used in their states to include the "cleaner" method of lethal injection.

It was not until the 1976 case of *Gregg v. Georgia* that the U.S. Supreme Court upheld a statute that appeared to be able to reduce juror discretion. Similar to *Furman v. Georgia* (1972), this case consolidated two others, *Jurek v. Texas* and *Proffitt v. Florida*. Troy Gregg was charged with committing armed robbery and murder, and, in accordance with the new Georgia statute, his trial was bifurcated. During the first phase of the trial, the jury found Gregg guilty of two armed robberies and murder. The judge then instructed the jurors that in the sentencing phase of the trial they could recommend a sentence of either death or life imprisonment for each count. Additionally, the judge told the jurors that they could not render a sentence of death unless they found beyond a reasonable doubt that at least one of three particular aggravating factors existed. (In general, an aggravating factor is a condition that makes the crime in question worse somehow; for example, if the victim was elderly, that can be an aggravating factor, as can the defendant's having a long criminal history.) The three possible aggravating factors in this case were as follows:

> a finding that the offense of murder was committed while the offender was engaged in the commission of two other capital felonies, that the offender committed the offense of murder for the purpose of receiving money and the automobile, and that the offense of murder was outrageously and wantonly vile, horrible and inhuman, in that they involved the depravity of the mind of the defendant. (*Gregg v. Georgia* 1976:3)

The jury found that two aggravating factors existed and recommended a sentence of death.

The Supreme Court upheld the new Georgia statute by a vote of seven to two, citing two reasons. First, the statute limits juror discretion by requiring that the state prove aggravating and mitigating factors at a separate penalty hearing. Second, it provides for the direct appeal of the capital conviction to the state's highest court. The Georgia statute thus became the model for death penalty laws across the United States. The first execution after the reinstatement of the death penalty occurred in Utah in 1977, when Gary Gilmore was executed by a firing squad.

METHODS OF EXECUTION

Currently, 38 states, the federal government, and the U.S. military authorize use of the death penalty. Although the primary method of execution used by 37 states, as well as the federal government and the military, is lethal injection, four other methods are approved: electrocution, lethal gas, hanging, and firing squad. Several states allow the use of more than one method as a matter of policy. For example, Arizona requires by statute that those sentenced to death after November 15, 1992, be executed by lethal injection. Individuals sentenced prior to that date may elect to die by lethal injection or by the gas chamber. Similarly, in Delaware, individuals sentenced before June 13, 1986, may elect to die by lethal injection or by hanging. All offenders sentenced after that date are executed by lethal injection.

One reason many states allow various methods of execution is so that they will have alternative methods already in place if their primary means are ruled unconstitutional. For example, Wyoming authorizes the use of the gas chamber if, and only if, lethal injection is forbidden. Oklahoma will employ electrocution if either lethal injection or the firing squad is ruled unconstitutional (Death Penalty Information Center 2002e). Table 1 lists the various

Table 1		Methods of Execution in the United States
Method	Number of Executions Since 1976	Jurisdictions That Authorize Use
Lethal injection	654	Alabama, Arizona, Arkansas, California, Connecticut, Delaware, Florida, Georgia, Idaho, Illinois, Indiana, Maryland, Mississippi, Missouri, Montana, Nevada, New Hampshire, New Jersey, New Mexico, New York, North Carolina, Ohio, Oklahoma, Oregon, Pennsylvania, South Carolina, South Dakota, Tennessee, Texas, Utah, Virginia, Washington, Wyoming, U.S. military, U.S. government
Electrocution	10	Alabama, Arkansas, Florida, [Illinois], Kentucky, Nebraska,[a] [Oklahoma], South Carolina, Tennessee, Virginia
Gas chamber	11	Arizona, California, Maryland, Missouri, [Wyoming]
Hanging	3	Delaware, New Hampshire, Washington
Firing squad	2	Idaho, [Oklahoma], Utah

SOURCE: Death Penalty Information Center (2002e).

NOTE: Square brackets indicate that the state authorizes the method only if a current method is found unconstitutional. For example, Illinois allows electrocution only if its primary method, lethal injection, is ruled unconstitutional.

a. Nebraska is the only state that requires electrocution as its primary method of execution.

Table 2 U.S. Executions by Race, Gender, and Age: 1608–2002

	Espy File 1608–1972		Death Penalty Information Center[a] 1976–2002	
	No.	%	No.	%
Race				
White	5,902	41	465	56
Black	7,084	49	281	34
Native American	353	2	13	2
Hispanic	295	2	54	7
Other	855	6	7	1
Total executions	14,489		820	
Gender				
Male	13,935	96	810	99
Female	554	4	10	1
Total executions	14,489		820	
Age at crime				
Under 18	341	2	21	3
18+	14,148	98	799	97
Total executions	14,489		820	

SOURCES: Espy and Smykla (1994), NAACP Legal Defense Fund (2002), and Death Penalty Information Center (2002g).

a. Executions as of December 17, 2002.

Table 3 Demographics of Defendants Currently on Death Row in the United States

Characteristics	Number	%
Race		
White	1,665	45
Black	1,603	44
Latino/a	347	9
Native American	40	1
Asian/Pacific Islander	41	1
Other	1	.03
Total	3,697	
Gender		
Male	3,643	98
Female	54	2
Total	3,697	
Juvenile		
Male	83	.02

SOURCE: NAACP Legal Defense Fund (2002).

methods of execution and the jurisdictions that authorize their use, as well as the number of people executed using each method since 1976.

THE DEMOGRAPHICS OF DEATH ROW: PAST AND PRESENT

Tables 2, 3, and 4 present the demographic data available on the offenders currently on death rows in prisons across the United States. The data displayed in these tables highlight the disparities and patterns of discrimination that exist in capital sentencing. Table 2 provides a historical overview of all the individuals executed in America from 1608 through 2002, with the population broken down by race, gender, and age. Table 3 presents demographic data on the current death row population, and Table 4 shows all executions carried out in the United States from 1977 through 2002, broken down by jurisdiction and race. (Table 4 begins with 1977 because the death penalty literature focuses especially on those executions that took place after the Supreme Court's pivotal decision in *Gregg v. Georgia* [1972].)

Female Offenders

It is noteworthy that the execution of female offenders is quite rare. From the first, Jane Champion's 1632 execution in the colony of Virginia in 1632, to the most recent,

the October 2002 execution of Aileen Wuornos in the state of Florida, there have been 564 documented executions of women in America (Death Penalty Information Center 2002g), the majority of which were carried out by hanging (Baker 1999). This figure represents 3% of the official number of executions that have ever occurred in the United States. The majority of the women who have been executed received the death penalty for crimes involving murder, witchcraft, or arson. Although the last two of these crimes are no longer punishable by death (arson is so punishable only if a homicide occurs as a result of the arson), cases of witchcraft and arson account for 51% of all women executed.

Female offenders have always been sentenced to death and executed at much lower rates than have their male counterparts. This is not surprising, given that women are less likely to be arrested for murder. Women account for only approximately 13% of all murder arrests, and they receive an even smaller proportion of imposed death sentences (2%) (Bohm 1999). Furthermore, since the *Furman* case in 1972, death sentences have been imposed on female offenders only 139 times. Additionally, women account for less than 2% (8) of the 749 executions conducted since 1976.

Given that women do commit murder, the question remains: Why are women less likely than men to be sentenced to death? It has been suggested that the death penalty statutes are written to favor female defendants. For example, when a woman is charged with a homicide, prosecutors are less able to demonstrate the presence of the kinds of aggravating circumstances required to sentence a person to death. Women are less likely than men to have past criminal records, to premeditate their crimes, or to be involved in felony murders. Female defendants are also more likely than males to bring up one or more mitigating factors in their defense, such as suffering from emotional disturbances or being under the influence of other persons who participated in the offenses. In capital murder cases, jurors and judges also tend to be more lenient toward female offenders because they believe that women are more likely than men to be rehabilitated (Streib 1993).

As of the end of 2002, 54 women were on death rows in U.S. prisons; this figure represents approximately 1.5% of the total 3,697 persons on death row in the United States at the time. (The discrepancy between the 139 death sentences imposed, as mentioned above, and the 54 remaining females on death row is the result of trial reversals and sentence commutations; see Death Penalty Information Center 2002g.) The majority of the 54 women on death row are white (54%); 33% are black, 11% are Latina, and 2% are Native American. As of 2002, 40% of these women were between the ages of 30 and 39, 29% were between the ages of 40 and 49, 13% were younger than 30, and the remaining 18% were 50 years of age or older. Among them, these 54 women were responsible for the murders of 81 victims, of whom 65% were white, 12% were black, 4% were Asian or Asian American, and 17% were Latino/a. Their victims were more often male than female, 53% versus 47%. Finally, most of their victims were between the ages of 18 and 49 (49%) (Death Penalty Information Center 2002g).

Minority Offenders

Many observers have argued that the use of the death penalty is racially biased, given the disproportionate numbers of minority group members who receive this penalty. Since the moratorium on capital punishment ended in 1976, 55.5% of those executed (406 individuals) have been white; 35.5% (260 people) have been black, 7% (48 people) have been Latino/a, 2% (13 people) have been Native American, and 1% (5 people) have been Asian Americans (NAACP 2002). The current racial composition of the death row population is 46% white, 43% black, 9% Latino/a, and 1% other (NAACP 2002).

Table 4   U.S. Executions by Jurisdiction and Race: 1977–2002

Location	Total Executions	Race			
		White	Black	Hispanic	Other[a]
Texas	289	149	94	42	4
Virginia	87	43	41	2	1
Missouri	59	36	22		1
Oklahoma	55	34	13		8
Florida	54	31	19	3	1
Georgia	31	18	13		
South Carolina	28	18	10		
Louisiana	27	14	13		
Alabama	25	9	16		
Arkansas	24	17	6	1	
North Carolina	23	16	7		
Arizona	22	18		2	2
Delaware	13	6	6		1
Illinois	12	7	5		
California	10	7	1		2
Nevada	9	7		1	1
Indiana	9	6	3		
Utah	6	4	2		
Mississippi	6	3	3		
Ohio	5	3	2		
Washington	4	4			
Maryland	3	1	2		
Nebraska	3	1	2		
Pennsylvania	3	3			
Kentucky	2	2			
Montana	2	2			
Oregon	2	2			
Colorado	1	1			
Idaho	1	1			
New Mexico	1	1			
Tennessee	1	1			
Wyoming	1	1			
Federal	2	1		1	

SOURCE: Data as of February 2003 from Death Penalty Information Center Web site (http://www.deathpenaltyinfo.org).

a. Includes Native Americans, Asians, and unknowns.

Several studies have revealed patterns of discrimination in sentencing based on the races of the defendants and the victims. Baldus, Woodworth, and Pulaski (1990), for example, examined sentencing patterns in Georgia during the 1970s, using a sample of approximately 2,500 homicide cases. These analysts found that a defendant (white or black) who was found guilty of killing a white person was 4.3 times more likely to be sentenced to death than was a person who murdered a black person. Data from the NAACP Legal Defense Fund's (2002) Death Row U.S.A. study support Baldus et al.'s findings. The NAACP reports that 169 black defendants who were convicted of taking the lives of white persons have been executed, whereas only 11 whites convicted of killing black persons have been executed. The NAACP found that 81% of the victims in death penalty cases were white, although only 50% of all homicide victims are white. The U.S. courts' response to these empirical data has been to deny relief, arguing that a pattern of racial disparity does not prove racial bias in any particular case.

Youthful Offenders

The first execution of a juvenile offender in America occurred in 1642 with the execution of Thomas Graunger of Plymouth Colony, Massachusetts. Since that time, less than 2% of offenders, or fewer than 362 individuals, have been executed for crimes committed while they were juveniles (Death Penalty Information Center 2002a). However, the United States remains one of only three nations that executes offenders for crimes committed when they were juveniles; the other two are Iran and the Democratic Republic of the Congo.

The state's taking of an individual's life for an offense he or she committed as a juvenile remains one of the most controversial issues surrounding the use of the death penalty. This issue is best discussed within the context of three significant U.S. Supreme Court cases that have solidified the constitutionality of the use of the death penalty for juvenile offenders. In the case of *Thompson v. Oklahoma* (1988), the defendant, at age 15, killed his brother-in-law and mutilated the man's body. He was tried as an adult, found guilty, and was given the death sentence. The question before the Court was whether or not it would be constitutional for the state to execute an offender who was 15 years of age or younger at the time the crime was committed. The justices chose not to answer the question before them directly. Instead, they ruled that any state without a prescribed minimum age requirement in its death penalty statute could not execute a person younger than 16 years of age.

In the 1989 companion cases *Stanford v. Kentucky* and *Wilkins v. Missouri,* the Court addressed the use of the death penalty for offenders who were 16 or 17 years of age at the time their crimes took place. Stanford and Wilkins, ages 17 and 16, respectively, were tried as adults and convicted of capital murder. On appeal, the defendants raised several issues in opposition of their sentences of death. These issues still remain at the heart of the battle to end the use of the death penalty for juvenile offenders. First, they argued that the use of the death penalty for a minor is contrary to the evolving standards of decency that mark the progress of a mature, civilized society, citing statistics regarding the actual numbers of executed juveniles in U.S. history to support this contention. Second, they argued that because most jurisdictions recognize age 18 as the legal age to exercise the right to vote, buy alcohol, and serve in the military, age 18 should also serve as the minimum age for execution. Finally, they argued that when capital punishment is used for juveniles, it fails to serve the acknowledged purpose of punishment. That is, this form of punishment does not deter juveniles from committing crimes because juveniles possess less well-developed cognitive skills than do adults, juveniles have less fear of death, and juveniles are less responsible and, therefore, less blameworthy.

By a vote of five to four, the U.S. Supreme Court ruled that the Eighth Amendment does not prohibit the use of the death penalty for a criminal a 16- or 17-year-old defendant. The Court did not agree that a national consensus against use of the death penalty for juveniles has been established and opined that society should expect to see small numbers of executed juveniles because so few capital offenses are committed by those under 17. Finally, the majority stated that the Court found it difficult to accept the argument that the guideline for determining if a person is old enough to vote, drink, and serve in the military can also be used to establish whether an individual is capable of understanding that taking the life of another person is wrong. At present, of the 40 jurisdictions that allow use of the death penalty, 16 have established age 18 as the minimum age for death penalty eligibility, 5 use age 17 as the minimum age, and 18 have set the minimum at 16 years of age (Streib 2002).

Fourteen years after the Supreme Court's 1989 ruling, recent developments suggest that Justices Stevens, Souter, Ginsburg, and Breyer are ready to consider the constitutional question regarding the execution of juvenile offenders. This orientation comes in the wake of the Court's refusal to consider direct relief for Kevin Stanford. The justices, two of whom were not sitting on the Court at the time of the earlier cases described above, have stated that they believe executing juvenile offenders is a "shameful practice" that is "inconsistent with the evolving standards of decency in a civilized society" (*In re Stanford* 2002). Nationally, there is a movement to end the execution of juvenile offenders altogether. Indiana has recently banned the use of the death penalty for offenders under the age of 18, and public interest groups are rallying support for the cause in Arkansas, Georgia, and Kentucky (Death Penalty Information Center 2002a).

Post-*Furman,* the United States has witnessed the execution of 18 juvenile offenders (less than 3% of the total number of executions since 1977); all of these executions involved males. All but one of these juveniles were 17 years old at the time they committed their crimes; one was 16 years old. When they died, these 18 individuals were between the ages of 24 and 38; 50% were white, 44% were black, and 5.5% were Latino (Streib 2002). Texas executed 10 of the offenders, Virginia executed 3, and Georgia, Louisiana, Missouri, South Carolina, and Oklahoma each executed 1 individual. Gerald Mitchell, the person most recently executed for committing the crime of murder while a juvenile, received the ultimate punishment in October 2001 (Death Penalty Information Center 2002a).

CAPITAL PUNISHMENT AT THE FEDERAL LEVEL AND WITHIN THE U.S. MILITARY

Within the U.S. legal system there are three separate criminal jurisdictions: state, federal, and military. In this section, I discuss the use of the death penalty in the latter two jurisdictions. With the exception of the U.S. Supreme Court, the federal government has not played a large role in the actual implementation of the death penalty, nor has the military. However, the death penalty statutes of these two jurisdictions list more capital crimes than do any of the 38 states that currently allow for the use of the death penalty.

The Federal Death Penalty

The number of offenses for which the U.S. government has employed the death penalty exceeds the numbers of capital offenses recognized at the state level. In the past, the federal government has employed hanging, electrocution, and even the gas chamber in carrying out the death penalty, mostly for the crime of murder. There have also been federal executions for the crimes of rape, kidnapping, and espionage. Since the execution of Thomas Bird in 1790, 336 men and 4 women have been executed in accordance with federal statutes; the most recent federal execution occurred in 2001 (Death Penalty Information Center 2002b).

The federal death penalty statute has changed significantly over time. In 1972, with the U.S. Supreme Court's decision in *Furman v. Georgia,* the federal death penalty was ruled to be in violation of the Eighth Amendment as were state statutes. It was not until 1988, with the passage of the Anti-Drug Abuse Act, or the "drug kingpin statute," that the federal death penalty was brought in line with state statutes and was, therefore, deemed constitutional. This statute made the death penalty mandatory for many drug-related offenses, such as the murder of a law enforcement officer during any drug-related crime.

In January 1993, President George H. Bush authorized lethal injection as the sole method of execution for federal offenders. In 1994, Congress passed the Federal Death Penalty Act as part of the Violent Crime Control and Law Enforcement Act. This act increased to 60 the number of federal crimes for which the death penalty can be imposed. These include treason and espionage (even if a death does not occur), most homicides for which federal jurisdiction exists, and continuing criminal enterprise drug offenses that do not include homicide but do involve large quantities of drugs or drug-related money.

The Federal Death Penalty Act also states that the method of execution to be employed is that used in the state in which the federal sentence is handed down. If that state does not allow for the use of the death penalty, the U.S. government selects another state in which to carry out the execution. Since this law was enacted, both the number of federal prosecutions in which an offense punishable by death has been charged and the number of cases for which the U.S. attorney general has requested use of the death penalty have increased (Bohm 1999). Additionally, a federal death row offender is granted only one appeal as a matter of right for both conviction and sentencing. This

appeal is made directly to the U.S. Court of Appeals for the circuit in which the case was tried. All other reviews, such as reviews by the Supreme Court, are discretionary. Only the president of the United States has the power to pardon a federal death row inmate (Death Penalty Information Center 2002b).

The most recent addition to federal death penalty laws took effect when President Clinton signed into law the Anti-Terrorism and Effective Death Penalty Act of 1996, an act created in response to the 1995 Oklahoma City bombing of the Alfred P. Murrah Federal Building. This act, which applies at both the federal and state levels, added four federal offenses to the list of capital crimes, created stricter filing deadlines for appeals, allowed for only one habeas corpus appeal in federal court, and limited the number of evidentiary hearings in death row cases. It was believed that these changes would not only speed up the death penalty process but also decrease the costs of the process (Schabas 1997).

The ways in which decisions are made to seek the death penalty in federal cases have also changed over time. After the passage of the Anti-Drug Abuse Act of 1988, the Department of Justice instituted a policy requiring all U.S. attorneys to submit any case in which the death penalty was being requested to the U.S. attorney general for review and approval. From 1988 until 1994, when Justice Department policy changed, approval to seek the death penalty was sought in 52 cases and received in 47 of those cases (U.S. Department of Justice 2000).

In 1995, the Department of Justice adopted the death penalty protocol that is in use today. At present, U.S. attorneys are required to submit each case in which a defendant is charged with a death-eligible crime, even if the death penalty is not a prime objective, to the Attorney General's Review Committee on Capital Cases. This committee then makes a recommendation to the U.S. attorney general. Since this procedure has been in place, 682 death-eligible defendants have been evaluated, and the attorney general has authorized seeking the death penalty in 159 of those cases (U.S. Department of Justice 2000). Of these 159 defendants, 75% have been members of minority groups.

The U.S. Military and Capital Punishment

Although official records are unavailable, scholars believe that executions occurred in the military during the American Revolution. The first official records of military executions in the United States were kept by the Union Army during the Civil War, and these records indicate that 267 military personnel were executed. Of these, 53% were executed for desertion and 27% were executed for murder. Although executions were carried out in the U.S. military through both world wars, there are two noteworthy differences between the later executions and those recorded during the Civil War. First, the number of executions declined: only 35 documented executions occurred during World War I, and 147 executions occurred during

World War II. Second, the majority of those executed in the later period had been convicted of the crime of murder (Bohm 1999). From the end of World War II until 1961, only 12 U.S. military personnel were executed. The most recent military execution took place in 1961, when U.S. Army Private John Bennett was hanged after being convicted of rape and attempted murder.

The Uniform Code of Military Justice classifies the 21 offenses punishable by death into three categories. The first of these categories includes espionage, felony murder, and rape; the second comprises offenses committed during wartime, such as desertion and willful disobedience of a superior officer; and the final category is made up of crimes considered to be breaches of the military code of conduct during wartime, such as willfulness in causing great human suffering or a serious injury (Bohm 1999).

Before a death sentence can be administered through a U.S. military court, the case must meet four criteria. First, all members of the military panel must vote to convict on the basis of a capital offense. Second, the government must have proved beyond a reasonable doubt at least one aggravating factor. Third, the panel must unanimously agree that any aggravating factors outweigh any mitigating and extenuating circumstances. And finally, all members of the panel must consent to the death sentence (*U.S. v. Curtis* 1991; Sullivan 1998). Thus it is noteworthy that, post-*Furman,* the Armed Forces Court of Appeals ruled that the military death penalty statute was unconstitutional because it failed to specify aggravating factors (*U.S. v. Matthews* 1983). In response, President Ronald Reagan signed an executive order in 1984 establishing new guidelines for military death penalty cases, including a list of 11 aggravating factors that serve to actualize the viability of the death penalty (Death Penalty Information Center 2002f).

CAPITAL PUNISHMENT AND SOME PARTICULAR CLASSES OF OFFENDERS

Although public support for the death penalty has varied substantially since the 1970s, capital punishment has become a permanent fixture in U.S. society. However, since the Supreme Court's landmark decision in *Gregg v. Georgia* (1976), opponents of the death penalty have argued that certain classes of criminal offenders should not be executed. In this section I briefly discuss some of the controversial issues surrounding this topic.

Mentally Retarded Defendants

Since the reinstatement of the death penalty in 1976, 35 mentally retarded offenders have been executed, and it is estimated that at least 300 persons currently incarcerated on death rows in U.S. prisons experience some degree of mental retardation (Death Penalty Information Center 2002d). Some analysts argue that executing mentally retarded persons constitutes cruel and unusual punishment, because

these individuals are incapable of understanding their constitutional rights, are unable to assist in their own defense, and should not be held culpable for their actions (*Penry v. Lynaugh* 1989). This issue is further complicated by the lack of a single, uniform definition of *mental retardation.* For example, the American Association on Mental Retardation (AAMR) has changed its definition of mental retardation several times during the past two decades. Although this organization's various definitions have maintained some commonality, they have differed concerning how the impairment affects an individual's normal daily activities. The AAMR's (2002) most recent definition of mental retardation is as follows:

> Mental retardation is a disability characterized by significant limitations both in intellectual functioning and in adaptive behavior as expressed in conceptual, social, and practical adaptive skills. This disability originated before age 18. (P. 1)

In 1989, the Supreme Court granted certiorari in *Penry v. Lynaugh* to determine whether the execution of mentally retarded persons violates the Eight Amendment. The *Penry v. Lynaugh* case involved a woman who was brutally raped, beaten, and stabbed to death. Before she died, the victim described her assailant to the police, and the description led to the arrest of John Paul Penry, a parolee who had recently served prison time for rape. Penry confessed to the crime and he was charged with capital murder.

At Penry's competency hearing, professionals testified that although Penry was 22 years of age, his mental age was 6½ and his IQ level was 54, a level at which a person is generally considered incompetent. Despite this testimony, the jury found Penry competent to stand trial. At the trial, state experts testified that although Penry had limited mental capacity, he held the potential to honor the law. The experts also testified that they believed that Penry's low IQ scores underestimated his level of alertness. The jury found Penry guilty of capital murder and sentenced him to death.

In *Penry v. Lynaugh,* the defense argued that the application of the death penalty to a mentally retarded person with the mental capacity lower than that of a 7-year-old constitutes cruel and unusual punishment. The defense also argued that there was an emerging national consensus against executing the mentally retarded. However, by a vote of five to four, the justices stated that executing a mentally retarded person is not a violation of the Eighth Amendment and refuted the argument that a national consensus existed against executing the mentally retarded. At the present time, only two states, Maryland and Georgia, and the federal justice system prohibit the execution of mentally retarded persons. Although the Supreme Court overturned Penry's death sentence because the jury at his trial was not allowed to take his mental capacity into account, on retrial Penry was again sentenced to death. In early 2001, the Court reviewed an appeal in *Penry v. Johnson,* at which time Penry's death sentence was again overturned on the basis that the jury was not provided adequate instructions for considering mental retardation as a mitigating factor.

After *Penry,* more states enacted legislation prohibiting the execution of mentally retarded defendants; today 16 states forbid such executions. In the summer of 2002, the U.S. Supreme Court again agreed to review the constitutional basis for executing mentally retarded defendants, using the case of Daryl Atkins, who was sentenced to death in Virginia for the 1996 robbery and murder of a U.S. airman. His appeal challenged the "evolving standards of decency" clause set by the Court in *Penry,* asserting that a national consensus had emerged against the execution of mentally retarded persons. In delivering the majority opinion for the Court, Justice Stevens wrote that the execution of mentally retarded criminals constitutes cruel and unusual punishment and is, therefore, prohibited by the Eighth Amendment. Justice Stevens further stated that although a number of states no longer allow for the execution of mentally retarded criminals,

> it was not so much the number of these States that is significant, but the consistency of the direction of change. It provided powerful evidence that today society views mentally retarded offenders as categorically less culpable than the average criminal. The evidence carriers even greater force when it is noted that the legislatures addressing the issue have voted overwhelmingly in favor of prohibition. (*Atkins v. Virginia* 2002:1–2)

This Supreme Court ruling is certain to have two particular results: First, the 20 states that allow for the execution of mentally retarded persons must now develop standards by which to determine the mental capacity of defendants in capital murder cases; and second, a significant number of inmates currently on death row are likely to petition for retrial on the basis of claims of mental retardation.

Innocence and the Death Penalty

The possibility that innocent persons may be executed remains one of the most important arguments against the use of the death penalty. Although the states and the federal government have expended great effort to minimize the chances that this may occur, evidence reveals that they have not always been successful. Since 1973, 102 persons have been released from death rows in various states based on evidence of their innocence (Death Penalty Information Center 2002c), and this number may continue to increase. This phenomenon is due in part to the expansion of the use of the death penalty in states such as New York and Kansas as well as the shorter appeal processes currently in vogue (McCann 1996).

There are several possible ways for a convicted individual to be declared innocent. One of these is for a government official to admit error in the person's prosecution, but this is an event that has yet to occur. A convicted person may also be declared innocent through official exoneration—that is, official recognition that the he or she either was not involved in the crime or was convicted of a crime that did not occur. A finding of innocence may involve the dismissal of charges against the defendant or a verdict of not guilty at a retrial (Radelet and Bedau 1998).

Radelet and Bedau (1998), who conducted a historical analysis of death penalty cases, claim to have identified 416 cases involving 496 defendants who were convicted of capital crimes but were later found to be innocent. Among these 416 cases were 23 individuals who were innocent but had been executed and 22 people who were granted reprieves within 72 hours of their scheduled executions. Defenders of the death penalty challenge Radelet and Bedau's findings, claiming that reasonable, unbiased judges would not allow a death sentence to be imposed based on inadequate evidence. Moreover, no court has ever acknowledged that an innocent person has been executed in the United States. Although supporters of the death penalty concede that errors may have occurred, they assert that such errors are a modest price to pay, given the social benefits derived from the law.

According to researchers, wrongful convictions occur for several reasons. The most common of these is perjury on the part of prosecution witnesses. The second leading cause of wrongful convictions is eyewitness misidentification. Other factors include false confessions or guilty pleas by innocent defendants who have been pressured by the police to confess to crimes they did not commit, the failure of prosecutors to dismiss charges in weak cases (especially high-profile cases), and the lack of high-quality legal representation for defendants (Gross 1996; Ofshe and Leo 1997; Radelet and Bedau 1998).

Currently, a nationwide social movement is calling for a moratorium on all executions until death penalty practices can be more closely examined. Several states, including Florida, Illinois, and Maryland, have voluntarily stopped executions pending inquiries into sentencing practices. Additionally, in 2001, members of Congress reintroduced the Innocence Protection Act, a law designed to protect the innocent from wrongful conviction. This act includes measures designed to provide qualified attorneys to defendants in capital murder cases and greater access to DNA testing on behalf of defendants.

CONCLUSION

The United States is currently experiencing a decline in the use of capital punishment, and a modest decrease in the number of death row inmates has occurred since 1976, when capital punishment was reinstated. Only 13 of the 40 jurisdictions that allow capital punishment carried out any executions during 2002. Judges and lawmakers are also taking steps to ensure that the death penalty is administered fairly. More than 100 persons who had been convicted of capital crimes have been freed since 1973 based on evidence of their innocence, the Supreme Court has ruled that the execution of mentally retarded offenders is unconstitutional, and the justices have recently signaled their willingness to reconsider the execution of offenders whose crimes were committed while the offenders were minors. Several states have voluntarily halted the scheduling of executions pending evaluations of sentencing practices. Despite these developments, however, legal and public debate will undoubtedly continue as issues such the execution of minors, racial disparities in sentencing, and the potential for execution of the innocent continue to be subjects of intense scrutiny.

REFERENCES

American Association on Mental Retardation. 2002. *Mental Retardation: Definition, Classification, and Systems of Supports,* 10th ed. Washington, DC: American Association on Mental Retardation.

Anti-Drug Abuse Act. 1988. 21 U.S.C. 848 (e-r).

Atkins v. Virginia, (00–8452), 536 U.S. 304, 2002.

Baker, David V. 1999. "A Descriptive Profile and Socio-Historical Analysis of Female Executions in the United States, 1632–1997." *Women and Criminal Justice* 10(3):22–43.

Baldus, David, George Woodworth, and Charles Pulaski. 1990. *Equal Justice and the Death Penalty: A Legal and Empirical Analysis.* Boston: Northeastern University Press.

Beccaria, Cesare. [1767] 1975. *On Crimes and Punishment,* translated 1975 by Harry Paolucci. Indianapolis: Bobbs-Merrill.

Bedau, Hugo A. 1982. *The Death Penalty in America.* New York: Oxford University Press.

Bohm, Robert M. 1999. *Deathquest: An Introduction to the Theory and Practice of Capital Punishment in the United States.* Cincinnati, OH: Anderson.

Costanzo, Mark. 1997. *Just Revenge: Costs and Consequences of the Death Penalty.* New York: St. Martin's.

Death Penalty Information Center. 2002a. "Executions of Juvenile Offenders." Washington, DC: Death Penalty Information Center. Retrieved December 20, 2002 (http://www.deathpenaltyinfo.org/juvexec.html).

———. 2002b. "The Federal Death Penalty." Washington, DC: Death Penalty Information Center. Retrieved December 20, 2002 (http://www.deathpenaltyinfo.org/feddp.html).

———. 2002c. "Innocence and the Death Penalty." Washington, DC: Death Penalty Information Center. Retrieved January 3, 2003 (http://www.deathpenaltyinfo.org/innoc.html).

———. 2002d. "Mental Retardation and the Death Penalty." Washington, DC: Death Penalty Information Center. Retrieved January 3, 2003 (http://www.deathpenaltyinfo.org/dpicmr.html).

———. 2002e. "Methods of Execution." Washington, DC: Death Penalty Information Center. Retrieved December 23, 2002 (http://www.deathpenaltyinfo.org/methods.html).

———. 2002f. "The U.S. Military Death Penalty." Washington, DC: Death Penalty Information Center. Retrieved December 20, 2002 (http://www.deathpenaltyinfo.org/military.html).

———. 2002g. "Women and the Death Penalty." Washington, DC: Death Penalty Information Center. Retrieved December 28, 2002 (http://www.deathpenaltyinfo.org/womenstats.html).

Espy, M. Watt and John Ortiz Smykla, comps. 1994. "Executions in the United States, 1608–1991: The Espy File." Ann Arbor, MI: Inter-university Consortium for Political and Social Research. Retrieved May 15, 2003 (http://www.icpsr.umich.edu/nacjd).

Furman v. Georgia, 408 U.S. 238, 1972.

Gregg v. Georgia, 428 U.S. 153, 1976.

Gross, Samuel R. 1996. "The Risks of Death: Why Erroneous Convictions Are Common in Capital Cases." *Buffalo Law Review* 44:469–84.

In re Stanford, 01-10009, 2002.

Lifton, Robert and Greg Mitchell. 2000. *Who Owns Death? Capital Punishment, the American Conscience, and the End of Executions.* New York: HarperCollins.

McCann, E. Michael. 1996. "Opposing Capital Punishment: A Prosecutor's Perspective." *Marquette Law Review* 79: 649–67.

McGautha v. California, 402 U.S. 183, 1970.

NAACP Legal Defense Fund. 2002. "Death Row U.S.A." Washington, DC: NAACP. Retrieved October 21, 2002 (http://www.deathpenaltyinfo.org/deathrowusarecent.pdf).

Ofshe, Richard and Richard Leo. 1997. "The Social Psychology of Police Interrogations: The Theory and Classification of True and False Confessions." *Studies in Law, Politics and Society* 16:189–201.

Penry v. Johnson, 00–6677, 2001.

Penry v. Lynaugh, 492 U.S. 584, 1989.

Radelet, Michael L. and Hugo A. Bedau. 1998. "The Execution of the Innocent." Pp. 223–42 in *America's Experiment With Capital Punishment: Reflections on the Past, Present and Future of the Ultimate Penal Sanction,* edited by James R. Acker, Robert M. Bohm, and Charles S. Lanier. Durham, NC: Carolina Academic Press.

Randa, Laura E. 1997. *Society's Final Solution: A History and Discussion of the Death Penalty.* Lanham, MD: University Press of America.

Schabas, William A. 1997. *The Abolition of the Death Penalty in International Law,* 2d ed. New York: Cambridge University Press.

Stanford v. Kentucky, 493 U.S. 361, 1989.

Streib, Victor L. 1993. "Death Penalty for Female Offenders." Pp. 142–45 in *A Capital Punishment Anthology,* edited by Victor L. Streib. Cincinnati, OH: Anderson.

———. 2002. "The Juvenile Death Penalty Today: Death Sentences and Executions for Juvenile Crimes, January 1, 1973–November 15, 2002." Retrieved December 28, 2002 (http://www.law.onu.edu/faculty/streib/juvdeath.html).

Sullivan, Dwight H. 1998. "A Matter of Life and Death: Examining the Military Death Penalty's Fairness." *Federal Lawyer,* June.

Thompson v. Oklahoma, 487 U.S. 815, 1988.

U.S. v. Curtis, 32 M.J. 252, 1991.

U.S. v. Jackson, 390 U.S. 70, 1968.

U.S. v. Matthews, 16 M.J. 354, 1983.

U.S. Department of Justice. 2000. "The Federal Death Penalty System: A Statistical Survey (1988–2000)." Retrieved January 10, 2003 (http://www.usdoj.gov/dag/pubdoc/dpsurvey.html).

Violent Crime Control and Law Enforcement Act. 1994. P.L. No. 103-322, 108 Stat. 1796.

Witherspoon v. Illinois, 391 U.S. 510, 1968.

MILITARY EXECUTIONS

J. ROBERT LILLY

PROLEGOMENON: HISTORICAL BACKGROUND

The origins of military executions worldwide are lost to antiquity, yet for centuries such executions have remained a stable but underdeveloped topic in the fields of military history and jurisprudence. In England, the first laws concerning military executions were written by kings in their instructions for various expeditions, including the orders issued by Richard I for the Crusades in A.D. 1190. Over the centuries, laws regarding the power of courts martial to impose the death penalty for ordinary crimes and for such uniquely military matters as mutiny have fluctuated widely. As the U.S. Supreme Court has recognized, "the first comprehensive articles of war were those declared by Richard II at Durham in A.D. 1325. and Henry V at Mantes in A.D 1429." (*Loving v. United States* 1996:761). Except during times of political disorder, these rules lost force after the hostilities ended because they were not fixed codes. The American Congress enacted the first U.S. Articles of War in 1789.

From one perspective, military executions are nothing more than part of the hard facts of warfare. The deaths of thousands of enemy soldiers and noncombatant prisoners at the hands of their captors during the First, Second, and Third Crusades are illustrative.[1] Another approach to the subject, the one I take in this chapter, focuses on *intramilitary* executions—that is, killings carried out by a military body against its own members. An analysis of *extramilitary* executions would examine the execution deaths of enemy soldiers and civilians. In July 1945, for example, the U.S. Army executed five German POWs Fort Leavenworth, Kansas, for the murder of a fellow prisoner (Green 1995).

Although military organizations and governments have found it important to document the use of capital punishment within the military, it is far more interesting to examine the *how* and *why* of military executions. In this chapter I strike a balance between these two perspectives, because it is nearly pointless to discuss one without the other. The death of Christ as a prisoner is a useful beginning example.

It is quite clear that biblical scholars agree that Christ was put to death by crucifixion under the military authority of Pontius Pilate. It is also agreed that soldiers contributed to Christ's humiliation before his death—they placed the crown of thorns on his head, lashed him, and gambled for his garments. There is less agreement on the symbolic meaning of his death. Was it strictly a military exercise by the Roman Empire in what was then essentially an "outback" region? If so, it is rather difficult to see what military purpose was achieved by killing one man who had no army. The *how* and *why* of Christ's death, however, are laden with several messages. One message was the reaffirmation, to the public and to the Roman Empire itself, that the empire still had the power to impose order by killing non-Romans. The slow and painful death by crucifixion was also a public and ignominious degradation ceremony—long reserved for the execution of criminals—that put Christ in the same league as thieves and murderers (Brown 1994:945–47). By publicly crucifying Christ, the Roman Empire told others, including Christ's followers and potential followers, what might happen to them while simultaneously, although only temporarily, repairing the tear in the empire's social fabric caused by Christ and his followers (Lilly and Ball 1982). Today it is arguable that although Christ died as a direct result of military decisions, his death was more importantly the most significant symbolic development in a growing religious movement.

In the remainder of this chapter, with few exceptions, I focus primarily on the *who, offenses, places, numbers, methods,* and *by whom* of the U.S. military's executions of its own personnel. Most of the information provided here comes from the American Revolutionary War, the American Civil War, and World Wars I and II—no U.S.

---

1. As Father John "Jack" McGuire (1933–2001) commented regarding the Crusades during a 1999 interview at the Mary Mother Queen of Heaven Catholic Church in Erlanger, Kentucky, "They were a bad idea."

soldiers were executed by the military during the Korean and Vietnam Wars.

WHO

Lower Ranks

Those who were executed by the military from the time of the American Revolutionary War through World Wars I and II came primarily from the lower ranks of noncommissioned personnel. This is not surprising, given the fact that all branches of the military are rigidly controlled hierarchical organizations with power flowing downward. There is one notable exception, however. A 1919 dispatch from Dijon, France, near the end of World War I reported that the U.S. Army authorities at Is-sur-Tille "sentenced and hanged an American Lieutenant for an assault on a little girl who died in consequence of injuries received" ("Hang American Officer" 1919).

Consistent with the fact that almost all executed soldiers have come from the lower ranks is that overwhelmingly these individuals have not been regular army career troops; rather, they have been volunteers and draftees who were in the army for the duration of a particular war. One possible exception comes from World War II: Private Theron W. McGann (white), married, IQ 118, age 23, of the 32nd Signal Construction Battalion, was hanged in France on November 20, 1944, for the nighttime rape at gunpoint of Madame Yvone Emilienne Fugenia Vaudevire on August 5, 1944. McGann had previously served in the Oregon National Guard, 162nd Infantry (*U.S. v. Theron W. McGann* 1944). Arguably, this does not qualify him as a member of the regular army, but he did have previous military experience.

Race

Because the U.S. military was racially segregated until 1948, race illuminates much about who was executed during the 20th century. During World War II, nearly 80% of the 70 soldiers executed in the European Theater of Operations (ETO) were black, even though black soldiers constituted only approximately 10% of the troops. The exact racial distribution of the 35 American military personnel who were executed during World War I, between April 6, 1917 and June 30, 1919, is unknown (U.S. War Department 1919: 674; U.S. Congress 1923). However, 25 of these 35 executions took place within the United States, and of those, at least 17 involved black soldiers. Of these 17 black soldiers, 13 were executed in August 1917 for

participating in a riot in Houston, Texas (U.S. Committee on Public Relations 1917; Haynes 1976). During 1918, 3 more blacks were hanged for "'assaulting and outraging' a 17-year-old white girl on the cantonement grounds" ("Whole Army Division" 1918). Of 11 more soldiers executed during World War I in France, 8 (73%) were black.

TYPES OF OFFENSES

Throughout U.S. history, soldiers have been executed for crimes specific to the military, such as desertion, mutiny, and cowardice. They have also been executed for misdeeds defined as felonies by civilian authorities that are also prohibited by military law, such as murder and rape. During the American Revolutionary War, General George Washington approved hundreds of executions, some for desertion (Daniel Hearn, personal communication, May 26, 2002). On April 23, 1779, Privates Richard Hollowell and John Williams were shot at Washington's Morristown, New Jersey, camp for repeated desertion. During the American Civil War, according to Alotta (1989), more than "275 men were executed for military offenses by the Union Army, whether guilty or not" (p. 186). More than half of these deaths resulted from charges of desertion alone or from this offense and others, including cowardice. No soldier was executed for desertion again until World War II.

The U.S. Army has not executed any soldiers since 1961, when Private John A. Bennett (black) was hanged for raping an 11-year-old white girl in Austria. Fisher (1988) has made an unsubstantiated claim that Bennett is the only U.S. soldier ever to be executed for rape during peacetime. During World War I, the U.S. Army did not execute any soldiers for purely military offenses. In 1923, Colonel W. A. Bethel, judge advocate, concluded that this was evidence "of the good conduct and discipline of the American soldiers who served abroad in the World War" (U.S. Congress 1923:ix).

A complete listing of the capital crimes for U.S. service members is contained in the U.S. Uniform Code of Military Justice. A total of 15 offenses carry the death penalty, although that punishment applies to many of the offenses only in time of war.[2] Since the time of the American Revolutionary War, the number of capital offenses has generally increased through the enlargement of military jurisdiction rather than through the creation of more death penalty offenses (Dwight H. Sullivan, personal communication, 2002). Execution for espionage in time of peace under Article 106a is an exception to this general rule. Also, currently there is some doubt as to whether the

---

2. These offenses are as follows: desertion, Article 85; assaulting or willfully disobeying superior commissioned officer, Article 90; mutiny, Article 94; misbehavior before the enemy, Article 99; subordinate compelling surrender, Article 100; improper use of countersign, Article 101; forcing a safeguard, Article 102; aiding the enemy, Article 104; spying; espionage, Article 106a; willfully hazarding a vessel, Article 110; misbehavior of sentinel or lookout, Article 113; premeditated murder, Article 118; felony murder, Article 118; and rape, Article 120.

use of the death penalty in a case of the rape of an adult woman during an attempted murder is constitutional (Jackson 1986).

PLACE

Military Installations

During times of both war and peace, American military executions have almost invariably been held at military installations, except for naval executions at sea (Valle 1980). The executions approved by General Washington are thought to have occurred outdoors on parade grounds at military camps or forts (Daniel Hearn, personal communication, May 26, 2002). The same practice appears to have been followed by the Union Army, according to one historian's account (Alotta 1989:24–25). The major symbolic purpose of these executions was discipline by example.

The places where many of the 35 World War I executions were carried out are unknown, but we do know that at least the 17 of these that took place on U.S. soil were conducted outdoors within the confines of military camps before several, if not all, of the soldiers stationed there. An exception to this practice occurred in Gievres, France, where a white soldier's execution for murder took place in secrecy "as far as possible . . . at a distant point . . . not to disturb the activities of a busy camp" (U.S. Congress 1923:v).

During World War II, 18 American soldiers were executed at a 400-year-old prison in Shepton Mallet, a small town near Bath in southern England, for offenses committed in Ireland, England, and Wales. Except for two soldiers who were shot, these men were hanged inside a small, two-story, red-brick attachment built specifically by the U.S. Army for putting soldiers to death at rope's end.[3]

Crime Scenes

U.S. military executions in France during World War II occurred at one of two places—either inside a military prison, if the victim was a member of the military, or semi-publicly, at or very near the scene of the crime, if the victim was a civilian, depending on the conditions of war. After being driven in a command car from Seine Disciplinary Training Center, Private Thomas W. McGann went to his death by hanging in a courtyard off the main highway in the northern section of Saint-Lô, Manche, France. The site was a short distance from where he had raped Madame Vaudevire (*U.S. v. Theron W. McGann* 1944; Emmett Bailey, Jr., personal communication, February 23, 1998).[4] The building adjacent to the gallows had been bombed—only the walls were left standing. A hedge screened the northern side of the gallows, and a stone wall enclosed the rear area. According to one eyewitness account, as the chaplain intoned a prayer, "the rain soaked masonry wall began to crumble and collapse toward the assembled witnesses" (Bailey 1986).

The semipublic executions that were carried out in France delivered two important messages: that any misbehavior that seriously threatened military discipline would be dealt with harshly, and that the local populace could be reassured that the U.S. Army was mindful of the importance of good public relations and could be trusted to use strong efforts to keep its soldiers in line.[5] Sometimes the U.S. Army invited French civilians and local authorities to witness executions so that they could convey these messages to others after the offender's death. McGann's execution is illustrative. In addition to the army's 10-member execution team, 18 "Authorized Spectators" from the U.S. Army and 10 Frenchmen were in attendance. The latter group included 6 gendarmes from Saint-Lô (*U.S. v. Theron W. McGann* 1944). The rape victim's name does not appear on the witness list, but Sergeant Emmett Bailey was there, and he recalls that she was standing nearby (personal communication, February 23, 1998). In a terse letter from the First U.S. Army Headquarters dated December 11, 1944, the victim was informed that the commanding general expressed his regret for McGann's offense and that he wished to thank her for her cooperation. The letter also informed her that McGann was hanged by the neck until dead.

The execution of U.S soldiers at the scenes of their crimes, as was done in France, was a practice that had been used earlier in the North African Theater of Operation (NATO). Eight days after American forces invaded Sicily on July 9, 1943, Privates Harvey Stroud, Armstead White, Willie A. Pittman, and David White entered without invitation the house of Giovanni Morana at Marretta, near Gela, Sicily. In the house were Morana, his wife, their 3-year-old child, and their nephew and some other relatives who were visiting. The soldiers (all of whom were black) compelled the nephew and other relatives to leave the house, after which each of the soldiers in turn raped Giovanni's wife, Giovianana Incatasciato Morana, forcing her husband and daughter to watch the assaults. The soldiers were apprehended and were subsequently hanged in the vicinity of Gela on August 30, 1943 (*U.S. v. Pvt. Harvey Stroud* 1943).

---

3. This structure still stands and now contains a small in-prison store.

4. Emmett Bailey was a T/sergeant in the 3047th Quartermaster Registration Company, U.S. Army, from May 1943 to November 1945.

5. As far as I have been able to determine, no military execution has been open to the public without restrictions. Those who witnessed the semipublic executions in France, for example, were allowed to be present by invitation only. The execution of Private McGann had 38 official witnesses, all male—28 of these were members of the U.S. Army. The other witnesses were 10 French citizens, most of whom were gendarmes. McGann's trial transcript does not mention that his rape victim, Madame Vaudevire, was a witness, but Emmett Bailey recalls that she was present.

SELECTION PROCESS

Field Executions

Not all, probably not most, soldiers executed by their commanders in the Western world during the 20th century had the benefit of trials, nor were they likely executed with any thoughts about public relations. During World War II, approximately 10,000 German soldiers were executed in the field along the Russian front for a wide range of offenses, including the loss or misuse of equipment, desertion, and cowardice (Batov 2002). Stragglers, and especially deserters, who were caught wandering aimlessly and unable to explain their behavior were usually shot or hanged by the side of the road as examples to other retreating individual troops or units (Sajer 1972:335; Neumann 1958:243–45).

Peter Neumann, who had been a member of an SS unit, wrote in 1958 how, toward the end of the war, he and others had been ordered to "arrest all deserters and shoot them immediately, in case of resistance" (pp. 243–45). He described one incident involving a Mercedes containing a captain and two other officers that was stopped at a roadblock:

> Abject fear is written all over the faces of the three men. They are obviously Staff Officers who, having no effective command, must have decided to head for Minsk off their own bats. But at a time when all of our resources should be mustered to try and hold the Bolsheviks, it is nothing more or less than treason to run away without fighting. (P. 245)

Unable to convince Neumann and his unit that they were not running away, the officers were led to a field down the road and shot to death with machine pistols.

Mass Executions

Military history is replete with large-scale incidents of mutiny, desertion, cowardice, and retaliation that led to mass executions. As Bryant (1979) states, "Perhaps the most infamous of these was the sepoy mutiny in British India, which began in [May] 1857" (p. 166). Among other things that led to this mutiny was what the native Indian soldiers (sepoys) saw as yet another example of foreigners' lack of sensitivity toward them and their culture. The British, already the subject of smoldering resentment in India, contributed to the mutiny by introducing a new piece of technology—the Lee-Enfield rifle. To load the rifle, a sepoy had to first bite off the end of the cartridge, which was well greased with a combination of beef and pork fat. Because the Koran holds pork to be unclean, and because Hindus hold the cow as scared, the sepoys protested that having to touch this fat with their mouths constituted

pollution to their bodies. The manufacturer of the rifle had not anticipated offending two dominant religious groups, nor had the British plotted to use the grease as a means of the assaulting the groups' faiths, but this situation nevertheless contributed to an outbreak of rebellion among the sepoys. The first incident occurred at a military base in Meerut, where some native soldiers murdered their officers and departed for Delhi. Within a few weeks the rebellion spread quickly, with similar occurrences across the province of Oudh. In some instances British officers' wives and children were attacked. The brutality was horrific, and it came to include other European men, women, and children as well.

Despite evidence that some of the mutinous sepoys had refused to carry out any mass butchering of women and children, and the fact that some of the killings were committed by mercenaries, the British army overreacted. Some of the mutineers who were captured were subsequently court-martialed and either hanged or shot. Others were executed by being blown from the muzzle of a cannon.

During World War I, in the spring of 1917, the French army faced serious problems with soldiers fleeing in the face of the enemy and deserting. The French military authorities conducted courts-martial aplenty and meted out severe punishments, but the effects were minimal. At one point, in hopes of instilling discipline, the army executed representative soldiers from various units based on a lottery (Keegan 1976:275–77). The British experienced a similar problem during World War I, but did not execute any soldiers based on a lottery (Putkowski and Syles 1989; Babington 1983; Corns and Hughes-Wilson 2001).[6]

During the American Civil War, Confederate partisan leader John Singleton Mosby used a lottery to select 7 out of 27 Union soldiers for execution without trial near the northern Virginia village of Rectortown. Mosby took this action as a proportionate retaliation for "the similar execution on September 22, 1864, of seven members of his command by members of the Union Army" (Boyle 1994:148). Of the Union soldiers Mosby selected, one escaped en route to the Union lines, where Mosby wanted them hanged so that "the sight of their dangling corpses would create the greatest possible effect on the Union soldiers" (Boyle 1994:148).

METHODS

On Land

To date, army executions have relied on hanging and shooting—the needle has yet to be utilized. General George Washington is believed to have reserved hanging for enemy spies and used shooting for military personnel, notably deserters. Traditionally, hanging has been considered the

---

6. Only in recent years have the British executions been examined in detail. For a brief summary of French military executions, visit the Web site http://www.shotatdawn.uk.

more ignominious method because it causes greater suffering and is less instantaneous than shooting. During the Civil War, the Union Army used both methods of execution almost equally in cases of murder and rape. Soldiers convicted of desertion, pillaging, spying, or mutiny were almost always shot (Alotta 1989:192–201). Of the approximately 112 soldiers executed for desertion from the Union Army, 100 (89%) were shot.

During World War I, the U.S. Army continued to use the rope for nonmilitary offenses—each of the 11 executions carried out was accomplished by hanging. This method was used predominantly throughout World War II's ETO. Only 6 of the 70 soldiers executed there were shot—all others were hanged. In England there was one exception to the tradition of executing soldiers who had committed offenses that could be defined narrowly as military crimes. Private David Cobb (black) disobeyed an order to give up his rifle and shot Second Lieutenant Robert J. Cobner (white) while Cobb was on guard duty. He was hanged at Shepton Mallet on March 12, 1943. Almost a year later, on March 5, 1944, Private Alex F. Miranda (white) shot First Sergeant Thomas Evison through the forehead because, Miranda said, Evison was snoring too loudly. Miranda was subsequently executed at Shepton Mallet, but, unlike Cobb, he was shot, as was Private Benjamin Pygate (black), who had stabbed Private First Class James Alexander (black) to death in an intraracial fight following the closing of a pub. It is unclear why Cobb was executed by hanging. Was it because he was black in the then-segregated U.S. Army? According to some circa 1990s recollections that I encountered in Shepton Mallet, it is possible that hanging was preferred because the sound of a rifle shot within the prison walls disturbed and offended members of the local public, who were just on the other side of the prison walls when the noisy, nasty deed was done. The method of execution, it must be noted, was recommended during sentencing at the court-martial—prison authorities probably had little control over this matter.

During World War II, desertion, although potentially a capital offense, was always punished with imprisonment or dismissal, with one famous exception—the case of Private Eddie D. Slovik (white). Out of more than 4,000 desertions prosecuted by the U.S. Army in the ETO, only Slovik, a small-framed, poorly educated Polish American from Michigan, was executed (Huie 1954). The circumstances of Slovik's crime and death are illustrative of the power of contextual explanations and the symbolic value of punishment. Slovik deserted Company G, 109th Infantry, twice, once between August 25, 1944 and October 4, 1994 and again on October 8–9, 1944. During his absence, his company was engaged in combat against Germany soldiers in Belgium. On November 11, 1944, Slovik was found guilty of desertion. He was executed, shot to death, on January 31, 1945, at Sainte-Marie aux Mines, France.

What was a rather routine desertion in October 1944 took on greater significance as the U.S. Army continued to fight the Germans during the winter of 1944 in the Ardennes campaign against what was Hitler's final counteroffensive in northwest Europe. Launched in the severe winter of December 1944, it quickly became known as the Battle of the Bulge. With astonishing mobility, the U.S. Army was successful in what Churchill called the greatest American battle of the war, and with its victory hastened Germany's defeat later in early May 1945. However, the human cost for the United States was the highest for any its World War II battles. Estimates of American casualties at the Battle of the Bulge vary from 80,000 to 100,000. Weigley (1981), one of the foremost U.S. military historians, claims that "the total American casualties in the Ardennes battle was 80,987" (p. 574). Of this number, 10,276 were killed or died from their wounds.[7]

It has been argued that during the years between the beginning of World War II and the Battle of the Bulge, U.S. military authorities in Europe became increasingly hardened against deserters. By late 1944, military prisons and jails were full of deserters and soldiers who had gone AWOL, and the army needed men who in the early years of the war had been rejected as unfit to serve. Indeed, Slovik had been rejected by the U.S. Army, only to be drafted later. It was within these shifting circumstances that Slovik's refusal to fight provided the U.S. Army with a timely opportunity to use execution as a deterrent to future desertions.

Shipboard Executions

Although significantly less numerous than army executions—no more than 17 American sailors and marines have been executed since 1849—shipboard executions are an important dimension of capital punishment in the military (Valle 1980:102–42). Historically, capital crimes at sea have involved acts that posed real and imminent danger to the well-being of a vessel, its command, and its crew. In addition, shipboard discipline has often appeared to be rash, cruel, and inhumane, even by military standards.

Mutiny, or suspected mutiny, has been the offense that has led to most of the shipboard executions in the U.S. Navy. The 19th-century "Somers affair" is illustrative. On a return trip from Africa to New York in late November 1842, Commander Alexander Slidell Mackenzie of the new U.S. Navy brig Somers was informed that Acting Midshipman Philip Spencer and two others were plotting to kill the ship's officers and use the ship for piracy. Three days later, on December 1, 1842, without trial but based on his officers' unanimous opinion that the three should be put to death, Mackenzie had Spencer and the other two suspects hanged (Valle 1980:108–10). Because of laws enacted before 1800, as well as one enacted in 1800, that

---

7. Sulzberger (1997) reports that on the U.S. side 20,000 were killed; perhaps this figure includes the deaths of allied soldiers.

required conviction by court-martial before the death penalty could be inflicted, these executions were illegal. A court of inquiry exonerated Mackenzie, however, and later a court-martial acquitted him on a split vote in what today we would call a whitewash. Philip Spencer, who was executed on the *Somers,* was the 17-year-old son of Secretary of War John C. Spencer.

Mutiny is not the only capital shipboard crime. Interestingly, prior to 1861 sodomy was a death crime in the British Royal Navy, although it is not a capital offense today. On February 1, 1861, four crew members on the HMS *Africaine* were hanged for sodomy on the orders of the ship's captain, Edward Rodney. No American sailor or soldier has been executed for sodomy, but many have been court-martialed and dismissed for this behavior, including Lieutenant Gotthold Frederick Enslin, the first soldier dismissed from the U.S. military for homosexuality. He was drummed out of the army on March 11, 1778, at the Grand Parade in Valley Forge, Pennsylvania (Shilts 1993:11).

Shipboard executions of sailors and marines have always involved hanging, as far as I have been able to determine, with one notable exception. In A.D. 1190, King Richard I published an ordinance that spelled out six offenses for which the Crusaders would be punished; two of these carried penalties of death: "Whoever shall slay a man on ship board, he shall be bound to the dead man and thrown into the sea. If he shall slay him on land he shall be bound to the dead man and buried in the earth" (quoted in *Loving v. United States* 1996:761).

Executioners

During and since the Revolutionary War, the executions of American soldiers have been carried out by U.S. military personnel, with two well-documented exceptions. Before the U.S. Army developed its own group of hangmen in World War II's ETO, it relied on the professional skills of England's Home Office official civilian hangmen. Among others, these men included Thomas Pierrepoint and his nephew Albert, who conducted most of the first 17 executions in the ETO (Pierrepoint 1977; Lilly 1996; Lilly and Thomson 1997). Firing squads, although relatively rare, were made up of noncommissioned enlisted men commanded by an officer. Hangmen, by comparison, were usually prison commandants with officer rank in the ETO and other World War II theaters of operation.

Burials

The interments of the 70 soldiers executed in the European Theater of Operations and the combined 26 put to death in the North African Theater of Operations and the Mediterranean Theater of Operations illustrate that ignominious deaths suggest ignominious burials. The 18 American soldiers executed at Shepton Mallet were at first buried in unconsecrated land located "backstage," on the outside perimeter and adjacent to tool sheds and a compost heap in the large Brookwood Cemetery in London. Those executed in France, Algeria, and Italy were also initially buried in graves separated from those who had died honorably (Lilly 1996).

At war's end, the bodies of most of these executed soldiers were exhumed and reinterred in a walled-off, secret section of the World War I Oise-Anise American Cemetery in Fere-en Tadenonis, France. Approximately 5 were sent home to their next of kin. David Cobb was the first U.S. soldier executed in England, and both his mother and his estranged wife requested that his body be returned. It arrived on March 31, 1949, and was reburied in the North Highland Street Cemetery in Dothan, Alabama. The body of executed deserter Eddie Slovik was returned to the United States in 1987. The final places of burial for all of the other executed U.S. soldiers during World War II include the post cemeteries at Clark Air Force Base in Luzon, Philippine Islands (20 soldiers), various post cemeteries within the United States (25 soldiers), and the post cemetery at Schofield Barracks in Hawaii (5 soldiers). In addition, 6 executed soldiers are buried in various private cemeteries within the United States.[8]

A small number of the soldiers who have been buried in cemeteries for World War II's dishonorable troops were not executed, however. Louis E. Garbus was scheduled to be executed in a Brisbane gas chamber on March 5, 1943, for the rape of a 10-year-old girl. Instead, he killed himself by taking cyanide. He is buried at the Schofield Barracks post cemetery in Hawaii. Sergeant Willie Hall and Private E. Lewis were convicted of killing T/5 G. Robinson on January 16, 1944, in Bizerte, Tunisia, and were sentenced to life confinement. Before he could begin his sentence at the U.S. penitentiary in Lewisburg, Pennsylvania, however, Hall died, probably at the NATO U.S. Army Disciplinary Training Center in Casablanca, French Morocco. He is buried in France. Lewis was released from the U.S. penitentiary in Atlanta, Georgia, in December 1952. Joseph J. Mahoney (NATO) was convicted in September 1943 of sodomy against a 13-year-old boy in Palma di Montechiaro, Sicily. He was sentenced to 5 years at the U.S. penitentiary in Lewisburg, but for reasons currently unknown he died and never made the journey to the United States. Mahoney was interred first at El Alia Cemetery in Algiers, and his body was later moved to France.

---

8. Not all of the 18 soldiers executed in England made it to France. The body of the first U.S. soldier executed in the ETO, 21-year-old Private David Cobb, an African American from Dothan, Alabama, was returned home to a city-owned cemetery in 1949. Cobb's mother and his estranged wife requested his body only 10 days after his death. Ted Darcy, senior research analyst for the WFI Research Group, provided me with the information reported here on the final interments of those executed and the civilians buried in U.S. military cemeteries.

How Many

The U.S. Army executed relatively few of its own soldiers in the past century compared with Britain and France. During World War I alone, France executed approximately 600 soldiers, mostly for mutiny and desertion. Some historians think the actual number is greater, because during a retreat of Allied troops in 1914, summary executions occurred on the battlefield, as well as deaths by officers shooting their own men. Britain's military reportedly put 346 of its own to death during World War I (Corns and Hughes-Wilson 2001).[9] Canada, by comparison, executed 23 soldiers during same war, all for desertion. The U.S. Army has carried out at least 459 executions since the last U.S. Navy execution in 1849 (Sullivan 1998). In the 20th century, the U.S. military terminated approximately 160 of its soldiers—none by summary execution (U.S. Department of Justice 1992).

CONCLUSIONS: THE FUTURE?

One of the more striking features of First World Western nations during the past 100 years has been their abandonment of the power to execute citizens. This raises interesting and perplexing questions about the future of intermilitary executions. Put simply, will the armed forces of these nations continue to execute their own members? On the one hand, there is the time-honored argument that the military is a unique institution whose emphasis on efficiency through discipline requires the availability of executions as an essential element of social control, especially during war. However, there is mounting evidence that this logic is less convincing today than it has been in the past.

Military Executions:
Little Used and Ineffective

Because inter- and intramilitary executions are extremely rare, it is difficult for anyone to point to the use of such executions as an efficient tool for maintaining discipline and deterring crime. Of the 266,785 British soldiers convicted of military offenses during World War I, for example, only 2,675 were sentenced to death, and only 276 (10%) were actually executed (Davies 1996:352). During World War II, the U.S. Army sentenced 443 soldiers to death in the European Theater of War, but only 70 (16%) were executed.[10] The United States has not executed a soldier for a military offense in nearly 60 years, and Great Britain has not executed a soldier since before World War II.

Furthermore, there is no empirical evidence that the use of executions makes any difference in the efficiency or effectiveness of fighting armies. As Davies (1996) has pointed out, during World War I the Australians "fought bravely and effectively, despite lower standards of formal discipline and the absence of a deterrent death sentence for those who stepped out of line" (p. 350).

Abandoning Military Executions

Some nations, including Canada (1998) and the United Kingdom (2001), have abandoned military executions. Although at first glance this development may appear to have little if any implication for the U.S. military, as Sullivan and Fidell (2002) note, "no factor is likely to affect U.S. military justice more powerfully during the coming century than internationalization" (p. xxiii). As the United States continues to maintain troops abroad, the U.S. military will increasingly be subject to the human rights norms of its host nations. According to Sullivan and Fidell, "Some European nations have already indicated a reluctance to turn over U.S. servicemembers for trial by death-eligible courts martial" (p. xxiii). The United States will also likely find it increasingly difficult to prevent its peacekeeping soldiers from being called before the new International Criminal Court. At the time of this writing, the Bush administration views the new global court as a threat to national sovereignty, whereas many European critics view U.S. resistance to the court as an indication of opposition to universal human rights law. Whatever the outcome of this issue, it is all but certain that the U.S. military has conducted its last capital court-martial on European soil (Sullivan and Fidell 2002:xxiii).

There is little doubt that the world learned more about military executions during the late 20th and early 21st centuries than at any previous time. The reason for this is that the wars of the 20th century, especially World Wars I and II, are relatively recent, well documented, often controversial, and interesting enough to a number of broad audiences to encourage ongoing amateur and professional research. One important additional contribution to the military execution learning curve in recent years has been the availability of material on the Internet, especially the existence of Web sites devoted to the topics of military executions and civilian capital punishment (see, for example, http://www.shotatdawn.org.uk). (Of course, researchers should approach the material presented on such Web sites with considerable caution; depending on the source, it may be incomplete or misleading.)

Interest in military executions continues to expand, in part because, with the benefit of hindsight and close examination, we can increasingly understand these deaths as an integral part of the great human tragedy—war. As we know so well from recent research on wrongful death

---

9. The number of military executions carried out by the British during World War I is debatable. Corns and Hughes-Wilson (2001) put the number at 346, whereas Davies (1996) reports 276.

10. Of the 443 sentenced to death, 151 (34%) had been convicted of rape and 82 (19%) had been convicted of murder.

convictions in civil society, innocent soldiers undoubtedly have been found guilty of and executed for crimes they did not commit.

REFERENCES

Alotta, Robert I. 1989. *Civil War Justice: Union Army Executions Under Lincoln.* Shippensburg, PA: White Mane.

Babington, Anthony. 1983. *For Sake of Example: Capital Courts-Martial 1914–1920.* New York: St. Martin's.

Bailey, Emmett, Jr. 1986. "The Gentle Rain." Unpublished manuscript.

Batov, Omer. 2002. Review of *Berlin: The Downfall, 1945,* by Anthony Beevor. *Times Literary Supplement,* June 14, p. 28.

Boyle, William E. 1994. "Under the Black Flag: Execution and Retaliation in Mosby's Confederacy." *Military Law Review* 144(Spring):148–64.

Brown, Raymond E. 1994. *The Death of the Messiah: From Gethsemane to the Grave,* vol. 2. New York: Doubleday.

Bryant, Clifton D. 1979. *Khaki-Collar Crime: Deviant Behavior in the Military Context.* New York: Free Press.

Corns, Cathryn and John Hughes-Wilson. 2001. *Blindfold and Alone: British Military Executions in the Great War.* London: Cassells.

Davies, Christie. 1996. "The British State and the Power of Life and Death." Pp. 341–74 in *The Boundaries of the State in Modern Britain,* edited by S. J. D. Green and R. C. Whiting. Cambridge: Cambridge University Press.

Fisher, Thomas J. 1988. "Hanging Scarcely Recalled." *Kansas City Times,* November 11, pp. B1–6.

Green, Vincent. 1995. *Extreme Justice.* New York: Pocket Books.

"Hang American Officer for Assault." 1919. *New York Times,* May 1, p. 18:1.

Haynes, Robert V. 1976. *A Night of Violence: The Huston Riot of 1917.* Baton Rouge: Louisiana State University Press.

Huie, William Bradford. 1954. *The Execution of Private Eddie Slovik.* New York: Duell, Sloan & Pearce.

Jackson, Robert T. 1986. "Death: An Excessive Penalty for Rape of a Child?" *Army Lawyer,* September, p. 37.

Keegan, John. 1976. *The Face of Battle: A Study of Agincourt, Waterloo and the Somme.* New York: Penguin.

Lilly, J. Robert. 1996. "Dirty Details: Executing U.S. Soldiers During World War II." *Crime & Delinquency* 42:491–516.

Lilly, J. Robert and Richard A. Ball. 1982. "A Critical Analysis of the Changing Concept of Criminal Responsibility." *Criminology* 20:169–84.

Lilly, J. Robert and J. Michael Thomson. 1997. "Executing U.S. Soldiers in England, World War II: Command Influence and Sexual Racism." *British Journal of Criminology* 37:262–88.

Loving v. United States, 517 U.S. 748, 1996.

Neumann, Peter. 1958. *The Black Market.* New York: Ballantine.

Pierrepoint, Albert. 1977. *Executioner: Pierrepoint.* London: Coronet.

Putkowski, Julian and Julian Syles. 1989. *Shot at Dawn: Executions in World War One by Authority of the British Army Act.* London: Lee Cooper.

Sajer, Guy. 1972. *The Forgotten Soldier,* translated by Lily Emmet. New York: Ballantine.

Shilts, Randy. 1993. *Conducting Unbecoming: Gays and Lesbians in the U.S. Military.* New York: St. Martin's.

Sullivan, Dwight H. 1998. "Playing the Numbers: Court-Martial Panel Size and the Military Death Penalty." *Military Law Review* 158(December):1-30.

Sullivan, Dwight H. and Eugene R. Fidell. 2002. "Introduction." Pp. xvii-xxvi in *Evolving Military Justice,* edited by Dwight H. Sullivan and Eugene R. Fidell. Annapolis, MD: Naval Institute Press.

Sulzberger, C. L. 1997. *American Heritage New History of World War II,* rev. and updated by Stephen E. Ambrose. New York: Viking.

U.S. v. Private Harvey Stroud. 1943. Trial transcript. NATO [North Africa Theater of Operations] 423. CM [Court Martial] 311647.

U.S. v. Theron W. McGann. 1944. Pp. 277–84 in *Board of Review for the European Theater of Operations,* vol. 12.

U.S. Committee on Public Relations. 1917. "Thirteen Colored Soldiers Are Executed for Participating in Riots at House." *Official U.S. Bulletin,* December 19, p. 4.

U.S. Congress. 1923. Hearings before a special committee on charges of alleged executions without trial in France (67th Congress). Washington, DC: Government Printing Office.

U.S. Department of Justice. 1992. *Capital Punishment.* Washington, DC: Government Printing Office.

U.S. War Department. 1919. *Report of the Judge Advocate General, United States Army,* vol. 1. Washington, DC: Government Printing Office.

Valle, James E. 1980. *Rock and Shoals: Order and Discipline in the Old Navy.* Annapolis, MD: U.S. Naval Institute.

Weigley, Russell. 1981. *Eisenhower's Lieutenants: The German Campaign of France and Germany, 1944-1945.* Bloomington: Indiana University Press.

"Whole Army Division Sees Negroes Hanged: Four Soldiers Faint, While Another Runs Amuck During Execution at Camp Dodge." 1918. *New York Times,* July 6, p. 4, col. 5.

THE ABORTION ISSUE IN THE UNITED STATES

MICHAEL C. KEARL

On his second full day as president of the United States, George W. Bush took swift action to restrict U.S. funds to international family planning groups involved in abortion. He vowed to protect "every person at every stage and season of life," reversing the Clinton administration's policy of providing unrestricted family planning aid. On the same day, Bush also gave the following written statement to marchers observing the anniversary of the U.S. Supreme Court's decision that legalized abortion:

> The promises of our Declaration of Independence are not just for the strong, the independent or the healthy. They are for everyone, including unborn children. We share a great goal, to work toward a day when every child is welcomed in life and protected in law . . . to build a culture of life, affirming that every person at every stage and season of life, is created equal in God's image.

Exactly 28 years earlier, on January 22, 1973, the U.S. Supreme Court launched one of the great social and political battles of our times. In the case of *Roe v. Wade,* the justices declared, in a seven-to-two decision, that women have a constitutional right to abortion and that states do not have the right to regulate abortions, particularly abortions performed during the first trimester.

The issue of abortion has divided Americans as few other moral issues have. Indeed, on the cover of its October 3, 1988, issue, *U.S. News & World Report* referred to the battle over abortion as "America's New Civil War." This issue has produced powerful political coalitions with millions of followers, demonstrations in which hundreds of thousands of marchers have taken part, bombings and burnings of scores of clinics, and even assassinations of abortion providers. Politicians' attitudes toward abortion have become the political litmus test of their moral adequacy, and a number of office seekers have been selected or rejected solely because of their positions on this one issue.

Abortions have been practiced across both time and space. Anthropologist George Devereux (1954) has demonstrated the near universality of abortion in primitive, ancient, and preindustrial societies. Currently, an estimated 50 million abortions occur internationally each year, terminating 22% of all pregnancies and nearly half of all unplanned pregnancies. Three-fourths of the planet's women live in countries where they have access to legal abortions. The American rate of abortion is higher than that in many other parts of the world, particularly European countries. According to a 1999 report published by the Alan Guttmacher Institute, for every 100 pregnancies in the United States there are 25.9 abortions, compared with 62.6 in the Russian Federation, 43.7 in Vietnam, 34 in the Czech Republic, 27.4 in China, 26.4 in Australia, 25.2 in Sweden, 22 in Canada, 17.7 in France, 14.1 in Germany, 13.1 in Israel, 3.1 in Bangladesh, 2.4 in South Africa, and 2.1 in India.

Abortion was widely tolerated during the early years of the American nation. So how did it become such a divisive matter a century and a half later? Why has legalized abortion touched such a vital moral nerve in the United States and not so much in many other developed nations? Are the heated protests seen in the United States actually directed toward abortion per se, or is the issue some symbolic proxy for other underlying conflicts? As I will delineate in this chapter, the history of abortion in the United States involves central moral, religious, and social values as well as dynamics of race and class.

TRENDS IN THE PROCEDURE

One year after induced abortion became legal, a 1974 National Planned Parenthood Association survey found this procedure to be the second most commonly performed surgical procedure (after tonsillectomies) in the United States. By 1980, more than 1.5 million abortions were being performed annually in this country, representing the termination of nearly one-third of all pregnancies. By century's end, the total number of abortions in the United States since legalization had exceeded 34 million, more than the entire population of California. The Alan Guttmacher Institute (2000) has estimated that more than 4 in 10 American women will have abortions during their lifetimes.

The numbers of abortions peaked at 1.61 million in 1990 and declined throughout the 1990s to 1.33 million in 1997. The abortion rate (number of abortions per 100 women ages 15 to 44) dropped from a high of 29.3 in 1980 to 20 in 1995. These declines were due in part to increased contraceptive use, especially among teenagers, and in part to decreases in the numbers of service providers, which declined between 1992 and 1996 from 2,380 to 2,042 facilities (Henshaw 1998).

One reason for the high rate of abortions in the United States is the fact that American women have among the highest rates of unplanned pregnancies of all industrialized countries. According to the Alan Guttmacher Institute (1999), nearly one-half of all pregnancies in the United States are unplanned (and one-half of these are terminated by abortion), compared with 31.8% in Great Britain and 17% in the Netherlands. Interestingly, the nation with the most liberal abortion laws, the Netherlands, has the third-lowest abortion rate.

HISTORICAL EVOLUTION OF THE AMERICAN DEBATE

Abortions were being performed in North America long before the founding of the United States. Before 1840, according to the research of James C. Mohr (1978), the practice was largely tolerated if performed before "quickening" (fetal movement, which typically begins around the 20th week of pregnancy). Most abortions were performed on the unmarried and desperate of the "poor and unfortunate classes," but the practice gradually expanded to include upper- and middle-class, white, native-born Protestants (p. 11).

Although the first laws against abortion appeared during the 1820s, it was only in the mid-19th century that the practice became generally outlawed—largely at the behest of the medical profession (Shenkman 1988). Moral crusaders against abortion, many of them physicians, first appeared during the 1850s; their efforts influenced some state legislatures to criminalize the procedure during the first decade following the Civil War. Mohr (1978) argues that the physicians who participated in this anti-abortion movement were motivated less by moral concerns than by their own elitist fears of a drop in the birthrate among of society's "better" classes (at a time when approximately one in five pregnancies was deliberately aborted, according to an estimate made by a committee of the American Medical Association in 1871) and by their desire to enhance their own professional recognition and monopolize the provision of health care. "Given the primitive nature of medical practice" at the time, Kristin Luker (1984) notes, "persuading the public that embryos were human lives and then persuading state legislatures to protect these lives by outlawing abortion may have been one of the few life-saving projects actually available to physicians" (p. 31).

Concurrently affecting the issue during this period was the institutionalization of Victorian attitudes toward sexuality. The Comstock Law, passed in 1873, officially criminalized birth control devices, the distribution of information on birth control and sexuality, and abortion. Within two decades, state laws appeared raising the age of consent. California, one of the first states to enact such statutes, increased the age from 10 to 14 in 1889, from 14 to 16 in 1897, and from 16 to 18 in 1913. Tennessee went the furthest, making it a felony for anyone to have sex with any woman under age 21 (Dolhenty 1998).

When the 20th century began, all states had laws outlawing abortion (Insel and Roth 2000). Public opinion on the procedure, which had largely been indifferent, had shifted to firm opposition toward this illegal act, which was also deemed immoral. The objectivity of women on the matter was questioned as the issue became framed in terms of the rights of women against those of embryos (Luker 1984:40). On the other hand, a countercurrent was developing, championed by Margaret Sanger and her reproductive freedom movement, as women discovered empowerment with the suffragist movement. Believing in the public's right to be informed about birth control, Sanger opened the nation's first birth control clinic in 1916 and 5 years later founded the American Birth Control League, the predecessor of Planned Parenthood. Sanger's ideas, however, were to be tarnished by perceptions that Sanger was a supporter of eugenics and a racist. This linking of contraception and abortion has evolved into two dialectical extremes in which both are seen either as aspects of personal liberty or as the eugenic means for lowering the populations of society's "lesser persons."

With the sexual revolution in the 1920s, according to Leslie Reagan (1998), 15,000 American women were dying each year from illegal abortions. Abortion remained a common medical practice until 1940, when states began enforcing the laws more vigorously—producing the "back alley" abortions that led to *Roe*. In 1971, a year after abortions were decriminalized in New York, the state's maternal mortality rate dropped 45% (Pollitt 1997).

Beginning in the late 1960s, the United States experienced unprecedented increases in female participation in the labor force and a corresponding growth in feminist awareness. With the spread of contraceptives, women realized new control over their reproductive capacities, freedom from being shackled by unwanted pregnancies. In 1967, Colorado passed the first law legalizing abortion, permitting it in cases in which carrying a pregnancy to term would cause serious impairment to the mother's physical or mental health, in cases of severe fetal defects, and in situations where the pregnancy was the result of rape or incest. It was in this context in 1973 that the U.S. Supreme Court made two decisions that struck down the anti-abortion statutes then in force in Texas and Georgia. In *Roe v. Wade,* the Court deemed an unborn child not to be a person within the meaning and protection of the term *person* as stated in the 14th Amendment. Basing its ruling on a woman's right to privacy, the Court said that a decision to have an abortion during the first 3 months of pregnancy must be left to the woman and her doctor. In *Doe v. Bolton,* the Court struck down restrictions on the kinds of facilities where abortions can be performed, saying that the procedure cannot legitimately be confined to hospital settings.

THE POST–*ROE V. WADE* ERA

The legalization of abortion triggered a number of questions: Should any restrictions on abortion be decided by legislators or by judges? Can states require a minor to obtain parental consent before an abortion? Can states require that a woman take a 24-hour "cooling-off" period before having an abortion? Can the government direct physicians to warn women of the risks and consequences of abortion? Must women having abortions in their second trimester of pregnancy be required to undergo the procedure in a hospital (Gest 1982)?

The debate surrounding abortion spawned powerful social movements over the final quarter of the 20th century. Hundreds of thousands of abortion supporters and opponents marched in many demonstrations. In 1992, for instance, an estimated one-half million individuals marched from the White House to the Capitol Mall in demonstration of their support for abortion rights and against a restrictive Pennsylvania law requiring, among other things, that any woman seeking an abortion observe a 24-hour waiting period and that a married woman seeking an abortion inform her husband of her intent. National organizations emerged and cultivated grassroots connections throughout the country. Fueled in dialectical opposition were such key players as Planned Parenthood and the National Abortion Federation (a consortium of abortion providers) on one side and the National Right to Life Committee (which claimed at century's end to have 3.5 million supporters, 400,000 donors, and 3,000 chapters) on the other ("Pro-Life Resources" 2000).

Ironically, a century after physicians gave anti-abortion laws their support, medical groups were opposing laws intended to curb abortion. In 1982, the American Medical Association, the American College of Obstetricians and Gynecologists, the Nurses Association of the American College of Obstetricians and Gynecologists, and the American Academy of Pediatrics urged the U.S. Supreme Court to declare unconstitutional an Akron, Ohio, city ordinance that required hospital abortions for women past their third month of pregnancy, forbade abortions for those

under the age of 15 without parental consent, and required physicians to read to their patients an account of the procedure's dangers. These organizations argued that such measures "interfere significantly with a woman's ability to exercise her constitutional right to decide whether or not to terminate her pregnancy" (quoted in Greenhouse 1982:1). The moral relativity of scientific medicine once again came to clash with the moral certainty of religion.

BATTLES FOR THE MORAL HIGH GROUND

The essence of power is persuasion, and the key to understanding this is to grasp how particular perspectives on life, or frames, are imposed on people's consciousnesses. Set the frame, and one sets the gestalt by which individuals make sense of their existence. Frames structure experience and give it meaning; they thereby guide social action (Goffman 1974).

The variability of the frames through which abortion is viewed is in part a result of Americans' deep ambivalence about the matter. As Roger Rosenblatt (1992) has noted, as of 1990, polls revealed that 73% of Americans favored abortion rights, yet 77% regarded abortion as "some form of murder"—in other words, many people live with the dissonance of supporting the legality of what they see as an immoral act. Add to this moral equation Cold War concerns over regime righteousness and reports in the late 1980s that in the godless Soviet state there were an estimated 2.08 abortions for every child born as opposed to 0.4 abortions for every American child born, and that in the Soviet Union an 8-minute abortion was available for 5 rubles ($7.50) whereas in the United States the average abortion cost $213 ("Life Beyond the Kremlin" 1988).

Also permitting various interpretations of abortion are such underlying issues as women's place in contemporary society, attitudes toward sexuality, the selfishness of excessive individualism, and the nature of social support for mothers and children in a society of increasing illegitimacy (at the beginning of the 21st century, roughly one-third of the nation's children were born out of wedlock—a proportion 2.5 times that of two decades earlier) and high rates of divorce that produce millions of impoverished, unloved, and undersocialized youth. Some saw the U.S. Food and Drug Administration's approval of the so-called morning-after abortion pill, mifepristone or RU-486, in 2000 as yet another example of the no-fault, me-first, pill-taking ethos of modern consumer society.

These frames have shaped the language of the debate on abortion and the very labels the competing groups apply to themselves, triggering deep-seated feelings. Following the shootings of two Brooklyn, Massachusetts, abortion clinic receptionists in late 1993, for instance, a Planned Parenthood blamed the murders on pro-life rhetoric in a newspaper ad with the headline "Words Kill."

In an informal exploration of when the group labels attached to the opposing sides in the abortion debate first entered American parlance, I found the term *pro-life* first appearing in the *New York Times* on November 28, 1972, and the term *pro-choice* first appearing in the *Washington Post* on June 28, 1977. It is unclear whether these labels were classifications made by journalists before they were employed as self-referents by these groups.

Abortion is, by definition, "feticide." As Naomi Wolf (1995) notes in developing her argument that the pro-choice movement needs to frame its defense of abortion rights morally, "The death of a fetus is a real death" (p. 26). Is abortion "homicide" or simply a "reproductive health procedure"? Consider the bias of the term *unborn child.* Karen W. Kramer (1990) points out that the terminology of the abortion debate became polarized over the 20-year period of her study. Her content analysis of articles on abortion shows that the proportions of references to "unborn child," "unborn infant," and "unborn baby" in sources associated with the pro-life movement increased during this period. Similarly, references to "fetus," "embryo," and "egg" increased in sources associated with the pro-choice movement during the period.

From these framings and attributions, some extreme analogies have emerged. Some observers have likened abortion to the Holocaust. One commentator has written that the "denial of abortion is like forcing a person to spend nine months intravenously hooked up to a medically endangered stranger who happens to be a famous violinist" (Pollitt 1997:112). Seeking legitimacy, pro-choice advocates have cited evidence of biblical approval of abortion (for examples, see Brian McKinley's "Why Abortion is Biblical" Web site at http://elroy.net/her/abortion.html). Pro-life proponents have countered with quotations from early, well-known feminists who abhorred the practice. For instance, the Women and Children First organization's Web site devoted to *Roe v. Wade* (http://roevwade.org) quotes Susan B. Anthony referring to abortion as "child-murder" and Simone de Beauvoir's claim that "the woman who has recourse to abortion disowns feminist values." In a blow to the pro-choice movement, Norma McCorvey, aka "Jane Roe," gained a great deal of publicity when she defected from the movement in 1995 to become a born-again Christian and anti-abortion spokeswoman.

The Shifting Battle Lines

Like players in a game of chess, both sides in the abortion debate have strategically employed wide-ranging ethical issues to legitimate their moral positions and to neutralize the claims of the other. Over time, both sides have expanded their focus to proclaim abortion's effects on the moral order of the broader culture. Anti-abortionists have developed slippery-slope theses, arguing that the availability of legal abortion increases sexual permissiveness and godlessness and diminishes respect for human life. By contrast, pro-choice proponents have asserted that abortion restrictions are patriarchal tools of oppression.

The issue has expanded into debates concerning sex education, sexual abstinence, birth control, and even AIDS. It has also produced violence and death. According to the National Abortion Federation, between 1977 and 1998 there were more than 1,700 attacks against abortion providers in the United States and at least 6 fatal shootings. Following the first murder of an abortion provider in 1993, the Reverend David Trosch, a Catholic priest in Mobile, Alabama, and founder of Life Enterprises Unlimited, was one of the signers of a declaration that labeled the death a "justifiable homicide." After the terrorist attacks on the World Trade Center and the Pentagon on September 11, 2001, and the subsequent anthrax deaths, hundreds of abortion clinics throughout the country received letters and packages containing threats and powdery substances. Most of the letters were signed by the Army of God and warned that the recipients would soon experience anthrax symptoms: "You have chosen a profession, which profits from the senseless murder of million of innocent children each year. We are going to kill you. This is your notice. Stop now or die" (quoted in Lewin 2001).

Fetal Rights: When Does Personhood Begin?

At what point of fetal development does the human organism become a "person," a social member in full standing? The Catholic Church teaches that "ensoulment" occurs at the moment of conception. Until a few centuries ago in the West, personhood was often not conferred until a child had survived to the age of several years. Rates of infant mortality were so high that it was not unusual for families to postpone the naming of small children, and infants' deaths did not merit funerary attention.

Owing to recent medical advances and insight, however, citizenship rights have been extended to the womb. For example, a death certificate must be completed for a fetus if death occurs within the third trimester of pregnancy. In a 1994 case, a man who caused a woman to miscarry her 2-month-old fetus—which was incapable of surviving outside her womb and was of a legally abortable age—was convicted of murder. The California Supreme Court upheld the conviction in a six-to-one decision. Writing for the majority, Chief Justice Malcolm Lucas stated, "The third-party killing of a fetus with malice aforethought is murder . . . as long as the state can show that the fetus has progressed beyond the embryonic stage of seven to eight weeks" (*People v. Davis* 1994:815). In contrast, the Minnesota Supreme Court ruled in a 1985 case involving the death of an 8½-month-old fetus in an auto accident that the man accused in the accident could not be charged with the death, reasoning that it was not a human being who had died, as the victim had not yet been born.

There have also been cases in which matters of fetal rights have been, from the pro-choice perspective, employed to curtail women's rights. Women, for instance, have been charged with contributing to their infants' deaths or with causing fetal injury through drug abuse. A Massachusetts judge had a pregnant woman taken into state custody through an order of protection on behalf of the fetus she carried. Until the practice was halted by the U.S. Supreme Court's *Ferguson v. City of Charleston* decision, the Medical University of South Carolina was testing pregnant women for drug use and, in violation of the Fourth Amendment, was turning over positive results to the police.

During the late 1990s, pro-life forces shifted the focus of abortion politics to late-term abortions. Medically referred to as *dilation and extraction,* this procedure involves inducing a partial breech delivery, cutting the fetus's skull, and then suctioning its contents. Anti-abortionists labeled this late-second- and third-trimester procedure *partial-birth abortion* and successfully created divisions within the ranks of abortion proponents by disseminating gruesome descriptions. However, they rarely mentioned the extreme rarity of the procedure (less than 1% of all abortions take place after the 21st week of pregnancy) and the fact that it is usually performed on fetuses known to have serious fatal birth defects (Blank 2001). In the 2000 case of *Stenberg v. Carhart,* the U.S. Supreme Court, by a vote of five to four, overturned a Nebraska law making the procedure illegal.

In early 2002, President Bush declared that embryos and developing fetuses qualify for a government health care program. He asserted that this stance had nothing to do with the abortion issue—rather, he framed it as a strategy to accelerate low-income women's eligibility for subsidized prenatal care by qualifying them from the moment of conception—but it nevertheless amounted to federal recognition that life begins at the moment of conception.

The Death of the Unborn to Save the Unborn

One way of checkmating an absolutist opponent is to place him or her in a no-win moral predicament. Concurrent with the heating up of the abortion debate has been an increase in the use of fertility drugs and the implanting of multiple embryos following in vitro fertilization, producing a rise in the numbers of multiple births. In some instances, women have become pregnant with more fetuses than they could safely carry—in one case octuplets. Given the pro-life focus on the rights of the fetus, what are the rights of the fetuses in such cases, if all are doomed unless their numbers are reduced through selective abortion?

The Biological and Psychological Damage Wrought to Aborting Females

To counter pro-choice attempts to frame the abortion controversy in terms of women's rights, the pro-life movement has given publicity to studies purporting that women who elect abortions are subject to various harms. Stories have been disseminated that focus on lifelong guilt and on

assertions that "post-abortion syndrome" is an emerging public health issue (Speckhard and Rue 1992). Pro-life interests have also asserted that studies have found that the damage caused by abortion is biological as well as psychological, as illustrated by findings indicating that women who have had induced abortions have a 30% higher risk of breast cancer than do women who have not had abortions (Brind et al. 1996).

On the other side of the debate, psychiatrist Paul Dagg (1991) has reported that more than one-third of the women in his study sample who were denied abortions and kept their babies (as most did) admitted to years of feeling strong resentment and anger toward their unwanted children. The children, in turn, were more likely than their wanted counterparts to drop out of school, commit crime, and suffer depression.

The Right Not to Be Born

Countering the anti-abortionists' focus on fetal rights, liberal newspapers gave significant coverage in 2001 to a decision made by France's highest appeals court that an individual born with a severe handicap is entitled to compensation if the mother was not given the opportunity to have an abortion—even if that would have meant the plaintiff's nonexistence. The case involved a woman who contracted German measles while pregnant and whose disease was not diagnosed. Eighteen years later, her child was deaf, nearly blind, and mentally retarded. To some observers, the court's granting of the award implied that the boy was worse-off alive than if he had never been born.

The Death of the Unborn to Extend the Lives of the Living

One of the first acts of the Clinton administration in 1993 was to abolish the Bush-administration's 5-year ban on federal financing of research using transplanted fetal tissue. Experiments using transplanted fetal tissue had shown promise for patients with Parkinson's disease, diabetes, thalassemia, severe combined immunodeficiency disease, and other ailments (Watanabe 1993). A panel of ethical, medical, and legal experts convened in 1987 by Case Western Reserve University's School of Medicine endorsed the transplantation of brain tissue from aborted fetuses to aid those suffering from such maladies. A year later, the morality of such procedures was deemed acceptable by an advisory committee of the National Institutes of Health. Anti-abortion groups, however, argued that such activity might encourage abortion.

In the late 1990s, debate shifted to the medical use of stem cells harvested from aborted fetuses and leftover embryos in fertility clinics. Human stem cells are yet-to-be specialized cells that hold the promise of being programmed to produce particular body parts, such as new hearts, lungs, and brain cells. With the hope of curing such maladies as Alzheimer's, Parkinson's, and leukemia, excitement over the research was considerable in the scientific community. Although stem cells are found in adult tissue, it was initially believed that the potential of such cells in adults was too specialized, unlike the all-purpose cells found in fetal tissue. Unfortunately, using this resource required the destruction of the fetus, which alarmed various pro-life groups, particularly the Vatican.

LONGITUDINAL ANALYSES OF AMERICANS' ABORTION ATTITUDES AND THE SOCIAL AND CULTURAL FACTORS UNDERLYING THE DEBATE

Given the aforementioned arguments, it should come as no surprise that Americans are almost evenly split in their attitudes toward legal abortion. In 2002, a Gallup poll found that 48% of Americans were "satisfied" with abortion policies in the United States, and 43% were dissatisfied. When asked if these policies should remain the same or be changed, 39% stated that they favored preserving the status quo, 39% favored making policies stricter, and 19% favored making policies less strict (Saad 2002). According to the combined 1972–2000 data from the General Social Surveys (GSS) conducted by the National Opinion Research Center (Davis and Smith 2000), support for the right of women to have a legal abortion "for whatever reason" (the least supported of the seven abortion questions asked in the GSS) peaked in 1994 at 45% and has consistently declined thereafter, to 38% in 2000. Cohort effects are not as great as one might expect, with virtually no difference in attitudes toward abortion among those born after 1940 and only a difference of

10 percentage points in support between those born after 1940 and those born during the 1920s and 1930s. The only cohorts that have significantly changed their position toward abortion as they have aged are those born during the 1950s and 1960s, and their attitudes have shifted in the liberal direction—more so for males than for females.

Figure 1 illustrates the remarkable consistency over time in Americans' attitudes toward abortion under varying conditions. Despite the fact that attitudes in 2000 were not that different from attitudes in 1972, there have been some fascinating shifts in how the abortion issue has resided in Americans' minds.

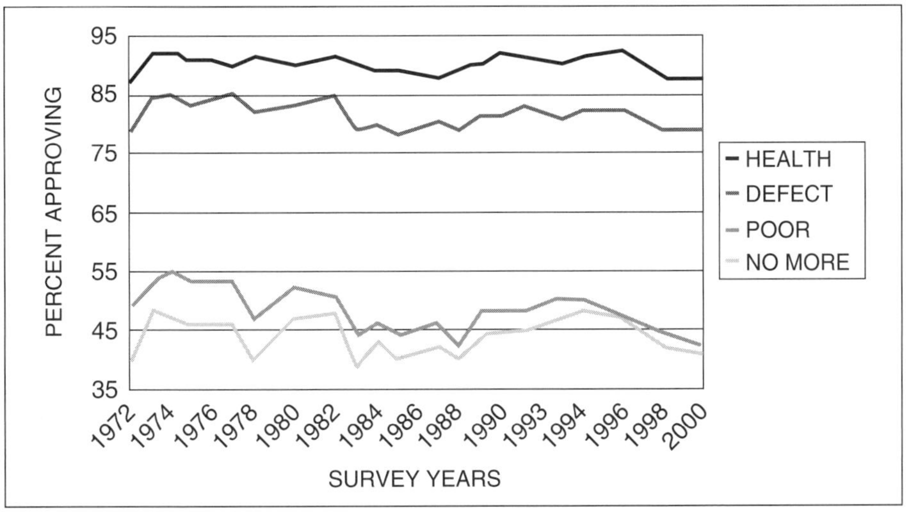

The Swinging Political Pendulum

With Ronald Reagan's election to the presidency, the pro-life movement allied itself firmly with the Republican Party, thereby knitting the religious right into the fabric of the GOP (Gailey 1986a). Not about to alienate this new constituency, the Reagan administration made it clear on numerous occasions that it intended to encourage the U.S. Supreme Court to review and overthrow the 1973 decision in *Roe v. Wade*. In opposing abortion, President Reagan initially referred to the procedure as "taking the life of a living human being"; later, he called it "murder" (Gailey 1986b).

Reagan's pro-life ideology also extended to the rights of severely deformed infants. In 1983, the president initiated a regulation with a directive to the attorney general and the secretary of Health and Human Resources that required all hospitals receiving federal funds to post the following notice: "Discriminatory failure to feed and care for handicapped infants in this facility is prohibited by Federal law." In addition, the notice stated that anyone having knowledge of the denial of "customary medical care" to handicapped infants should call the federal government, and a toll-free telephone number was provided for that purpose (Pear 1983). The following year, however, the administration had to back down from its attempt to force hospitals to maintain the lives of seriously deformed infants. Following the Reagan presidency, the abortion issue contributed to the greatest voting "gender gap" since 1920, as women defected from the Republican Party. A key plank in the 1988 Republican Party platform left no doubt about the party's position on abortion:

Figure 1 Percentages of Americans Approving of Legal Abortions (if mother's health at risk; if strong chance of serious birth defect; if family is poor and cannot afford more kids; if mother married and wants no more children)

SOURCE: Data from Davis and Smith (2000).

The unborn child has a fundamental individual right to life which cannot be infringed. We therefore reaffirm our support for a human life amendment to the Constitution, and we endorse legislation to make clear that the 14th Amendment's protections apply to unborn children . . . [a]nd we reaffirm our support for the appointment of judges at all levels of the judiciary who respect traditional family values and the sanctity of innocent human life.

To keep up the momentum gathered by the Reagan administration, President George H. Bush proclaimed January 20, 1991, National Sanctity of Human Life Day. However, with the Democrats' return to the White House 2 years later, much of the pro-life agenda underwent dismantling. Within months of President Clinton's taking office, federal employees were able to obtain abortions and have them paid for by their health insurance for the first time in a decade.

Figure 2 illustrates how individuals' views on abortion have over time become fused with party identification, as Democrats increasingly favor the right of women to have abortions on demand and Republicans have changed their position very little. During the 1977–83 period, strong Republicans were more likely to favor a woman's right to an abortion "for whatever reason" than were strong Democrats. By the 1984–88 period, the two groups were indistinguishable in their level of support for abortion rights. However, in the 1994–98 period, only 30% of strong Republicans answered the question "Do you think a woman should have the right to a legal abortion if she wants it for any reason?" in the affirmative, compared with nearly one-half of strong Democrats. Strong party identification came to require loyalty to the abortion stance of one's party—hence the longitudinal growth in support among strong Democrats and in opposition among strong Republicans. An unbridgeable chasm opened on the political landscape as Americans' moral ambivalence toward abortion became polarized by party.

Religion's Influence on Public Sentiment

As I have noted above, Americans' religiosity also fueled the explosiveness of the debate. In 1985, Dr. Russell Nelson, a member of the Council of the Twelve, the governing body of the Church of Jesus Christ of Latter-day Saints, stated regarding abortion that the loss of life from "the evils of war" was "dwarfed by the war on the defenseless" ("Mormon Leader" 1985). Bishop John J. O'Connor of Scranton, Pennsylvania, said in a 1984 television interview: "I always compare the killing of 4,000 babies a day in the United States, unborn babies, to the Holocaust. Now Hitler tried to solve a problem, the Jewish question. So kill them, shove them in the ovens, burn them. Well, we claim that unborn babies are a problem, so kill them. To me, it really is precisely the same" (quoted in Goldman 1984).

The more conservative the faith, the stronger the opposition to abortion. According to the combined 1998 and 2000 General Social Surveys, the proportions of persons favoring a woman's right to a legal abortion "for whatever reason" by religious group ranged from 28% of fundamentalist Protestants and 34% of Catholics to 43% of moderate and liberal Protestants and 76% of Jews. Interestingly, over the 23-year period that the GSS has included this abortion question, the greatest shift in attitudes has been found among those with no religious affiliation, whose support has declined by 10 percentage points.

The divisiveness of the abortion question is illustrated by the splits that exist even among those sharing the same religious faith. Within all religious groups but the moderate Protestant denominations and Jews, profound differences in responses to this question have been found between those who are strongly religious and those who are not strongly religious: 19% versus 35% favoring among fundamentalist Protestants, 20% versus 42% among Catholics, and 35% versus 50% among liberal Protestants.

Survey data consistently show that those who are better paid and better educated are more likely to favor abortion. Returning to the combined 1998 and 2000 General Social Surveys, for instance, we find that 51% of those with 4 or more years

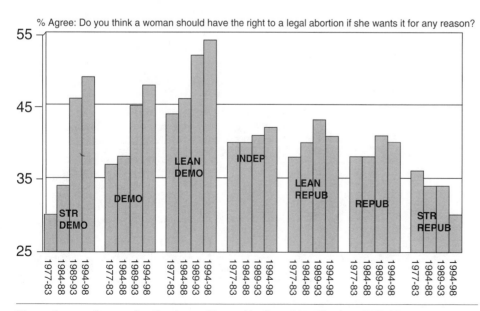

% Agree: Do you think a woman should have the right to a legal abortion if she wants it for any reason?

Figure 2   Support for Abortion on Demand by Party Identification, 1977–98

SOURCE: Data from Davis and Smith (2000).

of college education favored a woman's right to an abortion "for whatever reason," compared with only 29% of high school dropouts. Support also increases with income, from 35% among those making less than $10,000 a year to 54% among those making $90,000 or more. However, the more conservative individuals' religious faith, the less impact such liberalizing factors have.

The Controversy's Connections to the Feminist Movement and Matters of Sex

The abortion debate is thoroughly interwoven with the much broader issue of women's position in society and the exercise of power over women's reproductive lives. It is not coincidental that the abortion controversy heated up around the same time the ERA movement gained momentum in the 1970s. According to one feminist perspective, constraints on abortion rights are the newest mechanism by which patriarchal society controls women. Members of the pro-life movement, attempting to maintain their framing of the debate in terms of fetal rights, have countered with the argument that abortion actually reinforces patriarchy. For example, the Women and Children First organization (see the Web site at http://roevwade.org) asserts the following:

- Abortion promotes patriarchy, as its legal status was handed down by nine old men, abortion facilities are owned and operated primarily by men, abortionists are primarily men, and the people making millions of dollars from abortion each and every year—by exploiting women—are men.

- Abortion supports patriarchy because of sex-selection abortions. Abortion allows women (or forceful men) to choose to abort children on the basis of sex (i.e., unwanted females). In India, for instance, out of 8,000 abortions, 7,999 were female.

When one examines the relationship between Americans' attitudes toward abortion and the statement "women should take care of running their homes and leave running the country up to men" (using the combined 1977–98 GSS), one finds that those who disagree that a woman's place is at home are roughly twice as likely to endorse the right of a woman to have an abortion for whatever reason (variable ABANY) as are those who agree that home is the woman's place (Davis and Smith 2000). When Americans were asked about the accessibility of information on birth control ("In some places in the U.S., it is not legal to supply birth control information. How do you feel about this—do you think birth control information should be available to anyone who wants it, or not?"), of those who said such information should be available, 40% approved of ABANY, as opposed to only 11% of those who said such information should not be available.

Again looking at the GSS 1977–98, those favoring sex education in the public schools were 2.5 times more likely to approve of ABANY than those opposing such education. Similarly, when asked if methods of birth control should be available to teenagers between the ages of 14 and 16, 60% of those who strongly agreed approved of ABANY, as opposed to 23% of those who strongly disagreed.

The Abortion Conflict as Another Facet of the Battle Between the Haves and the Have-Nots

Before *Roe v. Wade,* social class largely determined the quality of the abortion experience. Women who were well connected had relatively easy access to safe, clean procedures, whereas women from the lower classes who sought abortions were forced to rely on providers whose methods were less medically safe, and they were thus more likely to be maimed or to die as a result. Three decades after abortion's legalization, poor women were three times more likely to have abortions than those financially better-off (National Abortion Federation 1990). Ironically, according to a survey Richard Wirthlin conducted for *Reader's Digest* in 1992, opposition to federal funding of abortions increases as individuals' position in the social hierarchy decreases. In Wirthlin's survey, those respondents making more than $60,000 annually favored federal funding of abortions by a 57-41 margin; those making less than $15,000 opposed it by a margin of 63-27 (cited in Gergen 1993).

This relationship between social class and support for abortion is evident in the data displayed in Table 1. The higher Americans' social class identifications, the more likely they are to support abortion on demand. However, class differences have contracted significantly over time, more so for men than for women, as support for abortion rights has dramatically increased among those of the lower class and waned among those identifying with the upper class.

On the surface, such patterns of class support might suggest that those at the top of the social hierarchy support abortion rights because they hope to check the proliferation of minorities and the poor, whereas those at the bottom fear that these "rights" are, in actuality, a mechanism for diminishing their likelihood of reproducing. But if this were an accurate portrayal of the unspoken reasoning of the upper classes, wouldn't the Republic Party endorse abortion rights? And what of the tensions between feminists and minorities within the Democratic Party?

It is not hard to understand why some members of minority groups harbor suspicions that abortion represents racial genocide. Indeed, by the late 1980s, 70% of Planned Parenthood clinics, the nation's largest chain of abortion facilities, were concentrated in black and Hispanic neighborhoods (Keath 1989). There also remain memories of the founder of Planned Parenthood, Margaret Sanger, who in her book *The Pivot of Civilization* (1922) warned against free maternity care for the poor and "dysgenic" races, those "stocks that are most detrimental to the future of the race and the world" (pp. 116–17). Black women are more

Table 1   Percentages Agreeing Women Should Have the Right to a Legal Abortion If Wanted "for Any Reason" by Year, Social Class, and Sex

	Sex	Lower Class	Working Class	Middle Class	Upper Class	Total
1977–80	M	28	33	42	68	37
	F	27	34	40	49	
1982–85	M	33	36	42	53	38
	F	22	35	41	43	
1986–89	M	35	35	47	67	39
	F	25	35	40	41	
1990–94	M	46	40	51	50	45
	F	33	42	47	57	
1996–2000	M	46	36	47	50	42
	F	39	39	45	48	
Latest-earliest	M	+18.2	+2.4	+4.6	−17.7	+4.7
difference	F	+12.4	+4.8	+5.1	−1.4	

SOURCE: Data from Davis and Smith (2000).

than three times as likely as white women to have abortions, and Hispanic women have roughly twice as many abortions as white women. Whereas about 16% of pregnancies among non-Hispanic white women end in abortion, the proportion for Hispanic women is 22% and that for non-Hispanic black women is 38% (Ventura et al. 2000:11). The General Social Surveys, however, reveal that although there were significant racial differences in attitudes toward abortion in the early 1980s—with blacks, particularly black males, most opposed—by century's end the differences had become insignificant.

In a curious turn of events, the beginning of the 21st century saw the publication of an academic thesis that has drawn condemnation from both sides of the abortion controversy. In 2001, John Donahue and Steven Levitt reported a causal connection between crime and abortion rates in an article in Harvard University's *Quarterly Journal of Economics*. Arguing that crime is largely the product of the unwanted children brought into the world by young, poor, undereducated, and unmarried females, Donahue and Levitt demonstrated statistically how state abortion rates are correlated with crime rates 15 to 18 years later. They note, "According to our estimates, legalized abortion may account for as much as one-half of the overall crime reduction . . . [suggesting] that the social benefit to reduced crime as a result of abortion may be on the order of $30 billion annually" (p. 414).

CONCLUSION: ABORTION AS A CORE COMPONENT OF AN EMERGING AMERICAN DEATH IDEOLOGY

As the above discussion has shown, over the final quarter of the 20th century, although Americans' attitudes toward

abortion changed little overall, there were shifts in the compositions of the so-called pro-life and pro-choice movements. Positions on the issue of abortion became increasingly melded with political party identification, whereas class and racial differences contracted to near insignificance. Religious faith and religiosity were, and remain, the most potent predictors of opposition to abortion in the United States. Interestingly, over this period, attitudes toward abortion became increasingly fused in Americans' minds with two other death-related moralities: those surrounding euthanasia and the right of the terminally ill to end their lives.

In the early 1980s, my colleague Richard Harris and I demonstrated the existence of an American death ideology and demonstrated the robust correlations of a scale measuring that ideology with a wide assortment of measures of contemporary individualism (Kearl and Harris 1981–82). We found, contrary to Granberg's (1978) claims, that antiabortionism does not entail an underlying consistent ideology and that those scoring on the most permissive end of this scale—specifically, those who endorsed euthanasia, the moral right of the terminally ill to commit suicide, and abortion—were most likely to condone homosexual lifestyles, to favor the legalization of marijuana, to consider it acceptable for a man and woman to have sexual relations before marriage, to disagree that a woman's place is in the home, to not believe in life after death, and to be divorced. We took this as empirical support for the key proposition of thanatological determinists (e.g., Becker 1973; Bauman 1992) that an individual's orientation toward matters of death lies at the very core of his or her entire moral framework.

Let's examine the status of this ideology over the 20 years since its detection. Specifically, to be considered are longitudinal trends in Americans' responses to the following three questions posed by the General Social Surveys (Davis and Smith 2000):

- Do *you* think it should be possible for a woman to obtain a *legal* abortion if the woman wants it for any reason? (variable ABANY; % yes 1977 = 36.6, 2000 = 38.0)

- Do you think a person has the right to end his or her own life if this person has an incurable disease? (SUICIDE1; % yes 1977 = 37.9, 2000 = 54.8)

- When a person has a disease that cannot be cured, do you think doctors should be allowed by law to end the patient's life by some painless means if the patient and his family request it? (LETDIE1; % yes 1977 = 59.7, 2000 = 64.4)

These three variables, listed in decreasing degree of difficulty to agree, form a Guttman scale: one first agrees with euthanasia, next with the right of the terminally ill to commit suicide, and finally with abortion. As the data displayed in Table 2 show, whereas in the 1977–80 period 22.8% of Americans agreed with euthanasia, suicide, and abortion, by the 1996–2000 period 34.3% agreed with all items—in other words, there was a 50% increase. The figures in the bottom row of the table show that this death ideology (e.g., if one disagrees with abortion then one disagrees with suicide and euthanasia, or if one disagrees with euthanasia then one also disagrees with suicide and abortion) has generally increased in consistency over time.

The data in Table 3 illustrate how this death ideology has polarized those at both ends of the political spectrum. Whereas in the 1977–80 period 33% of liberals and 19% of conservatives approved of all three death items, for a difference of 14.8 percentage points, by century's end this difference had nearly doubled. In addition, within each category of political ideology, the differences between the sexes increase the further to the right one goes. Among liberals, the sex difference in disagreeing with all three items is about 1.4%, increasing to 9.0% for moderates and to 14.2% among conservatives. Among conservatives, this sex difference peaked in the late 1980s. It is because of the fusing of moral beliefs toward abortion, euthanasia, and suicide among the terminally ill that President George W. Bush's decision on stem cell research became one of the defining events of the first year of his presidency—there was no middle ground, so thoroughly polarized had Americans' moral calculus become.

Table 2 Consistent Agreement-Disagreement With Elements of the American Death Ideology Over Time

	1977–80	1982–86	1987–90	1991–94	1996–2000
ABANY-LETDIE1: % yes-yes, % no-no	25.8, 32.5	28.9, 30.6	31.4, 27.4	36.0, 27.2	33.4, 27.0
ABANY-SUICIDE1: % yes-yes, % no-no	21.1, 48.3	24.8, 43.2	26.8, 39.9	33.9, 33.7	31.5, 33.7
LETDIE1-SUICIDE1: % yes-yes, % no-no	32.2, 35.2	40.7, 30.9	45.5, 28.1	53.5, 26.9	52.5, 26.9
%AGREE ALL, %DISAGREE ALL	22.8, 36.2	26.9, 32.7	29.5, 29.3	36.8, 27.8	34.3, 27.3
Guttman Scale of Reproducibility	80.6	82.5	83.9	86.2	85.2

SOURCE: Data from Davis and Smith (2000).

Table 3 Percentages Agreeing With Abortion, Suicide, and Euthanasia by Where Individuals Place Themselves on the Political Spectrum

	1977–80	1982–86	1987–90	1991–94	1996–2000	% Change
Liberals	33.4	41.0	42.3	56.9	51.9	18.5
Moderates	20.5	25.6	28.7	34.0	33.8	13.3
Conservatives	18.6	21.7	21.7	24.7	22.7	4.1
% difference (liberal-conservative)	14.8	19.3	20.6	32.2	29.2	

SOURCE: Data from Davis and Smith (2000).

REFERENCES

Alan Guttmacher Institute. 1999. "Abortion in Context: United States and World Wide." New York: Alan Guttmacher Institute. Retrieved June 2, 2003 (http://www.agi-usa.org/pubs/ib_0599.html).

———. 2000. "Facts in Brief." New York: Alan Guttmacher Institute. Retrieved June 2, 2003 (http://www.agi-usa.org/pubs/fb_induced_abortion.html).

Bauman, Zygmunt. 1992. *Morality, Immortality, and Other Life Strategies.* Stanford, CA: Stanford University Press.

Becker, Ernest. 1973. *The Denial of Death.* New York: Free Press.

Blank, Chris. 2001. "The Partial-Birth Fraud." *American Prospect,* September 24–October 8. Retrieved June 2, 2003 (http://www.prospect.org/print/v12/17/black-c.html).

Brind, Joel, Vernon M. Chinchilli, Walter B. Severs, and Joan Summy-Long. 1996. "Induced Abortion as an Independent Risk Factor for Breast Cancer: A Comprehensive Review and Meta-Analysis." *Journal of Epidemiology and Community Health* 50:481–96.

Dagg, Paul K. B. 1991. "The Psychological Sequelae of Therapeutic Abortion—Denied and Completed." *American Journal of Psychiatry* 148:578–85.

Davis, James A. and Tom W. Smith. 2000. *General Social Surveys, 1972–2000* [machine-readable data file] (principal investigator, James A. Davis; director and co–principal investigator, Tom W. Smith; co–principal investigator, Peter V. Marsden; NORC ed.). Chicago/Storrs, CT: National Opinion Research Center (prod.)/Roper Center for Public Opinion Research, University of Connecticut (dist.).

Devereux, George. 1954. "A Typological Study of Abortion in 350 Primitive, Ancient and Pre-Industrial Societies." In *Therapeutic Abortion,* edited by Harold Rosen. New York: Julian.

Dolhenty, Jonathan. 1998. "The Crazy-Quilt of Our Age of Consent Laws." Radical Academy. Retrieved May 29, 2003 (http://radicalacademy.com/ageofconsent.htm).

Donahue, John J. and Steven D. Levitt. 2001. "The Impact of Legalized Abortion on Crime." *Quarterly Journal of Economics* 116:379–420.

Gailey, Phil. 1986a. "Abortion Knits Religious Right Into G.O.P. Fabric." *New York Times,* June 19, p. 12.

———. 1986b. "Reagan Calls Abortion 'Murder' and Bars a Test." *New York Times,* June 24, p. 9.

Gergen, David. 1993. "Clinton's Abortion Problem." *U.S. News & World Report,* April 19, p. 74.

Gest, Ted. 1982. "What the Supreme Court Heard on Abortion." *U.S. News & World Report,* December 13, p. 83.

Goffman, Erving. 1974. *Frame Analysis: An Essay on the Organization of Experience.* New York: Harper Colophon.

Goldman, Ari. 1984. "Bishop Defends a Holocaust Analogy." *New York Times,* March 14, p. 17.

Granberg, Donald. 1978. "Pro-Life or Reflection of Conservative Ideology? An Analysis of Opposition to Legalized Abortion." *Sociology and Social Research* 62:414–29.

Greenhouse, Linda. 1982. "Medical Groups Opposing Curbs in Abortion Law." *New York Times,* August 31, pp. 1, 8.

Henshaw, Stanley. 1998. "Abortion Incidence and Services in the United States 1995–1996." *Family Planning Perspectives* 30:263–71.

Insel, Paul M. and Walton T. Roth. 2000. *Core Concepts in Health,* 8th ed. Mountain View, CA: Mayfield.

Kearl, Michael and Richard Harris. 1981–82. "Individualism and the Emerging 'Modern' Ideology of Death." *Omega* 12:269–80.

Keath, Greg. 1989. "Abortion Is Not a Civil Right." *Wall Street Journal,* September 27, p. A22.

Kramer, Karen W. 1990. "The Press and Symbols: The *New York Times* and Abortion from *Roe* to *Webster.*" Senior thesis, Princeton University.

Lewin, Tamar. 2001. "F.B.I. Identifies Suspect for Fake Anthrax Mailings to Abortion Clinics." *New York Times,* November 30, p. B6.

"Life Beyond the Kremlin." 1988. *New York Times,* May 30, p. 5.

Luker, Kristin. 1984. *Abortion and the Politics of Motherhood.* Berkeley: University of California Press.

Mohr, James C. 1978. *Abortion in America: The Origins and Evolution of National Policy, 1800–1900.* New York: Oxford University Press.

"A Mormon Leader Describes Abortion as 'War on Unborn.'" 1985. *New York Times,* April 8, p. 9.

National Abortion Federation. 1990. "Women Who Have Abortions" (October). Washington, DC: National Abortion Federation.

Pear, Robert. 1983. "Judge Strikes Rule Requiring Care for Infants With Defects." *New York Times,* April 15, pp. 1, 11.

People v. Davis, 7 Cal. 4th 797, May 16, 1994.

Pollitt, Katha. 1997. "When Abortion Was a Crime." *Atlantic Monthly,* May, pp. 111–15.

"Pro-Life Resources: Outreach." 2000. *National Right to Life News,* January, p. 12.

Reagan, Leslie. 1998. *When Abortion Was a Crime: Women, Medicine, and Law in the United States, 1867–1973.* Berkeley: University of California Press.

Republican Party. 1988. "Party Platform." Reprinted by CNN.com. Retrieved June 11, 2003 (http://www.cnn.com/allpolitics/1996/conventions/san.diego/facts/abortion/1984-88.shtml).

Rosenblatt, Roger. 1992. *Life Itself: Abortion in the American Mind.* New York: Random House.

Saad, Lydia. 2002. "Americans Still Not Content With Abortion Laws: But Majority Would Keep Abortion Legal." New York: Gallup News Service. Retrieved May 29, 2003 (http://www.gallup.com/poll/releases/pr020122.asp).

Sanger, Margaret. 1922. *The Pivot of Civilization.* New York: Brentano's.

Shenkman, Richard. 1988. *Legends, Lies and Cherished Myths of American History.* New York: William Morrow.

Speckhard, Anne C. and Vincent Rue. 1992. "Post-Abortion Syndrome a Growing Health Problem." *Journal of Social Issues* 48:95–119.

Ventura, S. J., W. D. Mosher, S. C. Curtin, J. C. Abma, and S. Henshaw. 2000. *Trends in Pregnancies and Pregnancy Rates by Outcome: Estimates for the United States, 1976–96* (NCHS Series 21, no. 56). Washington, DC: U.S. Department of Health and Human Services.

Watanabe, Myrna E. 1993. "With Five-Year Ban on Fetal Tissue Studies Lifted, Scientists Are Striving to Make Up for Lost Time." *Scientist,* October 4, p. 14.

Wolf, Naomi. 1995. "Our Bodies, Our Souls." *New Republic,* October 16, pp. 26–35.

Dying of AIDS
and Social Stigmatization

Robin D. Moremen

The Centers for Disease Control and Prevention (CDC 2001) describes acquired immunodeficiency syndrome, or AIDS, as a "specific group of diseases or conditions which are indicative of severe immunosuppression related to infection with the human immunodeficiency virus (HIV)" (p. 1). HIV suppresses the immune system by attacking the T4 lymphocytes, preventing them from recognizing and destroying even the most innocuous of foreign invaders. Once the immune system breaks down, opportunistic infections such as *Pneumocystis carinii* pneumonia, toxoplasmosis, Kaposi's sarcoma, candidiasis, cytomegalovirus retinitis, mycobacterium tuberculosis, and herpes simplex may take hold (Stine 1998). If the progression of such infections is not checked by therapeutic agents, a person with AIDS (PWA) may become debilitated and die a slow, painful death from a foreign agent that would be rendered harmless in a person with an intact immune system. According to CDC (2000a) estimates, from 1981 through the end of 2000, 21.8 million people worldwide had died of AIDS, and 450,000 of these deaths occurred in the United States. The number of deaths increased each year from the beginning of the epidemic in 1981 until 1995, then declined in 1996–97 and leveled off thereafter, due to the introduction of highly active antiretroviral therapy. Mortality from AIDS in the United States varies with sociodemographic factors: The decline in deaths has been greatest among white men who have sex with men and live in the Northeast; it has been less dramatic for women, for blacks and Hispanics, for residents of the South, and for those whose risk exposure is heterosexual contact (CDC 2002a).

Many speak of AIDS in the medical and demographic terms described above. Were it that simple, AIDS would take its place in the panoply of potentially deadly diseases, and that would be the end of the discussion. However, humankind is neither fair nor just in this regard; certain diseases, and the people who acquire them, have been—and still are—singled out for negative evaluation and treatment. Like lepers, epileptics, and syphilitics before them, people with AIDS have had to endure a deeply discrediting attribute, or stigma, associated with themselves and their disease, a kind of spoiled identity (Goffman 1963). This spoiled identity is not an intrinsic part of the disease; rather, it is ascribed by others, foisted on the ill by a society keen on keeping "those people" away from "the rest of us."

Stigmas often grow out of fear and loathing reactions by members of society who are ignorant about, and judgmental of, individuals whose lives and actions are somehow different from the "correct" and "proper" kinds of behavior espoused by the dominant group. The aversion to AIDS in U.S. society has grown out of some Americans' fear and loathing of death, incurable disease, and marginalized groups such as homosexuals, prostitutes, injecting drug users, and impoverished whites, blacks, and Latinos. This fear and loathing have created a toxic mix of social stigmatization for PWAs. In the remainder of this chapter, I explore the nature of stigmas, stigmatizing illnesses, homophobia and AIDS-related stigma, stigma management and the construction of a positive AIDS identity, and the relationships among fear, stigma, and AIDS.

GOFFMAN AND SOCIAL STIGMATIZATION

Erving Goffman (1963) is recognized as one of the first to draw our attention to the nature of stigma, although—according to *Webster's Dictionary*—the term itself is quite old, referring to a distinguishing mark burned or cut into the flesh, as of a slave or criminal. Over time, the term *stigma* has come to mean an attribute that is deeply discrediting, an undesired differentness from what society anticipates as "normal" (Goffman 1963). As a result of this differentness, stigmatized persons are excluded from normal social interaction. In order for social stigmatization to occur, a fairly clear boundary must exist between the acceptable and the unacceptable. The more rigid the boundary, the more likely it is that those who deviate from the acceptable will be discredited or seen as defective or abnormal. Once stigmatized, a person is viewed as "not quite human," which justifies society's exclusion and discriminatory action.

Goffman identifies three kinds of stigmas: (a) stigmas of the body, such as blemishes and deformities; (b) stigmas of the character, such as promiscuity and immorality; and (c) stigmas of social collectivities, such as being poor or a member of a marginalized racial or ethnic group. All three of Goffman's categories may be linked to persons with AIDS.

Stigmas of the body. Should the immune system become compromised and opportunistic infections take hold, a PWA may suffer from physical wasting or may develop skin lesions associated with histoplasmosis, herpes simplex, Kaposi's sarcoma (KS), or *Candida albicans.* According to Goffman (1963), such deformities and blemishes are evidence of stigmas of the body. Western cultural standards of attractiveness and acceptable body image are fairly rigid, and the weight loss associated with wasting syndrome and the lesions associated with herpes and KS do not conform to these standards.

Stigmas of the character. In Western society, AIDS was first associated with men having sex with men and with the injection of illegal substances. Because Western society has firm proscriptions against homosexuality and intravenous drug use, AIDS became associated with Goffman's second category of stigma, stigmas of character. Had the syndrome been associated initially with heterosexuals and the Boy Scouts, persons with AIDS undoubtedly would have avoided such negative characterological stigmatization.

Stigmas of social collectivities. After first appearing in gay men and injecting drug users, AIDS found its way into poor communities of color. This conforms to Goffman's last category of stigma, stigmas of collectivities. Goffman argues that stigmas may be transmitted through lineages and social groupings, such that all members of a race, nation, religion, or social group may share a tribal stigma. This has been evident in U.S. society's negative response to people of Haitian descent when it was discovered that some members of the black Haitian immigrant community were HIV-positive.

Self-isolation. Goffman (1963) argues that stigmatized persons may begin to self-isolate because society fails to accord them the respect and appreciation they expect and anticipate. For some HIV-positive individuals, such isolation may begin as soon as they learn of their HIV status. They may isolate themselves out of fear that others will learn of their HIV status and disengage from them, causing them to lose their jobs, their health insurance, their homes, their friends, their partners, and their families. Stories in the news media about PWAs being expelled from homes, schools, churches, and jobs only serve to reinforce this belief. Sometimes the shock of a positive HIV test result is so severe that individuals have thoughts of suicide (Adam and Sears 1996).

Psychic pain. Lacking the beneficial effects of daily social interaction with others, Goffman (1963) suggests, people who isolate themselves may become suspicious, depressed, hostile, anxious, and bewildered. PWAs may suffer from emotional, mental, and spiritual pain as well as physical debilitation (Dunbar et al. 1998). They may be shunned, feared, or cut off from the very people who might best offer them social support. The psychological literature is replete with evidence that social support acts as a buffer against stress and increases physical and mental well-being. These are benefits that PWAs may not experience.

Stigmas by association. Goffman (1963) also contends that stigmas may spread by association, from stigmatized persons to those with whom they have close connections. Therefore, others may avoid such relations with stigmatized individuals or terminate previously existing relations. Some people may shun persons with AIDS for fear that they, too, will be burdened with stigma and that others may assume they are also PWAs or, worse still, promiscuous gay persons with AIDS. Thus, in addition to self-isolation, stigmatized individuals may find that others—friends, neighbors, relatives, associates, partners, and family members—sever connections with them out of egoism and self-concern.

AIDS-related stigma. Although AIDS-related stigma has lessened in the United States in recent years, some individuals continue to be stigmatized. Those most likely to suffer AIDS-related stigma are individuals on the margins of society: gay men, intravenous drug users, women (particularly female sex workers), people of color, and people who are economically disadvantaged. The CDC (2002b) reiterates this point in its HIV Prevention Strategic Plan, which it issued on World AIDS Day in 2002:

Stigma associated with HIV/AIDS continues to profoundly affect prevention efforts, leading people to deny risk . . . avoid testing . . . delay treatment . . . and suffer needlessly. While stigma's pernicious effects are perhaps most obvious in countries other than the U.S., where people may be shunned and physically harmed, stigma negatively affects Americans as well. It is found at the structural level, in the form of laws and regulations, as well as more explicitly at community and individual levels.

Homophobia continues to hamper prevention efforts at all levels: from the individual at risk or infected, who may deny his risk because of internal conflicts, to the broader culture, which delivers anti-gay messages, institutionalizes homophobia through structural mechanisms, such as laws that regulate intimate sexual behavior, and lags in its support of sensitive and honest prevention for gay and bisexual youth, young adults and older men.

Stigma associated with addiction and illicit drug use also results in laws and other restrictions on effective prevention. Likewise, persistent social and institutional racism and gender and economic inequities stifle effective HIV prevention. For each of these groups at risk, stigma, stereotyping and prejudice must be addressed for prevention to be most effective. Political leadership and will are necessary to address these underlying issues, so critical to prevention's success.

Although most persons in the United States do not hold stigmatizing views of PWAs, approximately 20% of Americans still do (CDC 2000b). Such views are most common among people who are male, white, heterosexual, and 55 years of age and older, who have only a high school education, who have annual incomes of less than $30,000, who are in poor health, and who are generally misinformed about AIDS transmission (CDC 2000b; Herek 1999). Leaders of the Christian Right also work to keep AIDS-related stigma alive (Herek and Capitanio 1999).

STIGMATIZING ILLNESSES AND HIV/AIDS

Rose Weitz (1991) has written extensively about stigmatizing illness and HIV/AIDS. She begins with the premise that people who are ill are generally deemed less socially worthy than people who are healthy, and that most people who are ill are blamed somehow for their illness. This premise dates back to Talcott Parsons's (1951) notion of the "sick role," a concept he uses to describe the role in society of people who deviate from the social norm of wellness. Weitz argues that society views some illnesses as especially horrible because of the blame and dread they evoke, and this leads to the stigmatization of those who contract such illnesses. She maintains that the six conditions discussed below must be present for blame, dread, and stigma to occur; HIV/AIDS continues to conform, in some ways, to all six of these conditions.

Blame, dread, and stigma are greatest when the illness is connected to already stigmatized groups. AIDS was first identified in stigmatized populations—gay men, drug users, black Haitian immigrants, and prostitutes—and many in mainstream society felt, at least initially, that AIDS was fitting punishment for individuals who engaged in unacceptable behaviors, as defined by the dominant group. As the epidemic progressed and PWAs were identified who did not fall into these stigmatized categories (e.g., individuals who contracted AIDS from blood transfusions), a rhetoric of "innocent" versus "guilty" victims emerged; this dichotomy persisted into the late 1990s (Herek and Capitanio 1999). Thus AIDS stigma has been greater for those who are held responsible for their disease than for those deemed innocent victims (Herek and Capitanio 1999; Leiker, Taub, and Gast 1995).

Stigma is especially likely if the illness is linked to sexuality, and most especially to stigmatized sexuality. Western culture views sexuality with both fear and fascination. Sexual drives are among our most basic, but we refrain from discussing sexual behavior openly, especially "deviant" sexual behavior that is likely to result in sexually transmitted diseases such as HIV/AIDS. The Christian Right has done its best to prevent AIDS education programs from disseminating explicit information about the sexual behaviors linked to HIV transmission on the premise that these behaviors are deviant (Herek and Capitanio 1999). Furthermore, numerous studies have found that persons who are knowledgeable about HIV/AIDS and safe-sex methods do not necessarily put what they know into practice. This is particularly true of adolescents and the elderly; the former consider themselves invincible, and the latter cannot envision themselves as being at risk. One of the biggest public health gains made in the second decade of the AIDS epidemic was the increased public acceptance of frank talk about sexuality for all age groups, specifically in reference to the relationship between certain sexual practices and HIV transmission.

Stigma is highly likely when there is no vaccine available and the illness is viewed as contagious. To date, no vaccine or cure for AIDS exists, although the introduction of highly active antiretroviral therapy in 1996 has dramatically increased the survival time of persons living with HIV/AIDS (CDC 2002a). Many believe that HIV/AIDS will not be cured, but will become a chronic infectious disease that can be managed, not unlike diabetes, multiple sclerosis, or asthma (Moremen 1999). HIV *is* contagious, but the major route of transmission is the exchange of body fluids, not casual contact. In early studies, the CDC found that the level of people's fear concerning casual contact with PWAs was extremely high, and more recent studies appear to indicate that this is still the case (Herek and Capitanio 1999). Approximately a quarter of Americans continue to hold the belief that they may magically contract HIV by touching a sweater worn by a PWA or by drinking from the same glass as a PWA (CDC 2000b; Herek and Capitanio 1999). Beliefs such as these serve to fuel the fires of stigma against PWAs.

Stigma is especially likely if the illness brings about visible, disfiguring, or dehumanizing changes in the sick individual. Visibly disfiguring conditions have always evoked horror and loathing, whether associated with infectious disease or not. Historically, people with disfiguring conditions have been isolated, quarantined, exiled, exploited, or locked up (e.g., the Elephant Man, people with disabilities, people with leprosy or epilepsy). By removing the affected from public view, the unaffected avoid having to acknowledge the frailty of the human condition or accept that they are one accident or illness away from disability and death themselves. Although highly active antiretroviral therapy has lowered the incidence in PWAs of disfiguring conditions such as bodily wasting and Kaposi's sarcoma, these conditions still afflict 28% and 21%, respectively, of all persons who die of AIDS (Stine 1998; CDC 1999). With each new infection, a person living with AIDS typically experiences a 5% loss of body weight; this problem is most prevalent among PWAs who are female and among those who are economically disadvantaged (Stine 1998:147). Disfiguring conditions such as wasting and KS may evoke fear and loathing of persons in the advanced stages of AIDS.

Stigma is great if the illness results in death or significant disability and appears to have consequences for society as a whole. Prior to the introduction of antiretroviral therapy, HIV infection uniformly progressed to AIDS, resulting in disability and death. Now, for those HIV-positive persons who can afford the medications, the opportunistic infections associated with AIDS may be held off for years, possibly even decades. For those who cannot afford the medications, or who have greater difficulty accessing regular sources of care (e.g., sex workers, injection drug users, the uninsured, poor women of color), early death is far more likely. In the early years of the epidemic, AIDS did not appear to have consequences for society as a whole because it was associated mainly with marginalized groups or people in foreign lands; however, as AIDS entered the heterosexual population in the United States and the number of cases worldwide increased, the social consequences of this global epidemic, in which everyone is potentially at risk, became difficult to ignore. That AIDS has consequences for all of society only increases the fear associated with the disease.

Stigma is exacerbated by mysteries regarding the origin and progression of the illness. The origin of AIDS remains speculative, as does the progression of the illness. Why is it that some people remain HIV-positive for decades without progressing to full-blown AIDS and others progress to AIDS almost immediately? Studies are currently being conducted on individuals known as "nonprogressors"— those who are HIV-positive but appear to remain illness-free indefinitely (Haynes, Pantaleo, and Fauci 1996). Some researchers have speculated that nonprogressors may have a missing link in their viral DNA, but this explanation is theoretical at best. Questions for which we have no answers intensify the mystery surrounding HIV/AIDS and only add to the associated stigma.

AIDS AND HOMOPHOBIA

Many gay activists, journalists, and scholars draw a direct link between AIDS-related stigma and homophobia, arguing that fear and hatred of homosexuality and homosexuals is the primary source of stigma associated with AIDS and that this association is responsible for the lackluster response to HIV/AIDS in the early 1980s in the United States (Altman 1987; Gunther 1995; Herek and Capitanio 1999; Leiker et al. 1995; Shilts 1988). Because AIDS was initially identified as a "gay disease," social, political, medical, and economic resources were denied to those who needed them most; this had tragic consequences for persons with AIDS in the early years of the epidemic.

Gunther (1995) asserts that the link between homophobia and AIDS has resulted in three categories of AIDS-related stigmas, each of which includes aspects of the others: (a) fear of the disease itself, (b) fear and hostility toward those most affected and deemed most responsible for the disease, and (c) fear and hostility toward the specific behaviors that transmit the disease (on all these points, see also Herek 1999; Herek and Capitanio 1999; Leiker et al. 1995).

Fear of the disease itself. In the early years of the epidemic, AIDS was a disease of gay men that seemed to appear out of nowhere. No one understood how it was transmitted, no one understood how or why gay men were dying, and the physical attributes of the disease were visually terrifying. The high degree of uncertainty about the disease resulted in fear of the disease itself. This argument is not unlike Weitz's (1991) argument, noted above, that society fears mysterious sexually transmitted diseases in stigmatized populations.

Fear and hostility toward those most affected and deemed most responsible for the disease. Once AIDS was associated with specific groups of people—and not yet associated with specific behaviors of *all* groups of people—it was easy for society to move from fearing the disease itself to fearing and blaming the people most affected by the disease: men who have sex with men. Because gay and bisexual men were the first AIDS casualties, it did not take long for society to link the disease to stigmatized activities associated with gay sex. This resulted in a cascade of condemnatory language from the Christian Right; AIDS served as a symbolic vehicle for heterosexuals to express preexisting sexual prejudice (Herek and Capitanio 1999).

When it became apparent that Haitian immigrants— many of whom were heterosexual—also were casualties of the epidemic in numbers that were out of proportion to the size of this group in the population, race-related stigmas were added to gay-related stigmas. African Americans— by their skin-color association with Haitians—other immigrant groups, and ethnic minorities such as Latinos/Latinas found themselves the victims of fear and hatred as well, as race-related stigmas spread. When injecting drug users were added to the mix, the triumvirate of risk groups associated with AIDS was complete.

Risk-group thinking allowed people who were not members of particular groups to wall off their fears of contracting AIDS, at least temporarily, and provided further impetus for them to blame those who were members of the risk groups for bringing the disease into society (Herek and Capitanio 1999). Furthermore, members of risk groups were stigmatized to begin with, so the social, economic, political, and medical inaction of society in regard to AIDS was justified—"those people" deserved their fate. This "we/they" thinking—which *began* with gay men and then was transferred to other groups of marginalized people—proved extremely ineffective in containing the spread of the disease, but it helped the members of white, middle-class, heterosexual society feel better about themselves for a brief period.

Fear and hostility toward the specific behaviors that transmit the disease. Just as specific groups of people became feared and hated because of their association with HIV/AIDS, specific risk-group behaviors suffered the same fate as well (i.e., men having anal intercourse with other men, men and women having multiple sex partners, female sex workers having sex for money, and individuals using needles to inject drugs). With the exception of promiscuity (i.e., having multiple sex partners), all of these behaviors were subject to prosecution—thus society had already decided to put the weight of the law behind its labeling of these behaviors as deviant.

Society in general viewed the sexual behaviors of gay men as deviant, so society felt no obligation to treat PWAs in a caring and compassionate manner. The argument went that society had no obligation to care for individuals who brought about their own demise; persons with AIDS were not innocent, unwitting victims of an illness, but willing conspirators in their own doom. Even though society provided compassionate care to people who were dying because they ate, drank, or smoked too much, it had no obligation to respond similarly to gay men with AIDS, because they participated in sexual behaviors that elicited both fear and loathing on society's part.

In some respects this is a "good news/bad news" story. The good news is that the individuals most blamed for the epidemic (i.e., gay men) were also the people who were most successful at raising AIDS awareness and garnering funds for research and education/prevention efforts (Herek and Capitanio 1999). Gay men also have been quite successful in constructing a more positive AIDS-related identity for themselves. The bad news is that a large segment of the heterosexual community, even today, continues to associate AIDS primarily with homosexuality (or bisexuality), and this association is correlated with higher levels of sexual prejudice (i.e., antigay attitudes) (Herek and Capitanio 1999; Leiker et al. 1995).

STIGMA MANAGEMENT AND THE CONSTRUCTION OF A POSITIVE AIDS IDENTITY

Society constructs the discrediting labels and identities associated with stigmas, and so may also deconstruct and manage such labels and identities. Stigmatized individuals may influence the ways others see them by employing adaptive strategies and identity management. Sandstrom (1990, 1998), Siegel and Krauss (1991), Siegel, Lune, and Meyer (1998), and Tewksbury (1994) all speak to these issues in relation to gay men living with HIV/AIDS, but in many respects what they have to say applies to all PWAs.

Adaptive strategies for living with *HIV disease* include dealing with the possibility of a curtailed life span, dealing with reactions to a stigmatizing illness, and developing strategies for maintaining physical and emotional health (Siegel and Krauss 1991). Adaptive strategies for living with *advanced symptoms of AIDS* are somewhat different, but related. These include coming to terms with debilitation and a shrinking future; confronting the threats of suffering, dependence, and death; and building a postmortal self (Sandstrom 1998).

For those living with HIV/AIDS, identity management often occurs along a continuum from reactive to proactive, depending on the extent to which an individual accepts or challenges the stigma associated with HIV/AIDS (Siegel et al. 1998). Reactive strategies include attempts to hide one's HIV status, such as passing, covering, isolating, or distancing oneself from AIDS-related stigma (Sandstrom 1990; Siegel et al. 1998). Proactive strategies include building and embracing an AIDS identity and engaging in public educational efforts and social activism to change the social and political conditions associated with HIV/AIDS (Sandstrom 1990; Siegel et al. 1998). Following the path of gay men and lesbians in the gay rights movement, some HIV-positive individuals have proudly laid claim to their identities both as gay men and as people living with HIV/AIDS (Tewksbury 1994). Adopting the self-reference of a "person living with AIDS" places an emphasis on personhood and on living, not on objectification, illness, death, and victimhood (Tewksbury 1994). Interestingly, Tewksbury (1994) has found that heterosexual men living with AIDS have the greatest difficulty managing their identities (compared with gay men and heterosexual women with AIDS) because they have the least prior experience in adjusting to a marginalized and socially devalued status.

Women with AIDS appear to adopt a strategy that falls somewhere between the strategies of heterosexual men and those of gay men, largely because women face different issues. Many HIV-positive women report histories of trauma, including having been physically and sexually assaulted; they also describe histories of severe substance abuse and earned income through the sex industry, and often they are attempting to provide for children and other dependents (Adam and Sears 1996; Blankenship 1997; Dunbar et al. 1998). Despite these lifelong hardships, HIV-positive women are less apt to manipulate language to disguise their disease and are more likely to devote energies to their additional roles, such as being mothers (Tewksbury 1994). Like gay males, women experience social devaluation in society more generally and do not find HIV disease as identity altering as do their heterosexual male counterparts (Tewksbury 1994). Some women report being able to use the pain and despair of the HIV diagnosis as an opportunity for self-awareness and growth, and describe a profound healing in their lives that makes room for a richer existence (Dunbar et al. 1998). Gay men and heterosexual women living with HIV/AIDS appear to be adopting strategies that wrestle AIDS-related stigma to the ground and redefine it in terms of personal and collective empowerment.

FEAR, STIGMA, AND AIDS

The social stigmatization associated with AIDS is often tied up with fear, particularly fear of death, fear of incurable disease, and fear of marginalized groups.

Fear of Death

Becker (1973) argues that the United States is a death-denying society. Whether the fear of death is learned (healthy-minded argument) or innate (morbid-minded argument), it pervades our everyday existence, and it is only by repressing this fear that we can get on with the business of living. If we were to stare into the chasm of death on a daily basis, we would be immobilized. Thus we deny death's existence (employing our many euphemisms for death) even as we remain fascinated with death in private (as our death-saturated popular culture shows) (Gorer 1965). Like sex, death is a topic we do not discuss openly, nor do we prepare for death at home. We remove the dying to hospitals and nursing homes, and when they finally cease to live, we ship them off to funeral parlors, where they are made to look less dead. Over the past two centuries, we have come to view the members of the medical profession as our high priests; it is their job to "cure" us of death so that we are never forced to confront our fears. And when they fail to do so (as they inevitably must) our fears surface again, only to be pushed down by the next wave of denial. If we consider any death to be good, it is a death that comes at the end of a good long life; an early or unexpected death is considered a particularly bad death. A death preceded by a great deal of pain and debilitation is considered a bad death as well.

If we considered death to be a normal, inevitable, expected, and cherished part of life, our fears about it would not necessarily dictate our responses to those who are dying. But because we stubbornly refuse to stare into the abyss, we bring our fears with us to the beds of the dying. They remind us only too well of our own unutterable fate. In our attempts to deny death, we often deny the dying as well. This is part of the fear that we bring to those with advanced symptoms of AIDS. In them we see our own failure to beat back death. In their wasting bodies, we see the reflection of our own mortality. And because we reject this vision, we often reject them. It is from these origins that stigmas are born. We differentiate ourselves from their experience—they are the dying and we are the living. We are not like them.

Fear of Incurable Disease

The mysteries of incurable disease have always elicited fear in human beings. From the bubonic plague in the 13th century to the polio epidemic in the 20th century, people have reacted with fear and panic when faced with diseases that appear to be unknowable and incurable. Diseases provoke such fear particularly if they are contagious (e.g., smallpox) or if they are debilitating and result in slow, painful death (e.g., amyotrophic lateral sclerosis, or Lou Gehrig's disease). A case in point: We know that men seek treatment for any medical problem far less frequently than do women, but women are *not* more likely than men to seek prompt medical care for cancer or ischemic heart disease (Waldron 1985). It turns out that women, like men, are afraid of being diagnosed with any disease that may be incurable or lead to death. Although medical professionals may perform surgery to bypass arteries and infuse poisonous chemicals into the bodies of people with cancer, they have no cures for many of the chronic conditions that plague modernity, and ultimately we know this, whether or not we wish to admit it. A diagnosis of cancer, in particular, strikes fear in the heart of anyone who receives it. Those who are told they are HIV-positive experience a similar dread. In such cases, most people's initial, knee-jerk response is, "I'm going to die!" whether or not this is true. People respond this way because they associate incurable disease with death, and both elicit the most basic of existential fears.

The fear of disease is exacerbated when the death it causes is slow, bringing pain and debilitation. The misfortune of dying of AIDS is that the virus chips away at the immune system until nothing is left to defend the body from within. Organ systems die by degrees, with the body taking on an emaciated appearance toward the end. Often this is accompanied by extreme pain and demented cognition. No one would knowingly choose this for themselves, yet thousands of persons with AIDS have had to experience this kind of death. The gruesomeness of this particular death fuels the fear and revulsion that the fear of death itself initiates. Add to this mix the fear of marginalized groups that society imposes, and the social stigmatization of AIDS is complete.

Fear of Marginalized Groups

In social hierarchies, there are always dominant and submissive groups. Those at the top have access to the power and resources they need to maintain their dominance, and those at the bottom are marginalized because they lack access to the same power and resources. Once those at the top have acquired their power and resources, which they may do through no particular efforts of their own, they maintain their control by reinforcing the differentiation between themselves and those below. One way they do this is by defining themselves as superior and those beneath them as inferior. In addition to their access to power and resources, those at the top of a society usually have the opportunity to define that society's reality. Part of this definitional prerogative is the determination of what is acceptable and what is unacceptable. Invariably, dominant groups identify their own characteristics, behaviors, and belief systems as acceptable and those of less powerful groups as unacceptable.

Race, class, gender, religion, sexual orientation, and able-bodiedness are some of the dimensions along which power and privileges are differentiated in the United States, such that if you are white, middle- or upper-class, Christian, heterosexual, able-bodied, and male, you are most likely on top, and keeping those who are nonwhite, poor, non-Christian, gay, disabled, and female beneath you reinforces your position of privilege. These dimensions intersect and multiply, both for individuals at the top and individuals at the bottom. Thus, to be white is to have power, but to be wealthy and male *and* white is to have even more power; conversely, to be poor is to have no power, but to be black and female *and* poor is to have even less power.

When a disease that causes agonizing death arises among those at the bottom of society, the marginalized existence and generalized unacceptability of individuals afflicted with the disease are only reinforced. And in order to distract from the inequality built into the system, the powerful blame the victims for their illness, denounce them as deviants, and deny them access to resources. If they were to do otherwise, the very existence of the hierarchy would be called into question, and that is something those at the top cannot tolerate. Most unfortunately for persons with AIDS in the United States, the first victims were people at the bottom of society, and thus the entire course of the illness has been defined, from the outset, by their marginalized existence. Our fears of death, incurable disease, and marginalized groups have combined to produce the social stigmatization attached to dying of AIDS.

FUTURE TRENDS

What will it take to bring about change in the social stigmatization of people living with and dying of AIDS? Some would argue, and quite rightly, that the social stigmatization of PWAs is less evident now than it was a decade ago. Antiretroviral drugs allow people with HIV/AIDS to live longer and perhaps delay revelation of their illness. Surveys have found that most Americans are fairly knowledgeable about HIV/AIDS and supportive of PWAs (CDC 2000b), but AIDS-related stigma still exists. Continued progress in three areas will help to lessen the social stigmatization of persons with AIDS: changes in societal attitudes about death, the continued management of HIV/AIDS as a chronic illness, and societal recognition of the inequity of associating HIV/AIDS with marginalized existence.

The hospice and palliative care movements have begun to humanize and naturalize death. We have a long way to go to overcome our existential fears, but these movements, which change the settings where death takes place and acknowledge the need for comfort care, not cure, represent a step in the right direction. Antiretroviral therapies are extending the lives of people with HIV/AIDS, such that we have now begun to think of AIDS as a manageable disease as opposed to one that is always fatal. (This, unfortunately, is strictly a Western phenomenon. People with AIDS in developing countries are not able to afford AZT, much less the combination of drugs that will extend their lives, and drug companies appear to be more concerned about profits than about care. Until this changes, a staggering majority of AIDS deaths will take place in non-Western cultures.) As AIDS education and prevention efforts have proceeded in the United States, there has been more openness about sexuality and the sexual practices most linked with HIV/AIDS, and as needle-exchange programs have advanced, the sharing of infected needles has declined. Both of these efforts remain extremely controversial in some segments of society (e.g., the Christian Right), therefore we need to remain vigilant and not let complacency or harassment undo the good that has been done thus far. Finally, over time, Americans are slowly recognizing that AIDS is not associated exclusively with members of marginalized groups. People living with AIDS are pursuing empowerment strategies, and many members of mainstream society realize that they, too, are at risk.

All of these are positive first steps; however, we still need to work to dismantle the structures that led to the social stigmatization of persons with AIDS in the first place. This work will require a kind of acceptance and tolerance that societies heretofore have not exhibited, as well as a leveling of the hierarchical structures that reinforce and maintain the stigmatization of marginalized groups. That is a tall order for a small planet.

REFERENCES

Adam, Barry D. and Alan Sears. 1996. *Experiencing HIV: Personal, Family, and Work Relationships.* New York: Columbia University Press.

Altman, Dennis. 1987. *AIDS in the Minds of America: The Social, Political, and Psychological Impact of a New Epidemic.* Garden City, NY: Anchor.

Becker, Ernest. 1973. *The Denial of Death.* New York: Free Press.

Blankenship, Kim. 1997. "Social Context and HIV: Testing and Treatment Issues Among Commercial Street Sex Workers." Pp. 252–70 in *The Gender Politics of HIV/AIDS in Women: Perspectives on the Pandemic in the United States,* edited by Nancy Goldstein and Jennifer L. Manlowe. New York: New York University Press.

Centers for Disease Control and Prevention (CDC). 1999. "Surveillance for AIDS-Defining Opportunistic Illnesses, 1992–1997." *Morbidity and Mortality Weekly Report* 48(SS-2):1–22.

———. 2000a. *HIV/AIDS Surveillance Report,* vol. 12, no. 2. Atlanta, GA: CDC.

Centers for Disease Control and Prevention (CDC). 2000b. "HIV-Related Knowledge and Stigma: United States, 2000." *Morbidity and Mortality Weekly Report* 49:1062–64.

———. 2001. *HIV/AIDS Surveillance Report,* vol. 13, no. 2. Atlanta, GA: CDC.

———. 2002a. "Deaths Among Persons With AIDS Through December 2000." In *HIV/AIDS Surveillance Supplemental Report,* vol. 8, no. 1. Atlanta, GA: CDC.

———. 2002b. "Stigma and Discrimination: Links for World AIDS Day 2002." Atlanta, GA: CDC. Retrieved December 29, 2002 (http://www.cdc.gov/hiv/wad.htm).

Dunbar, Heather T., Charles W. Mueller, Cynthia Medina, and Tamra Wolf. 1998. "Psychological and Spiritual Growth in Women Living With HIV." *Social Work* 43:144–54.

Goffman, Erving. 1963. *Stigma: Notes on the Management of Spoiled Identity.* New York: Simon & Schuster.

Gorer, Geoffrey. 1965. *Death, Grief and Mourning.* Garden City, NY: Doubleday.

Gunther, Herbert Chao. 1995. *The Impact of Homophobia and Other Social Biases on AIDS.* San Francisco: Public Media Center.

Haynes, Barton F., Giuseppe Pantaleo, and Anthony S. Fauci. 1996. "Toward an Understanding of the Correlates of Protective Immunity to HIV Infection." *Science* 271:324–28.

Herek, Gregory M. 1999. "AIDS and Stigma." *American Behavioral Scientist* 42:1106–16.

Herek, Gregory M. and John P. Capitanio. 1999. "AIDS Stigma and Sexual Prejudice." *American Behavioral Scientist* 42:1126–43.

Leiker, Jason J., Diane E. Taub, and Julic Gast. 1995. "The Stigma of AIDS: Persons With AIDS and Social Distance." *Deviant Behavior* 16:333–51.

Moremen, Robin D. 1999. "Long-Term Care and 'Managed' AIDS: The Challenge We Face." *Research in the Sociology of Health Care* 16:171–85.

Parsons, Talcott. 1951. *The Social System.* New York: Free Press.

Sandstrom, Kent L. 1990. "Confronting Deadly Disease: The Drama of Identity Construction Among Gay Men With AIDS." *Journal of Contemporary Ethnography* 19:271–94.

———. 1998. "Preserving a Vital and Valued Self in the Face of AIDS." *Sociological Inquiry* 68:354–71.

Shilts, Randy. 1988. *And the Band Played On: Politics, People, and the AIDS Epidemic.* New York: Penguin.

Siegel, Karolynn and Beatrice J. Krauss. 1991. "Living With HIV Infection: Adaptive Tasks of Seropositive Gay Men." *Journal of Health and Social Behavior* 32:17–32.

Siegel, Karolynn, Howard Lune, and Ilan H. Meyer. 1998. "Stigma Management Among Gay/Bisexual Men with HIV/AIDS." *Qualitative Sociology* 21:3–24.

Stine, Gerald J. 1998. *Acquired Immune Deficiency Syndrome: Biological, Medical, Social, and Legal Issues.* Upper Saddle River, NJ: Prentice Hall.

Tewksbury, Richard. 1994. "'Speaking of Someone With AIDS . . .': Identity Constructions of Persons With HIV Disease." *Deviant Behavior* 15:337–55.

Waldron, Ingrid. 1985. "What Do We Know About Causes of Sex Differences in Mortality?" *Population Bulletin of the United States* 18.

Weitz, Rose. 1991. *Life With AIDS.* New Brunswick, NJ: Rutgers University Press.

Medical Euthanasia

Gail C. Walker

Each of us will eventually arrive at the end of a unique life and die an individual death. The natural boundaries of that life are marked by the events of birth and death in a most personal and private way. The symbolic significance that an individual attaches to death can affect many aspects of the way that person dies, including decisions regarding when and under what circumstances he or she dies, from what cause or reason, whether the decisions made by and for the individual are harmonious with the philosophical and ethical values that have defined important dimensions of that person's life, and how the individual and his or her loved ones evaluate the quality of the death experience. As Feifel (1990) points out, "Recognition of personal mortality is a major entryway to self-knowledge." Each person lives in a social context, however, and individual freedom in choices about life and death is limited by prevailing public policy, standard medical procedures and practices, and social conceptualizations about what constitutes "the common good." Society views individual decisions about life and death as affecting the whole community, and social policies within a democratic tradition often attempt to balance considerations of individual autonomy with respect for the rights and perspectives of others. Public policy should reflect more than the findings of opinion polls, financial expediency, and assertions of individual rights, but because there is currently no consensus as to what constitutes the common good in the area of death-related issues, it is difficult to determine what courses of action are best for both individuals and the larger society.

The right to die, physician-assisted suicide, hastened death services for terminally ill and nonterminally ill patients, and medical euthanasia have all recently been topics of discussion in social, medical, and legal forums. Surely there are few questions of equal importance: Under what circumstances is it appropriate to kill a fellow human being? A teaching story in the Bible says:

> Now Cain said to his brother Abel, "Let's go out to the field." And while they were in the field, Cain attacked his brother Abel and killed him. Then the Lord said to Cain, "Where is your brother Abel?" "I don't know," he replied. "Am I my brother's keeper?" (Genesis 4:8–10)

There have been many answers to Cain's question over the centuries. Although Cain killed Abel in anger and was punished with exile, societies have long recognized legitimate exceptions to the primary rule against killing. These have included killing in the time of war, in self-defense, and in the defense of others. Setting aside the circumstances of self-defense, war, and murder motivated by passion and opportunistic greed, the issue of medical euthanasia has focused attention on the legal, moral, and ethical considerations that derive from the essential dilemmas that accompany the technological advances made by modern medicine. The concepts of passive euthanasia, physician-assisted suicide (PAS), and active euthanasia have formed an arena in which scholars and medical professionals have examined the conflicted issues accompanying compassionate care for terminal patients, beneficence and autonomy, patients' rights to self-determination, comprehensive palliative care, and the limits of palliative care in management of pain and chronic suffering. In the modern era, advances and limitations in life-sustaining medical technologies have fostered an examination of assisted death and killing for merciful reasons.

Discussions of medical euthanasia involve several fundamental philosophical perspectives, which sometimes results in polarized and seemingly irreconcilable points of view for patients, their family members, physicians, and health care staff as well as conflicts in public policy standards and conflicts in general public opinion. As Battin (1995) notes, the central philosophical question in the ethical debate about suicide and its extension into PAS and euthanasia is, "What role may the individual play in his or her own death?"

Issues of paramount importance that have arisen in the shifting social and legal discussions of PAS and euthanasia include concerns about individuals' understanding of the medical management procedures that may take place during the actual process of dying, the identification and elimination of barriers to compassionate and comprehensive end-of-life care through the provision of palliative care and hospice services, and discussion of terminal patients' constitutional rights and protections. The pivotal decision is whether a person has a right to life or a right to choose hastened death under certain circumstances.

VITALISM AND RELATIVISM

Vitalism is the term typically attached to the idea that life itself is the fundamental value and must always be preserved and protected, regardless of considerations of quality (Fulton and Metress 1995). A corollary perspective is the "sanctity of life" view, which holds that all human life is equally valuable, regardless of quality considerations. In these views, the "right to life" is the fundamental human right upon which all other rights depend.

Public debate has yet to resolve the question of whether individuals have a corresponding "right to die." *Relativism,* or the "quality of life" ethic, takes into consideration an individual's life expectancy, medical prognosis, and level of functioning in activities of daily living as well as the risk and benefit levels of treatment options (Fulton and Metress 1995). Health care professionals must make quality-of-life judgments in order to act in their patients' interests (Kuhse and Singer 1989). The American emphasis on individualism has reinforced the perspective of relativism in U.S. public policy. Attempting to balance the benefits and burdens of quality-of-life considerations takes social policy onto a slippery slope, as reasonable choices in some circumstances might lead to unreasonable and unethical outcomes in other situations.

The slippery slope paradigm suggests that although society may condone actions that are ethically or morally appropriate in their own right, there is a risk that such actions may lead to other actions that are ethically or morally inappropriate. For instance, would policies that allow suicide under certain situations pave the way for policies that transform the option into an obligation, especially for individuals who are uninsured or underinsured, elderly, or incompetent? The movement to establish legal status for advance directives, living wills, and health care proxies was originally aimed at allowing more patient control of end-of-life decisions, because physicians were doing too much to prolong life and inadvertently also prolonging the process of dying. The possibility of a lingering death produced by high-technology medical intervention created a context in which patients became more receptive to the idea that physicians should be allowed to help them die. Although some people in intolerable health circumstances request hastened death services, others fear the implications of the legalization of medical euthanasia. Some patients now use advance directives to protect themselves from the premature withdrawal of medical treatment as a cost-saving measure by hospitals, health insurance companies, or family members. In an analysis of the coverage of the issue of euthanasia in American magazines from 1896 to 1976, Wallen (1996) clarifies the roots of the modern controversy. Apparently, Wallen notes,

> the euthanasia argument shifted its emphasis at mid century from the right to choose and its attendant corollaries to the right to die with its corresponding issues. Underlying this shift is the subliminal acknowledgment that America, through an unwritten contract with techno-medicine, has exchanged its self-determination for the promises of biological restructuring and prolongation of human life. Such a contract denies individual freedom to determine the importance of one's quality of life versus quantity of life. Americans since 1976 have been searching for ways to recapture their self-determination in the end-of-life decision making process.

DEATH WITH DIGNITY

What does it mean to die with dignity? Thoughtful and compassionate individuals are found on all sides of this debate. Dying with dignity can involve the terminal person's ability to maintain some control over the manner and timing of death. If health care professionals see the death of the patient only as a medical failure, they may neglect to create the conditions necessary for a "good death." For many people, a good death involves relief from suffering.

For some people, death with dignity comes through the endurance of suffering, even extraordinary suffering. As Humphry (1992) asks, "Does suffering ennoble? Is suffering a part of life and a preparation for death?" (p. 83). Although some view suffering as having redemptive value or other eventual benefit to the one who suffers, medical pain reduction has immediate benefit to the patient and family. Suffering can be eliminated, managed, or made tolerable through the sophisticated use of pain medications and comfort measures, although a side effect of the administration of increasing levels of pain medications is the suppression of respiration and thus the possibility or probability of ending life. Physicians and health care workers often discuss the implications of the Hippocratic Oath as it applies to their duty to carry out the basic commitment to save life and at the same time respect the moral imperative to prevent suffering, attempting to reduce a moral equation to an acceptable common denominator. A dynamic tension between conflicting understandings of human suffering and competing sources of moral authority has influenced the transformation of public opinion and public policies regarding euthanasia and assisted suicide (Turner 1997).

The essential social, moral, and ethical dilemma is how to find a balance between the advantages derived from modern knowledge and applications of technology within the context of personal autonomy and the right to self-determination as guided by personal values about life and death. As Jennings (1991) notes, in the euthanasia debate, the principle of autonomy has been extended into an "assertion of sovereignty over the timing and circumstances" of death and "society's unwillingness to impose a conception of 'good' on individuals whose personal values and conceptions of the good may differ." Clouser (1991) asserts that general acceptance of a patient's right to self-determination and limited acceptance of the morality and rationality of assisted suicide should not blur the emphasis on palliative care.

PALLIATIVE CARE

In the United States, within the context of a pluralistic cultural environment, a social consensus has evolved that a patient (directly or through a proxy) has the right to refuse life-sustaining treatments. This consensus has promoted the provision of hospice services and palliative care programs to improve individuals' quality of life during the dying process and has also fueled debates concerning the legalization of PAS and euthanasia. MacDonald (1994) suggests that the emphasis on euthanasia diverts attention from a more fundamental ethical concern, which is the allocation of resources to ensure the provision of excellent palliative care.

The goals of palliative care are to relieve suffering and to improve the quality of an individual's remaining life. In the palliative medical care of terminal patients, the patients' autonomous medical instructions and health care proxy decisions guide the process of comprehensive management of pain and determination of appropriate points in the dying process when treatments should be accelerated, withheld, or withdrawn. Palliative care includes the appropriate administration of narcotics, and, if morphine is insufficient to contain the pain, tranquilizers or anesthetics enable the patient to sleep without feeling pain. The acts of palliative care workers respect a patient's rights to self-determination, autonomy, and privacy and are often consistent with the training and social perspective of the practicing physician. Although the determination of appropriate professional, ethical, and legal conduct and clarification of intent can be complex in particular cases, specialists in palliative care generally do not practice PAS or active euthanasia (Foley 1991).

Battin (1991) investigated attitudes toward end-of-life dilemmas in the United States, Holland, and Germany, which all have aging populations; the majority of deaths in all three countries are attributable to deteriorative diseases. In Holland, health care workers can provide voluntary active euthanasia; in Germany, patients have legal access to assisted suicide, often outside of medical settings; and in the United States, the withholding and withdrawing of life-sustaining treatments are legal options. As Battin notes, the AIDS epidemic has underscored the fact that members of younger as well as older generations die of terminal illnesses. As the numbers of individuals dying of AIDS increased, it became clear that existing hospice programs were ill equipped to face the challenge of coping with the increase in demand for their services and with the varieties of distressing symptoms the disease presented for management.

When patients' pain is managed effectively and hospice services are provided, requests for assisted death are often reduced. Bernhoft (1993) suggests that requests for euthanasia services from terminally ill patients are often the result of treatable depression or the undertreatment of pain and advocates the provision of high-quality care for the terminally ill within a hospice framework, funded through hospice insurance. Byock (1993) asserts that patient requests for assisted suicide services or euthanasia often decrease when patients' suffering is controlled and patients are reassured that they will not be abandoned in the dying process—two of the central tenets of hospice care. The World Health Organization (1989) has suggested that a physician should not be allowed to consider assisted suicide or euthanasia for a patient until palliative care and pain relief have been addressed.

Even with the provision of opioid analgesia and hospice care, the presence of intractable pain and their poor physical functioning motivate some patients to request PAS or euthanasia (Emanuel et al. 1998). In one study, approximately 33% of patients with multiple sclerosis reported that they had thought about requesting PAS under certain conditions; the factors that they said would motivate them to make such requests included unbearable pain, inability to participate in the activities of daily living that bring them pleasure, knowing that they are causing a financial burden to family members or caregivers, and pronounced emotional distress (Berkman et al. 1999). Logue (1994) notes that some competent patients, and the families of incompetent patients, have clearly rejected palliative care procedures in both hospice and nonhospice settings due to current medical limitations in pain management and symptom control. Foley (1991) acknowledges that current palliative care programs may be insufficient to meet the needs of cancer patients in advanced stages of the disease, but asserts that medical professionals should work on providing competent care for dying patients through high-quality programs for symptom control, management of pain and psychological distress, and improvement of quality of life before examining options to terminate life. Logue suggests that policy makers should consider options beyond passive euthanasia, consistent with patient autonomy and the right to die, that may be medically necessary to alleviate patient suffering.

In a survey that Arena (1999) conducted with a small sample of family members of patients whose dying was prolonged medically, the respondents expressed dissatisfaction with the norms that regulate how we die. They found these norms to be inadequate to meet the needs of the terminally ill, and they suggested that instruction regarding end-of-life care should be included in the basic educational curricula of all health care professionals, especially instruction focused on the improvement of pain management and communication with dying patients and their loved ones. Many scholars and other observers have promoted the notion that health care professionals should give careful consideration to alternative treatment possibilities rooted in palliative care and hospice care, with special emphasis on sharing control over medical decisions with patients and their family members (Task Force on Physician-Assisted Suicide 1995; Uzych 1996). In contrast, Seale and Addington-Hall (1995) examined the results of three surveys of family members and friends of hospice patients and found that, when levels of patient dependency and distress were controlled for, the majority of survivors thought it would have been a better outcome if their loved ones had died earlier. Measures of quality of care, symptom relief, and care in other institutions showed a weak association with euthanasia requests, whereas measures of unmet needs for symptom treatment and residential services were more strongly associated with such requests.

An additional aspect of palliative care is the provision of mental health services to family care providers after a patient's death; such preventive psychological and social interventions can affect the psychological outcomes for the bereaved. Kelly et al. (1999) examined grief responses among family caregivers following patients' deaths and found the severity of those responses to be significantly related to preexisting psychological symptoms at the time of referral to palliative home care service; relationship with the patient; reported greater numbers of adverse life events, including previous bereavements and separation experiences; pattern and effectiveness of coping responses; and severity of the patient's illness. Billings and Kolton (1999) found that the major factors influencing family satisfaction with bereavement care following a family member's death in a hospital were considerations about respect for the privacy, dignity, and comfort of the patient; effective communication with the family; quality of the emergency ward care; proper attention given to advance directives; and the provision of bereavement support. Of these factors, bereavement support services were most often described as inadequate, with hospital social workers and chaplains unable to contact approximately one-third of the relatives after the death. Smokowski and Wodarski (1996) suggest that medical social workers can fill a unique need by developing and implementing programs aimed at providing comprehensive care for the terminally ill.

THE WISH TO DIE

In a study of cancer patients, Chochinov et al. (1999) found that those who were receiving palliative care reported a relatively stable will to live, although for some patients fluctuations in the will to live were substantial. These researchers note that the "main predictor variables of will to live were depression, anxiety, shortness of breath, and sense of well-being, with the prominence of these variables changing over time" (p. 3). According to Quill (1993), patients may express a wish to die when they suffer from incurable progressive medical illnesses, when they are tired of aggressive medical treatment programs, when they

develop unrecognized physical symptoms (or their physical symptoms are undertreated), when they have psychosocial problems, when they experience spiritual crises, when they have clinical depression features, and especially when they have unrelenting and intolerable suffering.

In a study of patients with diagnosed HIV, Breitbart, Rosenfeld, and Passik (1996) found that 63% expressed a preference in favor of legalized PAS and 55% had considered seeking such services when their disease process had become debilitating. Predictor variables in subjects who favored legalization of PAS included high scores on measures of psychological distress, previous experience with the terminal illness of a family member, low participation in religious activities, and perceived low levels of social support. Breitbart et al. found no correlations between endorsement of assisted suicide and pain severity, functional impairment, physical symptoms, or extent of the disease process. However, Rosenfeld et al. (1999) found that attitudes toward hastened death among HIV/AIDS patients were significantly correlated with pain intensity and distress from physical symptoms.

Fins et al. (1999) investigated end-of-life decision making and found that appropriate transitions from life-sustaining treatment to comfort care and palliative services were associated with presence of a health care proxy, "do not resuscitate" orders, and comfort care plans, although 41% of the patients continued to receive antibiotics and 30% continued to have blood drawn, and only 13% of patients on ventilators and 19% on nutrition and hydration opted to request withdrawal of these procedures prior to death. Singer, Martin, and Kelner (1999) surveyed patients about end-of-life care and found that the areas of importance the patients identified were adequate pain and symptom management, the avoidance of prolongation of the dying process, the achievement of control and the balancing of burden, and the strengthening of relationships with loved ones in the available time.

The aims of palliative care are to relieve patient suffering and to improve the quality of remaining life, not to hasten death. However, the provision of pain relief through palliative analgesic administration may simultaneously hasten or cause a patient's death, and the appropriate ethical choice may be difficult to determine. In some instances, hastened death resulting from the use of palliative analgesia for a terminally ill patient can be not only an ethical outcome but an obligatory one (Cavanaugh 1996). The clinical practice of "slow euthanasia" (Billings and Block 1996)—that is, the practice of using treatment methods that lead to pain management and an eventual comfortable death for the patient—is more acceptable than more overt forms of euthanasia to patients and their family members, to health care professionals and the medical community, and, by extension, to the general public. As Saunders (1989–90) notes:

We are not so poor a society that we cannot afford time, and trouble and money to help people live until they die. We owe it to all those for whom we can kill the pain. . . . to make voluntary [active] euthanasia lawful would be an irresponsible act, hindering help, pressuring the vulnerable, abrogating our true respect and responsibility to the frail and the old, the disabled and the dying.

Gostin (1993) suggests that the euthanasia debate has three levels—the cessation of life-sustaining treatment, patient suicide, and physician-assisted suicide—and advocates that we maintain the ethical and legal distinction between passive and active euthanasia while allowing assisted suicide as an appropriate part of the continuum of end-of-life choices. Bachman, Alcser, Doukas, and Lichtenstein (1996) assert that also appropriate to the debate are concerns about "whether public opinion polls reflect ethical positions, the percentage of physicians who would participate in assisted suicide if it were legal, and the effects of cost-conscious managed health care plans on decisions regarding euthanasia for terminally ill patients." Wilson and Chochinov (1996) report:

> In jurisdictions in which assisted suicide has received legislative recognition, relatively more physicians express a willingness to perform it; where it is currently practiced, the rate of actual participation is very high. This suggests that legislation leads to more participation than before-the-fact surveys may indicate.

INFORMED CONSENT AND THE PATIENT SELF-DETERMINATION ACT

The principle of "informed consent" means that patients must have information about treatments, including possible side effects, and their own prognoses in order to make decisions concerning their health care that are appropriate to their own situations and their own values and preferences. Under the Patient Self-Determination Act of 1990, health care professionals must provide patients with information on their rights to receive or refuse medical treatments, to formulate advance directives, to appoint health care proxies, to execute living wills, and to select levels of medical intervention, especially in regard to cardiopulmonary resuscitation, mechanical breathing, artificial nutrition and hydration, major surgery, kidney dialysis, chemotherapy, minor surgery, invasive diagnostic tests, the use of blood or blood products, antibiotics, simple diagnostic tests, and pain medications.

A patient's health care proxy is a legally designated agent who is empowered to make medical decisions on behalf of the patient if the patient should become incompetent or otherwise unable to exercise his or her rights to autonomy and self-determination and to give or refuse informed consent. The health care proxy is obligated to follow the patient's wishes as expressed through living wills, medical directives, or other instructions; he or she must act consistently in the patient's best interests, but may not pursue or promote any illegal course of action.

"IT'S OVER, DEBBIE": A CASE OF INVOLUNTARY EUTHANASIA

In 1988, a brief anonymous report in the *Journal of the American Medical Association* focused the controversy over active euthanasia on the issue of informed consent. The journal article was written by a physician who related how he was called to the hospital room of a 20-year-old woman who was apparently dying of ovarian cancer; the patient was attached to an IV and receiving nasal oxygen. The alcohol drip sedation the woman was receiving had caused her to vomit profusely, and she reportedly said to the doctor, "Let's get this over with." The physician, who wrote, "I could not give her health, but I could give her rest," instructed a nurse to prepare a syringe of morphine sulfate, which he then injected into the patient's IV. Within 4 minutes, the patient ceased breathing ("It's Over" 1988).

The medical community's response to this article was immediate and varied. The controversy ranged from the nature of this particular case (in which the act was both surreptitious and involuntary, suggesting the possibility of a criminal charge of felony premeditated murder) to the larger issue of whether there is an appropriate role for physicians in direct active euthanasia. In a small follow-up study, Anderson and Caddell (1993) surveyed oncology medical professionals and found that 60% indicated they agreed with the anonymous physician's actions and at least some supported physician-assisted euthanasia.

JACK KEVORKIAN: ASSISTED SUICIDE AND ACTIVE EUTHANASIA

In January 1990, Dr. Jack Kevorkian sent a letter to the Michigan Department of Licensing and Regulation in which he stated, "I have begun a unique medical practice: to assist in the rational suicide of patients who are suffering from eminently [*sic*] terminal illness, severely crippling or painful disease or deformity or trauma, and who, on their own, have decided that the quality of life for them has degenerated to intolerable levels" (quoted in "The People of the State of Michigan" 1991:110). In June 1990, Kevorkian assisted in the suicide of Janet Adkins, 54, who had been diagnosed as being in the early stages of Alzheimer's disease (Gibbs 1990). Murder charges were brought against Kevorkian for Adkins's death, but the charges were dismissed in December 1990. By late 1998, Kevorkian admitted that he had participated in approximately 130 deaths (Goodman 1998). Many questions arose about Kevorkian's activities. Although he was tried four times on criminal charges, he was not found guilty of criminal conduct related to his assisted suicide activities. However, Michigan authorities did revoke his medical license.

Those who criticized Kevorkian's actions had moral and religious objections to his ending the lives of others, to his confusing the role of physician as healer with the role of agent of assisted death (Kevorkian was a pathologist), and to the manner in which he conducted his assisted death services. Many complained that he provided his services without obtaining adequate medical information on his clients, without conducting sufficient consultations with his clients, and without ensuring that sufficient safeguards were in place to protect his clients. He was criticized especially for failing to suggest to his clients alternate methods for the management of physical pain. In addition, Kevorkian's clients were predominantly females who fit the general psychological profile of suicide attempters, and only 28.3% of them were terminally ill (Kaplan, Lachenmeier, et al. 1999–2000; Kaplan, O'Dell, et al. 1999–2000). Other criticisms of Kevorkian's approach to assisted death included factors related to his personality, such as his delight in being the subject of publicity, his "Dr. Death" persona, and his failure to follow his own purported guidelines and standards in carrying out assisted deaths (these consisted of prior client consultations with psychiatric and pain specialists, a 24-hour waiting period, the provision of extensive patient counseling, and the immediate halt to all assisted death actions at any sign of patient ambivalence).

On September 17, 1998, Kevorkian videotaped his own actions as he provided euthanasia services by lethal injection to Thomas Youk, who suffered with advanced amyotrophic lateral sclerosis (Lou Gehrig's disease). The tape was subsequently aired on the CBS television newsmagazine *60 Minutes,* and soon after, Kevorkian was charged with first-degree murder and criminal assisted suicide. The assisted suicide charge was subsequently dropped, and the testimony of Youk's family was irrelevant to the remaining murder charge. During the trial in March 1999, Kevorkian acted as his own lawyer and neglected to call any witnesses in his own defense. The jury found him guilty of second-degree murder and delivery of a controlled substance, and he was sentenced to a prison term of 10 to 25 years for the murder conviction and a concurrent 3 to 7 years for delivery of a controlled substance, with eligibility for parole in less than 7 years. At Kevorkian's sentencing, Judge Jessica Cooper of Oakland County, Michigan, stated:

> This trial was not about the political or moral correctness of euthanasia. It was about you, sir. It was about lawlessness. It was about disrespect for a society that exists and flourishes because of the strength of the legal system. No one, sir, is above the law. No one. You were on bond to another judge when you committed this offense; you were not licensed to practice medicine when you committed this offense, and you hadn't been licensed for eight years. And you had the audacity to go on national television, show the world what you did and dare the legal system to stop you. Well, sir, consider yourself stopped. (Quoted in "Judge Assails 'Lawlessness'" 1999)

TIMOTHY QUILL: PHYSICIAN-ASSISTED SUICIDE

In an article published in the *New England Journal of Medicine* in 1991, Dr. Timothy Quill reported his participation in the assisted suicide of a 45-year-old patient, "Diane," who suffered from acute myelomonocytic leukemia. Diane had refused traditional treatment protocols and entered a hospice program, conveying that she wanted to live fully and well in her remaining time and then end her life with dignity in the least painful way possible. After conferring with the Hemlock Society, she requested a prescription for barbiturates under the guise of complaints of insomnia. After several months had passed and her disease had progressed, she said her good-byes to family, friends, and physician. Two days later, her husband announced that Diane was dead. A Rochester, New York, grand jury reviewed the case and determined that no criminal conduct had occurred. Quill was charged with and subsequently cleared of medical misconduct by the New York State Medical Board. In his own defense, Quill (1993) has suggested that physicians should provide terminal patients more than pain management prescriptions and referrals to hospice services. In his view, physicians should accept the responsibility of providing continuing care to their terminal patients as they face the dying trajectory.

Criticisms of Quill's actions in the case of Diane focused on several issues, including whether voluntary euthanasia is appropriate care for the terminally ill (Levy 1991), whether Diane's statistical one-in-four chance of survival was sufficiently low for her physician to go along with her wish to forgo the uncertainties of treatment (Ross 1991), whether society has shown a predisposition to accept death as an outcome rather than develop more effective systems for end-of-life care (Lynn and Teno 1991), and whether cases such as Diane's represent the progressive slide of social values down the slippery slope of medical expediency (O'Conner 1991).

ATTITUDES ABOUT THE RIGHT TO DIE

In 1990, the Times Mirror Center for the People and the Press published the results of a national poll regarding public attitudes about the right to die. In his review of this poll, Kastenbaum (1998) notes that a significant majority of the respondents agreed that there are circumstances in which a person should be allowed to die, that people do have the right to make their own decisions about life-sustaining treatment, and that stopping treatment is a reasonable course of action in cases where individuals are suffering great physical pain or are unable to function in activities of daily living because of an incurable disease. The Americans surveyed strongly approved of right-to-die legislation that allows patients or their proxies to make decisions about the withdrawal or withholding of medical treatment. A slight majority agreed that a person has the moral right to end his or her own life if he or she is afflicted with an incurable disease or is suffering great pain with no hope of improvement. However, a strong majority disagreed that a person has the moral right to end his or her own life if he or she has become a burden to family or if life itself has become a burden. In general, the results of this poll suggest that Americans consider the specific circumstances of each case to be of paramount importance in the determination of an individual's right to die.

In comparing the results of a survey of health care workers concerning their attitudes about the right-to-die issue with national poll results, I found that, like the general public, the majority of health care workers endorse the concept of an individual's right to self-determination (Walker 1997). Health care staff were significantly more likely than members of the general public to agree that there are circumstances in which a person should be allowed to die and that people should have the right to make their own decisions about receiving life-sustaining treatment; that they themselves would ask a physician to stop treatment if they were in great pain or unable to function; that they approve of right-to-die legislation that allows medical treatment to be withdrawn or withheld, with patient consent; and that a person has the moral right to end his or her own life if afflicted with an incurable disease. However, a significantly smaller proportion of health care workers, compared with the general public, agreed that an individual is sometimes justified in killing his or her spouse because that person is suffering great pain from a terminal illness or that a person has the moral right to end his or her own life if he or she has become a burden on the family or if life has become a burden.

RATIONAL SUICIDE

Suicidal ideation and behavior often result from an individual's feelings of despair, depression, and hopelessness. If a desire for suicide derives from irrational motives, intervention in the suicidal process seems morally justifiable. But the question arises: Can suicide be a rational action when the alternative is unrelenting physical pain accompanying terminal illness? If so, rational suicide in the form of euthanasia may be considered a morally appropriate and legitimate exercise of an individual's right to self-determination.

In assisted suicide, although the individual's immediate cause of death results from his or her own actions, the individual has obtained the means for taking those actions with the cooperation of another person. The individual acts as the agent of his or her own death, which implies that the action involves the individual's consent, the absence of coercion, and the individual's voluntary assumption of the moral and legal consequences. It is not illegal to commit suicide in any jurisdiction of the United States; however, assisting in the death of another person is illegal, and a person who does so may be charged with accessory to suicide, homicide, or murder.

People's assessments of the moral appropriateness of suicide may depend on the religious and cultural context of the action. Today, most of the world's organized religions oppose or forbid suicide based on the extension of the belief that all life comes from God. From this viewpoint, the individual has temporary custody of the "divine spark" of life and is under a moral imperative to cherish and care for the gift. The Bible says: "Don't you know that you yourselves are God's temple and that God's Spirit lives in you? If anyone destroys God's temple, God will destroy him; for God's temple is sacred, and you are that temple" (First Corinthians 3:16–17). The Roman Catholic Church's Declaration on Euthanasia states that "intentionally causing one's own death, or suicide, is . . . equally as wrong as murder . . . a rejection of God's sovereignty and loving plan" (Sacred Congregation for the Doctrine of the Faith 1982:512; quoted in Corr, Nabe, and Corr 2000:480). According to Feldman and Rosner (1984), Judaism teaches that "human life [should] be treated as an end in itself. . . . Even individual autonomy is secondary to the sanctity of human life and therefore, a patient is not permitted to end his or her life" (p. 106; quoted in Corr et al. 2000:479). The Koran states, "Do not destroy yourselves" (4:29). In Hinduism and Buddhism, suicide is condemned because "the evil encompasses the karmic consequences of the act which impede the progress of liberation" (Crawford 1995:68; quoted in Corr et al. 2000:480).

In euthanasia, death is caused not directly by the individual but by the actions of another, an agent with beneficent intent to provide the individual with a "good death." Euthanasia is distinguished from homicide by the intent of the agent of death. Homicide, or murder, generally results from malevolent intent, whereas the intent of euthanasia is to relieve current suffering or prevent greater suffering. Criminal charges of homicide, manslaughter, or murder are more likely to be brought against the provider agent in a case of euthanasia if the individual who died was not already near death.

DISTINCTIONS IN EUTHANASIA

The roots of the term *euthanasia* are found in the Greek words *eu,* meaning "good" or "easy," and *thanatos,* meaning "death." Thus the term originally referred to a painless and peaceful dying. Over time, however, it has come to be applied to the act or practice of killing hopelessly sick or injured individuals or animals for reasons of mercy, in order to avert continued or increased suffering. The "good death" of euthanasia may be synonymous with "death with dignity" in individual cases. For many people, a death in which the dying process is pointlessly prolonged, causing needless pain and suffering, constitutes a "bad death." In clinical practice, prolonging life for the net effect of prolonging suffering can be seen as a violation of a fundamental rule of medicine: *Primum non nocere* ("First do no harm") (Fulton and Metress 1995).

Many observers make critical distinctions about hastened or assisted death along the dimensions of voluntary versus involuntary and active versus passive. In passive euthanasia, medical personnel withhold or withdraw treatment from a terminally ill or seriously injured patient and allow the patient to die due to the disease or injury. Some ethicists consider the withdrawal or withholding of medical treatment, especially nutrition and hydration, to be an act of omission. In contrast, active euthanasia is an act of commission, in which the intent of the course of action is the death of the patient, whether that patient dies through lethal injection or some other means or is actively assisted in the dying process. In voluntary euthanasia, a competent patient gives informed consent to withhold treatment, whether in a verbal expression of intent, through a living will, or through a statement of medical wishes made while the patient was competent and later expressed by a health care proxy. In involuntary euthanasia, others make decisions on behalf of the incompetent patient, and they may or may not have verbal or written expressions of the patient's wishes to guide the process. Unforeseen circumstances often create uncertainties for competent patients, the proxies of incompetent patients, and attendant physicians, health care staff, and family members.

The distinctions noted above are consequential for the discussion of PAS and euthanasia. The legal system and public opinion in the United States generally have been more tolerant of passive euthanasia, the practice of allowing a person to die by withholding or withdrawing life support when further procedures will only prolong suffering in the dying trajectory or maintain the person in a persistent vegetative state, than they have been toward the practice of active euthanasia.

RELIGIOUS TRADITIONS

As Albright and Hazler (1995) point out, widely differing religious, moral, governmental, and personal views of death, especially in light of medical and technological advances in prolonging and sustaining life, have resulted in widely divergent opinions and ethical perspectives on euthanasia. People's ethical and moral perspectives are often guided by their religious beliefs. Corr et al. (2000) summarize the perspectives on euthanasia of the major world religions as described below.

In Judaism, a central belief is that all life comes from God and is of infinite value; therefore, the duty is to preserve life, and active euthanasia is morally unacceptable. This tenet is derived from the Mishnah:

> They do not close the eyes of a corpse on the Sabbath, nor on an ordinary day at the moment the soul goes forth. And he who closes the eyes of a corpse at the moment the soul goes forth, lo, this one sheds blood. (Shabbat 23:5; quoted in Corr et al. 2000:498)

Supportive text can be found in the Babylonian Talmud:

> The rabbis taught: Who closes the eyes of a dying man is like a murderer, for it is the same as a candle which is about to go out. If a man lays a finger on the dying flame, it immediately becomes extinguished, but if left alone would still burn for a little time. The same can be applied to the case of an expiring man; if his eyes were not closed, he would live a little longer, and hence it is like murder. (Tract Sabbath; quoted in Corr et al. 2000:498)

In Christianity, a core belief is that all life comes from God and is therefore sacred; the duty is to be compassionate and to provide proper care to ourselves and others in a loving way. Among the many denominations that represent modern Christian belief there are various doctrinal perspectives on appropriate moral conduct in end-of-life situations, but most place an emphasis on palliative care. In the Bible, Jesus says that the first commandment is to

> love the Lord your God with all your heart and with all your soul and with all your mind and with all your strength. The second is this: "Love your neighbor as yourself." There is no commandment greater than these. (Mark 12:30–31)

In the theological tradition of the Catholic Church, physician-assisted suicide is viewed as a variant of euthanasia, which is seen as a breach of an individual's ethical responsibilities to self, the larger society, and God (O'Rourke 1991). In a survey of nurses, Nagy (1990) found general support for passive euthanasia and strong opposition to active euthanasia. The sample split sharply along religious lines, however, with Catholics indicating greater opposition to any form of euthanasia.

In the Islamic faith, Allah is the source of all life, and suffering reminds human beings of their misdeeds and brings them closer to God. Therefore, human interference through euthanasia thwarts the divine plan for each person. Mohammed instructs the faithful in the Koran, "Do not destroy yourselves" (4:29). The 1981 Islamic Code of Medical Ethics extends this principle:

> [The] doctor is well advised to realize his limit and not transgress it. If it is scientifically certain that life cannot be restored, then it is futile to diligently [maintain] the vegetative state of the patient by heroic means. . . . It is the process of life that the doctor aims to maintain and not the process of dying. In any case, the doctor shall not take positive measures to terminate the patient's life. (First International Conference on Islamic Medicine [1981] 1991:10; quoted in Corr et al. 2000:500)

In Hinduism, all reality flows from Brahmin, a featureless entity that arises from all that is. The reincarnation cycle is governed by the effects of karma, the consequences of the actions that individuals perform. Ending or maintaining life through medical intervention can interfere with the workings of karma, and suffering is one way to pay karmic debt. Therefore, assisted suicide and euthanasia can be undesirable courses of action, accumulating further karmic consequences for the recipient and the agent of hastened death.

A related principle is ahimsa, or the avoidance of violence, based on the idea that life is sacred. As Mohandas Gandhi explained: "Ahimsa does not simply mean non-killing. Himsa means causing pain to or killing any life out of anger, or from a selfish purpose, or with the intention of injuring it. Refraining from so doing is ahimsa" (quoted in Crawford 1995:115; as quoted in Corr et al. 2000:501). Gandhi (1980) also said, "Should my child be attacked with rabies and there was no helpful remedy to relieve his agony, I should consider it my duty to take his life" (p. 84; quoted in Corr et al. 2000:501).

In Buddhism, there is no God the creator. Karma drives the reincarnation cycle, and salvation lies in ending the cycle of death and rebirth. To desire an end of suffering is not unworthy, as Rinpoche ([1986] 1993) relates:

> The person who decides that they have had enough suffering and wish to be allowed to die is in a situation that we cannot call virtuous or non-virtuous. We certainly cannot blame someone for making that decision. It is not a karmically negative act. It is simply the wish to avoid suffering, which is the fundamental wish of all living beings. On the other hand, it is not a particularly virtuous act either. . . . Rather than being a wish to end one's life, it's a wish to end suffering. Therefore it is a karmically neutral act. (P. 374)

However, active euthanasia can be an unacceptable course of action. In the *Vinaya-Pitaka,* or *Book of Discipline,* the Buddha says:

> Whatever monk should intentionally deprive a human being of life or should look about so as to be his knife-bringer, or should praise the beauty of death, or should incite [anyone] to death, saying, "Hullo there, my man, of what use to you is this evil, difficult life? Death is better for you than life," or who should deliberately and purposefully in various ways praise the beauty of death or incite [anyone] to death: he also is one who is defeated, he is not in communion. (Quoted in Corr et al. 2000:502)

ARGUMENTS CONCERNING THE PRACTICE OF EUTHANASIA

In brief, the philosophical and moral debate about voluntary active euthanasia revolves around fundamental differences in perspectives (Parakh and Slesnick 1992; Rachels 1986). Those who support the practice of euthanasia employ three main arguments: the "mercy" argument, the "Golden Rule" argument, and the "enhancement of liberty" argument. The mercy argument extends compassion for the suffering person to include prevention of further suffering. The Golden Rule argument, as paraphrased from the Books of Matthew (7:12) and Luke (6:31) in the Bible, is that people should "do unto others" as they would have others do unto them—by implication, they should deliver others from misery. The enhancement of liberty argument, also referred to as the "autonomy," "right to die," or "quality of life" argument, is that a competent person should have the right to refuse medical treatment and even to request assistance in ending his or her own life. Each of these arguments is consistent with the secular philosophy of relativism.

Those who oppose the practice of euthanasia employ three main arguments also: the "Thou shalt not kill" argument, the "hope for a cure" argument, and the "slippery slope" argument. The religious prohibition "Thou shalt not kill" has been also translated as "Thou shalt not murder," emphasizing the overriding principle of preservation of life while excluding acts of justifiable killing, such as killing in self-defense or defense of others and killing in time of war. In essence, this central argument against the practice of euthanasia is consistent with the civil and religious prohibition against killing, even of oneself, regardless of circumstances, and the secular philosophical perspective of vitalism.

Those who use the "miraculous recovery" or hope for a cure argument take the point of view that medical diagnoses and prognoses are never certain and the possibility always exists that promising lines of research may yield improved treatments that could provide reasonable hope for an individual's recovery. However, the actual effect of adhering to this principle could be for both patient and medical personnel to become accustomed to suffering "because of moral uncertainty or unclarity" (Corr et al. 2000:497).

Those who make the slippery slope argument assert that the social acceptance of assisted or hastened death could contribute to abuses in other applications. For instance, the social legitimation of public policy and medical practice to allow euthanasia, and the availability of venues to provide euthanasia and hastened death services in appropriate situations to qualified patients, could lead to a progression from voluntary to involuntary euthanasia or to the inappropriate application of involuntary euthanasia in some cases, motivated by monetary considerations such as inheritance or the desire to avoid the emotional and financial costs of caring for terminally ill persons. The practice of involuntary euthanasia of terminally ill or critically injured patients could in turn be extended to persons in a persistent vegetative state, patients who are seriously injured and comatose, disabled and impaired persons, socially marginal individuals in custodial care situations, and, by implication, other socially marginal individuals or groups in the larger society. Indeed, Nazi doctors and health care staff participated in what was called euthanasia in following Hitler's policy of *Vernichtung lebensunwerten Lebens,* or the "extermination of valueless life" (Kastenbaum 1998:238). The Nazis defended their elimination of the infirm, a large proportion of the institutionalized population, homosexuals, and criminals as "mercy killing" and as a practice promoting economic efficiency. With the participation of government agents and physicians, these "measures of expediency" derived from policies socially identified as euthanasia were extended to the genocide of Jews, Romanies (so-called Gypsies), and millions of other people (Friedlander 1995).

Medical objections to the practice of active euthanasia have included the argument that taking a patient's life is inconsistent with the responsibilities and values of a healer. It is difficult, however, for doctors and other health care workers to witness unrelieved suffering and hear individuals' pleas for assistance in dying and remain professionally and personally detached. Physicians who decide to relieve suffering may be mistaken about the potential for recovery in individual cases. Doctors can face serious legal consequences for participating in assisted death or "death by request" actions, and if euthanasia or hastened death services are ever to be legalized, clear procedural guidelines will be necessary to safeguard physicians providing such services from potential malpractice suits and criminal charges. Regardless of the law and public policy, however, some physicians hold religious or ethical convictions that would prevent them from taking a person's life under any professional circumstances.

Some who argue against the practice of euthanasia have proposed that people who ask for assistance in dying are asking too much of others, and that each act of euthanasia results in the loss of the benefits to society of the exchange between the patient and others in the time of the natural life-to-death process (Travis 1991). When a person's death is brought about before his or her illness has run its fatal course, that person may be deprived of a valuable period of good life, and his or her family and friends may be deprived of the shared intimacy of the dying process, losing an irreplaceable time in which to express reciprocal love and provide companionship. Yet some patients will prolong their time for living and renegotiate their conditions of dying once they are assured that hastened death services are a viable option.

MEDICAL CONSIDERATIONS

Brescia (1991) asserts that recognizing the onset of the dying process is crucial to the physician's ability to make further decisions about a patient's medical care. Such recognition can prevent a patient from undergoing useless treatments or unnecessary procedures or from taking inadequate medications; it is "not an excuse to balance death with suffering or to request the frail ill to move aside."

From a counselor's perspective, the issues of autonomy, nonmaleficence, and beneficence are of paramount importance in discussions with patients about euthanasia decisions (Albright and Hazler 1995). Maier and Newman (1995) suggest that the factors of informed consent, competence, intent, and the physical and emotional status of the terminally ill patient are particularly relevant in euthanasia decisions. Shapiro and Miller (1994) investigated how medical students approach clinical ethical dilemmas related to euthanasia and found that the principles of patient autonomy and rights, economic constraints, and utilitarianism were issues of paramount concern. In general, they found that men were more likely than women to address utilitarian and cost-containment issues from a logical perspective and that women were more likely than men to incorporate patient and family rights from a social issues perspective.

PSYCHOLOGICAL CONSIDERATIONS

The diagnosis and management of psychiatric disorders in medically ill patients merits serious professional, ethical, and legal consideration in any discussion of euthanasia, as such disorders can influence individuals' ability to cope with the crises embedded in illness processes and considerations of mortality (Kelly and Varghese 1996). A patient's decision to pursue assisted suicide options must be both rational and autonomous, and must not be motivated primarily by depression (Weir 1992). Neither physicians nor psychiatrists want to enable the mentally ill to commit assisted suicide, and one of the safeguards often recommended for any legalized form of voluntary euthanasia is mandatory psychiatric review that is especially sensitive to patient ideation and symptoms indicative of major depression and/or delirium that can interfere with rational decision-making processes (Ryan 1995).

After Oregon passed a law permitting physician-assisted suicide in 1994, about two-thirds of surveyed psychiatrists in that state agreed that a physician should be permitted to write prescriptions for lethal medications for qualified patients, whereas one-third were opposed to the practice. Only 6% of those surveyed thought they could evaluate in a single session whether a patient had a psychiatric disorder that was resulting in impaired judgment in relation to an assisted suicide request (Ganzini et al. 1996). Groenewoud et al. (1997) found in a sample of 552 Dutch psychiatrists that 64% thought PAS requests from patients with mental disorders could be acceptable; 12% had provided hastened death services in the past, and an additional 45% were willing to assist in such services. The psychiatrists who said that they refused to assist noted that the following factors affected their decisions: belief that the mental disorder was treatable, doubt that the patient's suffering was unbearable or hopeless, and opposition to suicide in principle. Most, but not all, of the mentally disordered patients who had received PAS or euthanasia assistance from the Dutch psychiatrists were terminally or seriously physically ill as well.

As noted above, some have argued that the legalization of euthanasia could result in the failure of civil protections for vulnerable segments of the population or the actual abuse and exploitation of "marginal" individuals with limited social and practical support systems. Werth (1999) provides information on the professional standards of the American Counseling Association, the American Psychiatric Association, and the National Association of Social Workers concerning ethical conduct in assisted death services.

ACTIVE EUTHANASIA:
THE NETHERLANDS EXPERIENCE

Both opponents and proponents of physician-assisted suicide and euthanasia have referenced the model used in the Netherlands. Although Dutch law states that anyone who takes a life can be punished, a series of legal decisions made from 1970 to 1990 made it clear that physician-assisted euthanasia would not be prosecuted under certain conditions. In 1993, the Dutch legislature passed a bill under which physicians are allowed to take active steps to end the lives of patients who request a "dignified death." The guidelines include the following requirements: The patient has a confirmed terminal diagnosis; the patient has made a written request affirming a wish to die; the patient is enduring unbearable and incurable physical suffering; and the appropriate documentation is provided to the coroner (Cox 1993; Dupuis 1993). The means of hastened death include refusal of treatment by the patient, physician decision to forgo medical intervention, indirect euthanasia through accelerated pain management procedures, assisted suicide, and active euthanasia at the request of the patient. Koenig (1993) points out that 85% of assisted suicides in the Netherlands occur among the elderly, who seek assistance primarily from general practitioners.

Proponents argue that the availability of direct life-termination procedures allows terminally ill patients to choose more humane ways to die and may actually contribute to life extension, because patients are freed of fears about painful incapacitation and the eventual inability to commit suicide. In a study of AIDS patients in the Netherlands, Bindels et al. (1996) found that more than one-third had made a decision to utilize physician-assisted hastened death services as "an extreme form of palliation, applied in the terminal phase of the disease" (p. 499).

Hendin (1995) notes that legalization of PAS and euthanasia in the Netherlands has promoted a transformation of suicide and assisted death into a preferred mode of managing patients with serious or terminal illness. A survey commissioned by the Dutch government found that of the 130,000 deaths occurring in the Netherlands in 1990, approximately 2,300 were reported cases of active euthanasia and 400 were assisted suicides; the researchers estimate that an additional 1,000 people had hastened deaths without making formal requests for such intervention, and in nearly 1,900 deaths physicians increased dosages of pain-relieving drugs with the explicit purpose of hastening death (van der Maas, van Delden, and Pijnenborg 1992). Additional concerns arose in 1995 when a physician provided lethal medication to an infant who had been born with terrible and unrelenting pain from a spinal column defect, with authorization from the parents (Kastenbaum 1998). The controversy derived from the fact that the infant was not terminally ill and the decision involved the substituted judgment of the parents as surrogates about the quality and conditions of the newborn's life.

Do these latter cases represent a slide of social values down the slippery slope of expediency? Relevant issues from the Dutch experience include the viability as euthanasia candidates of patients who are not physically ill, the provision of euthanasia services to competent patients without consultation or informed consent, and the possibility that the appropriate medical application of euthanasia might become inappropriately available to patients with suicidal depression, to family members with ambiguous agendas and mixed motives, to health care proxies facing unforeseen complications and decisions to be made on behalf of patients, and to the health care providers responsible for allocations of resources, involving complex decisions balancing extent and kind of medical interventions and quality-of-life assessments for individual patients.

On November 28, 2000, the lower house of the Dutch Parliament approved a bill legalizing euthanasia (Deutsch 2000), adopting the informal guidelines already in practice and clearing the way for the upper house of the Parliament to endorse the euthanasia legislation in 2002 (Visser and Meijburg 2003). Dutch officials stressed that the Netherlands is not interested in becoming the international provider of euthanasia services; indeed, foreigners would not be able to meet the criterion of a long-term doctor-patient relationship.

Does the Dutch model provide a preview of the possible progression of outcomes in the American experience?

QUESTIONS

From the physician's perspective, assisted suicide may sometimes seem necessary and justifiable, a reasonable, compassionate, even merciful action to end a patient's life in the face of known terminal circumstances and disease or trauma trajectory, overwhelming suffering, or the presence of an unrelenting persistent vegetative state. The patient's pain and suffering are often the primary motives for a PAS request, but they may not be the only ones. Palermo (1995) includes among the possible motives the collaborating factor of the physician's loss of professional authority and influence over the progression of the terminal trajectory and suggests that PAS reflects a utilitarian approach to limiting suffering by eliminating the one who suffers.

Such concerns have shaped the public examination of fundamental questions regarding assisted death and medical euthanasia. Is rational or assisted suicide legal, moral, and/or ethical? Should hastened death services be restricted to terminally ill patients, or should persons suffering from debilitating conditions or from intolerable life circumstances be considered qualified candidates? Can we be sure that a patient is making an assisted death decision that is not influenced by the pressures of family concerns or economic circumstance? Can we implement sufficient safeguards to differentiate patient psychological distress from physical suffering? How many consultations are adequate to determine the advisability or need of assisted death in a given case? What kinds of people should serve on euthanasia review boards? The public debate in the United States has generally focused on two central issues: Should physician-assisted suicide and/or euthanasia be permitted, and, if so, what kind of legal and medical regulation should be required?

GUIDELINES

Quill, Cassel, and Meier (1992) have proposed a number of clinical criteria to guide physician decision making about assisted suicide. These include the following requirements: The patient must clearly and repeatedly express a wish to die of his or her own free will and at his or her own initiative, the patient's judgment must be undistorted; the patient must have an incurable medical condition that involves unrelenting and intolerable suffering, the physician must exhaust the known protocols of comfort care, the physician-assisted suicide must occur only within the parameters of a meaningful medical relationship, the physician must obtain due consultation with another physician who is well versed in comfort care, and the physician must maintain appropriate documentation. Klagsbrun (1991) notes that any documentation of physician-assisted suicide should include verification that the patient does not have treatable depression or symptoms of pain and discomfort that are responsive to palliative care and that the patient's discussion with the physician should have "duration, depth, and intimacy."

Compassion in Dying, a nonprofit organization operating in Washington State, has proposed guidelines and safeguards for physician-assisted hastened death. According to Kastenbaum's (1998) summary of these guidelines, they limit eligibility for assisted death to competent terminally ill adult patients experiencing severe and intolerable suffering. The patient must fully understand his or her diagnosis and prognosis. The request for assisted death services must not result from economic considerations or inadequate palliative care. An independent mental health evaluation must be obtained in order to verify that the patient understands the consequences of the decision and that the request is not motivated by emotional distress or depression. The consent of the patient's family and confirmation by an independent physician are also required. The patient must make three written and signed requests for hastened death, with at least a 48-hour interval between the second and third requests. Finally, any indication of indecision on the part of the patient or opposition from the patient's immediate family must cancel the process.

POLICY STATEMENTS REGARDING PAS AND EUTHANASIA

Cultural trends in the United States since early in the 20th century have included intervention in and medical management of the process of individual death.

Increasingly, this has included the incorporation of the use of sophisticated technologies that can aid in symptom management, improve palliative care, and prolong the dying trajectory. Because of the bureaucratization necessary at this level of intervention, end-of-life decision making has become a matter not only of individuals' rights to self-determination but of public moral deliberation and social policy. The possibility of the legalization, or at least decriminalization, of PAS and voluntary active euthanasia as a matter of public policy, in recognition of the intensely personal and painful nature of this decision at the end of life, has brought the matter to public debate. As one author has noted, "For me and many others, the right to die in a manner of one's own choosing is the ultimate civil liberty" (Humphry 1992:75). When Elisabeth Kübler-Ross (1974) was asked about pending legislation on euthanasia, she replied:

> I find it sad that we have to have laws about matters like this. I think that we should use our human judgment, and come to grips with our own fear of death. Then we could respect patients' needs and listen to them, and would not have a problem such as this. (P. 84)

In the Netherlands, the 1984 policy statement of the General Board of the Royal Dutch Medical Association, which discusses the legalization of euthanasia and assisted suicide, notes that the physician is the appropriate agent to provide life-ending intervention within a medical context, that physicians who reject the provision of assisted death services in principle or have situational objections in specific cases must be prepared to refer patients requesting those services to other physicians, and that the acceptability of euthanasia should not be evaluated according to the cause of suffering or the phase of dying (General Board of the Royal Dutch Medical Association 1996).

There are crucial distinctions, both medically and legally, among the courses of action taken depending on whether the intent is to allow a person to die, to assist in patient suicide, or to perform active euthanasia. The National Council on Death and Dying was established "to address the dilemma of freeing people from meaningless suffering while enhancing the valuing of life" (Clouser 1991). An intense medical, social, and legal debate has questioned whether PAS represents abandonment of the patient or justified killing, breach of the commitment to "do no harm" or prevention of greater suffering, appropriate management of sophisticated technologies or a failure of those same technologies to improve care of the dying.

The ethics committee of Maison Michel Sarrazin (1994) in Quebec has considered the clinical, institutional, ethical, and legal dimensions of euthanasia policy and has recommended that prohibitions against the practice be maintained. The Committee on Bioethical Issues of the Medical Society of the State of New York also officially opposes physician participation in assisted suicide and euthanasia, noting that 57% of surveyed New York physicians endorse the legal prohibition of euthanasia (Rosner et al. 1992). After a discussion of the issues, the New York State Task Force on Life and the Law (1994) voted unanimously to oppose the legalization of physician-assisted suicide.

U.S. CONSTITUTIONAL ISSUES AND ARGUMENTS

Is there a legal distinction between a patient's refusing life-support technologies or refusing nutrition and hydration and a patient's actively seeking physician-assisted suicide or hastened death through some form of euthanasia? The judicial assertion that the withdrawal of life-sustaining treatments or the administration of high levels of pain relief medications is equivalent to physician-assisted death services has been challenged (Orentlicher 1996).

In the United States, the courts' consideration of the assertion of a constitutional right to die from assisted suicide or euthanasia has been restricted to the terminally ill. The federal appeals courts have essentially ruled that the constitutional "due process" and "equal protection" clauses extend the patient's right to self-determination through refusing unwanted life-sustaining treatments to the right to seek physician-assisted suicide services (Sullivan 1997). In his ruling in a 1996 case, Judge Stephen Reinhardt of the Ninth Circuit Court of Appeals applied the "liberty interest" clause of the 14th Amendment and stated that the competent terminally ill adult may have an overriding interest in choosing a humane death instead of life in a state of helpless incompetence (*Compassion in Dying v. State of Washington* 1996). Judge Roger J. Miner of the Second Circuit Court of Appeals applied the "equal rights" clause of the 14th Amendment in another 1996 case, saying that the state has no interest in prolonging life for a person who is already in the process of dying (*Quill v. Vacco* 1996). The net effect of these rulings has been to bring legal reasoning closer to the social values attached to relief of patient suffering.

As Scofield (1991) notes, although the move toward legalizing assisted suicide appears to be supported by the constitutional "right to privacy," it actually constitutes a more radical change in law and social practice than is immediately apparent. Scofield suggests that in light of the complexities involved, acceptance of assisted suicide represents a "dubious advance in patient rights or social justice."

THE U.S. SUPREME COURT RULING

Legal challenges to state bans on physician-assisted suicide and hastened death services arose through the Ninth Circuit Court of Appeals in *Compassion in Dying v. State of Washington* (1996) and the Second Circuit Court of Appeals in *Quill v. Vacco* (1996). On April 2, 1996, the

Second Circuit Court rejected New York State laws banning physician-assisted suicide. Soon after, the American Medical Association filed an amicus brief with the U.S. Supreme Court, opposing the legalization of physician-assisted suicide (Gianelli 1996).

On June 26, 1997, the U.S. Supreme Court unanimously upheld state laws that ban physician-assisted suicide (Savage 1997). In its ruling, the Court did not deny the terminally ill the option of obtaining pain medications in dosages that could hasten death, as long as the drugs are not prescribed explicitly to cause death. The Court made it clear that it would not go beyond a 1990 ruling that supported terminally ill patients' constitutional right to reject life-support technologies and procedures, but distinguished that aspect of the patient's right to autonomous self-determination from a constitutional "right to die" in the form of physician-assisted suicide. The Supreme Court's ruling did not countermand the existing procedure that allows physicians to provide adequate pain relief even if the indirect effect of that action is to shorten life, a procedure known as "slow euthanasia."

Even though terminally ill patients do not have a constitutional right to assisted death, the states retain the right to enact laws that legalize it. The Supreme Court's ruling did not preclude states from passing legislation that would establish guidelines under which physicians may be allowed to hasten the deaths of patients in their care. Five of the nine justices suggested they might support such a claim in the future (Savage 1997). As Chief Justice William Rehnquist wrote, "Throughout the nation, Americans are engaged in an earnest and profound debate about the morality, legality, and practicality of physician-assisted suicide" (quoted in Denniston 1997:1A).

OREGON'S DEATH WITH DIGNITY ACT

Although the U.S. Supreme Court unanimously upheld state laws that ban physician-assisted suicide on June 26, 1997, the Oregon Death With Dignity Act of 1994 was renewed by referendum on October 27, 1997 (Chin et al. 1999). Oregon is currently the only U.S. state that allows physician-assisted suicide. Under the Oregon law, physicians can prescribe lethal medication for patients who are at least 18 years of age, who have made three requests for hastened death (at least one of which has been written and signed in the presence of witnesses), and who have a life expectancy of 6 months or less, with notification of the family and after the provision of counseling, if appropriate; in addition, the drugs cannot be provided until at least 15 days after the initial request has been made ("Physician-Assisted Suicide" 1995).

Chin et al. (1999) conducted a study of the 23 people prescribed lethal medications in 1998 under the Oregon Death With Dignity Act and found that 15 died from the medications, 6 died from the disease process, and 2 were still alive at the time of their study. The researchers compared the PAS patients to patients in a matched control sample and found that the PAS patients were more likely to have never married and more likely to be concerned about loss of autonomy and loss of control about body functions, but there was no difference between the two groups of patients in regard to fear of intractable pain, concerns about financial losses, level of education, or extent of health care coverage.

In a study that compared the attitudes of medical students in Oregon with those of medical students living outside of Oregon, Mangus, Dipiero, and Hawkins (1999) found that more than 60% of both groups were in favor of legal PAS and expressed a willingness to participate in legal hastened death practices, although the Oregon medical students expressed significantly more hesitancy about actually providing patients with lethal prescriptions.

ATTITUDES OF THE GENERAL PUBLIC TOWARD PAS AND EUTHANASIA

The findings of several studies indicate that approximately two-thirds of Americans currently endorse physician-assisted suicide (e.g., Blendon, Szalay, and Knox 1992; Bachman et al. 1996). In a 1990 poll conducted by the *New York Times* and CBS News, 53% of respondents agreed that a physician should be allowed to assist in the suicide of a terminally ill patient (Malcolm 1990). Among surveyed Canadian adults, 85% approve of withdrawing or withholding life-sustaining treatment for competent and consenting patients who are not likely to recover; in addition, 58% support PAS and 66% endorse euthanasia (Singer et al. 1995).

Using data gathered by the National Opinion Research Center's General Social Surveys from a sample of 16,455 adults over the period from 1977 to 1994, Kearl (1996) found that support for PAS and euthanasia services for terminally ill patients decreases with age, yet there has been an increase in support over time in all age groups. He also found that respondents concerned with control issues showed stronger support for both PAS and euthanasia. According to Caddell and Newton (1995), the practices of active euthanasia and PAS are most strongly supported by highly educated, politically liberal American adults who have a relatively weak religious orientation; those in this group also prefer that a physician administer hastened death services rather than that terminally ill patients commit suicide.

ATTITUDES OF PHYSICIANS AND HEALTH CARE WORKERS TOWARD PAS AND EUTHANASIA

It can be difficult to determine accurately the attitudes of health care professionals toward the practices of PAS and euthanasia. The inherent limitations of surveys on attitudes toward medical euthanasia include widely divergent definitions of PAS and euthanasia, selectivity of respondents and nonrespondents, sampling error, and embedded researcher points of view, which can strongly influence interpretation of findings. To date, the instruments used to assess these attitudes have employed hypothetical scenarios and anecdotes about situations that have developed in clinical practice. Respondents to questionnaires designed to assess medical professionals' willingness to provide assisted and hastened death services if it were legal to do so and/or their actual current practice of PAS and medical euthanasia face potential legal repercussions if the confidentiality of their responses is insufficiently protected. Physicians may be more conservative toward euthanasia than are members of the general public, and their opinions often reflect the various individual medical circumstances presented and the amount and kind of psychiatric morbidity indicated in the patient who requests assisted death services (Chochinov and Wilson 1995).

Bachman et al. (1996) found that among surveyed physicians in Michigan, 40% endorsed legalization of PAS, 37% supported no government regulation, 17% favored prohibition of the practice, and 5% were uncertain. The lowest rates of support were found among strongly religious respondents. When the physicians in Bachman et al.'s sample were asked about their willingness to provide PAS if it were legal, 35% expressed a willingness to provide assisted death services if requested, 22% said they would provide voluntary euthanasia or PAS, and 13% said they would restrict hastened death services to only PAS. In a survey of Washington State physicians, Cohen et al. (1994) found that 54% favored legalizing euthanasia in some circumstances, although only 33% were willing to participate personally in these practices, and 48% thought euthanasia could not be ethically justified; 53% supported physician-assisted suicide in some situations, and 40% were willing to assist in patient suicide. In a follow-up study, Dickinson et al. (1998) compared the attitudes of physicians from South Carolina with Cohen et al.'s Washington State sample and found overall strong similarity in the profile of physicians' attitudes in the two states. However, the researchers note that attitudes toward PAS and euthanasia were polarized.

In a survey of primary care physicians, Duberstein et al. (1995) found that 51% were opposed to PAS under any circumstances, 31% approved of legalization of PAS under certain circumstances, and 61% thought that suicide could be a rational option in certain circumstances. In addition, internists were less likely than family and general practitioners to be willing to provide euthanasia services, younger physicians were more likely to intervene to prevent a patient's suicide, and female physicians were more likely to agree that suicide could be a rational decision on the part of a patient. According to Foley ([1997] 1998), physicians who endorse physician-assisted suicide and direct medical euthanasia tend to view these practices as compassionate responses to a real medical need for competent but limited technological intervention in the care of terminal patients. Physicians who oppose these practices tend to view them as either morally wrong or extremely difficult to regulate.

In an investigation of Swedish physicians with specialties in the care of dying adult patients and palliative care and physicians from the Swedish Association for the Study of Pain, Valverius, Nilstun, and Nilsson (2000) found that half had discussed palliative care with dying patients, more than half had received patient requests for hastened death, approximately one-third had been asked for active euthanasia, and 10% had been asked for assisted suicide services. Although the physicians reported no cases of active euthanasia and only a few cases of assisted suicide, one-third of the physicians said that they had hastened a patient's death through the administration of sufficient dosages of analgesic or other drugs.

Meier et al. (1998) conducted a national survey of physicians in specialties in which requests for PAS and euthanasia are likely and found that a substantial proportion had received such requests (18.3% for PAS, 11.1% for active euthanasia) and approximately 6% had complied, either through the provision of prescriptions to be used to hasten death or lethal injection. In a survey of oncologists, Emanuel et al. (1998) found that approximately 16% had participated in PAS or euthanasia; of those participating physicians, approximately 53% were comfortable with their decisions, approximately 24% regretted their actions, and approximately 40% reported fearing prosecution as a result. Additionally, only approximately 34% of the oncologists who had participated in PAS and euthanasia reported that they had adhered to proposed guidelines in having the patients make repeated requests for hastened death, establishing the presence of extreme physical pain and suffering, and consulting with colleagues regarding this action; approximately 16% of patients who had received PAS or euthanasia had not participated in the decision-making process.

In a study of patients with HIV infection, Breitbart et al. (1996) found that 63% reported support for PAS and 55% had considered PAS options for themselves. The AIDS patients' predictor factors for interest in PAS were not related to pain severity, functional impairment, or symptom progression; rather, they were related to heightened psychological distress, previous experience with another's terminal illness, and Caucasian ethnicity with low religious identification and perceived low levels of social support. In a study of physicians who provide medical care to patients infected with HIV, Slome et al. (1997) found that 48% were willing to provide assisted suicide services to AIDS patients (in contrast to the 28% who had said they were willing in a 1990 survey of consortium physicians) and that 53% had already done so at least once. Voigt (1995) suggests that physicians who treat HIV-infected patients should approach discussions about euthanasia with their patients by "opening the door, discussing diagnostic realities, determining patient fears, evaluating depression, determining expectations, establishing supports, discussing options, and discussing problems from the patient's and the survivor's perspective."

Schwartz et al. (1999) conducted a survey of psychiatrists, internists, and family practitioners in Connecticut to investigate the influences of religious values, professional practice patterns, and ability to diagnose patient depression on attitudes toward PAS. The researchers found that although psychiatrists showed significantly more support for PAS than did internists or family practitioners, most respondents in all three groups of physicians were concerned about the effects of patient depression on requests for assistance in dying.

In a survey of registered nurses, Shuman et al. (1992) found that opposition to euthanasia was associated with strong religious beliefs, more years of experience, and the viewpoint of "death as an end"; nurses expressing support for euthanasia tended to be those who worked with dying patients, were politically liberal, and believed in a patient's right to self-determination in health care decisions. Sorbye, Sorbye, and Sorbye (1995) conducted a survey of nursing students and found that the factors most strongly associated with restrictive attitudes about voluntary active euthanasia were religious belief, conservative political views, and the perception of life as meaningful.

Asch (1996) surveyed critical care nurses and found that 17% reported they had received euthanasia or assisted suicide requests from patients or family members, 16% had provided hastened death services, and an additional 4% had withheld ordered life-sustaining treatment. In Young et al.'s (1993) sample of oncology nurses, 47% approved of legalization of physician-assisted death services and 16% expressed a willingness to administer physician-ordered lethal injections to competent terminally ill patients who requested such services.

In a survey of hospital social workers' attitudes, Csikai (1999) found support for both euthanasia and PAS as ethical practices that should be legal in certain situations. Many of Csikai's respondents said that they would be willing to participate in appropriate situations, and almost 25% reported already having been asked by patients or patients' family members for hastened death services.

In July 1, 1996, the Northern Territory of Australia passed the Rights of Terminally Ill Act, which legalized euthanasia. The law stood for 9 months, until its repeal on March 25, 1997 (Street and Kissane 1999–2000). Stevens and Hassan (1994) surveyed Australian nurses concerning the moral, ethical, and legal dimensions of euthanasia decisions and found that 60% endorsed legalization of active euthanasia under certain conditions, 19% had already acted to provide euthanasia to some patients, and 82% agreed that guidelines for medical practitioners about withholding and withdrawing medical treatment should be clarified. Kuhse and Singer (1993) also surveyed Australian nurses and found that among the nurses in their sample, 55% had been asked for active or passive euthanasia services by patients, 23% had been asked for assistance with such services by physicians, and 85% had assisted with hastened death actions. More than 75% of the surveyed nurses endorsed the euthanasia model as practiced in the Netherlands, and 67% thought euthanasia assistance to be a proper course of action for qualified patients under these guidelines.

In Hayes et al.'s (1999) survey of medical students in a third-year clinical clerkship who were enrolled in a pilot medical ethics program, respondents reported participating in end-of-life decision making, with evaluation of patient quality-of-life considerations and autonomy issues. They also reported having concerns about actual and potential legal liability and expressed polarized attitudes about PAS. These findings suggest that medical ethics programs need to prepare future physicians for clinical practice that is consistent with ethical guidelines and end-of-life legislation. This includes focusing on pain management and symptom relief, clarification of legal issues, training in how to resolve conflicts that arise from clashes between personal values/beliefs and public opinion and public policy, and encouragement of appropriate role-modeling behaviors in mentoring residents and attending physicians.

To summarize: Among practicing physicians and nurses in the United States, approximately 43% endorse legalization of PAS and 34% favor prohibition of PAS, 54% favor legalization of euthanasia in some circumstances, an additional 37% support no governmental regulation of this aspect of medical practice, and 28% would provide hastened death services or are already practicing PAS and/or euthanasia. Government regulation of PAS and medical euthanasia may be necessary, given the surreptitious practices revealed by recent surveys of physicians and health care workers.

POSTSCRIPT

The issues I have discussed in this chapter came into sharp focus for me recently. On Monday of my university's fall break in 2002, I was told that I had diverticulitis, a digestive difficulty common in midlife. On Tuesday, the diagnosis was changed to "pelvic mass," on Wednesday to "ovarian cancer," and on Thursday to "metastasized ovarian cancer with a compromised lymph system and liver." The physicians related survival statistics of a few weeks or at best a few months. As I sit at my kitchen table on this beautiful autumn afternoon, bathed in the toxic sweat of terminal illness and fighting down nausea, my perspective has been clarified. The patient's right to self-determination must include the right to preauthorize or to eliminate euthanasia as an option for ethical and humane end-of-life care. No one else can determine how much pain I can stand, or for how long. Even I do not know at this moment, but I do know this: No one else should dare to stand between me and my God.

REFERENCES

Albright, D. E. and R. J. Hazler. 1995. "A Right to Die? Ethical Dilemmas of Euthanasia." *Counseling and Values* 39(3): 177–89.

Anderson, J. G. and D. P. Caddell. 1993. "Attitudes of Medical Professionals Toward Euthanasia." *Social Science & Medicine* 37:105–14.

Arena, D. M. 1999. "Perspectives Toward Euthanasia Among Individuals Who Have Experienced the Prolonged Dying of a Loved One (Death)." *Dissertation Abstracts International* 60(6B):2603.

Asch, D. A. 1996. "The Role of Critical Care Nurses in Euthanasia and Assisted Suicide." *New England Journal of Medicine* 334:1374–79.

Bachman, J. G., K. H. Alcser, D. J. Doukas, and R. L. Lichtenstein. 1996. "Physician-Assisted Suicide: Reply." *New England Journal of Medicine* 335:519–20. Abstract obtained from APA/PsycINFO, 1999, Abstract No. 1996-05811-004.

Bachman, J. G., K. H. Alcser, D. J. Doukas, R. L. Lichtenstein, A. D. Corning, and H. Brody. 1996. "Attitudes of Michigan Physicians and the Public Toward Legalizing Physician-Assisted Suicide and Voluntary Euthanasia." *New England Journal of Medicine* 334:303–9.

Battin, M. P. 1991. "Euthanasia: The Way We Do It, the Way They Do It." *Journal of Pain and Symptom Management* 6:298–305.

———. 1995. *Ethical Issues in Suicide.* Englewood Cliffs, NJ: Prentice Hall. Abstract obtained from APA/PsycINFO, 1999, Abstract No. 1995-97196-000.

Berkman, C. S., P. F. Cavallo, W. C. Chestnut, and N. J. Holland. 1999. "Attitudes Toward Physician-Assisted Suicide Among Persons With Multiple Sclerosis." *Journal of Palliative Medicine* 2:51–63.

Bernhoft, R. 1993. "The Human Costs of Euthanasia: A Risk/Benefit Analysis of Physician-Assisted Suicide." *Clinical Therapeutics* 15:1185–88.

Billings, J. A. and S. D. Block. 1996. "Slow Euthanasia." *Journal of Palliative Care* 12(4):21–30.

Billings, J. A. and E. Kolton. 1999. "Family Satisfaction and Bereavement Care Following Death in the Hospital." *Journal of Palliative Medicine* 2:33–49.

Bindels, P. J. E., A. Krol, E. van Ameijden, D. K. F. Mulder-Folkerts, J. A. R. van den Hoek, G. P. J. van Griensven, and R. A. Coutinho. 1996. "Euthanasia and Physician-Assisted Suicide in Homosexual Men With AIDS." *Lancet* 47:499–504

Blendon, R. J., U. S. Szalay, and R. A. Knox. 1992. "Should Physicians Aid Their Patients in Dying? The Public Perspective." *Journal of the American Medical Association* 267:2658–62.

Breitbart, W., B. D. Rosenfeld, and S. D. Passik. 1996. "Interest in Physician-Assisted Suicide Among Ambulatory HIV-Infected Patients." *American Journal of Psychiatry* 153:238–42.

Brescia, F. J. 1991. "Killing the Known Dying: Notes of a Death Watcher." *Journal of Pain and Symptom Management* 6:337–39. Abstract obtained from APA/PsycINFO, 1999, Abstract No. 1991-34483-001.

Byock, I. R. 1993. "Consciously Walking the Fine Line: Thoughts on a Hospice Response to Assisted Suicide and Euthanasia." *Journal of Palliative Care* 9(3):25–28.

Caddell, D. P. and R. R. Newton. 1995. "Euthanasia: American Attitudes Toward the Physician's Role." *Social Science & Medicine* 40:1671–81.

Cavanaugh, T. A. 1996. "The Ethics of Death-Hastening or Death-Causing Palliative Analgesic Administration to the Terminally Ill." *Journal of Pain and Symptom Management* 12:248–54.

Chin, A. E., K. Hedberg, G. K. Higginson, and D. W. Fleming. 1999. "Special Report: Legalized Physician-Assisted Suicide in Oregon—the First Year's Experience." *New England Journal of Medicine* 340:577–83.

Chochinov, H. M., D. Tataryn, J. J. Clinch, and D. Dudgeon. 1999. "Will to Live in the Terminally Ill. *Lancet* 354:816–19. Abstract obtained from Network Project, Memorial Sloan-Kettering Cancer Center, *Network News,* Winter 2000:2–3.

Chochinov, H. M. and K. G. Wilson. 1995. "The Euthanasia Debate: Attitudes, Practices and Psychiatric Considerations." *Canadian Journal of Psychiatry* 40:593–602.

Clouser, K. D. 1991. "The Challenge for Future Debate on Euthanasia." *Journal of Pain and Symptom Management* 6:306–11. Abstract obtained from APA/PsycINFO, 1999, Abstract No. 1991-34487-001.

Cohen, J. S., S. D. Fihn, E. J. Boyko, A. R. Jonsen, and R. W. Wood. 1994. "Attitudes Toward Assisted Suicide and Euthanasia Among Physicians in Washington State." *New England Journal of Medicine* 331:89–94.

Compassion in Dying v. State of Washington. 79 F. 3d 790, 9th Cir. 1996.

Corr, C. A., C. M. Nabe, and D. M. Corr. 2000. *Death and Dying, Life and Living,* 3d ed. Belmont, CA: Wadsworth.

Cox, D. W. 1993. *Hemlock's Cup.* New York: Prometheus.

Crawford, S. C. 1995. *Dilemmas of Life and Death: Hindu Ethics in a North American Context.* Albany: State University of New York Press.

Csikai, E. L. 1999. "Hospital Social Workers' Attitudes Toward Euthanasia and Assisted Suicide." *Social Work in Health Care* 30(1):51–73.

Denniston, L. 1997. "No Right to Assisted Suicide." *Baltimore Sun,* June 27, pp. 1A, 6A.

Deutsch, A. 2000. "Dutch Parliament Passes Bill to Legalize Euthanasia." *Hornell* (New York) *Tribune,* November 29, p. 9A.

Dickinson, G. E., C. J. Lancaster, E. D. Sumner, and J. S. Cohen. 1998. "Attitudes Toward Assisted Suicide and Euthanasia Among Physicians in South Carolina and Washington." *Omega* 36:201–18.

Duberstein, P. R., Y. Conwell, C. Cox, C. A. Podgorski, R. S. Glazer, and E. D. Caine. 1995. "Attitudes Toward Self-Determined Death: A Survey of Primary Care Physicians." *Journal of the American Geriatrics Society* 43:395–400.

Dupuis, H. M. 1993. "Euthanasia in the Netherlands." *Annals of Oncology* 4:447–50.

Emanuel, E. J., E. R. Daniels, D. L. Fairclough, and B. R. Clarridge. 1998. "The Practice of Euthanasia and Physician-Assisted Suicide in the United States: Adherence to Proposed Safeguards and Effects on Physicians." *Journal of the American Medical Association* 280:507–13.

Feifel, H. 1990. "Psychology and Death: Meaningful Rediscovery." *American Psychologist* 45:537–43. Abstract obtained from APA/PsycINFO, 1999, Abstract No. 1990-18655-001.

Feldman, D. M. and F. Rosner, eds. 1984. *Compendium on Medical Ethics,* 6th ed. New York: Federation of Jewish Philanthropies of New York.

Fins, J. J., F. G. Miller, C. A. Acres, M. D. Bacchetta, L. L. Huzzard, and B. D. Rapkin. 1999. "End-of-Life Decision-Making in the Hospital: Current Practice and Future Prospects." *Journal of Pain and Symptom Management* 17:6–15.

First International Conference on Islamic Medicine. [1981] 1991. "Islamic Code of Medical Ethics." In *Choosing Death: Active Euthanasia, Religion, and the Public Debate.* Philadelphia: Trinity.

Foley, K. M. 1991. "The Relationship of Pain and Symptom Management to Patient Requests for Physician-Assisted Suicide." *Journal of Pain and Symptom Management* 6:289–97.

———. [1997] 1998. "Competent Care for the Dying Instead of Physician-Assisted Suicide." Pp. 135–39 in *Annual Editions: Death, Dying, and Bereavement,* 4th ed., edited by G. E. Dickinson, M. R. Leming, and A. C. Mermann. Guilford, CT: Dushkin/McGraw-Hill.

Friedlander, H. 1995. *The Origins of Nazi Genocide.* Chapel Hill: University of North Carolina Press.

Fulton, G. B. and E. K. Metress. 1995. *Perspectives on Death and Dying.* Boston: Jones & Bartlett.

Ganzini, L., D. S. Fenn, M. A. Lee, R. T. Heintz, and J. D. Bloom. 1996. "Attitudes of Oregon Psychiatrists Toward Physician-Assisted Suicide." *American Journal of Psychiatry* 153:1469–75.

General Board of the Royal Dutch Medical Association. 1996. "Vision of Euthanasia." *Giornale Italiano di Suicidologia* 6(1):9–29.

Gandhi, M. 1980. *All Men Are Brothers: Autobiographical Reflections.* New York: Continuum.

Gianelli, D. M. 1996. "AMA to Court: No Suicide Aid." *American Medical News,* November 25, pp. 27–28.

Gibbs, N. 1990. "Dr. Death's Suicide Machine." *Time,* June 18, 69–70.

Goodman, D. 1998. "Kevorkian Offers Kidneys Harvested From Assisted Death." *Evening Tribune* (Hornell, NY), June 8, p. A3.

Gostin, L. O. 1993. "Drawing a Line Between Killing and Letting Die: The Law, and Law Reform, on Medically Assisted Dying." *Journal of Law, Medicine & Ethics* 21:94–101.

Groenewoud, J. H., P. J. van der Maas, G. van der Wal, M. W. Hengeveld, A. J. Tholen, W. J. Schudel, and A. van der Heide. 1997. "Physician-Assisted Death in Psychiatric Practice in the Netherlands." *New England Journal of Medicine* 336:1795–1801.

Hayes, R. P., A. S. Stoudemire, K. Kinlaw, M. L. Dell, and A. Loomis. 1999. "Changing Attitudes About End-of-Life Decision Making of Medical Students During Third-Year Clinical Clerkships." *Psychosomatics* 40:205–11.

Hendin, H. 1995. "Assisted Suicide, Euthanasia, and Suicide Prevention: The Implications of the Dutch Experience." Pp. 193–204 in *Suicide Prevention: Toward the Year 2000,* edited by M. M. Silverman and R. W. Maris. New York: Guilford.

The Holy Qur'an, 5th ed. 1963. Edited by M. M. Ali. Lahore, Pakistan: Ahmadiyyah Anjuman Isha'at Islam.

Humphry, D. 1992. *Dying With dignity: Understanding Euthanasia.* New York: Birch Lane.

"It's Over, Debbie." 1988. *Journal of the American Medical Association* 259:272.

Jennings, B. 1991. "Active Euthanasia and Forgoing Life-Sustaining Treatment: Can We Hold the Line?" *Journal of Pain and Symptom Management* 6:312–16. Abstract obtained from APA/PsycINFO, 1999, Abstract No. 1991-33850-001.

"Judge Assails 'Lawlessness' of Kevorkian, Gives Him 10–25 Years." 1999. *St. Louis Post-Dispatch,* April 14, p. A1.

Kaplan, K. J., F. Lachenmeier, M. Harrow, J. C. O'Dell, O. Uziel, M. Schneiderhan, and K. Cheyfitz. 1999–2000. "Psychosocial Versus Biomedical Risk Factors in Kevorkian's First 47 Physician-Assisted Deaths." *Omega* 40:109–63.

Kaplan, K. J., J. O'Dell, L. J. Dragovic, C. McKeon, E. Bentley, and K. J. Telmet. 1999–2000. "An Update on Kevorkian-Reding 93 Physician-Assisted Deaths in Michigan: Is Kevorkian a Savior, Serial-Killer or Suicidal Martyr?" *Omega* 40:209–29.

Kastenbaum, R. J. 1998. *Death, Society, and Human Experience,* 6th ed. Boston: Allyn & Bacon.

Kearl, M. C. 1996. "Dying Well: The Unspoken Dimension of Aging Well." *American Behavioral Scientist* 39:336–60.

Kelly, B., P. Edwards, R. Synott, C. Neil, R. Baillie, and D. Battistutta. 1999. "Predictors of Bereavement Outcome for Family Carers of Cancer Patients." *Psychooncology* 8:237–49.

Kelly, B. J. and F. T. Varghese. 1996. "Assisted Suicide and Euthanasia: What About the Clinical Issues?" *Australian and New Zealand Journal of Psychiatry* 30:3–8.

Klagsbrun, S. C. 1991. "Physician-Assisted Suicide: A Double Dilemma." *Journal of Pain and Symptom Management* 6:325–28. Abstract obtained from APA/PsycINFO, 1999, Abstract No. 1991-34515-001.

Koenig, H. G. 1993. "Legalizing Physician-Assisted Suicide: Some Thoughts and Concerns." *Journal of Family Practice* 37:171–79.

Kübler-Ross, E. 1974. *Questions on Death and Dying.* New York: Macmillan.

Kuhse, H. and P. Singer. 1989. "The Quality/Quantity-of-Life Distinction and Its Moral Importance for Nurses." *International Journal of Nursing Studies* 26:203–12.

———. 1993. "Voluntary Euthanasia and the Nurse: An Australian Survey." *International Journal of Nursing Studies* 30:311–22.

Levy, M. H. 1991. [Letter]. *New England Journal of Medicine* 325:658.

Logue, B. J. 1994. "When Hospice Fails: The Limits of Palliative Care." *Omega* 29:291–301.

Lynn, J. and J. Teno. 1991. [Letter]. *New England Journal of Medicine* 325:659.

MacDonald, N. 1994. "From the Front Lines." *Journal of Palliative Care* 10(3):44–47.

Maier, D. M. and M. J. Newman. 1995. "Legal and Psychological Considerations in the Development of a Euthanasia Statute for Adults in the United States." *Behavioral Sciences and the Law* 13(1):3–25.

Maison Michel Sarrazin (Sillery, Quebec). 1994. "Position on Euthanasia." *Journal of Palliative Care* 10(4):23–26.

Malcolm, A. H. 1990. "Giving Death a Hand: Rending Issue." *New York Times,* June 9, p. 6.

Mangus, R. S., A. Dipiero, and C. E. Hawkins. 1999. "Medical Students' Attitudes Toward Physician-Assisted Suicide." *Journal of the American Medical Association* 282:2080–81.

Meier, D. E., C. A. Emmons, S. Wallenstein, T. Quill, R. S. Morrison, and C. K. Cassel. 1998. "A National Survey of Physician-Assisted Suicide and Euthanasia in the United States." *New England Journal of Medicine* 338:1193–1201.

The Mishnah: A New Translation. 1988. Translated by J. Neusner. New Haven, CT: Yale University Press.

Nagy, M. H. 1990. "Clinical Imperatives Versus Ethical Commitments in Euthanasia: The Perspectives of Nurses." *Loss, Grief and Care* 4(1–2):99–128.

New Edition of the Babylonian Talmud, vol. 2. 1896. Translated by M. L. Rodkinson. New York: Talmud Publishing.

New York State Task Force on Life and the Law. 1994. *When Death Is Sought: Assisted Suicide and Euthanasia in the Medical Context.* Albany: New York State Task Force on Life and the Law.

The NIV Study Bible: New International Version. 1985. Edited by K. Barker. Grand Rapids, MI: Zondervan.

O'Conner, N. K. 1991. [Letter]. *New England Journal of Medicine* 329:659.

Orentlicher, D. 1996. "The Legalization of Physician-Assisted Suicide." *New England Journal of Medicine* 335:663–67.

O'Rourke, K. (1991). Assisted suicide: An evaluation. *Journal of Pain and Symptom Management,* 6(5), 317–324.

Palermo, G. B. 1995. "Should Physician-Assisted Suicide Be Legalized? A Challenge for the 21st Century." *International Journal of Offender Therapy and Comparative Criminology* 39:367–76.

Parakh, J. S. and L. L. Slesnick. 1992. "Difficult Decisions: Euthanasia." *Science Teacher* 59(5):46–49.

Patient Self-Determination Act of 1990, Pub. L. No. 101–508, secs. 4206 and 4751, 104 Stat. 519.

"The People of the State of Michigan v. Jack Kevorkian." 1991. *Issues in Law and Medicine* 7(1):107–21.

"Physician-Assisted Suicide Initiative Passes in Oregon." 1995. *Western Bioethics News,* January, pp. 2–3.

Quill, T. E. 1991. "Death and Dignity: A Case of Individualized Decision Making." *New England Journal of Medicine* 324:691–94.

———. 1993. "Doctor, I Want to Die. Will You Help Me?" *Journal of the American Medical Association* 270:870–75.

Quill, T. E., C. K. Cassel, and D. E. Meier. 1992. "Care of the Hopelessly Ill: Potential Clinical Criteria for Physician-Assisted Suicide." *New England Journal of Medicine* 327:1380–84.

Quill v. Vacco. 80 F. 3d 716, 2d Cir. 1996.

Rachels, J. 1986. *The End of Life: Euthanasia and Morality.* New York: Oxford University Press.

Rinpoche, S. [1986] 1993. "The Gem Ornament." In S. Rinpoche, *The Tibetan Book of Living and Dying.* New York: HarperCollins.

Rosenfeld, B., W. Breitbart, K. Stein, J. Funesti-Esch, M. Kaim, S. Krivo, and M. Galietta. 1999. "Measuring Desire for Death Among Patients With HIV/AIDS: The Schedule of Attitudes Toward Hastened Death." *American Journal of Psychiatry* 156:94–100.

Rosner, F., P. Rogatz, R. Lowenstein, H. M. Risemberg, A. J. Bennett, A. Buscaglia, E. J. Cassell, P. B. Farnsworth, A. L. Halpern, J. B. Henry, B. Kabakow, P. R. Kark, A. B. Landolt, L. Loeb, P. J. Numann, F. V. Ona, P. H. Sechzer, P. P. Sordillo, and J. R. Wolpaw. 1992. "Physician-Assisted Suicide." *New York State Journal of Medicine* 92:388–91.

Ross, M. T. 1991. [Letter]. *New England Journal of Medicine* 325:658.

Ryan, C. J. 1995. "Velcro on the Slippery Slope: The Role of Psychiatry in Active Voluntary Euthanasia." *Australian and New Zealand Journal of Psychiatry* 29:580–85.

Sacred Congregation for the Doctrine of the Faith. 1982. "Declaration on Euthanasia." Pp. 510–17 in *Vatican Council II: More Postconciliar Documents,* edited by A. Flannery. Grand Rapids, MI: Eerdmans.

Saunders, C. 1989–90. "A Commitment to Care." *Raft: The Journal of the Buddhist Hospice Trust* 2:10.

Savage, D. G. 1997. "High Court Refuses to Grant Constitutional 'Right to Die.'" *Los Angeles Times,* June 27, p. A1.

Schwartz, H. I., L. Curry, K. Blank, and C. Gruman. 1999. "The Physician-Assisted Suicide Policy Dilemma: A Pilot Study of the Views and Experiences of Connecticut Physicians." *Journal of the American Academy of Psychiatry and the Law* 27:527–39.

Scofield, G. R. 1991. "Privacy (or Liberty) and Assisted Suicide." *Journal of Pain and Symptom Management* 6:280–88. Abstract obtained from APA/PsycINFO, 1999, Abstract No. 1991-34545-001.

Seale, C. and J. Addington-Hall. 1995. "Euthanasia: The Role of Good Care." *Social Science & Medicine* 40:581–87.

Shapiro, J. and R. Miller. 1994. "How Medical Students Think About Ethical Issues." *Academic Medicine* 69:591–93.

Shuman, C. R., G. P. Fournet, P. F. Zelhart, B. C. Roland, and R. E. Estes. 1992. "Attitudes of Registered Nurses Toward Euthanasia." *Death Studies* 16:1–15.

Singer, P. A., S. Choudhry, J. Armstrong, E. M. Meslin, and F. H. Lowy. 1995. "Public Opinion Regarding End-of-Life Decisions: Influence of Prognosis, Practice and Process." *Social Science & Medicine* 41:1517–21.

Singer, P. A., D. K. Martin, and M. Kelner. 1999. "Quality End-of-Life Care: Patients' Perspectives." *Journal of the American Medical Association* 281:163–68.

Slome, L. R., T. F. Mitchell, E. Charlebois, and J. M. Benevedes. 1997. "Physician-Assisted Suicide and Patients With Human Immunodeficiency Virus Disease." *New England Journal of Medicine* 336:417–21.

Smokowski, P. R. and J. S. Wodarski. 1996. "Euthanasia and Physician Assisted Suicide: A Social Work Update." *Social Work in Health Care* 23(1):53–66.

Sorbye, L. W., S. Sorbye, and S. W. Sorbye. 1995. "Nursing Students' Attitudes Towards Assisted Suicide and Euthanasia: A Study From Four Different Schools of Nursing." *Scandinavian Journal of Caring Sciences* 9(2):119–22.

Stevens, C. A. and R. Hassan. 1994. "Nurses and the Management of Death, Dying and Euthanasia." *Medicine and Law* 13:541–54.

Street, A. and D. Kissane. 1999–2000. "Dispensing Death, Desiring Death: An Exploration of Medical Roles and Patient Motivation During the Period of Legalized Euthanasia in Australia." *Omega* 40:231–48.

Sullivan, J. G. 1997. "A Terminal Case." *Contemporary Long-Term Care,* February, pp. 42–49.

Task Force on Physician-Assisted Suicide for the Society for Health and Human Values. 1995. "Physician-Assisted Suicide: Toward a Comprehensive Understanding." *Academic Medicine* 70:583–90.

Times Mirror Center for the People and the Press. 1990. *Reflections of the Times: The Right to Die.* Washington, DC: Times Mirror Center for the People and the Press.

Travis, R. 1991. "Two Arguments Against Euthanasia." *Gerontologist* 31:561–62.

Turner, L. 1997. "Euthanasia and Distinctive Horizons of Moral Reasoning." *Morality* 2(3):191–205.

Uzych, L. 1996. "Re: Euthanasia." *Canadian Journal of Psychiatry* 41:315.

Valverius, E., T. Nilstun, and B. Nilsson. 2000. "Palliative Care, Assisted Suicide and Euthanasia: Nationwide Questionnaire to Swedish Physicians." *Palliative Medicine* 14(2):141–48.

van der Maas, P. J., J. J. M. van Delden, and L. Pijnenborg. 1992. "Euthanasia and Other Medical Decisions Concerning the End of Life: An Investigation Performed Upon Request of the Commission of Inquiry Into the Medical Practice Concerning Euthanasia." *Health Policy* 22 (1–2):3–262.

Vinaya-Pitaka: The Book of Discipline, vol. 1. 1949. Translated by I. B. Horner. London: Luzac.

Visser, J. J. F. and H. H. V. Meijburg. 2003. "The Long Road to Legalizing Physician-Assisted Death in the Netherlands." *Illness, Crisis, and Loss* 11(2):113–21.

Voigt, R. F. 1995. "Euthanasia and HIV Disease: How Can Physicians Respond?" *Journal of Palliative Care* 11(2):38–41. Abstract obtained from APA/PsycINFO, 1999, Abstract No. 1996-93646-001.

Walker, G. C. 1997. "The Right to Die: Health Care Workers' Attitudes Compared With a National Public Poll." *Omega* 35:339–45.

Wallen, G. F. 1996. "Shades of Grey: The Euthanasia Controversy and the Rights of the Conscious and Rational Terminally Ill Adult Patient as Seen in Popular American Magazines, 1896–1976." *Dissertation Abstracts International* 57(4A):1793.

Weir, R. F. 1992. "The Morality of Physician-Assisted Suicide." *Law, Medicine, and Health Care* 20(1–2):116–26.

Werth, J. L. 1999. "Mental Health Professionals and Assisted Death: Perceived Ethical Obligations and Proposed Guidelines for Practice." *Ethics and Behavior* 9:159–83.

Wilson, K. G. and H. M. Chochinov. 1996. "Physician-Assisted Suicide." *New England Journal of Medicine* 335:518–19. Abstract obtained from APA/PsycINFO, 1999, Abstract No. 1996-05811-002.

World Health Organization. 1989. *Cancer Pain Relief and Palliative Care.* Geneva: World Health Organization.

Young, A., D. Volker, P. T. Rieger, and D. M. Thorpe. 1993. "Oncology Nurses' Attitudes Regarding Voluntary, Physician-Assisted Dying for Competent, Terminally Ill Patients." *Oncology Nursing Forum* 20:445–51.

PHYSICIAN-ASSISTED DEATH

MONIKA ARDELT

Physician-assisted death is not a new invention. Voluntary euthanasia and physician-assisted suicide were commonly practiced in ancient Greece and Rome to spare people of high social rank from prolonged suffering. The Hippocratic Oath, with its stance against physician-assisted death, represented a minority opinion among Greek physicians at the time it was written (Brogden 2001).

In modern times, the topic of physician-assisted death has gained prominence in the United States owing in part to the publicized deaths assisted by Dr. Jack Kevorkian and in part to Americans' general concerns about suffering painful, slow, and undignified death under medical care that appears to be able to prolong dying but not necessarily living (Benoliel and Degner 1995; Lattanzi-Licht and Connor 1995). At the core of the controversy concerning physician-assisted death is the individual's right to choose death versus society's obligation to protect its most vulnerable members from hastened and not completely voluntary death. The debate is often restricted to cases involving persons with terminal illnesses, but sometimes it is expanded to include people whose quality of life has become "unbearable" (Girsh 2000; Koch 2000; Ogden 2000).

DEFINITION OF PHYSICIAN-ASSISTED DEATH

The term *physician-assisted death* may be used to refer to euthanasia or to physician-assisted suicide. *Euthanasia,* a word from ancient Greek, can be translated as "a good death." Euthanasia can be active or passive and may be voluntary, involuntary, or nonvoluntary. In passive euthanasia, the patient does not receive life-supporting therapy, and this often results in the patient's death. In voluntary passive euthanasia, the patient refuses life-supporting therapy or such therapy is withdrawn at the patient's request. Involuntary passive euthanasia occurs when life-supporting therapy is withheld or withdrawn against the patient's wishes. If the patient's preferences are not known and the illness has progressed to a point where communication with the patient is no longer possible, withholding or withdrawal of life-supporting therapy is considered to be nonvoluntary euthanasia. In active euthanasia, by contrast, the physician performs an active intervention with the intent of ending the patient's life. If the patient requests that intervention, the euthanasia is voluntary; if the patient does not want to die, it is involuntary; and if the patient's wishes are unknown, it is nonvoluntary.

Although one could argue that taking a person off life-support could be considered an active intervention, the primary distinction between passive and active euthanasia is the *intention* to end a person's life (Sulmasy 2000; Kass and Lund 1996). If a person does not die after life-support has been removed, the intervention would not be deemed a failure. However, if a person continues to live after active euthanasia has been performed, the procedure would be considered unsuccessful. Finally, in physician-assisted suicide, the physician actively provides the patient with the means to end his or her life, usually by prescribing or providing a lethal dose of a medication that the patient independently ingests. In such a case, the physician might or might not be present at the time the patient decides to die.

Voluntary passive euthanasia is a legal and generally accepted practice in the United States. In 1990, the U.S. Supreme Court granted competent adults the right to refuse medical treatment. In the same year, the U.S. Congress passed the Patient Self-Determination Act, which requires all hospitals that receive federal funding to inform patients of their rights to demand or refuse medical treatment. Physician-assisted suicide and active euthanasia, however, are much more controversial. In 1997, the U.S. Supreme Court ruled that there is no constitutionally protected right to physician-assisted suicide but left it to the individual states to regulate physician-assisted death. To date, physician-assisted suicide is legal only in the state of Oregon, and active euthanasia remains illegal throughout the United States. In the Netherlands and Belgium, physician-assisted suicide and active euthanasia are legal under certain conditions, and in Switzerland assisted suicide is prosecuted only if the person who assisted in the suicide acted for selfish reasons. In this chapter, I use the term *physician-assisted death* to refer only to physician-assisted suicide and active euthanasia, with primary emphasis on physician-assisted suicide.

ARGUMENTS IN FAVOR OF PHYSICIAN-ASSISTED DEATH

Most people in the United States support physician-assisted death under two conditions: that it is voluntary and that the patient has a terminal or incurable illness. According to data from the General Social Surveys (surveys with a national U.S. probability sample conducted almost every year by the National Opinion Research Center), the proportion of U.S. residents who support the right of a person to end his or her own life if that person has an incurable disease increased from 39% in 1977 to 63% in 1998. During the same period, the proportion of people who agree that physicians should be allowed by law to end the life of a person with an incurable disease if the patient and the family request it increased from 62% to 71% (Davis and Smith 2000). These data indicate that U.S. residents support active voluntary euthanasia even more than they support physician-assisted suicide. Similarly, in a 1996–97 study of 988 terminally ill patients, Emanuel, Fairclough, and Emanuel (2000) found that 60% were in favor of physician-assisted suicide or euthanasia for a person with an incurable disease, even though only 11% had seriously thought about physician-assisted suicide or euthanasia for themselves. Relief from suffering and the maintenance of self-determination and control at the end of life are the arguments most often cited in favor of physician-assisted death.

Relief From Suffering

Many people are afraid of having to suffer excruciating pain and prolonged agony at the end of life and of being forced to continue an existence that has lost all meaning. If death is inevitable, physician-assisted death might provide the "good death" that otherwise appears to be impossible (Girsh 2000). Indeed, in their study of terminally ill patients, Emanuel, Fairclough, and Emanuel (2000) found that those with pain, substantial caregiving needs, and depressive symptoms were most likely to contemplate physician-assisted suicide or euthanasia. Yet emotional suffering might be more salient than physical suffering (Girsh 2000; Quill et al. 1998). In follow-up interviews conducted with their terminally ill respondents 2 to 6 months after their initial interviews, Emanuel et al. found that only those patients with depressive symptoms and those who experienced shortness of breath had changed their minds and started to contemplate physician-assisted suicide and euthanasia, whereas

increased pain or a decline in physical functioning did not lead to the desire for a hastened death. On the other hand, 50% of the patients who initially reported considering physician-assisted suicide or euthanasia were no longer doing so 2 to 6 months later. This suggests that patients' desires for physician-assisted suicide and euthanasia might not be particularly stable, and that therapeutic interventions designed to alleviate symptoms of depression and dyspnea might reduce requests for physician-assisted death.

Self-Determination and Control

The second major argument for physician-assisted death is that a person should have the right to choose a quick and painless death if he or she has an incurable illness and there is no hope for a recovery (Girsh 2000; Lenzer 1999). Many sick people are afraid that a progression of their disease will rob them of their dignity and mental faculties, and they do not want to become completely dependent on others. They prefer to die at a time of their choosing rather than witness their own terminal decline and a loss of self (Lavery et al. 2001).

Consistent with the principle of self-determination and control, physician-assisted death should be completely voluntary, both on the side of the patient and on the side of the physician (Girsh 2000; Lenzer 1999; Quill et al. 1998). Nobody should be pressured to engage in physician-assisted death, and patients should be free from depression when they make requests for such services. Patients should continue to have the right to request treatment even if that treatment is considered medically futile. Furthermore, no physician or health care provider should be forced to take part in physician-assisted death.

ARGUMENTS AGAINST PHYSICIAN-ASSISTED DEATH

Arguments against physician-assisted death revolve around ethical, moral, and religious considerations. In addition, some who oppose physician-assisted death make the "slippery slope" argument—that is, they are concerned that the legalization of physician-assisted suicide for terminally ill patients (a) might give way to active euthanasia and physician-assisted suicide for chronically ill persons and those who suffer from psychological distress, and (b) might pressure members of vulnerable populations into seeking early death.

Ethical, Moral, and Religious Considerations

Many physicians feel that it is unethical, morally wrong, and against the Hippocratic Oath to end a patient's life intentionally, even if the patient requests it. According to the American Medical Association's Code of Medical Ethics, physician-assisted death contradicts the physician's role as a healer (Kass and Lund 1996). Furthermore, patients might not be able to trust their doctors completely if doctors have the power to take their patients' lives, particularly in a climate of cost-saving incentives for physicians.

Moreover, physician-assisted suicide might place an undue moral and ethical burden on patients' family members and friends (Emanuel, Fairclough, and Emanuel 2000). For example, if a physician is not present at the time of a patient's suicide attempt, the patient might ask a family member or friend to help with the preparation and administration of the lethal medication. If death then does not come quickly, the family member or friend might also feel compelled to take steps to accelerate the dying process, such as by placing a plastic bag over the patient's head (Ogden 2000). A survivor who participates in such actions might suffer feelings of guilt and a prolonged and complicated bereavement process (Miller and Meier 1998).

Most religions also condemn physician-assisted suicide and active euthanasia. Life is considered to be a gift from God, and as such it is sacred. It is not for human beings to decide when life is no longer worth living if death does not come swiftly and naturally. It is permissible only for a patient to forgo or terminate a treatment that is unlikely to cure or benefit the patient but causes an extreme burden for either the patient or the community (Alexander 2000; Hai and Husain 2000; Kavesh 2000; Rowell 2000). This position is clearly in stark contrast to the argument for autonomy and control at the end of life. For many Christians, Jews, and Muslims, the sanctity of life and the sovereignty of God are absolute and override any individual's desire to end his or her life prematurely (Alexander 2000; Hai and Husain 2000; Kavesh 2000). As Rowell (2000) notes, according to the beliefs of most religions, "human freedom does not extend to a right to bring about our death at a time or in a manner specified by us" (p. 159).

Furthermore, caring for the terminally ill is an important practice in the lives of religious persons. They are asked to provide care that is not only restricted to the physical needs of the dying person but also addresses existential and spiritual needs, such as the meaning of suffering and death. This, in turn, can strengthen the relationship and the emotional bond between patient and caregiver. From a religious perspective, care for the dying is not primarily a burden; rather, it is an opportunity for the caregiver to develop compassionate love and to grow spiritually by sharing another person's pain and suffering and by providing selfless service to a person in need. The dying patient, on the other hand, might learn to find meaning in suffering, vulnerability, and dependency and to accept and give selfless love. In this context, physician-assisted death is seen as depriving terminally ill persons and their caregivers of a chance for spiritual growth and a deeper understanding of life (Alexander 2000; Koch 2000).

The Slippery Slope Argument

Many who oppose physician-assisted death are concerned that the legalization of physician-assisted suicide for the terminally ill might lead to the acceptance of physician-assisted suicide for the chronically ill, the disabled, and the psychologically distressed, as well as to the acceptance of active euthanasia for people whose quality of life appears to be extremely low but who do not have the capability to chose for themselves (Brogden 2001). If physician-assisted suicide is to be restricted to terminally ill patients, physicians need to be able to predict with a certain amount of accuracy how long a patient with a life-threatening illness is expected to live. Yet, in a 1999 study of Oregon physicians, Ganzini et al. (2001) found that 27% of physicians who had received requests for physician-assisted suicide and who were willing to prescribe lethal medications were not confident that they could predict whether a patient had a life expectancy of 6 months or less.

Those who make the slippery slope argument also point out that if unbearable suffering is the main reason for the legalization of physician-assisted suicide, it is not clear why such practices should be restricted to those who suffer physical symptoms at the end of life. Chronically ill and disabled people might suffer just as much as or even more than people with terminal illnesses, and they typically have to endure their suffering much longer (Lenzer 1999). For example, illnesses such as ALS, multiple sclerosis, AIDS, and neurological diseases progress slowly and can take years to lead to death. If physician-assisted suicide were to become legal, it is not clear how it could be justified for patients with severe pain and a life expectancy of less than 6 months but denied for patients with equally severe physical symptoms but the "wrong" kind of disease (Caplan, Snyder, and Faber-Langendoen 2000; Kamisar 1996). In fact, 75% of the people Dr. Kevorkian helped to die did not suffer from terminal illnesses (Roscoe et al. 2001).

Moreover, "suffering" might be more of an indicator of psychological distress than of physical pain, although there might be a certain reciprocal relationship between the intensity of pain and the experience of psychological distress (Drickamer, Lee, and Ganzini 1997; Holstein 1997). A quadriplegic, for instance, might suffer little physical pain but feel unable to bear the dependency and helplessness that such a life entails. Would it be fair to deny depressed and distraught patients the option of ending their lives (Kamisar 1996)? Indeed, supporters of physician-assisted death in the Netherlands argue that physical *and* mental suffering should be considered valid criteria for physician-assisted death (Koch 2000).

Furthermore, some individuals may not be able to ingest lethal doses of medication on their own, either because their illnesses have progressed to a point where swallowing is difficult or because they regurgitate the medication. Would it be fair to deny such people the option of physician-assisted suicide solely on the basis of their physical incapability? An alternative solution might be to offer active voluntary euthanasia. In fact, in the Netherlands, euthanasia is preferred to physician-assisted suicide because it is considered to be the safer and more reliable way to induce death (Brogden 2001; Groenewoud et al. 2000).

Finally, if only voluntary physician-assisted death is permissible, would this not mean that people who appear to suffer from physical or mental anguish but are no longer able to communicate their preferences for physician-assisted suicide or euthanasia would be denied physician-assisted death? If mental competence is a prerequisite of physician-assisted death, will not people be forced to choose death earlier rather than later if there is the possibility that their illness might eventually rob them of their capacity to decide (Caplan et al. 2000)? Legal permission to practice nonvoluntary euthanasia could be perceived as a solution to these problems.

In the name of fairness, justice, compassion, and mercy, the legalization of physician-assisted suicide for the terminally ill could easily be extended to the chronically ill, the disabled, and the mentally distraught. It also might lead to the legalization of active voluntary euthanasia for people who are unable to take their own lives and the legalization of active nonvoluntary euthanasia for patients who are no longer capable of deciding for themselves.

Another concern of those who make the slippery slope argument is that members of vulnerable populations—such as severely ill elderly persons and poor persons as well as disabled persons—might feel pressured to ask for physician-assisted suicide rather than continue with lives of dependency, suffering, and hardship (Koch 2000). In short, there is concern that the "right to die" might turn into the "duty to die" (Alexander 2000; Brogden 2001; Hardwig 1997; Osgood 2000). Even if individuals are not openly subjected to pressure to end their lives, once the *option* of physician-assisted suicide is available, people whose quality of life has deteriorated considerably might not have the strength to ask for continuing care and treatment if death appears to be the more rational and less burdensome alternative. For example, in a survey of elderly patients and their relatives, Koenig, Wildman-Hanlon, and Schmader (1996) found that approximately 60% of the older patients were against physician-assisted suicide in cases of terminal illness, whereas almost 60% of their family members supported it. In addition, the family members were not very successful in predicting the patients' preferences or in agreeing among themselves about what the patients' preferences would be. If terminally ill patients and their family members do not discuss end-of-life decisions and preferences openly, older terminally ill patients might feel inclined to choose physician-assisted suicide if it were legal and some family members expressed support for it in order to relieve the family of emotional and economic burden (Brogden 2001; Osgood 2000). Interestingly, in their sample of terminally ill patients, Emanuel, Fairclough, and Emanuel (2000) found

that older respondents and those who felt appreciated by others were less likely to consider physician-assisted suicide or euthanasia, but patients with substantial care needs were more likely to do so. In a follow-up study, these researchers found that the former caregivers of deceased patients were more likely to support the hypothetical case of a terminally ill person who desired euthanasia to avoid being a burden to his or her family if they felt that their own caregiving experiences had adversely affected their lives. By contrast, African American and religious caregivers and those who experienced social support were less likely to favor euthanasia in the above hypothetical scenario.

The economic incentives for individuals to choose physician-assisted death are quite strong (Alexander 2000; Brogden 2001; Osgood 2000). Physician-assisted suicide and euthanasia are much cheaper than the costs of continuing care, for families, insurance companies, and society. In a medical climate that is characterized by skyrocketing costs for advanced technological treatments and an aging population with prolonged years of disability and illness on the one hand and strong incentives for physicians to save on medical expenditures on the other, physician-assisted suicide and euthanasia would be the ultimate cost-saving tools (Miller and Meier 1998). Although physician-assisted suicide would be voluntary, some individuals, particularly older adults who have become sick, disabled, and dependent, might feel guilty and selfish for using up valuable resources and asking to be cared for if they have the legal option to end their lives and thus relieve relatives, physicians, and society from financial, physical, and/or emotional burden (Brogden 2001; Osgood 2000).

In a society that does not provide universal health care and long-term care for its citizens, the legalization of physician-assisted suicide might mean that people are given the option to die but not the option to be healed and to be cared for when they are ill (Brogden 2001; Caplan et al. 2000; Kamisar 1996). Not surprisingly, African Americans, the poor, and people with less education, who often lack access to adequate health care services before they become eligible for Medicare at the age of 65, tend to endorse the legalization of physician-assisted suicide in much smaller numbers than do white Americans and those with a higher income and better educational background (Emanuel, Fairclough, and Emanuel 2000; Koenig et al. 1996; Mouton 2000).

RECENT EXPERIENCES WITH PHYSICIAN-ASSISTED DEATH

In Western industrialized societies, only Belgium, the Netherlands, and the U.S. state of Oregon have legalized the practice of physician-assisted death. Although physician-assisted death has not been formally legalized in Switzerland, since 1942 assisted suicide by a physician or another person has been prosecuted only if the person who assisted acted out of selfish motives. In Belgium, physician-assisted death was legalized on May 16, 2002, following the legalization of physician-assisted death in the Netherlands on April 10, 2001, after more than a decade of tolerance for the practice. In Oregon, physician-assisted suicide—but not euthanasia—became legal on October 27, 1997. The practice of physician-assisted death in the Netherlands and in Oregon has been extensively documented and studied, and both cases are closely watched, particularly with regard to the slippery slope argument, as discussed above.

The Case of the Netherlands

Until 2001, physician-assisted suicide and euthanasia were illegal in the Netherlands, although both procedures had been tolerated for more than a decade and were not criminally prosecuted when the following four conditions were met: (a) The patient's request was voluntary, well considered, and persistent; (b) the patient judged his or her suffering as unbearable and without any hope for improvement in repeated discussions with the primary physician; (c) an independent physician confirmed that the patient's suffering was permanent and incurable; and (d) the prescribing physician submitted a full report to the coroner after the patient's death (Koch 2000; Ogden 2000). On April 10, 2001, the Netherlands formally legalized physician-assisted suicide and active euthanasia under the above-stated conditions.

In the Netherlands, the availability of physician-assisted suicide and euthanasia is not restricted to terminally ill persons who suffer incurable pain. Many older adults and AIDS patients choose physician-assisted death before they suffer the loss of autonomy, control, and dignity that often accompanies the progression of illness (Koch 2000). Unbearable and hopeless suffering might also be defined as psychological pain, as the case of Nettie Boomsma shows. Boomsma was a clinically depressed 50-year-old divorced social worker who had lost both of her children. She was allowed to commit physician-assisted suicide in 1991 after refusing intensive psychological counseling and therapy. Although this case was considered controversial in the Netherlands, a spokesperson for the Justice Ministry there defended the decision by referring to a person's right to choose death even in the absence of a terminal illness or insurmountable physical pain (Koch 2000).

It appears that in the Netherlands the legal status of physician-assisted suicide has led to voluntary active euthanasia, and euthanasia for the terminally ill has led to euthanasia for the chronically ill and those who suffer psychological distress (Brogden 2001). In some cases, euthanasia has been performed without the patient's explicit and persistent request (van der Maas et al. 1991, 1996). However, the incidence of such cases did not increase between 1990 and 1995. In 1990, 0.8% of all deaths in the Netherlands occurred through euthanasia without the patient's explicit and persistent request, compared with 0.7% of all deaths in 1995. Moreover, in more than half of those cases the decision to perform euthanasia had been discussed with the patient at an earlier stage of the illness, or the patient had expressed the desire for euthanasia at an earlier time in case of excruciating suffering. In other cases, the patient was no longer able to communicate his or her wishes (van der Maas et al. 1991, 1996).

In 1990, active voluntary euthanasia accounted for approximately 1.8% of all deaths in the Netherlands, whereas physician-assisted suicide was reported in about 0.3% of all deaths (van der Maas et al. 1991). The comparable figures for 1995 were 2.4% and 0.3%, respectively (van der Maas et al. 1996). Euthanasia takes place more often than physician-assisted suicide in the Netherlands because it is considered a safer and more successful method of delivering death (Brogden 2001). For example, researchers who analyzed cases of physician-assisted suicide and euthanasia performed in 1990–91 and 1995–96 in the Netherlands found that complications and problems with completion of the procedure were reported in 7% and 16%, respectively, of all physician-assisted suicide cases, but only in 3% and 6%, respectively, of all euthanasia cases. Furthermore, in 18% of all physician-assisted suicide cases, euthanasia had to be performed to induce death (Groenewoud et al. 2000). The problems most commonly associated with physician-assisted suicide were the patient's inability to take the lethal medication and the patient's vomiting after ingesting the lethal drug. Most of the problems reported with euthanasia involved difficulties in inserting an intravenous catheter and spasm or myoclonus. For 19% of all physician-assisted suicides and 10% of all euthanasia cases, the time from the administration of the first lethal medication to the patient's death was longer than the reporting physician had expected it to be, with a median duration of 3 hours.

Voluntary euthanasia allows those patients to end their lives who have the desire to die but would be unable physically to swallow lethal doses of medication and keep the medication in their stomachs (Groenewoud et al. 2000). For the Dutch, this is a question of general fairness. People should have the right to decide for themselves when life is no longer worth living, be it for physical or psychological reasons, and they should have access to professional help to make the death-inducing procedure as safe and effective as possible (Koch 2000). In fact, most physicians in the Netherlands are willing to perform active euthanasia or physician-assisted suicide, and slightly more than 50% have already done so. Only 12% would refuse to engage in active euthanasia or physician-assisted suicide (van der Maas et al. 1996).

In the Netherlands, younger patients seek euthanasia and physician-assisted suicide more often than do older patients (van der Maas et al. 1991, 1996). Patients whose deaths resulted from euthanasia or physician-assisted suicide in 1990 listed the following concerns when asked about their decisions to end their lives: 57% feared a loss of dignity, 46% mentioned unworthy dying, 46% mentioned pain, 33% did not want to be dependent on others, and 23% were tired of life (van der Maas et al. 1991). Interestingly, only 5% of the patients mentioned pain as the sole reason to end their lives. Contrary to common beliefs, it appears that psychological factors play a larger role in end-of-life decisions than do physical factors.

To date, the Netherlands probably provides the best conditions for the availability of physician-assisted death (Koch 2000; van der Maas et al. 1996). The Dutch have access to universal health care and long-term care services, and many Dutch people have long-standing relationships with family physicians who make house calls and are trained to listen to patients' concerns in regard to end-of-life issues. In the Netherlands, individuals have no need to consider physician-assisted death for economic or care reasons. Home and hospice care, medications, life-supporting therapies, and hospital stays are all covered equally and without additional costs to patients or their families. Without these provisions, even the Dutch might hesitate to legalize physician-assisted suicide and active euthanasia. Corneliss-Claussen, a psychologist and member of the Dutch Voluntary Euthanasia Society, cautions that "if the socioeconomic circumstances in a country are different, and if there are lots of financial problems with getting good care, the people should be very, very, very careful about introducing these possibilities [of physician-assisted death]" (quoted in Koch 2000:292).

The Case of Oregon

In 1994, 51% of Oregon voters approved the Death With Dignity Act, a citizens' ballot initiative. This act would have allowed a person with a life expectancy of less than 6 months to obtain a physician's prescription for a lethal dose of medication with the intent of ending his or her own life in a humane and dignified manner. The implementation of the Death With Dignity Act, however, was delayed by legal proceedings. In 1997, 60% of Oregon voters rejected a measure that would have repealed the Death With Dignity Act, and on October 27, 1997, Oregon became the first U.S. state to legalize physician-assisted suicide. The act does not require any physician or health care system to take part in physician-assisted suicide. On March 24, 1998, a woman with terminal breast cancer became the first person to die after receiving a physician's prescription for lethal medication under the Oregon Death With Dignity Act.

The Oregon law states that only a person diagnosed with a terminal illness and a life expectancy of 6 months or less can request physician-assisted suicide. Moreover, the patient must be 18 years or older, a resident of Oregon, and mentally capable of making health care–related decisions. For a physician to be protected from criminal prosecution for prescribing a lethal dose of medication, the physician and patient must meet the following additional requirements (Oregon Department of Human Services 2001):

- The patient must make at least two oral requests and one written request to the prescribing physician for the lethal

medication. In addition, the oral requests must be made at least 15 days apart, and the written request must be witnessed by at least two persons.

- The prescribing physician must inform the patient of available alternatives to physician-assisted suicide, including hospice and palliative care.

- Two physicians (the prescribing physician and a consulting physician) must confirm (a) the patient's terminal diagnosis and prognosis, (b) that the patient is mentally capable of making end-of-life decisions, and (c) that the patient's judgment is not clouded by any depressive disorder. If one of the two physicians suspects that the patient might suffer from depressive symptoms, the patient is required to be evaluated by a psychologist or psychiatrist.

- The prescribing physician must ask the patient to inform his or her next of kin of his or her desire to commit physician-assisted suicide. However, the patient is not required to comply with that request.

- The physician must report the prescription for lethal medication to the Oregon Health Division.

From 1998 through 2002, 129 people (16 in 1998, 27 each in 1999 and 2000, 21 in 2001, and 38 in 2002) died in Oregon after ingesting lethal medication provided by physicians under the protection of the Death With Dignity Act (Hedberg, Hopkins, and Kohn 2003; Hedberg, Hopkins, and Southwick 2002; Oregon Department of Human Services 2001; Sullivan, Hedberg, and Hopkins 2001). Physician-assisted suicide accounted for 0.06% of all deaths in Oregon in 1998, 0.09% of all deaths in 1999 and 2000, 0.07% of all deaths in 2001, and 0.13% of all deaths in 2002. In 1998, the persons who committed physician-assisted suicide in Oregon were more likely to be never married or divorced and less likely to be married than were Oregon residents who died of similar causes. They were also more likely to have expressed concern to their physicians about loss of autonomy and control of bodily functions as a consequence of their illness, but they were less likely to be completely disabled and bedridden than were persons in a matched control group of patients similar in age, underlying illness, and date of death. There were no significant differences between the two groups in regard to sex, race, or education level (Chin et al. 1999). In 1999 and 2000, the persons who engaged in physician-assisted suicide were not demographically different from Oregon residents who died of similar causes with the exception of education level. In both years, individuals who were at least college graduates had a higher likelihood of seeking physician-assisted suicide than did those with less education (Sullivan, Hedberg, and Fleming 2000; Sullivan et al. 2001). In 2001, the people who committed physician-assisted suicide were again more likely to be college graduates, but they were also more likely to be female and divorced than were Oregon residents who died of similar causes (Oregon Department of Human Services 2002). Overall, the 129 patients who died as a result of physician-assisted suicide from 1998 through 2002 were more likely than Oregon residents who died of similar causes during that time frame to be younger, divorced, and college graduates (Oregon Department of Human Services 2003).

In Oregon, complications associated with physician-assisted suicide appear to be less frequent than in the Netherlands. Vomiting after ingestion of the lethal medication occurred in only 4 of the 129 physician-assisted suicide cases that took place between 1998 and 2002, and seizures were not reported in any of the cases. The interval between the ingestion of the lethal dose and the time of death ranged from 4 minutes to 37 hours, with a median of 30 minutes (Hedberg et al. 2002; Oregon Department of Human Services 2003; Sullivan et al. 2001).

Most Oregon patients who ended their lives through physician-assisted suicide from 1998 through 2002 stated in conversations with their physicians that they were concerned about a loss of autonomy (7594%; total average = 85%), a decreasing ability to participate in activities that make life enjoyable (6984%; total average = 79%), and a loss of control of bodily functions (47–78%; total average = 58%). Only 2 of the 16 patients (12%) in 1998 mentioned concerns that they might be a burden to their family, friends, and caregivers; in 1999, 7 of the 27 patients (26%) mentioned this concern; in 2001, 4 of the 17 patients (24%) on whom data are available mentioned it; and in 2002, 14 of the 38 patients (37%) mentioned it; but in 2000, 17 of the 27 patients (63%) brought up this concern. Worries over inadequate pain control and the financial implications of their treatment appeared to be less relevant. Only 6–30% (total average = 22%) of the patients voiced any concerns over inadequate pain control, and only 3 of the 129 patients who died as a consequence of physician-assisted suicide between 1998 and 2002 expressed any concern about the financial implications of their treatment (Oregon Department of Human Services 2002, 2003; Sullivan et al. 2001).

In contrast to public perception in the United States, and comparable to the case of the Netherlands, the occurrence or fear of agonizing pain does not seem to be the primary reason patients in Oregon with terminal diagnoses have chosen physician-assisted suicide. Rather, psychological and social issues have been more important. Patients who choose physician-assisted suicide are most afraid that they will become dependent on others and lose their autonomy and control.

It is interesting to note that the legalization of physician-assisted suicide in Oregon has had the positive side effect of improving end-of-life care in that state (Cassel and Demel 2001). In 1993, only 21% of all Oregon deaths occurred under the care of hospice, compared with an estimated 36% in 2000. Moreover, from 1997 through 2000, the use of morphine for medical purposes increased by 50% (Steinbrook 2002). Correspondingly, in a survey of Oregon physicians in 1999, 30% reported that they had increased their numbers of hospice referrals since 1994,

76% stated that they had improved their knowledge of the use of pain medication at the end of life, and 69% reported that they had tried to improve their recognition of depressive symptoms in terminally ill patients (Ganzini et al. 2001).

In the same survey, 51% of the responding physicians said that they supported the legalization of physician-assisted suicide, whereas 31% opposed it. Yet, in contrast to the Netherlands, only 34% of the Oregon physicians stated that they were willing to prescribe a lethal dose of medication for a terminally ill patient; 46% were unwilling to do so, although only 30% said that they believed physician-assisted suicide is unethical or immoral. The data from this survey also showed that 14% of physicians had increased their willingness to participate in physician-assisted suicide from 1994 to 1999, and only 8% were less willing to do so in 1999 than they were in 1994 (Ganzini et al. 2001). This suggests that the acceptance of physician-assisted suicide might increase among physicians in Oregon the longer the Death With Dignity Act is in effect.

ALTERNATIVES TO PHYSICIAN-ASSISTED DEATH

Hospice and Palliative Care

Hospice care is often mentioned as an alternative to physician-assisted death. Founded in 1967 in England by Dame Cicely Saunders, the hospice movement has grown into a $1.5–$2 billion industry with more than 2,500 care providers in the United States (Beresford 1997; Lattanzi-Licht and Connor 1995). Hospice care is generally available for people with a life expectancy of 6 months or less who have decided to forgo curative treatment in favor of comfort care (Cassel and Demel 2001). As Lattanzi-Licht and Connor (1995) describe it, hospice "is a coordinated interdisciplinary program of pain and symptom control and supportive services for terminally ill persons and their families. A hospice program addresses physical, emotional, social, and spiritual needs. . . . It is a return to a more human, family-oriented philosophy of care aimed at controlling symptoms and improving the quality of life for individuals with a terminal illness" (p. 143). Ideally, hospice care does not consist only of symptom control and pain relief but also helps dying patients and their families to achieve closure and find meaning and purpose in dying (Connor 1998).

It is surprising to note, however, that 73–92% (total average = 83%) of the patients who decided to end their lives through physician-assisted suicide from 1998 to 2002 in Oregon were also receiving hospice care (Oregon Department of Human Services 2002, 2003; Sullivan et al. 2001). This suggests that hospice might not be the ultimate solution for everyone. Furthermore, we do not know how well the hospice philosophy of physical, emotional, social, and spiritual care can be realized in individual cases, and hospice care is not available for chronically ill and disabled persons with life expectancy of more than 6 months.

Many physicians argue that palliative care and better pain control should be offered to every patient, independent of the type and progression of the illness (Cassel and Demel 2001; Quill et al. 1998). In most cases, pain is treatable or can at least be alleviated to a point that it is no longer unbearable. Death is accepted if it is a consequence of increased pain medication, the so-called double effect, but the intention of the physician is only to relieve suffering and pain, and not to cause death (Kass and Lund 1996; Quill, Lee, and Nunn 2000). However, as the case studies of the Netherlands and Oregon have shown, patients opt for physician-assisted death less often because of unbearable pain than out of the fear of losing autonomy and control. Suffering tends to result from a combination of physical symptoms, pain, and concerns about psychosocial, existential, and spiritual issues (Holstein 1997; Quill and Byock 2000).

An essential part of successful palliative care, therefore, is the doctor-patient relationship. To alleviate suffering, physicians should be allowed and encouraged to take the time to truly listen to patients and caregivers, not only to their reports of physical symptoms but also to their concerns and to their expressions of fears, hopes, and desires (Holstein 1997; Quill 2001; Tulsky, Ciampa, and Rosen 2000). For example, a study of terminally ill patients and their caregivers found that caregivers of patients whose physicians listened to the caregivers' concerns and opinions about the patients' illness and treatment were less likely than other caregivers to be depressed and to report that caregiving had an adverse effect on their personal lives (Emanuel, Fairclough, Slutsman, et al. 2000). Yet, because physicians might lack the appropriate training and might not have the necessary skills or patience to listen attentively, successful palliative care might require the same kind of multidisciplinary teams of physicians, nurses, social workers, and spirituals advisers as does hospice care (Quill et al. 1998; Tulsky et al. 2000).

Wong and Stiller (1999) suggest that loss of meaning might be the primary source of a patient's suffering and the request for physician-assisted death at the end of life. They argue that a sole focus on *physical* symptoms is insufficient to relieve suffering. Instead, palliative care needs to include palliative counseling, which addresses end-of-life issues and the meaning of suffering and death. Through palliative counseling, people who are dying might learn to find dignity and meaning in their lives even if they have lost their autonomy and have become dependent on others. Hence physical and emotional suffering at the end of life might not only be a problem of the individual but might also indicate a failure of society and the community to provide adequate physical, emotional, and social support (Holstein 1997; Rowell 2000; Wong and Stiller 1999).

Terminal Sedation and Voluntary Refusal of Nutrition and Fluids

Not all suffering at the end of life can be relieved by palliative care. For people who suffer excruciating pain, unbearable shortness of breath, or other symptoms that cannot be eased by comprehensive palliative care, terminal sedation might be the best legally available alternative to physician-assisted death (Quill et al. 1998). In terminal sedation, the patient is sedated until he or she loses consciousness. Without artificial nutrition and other life-prolonging interventions, death tends to follow quickly (Quill et al. 2000).

The main difference between active euthanasia and terminal sedation is the intent to relieve intolerable pain and suffering rather than to end the patient's life, although the act of sedating the patient might hasten death (Quill and Byock 2000). However, the success of terminal sedation depends only on easing the patient's suffering and not on the death of the patient. The patient is given only enough medication to achieve and maintain unconsciousness, and no additional medication is administered to expedite death (Quill et al. 2000). By contrast, if active euthanasia does not lead to the death of the patient, the intervention is considered a failure. Yet, because terminal sedation and active euthanasia in practice might be differentiated only by the *intention* of the physician, terminal sedation should be considered an intervention of "last resort" and applied only after all other palliative care options have been exhausted (Quill et al. 1998). The patient must be fully informed about the consequences of the procedure, and his or her consent must be completely voluntary. If the patient is not competent to make an informed decision but suffering appears to be extreme and persistent, the physician should consult the patient's advance directives and discuss the patient's wishes and values with family members and the health care team before terminal sedation is initiated (Quill and Byock 2000).

Voluntary refusal of nutrition and fluid is another legal alternative to physician-assisted death for patients with terminal or incurable illnesses who insist on ending their lives. The voluntary cessation of eating and drinking is a self-determined and autonomous act on the part of the patient, yet, in contrast to physician-assisted death, it does not require direct intervention by a physician to end the patient's life (Brogden 2001; Miller and Meier 1998). The advantage of this alternative is that the patient does not have to ask a physician or family members to participate in the delivery of death, and so potential ethical or moral dilemmas are avoided (Quill and Byock 2000). Furthermore, death comes gradually, giving the patient enough time to change his or her mind (Miller and Meier 1998). The physical discomforts associated with the cessation of eating and drinking can be treated with palliative care, although hunger appears to be rare after an initial period of fasting, and symptoms of dry mouth and throat can be alleviated through assiduous mouth care (Quill and

Byock 2000). On the contrary, prolonged fasting is often accompanied by mild euphoria. The disadvantage of this course of action is that the dying process can take several days or even weeks, and the patient might suffer from confusion or delirium in the later stages of the process (Quill and Byock 2000).

Quill and Byock (2000) suggest the following clinical guidelines for terminal sedation and voluntary refusal of nutrition and fluid: First, the patient has been diagnosed with a terminal illness. Second, the patient has received comprehensive palliative care, but suffering is still severe and persistent. Third, the patient is not under psychological or spiritual distress. In general, terminal sedation and voluntary refusal of nutrition and fluid should be used only in extreme circumstances and when all other interventions to relieve the patient's suffering have failed.

Universal Health Care and Long-Term Care

As long as universal health care and long-term care are not provided in the United States, it might be difficult to argue that people would not feel pressured to request physician-assisted death if it became legally available (Brogden 2001; Koch 2000). Although only three of the persons who have engaged in physician-assisted suicide in Oregon so far have said that the "financial implications of the treatment" they faced were a factor, approximately one-third of the people who have committed physician-assisted suicide since the implementation of the Death With Dignity Act have mentioned relieving the burden on family, friends, and caregivers as one reason to end their lives (Oregon Department of Human Services 2003).

A possible alternative to physician-assisted death might be to provide government-sponsored financial, social, and emotional assistance to patients and to family members who care for terminally ill and disabled persons at home (Emanuel, Fairclough, Slutsman, et al. 2000). A patient who feels appreciated rather than a burden to the family and whose physical and psychosocial needs are adequately addressed will rarely consider physician-assisted suicide or euthanasia (Brogden 2001; Emanuel, Fairclough, and Emanuel 2000). Hospice-type care should be available not only for the terminally ill who have decided to forgo all further curative treatment, but for all persons with long-term care needs. This might take the form of professional help by health care providers and social workers who periodically visit the patient and his or her family at home, respite for family caregivers, and adult day-care centers. Furthermore, caregivers should not be forced to give up their jobs, thus losing their income and their own health insurance, if they decide to care for terminally ill and physically dependent relatives at home. Rather, under the provision of universal long-term care, family caregivers could be subsidized for their caregiving work and covered under a government-sponsored health insurance program such as Medicare.

CONCLUSION

Given the issues at stake, it is likely that the legalization of physician-assisted death will remain controversial. Although many cite untreatable and unbearable pain as the primary reason for the legalization of physician-assisted suicide, experiences in the Netherlands and in Oregon have shown that only a minority of patients who end their lives through physician-assisted suicide or active euthanasia mention unbearable pain and concerns over inadequate pain control as their primary motivation.

Physician-assisted death may be perceived either as the ultimate victory of personal control and autonomy over the inherently unpredictable process of dying or as the ultimate failure of society to protect its most vulnerable members and the sanctity of life. What does it say about a society if its people choose physician-assisted death when they can no longer conform to the Western ideal of autonomy and physical independence and feel that they have become a burden to others? Does this not imply that we have failed in our societal duty to care for the sick, dependent, and dying (Holstein 1997)? If physician-assisted death were to become legal, would that not send a message to people covered under the law that their lives are no longer worth living? Would they feel guilty about not wanting to end their lives if they needed a large amount of care and used up valuable resources yet had the legal right to free others of their burden? Does compassion for the dying consist in a law that allows them to end their lives at the time of their choosing, or rather in the promise not to abandon them during illness, suffering, and despair? As Holstein (1997) notes:

> "Death with dignity" means more than the ability and the opportunity to make choices about our own life and death. Dignity is a socially conditioned value resting upon the belief that others hold us in high regard. "Death with dignity" should rest on the fundamental knowledge that intimates, caregivers, and even strangers think well of me and recognize me, lying in that bed, to be as fully human as they are. (P. 850)

In a society with inadequate medical care for many and limited social and economic support for patients and caregivers in need, it could be dangerous to introduce physician-assisted death as an acceptable solution to end-of-life issues (Brogden 2001; Koch 2000; Osgood 2000). Before focusing on an individual's right to choose physician-assisted death, we should guarantee that every person has access to adequate health care and long-term care, including physical, emotional, and spiritual care at the end of life (Caplan et al. 2000). Just as it takes a village to raise a child, it also takes a village to help a person die a "good death."

REFERENCES

Alexander, Marc R. 2000. "Catholic Perspectives on Euthanasia and Assisted Suicide: The Human Person and the Quest for Meaning." Pp. 165–79 in *Cultural Issues in End-of-Life Decision Making,* edited by Kathryn L. Braun, James H. Pietsch, and Patricia L. Blanchette. Thousand Oaks, CA: Sage.

Benoliel, Jeanne Quint and Lesley F. Degner. 1995. "Institutional Dying: A Convergence of Cultural Values, Technology, and Social Organizations." Pp. 117–41 in *Dying: Facing the Facts,* 3d ed., edited by Hannelore Wass and Robert A. Neimeyer. Washington, DC: Taylor & Francis.

Beresford, Larry. 1997. "The Future of Hospice in a Reformed American Health Care System: What Are the Real Questions?" *Hospice Journal* 12:85–91.

Brogden, Mike. 2001. *Geronticide: Killing the Elderly.* Philadelphia: Jessica Kingsley.

Caplan, Arthur L., Lois Snyder, and Kathy Faber-Langendoen. 2000. "The Role of Guidelines in the Practice of Physician-Assisted Suicide." *Annals of Internal Medicine* 132:476–81.

Cassel, Christine K. and Beth Demel. 2001. "Remembering Death: Public Policy in the USA." *Journal of the Royal Society of Medicine* 94:433–36.

Chin, Arthur E., Katrina Hedberg, Grant K. Higginson, and David W. Fleming. 1999. "Legalized Physician-Assisted Suicide in Oregon: The First Year's Experience." *New England Journal of Medicine* 340:577–83.

Connor, Stephen R. 1998. *Hospice: Practice, Pitfalls, and Promise.* Washington, DC: Taylor & Francis.

Davis, James A. and Tom W. Smith. 2000. *General Social Surveys, 1972–2000* [machine-readable data file] (principal investigator, James A. Davis; director and co–principal investigator, Tom W. Smith; co–principal investigator, Peter V. Marsden; NORC ed.). Chicago/Storrs, CT: National Opinion Research Center (prod.)/Roper Center for Public Opinion Research, University of Connecticut (dist.).

Drickamer, Margaret A., Melinda A. Lee, and Linda Ganzini. 1997. "Practical Issues in Physician-Assisted Suicide." *Annals of Internal Medicine* 126:146–51.

Emanuel, Ezekiel J., Diane L. Fairclough, and Linda L. Emanuel. 2000. "Attitudes and Desires Related to Euthanasia and Physician-Assisted Suicide Among Terminally Ill Patients and Their Caregivers." *Journal of the American Medical Association* 284:2460–68.

Emanuel, Ezekiel J., Diane L. Fairclough, Julia Slutsman, and Linda L. Emanuel. 2000. "Understanding Economic and Other Burdens of Terminal Illness: The Experience of Patients and Their Caregivers." *Annals of Internal Medicine* 132:451–59.

Ganzini, Linda, Heidi D. Nelson, Melinda A. Lee, Dale F. Kraemer, Terri A. Schmidt, and Molly A. Delorit. 2001. "Oregon Physicians' Attitudes About and Experiences With End-of-Life Care Since Passage of the Oregon Death With Dignity Act." *Journal of the American Medical Association* 285:2363–69.

Girsh, Faye J. 2000. "Voluntary Euthanasia Should Be Legalized." Pp. 69–77 in *Euthanasia,* edited by James D. Torr. San Diego, CA: Greenhaven.

Groenewoud, Johanna H., Agnes van der Heide, Bregje D. Onwuteaka-Philipsen, Dick L. Willems, Paul J. van der Maas, and Gerrit van der Wal. 2000. "Clinical Problems With the Performance of Euthanasia and Physician-Assisted Suicide in the Netherlands." *New England Journal of Medicine* 342:551–56.

Hai, Hamid Abdul and Asad Husain. 2000. "Muslim Perspectives Regarding Death, Dying, and End-of-Life Decision Making." Pp. 199–211 in *Cultural Issues in End-of-Life Decision Making,* edited by Kathryn L. Braun, James H. Pietsch, and Patricia L. Blanchette. Thousand Oaks, CA: Sage.

Hardwig, John. 1997. "Is There a Duty to Die?" *Hastings Center Report* 27:34–42.

Hedberg, Katrina, David Hopkins, and Melvin Kohn. 2003. "Five Years of Legal Physician-Assisted Suicide in Oregon." *New England Journal of Medicine* 348:961–64.

Hedberg, Katrina, David Hopkins, and Karen Southwick. 2002. "Legalized Physician-Assisted Suicide in Oregon, 2001." *New England Journal of Medicine* 346:450–52.

Holstein, Martha. 1997. "Reflections on Death and Dying." *Academic Medicine* 72:848–55.

Kamisar, Yale. 1996. "The Reasons So Many People Support Physician-Assisted Suicide—and Why These Reasons Are Not Convincing." *Issues in Law and Medicine* 12:113–31.

Kass, Leon R. and Nelson Lund. 1996. "Courting Death: Assisted Suicide, Doctors, and the Law." *Commentary* 102:17–29.

Kavesh, William. 2000. "Jewish Perspectives on End-of-Life Decision Making." Pp. 181–97 in *Cultural Issues in End-of-Life Decision Making,* edited by Kathryn L. Braun, James H. Pietsch, and Patricia L. Blanchette. Thousand Oaks, CA: Sage.

Koch, Tom. 2000. "End-of-Life Issues: A Disability Perspective." Pp. 285–301 in *Cultural Issues in End-of-Life Decision Making,* edited by Kathryn L. Braun, James H. Pietsch, and Patricia L. Blanchette. Thousand Oaks, CA: Sage.

Koenig, Harold G., D. Wildman-Hanlon, and Kenneth Schmader. 1996. "Attitudes of Elderly Patients and Their Families Toward Physician-Assisted Suicide." *Archives of Internal Medicine* 156:2240–48.

Lattanzi-Licht, Marcia and Stephen R. Connor. 1995. "Care of the Dying: The Hospice Approach." Pp. 143–62 in *Dying: Facing the Facts,* 3d ed., edited by Hannelore Wass and Robert A. Neimeyer. Washington, DC: Taylor & Francis.

Lavery, James V., Joseph Boyle, Bernard M. Dickens, Heather Maclean, and Peter A. Singer. 2001. "Origins of the Desire for Euthanasia and Assisted Suicide in People With HIV-1 or AIDS: A Qualitative Study." *Lancet* 358:362–67.

Lenzer, Anthony. 1999. "Physician-Assisted Suicide: Policy Dilemmas." Pp. 281–95 in *End of Life Issues: Interdisciplinary and Multidimensional Perspectives,* edited by Brian de Vries. New York: Springer.

Miller, Franklin G. and Diane E. Meier. 1998. "Voluntary Death: A Comparison of Terminal Dehydration and Physician-Assisted Suicide." *Annals of Internal Medicine* 128:559–62.

Mouton, Charles P. 2000. "Cultural and Religious Issues for African Americans." Pp. 71–82 in *Cultural Issues in End-of-Life Decision Making,* edited by Kathryn L. Braun, James H. Pietsch, and Patricia L. Blanchette. Thousand Oaks, CA: Sage.

Ogden, Russel. 2000. "End-of-Life Issues in the HIV/AIDS Community." Pp. 265–83 in *Cultural Issues in End-of-Life Decision Making,* edited by Kathryn L. Braun, James H. Pietsch, and Patricia L. Blanchette. Thousand Oaks, CA: Sage.

Oregon Department of Human Services. 2001. *Oregon's Death With Dignity Act: Three Years of Legalized Physician-Assisted Suicide.* Portland: Oregon Department of Human Services.

———. 2002. *Fourth Annual Report on Oregon's Death With Dignity Act.* Portland: Oregon Department of Human Services.

———. 2003. *Fifth Annual Report on Oregon's Death With Dignity Act.* Portland: Oregon Department of Human Services.

Osgood, Nancy J. 2000. "Ageism and Elderly Suicide: The Intimate Connection." Pp. 157–73 in *Death Attitudes and the Older Adult: Theories, Concepts, and Applications,* edited by Adrian Tomer. Philadelphia: Brunner-Routledge.

Quill, Timothy E. 2001. *Caring for Patients at the End of Life: Facing an Uncertain Future Together.* New York: Oxford University Press.

Quill, Timothy E. and Ira R. Byock. 2000. "Responding to Intractable Terminal Suffering: The Role of Terminal Sedation and Voluntary Refusal of Food and Fluids." *Annals of Internal Medicine* 132:408–14.

Quill, Timothy E., Barbara C. Lee, and Sally Nunn. 2000. "Palliative Treatments of Last Resort: Choosing the Least Harmful Alternative." *Annals of Internal Medicine* 132: 488–93.

Quill, Timothy E., Diane E. Meier, Susan D. Block, and J. Andrew Billings. 1998. "The Debate Over Physician-Assisted Suicide: Empirical Data and Convergent Views." *Annals of Internal Medicine* 128:552–58.

Roscoe, Lori A., Julie E. Malphurs, L. J. Dragovic, and Donna Cohen. 2001. "A Comparison of Characteristics of Kevorkian Euthanasia Cases and Physician-Assisted Suicides in Oregon." *Gerontologist* 41:439–46.

Rowell, Mary. 2000. "Christian Perspectives on End-of-Life Decision Making: Faith in a Community." Pp. 147–63 in *Cultural Issues in End-of-Life Decision Making,* edited by Kathryn L. Braun, James H. Pietsch, and Patricia L. Blanchette. Thousand Oaks, CA: Sage.

Steinbrook, Robert. 2002. "Physician-Assisted Suicide in Oregon: An Uncertain Future." *New England Journal of Medicine* 346:460–64.

Sullivan, Amy D., Katrina Hedberg, and David W. Fleming. 2000. "Legalized Physician-Assisted Suicide in Oregon: The Second Year." *New England Journal of Medicine* 342:598–604.

Sullivan, Amy D., Katrina Hedberg, and David Hopkins. 2001. "Legalized Physician-Assisted Suicide in Oregon, 1998–2000." *New England Journal of Medicine* 344:605–7.

Sulmasy, Daniel P. 2000. "Voluntary Euthanasia Is Unethical." Pp. 24–32 in *Euthanasia* edited by James D. Torr. San Diego, CA: Greenhaven.

Tulsky, James A., Ralph Ciampa, and Elliott J. Rosen. 2000. "Responding to Legal Requests for Physician-Assisted Suicide." *Annals of Internal Medicine* 132:494–99.

van der Maas, Paul J., Johannes J. M. van Delden, Loes Pijnenborg, and Caspar W. Looman. 1991. "Euthanasia and Other Medical Decisions Concerning the End of Life." *Lancet* 338:669–74.

van der Maas, Paul J., Gerrit van der Wal, Ilinka Haverkate, Carmen L. M. de Graaff, John G. C. Kester, Bregje D. Onwuteaka-Philipsen, Agnes van der Heide, Jacqueline M. Bosma, and Dick L. Willems. 1996. "Euthanasia, Physician-Assisted Suicide, and Other Medical Practices Involving the End of Life in the Netherlands, 1990–1995." *New England Journal of Medicine* 335:1699–1705.

Wong, Paul T. P. and Catherine Stiller. 1999. "Living With Dignity and Palliative Care." Pp. 77–94 in *End of Life Issues: Interdisciplinary and Multidimensional Perspectives,* edited by Brian de Vries. New York: Springer.

PART IV

Passing Away

Dying as Social Process

DEATH AWARENESS AND ADJUSTMENT ACROSS THE LIFE SPAN

BERT HAYSLIP, JR.

ROBERT O. HANSSON

For many of us, our own death seems distant. Indeed, it is comparatively rare for young adults to die, and when they do, their deaths are most often violent. For children and adolescents, death sometimes comes in the form of accidents or disease; it also touches young lives when parents and (more often) grandparents die. As young adults, most of us face the loss of important persons in our lives—our parents and grandparents—and these losses remind us that we too will not live forever. For those who are middle-aged, the physical realities of aging as well as the increased likelihood of losing parents or age peers due to cancer or heart disease bring death closer. For older persons, death is almost a fact of life. The reality of death is perhaps most evident when we lose loved ones, especially others with whom we have shared our lives (see de Vries, Bluck, and Birren 1993).

In this chapter, we explore the salience of death across the life span. We assume that both age-related and individual differences exist in people's awareness of death. Such awareness is highly relevant to our individual lives and contributes to the meaning we assign to life. Indeed, idiosyncratic variations in the meanings we assign to death can either enhance or suppress our attention to death-related experiences, which may or may not covary with age. The meaning of death may also be rooted in historical events that shape the nature of death itself and our responses to it, and each of these events may have differential impacts on persons, varying by birth cohort (Hayslip and Peveto forthcoming). These distinctions parallel those made by Baltes (1987, 1997) in differentiating age-normative, history-normative, and nonnormative influences on developmental change across the life span.

MEANINGS OF DEATH

What death means to us personally dictates how we live our lives as well as how we react to death. Death is often seen as the ultimate loss. As Kastenbaum (1998) has noted, death may involve losses of several kinds:

1. The loss of our ability to have experiences

2. The loss of our ability to predict subsequent events (after death)

3. The loss of our bodies

4. The loss of our ability to care for persons who are dependent on us

5. The loss of a loving relationship with our family

6. The loss of the opportunity to complete treasured plans and projects

7. The loss of being in a relatively painless state

In addition, for some, death may mean punishment for one's sins (Kalish 1985). To the meanings of death listed above, Kastenbaum (2001) has added death as cycling/recycling (as death winds in and out of life), as enfeebled life (the dead are simply less alive or are a less vigorous form of life), as a continuation of life, and as nothingness. As we have noted, the meanings we attach to death reflect not only our unique life experiences but our shared cultural values about living and dying. In this respect, it is important to note that the tendency to personalize death (in which death represents a living person who has preceded one in death and with whom one will eventually be reunited) is commonplace among children and older adults (Cook and Oltjenbruns 1998; Kastenbaum 2001).

THE MEANING OF LIFE
AND RESPONSES TO DEATH

What individuals perceive as meaningful about life varies by age. For example, Reker, Peacock, and Wong (1987) found that, in general, older persons in their study sample reported more purpose in life than did the young; the older persons were also more death accepting. Yet the oldest-old (75+ years) and the young (16–29 years) experienced the most meaninglessness in life, had the fewest goals, and felt the most free-floating anxiety. One of our responses to death may be to use our time judiciously; that is, the awareness of death may help us to order our lives (Kastenbaum 1998). Without such orderliness, nothing would be any more important than anything else, and, indeed, it is often only when we nearly lose someone that we truly appreciate how special he or she is to us. However, it is important to point out that for some persons, simply living life on a day-to-day basis is more important than being preoccupied with future goals and plans. For example, Reker et al. found that older persons were less likely than younger persons to see life in terms of reaching goals and thinking about the future.

The personal meaning that death has for an individual likely influences how he or she responds to death, and this response may or may not heighten the individual's awareness of death-related experiences. In this respect, although fear and anxiety (see Hayslip 2003) are not the only ways in which we respond to death, they have received considerable research attention in the past 20 years (Neimeyer 1997–98). Whereas some might express anxiety over the variety of losses thought to accompany death, others may fear the loss of control over their everyday lives that may come about as a function of dying. People who are dying are often isolated from others in institutional settings, such as nursing homes or hospitals (Marshall and Levy 1990), and these settings can be depersonalizing.

Our feelings about death may determine the quality of the life we have left to live, and some evidence suggests that this response, too, covaries with age. In this context, one response to death or dying may be termed *overcoming* (Kastenbaum 1992). "Overcomers" see death as the enemy, as external, or as a personal failure, in contrast with others who have a participatory response to death. "Participators" see death as internal, as an opportunity to be reunited with a loved one, and as a natural consequence of having lived. As people age and approach death, they become more participatory in orientation (Kastenbaum and Aisenberg 1976), although some recent research has shown this relationship to be somewhat weaker than originally thought (Kastenbaum and Herman 1997).

INDIVIDUAL MEANING MAKING

Many person-specific and contextual variables influence death awareness. One organizing principle for understanding the role of such variables is that each somehow shapes an individual's perceived meaning of his or her own death or the death of a loved one. We want to emphasize, however, that understanding and assigning meaning to a death (one's own or that of a loved one) is likely to be an active and complex process. In this section, we explore how this process unfolds for individuals but also as a collective effort on the part of families and communities.

Weiss (1988) has noted that the need to find a satisfactory explanation for the loss of a loved one (cognitive acceptance) is one of the fundamental processes involved in grief recovery. Thus bereavement researchers have focused considerable attention on the systematic examination of how people try to make sense of their losses to death and how such efforts relate to individuals' eventual adjustment or recovery (Neimeyer 2001).

Davis and Nolen-Hoeksema (2001) have suggested that the process of meaning making can serve two important coping functions. They note, for example, that an unexpected, untimely, or traumatic death can threaten one's basic assumptions about the world and about how life works. One may find old understandings and values challenged and thus less comforting than they previously were. A first coping function, then, is to find or reconstruct a personal meaning for the death that helps to reestablish predictability and one's sense of security. To be satisfactory, such a meaning appears to require more than just a causal (medical) explanation for the death; instead, it demands a more philosophical, perhaps spiritual, explanation. Indeed, many people find satisfactory meanings with relative ease in the case of relatively "normative" deaths (e.g., "on time" deaths of the very old), and persons who possess helpful spiritual or religious beliefs often find satisfactory meanings in those beliefs. Not all bereaved, however, feel the need to search for meaning in a death. And those who do want a satisfactory explanation tend to find one fairly early on in their bereavement or not at all.

A second coping function of the meaning-making process is to help the bereaved individual to understand that in successfully dealing with a death, there is the possibility for personal growth or mastery, for an adaptive broadening of personal and philosophical perspectives, and for an increased appreciation of other important personal relationships. Davis and Nolen-Hoeksema (2001) report that in their research they have found that these perceived benefits of coping with a death are more consistently associated with eventual adjustment than is successfully finding a meaning in the death.

FAMILY MEANING MAKING

In the above discussion of meaning making, we have assumed an individual's frame of reference. Yet people's understandings of important life events and their implications are social (collective) constructions as well. For example, a death usually results in consequences for an entire family, and most families have long-established patterns of behavior that precede their need to cope with a death, through which they work collectively to arrive at or negotiate shared understandings of any traumatic life event. For example, family members will often support one another as they try to think through a problem (Nadeau 1998, 2001).

The process and group dynamic involved in family meaning making when a death occurs is especially interesting, given that individual family members often enter this time with quite different feelings about the death and different perceptions regarding its cause and potential implications. A concerted family process then may have positive effects, helping family members to find an explanation that comforts, allowing naturally occurring coping and support processes within the family to proceed, and diffusing any members' needs to blame someone or something. In this respect, a common strategy for family meaning making involves storytelling; that is, family members may share their personal understandings of the events or meanings surrounding the death. They search for commonalities, encourage shy or isolated members to participate, and help one another to recharacterize any troubling aspects of the event and to draw connections between co-occurring events or between perceptions of different family members (Nadeau 2001). Those who benefit the most from such a process are usually younger family members who lack the life experience, maturity, or resources necessary to cope with such events on their own.

Of course, families vary in the resources they bring to the meaning-making process. The members of some families may not be able to benefit from the perspectives of older and more experienced members because of limited family composition, for example. Some families are widely separated geographically, and members are not in frequent or meaningful contact. Some families lack a foundation of shared values or rituals, or lack cohesion or consensus regarding how they should try to adapt to change and stressful life events (Hansson et al. 1999; Nadeau 2001).

COMMUNITY MEANING MAKING

The meanings and implications of death can of course also be examined on a larger scale. Some deaths, such as the death of a president (e.g., John F. Kennedy) or the deaths of disaster victims (e.g., those killed in the terrorist attacks on the World Trade Center and the Pentagon on September 11, 2001), can disquiet a community or a nation and result in a collective search for meaning. Such efforts often focus on healing the community as well as reaffirming purpose and a sense of future. There is often a need to memorialize the dead, but in a way that addresses the diverse needs found within the community.

In the case of a large disaster, there are likely to be progressive layers of victims in addition to those who died.

These may include the immediate victims' family members, responding emergency personnel, members of the community who were not directly affected, and persons who, but for chance, might also have become victims (Taylor 1991). It is no small feat, therefore, for members of a community who are so differently touched by a disaster to find common understandings and meanings on which to rebuild—but communities try. An excellent example can be taken from the experience of the people of Oklahoma City after the 1995 bombing of the Alfred P. Murrah Federal Building. This community organized to create a memorial to the dead that might accommodate the diverse needs of the many levels of victims of the event. The strategy of those who worked on creating the memorial was to involve community members in conceptualizing and planning the memorial, and they systematically queried the community regarding priorities. In particular, they asked, "When you are at the memorial, what feeling(s) do you want to have?" (the response options included "pride," "anger," "fear," "hope," "solemnity," "courage," "concern," "inspiration," "peace," "healing," and "spirituality"). They then asked, "What should the memorial do?" (suggestions included "provide the names of the lost," "honor those who helped," "be for the whole nation," and "include something for the children") (DelCour 1996; Thomas 1996).

The Oklahoma City experience illustrates how death can bring a community together. However, the meanings attached to death can also divide communities. A profound example of this is the worldwide "death with dignity" movement (Hillyard and Dombrink 2001). Many people believe that a terminally ill adult who is in extreme pain yet intellectually competent should be allowed to request and receive a physician-assisted death. They see such assistance as consistent with our culture's values regarding personal autonomy and the alleviation of suffering, and they argue that issues of liberty and privacy rights have been extended to the individual's physical being in other areas of the law. Others, however, view the notion of physician-assisted death as a contradiction of many of the fundamental values of our culture, including religious beliefs regarding the sacredness of life. In addition, physicians typically view their calling as a responsibility to protect life, and many worry that a confusion of this role with the role of facilitator of death could weaken the trust that is necessary between doctors and patients. Many people have also expressed concern about the potential for abuse of physician-assisted death, especially in regard to vulnerable populations.

In this case, then, it is not so much a matter of finding meaning in death as it is a debate over competing meanings and rights, the stuff of political turmoil. In this context, the death with dignity movement has made considerable progress in recent years. After failures to establish physician-assisted death laws in several western states, Oregon passed its Death With Dignity Act in 1994. Moreover, after several unsuccessful court challenges, taken all the way to the level of the U.S. Supreme Court, as well as the implementation of important procedural controls, Oregon deaths under this law are now being recorded. At the foundation of this movement, however, have been efforts on both sides to organize political and ideological allies and to frame for public consumption particular views and interpretations of the meanings of such deaths. It is unlikely that Americans will arrive at a comfortable, shared understanding of this aspect of the community's experience with death within our generation, and the many other nations that have dealt with the issue have had similar experiences (Hillyard and Dombrink 2001).

LIFE-SPAN ISSUES IN COLLECTIVE MEANING MAKING

Each of the kinds of collective efforts to find meaning in death that we have discussed involves persons of many ages, and individual reactions reflect the age-related patterns described below. However, collective efforts also involve social processes and the framing of meanings by the older persons in the community, who have the most experience, authority, and wisdom. Where that process fosters community cohesion, survival, and prosperity, a pattern should stabilize. Where divides between meanings are too broad, however, the topic of death can be a potent and polarizing influence. Here we would expect the lines to be drawn not in terms of life-span-related competence, but more along ideological lines.

We turn now to a discussion of the many variables that influence individuals' awareness of death across the life span and thus affect the meanings they assign to mortality. In this context it is important to note that such variables not only influence but are also influenced *by* the meaning(s) individuals attach to their own and others' deaths.

Awareness of Death in Children and Adolescents

A given child's awareness of death is largely a function of the interaction between that child's development in the ability to think abstractly and his or her accumulation of death-related experiences. According to classic studies conducted by Nagy (1948) and by Speece and Brent (1996), children's developmental changes include at least semiregular changes in their understanding of death. Nagy's work suggests that children progress through three phases in their understanding of death. In the initial phase, death is not real to them—they believe the dead to have lifelike properties (e.g., death is like sleep). In the second phase, death is personalized and/or externalized, and in the third phase children reach a mature understanding of death as internal (to the person), universal, unavoidable, and irreversible. Speece and Brent's perspective differs slightly from Nagy's in that they identify a variety of aspects of an understanding of death (e.g., beginning with universality, inevitability, and unpredictability, followed

by irreversibility, causality, nonfunctionality, or the loss of the body's physical functions through death, and noncorporal continuation, or the ability to separate the ideas of life and death from the physical death of the body), which appear in a sequential, developmental, manner. Kastenbaum (2001) argues that children first understand the deaths of others before they comprehend their own deaths, but Speece and Brent do not agree. Despite the developmental shifts that all children go through, it is important to note that there are individual differences among children of given ages in their understanding and awareness of death (DeSpelder and Strickland 2002).

In addition to developmental differences among children, which often covary with their level of (Piagetian) cognitive development, death-related experiences also help to account for differences in children's understanding of death, as do individual differences in personality and the extent to which particular families communicate openly about death (Kastenbaum 2001). Additionally, children's awareness of death is affected by several other factors, including their patterns of play, their use of death-related humor and games (e.g., peekaboo, hide-and-seek), their exposure to death via the media, their experiences with the loss of family pets, and their parents' and teachers' use of "teachable moments" (Kastenbaum 2001).

Experiences with the deaths of grandparents, friends, heroes (sports figures, rock stars), and parents are particularly powerful influences on children's awareness of death, as are culturally relevant experiences such as the Columbine High School shootings in 1999, the Oklahoma City bombing in 1995, the space shuttle *Challenger* disaster in 1986, the terrorist attack on the World Trade Center in 2001, and the deaths of such public figures as Kurt Cobain, Dale Earnhardt, Sr., Selena, Princess Diana, John F. Kennedy, Robert Kennedy, Martin Luther King, Jr., and John F. Kennedy, Jr.

It is clear that the death of a parent has a profound impact on children and adolescents (e.g., Fristad et al. 2000–2001; Servaty and Hayslip 2001; Thompson et al. 1998), and Oltjenbruns (2001) notes that children often reexperience grief related to parental death as they mature. For example, for a young child a parent's death may signal the loss of safety, but during his or her adolescence, that same child may experience struggles with identity that are influenced by the parent's death. To the extent this occurs, it appears to be helpful for the child, in concert with the surviving parent, to attempt to "reconstruct" the deceased parent (Oltjenbruns 2001; Silverman, Nickman and Worden 1992).

When an adolescent experiences the loss of a parent, impaired school performance and disrupted, conflictual relationships with peers are often two results (Worden 1996). For some children and adolescents, the impact of a parent's death can be far-reaching (see Balk and Corr 2001; Kastenbaum 2001; Oltjenbruns 2001). Some may display a hypersensitivity to death, and especially to the loss of other family members (see Zall 1994).

Similar negative outcomes have been observed in children who have lost siblings to death (see Oltjenbruns 2001). Nevertheless, it should be noted that the impacts on children of either a parent's or a sibling's death covary with a number of factors, such as quality of the relationship and the nature of the death (e.g., through cancer, AIDS, suicide, murder). Moreover, as Kastenbaum (2001) notes, death has specific connotations for children depending on who dies (e.g., a pet, a parent, a friend, a grandparent). Likewise, some children may be unable or unwilling to let others know how they may be thinking about their own death or the deaths of others (Kastenbaum 2001).

For adolescents, awareness of death is often tied to the deaths of friends (see Balk and Corr 2001), parents, or grandparents and is intimately bound to their efforts to define themselves as unique individuals and to establish intimate relationships with others (Corr, Nabe, and Corr 2003). Of special significance are the deaths of age peers via suicide; such deaths may be especially difficult for adolescents who feel emotionally and interpersonally isolated from otherwise available sources of support. They may feel guilty for having failed to prevent the suicide or feel that they should have died instead, or they may feel they are being rejected by their friends who hold them responsible for the death (see also Corr et al. 2003). Balk and Corr (2001) note that family patterns of communication are often disrupted when a child dies; the impact of a sibling's death on an adolescent varies depending on whether the one who died was younger or an older adolescent (Balmer 1992).

Awareness of Death in Young Adulthood

For young adults, death comes, for the most part, unexpectedly. Rather than dying because of disease, young adults die often by accident or through violence (Corr et al. 2003). Although it is the rare younger person who dies of cancer or heart disease, potentially fatal illnesses such as AIDS are increasing among young adults (Cook and Oltjenbruns 1998). In most cases, however, deaths among young adults are due to homicides, auto or motorcycle accidents, and, in some cases, war (Cook and Oltjenbruns 1998).

Regardless of the cause of death, the process of dying disrupts the young adult's relationships with parents, children, and spouse, interferes with future goals and plans, and often undermines the individual's sense of attractiveness and sexuality (Corr et al. 2003). Understandably, a terminal illness or a sudden death leaves family members and friends feeling frustrated, angry, and lonely. Because death in young adulthood is nonnormative, young adults in the process of dying often feel angry and cheated because they are never going to reach the personal or career goals they have set for themselves. If they have children, they experience the sadness of knowing they will not see their children grow up, marry, and raise their own children (Rando 1984).

Terminal Illness

Young adults who suffer from AIDS or terminal cancer face many difficulties. At present AIDS is without a cure, although recent advances in drug treatment have improved the quality and quantity of life for persons with HIV/AIDS. Persons living with AIDS (PLWAs) and their families are sometimes isolated, and some feel both shame and guilt over having contracted a disease that many persons often inaccurately associate with homosexuality. PLWAs are sometimes discriminated against at work, have difficulty getting insurance coverage, and sometimes even have problems in getting adequate medical care. As a result, they often deny their diagnosis or hide their symptoms from others. Additionally, PLWAs who keep to themselves inadvertently deny others the opportunity to offer them support. Both PLWAs and their families grieve over the many losses death brings, with male children of PLWAs reporting the highest levels of distress (Rotheram-Borus, Stein, and Lin 2001). Yet, ironically, PLWAs are not permitted to grieve openly as others do because they are blamed for their illness. We term this special sense of loss *disenfranchised grief* (Corr 1998–99; Doka 1989). Others may not offer support to help PLWAs cope with their loss because they feel that these persons contracted the AIDS virus through their own immoral or illegal behavior—that is, "They had it coming to them, so they have nothing to be sad about." Thus the grief of PLWAs and their families is disenfranchised. Both those who die of AIDS and their survivors may be stigmatized, which makes their adjustment both before and after death more difficult.

Young adults with cancer are also often isolated and often discriminated against at work (even if they are in remission), but they face problems that are different from those faced by PLWAs. They may have to cope with seemingly endless visits to physicians, painful diagnostic procedures, disfiguring surgery, and/or chemotherapy or radiation therapy. Moreover, there is no guarantee that these treatments will be effective or, if the cancer is in remission, that it will not return. Despite their illness, young adults with cancer have the same needs for intimacy, autonomy, and dignity as other young adults, and these needs must be met (Cook and Oltjenbruns 1998). Many struggle to maintain a semblance of a family and social life, a difficult task for someone who is weakened by cancer or its treatment or whose appearance has changed due to surgery, chemotherapy, or radiation therapy.

Loss of a Child

A young adult who loses a child through death, particularly if the child dies at a relatively young age, may experience great personal distress for as long as 5 years after the death (Murphy et al. 1999). When a child dies in a hospital, the parents are sometimes physically separated from their dead child by hospital staff, especially if the child has died in childbirth or shortly thereafter; a funeral may not be held for such a child because it is assumed that it would be too upsetting, further interfering with the parents' healthy expression of feelings.

When a child dies, the parents may assume that they are responsible, that they should have done something to prevent their child's death. The parents often feel alone, angry, and resentful toward others, and each spouse may feel disappointed in the another. Ultimately, a child's death challenges feelings of "parental omnipotence"—the parents' feeling that, because they are parents, they should be able to "fix" everything in their child's life. The greatest fear of a young parent is that his or her child may die suddenly and that the parent will be powerless to prevent it. The death of a very young child can have serious consequences for the family as a whole, leading to divorce, physical or mental illness, and school difficulties (Cook and Oltjenbruns 1998).

Research has shown that among couples who have lost children to death, wives become less angry over time, but husbands' anger increases; husbands are also more likely to use denial as a coping mechanism (Bohannon 1990–91). Indeed, a father who loses a child does grieve, but it may take him longer to admit his grief to himself and to others (DeFrain et al. 1990–91). Families in which an atmosphere of open communication exists between husband and wife and between parents and children are most successful in accomplishing the grief work that follows the death of a child. Parents who lose a child need to make sense of the death; coming to an understanding of why the child died and accepting that the death was not their fault can help them do so (Kotch and Cohen 1985–86). Some families seek professional help in working through their grief, and community support is also very important. One well-known support organization is the Compassionate Friends, which brings parents who have lost children together to share their feelings as well as to help one another cope with the death of their loved sons or daughters.

Rubin and Malkinson (2001) argue that parents who have lost children to death grieve along two dynamic dimensions: personal functioning (e.g., well-being, quality of the marriage) and relationship to the dead child (e.g., idealizing the child after death). According to these researchers, the age of the child and the parent's age interact to dictate the impact of child loss, and the death of a child requires a parent's "lifelong accommodation" (p. 233) to the varying meaning of the loss and his or her relationship to the child who died.

Awareness of Death in Middle Adulthood

For adults who are in their 40s and 50s, the possibility of their own death or the death of a spouse becomes real. Cancer, heart disease, stroke, heart attack, and rarer diseases such as amyotrophic lateral sclerosis and multiple sclerosis are the major killers of middle-aged adults (see Hayslip and Panek 2002). For men, lung, colorectal, and prostate cancers become major concerns, and for women, lung, breast, and colorectal cancers are prominent concerns (American Cancer Society 1998).

When individuals in middle adulthood face terminal illness, they are likely to reevaluate life and its meaning (see DeSpelder and Strickland 2002). They often assess the quality of their relationships as well as their achievements and goals with a finality that was never present before—because they can never achieve those goals or fulfill the potential of their relationships. For these reasons, they may place importance on continuing to carry out their life roles (as father, mother, spouse, mentor, friend, worker). Ultimately, they must make plans for the future and settle "unfinished business" (Kübler-Ross 1969). They must put their legal affairs in order—insuring the security of a business, for example, or making arrangements to ensure that a child's education is paid for. It is critical that they take steps to be sure their obligations and responsibilities to loved ones do not go unmet after they die.

Like young adults who deal with terminal cancer, middle-aged persons who face the disease must make a series of adjustments—seeking appropriate treatment, coping with its side effects, dealing with remissions and relapses, and accepting the end of life (Cook and Oltjenbruns 1998). When an individual's cancer is incurable, he or she goes through the process described above.

Death also affects middle-aged individuals through the loss of one or both parents (see also Moss, Moss, and Hansson 2001). Because such deaths are often anticipated—that is, the loss of an elderly parent is viewed as "normal"—adult children's grief may be disenfranchised. The life circumstances of the middle-aged child and the older parent who has died (e.g., quality of life, living arrangement) also mediate the impact of a parent's death in adulthood (Moss et al. 2001).

When one loses a parent to death, one's awareness of one's own mortality increases. The fact that a parent is still alive serves as a "psychological buffer" against death (Moss and Moss 1983). As long as one of one's parents is alive, one can still feel protected, cared for, approved, and even scolded. Stripped of this "protection," one must acknowledge that one is now a senior member of the family and that death is a certainty. Although adult children certainly mourn and grieve over the loss of their fathers, their mothers may represent the last evidence of their families of origin, as women typically outlive men.

The death of a parent may also have special significance for men versus women. For an adult male, a father's death may represent the loss of a trusted friend, a role model, and a valued presence in the role of grandparent, especially if the son has male children of his own, as his identity is in part tied to his father's identity. An important part of raising his own son may be telling stories about his own father and encouraging his son to feel closer to his grandfather. For an adult female, a mother's death may heighten her own feelings as a mother, particularly if she and her mother have remained close over the years and have shared child-raising experiences. A parent's death thus symbolizes many things—the adult child's own mortality, independence from authority, attachment, and love. For many middle-aged persons, the deaths of their parents may coincide with other personal, marital, or work crises; in some cases, the loss of a parent can intensify a couple's marital difficulties (Douglas 1990–91).

Awareness of Death in Late Adulthood

Late adulthood is often a period during which individuals come to think in terms of loss—loss of good health, loss of relationships with others, and loss of status in the community as independent and productive persons (Kastenbaum 1998). Perhaps the most important losses that accompany getting older are the loss of a spouse and, ultimately, the loss of one's own life. Older people are likely to have had more death experiences (losses of parents, siblings, and friends) than younger people. This can have several consequences: First, for older people the future seems finite rather than infinite; second, older people may see themselves as less worthy than younger people because their futures are limited; third, older people may find that desirable roles are closed off to them; and fourth, not knowing what to do with their "bonus time" on earth, older people may think that they have already "used up" the years available to them. In addition, as more of their friends and relatives die, older persons become increasingly attuned to sadness and loneliness, as well as to signals from their bodies that say that death is near.

Death is further normalized in later life through its association with integrity (Erikson 1963), in terms of its being a developmental task of later life (see Hayslip and Panek 2002), and as a stimulus for life review (Butler, Lewis, and Sunderland 1998). It is in this context that an awareness of death may affect the quality of an individual's life and relationships with others. For example, women may be anticipatorily socialized into the role of widow prior to their husbands' deaths (Lopata 1996). Likewise, grandparents who are raising their grandchildren (due to various family circumstances) may have fears about their grandchildren's welfare in view of their own perceived imminent death (Hayslip et al. 1998).

Kastenbaum (1998) suggests that for some persons, the principle of compensation may preserve a sense of continuity and fairness about life and death. This principle suggests that, just as we may have been compensated by the "Tooth Fairy" for each lost tooth as children, older persons and terminally ill persons are compensated for the loss of health and ultimately the loss of life itself by the promise of eternity. We assume that persons who are near to death acquire a kind of spiritual wisdom that lets them view death more positively. The principle of compensation reinforces the practice of regressive intervention—that is, the stance that there is nothing more we can do for an old person. It is important to note, however, that older persons who are dying rarely say that they view the afterlife as a compensation for death (Kastenbaum 1998).

Indeed, many ideas about aging tend to reinforce the association between older persons and death, leading to the conclusion that death and dying are "more natural" or "more appropriate" for older persons than for the young. For example, integrity (a sense of completeness) and disengagement (withdrawal from others) have both been described as attributes of later life (Cumming 1963; Erikson 1963). Instead of seeing disengagement or integrity/life review as characteristic of all elderly persons, we might instead view these as being characteristic of some persons more than others irrespective of age, consistent with personality traits or specific life experiences. In contrast to this negative outlook regarding older persons and death, Cicirelli (1997) found that despite a low quality of life, older persons stated their preference to maintain life at all costs if they were to have a terminal illness. Only a minority of the older persons in Cicirelli's sample said that they would wish to end their lives through suicide, euthanasia, or physician-assisted suicide. Wong (2000) argues that persons who age "successfully" (Rowe and Kahn 1995) approach death more adaptively if they hold either neutral acceptance (using what time is left to accomplish something worthwhile and significant) or positive acceptance (self-actualization, the promise of a rewarding afterlife).

Generativity and Death

An awareness of limited time left in life also appears to be related to a shift in priorities regarding personal and social goals for that remaining time. Lang and Carstensen (2002) found that persons (typically older adults) who view their remaining time in this world as limited tend to place greater importance on two forms of goals. The first of these is generativity (implying a wish to help others, to share one's life experience with others, to leave one's mark on the world). An increased desire to contribute to future generations, then, may provide a comforting sense of "immortality" (McAdams, Hart, and Maruna 1998). The second goal that becomes more important involves emotion regulation (a need to understand one's own feelings more fully and to have some control over them).

Grief in Late Adulthood

In general, several factors seem to put a bereaved person at risk for both psychological and health-related difficulties: The death that caused the bereavement was sudden or especially violent, the bereaved person has feelings of ambivalence toward and was dependent on the person who died, the health of the bereaved person was poor prior to the death, there are other coexisting crises in the bereaved person's life, the person who died was the bereaved person's parent or child, and there is a lack of social support for the bereaved person (Stroebe and Schut 2001). Lund et al. (1986–87) found that, compared with other elderly persons in their study sample, those who were poor copers expressed lower self-esteem prior to bereavement and shortly after the death they had more confusion, expressed a greater desire to die, cried more, and were less able to keep busy.

Whether older persons and younger persons "grieve" in different ways in the process of adjusting to loss is a matter of some disagreement. Some scholars discuss "stages" of grief, such as a first phase of initial shock/disbelief, a second phase of working through one's feelings and reviewing one's relationship with the deceased, and a restructuring phase, when "life moves on," which may last for varying periods of time (Cook and Oltjenbruns 1998; Corr et al. 2003; DeSpelder and Strickland 2002). However, reactions to losses through death are highly variable; an older person's loss of a spouse, for example, must be understood in light of the interpersonal context in which older widows and widowers function (Moss et al. 2001).

Loss of a Spouse in Later Life

Clearly, older people are much more likely than younger people to have to deal with the loss of a spouse to death. Indeed, widowhood is a normative experience in later life. Between ages 65 and 75, 35% of women are widowed, versus 9% of men. For those ages 75–84, the figures are 60% and 19%, respectively. Among those age 85 and older, 80% of women are widowed, versus 39% of men (U.S. Bureau of the Census 1993). It is not surprising, then, that older widows outnumber older widowers by a ratio of six to one (U.S. Bureau of the Census 2000).

Relative to our knowledge about widows, we know comparatively little about how men cope with the loss of a spouse (see Lund 2000). Given the above-noted imbalance in the numbers of widowers versus widows, it would appear that support for widowers from other men who have lost their wives is likely to be scarce (Lund 2000). However, in a 2-year longitudinal study, Lund, Caserta, and Dimond (1986) found that widows and widowers tended to face common problems in bereavement, suggesting that the loss of a spouse represents a similar adjustment for men and women.

Given the many losses that older persons may face, it is important to note here that anyone who has to deal with several closely spaced deaths might not have the opportunity to do the grief work necessary to "work through" one loss before being confronted by another; this situation has been called *bereavement overload*. A person experiencing such overload may appear depressed or apathetic, or may suffer from physical problems (Kastenbaum 1978). In addition, when a person experiences a loss through sudden death, he or she may suffer from acute grief and thus may have particular difficulty coping with the loss (Cook and Oltjenbruns 1998).

It is commonly believed that younger persons who lose spouses through death have a more difficult time adjusting than do older individuals. For a young person, one consequence of a spouse's death may be increased child-care or work responsibilities for which the widowed spouse is unprepared. Also, as widowhood in young adulthood is relatively uncommon, the newly widowed person may not be able to look to others of his or her own age as models for how to survive alone. Although some researchers have found evidence that younger persons who are widowed make poorer adjustments than do older persons, others have not. For example, Thompson et al. (1991) discovered that although older bereaved spouses were initially more distressed than older nonbereaved spouses, 2 years later there were few differences between the groups. Sable (1991) found that older women's grief over losing their spouses subsided within 3 years. Yet, although many older widows eventually move on with their lives, others do not seem to be able to do so, perhaps because of lack of emotional support from others or the presence of other stressors. In Sable's study of bereaved women, 78% said that they thought they would never get over their loss; they simply learned to live it. Moreover, older women adjusted to loss more negatively than did younger women. This is contrary to many people's assumptions that because older women are more prepared for their husbands' eventual deaths they can adjust more quickly and completely when they are widowed.

When an older spouse dies, both the surviving spouse and the couple's adult children suffer a loss. Bass et al. (1990) found that the spouses in their study sample were more negatively affected by the death of an aged relative (spouse) than were the adult children, yet the spouses tended to become more socially active after the death than did their children, perhaps in an effort to rebuild support from others that was lacking prior to the spouse's death. Although the adult children reported trying to prepare themselves emotionally for the parent's death, this seemed to make adjustment more difficult. Findings such as these should alert us to our own biases about anticipatory grief (i.e., that one can be prepared emotionally for a death and thus make things easier). They should also help us to recognize the tremendous psychological burden a spouse carries in caring for a dying husband or wife.

The Loss of an Adult Child

Approximately 10% of adults over the age of 60 experience the death of a grown child (Moss, Lesher, and Moss 1986–87). Not only is the death of an adult child untimely, but it severs forever a lifelong parent-child bond (Blank 1997). Because this kind of loss is comparatively rare, those who experience such losses are unlikely to find others who have had similar losses available to provide needed emotional support (Moss et al. 1986–87). When an adult child dies, the relationships among all family members are affected. Each surviving sibling must deal with his or her own loss, and this influences the relationships of all the siblings with one another as well as with their older parents. Guilt, anger, and depression may cloud family relationships, impede communication, and disrupt family helping patterns and family rituals (see Rubin and Malkinson 2001). For the surviving parents, hope for the future may be eroded. When one's child dies, one's own mortality (and immortality) is shaken; one can no longer share in the joy of the child's life. Indeed, grandparents also experience significant grief over the death of a grandchild (Reed 2000).

When elderly parents and grandparents experience the death of an adult child/grandchild, their grief reactions are often very intense and prolonged (Cook and Oltjenbruns 1998; Murphy et al. 1999). Older persons who lose adult children through death experience a special sense of failure that many find difficult to deal with. Very few adults expect to bury their own children. Moss et al. (2001) provide a review of the comparatively scarce literature substantiating the negative impact of sibling death on older persons (relative to those whose spouses have died), as well as the impacts on elderly parents of the loss of an adult child, which can be quite variable. This is similarly true for grandparents who grieve for their dead grandchildren (see Fry 1997; Reed 2000).

CONCLUSION

In view of the above discussion of the factors that influence death awareness across the life span, we would be prudent to remind ourselves of the idiosyncratic meanings death has for children and adults, as well as to recognize the variability in how persons respond to such meanings as they experience both similar and different developmental transitions. Death awareness is at once an individual, familial, community, and cultural phenomenon, and its various elements interact dynamically. Thus death awareness might be best thought of as something individuals construct and reconstruct based on the interaction of developmentally significant life experiences (e.g., the death of a parent), cultural shifts in mortality rates, changes in funeral rituals (Irion 1990–91; Hayslip, Sewell, Riddle 2003), and cultural shifts in causes of and beliefs about death (Ariès 1981). Given such factors, we must recognize that each individual has a personal understanding of what death means and that a person's awareness of this meaning influences his or her responses to mortality—both his or her own and that of others.

REFERENCES

American Cancer Society. 1998. *What You Need to Know About Cancer.* Washington, DC: American Cancer Society.

Ariès, P. 1981. *The Hour of Our Death,* translated by H. Weaver. New York: Alfred A. Knopf.

Balk, D. and C. A. Corr. 2001. "Bereavement During Adolescence: A Review of Research." Pp. 199–218 in *Handbook of Bereavement Research: Consequences, Coping, and Care,* edited by M. S. Stroebe, R. O. Hansson, W. Stroebe, and H. Schut. Washington, DC: American Psychological Association.

Balmer, L. 1992. "Adolescent Sibling Bereavement: Mediating Effects of Family Environment and Personality." Ph.D. dissertation, York University, Toronto.

Baltes, P. B. 1987. "Theoretical Propositions of Life-Span Developmental Psychology: On the Dynamics Between Growth and Decline." *Developmental Psychology* 23:611–26.

———. 1997. "On the Incomplete Architecture of Human Ontogeny: Selection, Optimization, and Compensation as Foundation of Developmental Theory." *American Psychologist* 52:366–80.

Bass, D. M., L. S. Noelker, A. L. Townsend, and G. T. Deimling. 1990. "Losing an Aged Relative: Perceptual Differences Between Spouses and Adult Children." *Omega* 21:21–40.

Blank, J. 1997. *The Death of an Adult Child: A Book for and About Bereaved Parents.* Amityville, NY: Baywood.

Bohannon, J. R. 1990–91. "Grief Responses of Spouses Following the Death of a Child: A Longitudinal Study." *Omega* 22:109–22.

Butler, R. N., M. Lewis, and A. Sunderland. 1998. *Aging and Mental Health: Positive Psychosocial and Biomedical Approaches.* New York: Springer.

Cicirelli, V. G. 1997. "Relationship of Psychosocial and Background Variables to Older Adults' End of Life Decisions." *Psychology and Aging* 12:72–83.

Cook, A. S. and K. A. Oltjenbruns. 1998. *Dying and Grieving: Life-Span and Family Perspectives.* New York: Holt, Rinehart & Winston.

Corr, C. A. 1998–99. "Enhancing the Concept of Disenfranchised Grief." *Omega* 38:11–20.

Corr, C. A., C. M. Nabe, and D. M. Corr. 2003. *Death and Dying, Life and Living,* 4th ed. Belmont, CA: Wadsworth.

Cumming, E. 1963. "Further Thoughts on the Theory of Disengagement." *International Social Science Journal* 15:377–93.

Davis, C. G. and S. Nolen-Hoeksema. 2001. "Loss and Meaning: How Do People Make Sense of Loss?" *American Behavioral Scientist* 44:726–41.

DeFrain, J., L. Martens, J. Stork, and W. Stork. 1990–91. "The Psychological Effects of a Stillbirth on Surviving Family Members." *Omega* 22:81–108.

DelCour, J. 1996. "Memorial Survey Deadline Drawing Near." *Tulsa World,* January 28, p. A3.

DeSpelder, L. A. and A. L. Strickland. 2002. *The Last Dance: Encountering Death and Dying,* 6th ed. New York: McGraw-Hill.

de Vries, B., S. Bluck, and J. E. Birren. 1993. "Understanding Death and Dying From a Life Span Perspective." *Gerontologist* 33:366–72.

Doka, K. J. 1989. "Loss Upon Loss: The Impact of Death After Divorce." *Death Studies* 10:441–49.

Douglas, J. D. 1990–91. "Patterns of Change Following a Parent's Death in Mid-Life Adults." *Omega* 22:123–39.

Erikson, E. H. 1963. *Childhood and Society,* 2d ed. New York: W. W. Norton.

Fristad, M., J. Cerel, M. Goldman, E. Weller, and R. Weller. 2000–2001. "The Role of Ritual in Children's Bereavement." *Omega* 42:321–39.

Fry, P. S. 1997. "Grandparents' Reactions to the Death of a Grandchild: An Exploratory Factor Analysis." *Omega* 35:119–40.

Hansson, R. O., N. A. Vanzetti, S. K. Fairchild, and J. O. Berry. 1999. "The Impact of Bereavement on Families." Pp. 99–118 in *End of Life Issues: Interdisciplinary and Multidimensional Perspectives,* edited by B. de Vries. New York: Springer.

Hayslip, B., Jr. 2003. "Death Denial: Hiding and Camouflaging Death." In *Handbook of Death and Dying,* vol. 1, edited by C. D. Bryant. Thousand Oaks, CA: Sage.

Hayslip, B., Jr. and P. Panek. 2002. *Adult Development and Aging.* Melbourne, FL: Krieger.

Hayslip, B., Jr. and C. Peveto. Forthcoming. *Historical Shifts in Attitudes Toward Death, Dying, and Bereavement.* New York: Springer.

Hayslip, B., Jr., K. W. Sewell, and R. B. Riddle. 2003. "The American Funeral." In *Handbook of Death and Dying,* vol. 2, edited by C. D. Bryant. Thousand Oaks, CA: Sage.

Hayslip, B., Jr., R. J. Shore, C. E. Henderson, and P. L. Lambert. 1998. "Custodial Grandparenting and the Impact of Grandchildren With Problems on Role Satisfaction and Role Meaning." *Journal of Gerontology: Social Sciences* 53B:S164–73.

Hillyard, D. and J. Dombrink. 2001. *Dying Right: The Death With Dignity Movement.* New York: Routledge.

Irion, P. 1990–91. "Changing Patterns of Ritual Response to Death." *Omega* 22:159–72.

Kalish, R. A. 1985. "The Social Context of Death and Dying." Pp. 149–72 in *Handbook of Aging and the Social Sciences,* 2d ed., edited by R. H. Binstock and E. Shanas. New York: Van Nostrand Reinhold.

Kastenbaum, R. J. 1978. "Death, Dying, and Bereavement in Old Age: New Developments and Their Possible Implications for Psychosocial Care." *Aged Care and Services Review* 1:1–10.

———. 1992. *The Psychology of Death.* Boston: Allyn & Bacon.

———. 1998. *Death, Society, and Human Experience,* 6th ed. Boston: Allyn & Bacon.

———. 2001. *Death, Society, and Human Experience,* 7th ed. Boston: Allyn & Bacon.

Kastenbaum, R. J. and R. Aisenberg. 1976. *The Psychology of Death.* New York: Springer.

Kastenbaum, R. J. and C. Herman. 1997. "Death Personifications in the Kevorkian Era." *Death Studies* 21:115–30.

Kotch, J. B. and S. R. Cohen. 1985–86. "SIDS Counselors' Reports of Own and Parents' Reactions to Reviewing the Autopsy Report." *Omega* 16:129–39.

Kübler-Ross, E. 1969. *On Death and Dying.* New York: Macmillan.

Lang, F. R. and L. L. Carstensen. 2002. "Time Counts: Future Time Perspective, Goals, and Social Relationships." *Psychology and Aging* 17:125–39.

Lopata, H. 1996. *Current Widowhood: Myths and Realities.* Thousand Oaks, CA: Sage.

Lund, D. 2000. *Men Coping With Grief.* Amityville, NY: Baywood.

Lund, D., M. S. Caserta, and M. F. Dimond. 1986. "Gender Differences Through Two Years of Bereavement Among the Elderly." *Gerontologist* 26:314–20.

Lund, D., M. F. Dimond, M. S. Caserta, R. Johnson, J. Poulton, and J. Connelly. 1986–87. "Identifying Elderly With Coping Patterns Two Years After Bereavement." *Omega* 16:213–24.

Marshall, V. W. and J. A. Levy. 1990. "Aging and Dying." Pp. 245–67 in *Handbook of Aging and the Social Sciences,*

edited by R. H. Binstock and L. George. New York: Academic Press.

McAdams, D. P., H. M. Hart, and S. Maruna. 1998. "The Anatomy of Generativity." Pp. 7–43 in *Generativity and Adult Development,* edited by D. P. McAdams and E. de St. Aubin. Washington, DC: American Psychological Association.

Moss, M. S., E. L. Lesher, and S. Z. Moss. 1986–87. "Impact of the Death of an Adult Child on Elderly Parents: Some Observations." *Omega* 17:209–18.

Moss, M. S. and S. Z. Moss. 1983. "The Impact of Parental Death on Middle–Aged Children." *Omega* 14:65–75.

Moss, M. S., S. Z. Moss, and R. O. Hansson. 2001. "Bereavement and Old Age." Pp. 241–60 in *Handbook of Bereavement Research: Consequences, Coping, and Care,* edited by M. S. Stroebe, R. O. Hansson, W. Stroebe, and H. Schut. Washington, DC: American Psychological Association.

Murphy, S., A. Das-Gupta, K. Cain, L. Johnson, J. Lohan, L. Wu, and J. Mekwa. 1999. "Changes in Parents' Mental Distress After the Violent Death of an Adolescent or Young Adult Child: A Longitudinal Prospective Analysis." *Death Studies* 23:129–59.

Nadeau, J. W. 1998. *Families Making Sense of Death.* Thousand Oaks, CA: Sage.

———. 2001. "Meaning Making in a Family Bereavement: A Family Systems Approach." Pp. 329–47 in *Handbook of Bereavement Research: Consequences, Coping, and Care,* edited by M. S. Stroebe, R. O. Hansson, W. Stroebe, and H. Schut. Washington, DC: American Psychological Press.

Nagy, M. 1948. "The Child's Theories Concerning Death." *Journal of Genetic Psychology* 73:3–27.

Neimeyer, R. A. 1997–98. "Death Anxiety Research: The State of the Art." *Omega* 36:97–120.

———, ed. 2001. *Meaning Reconstruction and the Experience of Loss.* Washington, DC: American Psychological Association.

Oltjenbruns, K. A. 2001. "The Developmental Context of Childhood Grief." Pp. 169–97 in *Handbook of Bereavement Research: Consequences, Coping, and Care,* edited by M. S. Stroebe, R. O. Hansson, W. Stroebe, and H. Schut. Washington, DC: American Psychological Association.

Rando, T. A. 1984. *Grief, Dying, and Death: Clinical Interventions for Caregivers.* Champaign, IL: Research Press.

Reed, M. 2000. *Grandparents Cry Twice: Help for Bereaved Parents.* Amityville, NY: Baywood.

Reker, G. T., E. J. Peacock, and T. P. Wong. 1987. "Meaning and Purpose in Life: A Life-Span Investigation." *Journal of Gerontology* 42:44–49.

Rotheram-Borus, M., J. Stein, and Y. Lin. 2001. "Impact of Parent Death and an Intervention on the Adjustment of Adolescents Whose Parents Have HIV/AIDS." *Journal of Consulting and Clinical Psychology* 69:763–73.

Rowe, J. and R. Kahn. 1995. *Successful Aging.* New York: Dell.

Rubin, S. and R. Malkinson. 2001. "Parental Response to Child Loss Across the Life Cycle: Clinical and Research Perspectives." Pp. 219–40 in *Handbook of Bereavement Research: Consequences, Coping, and Care,* edited by M. S. Stroebe, R. O. Hansson, W. Stroebe, and H. Schut. Washington, DC: American Psychological Association.

Sable, P. 1991. "Attachment, Loss of Spouse, and Grief in Elderly Adults." *Omega* 23:129–42.

Servaty, H. and B. Hayslip, Jr. 2001. "Adjustment to Parental Loss Among Adolescents." *Omega* 43:311–30.

Silverman, P., S. Nickman, and J. Worden. 1992. "Detachment Revisited: The Child's Reconstruction of a Dead Parent." *American Journal of Orthopsychiatry* 62:494–503.

Speece, M. and S. Brent. 1996. "The Development of Children's Understanding of Death." Pp. 29–50 in *Handbook of Childhood Death and Bereavement,* edited by C. A. Corr and D. M. Corr. New York: Springer.

Stroebe, W. and H. Schut. 2001. "Risk Factors in Bereavement Outcome: A Methodological and Empirical Review." Pp. 349–71 in *Handbook of Bereavement Research: Consequences, Coping, and Care,* edited by M. S. Stroebe, R. O. Hansson, W. Stroebe, and H. Schut. Washington, DC: American Psychological Press.

Taylor, A. J. W. 1991. "The Field of Disasters and Disaster Stress." *British Journal of Guidance and Counseling* 19:1–7.

Thomas, J. 1996. "Unfinished Task: Memorial in Oklahoma City." *New York Times* (on-line), April 6.

Thompson, L. W., D. Gallagher-Thompson, A. Futterman, M. J. Gileski, and J. Peterson. 1991. "The Effects of Late-Life Spousal Bereavement Over a 30-Month Interval." *Psychology and Aging* 6:434–41.

Thompson, M., N. Kaslow, J. Kingree, M. King, L. Bryant, and M. Rey. 1998. "Psychological Symptomatology Following Parental Death in a Predominantly Minority Sample of Children and Adolescents." *Journal of Clinical Child Psychology* 27:434–41.

U.S. Bureau of the Census. 1993. *Marital Status and Living Arrangements* (Current Population Reports). Washington, DC: Government Printing Office.

———. 2000. *Statistical Abstract of the United States.* Washington, DC: Government Printing Office.

Weiss, R. S. 1988. "Loss and Recovery." *Journal of Social Issues* 44(3):37–52.

Wong, P. 2000. "Meaning and Successful Aging." Pp. 23–35 in *Death Attitudes and the Older Adult,* edited by A. Tomer. Washington, DC: Taylor & Francis.

Worden, W. J. 1996. *Children and Grief: When a Parent Dies.* New York: Guilford.

Zall, D. 1994. "Long Term Effects of Childhood Bereavement: Impact on Roles as Mothers." *Omega* 29:219–30.

Dying as Deviance

An Update on the Relationship Between Terminal Patients and Medical Settings

Charles Edgley

Much has been written about death and dying as historically forbidden topics of conversation. As human beings, we will, as the argument goes, do almost anything to avoid talking about either our own deaths or the impending deaths of others (Feifel 1963; Becker 1973; Sudnow 1967; Kübler-Ross 1969). Whether this human tendency is the result of a natural aversion to death, what Becker (1973) calls the "morbidly-minded argument," or whether it is simply a social convention in this culture (Knutson 1970), it has often been observed that Americans are uncomfortable around the topic of death. Moreover, the status of death and dying as forbidden topics of research is as important as their status as taboo topics for discussion. But since about 1980, much of this, many observers believe, has changed. Rather than being regarded as morbid curiosity seekers, social scientists who conduct research on death and dying have been increasingly sought out for the data their studies have produced. These data have been used to justify both medical and public policy about the dying and have seemingly brought death from the netherworld into the open. Bookstores, both "New Age" and mainstream, now routinely devote entire sections to death, dying, and bereavement. The result is a kind of "Happy Death" movement, as Lyn Lofland (1978) calls it, in which dying is regarded as a problem that we can resolve by talking about it, moving its venue, or legislating its elements, rather than as a predicament to be endured. Indeed, Levine and Scotch (1970) note that dying is emerging as a new social problem to be resolved.

Scholarship on the problems of death and dying, including research concerning the relationships between dying patients and their physicians, nurses, and other health care providers, so novel three decades ago, continues to escalate. Scholarly and professional social science journals have increased the numbers of papers they publish on the

subject, and numerous centers have been established whose purpose it is to explore both the social and personal meanings of death processes. Conferences on death studies abound, and the hospice movement alone has spawned a host of work on the problems of dying. Journals devoted to the subjects of death and dying have proliferated. *Omega, Advances in Thanatology, Mortality, Essence, Death Studies,* and the *Journal of Thanatology* are but a few of the academically oriented periodicals composed exclusively of reports on death-related research. However, although a large body of evidence makes it clear that there is legitimate scholarly interest in death-related problems, the taboos associated with death still exist, as I will show in this chapter. Moreover, these taboos are especially abundant in medical settings, which remain dedicated to viewing death as an enemy to be vanquished rather than to addressing the complex existential needs of human beings at the edge of life.

In the midst of the new acceptability of death studies, older efforts such as those of Glaser and Straus (1965, 1968) have taken on new significance. Much of Glaser and Straus's pioneering work dealt with the interactional framework in which dying takes place. Doctors, nurses, the dying patient, and the patient's family members and friends are all part of an interpersonal network in which the dying act occurs. Glaser and Straus suggest that in many ways this network constructs meanings that are morally negative. Following this line of analysis, I believe that a fruitful way to understand dying is to analyze the interactions within this network from the standpoint of the sociology of deviance.

Sociologists have defined deviance variously in terms of the act, the actor, and the audience reaction to the actor. In this chapter, I draw on and revisit earlier research by Wheeler, Edgley, and Orlando (1977) that formulated a framework for examining the social situation of the dying person in a medical setting.[1] More important, I update the logic of that research in order to explore the dilemmas of terminal patients caught between the existential demands of dying and the problems and concerns of hospitals and other institutional settings in which most dying takes place. In that earlier research, my colleagues and I built a concept of deviance based on the responses of others. We designed our research to test the hypothesis that the reactions of two of the terminal patient's most important audiences, physicians and nurses, place the patient in a deviant role. We then compared the attitudes of physicians and nurses to see if there were differences in how they viewed the dying person. Finally, we explored some tentative interpretations of those audiences' reactions to terminal patients. I begin by reviewing that research.

DEVIANCE AND THE RESPONSES OF OTHERS

Early theories of deviance presumed that deviants possess certain inherent traits that differentiate them from nondeviants. Persons were deviant, in this view, because of defects in their bodies, their brains, their genes, their psychologies, or their socialization. Other theorists, following a functionalist analysis of the relationship between acts and society, traced the deviant trait from the actor to the act, assuming that all deviant acts are harmful or injurious to society and are therefore deviant (Gibbs 1966:9). From this perspective, society seeks to maintain itself in a state of equilibrium, and acts that violate the social order, either normatively or even statistically, constitute deviance.

The labeling school of deviance, primarily a construction of sociologists, began in the 1960s to suggest that the reactions of a person's audiences constitute the main criterion for defining deviance, and that deviance lies neither in the actor nor in the inherent qualities of the act. Howard S. Becker (1963), a leading proponent of this way of thinking, cuts the Gordian knot with his simple assertion that "deviant behavior is behavior that people so label." He further takes the matter out of both the actor and the act by suggesting that "deviance is not a quality of the act the person commits, but rather a consequence of the application by others of rules and sanctions to an offender. The deviant is one to whom that label has successfully been applied" (p. 9). Erikson (1962) also defines deviance in a similar way when he says, "It is the audience which eventually decides whether or not any given action or actions will become a visible case of deviation" (p. 308). Kitsuse (1962) agrees, arguing that "forms of behavior per se do not differentiate deviants from nondeviants; it is the

responses of the conventional and conforming members of the society who identify and interpret behavior as deviant which sociologically transforms persons into deviants" (p. 253).

Gabriel Tarde (1898), a 19th-century sociologist, and Frank Tannenbaum (1979), an early contributor to dramaturgical analysis, writing in the 1930s, suggested that the source of deviance lies in the audience of the actor and not in the actor, but neither scholar developed the logical force of the concept further. In 1951, Edwin Lemert laid a systematic foundation for the current labeling approach. Lemert explains that a continuing pattern of deviance is caused by societal reactions to the discovery and subsequent labeling of the actor's deviation. He sees two types of deviance: primary and secondary. Primary deviance is the act itself and is inherently meaningless without the response of defining audiences. Lemert then suggests that the labeling of a person's behavior as deviant, along with the degree and visibility of the deviance, encourages the actor to adopt a deviant role and encourages others to define the actor as deviant. In essence, primary deviations become secondary ones as they are organized and solidified into a pattern of deviant conduct, and it is this secondary deviation that occupies much of society's attention.[2]

In attempting to refine the labeling perspective, Edwin Schur (1971) defines deviant behavior as "deviant to the extent that it comes to be viewed as involving a *personally discreditable* departure from a group's normative expectations, and elicits interpersonal or collective reactions that serve to 'isolate,' 'correct,' or 'punish' *individuals* engaged in such behavior" (p. 24). And lastly, Rubington and Weinberg (1971) state two fundamental positions taken by exponents of the labeling perspective:

Definition. A social problem or social deviant is defined by societal reactions to a presumed violation of expectations. If in other perspectives behavior and situations themselves were problematic, in this perspective what is problematic are the very conditions under which they come to be defined.

Causes. The cause of the social problem is know-aboutness. For, societal reactions cannot occur until the alleged behavior or situation is known. (P. 169)

THE CONCEPTUAL BASIS FOR DEVIANCE

Kitsuse (1972) insists that it is necessary to specify what society's morally negative reactions are directed toward. Unlike other labeling theorists, who stress behavior or acts as the objects of the labeling process, Kitsuse asserts that

---

1. It is important to note, as a backdrop to this chapter, that unlike in the past, when most people died at home, death is now an almost completely institutionalized affair. The vast majority of Americans now die in hospitals.

2. As I will show, this is precisely what happens as the primary deviation (a diagnosis of terminal illness) becomes organized into a secondary role (the dying patient).

"deviants are produced by the differential treatment of persons by others. . . . A person may be treated as deviant simply for what he is thought to be" (p. 240). It is in this sense that deviance does not even have to be directed toward concrete acts themselves; it may simply be a label applied to those persons *identified* as deviant. Given the assumptions and requirements of a situational context, this point will gain added salience later, when I focus the application of this framework on problems of dying in hospital settings.

Both Goffman and Kitsuse thus look at persons as the significant objects of the reactions, and not behavior or attributes.[3] According to Goffman (1963), a person's virtual social identity is always defined in the context of others. We place an individual in a category that has been socially defined and then anticipate this social identity. When the person actually possesses attributes that make him or her different from our moral expectations, the person becomes stigmatized in some manner.

From this perspective Wheeler et al. (1977) suggested that a deviant is a person who elicits aversive attitudes from audiences of sufficient strength to set him or her apart from others clearly. For the purpose of our research, deviants were persons who elicit aversive feelings and avoidance from those they encounter in the course of everyday life. This perspective, now the dominant one in sociologically informed studies of deviance, has been used only reluctantly by researchers examining medical settings. Because medicine has historically occupied a privileged position in sociological studies (Friedson 1970), researchers have always had a tendency to view medical venues in terms of their stated values rather than analytically in terms of a morally charged framework such as deviance and respectability. But social orders and their requirements remain, and medical environments, where life and death are on the line every day, are especially charged with such moral meanings.

THE PROBLEM

In the early research from which this update is derived, my colleagues and I attempted to test the hypothesis that the dying person's audiences (e.g., physicians and nurses) express aversive attitudes toward the dying person, and that these aversive attitudes are associated with avoidance of the dying person (Wheeler et al. 1977). We also compared the attitudes of nurses with the attitudes of physicians to see if there were any differences in how the two groups react to dying patients. Having determined that dying patients do represent a deviant category, we concluded the study by trying to understand why dying is a form of deviance in medical settings. From the idea that certain persons elicit aversive attitudes from their audiences, we shaped the following hypothesis:

> Dying persons elicit aversive attitudes from physicians and nurses that are significantly more aversive than the attitudes elicited by a nondeviant category of person, such as the executive.

This research successfully provided a basis for examination of the entire social situation of the dying person. The attitudes of the medical community toward the dying person had not, at that time, been sufficiently documented, and our research shed considerable light on the social interactions between dying patients and the medical teams surrounding them.

REVIEW OF THE LITERATURE

The literature on death and dying suggests that attitudes and responses toward the dying are frequently negative in character. Kübler-Ross (1969), recounting the reactions of nurses to dying patients, reports that they express anger, depression, and resentment. For example, one nurse pointed out the "absolute absurdity of wasting precious time on people who cannot be helped any longer"; another reported that when "these people die on me" it always made her feel very bad, and yet another said she got especially angry when "they died on me while other members of the family were present" (p. 252).[4] Kübler-Ross observes that the nurses' catharsis is "a courageous expression of their dislike for this kind of work mixed with a sense of anger, as if these patients committed an angry act against them by dying in their presence" (p. 252).

Glaser and Straus (1965:83) link the attitudes of medical personnel toward patients who know they are dying to the patients' conduct. For example, the following are some of the canons that dying patients are expected to obey:

1. They should not attempt to act in a way that brings about or hastens their own death.

2. They should maintain their composure.

3. They should face death with dignity.

4. They should not withdraw from the living.

5. They should cooperate in their own care.

6. They should not, if possible to avoid doing so, do anything that would distress or embarrass the staff.

---

3. This insistence that deviance be moved from an individual framework of attributes (psychological, biological, or social) to moral meanings constructed by others is the most fundamental contribution labeling theorists have made to the study of deviance.

4. The frustration stated by this nurse is reminiscent of the kind of triage training that medical personnel undergo. In traumatic situations such as plane crashes, earthquakes, and other circumstances where large numbers of people are affected, trauma teams sort victims in terms of those who are most and least likely to live. When time and resources are at stake, those who can be saved take precedence over those who are most likely to die.

"A patient who does most of these things," Glaser and Straus observe, "will be respected" (p. 86). In contrast, those who do not meet their obligations become objects of staff hostility and scorn.

The increasing trend toward dying in hospitals and nursing homes cannot be attributed entirely to the improvement of modern medical technology. It is at least partially attributable to society's attempt to isolate death and dying and thus minimize their disturbing effect. Blauner (1966:384) has suggested such a connection, observing that modern death control is bureaucratized in order to reduce the disturbance and disruption of the social order associated with death and dying. The coming of the hospice movement, with its efforts to renaturalize death, has done little to alter the role death plays in bureaucratized settings, including, ironically, hospice itself. As hospice has grown into a modern, institutionalized movement, it has itself become increasingly bureaucratized, with a hierarchy of personnel, increasing numbers of rules, and a value system that includes elements of coercion and control.[5] Dying patients are further isolated within the structure of the hospital itself. LeShan observed nurses during their work routines, timing them as they responded when patients summoned them, and discovered that nurses took significantly longer to respond to the calls of dying patients than to those of other patients. When he brought this fact to the nurses' attention, they indicated that they were not aware of it (Bowers, Jackson, Knight, and LeShan 1981:6–7).[6]

Kasper (1959), referring to the needs and care typically associated with the hopelessly ill, observes that "the dying are . . . not neglected, but they are very rarely approached with hope or even interest, because, I suppose, they simply will not feed the doctor's narcissism by responding and getting well" (p. 264). Recalling an incident in which a surgeon remarked during the performance of an operation on a 9-year-old boy "that it was a shame that this boy would not live to marry and have sons of his own," Kasper describes the reaction of the interns, residents, and nurses who heard the remark in the following manner: "The consensus seemed to be that it was, at least, in bad taste and might even be explained by assuming that the surgeon had been drinking before surgery" (p. 265). This story clearly illustrates the social norm typical of medical personnel, which forbids personal involvement with dying patients (Wheeler et al. 1977).

Glaser and Straus (1965:226–27) treat nurses' avoidance of dying patients as a strategy for maintaining composure. Indeed, they conclude that it is a general strategy

and appropriate under many different circumstances. They suggest that nurses adhere to a general defense strategy by which they maintain their composure during their care of dying patients: "This general strategy is a developmental process, comprising a progressive accumulation of strategies (pertaining to work, to talk with the patient, and to collective moods that develop among the nurses) which serve to reduce involvement in the patient as he approaches death" (p. 227).

Kalish (1966), using a modified form of the Bogardus Social Distance Scale, discovered that more than a third of his sample of 203 college students would not willingly allow a person dying of an incurable disease to live in their immediate neighborhoods. Furthermore, three out of five would not give such a person employment in the field they wish to enter. He found rejection of the person in constant pain to be even greater: "For this sample the only relationship that demands close and immediate personal interaction, the dating relationship, finds the person in pain almost completely rejected" (p. 153). It would appear that the person dying in uncontrolled pain experiences the most extreme form of avoidance.

THE MEDICAL SETTING: COPING WITH DEATH

People who work in health care, and others whose duties bring them into close contact with the critically ill, develop strategies for coping with unpleasant patient situations that they cannot physically avoid. Bowers et al. (1981) identify various "masks" that physicians hide behind to protect themselves against genuine person-to-person encounters with patients. First is the "mask of professional language," which violates the function of language, "for rather than communicating meaning it denies it" (p. 53). Second is the "mask of cynicism," through which the "things sacred to the patient are profaned or made common in the attitude of the physician" (pp. 53–54). The horseplay and profanity that medical students typically employ when they first approach their work with cadavers are only the beginning of a series of such defenses that physicians employ throughout their career.

Third is the "mask of materiality." In this strategy, the physician keeps something material—an oxygen mask, a stethoscope, a hypodermic needle—between him- or herself and the patient. As Bowers et al. explain, "Whatever it is, it becomes a focus of attention which screens the patient's feelings and anxiety from the tenderness of the

---

5. For example, proponents of the hospice movement argue on the one hand that hospice exists to help dying patients die in their own way, on their own terms, and according to their own values. On the other hand, within hospice practice there is a strong taboo against terminally ill patients' taking their own lives, and certainly against any form of assisted suicide. Clearly, dying emerges, like other behavior, in the context of a negotiated order in which the dying patient's needs are only one side of the equation.

6. It is clearly not meanness that motivates such actions; rather, it is ignorance. Hospitals are devoted to the heroic struggle to save lives. Dying patients represent a challenge to these values, and it is wholly natural to these settings that staff should regard the dying as doing something against the program.

physician's soul and makes it possible for the physician to go on about his tasks with protection against a full encounter with the patient" (p. 54).

The fourth mask is the "mask of impersonality." The patient loses his or her identity as a person and becomes a case or a disease. The nurse who replies to a physician's order to check how many patients are waiting by saying that "the heart and lung are still here" illustrates the use of this mask. Bowers et al. note that "the tendency to refer to the disease rather than the patient is a way of taking ahold of only that part of the being where security exists" (p. 54).

The "mask of ritualized action" is the fifth mask. For example, taking the pulse of a patient "is a point of contact that may be reassuring to the patient without really meaning much personally to the physician" (pp. 54–55). According to Bowers et al., ritualized actions "are structured types of behavior that stand between the person of the therapist and the person of the patient" (p. 55).

The sixth mask, the "mask of hospital routine, subtly strips the patient of those aspects of his life that measure his personality and his dignity" by making "the personal interests of the patient . . . secondary to the hospital routine" (p. 55). The seventh and final mask is the "mask of the 'it-it' relationship." In using this mask, in addition to making the person of the patient an "it" (i.e., a case or a disease), the physician also makes him- or herself an "it" by assuming "the role of the dispenser of precise medical knowledge" (p. 55). Note here that the "it-it" relationship with the dying patient is also the crux of all deviance labels. When persons are labeled deviant, they are transformed from persons into social categories that are defamed.

Bowers and her associates conclude that "at no point in the patient-physician relationship are the masks worn with such security as in the encounter with the dying patient" (p. 56). Thus the physician can avoid the dying patient psychologically and emotionally, even if he or she cannot always avoid the patient physically. Most deviance labels are asserted in the same way. Labels such as "criminal" or "mentally ill" accomplish the same purpose. They are ways of morally distancing ourselves from the miscreant, thereby making it easier to abandon them as objects of legitimate social concern. The necessity for doing so with the dying is, in some ways, more morally compelling than with other, more common, deviant labels. Members of the labeling audience can always tell themselves that they will never become criminals or a mental patients. But everyone dies, and by treating the dying as objects of deviance, audience members can further participate in the ritual of denying their own death.

Avoidance may also be viewed as a means of controlling the dying patient. When individuals cannot modify the disposition of a situation, they can control its consequences for themselves by avoiding it. However, medical personnel often control the disruption or unpleasantness caused by the dying person through even more direct action. One of the control measures they use most

frequently with dying patients is to make decisions for them. As Kübler-Ross (1969:8) has observed, decisions concerning if, when, and where a dying patient should be hospitalized are often made by persons other than the patient. She eloquently describes the dying person's hospital career:

> Our presumed patient has now reached the emergency room. He will be surrounded by busy nurses, orderlies, interns, resident, a lab technician who takes the cardiogram. He may be moved to X-ray and he will overhear options of his condition and discussions and questions to members of the family. He slowly but surely is beginning to be treated like a thing. He is no longer a person. Decisions are made often without his opinion. If he tries to rebel he will be sedated and after hours of waiting and wondering whether he has the strength, he will be wheeled into the operating room or intensive treatment unit and become an object of great concern and great financial investment. He may cry for rest, peace, and dignity, but he will get infusions, transfusions, a heart machine, or tracheotomy if necessary. He may want one single person to stop for one single minute so that he can ask one single question—but he will get a dozen people around the clock, all busily preoccupied with his heart rate, pulse, electrocardiogram or pulmonary function, his secretions or excretions but not with him as a human being. He may wish to fight it all but it is going to be a useless fight since all this is done in the fight for his life, and if they can save his life they can consider the person afterwards. Those who consider the person first may lose precious time to save his life! At least this seems to be the rationale or justification behind all of this—or is it? Is the reason for this increasingly mechanical, depersonalized approach our own defensiveness? Is this approach our own way to cope with and repress the anxieties that a terminally or critically ill patient evokes in us? Is our concentration on equipment, on blood pressure, our desperate attempt to deny the impending death which is so frightening and discomforting to us that we displace all our knowledge onto machines, since they are less close to us than the suffering face of another human being which would remind us once more of our lack of omnipotence, our own limits and failures, and last but not least perhaps our own mortality? (Pp. 8–9)

In addition to demonstrating that others make decisions for dying patients, Kübler-Ross suggests that drugs are often used to control them and reinforces the typology of masks as a means of avoidance. Bowers et al. (1981) also suggest that drugs play an important role in managing the patient for the benefit of the staff:

> In addition to the usual masks, there is the sedation which can be administered in order to take the patient and his unacceptable behavior farther away from any relationship that might exist between him and those around him. In effect, administering a sedation [sic] is often tantamount to saying to the patient, "If you must die, please go off and do it quietly while I am not looking." It amounts to a request to the patient to put on a mask that meets his obligation in the "it-it" relationship comparable to the masks the physician wears in avoiding genuine encounter with the person who is ill. (P. 56)

In the Wheeler et al. (1977) study, my colleagues and I used a self-administered questionnaire to test the hypothesis that dying patients represent a form of deviance in hospital settings. We drew two samples, one of physicians and the other of nurses. The physician sample was composed of 68 private practitioners and 13 members of the attending staff of a large teaching hospital; the nurse sample comprised 133 nurses working in the same teaching hospital. The questionnaire was divided into four parts. The first part gathered demographic information, the second and third parts were composed of attitude scales, and the final part consisted of 12 statements designed to elicit information about the respondent's attitudes, beliefs, and behavior regarding the dying person.

The second part of the questionnaire used a semantic differential scale to measure the meanings and attitudes elicited by six "person concepts"—a dying person, an alcoholic, a person who has tuberculosis, an atheist, an emotionally disturbed person, and an executive. The scale measured three dimensions: evaluation, potency, and activity. The respondent rated the object or person concept on a 7-point scale, the two poles of which were defined by polar adjectives. For example:

Desirable __ __ __ __ __ __ __ Undesirable

A score of 1 was assigned to the most positive response and 7 to the most negative. We then computed a composite score by squaring the three factor scores, summing the squares, and extracting the square root of the sum of the squares. We tested four minor hypotheses to determine if age, nursing certification, medical specialization of doctor, and type of nurse were associated with aversive attitudes and avoidance behavior.

The third part of the questionnaire consisted of a modified social distance scale composed of items ranging from intimate relationships to complete avoidance. Social distance scores ranged from 1 through 7, with a higher score showing greater social distance between the respondent and the person concept he or she was rating.

We measured attitudes elicited by dying persons, executives, and the four other person concepts by asking respondents to rate their feelings toward these person concepts on a semantic differential scale and social distance scale. We reasoned that if respondents rated the dying person negatively and the executive, traditionally nondeviant, positively while at the same time rating traditionally deviant types negatively, one could argue that the dying person elicited attitudes more similar to those elicited by deviant types than to those elicited by nondeviant types. We tested attitudes elicited by all six person concepts to see if they were significantly different from one another.

Our major hypothesis stated that dying persons elicit attitudes from physicians and nurses that are significantly more aversive than the attitudes elicited by a nondeviant category of persons, such as the executive. That proved to be the case: Both nurses and physicians ranked executives more favorably and dying patients more aversively. Nurses tended to rank alcoholics slightly more aversively than dying persons, whereas physicians ranked the emotionally disturbed and the alcoholic slightly more aversively than the dying patient. Indeed, both the doctors and the nurses, on standard social distance scales, suggested they would rather spend time working with tubercular patients, atheists, or even the emotionally disturbed than they would with dying patients.[7] Of course, the fact that they rated the dying patient more aversively does not mean that they viewed the patient as "deviant." We were reluctant to claim that our study actually documented deviance, suggesting instead that we had merely shown aversive attitudes toward the dying, but the direction of the data are nonetheless clear and pointed.

DYING AS DEVIANCE: THE CURRENT SITUATION

The literature discussed above is now almost 30 years old. Has the situation changed? If so, how? These issues are the subject of the remainder of this chapter. Although there has been no empirical follow-up to the Wheeler et al. study, several clues suggest that there continues to be a stigma against the dying that is regularly constructed in medical settings. One such clue comes from the logical force of Glaser and Straus's conceptualization of awareness contexts and the subsequent research this rich concept has spawned. Awareness contexts represent a powerful way of assessing any possible changes in the way dying patients are treated. Awareness contexts are inherently tied to the

---

7. In the method we employed in the Wheeler et al. (1977) study, the independent variable was the person concepts and the dependent variable was the attitudes elicited by dying persons and executives. We measured attitudes using the semantic differential scale (P scores) and social distance scales. P scores on the semantic differential scale higher than 6.93 were considered aversive. The neutral points were considered aversive, and less than 6.93 were nonaversive. Because the social distance scale had no neutral point, only the two extreme positions, 6 and 7, could be considered aversive. We used both the semantic differential scale and the social distance scale in a comparative manner. Six person concepts were rated: Besides the dying person and the executive, the others were an alcoholic, a person who has tuberculosis, an atheist, and an emotionally disturbed person. We also tested four additional independent variables to determine their influence on attitudes and avoidance: age of physician, age of nurse, medical specialization of physician, and whether the nurse was a registered nurse or a licensed practical nurse. For doctors, age was divided into three categories: 30–39, 40–49, and 50 and older. Medical specialization for doctors was divided into family practice, internal medicine, surgery, and other. For nurses, age was divided into three categories: 19–39, 40–49, and 50 and older. Nurses were divided into two categories: registered nurse and licensed practical nurse. Aversive attitudes were operationalized by the P score in the following manner: 5.5–7.4 = nonaversive to mildly aversive, 7.5–9.4 = moderately aversive, and 9.5–11.4 = highly aversive. The social distance scale operationalized attitudes as follows: 1–2 = nonaversive, 3–5 = moderately aversive, and 5–7 = highly aversive.

labeling process, for, as noted above, the direct cause of all deviance from a societal point of view is "know-aboutness." Societal reactions cannot occur until the alleged behavior or situation is known, and this "knowing" is what awareness contexts are all about.

As Glaser and Straus articulate, the following four possibilities, which are characteristic of all social situations, have particular salience for the dying:

Open awareness: In this awareness context, both the medical team and the patient know the person is dying, and (most important) both act on what they know. All aspects of the patient's condition are "open."

Closed awareness: In this context, one side knows and the other side is kept unaware. In the case of dying, the medical team is typically in possession of the relevant information about the dying person, and the patient is, for a variety of reasons, kept unaware. The deviance framework discussed above both establishes and encourages closed awareness.

Suspicion awareness: In this context, one side knows and the other side suspects the truth of the situation but does not know for sure. In the case of the dying patient, the medical team is in possession of information and withholds it from the dying patient, who tries to confirm his or her suspicions about the situation.

Mutual pretense: Occupying a position somewhere between open and closed awareness, mutual pretense has elements of both. Both sides know the truth, but both act as if something else is the case. Both the medical team and the patient know that the patient is dying, but both sides act as if he or she is merely ill.

Recent studies suggest that there are far more institutional (and legal) reasons for telling patients the truth than for keeping it from them, and as a result, doctors and nurses both are inclined toward more openness in communicating with the terminally ill and their families about the dying patient's condition. Seale (1991) notes that, influenced at least partially by the hospice movement, professionals now have a general preference for open awareness. However, that preference is "tempered by the consideration that bad news needs to be broken slowly, in a context of support, while recognizing that not everyone wishes to know all" (p. 943).

THE AMBIGUITIES OF OPEN AWARENESS

Although it is clear that today there is far more open awareness than has been the case in the past with dying patients, there are still substantial ambiguities even (perhaps *especially*) when the awareness context is open. Open awareness can lead to a host of conflicts that closed awareness

effectively shuts off. For example, a patient may want to die in a way that may be difficult for the medical team to arrange. He or she may want to die without pain, in private, and "with dignity," yet all of these concepts may have entirely different meanings for the dying person than they do for the medical team. In this sense, deviant labels arise directly because of the disparity between what the dying patient wants and what those who attend to the patient require.

Those dying patients who sense the implicit demands of the medical staff and comply with them are rewarded with labels such as "good patient," whereas those who diverge from the staff program are greeted with deviant labels such as "difficult" or "demanding." Pain management remains a negotiated order in which the patient and medical staff deal with each other from different moral frameworks. Study findings have repeatedly suggested that medical personnel continue to have both medical and legal concerns about patients becoming addicted and are reluctant to prescribe appropriate drugs in adequate dosages. Moreover, patients themselves often feel they should endure pain as a sign of moral strength and subscribe to various myths about the subject because they have not been educated to the contrary (DeSpelder and Strickland 1999:182). These disparities between what the dying patient wants and what staff are able and willing to provide constitute a major arena in which deviant labels can arise.

AWARENESS CONTEXTS AS MORAL MATTERS

Establishing and maintaining an awareness context with terminally ill patients is an intensely moral matter. Awareness contexts do not and cannot flow naturally from any particular biophysical state, no matter how dire the diagnosis is. They are inherently social. This is a fundamental tenet of interactionist approaches to relationships between the self and others, and one reason researchers working within this theoretical tradition insist on maintaining a distinction between biophysical and social states of affairs (Friedson 1970; Miller 1978).

Moreover, the new openness and naturalization of dying in medical settings has led some scholars to suggest a reversal of taboos. Previously, medical staff shunned the dying patient as if he or she were engaged in deviant behavior. But now, as Armstrong (1987; cited in Seale 1991) has suggested, the current medical enthusiasm for breaking the silence and ending the taboo has led to a kind of "medical interrogation" in which patients are maneuvered into "confessing" their own death. Those who choose not to participate in this new "openness" are treated as if they have done something wrong. This seems to be exactly what happened with those trained in the tradition of Kübler-Ross. *Descriptions* of the process that dying patients tend to follow have been transformed in treatment settings into *prescriptions* for the dying. To die in denial, in this new "open" setting, is to do something morally wrong.

There is also the dance that takes place between the medical team and the dying patient as the team tries to establish whether or not the patient even wishes to be in open awareness about his or her condition. For the patient terminally ill with cancer, the nature of the disease itself makes it difficult to maintain a stance of closed awareness, but many other serious illnesses contain considerable prognostic latitude for both the doctor and the patient. In his study of British physicians, Seale (1991) compared how doctors and dying patients communicated with one another in 1969 against such communication in 1987. He found that doctors in 1987 were more likely to tell their dying patients the truth, but he also found that they tended to wait to be asked and generally backed off and let the patients guide them on the issue of how much to tell and when. Seale's findings support Glaser and Straus's (1965) contention that awareness of dying is a definition of the situation intimately related to issues of time.[8] Finally, Seale's findings demonstrate another aspect of deviance: distinguishing between those who are morally entitled to the truth and those who can be kept in the dark:

> Results show that instances where the relatives were given information and the dying are not are still quite common. Patients are still highly likely to be left to guess for themselves that they are dying and the emotional isolation that this produces can only be guessed at in the absence of patients' own stories. (P. 951)[9]

CONCLUSION

In spite of the many changes that have occurred in medicine's sophistication regarding the diagnosis and treatment of fateful diseases, there remains a fundamental disparity between the social situation of dying patients and that of those who treat them. A deviance framework offers unique insights into this disparity and how the incongruity it causes is handled in medical settings. Death and dying may be routine medical events, but the social situation in which they are handled is fraught with the problematics of the construction of meaning. And as in other settings, those persons whose actions and identities most align with the purposes of the institution are dealt with differently than others. Clearly, in medical settings, the dying represent a category of identity that is strongly at variance with the purposes of the institution and are therefore most likely to be confronted by both aversive reactions and negative moral meanings.

REFERENCES

Armstrong, D. 1987. "Silence and Truth in Death and Dying." *Social Science & Medicine* 24:651–58.

Becker, Ernest. 1973. *The Denial of Death.* New York: Free Press.

Becker, Howard S. 1963. *Outsiders.* New York: Free Press.

Blauner, Robert. 1966. "Death and Social Structure." *Psychiatry* 29:378–94.

Bowers, Margaretta K., Edgar N. Jackson, James A. Knight, and Lawrence LeShan. 1981. *Counseling the Dying.* San Francisco: Harper & Row.

DeSpelder, Lynne Ann and Albert Lee Strickland. 1999. *The Last Dance: Encountering Death and Dying,* 5th ed. Mountain View, CA: Mayfield.

Erikson, K. T. 1962. "Notes on the Sociology of Deviance." *Social Problems* 9:307–14

Feifel, Herman. 1963. "Death." Pp. 8–21 in *Taboo Topics,* edited by Norman L. Farberow. New York: Atherton.

Friedson, Eliot. 1970. *Profession of Medicine: A Study of the Sociology of Applied Knowledge.* New York: Harper & Row.

Gibbs, Jack. 1966. "Conceptions of Deviance: The Old and the New." *Pacific Sociological Review* 9:9–14.

Glaser, Barney G. and Anselm L. Straus. 1965. *Awareness of Dying.* Chicago: Aldine.

———. 1968. *Time for Dying.* Chicago: Aldine.

Goffman, Erving. 1963. *Stigma: Notes on the Management of Spoiled Identity.* Englewood Cliffs, NJ: Prentice Hall.

Kalish, Richard A. 1966. "Social Distance and the Dying." *Community Mental Health Journal* 2:152–55.

Kasper, August M. 1959. "The Doctor and Death." Pp. 259–70 in *The Meaning of Death,* edited by Herman Feifel. New York: McGraw-Hill.

Kitsuse, John L. 1962. "Societal Reaction to Deviant Behavior: Problems of Theory and Method." *Social Problems* 9:247–56.

———. 1972. "Deviance, Deviant Behavior, and Deviants: Some Conceptual Problems." In *An Introduction to Deviance: Readings in the Process of Making Deviants,* edited by William J. Filstead. Chicago: Markham.

Knutson, A. L. 1970. "Cultural Beliefs on Life and Death." In *The Dying Patient,* edited by Orville G. Brim, Jr., Howard E. Freeman, Sol Levine, and Norman A. Scotch. New York: Russell Sage Foundation.

Kübler-Ross, Elisabeth. 1969. *On Death and Dying.* New York: Macmillan.

Lemert, Edwin. 1951. *Social Pathology.* New York: McGraw-Hill.

Levine, Sol and Norman A. Scotch. 1970. "Dying as an Emerging Social Problem." In *The Dying Patient,* edited by Orville G. Brim, Jr., Howard E. Freeman, Sol Levine, and Norman A. Scotch. New York: Russell Sage Foundation.

Lofland, Lyn. 1978. *The Craft of Dying: The Modern Face of Death.* Beverly Hills, CA: Sage.

Miller, R. S. 1978. "The Social Construction and Reconstruction of Physiological Events: Acquiring the Pregnancy Identity."

---

8. Indeed, Glaser and Straus's companion volume to *Awareness of Dying* (1965) is titled *Time for Dying* (1968).

9. Schou (1993) reports similar findings from her recent study of awareness contexts and the construction of dying among cancer patients. In a longitudinal ethnographic study of the experiences of 33 cancer patients in Northern England, she found that a complex interaction occurs between the dominant discourse of medicine and the narrative knowledge created by the dying person, and in each case how much the individual knows about his or her own dying is contingent on this interaction.

Pp. 119–28 in *Studies in Symbolic Interaction: An Annual Compilation of Research,* vol. 1, edited by Norman K. Denzin. Greenwich, CT: JAI.

Rubington, Earl and Martin S. Weinberg. 1971. *The Study of Social Problems: Five Perspectives.* New York: Oxford University Press.

Schou, Kirsten Costain. 1993. "Awareness Contexts and the Construction of Dying in the Cancer Treatment Setting: 'Micro' and 'Macro' Levels of Narrative Analysis." Pp. 238–63 in *The Sociology of Death: Theory, Culture, Practice,* edited by David Clark. Oxford: Blackwell.

Schur, Edwin M. 1971. *Labeling Deviant Behavior: The Sociological Implications.* New York: Harper & Row.

Seale, Clive F. 1991. "Communication and Awareness About Death: A Study of a Random Sample of Dying People." *Social Science & Medicine* 32:943–52.

Sudnow, David N. 1967. *Passing On: The Social Organization of Dying.* Englewood Cliffs, NJ: Prentice Hall.

Tannenbaum, Frank. 1979. "Definitions and the Dramatization of Evil." Pp. 160–65 in *Deviant Behavior: Readings in the Sociology of Deviance,* edited by Delos H. Kelly. New York: St. Martin's.

Tarde, Gabriel. 1898. *Études de Psychologie Sociale.* Paris: V. Giard & E. Briere.

Wheeler, Alban, Charles Edgley, and Lucille Orlando. 1977. "Dying as Deviance: Medical Practice and the Terminal Patient." Presented at the annual meeting of the Midwest Alpha Kappa Delta National Honor Society, February, Richmond, VA.

THE DYING PROCESS

GRAVES E. ENCK

Asking Samuel Johnson in 1769, when he was 60 years old, if one should "fortify" the mind against "the approach of death" would have elicited this passionate rebuff: "No, Sir, let it alone. It matters not how a man dies, but how he lives. The act of dying is not of importance, it lasts so short a time" (Boswell [1799] 1953:427). By the end of the 19th century in the United States, the same rebuff would have been appropriate. Life expectancy for a female born in 1900 was 46.3 years, and for a male it was 48.3 years (Fukuyama 2002:57). People died at home, primarily from infections, accidents, and childbirth, with death preceded by little, if any, disability, and their families paid the medical expenses (Lynn, Schuster, and Kabcenell 2000:4). One century changed everything. The maturing of the scientific method and its application in the 20th century to the environment, to public health, and to our own bodies brought us longevity, dramatic decreases in deaths from infectious diseases, and the "new reality . . . that most of us will die from complications of a serious chronic illness that we will 'live with' for years" (Lynn and Harrold 1999:2). Life expectancy for a female born in 2000 is 79.9 years, and for a male it is 74.2 years (Fukuyama 2002:57). People die in hospitals from failing hearts, malignant organs, brains destroyed by strokes, minds wandering in confused dementia, with death preceded by an average of more than 4 years of disability, and Medicare pays most of the medical expenses (Lynn et al. 2000:4).

Our language has made a partial concession to the "new reality." The "dying act" has become the "dying process," the new abstract noun denoting that death now requires, as *The Compact Edition of the Oxford English Dictionary* puts it, "a lapse of time." We still cling to Samuel Johnson's era when a friend or a colleague dies suddenly without discomfort or in sleep after a short illness, and we say, longingly, "If you have to go, that's the way to go," while knowing that dying is no longer "so short a time" for most Americans. For most of us, death will come at the end of an interval of time whose beginning is vague, whose ending is unpredictable, whose distinguishing feature

will be a series of irreversible changes brought about by "the generic death-dealing laws of biology common to all organisms," laws to which we are held "captives against our will" (Callahan 1993:164).

Time runs throughout our descriptions of disease. We call modern diseases "chronic," after the Greek *chronos*, meaning "time," or "progressive," the forward course of events through time. Death and dying are now modified by time-laden adjectives: *date-fixed dying, accelerated dying, curtailed dying, physician-assisted suicide, euthanasia, autoeuthanasia, elective death, hastened death, a planned closure, anticipatory self-destruction, preemptive suicide.* Questions about time come to mind, without reflection. The surgeon calls to tell me his findings. My mother's colon cancer, discovered too late, has escaped into the bloodstream; it is now a "systemic disease." "How long?" I ask without thinking. "Six to eighteen months without treatment, which, if done, should not be aggressive at her age of 87." She died six months and two weeks after that call. I saw the surgeon in a local hospital several weeks after she died and asked him how he could estimate so accurately. An older, experienced surgeon, he simply said, "You see something often enough, and you just know."

THE DYING TRAJECTORY

Barney Glaser and Anselm Straus would have understood his words perfectly. One can only imagine how often in 6 years of hospital observations they heard similar comments from physicians and nurses caring for dying people and acting as modern futurists, developing a "fan of probable futures" (Bell 1997:81) for their patients, each vane of which had its distinctive name: "short reprieve," "abrupt surprise," "swift death," "expected lingering while dying," "suspended-sentence," "entry-reentry." These were names given to "dying trajectories," as Glaser and Straus (1968) called them, staff expectations of when a patient would die projected onto a mental plane as a graph having "shape" and "duration," like the graph of a projectile's course.

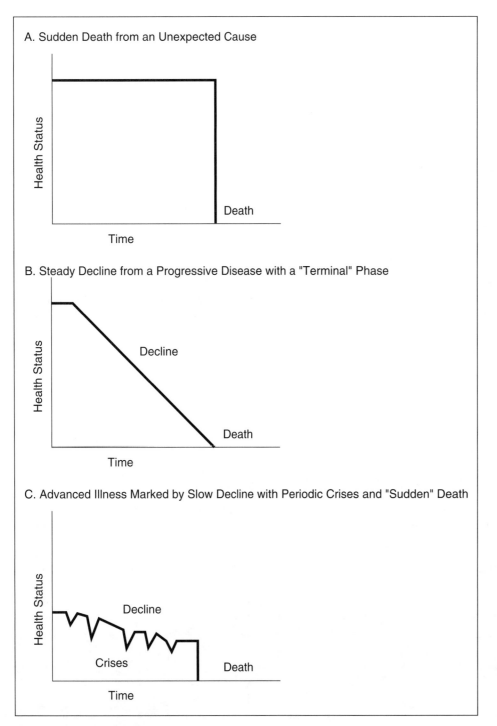

A. Sudden Death from an Unexpected Cause

Health Status

Death

Time

B. Steady Decline from a Progressive Disease with a "Terminal" Phase

Health Status

Decline

Death

Time

C. Advanced Illness Marked by Slow Decline with Periodic Crises and "Sudden" Death

Health Status

Decline

Crises

Death

Time

Figure 1   Prototypical Death Trajectories

SOURCE: Institute of Medicine, *Approaching Death: Improving Care at the End of Life,* copyright 1997 by the National Academy of Sciences. Reprinted with permission from the National Academy Press, Washington, D.C. (Computerized reproduction created by Rebecca Maxwell, University of Memphis.)

Foley (1996), director of the Open Society Institute's Project on Death in America, could say in her congressional testimony on the physician-assisted suicide debate that one of the factors driving the debate was "changes in the trajectory of dying, with large numbers of patients with cancer and AIDS alive for months and years following the diagnosis of an incurable illness" (p. 2). The Institute of Medicine (1997) uses the "dying trajectory" to "illuminate similarities and differences in patient experiences as they approach death," identifying three "prototypical death trajectories" (pp. 28, 29).

Brief vignettes illustrate each trajectory. Trajectory A describes sudden death from accident or heart attack, as illustrated by the death of Henri J. M. Nouwen, Catholic priest and author, who wrote in 1994, at age 62, that he was not prepared to die but knew that "the ten, twenty or thirty years" he had left would pass quickly (Nouwen 1994:4). Father Nouwen suffered a sudden, fatal heart attack just 2 years later.

Trajectory B is typical for cancer, thought to have "a more predictable trajectory from the point at which cure becomes unlikely until death than other chronic diseases" (Institute of Medicine 2001:13), as illustrated by the death of former French President François Mitterand. Diagnosed under a fictitious name with prostate cancer in 1981, shortly after his election, and given 3 months to live, he served two terms as president, keeping the disease a secret for most of that time (Zhamkin 2002:2). Only near the end of his presidency did he tell Marie de Hennezel, a psychologist in a palliative care unit, "The process has begun. The illness is fatal. I know . . ." (quoted in Hennezel 1998:161). Heeding her reminder that he must not "start

Dying "takes place over time," they wrote (p. 5). This imaginary lapse of time became the guiding principle for organizing daily medical work with the dying.

The "dying trajectory" has had lasting influence, gradually being transformed from a projection to a description of the course of a fatal disease, such that Dr. Kathleen dying before death comes," he spent the last year of his life sharing his reflections with Franz-Olivier Giesbert, published in 1998 as *Dying Without God,* and writing the foreword to Hennezel's book, in which he described the "separate time" of the dying when "they discover the freedom of being true to themselves" (p. ix).

Trajectory C describes death from a long chronic disease with intermittent crises, with death resulting from one of these or from a subsequent problem, as illustrated by the following hypothetical case. Any one of us might have a heart attack at age 60, followed by years of progressive heart failure, made worse at some point by diabetes and hypertension, finally dying at 80 of a stroke and its complications (Lynn and Harrold 1999:2).

WHY AND WHERE WE DIE

We see examples of all three trajectories in the statistics we gather about why and where we die. The usefulness of the "dying trajectory" is as a lens through which to look at these statistics and try to construct the imaginary graph by which a human being progressed from a healthy status to death across a "lapse of time." For each graph, we try to imagine the life activities that filled the days from diagnosis to death, if such time were available. Perhaps our own experience with a dying parent or friend, wife, lover, or colleague helps our imagination construct what neither these numbers nor the trajectories that describe them can give us. The current statistics on cause of death illustrate the changing time and shape of dying; the statistics on where we die illustrate the consequences of those changes.

In their report of final death statistics for 1999, Hoyert et al. (2001) list the 15 leading causes of death. Reading the list slowly and reflectively allows one to use one's imagination to draw the "dying trajectory" for each cause and compare it to the "prototypes." The percentage in parentheses following each cause here is the proportion of deaths from that cause accounted for by "older Americans," those 65 years old and older: heart disease (83.7%), cancer (70.9%), stroke (88.8%), chronic respiratory disease (87.1%), accidents (32.9%), diabetes (75.8%), influenza and pneumonia (89.9%), Alzheimer's disease (98.8%), kidney disease (84.3%), septicemia (80.3%), suicide (18.8%), chronic liver disease (40%), hypertension (85%), homicide (5.2%), aortic aneurysm (84%). These 15 causes accounted for 84% of the 2,391,399 American deaths in 1999. Older Americans accounted for 75.2% of all deaths in that year. The three leading causes of death—heart disease, cancer, and stroke—accounted for 60.3% of all American deaths.

Some variations in dying trajectory are known within some of these categories. Among the deaths from heart disease, 27.5% were deaths from "acute myocardial infarction," heart attack, with half or more of the victims probably dying within an hour of the attack (Nuland 1994:17). Accidents have a "trimodal" dying trajectory:

"immediate death," death occurring within minutes; "early death," death occurring within the first few hours; and "late death," death occurring days or weeks after the injury (Nuland 1994:145).

The time required for dying and the shape that dying takes affect where we die. In a recent review, Hempstead (2001:1) found studies of patients' preferences for place of dying but few systematic studies of death certificates to determine where we actually die. Her comparative review of New Jersey death certificates from 1989 and 1998 provides one indication of changing patterns: There was a decline in the proportion of deaths accounted for by hospital inpatients (from 61% to 49%) and an increase in the proportion of deaths occurring in a residence (17.8% to 24.6%) or a nursing home (8.6% to 16.4%), with important variations by age, race, county of residence, and cause of death (p. 1). For "older Americans," in 1998, the majority of deaths among those 65 to 79 occurred in institutions (hospital inpatient, 53.02%; nursing home, 10.4%), whereas 27.8% occurred in residences. The majority of deaths among those 80 and above also occurred in institutions (hospital inpatient, 46%; nursing home, 27.7%), with 20.8% occurring in residences (p. 5).

These data support the Institute of Medicine's (1997) profile of American dying. Three-fourths of the dying are "elderly," most of them covered by Medicare or other government health care programs for older, disabled, or poor people. Although the proportion of people dying at home is increasing, most die in institutions, mainly in hospitals, with a smaller number dying in nursing homes. People cared for in hospice programs account for a minority of all deaths, the majority of these caused by cancer (p. 260). As a result, "death at home in the care of family has been widely superseded by an institutional, professional and technological process of dying" (p. 33).

These 20th-century changes in dying trajectory created what Dr. Sherwin Nuland (1994) of Yale University calls "the method of modern dying," dying that occurs "in the modern hospital, where it can be hidden, cleansed of its organic blight, and finally packaged for modern burial. We can now deny the power not only of death but of nature itself" (p. xv). For a visitor to a modern hospital, writes Virginia Morris (2001), no one dies there, the handling of the body ensuring that death is concealed. When death occurs, the body is hidden from public view, wrapped in plastic, placed beneath a draped gurney disguised as an empty gurney or as a laundry cart, taken to the morgue, then to the back entrance to the hospital and taken away by undertakers in unmarked vehicles. "No one in the hospital is reminded that death occurs here, or that it occurs at all for that matter" (p. 52).

Other than cause of death, all we know about the 2,391,399 Americans who died in 1999—each now a "faceless Nobody, not a qualified Each" (Hillman 1999:38)—is that they died from the "weapons of every horseman of death" that kill and have always killed human beings: Their circulation stopped, their tissues received too little oxygen, their brain function ceased, their organs failed, their vital centers were destroyed (Nuland 1994:xviii). Beyond that, we know nothing about the "process" of any single person's dying, for "we rarely witness the process of dying as it routinely occurs" (Morris 2001:49), and "there are few reliable accounts of the ways in which we die" (Nuland 1994:8). As Nuland (1994) notes, those who regularly see death seldom write about it, whereas "poets, essayists, chroniclers, wags and wise men often write about death, but have rarely seen it" (p. 8). Bill Moyers has recently shown us a sample of what we could know in *On Our Own Terms: Moyers on Dying*, a four-part series presented by the Public Broadcasting Service and sponsored by the Robert Wood Johnson Foundation. Americans for Better Care of the Dying, an organization working to improve end-of-life care, suggests that newspaper obituary writers could help by writing something about how dead persons lived during their last years or months. What did they do? What did their families do (Lynn et al. 2000:205)?

Nuland (1994:xi) provides an introduction to some of the clinical and biological events of the "lapse of time" with *How We Die,* his conversation with those of us who want to know what dying is like. As another reminder of the "new reality," he tells us that fewer than one in five of us will die under such "easy circumstances" as death in an undisturbed coma, a peaceful death after a long illness, or a sudden death without discomfort (p. 142). Instead, our dying will more likely be "a messy business," perhaps from one of the six common causes that form the core of his book: AIDS, cancer, ischemic heart disease, Alzheimer's, accident, and stroke. Together, these accounted for 1,404,061 (59%) of U.S. deaths in 1999. His description of how these "common avenues to death" (p. xviii) kill us makes a myth of our belief in a "good death" (p. xvi), one of the many "invented symbols and stories" we use "to cope with death" (Wetz 2001:245). For Nuland, "death with dignity" is the chief mythical story, serving as a defense against confronting the biological realities that eventually disintegrate "the dying person's humanity. I have not often seen much dignity in the process by which we die" (pp. xvi–xvii).

DEATH ON PUBLIC DISPLAY

The "messiness" of dying is usually seen only by the dying, by their families, and by medical personnel. The public has no access to dying as it occurs, but public access to the final evidence of death is now available. Dr. Gunther von Hagens, an anatomist, has worked for more than 20 years to perfect "plastination," a technology by which a donor's corpse is embalmed, dissected, filled with reactive plastics, and cured into a fully plastic specimen, "frozen at a point between death and decay" (Hagens 2001:20). The specimen is protected from decay and can be displayed in many forms, including full-body demonstrations of

skeletal and muscular systems, full-body demonstrations of organic systems, isolated specific organs, or slices of various organs or of the entire body. Numerous specimens of each form are being shown in an exhibition titled *Body Worlds: The Anatomical Exhibition of Real Human Bodies,* described by its creator as "the aesthetic and instructive presentation of the body's interior" (p. 32).

I had the good fortune to see the exhibition at the Atlantis Gallery in London in March 2002. Here were whole-body specimens, minus the skin, shown in various poses that illustrated the various systems of the body. Here also were individual organs and cross-sectional slices of the brain and other organs. Seeing the final outcomes of Nuland's "weapons of death" activates the imagination about how messy the final days of dying could have been. Here one sees the final state of failed organs and destroyed vital centers. Here, "finally, the supply of oxygen to the body [broke] down" and "the person who was alive a moment ago is now dead" (Wetz 2001:245).

Here is a pair of smoker's lungs, blackened by tar, sitting on either side of an enlarged heart, swollen by increasing demands to compensate for failing lungs. The small card that accompanies the lung exhibit says that smoking 20 cigarettes a day deposits the equivalent of a coffee cup full of tar in the lungs each year, shortening life by an average of 5 years. The exhibition catalog calls smoking "suicide on the installment plan" (Whalley 2001:68). Here is the liver that while filtering the blood trapped a cancer cell whose origin was elsewhere and now is covered with mounds of metastatic cancer. This could well have been my mother's liver, for she died of metastatic liver cancer from a cancer that began in her colon and entered her bloodstream before it was diagnosed. Here is a cross section of the brain of one who died from a stroke, the dark pool of blood preserved in the brain tissue. Here is the swollen sclerotic liver. Here is the cross section of the chest cavity with extensive tumor growth infiltrating the vertebra. Here is the opened heart showing the erosive death of the heart wall, the evidence of myocardial infarction. This could have been my heart had not a cardiologist's skill with angioplasty prevented it. Here is the full-body plastinate of a woman in the fifth month of pregnancy, the front wall of the uterus opened to show the fetus, 6.5 inches long. Here is the reclining woman in the eighth month of pregnancy, opened to show the fetus crowding her abdominal organs. Here is the newborn child with hydrocephalus. Here is the plastinated horseman sitting astride his plastinated horse, holding his plastinated brain in one hand and the plastinated brain of his horse in the other, strikingly symbolic of Nuland's "horseman of death."

"Here Death is happy to rush to the aid of the living." So reads a sign in the foyer of the Heidelberg Institute of Anatomy (Hagens 2001:34). So, also, does death rush to our aid in this exhibition. Death is on display here, democratized, presented in anonymous, skinless cadavers, preserved indefinitely. Here one sees that, "like the death of life in general, the death of the individual human being is neither mysterious nor profound. It is the end of a natural course. Admittedly, we can try to postpone this biological actuality with the aid of modern medicine and a healthy life-style, but we cannot avoid it" (Wetz 2001:245).

TRAGIC POSTPONEMENTS

But postponement and avoidance are at the center of our controversies about dying. Should a person who wants to die be forced to postpone it? Can one postpone death too long and thereby lose the chance to avoid a much worse death, one with greater suffering for all concerned? Should one consider no longer postponing a current cause of death to avoid a worse one? Is it rational to choose suicide to avoid the deterioration of aging and loss of personhood? Two widely publicized cases in England, which occurred simultaneously, involving two women of the same age who died 17 days apart, represent our greatest fears about our own death. Cases like these provoke others to write about choosing the right time for one's death. The case summaries are followed below by a review of three of those views.

The first case involved Miss B, age 43, an unidentified former social worker, paralyzed from the neck down in February 2001 by a ruptured blood vessel in her neck. She was kept alive with a ventilator, confined to a hospital bed, totally dependent on others. She insisted that she wanted to be allowed to die, a right guaranteed her by English law, a decision she was judged competent to make. The doctors in her hospital refused to remove the ventilator because it was against their medical ethics and because they thought they would be killing her, preferring instead that she try rehabilitation, even though she had little or no chance of any improvement. She sued, giving testimony as the judge sat at the foot of her bed. She won and was moved to another hospital where doctors would honor her request and honor English law. Within 3 weeks after she was moved, the ventilator was removed, and she died on April 24, 2002 (Dyer 2002b).

The second case was that of Diane Pretty, also age 43, diagnosed in 1999 with motor neuron disease. By 2001, she was also paralyzed from the neck down, unable to speak and wanting to avoid the asphyxiation that would be her inevitable death. Suicide is not a crime in England, but assisting someone with suicide is, punishable by a maximum of 14 years in prison. Because of the disease, she could not kill herself. She asked that her husband be protected from prosecution so he could help her die. The director of public prosecutions refused. She sued, appealing her case through the British courts, lost, and finally appealed to the European Court of Human Rights in Strasbourg. Her appeal was denied on April 29, 2002, 5 days after Miss B died. Diane Pretty died of asphyxiation on May 11, 2002, in the hospice that had cared for her (Dyer 2002a).

These two tragic cases illustrate the major concerns of two prominent writers on the end of life. Miss B is the prototypical nightmare for Dr. Daniel Callahan (2000), medical ethicist at the Hastings Center. He warns against the "'technological imperative' . . . the compulsive use of technology to maintain life when palliative care would be more appropriate" (p. 654). When the continued use of technology is equated with preserving the sanctity of life, the result is the very "trap" that imprisoned Miss B and her physicians (Callahan 1993:88). American patients have the right to terminate treatment at any point, but when stopping treatment is seen as an act of killing by those who stop it, then families and physicians suffer conflict and guilt, having lost sight of the fact that the disease is the cause of death and not those who decide to let it take its course (Callahan 1993:88).

Facing such a medical nightmare, Callahan (1993) cautions us against postponing one cause of death for a subsequent cause of death that could be worse. The goal he seeks and the goal we all seek is the "peaceful death" he eloquently describes (pp. 195–96), a death that can be missed through persistent technological interventions. At some point, which only the individual can decide, perhaps the "peaceful death" is found through letting a fatal disease take its course, the patient guided by a compassionate physician who can explain what such a death will entail and who will provide maximum comfort and care (pp. 198–99). For Callahan, the physician has no greater role, for physician-assisted suicide or euthanasia would break the moral rule against doctors killing and turn doctors into killers (pp. 79, 104).

Diane Pretty's case is the prototypical nightmare for Derek Humphry, who, having helped his wife to die in 1975 to end her suffering from bone cancer, was investigated by England's director of public prosecutions after publishing his account of her death in 1978. After moving to the United States, he became a leading advocate for physician-assisted suicide and euthanasia through founding the Hemlock Society, which he left in 1992 to found ERGO (Euthanasia Research and Guidance Organization). His views have been widely disseminated in his book *Final Exit* (1996). Should someone like Diane Pretty, finding herself suffering from an advanced case of incurable disease and an unacceptable quality of life, be legally permitted to get a prescription for a lethal dose of medication that she can take at her home, when she chooses, with the help she would require, and thereby end her suffering through "assisted dying"? Derek Humphry's answer is yes. While the public policy debate about "physician-assisted suicide" (legal in the United States only in Oregon) continues, *Final Exit* is intended to be a guidebook to "accelerated death" through "self-deliverance" for adults who voluntarily and rationally seek to end prolonged, untreatable suffering in the last stages of an incurable disease (pp. xv–xvi). Once the decision is made, setting the time for death is a gamble. "But when is the best time? Too soon is to waste the good aspects of life, and perhaps unkind to those who love and need you. Too late means you might lose control" (p. 101).

A critical part of the debate over physician-assisted suicide concerns the complications that may occur when patients attempt such suicides. Until recently, few scientific studies had documented the clinical outcomes of such attempts (Nuland 2000:583). In its fourth annual report concerning Oregon's Death With Dignity Act, the Oregon Department of Human Services (2002) says that of the 21 patients who took lethal medications prescribed under the act in 2001, one vomited after swallowing the medication and died 25 hours later; another patient lived 37 hours after swallowing the medication. Neither regained consciousness, and emergency services were not needed. In a recent study in the Netherlands of physicians assisting in suicide or performing euthanasia, Groenewoud et al. (2000) found among the 649 reported cases (a) 35 cases of technical problems, such as difficulty in finding a vein in which to inject the lethal drug; (b) 24 cases of complications, such as nausea or vomiting; and (c) 44 cases of problems with completion, such as the time taken to die being longer than expected or the patient not entering a coma or awakening from a coma (p. 553). In some cases, physicians' attempts to assist suicide through prescribing or supplying lethal medications resulted in complications that led to the physicians' helping the patients take "one or more" of the medications. In these cases, the authors state, "it is not clear at what point a physician's assistance with suicide becomes euthanasia" (p. 555).

Groenewoud et al. recommend that physicians who choose to assist their patients with suicide or euthanasia should have the technical skills to perform both procedures, particularly knowledge of and "care in choosing doses and administering medications" (p. 556). In an editorial published with the results of Groenewoud et al.'s study, Nuland (2000) agrees: "Doctors are unprepared to end life. If this is a burden to be taken on and if the medical profession accepts it as falling within the realm of individual conscience, then thorough training in techniques must be made available" (p. 583). He commends the Royal Dutch Medical Association for recommending that physicians be present for attempted suicides or acts of euthanasia, especially given the circumstances of the patients. "Is it really possible that debilitated, terminally ill people, in physical and mental anguish, will unfailingly succeed in attempts to end their lives without medical help? Can any experienced witness to dying believe such a thing?" (p. 584).

The third view on choosing the right time to die is that of philosopher C. G. Prado (1998), for whom Callahan and Humphry represent the first two steps in a "fundamental reconception of human life" that is beginning to challenge the belief that "suicide is irrational and cowardly" (p. xiii). The emerging view is that life is not "an unrenounceable gift" but is "lived at *our* discretion" (p. 138) and "has a *volitional* terminus" (p. xiv). The first step was social acceptance of a person's right to refuse treatment that

prolongs life, the foundation of Callahan's warning against the "technological imperative," a step that, in the view of advocates of assisted suicide, bears no "significant difference" from the second step represented by Humphry's quest for the national legalization of a suffering person's right to request and receive treatment that ends life (p. 138). The third step will be the eventual social acceptance of "preemptive suicide" as a rational choice to forfeit "worthwhile life for anticipatory reasons" (p. 152). The choice of "anticipatory self-destruction" will be made by "reflective aging individuals" who "are in their late sixties or early seventies" (p. 99), free of diagnosable terminal disease, who want to avoid the anticipated "reduction of the self through age-related loss of faculties, traits, values and interests" that define them as persons (p. 112), leaving them to live and eventually to die as unacceptable "lesser" versions of themselves (p. 116). They have decided that "the persons into whom age is turning them aren't ones they think should live" (p. 97). An example of what one would seek to avoid through preemptive suicide is the situation of a person who, when diagnosed in the early stages of senile dementia, is still capable of choosing suicide, but chooses, instead, to live and "then, for the sake of a very short time of reasonably aware life, spends a decade existing as a mindless organism requiring constant care" (p. 104, n. 4). Like Humphry, Prado notes that "timing is crucial" (p. 68). One must neither act too soon, giving up too much worthwhile life, nor wait too long, until personal losses make rational suicide impossible (pp. 85, 111, 152–53). An exact time that meets both conditions cannot be set.

Of these three, the attempt to justify physician-assisted suicide holds center stage in the United States, obscuring, Prado believes, the subtle shifts in attitude that will eventually make preemptive suicide a public issue as the number of aging Americans grows and degradations from dementia increase. His case could well be enhanced should we choose to accept medical technology's offer of what Francis Fukuyama (2002) calls "a devil's bargain: longer life, but with reduced mental capacity" (p. 8), the very combination that Prado (1998) calls the "anticipated diminishment of self" (p. 46).

ENHANCING CARE AT THE END OF LIFE

Dr. Kathleen Foley (1996) believes that efforts to legalize physician-assisted suicide distract us from the greater need for improvement in care of the dying. Rather than asking how we can legally secure a lethal dose of medication, we should be asking questions about how and where we will die, who will care for us and control our pain, what options for end-of-life care we will have and how will we pay for them, who will respect our values and our cultural, religious, and spiritual beliefs (p. 1). These are questions that we should ask whether we are "living with" serious illness or "dying of" it, the division between the two having become so blurred that "the point at which dying begins is often impossible to define" (Lynn et al. 2000:5; see also Callahan 2000:655). Curative care and palliative care blend together indistinguishably. The answers to these questions should be readily available, institutionalized in a health care system that can provide services, care, and comfort throughout the "living" and "dying" experience.

These questions are particularly important in light of the World Health Organization's (1990) definition of palliative care as "the active total care of patients whose disease is not responsive to curative treatment." Palliative care gives priority to controlling pain and other symptoms and to meeting psychological, social, and spiritual needs in order to provide "the best quality of life for patients and their families." Living is affirmed, and dying, neither hastened nor postponed, is regarded as "a normal process" during which the patient is helped to "live as actively as possible until death" and the family is supported throughout the patient's illness and throughout the time of grief.

In its advocacy for these values and goals in all end-of-life care efforts, Last Acts, a national grassroots coalition devoted to improving care and caring near the end of life sponsored by the Robert Wood Johnson Foundation, appointed a Palliative Care Task Force to develop core precepts of end-of-life care. These precepts, published in a booklet called "Precepts of Palliative Care," cover five areas: (a) respecting patient goals, preferences, and choices; (b) comprehensive caring; (c) utilizing the strengths of interdisciplinary resources; (d) acknowledging and addressing caregiver concerns; and (e) building systems and mechanisms of support (reprinted in Lynn et al. 2000:340–41). The list is too extensive for me to discuss here more than a small sample from two of the precepts, but this is sufficient to provide some idea of the problems palliative care tries to address and to describe the work of some who have and do influence that effort.

First, those giving palliative care place "a high priority on diagnosis and treatment of psychological distress" (Lynn et al. 2000:341). Glaser and Straus (1965) touched on the psychological distress of the dying when they reported the ambiguity of medical personnel about how much "awareness" the patient should have. The patient's "awareness context" consisted of who knew what about the situation. The degree of awareness governed the interactions of medical staff with the patient. The greatest ambiguity surrounded the "open awareness context," in which staff and patient knew the truth about the patient's "impending death" and acted accordingly (p. 11). In such a context, time could be comforting or distressing, depending on the patient's capacity to use it. Time could be comforting if the patient could use it to bring closure to life through personal acts of "proper dying" (p. 103). Such end-of-life activities might include writing letters, praying, reviewing life, planning the future for survivors, finishing unfinished work, and reconciling broken relationships (pp. 43, 103). Or time could be distressing if the patient could not face death, thus dying with more suffering than

would have occurred if he or she had been left unaware (p. 103). Dying in psychological peace could leave the family thankful for their shared experience; dying in psychological anguish could leave the family wishing that the patient had been left unaware (p. 104).

In the fall of 1965, the same year Glaser and Straus's *Awareness of Dying* was published, Dr. Elisabeth Kübler-Ross was looking for any dying patient in Billings Hospital at the University of Chicago, in response to a request from four seminary students who asked to watch her interview a dying patient as she had done once before, in 1962, while on the staff at the University of Colorado. Despite resistance and repeated denials that anyone in the hospital was "dying," she found one dying patient who would talk in the presence of the seminary students. She then continued to find other dying patients to interview, persuading them to talk about their dying in front of her initially cautious but curious medical students. By the middle of the next year, her interviews had become weekly seminars on death and dying, beginning a career that would have profound consequences for care of the dying (Kübler-Ross 1997:139–42).

From her talks with more than 200 dying patients, Kübler-Ross identified five psychological reactions to dying. She called them "stages of dying" and listed them in sequence: "denial" that one is dying, "anger" at those who are not dying, "bargaining" with God for an escape, "depression" at realizing that escape is impossible, and "acceptance" in a quiet contemplation of the end of life. After the publication of *On Death and Dying* (1969), the "stages of dying" became so well-known that today they "roll trippingly off the tongue of anyone in America familiar with the contemporary Western view of mental health" (Singh 1998:168). *On Death and Dying* was the early forerunner of what we know as "palliative care"—an attempt to focus terminal care "on the patient as a human being," keeping the focus on the patient's experiences, needs, and reactions, to learn from the patient the hospital's "strengths and weaknesses" in caring for the dying (p. xi).

Although subsequent investigations have demonstrated that patients do not exhibit the reactions Kübler-Ross described in a commonly prescribed order, the continuing legacy of her work has been the public's first glimpse of a dying person's "overwhelming feeling of loss on all levels of experience" that comes with acknowledging the loss of life and the end of all hopes for the future (Lynn and Harrold 1999:17, 19; Kübler-Ross 1997:132). Kübler-Ross made dying a legitimate research topic for subsequent researchers such as Dr. Kathleen Dowling Singh, psychologist and psychospiritual counselor, who credits her with opening the way for Singh's investigation of the "nearing death experience" among hospice patients, a time of spiritual transformation during which the dying person moves from "a sense of perceived tragedy to a sense of perceived grace" (Singh 1998:15). The "chaotic" stage of the experience, incorporating Kübler-Ross's stages of dying, is superseded by alternating experiences of "surrender" and "transcendence," culminating in the "qualities of grace" present in dying.

The definition of patient distress has gone far beyond Kübler-Ross's work, as illustrated by the comprehensive survey of barriers to and opportunities for palliative care jointly sponsored by the Institute on Medicine and the National Research Council, published as *Improving Palliative Care for Cancer* (Institute of Medicine 2001). The underlying belief of this volume's editors and contributors is that "death is inevitable, but severe suffering is not" (p. x). *Suffering* is now an all-encompassing term applied to all facets of distress—physical, psychological, social, and spiritual—for both the patient and the patient's family. Contemporary care for the dying falls short of the goal of providing total care in these areas, not because such a system of care is deteriorating under economic pressures, but because in many cases such a system of comprehensive end-of-life care has yet to be developed (Lynn et al. 2000:11). Recognition of these shortcomings has led to current efforts by various medical specialty societies to develop common core principles of end-of-life care, accompanied by guidelines for clinical practice in each area of patient and family need (Cassel and Foley 1999). These efforts among medical specialties must be complemented by a more aggressive role in legislation and funding initiatives for end-of-life care by the federal government than has occurred thus far (Institute of Medicine 2001:49–50).

A second precept of palliative care is that those providing such care identify with and honor "the preferences of the patient and family" (Lynn et al. 2000:341). One major medical study has shown how difficult it may be to bring physicians to the point of honoring patient preferences at the end of life. The Study to Understand Prognoses and Preferences for Outcomes and Risks of Treatments, or SUPPORT, part of a $29 million project funded by the Robert Wood Johnson Foundation, is considered to be "the most influential phenomenon in moving end-of-life care in the 1990's," reflecting the growing concern, shared by Daniel Callahan, over the use of all available technological means "to extend briefly the lives of people with untreatable, soon fatal conditions" (Institute of Medicine 2001:37–38).

The SUPPORT researchers speculated that the communication of patients' end-of-life preferences to their doctors by a trained medical professional who understood the preferences of patients and the concerns of doctors would improve decision making at the end of life, resulting in physicians' honoring their patients' preferences to avoid painfully prolonged, "mechanically supported" dying (SUPPORT 1995:1591). The two-phase study examined five outcomes of patient care at the end of life: physician understanding of patient preferences, pain control, frequency and timing of the writing of do-not-resuscitate orders, the number of days spent before death in an intensive care unit or in a coma or receiving mechanical ventilation, and use of hospital resources (p. 1592). During

Phase I, which lasted 2 years, the researchers observed the care of 4,301 patients with life-threatening diagnoses in five teaching hospitals in the United States to establish the characteristics of "usual medical care" (p. 1594). They noted deficiencies in all five characteristics of hospital dying, among them the following: Less than half of the physicians knew their patients' preferences to avoid cardiopulmonary resuscitation; of those who were aware, 46% waited until the last 2 days of their patients' lives to write do-not-resuscitate orders (p. 1594)

In Phase II, which also lasted 2 years, the researchers randomly assigned 4,804 seriously ill patients to either an intervention group or a control group. The patients in the intervention group had their preferences for each outcome and their prognoses communicated to their physicians by a specially trained nurse who talked with patients, patients' families, and physicians to ensure that the patients' wishes were known in advance. The patients in the control group received "usual medical care." The intervention failed to improve either patient care or patient outcomes over those resulting from "usual medical care" (p. 1591).

The results left the SUPPORT researchers—and us—"with a troubling situation. The picture we describe of the care of seriously ill or dying persons is not attractive" (p. 1597). Improved communication did not bring about the desired dying experience, in which the pain of the dying was controlled, patients and their families were included in discussions of end-of-life care, and dying was not prolonged against patients' wishes. The researchers concluded that, among other steps, "more proactive and forceful attempts at change" will be needed to reach these goals (p. 1597).

DYING IN THE 21ST CENTURY

Concurrent with the publication of the SUPPORT findings, the Institute of Medicine appointed the 12-member Committee on Care at the End of Life in late 1995 to study a range of topics related to end-of-life care and to recommend changes to improve the care of the dying. The committee, acknowledging that "evidence and experience both indicate that much dying is far harder than it should be" (Institute of Medicine 1997:259), made seven recommendations for improving care at the end of life (pp. 266–71), noting that implementing them would require the institutions and people who make decisions about the care of the dying to change their "attitudes, policies, and actions" (p. 271).

If these recommendations are followed, what kind of care at the end of life will my grandchildren, now ages 4, 3, and less than 1 week, receive in the last quarter of the 21st century should they live to their full life expectancy and be dying of chronic or progressive fatal diseases? In contrast to my likelihood of dying in a fragmented "system" of curative care dominated, as Callahan (1993) has said, by the "technological imperative" and the view of death as "medical failure" (p. 63), my grandchildren will be cared for in a comprehensive and integrated system of palliative care staffed by multidisciplinary teams of health professionals trained in the latest scientific knowledge about dying and committed to providing "reliable, skillful and supportive care" through the use of all available resources "to prevent and relieve pain and other symptoms" (Institute of Medicine 1997:267).

Now among the dying "elderly," my grandchildren are the beneficiaries of systemic reforms in professional training, medical research, and public policy that define the professional and institutional characteristics of their care. Beginning in undergraduate preparation, all health professionals who care for the dying now receive education that emphasizes "the relevant attitudes, knowledge and skills to care well for dying patients," a reform made possible, in part, by the corresponding emphasis that federal research agencies and academic medical centers place on "strengthening the knowledge base for end-of-life care" (pp. 268–69). Because of these reforms in training and research, palliative care is a separate medical specialty with its own "area of expertise, education and research" (p. 269).

These developments are complemented by reforms in public policy reflecting the coordinated efforts of policy makers, consumer groups, patients, providers of health care, and researchers working in various specialties. Their efforts changed the institutional context of dying by creating reliable ways to measure the outcomes of palliative care, developing ways to hold organizations that care for the dying accountable for the care they provide, devising new ways to finance "coordinated systems of excellent care," and changing the laws, regulations, and medical board policies that had hindered the use of the full range of opioids to relieve pain and suffering (p. 267).

These remarkable changes, which we can hardly imagine, came about first and foremost because Americans accepted the responsibility that the Institute of Medicine believes is primarily ours: to keep "the public discussion going" about "the goal of improving care for those approaching death and overcoming the barriers to achieving that goal" (p. 270). In accepting this responsibility, Americans confronted and overcame two national deficits in dealing with death: "This nation has not yet learned how to talk realistically but comfortably about the end of life nor has it learned how to value the period of dying as it is now experienced by most people" (p. 265). Throughout the 21st century, through continual discussions, citizens learned about dying in the "new reality." They talked about the dying people in their communities and about their families, reviewed the options available to the dying, and kept the obligations they had to their fellow citizens to do whatever they could to "make it possible for most people to die free from avoidable distress and to find the peace or meaning that is significant to them" (p. 270). Their commitment to these goals, complemented by the availability and affordability of effective palliative care, means that my dying grandchildren have a range of choices far beyond our current "limited choice between suicide or continued suffering" (p. 271).

Thinking about the future of my grandchildren or your grandchildren highlights the stake we all have in correcting the unacceptable conditions of the "new reality" we inherited from the 20th century. Our "probable future" is to die as "older" people from chronic diseases. As the "horseman of death" approaches and our sufferings intensify, we will need palliative care from a health care system that is unprepared to care for us. If we want and expect better end-of-life care for ourselves and for our loved ones, we must take advantage of what Dr. Joanne Lynn, physician and director of the RAND Center to Improve Care of the Dying, calls "an unprecedented opportunity to improve [the] system, to make a difference in how people die." If we do not respond, "we will find ourselves dying in the very system we allowed to drift" (Lynn et al. 2000:10).

Creating an alternative to dying in a system "adrift" begins with our finding the time and the interest to learn about dying in our own communities. How do our fellow citizens experience dying in our local health care systems? What do our local health care systems do to provide comprehensive and coordinated end-of-life care? What can we do and what should we do to encourage and support improvements in the care of the dying in our communities? Having answered these and other questions, we must then attempt to enlist the energies of others in our communities in pursuing the common goal of available palliative care for everyone, conscious of our common stake in avoiding unnecessary suffering. Perhaps we could begin on a small scale by organizing study groups to read and discuss "The Agitator's Guide: Twelve Steps to Get Your Community Talking About Dying," published by Americans for Better Care of the Dying (reprinted in Lynn et al. 2000:205–6).

Educating ourselves about dying in our local communities, however, is only the primer for the more extensive and more difficult effort we must make to educate ourselves about and to activate ourselves to eradicate the inequities in our national health care system that result in unnecessary burdens of chronic disease and suffering for many Americans, particularly for the poor of all races, members of racial and ethnic minority groups, and the medically underserved and uninsured. Cancer, the "'prototypical' disease for organizing end of life care" (Institute of Medicine 2001:13), provides an excellent example of the need for such an effort. Cancer is expected to become the leading cause of death in the 21st century (Institute of Medicine 1999:1), an expectation that carries ominous implications for minorities and the uninsured. The "unequal burden" of this disease is already known, for "individuals of all ethnic backgrounds who are poor, lack health insurance, or otherwise have inadequate access to high-quality cancer care typically experience higher cancer incidence and mortality rates and low rates of survival from cancer" (Institute of Medicine 1999:2). One explanation is found among the roughly 30 million uninsured working-age adults for whom the "less frequent or no use of cancer screening tests" results "in delayed diagnosis and premature mortality for cancer patients" (Institute of Medicine 2002:4).

Many of us—including, perhaps, the authors and readers of the chapters in this volume—probably medically insured and quite certainly socialized in a society where "the desire to evade and avoid the events associated with death" is pervasive (Institute of Medicine 2001:33), may initially find realistic discussions of dying and the unequal burden of suffering and premature death borne by many our fellow citizens uncomfortable. Our desire for a humane system of care at the end of life for ourselves, our children, and our grandchildren, however, is inseparable from our efforts to create a humane and just health care system for all Americans, one free of the "unequal burdens" of suffering and dying and one that provides all dying people and their families "the right care at the right time in the right way" (Institute of Medicine 1997:271). Surely we have the wisdom and knowledge to guide us. We need only have the courage to follow Goethe's injunction, selected by the Institute of Medicine's Committee on the Consequences of Uninsurance for the frontispiece of its 2002 publication *Care Without Coverage:* "Knowing is not enough; we must apply. Willing is not enough; we must do" (p. iii). The *Handbook of Death and Dying* that is published early in the 22nd century will record what we did.

REFERENCES

Bell, Wendell. 1997. *Foundations of Futures Studies,* vol. 1. New Brunswick, NJ: Transaction.

Boswell, James. [1799] 1953. *Life of Johnson.* London: Oxford University Press.

Callahan, Daniel. 1993. *The Troubled Dream of Life: In Search of a Peaceful Death.* New York: Touchstone.

———. 2000. "Death and the Research Imperative." *New England Journal of Medicine* 342:654–56.

Cassel, Christine K. and Kathleen M. Foley. 1999. "Principles for Care of Patients at the End of Life: An Emerging Consensus Among the Specialties of Medicine." Milbank Memorial Fund. Retrieved May 24, 2002 (http://www.milbank.org/endoflife/index.html).

Dyer, Clare. 2002a. "'Free at Last'—Diane Pretty Dies." *Guardian Unlimited Network,* May 13. Retrieved May 17, 2002 (http://www.guardian.co.uk/archive/article/0,4273,4412349,00.html).

———. 2002b. "Miss B Dies After Winning Fight to End Care." *Guardian Unlimited Network,* April 30. Retrieved May 17, 2002 (http://www.guardian.co.uk/archive/article/0,4273,4404143,00.html).

Foley, Kathleen M. 1996. "Medical Issues Related to Physician Assisted Suicide." Testimony before the House Judiciary Subcommittee on the Constitution, April 29. Retrieved April 27, 2002 (http://www.house.gov/judiciary/2167.htm).

Fukuyama, Francis. 2002. *Our Posthuman Future: Consequences of the Biotechnology Revolution.* New York: Farrar, Straus & Giroux.

Giesbert, Franz-Olivier. 1998. *Dying Without God: Francois Mitterand's Meditations on Living and Dying.* New York: Arcade.

Glaser, Barney G. and Anselm L. Straus. 1965. *Awareness of Dying.* Chicago: Aldine.

———. 1968. *Time for Dying.* Chicago: Aldine.

Groenewoud, Johanna H., Agnes van der Heide, Bregje D. Onwuteaka-Philipsen, Dick L. Willems, Paul J. van der Maas, and Gerrit van der Wal. 2000. "Clinical Problems With the Performance of Euthanasia and Physician-Assisted Suicide in the Netherlands." *New England Journal of Medicine* 342:551–56.

Hagens, Gunther von. 2001. "Anatomy and Plastination." In *KORPERWELTEN: Fascination Beneath the Surface,* edited by Gunther von Hagens and Angelina Whalley. Heidelberg: Institute for Plastination.

Hempstead, Katherine. 2001. "Trends in Place of Death in New Jersey: An Analysis of Death Certificates." *Topics in Health Statistics,* February. Retrieved January 15, 2002 (http://www.state.nj.us/health/chs/topicspod.pdf).

Hennezel, Marie de. 1998. *Intimate Death,* translated by Carol Brown Janeway. New York: Vintage.

Hillman, James. 1999. *The Force of Character and the Lasting Life.* New York: Random House.

Hoyert, Donna L., Elizabeth Arias, Betty L. Smith, Sherry L. Murphy, and Kenneth D. Kochanek. 2001. *Deaths: Final Data for 1999* (National Vital Statistics Reports, vol. 49, no. 8). Hyattsville, MD: National Center for Health Statistics.

Humphry, Derek. 1996. *Final Exit: The Practicalities of Self-Deliverance and Assisted Suicide for the Dying,* 2d ed. New York: Dell.

Institute of Medicine. 1997. *Approaching Death: Improving Care at the End of Life,* edited by Marilyn J. Field and Christine K. Cassel. Washington, DC: National Academy Press.

———. 1999. *The Unequal Burden of Cancer,* edited by M. Alfred Haynes and Brian D. Smedley. Washington, DC: National Academy Press.

———. 2001. *Improving Palliative Care for Cancer,* edited by Kathleen M. Foley and Hellen Gelband. Washington, DC: National Academy Press.

———. 2002. *Care Without Coverage: Too Little, Too Late.* Committee on the Consequences of Uninsurance, Mary Sue Coleman and Arthur Kellerman, cochairs. Washington, DC: National Academy Press.

Kübler-Ross, Elisabeth. 1969. *On Death and Dying.* New York: Macmillan.

———. 1997. *The Wheel of Life.* New York: Touchstone.

Lynn, Joanne and Joan Harrold. 1999. *Handbook for Mortals: Guidance for People Facing Serious Illness.* New York: Oxford University Press.

Lynn, Joanne, Janice Lynch Schuster, and Andrea Kabcenell. 2000. *Improving Care for the End of Life.* Oxford: Oxford University Press.

Morris, Virginia. 2001. *Talking About Death Won't Kill You.* New York: Workman.

Nouwen, Henri J. M. 1994. *Our Greatest Gift: A Meditation on Dying and Caring.* New York: HarperCollins.

Nuland, Sherwin B. 1994. *How We Die: Reflections on Life's Final Chapter.* New York: Alfred A. Knopf.

———. 2000. "Physician-Assisted Suicide and Euthanasia in Practice." *New England Journal of Medicine* 342:583–84.

Oregon Department of Human Services. 2002. *Fourth Annual Report on Oregon's Death With Dignity Act.* Portland: Oregon Department of Human Services.

Prado, C. G. 1998. *The Last Choice: Preemptive Suicide in Advanced Old Age,* 2d ed. Westport, CT: Praeger.

Singh, Kathleen Dowling. 1998. *The Grace in Dying: How We Are Transformed Spiritually as We Die.* New York: HarperCollins.

SUPPORT Principal Investigators. 1995. "A Controlled Trial to Improve Care for Seriously Ill Hospitalized Patients: The Study to Understand Prognoses and Preferences for Outcomes and Risks of Treatment (SUPPORT)." *Journal of the American Medical Association* 274:1591–98.

Wetz, Franz Josef. 2001. "The Dignity of the Individual." In *KORPERWELTEN: Fascination Beneath the Surface,* edited by Gunther von Hagens and Angelina Whalley. Heidelberg: Institute for Plastination.

Whalley, Angelina. 2001. "The Human Body: Anatomy and Function." In *KORPERWELTEN: Fascination Beneath the Surface,* edited by Gunther von Hagens and Angelina Whalley. Heidelberg: Institute for Plastination.

World Health Organization. 1990. "WHO Definition of Palliative Care." In *Cancer Pain Relief and Palliative Care,* report of a WHO Expert Committee (WHO Technical Report Series 804). Geneva: World Health Organization. Retrieved December 1, 2002 (http://www.who.int/dsa/justpub/cpl.htm).

Zhamkin, Vladimir. 2002. "The 20th Century, Year After Year: 1996." Voice of Russia. Retrieved April 29, 2002 (http://www.vor.ru/century/1996.html).

ON COMING TO TERMS WITH DEATH AND DYING

Neglected Dimensions of Identity Work

KENT L. SANDSTROM

During the past three decades, a growing number of studies have examined the challenges confronted by people diagnosed with life-threatening or potentially life-threatening illnesses. Many of these studies have focused on the psychosocial issues encountered by the terminally ill. In the process, they have revealed that some of the most troubling issues confronted by dying individuals include fears of social isolation and rejection; feelings of guilt, shame, anger, and grief; radical role changes; loss of future expectations and hopes; denial of death; and adjustment to physical and emotional devastation (Baider 1972; Furstenberg and Olson 1984; Oberfield 1984; Samarel 1995; Stulberg and Buckingham 1990; Stulberg and Smith 1988; Vachon 1998). Other studies, building on the observations of Elisabeth Kübler-Ross (1969, 1981), have highlighted the stages of adaptation the terminally ill usually pass through as they grapple with such issues. These stages include numbness and disbelief, denial and isolation, anger and resentment, bargaining, depression, and planning for the reality of death (Morin and Batchelor 1984; Moynihan, Christ, and Silver 1990; Nichols 1985).

In identifying these stages, researchers have attempted to formulate models that can be applied to the experiences of all severely or terminally ill people, often with the goal of helping these individuals and the clinicians who care for them. Kübler-Ross was clearly guided by these aims in developing her theory of the dying process. Inspired by conversations with more than 200 dying individuals, she crafted this theory not only to help terminally ill people understand their coping reactions but also to allow clinicians to recognize these reactions and intervene positively, particularly by assisting the dying in progressing toward a state of hopeful acceptance.

Although Kübler-Ross's model has been useful to clinicians and dying patients, a variety of studies have revealed its flaws and limitations (Corr 1993; Corr and Corr 2000; Fox 1981; Hennezel 1989; Kastenbaum 1985; Weisman and Warden 1975). For example, empirical tests have demonstrated that this model mistakenly suggests that dying people move through sequential stages of coping when, in fact, they usually experience cyclical and vacillating processes of adjustment and adaptation, moving back and forth among responses such as denial, anger, and acceptance (Kastenbaum 1998). Studies have also shown that those dying may experience several of the "stages" identified by Kübler-Ross simultaneously. Moreover, researchers have reported that a number of dying people never go beyond the first two stages of adaptation identified by Kübler-Ross, and many feel apathy, apprehension, and anticipation as well as acceptance of death when they reach the final days of their lives (Weisman and Kastenbaum 1968). In some cases, the dying may also respond to their impending mortality with rage, guilt, fear, uncertainty, disbelief, dissonance, struggle, stoicism, or surrender (Shneidman 1984; Yedidia and MacGregor 2001).

Given the limitations of Kübler-Ross's model (as well as similar stage-based approaches), researchers have formulated alternative theories of how people cope with dying and death. For instance, Kenneth Doka has devised an approach that applies the principles of human development to the end of life. Guided by these principles, Doka (1997) focuses on the dimensions of social, psychological, and spiritual growth that can arise for dying individuals. Doka also seeks to isolate and identify "the commonalities of human experience that emerge at the end of life, including the universal needs and opportunities that people confront as they die" (Yedidia and MacGregor 2001:808). In pursuing these aims, Doka follows in the footsteps of Kübler-Ross, striving to develop a broadly generalizable model that is useful to both clinicians and the dying.

In a related vein, Charles Corr (1995) has formulated a theory that emphasizes the universal tasks individuals must grapple with as they come to terms with death and dying. According to Corr, these tasks present themselves in four key areas: the physical, the psychological, the social, and the spiritual. Corr proposes that in the physical area, dying individuals must concern themselves with meeting their bodily needs (e.g., nutrition, hydration, elimination, obtaining shelter) and minimizing their pain or physical distress. In the psychological realm, they must grapple with the challenges of maintaining a sense of security, autonomy, and richness. To feel secure, dying persons must remain as free as possible from anxiety and fear. To feel autonomous, they must sustain a sense of control over their lives and key decisions. To preserve a sense of richness and vitality, they must have access to activities that allow them to feel satisfied or bountiful. In the third key area of task work, the social domain, dying individuals face a couple of major challenges. The first is to sustain and enhance the social relationships they value, and the second is to address the demands of surrounding social groups and organizations, such as families, clubs, churches, and governmental entities. Finally, in the fourth area of task work, the spiritual realm, dying individuals must grapple with the challenge of maintaining a sense of integrity or wholeness. They must also find a way to sustain a sense of hope.

In highlighting these areas of task work involved in coping with dying, Corr (1995) emphasizes that coping is an active process that consists of "efforts to manage what occurs in one's life to achieve a livable balance insofar as it is possible" (p. 309). He also stresses that coping with dying is not merely a phenomenon that arises at the end of an individual's life; rather, it is a process that encompasses all of a person's life. It is also a process engaged in by all of the significant others who are drawn into the person's experience of dying.

Corr's task-based model of dying has several advantages. First, it avoids making claims that people go through stages of adaptation or that the dying process has a linear character. Second, it offers a holistic picture of how people cope with dying, considering not only their emotional states or psychosocial responses but also other important dimensions of their lives. Third, it has both universal and specific applications. It applies broadly to all individuals by focusing on the four primary areas of death-related task work. At the same time, it applies uniquely to each individual by focusing on the specific tasks that a person faces in coping with dying and how he or she addresses them. Fourth, the model recognizes the coping engaged in by all the people involved in a particular dying experience, including not only the dying person but also his or her friends, family members, and caregivers. In addition, it regards dying individuals as active agents who determine which tasks are important to them and how, when, or

whether they will address these tasks. Finally, Corr's model offers guidance to helpers and caregivers as they interact with the dying person. It proposes that they should be attuned to the tasks that the dying individual chooses to address and should focus their efforts on how to best help him or her in the completion of these tasks.

Despite offering several advantages, Corr's framework shares a significant shortcoming with many other "psychosocial" theories of the dying process; that is, it fails to recognize or discuss some of the most important forms of identity work engaged in by individuals as they come to terms with death and dying. More specifically, Corr's model fails to consider how and why many dying individuals alter their goals for self and fashion new, valued, and enduring identities—identities that enable them to sustain a sense of vitality, efficacy, and continuity in the face of death.

In an effort to address this gap in Corr's model and the literature on dying, I focus the remainder of this chapter on the identity work that persons living with AIDS (PLWAs) engage in during the final phases of their illness career. Drawing on in-depth interviews with 31 PLWAs, I describe how they (a) build or rebuild vital and valued selves; (b) counteract the threats posed by debilitation, suffering, and dying; and (c) fashion and solidify identities that extend beyond death.

In exploring these themes, I highlight some of the most prominent identity-related challenges encountered by individuals grappling with life-threatening or potentially life-threatening health complications. I also consider the trials and transitions that shape the self-images and identity constructions of persons with AIDS, particularly as they come to grips with the threat of death. Finally, I examine how persons with AIDS fashion postmortal identities and sustain a sense of symbolic continuity as they enter the last stages of their lives. Through focusing on this dimension of identity work, I reveal how people with terminal illnesses construct enduring selves and futures that enable them to gain a measure of control and transcendence over death as an ultimate limit.

RESHAPING IDENTITY AND PRESERVING VITALITY IN THE FACE OF DEATH

After receiving an HIV diagnosis, individuals typically wrestle with issues of stigma and uncertainty (Sandstrom 1990, 1996; Weitz 1989, 1991). They worry about how, whether, or when to share the news of their health status with others and how to address the threat of devaluation it poses. They also worry about the unpredictable aspects of their HIV infection, such as when it might provoke serious symptoms, what symptoms or complications might emerge, what treatments will be available, and how both the symptoms and treatments will alter their lives and selves (Sandstrom 1998).

As their illness unfolds and its physical and social implications become more clear, persons with HIV/AIDS find that their concerns start to change. For many, the threat of stigma wanes, especially if they establish or solidify relationships with supportive networks of others. Most also discover that their struggles with uncertainty diminish. In fact, they begin to feel far more concerned about the certainties that accompany their health status—certainties such as the onset of problematic symptoms, the disruption of comfortable routines, and the shortening of their life span.

Sustaining a Vital and Valued Self

As they come to terms with the disruptions and losses provoked by their health condition, persons with AIDS, like others diagnosed with potentially terminal illnesses, reconfigure their lives and selves and search for ways to preserve a sense of vitality and self-worth. In the process, they utilize various strategies of identity work. One of these strategies is *compartmentalization.* When compartmentalizing their illness, persons with AIDS acknowledge its presence in their lives but downplay its salience for self, as Barbara (all interviewees' names are pseudonyms) revealed when describing how she incorporated her AIDS diagnosis into her self-conception:

> I don't really think about being a person with AIDS, or having AIDS, on a day-to-day basis. . . . I think of AIDS as being part of who I am but not as something that's at the top of my list of identities. Instead, it would be pretty much toward the bottom. I'll admit that I wear my "person with AIDS" button at times, like when I do educational talks at schools, but on a day-to-day basis I'm more likely to think of myself as other things—like a friend, a caring person, or a nurse.

Through compartmentalizing their diagnosis, persons with AIDS keep it at the margins of self and maintain a life beyond it. They find it difficult, however, to continue employing this strategy when serious health problems arise and impose constraints on their valued involvements or interactions. Under these circumstances, minimizing the salience of the illness requires them to stake their cherished images of self in the past. This, in turn, evokes an "emotionally divided self" (Denzin 1984), especially as they try to come to terms with the incongruity between their past images of self and a self currently immersed in illness. Greg touched on these themes when he remarked:

> I find myself adjusting to, like, who I am now as opposed to who I used to be. You know, like I used to be a guy who was involved with all this stuff and a leader in the community, and so on. And now I'm not. I don't have the energy to do that anymore. So now I almost think of myself as like a couple of different selves—and this, being sick with AIDS, is an other self.

Given the difficulties that can arise in compartmentalizing their illness, PLWAs often employ a second form of identity work: *embracement.* When engaging in embracement, they build or sustain a valued self by highlighting the unexpected "blessings" that have resulted from their illness (Sandstrom 1990). For example, some individuals emphasize how their diagnosis has motivated them to make positive changes in self. As Carrie observed:

> I feel like AIDS has been sort of a blessing because, well, it's helped me to grow a lot as a person. I've come out of my shell emotionally and I've grown a lot spiritually. I mean, it's ironic but because of AIDS I've learned how to enjoy life and enjoy people. . . . It's been a very positive experience for me. I just feel so much better about myself now. You know, I've come to acceptance with AIDS and with who I am. Before becoming infected, I had no self-esteem, you know, and now I'm okay with who I am. I can relate to other people in a more genuine way. I don't have to try to pretend to be somebody else or to make somebody else happy. I can just be my own person.

Others point out that their illness has been a gift because it has shown them how much their partners, friends, or family members care about them. Still others stress how their illness has been a blessing because it has led them to reflect more deeply on the meaning of their lives and to clarify their goals and priorities. For instance, when discussing the effects of his diagnosis, Curtis said:

> I think it has forced some changes. I think I've become a little more focused about things on a daily basis and less apt to waste my time with unnecessary anger, you know. And I just think that I've eliminated, uh, a lot of things that I don't need to deal with. It's helped me to set priorities, you know. I'm better able to sort out what's really important and what isn't. I think that I've changed in that respect.

Another way in which persons with AIDS highlight the benefits of their illness and preserve a sense of self-worth is by reexamining the significance of previously cherished involvements, such as their sexual involvements (Weitz 1991). As their illness unfolds and triggers health complications, many PLWAs experience declines in sexual interest and activity. In turn, they place greater emphasis on nonsexual interactions and relationships (Sandstrom 1996). Thus, rather than assessing their value or attractiveness in terms of their erotic activities or involvements, they accentuate the new and deeper forms of intimacy and self-worth they can realize through nonsexual friendships.

In addition to relying on embracement, persons with AIDS frequently sustain or rebuild valued selves by engaging in strategies of *empowerment* (Kayal 1993; Sandstrom 1990, 2000). One of the more common ways they do this is by participating in AIDS-related education or advocacy efforts. Through speaking at schools or churches, facilitating support groups for persons living with HIV, serving as volunteers in AIDS service organizations, or engaging in lobbying efforts, they challenge stigmatizing constructions of HIV/AIDS and assert their right to define what it means to be a person living with the disease. They also derive feelings of efficacy from their related accomplishments in the "war against AIDS and AIDS-related stigma."

Finally, those individuals who have lived with AIDS for a decade or more may gain a sense of empowerment and self-value from being "long-term survivors." On one level, they can derive feelings of pride and accomplishment from having endured the trials and tribulations of life with AIDS. On another level, they can bask in the recognition and admiration they receive from others because of their ongoing survival. Yet long-term survivors also discover that their persistence in the face of AIDS poses threats to self. As they outlive friends or acquaintances with the illness, they wrestle with troublesome feelings of "survivor guilt" (Lifton 1967). As Jay noted:

> You know, you watch others die and you can't help but think, "Why am I still alive?" I mean, I try to say, "God just has a different plan for all of us, and it's my plan to be here." But it's hard to get around that—the survivor guilt. It does pop up a lot and I can't help but say to myself, "Why did that person die, but not me?"

In addressing this question and resolving their related feelings, long-term survivors often attribute their longevity (and others' deaths) to fate or other uncontrollable factors. For example, Neil remarked:

> I feel proud of the fact that I've survived but I feel that it was still totally beyond my control anyway. I don't think that people who died sooner, you know, did anything wrong. Mostly I don't think it has anything to do with what they did or didn't do. It's just because, you know, they got something and they died. Um, so I see it [survival] as something people don't have a whole lot of control over. And I see myself as just being lucky.

Through adopting such an outlook, long-term survivors can alleviate feelings of survivor guilt and protect themselves from accepting too much responsibility for their unfolding health situation.

Coming to Terms With Serious Illness, Suffering, and Dying

As their illness unfolds and provokes symptoms such as chronic pain, nausea, fatigue, neurological problems, and opportunistic infections, PLWAs are confronted with bodily evidence that challenges their visions of themselves as vital and healthy persons and, correspondingly, deters them from using identity work strategies that highlight the beneficial aspects of their illness experience. As a result, they often turn to other adaptive strategies that allow them to sustain a sense of control, vitality, and self-value.

One of these adaptations is to become more absorbed in the present and avoid thoughts of the long-term implications of their health problems. Through recasting their visions of the future and living more fully in the moment, persons with AIDS derive a greater sense of control and

find new sources of personal satisfaction and fulfillment. Many start to see and appreciate "the little things" happening around them each day, thereby anchoring themselves in what Charmaz (1991) describes as an *intense present*. In the process, they discover a revitalizing sense of joy and transcendence, as Ryan conveyed:

> When I got really sick and truly realized that I had a limited amount of time left to live, I started to look at things differently. All of a sudden each new day was precious to me—it was a gift that offered special surprises. I started to see and experience each moment as sacred, at least in some respects.

Like others grappling with serious or life-threatening illnesses, PLWAs find that living in an intense present leads them to experience not only a rejuvenating sense of joy, vitality, and transcendence, but also an enhanced sense of urgency (Sandstrom 1998). As they strive to "make each day count," they feel more compelled to take risks, explore new vistas, build new or closer relationships, tie up loose ends, and take advantage of reasonably good health while it lasts. In many cases, they also feel motivated to accomplish something socially meaningful while they still can. For example, when reflecting on how AIDS-related health complications had affected his visions of and goals for the future, Todd remarked:

> The thing it's focused me on the most, one of my concerns, is that I haven't made a dent in the world. And so I've decided to do some advocacy things, like starting an employee resource group for gays and lesbians at my company. I've started a group now. And I've gotten on the local diversity council so I can train people on all aspects of diversity. And that's helped me a lot—it's helped to take the focus off the fact that I might be dying and it's made me feel like I'm making a contribution to the world.

Nevertheless, although a declining health situation can give persons with AIDS greater motivation to seek new ambitions and embrace new identities, it can also make it difficult, if not impossible, for them to do so. As a result, PLWAs may decide to pursue more proximate and tangible goals for self. Through realizing these goals, they can sustain a sense of efficacy and self-worth, as Jim described:

> I set goals that I can meet on a daily basis. I make it a point to do that now, even though it's hard because of my energy level. . . . I try to do something outside the house every day— weeding, gardening, painting, or cutting grass. That's a requirement for me—it forces me to get up and get dressed. And when I'm done weeding or whatever, I feel like I've accomplished something worthwhile.

If their health deteriorates to the point where it becomes difficult to attain even small goals, PLWAs worry about losing highly cherished bodily capacities, such as their ability to see, walk, think clearly, drive a car, and engage in sexual activity. Above all, they feel concerned about losing their autonomy and jeopardizing their relationships with loved ones, particularly as they become increasingly dependent on others. To alleviate these anxieties and enhance their sense of personal freedom and control, many PLWAs make arrangements that specify who will care for them and how they should be cared for if or when they become incapacitated. Some make arrangements for their most intimate others, such as spouses or lovers, to serve as their primary caregivers. Others plan to receive caregiving assistance from a variety of people, including nurses and hospice personnel as well as family and friends, so that no one individual will feel burdened or resentful. Ginger revealed the attitudes of those embracing this approach when she remarked:

> It's a huge responsibility for one person—to take care of someone when they're really sick and dying. I know that because I took care of my husband in that situation. But, you know, I'm not going to expect anyone to do that for me. I'm trying to set things up so a bunch of people will be involved. That way nobody will have to carry the load alone.

In addition to planning for their future care, persons with AIDS, like others who are terminally ill, take a number of other steps to enhance their control over the process of dying. For instance, some make plans to end their lives if or when symptoms progress to the point where they have virtually no hope for recovery. More frequently, however, persons with AIDS exercise control over their dying process by writing up advance directives for their end-of-life care or assigning durable power of attorney to individuals they trust to carry out their wishes.

Yet another way that PLWAs derive a sense of control over their dying and death is by focusing on the recent advances that have taken place in HIV-related medical treatments. They may point to the health-related comebacks they have experienced as a result of taking antiretroviral drugs or drug combinations. They may also stress the continued progress being made in the development of new and more effective medications, as Corey illustrated when he remarked:

> It's just a matter of getting the right meds, you know. I was just reading the paper the other day—they're working on meds that operate differently than the protease inhibitors. I guess they're more of a block to the virus. And, you know, even if those meds don't work out, my doctor says there are 14 agents out there now and I've only used 4. And if they can find the right combination then I'll be okay—find one that works for 2 or 3 years, then find something that works for another 3 years. By that time, they might have something else that works for 2 or 3 more years. That's the attitude I'm sticking with—it's the attitude my doctor gave me from the beginning.

Transcending Death Through Building a Valued Postself

As dying individuals come to terms with their prospective mortality, they commonly try to make sense of their lives and to sustain a sense of personal continuity, often through emphasizing those features of self they want others to remember (Unruh 1983). They also strive to gain a measure of control over the last chapters of their lives and over their postmortal future (Charmaz 1991; Marshall 1975). This struggle for control becomes closely linked to their struggles for meaning, vitality, and continuity (Sandstrom 1998). As Victor Marshall (1980) has observed, by effectively legitimating or making sense of their personal histories and prospective deaths, terminally ill individuals can gain an enhanced sense of control. Indeed, through giving redemptive meaning to their lives and deaths, and through defining death as an opening to another life and identity, the dying can gain mastery over death as a final limit. That is, they can transcend death, at least on a symbolic level (Becker 1973).

One of the most prominent ways in which people with terminal illnesses transcend death is by constructing what some scholars describe as a "postself" (Lifton 1967; Schmitt and Leonard 1986; Shneidman 1973, 1995). As Shneidman (1995) posits, the "postself relates to the concerns of living individuals with their own reputation, impact, influence after death—those personal aspects that still live when the person himself does not" (pp. 455–56). Through building and embracing a viable postself, dying individuals can sustain a sense of hope, esteem, and vitality in their daily lives. They can also solidify and preserve valued identities and assure themselves that their lives have had or will have lasting meaning and importance (Sandstrom 1998).

Like others dealing with the prospect of death, PLWAs often seek to anchor important identities in a postmortal future. Some do this by devoting extra attention to their interpersonal relationships in the hope that after they have died they will be remembered as a "special friend," "loving parent," "caring colleague," or "wonderful partner." They may also try to solidify these and other favorable identities by writing letters, poems, diaries, or memoirs that they plan to pass along to relatives, friends, or the wider public. In crafting these autobiographical narratives, they document and accentuate the pieces of personal history for which they wish to be remembered.

Along with these strategies, many PLWAs anchor a postself in the enduring contributions they have made through their labors as nurses, counselors, educators, writers, artists, clergy, or businesspeople. In some cases they also try to leave a legacy through their accomplishments as leaders or participants in gay or HIV-related advocacy efforts. For instance, Rachel and Lee stressed the impact they had made through confronting homophobia and promoting HIV-related support programs in the small towns where they had lived. Others emphasized how they had made a lasting difference through their HIV/AIDS education efforts, as Ryan noted:

> The biggest legacy I'll leave, I think, is the work I've done in AIDS education. The local media, like the TV station and the local newspapers, they know who I am. And most of the people in this city know who I am. And there'll be nice things

written about me when I die—but, you know, above all, I think they'll stress the role I played as an educator. That'll be my mark—that I taught a lot of people around here to see that AIDS wasn't a plague or a punishment; it's just a disease, and it doesn't discriminate.

As they come to terms with dying, many persons with AIDS anchor postmortal identities not only in the legacies they will leave behind, but also in religious or metaphysical beliefs that they will live on spiritually (Sandstrom 1998). Several of the PLWAs I interviewed did not conceive of death as the end of existence; rather, they saw it as "a gateway to a new realm of being." Some thought of this postmortal realm in traditional Christian terms (e.g., as heaven). More commonly, however, they embraced Eastern or alternative religious philosophies that emphasize the continuation of a person's "life force" after death, either in an ongoing cycle of death and rebirth or in a journey of self-discovery. Most important, belief in an afterlife enables persons with AIDS to sustain a sense of hope and continuity regarding their present and future. Through drawing on this belief, they can build or preserve an essential sense of self and anchor it in a future beyond death—a future that seems more pleasant or promising than the present. This gives death a less menacing meaning. Instead of representing the cessation of self, it is defined as an opening to new experiences and, implicitly, to an enhanced or transformed self.

Finally, although most of the individuals I interviewed did not embrace or draw upon traditional Christian views when articulating their images of an afterlife, a few did employ Christian imagery in their efforts to immortalize the self and sanctify their experiences as persons living with AIDS. For instance, Jay, Greg, and Nancy emphasized that PLWAs have a crucial spiritual role to play in the larger society. They saw people with AIDS as "modern-day prophets" who need to "spread the word" to others about the signs of "planetary illness" emerging around them, such as war, homophobia, racism, poverty, and environmental destruction. Others emphasized similar themes when stressing how they were called to educate others about the broader meaning and implications of AIDS. As Don described:

> I've lived with AIDS for years now and I feel like, um, I've got something important to say. . . . I feel like I've got a mission now—a mission to teach others about what AIDS really means. I tell people that AIDS really stands for *"Am I Doing Something?"* Am I doing something to change things? Am I doing something to make the world a more compassionate place? Those are the questions we need to ask if we want to stop the spread of AIDS and HIV.

Through embracing a sense of special mission, persons with AIDS can build revitalized selves, legitimate their unfolding biographies, and alleviate some of the painful or troubling feelings evoked by their health condition (Sandstrom 1990). They can also connect their illness experiences to larger religious meanings and social dramas, thereby granting these experiences a redeeming, significant, and enduring purpose.

CONCLUSION

Much of the literature on the dying process focuses attention on the psychosocial adaptations and tasks engaged in by persons with AIDS as they cope with the prospect of death. Although this literature offers helpful insights into the emotional states that dying individuals experience, the areas of task work they address, and the dimensions of growth they can realize, it largely overlooks how dying persons interpret their situation and reshape their lives and selves in light of their interpretations. As a result, it fails to consider some of the most central identity-related challenges confronted by people as they cope with dying, such as how to sustain a vital and valued sense of self, particularly when dealing with debilitating or life-threatening symptoms.

In recent years, thanatologists have become more receptive to approaches that focus on the perspectives, self-stories, and lived experiences of dying individuals (Kastenbaum 1998). These approaches have relied on ethnographic interviews and inductive strategies of data analysis (Sandstrom 1990, 1998; Yedidia and MacGregor 2001; Zlatin 1995). As a result, they have accentuated the narratives, life themes, and identity constructions drawn upon by dying persons as they come to terms with their situation. Guided by this approach, in this chapter I have highlighted the identity-related narratives and strategies that persons living with AIDS use to build or preserve valued selves. In doing so, I have portrayed how they derive a favorable or vitalizing sense of self from their intimate relationships, personal accomplishments, and long-term survival, as well as from identity constructions that highlight the beneficial and empowering aspects of their illness experience. I have also revealed the strategies that PLWAs use to sustain a sense of control, value, and continuity as their health declines and the threat of death looms larger. Drawing on their personal narratives, I have shown how individuals with AIDS, like others coping with dying, strive to build and affirm viable postselves, or identities that will endure after their deaths. They link these postselves to the legacies they will leave behind through their creative endeavors, community involvements, work accomplishments, and personal relationships. In some cases, they also anchor postselves in visions of an afterlife where they will be liberated from current limitations and realize transformed or enhanced selves. Ultimately, regardless of how they construct and embrace postmortal identities, persons with AIDS gain a measure of control and transcendence over their prospective deaths by doing so. They also derive a sense of hope, vitality, and continuity that helps them in their struggles to cope with the daily ramifications of their illness.

In addressing these themes this chapter refines and extends the literature on the dying process, particularly by demonstrating how and why dying individuals construct identities not only in terms of their prospective earthly futures but also in terms of a postmortal future. Through making this contribution, the chapter draws attention to an important but relatively neglected dimension of the lived experience and identity work of people diagnosed with life-threatening illnesses. It also suggests the need for further research.

REFERENCES

Baider, Lea. 1972. "Some Observations on the Process of Dying." *Australian Journal of Social Issues* 7:207–16.

Becker, Ernest. 1973. *The Denial of Death.* New York: Free Press.

Charmaz, Kathy. 1991. *Good Days, Bad Days: The Self in Chronic Illness and Time.* New Brunswick, NJ: Rutgers University Press.

Corr, Charles A. 1993. "Coping With Dying: Lessons That We Should and Should Not Learn From the Work of Elisabeth Kübler-Ross." *Death Studies* 17:69–83.

———. 1995. "A Task-Based Approach to Coping With Dying." Pp. 303–11 in *The Path Ahead: Readings in Death and Dying,* edited by Lynne A. DeSpelder and Albert L. Strickland. Mountain View, CA: Mayfield.

Corr, Charles A. and Donna M. Corr. 2000. "Anticipatory Mourning and Coping With Dying: Similarities, Differences, and Suggested Guidelines for Helpers." Pp. 223–51 in *Clinical Dimensions of Anticipatory Mourning,* edited by Therese A. Rando. Champaign, IL: Research Press.

Denzin, Norman K. 1984. "A Note on Emotionality, Self, and Interaction." *American Journal of Sociology* 89:402–8.

Doka, Kenneth. 1997. "The Quest for Meaning in Illness, Dying, Death and Bereavement." Pp. 241–56 in *Death and the Quest for Meaning,* edited by Stephen Strack. Northvale, NJ: Jason Aronson.

Fox, Renee. 1981. "The Sting of Death in American Society." *Social Science Review* 49:42–59.

Furstenberg, Anne-Linda and Miriam Meltzer Olson. 1984. "Social Work and AIDS." *Social Work in Health Care* 9(4):45–62.

Hennezel, Marie de. 1989. "Denial and Imminent Death." *Journal of Palliative Care* 5(3):27–31.

Kastenbaum, Robert J. 1985. "Dying and Death: A Life-Span Approach." Pp. 619–43 in *Handbook of the Psychology of Aging,* 2d ed., edited by James E. Birren and K. Warner Schaie. New York: Van Nostrand Reinhold.

———. 1998. *Death, Society, and Human Experience,* 6th ed. Boston: Allyn & Bacon.

Kayal, Philip. 1993. *Bearing Witness: Gay Men's Health Crisis and the Politics of AIDS.* Boulder, CO: Westview.

Kübler-Ross, Elisabeth. 1969. *On Death and Dying.* New York: Macmillan.

———. 1981. *Living With Dying.* New York: Macmillan.

Lifton, Robert Jay. 1967. *Death in Life: Survivors of Hiroshima.* New York: Random House.

Marshall, Victor. 1975. "Age and Awareness of Finitude in Developmental Gerontology." *Omega* 6:113–29.

———. 1980. *Last Chapters: A Sociology of Aging and Dying.* Monterey, CA: Brooks/Cole.

Morin, Stephen F. and W. F. Batchelor. 1984. "Responding to the Psychological Crisis of AIDS." *Journal of Health and Social Behavior* 28:140–57.

Moynihan, Rosemary, Grace Christ, and Les Gallo Silver. 1990. "AIDS and Terminal Illness." *Social Casework* 69:380–87.

Nichols, Stuart. 1985. "Psychosocial Reactions of Persons With AIDS." *Annals of Internal Medicine* 103:13–16.

Oberfield, Richard. 1984. "Terminal Illness: Death and Bereavement: Toward an Understanding of Its Nature." *Perspectives in Biology and Medicine* 28:140–55.

Samarel, Nelda. 1995. "The Dying Process." Pp. 89–116 in *Dying: Facing the Facts,* 3d ed., edited by Hannelore Wass and Robert A. Neimeyer. Philadelphia: Taylor & Francis.

Sandstrom, Kent. 1990. "Confronting Deadly Disease: The Drama of Identity Construction Among Gay Men With AIDS." *Journal of Contemporary Ethnography* 19:271–94.

———. 1996. "Redefining Sex and Intimacy: The Sexual Self-Images, Outlooks, and Relationships of Gay Men Living With HIV Disease." *Symbolic Interaction* 19:241–62.

———. 1998. "Coming to Terms With Bodily Loss and Disruption Evoked by AIDS." *Illness, Crisis, and Loss* 6:15–29.

———. 2000. "Sexually Transmitted Diseases—AIDS." In *Encyclopedia of Criminology and Deviant Behavior,* edited by Clifton D. Bryant. London: Taylor & Francis.

Schmitt, Raymond L. and Wilbert M. Leonard II. 1986. "Immortalizing the Self Through Sport." *American Journal of Sociology* 91:1088–1111.

Shneidman, Edwin S. 1973. *Deaths of Man.* New York: Quadrangle.

———. 1984. "Malignancy: Dialogues With Life-Threatening Illness." Pp. 195–218 in *Death: Current Perspectives,* 3d ed., edited by Edwin S. Shneidman. Mountain View, CA: Mayfield.

———. 1995. "The Postself." Pp. 454–60 in *Death: Current Perspectives,* 4th ed., edited by John B. Williamson and Edwin S. Shneidman. Mountain View, CA: Mayfield.

Stulberg, Ian and Stephan L. Buckingham. 1990. "Parallel Issues for AIDS Patients, Families, and Others." *Social Casework* 69:355–59.

Stulberg, Ian and Margaret Smith. 1988. "Psychosocial Impact of the AIDS Epidemic on the Lives of Gay Men." *Social Work* 33:277–81.

Unruh, David. 1983. "Death and Personal History: Strategies of Identity Preservation." *Social Problems* 30:340–51.

Vachon, Mary. 1998. "Psychosocial Needs of Patients and Families." *Journal of Palliative Care* 14(3): 49–56.

Weisman, Avery and Robert Kastenbaum. 1968. *The Psychological Autopsy: A Study of the Terminal Phase of Life* (Community Mental Health Journal Monograph No. 4). New York: Behavioral Publications.

Weisman, Avery and J. W. Warden. 1975. "Psychosocial Analysis of Cancer Deaths." *Omega* 6:61–75.

Weitz, Rose. 1989. "Uncertainty and the Lives of Persons With AIDS." *Journal of Health and Social Behavior* 30:270–81.

———. 1991. *Life With AIDS.* New Brunswick, NJ: Rutgers University Press.

Yedidia, Michael and Betsy MacGregor. 2001. "Confronting the Prospect of Dying: Reports of Terminally Ill Patients." *Journal of Pain and Symptom Management* 22:807–19.

Zlatin, Debbie M. 1995. "Life Themes: A Method to Understand Terminal Illness." *Omega* 31:189–206.

DEATH IN TWO SETTINGS

The Acute Care Facility and Hospice

SARAH BRABANT

The tremendous interest in the 6-hour PBS series *On Our Own Terms: Moyers on Dying* when it was first aired supported Bill Moyers's rationale for producing the groundbreaking program: "There was a growing realization that something has gone wrong with the way we provide care for the dying and support their caregivers, and the time has come to fix it" (quoted in Public Broadcasting Service 2001). An estimated 19 million Americans tuned in when the series was first broadcast in 2001; the ratings were 58% higher than the national PBS prime-time average (Public Broadcasting Service n.d.). Although the focus of *On Our Own Terms* is how we die, the series shows that where we die is parallel in importance, accentuating the contrast between death with hospice care and death in an acute care facility. The current attitude toward preferable place of death is reflected in a recent Time/CNN poll that showed that 70% of those polled wanted to die at home. In reality, 75% of Americans die in medical institutions, and more than a third spend a minimum of 10 days in an intensive care unit before they die (Cloud et al. 2000).

In the early part of the 20th century, dying in a hospital was limited to those without financial or social resources. Sick individuals with sufficient resources recovered or died at home, among family and friends. By 1994, 78% of Americans died in hospitals, medical centers, or nursing homes; only 17% died at home (Corr, Nabe, and Corr, 1997). Although statistics on causes of deaths in hospitals are readily available, information about precisely where deaths occur is not. Statistics collected in 1997 at the University of Virginia Health Sciences Center, however, show that 18% of the deaths in that medical center occurred on floor units, 27% on the hospice unit, and 55% in intensive care units or the emergency room (Chapple 1998).

The shift in place of death for most Americans from home to institution is generally attributed to two factors: the expansion of medical technology and demographic changes. The advancement of medical technology has occasioned the use of equipment and the employment of skilled technicians in caring for the dying that are beyond the reach of individual physicians. Concomitantly, the geographic mobility of the U.S. population has minimized the probability that relatives or long-time friends are available to care for an individual at the end of life. As a result, dying and death have been relegated to professionals and thus have become phenomena relatively unfamiliar to most Americans (DeSpelder and Strickland 1999).

Death in an acute care facility has come to be associated with painful and often futile attempts to ward off death, or at least to delay it (see, e.g., Cloud et al. 2000). Hospice care, first initiated in the United States in 1974, has become, for some, a preferable alternative. In contrast to the cure-centered, often impersonal approach of the general hospital (Kalish 1985:293), hospice care focuses on palliative measures when there is consensus that death will occur in the near future (e.g., within 6 months) and reversal of the dying process is improbable. In hospice care, inclusion of the patient's family as an integral part of the care unit is a basic objective (Zimmerman 1981:5–6). For a variety of reasons, however, ranging from accessibility to personal preference, less than 20% of those who die in the United States receive hospice care (Corr et al. 1997). Thus, with the exception of the relatively small number of Americans who die instantly as the result of trauma or system failure (less than 10%), most Americans in the near future can expect to die in an institutional setting.

The American cultural emphasis on "the good death," as reflected in movies and television programs, has resulted in considerable pressure on hospitals in general and nurses in particular to provide hospice-like care (often defined as palliative care) when death is near. As Chapple (1999) warns, however, the often abrupt shift from aggressive care to palliative care is similar to trying to "play baseball on the gridiron while the football game is in full swing." In such a situation, "a top priority is to avoid being trampled" (p. 28). This notion of game shift warrants sociological attention. Thus, in this chapter, rather than comparing philosophical, political, and/or technological end-of-life issues, I employ Goffman's (1959) use of the theater as an analogy to focus on the differences in human interactions between hospice and institutional (particularly acute care) settings in regard to end-of-life care.

THE THEATER AS ANALOGY

According to Goffman (1959):

> A social establishment is any place surrounded by fixed barriers to perception in which a particular kind of activity takes place. . . . Within the walls of a social establishment we find a team of performers who cooperate to present to an audience a given definition of the situation. (P. 238)

Three components of Goffman's definition of a social establishment are important to my discussion in this chapter: the individual as a member of a team of performers, the physical space wherein this performance takes place, and the performance itself. With respect to the concept of a team, Goffman (1959) writes:

> A team, then, may be defined as a set of individuals whose intimate co-operation is required if a given projected definition of the situation is to be maintained. Team is a grouping, but it is a grouping not in relation to a social structure or social organization but rather in relation to an interaction or series of interactions in which the relevant definition of the situation is maintained. (P. 104)

Goffman (1971) also observes that "social settings and social occasions are not organized in terms of individuals but in terms of participation units" (p. 21). Individual actors, then, come together to present a particular kind of drama that at least purports to be based in consensus with respect to norms, values, and beliefs. Critical to this notion of a team of performers are the presence of an audience for whom the performance is intended and the possibility of outsiders who view the performance without the consent or, perhaps, even the knowledge of the performers.

The presentation or performance takes place within a particular space or stage. This space is often divided into a front region, where the performance is presented, and a back region, where the performance is prepared. As Goffman (1959) notes, "Access to these regions is controlled in order to prevent the audience from seeing backstage and to prevent outsiders from coming into a performance that is not addressed to them" (p. 238). Finally, the performance is not simply the unfolding of a set of individual behaviors, but rather "a preestablished pattern of action" (p. 16). This preestablished pattern of action may be thought of as the drama and includes

historical as well as cultural components. Using Goffman's analogy of the theater, in the pages that follow I compare death under hospice care with death in an acute care facility with respect to the drama and the stage on which the drama is played out, the actors, and the performance. I then discuss the implications of the differences between the two for both those who provide care and those who receive it.

THE DRAMA AND STAGE

Until the middle of the 19th century, care of the sick and dying in the United States took place largely in the home. Public care was relegated to almshouses, which were places few people entered voluntarily. Over time, the successful treatment of injured soldiers in military hospitals changed public attitudes toward caring for the ill in public facilities and signaled the beginning of the modern hospital. Hospitals came to be seen as places for the curing of certain diseases, not as the end of the road for society's less desirables. Today's hospitals are primarily short-term, acute care facilities; their primary mission is to "treat specific diseases and to return people to society with more or less the same functional capacity they had before they became ill" (Corr et al. 1997:204). In such settings, death is a failure. As Ariès (1982) notes:

> When death arrives, it is regarded as an accident, a sign of helplessness or clumsiness that must be put out of mind. It must not interrupt the hospital routine, which is more delicate than that of any other professional milieu. It must therefore be discrete. (P. 586)

Indeed, for many years, death in hospitals was kept so discrete that when Elisabeth Kübler-Ross (1969) requested permission to talk to dying patients in one hospital in the late 1960s, she was told that no one was dying there.

Although the words *hospital* and *hospice* can be traced to the same medieval root, the attitude toward death in hospice care is quite different from that found in acute care facilities. In hospice care, death is anticipated, given that a life expectancy of 6 months or less is required for a patient's entry into the program. The purpose in hospice care, then, is not to avoid death or even to delay it, but rather to facilitate an individual's dying in a way that meets that person's unique needs (DeSpelder and Strickland 1999). In contrast, in an acute care facility death is an aberration, a failure on the part of the technology and/or the medical profession.

Thus the contrasting concepts of "letting nature take its course" and "aggressive intervention" characterize the fundamental difference between hospice care and other types of health care, particularly health care in acute care settings. Letting nature take its course is a process-oriented perspective; aggressive intervention is an event-oriented perspective. The dramas enacted in the two settings are thus quite different. Hospice care calls for a "wait and watch" performance. There is no specific goal other than pain control. Timing is unimportant, and the process of dying is allowed to proceed at its own pace. In contrast, the critical care unit focuses on the immediate event in order to maintain, stabilize, and/or improve the patient's condition as quickly as possible. Although both dramas demand skill, the first requires an ability to watch without doing; in contrast, the second requires an ability to assess and respond quickly.

Hospice care takes place within a variety of settings, including patients' homes, freestanding hospice units, and hospice-based programs within hospitals, in either discrete units or assigned beds (Zimmerman 1981:10). Regardless of the setting, inclusion of the patient's family and friends is fundamental, thus there is a need for sufficient physical space, a commodity often overlooked in both the social science literature and the nursing literature on hospice. This includes space in proximity to the patient, the site of the drama itself, as well as what Goffman (1959) calls "backstage" space. This latter is a place where "the performer can relax . . . drop his front . . . forgo speaking his lines, and step out of character" (p. 112). It also provides the performer space in which to practice the performance before the actual event.

In a hospital, the stage on which the drama is played out is commonly very small. In a floor unit there may be room only for the patient's bed and one or two chairs. Monitors and other medical equipment may take up so much space that no more than one or two persons may share the room at any one time with the patient and hospital personnel. In an acute care unit, the space around the patient's bed is devoted totally to technology. Additionally, the cost and complexity of this technology necessitate that the hospital allow minimum space between patients' beds. Thus two or more dramas may be performed on one small stage at the same time. Backstage space for patients' family members and friends is limited in both floor and critical care units, and even when it is available (e.g., a family waiting room), it often affords little privacy. Private areas (such as the hospital chapel) are often at some distance from the stage itself. This lack of backstage space precludes the release of emotions as an appropriate behavior. It also negates the performers' opportunity to practice before the actual performance.

THE ACTORS

At the heart of hospice care is the notion that "the terminally ill person's own preferences and lifestyle must be taken into account in all decision making" (Kastenbaum 2001:131). Thus, in hospice care, the patient is the lead actor. This does not mean that the dying patient's every wish will be granted, but it does mean that the patient will not endure thirst or pain or gasp for breath when there are means available to prevent it. It also means that all involved take seriously any written documents in which

the patient has expressed his or her wishes. This includes, of course, advance directives. Major areas of concern in hospice care are the patient's right to a sense of basic security and protection, the patient's access to opportunities for leave-taking with those most important to him or her, and the patient's opportunity to experience the end of life in a way that is most meaningful to him or her. Family and friends, as defined by the patient, are of secondary importance only with respect to the patient. These individuals have a right to information as well as the right to express their thoughts and feelings. They have a right to privacy with the patient both before and after death. Finally, the members of the patient's interdisciplinary care team have the right "to adequate time to form and maintain personal relationships with the patient" (Kastenbaum 2001:132).

Hall's (1998) description of an acute care setting provides a sharp contrast to the status of the patient in hospice care:

> If there was an ethics committee in place in any [of the hospitals in which I worked] it was largely invisible. Certainly it did not figure in the daily operations of the nursing unit; decisions were made on a pragmatic basis. Anything even approaching what might have been termed an ethical dilemma was arbitrated or flat out decided by the doctor or administrator. Those on the front line were not involved. . . . The question of patient rights was addressed by reading them to new patients and duly charting that a patient had refused medication. The number of times I saw a doctor badger a patient into treatments, procedures or medications they expressly said they did not want far exceeded the times that discussion among team members and patient occurred. And while the old fashioned approach definitely shows signs of wear—the newer doctors, especially those dealing with HIV/AIDS patients, showed far more inclination to take their patients' desires as well as their prognoses into account—for the most part, we operated on the assumption that "doctor knows best." (P. 4)

Thus differences between hospice care and institutional acute care with respect to the roles played by physicians and nurses warrant special attention.

The Physician

In hospice care, all health care is provided under the direction of a qualified physician. Basic to the hospice philosophy, however, is the notion of a holistic care plan that acknowledges the patient as an intellectual, emotional, and spiritual being as well as a physical one. Thus the physician directs a team of professionals that includes nurses, social workers, occupational and speech therapists, pastoral care professionals, and a variety of consultants (e.g., radiologists, psychiatrists). Although the hospice physician directs the team, he or she is considered a member of the team who assists the patient and his or her family in the dying journey by providing unique professional skills, not as the individual responsible for a particular outcome.

In contrast, a physician in an acute care facility is charged by society to produce "a cure so that a patient can return to normal activities or at least to near-normal activities" (Kalish 1985:278). The dying patient, then, becomes a source of conflict. As Kalish (1985) notes, if physicians "continue to treat a dying person, they are applying their costly skills and training to a situation that might be better handled by others; if they do not continue to treat the dying person, they then feel they have failed to fulfill the patient's [and society's] expectations" (p. 279).

The Nurse

In hospice care, nurses bear the primary burden of ensuring patient comfort (Markel and Sinon 1978). In a real sense, this is the traditional role of the nurse, which originally included not only concern for the patient but concern for his or her family and friends as well. The degree to which the inclusion of patients' family members and friends was an important component in nursing care in the first half of the 20th century is reflected in the suggested code of ethics presented by the American Nurses Association in 1926:

> Therefore the nurse must broaden her thoughtful consideration of the patient so that it will include his whole family and his friends, for only in surroundings harmonious and peaceful for the patient can the nurse give her utmost of skill, devotion and knowledge, which shall include the safeguarding of the health of those about the patient and the protection of property. (P. 600)

Advances in technology and drug therapy, and the concomitant division of labor into increasingly narrow specialties, however, have minimized both the time professional health care providers have to spend and their opportunities for interaction with patients' family members and friends. Indeed, research has shown that today it is not uncommon for nurses to regard their expertise with machinery as part of and even the ultimate expression of nursing care (Barr and Bush 1998). The care of family and friends has been delegated to others, such as social services or pastoral care workers. The American Nurses Association's (1985) most recent code of ethics includes the patient's family in the circle of care only when death is imminent:

> The measures nurses take to care for the dying client and the client's family emphasize human contact. They enable the client to live with as much physical, emotional, and spiritual comfort as possible, and they maximize the values the client has treasured in life. (P. 4)

In the critical care setting, however, this mandate becomes problematic. As Chapple (1999) observes:

> In reality, death in the intensive care unit (ICU) is neither simple nor natural. [Nurses] would like this to happen "naturally," but our interferences in Nature's course up to the point of making the decision to withdraw life support have eliminated the possibility. (P. 25)

THE PERFORMANCE

The Script

In an acute care facility, the possibility of the patient's dying may certainly occur to the patient, the nurse, and/or members of the patient's family. However, as Chapple (1999) notes, "death is not the mission of any ICU" (p. 25). Indeed, the goal of everyone concerned is to prevent death. Thus, until the decision is made to discontinue treatment and/or to withdraw life support, death is a taboo topic. Dying, then, has no place in the performance played out in the critical care area. In contrast, the primary players in hospice care—the patient, at least one family member, and the hospice team—are in agreement that death, although not the mission, is the prognosis, and dying is what the drama is all about.

In an institutional setting, then, the shift from an event-oriented drama to one of process necessitates a major shift in script (i.e., construction of reality) for most, if not all, of the players. One or more members of the patient's circle of family/friends may have already defined the patient as "dead" when he or she entered the hospital; others, however, may have hoped for continued life. Those who define the patient's situation as hopeless often avoid the hospital or spend their time in semibackstage places, such as the hospital cafeteria or parking lot. Those who are onstage generally at least give lip service to hope.

With the shift from event-oriented to process-oriented drama, there may be considerable inconsistency in construction of reality among those who are onstage. The nurse and the patient's mother, for example, may concur that the patient is dying; the patient's father, on the other hand, may not. Multiple scripts demand more space onstage as well as greater access to backstage space, neither of which is available in critical care units and both of which are often limited in floor units as well.

An example of the lack of appropriate backstage space in institutional settings and the need for such space comes from the case of John, a member of an AIDS support group I facilitated. John had been hospitalized for some weeks for treatment of an AIDS-related illness when, as a result of the physician's decision to discontinue treatment and provide palliative care only, the drama shifted from treatment to letting John die. Both John's mother and his partner had questioned continued treatment for several days; John's father, however, had continued to hope for a cure. I remember the moment when he walked into his son's room and suddenly realized that his son was dying. He began to shake uncontrollably, and the nurse suggested that I go with him to the nurses' break room. We had just entered the break room when another nurse came in and demanded that we leave immediately, saying that this was where she ate her lunch. We had, in a real sense, violated her backstage. Fortunately, I knew the hospital well and was able to guide John's father out onto the fire escape, where he sobbed for some 15 minutes or more.

The Performers

When the drama shifts and becomes event oriented rather than process oriented, the rights and obligations of the performers shift dramatically. In a critical care setting, the tasks of the primary actors are fairly simple. The patient is supposed to get well; the medical personnel are supposed to make this happen. Thus the patient is supposed to relinquish his or her rights to dignity, privacy, and control to the medical personnel. In return, the medical personnel are obliged to make every effort to maintain, stabilize, and improve the patient's heath. Although the role of the patient's family is to be supportive in this endeavor, family members' primary task often becomes one of not interfering as the series of events resulting from the illness or trauma occur and then are assessed and treated.

When death is inevitable, the task of the patient is to let go (not the same as giving up). Some thanatologists suggest that this is a conscious act on the part of the dying person. Certainly, numerous anecdotal reports support this notion (see, e.g., Callanan and Kelley 1992). Given this task, the patient's rights include the right to comfort, the right to respect, and, above all, the right to make the decision to let go in his or her own time and not in accordance with anyone else's needs or preferences. In addition, the patient has the right to choose companionship or privacy both during the process and at the time of death. Needless to say, in a critical care setting, lack of space, proximity of other ill patients, and frequent reminders from other units (e.g., emergency or recovery rooms) that a transfer is imminent do not enhance the probability that the patient's rights will be honored.

The primary task of the patient's significant others is to say good-bye in such a way that the patient is allowed to die in peace and the family members or friends are able to look back on this time with a sense of fulfillment about the way in which they said good-bye. In order to accomplish this task, family and friends have a right to information, guidance, and affirmation that they are doing what they need to do—that is, playing an acceptable/appropriate role in the drama.

The professional caregiver has an obligation to define the situation (this includes providing information about the drama itself as well as expected role behavior), to set the limits for the performance of both the drama and the roles within the drama, and to model the behavior expected of all of the performers. The professional caregiver also has the responsibility of taking care of him- or herself, in order not to become an added responsibility for the other performers. Coupled with these complex tasks is the professional's right to feel good about him- or herself,

as a professional and as a human being. The latter is especially important.

In contrast to a growing body of nursing literature that suggests that critical care nursing is more stressful than nursing in other areas because of a variety of external factors (e.g., the need to assess and act quickly), some researchers have suggested that personality characteristics may be an even more important factor (Milazzo 1988). Thus a nurse may feel that he or she has provided the best possible nursing care and at the same time feel that he or she has somehow failed as a human being. The demand to shift quickly from an event-oriented drama to a process-driven one may exacerbate this feeling of failure as a human being.

The problematic nature of the shift from an event-oriented drama to a process-oriented one is not limited to the major players. The process-oriented drama requires a large supporting cast. The team approach is basic to hospice care. Physicians, nurses, clinical nurse practitioners, social workers, physical therapists, chaplains, and volunteers are all important components in a comprehensive approach aimed at meeting the social, physical, emotional, intellectual, and spiritual needs of the dying person. All the players share equal billing. It is also important to remember that this team is in place before the patient is defined as dying. The team members know each other; they have been through dress rehearsals together.

Although the various players mentioned above may be available in any given institutional setting, their coming together as a team for a specific person is often problematic. In an event-driven drama, support staff are identified and called in only as needed. Trained to focus on event rather than process, team members may take some time to develop the ability to work together in a process-oriented drama. These individuals may not know each other; they may not have ironed out any problems that could arise when boundaries between professional turfs are questioned, and some or all may still be using an event-oriented script.

As Chapple (1999) notes, the objective in the acute care unit is clear: to save the patient's life. "The rules and strategies of cardiopulmonary resuscitation (i.e., airway, breathing, circulation) and Advanced Cardiac Life Support algorithms, constantly refined and updated, tell us how to play the game with the best chance of success" (p. 25). There are no rules and strategies when the decision to withdraw life support occurs. Those who played an active role in making this decision (i.e., physicians and ethicists) have now completed their part in the drama and withdraw from the stage. The nurse, then, becomes the director of the new game. Chapple continues:

> A decision to withdraw life support, ethically made, does not often address the hands-on management issues that surround the dying process. Without a shared understanding of outcomes and standards, chaotic care can result. Hospice personnel have

such a shared understanding of the terminal care they provide, but the context of hospice practice and the longer death trajectory of hospice patients makes translation of that understanding into ICU practice problematic. (P. 28)

Using the dramaturgical model, shifting from the event-oriented drama of aggressive intervention to the process-oriented drama of letting nature take its course is tantamount to trying to produce grand opera on a stage designed for intimate dinner theater. It is not going to work. The stage itself is too small, the supporting staff is not assembled, and few if any of the performers are reading from the same script. Time—to plan, to learn the script, and to rehearse—is essential if the process-oriented drama is to be successful.

Hospice care professionals have learned that a patient's entry into hospice within hours or even days of death is problematic (Head 2000). The director of one hospice program suggests that a patient needs a minimum of 2 months in hospice care in order to experience the maximum benefit of such care (Nelson Waguespack, personal communication, April 17, 2002). Hospice care may not be desirable for some patients in acute care units even when hospice care is readily available. Even though a hospital may have a hospice unit available, a patient may prefer to remain in the acute unit, where the patient and his or her family knows the staff and is familiar with the surroundings. Regardless of the reason, the pressure on nurses in hospital settings, especially in critical care units, to provide hospice care at the end of a patient's life is unreasonable. It is possible, however, for acute care units to provide components of hospice care.

A closer look at the hospice drama reveals two distinct themes. Although both come under the rubric of the peaceful death, they are, in fact, quite different. One is pain control; the other has to do with completion of unfinished business on the part of the patient and his or her family and friends. Because of the emphasis on symptom control in hospice care, hospice professionals are well trained in pain and symptom management for a number of terminal diseases (Davie 2001). In part because of this expertise, the terms *hospice care* and *palliative care* are often used interchangeably. Indeed, by 2000, the National Hospice Organization had changed its name to the National Hospice and Palliative Care Organization. As Hunter (2001) notes, however, hospice care and palliative care are not the same:

> Hospice is a formalized interdisciplinary program of end-of-life care doing business under the provisions of the Medicare Hospice Benefit [enacted in 1982]. Palliative medicine (or, as some call it, palliative care) is the branch of medicine that specializes in caring for patients who cannot be cured and for whom the focus of care is comfort and maximizing the quality of life. (P. 3)

Despite the advances made in both hospice care and palliative medicine, at the present time, as Beresford (2001) points out, there is "no third-party reimbursement (other than hospice care) specific to the provision of palliative care and there is no regulatory structure or standard-setting body for palliative care" (p. iii). This, then, is a legal, and probably political, issue that is outside of the set of responsibilities that a nurse may reasonably be expected to fulfill.

Concerning the second theme, completion of unfinished business on the part of the patient and his or her family and friends, however, nurses may be able to help to some degree. Chapple (1999) recommends the following:

> When we withdraw life support, we need a simple statement to acknowledge the fact that a new game has started on our inhospitable field to orient us to our new priorities of care: *Dying is a process, and attending to the dying process is an ethical end in and of itself.* (P. 30)

She suggests that nurses do three things: invite participation in the process, allow time to pass, and allow for unpredictability.

Invitation to Participate

Chapple suggests that in inviting patients and their families to participate in the dying process, nurses should share both power and powerlessness. Power includes access to information and control of situation. Nurses can share information about the dying process in general as well as about particular cases they have experienced. They can also invite the other participants to share experiences they may have had with both death and dying in the past as well as contribute suggestions for the process that is taking place at this time. How do the participants define life and death? What do they think happens following death? Do they wish to be present during the process and/or the death? Are there religious or cultural norms that they wish to consider? Sharing power also means acknowledging and affirming cultural differences. Sharing powerlessness means sharing both lack of information and lack of control in the given situation. It is easier for participants to acknowledge regrets, sadness, and fears when they know that these emotions are shared with and affirmed by others. For nurses, this is a time for listening, not talking. A simple nod in response to another's words is often sufficient.

Allowing others to participate includes letting others share in immediate tasks. Knowing that you did something, however trivial, to assist a loved one in his or her last hours is a tremendous asset in the grief work that follows a death. I remember one occasion when a father was waiting for his son to die from AIDS. The young man was in no apparent pain, but he showed no evidence of being aware of the presence of others. His father paced the room, his hands clenched together. At one point, I rose to adjust the damp cloth on the young man's head and the father asked if he could do that. I handed him the cloth, and as he stroked his son's face with it, he told me about the times he had bathed his son when he was a little boy and prepared him for bed. I asked if he would like to do this now. At first he voiced concern that he might hurt his son, but he allowed me to bring him a bowl of water, a washcloth, and towels. I asked if he wanted me to stay, and he said he did not, but he wanted me to remain nearby "just in case." He then proceeded to bathe his son, who died later that evening. At the wake, the father came up to me, smiled, and said proudly that his son died in clean pajamas. I do not believe that he will ever forget his son's dying; he will, however, always have the memory that it was he who made certain that his child died in clean pajamas.

The nurse's invitation to participate may not only be helpful to the patient's family members and friends, it may also alleviate constant intrusion into the nurse's work by these persons. By taking a few minutes to teach someone how to perform a simple procedure for the patient, the nurse can avoid repeated requests for service. Family and friends are often concerned about the cessation of feeding during the end stage of the dying process. Feeding, after all, is one of the ways we show others that we love them. This is particularly true in some cultures, notably so in the Acadian ethos. By allowing family members and friends to crush ice or Popsicles and place small bits on the patient's lips, the nurse can both provide immediate relief from the strain of watching a loved one die and create good memories for the survivors to draw on following the death.

Sometimes participation of this type is not feasible, especially in crowded critical care areas. Placing a cool cloth on the patient's forehead, wiping the patient's mouth, and moistening the patient's lips, however, are small tasks that, although perhaps unnecessary or relatively unimportant, allow family members and friends to participate in caring for their loved one.

Allowing Time to Pass

In my experience, most participants want to know when death can be expected to take place. When they ask, it is useful for the nurse to acknowledge that their wish to know is normal and then draw attention away from the death itself to the process leading toward death. When cure is the goal, it is the professional who determines both the procedures to be done and the timing of these procedures. When death is imminent, it is the dying person who controls the process. Focusing on what is transpiring at the moment with the patient as well as those who wait with him or her, rather than the approximate time of a future event, helps to keep the drama flowing smoothly. One way in which the nurse can do this is by facilitating communication between the patient and his or her family and friends.

It is important that the nurse encourage those gathered in attendance to talk *to* the patient rather than *about* him or her, even if the patient is nonresponsive. This is a time to reminisce about events that were important to all the

participants. It is a time to forgive past omissions or commissions, a time to say thank you, a time to express the meaning that someone has for another. As death approaches, the technique of co-breathing can help family members, friends, and patient alike. The nurse can encourage those around the bedside to breath in unison with the patient. If his or her breathing is rapid, co-breathers can breathe with every other breath instead.

Allowing for Unpredictability

Predicting when death will occur is often haphazard at best. I have often left a patient's bedside "knowing" that I have just been with him or her for the last time before death only to return later that day or even a week or two later and find him or her still alive or even improved. I remember clearly one night when a patient's parents, nurse, and I concurred that the end was near. I sat with the young man's parents that night as we watched his breathing grow more and more labored and irregular. Just as dawn began to break, he suddenly opened his eyes, looked out the window, and asked me why I was still at the hospital. I have to admit that I was at a loss for words.

Similarly, I have experienced the shock of learning that someone died when I thought that person's death was days, weeks, or even months away. In the early months of my work with AIDS patients, I remember, I was surprised when a physician asked me if I thought a particular patient's death was imminent. It was then that I learned that dying is definitely not an exact science.

IMPLICATIONS

Chapple (1999), then, suggests that health care professionals in acute care settings need to apply new rules when death is imminent. From a sociological perspective, the shift in drama requires a shift in roles as well (Brabant 2001). These new roles include the nurse as director, the nurse as educator, and the nurse as role model. The shift in drama also includes new roles for the patient and his or her family members and friends.

The Nurse as Director

It is important that nurses plan ahead as much as possible. Locating available space for backstage use is best done prior to need, not as the result of need. Some hospitals have "family rooms" for this purpose, but these areas are usually at a distance from patients' rooms or lack essential privacy. Nurses can alleviate the pressure of having to cope with disruptive behavior on the floor or in a critical care area, and/or the embarrassment of trying to use a particular backstage space at the wrong time, by knowing in advance if there is a patient room that is not occupied that shift, by having a screen available to create a private area in the waiting room or at the end of a hall, and by establishing consensus among staff on when or if the nurses' lounge is available.

Nurses should become acquainted with the members of the hospital's social service and/or pastoral care staff. In an event-oriented drama, patients and/or their family members are referred to these areas of the hospital for services just as they are transported to particular areas for specific procedures (e.g., X rays, lab work). The focus in the event-oriented drama is on getting a task accomplished. Family members may simply be told where to go in order to meet with someone to discuss some issue, such as outpatient care. In this situation it is the department and its service, not the specific person with whom they meet, that is important. In the process-oriented drama, the focus shifts, and continuity is important. When the nurse can say that he or she has asked a particular person from social services or pastoral care to come by in order to talk with a family member about some of the things the family member asked about earlier, the interaction becomes more personal. This support person may have only suggestions to offer, not answers, but he or she also will have time to sit and talk with the patient's loved one for a few minutes, whereas the nurse may not.

The Nurse as Educator

In the past, most people experienced the death of someone they knew while they were still in childhood. Today, it is not uncommon for an adult to have had no prior experience with death. When this is the case, the nurse may need to serve as death educator. What are the signs of approaching death? What will take place as death occurs? What behavior is appropriate? What will happen following the death itself? The things the nurse says at this time, and the way in which he or she says them, can have critical impacts on the patient's family members and friends, both at the time of death and thereafter.

Although we often use the words *death* and *dead* in ordinary speech (as when we talk about someone being a deadbeat or having a death wish, or say, "I laughed so hard I almost died"), we often use euphemisms when death actually occurs (e.g., "He passed away"; "She left us"). One such expression traditionally used by nurses is "The patient expired." The use of such euphemisms by health care professionals is detrimental for at least two reasons. First, it supports the notion that death is a failure, something that should not be mentioned openly. It thus adds to the stigma surrounding death. Second, the use of euphemisms may lead to some confusion about what has actually taken place. On occasion people have come to me in a very distraught state following the death of a loved one because they were concerned that their loved one felt abandoned or suffered physically while in the morgue. Statements such as "They will be taking John down to the morgue to await the people from the funeral home" are misleading. John is dead. The professional should make that clear by saying, "John's body will be taken to the morgue."

Finally, the first task of grief work is to acknowledge that the person is dead. This does not mean that one accepts the death as all right, just that one acknowledges that the person is no longer alive. The nurse, as society's representative, can promote this acknowledgment by using the correct words.

The Nurse as Role Model

The nurse not only directs the drama, he or she provides the model for all others who take active roles. In touching the patient, the nurse shows by example how the patient's family members and friends may proceed. If the nurse treats the patient as an object, those who witness this will probably do so as well. If the nurse treats the patient as a human being with rights to dignity and respect, those in attendance will often follow suit. If the nurse can express his or her feelings of regret, others may feel permission to do so as well.

As death approaches, the nurse's roles as director, educator, and model may commingle with his or her role as coparticipant. The relationship between the nurse and his or her patient is coming to a close. It is time to give the patient permission to die, and the nurse may be an important person in this ritual. He or she may also use this opportunity to model this behavior for others. The moment of death may well be the most difficult time for the nurse, for it is at this time that he or she must step aside and at he same time set limits for the behavior of others.

It is not always as easy as it sounds for the nurse to step aside. I have to admit that I have often resented relatives who appear just before death occurs and take center stage with last-minute reconciliations when I was the one who cared for their loved one during the long weeks or months that preceded the death. I have to remind myself that this is, after all, what I had hoped would take place. I need to step aside and give others the center stage.

At the same time, it is the professional who must set the limits for final good-byes. Removing any tubes that may still be present, wiping away secretions that may have occurred in the last moments of life, and arranging the linens all attest to a shift in the drama. Allowing those in attendance time with the body is important. The nurse, however, must set limits, in terms of both behavior and length of time. The nurse's work in educating the patient's family and friends and modeling behavior toward the patient prior to the death can often make this much easier for everyone concerned.

Current debates between hospice professionals and palliative care professionals represent the emergence of a new arena for end-of-life care (Hunter 2001). In a joint project, the National Hospice and Palliative Care Organization and the Center to Advance Palliative Care are now considering three possible models: (a) hospice as an independent entity in contractual relationship with one or more hospitals, (b) hospice as a program within a hospital or medical center, and (c) hospice as a consultant/support for palliative care in a hospital (Beresford 2001). The drama is changing, scripts are being rewritten, and roles are shifting. Ethical considerations, legal issues, and the costs of care all play a part in the emergence of this new drama. In the meantime, awareness of the need to shift from an event-oriented drama to a process-oriented one, and the impossibility of putting on a full-scale opera on a small stage with no rehearsal or supporting cast, allows nurses to facilitate end-of-life care for patients and their family members and friends.

The Patient

It is of utmost importance that medical personnel, particularly nurses, understand that they need to assume new roles with new obligations when the drama shifts from acute care to end-of-life care. Of equal importance, however, is the willingness of the patient and his or her family and friends to assume new roles with new obligations as well. As with acute care personnel, this requires planning.

First, every potential acute care patient (and that includes all of us) should have a living will that clearly outlines his or her wishes in the event that death is likely to take place in the near future due to an incurable injury, disease, or illness. A living will, however, may not anticipate all circumstances, and so a second component of last directives is critical. This includes the establishment of a durable power of attorney, which authorizes someone else to make end-of-life decisions for the patient if the patient is no longer capable of making these decisions. The selection of this person requires some thought. It is important that the person selected is one who is both capable of assuming and willing to assume the role of advocate. Such an individual needs to be able to shift from a supporting role to a lead role in the drama, to ask questions, to assess and reassess the situation, and to make decisions that may or may not be popular ones. He or she should be able to build a cast of supporting actors (e.g., social services, pastoral care) to assist him or her in carrying out this new role. This position is not for the timid or unassertive, no matter how close the friendship.

Finally, it is important that the patient's immediate family members are aware of the patient's wishes and are willing to support both those wishes and the person with the durable power of attorney. All of this requires that the patient be willing both to contemplate the issues around his or her own death and dying and to draw others into a discussion of these issues. Given the death taboo in our society, this is no easy task.

Head (2000:5) suggests that when a patient enters hospice care at the last moment, the patient and his or her family and health care team should hold realistic expectations, and the parameters for their satisfaction must be redefined. This is good advice for patients, their families and friends, and professionals in the acute care unit as well. It is not often possible to produce a full-scale end-of-life opera.

Such a production takes time, space, and a large cast of actors. It may, however, be feasible to produce one or more arias. This in itself is quite an accomplishment when all is said and done.

REFERENCES

American Nurses Association. 1926. "A Suggested Code." *American Journal of Nursing* 26:599–601.

———. 1985. *Code for Nurses With Interpretative Statements.* Washington, DC: American Nurses Publishing.

Ariès, Philippe. 1982. *The Hour of Our Death,* translated by Helen Weaver. New York: Vintage.

Barr, Wendy J. and Helen A. Bush. 1998. "Four Factors of Nurse Caring in the ICU." *Dimensions of Critical Care Nursing* 17:214–23.

Beresford, Larry. 2001. *Hospital-Hospice Partnerships in Palliative Care.* Alexandria, VA: National Hospice and Palliative Care Organization.

Brabant, Sarah. 2001. "Extending the Circle of Care When Death Is Imminent." Pp. 429–41 in *End of Life Nursing Care,* edited by Belinda Poor and Gail P. Poirrier. Boston: Jones & Bartlett.

Callanan, Maggie and Patricia Kelley. 1992. *Final Gifts: Understanding the Special Awareness, Needs, and Communications of the Dying.* New York: Poseidon.

Chapple, Helen S. 1998. "Dying in the Hospital: Ethical Management of Ethical Death." Presented at Association for Death Education and Counseling preconference workshop, March 19, Chicago.

———. 1999. "Changing the Game in the Intensive Care Unit: Letting Nature Take Its Course." *Critical Care Nurse* 19(3):25–33.

Cloud, John, Wendy Cole, Maggie Sieger, Dan Cray, Greg Fulton, Anne Moffett, and Dick Thompson. 2000. "A Kinder, Gentler Death." *Time,* September 18, pp. 60–67.

Corr, Charles A., Clyde M. Nabe, and Donna M. Corr. 1997. *Death and Dying, Life and Living.* Pacific Grove CA: Brooks/Cole.

Davie, Karen A. 2001. "A Message From NHPCO President Karen Davie." *Hospice Professional* 1(1):3.

DeSpelder, Lynne A. and Albert Lee Strickland. 1999. *The Last Dance: Encountering Death and Dying.* Mountain CA: Mayfield.

Goffman, Erving. 1959. *The Presentation of Self in Everyday Life.* Garden City, NY: Doubleday.

———. 1971. *Relations in Public: Microstudies of the Public Order.* New York: Harper & Row.

Hall, John W. 1998. "The Essential Compass." *Hospice,* Summer, pp. 4–6.

Head, Barbara. 2000. "Short Length of Stay: Lessons Learned." *Hospice Professional,* Winter, pp. 1–3, 5-6.

Hunter, Walter R. 2001. "Hospice and Palliative Medicine: Irreconcilable Differences or Destined for the Altar?" *Hospice Professional* 1(1):1–6.

Kalish, Richard A. 1985. *Death, Grief, and Caring Relationships.* Monterey, CA: Brooks/Cole.

Kastenbaum, Robert J. 2001. *Death, Society, and Human Experience,* 7th ed. Boston: Allyn & Bacon.

Kübler-Ross, Elisabeth. 1969. *On Death and Dying.* New York: Macmillan.

Markel, William M. and Virginia B. Sinon. 1978. *The Hospice Concept.* New York: American Cancer Society.

Milazzo, Nancy. 1988. "Stress Levels of ICU Versus Non-ICU Nurses." *Dimensions of Critical Care Nursing* 7:52–58.

Public Broadcasting Service. 2001. "On Our Own Terms." In *PBS 2001 Annual Report.* Alexandria, VA: Public Broadcasting Service. Retrieved June 6, 2003 (http//:www.pbs.org/insidepbs/annualreport2001/terms.html).

———. n.d. "On Our Own Terms: Moyers on Dying." *Community Action Newsletter* no. 17. Retrieved June 6, 2003 (http://www.pbs.org/wnet/onourownterms/community/news_17.html).

Zimmerman, Jack M. 1981. *Hospice: Complete Care for the Terminally Ill.* Baltimore: Urban & Schwarzenberg.

THE HISTORY OF THE HOSPICE APPROACH

MICHAEL R. LEMING

I'm afraid of the pain.
I don't want to be alone when I'm dying.
I'm afraid of a long, protracted period of suffering.
I don't want to die in a hospital. Let me die at home.
I'm not afraid for myself, but I am worried about the effect of my death on those I love.

—Frequent responses to the question, Does dying frighten you?

Of the eight different types of death fears, the three that cause the highest anxiety are the fear of pain, the fear of dependency, and the fear of isolation (Leming 1979–80). Among Americans, as the comments above reflect, it is the process of dying, and not the event of death, that causes the most concern. In this chapter, I examine the worldwide hospice movement that has developed as a response to fears related to the dying process and the ways in which death is typically handled in institutional settings. The three primary patient concerns that hospice care addresses specifically are problems related to symptom and pain control, the apprehension caused by having others in control of one's life, and anxiety about being alone at the time of death (Magno 1990).

Hospice should be thought of primarily as a concept of care—a way to provide humane and supportive care for dying patients and their families (Burns, Carney, and Brobst 1989:65). The philosophical origin of the hospice movement is found in the teachings of Jesus, who encouraged his followers with these words:

> Then I, the King, shall say to those at my right, "Come, blessed of my Father, into the Kingdom prepared for you from the founding of the world. For I was hungry and you fed me; I was thirsty and you gave me water; I was a stranger and you invited me into your homes; naked and you clothed me; sick and in prison, and you visited me." . . . "Whenever you did these things for the least of these my brothers, you were doing them for me!" (Matthew 25:34–36, 40)

The words *hospice, hospital, hostel,* and *hotel* are all derived from the same Latin root, *spitium,* which means "host" or "guest." According to Kenneth Cohen (1979),

"The first hospitals were actually an outgrowth of religion rather than of medicine" (p. 15). As early as the fourth century, Roman Emperor Julian expressed his concern about the emergence of the Christian movement. As a response to the Christian emphasis on humanitarianism, Julian encouraged the priests of the ancient Roman religion to "establish hospices (*xenodochia*) in every city and thereby not permit others to excel us in good deeds" (quoted in Phipps 1988:93).

In medieval times, the word *hospice* referred to a way station for travelers needing assistance. Sandol Stoddard (1978) and William Phipps (1988) describe some of the early medieval hospices. Probably the most famous hospice in the world is the Hospice of Great Saint Bernard in the Alps. This hospice, founded more than a thousand years ago, trains dogs to rescue travelers lost on the Alpine slopes. With the passing of time, the word *hospice* came to encompass houses maintained for the sick as well as for travelers.

As the secularization of the modern age has progressed, hospitals have come to be dominated by secular administrators and medical practitioners who have established the priority of providing medical cures for the acutely ill rather than caring for those who are incurable. In 1905, the Irish Sisters of Charity established St. Joseph's Hospice in Hackney (near London) to provide patient-centered care for the terminally ill. One-third of the beds at St. Joseph's Hospice are reserved for patients who are expected to live only 3 months or less (Phipps 1988:96). According to the medical director of St. Joseph's Hospice, J. F. Hanratty, M.D., many physicians find it difficult to care for patients whom they cannot cure and to accept palliative medical skills and treatments as authentic medical protocol. It is not uncommon to hear a medical practitioner tell a terminal patient, "There is nothing more I can do." Hanratty notes:

> At St. Joseph's "more" is done, and the "more" is sophisticated therapies to control, as much as possible, all of the patient's distressing symptoms. The practice at St. Joseph's Hospice is, first of all, to establish that the diagnosis is accurate and that death is not far distant. The management of terminal illness then requires a change of roles and attitude on the part of those caring for the patient. (quoted in Carr 1989:266)

St. Christopher's Hospice in London, England, played a pivotal role in the development of the modern hospice movement by disseminating the hospice concept of care—that of ministering to the spiritual and physical needs of dying patients. St. Christopher's was founded in 1967 by Dr. Cicely Saunders, who began her career as a nurse and subsequently became a social worker. However, it was not until Saunders became a physician and obtained a grant to work with the Sisters of Charity at St. Joseph's Hospice for several years that she began to influence the course of institutionalized health care for dying patients on an international scale. Queen Elizabeth II recognized Saunders's achievements in 1981 by honoring her with the status of dame.

The first modern hospice program in the United States was the Connecticut Hospice, the origins of which were directly related to St. Christopher's. In 1963, Dr. Cicely Saunders was invited to lecture in New Haven at the Yale University School of Medicine. Over the next several years, contacts between Saunders and personnel from the Yale Nursing and Medical Schools were frequent. Local leaders from various disciplines became involved in the development of a hospice in Connecticut, and their planning resulted in the establishment in 1971 of Hospice Inc., the name of which was later changed to the Connecticut Hospice.

The original intent of the planning group was to build an inpatient facility similar to St. Christopher's. Funding proved to be a problem, however, and the group decided to inaugurate a home-care program in 1974. To test the viability of home care, the National Cancer Institute provided funds for a 3-year demonstration project. As a result, an inpatient facility was eventually built with the help of both federal and state funds; this facility opened in Branford, Connecticut, in 1980.

After the inpatient facility was completed, the Connecticut Hospice, with the help of a foundation grant, organized a separate corporation—the Connecticut Hospice Institute for Education, Training, and Research, Inc. The institute offered special help to health care leaders who wanted to improve the quality of care offered to terminally ill patients and their families. In 1981, the institute was merged with its founding organization; today, it continues its educational work as the John D. Thompson Hospice Institute for Education, Training and Research, Inc., the teaching arm of the Connecticut Hospice. The institute's purpose is to "share the hospice philosophy, and experience and skills with students, caregivers, administrators, the lay community and all those who desire to improve the quality of care for patients experiencing an irreversible illness and their families" (Connecticut Hospice 1997).

Since that beginning, the number of hospice programs throughout the United States has increased dramatically. Currently, more than 2,800 programs across the country serve more than 400,000 patients annually. In 1978, the National Hospice Organization was formed to provide for coordination of hospice activities and to assure that high standards of care would always be demonstrated by any program calling itself a hospice. Instrumental in working toward an accreditation procedure, this organization, which was renamed the National Hospice and Palliative Care Organization (NHPCO) in February 2000, also provides educational programs, technical assistance, publications, advocacy, and referral services to the general public. In addition to the NHPCO, which serves most of the nation's hospices and more than 4,200 professional members (National Hospice Organization 1997), every state now also has its own hospice organization to promote education and standards of care.

As of 1997, the National Hospice Organization estimated that more than 25,000 people were employed in hospice care across the United States, serving an estimated 400,000 patients each year. The 2,800 hospice programs existing at that time each served an average of 140 patient-families per year, and in serving these patients, more than 96,000 volunteers contributed more than 5.25 million hours of their time each year.

THE NATURE OF THE CONTEMPORARY HOSPICE

Although there are different types of hospice institutions, all hospice programs are unified by a shared general philosophy of patient care. Hospice is a specialized health care program that serves patients with life-threatening illnesses. In 1996, approximately 78% of hospice patients in the United States had cancer, 10% had cardiovascular diseases, 4% had AIDS, 1% had renal or kidney disease, 1% had Alzheimer's disease, and the remaining 6% had a variety of other diseases (National Hospice Organization 1997). Nationally, in 1992, the average hospice patient spent 64 days in hospice care (National Hospice Organization 1997). More than 90% of hospice care hours are provided in patients' homes, with inpatient care available as needed. In hospice, the *patient-family* is the unit of care. The primary goals of hospice care are to promote patient-family autonomy, to assist patients in obtaining pain control and real quality of life before they die, and to enable families of patients to receive supportive help during the dying process and in the bereavement period.

Pain Management

A hospice program is basically a medical program with physician direction and nurse coordination. Hospice leaders have discovered that patients cannot achieve a good quality of life unless their physical pain and symptoms such as nausea, vomiting, dizziness, constipation, and shortness of breath are under control. A major emphasis of hospice, therefore, is pain and symptom management.

Traditional medical care is often based on a "PRN" (from the Latin phrase *pro re nata*) approach, which means that medication is given "as the situation demands." In practice, this means that often a person must first hurt and ask for relief before his or her pain can be stopped. This approach is responsible for much of the suffering experienced by terminally ill patients.

When Cicely Saunders first began working at St. Joseph's Hospice in 1958, she developed an alternative method of pain control that has become the standard in hospice care. She writes:

> Here [St. Joseph's], as elsewhere at that time, one saw people "earning their morphine," and it was wonderfully rewarding to introduce the simple and really obvious system of giving drugs to prevent pain happening—rather than to wait and give them once it had occurred. Here too there was the potential for developing ideas about the control of other symptoms, and also for looking at the other components of pain. But first of all I must salute the Sisters of St. Joseph's and the compassionate matter-of-factness of their dedicated care. Together we began to develop the appropriate way of caring, showing that there could be a place for scientific medicine and nursing. We could illustrate an alternative approach to the contrast between active treatment for an illness (as if to cure it were still possible) or some form of legalized euthanasia. (Saunders 1992:20)

Hospice physicians believe that a patient should not hurt at all. Regular medication is, therefore, given in advance, before the pain begins. The aim is to erase the memory of the pain the patient has experienced and to deal with the fear of pain in the future. Pain medications are standardized to the needs of the patient. The aim is to control the pain and other symptoms without sedating the patient. Every symptom is treated as a separate illness, for only when each symptom is under control can a patient begin to find fullness and experience a good quality of life.

Home and Inpatient Care

The hospice concept includes both home care and inpatient care. Ideally, hospice care represents a continuum that includes both forms of care, beginning with home care and moving to inpatient care when it becomes necessary. However, the major emphasis of hospice treatment is on home care.

Inpatient care usually becomes necessary for one of three reasons. The first is that a stay of a few days in an inpatient facility may be helpful in bringing the patient's pain and other symptoms under control. The second is that the family taking care of the patient at home may become exhausted and need a few days' rest while the patient is cared for elsewhere. The third reason is that home care becomes inappropriate at a given stage of the illness due to the patient's condition or home situation. When a patient is admitted to an inpatient facility, the hope is usually that he or she will be able to move back and forth from home care to inpatient care as needed at various stages of the illness.

The Hospice Team

Hospice care is provided by an interdisciplinary team, with the representatives of each discipline having something to contribute to the whole. All of the team members work together, each in his or her own area of expertise, and each interdisciplinary team includes several layers or levels of care. At the center of the team is the *patient and his or her family.* The hospice movement emphasizes the need for patients to make their own decisions with the supportive help of health care professionals and other trained persons. A vital part of this process is the *patient's own physician*—the professional who will continue to be in charge of the care of the patient and write medical orders when necessary.

The next layer of the team includes the hospice's professional caregiving staff. This consists first of *physicians,* who are required to direct medical care. *Nurses* constitute the next category. Registered nurses are responsible for coordinating the patient's care, and licensed practical nurses and nurse's aides are also included—especially in inpatient settings.

The *hospice social worker* is an important part of the team. The social worker spends considerable time working with the patient's family, encouraging and helping family members to communicate with each other. Although family members may be aware that the patient is dying, they may never have discussed this among themselves or with the patient. The social worker also spends time dealing with social problems in the family, such as alcoholism and marriage problems, and working with the young children or grandchildren of patients. In modern society, all too often, children are shielded from participation in events centering on the death of a family member.

Pastoral care is also a basic part of the team. A relatively large hospice may employ a *chaplain* who directs pastoral care to patients and their families, counsels other members of the caregiving team on spiritual issues, and tries to involve members of the clergy in the community in the care of their own people. In a small hospice program, all of the spiritual care may be provided by local clergy who work closely with the hospice staff.

Financial counseling is another significant aspect of the hospice team. Because patients and their families have often exhausted their financial resources at the time of care, the financial counselor helps the family in seeking forms of third-party reimbursement, such as those provided by Medicare and private insurance companies, as well as in finding other programs for which the patient may be eligible.

The next layer of the hospice team involves a variety of health care professionals and other key leaders in the community whose help may be called upon during the illness. A *psychiatrist* or *psychologist* may be needed to provide expert counseling help. *Nurses, home health aides,* and *homemakers* employed by public health nursing agencies—such as visiting nurse associations—may be needed to provide special continuing health care or to share in the provision of patient care. *Physical* and/or *occupational therapists* may be needed to work with the patient to ensure his or her maximum daily functioning. Finally, the services of a *lawyer* and/or *funeral director* may be required to help the patient settle personal affairs and provide for the needs of survivors after the death.

Artists are increasingly being recognized as important members of the hospice team. The Connecticut Hospice pioneered the development of an arts program based on the philosophy that the arts can help patients to find meaningful fulfillment during their last days. In many hospice programs, artists working in varied areas, such as metalwork, photography, pottery, drama, dance, and music, are paired with patients who are interested in such self-expression.

Trained *volunteers* constitute an essential part of the hospice team. Medicare reimbursement for hospice care is predicated on the requirement that volunteer time represent 5% of all patient care, thus no hospice can exist for long without a strong volunteer component. NHPCO-affiliated programs recruit volunteers from many sources: churches (94% recruit in churches), civic groups (80%), social groups (70%), professional organizations (65%), business and industry (47%), colleges (34%), and secondary schools (12%) (National Hospice Organization 1997).

Hospice volunteers include many different kinds of people, including housewives, students, retired persons, and professionals such as social workers, psychologists, teachers, gerontologists, members of the clergy, and architects (Chng and Ramsey 1984–85:240). Many volunteers have lost loved ones and find that hospice work provides them with an opportunity to serve others. Some volunteers are retired health care professionals, such as physicians or nurses. Others are nonprofessionals who are deeply interested in the needs of dying patients and their families. Each volunteer brings with him or her skills and experiences that can greatly enhance the life of a terminal patient (Chng and Ramsey 1984–85:240).

Before volunteers begin a hospice program's extensive training program, they are interviewed by the volunteer coordinator and may be asked to complete specially designed questionnaires that assess their feelings and sensitivity toward dying persons. Hospices also require volunteers to undergo an average of 22 hours of training before they are allowed to work directly with patients or patients'

families. In addition to this initial training, every hospice program requires volunteers to take part in regular in-service training to maintain and update their skills. The average hospice volunteer provides services for 3 years; 50% of volunteers stay for 6 or more years (National Hospice Organization 1997).

Some volunteers help with patient-care tasks, such as providing transportation, sitting with a patient to free family members to get out of the house for a while, carrying equipment, or providing bereavement counseling for family members after the death of the patient. However, according to Chng and Ramsey (1984–85), hospice volunteers primarily perform three roles: companion/friend, advocate, and educator. In 1992, the average hospice received 3,300 hours of service from volunteers. Nationwide, that translates into more than 5.25 million hospice volunteer hours—approximately two-thirds of which pertain directly to patient care (National Hospice Organization 1997).

In a national study of volunteers conducted in 1992, the National Hospice Organization (1993) found that 87% of volunteers were female and that 58% of these were 60 years of age or younger, compared with 53% of male volunteers. The vast majority of these volunteers had experienced the death of a significant other—most of them had had a parent who was cared for in a hospice program.

The hospice volunteer represents a double benefit in that the patient and family identify him or her as being knowledgeable, but without the kind of professional status that can create a social distance. In the hospice program where I volunteered, we referred to the volunteer's companion/friend role as being a "competent presence" or "safe place." As a stranger who provides a "listening ear," without emotional involvements or professional entanglements, the volunteer can support the patient and his or her family members in a way that no other participant in the social network of dying can.

The volunteer also functions in an advocate role by acting on behalf of the dying patient and the family. Sometimes patients and their loved ones are afraid to challenge or ask questions of physicians and other medical personnel. The volunteer who becomes a trusted friend and confidant can often speak up for the patient and family members and make their needs known to those responsible for their care. I once served as the primary volunteer for a male patient who was undermedicated. When the patient complained to his nurse regarding his pain, the nurse told him to "brave it out." Knowing the medical system, I was able to contact the appropriate individuals, who were, indeed, able to have the patient's pain medications reevaluated. As Chng and Ramsey (1984–85) observe:

> To be truly effective, the suggestions of the volunteer have to stem from knowledge and understanding of the intricate patient-family-institutional configurations. Under the careful guidance of professionals, the volunteer can serve a significant role as ancillary to professionals. (P. 240)

The final role served by the hospice volunteer is that of educator. Most individuals in our society have not had many personal experiences with death. The hospice volunteer can learn from each experience in working with dying patients and pass on insights that may be helpful to patients and their families. The volunteer can help the dying and their loved ones to understand that the dying process is usually complex, stressful, and disordered. In addition, most patients and their families have a strong need to have their feelings and experiences validated. The volunteer can assure patients and families who are having a difficult time understanding their feelings, emotions, and experiences during the dying process that they are "quite normal."

Within the community at large, there are a number of influences at work that either assist with patient care or help to make it possible. In hospice care, the patient's family members and friends are urged to participate in the patient's care as much as possible. When family members cannot provide as much care as may be needed at certain times, hospice personnel try to meet the patient's needs by exploring all possible options for doing so (National Hospice Organization 1988). The patient-family support system is the most significant factor in the dying process for many patients, but the system also often includes numerous close or distant relatives, friends, neighbors, members of local churches, and/or other civic groups.

Hospice programs are dependent on a high degree of community interest and support. To develop and maintain such interest and support, those who seek to establish a hospice program must undertake a well-planned public information campaign. They must sell the concept of hospice to the medical community and to other members of the larger community. Specific activities during this process require financial support (especially while the hospice program is being developed), and, in addition, those planning the hospice program must be willing to testify before regulatory agencies about the granting of hospice accreditation, Medicare certification, and/or approval to begin offering services to people in the area.

Patient-Centered Care

One of the distinguishing features of the hospice concept of care is that, whenever possible, hospice enables patients to make their own decisions about how and where they want to live their lives. Patient-centered care is non-judgmental, unconditional, and empowering.

One of the patients of the hospice program where I volunteered provides an example of this philosophy of care. This patient had adult children in town but lived as a single person with his dog. He had lung cancer and desired to die at home, alone. He was also a smoker and heavy alcohol drinker. Our hospice program agreed to honor the patient's desires whenever it was possible. Therefore, a hospice nurse visited his house every 4 hours, and members of the police department checked in on the patient every hour from 10:00 P.M. to 7:00 A.M. The patient's pain was kept

under control without sedation. A hospice volunteer (who also happened to be a licensed vocational nurse) visited the patient two or three times each day, and she, along with friends and family members, met the patient's requests for liquor and cigarettes. All visits from members of the hospice team never lasted longer than 10 minutes. The patient died as he wanted—in his home, free from pain, and in control of his own care.

Although not every member of the hospice team, or the patient's family, would have chosen to die as this patient did, everyone respected the patient's right to make decisions regarding his care. The hospice philosophy states that patients and their families have the right to participate in decisions concerning their care, and that caregivers should not judge those decisions based on their own beliefs.

Bereavement Care

Because the family is part of the unit of care, the responsibility of the caregiving organization does not stop when the patient dies. Hospice programs offer continuing bereavement follow-up to members of patients' families for as long as may be appropriate, and the vast majority of hospice patients and families accept these bereavement services.

Most hospice programs have bereavement teams, consisting primarily of interdisciplinary volunteers, that follow up on all family members after a patient dies or on those family members identified by the patient's interdisciplinary teams as possibly being at major risk for the development of serious problems. Often hospice programs offer such bereavement services to the community at large, not just to those families served directly by hospice.

Hospices work with a wide variety of community organizations (e.g., churches, hospitals, nursing homes, and community mental health agencies) in providing bereavement support. Among NHPCO-affiliated programs, 80% provide support group services, 67% offer memorial services, 63% provide educational programs to the community, 60% provide individual/family counseling; 43% provide crisis counseling, 35% provide specific services to children, and 15% provide emergency room support for children (National Hospice Organization 1997).

Hospice bereavement care has several goals (Boulder County Hospice 1985):

1. To assess the normal grief response

2. To assess individual coping mechanisms and stress levels

3. To assess support systems

4. To set up additional support (groups, individual therapy, visits by team members) when needed

5. To identify individuals at high risk and intervene appropriately

6. To make referrals for financial problems and medical care

In bereavement services, as in other aspects of hospice care, the art of listening is emphasized. Family members need someone who is willing to listen while they discuss their feelings. Bereavement team support may last for a year or more, although the team tries to encourage family members to stand on their own feet as soon as possible.

Persons Served by Hospice

Hospice care knows no age restrictions, but most patients (70%) are over 65 years of age—of the remaining, 29% are adults under 65, and 1% are children (National Hospice Organization 1997). Most hospices provide care for patients suffering from any illness with a time-limited prognosis. According to Bass, Garland, and Otto (1985–86):

> The "average" hospice patient is white, in his or her middle sixties, . . . is afflicted with a form of cancer and . . . is being taken care of by his or her spouse. The patients remain in the program for an average (mean) of forty-seven days. The profile of the "average" patient, while helpful in a number of ways, also conceals as much as it reveals. For example, while it is true that the average hospice patient is sixty-two years of age, there is a substantial segment of patients who are either much younger or older than this average. Further, evidence presented in our research suggests that younger-than-average patients have different experiences with hospice care (i.e., they remain in the program for a shorter period, receive fewer staff visits, and are more likely to die in a facility). (P. 67)

Patient eligibility criteria usually include a diagnosis of a terminal illness, a prognosis of 6 months or less, consent and cooperation of the patient's own physician, and a willingness to deal with the dying process in an open awareness context. Some 98% of hospices require that all patients sign informed consent forms, but only 40% require DNR (do not resuscitate) orders (National Hospice Organization 1997).

Home care for a patient is often most viable when a relative (or friend) who can be a primary caregiver lives in the home and can assume responsibility for patient care when the patient is unable to provide care for him- or herself. For inpatient care, hospices usually require that the patient need help with pain or symptom control. For these reasons, only 45% of hospices admit patients without primary caregivers, even though another 31% admit patients without caregivers on a case-by-case basis (National Hospice Organization 1997).

Special Aspects of Home Care

Given that 77% of American hospice patients die at home (National Hospice Organization 1997), one of the questions frequently raised by family members is what to do if an emergency develops in the middle of the night or on a holiday. Although most physicians and other health care professionals do not make house calls, hospice personnel do.

Home care for hospice patients is made viable by the fact that physicians and nurses are on call 24 hours a day, 7 days a week. This gives patients and their families confidence that they can manage at home.

Community physicians continue to be involved in the care of their patients, and usually remain primary caregivers, while the patients are receiving home care. Such community involvement relates the hospice program to the area in which it is located and tends to give hospice care greater visibility than is sometimes true of health care programs.

When a hospice patient is admitted for inpatient care, the patient's own physician turns over the care of the patient to a hospice physician but must be willing to resume care if the patient is able to return home. Whereas traditional medical care in recent years has tended to concentrate care in specialized hospitals or in nursing homes, hospice care returns the focus to the family.

Special Aspects of Inpatient Care

Because the family is the unit of care, inpatient hospice facilities must include sufficient space for large numbers of family members to congregate. In addition, such care requires a homelike environment—the aim is to make the facility as much like a home away from home as possible. Patients are encouraged to bring with them a few favorite possessions, such as photographs, a favorite chair, or plants.

No arbitrary time restrictions are placed on those wishing to see patients in a hospice facility—they may visit at any time of day or night. Visitors of any age, including young children, are welcome. Furthermore, family pets, such as dogs and cats, may visit as well. The goal of an inpatient hospice facility is to provide a homelike environment where the patient and his or her family can appreciate the joys of social relationships.

The inpatient facility of the Connecticut Hospice in Branford illustrates the above principles. The family room is off-limits to staff—it is provided solely for the comfort of family members. Hospice care places considerable emphasis on the tastiness, attractiveness, and nutritional value of the food prepared for patients, and the Connecticut Hospice employs a gourmet chef who trained in Paris to supervise the facility's food preparation. Kitchens complete with refrigerators, microwave ovens, stoves, and sinks are also available for use by patients' families. Washing machines are maintained for their use. Large living rooms with fireplaces are available. Twelve four-bed rooms for patients help to develop social support systems among family groups. The facility also includes four single bedrooms. Spacious corridors next to patient rooms are decorated with plants and provide areas for family gatherings. Beds may be moved around as family members desire—on a nice day, many are seen outside, on patios. A commons room and chapel are used not only for religious services but for presentations by various kinds of artists. A beauty parlor, operated by volunteers, is available to help patients feel better about themselves. The facility also includes a preschool for 3- and 4-year-old children of staff, volunteers, and people in the community. When a patient dies (14% of all hospice deaths in America occur within inpatient facilities; National Hospice Organization 1997), he or she is taken to a viewing room for the family members.

MODELS OF INPATIENT HOSPICE CARE

As of 1997, approximately 100 hospice inpatient facilities existed across the United States, with a total of 1,200 beds. Of these, approximately 72% were nonprofit facilities, 4% were government funded, and 15% were for-profit facilities; the funding status of the remaining 9% was unidentified. Among these inpatient facilities, 30% were independent community-based institutions; 51% were divisions of hospitals, nursing homes, or home health agencies; and 5% were divisions of hospice corporations; the remaining 14% fell into the "other" or "not identified" category (National Hospice Organization 1997).

The first model of hospice care, the *freestanding hospice,* is entirely independent—it works closely with other components of the health care system but employs its own staff and raises its own funds; 30% of hospices in the United States are of this type. The Connecticut Hospice is an example of an independent community-based facility. This 52-bed, freestanding inpatient facility and home-care program offers palliative care for those needing to have their pain and symptoms brought under control before returning home as well as intensive round-the-clock medical and nursing care for those who cannot be cared for at home.

The second model of inpatient hospice care is *hospice based in a hospital, nursing home,* or *home health agency;* 51% of all NHPCO-affiliated hospice programs are of this type. This model provides inpatient care within the physical plant of a hospital, nursing home, or home health agency. It also provides home care through its own home-care department, by arrangements made with a local public health nursing agency, or by its own staff employed for that purpose. The Northfield Hospice in Northfield, Minnesota, where I have served as a volunteer, is an example of a hospital-based program.

The third model of inpatient care is the *hospice corporation,* which provides inpatient care for profit through affiliated local and regional hospice agencies; 5% of all hospice programs in the United States are of this type. The largest and most well-known of these is the VITAS Healthcare Corporation, which has its headquarters in Miami, Florida; this corporation has provided palliative hospice care since 1978. VITAS has 19 affiliated programs in seven states (Florida, California, Texas, Illinois, Pennsylvania, Ohio, and Wisconsin). All VITAS hospice patients must have a prognosis of a life expectancy of 6 months or less and agree to a care plan that is palliative

rather than curative. The VITAS palliative care plan involves aggressive treatment of physical and emotional pain and symptoms. All such treatment focuses on enhancing the patient's comfort and quality of life. Like other hospice programs, VITAS employs a team approach, with teams made up of health care professionals and volunteers. Although VITAS is a for-profit corporation, it accepts Medicare and Medicaid as 100% coverage for its services, and patients have no additional out-of-pocket expenses. VITAS services are also paid for by private insurance plans. Annually, VITAS's approximately 4,900 full- and part-time employees serve more than 25,000 patients and their families (the average daily census is nearly 6,000 patients).

Hospice planning groups exist in virtually every major city, and in many smaller cities, across the United States. They range from discussion groups made up of interested citizens to fully developed freestanding hospice programs. Currently, there are more than 2,800 hospice programs in the United States. In the 1990s, the annual growth of new hospices averaged approximately 8%, and growth in the numbers of patients served by all hospices averaged 17% (National Hospice Organization 1997).

HOSPICE ISSUES

Some have called the development of hospice care a "people's movement." If existing health care programs had been meeting the needs of the dying and supporting their families throughout their periods of illness and bereavement, no one would have needed hospices. The hospice movement originated in local communities as a result of the desire of health care professionals and civic leaders to provide better care than was previously available. Many leaders of the movement envision eventually working themselves out of their jobs as the larger health care system adopts the principles of hospice care. In the meantime, however, hospices pose a number of critical issues for health care in the United States, in areas such as patient quality of life, the patient-family as the unit of care, the cost of hospice services, the training of professionals, and public attitudes.

Quality of Life

Proponents of the hospice movement proclaim that every human being has an inherent right to live as fully and completely as possible up to the moment of death. Some traditional health care professionals, emphasizing the curing of the patient at any cost, have ignored that right. Many physicians have been trained, for example, to emphasize restoring the patient to health. Accordingly, many patients are subjected to series of operations designed to prolong their lives even though curing them is sometimes impossible, as in the case of rapidly progressing cancer. Most hospice patients have had some surgery, chemotherapy, or radiation treatments. Some continue these even while they are hospice patients because the treatments provide some pain relief (radiation, for example, may reduce the size of a tumor and, therefore, reduce the patient's discomfort). There comes a point, however, if good quality of life is a goal, that the patient should refuse further surgery, seek ease of pain without curing, and attempt to live qualitatively rather than quantitatively. In hospice, cure goals for patients are changed to comfort goals, and all patients play a significant role in the health care decisions affecting them.

Because of this emphasis on quality of life, hospices pay attention to many different facets of pain reduction, including but not limited to physical pain. Hospice medical professionals have spent considerable time in developing a variety of methods of pain control that subdue not only what the patient describes as pain but also symptoms related to various illnesses. Much of this emphasis on pain control has developed despite the common practice in mainstream health care of sedating patients in pain. A patient who is "knocked out" or has become a "zombie" cannot experience a good quality of life. Hospice physicians try to find the point at which the patient's pain is managed, but the patient is not sedated. To provide this kind of pain management, hospices have had to conduct considerable retraining of health care workers.

Hospice staff and volunteers also deal with the social, psychological, financial, and spiritual pain of patients and their families. Outside of hospice care, a terminally ill patient may experience social abandonment or personal isolation that comes when friends and acquaintances stop visiting because they are unable to cope with issues of death, don't know about what to say or do, or simply are not aware of what the patient is experiencing. As Chng and Ramsey (1984–85) note, "In too many cases family members may inadvertently 'reject' the patient when confronted with the reality of death, while the professional staff may distance itself to avoid becoming too emotionally involved" (p. 237). Hospice workers can help a dying patient's family members and friends understand that the patient has a great need for social support and companionship at this time.

Patients and their families also often experience financial problems; many face large hospital and medical bills at a time when family income may also be diminished. In addition, many experience spiritual pain as they seek answers to existential questions and ponder the ultimate meaning and purpose of life in the face of suffering. "Why did God allow this to happen to me?" and "Why do bad things happen to good people?" are questions frequently asked by terminally ill patients and their families.

Hospice care makes the meeting of all the patient and family's needs—social, psychological, financial, and spiritual—a major priority. By doing this, hospice provides an alternative to the kind of health care found in most medical treatment centers. However, no health care professional can begin to meet the social, psychological, financial,

or spiritual needs of terminally ill patients (and their families) until he or she is comfortable with discussing death-related issues. If a physician, for example, is afraid of death or chooses to ignore it, he or she will find it difficult to enable patients to deal with the issues involved in dying.

The hospice movement also emphasizes the importance of the patient's environment to his or her quality of life (in this context, the term *environment* refers to the setting where provisions are made for the patient's needs). In hospice, patients receive care in their own homes or in inpatient facilities designed to be as homelike as possible. In contrast, the floor plans, decor, and furnishings found in most health care facilities have been designed for the convenience of staff rather than for the needs of patients.

A critical question is, What constitutes a good quality of life? What does an individual most want to accomplish or experience before he or she dies? When one of the patients I knew at Northfield Hospice was asked that question, he said that he had always wanted to take a helicopter ride. With the help of the local NBC television station, the hospice made his dream a reality. Like that patient, almost everyone has unfinished business in life. Some may wish to renew relationships with friends or family members with whom they've lost touch. Others may desire to put their own affairs in order, to write their memoirs, to plant a garden, to watch the sun set, or to plan their own funeral services.

The Patient-Family as Unit of Care

Traditional health care in the United States has long concentrated on the patient and ignored the patient's family. Perhaps many health care workers would say, if given an opportunity to state their opinions confidentially, that they would prefer that their patients' family members stay away. Traditional ideas about the appropriate ratios of physicians, nurses, social workers, or chaplains to those needing care have been based on the assumption that only the patients need attention. Although hospice staff, to be sure, are not given the responsibility of meeting the physical needs of all patients' family members, they do take tremendous care to address the social, psychological, and spiritual needs of patients' families.

Compared with the traditional health care system, hospices provide much higher ratios of professional staff members to patients served. For example, in the state of Connecticut, the public health code's regulations for hospice licensure stipulate that at all hours of the day and night, a hospice must have on duty at least one registered nurse for every six patients and at least one nursing staff member (licensed practical nurse or a nurse's aide and a registered nurse) for every three patients.

Family care, however, involves much more than numbers of staff. It requires that health care workers know how to cope with the fears, worries, tears, and turmoil of a terminally ill patient's family members; this includes knowing when to speak, when not to speak, and what to say. Hospice workers take the time to listen, to determine how they may be most helpful.

Hospice care is costly care due to the numbers of staff involved. It challenges society as a whole to give priority to such care because of the right of the dying to a good quality of life. In a traditional hospital setting, a nurse on a night shift must often struggle to meet the needs of perhaps an entire floor of patients; he or she is not able to take the time to sit with a dying patient for whom the nighttime is especially difficult. Nor does this nurse have the time to be of assistance to any dying patients' husbands, wives, or children as they struggle with grief.

In hospice care, each staff person is supported by the patient's interdisciplinary team as the various disciplines come into play in meeting family needs. For example, when a patient asks a night-shift nurse a question relating to spiritual care, the nurse might wish to give an answer at the time, but he or she can also rely on the team's chaplain as a resource to determine the best way to meet the patient's spiritual needs.

In hospice care, the patient-family unit is involved in all decision making concerning the patient's care. Caregivers who have worked mainly in traditional health care may find it difficult to adjust to such a system, as they may be accustomed to making decisions and having everyone go along with what they have decided.

Cost of Hospice Care

Even though hospice care is personalized to meet the needs of each patient (with each patient's care involving an entire team of professional and volunteer caregivers), it is also very cost-effective, because more than 90% of hospice care hours are provided in patients' homes, substituting for more expensive multiple hospitalizations. In a 1995 study commissioned by the National Hospice Organization (1997), the health care policy research organization Lewin-VHI found that for every dollar Medicare spent on hospice, $1.52 in expenditures was saved. Furthermore, in the last year of life, a hospice patient incurred an average of $1,786 less in costs than did an individual not in hospice care. When the time period examined was just the last month of life, the savings of the hospice patient totaled $3,192, as hospice home-care days often substituted for expensive hospitalizations.

Ideally, no prospective hospice patient may be turned away because of lack of money. Only 15% of all hospice programs are operated by for-profit organizations, and each year even these programs provide some care for patients who cannot afford to pay; in addition, most poor, underinsured, and uninsured families do receive some financial assistance. As of 1997, the sources of payment for hospice services broke down as follows: Medicare, 66.8%; private insurance, 14.6%; Medicaid, 9.1%; indigent

(nonreimbursed) care, 6.3%; and "other," 3.2% (National Hospice Organization 1997).

Medicare-eligible patients are insured for hospice care from Medicare-certified providers by the Medicare Hospice Benefit, which was enacted in 1982. To become Medicare certified, a hospice program must undergo a vigorous evaluation of the services it provides and must agree to provide the following services directly to patients: nursing care, medical social services, physician services, counseling, and volunteer services. As of 1997, 77% of all hospices in the United States were Medicare certified, and another 3% had pending applications (National Hospice Organization 1997).

The General Electric Company was the first major employer in the United States to provide a hospice benefit for its employees. Currently, coverage for hospice is included in the health insurance packages of more than 80% of employees in medium and large businesses. Furthermore, the majority of private insurance companies offer comprehensive hospice care benefit plans, and major medical insurance policies, provided through insurance companies and offered to employees as part of benefits packages, also underwrite hospice coverage in most instances. However, many hospice programs still rely on income from grants and donations to meet the needs of their patients and families as they provide services not covered by Medicare, Medicaid, and insurance reimbursements (National Hospice Organization 1997).

Proponents of the hospice movement hope to make it possible for any person of any age who suffers from a terminal illness to be eligible for coverage of the costs related to hospice care. They are also firm in their conviction that such care saves considerable money in the long run. Many patients who are currently hospitalized would not need to be if hospice services were available for them and their families. A basic question for Americans is whether, as a society, we believe enough in ensuring a good quality of life for the dying that we are willing to do whatever it takes to make that possible.

CONCLUSION

As the American way of life has become increasingly impersonal, dying has shifted from the home to the hospital or nursing home—away from kin and friends to a bureaucratized setting. The birth of the hospice movement in the United States might be considered a countermovement to this trend. As we seek out primary group relations in our largely individual-oriented society, more and more Americans are seeking to die in the setting of a familiar home rather than in the sterile environment of a hospital. Perhaps we are evidencing a return to a concern for each other—a new dignity in dying may be on the horizon.

Hospice represents a return to caring and compassion. It is a revival of neighbors helping neighbors—a concept so often lost in our urbanized society. Hospice consists of professionals literally going the extra mile, going to patients' homes when needed—medical personnel actually making house calls. Hospice, for example, encourages children under the age of 14 to be present with the terminally ill person rather than making them wait in the hospital lobby. Hospice is a grassroots movement springing up in small communities, as well as larger urban settings, to provide better health care. To paraphrase the words of Robert Kavanaugh (1972:19), the hospice concept of care helps us to unearth, face, understand, and accept our true feelings about death and provides us with opportunities for joyful living and dying as we choose. In short, hospice is a movement that can transform our awkwardness in death-related situations into a celebration of life.

With federal money now covering most hospice expenses, and with rigid government requirements in place for approval of hospice programs, the newest challenge for the hospice movement is to prevent hospice programs from being strangled by the bureaucracies from which they receive financial assistance. Hospice programs must also continue to make the patient-family unit the central focus of care, treating these clients in a nonjudgmental and unconditional manner and thus empowering them as autonomous human beings. Finally, given that 55% of all hospice programs do not admit patients who do not have primary caregivers, it is imperative that in the future hospice programs do more to make it possible to extend services to patients who are without such resources. These are the dying patients to whom Jesus was referring when he said, "Whenever you did these things for the least of these my brothers, you were doing them for me!" (Matthew 25:40).

REFERENCES

Bass, David M., T. Neal Garland, and Melinda E. Otto. 1985–86. "Characteristics of Hospice Patients and Their Caregivers." *Omega* 16:51–68.

Boulder County Hospice. 1985. *Bereavement Care Manual.* Boulder, CO: Boulder County Hospice.

Burns, Nancy, Kim Carney, and Bob Brobst. 1989. "Hospice: A Design for Home Care for the Terminally Ill." *Holistic Nursing Practice* 3(2):65–76.

Carr, William F. 1989. "Lead Me Safely Through Death." *America* 160(11):264–67.

Chng, Chwee Lye and Michael Kirby Ramsey. 1984–85. "Volunteers and the Care of the Terminal Patient." *Omega* 15:237–44.

Cohen, Kenneth. 1979. *Hospice: Prescription for Terminal Care.* Germantown, MD: Aspens Systems.

Connecticut Hospice. 1997. "About Hospice." Branford: Connecticut Hospice. Retrieved June 7, 2003(http://www.hospice.com/about.html).

Kavanaugh, Robert E. 1972. *Facing Death.* Baltimore: Penguin.

Leming, Michael R. 1979–80. "Religion and Death: A Test of Homans' Thesis." *Omega* 10:347–64.

Magno, Josefina B. 1990. "The Hospice Concept of Care: Facing the 1990s." *Death Studies* 14:3109–19.

National Hospice Organization. 1988. *The Basics of Hospice.* Arlington, VA: National Hospice Organization.

———. 1993. *1992 Annual Report.* Arlington, VA: National Hospice Organization.

———. 1997. "Hospice Fact Sheet." Arlington, VA: National Hospice Organization.

Phipps, William E. 1988. "The Origin of Hospices/Hospitals." *Death Studies* 12:91–99.

Saunders, Cicely. 1992. "The Evolution of the Hospices." *Free Inquiry* 12(Winter):19–23.

Stoddard, Sandol. 1978. *The Hospice Movement: A Better Way of Caring for the Dying.* New York: Vintage.

Dying in a Total Institution

The Case of Death in Prison

Francis D. Glamser

Donald A. Cabana

Over the past 100 years, Americans' common experience and social view of death have changed markedly. At the beginning of the 20th century, death was likely to occur at any age and was especially common among the very young. In 1900 in the United States, half of all deaths occurred among children under 15 years of age, and infant mortality rates were quite high by today's standards. Because deaths were usually the result of infections, diseases, or accidents, they could occur to anyone at any time, and they could occur suddenly. People usually died in bed at home.

Not only has the timing of death changed, but so have its causes and locations. Increasingly, death is caused by chronic diseases such as heart disease and cancer, which are concentrated among the elderly. Therefore, death is now most likely to occur in a hospital or nursing home. It is estimated that 45–50% of deaths in the United States occur in hospitals, and another 35% in nursing homes (Marshall 1980; Foley et al. 1995). This means that only about 25% of deaths occur in private homes.

These demographic and medical changes have served to remove death as a visible, normal part of life. In an earlier day, by the time a person reached adulthood, he or she had witnessed a great deal of death. Cemeteries adjacent to the churches and wakes held in private homes reinforced the omnipresence and inevitability of death. Now cemeteries are easily avoided, and wakes occur in funeral parlors, away from the eyes of the community. All of these changes make it easy for most Americans to deny death until well into middle age. People who are likely to die are placed in hospitals or nursing homes, and so are removed from their communities and the daily lives of others.

A similar situation exists in regard to prison inmates in general and to death in prisons in particular. We send criminals off to corrections facilities, many of which are located in remote areas, and the public does not have to think about them. When they die, the public does not have to know about it. Dying in prison is not something the average citizen ever thinks about. Older inmates and those with long sentences, however, think about it a great deal. For long-term inmates who have lost contact with the outside world, dying in prison is the ultimate confirmation of a wasted life. The fear of dying in prison haunts many inmates who see themselves as unlikely to survive their sentences.

Hospitals, nursing homes, and prisons are all what sociologists refer to as *total institutions,* a concept developed by Erving Goffman (1961). In such settings, all aspects of daily living are supervised and controlled by staff members. What inmates eat, when and where they sleep, what they wear, and what they are permitted to do are all beyond their control. Living under such circumstances is unpleasant at best. Dying in a total institution has become a common experience in the United States.

Until very recently, the issue of prison death was not very visible. Most inmates served relatively short terms, and few grew old enough in prison to produce a large number of deaths. As we will discuss below, a larger, older, and sicker inmate population has changed things. The increased incidence of a number of infectious diseases, such as AIDS, hepatitis, and tuberculosis, means that death in prison is no longer limited to the elderly. For many reasons, some practical and some humanitarian, the subject of dying in prison is worthy of investigation.

Life inside a penitentiary is a microcosm of the world that lies beyond prison walls. The world "inside" would, at first blush, give casual observers little cause to notice any similarities between themselves and the more than 2 million men and women who inhabit the nation's prisons and jails. A closer examination, however, reveals that prisoners and nonprisoners have many more traits in common than most citizens would be comfortable acknowledging. Like anyone else, inmates harbor hopes and dreams, suffer disappointments and failure, and dare to plan for the future, all the while haunted by their past missteps. Like the individuals who make up the rest of society, they are husbands and wives, fathers and mothers, ordinary people who, for various reasons, have been segregated and isolated from the general population.

Prison society, despite its many similarities to the outside world, is nevertheless a world unto itself. The captives live in an environment punctuated by brutality and violence, in a landscape often harsh and unforgiving. It is a world in which fear, especially the fear of death, often reigns supreme. As in any other community, inside the prison gates death is the great equalizer, and death frequently assumes forms and shapes that serve as a stark reminder of man's inhumanity to man and of human beings' great vulnerability.

Prisons possess unique qualities that separate them from the outside. They have their own language, argot, and slang. There is a clear socioeconomic pecking order, with customs and mores peculiar to the prison environment. Prisons even have their own systems of justice: There is the official system, the myriad rules, regulations, policies, and procedures promulgated by prison officials to govern inmate behavior and guide prison operations, and then there is the inmate system, one that leaves little room for error and is devoid of compassion or forgiveness. The inmate justice system is based on the simplest of predicates: The strong prevail, dominating the weak, with the weak finding a subclass of the weakest inmates to dominate. It is a system that enforces rules and regulations in a variety of ways: through fear tactics, intimidation, strongarming, threats, assault, extortion, and death. Enforcement of the rules is violent, frequently fatal, and can strike without warning.

One additional characteristic that helps define the nature of the penitentiary is magnification. Virtually every facet of prison life is affected by magnification. The unrelenting stresses in prison, feeding off of paranoia, fear, and violence, create an environment in which everything becomes exaggerated. The most insignificant events quickly become larger than life. A simple headache becomes a migraine, a stomachache becomes a malignancy, an unpaid debt involving a soda pop or a package of crackers becomes a death sentence.

Death and dying in a prison setting take on the numerous shapes and forms found in any society, with one noteworthy exception: executions. Death by violence, suicide, terminal illness, aging, and disease are common in prisons, but prison officials are currently being forced to cope with significant changes in the mix of causes of prison deaths. The graying of the nation's prison population will continue to have an impact on the role of death and dying inside the walls, but death by violence and suicide will always loom large.

Between 1988 and 1994, the number of prison deaths per year in the United States doubled, from 1,449 to 2,986, while the prison population increased by only 50%. Since 1994, the number of deaths annually has hovered around 3,000 (Camp and Camp 2000). Initially, this disproportionate increase can be explained by the rapid increase in deaths related to AIDS among inmates. More recently it reflects the culmination of the dramatic growth of the prison population in the United States over the past two decades and the higher proportion of long sentences. The net effect is that increasing numbers of inmates are growing old in prison, and more are dying. Although the proportion of prisoners who die in any one year is low (slightly more than 2 per 1,000), the prison system must respond to the absolute number of deaths.

The numbers and percentages of prisoners who are serving long sentences have been growing since the 1980s. The most dramatic growth has been in the absolute numbers of prisoners serving long sentences. Merianos et al. (1997) identify three long-term prisoner groups: natural lifers, life-sentenced prisoners, and those sentenced to 20 years or more. Although many prisoners assigned to the last two categories may not serve their entire terms, many of them will grow old in prison, and some of them will die there.

A look at the change in the numbers of prisoners serving long sentences between 1986 and 1995 makes it clear why the numbers of people dying in prison have remained high in spite of a great reduction in AIDS deaths. In 1986, approximately 85,000 prisoners were serving one of the three categories of long sentences noted above. They constituted 17% of the total prison population. By 1995, the number of long-term inmates had grown to more than 246,350, representing 25% of the total prison population (Merianos et al. 1997).

The aging of the prison population is partially the result of changes in sentencing policies throughout the United States. Increases in crime during the 1980s and early 1990s created a demand for longer sentences, truth in sentencing laws, and "three strikes" laws. Although most prisoners leave prison within a few years, the number of those who do not has been steadily increasing (Merianos et al. 1997).

Currently, more than 100,000 inmates age 50 or older are housed in state and federal prisons; of these, 35,000 are age 65 or older. Inmates age 50 or older now account for 8.6% of the prison population, up from 5.3% in 1991 (Camp and Camp 2000; Cohn 1999). Researchers have identified three categories of older prisoners: (a) inmates who are serving life sentences, who have grown old in prison; (b) inmates who have long histories of repeated incarcerations; and (c) inmates who have been convicted of criminal offenses late in life (see, e.g., Aday 1994). It is estimated that as many as 50% of older inmates are first-time offenders, most of whom were sent to prison at or above the age of 60. These older inmates have usually committed crimes against persons (Aday 1994).

Most first-time offenders, of course, are young; in 1999, the average age of initial incarceration was 31.8. However, the average age of first-time offenders has increased almost 2 years since 1991 (Camp and Camp 2000). As crime rates have increased over the past two decades and the U.S. population has aged, numbers of arrests of older people for serious offenses have increased greatly. Because judges now often have less latitude in sentencing than they had in the past, more of these older offenders go to prison, and some will die there.

NATURAL CAUSES

Because of lifestyle and socioeconomic factors, older inmates tend to be in poorer health than their counterparts on the outside, and they develop health problems much earlier. Inmates often come from the poorest segments of society, and they exhibit a high incidence of such health problems as hepatitis, tuberculosis, diabetes, hypertension, cancer, emphysema, asthma, arthritis, stroke, and, in recent years, acquired immune deficiency syndrome (AIDS). They are also more likely to have been exposed to alcohol abuse, heroin use, amphetamine use, and tobacco than persons on the outside (Marquart et al. 1997).

Given these kinds of health problems, which have their roots largely in lifestyle and environmental factors associated with poverty, a prisoner with a chronological age of 50 may exhibit the health problems of a much older person on the outside (Cohn 1999). Thus the mortality associated with an aging prison population begins to become evident in a relatively brief period of time.

The inmate who has grown old while serving time may be housed with the prison's general population or, increasingly, in a unit specifically designed for geriatric and/or disabled inmates. Such an inmate may die unexpectedly in the unit or in the acute care facility following complications of chronic illness. If the inmate unexpectedly expires in the housing unit, the unit officers begin CPR while summoning security and alerting the acute care facility. Sudden death is handled the same as other deaths. Health care personnel continue resuscitation efforts even as the inmate is removed by ambulance to the prison hospital. If the inmate expires, the prison's security department and administration are notified, and then the usual procedures for contacting the inmate's family are initiated.

An inmate who dies of terminal illness while in custody may have lingered for months. In these circumstances, prison officials must deal with the same issues that would be relevant for a terminally ill patient in the free world. Decisions and final instructions must be communicated by the inmate and/or his family concerning resuscitation and life-support measures. Very often, the inmate has either outlived all of his family members or has not had contact with them for many years. Like many geriatric inmates, those who are terminally ill often have no home but the penitentiary. In essence, the prison staff has become their family. The absence of family or friends

at the bedside of a dying inmate is a stark reminder of the custodial surroundings. The second author of this chapter (a former state penitentiary warden) recalls visiting with one older inmate who was dying of cancer and had but a few days to live. He recalls how profoundly saddened he was because he had known the inmate for more than 20 years. It was like losing a family member. Tearfully, the inmate laughed and said what a shame it was that a man lying on his deathbed had to call his warden the only family he had.

Because many inmates who are terminally ill have lost contact with family members, other inmates and prison staff must fulfill that role. This means that there are no family members to claim the body or make final arrangements. At the Louisiana State Penitentiary in Angola, when an inmate must be buried on the prison grounds because no one claims his body, the inmates build the casket as well as plan and conduct the funeral service, which can be very moving. When such services are held, inmates are permitted to attend, and some funerals are very well attended by both inmates and staff.

The data displayed in Table 1 show the growing importance of natural deaths in prisons over time as the prison population ages. As the table shows, the total numbers of deaths annually are roughly comparable over the period in question; that is, the absolute numbers of deaths overall are fairly stable. The table also shows that the proportion of deaths attributable to natural causes has been rising as the proportion attributable to AIDS has been falling. This shift is almost one for one in terms of both percentages and absolute numbers. Although the total number of inmate deaths per year was fairly stable between 1994 and 1999, these annual figures are more than double the number in 1988, when 1,449 prisoners died. The sharp rise in the numbers of inmate deaths between 1988 and 1994 was caused by the increasing incidence of AIDS among prisoners, especially in large states (e.g., New York, Florida, California, and Texas). The continuation of this higher level of mortality may be attributed to the growing population of older inmates, as indicated by the increased numbers of deaths from natural causes.

Table 1 Percentages of Prison Deaths by Cause, 1995–99

Cause	1995	1996	1997	1998	1999
Natural	53.6	58.8	66.5	68.6	73.2
AIDS	33.1	38.6	17.5	10.0	10.1
Suicide	5.4	5.1	5.8	10.4	5.8
Homicide	2.4	2.1	2.6	2.9	2.0
Other	5.5	5.4	7.5	8.1	8.7
Total deaths	3,345	3,284	3,040	2,991	3,213

SOURCE: Adapted from Camp and Camp (2000:30-33).
NOTE: Figures shown are totals for state, federal, and Washington, D.C., prisons. The "other" category includes unknown/other causes, executions, accidents, and escape attempts.

AIDS

As we have noted, the increase in prison deaths between 1988 and 1994 is related to the large increase in the numbers of inmates dying from AIDS-related causes. The late 1980s witnessed an epidemic of illicit drug use among the urban poor in the United States at the same time the human immunodeficiency virus (HIV) was spreading within the general population. Among needle-sharing drug users the virus spread easily, and many of the victims found their way into the prison system. At one point, 18% of men coming into New York State correctional facilities tested HIV-positive. As of 1999, it was estimated that 3% of all inmates in the United States were infected with HIV (Greifinger 1999).

AIDS-related deaths in U.S. prisons reached a peak of 1,010 in 1995. By 1999, the number had fallen to 242. This decrease can be attributed to the availability of better and more effective treatments for HIV/AIDS, in spite of the fact that inmate populations have continued to grow, as have the numbers of HIV-positive prisoners, although somewhat more slowly. The current HIV infection rate is 3.4% among female inmates in state prisons; among male inmates, the rate is 2.1% (Kohn, Hasty, and Henderson 2001). The rate of HIV infection among prisoners is approximately 20 times that found in the general population (Marquart et al. 1997).

SUICIDE

Suicide poses a constant threat in the prison setting, especially in the late fall and early winter months, which include the holiday season. Inmate suicides can be profoundly disturbing for several reasons. First, of course, they are extremely unpleasant. Inmates frequently hang themselves with shoestrings (a slow, agonizing death by strangulation), slash their wrists, arms, or throats, or even run themselves headfirst into concrete walls.

In such situations, when an inmate is found without any visible signs of life, the officers must immediately notify both prison health care and security officials. If the inmate has obviously been dead for more than 5 minutes, resuscitation efforts are not initiated. The area is sealed off to maintain the integrity of evidence, and the coroner is summoned to initiate an investigation and to determine officially whether the death is a result of suicide or foul play. The inmate's body is not disturbed until the coroner and prison investigators have thoroughly examined the body and the scene.

Occasionally, however, even the most stringent rules of evidence and procedure are not followed. A young inmate in a southern prison known to the second author was serving a life sentence for murdering his wife's lover. The young man had been on antidepressants and was on suicide watch continuously. Despite the prison's best efforts, the inmate committed suicide early one morning by hanging himself with a shoelace and slashing his wrists and arms. In his shirt pocket was found a copy of divorce papers that he had received the day before. Also in his pocket was a picture of himself with his wife and 3-year-old daughter. On the back of the photograph he had penned the words "so much pain." The prison officers, who had worked with the young man and liked him, were so upset by his death that, with the warden's permission, they cut him down before the coroner arrived. In their view, leaving him to hang there was unnecessarily degrading.

In most cases, however, the scene is secured and evidence is collected, including photographs. The position of the body and any objects around the body that could have resulted in death (e.g., pills, rope, sheets, razor blades, shoestrings) are examined as part of the effort to determine the cause of death. If the coroner finds the death to be a suicide, the body is shipped to the state medical examiner for an autopsy, as required by law. The prison investigators then continue to collect evidence and interview other inmates and staff. A key aim of the investigation is to determine whether or not staff interventions could have prevented the death.

Any inmate who expresses or is reported to have expressed suicide ideation is placed on suicide watch. The ramifications of such a move can be profound for the inmate, who may be moved to a bare cell in an electronically monitored psychiatric unit where professional health care staff can observe him or her. Living this way indefinitely can become debilitating for the inmate, but the primary purpose of suicide watch is to prevent the inmate's death.

Suicide is the third leading individual cause of inmate deaths in state and federal correctional facilities, accounting for about 6% of all deaths (Camp and Camp 2000). However, suicide remains the leading cause of death in jails among inmates who are facing the initial stages of incarceration and who are often under the influence of drugs or alcohol (Hayes 1995). It is interesting to note that in Australia, suicide is the leading cause of death among prison inmates, at 47% (Dalton 1999). The reasons for the high proportion of deaths attributable to suicide in that country's prisons are unknown, but it may be a function of Australia's relatively young inmate population and the very low incidence of AIDS among prisoners. It may also reflect a relatively good state of health among persons who enter the prison system.

Although in the United States suicide is much less common in prisons than in jails, it remains a relatively constant cause of death in U.S. prisons. In general, prisoners who commit suicide do so in the early years of their confinement. They are usually housed alone at the time of their suicide, and they often have histories of prior attempts and/or mental illness. Precipitating events may include new legal problems, marital or relationship difficulties, and conflicts with other inmates (Hayes 1995).

The numbers of suicides in most state correctional systems are relatively low compared with deaths due to health-related causes. In 1999, 39 states reported 5 or fewer suicides in state prisons, and only 5 states reported 10 or more suicides (Camp and Camp 2000). These low numbers may be attributed to increasing awareness of suicide prevention in the corrections field (Hayes 1995). Lindsay Hayes provides an excellent overview of a prison suicide prevention program in a 1995 article on suicide in adult correctional facilities. He reviews and explains the importance of inmate assessment, communication among staff members and inmates, housing decisions, inmate supervision, prompt intervention, reporting, and follow-up.

EXECUTION

Nothing is more surreal in the penitentiary than a death by execution. It is a time of stress and tension for inmates and staff alike. The violent murders that take place in prisons are shocking, the deaths of terminally ill and geriatric inmates are sad conclusions to largely failed lives, and inmate suicides are testimony to the fragile nature of our existence. All of these kinds of deaths, in their own way, have profound effects on prison staff who have come to know the victims over the course of their years in prison. However, executions are different from any other kind of death. It is interesting, but perhaps not surprising, that most wardens who are called on to carry out executions are ambivalent, at best, about the death penalty.

Condemned prisoners may spend a decade or longer awaiting their fate. In theory, prison staff are not supposed to get close to inmates. In practice, it is all but unavoidable. For this reason alone, most wardens do not permit death row officers to be part of the execution team.

Over the years, prison officials have developed procedures for carrying out executions; in any given prison, these procedures are referred to collectively as the execution protocol. The protocol consists of every eventuality that must be covered for an execution to be carried out properly. The amount of planning required is enormous. The warden must designate staff volunteers for various duties on the execution team. This task alone is both time-consuming and stressful, as the warden attempts to strike a delicate balance in selecting staff who are volunteers, but not eager volunteers.

The inmate must be asked to decide on a menu for a last meal and on funeral arrangements following the execution. If the inmate has no family or anyone else to claim the body, the prison must arrange for burial in a prison cemetery. The warden must also determine if the inmate wishes to be sedated just prior to the execution. Such topics are not the stuff of normal conversation.

Arrangements must be made for the inmate's family, if any, to have a final visit. The second author, a former warden, recalls a mother's tearful good-bye with a son who was scheduled for execution in a few days. As she turned to leave, she looked at the warden and pleaded with him not to kill her child. He has described that moment as the single most difficult of his long career in corrections.

If prison officials are not already deeply stressed by the plethora of details they must attend to in preparing for an execution, they are likely to become so when they conduct the execution rehearsals. The various U.S. states employ five different methods of execution: electrocution, hanging, firing squad, gas chamber, and lethal injection. Each method has its own idiosyncratic nuances that prison officials must contend with, and each gives officials cause for concern, because nothing, absolutely nothing, causes more stress than the possibility of a botched execution. Endless questions and scrutiny from the media, the knowledge that the inmate died a needlessly agonizing death, criticisms from capital punishment opponents and self-serving politicians—all these add up to a warden's worst nightmare. So regardless of the method employed, rehearsals are a grotesque necessity.

Hanging a condemned inmate correctly is practically a science. The knot must be placed in exactly the right location under the jaw, the weights must be precise, the trapdoor must operate efficiently. The electric chair, under the best of circumstances, is ripe for human and/or mechanical errors. If the wiring is not done correctly, the chair will either not work at all or, worse yet, severely burn and otherwise injure the condemned prisoner without causing unconsciousness. The gas chamber is the most dangerous and complex of the five methods. Most prisons that use gas chambers for executions include in their execution protocols checklists of some 40 procedures that must be done correctly and in a particular order. One mix-up, one batch of chemicals in the wrong proportions, and the prison officials' worst fears will come true. Lethal injection and the firing squad pose fewer risks for error than do other methods, but neither is completely foolproof.

Following an execution, the coroner is required to establish the cause of death. Once the inmate has been pronounced dead, the body is stripped, bathed, and dressed in clean prison clothing. If the gas chamber is the instrument of death, officials are required to wait from 10 to 15 minutes after the inmate expires before the chamber can be unsealed. At that time, officers dressed in protective rubber gear and wearing gas masks to prevent contact with the cyanide poisoning unceremoniously wash the body down with a garden hose. The body is then dressed and turned over immediately to a private funeral home.

In terms of total numbers, execution ranks between suicide and homicide as a cause of death in U.S. prisons. In 1999, the 95 executions carried out accounted for 3% of all deaths in prisons. More than half of all executions that year occurred in two states: Texas (35) and Virginia (14). The most common number of executions in a state for 1999 was zero, as was the case in 33 states. Only 5 states reported more than 4 executions that year. As a cause of death in prison in any given state, execution is uncommon (Camp and Camp 2000).

HOMICIDE

As in any other community, in prisons violent death occurs in many different ways; in prisons, however, such deaths often include a degree of brutality and callousness seldom found in the outside world. The perpetrators of violent deaths in prisons frequently intend to degrade and disrespect their victims. Although inmates and staff frequently claim to be immune to the effects of violence, some violent deaths in prisons can shake even the most hardened officers and inmates. In one incident that took place in a midwestern maximum-security prison, a long-simmering dispute between two inmates spilled over at the breakfast table one morning. Seated at one end of the dining hall, the two men began to quarrel. Challenges and threats were issued, and without warning each one pulled out a shank, a homemade knife. Almost before officers had time to react, other inmates sitting nearby began to scatter, some shouting encouragement to the two combatants, others excitedly calling the officers to intervene. As quickly as it started, the dispute ended with one of the men being decapitated. When all the other prisoners had put as much distance as possible between themselves and the assailant, there remained one man sitting at the table where the murdered, headless inmate was slumped forward into his tray of food. The man was an older prisoner, his craggy features and prison-made tattoos betraying the ravages of his long sentence. Unaffected by the commotion around him, he continued to eat his breakfast. Suddenly, to the horror of staff and inmates alike, he grabbed the decapitated head by the hair and disgustedly tossed it over his shoulder, cursing it for getting blood on his food. The most chilling aspect of violent death in prison is the unwritten maxim of the inmate code: Don't interfere.

Most states have very stringent laws concerning the investigation of violent death in prison. Wherever the death occurs, whether in a cell or out on the prison yard, the area must be handled as any other crime scene would. Physical evidence must be gathered and preserved, a chain of evidence maintained, witnesses (both inmate and staff) interviewed, and proper authorities notified. Although prison internal affairs investigators may conduct the preliminary investigation, once it becomes clear that a crime has been committed, an independent law enforcement agency (usually the state police) is called in. Violent death scenes present a dilemma for prison officials. On the one hand, officials are required to make sure such scenes are handled as any murder scene would be; on the other hand, they want to return a sense of normalcy to prison operations as quickly as possible. Neither inmates nor staff want to have to see the body of a murdered inmate lying around for several hours, but very often that is exactly what happens. The body cannot be moved until the coroner arrives and officially pronounces the inmate dead. Following removal of the body from the crime scene, it is transported to the prison hospital, where it is bathed, given a change of clothing, fingerprinted, photographed, and tagged. The body is then transported to a state medical examiner for an autopsy. Only after an autopsy is completed is the body released to a funeral home of the inmate's family's choice for burial. If no one claims the body, prison officials must provide a funeral service and burial in the prison cemetery.

For prison officials, perhaps the most difficult part of a violent death in prison is the responsibility of contacting the deceased inmate's family. Frequently this task is left to a prison chaplain, but not when the murder victim is a prison employee, an eventuality that all wardens dread.

The general public tends to overestimate the frequency of homicide as a cause of death in prisons. Since 1994, homicides have accounted for less than 3% of all prison deaths in the United States, and in 1999 only 21 states recorded 1 or more homicides in correctional facilities. Of the 3,213 inmate deaths in 1999, only 65 were homicides (Camp and Camp 2000). That said, some states and some specific facilities have much higher than average prison homicide rates. The states in which this was true in 1999 include California, Colorado, Maryland, Mississippi, Oklahoma, Oregon, South Carolina, and Tennessee. Because the absolute numbers of prison homicides tend to be very low (only 5 states had 4 or more in 1999), small variations from one year to the next can have large, perhaps misleading, effects on percentages. On the other hand, some facilities do have reputations for being particularly dangerous.

The importance of prison management and leadership in controlling inmate violence may be seen in the case of the Louisiana State Penitentiary at Angola, which used to be one of the most dangerous corrections facilities in the United States. Angola houses more than 5,000 long-term inmates, of whom 85% are unlikely to leave alive. One career guard told the first author that he could remember the bad old days, when killings occurred almost once a month. Now, a year can pass without a homicide, as was the case in 1999.

END-OF-LIFE CARE

The dramatic increase in prison deaths that began in the late 1980s, primarily as a result of the AIDS epidemic, generated a great deal of interest in end-of-life care for prisoners. Continued high levels of mortality brought about by longer sentences and an aging prison population mean that prisons must have procedures in place to deal with the needs of dying prisoners. One response to those needs is hospice care.

The aim of hospice care is to assist dying persons to die with dignity and with a minimum of pain. Hospice programs provide emotional support for terminally ill patients and their family members in the final months of life. Such programs are now available in most communities, but their introduction into prisons is relatively recent. As of 2001, 19 states had at least one hospice program in a correctional setting, and 14 additional states had programs under development ("Growing Movement" 2002).

Offering hospice care in a prison involves dealing with many problems not encountered in home hospice care. Issues of security, drug use, inmate autonomy, visitation, and volunteer selection can all present challenges in a prison setting. Getting inmates to enroll in a hospice program can also be problematic. Admitting that one's condition is terminal means accepting dying in prison—something most inmates fear. For younger prisoners who assume or hope they will be released someday, the fear of death is the fear of a sudden and violent death that will deny them a chance at freedom. Older inmates see dying in prison as the final degradation and the ultimate confirmation of a failed life. They will die in isolation, with no chance for redemption or reconciliation. Furthermore, accepting help amounts to an admission of vulnerability, which is difficult for inmates who have learned the importance of appearing tough (Price 1999). The National Prison Hospice Association addresses the special problems associated with hospice programs in correctional settings.

COMPASSIONATE RELEASE

In an earlier day, when prison deaths were not as common and the numbers of sick and aged prisoners were not as high as they have been in recent years, parole boards might have released older dying prisoners to spend their final days outside the prison walls. Today, because of increases in the numbers of prisoners sentenced to life without the possibility of parole, and particularly because of growing public sentiment against parole, such compassionate releases have become far less common.

Faced with the highest prison HIV infection rate in the country, the New York State Legislature passed the Medical Parole Law in 1992. This law was designed to allow dying prisoners who are no threat to the community to be released early. For an inmate to qualify for possible release, the law requires that a physician certify that the inmate is so debilitated as to be beyond self-care and is unlikely to recover. The physician must also certify that the inmate is incapacitated to the point of being incapable of presenting a threat to society. The state parole board then reviews the case. Only about 20% of all requests for release made under this law are granted (Beck 1999).

Death maintains a constant presence in prison, whether through violence, aging, disease, or the purposeful, methodical means ordered by the courts. Executions may make the news briefly, but most of the dying that occurs in prisons is hidden from view. It is experienced by people who, by and large, have already been removed from the outside community and from public consciousness. However, it is not removed from the staff or inmates of our prisons. For these people it is real, and it affects them deeply.

REFERENCES

Aday, Ronald. 1994. "Aging in Prison: A Case Study of New Elderly Offenders." *International Journal of Offender Therapy and Comparative Criminology* 38:80–91.

Beck, John. 1999. "Compassionate Release From New York State Prisons: Why Are So Few Getting Out?" *Journal of Law, Medicine & Ethics* 27:216–33.

Camp, Camille and George Camp. 2000. *The 2000 Corrections Yearbook: Adult Corrections.* Middletown, CT: Criminal Justice Institute.

Cohn, Felicia. 1999. "The Ethics of End-of-Life Care for Prison Inmates." *Journal of Law, Medicine & Ethics* 27:252–59.

Dalton, Vicki. 1999. "Death and Dying in Prison in Australia: National Overview, 1980–1998." *Journal of Law, Medicine & Ethics* 27:269–75.

Foley, Daniel, Toni Miles, Dwight Brock, and Caroline Phillips. 1995. "Recounts of Elderly Deaths: Endorsements for the Patient Self-determination Act." *Gerontologist* 35:119–21.

Goffman, Erving. 1961. *Asylums: Essays on the Social Situation of Mental Patients and Other Inmates.* Garden City, NY: Doubleday.

Greifinger, Robert. 1999. "Commentary: Is It Politic to Limit Our Compassion?" *Journal of Law, Medicine & Ethics* 27:234–37.

"A Growing Movement." 2002. *Correct Care* 16(Spring):18.

Hayes, Lindsay. 1995. "Prison Suicide: An Overview and a Guide to Prevention." *Prison Journal* 75:431–56.

Kohn, Carol, Susan Hasty, and C. W. Henderson. 2001. "Aids Deaths in Prisons Fall Sharply." *AIDS Weekly*, July 6, pp. 15–16.

Marquart, James, Dorothy Merianos, Jamie Hebert, and Leo Carroll. 1997. "Health Condition and Prisoners: A Review of Research and Emerging Areas of Inquiry." *Prison Journal* 77:184–208.

Marshall, Victor. 1980. *Last Chapters: A Sociology of Aging and Dying.* Monterey, CA: Brooks/Cole.

Merianos, Dorothy, James Marquart, Kelly Damphousse, and Jamie Hebert. 1997. "From the Outside In: Using Public Health Data to Make Inferences About Older Inmates." *Crime & Delinquency* 43:298–313.

Price, Cheryl. 1999. "To Adopt or Adapt? Principles of Hospice Care in the Correctional Setting." *NPHA News, Newsletter 6*, Spring.

FORMAL AND INFORMAL CAREGIVING AT THE END OF LIFE

PAMELA J. KOVACS

DAVID P. FAURI

Persons admitted to health care institutions for acute, chronic, and emergency care who are dying receive care from a range of persons—professional staff, volunteers, family members, and friends. Institutionally based care is provided in hospitals, nursing homes, and hospice and palliative care units. Home-based care is also an option, with the assistance of home health care services, hospice, and family and other loved ones. The responsibilities of caregiving are often shared between formal and informal caregivers, including medical professionals, specialized auxiliary staff, volunteers, and family members. Health care professionals, especially in institutional settings, are increasingly limited by time and cost constraints in tending to the medical as well as the psychosocial needs of dying patients and their families.

Regardless of cause or setting, and depending on the nature and circumstances surrounding the death, a variety of caregivers may be involved in helping with the dying process. The word *caregiver* is used to describe both those who provide help on a formal basis (e.g., professionals and trained volunteers) and those whose help is provided more informally (e.g., family members, friends, neighbors, and others who are not associated with health care organizations but who have personal connections to the patient and/or family). (We use the hospice definition of *family:* "All those in loving relationships with the person who is dying, the people who can be counted on for caring and support, regardless of blood or legal ties"; Lattanzi-Licht, Mahoney, and Miller 1998:29.) By improving our understanding of the complexity of caregiving, we can enhance the care of the dying and better support those who provide that care.

In this chapter, we examine the variety of roles performed by formal and informal caregivers in assisting persons who are dying in health care institutions or at home with hospice and home health care services. We explore the influence of the institutional setting on caregivers and the roles of formal and informal caregivers, including how these are influenced by social, cultural, and technological factors. Although caregivers often derive professional and/or personal satisfaction from providing care to dying persons, they may experience stress themselves; therefore, we address how caregiver support in the form of resources and training can aid them in their efforts to provide compassionate and effective care.

In our multicultural society, professional caregivers face the challenge of maintaining cultural sensitivity and competence in their work with patients and families. We acknowledge that extensive variation exists among cultures in regard to the dying process, and we discuss this briefly, but other chapters in this handbook address the impact of culture on dying more directly. We discuss the more traditional caregiving model in health care institutions, which originates from a Western or Eurocentric tradition, because that is the reality most Americans experience.

THE CHANGING ROLE OF HEALTH CARE INSTITUTIONS IN THE DYING PROCESS

In 2000, the majority of deaths in the United States occurred in health care institutions, mainly hospitals (50%) and nursing facilities (25%). The remaining 25% died at home. Of those deaths occurring at home, some were sudden deaths and accidents and approximately 14% were anticipated deaths under hospice care (National Hospice and Palliative Care Organization 2002). Prior to the 20th century, it was more common for death to occur at home, with care provided by family members and neighbors, perhaps supplemented by visits to the home from a local physician. This change in place of death has affected the roles that formal and informal caregivers play in the dying process. In the past, generations of family members surrounded the dying person, keeping a "vigil," and managed funeral preparations, including preparing the body. Visitation and viewing of the body often took place in the home rather than in a funeral parlor. The modern-day use of the term *funeral home* and the decor found in such facilities draws heavily on the family home setting, suggesting comfort and warmth.

Caregiving in this earlier era was less of an option and more of an understood personal and family responsibility. In contrast, with advancements in modern medicine, people began to observe rather than participate as caregivers in the dying process, deferring more often to professionals in institutional settings. A desire to return to these home-based practices of caring for the dying has spurred the growth of the hospice movement in the United States since 1974; today, more than 3,000 hospices are in operation across the country, serving most communities. However, for a variety of reasons, including availability, the wishes of patients and their families, and causes of death, hospice was involved in fewer than 15% of all U.S. deaths in 2000 (National Hospice and Palliative Care Organization 2002). Hence the majority of Americans die somewhere other than home.

Several factors account for the shift in American society from traditional family caregiving to institutionally based caregiving. First is the belief that life can be prolonged in health care institutions through scientifically based care (Fins 1999). The technology of medical monitoring and treatment has become standard for persons who are seriously ill or dying. Second is a general discomfort with discussing and acknowledging death, which in some cases leads to denial about the reality of impending death. Like mental illness, physical illness and decline are viewed as unpleasant and uncomfortable reminders of our vulnerability and mortality. Medical institutions provide the benefits of science and technology for the dying while at the same time separating family members and loved ones from aspects of death that may be physically and/or emotionally difficult. Medical professionals are looked to for help in managing death and easing the dying process for the patient and family. The third factor contributing to the prominence of institutional caregiving is the increasing mobility of the U.S. population. Fewer families experience the immediate and local support of multigenerational, extended families today than in the past. As young people move away and older family members remain behind or relocate during retirement, the availability of family caregivers is often compromised, causing greater dependence on formal caregivers. Fourth, due to the trend toward smaller family size, fewer adult children are available to share the caregiving responsibilities for older adults (Moen, Robison, and Fields 1994). The fifth contributing variable is the fact that more Americans are living longer,

often outliving those who would be their caregivers (spouses or partners, adult children, and friends) at the very time their caregiving needs increase.

Health care institutions are formalized in nature, with emphasis on routine and prescribed ways of accomplishing goals. The institutional setting provides symbolic functions concerning how care is given and how death is processed. Caregiving for the dying in medical institutions involves a specialized, structured social process governed by professionals and influenced by their training and prescribed roles, as well as by the rules and procedures of the institutional setting (Rosenberg 1987).

The quality of care that professional caregivers provide to the dying person and the support they provide to the patient's family and loved ones depend on the professionals' orientation toward death and dying, their roles in the process, and the degree to which the institution supports their work in this area. Providing health care under the pressures of cost control and managed care puts a premium on efficiency in staff utilization. This creates stress for professional care providers when they see the need to take time with a dying patient and the patient's family members but find it difficult to do so because of demands to see other patients or to justify time spent with family members.

Standardized care and routines in institutions replace the more personalized care provided in a home setting. As hospitals experience financial pressures, private spaces where patients' family members can meet together or with staff are often limited; this results in an environment that is not very conducive to addressing the social and emotional needs of grieving families. Also, in most institutional settings the primary relationship is that between the medical staff and the patient, and any relationship between staff and the patient's family may be to some degree peripheral or secondary. Societal respect for scientifically based professional medical practice reinforces this arrangement. Ideally, however, for dying persons who are no longer responding to or who no longer desire aggressive, curative care, the focus of medical attention shifts to palliative care. The need is not necessarily for less care, but for care with a different focus, one with increased attention to the physical, psychosocial, and spiritual needs of the patient and his or her family. Such care is best provided by a multidisciplinary team of professional (formal) caregivers that includes a physician, nurse, nursing assistant, social worker, chaplain, and volunteer trained in palliative care.

CHARACTERISTICS OF CAREGIVING

Caregiving is multidimensional. For a particular patient it can often involve an array of caregivers, both formal and informal, and possibly in more than one setting. Even in an institutional setting, where professional staff members assume the major caregiving responsibility, family members and friends of the patient may continue with informal caregiving functions such as emotional support and other comfort measures.

Formal and Informal Caregivers

Ideally, caregiving for a dying person is provided through a team approach in which the team of caregivers includes professionals associated with health care institutions and family members and friends of the patient who are based in the home and community. Professionals are the designated *formal* caregivers, with socially sanctioned and prescribed roles for which they have received appropriate training and for which they are appropriately compensated. Formal caregivers in traditional institutional settings are medical professionals trained to cure, rehabilitate, and restore functioning. Hospice and other home-based care professionals often bridge the gap between institution and home with more training in palliative care.

In contrast, *informal* caregivers are family, friends, neighbors, and others who assist the patient with daily living tasks and provide emotional support, generally without payment (Hogstel 2001). According to the Family Caregiver Alliance (2002), in 1997 22.4 million U.S. households (23%, or nearly one out of four) were involved in caregiving to persons age 50 and older; it is expected that by the year 2007, that number could climb to 39 million.

The array of persons providing care to a given patient may vary over time, depending on the physical and psychosocial needs of the patient and his or her family as well as the resources available. Prior to a patient's admission to a medical setting, the family has often carried major responsibility for care in the home setting. In an institutional setting, professional staff assume major responsibility, and in some cases hospice staff become the major source of caregiving.

Terminal illness, in contrast with death in an emergency situation or within a hospital intensive care unit, requires that formal and informal caregivers provide care over a longer period of time. Once hospice is involved, the unit of care shifts from the patient alone to the patient and his or her family. This can be a major factor in alleviating some of the stresses that family caregivers experience. At the same time, stress in the relationship between the patient's family and medical staff can result if family members feel that the medical staff have referred the patient to hospice care "too late." Delayed referral may result when it is difficult to predict the patient's expected length of survival or when the patient and/or family members have difficulty accepting the hospice referral.

Gender and Caregiving

Although men are increasingly assuming greater roles in family caregiving, women in their mid-40s and older continue to provide approximately 75% of the care for older family members in the United States (Family Caregiver Alliance 2002). To date, it is unclear what impact women's increased participation in the workforce has had on their involvement in family caregiving responsibilities. Moen et al. (1994) conducted a study of 293 women from four birth cohorts and found that women in all cohorts were equally likely to become caregivers, regardless of whether or not they were employed, confirming the idea that many women assume family caregiving roles in addition to full- and part-time employment. To accommodate their employment, some women are involved as managers of caregiving rather than as direct providers of care (both for children and for sick family members); others are more apt to share the responsibilities with other family members. As Conner (2000) reports, "The research findings on the effect of employment on women's caregiving activities are mixed and somewhat contradictory" (p. 101). Some studies suggest that employment can moderate the effects of the caregiving experience on women, providing a socially acceptable limit on what care recipients might expect of caregivers; others suggest that the ability to juggle conflicting demands can be particularly rewarding and self-enhancing. Some researchers have speculated that in order to make time for caregiving, women who are also employed reduce their level of involvement in voluntary and social activities, whereas others have found that some women increase their participation in voluntary social activities that serve as a means of relieving the stress associated with caregiving.

Less is known about the experiences of male caregivers, because women are more often the subjects of research. Although daughters tend to provide more care for aging parents than do sons, this may change as the elderly population grows in this time of smaller family size and changing gender roles, making caregiving an expected role for all family members, at least in the dominant Western culture.

Ethnicity and Culture

Aside from gender differences, ethnic and cultural differences also influence caregiving practices. According to Hoffmann and Mitchell (1998), across cultures, "the family unit invokes a strong sense of belonging" (p. 5). Because caregiving is learned within the family, which is a cultural environment, it is understandable that the behaviors and roles related to caregiving are influenced by cultural values and practices (Phillips et al. 1996). Still, one must carefully examine generalizations about ethnic groups, because tremendous diversity exists *within* as well as *among* groups, depending on degree of acculturation, urban and rural experiences, socioeconomic status, personal values, and other factors. With this word of caution, we offer the following descriptions of the values and practices associated with caregiving within some of the primary ethnic groups in the United States.

Two important characteristics of African American families may affect the delivery of family caregiving: (a) African Americans are more likely than whites to live in extended family households, allowing caregiving responsibilities to be shared by more family members; and (b) compared with white families, family roles in African American families tend to be more flexible and egalitarian, with men and women sharing household and family caregiving responsibilities (Conner 2000).

Hispanic and Asian American family values tend to stress respect for older people and the importance of family obligation, with strong intergenerational linkages. The Family Caregiver Alliance (2002) reports that among Americans between ages 45 and 55, a much higher proportion (42%) of Asian Americans provide care for older relatives than do white, non-Hispanic Americans (19%). A similar emphasis on respect for and inclusion of older family members is seen in Native American populations, especially those living in rural areas (Conner 2000), although there has been a shift toward greater dependence on community services to meet the needs of elders as more Native Americans have moved off the reservations to urban areas.

In their study of caregiver burden, Hoffmann and Mitchell (1998) found that this term is not universally recognized in all cultures. For example, historically the Amish view the opportunity to provide elder care as a gift, and Puerto Rican families guarantee their members protection and caregiving for life. More research examining family caregiving in various racial and cultural minority groups is needed if we are to gain a fuller understanding of the impacts of poverty and socioeconomic status on such caregiving as well as the degree to which family members in these groups assume the values and practices of the dominant culture.

CARING FOR THE CAREGIVERS

Ideally, persons who are dying in an institutional setting are given social support through the trajectory of the dying process, surrounded and supported by institutionally based caregivers, including professional staff and volunteers, and by their families and members of their community. A major distinguishing factor in the traditional management of illness in the institutional setting is that the patient receives care from professional medical staff in a setting that is organized specifically around the provision of this care (Corbin and Straus 1988). In institutional settings, patients' family members may be relegated to corridors and waiting areas. Yet they are primary providers of care at various points in the dying process, especially in the home setting, and they can continue to give emotional support in the institutional setting. In the home setting, the work of caregivers is much more variable and ranges from help with activities of daily living to emotional support and psychological processes such as "saying good-bye" and tending to unresolved conflicts. In the institutional setting, the

Caregiving Provided for the Patient by		
Informal Caregivers	and	**Formal Caregivers**
Family and Friends		Professional Staff and Volunteers
Results in Caregiving Needed by		
Family and Friends	and	Professional Staff and Volunteers

Figure 1   Caring for the Caregivers

work related to daily living is taken care of by professional caregiving staff, but the emotional support of the family is still important. Health care professionals are increasingly recognizing this fact, as evidenced by recent trends toward the integration of palliative care in institutional settings that recognizes the value of addressing the psychosocial and spiritual, as well as the physical, needs of patients.

The experience of caregiving, especially as it relates to the final stage of life, affects all participants. Just as they provide care for patients, formal and informal caregivers also need to receive care in order to maintain their emotional and physical stability, so that they can continue to be effective caregivers (see Figure 1).

Stressors and Caregiving

Caregiving, whether formal or informal, can be very demanding; in addition to consuming the caregiver's time, it drains his or her physical and emotional energy. It should be recognized, however, that caregiving can also be a rewarding experience for both formal and informal caregivers. Formal caregivers can realize a sense of professional competence and fulfillment through their work, and informal caregivers may find that they experience increased family closeness and growth in their personal feelings of self-confidence. For both types of caregivers, the presence of social supports, personal coping mechanisms, previous preparation or current instruction in caregiving, and positive beliefs and cultural values about caregiving can help to minimize caregiver burden.

Caregivers may experience major stresses owing to emotional, physical, or financial pressures and relationships. Stressors may be immediate and short-term, or, especially in the case of families, they may be reflective of long-term relationships. Figure 2 presents a summary of the potential stressors related to formal and informal caregiving. It is normal for an individual to experience stress in a caregiving role, and the degree of that stress and the caregiver's capacity to cope depend on a variety of factors. A person's position on the continuum of caregiver stress fluctuates depending on life experiences, the availability of support and resources, and the person's preparation for the role of caregiver. A thorough patient and family assessment and care plan for the dying patient should include an assessment of informal caregiver status. It is important that the

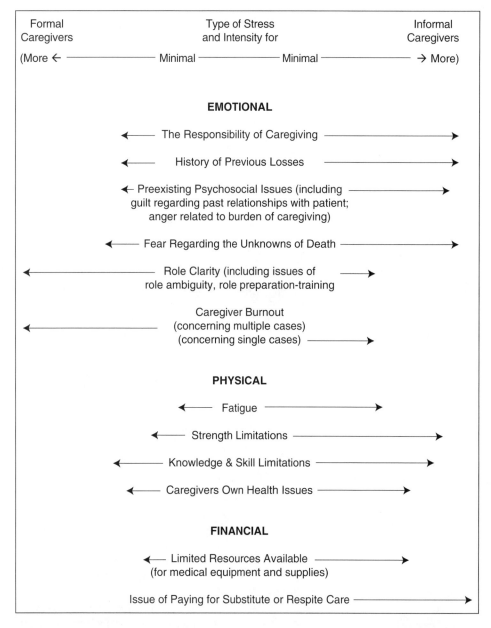

Formal Caregivers	Type of Stress and Intensity for	Informal Caregivers
(More ←	——— Minimal ——— Minimal ———	→ More)

EMOTIONAL

← The Responsibility of Caregiving →

← History of Previous Losses →

← Preexisting Psychosocial Issues (including guilt regarding past relationships with patient; anger related to burden of caregiving) →

← Fear Regarding the Unknowns of Death →

← Role Clarity (including issues of role ambiguity, role preparation-training →

Caregiver Burnout (concerning multiple cases) (concerning single cases) →

PHYSICAL

← Fatigue →

← Strength Limitations →

← Knowledge & Skill Limitations →

← Caregivers Own Health Issues →

FINANCIAL

← Limited Resources Available (for medical equipment and supplies) →

Issue of Paying for Substitute or Respite Care →

Figure 2   Stressors and Caregiving

care plan include attention to monitoring and minimizing caregiver stress, the goal being to bring caregivers as close as possible the center of the continuum shown in Figure 2. The goal is to minimize rather than eliminate stress, given the inherent nature of stress during such a challenging time of life.

Support for Formal Caregivers

Like caregiving, the provision of support for formal caregivers is multidimensional. It might include structured institution-based activities, active support groups for professional staff and volunteers, peer and individual supervision, and professional training and continuing education in end-of-life care. Some examples of institutional support include groups for staff and volunteers, supervisory

support in an atmosphere in which it is safe to discuss the challenges of the work, and memorial services that provide time for staff and family to honor individuals who have died, as well to acknowledge the work and personal involvement of the caregivers. Hospice and palliative care programs to varying degrees include such supports for staff. Until recently, similar support was more limited in acute and critical care settings (Fauri, Ettner, and Kovacs 2000). As Curtis and Rubenfeld (2001) suggest in regard to critical care, "The challenge to clinicians and educators in this area is to span two cultures: the rescue culture of critical care and the hospice culture of palliative medicine" (p. 4). Clinicians, as well as patients and their families, need support and training in making the transition from attempting to cure, rescue, and prolong life to providing comfort and allowing death with dignity. In a survey of nursing homes, however, Murphy, Hanrahan, and Luchins (1997) found minimal support available to residents, their families, or staff members following deaths in these institutions. Recent initiatives through the Robert Wood Johnson Foundation's Promoting Excellence in End-of-Life Care program and the Soros Foundation's Project on Death in America address the need for education and support in nursing homes and other long-term care facilities.

Professional caregivers often experience stress as a result of unclear boundaries between themselves and patients' families and in their relationships with professional colleagues. To a degree, this is set up within the curative role expected of medical staff. For example, when working with dying children, professional caregivers often have "unrealistic expectations and grandiose feelings of indispensability" (Lattanzi-Licht 1991:298). Also, caregiver strain among professionals on hospice teams has been attributed to role blurring and lack of clear role definition among nurses, social workers, and chaplains. Peer support groups and individual supervision are useful vehicles for clarifying such issues, processing feelings, and offering general professional support.

In addition to institutional activities and resources, a critical source of support for formal caregivers is professional training and continuing education, because it creates confidence and increases competence. Recent trends reflect the desire of many organizations to help professionals and the general public feel more comfortable and competent with end-of-life care issues. Several important public and private initiatives have focused on the education of physicians, nurses, social workers, chaplains, and others who provide care to the dying (see, e.g., McPhee et al. 2000). Initiatives to improve palliative care education for professionals and the public include the American Medical Association's Education for Physicians in the End-of-Life Care Program (EPEC) and a similar program for nurses (ELNEC); the U.S. Department of Veterans Affairs's Faculty Scholars in End-of-Life Care Program; the Soros Foundation's Project on Death in America; two programs funded by the Robert Wood Johnson Foundation, Last Acts and Community-State Partnership; and the Public Broadcasting Service's project tied to the Bill Moyers series *On Our Own Terms: Moyers on Dying*. All of these are examples of broad-based efforts to enhance end-of-life care through professional and public education, state policy, and community awareness.

Addressing the individualized support needs of professional caregivers presents a challenge, given the wide range of personal and professional comfort levels and expertise with death and dying. Harper (1977) has developed a model of the stages of development that identifies an adaptation process that professionals experience over time as they become more comfortable in this work. Harper has focused in her work on professionals working in oncology, and although empirically based studies are not available, chapters she has written on her model continue to be included in edited volumes addressing end-of-life care (Harper 1989, 1993). Harper's model contains the following five stages, in 3-month increments, related to "coping with professional anxiety in terminal illness" (Harper 1977:29):

- Initially one intellectualizes as a way of dealing with anxiety and lack of knowledge (0–3 months).

- Next, one simply tries to survive emotionally (3–6 months).

- There occurs a feeling of depression often related to painful experiences (6–9 months).

- Eventually, after 9–12 months of this work, one experiences "emotional arrival" as skills are acquired and enhanced.

- In the final stage, achieved between 12 and 24 months, one can feel deep compassion in this work because of self-realization, self-awareness, and self-actualization.

Support for Informal Caregivers

Informal caregivers also need support. Most often, for assistance in caregiving an informal caregiver depends on family members, friends, and others in his or her community, many of whom are also personally affected by the patient's impending death. Hospice recognizes the need to support informal caregivers, and most programs provide respite care to give caregivers time away from this emotionally draining work. Respite may be provided by a volunteer or staff member for a few hours, or, when the physical needs of the patient are especially demanding, the patient may be admitted to an inpatient unit for a period to provide relief for the informal caregivers.

Much of the research on caregiving has focused on generational issues, in particular the "sandwich generation" phenomenon of adult children caring for both their own children and their older parents (Pearlin, Pioli, and McLaughlin 2001). Increasingly, however, older spousal caregivers may be forced to restructure their lives to accommodate the demands of caregiving, suggesting that this phenomenon of fitting in caregiving while managing other roles is not limited solely to the younger generation of adult children.

Information and education about how best to care for the patient are important forms of support for informal caregivers. Knowledge about the following topics can help to prepare and support informal caregivers: medication; moving, bathing, and assisting the patient safely and comfortably; nutritional needs; and the dying process itself. Assistance with legal and financial matters such as funeral arrangements, living wills, power of attorney, and DNR (do not resuscitate) orders is another form of support for those in the caregiving role. Hospice families receive this information because in the hospice approach family caregivers are considered an important part of the care team and a link from the home to the hospice team. An informed family is better able to provide care and is usually more comfortable doing so. Time invested in educating family members often helps ease their fears, increases their competence, and may minimize emergency calls. Hospice professionals must recognize, however, that for some people, such information may be overwhelming rather than comforting. The identification of those members of the family system with whom it is most appropriate to share this information is an important part of the patient and family's psychosocial assessment.

Providing informal caregivers with informational support and education takes time, and in busy, short-staffed, fast-paced hospital units, staff usually do not have much time or incentive to answer questions and help to educate patients' family members. As more health care staff are trained in palliative care, addressing the psychosocial and spiritual needs of patients and families through education, counseling, and other supportive measures should become more fully integrated in traditional care.

Support groups are another source of information support. In such groups, family caregivers can learn how others manage their caregiving roles as well as receive emotional support. Unfortunately, scheduling support group meetings is challenging in hospital settings, given short lengths of stay, limited meeting space and time, and families' sporadic visitation schedules. The establishment of support groups is more feasible in nursing home and hospice settings, due to the longer time frame in which care takes place.

Concern about the stress that family caregivers experience, often referred to as *caregiver burden,* has been addressed in the professional literature since the 1980s. Terms such as *caretaker role fatigue, spousal burnout,* and *role engulfment* refer to an imbalance between the physical and mental resources needed to care for the recipient and those available within the family unit or community (Hoffman and Mitchell 1998). The demands of caregiving often result in depression, anxiety, sleeplessness, and other signs of emotional strain. In addition, caregivers might experience financial hardship and deterioration of their own health, which in turn affects other family members and the patient.

The need to alleviate the physical and emotional stress associated with caregiving has led to the development of support groups, the publication of self-help literature, and other activities designed to minimize caregiver isolation and reduce stress. There has also been a policy response to the increasing involvement and importance of family caregivers, indicating a new appreciation of the associated role strain. In 2000, the U.S. Congress provided funding for the National Family Caregiver Support Program under Title III of the Older Americans Act. This program encourages support for caregivers through training, counseling, and information, as well as respite care for family members who are providing support for older relatives at home (AARP 2002).

The physical, emotional, and financial strains inherent in being a caregiver are a reality. Conner (2000:248), however, questions whether caregiving must be defined only as a burden and identifies potential rewards in this "opportunity." She suggests that many caregivers derive enhanced self-esteem from managing the multiple roles associated with caregiving and that through these multiple roles caregivers are often linked to the greater community. Family caregiving is a sign of the strength of the family at a time when rates of divorce, poverty, juvenile crime, and substance abuse as well as other statistics indicate a decline in the American family. Lattanzi-Licht et al. (1998) describe this complexity: "Most [hospice] families relate to the dying process as both a difficult and valuable time. . . . the majority of family members who care for a loved one describe high feelings of self-satisfaction and little regret" (pp. 30–31).

NEGOTIATING CAREGIVING AMONG STAFF MEMBERS

The setting in which caregiving takes place influences the nature of caregiving roles. Traditionally, health care institutions are organized around the medical model, with a social order that places the physician at the top of a hierarchy of care. Straus et al. (1964) suggest that this order is negotiated and based on each person's "definition of the situation" (Wiener 2000). The diverse and sometimes divergent perspectives of the participants shape a social order that is negotiated through an ongoing process of bargaining, maneuvering, restraining, and compromising. Staff representing a variety of professions bring differing expectations of team members' caregiving roles to the team setting. Although this creates a rich environment in which team members can engage in critical thinking about their beliefs and practices and how they can contribute to improved patient care, this negotiation process can be challenging. It can take many different courses, depending upon the people involved, the professions represented, and the setting. In traditional settings, the unit of care, or "unit of attention," is the patient, as care tends to focus on "cure-oriented" therapies and interventions; negotiation in such settings involves primarily those who provide or control the interventions. In a less traditional model of care, such as hospice, however, the unit of care is the patient *and* the patient's family, and negotiation therefore also involves informal caregivers. These different perspectives help shape the nature of the care.

In an institutional setting, caregiving is the responsibility of physicians, nurses, unit support staff, and ancillary service staff (e.g., social workers, chaplains, physical therapists, occupational therapists), with limited assistance from volunteers. Emergency medical technicians, emergency room personnel, and organ recovery and transplant staff also become involved when appropriate. Medical professionals, in particular physicians and nurses, have technical expertise and authority, status, and knowledge of institutional processes. Dying patients and their families often defer to this expertise, leaving medical staff in a control position in care planning and decision making. This might be expected in matters related to medical treatment and physical processes, but it can also extend into areas related to the psychosocial and spiritual aspects of end-of-life care.

It is often stressful for medical staff to help grieving families and to devote time to anything beyond immediate patient medical requirements. Following the death of a patient, family members and friends often face grief in the unfamiliar institutional setting (VonBlock 1996; Wells 1993). This may elicit bereavement needs that not all staff are prepared to address, but increasingly hospitals have staff members trained in bereavement matters or bereavement teams headed by clergy or social workers. Staff with this training can best assist the dying patient, the patient's family, and medical staff with bereavement care by becoming involved in the case as early as possible (Fauri et al. 2000).

Traditionally, medical practice in an institutional setting is intended to extend life, in a quantitative sense. Physicians spend considerable energy organizing and directing treatment for their patients (Straus et al. 1964). Persons who have been trained to cure or rehabilitate often perceive a patient's death to be a failure. Health care professionals trained in palliative care, however, consider comfort care and symptom management to be part of standard medical care. Once a decision is made that palliation is the appropriate focus in the patient's care, medical care shifts in orientation. Palliative care enhances the quality of life remaining, and for formal caregivers, this requires a shift in emphasis to "comfort care." It also requires rearrangement of the order negotiated for treatment. For example, management of pain through medication and pain control procedures is emphasized, requiring continuing assessment and adjustment of medication and pain control procedures by medical staff. As refocusing takes place, the presence of family and other loved ones can be critical to the emotional well-being of the patient. Family members and friends are better able to provide emotional support to the patient when they have the comfort of knowing that the patient's pain and symptoms are being managed.

CONCLUSION

There was a time when caring for dying patients and their families was an integral part of family and community life as well as the practice of medicine. As medical care became more specialized and technological advances facilitated a societal desire to avoid death and prolong life, the care of the dying became more fragmented. Health care institutions play a key role in the lives of dying patients; hence the importance of support for professional caregivers.

We recommend that support, resources, and training be readily available for formal caregivers, including increased, ongoing, and culturally sensitive training in end-of-life care for physicians, nurses, clergy, social workers, pharmacists, nutritionists, and other allied health professionals who assist patients and families during any part of their experience with life-limiting illness. Formal caregivers need the opportunity for bereavement support through structured support groups, individual and peer supervision, and time off as needed for personal care and professional development. Formal caregivers need to have time and opportunities to clarify role confusion and ambiguity associated with stress and occupational burnout.

Informal caregivers need education and emotional support in order to perform their roles. These forms of support are often provided by local health care organizations, community associations, private practitioners, and national organizations. Through participation in family caregiver support groups, as well as through less formal individual conversations with health care professionals, informal caregivers have opportunities to ask questions and share their fears; they can learn how to change dressings, administer medications, bathe a dying relative, and deal with their guilt when they cannot fulfill the roles they believe they should. Informal caregivers need societal and financial support

such as that reflected in the National Family Caregiver Support Program, which helps families provide care for older relatives. Parents, adult children, and other caregivers need family leave time from work and flexible work schedules that will allow them to balance multiple roles. They may also benefit from spiritual guidance or counseling. The recent focus on death and dying in the mass media, increased training in end-of-life care in the medical professions, and important policy initiatives addressing the rights of the dying and encouraging respite care for caregivers are all positive signs. Much needs to be done, however, to maintain this momentum, given the societal desire to deny and "cure" death.

Caring for the dying will always be one of life's most challenging privileges. With proper support, resources, and training, both formal and informal caregivers are better able meet this challenge in a way that enhances not only the lives of persons who are dying, but their own lives as well.

REFERENCES

AARP Research Center. 2002. "Caregiving and Long-Term Care." Washington, DC: AARP. Retrieved June 8, 2003 (http://research.aarp.org/health/fs82_caregiving.html).

Conner, Karen A. 2000. *Continuing to Care: Older Americans and Their Families in the 21st Century.* New York: Falmer.

Corbin, Juliet M. and Anselm L. Straus. 1988. *Unending Work and Care: Managing Chronic Illness at Home.* San Francisco: Jossey-Bass.

Curtis, J. Randall and Gordon D. Rubenfeld. 2001. *Managing Death in the Intensive Care Unit: The Transition From Cure to Comfort.* New York: Oxford University Press.

Family Caregiver Alliance. 2002. "Fact Sheet: Selected Caregiver Statistics." San Francisco: Family Caregiver Alliance. Retrieved June 8, 2003 (http://www.caregiver.org/fact-sheets/selected_caregiver_statistics.html).

Fauri, David J., Barbara Ettner, and Pamela J. Kovacs. 2000. "Bereavement Services in Acute Care Settings." *Death Studies* 24:51–64.

Fins, Joseph J. 1999. "Death and Dying in the 1990s: Intimations of Reality and Immortality." *Generations: Journal of the American Society on Aging* 23:81–86.

Harper, Bernice. 1977. *Death: The Coping Mechanism of the Health Professional.* Greensboro, SC: Southeastern University Press.

———. 1989. "Serving the Dying Client." Pp. 131–40 in *Communication Disorders in Aging,* edited by Raymond H. Hull and Kathleen M. Griffin. Newbury Park, CA: Sage.

———. 1993. "Staff Support." Pp. 184–97 in *Hospice Care for Children,* edited by Ann Armstrong-Dailey and Sarah Zarbock Goltzer. New York: Oxford University Press.

Hoffmann, Rosemary L. and Ann M. Mitchell. 1998. "Caregiver Burden: Historical Development." *Nursing Forum* 33(4):5–11.

Hogstel, Mildred O. 2001. *Gerontology: Nursing Care of the Older Adult.* Independence, KY: Delmar Learning.

Lattanzi-Licht, Marcia. 1991. "Professional Stress: Creating a Context for Caring." Pp. 293–302 in *Children and*

Death, edited by Danai Papadatou and Costas Papadatos. New York: Hemisphere.

Lattanzi-Licht, Marcia, John J. Mahoney, and Galen W. Miller. 1998. *The Hospice Choice: In Pursuit of a Peaceful Death.* New York: Fireside.

McPhee, Stephen J., Michael W. Rabow, Steven Z. Pantilat, Amy J. Markowitz, and Margaret A. Winker. 2000. "Finding Our Way: Perspectives on Care at the Close of Life." *Journal of the American Medical Association* 284:2512–13.

Moen, Phyllis, Julie Robison, and Vivian Fields. 1994. "Women's Work and Caregiving Roles: A Life Course Approach." *Journal of Gerontology: Social Sciences* 49:S176–86.

Murphy, Kathleen, Patricia Hanrahan, and Daniel Luchins. 1997. "A Survey of Grief and Bereavement in Nursing Homes: The Importance of Hospice Grief and Bereavement for the End-Stage Alzheimer's Disease Patient and Family." *Journal of the American Geriatrics Society* 45:1104–7.

National Hospice and Palliative Care Organization. 2002. "NHPCO Facts and Figures." Washington, DC: National Hospice and Palliative Care Organization. Retrieved June 8, 2003 (http://www.nhpco.org/public/articles/facts&figures9-2002.pdf).

Pearlin, Leonard, Mark F. Pioli, and Amy E. McLaughlin. 2001. "Caregiving by Adult Children: Involvement, Role Disruption, and Health." Pp. 238–54 in *Handbook of Aging and the Social Sciences,* 5th ed., edited by Robert H. Binstock and Linda K. George. New York: Academic Press.

Phillips, Linda, Isela Luna, Cynthia K. Russell, Gloria Baca, Young Mi Lim, Sandra L. Cromwell, and Esperanza Torres de Ardon. 1996. "Toward a Cross-Cultural Perspective of Family Caregiving." *Western Journal of Nursing Research* 18:236–51.

Rosenberg, Charles E. 1987. *The Care of Strangers: The Rise of America's Hospital System.* New York: Basic Books.

Straus, Anselm L., Leonard Schatzman, Rue Bucher, Danuta Ehrlich, and Melvin Sabshin. 1964. *Psychiatric Ideologies and Institutions.* New York: Free Press.

VonBlock, L. 1996. "Breaking the Bad News When Sudden Death Occurs." *Social Work in Health Care* 23(4):91–97.

Wells, Paula J. 1993. "Preparing for Sudden Death: Social Work in the Emergency Room." *Social Work* 38:339–42.

Wiener, Carolyn L. 2000. "Applying the Straussian Framework of Action, Negotiation, and Social Arenas to a Study of Accountability in Hospitals." *Sociological Perspectives* 43(4):S59–71.